DATE DUE

			PRINTED IN U.S.A.

Literature Criticism from 1400 to 1800

Guide to Gale Literary Criticism Series

When you need to review criticism of literary works, these are the Gale series to use:

If the author's death date is: **You should turn to:**

After Dec. 31, 1959
(or author is still living)

CONTEMPORARY LITERARY CRITICISM

for example: Jorge Luis Borges, Anthony Burgess,
William Faulkner, Mary Gordon,
Ernest Hemingway, Iris Murdoch

1900 through 1959

TWENTIETH-CENTURY LITERARY CRITICISM

for example: Willa Cather, F. Scott Fitzgerald,
Henry James, Mark Twain, Virginia Woolf

1800 through 1899

NINETEENTH-CENTURY LITERATURE CRITICISM

for example: Fedor Dostoevski, Nathaniel Hawthorne,
George Sand, William Wordsworth

1400 through 1799

*LITERATURE CRITICISM FROM 1400 TO 1800
(excluding Shakespeare)*

for example: Anne Bradstreet, Daniel Defoe,
Alexander Pope, François Rabelais,
Jonathan Swift, Phillis Wheatley

SHAKESPEAREAN CRITICISM

Shakespeare's plays and poetry

Antiquity through 1399

CLASSICAL AND MEDIEVAL LITERATURE CRITICISM

for example: Dante, Homer, Plato, Sophocles, Vergil,
the Beowulf Poet

Gale also publishes related criticism series:

CHILDREN'S LITERATURE REVIEW

This series covers authors of all eras who write for the preschool through high school audience.

SHORT STORY CRITICISM

This series covers the major short fiction writers of all nationalities and periods of literary history.

ISSN 0740-2880

Volume 8

Literature Criticism from 1400 to 1800

Excerpts from Criticism of the Works
of Fifteenth-, Sixteenth-, Seventeenth-, and
Eighteenth-Century Novelists, Poets, Playwrights,
Philosophers, and Other Creative Writers, from
the First Published Critical Appraisals
to Current Evaluations

James E. Person, Jr.
Editor

Robin DuBlanc
Associate Editor

Gale Research Company
Book Tower
Detroit, Michigan 48226

STAFF

James E. Person, Jr., *Editor*

Robin DuBlanc, *Associate Editor*

James P. Draper, Jay P. Pederson, *Senior Assistant Editors*

Claudia Loomis, Peter Wehrli, Shannon J. Young, *Assistant Editors*

Jeanne A. Gough, *Permissions and Production Manager*

Lizbeth A. Purdy, *Production Supervisor*
Kathleen M. Cook, *Assistant Production Coordinator*
Cathy Beranek, Suzanne Powers, Kristine Tipton, Lee Ann Welsh, *Editorial Assistants*

Linda M. Pugliese, *Manuscript Coordinator*
Donna Craft, *Assistant Manuscript Coordinator*
Jennifer E. Gale, Maureen A. Puhl, Rosetta Irene Simms, *Manuscript Assistants*

Victoria B. Cariappa, *Research Supervisor*
Maureen R. Richards, *Research Coordinator*
Mary D. Wise, *Senior Research Assistant*
Joyce E. Doyle, Kevin B. Hillstrom, Karen D. Kaus, Eric Priehs,
Filomena Sgambati, Laura B. Standley, *Research Assistants*

Janice M. Mach, *Text Permissions Supervisor*
Kathy Grell, *Text Permissions Coordinator*
Mabel E. Gurney, Josephine M. Keene, *Senior Permissions Assistants*
Eileen H. Baehr, H. Diane Cooper, Anita L. Ransom, Kimberly F. Smilay, *Permissions Assistants*
Melissa A. Kamuyu, Martha A. Mulder, Lisa M. Wimmer, *Permissions Clerks*

Patricia A. Seefelt, *Picture Permissions Supervisor*
Margaret A. Chamberlain, *Picture Permissions Coordinator*
Pamela A. Hayes, Lillian Tyus, *Permissions Clerks*

Library of Congress Catalog Card Number 83-20504
ISBN 0-8103-6107-8
ISSN 0740-2880

Computerized photocomposition by
Typographics, Incorporated
Kansas City, Missouri

Printed in the United States of America

10 9 8 7 6 5 4 3 2

Contents

Preface

"If I have seen farther," wrote Sir Isaac Newton, echoing Fulbert of Chartres and commenting on his own indebtedness to the sages who preceded him, "it is by standing on the shoulders of giants," a statement as applicable to ourselves today as it was to Newton and his world. Many of the political and intellectual foundations of the modern world can be found in the art and thought of the fifteenth through eighteenth centuries. During this time the modern nation-state was born, the sciences grew tremendously, and many of the political, social, economic, and moral philosophies that are influential today were formulated. The literature of these centuries reflects this turbulent time of radical change: the period saw the rise of drama equal in critical stature to that of classical Greece, the birth of the novel and personal essay forms, the emergence of newspapers and periodicals, and significant achievements in poetry and philosophy. Much of modern literature reflects the influence of these centuries' developments. Thus the literature of this period provides insight into the universal nature of human experience, as well as into the life and thought of the past.

Literary criticism can also give us insight into the human condition, as well as into the specific moral and intellectual atmosphere of an era, for the criteria by which a work of art is judged reflect contemporary philosophical and social attitudes. Literary criticism takes many forms: the traditional essay, the book or play review, even the parodic poem. Criticism can also be of several kinds, including descriptive, interpretive, textual, appreciative, and generic, among others. Collectively, the range of critical response helps us understand a work of art, an author, an era.

Scope of the Series

Literature Criticism from 1400 to 1800 (LC) is designed to serve as an introduction to the authors of the fifteenth through eighteenth centuries and to the most significant commentators on these authors. The works of the great poets, dramatists, novelists, essayists, and philosophers of those years are considered classics in every secondary school and college or university curriculum. Because criticism of this literature spans a period of up to six hundred years, an overwhelming amount of critical material confronts the student. To help students locate and select criticism on the works of authors who died between 1400 and 1800, *LC* presents significant passages from the most noteworthy published criticism on authors of these centuries. Each volume of *LC* is carefully compiled to represent the critical heritage of the most important writers from a variety of nationalities. In addition to major authors, *LC* also presents criticism on lesser-known writers whose significant contributions to literary history are reflected in continuing critical assessments of their works.

The need for *LC* among students and teachers of literature of the fifteenth through eighteenth centuries was suggested by the proven usefulness of Gale's *Contemporary Literary Criticism (CLC), Twentieth-Century Literary Criticism (TCLC),* and *Nineteenth-Century Literature Criticism (NCLC),* which excerpt criticism of creative writing from the nineteenth and twentieth centuries. Because of the different time periods covered, there is no duplication of authors or critical material between any of Gale's literary criticism series. For further information about these series, readers should consult the Guide to Gale Literary Criticism Series preceding the title page of this volume. Here, the reader will note that there is a separate Gale reference series devoted to Shakespearean studies. For though belonging properly to the literary period covered in *LC,* William Shakespeare has inspired such a tremendous and ever-growing corpus of secondary material that the editors have deemed it best to give his works the extensive critical coverage best served by a separate series, *Shakespearean Criticism.*

Each author entry in *LC* provides an overview of major criticism on an author. Therefore, the editors include approximately twelve authors in each 550-page volume (compared with approximately forty authors in a *CLC* volume of similar size) so that more attention may be given each author. Each author entry represents a historical survey of the critical response to an author's work: early criticism is presented to indicate initial responses, later selections represent any rise or decline in the author's literary reputation and describe the effects of social or historical forces on the work of an author, and retrospective analyses provide students with a modern view. The length of an author entry is intended to represent the author's critical reception in English or foreign criticism in translation. Articles and books that have not been translated into English are therefore excluded. Every attempt has been made to identify and include excerpts from the seminal essays on each author's work, and to include recent critical commentary providing modern perspectives on the writer. An author may appear more than once in the series because of the great quantity of critical material available, or because of a resurgence of criticism generated by such events as an author's anniversary celebration, the republication of an author's works, or the publication of a newly translated work.

Organization of the Book

An author entry consists of the following elements: author heading, biographical and critical introduction, list of principal works, excerpts of criticism (each followed by a bibliographical citation), and an additional bibliography for further reading. Also, most author entries reproduce author portraits and other illustrations pertinent to the author's life and career.

- The *author heading* consists of the author's full name, followed by birth and death dates. The unbracketed portion of the name denotes the form under which the author most commonly wrote. If an author wrote consistently under a pseudonym, the pseudonym will be listed in the author heading, with the real name given in parentheses on the first line of the biographical and critical introduction. Also located at the beginning of the introduction to the author entry are any name variations under which an author wrote, including transliterated forms for authors whose native languages use nonroman alphabets. Uncertain birth or death dates are indicated by question marks.

- The *biographical and critical introduction* contains background information designed to introduce the reader to an author and to the critical discussion surrounding his or her work. Parenthetical material following many of the introductions provides references to biographical and critical reference series published by Gale, including *Children's Literature Review, Dictionary of Literary Biography, Something about the Author,* and *Yesterday's Authors of Books for Children.*

- Most *LC* entries include *portraits* of the author. Many entries also contain illustrations of materials pertinent to an author's career, including selected holographs of manuscript pages, title pages, letters, or representations of important people, places, and events in an author's life.

- The *list of principal works* is chronological by date of first book publication and identifies the genre of each work. In the case of foreign authors whose works have been translated into English, the title and date of the first English-language edition are given in brackets following the foreign-language listing. Unless otherwise indicated, dramas are dated by first performance, not first publication.

- *Criticism* is arranged chronologically in each author entry to provide a useful perspective on changes in critical evaluation over the years. All titles by the author featured in the critical entry are printed in boldface type to enable the user to ascertain without difficulty the works being discussed. Also for purposes of easier identification, the critic's name and the composition or publication date of the critical work are given at the beginning of each excerpt. Unsigned criticism is preceded by the title of the source in which it appeared. When an anonymous essay has been attributed to a critic, the critic's name appears in brackets at the beginning of the excerpt and in the bibliographical citation. Publication information (such as publisher names and book prices) and parenthetical numerical references (such as footnotes or page and line references to specific editions of works) have been deleted at the editor's discretion to provide smoother reading of the text.

- Critical essays are prefaced by *explanatory notes* as an additional aid to students using *LC*. The explanatory notes may provide several types of useful information, including: the reputation of a critic, the importance of a work of criticism, the specific type of criticism (biographical, psychoanalytic, structuralist, etc.), the intent of the criticism, and the growth of critical controversy or changes in critical trends regarding an author's work. In some cases, these notes cross-reference the work of critics who agree or disagree with each other. Dates in parentheses within the explanatory notes refer to a book publication date when they follow a book title and to an essay date when they follow a critic's name.

- A complete *bibliographical citation* designed to facilitate location of the original essay or book by the interested reader follows each piece of criticism.

- The *additional bibliography* appearing at the end of each author entry suggests further reading on the author. In a few rare cases it includes essays for which the editors could not obtain reprint rights.

An appendix lists the sources from which material in each volume has been reprinted. It does not, however, list every book and periodical consulted in the preparation of the volume.

Cumulative Indexes

Each volume of *LC* includes a cumulative index to authors listing all the authors that have appeared in *Contemporary Literary Criticism, Twentieth-Century Literary Criticism, Nineteenth-Century Literature Criticism, Literature Criticism from 1400 to 1800,* and *Classical and Medieval Literature Criticism,* along with cross-references to the Gale series *Short Story Criticism, Children's Literature Review, Authors in the News, Contemporary Authors, Contemporary Authors Autobiography Series, Contemporary Authors Bibliographical Series, Dictionary of Literary Biography, Something about the Author, Something about the Author Autobiography Series,* and *Yesterday's Authors of Books for Children.* Readers will welcome this cumulative author index as a useful tool for locating an author within the various series. The index, which includes authors' birth and death dates, is particularly valuable for those authors who are identified with a certain period but whose death dates cause them to be placed in another, or for those authors whose careers span two periods. For example, F. Scott Fitzgerald is found in *TCLC,* yet a writer often associated with him, Ernest Hemingway, is found in *CLC.*

Each volume of *LC* also includes a cumulative nationality index, in which authors' names are arranged alphabetically under their respective nationalities and followed by the numbers of the volumes in which they appear. In addition, each volume of *LC* includes a cumulative index to titles, an alphabetical listing of the literary works discussed in the series since its inception. Each title listing includes the corresponding volume and page numbers where criticism may be located. Foreign-language titles that have been translated are followed by the titles of the translations—for example, *El ingenioso hidalgo Don Quixote de la Mancha (Don Quixote).* Page numbers following these translated titles refer to all pages on which any form of the titles, either foreign-language or translated, appear. Titles of novels, dramas, nonfiction books, and poetry, short story, or essay collections are printed in italics, while all individual poems, short stories, and essays are printed in roman type within quotation marks. In cases where the same title is used by different authors, the author's surname is given in parentheses after the title, e.g., *Poems* (Bradstreet) and *Poems* (Killigrew).

Acknowledgments

No work of this scope can be accomplished without the cooperation of many people. The editors especially wish to thank the copyright holders of the excerpts included in this volume, the permissions managers of many book and magazine publishing companies for assisting us in locating copyright holders, and Anthony Bogucki for assistance with copyright research. We are also grateful to the staffs of the Detroit Public Library, the Library of Congress, University of Detroit Library, University of Michigan Library, and Wayne State University Library for making their resources available to us.

Suggestions Are Welcome

Readers who wish to suggest authors to appear in future volumes, or who have other suggestions, are cordially invited to write the editor.

Additional Authors to Appear
in Future Volumes

Abravenel, Isaac 1437-1508
Abravenel, Judah 1460-1535
Addison, Joseph 1672-1719
Agricola, Johannes 1494?-1566
Akenside, Mark 1721-1770
Alabaster, William 1567-1640
Alarcón y Mendoza, Juan Rúiz
    1581-1634
Alberti, Leon Battista 1404-1472
Alembert, Jean Le Rond d' 1717-1783
Amory, Thomas 1691?-1788
Anton Ulrich, Duke of Brunswick
    1633-1714
Aretino, Pietro 1492-1556
Ascham, Roger 1515-1568
Aubigne, Théodore Agrippa d'
    1552-1630
Aubin, Penelope 1685-1727?
Aubrey, John 1620-1697
Bâbur 1483-1530
Bacon, Sir Francis 1561-1626
Bale, John 1495-1563
Barber, Mary 1690-1757
Baretti, Giuseppi 1719-1789
Barker, Jane 1652-1727?
Bartas, Guillaume de Salluste du
    1544-1590
Baxter, Richard 1615-1691
Bayle, Pierre 1647-1706
Beaumarchais, Pierre-Augustin Caron
    de 1732-1799
Beaumont, Francis 1584-1616
Belleau, Rémy 1528-1577
Berkeley, George 1685-1753
Bessarion, Johannes 1403-1472
Bijns, Anna 1493-1575
Bisticci, Vespasiano da 1421-1498
Blackmore, Sir Richard 1650-1729
Boccalini, Traiano 1556-1613
Bodin, Jean 1530-1596
Bolingbroke, Henry St. John
    1678-1751
Boyle, Roger 1621-1679
Bradford, William 1590-1657
Brant, Sebastian 1457-1521
Bredero, Gerbrand Adriaanszoon
    1585-1618
Breitinger, Johann Jakob 1701-1776
Breton, Nicholas 1545-1626
Broome, William 1689-1745
Brown, Thomas 1663-1704
Browne, Sir Thomas 1605-1682
Bruni, Leonardo 1370-1444
Bruno, Giordano 1548-1600
Buffon, George-Louis Leclerc, Comte
    de 1707-1788

Burgoyne, John 1722-1792
Burnet, Gilbert 1643-1715
Burton, Robert 1577-1640
Butler, Samuel 1612-1680
Byrd, William, II 1674-1744
Byrom, John 1692-1763
Calderón de la Barca, Pedro 1600-1681
Camden, William 1551-1623
Campion, Thomas 1567-1620
Carew, Richard 1555-1620
Carew, Thomas 1594-1640
Carver, Jonathan 1710-1780
Casanova di Seingalt, Giacomo
    Girolamo 1725-1798
Castiglione, Baldassare 1478-1529
Castillejo, Cristobalde 1492-1550
Cavendish, William 1592-1676
Caxton, William 1421?-1491
Centlivre, Susanna 1667?-1723
Chapman, George 1560-1634
Chartier, Alain 1390-1440
Chaucer, Geoffrey 1340?-1400
Christine de Pizan 1365?-1431?
Cibber, Colley 1671-1757
Cleveland, John 1613-1658
Collyer, Mary 1716?-1763?
Colonna, Vittoria 1490-1547
Commynes, Philippe de 1445-1511
Condillac, Etienne Bonnot, Abbé de
    1714?-1780
Cook, James 1728-1779
Corneille, Pierre 1606-1684
Cortés, Hernán 1485-1547
Cotton, John 1584-1652
Courtilz de Sandras, Gatiende
    1644-1712
Cowley, Abraham 1618-1667
Cranmer, Thomas 1489-1556
Crashaw, Richard 1612-1649
Crébillon, Prosper Jolyot de 1674-1762
Cruden, Alexander 1701-1770
Curll, Edmund 1675-1747
Dampier, William 1653-1715
Daniel, Samuel 1562-1619
Davenant, Sir William 1606-1668
Davidson, John 1549?-1603
Da Vinci, Leonardo 1452-1519
Day, John 1574-1640
Dekker, Thomas 1572-1632
Delany, Mary Pendarves 1700-1788
Denham, Sir John 1615-1669
Dennis, John 1657-1734
Deloney, Thomas 1543?-1600?
Descartes, René 1596-1650
Desfontaines, Pierre François Guyot,
    Abbé 1685-1745

Diaz del Castillo, Bernal 1492?-1584
Diderot, Denis 1713-1784
Donne, John 1572-1631
Drummond, William 1585-1649
Du Guillet, Pernette 1520?-1545
Dunbar, William 1460?-1520?
Elyot, Thomas 1490-1546
Emin, Fedor ?-1770
Erasmus, Desiderius 1466-1536
Etherege, Sir George 1635-1691
Eusden, Laurence 1688-1730
Evelyn, John 1620-1706
Fabyan, Robert ?-1513
Fairfax, Thomas 1621-1671
Fanshawe, Lady Anne 1625-1680
Fanshawe, Sir Richard 1608-1666
Farquhar, George 1678-1707
Fénelon, François 1651-1715
Fergusson, Robert 1750-1774
Ficino, Marsillo 1433-1499
Fletcher, John 1579-1625
Florian, Jean Pierre Claris de
    1755-1794
Florio, John 1553?-1625
Fontaine, Charles 1514-1565
Fontenelle, Bernard Le Bovier de
    1657-1757
Fonvizin, Denis Ivanovich 1745-1792
Ford, John 1586-1640
Foxe, John 1517-1587
Franklin, Benjamin 1706-1790
Froissart, Jean 1337-1404?
Fuller, Thomas 1608-1661
Galilei, Galileo 1564-1642
Garrick, David 1717-1779
Gascoigne, George 1530?-1577
Gay, John 1685-1732
Gibbon, Edward 1737-1794
Gildon, Charles 1665-1724
Glanvill, Joseph 1636-1680
Góngora y Argote, Luis de 1561-1627
Gosson, Stephen 1554-1624
Gottsched, Johann Christoph
    1700-1766
Gower, John 1330?-1408
Gracian y Morales, Baltasar 1601-1658
Graham, Dougal 1724-1779
Greene, Robert 1558?-1592
Griffith, Elizabeth 1727?-1793
Guarini, Giambattista 1538-1612
Hakluyt, Richard 1553-1616
Hall, Edward 1498-1547
Harrington, James 1611-1677
Hartley, David 1705-1757
Helvetius, Claude Arien 1715-1771
Henslowe, Philip ?-1616

Herbert, George 1593-1633
Herrick, Robert 1591-1674
Heywood, Thomas 1574-1641
Hobbes, Thomas 1588-1679
Hogarth, William 1697-1764
Holbach, Paul Heinrich Dietrich 1723-1789
Holinshed, Raphael ?-1582?
Hooker, Richard 1544-1600
Hooker, Thomas 1586-1647
Howard, Henry, Earl of Surrey 1517-1547
Hung Sheng 1646-1704
Hutcheson, Francis 1694-1746
Ibn Khaldun, Abd al-Rahman ibn Muhammad 1332-1406
Iriarte, Tomas de 1750-1791
Isla y Rojo, José Francisco de 1703-1781
James I, King of Scotland 1394-1437
Jami, Nur ud-din 'Abd-ur-rahman ibn Ahmad 1414-1492
Johnson, Samuel 1709-1784
King, William 1662-1712
Knox, John 1514?-1572
Kochanowski, Jan 1530-1584
Kyd, Thomas 1558-1594
La Bruyére, Jean de 1645-1696
La Fontaine, Jean de 1621-1695
Langland, William 1330?-1400
Lanyer, Aemilia 1569-1645
La Rochefoucauld, Francois de 1613-1680
Law, William 1686-1761
L'Estrange, Sir Roger 1616-1704
Let-we Thon-dara 1752-1783
Lipsius, Justus 1547-1606
Littleton, Sir Thomas 1422-1481
Lo Kuan-Chung c.1400
Lodge, Thomas 1558-1625
Lope de Vega 1562-1635
Lopez de Ayala, Pero 1332-1407?
Lovelace, Richard 1618-1657
Loyola, Ignacio de 1491-1556
Luther, Martin 1483-1546
Lydgate, John 1370?-1452
Lyly, John 1554-1606
Lyttelton, George 1709-1773
MacDomhnaill, Sean Clarach 1691-1754
Macpherson, James 1736-1796
Maitland, Sir Richard 1496-1586
Malory, Sir Thomas ?-1471
Mandeville, Bernard de 1670-1733
Marat, Jean Paul 1743-1793
Marie de l'Incarnation 1599-1672
Marlowe, Christopher 1564-1593
Marston, John 1576-1634
Massinger, Philip 1583-1640
Mather, Cotton 1663-1728

Mather, Increase 1639-1723
Metastasio, Pietro 1698-1782
Michelangelo Buonarrotti 1475-1564
Middleton, Thomas 1580-1627
Milton, John 1608-1674
Molière 1622-1673
Montagu, Lady Mary Wortley 1689-1762
Montfort, Hugo von 1357-1423
More, Henry 1614-1687
More, Sir Thomas 1478-1535
Morton, Thomas 1575-1647
Muret, Marc-Antoine de 1526-1585
Nashe, Thomas 1567-1601
Nawa i 1441-1501
Newton, Sir Isaac 1642-1727
North, Sir Thomas 1535?-1601?
Norton, Thomas 1532-1584
Oldham, John 1653-1683
Otway, Thomas 1652-1685
Pade-tha-ya-za 1684-1754
Painter, William 1540?-1594
Paracelsus 1493-1541
Parr, Catharine 1512-1548
Pascal, Blaise 1623-1662
Pasek, Jan Chryzostom 1636-1701
Peele, George 1556-1596
Pembroke, Mary Sidney, Countess of 1561-1621
Penn, William 1644-1718
Pepys, Samuel 1633-1703
Pico della Mirandola, Giovanni 1463-1494
Poliziano, Angelo 1454-1494
Quarles, Francis 1592-1644
Quevedo y Villegas, Francisco Gomez de 1580-1645
Racine, Jean 1639-1699
Raleigh, Sir Walter 1552-1618
Reuter, Christian 1665-1712
Revius, Jacobus 1586-1658
Reynolds, Sir Joshua 1723-1792
Rochester, John Wilmot, Earl of 1648-1680
Rojas Zorilla, Francisco de 1607-1648
Roper, William 1498-1578
Rousseau, Jean-Baptiste 1671-1741
Rousseau, Jean-Jacques 1712-1788
Rowe, Elizabeth 1674-1737
Rutherford, Samuel 1600?-1661
Sackville, Thomas 1536-1608
Saint-Simon, Louis de Rouvroy 1675-1755
Santeuil, Jean Baptiste de 1630-1697
Savage, Richard 1696-1742
Savonarola, Girolamo 1452-1498
Scarron, Paul 1610-1660
Scott, Sarah 1723-1795
Selden, John 1584-1654
Sévigné, Madame de 1626-1696

Sewall, Samuel 1652-1730
Shadwell, Thomas 1642-1692
Shaftesbury, Anthony Ashley Cooper, Earl of 1671-1713
Shenstone, William 1714-1763
Shirley, James 1596-1666
Sidney, Sir Philip 1554-1586
Skelton, John 1464?-1529
Smith, Adam 1723-1790
Smith, Captain John 1580-1631
Spee, Friedrich von 1591-1635
Spinoza, Benedictus de 1632-1677
Sprat, Thomas 1635-1713
Stanhope, Philip 1694-1773
Steele, Sir Richard 1672-1729
Suckling, Sir John 1609-1642
Swedenborg, Emanuel 1688-1772
Takeda Izumo 1690-1756
Tasso, Bernardo 1494-1569
Taylor, Edward 1645-1729
Taylor, Jeremy 1613-1667
Temple, Sir William 1629-1699
Tencin, Madame de 1682-1749
Teresa de Jesús 1515-1582
Testi, Fulvio 1593-1646
Thomas à Kempis 1380?-1471
Thomson, James 1700-1748
Tourneur, Cyril 1570-1626
Traherne, Thomas 1637-1674
Trai, Nguyen 1380-1442
Tristan 1601-1655
Tyndale, William 1494?-1536
Urquhart, Sir Thomas 1611-1660
Ussher, James 1581-1656
Vasari, Giorgio 1511-1574
Vaughan, Henry 1621-1695
Vaughan, Thomas 1622-1666
Vico, Giambattista 1668-1744
Villiers, George 1628-1687
Villon, François 1431-1463
Voltaire 1694-1778
Waller, Edmund 1606-1687
Walton, Izaak 1593-1683
Warburton, William 1698-1779
Warner, William 1558-1609
Warton, Thomas 1728-1790
Webster, John 1580-1638
Weise, Christian 1642-1708
Wesley, John 1703-1791
Whetstone, George 1544?-1587?
White, Gilbert 1720-1793
Wigglesworth, Michael 1631-1705
Williams, Roger 1603-1683
Winckelman, Johann Joachim 1717-1768
Winthrop, John 1588-1649
Wyatt, Sir Thomas 1503-1542
Yuan Mei 1716-1797
Zólkiewski, Stanislaw 1547-1620
Zrinyi, Miklos 1620-1664

Readers are cordially invited to suggest additional authors to the editors.

Michael Drayton

1563-1631

English poet and dramatist.

A skilled Elizabethan poet, Drayton is distinguished less by genius than by his consistently high level of achievement in virtually every poetic genre he attempted: the ode, eclogue, epistle, sonnet, fairy poem, and epic. His greatest poems are usually considered the frequently anthologized sonnet "Since there's no help, come let us kiss and part," the thematic collections *Englands Heroicall Epistles* and *The Muses Elizium,* the mock-heroic poem *Nimphidia, the Court of Fayrie,* and his long chorographic epic, *Poly-Olbion.* Despite the differing ing meters and forms of these works, each displays the essential qualities associated with Drayton's artistry: implicit dedication to his vocation and profound reverence for his native land. Recognized in his day as a poet worthy of comparison with his contemporaries Shakespeare, Edmund Spenser, and Ben Jonson, Drayton was later consigned to relative obscurity, but is respected today as a competent—and occasionally inspired—poet.

Drayton was born in Hartshill, Warwickshire into a prominent family of tradespeople. At ten he began service as a page in Sir Henry Goodere's household in nearby Polesworth; Sir Henry is believed responsible for much of Drayton's early education and introduction to the classics, and for encouraging the boy in his pronounced interest in crafting poetry. Biographers believe that Drayton fell in love with Sir Henry's daughter Anne, and surmise that is she whom he celebrated (under the name "Idea") as the ideal woman in his pastoral poems and love sonnets. Perhaps as early as the late 1580s and certainly by the early 1590s, Drayton moved to London to launch his career as a poet. His first work, a compendium of biblical paraphrases entitled *The Harmonie of the Church,* appeared in 1591 to little acclaim, for it was considered then, as it is now, undistinguished and antiquated. His next publication, however, established him as a learned and capable versifier; the pastoral series *Idea the Shepheards Garland,* while signaling his debt to Spenser's *Shepheardes Calendar* (1579), also earned Drayton personal recognition. For the remainder of the decade Drayton wrote love poetry and pastorals but also found success with historic verse, namely *Mortimeriados* and *Englands Heroicall Epistles.* Notwithstanding his popular success, Drayton's financial compensation was slight and circumstances forced the poet to work extensively during the years 1597 to 1602 for Philip Henslowe's theatrical companies. He assisted in the composition of a host of plays—perhaps as many as thirty—but the only extant piece is *The First Part of the True and Honorable Historie, of the Life of Sir John Old-Castle* (at one time believed written by Shakespeare), which was produced in 1599.

Shortly following the death in 1603 of Elizabeth I, Drayton, in obeisance to tradition, issued a commendatory poem to the new ruler, James I. However, his neglect to mention the glory of the late queen's reign displeased James and thus greatly hindered his chances for royal recognition, sponsorship, and advancement. Drayton's disappointment was somewhat relieved the same year, when his new patron, Sir Walter Aston, bestowed upon him the rank of esquire (a distinction of which the common-born poet was very proud). Nonetheless, the obscure, unpopular work of his next few years, which included

the satire *The Owle,* reflects his overall disappointment and resentment. However, in 1606 Drayton regained popular approval with his *Poemes Lyrick and Pastorall.* This collection contained the first Horatian odes to appear in English as well as revisions of some of his earlier works, for Drayton considered the task of revision essential as he mastered new levels of skill and aesthetic understanding. During the next several years he was occupied with the composition of his most ambitious work, *Poly-Olbion,* the first part of which he published in 1612. Intended as a patriotic paean to Britain, the work received small recognition beyond Drayton's literary circle (much to the poet's dismay and pique). He was far more successful in 1619 when he published his newly revised and expanded *Poems.* Three years later Drayton issued the second part of *Poly-Olbion,* explaining in a preface his intentions for the poem and venting his strong censure of those who had failed to appreciate the first part. In his last decade, Drayton published some of what critics consider his most original and technically perfect verse, including the fairy romance *Nimphidia* and the nymphal sequence *The Muses Elizium.* By the time of his death in 1631, Drayton, highly honored for his talent and respected for his conscientious dedication to his craft, was buried in Westminster Abbey beside Geoffrey Chaucer and Spenser.

The remarkable diversity of Drayton's work combined with his frequent and extensive revision creates difficulties for the scholar who seeks to describe Drayton's poetry succinctly. By turns a pastoralist, Elizabethan sonneteer, classical odist, and celebrator of Great Britain in epic, Drayton defies facile categorization. Still, Oliver Elton, a leading scholar of Drayton's work, has isolated one common thread running throughout his poetry: his devotion to his native land. As Elton has written: "No man tried in so many forms to utter the passion for England, the passion of England for itself." Drayton's many historical poems, including *Mortimeriados* (later revised as *The Barrons Wars*) and *The Battaile of Agincourt,* treat momentous events in British history. Even Drayton's pastorals, critics contend, are patriotic in the sense that his idyllic landscapes are recognizably English. Drayton's most overt panegyric to Britain is also the poem most closely associated with his name: *Poly-Olbion.* Although it is not generally considered his best, the poem is assuredly his longest and most ambitious: thirty "songs" of from 300 to 500 Alexandrine lines each, describing the topography, archaeology, history, and culture of England and Wales. (A planned inclusion of Scotland never materialized.) Using as his primary source antiquary William Camden's *Britannia* (sixth ed., 1607), Drayton documented with painstaking minuteness the land, history, and people of Great Britain, making frequent use of personification and lyric catalogue. He employed scholar John Selden to provide explanatory notes to his numerous historical and geographical allusions and an engraver to provide maps for each song. From its inception the work has had its detractors, who charge that the epic is too detailed and encumbered by awkward, windy grammatical passages—an inherent pitfall, some believe, of the Alexandrine form—and thus virtually impossible to read straight through from beginning to end. However, scholars today recognize *Poly-Olbion* as an ambitious project that, if uncomfortably lengthy, is nonetheless an astonishingly rich, exuberant, and thoroughly original achievement in English literature.

Drayton's interest in Britain's history is also evident in *Englands Heroicall Epistles,* a series of paired letters between famous English couples. This work represents a shift for Drayton from cautiously imitating such contemporary forms and trends as the pastoral eclogue and the love sonnet to cultivating ancient models (in this case Ovid's *Heroides*) and adapting them to suit the language, tastes, and common heritage of English people. Further, while *Heroides* contains the one-sided laments of a group of famous women, Drayton's *Epistles* presents paired letters, with the result that a complete dialogue is maintained and a more entertaining drama unfolded. As Barbara C. Ewell has written: "Instead of a single, idealized version of the past, *Englands Heroicall Epistles* offers a variety of interpreters and interpretations, none perfect or complete, but each fascinating, each illuminating its fraction of the whole of reality."

Of Drayton's other works, two late poems are considered of special importance: his fairy poem *Nimphidia* and the pastoral *The Muses Elizium.* Critics call *Nimphidia* an unusual poem, but an imaginative and enjoyable one. Kathleen Tillotson has commented that "in its peculiar blend of diminutive fairies and mock-heroic (and mock-romantic) adventures, it is original and unique." *The Muses Elizium* hearkens back to the pastoral subject matter and Spenserian influence of Drayton's earliest efforts, yet in its tone of peaceful reconciliation with an imperfect world and its mastery of syntax, rhythm, and thematic transition (a mastery which came late to Drayton, whose handling of poetic technicalities has frequently been deemed ragged or ambiguous in his other works), the work has been called Drayton's maturest and most fully realized. As Tillotson has stated: *"The Muses Elizium . . .* is the ideal culmination of his career; a vision as complete in its own way as Shakespeare's late plays. . . . Drayton has at last found a form entirely congenial to all his powers, and this late-found harmony releases his poetry into song, all the gnarls and knots of his style smoothed away."

During his lifetime, Drayton was renowned as the "golden-mouthed" poet. Most of his works met with popular approval, with the notable exception of *Poly-Olbion,* and even public indifference to that epic was tempered by the praise it received from Drayton's literary peers. However, Drayton's contemporaries on the whole preferred *Englands Heroicall Epistles* and *Nimphidia* to his other works, a judgment corroborated by subsequent critical history: as Drayton's reputation declined, only these two poems escaped the virtual eclipse of the others. For indeed the popular appeal of Drayton's works tapered off dramatically following his death and few remembered—much less read—the poet. Late seventeenth-century critics, when they spoke of Drayton at all, treated him as a literary curiosity: only forty years after Drayton's death, Edward Phillips referred to him as "antiquated" and to his work as "old fashion'd." In the middle of the eighteenth century, an edition of Drayton's collected works was published, prefaced by a laudatory survey of his poetry wherein the critic (probably Charles Coffey) asserted that "we need not wonder that he was in his Lifetime esteemed the Delight of the Muses, and one who did Honour to his Age and Country," but the new edition sparked only a limited revival of interest in Drayton's work and even this soon faded. In the nineteenth century, while he did not regain his stature as a popular poet, Drayton was praised by such eminent critics as Charles Lamb and George Saintsbury; the former, in a tribute to *Poly-Olbion,* honored Drayton as "Panegyrist of my native Earth," while the latter allowed that "he is a poet of surprisingly high merit." Further, as Russell Noyes has revealed in his study of Drayton's critical history, many of the leading poets of the century, including William Wordsworth, John Keats, and Alfred, Lord Tennyson, were acquainted with Drayton's poetry and to some extent indebted to it. The twentieth century has given rise to more investigative, in-depth appraisals of Drayton's poetry. Recent studies such as Ewell's of *Englands Heroicall Epistles* and Stella P. Revard's of *Poly-Olbion* indicate renewed critical interest in the themes, design, and poetics of these works, and many of Drayton's other works have received similar attention. In general, twentieth-century scholarship confirms a judgment figuratively articulated by William Hazlitt in the preceding century: "[Drayton's] mind is a rich marly soil that produces an abundant harvest, and repays the husbandman's toil, but few flaunting flowers, the garden's pride, grow in it, nor any poisonous weeds."

Thus, Drayton is respected as a journeyman poet, a highly competent and conscientious poet who, though he rises infrequently to genius, disappoints as rarely. Elton has maintained: "He seldom writes a perfect poem, or one without perfect lines." When evaluated against the masters of his own day, some claim that Drayton emerges as more than just a highly trained poet. His sonnets have been favorably compared with Shakespeare's, his odes with Jonson's, his pastorals with Spenser's; though his overall achievement is equal to none of these writers, nor that of his classical mentors, his poetical career represents one of the most sustained and distinguished in English history. In the words of Elton: "If he does not rank without question among the highest, he is an athlete, suspected of half-Olympian and half-terrestrial blood, who is of commanding stature and can lift many weighty burdens; with a sturdy, dignified beauty of his own, and a soft, musical grace; and speaking now and then with something of the divine accent.''

PRINCIPAL WORKS

The Harmonie of the Church. Containing the Spirituall Songes and Holy Hymnes, of Godly Men, Patriarkes and Prophetes: All, Sweetly Sounding, to the Praise and Glory of the Highest (poetry) 1591

Idea the Shepheards Garland, Fashioned in Nine Eglogs. Rowlands Sacrifice to the Nine Muses (poetry) 1593; also published in *Poemes Lyrick and Pastorall* as *Eglogs* [revised edition], 1606

Peirs Gaveston, Earle of Cornwall. His Life, Death, and Fortune (poetry) 1593

Ideas Mirrour. Amours in Quatorzains (poetry) 1594; also published as *Idea* [revised and enlarged editions], 1599, 1600, 1602, 1605, 1619

Endimion and Phoebe. Ideas Latmus (poetry) 1595; also published in *Poemes Lyrick and Pastorall* as *The Man in the Moone* [revised edition], 1606

Mortimeriados. The Lamentable Civell Warres of Edward the Second and the Barrons (poetry) 1596; also published as *The Barrons Wars in the Raigne of Edward the Second* [revised edition], 1602

Englands Heroicall Epistles (poetry) 1597; revised and enlarged editions, 1598, 1599, 1600

The First Part of the True and Honorable Historie, of the Life of Sir John Old-Castle, the Good Lord Cobham (drama) 1599

To the Majestie of King James (poetry) 1603

The Owle (poetry) 1604

Poems (poetry) 1605

Odes (poetry) 1606

Poems Lyrick and Pastorall (poetry) 1606

Poly-Olbion; or, a Chorographicall Description of Tracts, Rivers, Mountaines, Forests, and Other Parts of This Renowned Isle of Great Britaine, with Intermixture of the Most Remarkable Stories, Antiquities, Wonders, Rarityes, Pleasures, and Commodities of the Same: Digested in a Poem (poetry) 1612

Poems (poetry) 1619

The Second Part; or, A Continuance of Poly-Olbion from the Eighteenth Song. Containing All the Tracts, Rivers, Mountaines, and Forrests: Intermixed with the Most Remarkable Stories, Antiquities, Wonders, Rarities, Pleasures, and Commodities of the East, and Northerne Parts of this Isle, Lying betwixt the Two Famous Rivers of Thames, and Tweed (poetry) 1622

The Battaile of Agincourt (poetry) 1627

Elegies upon Sundry Occasions (poetry) 1627; published in *The Battaile of Agincourt*

The Moone-Calfe (poetry) 1627; published in *The Battaile of Agincourt*

Nimphidia, the Court of Fayrie (poetry) 1627; published in *The Battaile of Agincourt*

The Shepheards Sirena (poetry) 1627; published in *The Battaile of Agincourt*

The Muses Elizium, Lately Discovered, by a New Way over Parnassus. The Passages Therein, Being the Subject of Ten Sundry Nymphalls (poetry) 1630

The Works of Michael Drayton. 5 vols. (poetry and drama) 1931-41

WILLIAM ALEXANDER   (poem date 1600)

[*Alexander, a friend of Drayton, was a Scottish poet, dramatist, and statesman. His chief works include the sonnet collection Aurora (1604) and the long poem Doomsday (1614). In the following poem (first published in the 1600 edition of Englands Heroicall Epistles), Alexander salutes the Ovidian cast of the work.*]

> Now I perceive *PYTHAGORAS* divin'd,
> When he that mocked *Maxim* did maintaine,
> That Spirits once spoyl'd, revested were againe,
> Though chang'd in shape, remaining one in Mind;
> These Love-sicke Princes passionate estates,
> Who feeling reades, he cannot but allow,
> That *OVIDS* Soule revives in *DRAYTON* now,
> Still learn'd in Love, still rich in rare Conceits,
> This pregnant Spirit affecting further Skill,
> Oft alt'ring Forme, from vulgar Wits retir'd,
> In divers Idyoms mightily admir'd,
> Did prosecute that sacred Studie still;
>   While to a full Perfection now attain'd,
>   He sings so sweetly, that himselfe is stain'd.

> *William Alexander, '' 'Englands Heroicall Epistles':*
> *To M. Michael Drayton,'' in* The Works of Michael
> Drayton, *Vol. II, edited by J. William Hebel, Basil*
> *Blackwell, 1932, p. 131.*

J. SELDEN   (poem date 1610)

[*An English historian, antiquary, and statesman, Selden wrote the comprehensive, scholarly annotations to the first part of Poly-Olbion. In the following poem, which was included in a 1610 edition of Drayton's Poems, Selden addresses the poet, according him high praise.*]

> I must admire thee (but to praise were vaine,
> What ev'ry tasting palat so approves)
> Thy Martiall *Pyrrhique*, and thy *Epique* straine
> Digesting *Warres* with heart-uniting *Loves;*
> The two first Authors of what is compos'd
> In this round Systeme *All;* it's ancient lore
> (All Arts in *Discords* and *Concents* are clos'd.
> And when unwinged soules the Fates restore
> To th' earth for reparation of their flights,
> The first *Musicians, Schollers, Lovers* make;
> The next ranke destinate to *Mars* his Knights;
> The following rabble meaner titles take)
> I see thy Temples crown'd with *Phœbus* rites:
>   Thy *Bay's* to th'eye, with *Lilly* mixt and *Rose,*
>   As to the eare a *Diapason* close.

> *J. Selden, ''Upon the 'Barons Warres', the 'Epistles'*
> *and 'Sonnets','' in* The Works of Michael Drayton,
> *Vol. II, edited by J. William Hebel, Basil Blackwell,*
> *1932, p. 8.*

MICHAEL DRAYTON   (essay date 1612)

[*The following excerpt is taken from Drayton's ''To the Generall Reader'' prefaced to the 1612 edition of the first part of Poly-Olbion. Here, he challenges his readers to exert themselves to appreciate the poem despite its difficulties. That Drayton's audience failed to meet his expectations is apparent from his address to the reader of the second part of Poly-Olbion (see essay dated 1622).*]

In publishing this Essay of my Poeme [*Poly-Olbion*], there is this great disadvantage against me; that it commeth out at this time, when Verses are wholly deduc't to Chambers, and nothing esteem'd in this lunatique Age, but what is kept in Cabinets, and must only passe by Transcription; In such a season, when

Map from Poly-Olbion *(1612)*

the Idle Humerous world must heare of nothing, that either savors of Antiquity, or may awake it to seeke after more, then dull and slothfull ignorance may easily reach unto: These, I say, make much against me; and especially in a Poeme, from any example, either of Ancient, or Modern, that have proved in this kind: whose unusuall tract may perhaps seeme difficult, to the female Sex; yea, and I feare, to some that think themselves not meanly learned, being not rightly inspired by the Muses: such I meane, as had rather read the fantasies of forraine inventions, then to see the Rarities and Historie of their owne Country delivered by a true native Muse. Then, whosoever thou be, possest with such stupidity and dulnesse, that, rather then thou wilt take paines to search into ancient and noble things, choosest to remaine in the thicke fogges and mists of ignorance, as neere the common Lay-stall of a Citie; refusing to walke forth into the *Tempe* and Feelds of the Muses, where through most delightfull Groves the Angellique harmony of Birds shall steale thee to the top of an easie hill, where in artificiall caves, cut out of the most naturall Rock, thou shalt see the ancient people of this Ile delivered thee in their lively images: from whose height thou mai'st behold both the old and later times, as in thy prospect, lying farre under thee; then convaying thee downe by a soule-pleasing Descent through delicate embrodered Meadowes, often veined with gentle gliding Brooks; in which thou maist fully view the dainty Nymphes in their simple naked bewties, bathing them in Crystalline streames; which shall lead thee, to most pleasant Downes, where harmlesse Shepheards are, some exercising their pipes, some singing roundelaies, to their gazing flocks: If as, I say, thou hadst rather, (because it asks thy labour) remaine, where thou wert, then straine thy selfe to walke forth with the Muses; the fault proceeds from thy idlenesse, not from any want in my industrie. . . . Thus wishing thee thy hearts desire, and committing my Poeme to thy charitable censure, I take my leave. (pp. v-vi)

> *Michael Drayton, "To the Generall Reader," in his* The Works of Michael Drayton: Poly-Olbion, Vol. IV, *edited by J. William Hebel, Basil Blackwell, 1933, pp. v-vi.*

MICHAEL DRAYTON   (essay date 1622)

[Drayton was hurt and disappointed by the tepid response to the first part of Poly-Olbion, *attributing it to his readers' ignorance and failure to "straine [themselves] to walke forth with the Muses" (see excerpt dated 1612). In his address to the reader of the second part of* Poly-Olbion, *curtly titled "To Any That Will Read It," Drayton expresses his outrage over the unenthusiastic public response to the poem and slings a few barbs at his unappreciative audience.]*

When I first undertook this Poem [**Poly-Olbion**], or, as some very skilful in this kind have pleased to term it, this Herculean labour, I was by some virtuous friends persuaded, that I should receive much comfort and encouragement therein; and for these reasons: First, that it was a new, clear, way, never before gone by any; then, that it contained all the Delicacies, Delights, and Rarities of this renowned Isle, interwoven with the Histories of the Britans, Saxons, Normans, and the later English: And further that there is scarcely any of the Nobility or Gentry of this land, but that he is some way or other by his Blood interested therein. But it hath fallen out otherwise; for instead of that comfort, which my noble friends (from the freedom of their spirits) proposed as my due, I have met with barbarous ignorance, and base detraction; such a cloud hath the Devil drawn over the world's judgment, whose opinion is in few years fallen so far below all ballatry, that the lethargy is incurable: nay, some of the Stationers, that had the selling of the First Part of this Poem, because it went not so fast away in the sale, as some of their beastly and abominable trash, (a shame both to our language and nation) have either despitefully left out, or at least carelessly neglected the Epistles to the Readers, and so have cozened the buyers with unperfected books; which these that have undertaken the Second Part, have been forced to amend in the First, for the small number that are yet remaining in their hands. And some of our outlandish, unnatural English, (I know not how otherwise to express them) stick not to say that there is nothing in this Island worthy studying for, and take a great pride to be ignorant in any thing thereof; for these, since they delight in their folly, I wish it may be hereditary from them to their posterity, that their children may be begg'd for fools to the fifth generation, until it may be beyond the memory of man to know that there was ever other of their families: neither can this deter me from going on with Scotland, if means and time do not hinder me, to perform as much as I have promised in my First Song:

> Till through the sleepy main, to *Thuly* I have gone,
> And seen the Frozen Isles, the cold *Deucalidon,*
> Amongst whose iron Rocks, grim *Saturn* yet remains
> Bound in those gloomy caves with adamantine chains.

And as for those cattle whereof I spake before, *Odi profanum vulgus, et arceo* [''I loathe the uncouth, vulgar throng, and I keep them at a distance''], of which I account them, be they never so great, and so I leave them. To my friends, and the lovers of my labours, I wish all happiness. (pp. ix-x)

> *Michael Drayton, ''To Any That Will Read It,'' in his* The Second Part; or, A Continuance of Poly-Olbion from the Eighteenth Song, *John Marriott, John Grismand, and Thomas Dewe, 1622, pp. ix-x.*

WILLIAM BROWNE   (poem date 1622)

[*A minor English poet, Browne is remembered for his* Britannia's Pastorals *(1613-16). In the following tributary poem to his friend, originally published with the second part of* Poly-Olbion *in 1622, he hails Drayton as one of the last of the great Elizabethan poets.*]

> Englands brave *Genius,* raise thy head; and see,
> We have a *Muse* in this mortalitie
> Of *Vertue* yet survives; All met not Death,
> When wee intoomb'd our deare *Elizabeth.*
> Immortall *Sydney,* honoured *Colin Clout,*
> Presaging what wee feele, went timely out.
> Then why lives *Drayton,* when the *Times* refuse,
> Both *Meanes* to live, and *Matter* for a *Muse?*
> Onely without *Excuse* to leave us quite,
> And tell us, Durst we act, he durst to write.

Now, as the people of a famish'd *Towne,*
Receiving no *Supply,* seeke up and downe
For mouldy Corne, and Bones long cast aside,
Wherewith their hunger may bee satisfide:
(Small store now left) we are inforc'd to prie
And search the darke Leaves of Antiquitie
For some good *Name,* to raise our *Muse* againe,
In this her *Crisis,* whose harmonious straine
Was of such compasse, that no other Nation
Durst ever venture on a sole Translation;
Whilst our full language, Musicall, and hie,
Speakes as themselves their best of *Poesie.*
   Drayton, amongst the worthi'st of all those,
The glorious *Laurell,* or the *Cyprian Rose*
Have ever crown'd, doth claime in every Lyne,
An equall honor from the sacred *Nyne:*
For if old *Time* could like the restlesse Maine,
Roule himselfe backe into his Spring againe,
And on his wings beare this admired *Muse,*
For *Ovid, Virgil, Homer,* to peruse.
They would confesse, that never happier *Pen,*
Sung of his *Loves,* his *Countrey,* and the *Men.*

> *William Browne, ''To My Honor'd Friend Mr. Drayton,'' in* The Works of Michael Drayton: Poly-Olbion, Vol. IV, *edited by J. William Hebel, Basil Blackwell, 1933, p. 393.*

BEN JONSON   (poem date 1627)

[*The first (though unofficial) poet laureate of England, Jonson was among the most prominent writers of the Elizabethan Age. He is especially esteemed for such satirical plays as* Every Man in His Humor *(1598),* Volpone *(1605-06), and* The Alchemist *(1610). He also distinguished himself as a writer of court masques and in several varieties of verse, displaying always an unrivaled classical learning. His poem, ''The Vision of Ben Jonson, on the Muses of His Friend M. Drayton,'' was first published in* The Battaile of Agincourt *in 1627. While some critics believe that Jonson's admiration for Drayton and his work was sincere, others detect more than a hint of irony in the following lines.*]

> It hath beene question'd, MICHAEL, if I bee
> A Friend at all; or, if at all, to thee:
>   Because, who make the question, have not seene
> Those ambling visits, passe in verse, betweene
> Thy *Muse,* and mine, as they expect. 'Tis true:
> You have not writ to me, nor I to you;
> And, though I now begin, 'tis not to rub
> Hanch against Hanch, or raise a riming *Club*
> About the towne: this reck'ning I will pay,
> Without conferring symboles. This's my day.
>   It was no Dreame! I was awake, and saw!
> Lend me thy voyce, O FAME, that I may draw
> Wonder to truth! and have my Vision hoorld,
> Hot from thy trumpet, round, about the world.
>   I saw a Beauty from the Sea to rise,
> That all Earth look'd on; and that earth, all Eyes!
> It cast a beame as when the chear-full Sun
> Is fayre got up, and day some houres begun!
> And fill'd an Orbe as circular, as heaven!
> The Orbe was cut forth into Regions seaven.
> And those so sweet, and well proportion'd parts,
> As it had beene the circle of the Arts!
> When, by thy bright **Ideas** standing by,
> I found it pure, and perfect *Poësy,*
> There read I, streight, thy learned **Legends** three,
> Heard the soft ayres, between our Swaynes & thee,
> Which made me thinke, the old *Theocritus,*
> Or Rurall *Virgil* come, to pipe to us!
> But then, thy' epistolar *Heroick* Songs,
> Their loves, their quarrels, jealousies, and wrongs,

Did all so strike me, as I cry'd, who can
With us be call'd, the *Naso,* but this man?
And looking up, I saw *Minervas* fowle,
Pearch'd over head, the wise *Athenian* Owle:
I thought thee then our *Orpheus,* that wouldst try
Like him, to make the ayre, one volary:
And I had stil'd thee, *Orpheus,* but before
My lippes could forme the voyce, I heard that Rore,
And Rouze, the Marching of a mighty force,
Drums against Drums, the neighing of the Horse,
The Fights, the Cryes, and wondring at the Jarres
I saw, and read, it was thy **Barons Warres!**
O, how in those, dost thou instruct these times,
That Rebells actions, are but valiant crimes!
And caried, though with shoute, and noyse, confesse
A wild, and an authoriz'd wickednesse!
Sayst thou so, *Lucan?* But thou scornst to stay
Under one title. Thou hast made thy way
And flight about the Ile, well neare, by this,
In thy admired *Periégesis,*
Or universall circumduction
Of all that reade thy **Poly-Olbyon.**
That reade it? that are ravish'd! such was I
With every song, I sweare, and so would dye:
But that I heare, againe, thy Drum to beate
A better cause, and strike the bravest heate
That ever yet did fire the *English* blood!
Our right in *France!* if ritely understood.
There, thou art *Homer!* Pray thee, use the stile
Thou hast deserv'd: And let me reade the while
Thy Catalogue of Ships, exceeding his,
Thy list of aydes, and force, for so it is:
The Poets act! and for his Country's sake
Brave are the Musters, that the Muse will make.
And when he ships them where to use their Armes,
How do his trumpets breath! What loud alarmes!
Looke, how we read the Spartans were inflam'd
With bold *Tyrtæus* verse, when thou art nam'd,
So shall our *English* Youth urge on, and cry
An *Agincourt,* an *Agincourt,* or dye.
This booke! it is a *Catechisme* to fight,
And will be bought of every Lord, and Knight,
That can but reade; who cannot, may in prose
Get broken peeces, and fight well by those.
The miseries of *Margaret* the Queene
Of tender eyes will more be wept, then seene:
I feele it by mine owne, that over flow,
And stop my sight, in every line I goe.
But then refreshed, with thy **Fayerie Court,**
I looke on *Cynthia,* and *Sirenas* sport,
As, on two flowry Carpets, that did rise,
And with their grassie greene restor'd mine eyes.
Yet give mee leave, to wonder at the birth
Of thy strange **Moon-Calfe,** both thy straine of mirth,
And Gossip-got acquaintance, as, to us
Thou hadst brought *Lapland,* or old *Cobalus,*
Empusa, Lamia, or some Monster, more
Then *Affricke* knew, or the full *Grecian* store!
I gratulate it to thee, and thy *Ends,*
To all thy vertuous, and well chosen Friends,
Onely my losse is, that I am not there:
And, till I worthy am to wish I were,
I call the world, that envies mee, to see
If I can be a Friend, and Friend to thee.

(pp. 3-5)

Ben Jonson, "The Vision of Ben Jonson, on the Muses of His Friend M. Drayton," in The Works of Michael Drayton, Vol. III, edited by J. William Hebel, Basil Blackwell, 1932, pp. 3-5.

MICHAEL DRAYTON   (poem date 1627)

[*In the following excerpt from the poem "To My Most Dearely-Loved Friend Henery Reynolds Esquire, of Poets and Poesie" (originally published in 1627 with* The Battaile of Agincourt), *Drayton describes his early love for poetry.*]

For from my cradle (you must know that) I,
Was still inclin'd to noble Poesie,
And when that once *Pueriles* I had read,
And newly had my *Cato* construed,
In my small selfe I greatly marveil'd then,
Amongst all other, what strange kinde of men
These Poets were; And pleased with the name,
To my milde Tutor merrily I came,
(For I was then a proper goodly page,
Much like a Pigmy, scarse ten yeares of age)
Clasping my slender armes about his thigh.
O my deare master! cannot you (quoth I)
Make me a Poet, doe it; if you can,
And you shall see, Ile quickly be a man,
Who me thus answered smiling, boy quoth he,
If you'le not play the wag, but I may see
You ply your learning, I will shortly read
Some Poets to you; *Phœbus* be my speed,
Too't hard went I, when shortly he began,
And first read to me honest *Mantuan,*
Then *Virgils Eglogues,* being entred thus,
Me thought I straight had mounted *Pegasus,*
And in his full Careere could make him stop,
And bound upon *Parnassus* by-clift top.
I scornd your ballet then though it were done
And had for Finis, *William Elderton.*

(pp. 226-27)

Michael Drayton, "To my Most Dearely-Loved Friend Henery Reynolds Esquire, of Poets and Poesie," in his The Works of Michael Drayton, Vol. III, edited by J. William Hebel, Basil Blackwell, 1932, pp. 226-31.

WILLIAM DRUMMOND   (letter date 1631?)

[*Drummond was a Scottish man of letters who is best remembered for his political and elegiac poetry and a prose meditation on death. He was a correspondent of Drayton, although the two never met. In the following excerpt from a letter to the Earl of Stirling, apparently written soon after Drayton's death, Drummond expresses his sorrow.*]

The Death of M. D. your great freind, hath beene very greevous to all those which love the Muses heere; cheeflie that hee should have left this World before he had perfected the Northern part of his **Polyolbion**: that it brake off that noble worke, of the Northern part of the **Polyolbion** which had beene no litle honour to our Country. All wee can doe to him is to honour his Mem-orye. (p. 93)

If the date of a Picture of his be just, he hath lived three score and eight yeeres, but shall live by all likelihead so long as men speake English after his death. I, who never saw him, save by his letters and poesie, scarce beleive hee is yet dead; and would fain misbelieve veritye, if it were possible. (p. 94)

William Drummond, in a letter to the Earl of Stirling in 1631? in Archaeologia Scotica, Vol. IV, 1857, pp. 93-4.

EDWARD PHILLIPS   (essay date 1675)

[*Phillips was an English literary scholar whose major works include a philological dictionary entitled* The New World of English

Words *(1658) and the biographical survey* Theatrum Poetarum *(1675). In the following excerpt from the latter work, taken from the 1800 edition augmented by Sir Samuel Edgerton Brydges and entitled* Theatrum Poetarum Anglicanorum, *Phillips provides a terse judgment of Drayton.*]

Michael Drayton, contemporary of Spencer and Sir Philip Sydney, and for fame and renown in poetry, not much inferior in his time to either: however, he seems somewhat antiquated in the esteem of the more curious of these times, especially in his *Polyolbion,* the old fashion'd kind of verse whereof, seem somewhat to diminish that respect which was formerly paid to the subject, as being both pleasant and elaborate, and thereupon thought worthy to be commented upon by that once walking library of our nation, Selden; his *England's Heroical Epistles,* are more generally lik'd; and to such as love the pretty chat of nymphs and shepherds, his *Nymphals* and other things of that nature, cannot be unpleasant. (p. 262)

> Edward Phillips, "Michael Drayton," in his Theatrum Poetarum Anglicanorum, *edited by Sir Samuel Edgerton Brydges, J. White, 1800, pp. 262-67.*

CHARLES COFFEY? (essay date 1745?)

[*Coffey was an Irish dramatist whose best-known play is the ballad opera* The Devil to Pay; or, The Wives Metamorphosed *(1731). He is thought to be the editor of* The Works of Michael Drayton, Esq., *the first edition of Drayton's collected works to appear after the poet's death (Coffey's own death in 1745 preceded by three years the publication of the work). In the following excerpt from his introduction to the work, the critic admiringly surveys Drayton's oeuvre.*]

It is not a little strange that a Person who raised to himself so high a Reputation by his Writings, and who was besides so great a Lover of his Country, and so much esteemed by Men of the best Heads and brightest Wits of the Age in which he lived, should, notwithstanding, have so little Regard shewn to his Memory, as to have scarce a single Incident of his Life recorded by any other Pen than his own. (p. 1)

[*Drayton's*] first Essays were the natural Flights of a young and sprightly Genius, well seasoned with Learning, and not at all deficient in Judgment; so that he had no Reason in his riper Years to be ashamed of these early Performances, as the Reader will perceive by consulting his *Idea* and his *Elegies,* most of which were written when he was a young man. In these he discovered much of that laudable Fondness for his Country, which is incident to every good Mind, as particularly appears by the following short and beautiful Poem on the River *Ankor,* which runs through the Forest of *Arden,* in *Warwickshire,* the Scene of his juvenile Pleasures, and of his first Correspondence with the Muses, which with respect to the natural and unaffected Vivacity of the Thoughts, Elegance of Composition, and Harmony of Numbers, might pass for no mean Testimony of Poetic Genius even at this Day. The Lines are these;

> Clear *Ankor,* on whose silver-sanded Shore
> My soul shrin'd Saint, my fair *Idea* lies,
> O blessed Brook, whose milk-white Swans adore
> Thy crystal Stream refined by her Eyes,
>
> Where sweet myrrh-breathing Zephyr in the Spring
> Gently distills his Nectar-dropping Showers,
> Where Nightingales in *Arden* sit and sing
> Amongst the dainty Dew-impearled Flowers;
> Say thus, fair Brook, when thou shalt see thy Queen,

> Lo, here thy Shepherd spent his wand'ring Years;
> And in these Shades, dear Nymph, he oft had been,
> And here to thee he sacrific'd his Tears:
> Fair *Arden,* thou my *Tempe* art alone,
> And thou, sweet *Ankor,* art my *Helicon.*

His Affection for Poetry, however strong, did not hinder his Application to other Branches of Learning; but more especially to History, and particularly that of his own Country, in which he became as knowing as any Man of his Time; and with great Industry and Pains set himself to enquire into the secret Springs and Motions, by which the most remarkable Events, and most surprising Revolutions had been brought about. In these Enquiries, it was natural for him to take Notice of the singular Turns of Fortune that had befallen the most eminent Persons flourishing in different Ages; and where he found their Stories had not been fully represented to the World, or their Characters set in a true Light, he was desirous of rendering that Service to Posterity, and of preserving from Oblivion the Actions of those whose Persons had been persecuted by Fortune.

He had before him the Example of *Lydgate,* the famous Monk of *Bury,* who translated into *English* Verse the celebrated Work of *Boccace;* and the Continuation of what Work under the Title of *The Mirrour for Magistrates,* written by some of the prime Wits in the Reign of Queen *Elizabeth;* wherein this Method of celebrating famous Persons is chiefly applied to those who have flourished in this Island, and has undoubtedly the Source of our Historical Plays.

This it was that put him upon writing his *Legends,* of which he first published three, and then added a fourth.... These Historical Poems, adorned and heightened with all the Ornaments of a lively Fancy, and thick sown with short judicious Reflections, flowing from a sound Judgment in Men and Things, were received as they deserved with universal Applause, and gained their Author the Reputation which he had so long sought, of being a great Poet, and this too from the best Judges, of whom there were not a few in those Times.

This emboldened him to take a higher Flight, and to attempt a new Kind of Writing, at least in our Language. These he entitled *England's Heroical Epistles.* As to the Matter of them, it was all borrowed from true History, and the principal Facts in them are supported by Annotations drawn from the Chronicles that were then published. As for the Form, he professes to have imitated *Ovid,* and it must be allowed that the Characters are finely supported.

This Work, which appeared, as we learn from the Notes, while the Earl of *Essex* was in the Height of Favour with Queen *Elizabeth,* added much to that Fame which he had already acquired; and procured him, according to the Mode of that Age, the Commendations of the greatest Wits in his own Country and in *Scotland:* amongst the former was Sir *Edmund Scory;* and amongst the latter Sir *William Alexander* [see poem dated 1600], afterwards Earl of *Sterling,* who was himself one of the finest Gentlemen, as well as one of the politest Scholars and best Poets that Kingdom had to boast: so that now the Character of our Author was thoroughly established, and the Praises bestowed upon him incited him to proceed in his Career, and to undertake a larger and more difficult Work, in which he might have an Opportunity of shewing to how good Purpose he had spent his Time in the Study of *Homer* and *Virgil,* those two great Lights of *Greek* and *Roman* Poesy; and how much he possessed of that Fire and Spirit which enabled *Lucan* to raise his own Reputation by singing his Country's Ruin.

This was his Historical Poem of the **Barons Wars,** divided into *six Cantos,* containing the History of the Reign of *Edward* the Second, with which he had rendered himself perfectly acquainted, by the Perusal of all our ancient Authors. (pp. 3-7)

The Characters are finely drawn, and I am satisfied very justly too; for besides his own Knowledge in the History of *England,* which was very great, he had the Advice and Assistance of the most able and knowing Men of that Time; when the collecting and comparing our ancient and original Writers was a favourite and fashionable Stile.

It is therefore much to be regretted, that these Cantos were not illustrated by Annotations in the same Manner as his *Epistles,* from whence we might have been more particularly acquainted with the Grounds on which he went; since that he seldom or never proceeded without, appears from the Pains he took to compare Sir *Thomas More*'s Description of the Person of *Jane Shore* with her original Picture, of which he has given us a curious and exact Account, that had been otherwise buried in Oblivion.

As to the Manner of his Poem, it was written originally in Stanzas of seven Lines, which he afterwards changed very judiciously for the Octavo, or more musical Stanza of eight Lines. As he followed the *Italian* Mode in the Structure of his Verse, so he followed it likewise in the Division of his Work, not into Books but into Cantos; being led thereto, as he tells us himself in his learned Preface, by the Example of *Edmund Spenser.* It is no Wonder therefore, that a Work written with so much Art as well as Truth, and which was equally valuable whether considered as a Poem or a History, was universally admired in an Age when there flourished so many Persons of true Taste and exalted Genius, who knew how to set a just Price upon the Labour both of the Poet and Historian. (pp. 8-9)

The next Thing he published was the largest and most elaborate Performance of his whole Life, being the first Part of his **Poly-Olbion,** containing eighteen Songs. It was published in 1612, in Folio. This Work, which is a Poetical Description of *England,* is one of the most learned and laborious, as well as one of the most ingenious entertaining and accurate Pieces that is to be found in our Language; and therefore the great SELDEN did not disdain to let his Commentaries accompany the Songs of his Friend, which as they are exceeding judicious, and contain an infinite Variety of curious and recondite Learning, so they gave such a Weight and Authority to this Piece, as have supported it in the Esteem of all good Judges above a Century.

To say the Truth, and what is barely the Truth, it is not easy to conceive a harder Task than that which our Author imposed upon himself when he set about this Undertaking; and yet it would be full as great a Difficulty to imagine a Thing of this Kind brought to a higher Degree of Perfection. This will appear still more wonderful to the critical and learned Reader, when he considers the Time in which it was wrote, and how few Helps the Author had towards compleating so vast a Design in comparison of what he might have had, if he had lived in later Times. The true Way of judging of the Merit of this Book, is to compare it with *Cambden*'s celebrated Work in Prose, from whence it will appear how little Mr. *Drayton* borrowed from others, and what infinite variety of curious Facts he inserted from our old Manuscript History, and how judiciously they are applied. We need not therefore be surprized that not only the Writers next in Point of Time, such as *Weever* and *Fuller,* borrow from him so largely, or the later Antiquaries,

such as *Musgrave, Kennet, Wood,* and *Hearne,* cite him as a most authentick Author. (pp. 12-13)

The second Part of the **Poly-Olbion,** containing the twelve last Songs, was published ten Years after the former; to render the Work in every Respect compleat, except having such a Body of learned Notes as accompanied the former, of which if either Mr. *Selden* had then had Leisure, or any other Antiquary of great Abilities would have taken the Pains, they had undoubtedly been very capable of the like Illustrations. As it was, they were celebrated by *Ben Johnson* [see poem dated 1627] and other excellent Judges, as equal in every Respect to the Hopes that had been raised by the former Part, and will certainly do Honour to the Author's Memory, as long as there are any who love and honour their native Country so much as to make it their Business to enquire into her past as well as present State; for such will find themselves under a Necessity of recurring to Mr. *Drayton,* who as he had no Example, except it may be one or two short *Latin* Poems, by the incomparable *John Leland,* so he has not hitherto had any Imitator, notwithstanding the Praises his Work obtained, and the high Price it has born.

The **Battle of Agincourt** was the next Work our Author published, which is an Historical Poem of that glorious Expedition of King *Henry* the Fifth, by which he laid the Foundation of the Conquest of *France,* which he afterwards happily achieved: it is written in the same *Stanza* with his **Barons Wars,** but being one single Action is not divided into *Cantos.* In this, as in all his other Works, the Author pays a deep Respect to History, and varies from it as little as possible.... (pp. 14-15)

In this Poem of our Author, the Language is much purer and more correct than in his former Writings: but there are not so many Reflections, or such high Flights of Fancy as in his preceding Pieces. (p. 15)

This was followed by his **Miseries of Queen Margaret,** the unfortunate Wife of that still more unfortunate Monarch *Henry* VI. It is written in the same *Stanza* with the former, and is like it an entire Piece, tho' much the larger of the two; the Design of this Poem is to shew "that Calamities are, generally speaking, either a just Punishment of Vices, or the natural Consequences of Indiscretions; from which, those who move in a superior Sphere are so far from being secure, that on the contrary they stand but so much the more exposed, and usually feel the quickest and severest Reverses of Fortune." It is for this Reason that we find more Reflections in this than in the former, more indeed than I think are to be found in any other of his Works; but as they are short, judicious, and perfectly well applied, they are so far from being Blemishes to this Poem, that they may be justly stiled its greatest Beauties, as they rise naturally from the Subject, and are perfectly consistent with the Author's Purpose.

He had touched upon this Topick before in his **Heroick Epistles;** and both here and there he keeps close to Historical Facts, and shews that *Truth* is as susceptible of the Graces of Poetry as *Fiction;* and that it is in the Power of a great Genius to move the Passions as strongly by a natural Representation of Facts that have really happened, as it is possible to do by having Recourse to Invention; which is an Excellency so much the more worth observing, as it is certainly very uncommon; for as our Author and some other judicious Critics observed, tho' there is much sound Sense, great Smoothness of Numbers, and a commendable Correctness of Language in Mr. *Daniel*'s Historical Poems, yet they have for all that an apparent Flatness and a perfectly Prosaic Turn.

We come now to the lighter Works of our Author; which, however, are very far from being inferior to the rest; indeed so far from it, that if I durst trust my own Judgment, I would venture to assure the Reader that there are hardly any finer Poems in our Language than those three of which I am next to speak. His **Nymphidia, or Court of Fairy,** is in every Respect singular and exquisite. It is a *Fairy Tale* most happily imagined, written with great Fire and Spirit, heightened by the most pleasing Imagery, most admirably conducted, and very artfully concluded. There is in it all that Enthusiasm, which is, properly speaking, the Soul of Poetry, and of which our Author had given but few Specimens in his former Works. Hence it appears that in all his other Pieces, that grave and solemn Air, that strict Regard to Characters, and prudent Attention to his Subjects, were all the Effects of a well-regulated Judgment, and not at all owing to a Barrenness of Invention, Want of Genius, or an exhausted Fancy. For in this single Poem we may discern the Liveliness of *Spenser*, the happy Power of *Shakespear*, and all the Skill of *Johnson*.

There is besides all this, a Vein of Irony or Humour runs through the whole that seems peculiar to our Author, and of which we could never have imagined him Master from the Perusal of his larger Works. The Measure of the Verse is very luckily adapted to the Nature of the Tale, and tho' the Language is intermixed with many old Words and obsolete Phrases, yet these are introduced on purpose, and with such Dexterity, that they give a certain Air of Antiquity to the Narration, which is none of its meanest Beauties. There is no doubt that many of our modern Readers will imagine that I am strongly prejudiced in our Author's Favour, and that I have carried my Commendations of this Fairy Tale much beyond its real Merit; to these, all I can say is this, that if they will peruse it with a reasonable Degree of Attention, they will find I have rather fallen short of Truth, and this too without making any Allowances for the Time in which it was written, which for any thing in the Sentiment, Method, or Diction, might have been no longer ago than yesterday.

His Pastorals intituled **The Quest of Cynthia** and **The Shepherd's Sirena,** are exquisite Performances, and will appear such to every true Judge, as they have all the Beauties, and all the Graces of which that Kind of Poetry is susceptible. They have each a little Plot, finely imagined, regularly conducted, and prettily concluded. The Numbers are so just, so elegant, and so flowing, that perhaps we have not in this Respect two finer Pieces in our Tongue. There is indeed a little Sprinkling of antiquated Words, but the Choice is so judiciously made that it does not obscure the Sense, as in *Spenser* often, and sometimes even in *Shakespear,* but gives it that natural Rudeness, that pleasing Rusticity, which makes the *Doric* Dialect so charming in the Works of *Theocritus*, and is indeed essentially necessary to Pastoral.

In a Word, and not to dwell too long upon Pieces we should not have dwelt on at all, if it had not been to excite the Reader's Curiosity for his own Profit, let us conclude with observing, that these are in all Respects our Author's Master-Pieces, the perfectest Poems that ever fell from his Pen, and which fully refute the Notion that the Harmony of Numbers in *English* Poesy was unknown 'till *Waller* stole the Secret from *Fairfax;* whereas any Critic who has an Ear, must allow that there is hardly a Poem in *Waller* more harmonious than these of Mr. *Drayton,* or in every other Circumstance more correct.

At length we are arrived at what seems to have been his latest Work, which is his **Moon-Calf,** a Satire in which surely there wants not either Wit, Spirit, or that warm Poetic Madness, which himself has elsewhere celebrated, as that which distinguishes the true *Genius,* and can never be either counterfeited or imitated. He feigns that the WORLD was in Labour, and brought forth by the EVIL FIEND an Androgynous Monster, which being divided, produced an *effeminate* Man, and a *masculine* Woman. He takes Occasion from thence to inveigh bitterly against the Manners of the Age in which he liv'd, and to lay open its Vices, not with Freedom barely, but with Fury. In short, his Indignation, or to speak plainly, his Resentment, is very conspicuous, and we cannot help discerning how much his Spleen is gratified, while he seems to be intent only on the great Work of Reformation.

This, however, is no Detriment to his Reader; it adds to the Poignancy of his Satire, and gives such a Fertility to his Invention as is truly amazing, but it must be acknowledged that there is a Roughness in the Verse, perhaps beyond what even Satire might excuse; but which, however, may be in some Measure qualified, if we consider this Performance as an absolute *Original,* for which the Author could not have the least Hint from any of our old Poets, or from his Cotemporaries, any more than from the Ancients; that the Fiction is extremely bold, breaks out into a vast Extent, and is notwithstanding thoroughly executed. It was the last Blaze of his Poetic Flame, and therefore glaringly strong, and glittering with an irregular Splendor. (pp. 15-20)

[His] *Elegies* were written at several Times, and upon several Occasions; and therefore no wonder that they are written in different Manners. There are, however, few that deserve to be particularly mentioned. In his Epistolary Poem to Mr. *William Brown* [**"To My Noble Friend Master William Browne, of the Evill Time"**], who seems to have been his Companion in Misfortunes, he sooths his Discontent by shewing him the Follies and Vices of those Times in which they had been shipwreck'd, and generously concludes, that to suffer in such an Age was to triumph. His Elegy inscribed to *Henry Reynolds,* Esq [**"To My Most Dearely-Loved Friend Henry Reynolds Esquire, of Poets and Poesie"**]; is as its Title bears a very clear and candid Criticism upon Poets and Poetry; and for that Reason alone deserves to be read, as it gives us the true Character of the most eminent of those that flourished in his Time; the best of which, such as *Spenser, Shakespear,* and *Johnson,* appear to have been his intimate Acquaintance, and indeed the latter paid him greater Honours in his Poetical Capacity than any other Man. (p. 20)

After this short, and in some Measure, superficial View of his numerous Poetical Performances, we need not wonder that he was in his Lifetime esteemed the Delight of the Muses, and one who did Honour to his Age and Country. (pp. 21-2)

In a Word, all the great and good Men of his Time were his Friends at least, if not his Patrons. That he did not thrive, arose from no great Singularity in that Age in which he flourish'd; for the Men of Interest were not then remarkably great or good, that is to say, they were not either proper Judges of Merit, or real Friends to Virtue. Our Poet had deserved well of his Prince, and he trusted to that, but he could not flatter his Favourites; the Names of *Salisbury, Somerset,* or *Buckingham,* do not so much as once occur in his Writings, which shews that though he was an excellent Poet, he was a very indifferent Courtier.

When this shall be attentively consider'd, it will undoubtedly raise the Reputation of our Author to its deserved Height, in every virtuous Reader's Judgment. We do not take his good

Qualities upon trust, but are the natural and proper Judges of them. (pp. 22-3)

In Queen *Elizabeth*'s Reign, Greatness resided in her, and the most exalted Statesman never failed of receiving from Time to Time such Lessons of sovereign Authority, as kept him in his primitive Humility, and hindered him from forgetting his Power was only derivative. Poets therefore made their Court to the Queen, by making their Works useful to her Subjects; and here *Drayton* was in his Element. But under King *James*, a Prince of a mild and placid Temper, all his Ministers were the Slaves of those above, and Tyrants to all below them. They courted the King by offering him Incense, as if he had been an Idol; and in their Turns they expected Incense too, which if they received, they snuffed from whatever Hand it came. But it is the Curse of Idolatry to take its Priests, like those *Jeroboam* made for his Golden Calves, *from amongst the meanest of the People;* and our Author was not, nor would make himself one of these, and to his immortal Honour be it spoken, he starved with Truth and Virtue, instead of rising by Vice, or paying Court to Folly. (p. 23)

> *Charles Coffey?, "An Historical Essay on the Life and Writings of Michael Drayton, Esq.," in* The Works of Michael Drayton, Esq., *Vol. 1, 1748. Reprint by W. Reeve, 1753, pp. 1-26.*

THEOPHILUS CIBBER　(essay date 1753)

[*Cibber was the son of the English actor and dramatist Colley Cibber, and an actor and playwright himself. He is best known for his comedies and farces and for his revision of Shakespeare's* Henry VI. *In the following excerpt, he remarks on Drayton's career, reputation, and influence.*]

[Drayton] was distinguished as a poet about nine or ten years before the death of Queen Elizabeth, but at what time he began to publish cannot be ascertained. In the year 1593, when he was but 30 years of age, he published a collection of his *Pastorals;* likewise some of the most grave poems, and such as have transmitted his name to posterity with honour, not long after saw the light. His *Baron's Wars,* and *England's heroical Epistles;* his [*Legends*] of Robert of Normandy; Matilda and Gaveston, for which last he is called by one of his cotemporaries, Tragædiographus, and part of his *Polyolbion* were written before the year 1598, for all which joined with his personal good character, he was highly celebrated at that time, not only for the elegance and sweetness of his expressions, but his actions and manners, which were uniformly virtuous and honourable; he was thus characterised not only by the poets, and florid writers of those days, but also by divines, historians, and other scholars of the most serious turn and extensive learning. (pp. 213-14)

It is easy for those who are conversant with our author's works to see how much the moderns and even Mr. Pope himself copy Mr. Drayton, and refine upon him in those distinctions which are esteemed the most delicate improvements of our English versification, such as the turns, the pauses, the elegant tautologies, &c. (p. 218)

He was honoured with the patronage of men of worth, tho' not of the highest stations; and that author cannot be called a mean one, on whom so great a man as Selden (in many respects the most finished scholar that ever appeared in our nation) was pleased to animadvert. His genius seems to have been of the second rate, much beneath Spencer and Sidney, Shakespear

and Johnson, but highly removed above the ordinary run of vesifyers. (p. 219)

> *Theophilus Cibber, "The Life of Michael Drayton," in his* The Lives of the Poets of Great Britain and Ireland, Vol. 1, 1753. *Reprint by George Olms Verlagsbuchhandlung, 1968, pp. 212-19.*

OLIVER GOLDSMITH?　(essay date 1758)

[*Goldsmith is considered one of the most important writers of the Augustan Age. He distinguished himself during his lifetime as an expressive narrative poet and has since been acclaimed for the novel* The Vicar of Wakefield *(1766), in which he pioneered the use of the protagonist as narrator, and for the influential drama* She Stoops to Conquer *(1773), which helped to introduce a new era of robust comedy to a theater overwhelmed by sentimentalism. The following excerpt is taken from an essay thought to be Goldsmith's, wherein the critic rates several poets, including Drayton, in the areas of genius, judgment, learning, and versification.*]

This scale is supposed to consist of 20 degrees for each column, of which 19 may be attained in any one qualification, but the 20th was never yet attain'd to.	Genius.	Judgment.	Learning.	Versifications.
Chaucer	16	12	10	14
Spencer	18	12	14	18
Drayton	10	11	16	13
Shakespear	19	14	14	19
Johnson	16	18	17	8
Cowley	17	17	15	17
Waller	12	12	10	16
Fairfax	12	12	14	13
Otway	17	10	10	17
Milton	18	16	17	18
Lee	16	10	10	15
Dryden	18	16	17	18
Congreve	15	16	14	14
Vanburgh	14	15	14	10
Steel	10	15	13	10
Addison	16	18	17	17
Prior	16	16	15	17
Swift	18	16	16	16
Pope	18	18	15	19
Thomson	16	16	14	17
Gay	14	16	14	16
Butler	17	16	14	16
Beaumont and Fletcher	14	16	16	12
Hill (Aaron)	16	12	13	17
Rowe	14	16	15	16
Farquhar	15	16	10	10
Garth	16	16	12	16
Southern	15	15	11	14
Hughes	15	16	13	16

By *Genius* is meant those excellencies that no study or art can communicate: such as elevation, expression, description, wit, humour, passion, &c.

Judgment implies a preserving that probability in conducting or disposing a composition that reconciles it to credibility and the appearance of truth, and such as is best suited to effect the purpose aim'd at.

By *Learning*, is not meant learning in an academical or scholastic sense, but that species of it which can best qualify a poet to excel in the subject he attempts.

Versification is not only that harmony of numbers which renders a composition, whether in rhime or blank verse, agreeable to the ear, but a just connection between the expression and the sentiment, resulting entirely from the energy of the latter, and so happily adapted, that they seem created for that very purpose, and not to be altered but for the worse. (p. 6)

> *Oliver Goldsmith?, ''The Poetical Scale,'' in* The Literary Magazine, *Vol. III, January, 1758, pp. 6-8.*

OLIVER GOLDSMITH   (essay date 1762)

[*The following excerpt is taken from Goldsmith's* The Citizen of the World *(1762), a series of fictional letters written by ''a Chinese Philosopher, Residing in London, to his Friends in the East.'' Here, as his protagonist is guided through Westminster Abbey by a chance-met gentleman, Goldsmith succinctly and contemptuously dismisses Drayton.*]

As we walked along to a particular part of the temple, There, says the gentleman, pointing with his finger, that is the poets' corner; there you see the monuments of Shakespear, and Milton, and Prior, and Drayton. Drayton, I replied, I never heard of him before. . . . (p. 34)

> *Oliver Goldsmith, ''An Account of Westminster Abbey,'' in his* The Citizen of the World *and* The Bee, *edited by Austin Dobson, J. M. Dent & Sons Ltd., 1934, pp. 32-6.*

SIR SAMUEL EGERTON BRYDGES   (essay date 1800)

[*Brydges was an English writer whose creative work is considered mediocre but whose bibliographic skills have been highly praised. In the following excerpt, he summarizes Drayton's poetic successes and failures.*]

Drayton's taste was less correct, and his ear less harmonious than [Samuel] Daniel's—but his genius was more poetical, though it seems to have fitted him only for the didactic, and not for the bolder walks of Poetry. The *Poly-olbion* is a work of amazing ingenuity, and a very large proportion exhibits a variety of beauties, which partake very strongly of the poetical character; but the perpetual personification is tedious, and more is attempted than is within the compass of poetry. The admiration in which the *Heroical Epistles* were once held, raises the astonishment of a more refined age. They exhibit some elegant images, and some musical lines.—But in general they want passion and nature, are strangely flat and prosaic, and are intermixed with the coarsest vulgarities of idea, sentiment, and expression. His *Barons Wars* and other historical pieces are dull creeping narratives, with a great deal of the same faults, and none of the excellencies which ought to distinguish such compositions. His *Nimphidia* is light and airy, and possesses the features of true poetry. (pp. 265-66)

> *Sir Samuel Egerton Brydges, ''Michael Drayton,'' in* Theatrum Poetarum Anglicanorum *by Edward Phillips, edited by Sir Samuel Egerton Brydges, J. White, 1800, pp. 262-67.*

CHARLES LAMB   (essay date 1818)

[*An essayist, critic, and poet, Lamb is credited with initiating the revival of interest in Elizabethan and Restoration drama in nineteenth-century England. His critical comments on the plays of John Webster, Jeremy Taylor, Thomas Heywood, and John Ford, recorded in the form of notes to his anthology,* Specimens of the English Dramatic Poets, Who Lived About the Time of Shakespeare *(1808), demonstrate a literary taste and refinement new in his time. Unlike some of his contemporaries, Lamb never tried to construct an all-embracing, systematic critical theory. Instead, his method was to point out fine passages in particular works and convey his enthusiasm to his readers. Concurrently with William Hazlitt, Lamb developed and utilized in his criticism the innovative techniques of evocation, metaphor, and personal reference. Lamb is chiefly remembered for his* Elia: Essays Which Have Appeared under That Signature in the ''London Magazine'' *(1823) and* The Last Essays of Elia *(1833), a series of familiar essays which are admired for their breadth, quaint style, and intimate tone. In the following excerpt from an 1818 appraisal of the anonymous play* The Merry Devil of Edmonton *(1608), Lamb is drawn into tangential praise of* Poly-Olbion.]

The scene in this delightful comedy [*The Merry Devil of Edmonton*], in which Jerningham, ''with the true feeling of a zealous friend,'' touches the griefs of Mounchensey, seems written to make the reader happy. Few of our dramatists or novelists have attended enough to this. They torture and wound us abundantly. They are economists only in delight. Nothing can be finer, more gentlemanlike, and nobler, than the conversation and compliments of these young men. How delicious is Raymond Mounchensey's forgetting, in his fears, that Jerningham has a ''Saint in Essex;'' and how sweetly his friend reminds him! I wish it could be ascertained, which there is some grounds for believing, that Michael Drayton was the author of this piece. It would add a worthy appendage to the renown of that Panegyrist of my native Earth; who has gone over her soil, in his *Polyolbion,* with the fidelity of a herald, and the painful love of a son; who has not left a rivulet, so narrow that it may be stept over, without honorable mention; and has animated hills and streams with life and passion beyond the dreams of old mythology. (pp. 44-5)

> *Charles Lamb, ''Characters of Dramatic Writers, Contemporary with Shakspeare,'' in* The Works of Charles and Mary Lamb: Miscellaneous Prose, 1798-1834, *Vol. I, edited by E. V. Lucas, Methuen & Co., 1903, pp. 40-55.*

WILLIAM HAZLITT   (lecture date 1820)

[*An English essayist, Hazlitt was one of the most important critics of the Romantic Age. He was a deft stylist, a master of the prose essay, and a leader of what was later termed ''impressionist criticism''—a form of personal analysis directly opposed to the universal standards of critical judgment accepted by many eighteenth-century critics. Hazlitt, like Samuel Taylor Coleridge before him, played a substantial role in the reinterpretation of Shakespeare's characters during the nineteenth century, and he contributed significantly to the revival of a number of Elizabethan dramatists, including John Webster and Thomas Heywood. Although he has often been considered a follower of Coleridge, he is closer in spirit and critical methodology to Charles Lamb. Like Lamb, Hazlitt utilized the critical techniques of evocation, metaphor, and personal reference—three innovations that greatly altered the development of literary criticism in the nineteenth and twentieth centuries. In the following excerpt from a lecture given in 1820, Hazlitt offers a short, mixed review of Drayton's poetry.*]

Michael Drayton's **Poly-Olbion** is a work of great length and of unabated freshness and vigour in itself, though the monotony of the subject tires the reader. He describes each place with the accuracy of a topographer, and the enthusiasm of a poet, as if his Muse were the very *genius loci*. His **Heroical Epistles** are also excellent. He has a few lighter pieces, but none of exquisite beauty or grace. His mind is a rich marly soil that produces an abundant harvest, and repays the husbandman's toil, but few flaunting flowers, the garden's pride, grow in it, nor any poisonous weeds. (p. 192)

> *William Hazlitt, "On Miscellaneous Poems," in his* Lectures on the Literature of the Age of Elizabeth, and Characters of Shakespear's Plays, *George Bell and Sons, 1884, pp. 172-212.*

SAMUEL TAYLOR COLERIDGE   (conversation date 1831)

[*Coleridge was at the intellectual center of the English Romantic movement and is considered one of the greatest poets and literary critics in the English language. Besides such classic poems as* The Rime of the Ancient Mariner *(published in* Lyrical Ballads, *1798), his most important contributions include his prominent role in the formulation of Romantic theory, his introduction of the ideas of the German Romantics to England, and his Shakespearean criticism, which overthrew the last remnants of the neo-classical approach to William Shakespeare and focused on the dramatist as a masterful portrayer of human character. The following excerpt is from Coleridge's conversation of September 11, 1831, as reported by his nephew Henry Nelson Coleridge. Here, he gives his opinion of Drayton.*]

Drayton is a sweet poet, and Selden's notes to the early part of the **Polyolbion** are well worth your perusal. Daniel is a superior man; his diction is pre-eminently pure. . . . (p. 265)

Yet there are instances of sublimity in Drayton. When deploring the cutting down of some of our old forests, he says, in language which reminds the reader of Lear, written subsequently, and also of several passages in Mr. Wordsworth's poems:—

> our trees so hack'd above the ground,
> That where their lofty tops the neighbouring countries crown'd,
> Their trunks (like aged folks) now bare and naked stand,
> As for revenge to Heaven each held a wither'd hand.

That is very fine. (p. 266)

> *Samuel Taylor Coleridge, "Drayton and Daniel," in his* Specimens of the Table Talk of the Late Samuel Taylor Coleridge, *Vol. I, edited by H. N. Coleridge, John Murray, 1835, pp. 265-67.*

ROBERT SOUTHEY   (essay date 1839)

[*An English man of letters, Southey was a prominent literary figure of the late eighteenth and early nineteenth centuries and a key member of the Lake School of poetry, which numbered among its more outstanding exponents William Wordsworth and Samuel Taylor Coleridge. As a poet, Southey composed short verse, ballads, and epics and experimented with versification and meter. His prose writings include ambitious histories, biographies, and conservative social commentaries; critics often praise these writings more than his poetry. Today Southey is primarily remembered for his biographies of such figures as Horatio Nelson, Thomas More, and John Wesley and as a conservative theorist. In the*

following excerpt, Southey pronounces Poly-Olbion *and its author deserving of modern respect.*]

> Do, pious marble, let thy readers know
> What they and what their children owe
> To Drayton's name, whose sacred dust
> We recommend unto thy trust.
> Protect his memory, and preserve his story;
> Remain a lasting monument of his glory;
> And when thy ruins shall disclaim
> To be the Treasurer of his name,
> His name that cannot fade, shall be
> An everlasting monument to thee.
>
> EPITAPH IN WESTMINSTER ABBEY.

The Poet Crabbe has said that there subsists an utter repugnancy between the studies of topography and poetry. He must have intended by topography when he said so, the mere definition of boundaries and specification of land-marks, such as are given in the advertisement of an estate for sale; and boys in certain parts of the country are taught to bear in mind by a remembrance in tail when the bounds of a parish are walked by the local authorities. Such topography indeed bears as little relation to poetry as a map or chart to a picture.

But if he had any wider meaning, it is evident, by the number of topographical poems, good, bad and indifferent, with which our language abounds, that Mr. Crabbe's predecessors in verse, and his contemporaries also, have differed greatly from him in opinion upon this point. The **Poly-olbion**, notwithstanding its common-place personifications and its inartificial transitions, which are as abrupt as those in the *Metamorphoses* and the *Fasti,* and not so graceful, is nevertheless a work as much to be valued by the students and lovers of English literature, as by the writers of local history. Drayton himself, whose great talents were deservedly esteemed by the ablest of his contemporaries in the richest age of English poetry, thought he could not be more worthily employed than in what he calls the Herculean task of this topographical poem; and in that belief he was encouraged by his friend and commentator Selden, to whose name the epithet of learned was in old times always and deservedly affixed. . . . I would not say of this Poet, as Kirkpatrick says of him, that when he

> ———his Albion sung
> With their own praise the echoing vallies rung;
> His bounding Muse o'er every mountain rode
> And every river warbled where he flowed;

but I may say that if instead of sending his Muse to ride over the mountains, and resting contented with her report, he had ridden or walked over them himself, his poem would better have deserved that praise for accuracy which has been bestowed upon it by critics who had themselves no knowledge which could enable them to say whether it were accurate or not. Camden was more diligent; he visited some of the remotest counties of which he wrote.

This is not said with any intention of detracting from Michael Drayton's fame: the most elaborate criticism could neither raise him above the station which he holds in English literature, nor degrade him from it. He is extolled not beyond the just measure of his deserts in his epitaph which has been variously ascribed to Ben Jonson, to Randolph, and to Quarles, but with most probability to the former, who knew and admired and loved him.

He was a poet by nature, and carefully improved his talent;— one who sedulously laboured to deserve the approbation of such as were capable of appreciating, and cared nothing for the censures which others might pass upon him. "Like me that list," he says,

> my honest rhymes,
> Nor care for critics, nor regard the times.

And though he is not . . . one of those whose better fortune it is to live in the hearts of their devoted admirers, yet what he deemed his greatest work will be preserved by its subject; some of his minor poems have merit enough in their execution to ensure their preservation, and no one who studies poetry as an art will think his time misspent in perusing the whole,—if he have any real love for the art which he is pursuing. The youth who enters upon that pursuit without a feeling of respect and gratitude for those elder poets, who by their labours have prepared the way for him, is not likely to produce any thing himself that will be held in remembrance by posterity. (pp. 32-6)

> *Robert Southey, "Remarks on an Opinion of Mr. Crabbe's: Topographical Poetry, Drayton," in his* The Doctor, &c., *Vol. II, Longman, Rees, Orme, Brown, Green, Longman, 1839, pp. 32-6.*

ISAAC DISRAELI (essay date 1841)

[*Although probably most famous as the father of British prime minister and novelist Benjamin Disraeli, Isaac Disraeli was an essayist who wrote several interesting and important works on eighteenth-century literature. In the following excerpt, he considers the strengths and weaknesses of* Poly-Olbion *and of Drayton's poetry in general.*]

The *Poly-Olbion* of Drayton is a stupendous work, "a strange Herculean toil," as the poet himself has said, and it was the elaborate production of many years. The patriotic bard fell a victim to its infelicitous but glorious conception; and posterity may discover a grandeur in this labour of love, which was unfelt by his contemporaries. (p. 218)

The grand theme of this poet was his fatherland! The muse of Drayton passes by every town and tower; each tells some tale of ancient glory, or of some "worthy" who must never die. The local associations of legends and customs are animated by the personifications of mountains and rivers; and often, in some favourite scenery, he breaks forth with all the emotion of a true poet. The imaginative critic has described the excursions of our muse with responsive sympathy. "He has not," says Lamb, "left a rivulet so narrow that it may be stepped over without honourable mention, and has associated hills and streams with life and passion beyond the dreams of old mythology" [see excerpt dated 1818]. But the journey is long, and the conveyance may be tedious; the reader, accustomed to the decasyllabic or heroic verse, soon finds himself breathless among the protracted and monotonous Alexandrines, unless he should relieve his ear from the incumbrance, by resting on the cæsura, and thus divide those extended lines by the alternate grace of a ballad-stanza. The artificial machinery of Drayton's personifications of mountains and rivers, though these may be often allowed the poet, yet they seem more particularly ludicrous, as they are crowded together on the maps prefixed to each county, where this arbitrary mythology, masculine and feminine, are to be seen standing by the heads of rivers, or at the entrances of towns.

This extraordinary poem remains without a parallel in the poetical annals of any people. . . . (pp. 218-19)

[Though] this poet devoted much of his life to this great antiquarian and topographic poem, he has essayed his powers in almost every species of poetry; fertility of subject, and fluency of execution, are his characteristics. He has written historical narratives too historical; heroic epistles hardly Ovidian; elegies on several occasions, or rather, domestic epistles, of a Horatian cast; pastorals, in which there is a freshness of imagery, breathing with the life of nature; and songs, and satire, and comedy. In comedy he had not been unsuccessful, but in satire he was considered more indignant than caustic. There is one species of poetry, rare among us, in which he has been eminently successful; his *Nymphidia, or Court of Faerie,* is a model of the grotesque, those arabesques of poetry, those lusory effusions on chimerical objects. There are grave critics who would deny the poet the liberty allowed to the painter. The *Nymphidia* seems to have been ill understood by some modern critics. The poet has been censured for "neither imparting nor feeling that half-believing seriousness which enchants us in the wild and magical touches of Shakespeare;" but the poet designed an exquisitely ludicrous fiction. Drayton has, however, relieved the grotesque scenes, by rising into the higher strains of poetry, such as Gray might not have disdained.

It was the misfortune of Drayton not to have been a popular poet, which we may infer from his altercations with his booksellers, and from their frequent practice of prefixing new title pages, with fresher dates, to the first editions of his poems. That he was also in perpetual quarrel with his muse, appears by his frequent alteration of his poems. He often felt that curse of an infelicitous poet, that his diligence was more active than his creative power. Drayton was a poet of volume, but his genius was peculiar; from an unhappy facility in composition, in reaching excellence he too often declined into mediocrity. A modern reader may be struck by the purity and strength of his diction; his strong descriptive manner lays hold of the fancy; but he is always a poet of reason, and never of passion. He cannot be considered as a poet of mediocrity, who has written so much above that level; nor a poet who can rank among the highest class, who has often flattened his spirit by its redundance. (pp. 221-22)

> *Isaac Disraeli, "Drayton," in his* Amenities of Literature: Consisting of Sketches and Characters of English Literature, *Vol. II, 1841. Reprint by Routledge, Warnes, and Routledge, 1859, pp. 218-23.*

GEORGE SAINTSBURY (essay date 1880)

[*Saintsbury has been called the most influential English literary historian and critic of the late nineteenth and early twentieth centuries, his numerous literary histories and studies of European literature establishing him as a leading critical authority. Saintsbury adhered to two distinct sets of critical standards: one for the novel and the other for poetry and drama. As a critic of novels, he maintained that "the novel has nothing to do with any beliefs, with any convictions, with any thoughts in the strict sense, except as mere garnishings. Its substance must always be life not thought, conduct not belief, the passions not the intellect, manners and morals not creeds and theories. . . . The novel is . . . mainly and firstly a criticism of life." As a critic of poetry and drama, Saintsbury was a radical formalist who frequently asserted that subject is of little importance and that "the so-called 'formal' part is of the essence." René Wellek has praised Saintsbury's critical qualities: his "enormous reading, the almost universal scope of his subject matter, the zest and zeal of his exposition" and "the audacity with which he handles the most ambitious and unattempted arguments." In the following excerpt, Saintsbury briefly surveys Drayton's poetry, commenting on its variety and its uneven merit.*]

13

The sentence which Hazlitt allots to Drayton is perhaps one of the most felicitous examples of short metaphorical criticism [see excerpt dated 1820]. 'His mind,' says the critic, 'is a rich marly soil that produces an abundant harvest and repays the husbandman's toil; but few flaunting flowers, the garden's pride, grow in it, nor any poisonous weeds.' Such figurative estimates must indeed always be in some respects unsatisfactory, yet in this there is but little of inadequacy. It is exceedingly uncommon for the reader to be transported by anything that he meets with in the author of the *Polyolbion*. Drayton's jewels five words long are of the rarest, and their sparkle when they do occur is not of the brightest or most enchanting lustre. But considering his enormous volume, he is a poet of surprisingly high merit. Although he has written some fifty or sixty thousand lines, the bulk of them on subjects not too favourable to poetical treatment, he has yet succeeded in giving to the whole an unmistakeably poetical flavour, and in maintaining that flavour throughout. The variety of his work, and at the same time the unfailing touch by which he lifts that work, not indeed into the highest regions of poetry, but far above its lower confines, are his most remarkable characteristics. The *Polyolbion,* the *Heroical Epistles,* the *Odes,* the **"Ballad of Agincourt,"** and the *Nymphidia* are strikingly unlike each other in the qualities required for successful treatment of them, yet they are all successfully treated. It is something to have written the best war song in a language, its best fantastic poem, and its only topographical poem of real value. Adverse criticism may contend that the *Nymphidia* and the *Polyolbion* were not worth the doing, but this is another matter altogether. That the **"Ballad of Agincourt"** was not worth the doing, no one who has any fondness for poetry or any appreciation of it will attempt to contend. In the lyric work of the *Odes,* scanty as it is, there is the same evidence of mastery and of what may be called thoroughness of workmanship. Exacting critics may indeed argue that Drayton has too much of the thoroughly accomplished and capable workman, and too little of the divinely gifted artist. It may be thought, too, that if he had written less and concentrated his efforts, the average merit of his work would have been higher. There is, at any rate, no doubt that the bulk of his productions, if it has not interfered with their value, has interfered with their popularity.

The Barons' Wars, which, according to some theories, should have been Drayton's best work, is perhaps his worst. The stanza, which he has chosen for good and well-expressed reasons, is an effective one, and the subject might have been made interesting. As a matter of fact it has but little interest. The somewhat 'kite-and-crow' character of the disturbance chronicled is not relieved by any vigorous portraiture either of Mortimer or of Edward or of the Queen. The first and last of these personages are much better handled in the *Heroical Epistles.* The level of these latter and of the *Legends* is decidedly high. Not merely do they contain isolated passages of great beauty, but the general interest of them is well sustained, and the characters of the writers subtly differenced. One great qualification which Drayton had as a writer of historical and geographical verse was his possession of what has been called, in the case of M. Victor Hugo, *la science des noms* [''the science of names'']. No one who has an ear can fail to recognise the felicity of the stanza in **"Agincourt"** which winds up with 'Ferrars and Fanhope,' and innumerable examples of the same kind occur elsewhere. Without this science indeed the *Polyolbion* would have been merely an awkward gazetteer. As it is, the 'strange herculean task,' to borrow its author's description of it, has been very happily performed. It may safely be assumed that very few living Englishmen have read it through.

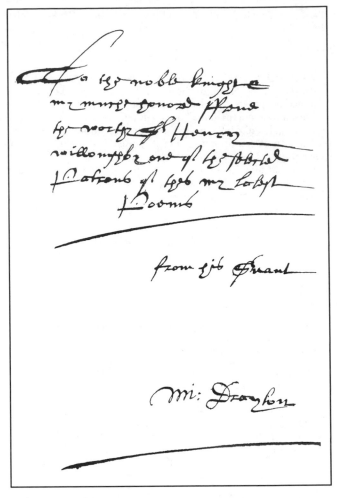

A sample of Drayton's handwriting.

But those who have will probably agree that there is a surprising interest in it, and that this interest is kept up by a very artful admixture of styles and subjects. Legends, fancy pieces such as that of the Marriage of Thame and Isis, with its unmatched floral description, accounts of rural sports and the like, ingeniously diversify the merely topographical narrative. Had the *Polyolbion* been its author's only work, Goldsmith's sneer [see excerpt dated 1762] would still have been most undeserved. But the variety of Drayton's performance is almost as remarkable as its bulk. This variety it is impossible to represent fully . . . in this notice. . . . But to the foregoing remarks it may be added that Drayton was master of a very strong and at the same time musical decasyllabic line. His practice in Alexandrines and in complicated stanzas seems to have by no means injured his command of the ordinary heroic couplet. His series of *Sonnets to Idea* is perhaps his least successful work if we compare him with other men, just as *The Barons' Wars* is his worst performance if his own work only be considered. The *Nymphidia* has received higher praise than any other of his poems, and its fantastic conception and graceful tripping metre deserve this praise well enough. The curious poems of *The Owl* and *The Man in the Moon* show, if they show nothing else, his peculiar faculty of raising almost any subject to a certain poetical dignity by dint of skilful treatment. Lastly, his prose Prefaces deserve attention here, because many of them display the secret of his workmanlike skill. It is evident from them that Drayton was as far as possible from holding the false and foolish improvisation-theory of poetry, and they testify to a most careful study of his predecessors and contemporaries, and to deliberate practice in the use of the poet's tools of language and metre. (pp. 526-28)

> George Saintsbury, "Michael Drayton (1563-1631)," in *The English Poets: Chaucer to Donne*, Vol. I, edited by Thomas Humphry Ward, 1880. Reprint by The Macmillan Company, 1920, pp. 526-28.

RICHARD GARNETT (essay date 1893)

[*In the following excerpt from his introduction to* The Battaile of Agincourt, *Garnett appraises Drayton as an epic and pastoral poet.*]

In the mighty series of Shakespeare's historical plays, including in the enumeration Marlowe's *Edward the Second* and the anonymous *Edward the Third*, England possesses a national epic inferior to that of no country in the world, although the form be dramatic. In one respect, indeed, this epic is superior to any but the Homeric poems, standing one remove less apart from the poetry of the people. The impression of primitive force which the Homeric poems convey by their venerable language is equally well imparted by Shakespeare's spontaneity and his apparent and probably real innocence of all purely literary intention.

Epic poets, however gifted, could be but gleaners after such a harvest. Yet not every excellent poet, even of that dramatic age, was endowed with the dramatic faculty, and two of especial merit, singularly devoid of dramatic gift, but inferior to none in love of their country and self-consecration to its service, turned their attention to the epic. These were Samuel Daniel and Michael Drayton. The latter is our subject, but something should also be said of the former. Drayton not unfairly hit the blot in his successful rival when he said of him:

> His rimes were smooth, his meeters well did close,
> But yet his maner better fitted prose.

This is one way of putting it; from another point of view Daniel may be regarded as almost the most remarkable literary phenomenon of his time; he is so exceedingly modern. He outran the taste of his own period by a hundred years, and without teacher or example displayed the excellences which came to be preferred to all others in the eighteenth century. "These poems of his," says his editor in that age (1718), "having stood the test of above a century, and the language and the versification being still pure and elegant, it is to be hoped they will still shine among his countrymen and preserve his name." At this time, and for long afterwards, Drayton, save for an occasional reprint of his *Nimphidia* among miscellaneous collections, was utterly neglected. Even after the editions of 1748 and 1753 he is alluded to by Goldsmith as a type of the poet whose best title to fame is his tomb in Westminster Abbey [see excerpt dated 1762].

The nineteenth century has reversed this with other critical verdicts of the eighteenth, and, with all due respect to Daniel, Drayton now stands higher. Yet, where the two poets come most directly and manifestly into competition, Drayton's superiority is not so evident. As a whole, Daniel's *Civil War* is a better poem than Drayton's *Barons' Wars*. The superiority of the latter lies in particular passages, such as the description of the guilty happiness of Isabella and Mortimer. . . . This is to say that Drayton's genius was naturally not so much epical

as lyrical and descriptive. In his own proper business as a narrative poet he fails as compared with Daniel, but he enriches history with all the ornaments of poetry; and it was his especial good fortune to discover a subject in which the union of dry fact with copious poetic illustration was as legitimate to the theme as advantageous to the writer. This was, of course, his *Polyolbion*, where, doing for himself what no other poet ever did, he did for his country what was never done for any other. Greece and Rome, indeed, have left us versified topographies, but these advance no pretension to the poetical character except from the metrical point of view, though they may in a sense claim kinship with the Muses as the manifest offspring of Mnemosyne. If any modern language possesses a similar work, it has failed to inscribe itself on the roll of the world's literature. The difficulties of Drayton's unique undertaking were in a measure favourable to him. They compelled him to exert his fancy to the uttermost. The tremendous difficulty of making topography into poetry gave him unwonted energy. He never goes to sleep, as too often in the *Barons' Wars*. The stiff practical obstacles attendant upon the poetical treatment of towns and rivers provoke even the dragging Alexandrine into animation; his stream is often all foam and eddy. The long sweeping line, of its wont so lumbering and tedious, is perfectly in place here. It rushes along like an impetuous torrent, bearing with it, indeed, no inconsiderable quantity of wood, hay, and stubble, but also precious pearls, and more than the dust of gold. Its "swelling and limitless billows" mate well with the amplitude of the subject, so varied and spacious that, as has been well said, the *Polyolbion* is not a poem to be read through, but to be read in. Nothing in our literature, perhaps, except the *Faery Queen*, more perfectly satisfies Keats's desideratum: "Do not the lovers of poetry like to have a little region to wander in, where they may pick and choose, and in which the images are so numerous that many are forgotten and found new in a second reading: which may be food for a week's stroll in the summer? Do they not like this better than what they can read through before Mrs. Williams comes down stairs? a morning work at most?"

The *Polyolbion* was completed by 1619, though the concluding part was not published until 1623. *The Battaile of Agincourt,* . . . appeared with others in 1627. As none of the pieces comprised in it had appeared in the collected edition of Drayton's works (the *Polyolbion* excepted) which he had published in 1620, it is reasonable to conclude that they had been composed between that date and 1627. They prove that his powers were by no means abated. *Nimphidia*, in particular, though lacking the exquisite sweetness of some of his lyric pastorals, and the deep emotion of passages in his *Heroicall Epistles*, excels all his other productions in airy fancy, and is perhaps the best known of any of his poems. Nor does the *Battaile* itself indicate any decay in poetical power, though we must agree with Mr. Bullen that it is in some parts fatiguing. This wearisomeness proceeds chiefly from Drayton's over-faithful adherence, not so much to the actual story, as to the method of the chronicler from whom his materials are principally drawn. It does not seem to have occurred to him to regard his theme in the light of potter's clay. Following his authority with servile deference, he makes at the beginning a slip which lowers the dignity of his hero, and consequently of his epic. He represents Henry the Fifth's expedition against France as originally prompted, not by the restless enterprise and fiery valour of the young king, much less by supernatural inspiration as the working out of a divine purpose, but by the craft of the clergy seeking to divert him from too nice inquiry into the source and application of their revenues. Henry, therefore, without, as modern investigators think, even sufficient historical authority, but in any case without poetical justification, appears at the very beginning of the poem that celebrates his exploits in the light of a dupe. Shakespeare avoids this awkwardness by boldly altering the date of Henry's embassy to France. His play opens, indeed, with the plots of the ecclesiastics to tempt the king into war, but it soon appears that the embassy claiming certain French dukedoms has been despatched before they had opened their lips, and that they are urging him to a course of action on which he is resolved already. Spenser or Dryden would have escaped from the difficulty in a manner more in accordance with epic precedent by representing Henry's action as the effect of a divine vision. Edward the Third or the Black Prince would have risen from the grave to urge him to renew and complete their interrupted and now almost undone work; or the ghosts of chiefs untimely slain would have reproached him with their abandoned conquests and neglected graves. Drayton has merely taken the story as he found it, without a thought of submitting its dross to the alchemy of the re-creative imagination of the poet. The same lack of selection is observable in his description of the battle itself. He minutely describes a series of episodes, in themselves often highly picturesque, but we are no better able to view the conflict as a whole than if we ourselves had fought in the ranks. As in painting, so in poetry, a true impression is not to be conveyed by microscopic accuracy in minutiæ, but by a vigorous grasp of the entire subject.

Notwithstanding these defects, which one might have thought would have been avoided even by a poet endowed with less of the bright and sprightly invention which Drayton manifests in so many of his pieces, *The Battaile of Agincourt* is a fine poem, and well deserving the honour of reprint. It is above all things patriotic, pervaded throughout by a manly and honourable preference for England and all things English, yet devoid of bitterness towards the enemy, whose valour is frankly acknowledged, and whose overweening pride, the cause of their disasters, is never made the object of ill-natured sarcasm. It may almost be said that if Drayton had been in some respects a worse man, he might on this occasion have been a better poet. He is so sedulously regardful of the truth of history, or what he takes to be such, that he neglects the poet's prerogative of making history, and rises and falls with his model like a moored vessel pitching in a flowing tide. When his historical authority inspires, Drayton is inspired accordingly; when it is dignified, so is he; with it he soars and sings, with it he also sinks and creeps. Happily the subject is usually picturesque, and old Holinshed at his worst was no contemptible writer. Drayton's heart too was in his work, as he had proved long before by the noble ballad on King Harry. . . . If he has not shown himself an artist in the selection and arrangement of his topics, he deserves the name from another point of view by the excellent metrical structure of his octaves, and the easy fluency of his narrative. One annoying defect, the frequent occurrence of flat single lines not far remote from bathos, must be attributed to the low standard of the most refined poetry in an age when "the judges and police of literature" had hardly begun either to make laws or to enforce them. It is a fault which he shared with most others, and of which he has himself given more offensive instances. It is still more conspicuous in the most generally acceptable of his poems, the *Nimphidia*. The pity is not so much the occasional occurrence of such lapses in *The Battaile of Agincourt,* as the want of those delightful touches in the other delightful poems which give more pleasure the more evidently they are embellishments rather springing out of the author's fancy than naturally prompted by his subject. (pp. viii-xvi)

Ben Jonson may be suspected of a sneer when he congratulates Drayton on . . . outdoing Homer, as he had previously outdone, or at least rivalled, Virgil, Theocritus, Ovid, Orpheus, and Lucan [see poem dated 1627]. Ben might have said with perfect sincerity that Drayton's descriptions are fine pieces of work, showing great command of language, and only open to criticism from some want of proportion between them and the poem of which they are but subordinate episodes. This censure would have been by no means just if the whole piece had been executed on the scale of the description of the siege of Harfleur. It is difficult to imagine what could have tempted Drayton to spend so much time upon an episode treated by Holinshed with comparative brevity. Some of the stanzas are exceedingly spirited, but as a whole the description certainly fatigues. If the same is to some extent the case with the description of the Battle of Agincourt itself, the cause is not so much prolixity as the multitude of separate episodes, not always derived from the chroniclers, and the consequent want of unity which has been already adverted to. The result is probably more true to the actual impression of a battle than if Drayton had surveyed the field with the eye of a tactician, but here as elsewhere the poet should rather aim at an exalted and in some measure idealized representation of the object or circumstance described than at a faithful reproduction of minor details. Even the Battle of the Frogs and Mice in Homer is an orderly whole; while Drayton's battle seems always ending and always beginning anew, a Sisyphian epic. What, however, really kindles and vivifies the unequal composition into one glowing mass is the noble spirit of enthusiastic patriotism which pervades the poet's mind, and, like sunlight in a mountainous tract, illuminates his heights, veils his depressions, and steeps the whole in glory. (pp. xix-xx)

Comparisons between modern and ancient poets must necessarily be very imperfect; yet our Drayton might not inaptly be termed the English Theocritus. If not so distinctly superior to every other English pastoral poet as Theocritus was to every other Greek, he yet stands in the front rank. He is utterly free from affectation, the great vice of pastoral poetry; his love of the country is sincere; his perception of natural phenomena exquisite; his shepherds and shepherdesses real swains and lasses; he has happily varied the conventional form of the pastoral by a felicitous lyrical treatment. Paradoxical as it may appear, Drayton was partly enabled to approach Theocritus so nearly by knowing him so imperfectly. Had he been acquainted with him otherwise than through Virgil, he would probably have been unable to refrain from direct imitation; but as matters stand, instead of a poet striving to write as Theocritus wrote in Greek, we have one actually writing as Theocritus would have written in English. But the most remarkable point of contact between Drayton and Theocritus is that both are epical as well as pastoral poets. Two of the Idylls of Theocritus are believed to be fragments of an epic on the exploits of Hercules; and in the enumeration of his lost works, amid others of the same description, mention is made of the *Heroines,* a curious counterpart of Drayton's *Heroicall Epistles.* Had these works survived, we might not improbably have found Drayton surpassing his prototype in epic as much as he falls below him in pastoral; for the more exquisite art of the Sicilian could hardly have made amends for the lack of that national pride and enthusiastic patriotism which had died out of his age, but which ennobled the strength and upbore the weakness of the author of *The Battaile of Agincourt.* (pp. xxii-xxiii)

Richard Garnett, in an introduction to The Battaile of Agincourt *by Michael Drayton, Charles Whittingham & Co., 1893, pp. vii-xxiii.*

EDMUND GOSSE (essay date 1894)

[*Gosse's importance as a critic is due primarily to his introduction of Henrik Ibsen's "new drama" to an English audience. He was among the chief English translators and critics of Scandinavian literature and was decorated by the Norwegian, Swedish, and Danish governments for his efforts. Among his other works are studies of John Donne, Thomas Gray, Sir Thomas Browne, and important early articles on French authors of the late nineteenth century. Gosse was largely a popularizer, with the consequence that his commentary is not considered in the first rank of modern critical thought. However, his broad interests and knowledge of foreign literatures lend his works much more than a documentary value. In the following excerpt. Gosse evaluates Drayton's poetic career.*]

During the eighteenth century, at least, no non-dramatic poet of [the Jacobean] period was so much read or so often reprinted as Drayton. Joseph Hunter expressed no opinion shocking to his generation when he claimed for Drayton a place in the first class of English poets. His ease, correctness, and lucidity were attractive to our elder critics, and outweighed the lack of the more exquisite qualities of style. If Drayton can no longer be awarded such superlative honours as were formerly paid to him, he is nevertheless a poet of considerable originality and merit, whose greatest enemy has been his want of measure. His works form far too huge a bulk, and would be more gladly read if the imagination in them were more concentrated and the style more concise. Drayton attempted almost every variety of poetic art, and his aim was possibly a little too encyclopædic for his gifts. (p. 93)

Probably in 1606, Drayton issued one of the most charming of his books, **Poems Lyric and Pastoral**, consisting of odes, eclogues, and a curious romance called **The Man in the Moon**. The *Odes* doubtless belong to his youth; they are particularly happy in their varied versification, of which two brief specimens may suffice. This stanza exemplifies the **"Ode on the New Year"**—

> Give her the Eoan brightness,
> Wing'd with that subtle lightness,
>   That doth transpierce the air;
> The roses of the morning,
> The rising heaven adorning,
>   To mesh with flames of hair.

and this the **"Ode to his Valentine"**—

> Muse, bid the morn awake,
>   Sad winter now declines,
> Each bird doth choose a make,
>   This day's Saint Valentine's,
> For that good bishop's sake,
>   Get up and let us see,
>   What beauty it shall be,
> That fortune us assigns.

These are fresh and lively, without any strong grip on thought. By far the best of the odes, however, is the noble **Battle of Agincourt,** which is Drayton's greatest claim to the recognition of posterity, and the most spirited of all his lyrics.

In a bold preface to his **Eclogues**, Drayton promises something new; but these pastorals are not to be distinguished from Elizabethan work of the same kind, except by the fine lyrics which are introduced in the course of them. Of these the best is the very remarkable birthday ode to Beta in the third eclogue. . . . (pp. 95-6)

For the rest, these pieces present a vague but pretty impression of nymphs singing and dancing in the flowery meadows around a middle-aged swain who deplores to them his want of material success and courtly recognition.

Passing, for the moment, the **Poly-Olbion,** we come in 1627 to a miscellaneous volume, consisting of seven independent poetical works not before given to the public. Of these two, **The Battle of Agincourt** (not to be confounded with the ode) and **The Miseries of Queen Margaret,** are fragments of that epic in *ottava rima* which Drayton was always projecting and never completed. **Nimphidia, or the Court of Fairy,** is a fantastic little romance, perhaps closer to being a masterpiece than any other which Drayton composed, dealing with the loves of Pigwiggin and Queen Mab in a style of the most airy fancy. **The Moon-Calf** is as clumsy as its predecessor is elegant and exquisite; this is a kind of coarse satirical fable in the heroic couplet. **The Quest of Cinthia** is a long ballad, so smooth, and it must be confessed, so conventional, that it might almost have been written a century and a half later. **The Shepherd's Sirena** is a lyric pastoral of much lightness and charm, and the volume closes with some **Elegies** of various merit.

At least as early as 1598, as we learn from Francis Meres, Drayton had designed a heroic and patriotic poem of great extent. It was to celebrate the kingdom of Great Britain with the exactitude of Camden, but with the addition of every species of imaginative ornament. (pp. 97-8)

As the poet says, the composition of **Poly-Olbion** was "a Herculean toil," and it was one which scarcely rewarded the author. He had a great difficulty in finding a publisher for the complete work, and he told the sympathetic Drummond—"my dear sweet Drummond"—that the booksellers were "a company of base knaves." The work is written in a couplet of twelve-syllable iambic lines, in imitation of the French Alexandrine, but with an unfailing cæsura after the third foot, which becomes very tiresome to the ear. (pp. 98-9)

At the same time, it must be confessed that the entire originality of the poem, its sustained vivacity, variety and accuracy, and its unlikeness to any other work of the age, give an indubitable interest to **Poly-Olbion,** which will always be referred to with pleasure, though seldom followed from "the utmost end of Cornwall's furrowing beak," to the fall of Esk and Eden into the Western Sands.

The confidence of Drayton in his own divine mission is sublime and pathetic. However unlucky he may be, he invariably takes the attitude of a poet of unquestioned eminence. In his **Man in the Moon,** the shepherds give Rowland (Drayton's accepted pseudonym) the office of their spokesman, because he was—

> By general voice, in times that then was grown,
> So excellent, that scarce there had been known,
> Him that excell'd in piping or in song.

His popularity might account for, yet scarcely excuse this attitude; but, in spite of this egotism, Drayton is a writer who commands our respect. He is manly and direct, and his virile style has the charm of what is well-performed in an easy and straightforward manner. He had studied the earlier poets to good effect. His critical knowledge of literature was considerable, and his acquaintance with natural objects exceptionally wide. His vocabulary is rich and uncommon; he has a pleasing preference for technical and rustic words. His variety, his ambition, his excellent versification claim our respect and admiration; but Drayton's weak point is that he fails to interest his reader. All is good, but little is superlatively entertaining. His most perfect poem was introduced by him, without any special attention being drawn to it, in what is supposed to be the sixth edition of his *Poems,* the folio of 1619. It is the following touching and passionate sonnet ["**Since there's no help, come let us kiss and part**"]:—

> Since there's no help, come let us kiss and part,—
> Nay, I have done, you get no more of me;
> And I am glad, yea glad with all my heart,
> That thus so cleanly I myself can free.
>
> Shake hands for ever, cancel all our vows,
> And when we meet at any time again,
> Be it not seen in either of our brows,
> That we one jot of former love retain.
>
> Now at the last gasp of love's latest breath,
> When, his pulse failing, passion speechless lies,
> When, faith is kneeling by his bed of death,
> And innocence is closing up his eyes,—
>
> —Now if thou wouldst, when all have given him over,
> From death to life thou mightst him yet recover!

(pp. 99-101)

Edmund Gosse, "Campion — Drayton — Drummond— Sir John Beaumont," in his The Jacobean Poets, *Charles Scribner's Sons, 1894, pp. 89-115.*

FRANCIS THOMPSON   (essay date 1899)

[*Thompson was one of the most important poets of the Catholic Revival in nineteenth-century English literature. Often compared to the seventeenth-century metaphysical poets, especially Richard Crashaw, he is best known for his poem "The Hound of Heaven" (1893), which displays his characteristic themes of spiritual struggle, redemption, and transcendent love. Like other writers of the fin de siècle period, Thompson wrote poetry and prose noted for rich verbal effects and evidence of a devotion to the values of aestheticism. In the following excerpt from an essay first published in 1899, Thompson critiques Drayton's technical skills.*]

[Drayton] is known to every schoolboy (not merely him too famous in Macaulay's pages) by the rousing "**Ballad of Agincourt**"; yet, unfortunate enough, he is further known in literary histories chiefly as the author of that very fearsome production—the *Polyolbion.* Not twenty Charles Lambs [see excerpt dated 1818] could get any unleisured man to read it. In reality he is one of the most masculine and individual among our minor poets. Whatever he does is burly, forthright, with a true English independence. Other ways may be better, he seems to say, but he will do things his own way. And his own way is mostly worth doing.

Yet Drayton, it must grudgingly be confessed, is a clumsy workman. Like most clumsy workmen who have something to say, he offends by awkward or downright unintelligible ellipses. Clumsy workmen who have nothing to say sin in quite other fashion. But inexpert craftsmen who are full of matter almost invariably try to bring their matter within metrical compass by the omission of connecting words—what is technically called ellipsis. It takes a great artist to use ellipsis well. Shakespeare is a master of it; yet even Shakespeare sometimes faults by excessive and crabbed ellipsis. Donne, a very pregnant writer, who, like Drayton, is not a good craftsman, is full of violent and knotty ellipses. But he has at least the palliation that his ellipses are scholarly, and result from an indiscreet

imitation of the Latin, where the inflected character of the language permits bold ellipsis inadmissible to an uninflected language like the English. Drayton's ellipses are not scholarly; they are thoroughly indigenous and awkward, as well as crabbed; the mere untaught expedients of a man who finds it difficult to shepherd his thick-coming ideas into the strait pen of a defined stanza. For this reason—whether or not he be at his best poetically—he is least clumsy in expression where he employs continuous metre (as in his pastorals) which permits him to take what compass he pleases in his utterance—gives him, in fact, room to turn round in. And Drayton, like the sturdy, strong, not unbovine Anglo-Saxon he is, needs a good deal of room to turn round in. This lack of adroitness hampers him in his sonnets, which abound in lumbering and quite unclassical ellipses, making them difficult reading. He is still more clod-paced in his *Odes,* and other poems written in brief stanzas of curt lines. Yet he is curiously fond of such measures—doubtless from his instinctive love of pregnancy. His virile abundance of idea well qualifies him for these stern, short metres—indeed, almost calls for them. But unluckily his indexterity of execution no less disqualifies him. He is like a man of pithy temperament but thick utterance. So that most readers had better take refuge in his pastorals, with their charming simplicity and flowing expression. Those only who are willing to wrestle with maladroit and knotty expression for the sake of masculine substance—whose teeth are sound enough to crack a tough nut for the sake of a nutritious kernel—should adventure upon the sonnets and the poems in curt stanza form. (pp. 68-9)

Yet this poet, whom we have in effect compared to a broad-shouldered Saxon farmer, needing much room to "come about" (in nautical phrase), can be delightfully dainty on occasion, full of pretty fancy—nay, even a certain arch caprice. So it was with rough old Ben, but Jonson had a classic elegance and accomplishment in his lighter moods, which is lacking to the less learned Drayton. Charming is the fancy and whimsy of *Nymphidia,* Drayton's mock-heroic fairy poem. Hark how the very metre seems to trip along on little feet, most apt for a fay story:

> Hence shadows, seeming idle shapes,
> Of little frisking elves and apes
> To earth do make their wanton scapes,
>   As hope or pastime hastes them;
> Which maids think on the hearth they see
> When fires well-near consumèd be,
> There dancing fays by two and three,
>   Just as their fancy casts them.

He has, indeed, a happy instinct for minor metres; witness the most graceful measure of the song in *The Shepherd's Sirena.* Pity it is these things are flawed at intervals by his awkward twists of expression. His pastorals have a sweet and clean rusticity about them, if they lack the downright realism of Allan Ramsay, and are full of the open air. Old Walton might have quoted his praise of fishing in the "**Sixth Nymphal**" [of *The Muses Elizium*]. There is much that is fine in the ode "**To the Virginian Voyage**," with its prophecy fulfilled so splendidly in later times:

> And in regions far,
> Such heroes bring ye forth
>   As those from whom we came;
>   And plant our name
> Under that star
> Not known unto our North.

One sonnet of Drayton's is famous: **"Since there's no help, come let us kiss and part."** But the others are by no means so vastly inferior, for all the faults we have already noted in them. (pp. 69-70)

Francis Thompson, "Daniel and Drayton," in his Literary Criticisms, *edited by Rev. Terence L. Connolly, S. J., E. P. Dutton and Company, Inc., 1948, pp. 67-72.*

W. J. COURTHOPE (essay date 1903)

[*Courthope was an English educator, poet, literary critic, and biographer whose most notable work is his six-volume* History of English Poetry (1895-1910). *Described by Stuart P. Sherman as a confirmed classicist in poetical theory, Courthope reacted against Romantic theory and practice and advocated a return to the heroic couplet and the satiric poetry characteristic of the age of Alexander Pope, whose collected works he edited. Courthope's criticism tends to center on the extent to which authors reflect the English character and traditions that encouraged the growth of the British empire. In the following excerpt, he discusses Drayton's poetry, noting where it is initiative and constrained, and where original and independent.*]

In fineness of fancy, in delicacy of humour, as well as in manly vigour of diction, [Drayton] has few superiors among his contemporaries, and, with the exception of Ben Jonson, there were none of them who equalled him in versatility of invention and in the extent of his learning. He tried many kinds of poetry, and wrote well in them all.

Some critics of his time charged him, as they did [Samuel] Daniel, with imitation. Their criticism was superficially just. The **Shepherd's Garland** was imitated from the *Shepherd's Calendar.* Many, if not most, of the sonnets in **Idea's Mirror** are based on conceits first invented by Daniel or Constable. **Endimion and Phoebe** was inspired by Marlowe's *Hero and Leander;* and if Drayton had not witnessed the same poet's *Edward II.,* he would perhaps never have conceived the character of Mortimer, the hero of his **Baron's Wars.** When his critics spoke of him as an imitator, they were probably thinking of his **England's Heroical Epistles,** which were, of course, suggested by the *Heroides* of Ovid. Spencer and Shakespeare both supplied him with some fundamental ideas. From the episode of the marriage of the Thames and the Medway in the *Faery Queen* he got the structural design of the **Polyolbion,** and from the description of Queen Mab in *Romeo and Juliet* the framework of **Nymphidia.**

All this is just what we should expect from the account Drayton gives us of his early inclination to verse-making: he became a poet by reading and admiring the works of other poets [see excerpt dated 1627]. His genius, receptive and many-sided, required to be set in motion from without, but, once supplied with materials, it stamped on them the impress of its own character. He imitated after the fashion of the best poets. Seed, sown by the hands of others in the quick soil of his imagination, brought forth a new variety of fruit. The ideas he borrowed were reinvested to advantage, and the poetical fortune he made out of them was honestly earned by his own judgment and invention.

What he lacked was loftiness and resolution of artistic purpose. With more respect for himself and his art, he would have been able to turn his many fine qualities towards some worthy end. As it was, he could not "himself above himself erect himself." Instead of leading the taste of his day, he sought to follow it,

and to make his art an instrument of his own promotion. Unfortunately for him, the taste of the Court was in itself so frivolous and uncertain that it could not guide his invention into right channels. Since Sidney's disappearance the great ideal of chivalry had decayed, and the garb of romantic allegory and Arcadianism, in which that poet and Spenser had sought to ennoble courtly manners, had fallen out of fashion. Those of the courtiers who were conscious of great merit attempted to mark their pre-eminence by external magnificence and the ostentatious patronage of letters. The praises of ingenious poets were eagerly sought for: hence the leading motive of all Drayton's earlier poems, **The Shepherd's Garland, Idea's Mirror, Endimion and Phoebe,** and even **Mortimeriados,** was to gratify the vanity, while pleasing the imagination, of the Countess of Bedford and her circle. Poetry cannot rise above the taste that inspires it, any more than water can rise above its own level.

England's Heroical Epistles display more independence of spirit, and therefore deservedly achieve a higher artistic success. There was some originality in the design of applying Ovid's invention of poetical letter-writing to famous characters in English history, and considerable versatility of imagination is shown in conceiving the different situations of the various lovers. But there are traces of mechanical workmanship in the execution of the design. Ovid divides the six epistles of his *Heroides* between the letters, with the answers to them, of three pairs of lovers. Drayton follows this plan through all of his twenty-four epistles, with the result that his style necessarily becomes monotonous. Nevertheless, these poems contain vigorous and harmonious passages, of which the best is perhaps the following from the epistle of Surrey to the Lady Geraldine:—

> When time shall turn those amber locks to gray,
> My verse again shall gild and make them gay,
> And trick them up in knotted curls anew,
> And to thy autumn give a summer's hue:
> That sacred power that in my ink remains
> Shall put fresh blood into thy withered veins,
> And on thy red decayed, thy whiteness dead,
> Shall set a white more white, a red more red.
> When thy dim sight thy glass cannot descry,
> Nor thy crazed mirror can discern thine eye,
> My verse, to tell the one what th' other was,
> Shall represent them both, thine eye and glass,
> When both thy mirror and thine eye shall see
> What once thou saw'st in that, that saw in thee;
> And to them both shall tell the simple truth,
> What that in pureness was, what thou in youth.

The reader will observe in this passage how characteristically Drayton borrows the idea from Daniel, but fits it to his own epistolary method, and also with what rare art he has adapted the leading features of Ovid's elegiac verse to the English decasyllabic line. In his terse epigrams and antitheses we have the germs of the style which reached its last development in Pope's treatment of the heroic couplet.

The freedom and fluency with which **England's Heroical Epistles** are written give the measure of the advance made by Drayton when disembarrassed of the necessity of paying compliments in verse. Fresh energy was added to his style after his quarrel with the Countess of Bedford, and it is artistically instructive to compare the insincerity of such a sonnet as that beginning **"Wonder of Heaven"** in **Idea's Mirror** with the manly directness of the sonnets prefatory to the later collection, **Sonnets under the Title of Idea,** and still more with the famous and splendid lines in which it is now clear that he symbolised, under the imagery of lovers' parting, his final rupture with his patroness:—

> Since there's no help, come let us kiss and part!
> Nay, I have done, you get no more of me,
> And I am glad, yea, glad with all my heart,
> That thus so cleanly I myself can free;
> Shake hands for ever, cancel all our vows,
> And, when we meet at any time again,
> Be it not seen in either of our brows
> That we one jot of former love retain.
> Now, at the last gasp of love's failing breath,
> When, his pulse failing, passion speechless lies,
> When faith is kneeling by his bed of death,
> And innocence is closing up his eyes,
>   Now if thou wouldst, when all have given him over,
>   From death to life thou mightst him still recover.

Had Drayton valued his art at the same rate as he here values himself, he might have produced some great poems. But it was not to be. The necessities of living were too strong for him. He was forced now to write down to the public taste. *Mortimeriados,* originally designed for the amusement of the Countess of Bedford, was based, after Marlowe's fashion, upon the character of Mortimer. When the Countess had to be deprived of her share of the inspiration, the poem was converted, for the benefit of the general reader, into a formal epic on *The Baron's Wars.* It thus became a rival of Daniel's *Civil Wars,* and consequently liable to the sentences which Drayton himself passed on the latter composition. In the same way—as we see from the preface [see excerpt dated 1612]—the *Polyolbion* was evidently designed to catch the interest of the numerous readers who were patriotically interested in the archaeology of their own counties. The conception was not primarily poetical; and in spite of its vast learning and accurate descriptions, in spite, too, of the mythological impersonations, by means of which the poet seeks to raise the narrative out of the sphere of prose, nothing can save the work from the censure of being "antiquity in verse." There are passages in the thirty songs, which constitute the poem, full of ingenious fancy; but, as a whole, the mechanical conduct of the action and the monotony of the Alexandrine verse . . . make it unreadable.

The admirable ballad on the battle of Agincourt was evidently struck off at a heat under the inspiration of the metrical tune in Thomas Heywood's song, "Agincourt, Agincourt! know ye not Agincourt?" but the epic narrative of the battle, which Drayton afterwards built out of the ballad, is nothing more than versified prose. Only once again in his later years did he soar into a divine region above the heavy and gross atmosphere of hack-writing. This was in the delightful fairy epic *Nymphidia,* in which he burlesques the action both of *A Midsummer Night's Dream* and the *Orlando Furioso.* Many years before he had struck upon the happy thought of imitating Chaucer's lay of Sir Thopas in the pastoral ballad of Dowsabell, which is the only valuable portion of *The Shepherd's Garland.* In a development of this metre he now found an epic vehicle for the narrative of the madness of the fairy king Oberon, caused by a not unwarranted jealousy of Pigwiggen, one of his knights, whose relations with Queen Mab seem to have resembled those existing between Launcelot and Guinevere. The action of the poem is made up of the adventures arising out of an assignation granted by the Queen to Pigwiggen, which Oberon, hearing of, resolves to interrupt. Oberon's madness is, on an elfin scale, the exact counterpart of Orlando's, the relative heroic proportion being preserved throughout, and the incidents imagined with the most excellent humour and invention. (pp. 40-5)

W. J. Courthope, "Spenser's Successors: Michael Drayton, William Browne," in his A History of English Poetry, Vol. III, Macmillan and Co., Limited, 1903, pp. 27-53.

OLIVER ELTON (essay date 1905)

[*Elton was an English academic and literary historian. In such works as the six-volume* Survey of English Literature (1912-28) *and* The English Muse (1933), *he examined English literature from the Anglo-Saxon period through the early twentieth century. In the following excerpt from his critical study of Drayton, he discusses the progression of the poet's career and notes the endurance of his achievement.*]

More than the masters, the explorers of unknown forms, the original breakers-up of the wilderness, Drayton has the title of an Elizabethan poet, of a representative. He tells of the current achievements and aims of his age in poetic art. What others lend him, he appropriates with power and redelivers, and he comes honestly by the pleasure that his work gives him. The rarer part of a truly originative mind like Spenser's—his nicety of colour or his sense of the terror of the sea—only isolates him from contemporary feeling: it is usually best felt by far posterity, and it offers no hold to discipleship. Drayton was no such weaver of new hues and stories upon the arras of dreams; his delight is to utter sincerely the ruling Elizabethan thoughts and ardours, though he too . . . struck, after a while, on some fortunate inventions, and heard rhythms of his own. He tried nearly every kind of verse that was the mode during the last ten years of the queen's reign, except moral allegory. He wrote pastoral, sonnet, paraphrase, Ovidian fable, narrative chronicle, legend, and panegyric. If no other poetry were left but his, we could discover from it many of the imaginative interests of those years. . . . [Drayton] treads at high noon upon the frequented roads of poetry, shunning twilight and the woven shadows of the forest. His inequality is that which besets almost all of his generation except Spenser. Like others, he seldom writes a perfect poem, or one without perfect lines. Some of the species he attempted proved unresourceful in his hands, like the legend, the chronicle, and the satire; others, like the ode and pastoral, prospered; and in one style, that of the *Heroical Epistles,* he found an unborrowed tune. He frankly submits to the sway exercised by Sidney, by Spenser, and by Daniel, upon the last verse written under the Tudors, but his artistic tie with each of them is different, and tells upon different parts of his poetry.

The praise of Spenser is found in the verse of Drayton at intervals over five-and-thirty years, and if the influence fades, admiration remains. The younger poet was ever revising, and knew of the knots and obstacles in his own talent, naturally level and sturdy rather than gracious or dexterous, and he was put to shame by the sure hand of the always poetical Spenser. In *Endimion and Phoebe* he cries:

> Dear Colin, let our Muse excusèd be,
> Which rudely thus presumes to sing by thee;
> Although the strains be harsh, untuned, and ill,
> Nor can attain to thy divinest skill.

And writing in the reign of Charles he still honours 'Colin'

> On his shawm so clear
> Many a high-pitched note that had.

And to the last he regarded 'grave, moral Spenser' as 'in all high knowledge surely excellent,' and awarded him a kind of Homeric scope for the bravery of his invention:

> I am persuaded there was none
> Since the blind bard his Iliads up did make,
> Fitter a task like that to undertake.

And this loyalty, filial, not servile, had its reward when Drayton began himself to be called 'golden-mouthed,' or to be commended for the 'purity and preciousness of his phrase': epithets that we can still apply to him at his best. Spenser . . . served Drayton most in the fields of the pastoral and the sonnet; the debt extends to subject and to cadence as well as to many a strain of sentiment, whether pessimistic, defiant, or Platonic. And he also infected Drayton with his lofty and proud conception of what the poet's calling really is, when it is confronted with the brute and bastard ambitions of the world. (pp. 26-30)

By one of the chances of history, the pastoral eclogue, arranged in a cycle of months, had served, rather than any larger form, to announce in 1579 the coming of the new poetry. The *Shepherd's Calendar,* with the variety of its adventures in rhythm, and its flashes of the nobler style, had at once caught attention, and found imitators. Of Thomas Watson little can be said; but, fourteen years after, Drayton was the first worthy pastoral follower of Spenser, and began his true poetical life as Spenser's student. ***Idea, the Shepherd's Garland, fashioned in nine Eglogs; Rowland's Sacrifice to the Nine Muses,*** was published in 1593. Drayton here turns away from the shepherd dialect that, to speak the truth, makes the *Calendar* tiresome, as well as from that habit of prudently obscure invective against Church or State, which is traceable at last to the Latin pastorals of Petrarch. But, like Spencer, he uses the eclogue in one of its most primitive extensions, for eulogy. The third number contains an ode to Elizabeth, which may well compare with the earlier "April." Splendour and onset are not wanting here, and the lengthy lines, which Drayton always favoured, have the weight of a broad and tumbling wave. (pp. 31-2)

[In the eighth eclogue] Drayton first uses the jingle of the old rhymed romances in a sportive way to which he afterwards—thirty and more years afterwards—gave his fullest finish in ***Nymphidia*** and the ***Shepherd's Sirena.*** This echo of Chaucer's *Sir Thopas* may have come to him through Spenser; and he finds just the right, flat sheep-bell tinkle, and the right, faded-archaic diction, *miniveer, Dowsabel, Chanteclere,* that is the far echo of a burlesque of something itself long perished. Otherwise there is, one may fear, some commonness and extravagance in ***The Shepherd's Garland;*** in the celebrations of Sidney under the name of Elphin, and of his sister under that of Pandora, and in many other places. But thirteen years later, in 1606, Drayton re-edited these pastorals thoroughly, and did them good, although he inserted new enigmas. . . . The improvements in this version show the unabated sway of Spenser and his perennial power to ennoble Drayton's language. In the renewed praises of Sir Philip Sidney, whose worth and honour, we are told, some have been rashly censuring, a few lines have the plangency of their original, the "Ruins of Time":

> And, learned shepherd, thou to time shalt live
>   When their great names are utterly forgotten,
> And fame to thee eternity shall give
>   When with their bones their sepulchres are
>   rotten.
>
> Nor mournful cypress nor sad widowing yew
>   About thy tomb to prosper shall be seen,
> But bay and myrtle which be ever new,
>   In spite of winter flourishing and green.

Drayton shows also more of that power of pure singing, which came to him late and slow. He could not learn it from Spenser who hardly practised in short lyric measures. More than once we have a presentiment of the music that the long-living Drayton was to discover in himself twenty years later still; the riches of lyrical sound, the magic of Carew and the age of Charles. To the pastoral, of a lighter and more lovely shape, he was to return in his old age, as *The Muses' Elizium* testifies. (pp. 35-7)

[There] were reasons why Drayton should suffer eclipse during the day of Dryden and Pope; for he had begun to be obscured even earlier. He had overlived the bitter end of the great patriotic age of which he tried to be the voice; he had produced much that died at once; and his instinct to absorb and copy, though he is far too strong to be called a mimic, did not always enable him to shape his materials. In his big work [*Polyolbion*] he attempted so much that it is hard to rescue attention for its noble episodes. He left no school, though he had created some original forms like the ***Heroical Epistles,*** the ***Odes,*** and the ***Nymphidia.*** The last of these leaves a tiny wake behind it in the history of our poetry.

But the change of poetical taste also unduly marred his fame. He and not Milton is the last Elizabethan in the truer sense. He had sounded the bugle-calls of the older generation; he had sung his fervent and chivalrous love and his hope of enduring verse, and his love for the land and all its ancient things. In the middle of the seventeenth century the themes of Milton and those around him were different, and Drayton's somewhat fitful executive talent failed to buoy up his reputation. But with Marlowe and Chapman to share his oblivion he was in good society.

If Drayton left no school, he had never been vowed to any. He touched and studied poets, from Spenser to Carew, who were of different worlds. During his first twenty years we can tell from his verse what kinds of non-dramatic poetry were in acceptance, and how a gallant and capable craftsman could realise them. He was justified in his courage, but it is curious to see the frequent struggle of his strong and stiff-grained spirit with subjects that call for a sure and supple hand. Often he seems to prevail, in the English way, by pure force of toil and character. But the variety of his successes is imposing. He wrote hardly anything that is not luminous here and there, that fails of articulate and beautiful passages, and he wrote much that is sustained. If we are to name his most insuperable flaw, apart from his bluntness, it can be seen by any pedagogue; it is that want of clear and right grammar, which raises smoke and friction in the axles of his chariot. But in youth and age he was often a master of the eclogue and its enchanting artifice. As sonneteer he could step into the circle of Shakespearean splendour and intensity, and once he leapt full into the centre, having murmured the right incantation. He had his days of decorative felicity, when he made ***Endimion and Phoebe,*** and not then only. He moved easily in the Ovidian declamatory style, harping on love and *desiderium* ["ardent desire"]. Even in satire and religious verse, his least fortunate field, he struck out flashes. No man tried in so many forms to utter the passion for England, the passion of England for itself. In some he failed, but he went on undismayed to others not less exacting. He is least impeded and bravest and most musical in several of his odes. Age brought him a lighter hand; he achieves the pitch of good-natured and manly gaiety in his epistles on himself and his friends. But he is latterly happiest in lyric of the gallant, faintly mannered, not too vehement kind, where he is thinking of his cadence and enjoying it. Historians have begun to talk as if they were ashamed of Drayton, but theirs is the sacrifice.

His importance in the musical, and not only in the mechanic, evolution of our verse is real and distinct. He gave an accent of his own to nearly every measure that he practised; and he practised sextain, rhyme royal, sonnet, Italian octave, heroic couplet, short-lined ode, octosyllabic couplet, dithyrambic stanza, and alexandrines. There is not one of these that he did not sometimes write as well as any poet of the English Renaissance. It was in the ode and the couplet that his tunes, if not very subtle or abstrusely harmonised, were most his own, and most fertile as examples. The angel of rhythm visits him forgetfully and capriciously, and like Wordsworth he goes on doggedly in its absence. But he has notes at first of the shawm and trumpet, and latterly of the flute as well.

> Near to the silver Trent
>   Sirena dwelleth,
> She to whom nature lent
>   All that excelleth:
> By which the Muses late,
>   And the neat Graces
> Have for their greater state
>   Taken their places;
> Twisting an anadem
>   Wherewith to crown her,
> As it belonged to them
>   Most to renown her.

The slight ruggedness in these verses is not unpleasing, and saves their nerve. And elsewhere Drayton is among the first to strike out the tune that is heard all through the seventeenth century in Cowley, in Rochester, in Dryden, down to the darker days of lyric:

> I pray thee, love, love me no more,
>   Call home the heart you gave me,
> I but in vain that saint adore
>   That can, but will not save me;
> *These poor half-kisses kill me quite;*
>   Was ever man thus served,
> Amidst an ocean of delight
>   For pleasure to be starved?

To learn to write this after sixty shows a great vitality of assimilation or invention; how far Drayton has travelled in his musical art from his Spenserian days, or from the style of 1597,—from this!—

> When heaven would strive to do the best it can,
> And put an angel's spirit into man,
> The utmost power it hath, it then doth spend,
> When to the world a Poet it doth intend. . . .
> When Time shall turn those amber locks to grey,
> My verse again shall gild and make them gay,
> And trick them up in knotted curls anew,
> And to thy autumn give a summer's hue:
> That sacred power, that in my ink remains,
> Shall put fresh blood into thy withered veins,
> And on thy red decayed, thy whiteness dead,
> Shall set a white more white, a red more red.

And yet . . . this earlier oratory has its own line of descendants, and will startle those who think that it began with Sandys or with Waller. We cannot say of Drayton, in the pedigree of literature, as we must of so many poets, *obiit sine prole* ["he died without progeny"]. Nor is his interest at all purely of the damning historical kind, which is only another name for a second death, unless it be reinforced by absolute excellence: for to this excellence he often attains, and in the register of the poets he is himself, not simply one of our ancestors who

made experiments. If he does not rank without question among the highest, he is an athlete, suspected of half-Olympian and half-terrestrial blood, who is of commanding stature and can lift many weighty burdens; with a sturdy, dignified beauty of his own, and a soft, musical grace; and speaking now and then with something of the divine accent. (pp. 150-56)

Oliver Elton, in his Michael Drayton: A Critical Study, *revised edition, 1905. Reprint by Russell & Russell, 1966, 216 p.*

ROBERT HILLYER   (essay date 1923)

[*Hillyer was an American poet, novelist, and literary scholar best known for his championing of the heroic couplet in such works as his poetry collection* Sonnets and Other Lyrics *(1917) and his critical study* In Pursuit of Poetry *(1960). His* Collected Verse *(1933) won the Pulitzer Prize. In the following excerpt, Hillyer examines the* Idea *sonnets, comparing them favorably with other Elizabethan love poetry.*]

[The] sonnets of Shakespeare are with difficulty detached from all the nonsense—pestiferous nonsense, as Mr. Machen would say—that has been written about Mr. W. H. and the Dark Lady. Shakespeare did unlock his heart! He didn't! Mr. W. H. was Willy Hughes, the Earl of This and That, William Himself! The Dark Lady was Mary Fitton (a blonde, by the way); she was an abstraction; she was Anne Hathaway suddenly restored to favour! Such goings-on as these have presented a pretty spectacle indeed to the poor wretches who would fain enjoy the poems themselves. There is no excuse for it; nowhere in criticism can be found a more shoddy and lewd suburb of the intellectual city.

In protest, let us ignore absolutely the origin of Drayton's sonnets, and, strangely enough, consider them as literature. Grouped under the vague title **Idea,** they are the least vague and the most outspoken poems of their time. The segregation, under various absurd names, of the single **"Sonnet LXI,"** **"Since there's no help,"** tacitly implies that the rest of the series is negligible. This is far from the truth. Mr. Symons, the most sensitive of modern critics of the Elizabethan period, concedes that "there are a dozen others only less fine than this one." Let us add, there are a dozen others more interesting.

Out of the sixty-three which compose the cycle, about one-fifth are unadulterated conceits, banal when they were written, unreadable now. But in most of the sonnets, conceit has yielded to a chemical change in the crucible of the poet's mind. They are, indeed, the old components, but entirely reorganized, sometimes with a nimble satire, sometimes with a vigour that recalls Donne, always with the steady heat of honest passion. Take, for example, the classic conception of the poet conferring immortality on the beloved; a favourite theme with the Elizabethans, familiar in its Shakespearean dress:

> So long as men can breathe or eyes can see,
> So long lives this, and this gives life to thee.

Drayton is not content with the conception in itself; he must vent his scorn of the minxes he beholds in the streets of the city; he must condescendingly inform his chosen lady of the happiness of her fate in being enshrined in his verses:

> How many paltry, foolish, painted things
> That now in coaches trouble every street,
> Shall be forgotten, whom no poet sings,
> Ere they be well wrapp'd in their winding-sheet!
> Where I to thee eternity shall give,
> When nothing else remaineth of these days,

And Queens hereafter shall be glad to live
Upon the alms of thy superfluous praise.
Virgins and matrons reading these my rhymes,
Shall be so much delighted with thy story,
That they shall grieve they liv'd not in these times,
To have seen thee, their sex's only glory;
    So shalt thou fly above the vulgar throng,
    Still to survive in my immortal song.

There is an irritable intensity to this, a nervous exaggeration, which quickens the old, arrogant thought with a new liveliness.

"Sonnet LIX" [**"As Love and I, late harbour'd in one Inne"**] is a riot of proverbs and euphuisms—all that we are accustomed to condemn as lapses of taste in the literature of the period. Yet, after Love and The Lover have exchanged their witticisms through the three quatrains, the poet himself, unable to support any longer this parody on his passion, impatiently cuts into the banter with,

    And having thus a while each other thwarted,
    Fools as we met, so fools again we parted.

This trick of reappearing, with heart bare, after playing with verbal masques of emotion, is frequent with Drayton:

    Thus am I still provoked to every evil
    By this good, wicked Spirit, sweet Angel-devil.

    Now if thou wouldst, when all have given him over,
    From death to life thou mightst him yet recover.

After performing the usual tricks with the word heart, he cries

    Why talk I of a heart when thou hast none?—
    Or if thou hast, it is a flinty one.

Then, having worn out his patience with conceits from Roman mythology,

    I conjure thee by all that I have nam'd
    To make her love, or, Cupid, be thou damn'd.

It is not in the couplets alone that the lover pushes his fist through the scenery and peers out to see how goes the play. Here he devotes the fourteen lines to some homely episode of his suit; there he gives us a glimpse of some contemporary event or fashion. Now and then a whole poem is given over to smooth, lyric numbers; more frequently the sonnet-form strains under a gust of anger or of spite. The atrabilious fancy of **"Sonnet VIII"** [**"There's nothing grieves me, but that Age should haste"**] affords us, I suspect, far keener insight into a lovesick mind than the lachrymose offerings of more conventional poets. . . . (pp. 488-89)

This sonnet shows, especially in the second verse, the extremely uneven quality of Drayton's technique. He was not a born versifier; his expression tends to falter. He was aware of this himself, and, we are told, revised his work constantly. But judging from *Idea,* we may conclude that the revision was occasioned less by a desire for smooth measures than a passion for complete sincerity. Drayton was so eager to pack everything into fourteen lines that the unyielding words burst with the pressure of such a mass of meaning. Damaging as this method was to the technical quality of his verse, it contributed to the higher quality which transcends technique; which, when blent with perfection of technique, becomes what we vaguely term supreme poetry. These sonnets are not supreme poetry; they stutter with intensity; they fumble with nervous impatience. But they are interesting poetry of the highest order, and they are, beyond all doubt, genuine statements. . . .

Perhaps I have neglected the more conventionally poetic in favour of the more distinctive sonnets. For the man draped his mind so carelessly that one is more absorbed by the dazzle of naked thought than the drapery itself. But one can not forget "So doth the ploughman gaze the wandering star," and many another single line of flawless beauty. Beside such passages, beside the whimsical outpouring of every mood, there are moments of grave meditation which would harmonize with the more solemn music of Spenser's sequence.

Breaking the self-imposed regulation with which we began, let us admit that Drayton's suit, unlike Spenser's did not end in marriage, nor was his horizon ever gilded with the hope of success. "I ever love where never hope appears." Remembering Byron's

    Think you, if Laura had been Petrarch's wife,
    He would have written sonnets all his life?

we may find consolation where Drayton found only bleak failure, for failure has induced in his work an angry vigour which is the essence of the cycle even more than the nobler, tragic mood with which the famous Sonnet LXI has made us familiar.

It is unfortunate that one poem, not representative of the series, should have received its due praise only at the expense of the others. For although Sidney's sonnets are more romantic, and Spenser's more exalted, than Drayton's; nevertheless, the sonnets to *Idea* are the most varied, the liveliest, perhaps the greatest, of all the sonnets of that age except those of Shakespeare. (p. 489)

    Robert Hillyer, "The Drayton Sonnets," in The Freeman, *New York, Vol. VI, No. 151, January 31, 1923, pp. 488-89.*

J. C. SQUIRE (essay date 1924)

[*Squire was an English man of letters who lent his name to the "Squirearchy," a group of poets who struggled to maintain the Georgian poetry movement of the early twentieth century. Typified by such poets as Rupert Brooke and John Drinkwater, Georgian poetry was a reaction against Victorian prolixity, turn-of-the-century decadence, and contemporary urban realism. Squire and the Georgians wished to return to the nineteenth-century poetic tradition of William Wordsworth and the Lake Poets, concerning themselves primarily with the traditional subjects and themes of English pastoral verse. Squire was also a prolific critic who was involved with many important English periodicals; he founded and edited the* London Mercury, *served as literary and, later, acting editor of the* New Statesman, *and contributed frequently to the* Illustrated London News *and the* Observer. *His criticism, like his poetry, is considered traditional and good-natured. In the following introduction to a 1924 edition of* Nimphidia, *Squire comments on the poem's nonsensical appeal.*]

Michael Drayton's *Nimphidia* is one of the most charming pieces of English fairy poetry; sister of the fairy scenes in *A Midsummer Night's Dream,* and mother of the *Night-Piece to Julia.* It is an odd thing that not one reader knows it for a hundred who are familiar with the same poet's *Agincourt.* Its fancies are extraordinarily pretty and varied, and it is marked by a peculiarly charming whimsicality.

The note of *Drayton's* humour is sounded in the opening stanzas:

    Olde CHAUCER doth of *Topas* tell,
    Mad RABLAIS of *Pantagruell,*
    A latter third of *Dowsabell,*
    With such poore trifles playing:
    Others the like have laboured at
    Some of this thing, and some of that,
    And many of they know not what;
        But that they must be saying . . .

He proceeds to *Oberon*'s palace in the air, made of spiders' legs, cats' eyes, and bats' skins gilt with moonshine. *Oberon* is jealous of *Pigwiggen* (as good a name as *Bottom*), who has given Queen *Mab* a bracelet made of emmets' eyes, 'a thing he thought that she would prize.' *Pigwiggen* makes an assignation at a cowslip flower. The Queen flies thither in her gnat-drawn snail-shell with wheels made of cricket bones. *Hop, Mop, Drop, Pip, Trip, Skip,* and her other monosyllabic attendants find her gone and give chase on a grasshopper. *Oberon* becomes enraged, and successively engages in erroneous strife with a wasp, a glow-worm, and a swarm of bees. He meets *Puck,* who leads him to his faithless consort. There is a grand battle, and in the end *Proserpina* wipes all trace of these untoward events from the memories of those who have taken part in them.

The detail is excellent all the way, and the metre moves trippingly. Sheer nonsense has seldom been more delightfully written. (pp. 5-6)

> *J. C. Squire, in a preface to* Nimphidia: The Court of Fayrie *by Michael Drayton, edited by J. C. Squire, Basil Blackwell, 1924, pp. 5-6.*

EDMUND BLUNDEN   (essay date 1931)

[*Blunden was associated with the Georgians, an early twentieth-century group of English poets who reacted against the prevalent contemporary mood of disillusionment and the rise of artistic modernism by seeking to return to the pastoral, nineteenth-century poetic traditions associated with William Wordsworth. In this regard, much of Blunden's poetry reflects his love of the sights, sounds, and ways of rural England. As a literary critic and essayist, he often wrote of the lesser-known figures of the Romantic era as well as of the pleasures of English country life. In the following excerpt, he discusses* Poly-Olbion's *eloquent expression of patriotism as well as the poem's faults of excessive length and monotony.*]

When, in 1622, the author of *Polyolbion* put forth the second part of his poem, he was not in the best of tempers. His first part had contained a notice "To the General Reader," not so conciliatory as it might have been, with its "If, as I say, thou hadst rather (because it asks thy labour) remain where thou wert, than strain thyself to walk forth with the Muses, the fault proceeds from thy idleness, not from any want in my industry" [see excerpt dated 1612]. That had been in 1612. So few had strained themselves during the next ten years that poor Drayton evidently began to think the reader anything but general. The publishers had already annoyed him by agreeing with him. The publishers were "a company of base knaves." His second part was at last printed, for three of these wretches, and enabled him to address a protest "To any that will read it" [see essay dated 1622]. It spoke of "outlandish, unnatural English," who openly, brazenly declared their self-satisfied ignorance. This bovine behaviour could only result in one thing—Drayton's contempt of such "cattle."

And, sad as the case is, *Polyolbion* has never in its three centuries employed overmuch the general reader. It has been seldom reprinted. When one considers that it contains more than fourteen thousand lines in that long-winded measure the Alexandrine, this melancholy attitude on the part of Drayton's friends the booksellers ought to cause no surprise. The truth is, they have done somewhat better by the unwieldy giant than with strict commercial restraint they might have done. (p. 36)

Perhaps some minds, at the outset, will maintain that Drayton set out to achieve the impossible; and no doubt an argument exists in justification of this. Of his intentions Drayton, unlike many poets, and particularly those of to-day, gives a plain statement. It is the explanatory title of his 1622 volume: "A Chorographicall Description of all the Tracts, Rivers, Mountains, Forests, and other Parts of this Renowned Isle of Great Britain, with intermixture of the most Remarkeable Stories, Antiquities, Wonders, Rarities, Pleasures, and Commodities of the same. Divided into two Bookes. . . . Digested into a Poem by Michael Drayton, Esquire." All the tracts, rivers, mountains, forests and other parts! The spirit not kindled at the same torch with Drayton's might be excused for considering the matter in a prose light, which transforms it with no great effort into a row of "Beauties of England and Wales"—all that Drayton actually accomplished—with numerous plates. But it was to be a poem, doubtless illustrating the principle of long poems which must have their prose passages, yet in the main, according to Drayton's further promises, leaving the hearer in a fantastic triumph.

> Walk forth into the *Tempe* and fields of the Muses, where through most delightful groves the angelic harmony of birds shall steal thee to the top of an easy hill, where, in artificial caves, cut out of the most natural rock, thou shalt see the ancient people of this Isle deliver thee in their lively images: from whose height thou mayest behold both the old and later times, as in thy prospect, lying far under thee; then conveying thee down by a soul-pleasing descent

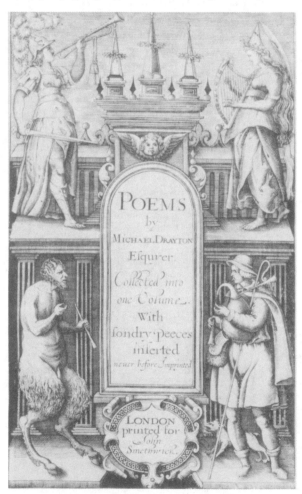

Frontispiece of Drayton's Poems *(1605).*

through delicate embroidered Meadows, often veined with gentle gliding Brooks; in which thou mayest fully view the dainty Nymphs in their simple naked beauties, bathing them in crystalline streams; which shall lead thee to most pleasant Downs, where harmless Shepherds are, some exercising their pipes, some——

Enough. We will try this, and give up our first objections.

There is much more, however, than a general difficulty in reading *Polyolbion*. The Alexandrine is one of the especial grievances which many must feel against their poet Drayton. Too often it suggests Pope's scornful metaphor, "a wounded snake"; and it is, unfortunately, when Drayton is carrying out his plan of describing "all" the map of Britain that his measure reveals the painfulness of his journey. It is not, as Hazlitt briefly says [see excerpt dated 1820], that the work itself conceived as a whole betrays a freshness abating from its first degree: but sometimes in the execution of his duty Drayton fills his notebook with monotonous details.

> And in that Isle again, which beareth *Ely*'s name,
> At *Ramsey*, *Merwin* so a veiléd maid became
>
> Amongst our Virgin-Saints, where *Elfled* is enroll'd,
> The daughter that is nam'd of noble *Ethelwold*,
> A great *East-Anglian* Earl, of *Ramsey* Abbess long,
> So of our Maiden-Saints, the female sex among.
> With *Milburg*, *Mildred* comes, and *Milwid*, daughters dear,
> To *Mervald*, who did then the *Mercian* sceptre bear.
> At *Wenlock*, *Milburg* died (a most religious maid.)
> Of which great Abbey she the first foundation laid:
> And *Thanet* as her Saint (even to this age) doth hery
> Her *Mildred*. *Milwid* was the like at *Canterbury*.

These passages are the stony ground of *Polyolbion*, but to their author they were evidently no less part of his happy kingdom than those which more closely resemble his Arcadian advertisement just now quoted.

Must it not be admitted, too, that his artificial machinery, working no doubt admirably well towards the completion of his design, at length tries the reader? "Our second Ovid" personifies so impersonally and so often that one longs at times for a river not in love, nor boasting, nor looking grim at another: for a mountain not making a speech. Geography without fable might, for the ease of the weaker sort, have been allowed more divers occasions amid the profusion; so great is Drayton's gift of natural description that his armoury of fancies, insomuch as it is for ever intervening, has much to be blamed for. But working largely by the map, and not like Camden, the other "nourrice of antiquitie," riding or walking over the places unfamiliar to him, Drayton cautiously avoided the conflict of precise though imaginative painting with local information; to style a stream clear or silver being safer than to see it twinkling through meeting willows at a venture. So vigilant is he in his tactics that he cannot call the Wey a "fern-crown'd Flood" without the footnote, "Coming by *Fernham*, so called of *fern* there growing."

One could pursue other charges against *Polyolbion* from the view of the reader; even that of incompleteness in regard to its own stated scope—of superstitions, sports and pastimes, trades, types, towns and relics unsung; but to do this would perhaps be to cause Drayton's pious shade an anxiety lest his poem had not been long enough. It becomes more congenial to agree with him that it is a poem, "genuine, and first in this kind," the utterance of a man gloriously seeking to use for his country's renown the peculiar powers which his country had

bred in him. Not different in amassed intensity, though in rapture less sudden, was this worship of Drayton's from that transfiguring patriotism which in 1798 changed the note of Coleridge's *Fears in Solitude* from

> We have been too long
> Dupes of a deep delusion

to

> O divine
> And beauteous island! thou hast been my sole
> And most magnificent temple.

Nor did Drayton speak this his mind on the one occasion: there is his "**Agincourt**," fiery with the very soul of "such acts"; his "**Virginian Voyage**," leading our eyes beyond the then awesome Atlantic to new English heroism; his *Nimphidia*, green thoughts in green shades of England. Here, however, the grand sum of his ancestral, his chivalrous, his adventurous, his pastoral pride was to be determined; the reckoning of his gratitude to his home paid to the uttermost farthing. How, then, is his poem to be judged—as an antiquarian relic, or a deed of unique fervour? The critic and the philanthropist in us may fall out over the answer; the heaviness of the achievement, in so many places, obscuring the singular effulgence of the sustaining impulse.

"What he deemed his greatest work will be preserved by his subject," wrote Southey [see excerpt dated 1839], who even as a poet had a Draytonian doggedness and severe laureateship. It may be so; it is certain that many know the name and realise the inspiration of *Polyolbion* who have not read a dozen lines of the poem. But to end there is to miss much more than strings of place-names and rhymed chronicles. A poet with the vitality of Drayton, a countryman with his shrewd eye to see and vocabulary to express, a reader of history as magnificence with advantages of comprehension gained from his own career, could not easily have set down song after song without many triumphs by the way. Of Drayton's minor poems Mr. Brett, their most recent editor [see Additional Bibliography], has said that to appraise them is to seem "criticising many poets, not one"; and the finest passages in his *Polyolbion* vary as much as, under their uniform dress, they could do. The fierce onset of "**Agincourt**," the rapt serenity of his farewell to the "**Virginian Voyage**," the "once upon a time" enchantment of *Nimphidia*, and the poetical table-talk (from the neat occasionally breaking into the brilliant), of "**To Henry Reynolds**" are to be rediscovered in that wide country *Polyolbion*. (pp. 37-41)

The Thirteenth Song of *Polyolbion* is, if not the best, considered separately, yet of the best; and that is clearly due to its theme, Warwickshire. The pictures of home fields and forests here are fresh and green.

> My native Country then, which so brave spirits hast bred,
> If there be virtue yet remaining in thy earth,
> Or any good of thine thou breath'd'st into my birth,
> Accept it as thine own:

and one knows that he here leaves his map and his ingenuity, and tells to himself again all the pleasures of the past. The woods and ridings are about him; the old sunshine holiday gives him leave to explore in his first liberty. There he meets old people whom he knew, as he met them once: the hunted hart breaks out of the covers,

> Whom when the plow-man meets, his team he letteth stand
> T'assail him with his goad: so with his hook in hand
> The shepherd him pursues, and to his dog doth hollow:
> When with tempestuous speed, the hounds and huntsmen
> follow.

These are better rustics than the china ones of his Preface "To the General Reader," exercising their pipes and singing roundelays to their gazing flocks. A longer glimpse of another real man follows; and even in the twentieth century it has been possible here and there to see his like, an ancient man, hovering on the verges of the parish, muttering to himself the philosophy that he keeps to himself, alive but already a legend.

> Suppose twixt noon and night, the sun his half-way wrought
> (The shadows to be large, by his descending brought)
> Who with a fervent eye looks through the twyring glades,
> And his dispersèd rays commixeth with the shades,
> Exhaling the milch dew, which there had tarried long,
> And on the ranker grass till past the noon-sted hong;
> When as the hermit comes out of his homely Cell,
> Where from all rude resort he happily doth dwell:
> Who in the strength of youth, a man-at-arms hath been;
> Or one who of this world the vileness having seen,
> Retires him from it quite: and with a constant mind
> Man's beastliness so loths, that flying human kind,
> The black and darksome nights, the bright and gladsome days
> Indiff'rent are to him, his hope on God that stays.
> Each little village yields his short and homely fare:
> To gather wind-fall'n sticks, his great'st and only care;
> Which every aged tree still yieldeth to his fire.

The picture is not left in the halfway stage, but, like all his kind, the old man finds a living by the "receipts" which he has inherited or invented, his special and supposedly useful knowledge providing for him just that pittance which enables him to be a recluse. He is traced, by Drayton, abroad looking for simples, gleaning the sunny clearings, and thinking his remedies "wondrous good." In brief, so kindly does the poet dream of his hermit that he with difficulty "inforces" the Muse on her course.

It is in this passage of the Hermit, I believe, that Drayton in the *Polyolbion* is found approaching the mood of his precious *Nimphidia* most nearly. If *Nimphidia* was not written in Arden or in a daydream of Arden, I have no other conjecture. Apart from the simples that Nimphidia mingled to bewitch Hobgoblin, and that the Hermit gathers also for his own ends, there is a sylvan friendliness, not without its smile, common to both pieces; and if his Hermit had existed in the flesh, and the fairy court only in their aerial shapes, he regards both through the brightness at the far end of the shady alley, whether dream or memory it matters not. For the fantastic jesting of *Nimphidia,* a kindred humorous play occurs in the One-and-Twentieth Song of *Polyolbion,* where Gogmagog, nervously pulling his beard, woos Granta.

> Sweeting mine, if thou mine own wilt be,
> C' have many a pretty gaud, I keep in store for thee.
> A nest of broad-fac'd Owls, and goodly Urchins too;
> Nay Nymph take heed of me, when I begin to woo:
> And better yet than this, a Bulchin twa years old,
> A curl'd-pate calf it is, and oft could have been sold:
> And yet beside all this, c' have goodly Bear-whelps twa,
> Full dainty for my Joy, when she's dispos'd to play:
> And twenty Sows of Lead, to make our wedding-ring;
> Bezides, at *Sturbridge Fayre,* chill buy thee many a thing:
> Chill zmouch thee every morn, before the Sun can rise
> And look my manly face, in thy sweet glaring eyes.

As *Polyolbion* proceeds, its fluent poetical passages do not by any means become rarer. The last twelve Songs, introduced by the enraged poet with his retaliation for years of neglect, "To any that will read it," are indeed full of vigour. Perhaps they even gained in strength and beauty when the poet found himself not cheered by the chorus of the high and mighty which

his first human imperfection had expected, but "left in the world alone." (pp. 41-3)

Phrases of weariness fall from him once or twice, as well they might; the Muse

> 　　　　　　　　　　　　　　　　must now
> As workmen often use, a while sit down and blow,

or again,

> 　　From my tirèd hand, my labour'd Canto ends.

And at the commencement of the Thirtieth and last Song, bidding himself go "cheerly on," he cannot repress some bitter exclamations upon the public ignorance. But that is all: the impulse of love and praise of the Happy Island, which first sent him forth on this universal pilgrimage, still bears him on in his eloquent sweet recountings, until finally, with the simplest farewell,

> My *England* I conclude, for which I undertook,
> This strange *Herculean* toil, to this my Thirtieth Book,

he takes his leave. (p. 46)

> Edmund Blunden, "The Happy Island," in his Votive Tablets: Studies Chiefly Appreciative of English Authors and Books, *1931. Reprint by Harper and Brothers, 1932, pp. 36-46.*

J. WILLIAM HEBEL　(essay date 1931)

[*An American scholar, Hebel edited the definitive collection of Drayton's works,* The Works of Michael Drayton *(5 vols., 1931-41). Following Hebel's death soon after the publication of the fourth volume, his task was continued and completed by Kathleen Tillotson and Bernard H. Newdigate. (For Tillotson's criticism, see the excerpt dated 1941; see Additional Bibliography for Newdigate's biography of Drayton.) In the following excerpt from the preface (dated 1931) to the second volume of* The Works of Michael Drayton, *Hebel appreciatively appraises the poet's sonnets and odes.*]

[In Drayton's collection *Poems* of 1619] he made his final and most thorough revision of his early poems, achieving at last, after many successive revisions, the text which satisfied his mature judgment. In general his judgment was good: the most successful of his early poems he left practically untouched, and he revised carefully the poems in which the facility of youthful enthusiasm had swept him into diffuse and turbid expression. In a few poems something of his earlier freshness is sacrificed, to be replaced by clearer, neater, more concise, and more grammatical writing. It is by the text of 1619 that Drayton evidently wished his early poems to be finally judged. When in 1631, the last year of his life, a part of the contents of the volume of 1619 was republished, he made no further textual changes. (p. v)

The volume of 1619 contains several of the poems by which, through their circulation in anthologies, Drayton has been most widely known. The Sonnet, **"Since ther's no helpe,"** and the two Odes, **"To the Virginian Voyage"** and the **"Ballad of Agincourt,"** are, as they deserve to be, familiar to all readers of English poetry. The anthologist, of course, cannot omit these poems, and he has room for little more; thus the merit of the rest of the volume, not easily accessible to many readers, has been unjustly obscured by the excellence of the popular favourites. That these few poems are all that readers will enjoy from Drayton's collection has been too quickly taken for granted.

As an example let us take the sonnet sequence, *Idea.* The general assumption seems to be that in the sequence there is a single masterpiece, the famous Sonnet "Since ther's no helpe," and that the other sonnets give no hint of the poetic qualities which produced the one success. One even hears at times the rumour that perhaps this sonnet is to be attributed to Shakespeare, thereby explaining the supposed discrepancy in quality between "Since ther's no helpe" and the remainder of the sequence. But no such discrepancy in quality really exists. In many of the other sonnets Drayton is also genuine in his emotion, forthright in his phrasing, and precise in his imagery. Even the conventional conceit of the immortality conferred upon his mistress by the poet's verses, Drayton makes live again in his direct utterance, summoning up the pageant of the Elizabethan street [in the 6th Sonnet, "**How many paltry, foolish, painted things**"] and giving a new air of reality to the poet's boast:

> How many paltry, foolish, painted things,
> That now in Coaches trouble ev'ry Street,
> Shall be forgotten, whom no Poet sings,
> Ere they be well wrap'd in their winding Sheet?

Likewise the note of reality attained in the 1st Sonnet ["**Like an adventurous sea farer am I**"] by the comparison of the 'Travels' in love with the voyages of discovery,

> Like an adventurous Sea-farer am I,
> Who hath some long and dangerous Voyage beene,

at once enlarges the imagination to that spaciousness which is the characteristic delight of Elizabethan poetry at its best. In the 20th Sonnet, "**An evill spirit your beautie haunts Me still,**" Drayton achieves an expression of one of the paradoxes of love, which rings true for Elizabethan and modern alike. In another mood he pays those compliments to his mistress which convention demanded of the sonneteer, tempering his directness with just the right mixture of exaggeration and artificiality, without which compliment loses half its charm. Tenderly he weaves together his love for his 'Idea,' Anne Goodere, and for the little stream which runs by Powlesworth, her home:

> Cleere *Ankor,* on whose Silver-sanded shore,
> My Soule-shrin'd Saint, my faire IDEA lies.

With the exception of a few failures in which conventional conceits have not been transmuted by the sincerity of Drayton's realism, or the delicacy of his sentiment, the whole sequence is a worthy setting for one of England's greatest sonnets. (pp. vi-vii)

The reader will find that the excellence of Drayton's odes is not to be sought in the "**Virginian Voyage**" and "**Agincourt**" alone; in other odes he will enjoy again

> the Trick,
> Of Ryming; with Invention quick,

and the hurry and tumble of the crisp expression. In *The Eglogues* there are charming pastoral scenes and delightful lyrics, to which let the lyric of 'daintie Daffadil' in "The Ninth Eglogue" bear witness. In *The Owle,* if the pleasure in the poetry is not great, there is the fascination of attempting to unravel the tangled skein of the dark conceit. Among the historical poems *Englands Heroicall Epistles,* extraordinarily successful with Drayton's contemporaries and retaining some popularity on through the eighteenth century, is perhaps best fitted to evoke in the modern reader something of the romance which the Elizabethans found in poems celebrating England's past. (p. viii)

J. William Hebel, in a preface to The Works of Michael Drayton, Vol. II, *edited by J. William Hebel, Basil Blackwell, 1932, pp. v-viii.*

VITA SACKVILLE-WEST   (essay date 1932)

[*Sackville-West was an English poet, novelist, and biographer associated with the Bloomsbury group, a circle of writers, artists, and intellectuals who held informal artistic and philosophical discussions in the Bloomsbury district of London from around 1907 to the early 1930s. The Bloomsbury group adhered to no uniform aesthetic or philosophic beliefs but did commonly express an aversion to moral prudery, a desire for greater social tolerance, and an aesthetic appreciation of beauty. The group included at various times Lytton Strachey, E. M. Forster, Clive Bell, John Maynard Keynes, and Virginia Woolf. Woolf is believed to have modeled the setting for her novel* Orlando *(1928) on Sackville-West's ancestral home, Knole Castle, which also provided the impetus for much of Sackville-West's own work, uniting her interests in the pastoral and in English history. Her long poem* The Land *(1926) reveals her connection with the Georgians, a group of English poets who, wishing to return to the nineteenth-century poetic traditions of William Wordsworth and the Lake Poets, wrote primarily of nature or serene country life. In the following excerpt, she attributes the unevenness of Drayton's verse to his own complex character.*]

"He wants one true note of a poet of our times, and that is this, he cannot swagger it well in a tavern, nor domineer in a pot-house." Thus wrote young, contemporary Cambridge of Michael Drayton. It seems a curious and somewhat irrelevant grievance to nourish against a poet, but the words "a poet of our times" are perhaps significant. Such qualifications as dominance in a pot-house were important to the Elizabethan and even the Jacobean mind. Yet Drayton was manly enough, direct and objective enough, as his robust though now unreadable epics testify. His ear was not always above reproach, though he was careful, too careful, to observe:

> That ev'ry lively Ceasure
> Shall tread a perfect Measure,
>   Set on so equall feet,

and his load of scholarship at moments becomes intolerable, peppering his pages with marginal notes and references; but of the author of "**Agincourt**" and "**The Virginian Voyage**" it can never be said that here was not a virile muse. (p. 186)

Drayton, like many another minor poet, is one who has both suffered from and benefitted by the modern short-cut of the anthology. Few lovers of poetry, however ardent, will be willing to wade through *The Barons Warres* or *England's Heroicall Epistles.* We should not advise them to do so. Even those two strange compositions, *The Owle* and *The Man in the Moone,* are scarcely adapted to an impatient modern taste. But the *Odes with other lyric poesies* may be read with delight, and indeed it surprises me to find that some of them should have escaped the attention of our avid anthologists. At least four if not five pieces among the *Odes* might find a worthy place: "**To the New Yeere,**" "**To his Rivall,**" "**The Cryer,**" "**To his coy love,**" and "**His defence against the idle Critick,**" with its most pertinent suggestions. But, by the usual irony of a poet's fate, Drayton owes such immortality as he possesses to the one sonnet, "**Since there's no help, come let us kiss and part.**" A first-class sonnet indeed; and even that has been attributed by some to Shakespeare.

Drayton has, in fact, enjoyed the usual share of good-luck and ill-luck. He dedicated the whole of a fairly long life to poetry;

he obtained a reverberating success among his contemporaries. That his name should live to-day on the merits of one sonnet is perhaps no more than a poet should exact. For the production of one perfect sonnet, sixty years is perhaps little room.

Why, then, is it so difficult, with the best will in the world, to read through Drayton's collected works? Some of them are impossible, and would defeat the sturdiest interest; but every now and then the page clears as though a ray of light had fallen across it. He had, I think, a complex mentality. The solemn and the fantastic were curiously and contrarily mixed in him. It is almost incredible that the author of **Nimphidia** and of the **Heroicall Epistles** should be one and the same person. The pedant and the poet were at war.

Pedantry cast aside, he could write such lines as these:

> Clear had the day been from the dawn,
>   All chequered was the sky,
> Thin clouds like scarfs of cobwebbed lawn
> Veiled Heaven's most glorious eye.
> The wind had no more strength than this,
> That leisurely it blew,
> To make one leaf the next to kiss,
>   That closely by it grew.
> The rills that on the pebbles played,
>   Might now be heard at will;
> This world the only music made,
>   Else everything was still.

Here is no pedantry. But it must be admitted that among the quicksands of boredom there are only a few solid places. They are, however, worth reaching. (pp. 186-87)

> *Vita Sackville-West, "Michael Drayton," in* The Spectator, *Vol. 149, No. 5432, August 6, 1932, pp. 186-87.*

KATHLEEN TILLOTSON (essay date 1941)

[*English scholar Tillotson, together with Bernard H. Newdigate, completed the editing of* The Works of Michael Drayton *begun by J. William Hebel (see excerpt dated 1931). In the following excerpt from her notes to* The Muses Elizium, *Tillotson investigates this, Drayton's final work, as "the ideal culmination of his career."*]

The Muses Elizium, published in Drayton's sixty-eighth year, is the ideal culmination of his career; a vision as complete in its own way as Shakespeare's late plays. It is 'the Poets Paradise': the muses, flowers, jewels, the beauties of the human body and the joys of country life are all there, not in laboured catalogue but enclosed and circumscribed in a perfect dramatic fantasy. Drayton has at last found a form entirely congenial to all his powers, and this late-found harmony releases his poetry into song, all the gnarls and knots of his style smoothed away. For the first time in a long poem, no effort is visible; indeed, his control is so easy and complete that it admits of play, the delight of the artist in the very materials of his craft. In the passage describing the horses of Apollo,

> That bear'st the morning on thy breast
> And leav'st the night behind thee

one feels the poet's infectious joy not only in his subject but in the metre he has lighted upon. So also in the choruses, and in the rhyming bouts of nymphs and shepherds. (The theme of emulation is recurrent, and Drayton rejoices in its challenge.)

Drayton is writing a new kind of pastoral. He has abandoned the presentation of real persons, the symbolizing of the poet

as shepherd, the intermittent realism of the shepherd's profession and environment, and the rustic-archaic diction. Neither Rowland nor Hodge could be at home in Elizium; the very names are now wholly classical. When a 'real' shepherd, Melanthus, is admitted, he is seen at one remove; he relates the details of a shepherd's life to the admiring nymphs, to whom it appears to have all the charm of novelty. *The Muses Elizium* is not in line with the work of seventeenth-century eclogue-writers, such as Browne, Wither and Brathwait. Drayton is nearer to the masques of Jonson, the masque in *The Tempest,* and pastoral dramas such as Fletcher's *Faithful Shepherdess;* the Nymphals, unlike Drayton's earlier ecologues, are formally scenic, and, as often in pastoral plays, their population is predominantly feminine. But Drayton's nymphs, unlike Fletcher's shepherdesses, exist in their own right, and are not there for purposes of love-intrigue. Indeed, the novelty of this pastoral is most evident in the complete absence of passion, whether in feeling or in words; the conceit of Venus's banishment in the seventh Nymphal is central. Here are no unhappy wooings or hopeless pangs: Lirope teases her rival wooers, who themselves regard the courtship with some humour; when there is a Prothalamion, the bridal pair are fairies; the nymphs praise each other's beauties lavishly, yet with no Sapphic fervour but rather a cool, gay, aesthetic detachment. This detachment is everywhere felt. It is not cold; but the hyperboles and the raptures are formalized—by the diction ('scaly brood' and 'dapper Elfe' are characteristic pointers), and by the precise metres with their short lines and frequent rhymes.

> She chid, she cherisht, she gave life,
> Againe she made to dye,
> She raisd a warre, apeasd a Strife,
> With turning of her eye.
> Some said a God did her beget,
> But much deceiv'd were they,
> Her father was a *Rivelet*,
> Her Mother was a *Fay*.

There is detachment too in the poet's delicate appreciation of the beauty of things (clouds are like scarves of cobweb lawn, grass is like spun silk); people are appreciated just in so far as they can compete with that beauty. Here one is often reminded of Herrick, and especially in the fairy wedding of the eighth Nymphal, which, whatever the truth of chronology, belongs to his poetic region.

An other-world or earthly paradise, more refined, more transparent than the usual world of pastoral, is a necessary setting for such a poem. But in 'Elizium' Drayton presents something more than the Homeric heavenly plain mingled with memories of Arcadia, the Bower of Bliss and the Garden of Adonis. (He has nothing to do with Spenser's main idea: only the rivulets here indulge in 'lascivious Gyres.') It is the *Muses'* Elysium, the *Poets'* Paradise, with Apollo as its tutelary deity. And to Drayton's surviving contemporaries at least, that word 'Elizium' would carry a hint of Elizabeth's reign, that long-ago golden age for poets, which was also (or seemed in retrospect) a golden age in Drayton's life and work. The symbolism must not be overpressed; but it is supported by other evidence of Drayton's homesickness for that age and his hatred of the 'iron times' in which he found himself. Elizium marches on Felicia, and that is Drayton's ironic name for the real world; the bowers of the nymphs may be 'free from the rude resort Of beastly people,' but faint rumours reach them of women who are loathsome and deformed and men who are mad past curing. And in the tenth and last Nymphal Drayton is outspoken in criticism. The nymphs see, and are at first frightened by an old satyr;

and the reader (remembering Spenser's satyrs, or, at the other extreme, Fletcher's) may at first expect conventional melodrama. But this satyr—who begins to seem 'not halfe so ugly'—is only an old weary refugee from Felicia, lamenting for its lost woodlands, and taking their destruction as an emblem of the general disrespect for antiquity. This had often in *Poly-Olbion* been Drayton's own sad theme, and the failure of his life's work in that poem had brought it home to him cruelly. The Nymphal ends with a promise of protection for the satyr and a curse on the Felicians; suggesting that Drayton, like the satyr, had been successful in his escape, partly perhaps by finding a second golden age in the protection of the house of Dorset. And from his deliberate punning on the two senses of 'satire' he clearly means us to conclude that the bitterness of his own satires has found its solvent in pastoral. (pp. 219-20)

> *Kathleen Tillotson, in an introduction to "The Muses Elizium": Nymphalls 1-10, in* The Works of Michael Drayton, Vol. V, *J. William Hebel, Kathleen Tillotson, Bernard H. Newdigate, eds., Basil Blackwell, 1941, pp. 219-23.*

MARIO PRAZ (essay date 1947)

[*Praz was an Italian critic, translator, and authority on the literature of the baroque and romantic periods. In his pioneering study,* La Carne, la morte e il diavolo nella letteratura romantica *(1930;* The Romantic Agony, *1933), he explored the tradition of sadism in literature, art, and music. His translations include works by Shakespeare, Ben Jonson, Charles Lamb, Jane Austen, Walter Pater, and T. S. Eliot. In the following excerpt from a review of* The Works of Michael Drayton, *edited by J. William Hebel, Kathleen Tillotson, and Bernard H. Newdigate, Praz offers a largely negative discussion of Drayton's poetry.*]

Once it was unfairly remarked about Dante that a large amount of his popularity in Italy was due to the topical references to Italian towns, families, etc. scattered throughout the *Divina Commedia*. This, which is only an amusing paradox as regards Dante, is nothing less than sober truth when we come to speak of Drayton's *magnum opus, Poly-Olbion.* While the late J. William Hebel, to whose industry we owe the tercentenary edition of the works of Michael Drayton, was editing *Poly-Olbion,* he found that copies of this poem which common report represented as being little read although widely known by name, were in continuous demand at the British Museum, and not only he received query after query from other students of the poem, but was able to form new friendships during his frequent visits to libraries to consult rare editions, a common love for *Poly-Olbion* supplying the basis. Can one love *Poly-Olbion* any more than one would the Brobdingnagian nurse in *Gulliver's Travels*? Because if the shape of a poem is there, and if the name of verse can be given by courtesy to its jog-trotting alexandrines, little do we find there of the poetic spirit, although Prof. Hebel says that "the poetry, not often aspiring to lyrical values", is, all the same, "quiet, sure, and strong in its fitness to the subject matter." But the topographical character of the poem makes it a favourite with antiquarians: "The poem yields information, not the less interesting because it is in verse form, about earlier conceptions of British history; about local legends, beliefs, and customs, about sports, pastimes and natural history; about farming, industry, and commerce—information to be checked with Selden's notes, and with Drayton's chief source, Camden's *Britannia*." "Perhaps the best way to enjoy *Poly-Olbion* is to make the poem a companion on a tour in England and Wales." It is curious that the characteristic of being a versified Baedeker, which adverse

critics urged against D'Annunzio's *Città del silenzio,* should be considered a merit by a lover of Drayton's *Poly-Olbion.* But how far does the poem succeed in "re-creating the romantic spell of Elizabethan England" is open to question. Doubtless the poem is quaint: "many pages will seem but a versified map overcrowded with nymphs of river, hill, and woodland", and old maps are quaint, although the quaintness of shepherds seated on hillocks, of towns represented like ladies balancing diminutive castles on their heads and of naked nymphs emerging newt-like from meandering rivers, is apt to pall no less than, in those old maps, the full-blown sailing ships bestriding the main. Any passage of the poem is enough to convey an idea of the whole; I choose at random this from Song XX:

> These Nymphs trick'd up in tyers, the Sea-gods to delight:
> Of Currall of each kind, the blacke, the red, the white;
> With many sundry shels, the Scallop large, and faire:
> The Cockle small and round, the Periwinkle spare,
> The Oyster, wherein oft the pearle Is found to breed,
> The Mussell, which retaines that daintie Orient seed:
> In Chaines and Bracelets made, with linkes of sundry twists,
> Some borne about their wasts, their necks, some on the wrists.
> Great store of Amber there, and Jeat they did not misse;
> Their lips they sweetned had with costly Ambergris.

This is one of the shortest and more bearable of Drayton's inventories: a long one will be found in Song XXIV, an interminable catalogue of Briton and Saxon saints, hermits, missionaries, etc. I imagine an antiquarian may grow very fond of such things, just as one would treasure auction sale catalogues; there is almost nothing on earth which may not be envisaged as worth collecting: one can collect pebbles as well as precious stones, matchbox pictures no less than old paintings. At its best Drayton's poem is like one of the early museums or *Wunderkammern*, full of curious fossils, skeletons of crocodiles, ostrich-eggs, and some objects of virtu to which the term of art would be more appropriate.

Poly-Olbion was just the kind of work one would expect a man like Drayton to take up with enthusiasm. Such a gigantic task supplied a vent to his insatiable thirst of versifying.... He had tried every literary *genre,* and, if we are to credit the words of a contemporary, William Browne [see poem dated 1622], had succeeded in all.... He had echoed all the fashions of the past and anticipated a few of the future, from the day in which he had petulantly begged his schoolmaster: "Make me a poet" [see excerpt dated 1627]. To begin with, his very conception of the poet, which included the historian and the antiquary, dated from the day of Ronsard and the Pléiade. His first work, **The Harmonie of the Church,** strikes one immediately as old-fashioned: the style recalls certain tiresome tricks of some of the translators of Seneca; he followed in the wake of *The Shepheardes Calender,* then in its fourth edition, with **The Shepheards Garland,** in a period when "writing pastorals was only less obvious than writing sonnets"; he published his first sequence of sonnets at the height of the vogue following Watson, Sidney, Daniel, Constable, Barnes, Lodge and Fletcher; and in his sonnets, although perhaps no single phrase can be said to be a translation of a continental sonnet, as is frequently the case with Elizabethan sonneteers, there is nothing which is not conventional and characterless; with **Endimion and Phoebe** he was earlier than usual in catching the fashion of the erotic narrative poem, of which *Venus and Adonis* is the most conspicuous instance; at the same time he fell under the influence of Du Bartas. Daniel's *Complaint of Rosamond* (1592) had started a vogue for historical legends, and Drayton responded at once with a series of **Legends,** "**Peirs Gaveston,**" with its flowing and nerveless verse, being the first and longest of the set. He is alternatively haunted by Marlowe, Shakespeare, Daniel, and brings all his inspirers down to the humdrum level of his own Muse. Minor writers are often more interesting for the student of manners and fashions than great authors; but the student of Elizabethan vogues, I am afraid, would hardly be more gratified by perusing Drayton's poems than, say, a student of the Regency would find his appetite satisfied by a water-gruel diet of Pierce Egan's *Life in London.* . . . In **"Robert of Normandy"** Drayton emulated the *Gerusalemme liberata*, in *Mortimeriados* he imitated Daniel's *Civil Wars* (1595): the poem drags on for nearly three thousand lines, of which the antiquarian may perhaps treasure the description of an elaborate bed in the crowded style of decoration loved by the Elizabethans:

> A stately Bed under a golden tree,
> Whose broad-leav'd branches covering over all,
> Spread their large Armes like to a Canapy,
> Dubbling themselves in their lascivious fall,
> Upon whose top the flying *Cupids* spraule,
> And some, at sundry cullored byrds doe shute,
> Some swarving up to get the golden fruite.
> A counterpoynt of Tyssue, rarely wrought,
> Like to *Arachnes* web, of the Gods rape,
> Which with his lifes strange history is wrought, etc.,

In one instance only Drayton departed from the lines of his contemporaries, and this initiative proved disastrous for him. The favourite subject for poets in the spring of 1603 were the death of Elizabeth and the accession of James. In his "gratulatorie poem" *To the Majesty of King James,* a conventional piece of journalism, Drayton omitted all reference to the deceased Queen and this omission, instead of winning him favour, brought about his disgrace. . . . *England's Heroicall Epistles* proved the most popular of Drayton's works, and earned for him the title of "our English Ovid". Mrs. Tillotson praises Drayton's handling of the *genre,* which she finds subtler than Ovid's ("the moment of correspondence is chosen for its maximum emotional value"), and the perfect control of the decoration. Their chief importance lies, however, in the epigrammatic antithesis of the couplet; on this development which was to have a far-reaching consequence in English poetry I am going to say a few words further on. In the *Heroicall Epistles,* then, Drayton, that whispering-gallery of the voices of other poets, actually seems to capture a voice from the future, the voice of Pope! From another point of view the *Heroicall Epistles* command attention: as Mrs. Tillotson remarks, "it may be said emphatically that in this work Drayton's imaginative treatment of history is worthy, both in conception and execution, to rank beside the historical plays of any of his contemporaries except Shakespeare, and much above any treatment of history in verse narrative." (pp. 97-100)

In that same year which saw the publication of the *Heroicall Epistles,* we find Drayton intent on polishing and remodelling his sonnets with numerous and minute revisions. An almost unique case in the annals of literature, he was an indefatigable craftsman, for all his facility to bend, like a reed, whatever way the wind of fashion blew. Had Drayton been a great poet, what wealth of material would be at our disposal for the study of his technique! As it is, the abundance of variant readings supplied by the editors does not invite to a close study. In some cases, as in the recast **"Pierce Gaveston,"** which exists in five distinct forms, all the additions in the 1595-6 text are "irrelevant to the narrative and indeed have very little content of any kind: they are apostrophes, sententiae, images, all in the same hypnotically rocking style, and interesting as illustrating

the extreme of dilution possible in Elizabethan verse." This remark of the editor makes one rather sceptical about the importance of variant readings in an author like Drayton.

In 1619 the sonneteering vogue had long died out, and Drayton's pertinacity was decidedly unfashionable. Only a progress in excellence could justify such obstinacy, but of all the sonnets one only has found its way into the anthologies, the famous **"Idea 61,"** proclaimed by Rossetti the best sonnet in the language, **"Since there's no helpe, Come let us kisse and part".** Lisle Cecil John's criticism (in *The Elizabethan Sonnet Sequences, Studies in Conventional Conceits,* 1938) sounds final: "Good poet [or should one say versifier?] though he sometimes could be, his sonnets often come off badly when placed side by side with those of his fellow craftsmen, for his quest for originality led him to unjustifiable hyperbole. His faults, however, probably spring from a lack of incentive other than a desire for poetic renown." (p. 101)

In the volume of odes (whose fashion dates from Ronsard), the **"Ballad of Agincourt"** (not a proper ode) shows a felicitous condensation of much epic material which Drayton had elsewhere diluted in long-winded poems; the **"Virginian Ode,"** based on reports of travellers, anticipates the magic of exoticism which culminated in Marvell's *Bermudas:*

> When as the Lushious smell
> Of that delicious Land,
>   Above the Seas that flowes,
>   The cleere Wind throwes,
> Your Hearts to swell
> Approching the deare Strand.

It is perhaps a far cry to Marvell's magic lines:

> He gave us this eternal Spring
> Which here enamels everything . . .
> He hangs in shades the orange bright
> Like golden lamps in a green night . . .

but the poet's reaction to such descriptions as Amadas' and Barlowe's bears witness that the call of the distant Eden was already at work. Those voyagers experienced "so sweet, and so strong a smel, as if we had bene in the midst of some delicate garden abounding with all kinde of odoriferous flowers, by which we were assured, that the land could not be farre distant."

"The Heart," in the volume of the *Odes,* brings us into the very centre of the metaphysical manner. Lines like:

> Were it cymented or sowne
> By Shreds or Pieces knowne,
> We each might finde our owne—

sound almost like Donne's. On the other hand the moralising speeches of Fame and Fortune in **"Robert of Normandie,"** published also in 1619, bring us back to mediaeval tradition, and the **"Legend of Great Cromwell"** conforms to the trite mediaeval pattern of the *De Casibus,* common to the collection of the *Mirror for Magistrates* in which that poem was included. These legends of 1619 are *exempla:* **"Gaveston"** illustrates the fate of minions, **"Matilda"** illustrates chastity, **"Robert of Normandie"** culminates in a debate between Fame and Fortune, **"Cromwell"** shows the precariousness of the rise of a new man. Mediaeval is also the framework of **"The Owle,"** where the combined conventions of the spring-time dream, the bird-fable and the debate, as a vehicle for comment on current affairs, derive from Chaucer's *Parlement of Foules.* Still, in conformity with the rhythm of seesaw which seems typical of Drayton's career, in the same year 1619, next to so many echoes of the past, we have again an anticipation of the future in the *Pastorals*. . . . [Of the ninth eclogue, Tillotson writes:] "It is in this Eclogue that Drayton attains the rare balance of actuality and formality which marks the highest achievements of Elizabethan pastoral." The metre of this ninth eclogue is the same as in Gray's celebrated "Elegy," and if the reader happens, in consequence, to be haunted by the memory of this latter poem, he will inevitably notice how Drayton misses the landscape and sees only the flowers, and these rather as bearers of emblematical senses than as natural objects. (pp. 101-02)

For Mrs. Tillotson "*The Muses Elizium*, published in Drayton's sixty-eighth year, is the ideal culmination of his career: a vision as complete in its own way as Shakespeare's late plays. It is 'the Poets Paradise': the muses, flowers, jewels, the beauties of the human body and the joys of country life are all there, not in laboured catalogue but enclosed and circumscribed in a perfect dramatic fantasy. Drayton has at last found a form entirely congenial to all his powers, and this late found harmony releases his poetry into song, all the gnarls and knots of his style smoothed away" [see excerpt dated 1941]. . . . [In] my opinion, Mrs. Tillotson's praise is a little extravagant, for the difference between the catalogues in this work and those in Drayton's other poems is after all not so great (see for instance the catalogue of precious stones in the ninth Nimphal). A tendency which is eventually to settle in the poetic diction of the next century is noticeable here and there. Thus in the sixth Nimphal we come across the *scaly brood* (l. 147) which we are going to meet again in Pope's *Windsor Forest (scaly breed)*. The account of the animals in *Noahs Floud* is "the latest and best of Drayton's catalogues, a masterpiece of humorous and tender observation." One will certainly remember the Ram which "to the Arke ushers his gentle Ewe" (l. 274), and the squirrel "that leapt so nimble betwixt tree and tree" behaving in the Ark like "a Ship-boy come to clime the Mast" (l. 324 ff.).

As I said, the work of Drayton which is the most interesting technically is the series of *England's Heroicall Epistles*. The treatment of the heroic couplet with an epigrammatic bias already distinctly foreshadows Pope. Miss Ruth C. Wallerstein, who in her essay on *The Development of the heroic couplet* (PMLA, 1935, pp. 166-209) has traced the progressive stages in the formation of a measure which Pope was to make his own, has laid much stress on Ben Jonson but underestimated the importance of Drayton's *Heroicall Epistles*. The antithetical movement, the rhyme falling in with the syntactical construction, are found throughout Drayton's epistles. (p. 104)

Other instances of this treatment of the heroic couplet could be given from *The Owle*. But it is chiefly in the *Epistles* that the antithetic and epigrammatic couplet recurs so frequently as to form the very pattern of the little poems, and to give to the play of feelings the curious geometrical effect of a game of cards or a ballet (or of both at the same time, if we may be allowed to bring in Stravinskij's *Jeu de cartes*). The Kings and Queens who in the *Heroicall Epistles* thus bandy passions and sentiments, acquire the artificial elegance of kings and queens on the "nice verdant carpet" of a gaming-table, "fittest arena for those courtly combatants to play their gallant jousts and tourneys in". If kings and queens of cards had a way of expressing their feelings, surely they would talk in heroic couplets like Drayton's, each couplet diagonally cut across by an antithesis like the cards themselves showing the same inverted bust above and below a diagonal line. The treatment of the couplet brings this Elizabethan world of kings and queens curiously near to the artificialities of the next century and to Pope.

While we turn page after page of passionate protestations, we quite naturally expect to come suddenly across the lines:

> Soon as thy letters trembling I unclose,
> That well-known name awakens all my woes.
> Oh name for ever sad! for ever dear!
> Still breath'd in sighs, still usher'd with a tear. . . .

Literature has its heights and hollows like the earth itself; in the Elizabethan region Drayton's poetry is certainly the most extensive expanse of flat country, but, wide as it is, it seems hardly noticeable among the peaks that screen it from our view to-day. Once we have read the four big volumes of Drayton's verse, we relegate them to the back row of our bookcase, only to be consulted by the curious antiquary. (p. 107)

> *Mario Praz, "Michael Drayton," in* English Studies, *Netherlands, Vol. XXVIII, No. 4, 1947, pp. 97-107.*

HALLETT SMITH   (essay date 1952)

[*Smith is an American scholar who specializes in Shakespearean and other Elizabethan literature. In the following excerpt, he discusses the influence of Spenserian pastoral on Drayton's* Idea the Shepheards Garland.]

The most ambitious of Spenser's followers is Michael Drayton, who published in 1593 a group of eclogues modeled on *The Shepheardes Calender* and called *Idea The Shepheards Garland Fashioned in Nine Eglogs*. Drayton plans his series with the same objectives of variety in style and mood, contrast of type, and seriousness of aesthetic and moral purpose which characterized Spenser, and in many instances the imitation is more direct and specific. His second eclogue, for example, is a debate between age and youth, and his third is a panegyric on Elizabeth under the name of Beta, filling out the rest of her name from Spenser's Eliza in the April eclogue. His first and last eclogues are complaints, as are Spenser's.

Drayton republished his pastorals in 1606 and 1619. He is especially interesting to the student of the history of English poetry because of the revisions he made for the edition of 1606. Some of these, at least, were made before 1600, as the revised versions appear in *England's Helicon* of that year. Drayton, in revising, cuts down the religious imagery, transforms his style into something more balanced, epigrammatic, and classical. He removes some of the archaic language, but on the whole, instead of moving away from discipleship to Spenser, he clearly moves closer to his master. This is a significant point, and Drayton provides the natural link between the pastoral tradition of the Elizabethans and the more domesticated and yet more classical school of the seventeenth century with its Browne, Herrick, and Milton.

Yet Drayton must not be dismissed as a mere historical link. His pastoral poetry deserves attention on its own merits. Probably the eighth eclogue in *The Shepheards Garland* represents him at his best. It is based upon the same structural principle as Spenser's "August," with two well-marked and contrasting parts. The first part is a treatment of the theme of the Golden Age, traditional enough in pastoral, but Drayton prefaces it with an interesting comment on contemporary kinds of poetry:

> Shepheard why creepe we in this lowly vaine,
> as though our muse no store at all affordes,
> Whilst others vaunt it with the frolicke swayne,
> and strut the stage with reperfumed wordes.

> See how these yonkers rave it out in rime,
> who make a traffique of their rarest wits,
> And in Bellonas buskin tread it fine,
> Like Bacchus priests raging in franticke fits.

This alternative of flamboyant stage poetry, as practiced by the Marlowes, Kyds, and Shakespeares of the time, is rejected by the shepherds, as is the poetry of the *Mirror for Magistrates* sort:

> My Muse may not affect night-charming spels,
> whose force effects th'Olympicke vault to quake,
> Nor call those grysly Goblins from their Cels,
> the ever-damned frye of Limbo lake.

When Drayton proceeds to his description of the Golden Age, he makes clear that it was the time when the pastoral ideal governed mankind. His description of the Golden Age is both pictorial-idyllic and moral; simplicity and beauty went hand in hand with innocence. When the aspiring mind destroyed the pastoral *otium* ["ease"] and the Golden Age was no more, poets began to write of "slaughtering broiles and bloody horror." The corruption of more recent times may be seen by the absence of the natural and simple in life. Paradoxically, it is ages other than the Golden Age which put an undue and immoral value upon gold. This position is sometimes misunderstood, since it seems almost like the position of the satirist. It is in reality no more than the criticism of life which inheres in pastoral itself. In the fifth eclogue, Drayton is more specific about the levels of poetry. Rowland, who represents Drayton himself, declines to sing heroic poetry, which is too high, or satire ("foul slander," as he calls it), which is too low but he will sing pastoral, which is the mean.

The second part of Drayton's eighth eclogue is the pleasant poem of "Dowsabell." For this, Drayton has imitated Spenser's trick in "March" of using Chaucer's Sir Thopas meter for comic effect. But the comic tone here mingles with one of sympathy and familiar recognition, for Dowsabell is a "naturalized" shepherdess, obviously an inhabitant of the Cotswold hills rather than of Arcadia. She is involved in the usual *pastourelle* situation, though she begins the wooing herself, and the conclusion is as pretty and naïve as the conclusion of Breton's "As it fell upon a day." The contrast between the two parts of the eclogue is therefore very effective; we have the seriousness of the pastoral judgment of life, with the Golden Age as criterion, and we have the precise, actual, identified situation in the Dowsabell lyric, treated with detached amusement.

Drayton is the most interesting of the followers of Spenser in pastoral, and he illustrates well enough the survival of interest in pastoral poetry, even though the style of it changed, on into the seventeenth century. (pp. 59-61)

> *Hallett Smith, "Pastoral Poetry: The Vitality and Versatility of a Convention," in his* Elizabethan Poetry: A Study in Conventions, Meanings, and Expression, *1952. Reprint by Harvard University Press, 1964, pp. 1-63.*

C. S. LEWIS (essay date 1954)

[*Lewis is considered one of the foremost Christian and mythopoeic authors of the twentieth century. Indebted principally to George MacDonald, G. K. Chesterton, Charles Williams, and the ancient Norse sagas, he is regarded as a formidable logician and Christian polemicist, a perceptive literary critic, and—perhaps most highly—as a writer of fantasy literature. Also a noted academic*

and scholar, Lewis held posts at Oxford and Cambridge, where he was an acknowledged authority on medieval and Renaissance literature. A traditionalist in his approach to life and art, he opposed the modern critical movement toward biographical and psychological interpretation, preferring to practice and propound a theory of criticism that stresses the author's intent. The following excerpt is taken from Lewis's English Literature in the Sixteenth Century, *in which he introduced the terms "Drab" (to characterize that poetry of the early Elizabethan period containing rough combinations of sound and rhythm and sparse, uninventive imagery) and "Golden" (to define poetry written largely between the period 1579 and 1603 and characterized by bright, musical, and "uncontorted" lines containing ageless imagery). Here, Lewis assesses Drayton as a "half Golden" poet.*]

[Michael Drayton is] a poet only half Golden, but in quite a different way from Greville, Davies, and Daniel. They began with Gold and moved away from it; he began with Drab, constantly relapsed into it, and in his old age, when the Golden period was over, at last produced his perfect Golden work, so pure and fine that no English poet has rivalled it. His weakness is the very opposite of Daniel's; he was in a sense too poetical to be a sound poet. His sensibility responded almost too quickly to every kind of subject—myth, the heroic past, tragic story, and (most of all) the fruitful, sheep-dotted, river-veined, legend-haunted expanse of England. He had an unquenchable desire to write poetry about them all, and he always seemed to himself to be succeeding because he mistook the heat which they aroused in him for a heat he was communicating to the reader. He himself has told us (in the **"Epistle to Henry Reynolds"** [see excerpt dated 1627]) how at the age of ten he hugged his 'mild tutor' begging to be made into a poet, and how the good man granted his request, in typically sixteenth-century fashion, by starting him on Mantuan. In that scene we have what is essential in Drayton the man: a man with one aim, devoted for life to his art, like Milton or Pope. If the Muse regarded merit he would have been one of our greatest poets.

His career began inauspiciously with *The Harmony of the Church*, drab scriptural paraphrases to which critics are too kind when they accuse them of 'wooden regularity' for they are in reality wooden without being regular. *Idea, The Shepherd's Garland* might be the work of a different man. These 'eglogs' are much influenced by Spenser's pastoral poetry but wisely refrain from his attempts at rustic realism. They were republished later with so many alterations as to make them a new book. But even the 1593 version shows promise: the lyrics, as always in Drayton, are the best part.

Idea's Mirror . . . makes us think that Drayton is now going on from strength to strength but with *Endimion and Phoebe* there is another check. In this perplexing poem the style of the erotic epyllion jostles with that of Du Bartas, and there is a similar wavering in Drayton's conception of his theme. He has, rightly, a feeling that this myth demands something more than a sensuous treatment, but has not quite made up his mind what that something more should be. I think he would like to have depicted the Platonic ascent from carnal to intelligible love, but has really no idea of what one would find at the top of the ladder. He has to fill up with astronomy and the theory of numbers. When he re-wrote it eleven years later as *The Man in the Moon* the discrepancy remained and was aggravated by a syntax so contorted as to be almost unreadable. In the earlier version the descriptive passages often have the prettiness that was intended. The movement of the couplets is a little monotonous.

His continual rewritings set us a problem. Detailed comparisons between versions are impossible in a short account, and if these are abandoned it becomes difficult to keep any kind of chronology. The *Legends* of "Matilda," "Pierce Gaveston," and "Robert of Normandy" were originally written between 1593 and 1596; that of "Cromwell" did not follow till 1607. All four reappeared in 1619, with much revision. The *Mortimeriados* of 1596, much altered, became the *Barons' Wars* of 1603. Drayton's second thoughts are often important, but cannot of course be more important than the poems in which they occur. The truth is that this enormous body of historical verse, including the *Agincourt* and *Miseries of Queen Margaret,* adds very little to his reputation. (pp. 531-32)

Drayton, like Daniel, takes his historical poetry seriously as history: his marginal notes are significant. At the same time he adopts all the rhetoric and (on occasion) the sensuous richness which his age considered proper to high poetry. But such purple patches, like the fig-leaf in sculpture, only emphasize what they are meant to hide. The whole layout of the poem remains that of prose history. We are told that public persons did this or that and for such and such reasons, but we are not shown them doing it. In the *Baron's Wars* we are well into the second canto before we reach anything like an epic scene with a concrete where and when. No 'historical estimate' should deter us from saying that this is bad, bad work: interesting only in so far as it shows us how necessary the introductory letter to the *Faerie Queene* still was. Drayton has learned no structural lessons from all the great narrative poets who preceded him. He has not advanced on the old rhyming chroniclers. If you are going to be as artless as they in *ordonnance* it would be better to be artless in style too. It offends less and gets over the ground more briskly. Comparison between Drayton's epic [*Battaile of Agincourt*] and his ["Ballad of Agincourt"] is instructive. The epic panoply adds nothing and loses all the race and relish of the humbler poem. The attempts to produce greatness and terror by such slaughter-house details as 'There drops a cheeke and there falls off a nose' are pitiable. The only good things in [*The Battaile of Agincourt*] occur in the speeches; notably in Gam's rodomontade

> I tell thee Woodhouse, some in presence stand
> Dare prop the Sunne if it were falling down.

It was not till 1597, when the first version of *England's Heroical Epistles* appeared, that Drayton's historical interests found successful poetic expression; so successful that his revisions in the later editions were less drastic than usual. The *Epistles* are of course modelled on Ovid's *Heroides* and we get rid of the epic chimera. They show a mingling of three styles, the genuinely Ovidian, the Golden, and the early Metaphysical. Thus the description of the grove in "Surrey to Geraldine" is pure Golden, the passage on gold in "Edward the Fourth to Mrs. Shore" faintly suggests an Elegy by Donne, and "Rosamond" is so like Ovid that we catch ourselves trying to remember the Latin. These styles, however, melt into one another without producing any discomfort; nor are conceit and hyperbole (common to them all) so managed as to exclude nature. Real passions at that time expressed themselves flamboyantly. Queen Isabel's remark on the element of fear in all sorrows is true and, I think, original; Henry II on kingship has pathos; the haggish malice of Elinor Cobham and the chivalrous patience of her husband are well brought out; Mortimer sustains his character of Stoic magnanimity successfully. One great virtue of the whole collection is the sweetness and vigour of its verse. The heroic couplet is here in its early perfection, looser than the Augustan mode but far from the meandering of the seventeenth

century or the Romantics. It can throw up every now and then a line of astonishing force—'And care takes vp her solitarie inne', or 'Where the disheuel'd gastly sea-nymph sings', or (of lipstick) 'On Beauties graue to set a crimson Hearse'.

With the exception of these *Epistles* nearly all Drayton's valuable work falls outside [the sixteenth century]: accounts of the interesting though very uneven *Polyolbion* and of *Nimphidia* (dear to some who do not care for 'faerie' and hateful to all who do) must be sought elsewhere. I cannot thus surrender either the *Shepherd's Sirena,* which appeared in the 1627 volume, or the *Muses Elizium.* No history of Golden poetry could possibly omit them. In these the unfashionable old poet who had long been fighting a rear-guard action against those who would

> exile
> All braue and ancient things foreuer from this Ile

and proclaiming in his solitude

> Antiquitie I loue nor by the worlds despight
> I cannot be remoou'd from that my dear delight,

received at last his reward and was allowed to conclude the Golden Age with something (as the poetess said) 'more gold than gold'. For in these last poems of his all that richness turns finer, more rarefied, more quintessential, than ever before. The *Shepherd's Sirena* is in one way like all Golden poetry: yet in

THE
HARMONIE
of the Church.

Containing,

The Spirituall Songes and
holy Hymnes, of godly men, Patriarkes and
Prophetes : all, sweetly sounding, to the praise
and glory of the highest.

Now (newlie) reduced into sundrie kinds of
English Meeter : meete to be read or sung,
for the solace and comfort of the godly.

By M. D.

LONDON.

Printed by Richard Ihones,
at the Rose and Crowne, neere Holborne
Bridge, 1 5 9 1,

b

Title page of Drayton's first published work (1591).

another way there is no poem at all like it. A hundred and twenty lines in the lulling incantatory metre of the *Phoenix and the Turtle,* lines full of winter and heartbreak, provide the base. Against this, silvery, cascading, the song stands out with startling beauty. Its incomparable music—which would be rather like Mr. de la Mare's if it were not so passionless and so free from his undercurrent of misgiving—depends on taking a metre which, of itself, is always threatening to develop into a commonplace dactylic tumble, and then delicately, deftly, variously holding it back from that development. The charm of this song is its inhumanity. We are nominally praising a woman, yet it is a river as much as a woman, or neither. It is almost 'about' nothing: as near to 'pure' poetry as the nature of language will allow. This 'purity' continues in the best parts of the *Muses Elizium.* Nothing more Golden had ever been produced. They teach nothing, assert nothing, depict almost nothing. . . . Their methods are those of Pastoral, but the last links with real shepherd life have been severed. But not the last images from actual nature. There is an exquisite mingling of impossible beauties with things really observed, 'either other sweetly gracing'. Thus on the one hand all seasons are blended so that the fruits hang 'Some ripening, ready some to fall, Some blossom'd, some to bloome'; the eyes of Lirope turn pebbles to diamond and tempest to calm; it is not beyond hope

> To swerue up one of Cynthias beames
> And there to bath thee in the streames
> Discouer'd in the Moone,

or that all the pearls of all the seas and either India should dissolve into a lake,

> Thou therein bathing and I by to take
> Pleasure to see thee clearer than the Waue.

But then, on the other hand, the reflection of a girl's yellow hair upon the lily wreath that surrounds it casts a light 'like the sunnes vpon the snow'; the 'west winde stroakes the violet leaues': an early morning sky is 'chequerd' with 'thin clouds like scarfs of Cobweb lawne': bees stagger homeward 'vp in hony rould More than their thighes can hould'. The power of this Elizian poetry to transform its material is perhaps best seen in the first 'Nimphall'. Taken in itself the subject of that poem is scarcely tolerable. Each nymph praises the other's beauty by preferring it to her own. The perversity of the original Greek models survives only in the fact that this preference is dissociated from all idea of envy or even of regret: we are left with two inhuman, inexplicable voices uttering their passion for beauty and, save for that, passionless. It is thus that real fairies (not the bric-à-brac of *Nimphidia* would speak if they existed. It is the ultimate refinement of Golden poetry, Gold 'to ayery thinnesse beate', without weight, ready to leave the earth. (pp. 532-35)

C. S. Lewis, "Verse in the 'Golden' Period," in his
English Literature in the Sixteenth Century, Exclud-
ing Drama, *1954. Reprint by Oxford at the Clarendon
Press, 1962, pp. 464-535.*

JOSEPH A. BERTHELOT   (essay date 1967)

[Berthelot is an American educator and the author of a critical study of Drayton. In the following excerpt from this work, he traces the development of Drayton's pastoral poetry.]

Under the guise of writing about lowly shepherds and their love life, the Renaissance poets propounded their views on many subjects. They wrote about their own lives, made topical references, satirized the church or politics, told simple stories, and experimented with the language and various poetic techniques. (p. 45)

[The] pastoral was by no means an English-born genre. In an address to the reader, Drayton pointed out its Classical and European roots. He gave appropriate credit to Theocritus, Vergil, and Sannazaro as the chief pastoralists in the Greek, Roman, and European traditions. The pastoral was a highly popular genre on the continent during the late Middle Ages and the Renaissance. The works in this genre of Mantuan, Petrarch, Guarini, Tasso, and Marot, all carried over and influenced the English in their own development of the pastoral.

The first important pastoral in England in this period was Spenser's *The Shepherd's Calendar* in 1579. In the 1590's Sir Philip Sidney and the Countess of Pembroke's (his sister) *Arcadia* as well as Thomas Lodge's *Rosalynde* made a strong and delightful impact on the English reader. Among the many pastorals arose romances, drama, satire, and elegy, all under the guise of the simple bucolic world.

In the same manner as he had done with the sonnet sequence, Drayton joined the ranks of the pastoralists in the early years of their popularity. In 1593 he published *Idea, The Shepheards Garland,* which was strongly influenced by Spenser's *Calendar.* Again just as he revised his sonnets until he arrived at new and original poems with greater maturity and polish, so he continued to work in the pastoral medium until he achieved like results. In 1595 he published *Endimion and Phoebe,* a pastoral with strong Ovidian strains. He completely revised the 1593 edition of his eclogues in 1606 under the title of *Eclogs,* and at the same time rewrote the Endimion story under the heading of *The Man in the Moon.*

Long after the tide of popularity for the pastoral had receded Drayton again published several new works in this genre: *The Quest of Cynthia; The Shepheards Sirena;* and *Nimphidia.* Finally in 1630, the year before his death, he published his pastoral masterpiece, *The Muses Elizium.* In these works Drayton moved from the Elizabethan pastoral of Spenser and Lodge into a Caroline fairy pastoral which was completely original with him.

In . . . his first pastoral work [*Idea, The Shepheard's Garland*] Drayton followed many of the same objectives which Spenser had had in the creation of *The Shepherd's Calendar.* Much of the style, the mood, the contrasting of types, and the love-sick debates are similar in both works. Thus Rowland bewails his unrequited love as did Colin. . . . The subjects and the sentiments are frequently the same in both works, and Drayton used many of the metrical patterns which occurred in Spenser's pastoral. Spenser had used archaisms to discover a language suitable for poetry; Drayton used many of the same archaisms, but added more of them from the Midland dialect.

However, Drayton did not merely copy Spenser. The two works have completely different purposes. Spenser had used the pastoral tradition, as handed down from Petrarch and Mantuan, to attack religious and political abuses. Drayton had no specific target for attack; he observed society and made general comments on it at times. In addition Drayton emphasized the English background of his characters by drawing a fictional world which could easily fit into the Cotswolds. Furthermore, Spenser developed his *Calendar* around the changing of the seasons and Colin's change from youth to age, while Drayton did not follow the seasons with any consistency. Actually the arrangement of the *Garland* was in a rough concentric pattern. ["Eclogue I" and "**Eclogue IX**"] were monologues of complaint; "**II**" and "**VII**" were debates on love between youth and age; and the center formed a core of four eclogues with panegyrics. Drayton, unlike Spenser, turned away from archaic dialect for the most part, and emphasized it only in the ballad in "**VIII.**"

In "**Eclogue I**" the shepherd "Rowland malcontent bewayles / the winter of his grief." But the tone of the poem is not merely that of unrequited love as in "January." Rowland's complaint is coupled with deep religious significance and imagery. He calls on "O Blessed Pan," here the Christian God, for merciful attention to his confession. The first half of the eclogue contains the ritualistic pattern of submission, contrition, and oblation:

> Let smoky sighs be pledges of contribution
> For Follies past to make my souls submission.

The eclogue opens in spring, and the freshness of the season provides a contrast for his melancholy and repentance. In the *Calendar* Colin moved from disappointment mingled with hope in "January" to complete despair in "December"; but Rowland does not show this progression. Rather he begins in "**I**" with pious repentance and ends in "**IX**" with hopeless love-sickness. The IXth eclogue takes place in winter, and the weather corresponds to Rowland's somber state. In this eclogue he calls on Phoebe and the stars to hear his complaint. In both "**I**" and "**IX**" Drayton used the sixain, *ababcc*, the metrical form of Spenser's "January" and "December". (pp. 45-7)

In general Drayton followed the leadership of Spenser in his first pastoral, but he also made several of his own contributions to the growth of the form. He dropped the extremes of political or religious satire, and made the pastoral primarily a series of discussion and songs in praise of love, friendship, and the Golden Age. He also restored a sense of humor to the pastoral which recalled some of the Theocritan comic idylls.

Specifically his first attempt at this genre had its drawbacks. The eclogues were filled with many awkward constructions and violent inversions of syntax. In order to maintain the meter and rhyme, he frequently had subjects without verbs and used participles as main verbs. Also many of the conceits were overly extravagant and strained. It would be his task in his coming revisions to eliminate these faults which were common to most of his early poetry. Of the entire series, "Dowsabell" [in "**Eclogue VIII**"] alone needed and received little revising.

Thirteen years after their first publication, a completely revised edition of the pastoral *Garland* appeared under the simple title of *Eclogs*. Drayton rewrote almost all of the songs, transposed the sequence, and added another eclogue to the set. Other changes included the dropping of the verse arguments which had prefaced each eclogue and the Latin tags from Ovid's *Amores* which had followed each eclogue. He also changed his rule against allowing the same character to appear in successive eclogues.

A few changes were made in this edition for the republication in 1619, but these were mostly for the purpose of improving the versification and the syntax. In each of the newer versions Drayton smoothed out the lines by cutting down on the complexity of the rhetoric. His efforts were not completely successful, but the trend of his revisions is easily observed. Drayton did strain the rhythm in a few places (i.e., Borrill's curse on love in 7:131-46), but this was the exception rather than the rule. An analysis of the 1619 variants shows that Drayton changed relatively few rhymes. Actually the basic revisions which Drayton made were paralleling the new Jacobean fashion in writing which was moving away from the extravagant and

self-conscious mannerisms of the Elizabethans. He reworked most of the heavy conceits to bring the rhetoric into better balance with the ideas which were the rational element of the poems. He also dropped many of the archaisms with the exception of "**Eclogue VII**", making a greater contrast and effectiveness in their use in the "Dowsabell" segment. In this edition Drayton was not really departing from the Spenserian influence; rather, he was following the master of *Colin Clouts Come Home Again*. For Spenser had, in this later work, led the pastoralists away from their fascination with rhetoric and bombast which had occupied their interests in the early 1590's.

In "**Eclogue I**" Drayton dropped his use of the repentance theme which had held such a dominant place in "**Eclogue I**" of the earlier edition. Instead of this religious emphasis, Rowland emphasizes his defiance as a poet who has failed to receive adequate recognition. Of course we are well aware of Drayton's bitter disappointment in not being recognized in some signal way at the accession of King James to the throne in 1603.

In the last eclogue Drayton made extensive internal changes with only seven of the seventeen stanzas recognizable from 1593. No longer is the emphasis on Rowland as the forlorn lover, but rather Rowland points to the stars as the cause of his difficulties. He also carries on the theme of "**Eclogue I**" as a poet of injured merit and frustrated ambition. He achieved an excellent mood of tranquillity in two of the stanzas in which he emphasizes his own poetic abilities:

> O Night, how still obsequious have I been
> To thy slow silence whispering in thine ear,
> That thy pale Sovereign often hath been seen,
> Stay to behold me sadly from her Sphere,
> 　　Whilst the slow minutes duly I have told,
> 　　With watchfull eyes attending on my Fold.
> How oft by thee the solitary Swain,
> Breathing his passion to the early spring,
> Hath left to hear the Nightingale complain,
> Pleasing his thoughts alone, to hear me sing!
> 　　The Nymphs forsook their places of abode,
> 　　To hear the sounds that from my Music flow'd.

In "**Eclogue II**" Drayton no longer attributed the virtues of the divinity to Idea, but he does make her the *primum mobile* of the universe; and the general emphasis shifts to the worship of women. The second song becomes a deification of love itself. In this latter song he introduced a new form of eight-line stanza with the first four lines, a pentameter quatrain, *abab*, and the second four, a ballad quatrain, tetrameter-trimeter, *cdcd*.

In his praise of Beta in "**Eclogue IV**" Drayton made a few very significant changes which strengthened the structure of the poem. He made the Thames a King, better to balance Beta, Queen of the Virgins. He deleted the stanzas on the Muses and the angels, so that all of the emphasis would fall on the homage of the nymphs. He also added certain dramatic qualities of action to the poem. The nymphs now enter singing and announce Beta's arrival; they sport on the strand while Beta reclines on the bank. Beta peers into the water and sees her own reflection, and thus the sea deities have better reason to spread her fame as it has been caught by the waters. These bits of action make the poem more realistic, and take away much of the artificiality caused by the conventions in such a panegyric.

In "**V**" he revised his panegyric to Idea, giving a new order to the jumble of praises of her features. Now the poem has a real sense of direction as he carefully praises her physical self in five stanzas leading to the stanzas which describe her real beauty, her virtues. Thus in an ascending order he moves from beauty to goodness. (pp. 52-4)

Three years after the original publication of *The Shepheards Garland* Drayton included another current trend in his pastoral poetry, that of the Ovidian or amatory. Among the many Ovidian poems which were published about this time were Christopher Marlowe's *Hero and Leander*—being circulated in manuscript by 1593—Shakespeare's *Venus and Adonis* and *The Rape of Lucrece,* and finally Drayton's *Endimion and Phoebe.*

In this work Drayton followed the lead of Shakespeare and Marlowe in the development of the Ovidian myth and combined with it DuBartas' expression of Platonic love as found in *Uranie.* The Drayton poem falls naturally into two parts. The first is a pastoral love story in which the goddess Phoebe disguises herself as a shepherdess and pursues Endimion until he in turn tries to catch her. Then she reveals her divinity, and the second part begins. Endimion is translated to Mount Latmus, the home of the Muses; and the poet gives a poetized scientific discourse on celestial numbers, astrology, and poetic inspiration. Endimion is taught to love natural beauty; but upon discovering Phoebe is absolute beauty, he is taken to heaven in order to visualize the Platonic ideal.

The first part of the poem is heavy with the Ovidian richness without being erotic. (pp. 55-6)

The last section of the poem is almost poetized science as Drayton turned from the Ovidian myth to an apology for poetry as the divine science. The joining of the two sections is not well done, and perhaps the poem would be a better pastoral if the second part had been omitted. (p. 57)

Endimion and Phoebe was never reprinted during Drayton's lifetime. Instead he rewrote the poem completely in 1606 with new title, *The Man in the Moon,* and cut the old version almost in half. The love story of the first part was dropped; instead the poem opens with a pastoral scene in which the shepherds are celebrating the feast of Pan. At their request Rowland tells a story relating how Phoebe disguised herself to protect Endimion from the radiance of her divinity. He gives a long description of the mantle she wears. On it is depicted the violence of the sea, and waterfowl and their habitations. This painting on the mantle recalls the medieval tradition which Chaucer used when he described the paintings lining the walls of the temple of Mars in "The Knight's Tale." The listing of the water-birds comes from Sylvester's translation of "La Semaine"; however, Drayton amplifies the catalog and gives such a realistic description of their habits as one might expect today from a member of the Audubon Society.

Phoebe comforts Endimion who is frightened by the pictures of violence on her mantle. She tells him of her ancestry and her powers as a goddess in ruling the tides of the sea, the fertility of the earth, and the minds of men. She then takes him on a much more orderly journey than in 1595. First they visit the haunts of the nymphs of the waters, the seas, the mountains, and the woods. From there they go on to the celestial spheres and the abode of the fixed stars and the angels. Finally, from the moon the poet looks down upon the earth where he sees the hidden vices of the miser, the lecher, the murderer, the thief, and the false lover.

The changes in the poem are numerous. Now the journey is taken only to instruct Endimion in the mysteries of the human condition and the universe. The melancholy which afflicts Endimion no longer proceeds from love, but from an inability to understand Phoebe and what she means. For in this new version he sees three contrasting worlds: the pleasant pastoral life of Rowland and the shepherds; the vicious underworld of the werewolves in the opening, and of evil men at the end; and the world of the nymphs and the celestial mysteries. The poet stands with the shepherds between the vicious and the celestial, and he has the duty to report the beauties of the latter and expose the evils of the former.

In 1595 the poem had the flavor of Spenser and Marlowe, but now it has changed to a Jacobean simplicity in its description and action. The extravagance of the Ovidian influence is gone, but the poem does not suffer from this absence. Actually the new structural unity and definite sense of direction which hold this poem together far outbalance the loss of the love story. It is not inferior to *Endimion and Phoebe;* it is rather another kind of poetic rendition. (pp. 58-9)

[*The Shepheards Sirena*] seems to be a pastoral poem about the Golden Age. The lilting lines have a base of winter and heartbreak. The whole object of the poem seems to be a description of love and sorrow, with the object a woman, a river, or neither. It is Drayton's closest approach to the pure poetry of emotion without a definite object.

This 383 line poem has an unusual metrical form. The basic meter which is used throughout, except for the 170 lines of the song, consists of tetrameter heptasyllabic quatrains with an *abab* rhyme scheme. The song has ten stanzas of twelve lines with a common five line refrain:

> On thy Bank,
> In a Rank,
> Let thy Swans sing her
> And with their Music,
> along let them bring her.

Since it is a song, the lines could be considered to be a variable of the normal eleven syllable couplet with a masculine internal rhyme after the third beat. With this in mind, the chorus becomes another long couplet. However, considering the lightness of the poem and the fact that the regular line only has seven syllables, the song gives a better visual impression and the rhymes are emphasized with these short line divisions.

The poem as a whole is a delightful piece of writing. Its major quality is the smoothness of the line which almost hypnotizes the reader into belief in the sorrow and passion described. It also seems to have affinities with such works as Brown's *Shepherd's Pipe* and Wither's *Shepherd's Hunting,* which have the same delicate pastoral atmosphere but a stronger satiric flavor.

The best poem in the 1627 edition was his fairy poem, *Nimphidia.* Written in eighty-eight rollicking eight-line stanzas, it has an *aaabcccb* rhyme scheme. The *a* and *c* lines are generally regular tetrameter and the *b* lines are trimeter with a feminine ending. This shortened line with the feminine rhyme causes the tempo of the poem to move at a fast pace. In this mock heroic tale we have a burlesquing of many of the features of the medieval romance besides this variation of the meter. As a fairy tale *Nimphidia* does not really belong in the pastoral genre. However, in a study of Drayton's works it does represent one stage in his own development of the pastoral. This genre was basically escapist in nature. Love and romance in a humble rustic setting was the tone set for the pastoral by Theocritus. In this poem Drayton investigated an area of the woodland landscape familiar to all Englishmen from their folklore. He wrote of the love and romance of the fairies who were the "natural" inhabitants of the English countryside. Drayton merely emphasized this one aspect of the pastoral world in this poem.

Further *Nimphidia* represents a stage in his move to a more Classical pastoral world which he would later describe in *The Muses Elizium*. In this latter poem Drayton reached his ultimate in the pastoral genre. He retained the fairyland of *Nimphidia* and peopled it with nymphs and swains. Elizium finally moves beyond the land of magic into a land of the ideal. With the exception of the eighth nimphall which does emphasize the diminutiveness of the fairies, Drayton's nymphs and swains think and act like shepherdesses and shepherds of the Theocritan idylls. By passing through the fairyland of Queen Mab, Drayton was able to discover the ideal homeland, Elizium, for a pastoral setting. (pp. 60-2)

Drayton has much of the world of Shakespeare's *Midsummer Night's Dream* in [his *Nimphidia*], but he adds the burlesque and emphasizes the diminutive. He has the delicate control of Herrick's fairy poetry, only on a greater scale. Drayton's fairy world is not idealized, but rather everything is described in delightful specific detail with the fairies possessing very human passions and emotions. Aside from Herrick, the best passage in literature which illustrates the same quality as found in Drayton's poem is Mercutio's speech about Queen Mab in Act one, scene four, of *Romeo and Juliet*.

The year before he died Drayton published his last pastoral, *The Muses Elizium,* which consisted of a verse argument describing Elizium and ten nimphalls. It is a combination of true pastoral elegance with fairy lightness. The majority of the characters in Elizium are not shepherds, but rather nymphs; yet in this new work he moved closer to the Classical form of the pastoral than in any of his previous writings. In itself *The Muses Elizium* was Drayton's masterpiece in the delicate Caroline manner. He had by this time solved most of the problems which he had observed in his craftsmanship over the previous thirty-nine years. His style had finally become smooth, and the language now flowed with less effort than before. In it he handled many different metrical forms with true ease and grace. Thus scattered throughout the work are ballad quatrains, *abab*; tetrameter couplets; pentameter couplets; hexameter couplets; pentameter quatrains, *abab*; a double three-line stanza, *aabccb*, with tetrameter in *a* and *c* lines and trimeter in *b* lines; double trimeter quatrains linked together by the rhyme *aaab cccb*. In all of these there is new ease in their use. (pp. 63-4)

The high point in the entire work comes in the eighth nimphall. Here we have the preparations for the wedding of the nymph Tita with a Fay. This nimphall stands along with *Nimphidia* as a prime example of Drayton's fairy poetry. In contradiction to the custom of the real world, the marriage is an ideal one; based upon name and family relationships, it is carefully and deliberately made. There is no thought of a marriage based on the kind of passion which Venus and Cupid might represent.

The emphasis is on ceremony and decoration. Thus the nuptial song leads only to the door of the wedding chamber; all comments about the nuptial couch are omitted. Again Drayton emphasized the diminutiveness and delicateness of the fairy dress and ornamentation. In their efforts to outdo the elfin world in beauty and grandeur, the nymphs take special care with the wedding gown:

> Of Pansie, Pink, and Primrose leaves,
> Most curiously laid on in Threaves:
> And all the embroidery to supply,
> Powdered with flowers of Rosemary:

> A trail about the skirt shall runn,
> The silke-worms finest, newly spunn:
> And every Seam the Nimphs shall sew
> With th'smallest of the Spinners clew:
> And having done their work, again
> These to the Church shall bear her Train:
> Which for our Tita we will make
> Of the cast slough of a Snake,
> Which quivering as the wind doth blow,
> The Sun shall it like the Tinsell show.

(pp. 67-8)

The Muses Elizium is Drayton's most perfect work and the culmination of his pastoral career. He took the best elements from his earlier pastoral works and united them in this his masterpiece. In this way he retained the careful attention to setting which was the mainstay of *Endimion and Phoebe*. He drew the holiday mood from the ninth eclogue of 1606. He kept the grace and lightness of his lyrics in the *Eclogs*. His satire he found in *The Man in the Moon* and *The Shepheards Sirena*. The nymphs, satyrs, hermits, and the other men in the sixth nimphall peopled the forests in *Poly-Olbion*. And finally, the over-all delicacy had its forerunner in *Nimphidia*.

As a pastoralist Drayton began with close imitation of his masters. But as he continued to write and experiment in this genre, his poetic talent grew until he created new and original pastoral forms. And as with *Idea*, his pastorals changed from the style of the Elizabethans to the new styles of a new age. (p. 69)

Joseph A. Berthelot, in his Michael Drayton, *Twayne Publishers, Inc., 1967, 172 p.*

WALTER R. DAVIS   (essay date 1969)

[*Davis is an American educator and the author of* A Map of Arcadia: Sidney's Romance in Its Tradition *(1965) and* Idea and Act in Elizabethan Fiction *(1969). In the following excerpt, he differentiates* Ideas Mirrour *(1594) from the revised* Idea *of 1619, revealing the comic undercurrents apparent in the later sonnet sequence.*]

Ideas Mirrour of 1594 is an exercise in the high, or even hieratic, style: its focus is on the sonnet-mistress, who is treated as a goddess, especially in the frequent "goddess-temple-altar" conceit, its diction is heightened, it is full of affective devices like repetition, apostrophe, and exclamation. . . .

Idea of 1619 . . . is a totally different sequence. Only 20 of the original 51 sonnets survive revision; hyperbole, religious phraseology, and "accents of despair" disappear in the re-writing of those which survive; and 43 new sonnets have been added. And the new sonnets have a totally new tonality. . . . (p. 204)

The purpose of this essay is to define the quality of the 1619 *Idea*; what will be stressed in it is not Drayton's growing mastery of the sonnet, nor the wisdom of his revisions (though they are excellent), but the nature of the final product. The thesis is that *Idea* is essentially a comic sonnet-sequence, its subject the unsuccessful attempt to avoid conventionality.

The prefatory sonnet **"To the Reader of these Sonnets"** is meant to fix the reader's expectations of the sequence:

> Into these Loves, who but for Passion lookes,
> At this first sight, here let him lay them by,
> And seeke else-where, in turning other Bookes,
> Which better may his labour satisfie.

No farre-fetch't Sigh shall ever wound my Brest,
Love from mine Eye a Teare shall never wring,
Nor in *Ah-mees* my whyning Sonnets drest,
(A Libertine) fantastickly I sing:
My Verse is the true image of my Mind,
Ever in motion, still desiring change;
And as thus to Varietie inclin'd,
So in all Humors sportively I range:
   My Muse is rightly of the *English* straine.
   That cannot long one Fashion intertaine.

This is a very unusual opening indeed, and on many counts. For one, the first quatrain makes an explicit refusal to exhibit the one essential trait Sidney had laid out and the other sonneteers had followed, that the love poet must show in his verse such a "forciblenesse or *Energia*" that his mistress will believe him to be really in love. The focus is to be not on the excellence of the mistress or on the sincerity of the lover's passion for her, but rather on his wandering mind. Such a focus on the mind, while running counter to that of Spenser, Daniel, and most of the other sonneteers, does have ample precedent in *Astrophel and Stella*; but there it served to indicate precisely what Sidney wanted, the sincerity of his lover in contrast to others. Here it does just the opposite: it distances this lover from his experience, and presents him quite frankly as a literary artist striving for variety rather than depth of expressiveness.

Furthermore, this lover whose mind we are asked to explore calls himself a "Libertine"; while that term lacks the narrow denotation of sexual profligacy it has in modern times (and was beginning to have in Drayton's time) and hence in no wise suggests a link between Drayton and the later French "libertine" poets Saint-Amant and Théophile, it does have considerable shock-value. Most saliently, it presents the lover as a free-thinker in regard to the religion of love, one who refuses to go through the ritual sacrifices of sighs and tears before the altar of the mistress. Secondly, it has the more general meaning of one who, untrammeled by set beliefs and codes (and here, if Drayton's capitalization is significant, we may detect a metaphorical link to the French *Libertins,* for whom distinctions of good and evil in nature did not apply), goes his own way, "sportively" ranging either among women, like Donne in "The Indifferent," or among all sorts of pleasures and states of mind.

The total effect of Drayton's introductory sonnet, the above considerations suggest, is to remove *Idea* from the amorous context of all other sonnet-sequences, and instead to invite the reader to experience the sequence as he would non-amorous verse like satire, as a "true image" of a fantastic mind (like that of the satyr thought to lie at the root of the satirical tradition in Elizabethan times), seeking variety in its sportiveness. Truly these sonnets are to be sonnets of a satirist or comedian; this sonnet itself insists on its lack of the "puling sighes" and "*aye me's*" Marston had mocked, and it veers toward satire in the couplet (as revised in 1619), which rather suddenly turns to the common satiric target of fashion and, in doing so, turns on the English reader, who has been divorced from the sentimentalist, to identify him with the fickle. The antic disposition of this fantastic lover reappears in many subsequent sonnets, which take up the mask of this one in order to complicate it. (pp. 204-06)

"Sonnet 24" [**"I heare some say, this Man is not in love"**] so complicates the mask of libertine as to become an explicit denial of the introductory sonnet; it seems almost a direct reply to William Drummond, who had taken the sonnet to the reader

so to heart as to remark that Drayton "by I know not what artificial *Similes* . . . sheweth well his mind, but not the Passion":

I heare some say, this Man is not in love:
Who? can he love? a likely thing, they say;
Reade but his Verse, and it will eas'ly prove.
O, judge not rashly (gentle Sir) I pray,
Because I loosely trifle in this sort,
As one that faine his Sorrowes would beguile:
You now suppose me all this time in sport,
And please your selfe with this Conceit the while;
Ye shallow Censures, sometimes see yee not,
In greatest Perils some Men pleasant be. . . .

The fantastical writer of the introductory sonnet is now seen to be the mask of the passionate sufferer, sportive ranging is a kind of indirect expression of real desire, and the reader who was warned *not* to seek passion in *Idea* is now told to do just the opposite: to seek the real passion beneath the antic mask. Here the satirical tone of the opening portions of the sequence is shown to be just what it had been in *Astrophel and Stella*: an indication of real emotional intensity (but compare *Astrophel and Stella* 54, where it is the lover's silence rather than his trifling that proves the depth of his passion). The unconventional pose finds here in Sonnet 24 a conventional base. Therefore **"Sonnet 31"** [**"Me thinkes I see some crooked Mimicke jeere"**] uses the libertine pose in an entirely new way; the opening is rather like that of 24:

Me thinkes I see some crooked Mimicke jeere,
And taxe my Muse with this fantasticke Grace,
Turning my Papers, askes, What have we heere?
Making withall some filthy Antike Face.

Now the reader, before mocked as imperceptive, is openly attacked: interestingly enough, it is he that has the antic face, not the poet. And the fantastic style is not now merely the surface of real experienced passion, but a proper style; the sonnet proceeds, deliberately trying to be as homely and cumbersome as it can be in order to prove that just these qualities form fit praise for Idea:

Since Sonnets thus in Bundles are imprest,
And ev'ry Drudge doth dull our satiate Eare;
Think'st thou my Love shall in those Ragges be drest,
That ev'ry Dowdy, ev'ry Trull doth weare?
   Up, to my Pitch, no common Judgement flyes,
   I scorne all Earthly Dung-bred Scarabies.

This sestet wittily insists and shows that the low style is really the high style, that Idea by being compared to dowdies and trulls is being more fully praised than would be otherwise possible. (pp. 207-08)

The central action of the libertine poet is not to show how silly love is but to show the supernal value of that woman who destroyed his right reason; and that action becomes curious insofar that various radical and unconventional poses are taken up only to end with the conventional motives. Satire becomes a mode of sentiment, and the lover both sees himself comically and praises seriously the mistress who has made his life a series of efforts to evade the conventional "ah-mees" only to find them constantly issuing from his lips in changed forms. The several directly comic sonnets in *Idea* revolve around the concept of love as folly: their rather paradoxical effect is at once to laugh at the lover and to turn his folly into the mistress' triumph.

Many of the comic sonnets locate the folly of love in the figure of Love himself by depicting Cupid in the manner of some of Sidney's and Greville's sonnets as a wayward and destructive child. **"Sonnet 22"** [**"With Fooles and Children good Discretion beares"**] presents Cupid and the lover as child and idiot, respectively, and exposes both to village scorn, while **"Sonnet 23"** [**"Love banish'd Heav'n, in Earth was held in scorne"**] shows Cupid as a cunningly ungrateful beggar, **"Sonnet 7"** [**"Love, in a Humor, play'd the Prodigall"**] as a drunken ruffian. **"Sonnet 36"** [**"Thou Purblind Boy, since thou hast beene so Slacke"**] is a direct address conjuring Cupid as a "purblind Boy" and consigning him to damnation, while **"Sonnet 48"** [**"Cupid, I hate thee, which I'de have thee know"**] treats him scornfully and colloquially as a "naked Starveling" and "Poore Rogue" who may be turned out of doors to become "some bungling Harpers Boy." But the folly of love is presented much more fully by action than by characterization or caricature, especially in the sonnets showing the ironic circularity of the lover's efforts. **"Sonnet 46"** [**"Plaine-path'd Experience, th'un-learneds guide"**] is a ruefully comic version of the "murder will out" theme introduced in **"Sonnet 2"** [**"My heart was slaine, and none but you and I"**]; at the inquest over his dead heart, Idea's approach makes the heart bleed; this proves her guilt, but does the dead heart no good at all:

> But what of this? Should she to death be led,
> It furthers Justice, but helpes not the dead.

"Sonnet 15" [**"Since to obtaine thee, nothing me will sted"**] takes up the lover's attempt to leave his folly satirically: he can cure his love by a charm composed of the heart of a chaste woman, the tears of an obedient mistress, the sighs of a constant wife, and so forth—thus by satire both mocking Idea, who assumedly lacks these traits, and mocking the lover's attempt, for such ingredients are nowhere to be found. (pp. 209-10)

The famous **"Sonnet 61,"** **"Since ther's no helpe,"** is Drayton's most successful exercise in destroying a pose in order to show the full force of love. The octave creates the pose of libertine indifferent by its conversational manner, its abrupt and clipped syntax, and its colloquial diction; the sense that this is a pose adopted in despair comes through only in the projected future meeting and the occasional over-insistence on nonchalance ("And I am glad, yea glad"). The sestet presents an absolute contrast with the octave, its urgency carried by anaphora and trochaic lines, periodic syntax suspending the final opportunity to save love till the last line, and the creation of a large affective image instead of mere statement. The pathos of the scene of Love's death is intensified by its slow development, the use of pathetic optics through spectators like Faith and Innocence (whose very abstractness shows the importance of the act's finality), and the insistence on process through present participles (forcing a focus on the moment which is absent in the insistence on past and future in the octave). The two very different styles of this sonnet produce a fascinatingly paradoxical effect. The speaker of the octave is above all a convincing human being, a man speaking to men; yet, just as fully, he is a man posing, pretending an indifference he cannot really feel. The speaker of the sestet is the standard Petrarchan stick-figure with his personifications and his pleading tone; yet his is just as obviously the voice of feeling, urgency, pain. In the plot traced by this masterful sonnet, the libertine is unmasked: the man attempting to live a carefree natural life unaffected by cant is shown at the end to be—alas—nothing but the conventional lover living out his life of tired but all-too-real clichés.

Although it is not the purpose of this paper to map out the structure of *Idea*, it must be noticed that the last two sonnets of the sequence, along with **"Sonnet 61,"** dwell on the failure of the lover to escape the conventional nets, on the circularity of his effort. **"Sonnet 62,"** **"When first I Ended, then I first Began,"** records fully the series of attempts to circumvent love and its straitening effects on the self, and characterizes those attempts as folly—"Wise in Conceit, in Act a very sot"— folly, whose main element is the effort to seem other than what one is: "What most I Seeme that surest am I Not." That the sonnet ends with the tired Petrarchan conceit of burning in ice and freezing in fire is the surest emblem of its imitative form. **"Sonnet 63"** [**"Truce, gentle Love, & Parly now I crave"**] ends by asserting directly what we have seen dramatized in so many of the sonnets: the failure of an affected tone which leads to the success of love or the mistress:

> Or if no thing but Death will serve thy turne,
> Still thirsting for subversion of my state;
> Doe what thou canst, raze, massacre, and burne;
> Let the World see the utmost of thy hate:
>   I send defiance, since, if overthrowne,
>   Thou vanquishing, the Conquest is mine owne.

Comedy is social in its orientation rather than cosmic; as such it celebrates "the golden mean" rather than "the dark voyage," and tends to view departures from conventional behavior as departures from nature rather than as heroic exploits. The man who, in tragedy, flees from social convention to find higher ideals of conduct or principle is seen through the comic lens as the unadaptable, the man with a rigid mechanical response like Sergius with his folded arms in *Arms and the Man* or Malvolio whose crossed garters symbolize his self-imprisonment in *Twelfth Night*. The clearest expressions of the conventions of love as germaine to the basis of society in Drayton's own time are of course Shakespeare's romantic comedies— *Loves Labours Lost*, for example, where the male rejection of love and its poses is equated, in the two songs that end the play, with rejection of nature, or *Much Ado About Nothing*, wherein Benedick, after sighing, "The world must be peopled"—a phrase that forms the farewell to his witty style— turns to, and starts to write stilted sonnets and enter a courtly code with his mistress. The tone proper to such social comedy is that tone achieved by Rosalind and Touchstone in *As You Like It*, the realistic but mordant tone of ironic acceptance of life in an imperfect world as both silly and valuable, a tone welcoming with a wry smile a world of values where the clichés of life remain stiff, not to be repealed.

The plot of *Idea* is the attempt to establish the uniqueness of individual experience and its failure, the attempt to escape from standard passionate suffering into a libertine pose and its failure, the attempt to range sportively inside an offhand fantastic style and its failure in returning to sighs and tears and all the rest of the Petrarchan panoply of emotions. Drayton's plot is in this way essentially a comic plot, its butt the lover himself who refuses to accept the everyday world of romantic cliché for what it is, but who must at length—sonnet by sonnet— realize his involvement in it and side with the readers who laugh at him. (pp. 214-16)

Walter R. Davis, " 'Fantastickly I Sing': Drayton's 'Idea' of 1619," in Studies in Philology, *Vol. LXVI, No. 2, April, 1969, pp. 204-16.*

GEOFFREY G. HILLER (essay date 1970)

[*In the following excerpt, Hiller describes Drayton's break with pastoral tradition in* The Muses Elizium.]

From the title-page of *The Muses Elizium* it is evident that Drayton was aware that his work was different from other pastorals: *The Mvses Elizivm, Lately discouered, By a New Way Over Parnassvs.* In his dedicatory epistle to Dorset he declared: 'I have often adventured upon desperate untrodden wayes, which hath drawn some severe censures, upon many of my Labours, but that neyther hath, nor can ever trouble me', implying that this work too was along a desperate, untrodden way. Drayton was not given to proclaiming the originality of his work in prefaces, but when he did he was justified. *Poly-Olbion,* for instance, does indeed follow 'a new, cleere way, never before gone by any' [see essay dated 1622]. In *The Muses Elizium* all the traditional devices of the pastoral convention are given a new turn.

Drayton's poem is unusual . . . in depicting at some length a world free from love (that is, the troublesome type of love which Cupid represents). The action of the vast majority of pastorals takes place in a world which has fallen from the Golden Age, where love between shepherds and shepherdesses was mutual and carefree. The chief complaint of the shepherd was invariably his unrequited love. Barnfield's shepherd, for instance, praises the contentment, peace, and purity of his life and then launches on a seven-stanza tirade against Love which mars his happiness:

> How happie were a harmles Shepheards life,
> If he had neuer knowen what Loue did meane.

A shepherd could, of course, take pleasure in love even if it were unrequited, but more often his attitude was that of Spenser's Thomalin:

> Of Hony and of Gaule in loue there is store:
> The Honye is much, but the Gaule is more.

It is the existence of the kind of love having gall as well as honey which differentiates the pastoral world from that of the Golden Age. *The Muses Elizium* is entirely free from this love. Venus and Cupid are banished as soon as they are discovered. The love which Elizium enjoys is neither that of the lovesick shepherd of Barnfield nor the sensual passion of Carew's ''Rapture'': no lovers die of grief or entwine their 'panting lims' in Drayton's Elizium. The only wanton pranks and 'lascivious Gyres' here are those of the meandering rills. And because no one is prevented, like Spenser's Colin Clout, from piping because of his love-grief, the chief occupation is singing. It is in fact the 'Poets Paradice', where poetry is not only sung but appreciated, a significant phenomenon for Michael Drayton. There is no necessity here to lament the passing of the happy Golden Age as Spenser and Drayton himself had done earlier in their pastorals.

In the lovesick world of many other pastorals nature mourns sympathetically with the grief-stricken shepherd and his sorrow is reflected in its wintriness; or, in a deliberate reversal of the pathetic fallacy, nature seems to rejoice in her spring or summer gladness while the shepherd grieves. Here, however, like the inhabitants of Elizium, the birds sing music, and the flowers only grow more beautiful with time, as time renews the strength and wit of the poets:

> There in perpetuall Summers shade,
> *Apolloes* Prophets sit
> Among the flowres that never fade,
> But flowrish like their wit . . .

Thus Drayton has put the conventional pathetic fallacy to a new use.

The first Nymphal contains a rival singing-match between two nymphs, Rodope and Dorida. But the combatants are not shepherds boasting of their own virtues or those of their mistresses, nor as in Brathwaite's *Shepheards Tales* (1621) are they shepherds holding a doleful contest to decide who has been treated most unkindly by a woman: they are both *nymphs* praising the beauty of *each other*. Phoebus, as wanton as the rivulets, pries through the thickets expecting to see goddesses consumed by sensual love, but there is no amorous sensuality in Elizium: Dorida saw Rodope's thigh only when 'the wind thy skirt up blew'. They appraise each other's anatomy in extravagant terms and in the systematic style of the medieval lyric and of Carew's ''Rapture'', but the boldness, the relish for the flesh is absent. And the contest is in fact pointless: they are both so beautiful that one would think

> That th'one of them the other was,
> And but themselves they seem'd.

Similarly, in the 'golden wishes' passage of the fourth Nymphal, two nymphs, Mertilla and Cloris, wish each other pastoral joys in terms normally used by the lovesick shepherd to his beloved.

In the second Nymphal Drayton has combined three of the traditional pastoral devices: the Professional Debate, the Hill v. Valley Debate, and the Invitation to Love. Of the first I shall speak later.

The hill-dweller debating with the valley-dweller was a not uncommon theme before 1630, but invariably it was a serious contest; in both Mantuan and Spenser it forms a basis for a heated religious discussion. The Invitation to Love had similarly always been a favourite topic of pastoral song, and there are many instances where the formula has been elaborated so that the lovers, often of different pastoral vocations, vie with each other in their gifts for the favour of the beloved. Occasionally the treatment was humorous, but the contestants themselves always took their rivalry seriously; Espilus and Therion's contest for the May Lady is an example. In Drayton, however, the singers themselves are enjoying the fun. Lalus, the valley-dweller and shepherd, describes his gifts, but his increasing extravagance is regularly deflated by Cleon, hill-dweller and goatherd, who scoffs at his rival's offerings before praising his own with similar hyperbole. Lirope the nymph laughs teasingly at the gifts of each of her 'Chapmen' suitors. She prefers her dog to any lamb or kid, and will be weighted down with all the proffered jewels! Her common sense recalls that of Raleigh's nymph in her reply to Marlowe's shepherd. Still without discriminating, Lirope finally holds out a scrap of hope to each suitor. There is no question of despair and neither suitor is really troubled by her refusals. In a later poem by Godolphin, ''Tom and Will were Shepherds twain'', two shepherds love Pastora who, like Lirope, cannot discriminate between them, but when she leaves them they break their pipes and abandon themselves to despair: such is the difference between Drayton's golden world and the conventional pastoral world.

The Professional Debate in the sixth Nymphal is closer to tradition. This may well be accounted for by the likelihood that the speeches of Silvius the woodman, Halcius the fisherman, and Melanthus the swain were written earlier as part of *Poly-Olbion.* At least the hexameter couplets and the debate construction suggest this; but the lives of the three men are depicted with extraordinary vivid detail, unsurpassed elsewhere in Drayton. Ever since Theocritus the different occupations of pastoral characters had been the cause of arguments among them: shepherds, goatherds, neatherds, foresters, and fishermen frequently held each other in contempt. Here, however, the contest is entirely friendly and no aspersions are cast by one on another. Each singer is intent on proving himself a gallant gentleman as well as a happy king of his domains. Moreover, since the victory of one over the others would be indecorous, the nymphs, after an amusing display of psychology as their minds change, award equal honours to all.

The pastoral festival in the third Nymphal shows Drayton at his gayest and wittiest; in his new-found self-confidence he can permit himself to laugh even at what he once treated seriously. In his ode **"The Sacrifice to Apollo"** he had proclaimed the power of liquor to promote poetic raptures, but in that work he showed a noticeable restraint and discretion, and a seriousness in his attitude to poetry. There, while the wine flowed freely, the drinkers were nevertheless '*Delphian* prophets' holding a 'learn'd Meeting': their jests were 'fayrely given, / Becomming well the place'. Here, however, the singers conduct 'Orgies'; they become 'soundly liquord', and with sweating brains pour forth their prophetic utterances. Doron and Dorilus in their song rejoice extravagantly in their poetic drunkenness and the metre gives the effect of reeling intoxication:

> DORON. Why *Dorilus* thou mak'st me mad,
> And now my wits begin to gad,
>   But sure I know not whither.
>
> DORILUS. O *Doron* let me hug thee then,
> There never was two madder men,
>   Then let us on together.

Drayton's earlier work is packed with references to the divine nature of poesy; now he is mocking at his own former seriousness. Classical mythology is also joyfully travestied: Hermes flounders through the Heliconian spring on his '*Tit*' (Pegasus) and bangs his head on Parnassus; Iris is a 'pert and sawcy Elfe'. In contrast with Drayton's serious account of the aspirations of the poet-shepherd in **Endimion and Phoebe,** the poet here may

> swerve up one of *Cynthias* beames,
> And there to bath thee in the streames,
> Discoverd in the Moone.

The next 'Bout' begins when Naiis challenges Cloe to verbal combat. Their song is in a metre which recalls the **"Ballad of Agincourt"**, but metrically it is a great improvement on the ode. Drayton has learned to avoid the intolerable monotony of the regular trochee at the beginning of each line and to make metrical accent coincide with speech stress for a particularly happy, apparently effortless effect:

> The Wood-Nimphes sit singing,
> Each Grove with notes ringing
> Whilst fresh Ver is flinging,
> Her Bounties abroad.

Florimel, the 'melancholy' nymph is then bidden to sing. Cloris and Mertilla make extravagant promises to her, parodying by their very hyperbole the conventional request to a shepherd to sing which so frequently begins a pastoral eclogue. These promises being also in vain, Claia with mock solemnity wishes that all the foulest weeds in Elizium be given to Florimel if she refuses to oblige. Florimel therefore complies in a song which is in every way heretical, in mocking at Platonic love, in swearing friendship is never true, women vacillate, and Time destroys Beauty. But the nymphs cannot endure to hear such falsities, which befit only Felicia, and call upon her to cease. Florimel, a 'mirthfull Gerle and given to sport and game', has brought the principles of Felicia to bear on Elizium and thus

betrayed it but the other Nymphals prove her song untrue: there *is* Platonic love, constancy, and eternal beauty in Elizium. The Nymphal ends with a hymn to the Muses, its sedateness contrasting with the comic songs preceding it. Many stanzas, particularly the first, sustain a certain grandeur, but generally there is a concentration on the comprehensive rather than on poetic quality (as in the tree and flower lists of the fifth Nymphal) and the refrain is a little empty and too clumsily phrased to be eight times repeated. The song is one of the few serious lapses in the whole work.

A further instance of the freshness and novelty which characterize **The Muses Elizium** is the fairy wedding of the eighth Nymphal. As Edgar Long has pointed out [in a 1916 article in *Studies in Philology*], Drayton was the first poet to introduce fairies into the formal pastoral eclogue. Fairies were being described as diminutive by the turn of the sixteenth century; in **Poly-Olbion** they are tiny enough to play barley-break on ears of corn, and the extreme smallness of the characters contributes to the mock-heroic comedy in **Nimphidia**. It was natural that diminutive fairies should rarely appear as companions of man-size pastoral characters, despite their common rural environment. Here Drayton has minimized the problem by describing the nymph Tita as so small that she is herself 'of the Fayry kinde' and by not allowing either her or the fay to appear in person. Over half the Nymphal is devoted to the cogitations of Mertilla and Claia on the 'curious things' with which they will bedeck the bride. Drayton indulges in a detailed description of their gifts, and the clothes and other appurtenances of Tita, enumerated entirely for the sake of the novelty of their minuteness in the manner of the nonpastoral poems of Steward and Herrick. Once again Drayton has broadened the bounds of the pastoral.

In the ninth Nymphal there is a hymn sung by the Muses to Apollo, the reigning deity, reminding the reader that Elizium is dedicated to poetry. The panegyric, almost operatic in its dignity, is one of Drayton's finest passages. In it he shows a skill, matured since **Poly-Olbion,** in using proper names for grandiose effect and in fitting them metrically into his lines with happy facility. Unfortunately there follows a rather dull catalogue of gems with which the nymphs are to build a shrine to the god.

I wish finally to consider the satirical passages in **The Muses Elizium.** Drayton's long career was marked by a series of hardships and disappointments. His (probably forced) withdrawal from the circle of Lucy Countess of Bedford, the years of hackwork for Henslowe, his rejection by King James in 1603, and above all the failure in popularity of **Poly-Olbion,** all increased his bitterness against the world. His fierce diatribes against popular poetasters, ignorant and malicious critics, and the vices of civilization in general increased in length and intensity through his life. Parts of his **Moone-Calfe** and the Elegies may have been written earlier, but he still considered himself justified in publishing them in 1627, and they contain some of his most vehement outbursts. But three years later, in **The Muses Elizium,** his satire for the most part has lost its sting. Elizium is entirely detached from Felicia, which is not only across Codrus's river but in a different world altogether, 'the rude resort / Of beastly people'. In the fourth Nymphal Cloris, who has travelled to see the cosmetic-covered Felicians, returns and is comforted by Mertilla:

> Let not thy noble thoughts descend
> So low as their affections . . .
> Such mad folks ne'r let us bemoane,
> But rather scorne their folly . . .

The stupidity of the Felicians, and their susceptibility to the wiles of Venus and Cupid, is now merely 'Something worth laughter'. The Felicians are mad past curing, however potent Clarinax's herbs may be. Drayton has finally come to terms with mankind by escaping from it. He is surely to be identified with the aged satyr in the tenth Nymphal who, having discovered 'a New Way Over Parnassus', is content to leave the doomed Felicians to their fate:

> I seeing the plagues that shortly are to come
> Upon this people cleerly them forsooke:
> And thus am light into Elizium,
> To whose straite search I wholly me betooke.

The satyr's age and ugliness at first make him incongruous in Elizium, but he is finally accepted by the nymphs, just as Drayton, now an old man of sixty-seven, was adopted into the Dorset family at Knole. It is true that the satyr delivers a final tirade against the Felicians for felling the forests, and for ignoring the songs sung of their brave ancestors, but despite its intensity the condemnation is spoken by one now detached from the evil world. The Nymphal ends abruptly and on a slight discord, but in terms of the poet's personal life the tenth Nymphal itself is not incongruous: by finding this route over Parnassus the once neglected and discontented poet has entered a Golden World of his own making.

It is the resignation and detachment gained through this imaginative withdrawal which paradoxically accounts for Drayton's over-all lightheartedness, felicity of expression, and confident ability to refurbish the older pastoral convention into a more lively, more dramatic form in his last pastoral work. (pp. 7-13)

> *Geoffrey G. Hiller, "Drayton's 'Muses Elizium': A New Way Over Parnassus," in* The Review of English Studies, *n.s. Vol. XXI, No. 81, February, 1970, pp. 1-13.*

RICHARD F. HARDIN (essay date 1973)

[*Hardin is an American educator and critic. In the following excerpt, he characterizes and judges Drayton as a poet of history and tradition, of nature, and of England. Hardin focuses on four odes: "To the Virginian Voyage," "Ballad of Agincourt," "An Ode Written in the Peake," and "A Hymne to His Ladies Birth-Place."*]

If the annual scholarly bibliographies are any indication, Michael Drayton is today the least fashionable of important Elizabethan poets. Those who know his poems recognize that the best of them deserve the attention of any literate reader, and that historians of the Jacobean age can learn from the social criticism that they contain. Yet neither literary historians nor social historians seem especially informed about his work today, the tendency being to shunt him off with Daniel, Campion, and "others" as one more star in a galaxy of able performers. (p. v)

His eclipse came with the "rediscovery" of Donne and the Metaphysicals in the decades just after the publication of the *Cambridge History*, when an increasing number of important critics began to view Drayton, "the Petrarchans," and even Spenser as so many pedantic weeds in the Muse's garden *ante Donne*. Eliot observed in "Imperfect Critics" [see Additional Bibliography] that the only good lines in Drayton's "dreary sequence of ideas" occur when he "drops his costume for a moment and talks in terms of actuality." Yvor Winters, in his notable revaluation of Elizabethan poetry, placed Drayton among the rhetorically obsessed, morally unenlightening family of

Petrarchans [see Additional Bibliography]. Followers of Eliot and Winters—through devotion to their masters, one feels, rather than first-hand acquaintance with Drayton's poetry—have perpetuated the view of Drayton as a tedious Petrarchan or a tiresome drudge. It is a view that still prevails in many quarters, notwithstanding the respect for Drayton evinced in such important studies as Rosemond Tuve's *Elizabethan and Metaphysical Imagery* [see Additional Bibliography] and Hallett Smith's *Elizabethan Poetry* [see excerpt dated 1952].

Drayton was surely a different kind of poet from Donne, and the sort of poetry for which Drayton was most applauded in his time, historical poetry, has little if any audience today, in contrast to the intensely personal, apolitical poetry of Donne. Donne's first audience, like his audience today, was an urbanized one: London professional men, intellectuals, members of the Establishment. Drayton wrote for a more geographically dispersed audience of country gentlemen and lesser aristocrats sharing his conservative political, religious, and intellectual outlook. Donne's poetry, except for a few occasional pieces, was written for the private enjoyment of a sophisticated coterie delighting in his mastery of wit, surprise, and conceit. Drayton, like Spenser, was a public poet moved by an educated faith in English destiny—truly "Elizabethan," as historians have come to understand that term, in his persistent desire to raise English poetry and national fame above that of other cultures, past and present.

My purpose in this essay is not to restore Drayton to the place of eminence he held in his time—no one can do that; rather, it is to impart a sense of his identity as a poet, particularly to explain how he is distinguished among his contemporaries by the intensity of his devotion to England and English traditions. (pp. v-vi)

The standard edition of Michael Drayton's works contains about two thousand pages of verse in four volumes. Even when we take into account the many revised poems, which comprise a large part of one volume, we are still left with a formidable amount of poetry. Add to this the scant critical attention that has been paid Drayton, and one hardly knows how to approach him. He wrote sonnets and other brief lyric poems, but he wrote the enormous *Poly-Olbion* as well, not to mention several long historical pieces. He attempted almost all the kinds of poetry known in his day, and did well in most of them: religious, heroic, pastoral, elegiac, and satiric. He had a hand in writing a number of plays, and he introduced two "new" kinds of poetry into England with his heroic epistles and odes.

From this wide range of poetry, the reader who wants a few poems containing the essence of Drayton should, I believe, choose the odes, first published in 1606, later augmented in the collected *Poems* of 1619. If need be, he can narrow the essential list still further to four odes, the first two of which are his best: **"To the Virginian Voyage," "Ballad of Agincourt," "An Ode Written in the Peak," and "A Hymn to His Lady's Birthplace."** (pp. 1-2)

Short as they are, these few poems exemplify the Drayton of the long historical and topographical works: the public poet who employed his talent for the celebration of his country; the conservative spokesman for the traditions and values of rural English gentlemen; the Elizabethan imbued with a sense of his country's destiny. In each of them, the object of praise is not so much the lady or the heroes of Agincourt and Virginia as it is England herself—the England who is chief actor and principal object of praise in *Poly-Olbion*. As in nearly all Drayton's

ODES.

WITH

OTHER LYRICK

POESIES.

BY

MICHAEL DRAYTON,

ESQVIRE.

LONDON,

Printed for IOHN SMETHVVICKE.

1 6 1 9.

Title page of a late edition of Drayton's Odes, *which was originally published in 1606.*

poems, there is in these a fundamental, radical Englishness, for their author was the most English poet of his age, if not of all others. At a later date his kind of patriotism in poets can often be attributed to simple-mindedness or crass hypocrisy, but in the early 1600s the current of nationalism in England was still fresh enough that a bit of her landscape or history could produce deep and powerful sentiments in the audience. For this reason, in discussing the four poems that I have chosen as representative . . . I often disregard the distinction usually made between the poet and the persona speaking in his poems. For the most part the two voices are virtually one and the same, as I believe they must be in the poetry of celebration.

"An Ode Written in the Peak" reflects Drayton's awareness of the classical tradition of the ode: like Martial's epigram on the villa of Faustinus at Baiae, or Horace's poems on his Sabine farm, it is a poem in praise of a place. But the difference between Drayton and his Roman antecedents is important, for they had written on a place belonging to someone, while Drayton wrote on a place that belonged to all England. As the earlier poets had associated the virtues of the place with its owner, Drayton extols the English virtues of the Peak; thus the contrast on which his poem is built, between the cold North and warm South, extends beyond England to the greater rivalry between the civilizations of southern and northern Europe.

The mood is one of celebration, but lightly recreative, like many passages elsewhere in Drayton. He begins by wondering whether any poet can work "Exposed to sleet and rain" in the wintery Peak:

> This while we are abroad,
> Shall we not touch our lyre?
> Shall we not sing an ode?
> Shall that holy fire,
> In us that strongly glowed,
> In this cold air expire?

As we should expect of the author of *Poly-Olbion,* he cannot avoid pointing out the local tourist attractions, the clear rivers and the caves, but most of all those two sovereign emblems of English gemütlichkeit, "Buckston's delicious baths," topped off with "Strong ale and noble cheer, / T'assuage breme Winter's scathes." The poem concludes on a pun: wherever the place, at whatever time, "The Muse is still in ure"—playing on the Latin sense (*uro,* "burn") to suggest that the holy fire of the opening stanza is always alive. Poetry does not thrive in one particular place and time, just as the poetry of the Northern culture can compete with that of the Mediterranean South, whether ancient or modern. National competition is a familiar theme in Drayton, perhaps most fully explored by Surrey and Geraldine in *England's Heroical Epistles.*

Another representative ode, **"A Hymn to His Lady's Birthplace"** (first printed in 1619), shows how the poem in praise of a person can be manipulated by Drayton into the kind of patriotic tribute he enjoyed writing. This expression of esteem for the daughter of his old patron might, for another poet, have been the occasion for a more intimate poem, but the **"Hymn"** is every bit as public as the other three odes. Like Spenser's *Prothalamion,* it shows a divided concern for the subject of his praise and the places with which she is associated, as if these places have a life and personality of their own. Coventry is elevated to a national shrine honoring Idea's (Anne Goodere's) birthplace, and as in the **"Ode Written in the Peak"** Drayton celebrates the local attributes (the city prospect, its walls and spires, the "trophies of the boar") but generalizes upon their patriotic implications.

Far superior to either of these as a patriotic poem is the ode **"To the Virginian Voyage,"** entered for publication when the patent for the Virginia colony was less than two weeks old. Behind this singular poem are two important influences—first, Richard Hakluyt, a favorite mine of information for Drayton and a guiding spirit behind his poetry. Hakluyt and he had much in common: both were country gentlemen in origin, both sought to make Englishmen aware of their national superiority through patient, sometimes plodding historical research. And if ever the first propagandist for English imperialism found a disciple it was Drayton. "Industrious Hakluyt," he calls him in the ode:

> Whose reading shall inflame
> Men to seek fame,
> And much commend
> To after-times thy wit.

Privately, Drayton must have wished the same for his own writings—if not in all his work, at least in this poem, one of the few great English poems of empire, drawing its strength from the very newness of that theme in the national culture.

A second influence in the poem is the ancient dream of the earthly paradise, the land of abundance and eternal spring that men had long believed lay far to the west of Europe. Columbus had been the first of many explorers to identify America with this mythical place, and in England the association had become fairly common by the seventeenth century. Some were convinced that Virginia lay on the threshold of Eden; Drayton portrays it as a natural paradise, "Earth's only paradise," where "the golden age / Still Nature's laws doth give." In a land where the profiteers had not yet enclosed the farmland and ravaged the forests—familiar topics in Drayton's later satire—Englishmen might hope to live in the same spirit of justice as had prevailed in primitive times.

Beside this return to natural justice, the earthly paradise would bring freedom from want. Drayton is lured by the same promise that had excited men like John Smith and Arthur Barlow about the new England:

> Where Nature hath in store
> Fowl, venison, and fish,
> And the fruitfull'st soil,
> Without your toil,
> Three harvests more,
> All greater than you wish.

At a later time, when Goldsmith could describe a nightmarish land across the Atlantic, where "crouching tigers wait their hapless prey, And savage men more murd'rous still than they," men might with reason dismiss this poem as naïve, infused as it was with the enthusiasm of a generation who, like Hakluyt and Drayton, never experienced the hazards of actual colonial life.

The heavy emphasis on material abundance in the ode, particularly Drayton's urging the voyagers "to get the pearl and gold," leads us to think that its author had only the material advancement of England in mind. The whole poem, however, with its promise of safe voyage and wealth, rises to one climactic stanza, the keystone of the arch. Drayton exhorts the voyagers to thank God for their success, to be happy,

> And in regions far
> Such Heroes bring ye forth,
> As those from whom we came,
> And plant our name
> Under that star
> Not known unto our North.

This Virginian voyage was not just another foraging excursion or exploratory trip, like the expeditions of the sixteenth century. If we exclude those often abortive attempts, it marks the beginning of a continued English presence in the New World. In the ode, particularly in the stanza I have just quoted, Drayton is doing nothing less than celebrating the birth of America. The voyagers are not only to enjoy their material prosperity, they are to increase and multiply: to bring forth "heroes," like the Englishmen of old whom Drayton so often celebrates in his historical poetry. Just as Nature's profusion in Virginia contrasts with her poverty in the Old World, the new race of Virginians will signal a return to the age of heroes. Drayton accepts the antiquarian paradox that the modern world is the world grown old, so that the phrase "New World" held a special significance for him. Indeed, the famous opening stanza can only be read in the light of this contrast between the heroes of the New World and the burnt-out men of the Old:

> You brave heroic minds,
> Worthy your country's name,
> That honor still pursue,
> Go, and subdue,
> Whilst loit'ring hinds
> Lurk here at home, with shame.

It is no coincidence that this and the previously quoted stanza echo the words of God to Adam: "Be fruitful and multiply, and fill the earth and subdue it." During the early seventeenth century, the idea became commonplace that English expansion was somehow a reenactment of that which God ordained for the elect of the Old Testament, from Adam and Noah to Abraham and Moses. Many puritan New Englanders thought of themselves as righteous outcasts from a modern Egypt, seeking a new Canaan.

The bulk of Drayton's writing is historical poetry, and I believe that the **"Virginian Voyage,"** even though it looks to the future rather than the past, fits into the overall scheme of the historical work. The whole Elizabethan impulse toward colonial expansion derives from the same spirit that Drayton's work and the historical drama of the Elizabethan stage may be said to embody. The wars with France in the fifteenth century had been an earlier stage of the development of a national identity, and the resulting desire to expand this time took the form of colonial expeditions. Thus there is a continuity between the spirit of the **"Virginian Voyage"** and the last poem in our representative list, the **"Ballad of Agincourt."**

Like many of his countrymen Drayton was disappointed in James I's failure to pursue an aggressive policy of colonial expansion and to assert himself militarily on the Continent as earlier English rulers had done. The ideal monarch in this respect was of course Henry V, who figures prominently in Drayton's long *Battle of Agincourt* and in the **"Ballad."** As is the case with all his historical verse, this poem passes judgment on the present and past, and does so in fact by holding up to contemporary Englishmen the example of their forefathers. It was probably Drayton's favorite among his own works, for in the preface to the odes he singles it out:

> [I] would at this time also gladly let thee understand, what I think above the rest, of the last ode of this number [i.e., the **"Ballad"**], or if thou wilt, ballad in my book: for both the great master of Italian rhymes, Petrarch, and our Chaucer, and other of the upper house of the Muses, have thought their canzons honored in the title of a ballad; which, for that I labor to meet truly therein with the old English garb, I hope as able to justify, as the learned Colin Clout his roundelay.

These remarks, beside showing Drayton's esteem for the poem, suggest that he called it a ballad because that kind of poetry had a venerable tradition in England, notwithstanding its abuse by contemporary hacks. Moreover, he meant the ballad to be sung: both the preface and the ensuing verse-history of the ode (**"To Himself, and the Harp"**) show that he thought of odes as necessarily accompanied by music. (pp. 2-7)

The **"Ballad of Agincourt"** is, in fact, the closest thing to an Anglo-Saxon war poem to be written in Drayton's age.... King Henry might be called the hero of the poem, but this would be misleading, for every Englishman is valorous. The listing of names and attributes of each prominent English leader lends the ode a heroic breadth that is difficult to attain in so short a poem. Even the typography conveys a sense of sustained monumentality:

> WARWICK in blood did wade,
> OXFORD the foe invade,
> And cruel slaughter made,
>
> Still as they ran up;
> SUFFOLK his ax did ply,
> BEAUMONT and WILLOUGHBY
> Bare them right doughtily,
> FERRERS and FANHOPE.

Nothing in the poem mitigates this relentless martial spirit, no sense of the irony or paradox of human warfare. The prevailing tone is, on the contrary, quite heartless. . . . Some may see the starkness of the poem as a fault—certainly it does not have the emotional complexity of a lyric by Donne or Shakespeare; the emotion itself, however, is not a simple one to account for in men, and I cannot think of another short poem in English that has conveyed it quite so successfully, in all its bare and terrible directness, as Drayton's ode. (pp. 7-8)

[Aside] from Shakespeare there are few moments in English poetry that impart so convincingly the mood of a man convinced of his nation's destiny as **"The Virginian Voyage"** and the **"Ballad of Agincourt."**

From these four odes, then, we may abstract the motives underlying almost all of Drayton's work: the desire to place English poetry in competition with that of the ancients and moderns of other countries; to revere the past and praise the natural beauty of England; to make clear to his English readers their virtues as a people. His poems are historical, topographical, encomiastic, occasionally indignant; but they are above all English. (pp. 8-9)

> *Richard F. Hardin, in his* Michael Drayton and the Passing of Elizabethan England, *The University Press of Kansas, 1973, 181 p.*

STELLA P. REVARD   (essay date 1977)

[*Revard is an American educator and author of* The War in Heaven: "Paradise Lost" and the Tradition of Satan's Rebellion *(1980). In the following excerpt, she discusses Drayton's unique blending of myth and reality, nature and anthropomorphism, English geography and English culture in* Poly-Olbion.]

Michael Drayton's **Poly-Olbion** is usually approached as a curiosity, the longest topological poem in English, curious in its antiquarian learning and still more curious in its apparent design to chart with a cartographer's accuracy every tract, river, mountain, forest, dell in Great Britain. Scholarly studies of **Poly-Olbion**—Gerhard Buchloh's *Michael Drayton, Barde, und Historiker, Politiker und Prophet* and Alice d'Haussy's *Poly-Olbion, ou L'Angleterre Vue Par Un Élizabéthain*—have for the most part attempted to evaluate the poem in terms of its use of antiquarian materials. Yet, though we must be aware how Drayton's work is rooted in the historical traditions of Elizabethan England, we must not forget its poetical design. Drayton divided **Poly-Olbion** not into chapters or books, but into songs, and consistently he subordinates whatever history he is recounting to the lyrical mode of these songs. In his preface, moreover, he promises readers pleasures of a poetical order [see excerpt dated 1612]. For our delight Drayton will create a perfect world of nature in which we may hear "harmless Sheapheards . . . some exercising their pipes, some singing roundelaies, to their gazing flocks" and may see "dainty Nymphes in their simple naked bewties, bathing them in Crystalline streams." It is my aim to examine the design of this perfect world of nature.

Before we inquire into overall design, however, it is wise to examine some particulars, for Drayton in writing topological pastoral is dealing with a very special kind of poetry. The nymphs and shepherds to whom he alludes in his preface are, of course, the actual features of the landscape anthropomorphized. Thus forest nymphs are not merely nymphs who inhabit forests, but the forests themselves; hill shepherds, not the conventional complainers upon hillsides, but the hills. This genre of pastoral, which is of venerable ancestry, had newly been given voice in Drayton's time by Spenser in *Colin Clouts Come Home Again* and in Book IV, canto ll of *The Faerie Queene*, the "marriage" of the Thames and the Medway. But Drayton's purposes in using topological pastoral are not those of his master Spenser. Whereas Spenser had used it as embellishment to complement the main action of the poem and had relegated it to set pieces, Drayton uses it as his principal device. Topological characters are the main characters in Drayton, topological "action" the only action of his poem. However these ladies and gentlemen of the landscape may resemble real or fictional heroines and heroes, they do not exist in Drayton's pastoral to call these to mind. Humanity has been excluded from **Poly-Olbion** except as topological characters themselves look at human beings and the world of men.

Thus, Drayton's kind of pastoral requires some adjustment on the part of the reader. Held together as it is by a series of dramatic incidents in which the persons of the landscape are described as and act like human beings, **Poly-Olbion** consistently tempts the reader to view it as a pastoral masque in which "hills" and "rivers" are merely human beings in fancy dress. For example, the reader at first regards Drayton's description of the love triangle involving the hill Clent, the forest Feckn'ham, and the river Salwarpe as the conventional conflict all too familiar in pastoral eclogue or romance. The forest Feckn'ham dotes upon the river, who takes no notice of her, being "from all affection free." The forest in turn is immoderately loved by the elderly hill Clent, who rues both her "fall" and her flight from him. Momentarily we see in Feckn'ham the fleeing maiden of *Orlando Furioso* or *The Faerie Queene*, who loves one knight distractedly only to be pursued by another. But only momentarily. What we really see is that the *forest* has left the *hill-top* barren of trees, which cluster instead about the nearby *river*. Feckn'ham, however fugitive her appearance, is not meant as the successor to Angelica or fair Florimell. Nor is Clent Roland as he loudly laments that the faithless forest has lavished her affections on an unworthy rival. How far from the world of romance we are as we hear a hill, vowing to forsake all pleasure, upbraid a "fallen" forest and threaten a river with vengeance: "Which when, most wilfull Nymph, thy chaunce shal be to see, / Too late thou shalt repent thy small regard of mee." Clent, of course, cannot carry out his threats; like the lover on Keats's storied urn frozen by art, Clent is frozen by nature. Drayton has created this little drama perhaps for the sheer fancy of it, perhaps to glance wryly at the absurdities of romance that it mimics. What is most important, however, is that in telling his story of rivalry and rejected love, he has taken care to "ground" it in topological truth. We see the landscape better, not worse, for Drayton's story. Consistently Drayton aims to transcend nature, to heighten it, to render it—as Sidney said the artist must—yet more golden, but never to deny it.

Throughout **Poly-Olbion,** the distinctive quality of Drayton's pastoral is the ease with which it combines the real and the fanciful. For example, there is no contradiction for Drayton in describing Milford Haven both as a busy harbor and as a nymph over whose bosom ships glide. He can also celebrate Yarmouth alternately for its fishing industry and its nymphs adorned with coral. And the river Tivy is notable for her beauty and for her beavers and salmon-falls. Drayton is like the old makers of tapestries who employ the faces of real persons in the most intricate of mythological designs. The challenge for Drayton obviously was to interweave as finely as possible the colors of myth and reality in each song.

Nowhere is this interweaving more skillful than in the thirteenth song, where the poet sings of his native Warwickshire. There in a single song we have geomorphic myth, social criticism, and natural idyll. The song begins with the introduction of the Forest of Arden, who as a venerable father speaks of the heritage of the land.

> Of all the Forrests heere within this mightie Ile,
> If those old *Britains* then me Soveraigne did instile,
> I needs must be the great'st; for greatnesse tis alone
> That gives our kind the place. . . .

But the Forest represents not only nostalgia for things past; as a bitter social reformer he denounces contemporary practices which have despoiled the land: cutting down trees, limiting and enclosing the forest, and setting villages so close by that deer are dislodged from their coverts. The lament for the lost beauty of the land is short-lived, however; what follows is an idyllic passage in which the present beauties of nature are evoked. Drayton describes the wood in early morning when men are preparing for a hunt. We hear first the choir of birds: "quirristers" are perched upon the "highest spray of every mounting pole" and "with their cleere open throats, / Unto the joyfull Morne so straine their warbling notes." Now Drayton once more interrupts with one of his most characteristic digressions, the catalogue. Having evoked a mirthful choir of forest birds who fill the air with the sound of their harmony, he now must characterize each one. And so he does, showing how nature has marked the "Woosell" with its golden bill or particularized the "Throstell" with the shrill sharps of its song. Curiously enough, Drayton's display of ornithological lore supports rather than destroys his forest idyll. The real birds with their individual color and characteristics remind us that Drayton is singing of an actual and not a mythical forest. Yet as he concludes the passage, it is myth that is liberally mixed with reality. The classical patroness of the hunt, Diana, appears wearing her bow and attired in green, not at all out of place in an English forest. The hunt she presides over is, of course, the classical hunt for the stag, the fittest quarry for the "chaste mightie Forrests Queene." The conclusion to this hunt is one of Drayton's most vivid pieces of realism. The stag at bay fights for his life, dealing deadly wounds to the "churlish throated hounds" with his sharp-pointed head. Only when we can bear it no more does Drayton soften this cruel and bloody picture with a touch of folklore. Conquered by the hunter, the stag weeps "precious tears" for his own death, tears, as Drayton tells us, which are medicinal. Drayton's pastoral in this Warwickshire passage has appealed to not one but many aspects of life. Surely inherent in his design, as the Greek word *poly* in his title implies, is the celebration of "manyness" and "muchness" of the land itself: its variety and wealth. As Drayton has shown us in this thirteenth song and as he continues to show throughout the poem, England is a land of abundant resources and experiences. She provides man with bodily sustenance and she sustains him with legend and history; she delights him with her manifold beauties and she inspires his poetry.

Yet Drayton's design in *Poly-Olbion* transcends poetical celebration of England's beauty and abundance. Drayton has so ordered his world of nature that we may see in it far more than the natural world beautified for so-called ornamental effect. Borrowing from Elizabethan thought its favorite principle of hierarchy, Drayton has hierarchically organized the world of *Poly-Olbion* so that it mirrors English society, wherein sovereigns reign and subjects offer obedience. In *Poly-Olbion* the kings and queens are the mountains and rivers who dominate the land. To the mountains, hills and valleys bow in recognition of their highest station; to the rivers, streams and brooks offer tribute as handmaidens and attendants who feed and swell their waters. These kings and queens necessarily are absolute in that their right to reign is geomorphically if not divinely determined. Theirs is a right, moreover, universally recognized and seldom contested. (pp. 105-08)

Drayton mirrors in his pastoral the Elizabethan world of intrigue and passion, yet in his world of nature, the passions of political life are exercised harmlessly. The perfect world of nature checks the less than perfect impulses of its anthropomorphic deities. Violence is rendered not only harmless, but absurd. We might liken Drayton's satiric technique here to that which he uses in the fairy pastoral *Nymphidia*. There Oberon may jealously rave, but his murderous intent is limited in that he is armed only with a sword made of a hornet's sting and a spear from a horse-fly's tongue. Would that the violence of men could be likewise limited! So in *Poly-Olbion* Drayton has created a world not without conflict, but one in which conflict truly is resolved for the better. The great rivers and mountains of the landscape reign with a kind of indisputable supremacy that even the great Elizabeth and her successor James might envy.

Yet the design of *Poly-Olbion* reaches beyond expressing perfectly in nature the peaceful hierarchy of persons and things the Elizabethans and Jacobeans so longed for in their own society. Drayton's aim in *Poly-Olbion* was to create, as it were, a tableau in which the geography of the land becomes one with the history, the morality, the aesthetics of the people who inhabit it. And he has unfolded this design slowly over the course of the first eighteen songs of Part 1. Moving geographically from Cornwall to Devon to Wales and eastward to the Midlands, he recounts progressively the history of Great Britain, interspersing historical account with geographical commentary in the form of topological myth, and adding descriptive flourish, dramatic incident, and moral exemplum. His historical survey is artfully linked with his geographical, beginning in "**Song 1**," when the "cleere Dert" opens the history, continuing with the Severne's account of the Britons and the Weaver's complementary account of the Saxons, and not concluding until "**Song 18**" when the Thames ends the narrative with the triumph of the kings of England. (pp. 110-11)

Drayton's treatment of the rivers . . . provides an example of the complexity of his design. There are two main rivers in the first part of *Poly-Olbion*: the Severne and the Thames, high queen and high king of Drayton's landscape. Upon them he lavishes his poetical attention. In "**Song 5**," he describes Severne as a queen upon the throne, naming her Sabrine for the nymph most closely connected with her. . . . In the strictest sense, the Severne represents for Drayton the heritage of Wales and the Briton past; she has been acknowledged queen of the Welsh countryside and patroness of Briton kings and queens. In this passage, however, the Severne also stands for Elizabeth, the most English of queens, and she is depicted—like Eliza in *The Shepherd's Calendar*—as a nymph of the pastoral world, queenly, beautiful, and chaste. But Drayton is not content with the triple role of pastoral-nymph, British patroness, and Tudor queen; he has yet another role for the Severne to play. In "**Song 5**," recounting the boundary dispute between England and Wales over the Isle of Lundy, he has Severne the queen serve as arbitress. In delivering her judgment, she enunciates the important principle of Tudor destiny. Lundy belongs neither to England nor Wales, but to both and is a sign of the unity rather than the division of the land. She goes on to predict that the two countries shall further be joined, "grafted in the stock of great *Plantaginet*." The new line of English kings from Henry of Monmouth on are sprung from the "stock" of Wales grafted to that of England. And this first union is but the prologue to the second, when the "Steward stem" shall be joined to the Tudor and thus the "three sever'd Realmes in one shall firmlie stand." The above is, of course, familiar doctrine for a sixteenth- or seventeenth-century Englishman. What makes it more than political propaganda in Drayton's poem is that Drayton has made it appear as the voice of the land itself. What better symbol of unity than a mighty and beautiful river which flows through both lands, serves in part as their boundary, and enriches them both!

As Drayton moves into the final sections of the first part of his poem, he again uses the symbol of a river to further his design. Songs 15 through 18 of *Poly-Olbion* are devoted to the description of the Thames: his ancestry, the marriage of his parents, his own birth, and his triumphal upbringing and maturity. We move from the Cotswolds to Oxford to London and to the sea—and in so doing we move from the rural to the intellectual to the international scene. Drayton is undoubtedly deeply indebted to Spenser for many of the descriptions in these three songs; most notably his marriage of the Isis and the Tame depends upon Spenser's marriage of the Thames and the Medway. Yet the aim of the two poets is quite different. Spenser through celebration of the fruitfulness of nature is presenting symbolically the triumph of love and in his marriage of the Thames and the Medway is preparing for the spousals of Marinell and Florimell. Drayton celebrates not the triumph of human love but that of his own historio-geographical design. The marriage of the rivers, Tame and Isis, which results in the birth of the Thames is not without its symbolic and historical implications. Again Drayton is alluding to Tudor myth, for the Isis represents Elizabeth of York and the Tame, Henry of Lancaster. This marriage is both a union of the red and white roses of Lancaster and York and a symbol of the commingling of the thousand traditions and strengths which have made England the land of abundance and beauty that she is. In presenting the wedding, Drayton has other purposes as well. He is intent first to describe accurately the surroundings (the Cotswolds, the Chiltern Hills, the country about Oxford), and second to offer in this wedding his praise of the English country scene and country life. The bride Isis, who takes her course through peaceful and lovely landscape, is made to represent the physical beauty of the land; the groom Tame represents its wealth. The Chiltern Hills and Alsbury Vale are the "parents" of Tame, and Drayton makes repeated reference to their rural prosperity: "*Alsbury's* a Vale that walloweth in her wealth." But Alsbury is also made the fussy rural matron: "lustie, frim, and fat, [who] holds her youthful strength." She cannot be kept from "prodigall expense" in setting forth her son. She "feedes her *Tame* with Marle, in Cordiall-wise prepar'd" and endeavors to match or exceed the "expense" which the Cotswolds have lavished upon the bride. Clearly Drayton is portraying both the wealth of this sheep-grazing district and those wealthy rustics who inhabit it. We also have for a moment domestic comedy between Alsbury, the willful wife and her more conservative husband, Chiltern, whose hoar and chalky head alternately calls to mind the white hair of an elderly countryman and the Chiltern's beechen woods. A typical anxious spouse, he chides his wife that her lavish expense breeds surfeit and cloys the stomach, besides being an extravagant waste.

Drayton's account of the wedding is, of course, more than a rural comedy. He is writing a prothalamion, and as he describes the approach of the bride, we are given passages of pure lyric description. The scene is Oxford, and its spires tower soberly over the meadows and lend a classic tone to the invocation to the rural muses.

> Yee Daughters of the Hills, come downe from every side,
> And due attendance give upon the lovely Bride:
> Goe strewe the paths with flowers by which shee is to passe.
> For be yee thus assur'd, in *Albion* never was
> A beautie (yet) like hers: where have yee ever seene
> So absolute a Nymph in all things, for a Queene?

To describe both bride and groom, Drayton constructs intricate contrasting catalogues of flowers. The Tame is dressed in those flowers which spring "from the replenisht Meads, and fruitfull Pastures neere," Primrose, Hare-bell, Woodbind, Daffadilly, Cowslip, Oxslip, Columbine—Drayton paints the wild meadows which border the Tame. For the Isis, he chooses those flowers which bloom in cultivated gardens along her route: Pansie, Mary-gold, Daysie, Button-batcheler, Sweet William. So simultaneously, he suggests the actual river-borders and a fanciful rural swain and his bride, adorned with flowers for a country wedding. The herbs are strewn, bride and bridegroom meet, a rural couple and coupling rivers, who join their "crystal" waters. "When as your crystall wasts you closely doe enfold, / Betwixt your beautious selves you shall beget a Sonne, / That when your lives shall end, in him shall be begunne." Thames, begotten of this union, will carry on the "being" of the parents. Here is the familiar Elizabethan commonplace: the progeny is the second self of the parents, who perpetuates their beauty and strength. This Thames, however, will not only carry on the rural heritage of his parents, but will achieve international fame: the rivers of Europe will esteem him highly and "the *Skeld*, the goodly *Mose*, the rich and Viny *Rheine*, / Shall come to meet the *Thames* in *Neptunes* watry Plaine." What begins in tone as a graceful wedding-song with the traditional compliments to beauty, joy, and fertility ends as a paean to England's eternity. The Isis and the Tame are no mere bridal pair, who may expect a human and therefore impermanent futurity in their offspring; their child is eternally begotten and possesses a continuity of time and place which links him alike to the Britons and Saxons long dead and to generations unborn. No mere symbol of Tudor monarchy, he is England itself.

Drayton's prothalamion concludes as the Charwell calls upon all of England's rivers to be present and to join in the celebration of England's unity by "uniting" one with another. . . . But the rivers which Drayton has described are symbols not merely for England's unity, but for the world's. Rivers mark the seats of towns and havens, lend their names to the land, trace the boundaries of nations, and divide the "tripartited Ile" of England and the globe itself. Nations take their fame from their rivers, as India from the Ganges or Spain from the Tagus, and finally from the rivers of one's native land, one learns a valuable lesson. As the rivers are fed from the land, so man. Like them, he is nourished in her bowels, grows and thrives as nature feeds him with the sacred power of goodness. Like them, he too must go forth to care for the land and to make it fertile through the power dispensed to him by nature herself. In showing how virtuous men, like the rivers, must nurture their land, Drayton once more has used topography to point a moral. (pp. 111-15)

With similar pastoral techniques Drayton continues his tour of England in *Poly-Olbion*, Part 2. Its twelve sequent songs survey the "northern parts of this isle." Still more nymphs and gods of landscape are introduced to us; still more local legends recounted (Robin Hood appears in **"Song 26"**); historical accounts continue (the battles of the Civil and Scottish wars are told); and catalogues abound, as diverse [as] those of marsh and sea birds or of Cambro-British and English saints. What is missing, however, in Part 2 is the sense of overarching design that characterized Part 1. Although Drayton is still partial to rivers as the dominant pastoral personalities, none of the rivers of Part 2 engage the interest nor are as symbolically vital as the Severne and Thames of Part 1. Nor does the poem move with the kind of narrative unfolding of Part 1, where the reader is made to feel the sense of historical and geographic progression as he journeys from Cornwall to Wales and finally to England. Nor is there a dramatic and lyric climax achieved such as occurred in Part 1 when the Isis and the Tame were wed with pastoral pageantry and the destiny of England assured with the begetting of Thames.

Yet despite the shortcomings of Part 2, Drayton does attempt in **"Song 30"** to unite both parts of his poem by evoking once more the perfect world of nature he had promised to create. He plants his paradise in Westmerland, for there wanders the brook Eden, whose name suggests the first perfect world.

> O my bright lovely Brooke, whose name doth beare the sound
> Of Gods first Garden-plot, th' imparadized ground,
> Wherein he placed Man, from whence by sinne he fell.
> O little blessed Brooke, how doth my bosome swell,
> With love I beare to thee. . . .

In Eden, however, Drayton appeals to more than the memory of paradise; he alludes to the glories of England which he has labored to include in his poem. Near Eden's bank, seventy-seven stones stand in a ring, each stone ten feet in height, and enclosed within these stones the bones of men long dead. The victory for which this monument was erected has been lost in the "dark oblivion" of time. Nearby, there is a "little rising Bank, which of the Table round, / Men in remembrance keepe, and *Arthurs* Table name." The world of nature guards the relics of man's past and renews man himself, doing, in effect, what Drayton has attempted to do in his poem. And on that note Drayton concludes his "strange *Herculean* toyle." "Faire Eden" meets the attending floods which "downe from the Westerne Sands into the Sea doe fall"; to this obscure little brook, Drayton has entrusted the task of bringing his pastoral design to a fitting conclusion. (pp. 116-17)

> *Stella P. Revard, "The Design of Nature in Drayton's 'Poly-Olbion'," in* Studies in English Literature, 1500-1900, *Vol. XVII, No. 1, Winter, 1977, pp. 105-17.*

WARREN W. WOODEN (essay date 1977)

[*In the following excerpt, Wooden describes the wide-ranging appeal of* Nimphidia *as children's literature.*]

Critical consensus no longer considers the prolific Drayton a major Renaissance poet. It is nevertheless true, as his modern editor [J. William Hebel, in **The Works of Michael Drayton**] remarks, that "Nymphidia has won wider and more continued popularity than any other poem of Drayton's." I suggest that much of the sustained popularity of Drayton's fairy poem lies in its particular appeal to children, and I propose to analyze the elements in the poem which contribute to this appeal.

Like his Warwickshire countryman William Shakespeare, Drayton was originally a country boy, widely read but without university training, who made his mark in London as a poet of talent and versatility. And again like his friend Shakespeare, Drayton appears to have written for the widest possible popular audience. Thus in the early seventeenth century, while Donne and the metaphysical poets wrote for and circulated manuscripts among an avant-garde intellectual coterie and Jonson and the Tribe of Ben wrote neoclassic verse for the cultivated and aristocratic, Drayton aimed at a far wider reading public. Consequently, he insisted on printing his verse—"attempting," one recent critic [Richard F. Hardin] persuasively argues, "to write for a national audience," not just for the Court or for Londoners but for an audience widely dispersed all through the country. Although we assume the *Nymphidia* was written with an adult audience in mind, the calculated breadth of appeal for which Drayton strove certainly contributed to the comparative accessibility of his work to children. As a fairy story treated in the mock-heroic mode, the *Nymphidia* is constructed to give pleasure to various strata of the reading public—the well educated and the casual reader, the courtier-sophisticate and the country-traditionalist. The first two stanzas of *Nymphidia* announce Drayton's intention to cultivate this wide range of appeal:

> Olde CHAUCER doth of *Topas* tell
> Mad RABLAIS of *Pantagruell,*
> A latter third of *Dowsabell,*
>   with such poore trifles playing:
> Others the like have laboured at
> Some of this thing, and some of that,
> And many of they know not what,
>   But that they must be saying.
>
> Another sort there bee, that will
> Be talking of the Fayries still
> Nor never can they have their fill,
>   As they were wedded to them;
> No Tales of them their thirst can slake,
> So much delight therein they take,
> And some strange thing they faine would make,
>   Knew they the way to doe them.

The first stanza announces the mock-heroic treatment of the subject, a technique specifically literary and presupposing the reader's familiarity with both ancient and modern classics of the heroic genre. Similarly, the range of allusion speaks to a well-educated audience, for Chaucer's English was rough going for many seventeenth-century readers and Rabelais was not widely available in English. But stanza two evokes the native, oral tradition of fairies—tricksters as familiar to children as to adults. Drayton then announces at the outset that he casts with a wide sweep, suggesting a readership of varied literary backgrounds and implicitly promising something for everyone including young readers.

Among the pleasures to be shared by readers of every background, for example, are those imparted by metre, rhyme, and stanza form. It seems likely that a modern critic's observation that "poetry, unlike other forms of literature, is common ground for both children and grown-ups," would have been axiomatic in the early seventeenth century, when poetry still dominated prose as *the* medium of literary expression. *Nymphidia* is composed of eighty-eight verses of a surprisingly versatile 8-line stanza rhyming *aaabcccb*. It is a development of the 6-line tail-rhyme stanza of Chaucer's *Sir Thopas* which was similarly designed to deflect the meter of the old heroic ballads and metrical romances to humorous purposes. Drayton's b-tail rhymes are double however and generally in trimeter as opposed to the tetrameter of the a- and c-lines. As one might expect, the effect of the short-line stanza built on triplets and punctuated with feminine rhymes is lively and mercurial. The poetic form complements the impetuous capering of the fairies and contributes significantly to the poem's sense of good fun. Drayton's absolute mastery of this frolicsome stanza is nowhere so evident as in the fairy Nymphidia's spell however, when the poet subdues his stanza for an incantation which might well have sent a pleasurable thrill through a young reader. A full appreciation of the comic effect of *Nymphidia*'s stanza form finally depends upon reading the poem aloud so that the triplets and feminine rhymes may receive full emphasis.

Despite Drayton's references to Chaucer and Rabelais and his indebtedness to the stanza form of *Sir Thopas,* it is the fairy poetry of Shakespeare to which *Nymphidia* is most directly indebted. As numerous critics have pointed out, the domestic difficulties of Oberon and his queen in *A Midsummer Night's Dream* suggests the plot of *Nymphidia,* where in place of the changling boy the complication is provided by a rival suitor for the Queen's favors. The main plot—a court intrigue featuring the maneuvering and folly of Oberon, Queen Mab, and the rival suitor, the fairy-knight Pigwiggen—furnishes the focal action. Almost as important as the plot however are the minutely detailed descriptive passages, a *sine qua non* of fashionable post-Shakespearean fairy poetry (see Jonson, Herrick, William Browne), which derive from the famous description of Mab and her chariot in *Romeo and Juliet.* The whole occurs in an English pastoral setting with the actions of the principals treated in mock-heroic fashion, paralleling the antics of the tiny creatures with the heroes of classic and romance. Further, the sophisticated reader is invited to delight in such mock-epic conventions poet and fairies blunder through as the invocation to a muse; Oberon's heroic frenzy, mad as Ajax or Orlando Furioso; the inventory of the hero's armor; the formal preparations for a trial by combat; and the intervention of a goddess in the climactic combat.

It seems likely that a large segment of Drayton's intended audience, including most youthful readers, would not be able to appreciate fully the literary humor of much of this mock-heroic. For the less sophisticated audience suggested by stanza two, however, Drayton offers pleasures of another kind. In addition to the broad-based appeal of the native fairy lore which Drayton generously loads into the interstices of the slender plot, the fairies' mock-heroic antics are genuinely humorous in their own right, without reference to literary models and allusions. The ''minifying'' technique, popularized by Shakespeare's Queen Mab passage, results in descriptive passages of ingenuity and charm and the English pastoral setting keeps the poem in contact with the contemporary countryside and its folklore. It is primarily these features of the *Nymphidia* which, once the poem was in the house, were capable of imparting a special kind of pleasure to children. Of course there is much in *Nymphidia,* as there is in *Gulliver's Travels,* which children will not understand, but Drayton has pitched his poem at such a broad audience that there is much more in the poem to which a child will respond with alacrity and delight.

The fairy folklore which informs *Nymphidia* draws directly on the familiar materials of childhood, the tales of fairies and sprites learned at mother's or nurse's knee and passed about from child to child. Thus, although Drayton's fairies may derive from a larger European tradition and may mock sophisticated codes of courtesy and conduct in their love and war, they are still, simultaneously, the fairies of the English countryside. Puck and Tom Thumb are here; the beauteous Queen Mab is still she of the Night-mare. The fairies engage in all the pursuits of traditional English fairy folklore—the pinching of mortals, the penny reward for cleanliness, the stealing of changelings. In combining the oral with the literary traditions of the fairy world, Drayton seeks to interest readers of every background, while incidentally providing for young readers a reassuringly familiar subject treated in a new way. Regardless of whether it was a part of Drayton's intent, in *Nymphidia* he created a bridge from the oral tradition of native folklore to the great world of European classical literature, a bridge most children of the time were constrained to cross in far more sober vehicles.

As the transition from one literary tradition to another might have challenged and excited the young reader of *Nymphidia,* so Drayton's descriptive technique, sharply detailed against the fantastic foreground, exerts a powerful imaginative appeal to the child in its equipoise of reality and fantasy. The stanzas describing the arming of the fairy knight Pigwiggen, who has challenged Oberon to combat, may serve as an example of this descriptive technique:

> And quickly Armes him for the Field,
> A little Cockle-shell his Shield,
> Which he could very bravely wield:
> Yet could it not be pierced:
> His Speare a Bent both stiffe and strong,
> And well-neere of two Inches long;
> The Pyle was of a Horse-flyes tongue,
> Whose sharpnesse naught reversed.
>
> And puts him on a coate of Male,
> Which was of a Fishes scale,
> That when his Foe should him assaile,
> No poynt should be prevayling:
> His Rapier was a Hornets sting,
> It was a very dangerous thing:
> For if he chanc'd to hurt the King,
> It would be long in healing.

Here the ingenuity of Drayton's description of his diminutive warrior equipped with rustic weapons and armor stimulates the imagination in the combination of the familiar and the fantastic. By carrying through this minifying technique—far more regularly than Shakespeare does in *A Midsummer Night's Dream,* though with less mathematical precision than Swift would employ in Lilliput—against the native pastoral background, Drayton goes far toward the creation of a self-contained universe of fairyland with an atmosphere and logic all its own. As in most successful fiction, this atmospheric unity derives largely from the key elements of the narrative: plot and character.

Despite rich descriptive passages and folklorist interpolations, *Nymphidia* possesses a clear plot furnished with plenty of action. Flirtatious Queen Mab is the central figure with Oberon and Pigwiggen, abetted by their agents Tom Thumb and Puck, in competition for her favor. The presumption of Mab's infidelity causes Oberon to run mad, after the fashion of Orlando Furioso. But in Drayton's miniaturized world, Oberon's frenzied encounters become increasingly farcical: he mistakes a glowworm for a devil, at a hive of bees he is thoroughly bedaubed with wax and honey, he tumbles off an ant he has mounted into more dirt and slime, he collides with a molehill which he takes for a mountain, he scales the molehill and falls down the other side into a lake. Oberon's mock-heroic misfortunes are harmless, simple and physical, of the pie-in-the-face variety which would delight a child who had never heard of Homer, Ariosto, or Cervantes. This plot pattern of sound and fury eventuating in laughter dominates the narrative, establishes the poem's tone, and dictates the happy ending, where

Proserpina (no less) intervenes in the trial by combat between Oberon and Pigwiggen, "For feare lest they too much should bleed, / Which wondrously her troubled," to set all right again through a judicious application of Lethe water. All exit "with mickle joy and merriment," in harmony with the atmosphere of good humor which pervades the poem. (pp. 34-9)

In sum, *Nymphidia* possesses all the attributes of a successful fairy tale for children, even while it is demonstrably something other and more than that. It has fallen into neglect in our own time as the work of what one critic aptly calls "today the least fashionable of important Elizabethan poets" [see excerpt by Hardin dated 1973]. If it is dismissed now as a narrative poem too long to fit comfortably into the standard anthologies of children's verse, it seems most unlikely *Nymphidia*'s rollicking good humor and capacity for imaginative stimulation would have escaped the notice of . . . [children of preceding ages]. It is a work which deserves a prominent place not just in the annals of fairy poetry, but in the history of early English children's literature. (p. 40)

> Warren W. Wooden, "Michael Drayton's 'Nymphidia': A Renaissance Children's Classic?" in Children's Literature: Annual of the Modern Language Association Seminar on Children's Literature and The Children's Literature Association, *Vol. 6, 1977, pp. 34-41*.

BARBARA C. EWELL   (essay date 1983)

[*Ewell is an American scholar of Renaissance and women's literature. In the following excerpt, she analyzes the theme of perception and reality in* Englands Heroicall Epistles.]

Though *Englands Heroicall Epistles* has always been the most popular of Michael Drayton's works and the subject of some critical attention, its central place in this prolific poet's canon has not been fully appreciated. I propose to explore two important but neglected features of this ill-mapped territory: the role of the letter in shaping the poem, both as a conscious poetic and as a principle of unity; and the poem's pivotal role in Drayton's development as a poet, for *Englands Heroicall Epistles* marks the transition from his early, staid, and derivative verse, whose end is the passive reflection of ideals, to the lively, distinctive poetry of his maturity, whose focus is the mind as it transmutes experience into art. This later work, especially *Idea* and *The Muses Elizium,* has earned Drayton the critics' regard and most clearly demonstrates the currency of his epistemological concerns. Such concerns, though credited to Donne, Herrick, and other seventeenth-century writers, are usually denied to the presumably conservative Drayton. But his later poetry indicates that he was indeed aware of the great intellectual transformations that had begun in his time, to be culminated in ours: the shift from viewing meaning as external and independent of the mind to seeing it as a projection of human consciousness. Thus, Drayton's best poetry and the poetics that accompanied it were quite current, developed from this nascent but very important Renaissance recognition of the powers of the mind.

The aesthetic principle that emerged and that underlies this later, superior work is best revealed in the poem where it takes shape. And the specific crucible of that transmutation from experience to art is the Ovidian letter itself.

That the epistolary method is central to the originality of *Englands Heroicall Epistles* should be no real surprise. Drayton's use of verse letters between fictional correspondents, although imitated from Ovid's *Heroides,* was a first in English and coincided with a burgeoning interest in letter writing, both as a practical art and as entertainment, which led ultimately, of course, to the development of the novel. Drayton goes to some lengths to underscore the epistolary character of the poems, providing immediate and realistic occasions for the missives as well as maintaining what Kathleen Tillotson calls the "illusion of actual letter-writing" that he had found in Ovid. This self-consciousness of the poems as letters is pervasive. For example, all but four epistles open with an explicit reference to their medium, commenting on the tools of ink and paper, on the "lines" the "hand" produces, or on the physical reception these might expect. The remaining poems imitate the structure of a letter with a formal salutation (as in those of Edward IV and Mary the French queen) or a stylized closing (as in Suffolk's and Duke Humphrey's). These devices underline Drayton's efforts at realism, but the ultimate significance of this self-consciousness lies in the recognition that each artifact reflects an individual and active mind. (pp. 231-33)

Various commentators have remarked that the letter by its nature is a form of self-creation, a means of "transforming the amorphous self into art." To write a letter is to define for a reader a specific image of the self, one shaped by selecting and interpreting details from that perpetual flux of events which is our experienced reality. In *Englands Heroicall Epistles,* the definition of these distinct selves is central to the poem. Though history is the poem's apparent subject, what preoccupies Drayton is, as Joan Grundy observes [see Additional Bibliography citation dated 1969], the personality and unique perspective of each letter writer, "the chaos in the mind." Of course Drayton wanted to give his readers accurate history, as the appended prose notes make clear. But his apologetic preface, "To the Reader," points out that the place for historical precision is his glosses, not the poems, where the "inter-woven Matters Historicall" are often "unexplained." Rather, Drayton's real focus is on the fictional selves which order that history and on the process by which those selves are created on paper. For the letters are not merely mirrors, but artifacts whose shapes reveal their creators like fossil stones exposing some invisible past.

By reporting certain details and not others, by choosing to give this information first and that last, by adopting this style or selecting that diction, each letter writer conveys not history but the shape of a self: the imprint of the priorities and biases that each brings to the life she or he inhabits. These highly individualized shapes, these selves, these vivid characterizations, embodied in language and impressed on the uncertain flux of history, become the focus of the poem and its most praised feature. Instead of a single, idealized version of the past, *Englands Heroicall Epistles* offers a variety of interpreters and interpretations, none perfect or complete, but each fascinating, each illuminating its fraction of the whole of reality.

Drayton's focus on the creation of a self, or of varied selves, has important implications for the development of his poetic. To define a self in language, to create an artifact, implies a certain permanence that Drayton, perhaps more than many artists, sought from poetry. Certainly his novice work, in attempting a direct reflection of ideals through ornamented language, explicitly seeks the stability of immortality. This recurrent longing for order, quite poignant amidst the apparent chaos of the close of the Elizabethan era, is only reexpressed in the letters. Here, though, order comes not from external ideals, which necessarily falsify human experience, but from within, from the very perceptions and language that engender the immortal artifacts themselves. Thus order and meaning are rooted in the created selves of the letters.

This transfer of order and identity from external sources to arbitrary ones, like language, was hardly unique to Drayton. Indeed, for him as for his age, which saw the dawn of autobiography and of a deliberately introspective poetry, language became a more reliable means of identifying the self than the failing external order. (pp. 234-35)

In the epistolary form Drayton found a response . . . to this dissolving certainty of value and identity. Each of the letters of *Englands Heroicall Epistles* is an effort to fix an identity, to reveal a mind in the act of giving shape and meaning to the welter of experience. Each has a set focus, but none is definitive; all are partial and incomplete, like people. In the process of defining these selves, however, Drayton also formulated a conception of poetry that transformed his own poetic practice. Instead of attempting to mirror eternal ideals in his poetry, the aesthetic principle to which all his previous verse attests, Drayton now focused on the imaginative processes by which experience, with all its uncertainty, is transmuted into linguistic artifact, into a fixed articulation of a specific perspective—into poetry. It is consciousness, then, that defines the shape of experience, that orders the history of the poem; it is these varied minds that are its center and subject. For, to concentrate on character and on the process of revealing unique selves is also to disclose a new relation between art and reality, between words and things: the processes of the mind rather than static ideals become the shaping force of human experience and the source of permanence and meaning, even as they open a dangerous way to distortion and manipulation.

But the letter form suggests even more than a new poetics and the ultimate subject of the poem; it also provides a key to its unity. Largely inconclusive and unsatisfying, the various attempts to define that unity have generally relied on external themes: the relationship between correspondents, the writers' attitudes toward Fortune, the degrees of Ovidian imitation, and, most recently, the role of Providence in English history. None of these really succeeds in justifying our persistent sense that the letters are a whole, joined by more than the superficial links of chronology. But there are features of the letter, and of the aesthetics that it implies, that may be helpful in understanding the relationships among these epistles. One such feature is the letter's dependence on a response for completion. . . . Thus, instead of one autonomous version of reality, we are given two dependent ones. And these, based on the elemental contrast of male and female (the only indisputably common feature of the epistles), are both unique and complementary. But Drayton does not stop there. This interdependent quality is, in fact, apparent throughout the letters: virtually every element of *Englands Heroicall Epistles* has its necessary complement, a circumstance that results in an intricate counterpoint of individuals, pairs of correspondents, groups of letters, themes, attitudes, situations, motives, and consequences. Letters, as Joseph Kestner has observed, "are . . . about their relationship with one another." And in *Englands Heroicall Epistles* this is especially so, for it is through their interdependence that Drayton has both unified the whole and emphasized the fragmentation of human truth. (pp. 236-38)

The first several pairs of letters set up what emerges as the central issue of the poem: how language affects experience. Manipulating conventional styles and poses (high and plain styles, Petrarchan and Ovidian rhetoric, for example), Drayton

Title page of a late edition of Englands Heroicall Epistles, *a work originally published in 1597.*

posits a variety of complementary ways in which the self manifests itself through language and, concomitantly, ways in which reality, or history, is shaped according to that manifestation, that individual mind. The opening exchange between Rosamond and Henry II (one of the most famous pairs) dramatizes the radically different shapes two minds can impose on the same reality. Rosamond, who writes first, sees everything through the dark glass of despair over her illicit liaison with the king. With its moralizing diction and images of bestial transformations, the language of her letter reveals a self deformed by sin and guilt: "A Monster both in Bodie and in Mind." Nature and art combine to mock her sin: brooks babble her shame; wily fish rebuke her gullibility; Lucrece's painted fidelity censures her frailty; passers-by stare their condemnation; her name reveals its Latin pun on her disgrace; and even flickering candles, which dim with her breath, protest her crime. For Rosamond, remorse has turned all her experience into moral recriminations.

To Henry, however, the world looks quite different. Shaped by the conceited, high style that befits his rank and extravagant affection, his letter systematically reassigns the meanings of Rosamond's experience. From emblems of guilt, they become romantic marks of her virtues. One by one, he reinterprets the accusing brook, the elusive fish, the incriminating gaze of passers-by, the name she blushes to bear. What appeared to

Rosamond a nightmare becomes, through the language of praise, a vision of her own potency. Indeed, Henry attests, she is herself an agent of transformation, converting his cares to comforts, his age to youth. Henry's Petrarchanism defines a pose whose art is precisely to create a goddess-artifact whose perfections will render him immortal. His language can reshape her being because his assumed self demands her deification to justify his passion. In his view, then, she herself is the force that inspires the transformation of a nightmare of guilt into a dream of eternal love. (pp. 238-39)

[Successive, paired] self-definitions are climaxed in the . . . penultimate pair of letters between Surrey the poet and his lady Geraldine. As befits one whose vocation is language, Surrey extols the powers and effects of poetry. But his letter, in its extremism, its one-sided adulation of language, is . . . a critique of his position (and of the younger Drayton, who once espoused it). . . . It remains for Geraldine to characterize the limitations that Surrey overlooks and to balance his excess.

Surrey's letter, which opens with a self-conscious defense of the "harsh-tun'd Cadences" of his "Native Tongue," reiterates the early Drayton's notion that the mode of poetry is praise and its effect immortality. The high style of Surrey's language changes everything to artifact: his recollection of his departure from Geraldine becomes an emblem of his emotions, her illness an omen, the tournament a masquelike celebration of her beauty, his memories of England a sign of poetry's power to renew. This artful perspective, with its idealized and stylized descriptions, gives the letter a stilted quality; but for poets like Surrey, these versions of reality far surpass mere experience in value and truth. Surrey, like the Drayton of *Ideas Mirrour,* thinks of himself as one of "great APOLLO's Heires" whose divine gift is to immortalize. Language is for the poet the ultimate reality, a power to create whole cities: "My Lines for thee a *Florence* shall erect." But like the Surrey of Thomas Nashe, from whose hyperbolic narrative Drayton borrowed, this Surrey is afflicted with a self-conscious attitudinizing that blinds him to the real distortions that language also manufactures. That Surrey posits such a stiffly artificial self suggests how far Drayton himself had come from an uncritical use of ornamental language in reflecting ideals.

Geraldine's letter offers the necessary corrective to this injudicious adulation of poetry and language—a corrective which Drayton himself must have been observing. Like the earlier Alice and Matilda, Geraldine despises and distrusts the emptiness elaborate language often conceals, a danger seemingly unnoticed by Surrey. She mocks those who value appearance over substance—the shallow courtiers and sycophants, for example, who admire her lover's verse only because "the better sort doe so." Geraldine's direct and unpretentious, even colloquial, language manifests her own devotion to a strict congruence of word and thing; in the end she even vows to retire from the duplicitous court to the simpler, more congruent life of "some Country Grange." For her, as for the wily Queen Mary, poetry is secondary to the reality it should—but often does not—reflect. What moves Geraldine is not Surrey's verses, but their flesh-and-blood author. That he should erect another Florence is less important to her than that he should establish his own estate by begetting a few heirs and thus turn poetic realities into physical ones. She herself attempts this transmutation by identifying Surrey as the "Wand'rer" Ulysses and then insisting that their lives complete the myth: "Then, as ULYSSES Wife, write I to thee, / Make no reply, but come thy selfe to mee." Since Geraldine would have language and act

correspond, she would have her allusion impose itself on experience: if figuratively she is Ulysses' wife, then Surrey must literally return to her side. What he would turn to art, she would transmute again into act. Importantly, however, for both the agency of power is language.

But whether the "experience" of Geraldine or the "artifice" of Surrey prevails is really less important here and elsewhere in the letters than that both views are possible. Once words and things become distinct, perception, embodied in language, governs reality; then language can either transform that reality so profoundly that its very truth may be questioned, or shape it so forcefully that it accomplishes one's own will and purposes. Although Drayton might still prefer the harmony that Matilda and Geraldine affirm or the positive ends that Surrey pursues, his poem as a whole insists that the truth is much more complex than these views, full of contradictions and powers and perils that must be acknowledged, if not adopted.

In the second half of the *Epistles,* Drayton moves from a concern with the explicit powers of language as art to the parallel but more general theme of how perception affects one's universe and one's destiny within it. What are the possible responses to a reality perceived as ordered or chaotic, benevolent or hostile? Here the basic dilemma of the correspondence between words and things is explored in terms of the relationship between the self and fate—a motif long recognized as central to the poem. Asserting an interiorized criterion of reality, Drayton implies that the self responds to a universe essentially of its own making, whether ordered or disordered, providential or meaningless. What one perceives as one's fate within that cosmos may or may not be "true" (confirmed by subsequent events), but that imagined fate is a direct consequence of one's notions of the relationship between words and things. Much as the conventions of art shape experience into artifacts that reflect various selves, the contrasting attitudes and realities of these epistles reveal the diverse versions of the universe that the self can project. In these letters, character is defined by one's perception of order and one's response to that particular vision. However, judgment on the quality of that vision is suspended in the poem. The reader must weigh it against the reality of history that, expounded in Drayton's notes, often exists in tension with the letter. Interestingly, the use of historical personages to embody specific constructions of value and meaning in some ways anticipates the process of Donne's *Anniversaries* and his verse epistles. In Donne, for example, as we reflect on the inflated significance of Elizabeth Drury, we become engaged in defining a specific perception of the cosmos and our epistemological relation to that essentially fictive reality. For both poets, form—the eulogy and the epistle—constitutes a mode of perception which reorders our ways of knowing the cosmos and its meaning. Thus the method of the poem—the letter shaping history as language shapes the self as art shapes experience—is extended to embrace a more fundamental epistemology: how we perceive the universe governs not only our response to it, but, to some extent, its reality as well; perception, in all its diversity, supersedes fact.

Drayton's most interesting comment on this diversity and relativity of perception occurs in a unique cluster of epistles in the latter half of the poem: the letters of Lady Eleanor Cobham and Duke Humphrey of Gloucester, and those of their archenemies, Queen Margaret and William de la Pole, Duke of Suffolk. Not only do all of the four writers comment on each other, but they do so from opposing (albeit uniformly tragic) views of the same set of events. This four-sided perspective on the reign of Henry VI is Drayton's most obvious dramatization of the multiplicity of ways in which the mind can shape reality.

In the opening letter, the mad Eleanor, exiled on the Isle of Man, would impose the chaos of her demented mind on the world at large. Thrust by slander from her position of eminence, she has experienced the power of language to misshape; she has been transformed from duchess to witch. She is preoccupied with the Druidic charms and potions she might use to infect her rival Margaret with her own frenzied, deranged view. Her ranting invective, grotesque and occult imagery, and abrupt shifts embody her twisted perspective, the chaos of a malicious world, into which she would cheerfully drag her enemy. But chaos brings disconnection and impotence, too; and Eleanor concludes in despair: "My wish is all thy EL'NOR can afford."

To her husband, however, this disordered view and the effort to control reality with the mind are deeply disturbing. In his letter Gloucester clings instead to the remnants of truth that are the foundations of his integrity. Believing that reality cannot be manipulated by language—even magic language—he finds comfort in what he considers the unshakable facts of his career and his relationships: "Whilst in these Brests we beare about this Life, / I am thy Husband, and thou art my Wife." His plain colloquial style mirrors that confidence in ordinary truth and the orderly turns of Fortune's wheel with which he directly opposes Eleanor's efforts to control fate with incantatory magic. What she would reshape with her mind, though to lethal ends, he would affirm as the unavoidable decrees of Providence, unalterable as fact.

Gloucester's steadfast confidence is echoed in the letter of his enemy, Suffolk. But the source of Suffolk's optimism is quite different from Gloucester's. Exiled like Eleanor, he believes with her that the mind is the chief ally against misfortune. Instead of projecting his vision outward as she does, however, he would withdraw from a disordered world to create his own stable universe within. A series of *sententiae* defines his Stoic faith:

> No Banishment can be to him assign'd,
> Who doth retaine a true-resolved Mind.
> Man in himselfe a little World doth beare,
> His Soule the Monarch, ever ruling there:
> Where-ever then his Body doth remaine,
> He is a King, that in himselfe doth raigne;
> And never feareth Fortunes hot'st Alarmes,
> That beares against her Patience for his Armes.

In control as the Duchess is not, Suffolk is the poem's arch-representative of the mind's positive potential to shape experience. Like earlier courtiers, he turns reality into art, literally in his courtship of Margaret and figuratively in bearing his exile with calm resignation. Yoking his romantic recollections of the past with sententious philosophizing, Suffolk steers a middle course between the illusory optimism of Gloucester and the bitter despair of Eleanor. His attitude in many ways reflects the seventeenth-century solution to the discrepancy between words and things: retreat to a private world governed and created by one's own thought.

But even this solution has its drawbacks, as the answering letter from Margaret makes clear. With good reason, this poor queen has as little faith as Gloucester in the power of mere language to control reality. Verbal failures—broken oaths and slanders—as well as other inversions of order ("Thus all goes backward, crosse comes after crosse") have made her as distraught as Eleanor in her experience of chaos. But her distrust of the mind's powers is as fatal as Eleanor's trust is impotent. For when Margaret does have premonitions of her lover's fate—

troubled dreams of his death by water—she foolishly dismisses them, taking comfort in her experience of the lack of correspondence between words and things: "It cannot hurt, although I thinke amisse." A direct challenge to Suffolk's complacent vision of a self-created world, Margaret's letter ironically affirms the external reality that will impinge itself perforce. Even as she denies the mind's power, she unknowingly confirms it.

Taken together, then, these four letters underline the ambivalent multiplicity of the self's perception of reality. Contrasting with and complementing one another, they epitomize the poem's fundamental assertion that in an uncertain world the self, through language, defines a multiplicity of realities, none absolute, each qualifying and qualified by others. Placed at the heart of Drayton's poem, these letters are a tentative statement of the relative reality that the poet was articulating.

The remaining pairs of letters continue the qualifying process; as with the principally amatory epistles, contrast governs the exploration of the varied possibilities of perception and response. (pp. 241-46)

[The pair of letters between Richard II and Isabella] is among the poem's most despondent, especially since it is juxtaposed with the buoyant letters of Katherine and Owen, which immediately follow. In Isabella's painful experience, misfortune has been the consequence of misread omens and mistaken perceptions. Even as Owen has correctly seen his good fortune in the stars, Isabella (whose letter rivals his for cosmic imagery) has been deceived by their promises. Her own eyes have been "faithlesse Spyes," mistaking the usurping Henry for her returning Richard. Like Eleanor, and Isabella, she tries to take comfort in curses, but her skepticism of the power of words remains. She concludes with apprehension of a future that cannot be discerned, whose hidden dangers "Heaven alone doth know." Richard's reply only deepens this mournful vision. With his life stripped of all its external marks of meaning—crown, wealth, birthright, and wife—he verbally extinguishes himself in negative definitions: "Comfort is now unpleasing to mine Eare, / Past cure, past care, my Bed become my Beere." For him, language indeed retains power, but of an intensely destructive nature. His self-negation even removes him from the pale of Providence: "Since now Misfortune humbleth us so long, / Till Heaven be growne unmindfull of our Wrong." In the end he is left with only the final realization of his non-being in death:

> Whilst I deprest before [Henry's] Greatnesse, lie
> Under the weight of Hate and Infamie.
>   *   *   *
> [I] Out-live mine Honour, burie my Estate,
> And leave my selfe nought, but my Peoples Hate.

But if these and most of the letters on this theme reflect a rather Jacobean despair, *Englands Heroicall Epistles* concludes on a high note of optimism. Although Lady Jane Grey and Lord Guildford Dudley face imminent execution with singular awareness, they (like Gloucester and Tudor) are confident of their own congruence with a benevolent Providence. To Lady Jane, "Conscience cleare" is the source of their serenity; the key to their response is patient submission to a certain reality beyond the false appearances of misfortune. Death, which was for Richard the ultimate negation, is for these two, as Lady Jane insists, "but an acted passion" and the way out of "our Soules prisons." Based on Foxe's famous *Book of Martyrs*, this final and popular pair of letters affirms in its homiletic tones and biblical allusions a staunch Protestant trust in "those Celestiall Joyes . . . / Which mortall Tongue's unable to expresse.'' The inner self and destiny are reunited here by the agency of the word, a gospel faith. But even as the perception of these saints establishes that congruence, the language embodying it is explicitly rejected for a reality beyond mere speech. As in Donne, we are forced to see what cannot be seen, to redefine what we know.

Drayton's exploration of the ways in which the mind shapes its reality culminates in this final affirmation. In the course of the poem, no perspective—confidence or despair, congruence or discrepancy—is left unqualified or is fully sanctioned. And although that of Jane Grey and Dudley, for example, seems preferable, even these two, who die as martyrs, are, after all, condemned as traitors. What matters, finally, is the perception of their death; and that perception, buttressed by Protestant theology as well as philosophical skepticism, helps in turn to define its reality.

Both by contrasting the ways in which one's perceptions of order affect the nature of one's fate and by exploring the effects of art on one's apprehension of reality, Drayton knits his poem together in several interesting ways. The very manner by which the letter form shapes historical material reiterates the epistemological concerns of the poem: how does one's perception of the self affect one's experience? how does method influence matter? how does the mind shape the history it would narrate? And as the individual letters pose these questions, the poem as a whole provides a response: the mind fashions its experience in ways as manifold as the language that can articulate it—in a plethora of styles and patterns, each reflecting a unique stance and self that define the way to meaning.

Drayton's recognition of the effect of persona and style, then, has profound implications for his later poetic. Freed from the static mediation of ideals, his subsequent poetry is newly conscious of itself as a way of perceiving, an act of transformation. By this recognition, moreover, Drayton places himself in the mainstream—rather than in the backwaters to which he is usually consigned—of seventeenth-century aesthetic thought. He, too, manifests the inward-looking epistemological interests that characterize the period. The consequences of this new conception of poetry are most immediately evident in the revisions Drayton undertook soon after he completed *Englands Heroicall Epistles*. For example, it is in the 1599 version of his sonnets that *Ideas Mirrour* becomes *Idea,* and the focus is shifted from an idealized mistress to a posturing, self-conscious sonneteer in search of the proper articulation of his unique experience. This and similar transformations, together with his later poems, reflect the poetic that had emerged in the writing of *Englands Heroicall Epistles.* For the mature Drayton, the act of poetry, like the mind itself, imposes an order on experience which reveals their (poetry's *and* the mind's) own nature; the method or act of shaping becomes the real center of the poem—a self-reflexive image of the process of making. Refined and transformed by later work, these notions are the primary interest and real merit of Drayton's best poetry. (pp. 247-50)

> *Barbara C. Ewell, "Unity and the Transformation of Drayton's Poetics in 'Englands Heroicall Epistles': From Mirrored Ideals to 'the Chaos in the Mind'," in* Modern Language Quarterly, *Vol. 44, No. 3, September, 1983, pp. 231-50.*

ADDITIONAL BIBLIOGRAPHY

Alpers, Paul J. "Spenser's Poetic Language." In his *The Poetry of "The Faerie Queene,"* pp. 70-106. Princeton: Princeton University Press, 1967.

Contains a brief comparison of the verse in *The Barrons Wars* with that of *The Faerie Queene.*

Boyd, Eva Phillips. "Trailing Michael Drayton: A Summer Idyl for Dryasdusts." *Sewanee Review* XLIV, No. 3 (July-September 1939): 303-19.

Narrative of an itinerant scholar's journey about the British countryside—the land that inspired Drayton's *Poly-Olbion.*

Brett, Cyril. Introduction to *Minor Poems of Michael Drayton,* by Michael Drayton, edited by Cyril Brett, pp. v-xxiv. Oxford: Clarendon Press, 1907.

Comprehensive critical and bibliographical survey of Drayton's works.

Bristol, Michael D. "Structural Patterns in Two Elizabethan Pastorals." *Studies in English Literature, 1500-1900* X, No. 1 (Winter 1970): 33-48.

Contrasts the structural pattern and thematic scheme of Edmund Spenser's *The Shepheardes Calender* (1579) and Drayton's *Idea the Shepheards Garland.*

Campbell, Thomas. "Michael Drayton." In his *Specimens of the British Poets; with Biographical and Critical Notices, and an Essay on English Poetry,* Vol. 3: *Drayton, 1631, to Phillips, 1664,* pp. 1-58. London: John Murray, 1819.

Selections from Drayton's poetry prefaced by a brief biography and critical appraisal. Campbell concludes that "[Drayton's] muse had certainly no strength for extensive flights, though she sports in happy moments on a brilliant and graceful wing."

Carter, Katherine D. "Drayton's Craftsmanship: The Encomium and the Blazon in *Englands Heroicall Epistles.*" *The Huntington Library Quarterly* XXXVIII, No. 4 (August 1975): 297-314.

Examines Drayton's use of two rhetorical devices, the blazon and the encomium, to dramatize the heroic personalities in *Epistles.*

Cawley, Robert Ralston. "Drayton and the Voyagers." *PMLA* XXXVIII, No. 3 (September 1923): 530-56.

Demonstrates the dependency of *Poly-Olbion* on Richard Hakluyt's *Principall Navigations, Voiages, and Discoveries of the English Nation Made by Sea or Over-land* (1598-1600).

Coleridge, Samuel Taylor. "Elizabethan and Jacobean Literature." In his *Coleridge's Miscellaneous Criticism,* edited by Thomas Middleton Rayser, pp. 231-79. Folcroft, Penn.: Folcroft Press, 1936.

Contains marginalia on Robert Anderson's sketch of Drayton in his *British Poets* (1807). Coleridge's principal comment is on the *Idea* sonnets, of which he writes: "The sonnets are not *metrically* sonnets, but poems in fourteen lines—and it would be difficult to point out one good one. . . . The best, I think, of these 'Ideas' is the 59th, which is original in conception, and humorously executed."

Eliot, T. S. "Imperfect Critics." In his *The Sacred Wood: Essays on Poetry and Criticism,* pp. 17-46. 1920. Reprint. London: Methuen & Co., 1972.

Contains a brief, derogatory reference to Drayton's *Idea* sonnets.

Fleay, Frederick Gard. "Michael Drayton" and "Shakespeare." In his *A Biographical Chronicle of the English Drama, 1559-1642,* Vol. I, pp. 137-61, Vol. II, 176-232. London: Reeves and Turner, 1891.

Two essays. The first is a general overview of Drayton's life and works, including a consideration of the dramas attributed to Drayton and a speculative inquiry into contemporary allusions in his poetry. The second article contains a comparative analysis suggesting that Shakespeare's sonnets were significantly influenced by Drayton's.

Grundy, Joan. "'Brave Translunary Things'." *Modern Language Review* LIX, No. 4 (October 1964): 501-10.

Analyzes Drayton's poetic theory through concentration on his use of the adjective "clear" in his verse.

———. "The Poetry of Drayton: 1) The Heroic" and "The Poetry of Drayton: 2) *Poly-Olbion.*" In her *The Spenserian Poets,* pp. 107-27, 128-42. New York: St. Martin's Press, 1969.

Illuminates two aspects of Drayton's work: his delineation of the heroic ideal and the thematic and technical unity of *Poly-Olbion*. Of that poem, Grundy writes: "*Poly-Olbion* is something better than a 'curiosity' to be ridiculed or patronised. Within the *corpus* of Drayton's work, it stands as his *Faerie Queene*."

Hardin, Richard F. "Convention and Design in Drayton's *Heroicall Epistles*." *PMLA* LXXXIII, No. 1 (March 1968): 35-41.
    Proposes that the essential character of *Epistles* is more Elizabethan than Ovidian.

Harner, James L. *Samuel Daniel and Michael Drayton: A Reference Guide*. Boston: G. K. Hall & Co., 1980, 338 p.
    Annotated bibliography of Drayton criticism from 1684 to 1979.

Hebel, J. William. "Drayton's *Sirena*." *PMLA* XXXIX, No. 4 (December 1924): 814-36.
    In response to Raymond Jenkins's 1923 article (see citation below), suggests different models for the characters of *The Shepheards Sirena*. Hebel posits that Drayton and Ben Jonson were rivals and considers Jonson's ostensibly commendatory poem to Drayton (see poem dated 1627) riddled with satiric barbs. For Jenkins's rebuttal, see the citation below dated 1927.

Hiller, Geoffrey G. "Drayton's *Muses Elizium*: 'A New Way Over Parnassus'." *The Review of English Studies* n.s. XXI (1970): 1-13.
    Highly favorable study of *The Muses Elizium* as Drayton's most original pastoral work.

Jenkins, Raymond. "Drayton's Relation to the School of Donne, as Revealed in the *Shepheards Sirena*." *PMLA* XXXVIII, No. 3 (September 1923): 557-87.
    Identifies real models for the allegorical characters of *The Shepheards Sirena*, viewing the poem as a defense of the Spenserian school against the school of John Donne. J. William Hebel disagrees, in his work cited above.

──────. "Drayton's *Sirena* Again." *PMLA* XLII, No. 1 (March 1927): 129-39.
    Refutation of J. William Hebel's essay (see citation above) in which he argues that Jonson was Drayton's prime satiric target in *The Shepheards Sirena*.

LaBranche, Anthony. "The 'Twofold Vitality' of Drayton's *Odes*." *Comparative Literature* XV, No. 2 (Spring 1963): 116-29.
    Discusses Drayton's pioneering resurrection and Anglicization of the classical ode.

Le Gallienne, Richard. "Michael Drayton." In his *Retrospective Reviews: A Literary Log*, pp. 50-6. London: John Lane, The Bodley Head, 1896.
    Evaluates selected poems of Drayton, particularly *The Battaile of Agincourt*, which Le Gallienne writes has "many faults of construction," though "it remains an inspiring piece of work."

Nagy, N. Christoph de. *Michael Drayton's "England's Heroicall Epistles."* Bern: Francke Verlag, 1968, 67 p.
    Monograph study of themes and compositional devices in *Epistles*. Nagy grounds his essay in an analysis of the numerous parallels between Drayton's work and Ovid's *Heroides*.

Newdigate, Bernard H. *Michael Drayton and His Circle*. Oxford: Basil Blackwell for Shakespeare Head Press, 1961, 239 p.
    Biography including an extended examination of how Drayton was influenced by early patrons, theatrical acquaintances, and literary colleagues.

Noyes, Russell. "Drayton's Literary Vogue Since 1631." *Indiana University Studies* XXII, No. 107 (March 1935): 3-23.
    Useful survey of Drayton's literary reputation from 1631 to the mid-nineteenth century.

Parsons, D. S. J. "The Ode of Drayton and Jonson." *Queen's Quarterly* LXXV, No. 4 (Winter 1968): 675-84.
    Discusses the qualified success of the two poets' reintroduction of the classical ode form.

Pearson, Lu Emily. "The Changing Moods of Michael Drayton's Sonnets." In her *Elizabethan Love Conventions*, pp. 188-201. Berkeley: University of California Press, 1933.
    Traces the progression of technique and theme in the *Idea* sonnets.

Petronella, Vincent F. "Double Ecstasy in Drayton's *Endimion and Phoebe*." *Studies in English Literature, 1500-1900* 24, No. 1 (Winter 1984): 87-104.
    Investigates Renaissance Neoplatonic themes in *Endimion and Phoebe*.

Pope, Alexander. Letter to Warburton. In his *The Correspondence of Alexander Pope*, Vol. IV, edited by George Sherburn, pp. 427-28. Oxford: Clarendon Press, 1956.
    1742 letter containing Pope's offhand remark that Drayton was "a very mediocre poet."

Rees, Joan. "Hogs, Gulls, and Englishmen: Drayton and the Virginian Voyages." *The Yearbook of English Studies* 13 (1983): 20-31.
    Discusses Drayton's poem of early colonization, "Ode to the Virginian Voyage."

Rowse, A. L. "A Topographical Elizabethan." *The New Statesman and Nation* XXII, No. 559 (8 November 1941): 412.
    Largely favorable appraisal of Drayton as a poet of "silvery charm."

Saintsbury, George. "*The Faerie Queen* and Its Group." In his *A History of Elizabethan Literature*, pp. 82-156. New York: Macmillan Co., 1924.
    Contains an overview of Drayton's life and works.

──────. "The Contemporaries and Followers of Spenser in Stanza and Couplet." In his *A History of English Prosody from the Twelfth Century to the Present Day*, Vol. II: *From Shakespeare to Crabbe*, pp. 88-128. New York: Russell & Russell, 1961.
    Includes a study of Drayton's prosody.

Thomas, Vivien. Introduction to *Michael Drayton: Selected Poems*, by Michael Drayton, edited by Vivien Thomas, pp. 7-12. Manchester: Carcanet, Fyfield Books, 1977.
    Surveys Drayton's original works and his numerous revisions.

Tuve, Rosemond. "The 'Garment' of Style and Functional Sensuous Imagery." In her *Elizabethan and Metaphysical Imagery: Renaissance Poetic and Twentieth-Century Critics*, pp. 61-78. Chicago: University of Chicago Press, 1947.
    Examines Drayton's revisions of his sonnets between 1594 and 1619.

Waldron, Francis Godolphon. "Michael Drayton." In his *The Biographical Mirrour, Comprising a Series of Ancient and Modern English Portraits, of Eminent and Distinguished Persons*, pp. 102-11. London: S. and E. Harding, 1795.
    Biographical sketch containing limited critical commentary. In his lengthiest judgment, Waldron remarks: "It is in the *Pastoral* and *Fairy* stiles of writing that Drayton eminently excels—may I be bold enough to say?—every other English poet, ancient or modern!"

Westling, Louise Hutchings. *The Evolution of Michael Drayton's "Idea."* Elizabethan & Renaissance Studies, Vol. 37, edited by James Hogg. Salzburg: Institut für Englische Sprache und Literatur Universität Salzburg, 1974, 187 p.
    Appraisal of Drayton's development as a sonneteer.

Whitaker, Lemuel. "Michael Drayton as a Dramatist." *PMLA* XVIII, No. 3 (1903): 378-411.
    Biographical examination of Drayton's theatrical career. Whitaker concludes: "There is no external evidence that he had a hand in any play now extant except *Sir John Oldcastle*."

Winters, Yvor. "Aspects of the Short Poem in the English Renaissance." In his *Forms of Discovery: Critical & Historical Essays on the Forms of the Short Poem in English*, pp. 1-120. Chicago: Alan Swallow, 1967.
    Contains a short examination of Petrarchan elements in Drayton's sonnets.

Gotthold Ephraim Lessing

1729-1781

German critic, dramatist, essayist, historian, biographer, and poet.

Lessing is considered the greatest aesthetic theorist of the German Enlightenment. Through his critical and dramatic works he helped free German literature from the conventional strictures of then-dominant French classical school. In his highly influential aesthetic study *Laokoon; oder, Über die Grenzen der Mahlerey und Poesie* (*Laocoon; or, The Limits of Poetry and Painting*) he defined and differentiated the provinces of the plastic arts and literature, arguing in lucid, pithy, and ironic prose against imposing the characteristics proper to one artistic medium upon the other. His *Die Hamburgische Dramaturgie* (*Hamburg Dramaturgy*) is a revolutionary plea for a drama based on imaginative inspiration and observation rather than on arbitrary rules. Lessing was also the author of Germany's first major comedy (*Minna von Barnhelm*) and earliest domestic tragedy (*Miss Sara Sampson*). In addition, he was a strong advocate of religious tolerance, and his dramatic poem *Nathan der Weise* (*Nathan the Wise*) is considered an outstanding example of progressive thinking and enlightened humanitarianism.

Lessing was born in Kamenz, a small town in Saxon Lusatia. He was sent by his father, the town's chief pastor, to St. Afra's School in Meissen, one of three German *Fürstenschulen*, elite schools for the nobility. There he excelled, augmenting the required courses with a self-directed study of the classics, winning a place at the University of Leipzig. Matriculating in 1746 as a theology student (at his father's desire), Lessing soon discovered a sphere more congenial to him. He ventured into the arts, particularly the theater, and wrote his first plays, *Damon; oder, Die wahre Freundschaft* and *Der junge Gelehrte*. Forced by mounting debts to flee Leipzig, Lessing took up residence in Berlin, where, at age seventeen, he resolved to become a professional writer. He supported himself by rendering translations and writing articles and reviews, while continuing to turn out plays, chiefly in the French style. In 1751, eager for more education, he left Berlin for the University of Wittenberg, where he was made master of arts in 1752. He then returned to Berlin, surviving, in an age of patronage, almost entirely without sinecure.

Lessing struggled constantly during the remainder of his life for security in his chosen career, literature. In Berlin he wrote his first commercially successful play, *Miss Sara Sampson,* and contributed frequently to the critical journal *Briefe, die neueste Litteratur betreffend.* In 1760, needing money, he took on official, but hardly rigorous, employment in Breslau, where he read the classics at leisure, wrote *Laocoon,* and composed *Minna von Barnhelm.* Leaving Breslau in 1765, he soon fell back into debt. Two years later, his financial problems were relieved by his appointment as the new Hamburg repertory company's in-house dramatic critic. In this position he founded and wrote a semi-weekly critical newsletter, *Hamburg Dramaturgy.* But the company failed at the end of its first season, and Lessing again found himself without a steady income. He was then hired as keeper of the Duke of Brunswick's library at Wolfenbüttel, where he engaged from time to time in religious and literary controversies and wrote one of his most

complex plays, *Emilia Galotti.* In 1776 he married the widow of his friend Engelbert Konig, but scarcely a year later both she and an infant child were dead. Embittered and disconsolate, Lessing spent his last years advocating humanism and religious tolerance. In 1779 he finished *Nathan the Wise* and the following year completed a final work, *Die Erziehung des Menschengeschlechts* (*The Education of the Human Race*). He died several months later, aged fifty-two.

Lessing considered himself primarily a critic: his dramatic, poetic, and theological work designed, in many cases, to illustrate his critical theories. His first major critical work, the collaborative *Briefe, die neueste Litteratur betreffend,* a series of essays written in the form of letters, pungently compares ancient and modern drama and treats such subjects as biographical fallacy, the inadequacies of the German theater, the nature of genius, and poetic forms. The famous seventeenth letter, a witty, trenchant, and colloquial attack on the classicist Johann Christoph Gottsched's continuing influence in the German theater, guided German aesthetics away from French standards, with an effect often described as incalculable. *Laocoon,* Lessing's next major critical essay, distinguishes the domain proper to literature from that proper to painting and sculpture, countering the inferences his contemporaries drew from Horace's *"ut pictura poesis"* ("as in painting, so in poetry")— that is, that the same aesthetic principles apply to both visual and written art. Lessing argued that the two media are not merely different manifestations of the same artistic expression, but require dissimilar artistic rendering because of the distinction between their functions prescribed by their very natures: the plastic arts represent "figures and colors in space" while poetry deals with "articulated sounds in time." In other words, painting and sculpture capture and describe their subjects as they exist in one particular place and time; poetry narrates actions as they occur and develop in a temporal sequence. Lessing's last major critical work, *Hamburg Dramaturgy*, treats the drama exclusively. The work, conceived as a "critical index" of the Hamburg repertory's performances and later called by J. G. Robertson the "greatest text-book of the theatre" to be written during the eighteenth century, discusses classical drama theories, noting where they are observed or transgressed in the company's productions. Lessing treated theoretical issues as well, focusing on Aristotelian dramatic theory, citing Shakespeare's mastery of it and the current misunderstanding and debasement of it.

For the most part, Lessing's dramas complement his critical theories. His first play, *Faust,* of which only a fragment exists, is based not on a classical theme but on the native German Faust legend. While *Miss Sara Sampson* adheres to the conventional structure of French drama, with five acts, scene divisions at entrances and exits, and the observance of the unities of time, place, and action, it is a pioneering play in its introduction of the *bürgerliches Trauerspiel,* bourgeois or domestic tragedy, to the German stage. The story of a virtuous Englishwoman deceived by a dishonorable lover, the sentimental *Miss Sara Sampson* is the first German tragedy to employ middle-class characters. The comedy *Minna von Barnhelm,* which followed *Miss Sara Sampson,* is generally considered Lessing's greatest play. Recognized as Germany's first modern comedy, the play is thought creative and original in its combination of serious moral and political undercurrents with witty and realistic characterization and action. *Emilia Galotti,* a domestic prose tragedy based on the Roman legend of Virginius's killing his daughter to protect her chastity, updates its classical theme to modern times and is notable as another of Lessing's domestic tragedies. Like his minor play *Die Juden,* Lessing's last drama, *Nathan the Wise,* a philosophical work in blank verse, expresses Lessing's commitment to racial, religious, and intellectual tolerance. Uniting classical form with Enlightenment ideas, *Nathan* presents, through the pleas of a Jew, a Christian, and a Mohammedan, a solution to the problems of prejudice.

Lessing was considered a genius and an acute and original thinker by distinguished contemporaries. The earliest commentators were quick to recognize his criticism as seminal. The plastic and poetic arts, claimed Johann Wolfgang von Goethe, were in *Laocoon* "illumined . . . as by a lightning flash; all the criticism which had hitherto guided and judged was thrown away like a worn-out coat." Almost without exception, others joined Goethe in extolling the novelty and positive impact of the criticism, especially the way it directed attention from the narrow conventions of the French classical school, promoting an independent German theater. For the dramas, however, critical reaction did not long remain exclusively positive. Though generally popular in their first performances, most of Lessing's plays were soon faulted for, as August Wilhelm Schlegel put it, demanding "not only in dialogue, but everywhere else also, a naked copy of nature." Some nineteenth-century commentators found the dramas dull and unimaginative, a circumstance put down to Lessing's strict policy of employing "natural" dialogue, everyday characters, and routine storylines. Still others, however, considered these

very qualities the foundation of Lessing's dramatic achievement, claiming for him preeminence as, in the words of Heinrich Heine, "the literary Arminius who delivered [the German] theatre from . . . foreign rule." Thus it may be said that early critics praised the theoretical works with one voice but were at odds about how successfully the theories were applied.

During the twentieth century Lessing's works have been subject to frequent and rigorous examination. The dramas, especially *Miss Sara Sampson, Minna von Barnhelm,* and *Nathan the Wise,* are now recognized as the beginning of an enduring German dramatic tradition, one in which German subjects predominate, verisimilitude is a ruling principle, and nonaristocratic characters interact in common domestic settings. This achievement has led to a new epithet for Lessing: the founder of the German theater. As a critical theorist, Lessing's influence on literature has been immense. Robert Waller Deering has claimed that Lessing "set more people to thinking than any other German writer." Thus today, owing to his complementary achievements in the drama and in criticism, Lessing is widely acknowledged a prominent architect of modern German literature, and his works remain at the pinnacle of German thought.

PRINCIPAL WORKS

Damon; oder, Die wahre Freundschaft (drama) 1747; published in journal *Ermunterungen zum Vergnügen des Gemüts*
Der junge Gelehrte in der Einbildung: Ein Lustspiel in drey Aufzügen (drama) 1748
Die alte Jungfer: Ein Lustspiel in drey Aufzügen (drama) 1749
Beiträge zur Historie und Aufnahme des Theaters [with Christlob Mylius] 4 vols. (essays, history, and criticism) 1750
Kleinigkeiten (poetry) 1751
Briefe, die neueste Litteratur betreffend [with Moses Mendelssohn and Christoph Friedrich Nicolai] (criticism) 1759-65
G. E. Lessings Fabeln: Drei Bücher, Nebst Abhandlungen mit dieser Dichtungsart verwandten Inhalts [translator and adaptor] (fables) 1759
    [*Fables from the German,* 1773]
Faust (unfinished drama) 1759; published in journal *Literaturbriefe*
Philotas: Ein Trauerspiel (drama) 1759
Der Misogyne; oder, Der Feind des weiblichen Geschlechts: Ein Lustspiel in zwey Aufzügen (drama) 1762
Miss Sara Sampson: Ein bürgerliches Trauerspiel in fünf Aufzügen (drama) 1764
Laokoon; oder, Über die Grenzen der Mahlerey und Poesie (criticism) 1766
    [*Laocoon; or, The Limits of Poetry and Painting,* 1836]
Die Hamburgische Dramaturgie. 2 vols. (criticism) 1767-68
    [*Hamburg Dramaturgy,* 1962]
Minna von Barnhelm; oder, Das Soldatenglück: Ein Lustspiel in fünf Aufzügen (drama) 1767
Briefe antiquarischen Inhalts. 2 vols. (essays) 1768-69
Der Freygeist: Ein Lustspiel in fünf Aufzügen (drama) 1768
Die Juden: Ein Lustspiel in einem Aufzuge (drama) 1768
Der Schatz: Ein Lustspiel in einem Aufzuge (drama) 1768
Emilia Galotti: Ein Trauerspiel in fünf Aufzügen (drama) 1772
    [*Emilia Galotti: A Tragedy in Five Acts,* 1801]
†*Der Geschichte und Litteratur: Aus den Schätzen der Herzoglichen Bibliothek zu Wolfenbüttel.* 3 vols. (essays and history) 1773-81

Anti-Goeze (essay) 1778
Ernst und Falk: Gespräche für Freymäurer (dialogues) 1778
[*Lessing's Masonic Dialogues*, 1927]
Nathan der Weise: Ein dramatische Gedicht, in fünf Aufzügen
(drama) 1779
[*Nathan the Wise: A Philosophical Drama*, 1781]
Die Erziehung des Menschengeschlechts (essay) 1780
[*The Education of the Human Race*, 1858]
Fragmente des Wolfenbüttel'schen Ungenannten: Anhang zu
dem Fragmente vom Zwecke Jesu und seiner Jünger
(history) 1784
[*Fragments from Reimarus, Consisting of Brief Critical Re-*
marks on the Object of Jesus and His Disciples, 1879]
Gotthold Ephraim Lessings Kollektaneen zur Literatur. 2 vols.
(criticism) 1790
G. E. Lessing's Leben des Sophocles: Herausgegeben von J.
J. Eschenburg (biography) 1790
G. E. Lessing's sämmtliche Schriften. 32 vols. (dramas, essays, poetry, dialogues, biography, criticism, and histories) 1825-28

*This work was revised by J. J. Johnstone as *The Disbanded Officer:*
or, The Baroness of Bruchsal in 1786.

†Lessing collaborated with Johann Joachim Eschenburg on the fifth
contribution to this series.

AUGUST WILHELM VON SCHLEGEL (lecture date 1808)

[*Schlegel was a German translator, critic, poet, and orientalist*
who, in collaboration with his brother, Friedrich von Schlegel,
gave direction to the German Romantic school. An early champion
of Shakespeare in Germany, August's translations of seventeen
of Shakespeare's plays number among the finest ever made into
German. In the following excerpt from a lecture originally deliv-
ered in Vienna in 1808 and later published in his celebrated Über
Dramatische Kunst und Literatur *(1809-11;* A Course of Lectures
on Dramatic Art and Literature, *1815), Schlegel surveys Lessing's*
career as a dramatist and critic.]

Lessing, . . . in his early dramatic labours, did homage to the
spirit of his age. His youthful comedies are rather insignificant;
they do not already announce the great mind who was afterwards to form an epoch in so many departments of literature.
He sketched several tragedies after the French rules, and executed several scenes in Alexandrines, but has succeeded with
none: it would appear that he had not the requisite facility for
so difficult a metre. Even his *Miss Sara Sampson* is a familiar
tragedy in the lachrymose and creeping style, in which we
evidently see that he had *George Barnwell* before his eyes as
a model. In the year 1767, his connexion with a company of
actors in Hamburgh, and the editorship of a periodical paper
dedicated to theatrical criticism, gave him an opportunity of
considering more closely into the nature and requisitions of
theatrical composition. In this paper he displayed much wit
and acuteness; his bold, nay, (considering the opinions then
prevalent,) his hazardous attacks were especially successful in
overthrowing the usurpation of French taste in Tragedy. With
such success were his labours attended, that, shortly after the
publication of his *Dramaturgie,* translations of French tragedies, and German tragedies modelled after them, disappeared
altogether from the stage. He was the first who spoke with
warmth of Shakspeare, and paved the way for his reception in
Germany. But his lingering faith in Aristotle, with the influence

which Diderot's writings had had on him, produced a strange
compound in his theory of the dramatic art. He did not understand the rights of poetical imitation, and demanded not
only in dialogue, but everywhere else also, a naked copy of
nature, just as if this were in general allowable, or even possible
in the fine arts. His attack on the Alexandrine was just, but,
on the other hand, he wished to, and was only too successful
in abolishing all versification: for it is to this that we must
impute the incredible deficiency of our actors in getting by
heart and delivering verse. Even yet they cannot habituate
themselves to it. He was thus also indirectly the cause of the
insipid affectation of nature of our Dramatic writers, which a
general use of versification would, in some degree, have
restrained.

Lessing, by his own confession, was no poet, and the few
dramas which he produced in his riper years were the slow
result of great labour. *Minna von Barnhelm* is a true comedy
of the refined class; in point of form it holds a middle place
between the French and English style; the spirit of the invention, however, and the social tone portrayed in it, are peculiarly
German. Every thing is even locally determined; and the allusions to the memorable events of the Seven Years' War
contributed not a little to the extraordinary success which this
comedy obtained at the time. In the serious part the expression
of feeling is not free from affectation, and the difficulties of
the two lovers are carried even to a painful height. The comic
secondary figures are drawn with much drollery and humour,
and bear a genuine German stamp.

Emilia Galotti was still more admired than *Minna von Barn-*
helm, but hardly, I think, with justice. Its plan, perhaps, has
been better considered, and worked out with still greater diligence; but *Minna von Barnhelm* answers better to the genuine
idea of Comedy than *Emilia Galotti* to that of Tragedy. Lessing's theory of the Dramatic Art would, it is easily conceived,
have much less of prejudicial influence on a demi-prosaic species than upon one which must inevitably sink when it does
not take the highest flight. He was now too well acquainted
with the world to fall again into the drawling, lachrymose, and
sermonizing tone which prevails in his *Miss Sara Sampson*
throughout. On the other hand, his sound sense, notwithstanding all his admiration of Diderot, preserved him from his declamatory and emphatical style, which owes its chief effect to
breaks and marks of interrogation. But as in the dialogue he
resolutely rejected all poetical elevation, he did not escape this
fault without falling into another. He introduced into Tragedy
the cool and close observation of Comedy; in *Emilia Galotti*
the passions are rather acutely and wittily characterized than
eloquently expressed. Under a belief that the drama is most
powerful when it exhibits faithful copies of what we know,
and comes nearest home to ourselves, he has disguised, under
fictitious names, modern European circumstances, and the
manners of the day, an event imperishably recorded in the
history of the world, a famous deed of the rough old Roman
virtue—the murder of Virginia by her father. Virginia is converted into a Countess Galotti, Virginius into Count Odoardo,
an Italian prince takes the place of Appius Claudius, and a
chamberlain that of the unblushing minister of his lusts, &c.
It is not properly a familiar tragedy, but a court tragedy in the
conversational tone, to which in some parts the sword of state
and the hat under the arm as essentially belong as to many
French tragedies. Lessing wished to transplant into the re-
nownless circle of the principality of Massa Carara the violent
injustice of the Decemvir's inevitable tyranny; but as by taking
a few steps we can extricate ourselves from so petty a territory,

so, after a slight consideration, we can easily escape from the assumption so laboriously planned by the poet; on which, however, the necessity of the catastrophe wholly rests. The visible caro with which he has assigned a motive for every thing, invites to a closer examination, in which we are little likely to be interrupted by any of the magical illusions of imagination: and in such examination the want of internal connectedness cannot escape detection, however much of thought and reflection the outward structure of a drama may display.

It is singular enough, that of all the dramatical works of Lessing, the last, *Nathan der Weise,* which he wrote when his zeal for the improvement of the German theatre had nearly cooled, and, as he says, merely with a view to laugh at theologists, should be the most conformable to the genuine rules of art. A remarkable tale of Boccacio is wrought up with a number of inventions, which, however wonderful, are yet not improbable, if the circumstances of the times are considered; the fictitious persons are grouped round a real and famous character, the great Saladin, who is drawn with historical truth; the crusades in the background, the scene at Jerusalem, the meeting of persons of various nations and religions on this Oriental soil,— all this gives to the work a romantic air, and with the thoughts, foreign to the age in question, which for the sake of his philosophical views the poet has interspersed, forms a contrast somewhat hazardous indeed,but yet exceedingly attractive. The form is freer and more conprehensive than in Lessing's other pieces; it is very nearly that of a drama of Shakspeare. He has also returned here to the use of versification, which he had formerly rejected; not indeed of the Alexandrine, for the discarding of which from the serious drama we are in every respect indebted to him, but the rhymeless Iambic. The verses in *Nathan* are indeed often harsh and carelessly laboured, but truly dialogical; and the advantageous influence of versification becomes at once apparent upon comparing the tone of the present piece with the prose of the others. Had not the development of the truths which Lessing had particularly at heart demanded so much of repose, had there been more of rapid motion in the action, the piece would certainly have pleased also on the stage. That Lessing, with all his independence of mind, was still in his dramatical principles influenced in some measure by the general inclination and tastes of his age, I infer from this, that the imitators of *Nathan* were very few as compared with those of *Emilia Galotti.* Among the striking imitations of the latter style, I will merely mention the *Julius von Tarent.* (pp. 510-13)

August Wilhelm von Schlegel, "Lecture XXX," in his Course of Lectures on Dramatic Art and Literature, *edited by Rev. A. J. W. Morrison, translated by John Black, revised edition, 1846. Reprint by AMS Press, Inc., 1973, pp. 506-29.*

MADAME THE BARONESS DE STAËL-HOLSTEIN (essay date 1810)

[A leader of the movement to eliminate the classical influence on French literature, Madame de Staël helped to bring Romantic thought to the forefront of French consciousness. The author of novels, philosophical essays, and criticism, she is best known for her controversial De l'Allemagne *(1810; Germany, 1813), a critical study highly sympathetic to German idealism. In the following excerpt from this work, she assesses Lessing's contribution to German literature.]*

Lessing wrote in prose with unexampled clearness and precision: depth of thought frequently embarrasses the style of the writers of the new school; Lessing, not less profound, had something severe in his character, which made him discover the most concise and striking modes of expression. Lessing was always animated in his writings by an emotion hostile to the opinions he attacked, and a sarcastic humor gives strength to his ideas.

He occupied himself by turns with the theatre, with philosophy, antiquities, and theology, pursuing truth through all of them, like a huntsman, who feels more pleasure in the chase than in the attainment of his object. His style has, in some respects, the lively and brilliant conciseness of the French; and it conduced to render the German language classical. The writers of the new school embrace a greater number of thoughts at the same time, but Lessing deserves to be more generally admired; he possesses a new and bold genius, which meets nevertheless the common comprehensions of mankind. His modes of perception are German, his manner of expression European. Although a dialectician, at once lively and close in his arguments, enthusiasm for the beautiful filled his whole soul, he possessed ardor without glare, and a philosophical vehemence which was always active, and which by repeated strokes produced effects the most durable.

Lessing analyzed the French drama, which was then fashionable in his country, and asserted that the English drama was more intimately connected with the genius of his countrymen. In the judgment he passes on Mérope, Zaïre, Semiramis, and Rodogune, he notices no particular improbability; he attacks the sincerity of the sentiments and characters, and finds fault with the personages of those fictions, as if they were real beings; his criticism is a treatise on the human heart, as much as on theatrical poetry. To appreciate with justice the observations made by Lessing on the dramatic system in general, we must examine . . . the principal differences of French and German opinion on this subject. But, in the history of literature, it is remarkable that a German should have had the courage to criticise a great French writer, and jest with wit on the very prince of jesters, Voltaire himself.

It was much for a nation, lying under the weight of an anathema which refused it both taste and grace, to become sensible that in every country there exists a national taste, a natural grace; and that literary fame may be acquired in various ways. The writings of Lessing gave a new impulse to his countrymen: they read Shakspeare; they dared in Germany to call themselves German; and the rights of originality were established instead of the yoke of correction. (pp. 169-70)

Among the writings of Lessing, one of the most remarkable is the *Laocoön*; it characterizes the subjects which are suitable both to poetry and painting, with as much philosophy in the principles as sagacity in the examples: nevertheless, it was Winckelmann who in Germany brought about an entire revolution in the manner of considering the arts, and literature also, as connected with the arts. (pp. 170-71)

Madame the Baroness de Staël-Holstein, "Lessing and Winckelmann," in her Germany, *Vol. I, 1859. Reprint by H. W. Derby, 1861, pp. 168-74.*

J. W. VON GOETHE (essay date 1811-22)

[Goethe was a German writer who is considered one of the greatest figures in world literature. A genius of the highest order, he distinguished himself as a botanist, physicist, and biologist; he was an artist, musician, and philosopher; and he had successful careers as a theater director and court administrator. Above all, he contributed richly to his nation's literature. Excelling in all

genres, Goethe was a shaping force in the major literary movements of the late eighteenth and early nineteenth centuries in Germany. In the following excerpt from his autobiography, Aus meinen Leben: Dichtung und Wahrheit *(1811-22;* Memoirs of Goethe: Written by Himself, *1824), Goethe describes the impact of* Minna von Barnhelm *and* Laocoon *on contemporary German literature.*]

[I must make] honourable mention of one work, the most genuine production of the Seven Years' War, and of perfect North German nationality; it is the first theatrical production caught from the important events of life, one of specific temporary value, and one which therefore produced an incalculable effect,—**Minna von Barnhelm.** Lessing, who, in opposition to Klopstock and Gleim, was fond of casting off his personal dignity, because he was confident that he could at any moment seize it and take it up again, delighted in a dissipated life in taverns and the world, as he always needed a strong counterpoise to his powerfully labouring interior; and for this reason also he had joined the suite of General Tauentzien. One easily discovers how the above-mentioned piece was generated betwixt war and peace, hatred and affection. It was this production which happily opened the view into a higher, more significant world, from the literary and citizen world in which poetic art had hitherto moved. (p. 238)

The mind can be highly delighted in two ways, by perception and conception. But the former demands a worthy object, which is not always at hand, and a proportionate culture, which one does not immediately attain. Conception, on the other hand, requires only susceptibility; it brings its subject-matter with it, and is itself the instrument of culture. Hence that beam of light was most welcome to us which that most excellent thinker brought down to us through dark clouds. One must be a young man to render present to oneself the effect which Lessing's **Laocoon** produced upon us, by transporting us out of the region of scanty perceptions into the open fields of thought. The so long misunderstood *ut pictura poesis* ["as in painting, so in poetry"] was at once laid aside, the difference between plastic and speaking art was made clear, the summits of the two now appeared sundered, however near their bases might border on each other. The plastic artist was to keep himself within the bounds of the beautiful, if the artist of language, who cannot dispense with the significant in any kind, is permitted to ramble abroad beyond them. The former labours for the outer sense, which is satisfied only by the beautiful; the latter for the imagination, which may even reconcile itself to the ugly. All the consequences of this splendid thought were illumined to us as by a lightning flash; all the criticism which had hitherto guided and judged was thrown away like a worn-out coat; we considered ourselves freed from all evil, and fancied we might venture to look down with some compassion upon the otherwise so splendid sixteenth century, when, in German sculptures and poems, they knew how to represent life only under the form of a fool hung with bells, death under the misformed shape of a rattling skeleton, and the necessary and accidental evils of the world under the image of the caricatured devil.

We were the most enchanted with the beauty of that thought, that the ancients had recognised death as the brother of sleep, and had represented them similar even to confusion, as becomes Menæchmi. Here we could first do high honour to the triumph of the beautiful, and banish the ugly of every kind into the low sphere of the ridiculous in the kingdom of art, since it could not be utterly driven out of the world.

The splendour of such leading and fundamental conceptions appears only to the mind upon which they exercise their infinite

activity—appears only to the age in which, after being longed for, they come forth at the right moment. Then do those at whose disposal such nourishment is placed, fondly occupy whole periods of their lives with it, and rejoice in a superabundant growth. . . . (pp. 270-71)

> *J. W. von Goethe, "Leipzig (continued)—German Literature," and "Art—Dresden—Return from Leipzig," in his* The Autobiography of Goethe, Truth and Poetry: From My Own Life, Books I.-XIII., Vol. I, *translated by John Oxenford, revised edition, George Bell and Sons, 1881, pp. 218-63, 264-302.*

FRIEDRICH von SCHLEGEL   (lecture date 1815)

[*A German essayist, critic, orientalist, and poet, Schlegel was the younger brother of the writer August Wilhelm von Schlegel. Widely considered the most penetrating mind among the founders of German Romanticism, Friedrich is perhaps best remembered for his historical criticism, including* Geschichte der alten und neuer Literatur *(1815;* Lectures on the History of Literature, Ancient and Modern, *1818) and* Die Philosophie des Lebens *(1828;* The Philosophy of Life and the Philosophy of Language, *1847). In the following excerpt from the former work, Schlegel assesses Lessing's critical works.*]

The criticism of Lessing had the effect of drawing our attention too much to the stage. With all his acuteness and erudition, of which none can be a greater admirer than myself, it may, I think, be doubted whether Lessing produced a favourable effect on the German theatre. The translations of Corneille and Voltaire soon gave place to that species of moral domestic pictures introduced into France by Diderot, and prose was even supposed, for a considerable time, to be necessary for a truly natural dialogue. This pernicious error, however, at last passed away. The enthusiasm for Shakespeare, to which Lessing greatly contributed, was more permanent; and from him we derived notions, both of nature and of poetry, far more profound and exquisite than were ever entertained by any of the school of Diderot.

As a critical writer, Lessing was better adapted for discovering and destroying particular errors in taste than for assigning to any one work, author, or species of writing, a true and just place in the scale of literary merit. He had not leisure nor patience to study the perfections of any one great work, as Winkelmann did; and without such mature consideration and quiet enthusiasm, no man can become an universal critic. We must learn to comprehend the essence of art from admiration of excellence, rather than from detection of error. Lessing is too much a philosopher, and too little an artist in his criticism. He wants that energy of fancy by which Herder was enabled to transport himself into the spirit and poetry of every age and people. It is this very perception and feeling of the poetical, in the character of natural legends, which forms the most distinguishing feature in the genius of Herder. The poetry of the Hebrews was that which most delighted him. He may be called the mythologist of German literature, on account of this gift, this universal feeling of the spirit of antiquity. His power of entering into all the shapes and manifestations of fancy, implies in himself a very high degree of imagination. His mind seems to have been cast in so universal a mould, that he might have attained to equal eminence, either as a poet, or as a philosopher. (pp. 412-13)

Lessing, so soon as his spirit had reached the height of its manly maturity, laid aside, as follies of his youth, the whole of his antiquarian, dramatic, and critical pursuits. The philosophical inquiry after truth was the object of all his later exertions, and he devoted himself to this noble pursuit with an earnestness of enthusiasm to which even his ardent mind had as yet been a stranger. In his earlier pursuits, he seems to have written rather by way of exercising his genius, and from the wish of overthrowing his adversaries, than from any profound love of his own cause. However much nature had fitted him to be a critic, his highest destination was for philosophy. He was too far above his age to be understood by it; and, moreover, he did not live to fill up the outline of the system which he embraced. (pp. 413-14)

In all [Lessing's] controversial writings, (and in none more than his *Education of the Human Race,* and his *Freemason Dialogues,*) we may discover things more intimately connected with the principal subjects of the higher philosophy, than any contemporary inquirer seems ever to have contemplated. Leibnitz was the only philosopher, near his own time, of whom he thought much, and him he considered as standing at a very great distance from those who at that time conceived themselves to be of the Leibnitzian school. He understood him better than any of them, because he studied Spinosa whom they neglected. The metaphysics of Lessing are, indeed, imperfect, and, in some respects, he seems not only to have overcome, but even not to have understood that greatest of all his adversaries; but I must confess that I think he saw farther than Kant, although not with so systematic an eye, into the deep places of philosophy. Had he lived longer and husbanded his strength, his influence and fame might have become very superior to what they are. The freedom and boldness of his spirit might have given a better direction to German philosophy than it received from Kant and his adherents. He is sometimes said to have been a Spinosist; but of this reproach he is by no means deserving. One of his most favourite notions was that of the metempsychosis—a doctrine obviously quite irreconcileable with the genius of a philosophy that denied the personal duration of the soul. Lessing's leaning was rather to the old oriental philosophy, and of this he himself makes no secret. I perfectly agree with those who maintain that enthusiasm cannot be guarded against with too much care and anxiety; for it is clear, that all the masterly learning of Leibnitz, and all the sound judgment of Lessing, could not preserve these great men from mistakes which are very easily discovered and ridiculed by their inferiors. (pp. 415-16)

> *Friedrich von Schlegel, "Lecture XVI," in his* Lectures on the History of Literature: Ancient and Modern, *revised edition, William Blackwood and Sons, 1841, pp. 407-30.*

THOMAS CARLYLE   (essay date 1827)

[A noted nineteenth-century essayist, historian, critic, and social commentator, Carlyle was a central figure of the Victorian age in England. In his writings, Carlyle advocated a Christian work ethic and stressed the importance of order, piety, and spiritual fulfillment. Known to his contemporaries as the "Sage of Chelsea," Carlyle exerted a powerful moral influence in an era of rapidly shifting values. In the following excerpt from an 1827 Edinburgh Review *study of contemporary German authors, Carlyle praises Lessing as the German writer most amenable to English taste.]*

[It] is to Lessing that an Englishman would turn with readiest affection. We cannot but wonder that more of this man is not known among us. . . . Among all the writers of the eighteenth century, we will not except even Diderot and David Hume,

there is not one of a more compact and rigid intellectual structure; who more distinctly knows what he is aiming at, or with more gracefulness, vigour and precision sets it forth to his readers. He thinks with the clearness and piercing sharpness of the most expert logician; but a genial fire pervades him, a wit, a heartiness, a general richness and fineness of nature, to which most logicians are strangers. He is a sceptic in many things, but the noblest of sceptics; a mild, manly, half-careless enthusiasm struggles through his indignant unbelief: he stands before us like a toilworn but unwearied and heroic champion, earning not the conquest but the battle; as indeed himself admits to us, that 'it is not the finding of truth, but the honest search for it, that profits.' We confess, we should be entirely at a loss for the literary creed of that man who reckoned Lessing other than a thoroughly cultivated writer; nay, entitled to rank, in this particular, with the most distinguished writers of any existing nation. As a poet, as a critic, philosopher, or controversialist, his style will be found precisely such as we of England are accustomed to admire most; brief, nervous, vivid; yet quiet, without glitter or antithesis; idiomatic, pure without purism; transparent, yet full of character and reflex hues of meaning. 'Every sentence,' says Horn, and justly, 'is like a phalanx;' not a word wrong-placed, not a word that could be spared; and it forms itself so calmly and lightly, and stands in its completeness, so gay, yet so impregnable! As a poet he contemptuously denied himself all merit; but his readers have not taken him at his word: here too a similar felicity of style attends him; his plays, his *Minna von Barnhelm,* his *Emilie Galotti,* his *Nathan der Weise,* have a genuine and graceful poetic life; yet no works known to us in any language are purer from exaggeration, or any appearance of falsehood. They are pictures, we might say, painted not in colours, but in crayons; yet a strange attraction lies in them; for the figures are grouped into the finest attitudes, and true and spirit-speaking in every line. It is with his style chiefly that we have to do here; yet we must add, that the matter of his works is not less meritorious. His Criticism and philosophic or religious Scepticism were of a higher mood than had yet been heard in Europe, still more in Germany: his *Dramaturgie* first exploded the pretensions of the French theatre, and, with irresistible conviction, made Shakspeare known to his countrymen; preparing the way for a brighter era in their literature, the chief men of which still thankfully look back to Lessing as their patriarch. His *Laocoon,* with its deep glances into the philosophy of Art, his *Dialogues of Freemasons,* a work of far higher import than its title indicates, may yet teach many things to most of us, which we know not, and ought to know. (pp. 51-3)

> *Thomas Carlyle, "State of German Literature," in his* Critical and Miscellaneous Essays: Collected and Republished, Vol. I, *Brown and Taggard, 1860, pp. 30-91.*

HEINRICH HEINE   (essay date 1835)

[Heine was a German poet, critic, dramatist, novelist, and travel writer who is widely considered one of the outstanding literary figures of nineteenth-century Europe. Best known for his Buch der Lieder *(1827;* Heinrich Heine's Book of Songs, *1856), Heine adopted a humorous, ironic tone, which pervades his poetry, prose, and commentaries on politics, art, literature, and society. In the following excerpt from* De l'Allemagne *(1835;* Germany, *1892), a collection of essays on contemporary German life and letters, he discusses Lessing as "the founder of modern German literature."]*

Lessing was the literary Arminius who delivered our theatre from . . . foreign rule. He showed us the nothingness, the laughableness, the flat and faded folly of those imitations of the French theatre, which were in turn imitated from the Greek. But he became the founder of modern German literature, not only by his criticism, but by his own works of art. This man pursued with enthusiasm and sincerity art, theology, antiquity, and archæology, the art of poetry, history; all with the same zeal and to the same purpose. There lives and breathes in all his works the same great social idea, the same progressive humanity, the same religion of reason, whose John he was, and whose Messiah we await. This religion he always preached, but alas! too often alone and in the desert. And there was one art only of which he knew nothing—that of changing stones into bread, for he consumed the greatest part of his life in poverty and under hard pressure,—a curse which clings to nearly all great German geniuses, and will last, it may be, till ended by political freedom. Lessing was more inspired by political feelings than men supposed, a peculiarity which we do not find among his contemporaries, and we can now see for the first time what he meant in sketching the duo-despotism in *Emilia Galotti.* He was regarded then as a champion of freedom of thought and against clerical intolerance; for his theological writings were better understood. The fragments *On the Education of the Human Race* . . . may give an idea of the vast comprehensiveness of Lessing's mind. The two critical works which exercised the most influence on art are his *Hamburgische Dramaturgie* . . . and his *Laocoön, or the Limits of Painting and Poetry.* His most remarkable theatrical pieces are *Emilia Galotti, Minna von Barnhelm,* and *Nathan the Wise.* (pp. 257-59)

[Lessing] was a man out and out, who, when he destroyed something old in a battle, at the same time always created something new and better. "He was," says a German author, "like those pious Jews, who during the second building of the Temple were often troubled by attacks of the enemy, and so fought with one hand while with the other they worked at the house of God." This is not the place where I can say more of Lessing, but I cannot refrain from remarking that he is, of all who are recorded in the whole history of literature, the writer whom I love best. (p. 259)

> *Heinrich Heine, "Book I," in his* Germany, Vol. I, *translated by Charles Godfrey Leland, William Heinemann, 1892, pp. 237-313.*

[JOHN STUART BLACKIE] (essay date 1840)

[*Blackie was a Scottish philologist, translator, and poet who was widely known in his day for his translations of the works of Aeschylus. He contributed many articles and reviews to periodicals, and enthusiastically promoted Gaelic culture in such works as* The Language and Literature of the Scottish Highlands (*1876*) *and* Life of Robert Burns (*1888*). *In the following excerpt, Blackie describes the "tangible results of Lessing's literary activity," relating them, in passing, to contemporary English literature and criticism.*]

Gotthold Ephraim Lessing was in no sense a child of gigantic impulse, a soul of potent thunder and lightning, like Martin Luther. He could not "bellow" like the great reformer, though he could cut as keenly, and more neatly and scientifically. Nevertheless there is something irregular, and to the superficial observer paradoxical, in his whole appearance; something that will not fall easily under any of the common critical categories; something that looks very unfinished and unsatisfactory upon

paper; lines innumerable; sketches finely conceived and powerfully drawn, but fragmentary, or zig-zag, working themselves now out of, now into, strange corners, and ending, to all practical purposes, so far as we can see—in nothing. The truth is that Lessing was more concerned to work on his own age than for posterity; at least circumstances so brought it about that he was continually engaged in critical, theological, philological, artistical battles, the fighting of which was not the less beneficial to his age and country, that the modern English critic can with difficulty interest himself in them, and, from feeling perfectly indifferent to the issue, somewhat hastily concludes that the man who laid so many pigmies low was himself a pigmy—at least a champion much overrated. The interest of battles literary and political ceases with the day; but the fruit of battles well-devised, and well fought, is eternal. Consubstantiation is forgotten, but the German Reformation remains; the Silesian war may force little sympathy now, but the Prussian kingdom can command respect: so Klotz, and Goetz, and Gottsched; shallow learning, sectarian bigotry, Frenchified pedantry, are things no longer named in Germany; but a German literature exists among the most erudite, the most humanized, and the most characteristic that are, of which literature Lessing was one of the noblest pioneers; and a German language is studied by all European thinkers, of which language Lessing was second—we will not say to Goethe—the most masterly handler.

Lessing has produced pieces finished and perfect in matter and form, which may not indeed, as Menzel thinks, "be sufficient to place him side by side with the greatest poets of all nations," but which must ever remain classical, so long as good taste, a clear understanding, and high-toned manly feeling, shall prevail over the literature of fermentation and excitement. But it is wiser and safer to base Lessing's reputation upon what he was and did to his own age as a great literary reformer, than upon what he is to us now, or will be to a distant posterity. Not that there is anything false or ephemeral about him; he is as true and real, as healthy and enduring, in what he has done as anything can be; but what he has done for us of the 19th century in England bears a very small proportion, in public and popular importance, to what he did for his own Germans of the 18th century. And not only what he *did,* but, as we already said, what he *was.* "Many wits have sparkled more brightly," says Goethe, "but where will you find such a CHARACTER?" Lessing was in his works, and is in his writings, the very beau-ideal of manliness; and this is the very thing which of all others, to the Germans of the last century, was the most necessary to be exhibited. Not only flat and barren as the sands of Brandenburg was the German literature of the year 1750, but there was something worse than that—effeminacy, puerility, childishness. Indeed the whole age was corrupt. In every petty princedom luxuriated a government of priests and Pompadours, French cooks and English dogs; and nothing of a stern sort to set against this glittering corruption but the icy sarcasm of Frederick, the stilted pedantry of university learning, and the stiff, stubborn rigidity of old Lutheran orthodoxy. How deeply disease was seated in that age, a healthy English eye reads without much difficulty in the works even of the greatest intellects that afterwards covered Europe with their fame. . . . In such a state of things Germany wanted nothing so much as one healthy, vigorous man; a man who, though he might be neither a Titan in poetic genius, nor an emperor in the world of books, was still in all necessary points a perfect MAN; with a clear eye to see things as they are, a healthy heart to enjoy them, a strong arm to smite down folly in high places, a mouth to speak unceremonious truth and the keen edge of wit to lancet the rottenness of the times. Such a man was Lessing. (pp. 234-36)

We now proceed to ask what are the tangible results of Lessing's literary activity; and here we stumble on the main difficulty of the case to the mere English student. English literature is the literature of character and action: German literature is the literature of thought and feeling. It is extremely difficult to make an Englishman, who is not heart and hand a German student, estimate the writings of Lessing as they ought to be estimated. Earnest and serious thought—a hungering and thirsting after speculative truth—a love of scientific investigation for its own sake—not profound piety merely, but an innate instinct to probe the philosophy of all religions—are qualities of mind necessary to the proper appreciation of most German writers, much more of a fragmentary and polemical writer like Lessing. (pp. 243-44)

Happily, in the first and most obvious phasis of his activity, Lessing stands forth from amid the cloudy envelopement of German speculation, as intelligible, tangible, and, we may say, thoroughly English a mind, as the English student might desire. We find him, as a dramatist, free from all that mock heroic extravagance, or dreamy, floating, uncharacteristic poetry that in many German dramas so reasonably offends our manly English taste. Lessing was the poet of reality, and of living, acting nature, so far as he knew it, or could know it in a *German* world. Of the three German minds of the last century, Goethe, Lessing, and Kant, the least artificial, and, so far as manner is concerned, the most thoroughly English, was Lessing; for Kant dressed up his practical philosophy in a scholastic phraseology, which created more appearance of mystery than really existed; and Goethe's much bespoken objectivity was of too delicate, voluptuous, and artistical a nature, to meet with any ready sympathy from the rude, rough, brawny Briton. Lessing was altogether free from every sort of philosophical or æsthetical mannerism. What it was given him to see, he saw plainly; and he said plainly what he saw. Hence the perfection of his dramas *within their own limits,* both as to matter and style. They are perfectly true, exact, and natural; and perfectly free from any sort of cant and humbug. Nothing false is admitted, however fine; nothing that when analyzed is mere phrase, however brilliant. He speaks directly *at* the thing, neither painting out nor building up—the real secret of the dramatic style. To the Germans such a man *was, is* invaluable. We with our Shakspeare, and a host of not unworthy satellites, may afford to look down upon him coolly enough; and yet, beyond Shakspeare, even we—born dramatists as we are—will find it difficult to produce many plays, that in perfect dramatic finish are more classical than Lessing's three ripe pieces—*Emilia Galotti, Minna von Barnhelm,* and *Nathan the Wise.* True, we may think them cold and even bare, when set against our master-pieces; but what is there that we English will not think cold after the fire and fury that we delight in on the stage? And what will we not consider bare, after that super-ornate style of poetry, which we seem to have made a law of, to compensate the habitual baldness of our prose? This, however, the admirer of Lessing must allow, that his genius was too pointed and exact, not sufficiently rich, luxuriant, and vehement, for high dramatic excellence. That he is not entitled to rank as a dramatic poet of a high order, the very smallness of the number of his classical plays sufficiently indicates. Fertility is not always great; but great geniuses are always fertile. Lessing himself seems very modestly to have been of opinion that he had no dramatic *genius* at all. The passage in [*Hamburgische Dramaturgie* in] which this self-condemnation occurs, is curious.

I am neither a player nor a poet. I am complimented indeed, not seldom, with the latter honourable title. But they do not know me. A few dramatic essays that I have ventured do not justify this forward generosity with the title of poet. Not every man who takes a pencil in his hand, and mixes colours, is a painter. The oldest of these essays of mine belong to a period of life when readiness and dexterity are often mistaken for genius.

(pp. 244-45)

This is showing one's weak side to the public (it was a *public* confession) in a style that, had a greater dramatist said it, might have fallen conveniently under the category of "fishing for a compliment." As it is, we must say that there is a great deal of meaning in it; that the word genius, however, is a very doubtful and dangerous word, and has been justly suspected by all sensible men in this country, from Reynolds to Walter Scott; and that taking Lessing on his own confession, it merely proves that his dramatic talent, however finished the works it might produce, was neither very ready, nor very exuberant. To us it is plain that Lessing's genius was decidedly dramatic. No one will read his first juvenile piece, *Der Junge Gelehrte,* a mere farce, without perceiving a fine eye for dramatic situation. Lessing's modest rating of his own talent, indeed, seems to have been of the utmost benefit to him, in forming his dramatic style. He was a close and intelligent student of stage effect. Neither Aristotle, in whom he was deeply read, nor natural genius, which he disclaimed, could teach him this. Wise was the man who could always believe that he had much need to be taught! (pp. 245-46)

[In *Hamburgische Dramaturgie*] Lessing opened that battery against Voltaire which was to pave the way for the canonization of Shakspeare in Germany, put an end to the unseemly coquetry with France, and unite England and Germany as closely in literary, as they are in physical kinship. Twenty years before Goethe, Lessing held up Shakspeare to his countrymen as the great dramatic model; forty years before Schlegel, he studied Calderon. Before Schlegel also, he studied and appreciated the Greek drama, placing himself—where alone it could be studied and appreciated—on Greek ground. (pp. 246-47)

Lessing's plays are not only valuable as perfect models of German style, but as living and characteristic pictures of the age in which he lived. *Emilia Galotti* is a stern record of the worthlessness and corruption of petty German princedoms in an age where portentous Dubarrydom (as Carlyle phrases it) reigned over the half of Europe. *Minna von Barnhelm* is a fine cabinet picture of honest honourable German soldiership during the famous seven years' war. The honesty belongs to Germany; the honour (so Menzel says) peculiarly also, as no one can doubt, to Lessing himself.

Nathan the Wise is that one of Lessing's dramatic trio which (looking not merely to the form but to the inner soul of it) is at once the least adapted to English taste, and the most characteristic of Lessing's genius; the perfect symbol—the bloom and ripe fruit of his whole potical existence, we may say; but altogether unfit for the present, though haply not for some future and more intellectual stage.

Southey, in Thalaba and Kehama, has endeavoured to show, and we think shown successfully, how something as analogous to the spirit of Christian faith, as Platonism, for example, may live and flourish in the soul of a Mahometan or a Hindoo; Lessing also, in the character of Nathan, a Jew, has done his difficult task better than most writers, for Cumberland's Jew is an utter failure, and so are all attempts to endue this race with Christian virtue, whether conversive or imaginative.

As to mere style, which in Lessing's works has been often and deservedly praised, no man possessed more largely than he the natural instinct of shaking himself free from all vain entanglements and useless adornments of words. Simplicity almost to barrenness; precision and point almost to the fault of habitual epigram, characterize every page. This appears particularly in his fables, which he composed upon a model exactly the reverse of La Fontaine. With a native Saxon impulse, he placed himself instinctively counter to everything French. In this, Coleridge did not surpass him. He knew also well, how completely the solidity and simplicity that becomes a German are identical with what we are accustomed to admire most in the classic works of Greek antiquity.

But Lessing, we think, erred in the opposite direction to La Fontaine, and gave us fables (in plain prose after the old Æsopian fashion), which, in aiming at condensation and precision, lose that honest breadth of simple narrative, which, within its own narrow limits, characterizes the ancient fable. (pp. 247-48)

Lessing wrote epigrams also—happily, not many. It is an idle work, a sort of shooting cleverly at nothing; for an epigram writer has no object, unless indeed he hits a person; and this, a wise man will rather let alone. . . .

Among the tangible results of Lessing's many-sided activity, we must not forget to mention, and we need only mention, the *Laocoon*. This admirable discourse on the limits of poetry and painting may be read even now with pleasure and profit by every lover of the arts. In the year 1766, in Germany, it was like all Lessing's works—a prophecy of better times; an anticipation of the present flourishing state of the science of antiquity in Germany; of that living archæology of sympathy and reproduction which the names of Böekh and Müller have so exalted. (p. 249)

To the theological student and inquirer into Christianity, the celebrated *Wolfenbüttel Fragments* . . . , with the controversy arising out of them, present a most attractive subject of study. Tangible literary result, indeed, is here none; but there is that which, with a candid mind, necessarily leads to a result,—a learned and well-pleaded statement on both sides of the most important case that can be brought before the moral faculties of man for decision. Lessing's connection with the theological literature of Germany, is indeed one of the main features of his literary existence. . . . When in Hamburg he praised the orthodox preacher, Goetze, and gave the go-by to the rationalist Alberti, who preached smooth moral doctrine to the fashionable taste of the time, as Blair not long afterwards did in Scotland. He also expressed himself very strongly against the irreligious tone, under the influence of the Great Frederick, then fashionable at Berlin. (p. 250)

We do not flatter ourselves to have succeeded by this hasty sketch in giving to the reader who has not studied him, a perfect idea of Lessing; but if the student wishes to know him properly, he must see him fighting his battles, and in those battles he is not to contemplate chiefly the matter of the dispute, but the fine play of the muscle, the sure aim of the stroke, the position of the combatant wisely chosen and maintained with a kingly attitude. A hireling fencer certainly he is not; but you will often be surprised, after much preparation, to see this Titan take his stand against Jove in behalf of some climbing boy, or a poor penniless beggar—some stray heroism on earth not loudly sounded, but recorded by an angel in heaven.

There are few men from whom the professional scholar and literary man can drink in a nobler spirit; few who can afford more valuable aid in that most difficult task—the formation of a literary character. Perhaps Fichte may lecture more scientifically, but Lessing gives us more varied and more interesting exemplifications; he is the very eye of inquiry, the sword of research; the Prometheus Purphoros of the multitudinous world of books, a world, which, if one is not taught to use it wisely, instead of being an inexhaustible armoury of Pallas, will eat into a man like a cancer, and ossify him to the very core. We therefore recur to what we set out with, and urge the study of Lessing upon our studious youth, not for that part of him which appears tangibly in finished works upon paper, neatly inventoried by historians of German literature; but for the spirit of truth-worship which breathes in all his works; for those high lessons in the noble art of intellectual gladiatorship, which his example supplies. We do not wish to overpraise him. We are no blind devotees of German literature. Where, indeed, shall we find in that region the breadth of easy strength, the "Lions at play," which a Rubens might paint, and a Shakspeare dramatize? If Goethe was a Hercules, Weimar was to him an Omphale, in whose arms the man of muscle, before he had performed half his feats, was fondled into effeminacy. The poet of Faust had mass and luxuriance, but he wanted manliness. Lessing wants mass and luxuriance, but he is a beau-ideal of vigour, intellectual and moral. Menzel is right when he eulogizes him as the manliest man that the Germans have; and they who study the art of studying under him must be accordingly. It is pleasing to trace in him, amid his unsettled notions, no wish to destroy what is beyond price in the eyes of many. Not a particle of the sneering infidelity, the literary baseness, the foul dishonesty of quotation, the vile flippancy, and the still viler raillery in the room of reason, that brands the school of Voltaire, debases Lessing. We cannot believe that he published the *Fragments* with the design of aiding the cause of religion; but we are quite assured that he would not have relished their modern termination in Strauss. . . . Archbishop Leighton rightly says, "Never be afraid to doubt, if only you have the disposition to believe; and doubt, in order that you may end in believing the truth." To this state the wise archbishop puts a limit. The student of Lessing must take this for a motto. (pp. 252-53)

[John Stuart Blackie], *"Lessing's Life and Writings," in* The Foreign Quarterly Review, *Vol. XXV, No. L, July, 1840, pp. 233-53.*

[GEORGE HENRY LEWES] (essay date 1845)

[*A popular nineteenth-century English miscellaneous writer, Lewes is perhaps best remembered for his personal and professional relationship with the novelist George Eliot. Largely unsuccessful as a fiction writer, Lewes turned to philosophy, science, and biography, achieving recognition for his* Biographical History of Philosophy (1845), *Comte's* Philosophy of the Sciences (1853), *and* Life and Works of Goethe (1855). *He was also an exceptionally able dramatic critic, writing, along with many reviews, his* Actors and the Art of Acting (1875). *In the following excerpt from another work, he surveys Lessing's literary career, focusing on Lessing's clearness of mind and the merits and faults of his dramas, critical essays, and poetical works.*]

The parent vice of German literature is want of distinct purpose; and as consequences of this, want of masculine character, and chastened style. It is this want of definite purpose—or call it want of culture—which generates their idle speculation, trivial research, spurious enthusiasm, and endless book-making. (p. 452)

Such, broadly stated, appear to us the radical defects of German literature. In Gottlob Ephraim Lessing, there is no trace of them. If he has one characteristic which separates him from his successors, it is that of distinct purpose; the prominent peculiarity of his works, as contrasted with those of his countrymen, is their direct and practical tendency. His mind is of a quality eminently British. Of all Germans, he is the least German; yet he created German literature, and is the idol of his country. He has the qualities Englishmen most admire, because the history of our nation shows that with such qualities we have achieved our greatness. His mind is both clear and strong, free from *schwärmerei*, (a word untranslatable, because the thing itself is un-English,) free from cant and affectation of all kinds. He valued books, but he valued action more. Few men have been so erudite, no man held erudition more cheaply. Nothing in his writings betrays that he ever thought of pandering either to morbid sensibility or irrational enthusiasm. Of how many German authors can this be said? If there be any German writer, communion with whom may be beneficial to Englishmen, that writer is Lessing;—not simply because he is one of the greatest of Germans, but because his greatness is of that kind which Englishmen best appreciate. He belongs, moreover, to that class of authors whose value consists in what they suggest or inspire more than in what they teach. The influence such men exercise, is indirect, but effective; and, consequently, the admiration they inspire is not always borne out by their works. If, therefore . . . , we use language which may appear too laudatory to those acquainted only with some of Lessing's works, our justification is, that our admiration is founded on an estimate of the entire man; and that we look at his works with reference to the time at which they were produced, and to the spirit pervading them. (pp. 453-54)

[Lessing's] whole life was a combat,—at one time against poverty—at another, against pedantry and folly. He had to fight for bread, and to fight for truth. The object of his life was to create a National Literature; and he created it. But he could only have achieved this by indomitable courage and activity, joined to many and rare abilities. He was made for a great polemic. The restless activity which urged him into all departments of literature, was accompanied by a rare acuteness in detecting every symptom of weakness, and every means of cure. He was aggressive, impetuous, but not destructive; for he never destroyed without at the same time erecting something better in the place of that which he demolished. His wit was inexhaustible—his erudition unfailing—his logic unfaltering—his style excellent. No polemic, except perhaps our Bentley, ever rivalled Lessing; and Bentley's field was extremely narrow in comparison; for Lessing carried his triumphant arms into the domains of philosophy, religion, the drama, and art in general, no less than into antiquity. All species of polemical warfare were welcome to him; for he succeeded in all. He was never at a loss for weapons, nor for skill to use them. He was the first German who gave to German literature its national tendencies and physiognomy. Klopstock had made it English. Wieland had made it French. Lessing made it German. With a daring hand, this iconoclast smote down the foreign idols from their pedestals, and, with a rarer talent, pointed out the way by which national idols might be formed.

The quality that most strikes the reader of Lessing, after his polemical tendency, is clearness. His intellect impresses you as being essentially clear, strong, direct. There is nothing mys-

tical, vapoury, or affected about him. His clearness is seen in his taste, no less than in his diction. He had no tolerance for obscure, shadowy grandeur. When all Germany was mad about Ossian, whom they ranked higher even than Homer, Lessing continued to proclaim the inexhaustible wealth of Homer, and had nothing but contempt for Ossian. He first saw the greatness of Shakspeare. He preferred Sophocles to Æschylus and Euripides; Racine to Corneille. But although he scouted mysticism, and very properly appealed to Greek simplicity, he was not so simple as to suppose that every kind of simplicity was either Greek or admirable. (pp. 455-56)

It was owing to this clearness that he fell into none of his countrymen's mistakes of confounding the means with the end. Thus his very erudition was practical, and all turned to practical purposes: immense as it was, it was all fruitful. His mind was a storehouse of knowledge, wherein each subject had its fit compartment; not a lumber-room, wherein all things were huddled together, without method and without purpose. His was not the erudition of foot-notes, that cheapest of all displays, in which a man quotes every book he reads, though far from having read every book he quotes. Lessing was one of the few Germans who did not read for reading's sake. In consequence of which, he never opened a book without finding something others had overlooked. As Glauber found a valuable salt in that which had been always thrown away, so did Lessing extract matter from the dullest book he took up.

The clearness of Lessing's mind is best seen in his style. To us it is very significant that German authors should have had so excellent a model, and nevertheless have written so heavily. Lessing's excellence has always been admitted, but it has not been imitated. The result has been, that (allowing for one or two great writers) German literature is, in respect of style, the most objectionable of any in Europe. With a model like Lessing, whose sentences are brief, pregnant, colloquial, and direct—admitting of no doubt as to meaning, yet eschewing all superfluous words—the Germans, with few exceptions, produce nothing but long lumbering sentences; the copiousness serving to darken, not to illustrate. Lessing's style we, on the whole, regard as the finest that has been written in Germany. It is superior, we think, to Göthe's, in being more colloquial, more vivacious, and more impetuous. There is that in Göthe's prose which betrays the care bestowed on it; though very beautiful, transparent, and harmonious, it wants somewhat of the freshness, and a great deal of the impetuosity of Lessing's. Schiller, again, writes with considerable power, and with care; but he wants precision and vivacity.

As a poet, Lessing has very slight pretensions; yet it is but justice to add, that no one ever held those pretensions more cheaply than he did himself. There is a passage in his *Dramaturgie* more truly modest, more honestly self-criticizing, than any thing of the sort in any other author we have met with. 'I am neither a dramatist nor a poet,' said he. 'It is true that people often do me the honour to account me the latter. But this is simply because they do not know me.' . . . This confession is to be received with some qualification. True, he was not a poet. He wanted the finer, subtler feelings, and the keen sensibility of the poetical temperament—qualities which cause that strange inter-penetration of thought and emotion justly considered the primary condition of all genuine poetry. He knew this well, and said so. He knew that in literature, many, as Plato says, bear the Thyrsus, but few are inspired by the God . . . ; and he was not one of the few. In as far, then, as the poet is necessary to the dramatist, Lessing was not a dramatist. In as far as knowledge of life, character, and passion, joined to a knowledge of the drama as an art, could make him a dramatist, he was one. If he did not attain that exalted station to which his young ambition once aspired—if he did not become the German Molière—if he could not rank himself beside the great Dramatists—he unquestionably deserves a place beside those second only to the great poets. He was the first to give the Germans a national drama. His plays became national idols; and have survived nearly a century of changes without much diminution of favour. They owe their success to sterling character, and admirable construction; which, after all, are the primary requisites of the acting drama. Of fancy there is none; of imagination but little; and that little not of the high poetical kind. His plays are all, except *Nathan der Weise,* written in prose—inimitable prose. *Nathan* is written in blank verse; but is not the more poetical on that account.

Amongst the *Gedichte* [''poems''] which occupy the first volume of his works, few, except the epigrams, are now read, and few deserve to be read. Perhaps the best of all is that which is strangely enough printed amongst the epigrams, beginning *Ein rundes, tolles, nettes Ding,* which has great vivacity and concision. Of the hundred and sixty epigrams there collected, not more than half are good; a few are perfect. Marial is his great model, and many of his epigrams are but translations from the Roman poet. These are admirably rendered. (pp. 456-58)

His Dramas should always be read with reference to the epoch at which they were produced. We do not say they are deficient in intrinsic excellence; but thinking that they do not quite equal their reputation, we are disposed to attribute some of their reputation to their having been the first efforts of a national drama. They have an interest as *Mémoires pour servir* [''useful reminders'']. Thus *Der Freigeist,* one of the earliest, as a comedy, is heavy, ill-conceived, and feebly executed; but it is a curious indication of the spirit of the times. The hero, a freethinker, is a man of many virtues. The leaven amidst these good qualities, is his uncompromising antipathy to Priests. He rejects the friendship and kindness of Theophan; insults him, and suspects him, only because he is a Priest. How truly is a large portion of the eighteenth century reflected in this antipathy! . . . In the conception of *Der Freigeist,* there is a token of Lessing's manly impartiality. Although a freethinker himself, he exposed the intolerance of freethinkers. He had no party spirit,—no sectarian prejudices. No one was ever so passionate in the search after truth, who was also so tolerant of the opinions of others.

If we have thus had occasion to notice Lessing's exemption from the intolerance of the age, we have next also to note a similar exemption from its sentimentality. *Miss Sara Sampson* is a domestic tragedy of the Kotzebue school—a school to which Göthe and Schiller, in their early pieces *Stella* and *Kabale und Liebe,* gave the sanction of their names. It has a subject so tempting for sentimentality, that Lessing's having escaped that temptation is really wonderful. It is not a good play; but it exhibits the developed skill of a dramatist in comparison with *Der Freigeist.* The plot is improbable, but admirably conducted, and exhibits some very interesting situations. There is little skill shown in the delineation of character. Marwood is a mere fury. Sara, though *naïve,* is somewhat commonplace. On the whole, it was a great play for the period; and elicited universal applause. (pp. 460-61)

Philotas was his next attempt. It is a tragedy (if it can be so called) in one act. Aridæus, a Grecian King, has taken prisoner Philotas, the son of his rival; his own son being also a prisoner

in the rival's camp. He proposed to Philotas an interchange. Philotas, remarking his absorbing love, and concluding that it would cause him to make any sacrifices for the sake of recovering his son, resolves to immolate himself for his country. He sends a message to his father, bidding him extort the object in dispute between the two countries, as the ransom of the son of Aridæus. He then kills himself to prevent his father's exchanging the prince for him. The character of the impetuous Philotas, half-boy, half-hero, is finely, even delicately sketched. The other characters are commonplace. A great fault was committed in writing this play in prose, which is incompatible with so ideal a subject, and such exalted motives.

Minna von Barnhelm succeeded. Of all German comedies, this has our preference. In no other have we seen such pure dramatic presentation of character, and that character so unmistakeably German. Major Tellheim is said to be a portrait of Lessing's admirable friend Kleist. It is handled with great skill; and although criticism might perhaps object to the Major's extreme sensitiveness, we have no doubt that even this was true to the life. The play is very amusing, except towards the close, where there is a little too much delay in bringing about a *dénouement* perfectly foreseen. Otherwise it is very animated. The dialogue is excellent—direct, rapid, and sparkling. The great charm of the piece is its German individuality. There you see the German character, not in what is most elevated, nor in what is fantastic and cloudy, but in its real strength;—its simplicity, honesty, warmth of feeling, and unaffected expression of feeling. Written whilst Lessing was with the army at Breslau, it breathes a generous spirit of admiration; and urges pointedly the justice of rewarding the brave defenders of 'Fatherland.' Its effect on the army was electrical; its effect on all Germany was, and continues to be, immense.

Emilia Galotti is generally ranked higher than *Minna,* but with very little justice. It is, doubtless, a remarkable production, full of purpose and interest, and alwyas successful on the stage. The plot is constructed with skill; the characters selected and contrasted with fine discrimination, and drawn with clear, sharp outlines. But, in spite of these merits, there is something in the play which is not genial; there is a want of that indefinable charm which *Minna* possesses—a charm that makes all the difference between creative and constructive genius. *Minna von Barnhelm* is a genuine comedy; we cannot call *Emilia Galotti* a genuine tragedy. The free spirit of mirth, the easy evolution of character, the adequacy of motive, current through the one, have no counterparts in the other. It is not that *Emilia* is deficient in strongly conceived character, or true and sufficient motive; it is that the want of a passionate fusion of the various elements into a poetical whole, causes the impression to be marred. The play is critical, not poetical. Moreover, there is a radical error in the conception, which surprises us in so great a critic. . . . In one word, the *dénouement* of *Emilia Galotti* does not, to us, seem justified by modern feelings.

In making these objections, we are far from meaning to imply that *Emilia Galotti* is an indifferent play; it is only not a great one. Judging it according to the tragedies which figure on the German stage, it may, however, be called great; so admirably are the characters presented. The weak, vacillating prince, eager to profit by the villanies of Marinelli, but not daring to face the consequences—prone to crime, but always throwing the blame of it on others—utterly unprincipled—destitute even of the energy to be consistently base—signing a death-warrant with the same levity as a *billet-doux*—may be pronounced so far one of the best creations of the drama. Almost as good, in its way, is the handling of that curious figure the Countess Orsina, with her mixture of frivolity and intensity, of voluptuousness and fiery passion. She is the prototype of Schiller's Julia, Princess Von Eboli, and Lady Milford; but Schiller has fallen many degrees short of his model. Marinelli, the supple courtier and smooth-faced villain, is drawn with effect. Odoardo is a more ambitious, but less successful sketch. (pp. 461-63)

Nathan der Weise is a work which still excites the deepest admiration in Germany; in fact, if you mention Lessing to a German, the chances are, that he will at once refer to *Nathan* for a proof of his genius, as he would to the *Faust* of Göthe for a proof of his. *Nathan* has not been a favourite elsewhere; and this difference in judgment would show that the work had some charm peculiarly national. In the dearth of great poems, *Nathan* is doubtless ranked high; for, as the Spaniards say, *en regno del ciegos el tuerto es Rey* (in the land of the blind the one-eyed is King) Perhaps also the nature of the subject . . . . the grand and beautiful spirit of tolerance which pervades it, may cause the Germans to forgive its want of poetry. It is undoubtedly a charming work; but not a fine poem. Its conception is philosophical, its execution epigrammatic and polemical. A. W. Schlegel, who always speaks of Lessing with quiet malice, says of *Nathan* that it 'is curious, as being the only drama not written for the stage; and therefore, being uninfluenced by his critical principles, is more conformable to the genuine rules of Art' [see excerpt dated 1808]. What those genuine rules are, we should be happy to learn: he does not explain; and how Lessing could have written any drama without being influenced by his critical principles, we are at a loss to conceive. (p. 464)

Nathan der Weise is not a great poem; it is nevertheless a very remarkable work, imbued with deep and generous feeling, and full of profound thought. It is a work that exercises a strong influence on the reader;—a work which, though polemical, is nevertheless so tolerant—because indeed it only contends for tolerance, and contends generously—that all classes, however diversified their opinions, must unite in admiration of it. The leading design is to inculcate tolerance of the opinions of others: not by destroying the groundwork of all belief—(which is too often the method of those who preach tolerance)—but by showing that all creeds, if sincere, and accompanied by benevolence, are to be honoured; because although each cannot be the true creed, yet each will, in that way, fulfil the object of all religion. This is the moral of that beautiful story of the three rings, which Lessing has taken from Boccaccio: this moral is further developed by the whole piece. The *dénouement*—where Recha and the Templar are discovered to be brother and sister, Saladin their uncle, and Nathan their spiritual father, the three families united into one family—is a type of the three religions, Christianity, Judaism, and Mahometanism, harmoniously united;— of unity of purpose, not excluding diversity of character. (pp. 464-65)

The character of Nathan himself, is by critics considered a masterpiece. He certainly rivets attention, and retains our sympathies. He is a fine philosophical figure, whose wisdom and tolerance endow him with a dignity which strongly impresses the reader. But it seems to us that there is a fundamental error in the conception. Nathan is meant for a Jew, he is always called a Jew, but he is only a Jew in name. His sentiments and his religion are not those of a Jew; it was therefore worse than superfluous to give him the name. . . . Lessing is constantly applauded for having chosen a representative of the most exclusive and fiercely bigoted of all races, as the exemplar

of tolerance; but this is surely either inconsistent or erroneous. Nathan is an exemplar of tolerance: but assuredly his tolerance is not that of a Jew. (p. 466)

It is curious to turn from the calm and far-reaching tolerance of *Nathan der Weise,* to the impetuous onset upon existing tastes in the *Hamburgische Dramaturgie*—the work which, of all critical works ever published, perhaps achieved the most instantaneous victory. It is difficult to appreciate the 'sensation' this work caused, now that its fundamental ideas have been long popularised in all shapes. But on a slight examination of the state of public opinion at the time that Lessing wrote, the importance of his views will only appear equalled by their audacity. . . . The *Dramaturgie* has long fulfilled its object, and almost outlived its interest. To the English reader there can be no interest in wading through critiques on German plays, and German actors no longer known; nor can there be much attraction in witnessing the assault upon a tragic system which no living Englishman would pronounce a model. For our own parts we think Lessing unjustly severe on the French poets; and not at all willing to admit their peculiar merits. The critic, however, cannot glance over the *Dramaturgie* without profit; and scholars no less than critics will do well to read his discussion of Aristotle's definition of Tragedy.

Perhaps the characteristics of Lessing's mind are nowhere more distinctly visible than in his treatise on the *Laokoon*. The clearness and the directness of the style, are qualities so rare in such works, that one is apt to think lightly of its ideas; a journey, so easily performed, does not seem difficult; ideas, so easily grasped, seem obvious. But, on closing the book, if you compare the state of your opinions on art with those entertained previous to the perusal, you will be able to estimate its value. We have heard very eminent men declare, that it taught them more about art than all the other works they had read upon the subject put together. It is a book essentially instructive. The admirable analytical sagacity with which the boundaries of each art are distinguished, opens a vast field of criticism. The clear and piercing glance thrown upon the fog and vapour of critical prejudice, has the aid of keen wit and apposite learning in the demolition of grave absurdities. The book is made up of digressions; and yet these digressions are so well planned as to form constituent parts. He tacks away from the port, only to fill his sails with wind. He gains the summit of a mountain by winding round it, where direct ascent would be impracticable. (pp. 466-68)

[*George Henry Lewes*], *"Lessing," in* The Edinburgh Review, *Vol. LXXXII, No. CLXVI, October, 1845, pp. 451-70.*

JAMES RUSSELL LOWELL   (essay date 1867)

[*Lowell was a celebrated American poet and essayist, and an editor of two leading journals, the* Atlantic Monthly *and the* North American Review. *He is noted for his satirical and critical writings, including* A Fable for Critics *(1848), a book-length poem featuring witty critical portraits of his contemporaries. Although often awkwardly phrased, and occasionally vicious,* A Fable *is distinguished by the enduring value of its literary assessments. Commentators generally agree that Lowell displayed a judicious critical sense, despite the fact that he sometimes relied upon impressions rather than critical precepts in his writings. Most literary historians rank him with the major nineteenth-century American critics. In the following excerpt from his 1867 review of Adolf Stahr's* G. E. Lessing: Sein Leben und Seine Werke *(1864;* The Life and Works of Gotthold Ephraim Lessing, *1866), Lowell assesses Lessing's critical and dramatic achievements.*]

My respect for what Lessing was, and for what he did, is profound. In the history of literature it would be hard to find a man so stalwart, so kindly, so sincere, so capable of great ideas, whether in their influence on the intellect or the life, so unswervingly true to the truth, so free from the common weaknesses of his class. Since Luther, Germany has given birth to no such intellectual athlete,—to no son so German to the core. Greater poets she has had, but no greater writer; no nature more finely tempered. Nay, may we not say that great character is as rare a thing as great genius, if it be not even a nobler form of it? For surely it is easier to embody fine thinking, or delicate sentiment, or lofty aspiration, in a book than in a life. The written leaf, if it be, as some few are, a safe-keeper and conductor of celestial fire, is secure. Poverty cannot pinch, passion swerve, or trial shake it. But the man Lessing, harassed and striving life-long, always poor and always hopeful, with no patron but his own right-hand, the very shuttlecock of fortune, who saw ruin's ploughshare drive through the hearth on which his first home-fire was hardly kindled, and who, through all, was faithful to himself, to his friend, to his duty, and to his ideal, is something more inspiring for us than the most glorious utterance of merely intellectual power. The figure of Goethe is grand, it is rightfully pre-eminent, it has something of the calm, and something of the coldness, of the immortals; but the Valhalla of German letters can show one form, in its simple manhood, statelier even than his.

Manliness and simplicity, if they are not necessary coefficients in producing character of the purest tone, were certainly leading elements in the Lessing who is still so noteworthy and lovable to us when eighty-six years have passed since his bodily presence vanished from among men. He loved clearness, he hated exaggeration in all its forms. He was the first German who had any conception of style, and who could be full without spilling over on all sides. . . . If ever a man stood firmly on his own feet, and asked help of none, that man was Gotthold Ephraim Lessing. (pp. 298-300)

[Lessing] could only feel his own strength, and make others feel it,—could only call it into full play in an intellectual wrestling-bout. He was always anointed and ready for the ring, but with this distinction, that he was no mere prize-fighter, or bully for the side that would pay him best, nor even a contender for mere sentiment, but a self-forgetful champion for the truth as he saw it. Nor is this true of him only as a critic. His more purely imaginative works—his *Minna,* his *Emilia,* his *Nathan*—were all written, not to satisfy the craving of a poetic instinct, nor to rid head and heart of troublous guests by building them a lodging outside himself, as Goethe used to do, but to prove some thesis of criticism or morals by which Truth could be served. His zeal for her was perfectly unselfish. "Does one write, then, for the sake of being always in the right? I think I have been as serviceable to Truth," he says, "when I miss her, and my failure is the occasion of another's discovering her, as if I had discovered her myself." (p. 301)

It is in the *Dramaturgie* that Lessing first properly enters as an influence into European literature. He may be said to have begun the revolt from pseudo-classicism in poetry, and to have been thus unconsciously the founder of romanticism. Wieland's translation of Shakespeare had, it is true, appeared in 1762; but Lessing was the first critic whose profound knowledge of the Greek drama and apprehension of its principles gave weight to his judgment, who recognized in what the true greatness of the poet consisted, and found him to be really nearer the Greeks than any other modern. This was because Lessing looked al-

ways more to the life than the form,—because he knew the classics, and did not merely cant about them. . . . In breadth of understanding, and the gravity of purpose that comes of it, he was far above Fletcher or Webster, but how far below either in the subtler, the incalculable, qualities of a dramatic poet! . . . Criticism can at best teach writers without genius what is to be avoided or imitated. It cannot communicate life; and its effect, when reduced to rules, has commonly been to produce that correctness which is so praiseworthy and so intolerable. It cannot give taste, it can only demonstrate who has had it. Lessing's essays in this kind were of service to German literature by their manliness of style, whose example was worth a hundred treatises, and by the stimulus there is in all original thinking. Could he have written such a poem as he was capable of conceiving, his influence would have been far greater. It is the living soul, and not the metaphysical abstraction of it, that is genetic in literature. If to do were as easy as to know what were good to be done! It was out of his own failures to reach the ideal he saw so clearly, that Lessing drew the wisdom which made him so admirable a critic. Even here, too, genius can profit by no experience but its own. (pp. 340-42)

[We must acknowledge] the truth of Lessing's own characteristic confession, that he was no poet. A man of genius he unquestionably was, if genius may be claimed no less for force than fineness of mind,—for the intensity of conviction that inspires the understanding as much as for that apprehension of beauty which gives energy of will to imagination,—but a poetic genius he was not. His mind kindled by friction in the process of thinking, not in the flash of conception, and its delight is in demonstration, not in bodying forth. His prose can leap and run, his verse is always thinking of its feet. Yet in his *Minna* and his *Emilia* he shows one faculty of the dramatist, that of construction, in a higher degree than any other German. Here his critical deductions served him to some purpose. The action moves rapidly, there is no speechifying, and the parts are coherent. Both plays act better than anything of Goethe or Schiller. But it is the story that interests us, and not the characters. These are not, it is true, the incorporation of certain ideas, or, still worse, of certain dogmas, but they certainly seem something like machines by which the motive of the play is carried on; and there is nothing of that interplay of plot and character which makes Shakespeare more real in the closet than other dramatists with all the helps of the theatre. It is a striking illustration at once of the futility of mere critical insight and of Lessing's want of imagination, that in the *Emilia* he should have thought a Roman motive consistent with modern habits of thought, and that in *Nathan* he should have been guilty of anachronisms which violate not only the accidental truth of fact, but the essential truth of character. Even if we allowed him imagination, it must be only on the lower plane of prose; for of verse as anything more than so many metrical feet he had not the faintest notion. Of that exquisite sympathy with the movement of the mind, with every swifter or slower pulse of passion, which proves it another species from prose . . . , he wanted the fineness of sense to conceive. If we compare the prose of Dante or Milton, though both were eloquent, with their verse, we see at once which was the most congenial to them. Lessing has passages of freer and more harmonious utterance in some of his most careless prose essays, than can be found in his *Nathan* from the first line to the last. In the *numeris lege solutis* ["freedom of meter"] he is often snatched beyond himself, and becomes truly dithryambic; in his pentameters the march of the thought is comparatively hampered and irresolute. His best things are not poetically delicate, but have the tougher fibre of proverbs. Is it not enough, then, to be a great prose-writer? They are as rare as great poets, and if Lessing have the gift to stir and to dilate that something deeper than the mind which genius only can reach, what matter if it be not done to music? Of his minor poems we need say little. Verse was always more or less mechanical with him, and his epigrams are almost all stiff, as if they were bad translations from the Latin. Many of them are shockingly coarse, and in liveliness are on a level with those of our Elizabethan period. . . . The prettiest of his shorter poems (**"Die Namen"**) has been appropriated by Coleridge, who has given it a grace which it wants in the original. His **Nathan,** by a poor translation of which he is chiefly known to English readers, is an Essay on Toleration in the form of a dialogue. As a play, it has not the interest of **Minna** or **Emilia,** though the Germans, who have a praiseworthy national stoicism where one of their great writers is concerned, find in seeing it represented a grave satisfaction, like that of subscribing to a monument. There is a sober lustre of reflection in it that makes it very good reading; but it wants the molten interfusion of thought and phrase which only imagination can achieve.

As Lessing's mind was continually advancing,—always open to new impressions, and capable, as very few are, of apprehending the many-sidedness of truth,—as he had the rare quality of being honest with himself,—his works seem fragmentary, and give at first an impression of incompleteness. But one learns at length to recognize and value this very incompleteness as characteristic of the man who was growing lifelong, and to whom the selfish thought that any share of truth could be exclusively *his* was an impossibility. At the end of the ninety-fifth number of the **Dramaturgie** he says: "I remind my readers here, that these pages are by no means intended to contain a dramatic system. I am accordingly not bound to solve all the difficulties which I raise. I am quite willing that my thoughts should seem to want connection,—nay, even to contradict each other,—if only there are thoughts in which they [my readers] find material for thinking themselves. I wish to do nothing more than scatter the *fermenta cognitionis* ["random thoughts"]." That is Lessing's great praise, and gives its chief value to his works,—a value, indeed, imperishable, and of the noblest kind. No writer can leave a more precious legacy to posterity than this; and beside this shining merit, all mere literary splendors look pale and cold. There is that life in Lessing's thought which engenders life, and not only thinks for us, but makes us think. Not sceptical, but forever testing and inquiring, it is out of the cloud of his own doubt that the flash comes at last with sudden and vivid illumination. Flashes they indeed are, his finest intuitions, and of very different quality from the equable north-light of the artist. He felt it, and said it of himself, "Ever so many flashes of lightning do not make daylight." We speak now of those more rememberable passages where his highest individuality reveals itself in what may truly be called a passion of thought. In the **Laocoön** there is daylight of the serenest temper, and never was there a better example of the discourse of reason, though even that is also a fragment.

But it is as a nobly original man, even more than as an original thinker, that Lessing is precious to us, and that he is so considerable in German literature. In a higher sense, but in the same kind, he is to Germans what Dr. Johnson is to us,—admirable for what he was. Like Johnson's, too, but still from a loftier plane, a great deal of his thought has a direct bearing on the immediate life and interests of men. His genius was not a St. Elmo's fire, as it so often is with mere poets,—as it was in Shelley, for example, playing in ineffectual flame about the

points of his thought,—but was interfused with his whole nature and made a part of his very being. To the Germans, with their weak nerve of sentimentalism, his brave common-sense is a far wholesomer tonic than the cynicism of Heine, which is, after all, only sentimentalism soured. His jealousy for maintaining the just boundaries whether of art or speculation may warn them to check with timely dikes the tendency of their thought to diffuse inundation. Their fondness in æsthetic discussion for a nomenclature subtle enough to split a hair at which even a Thomist would have despaired, is rebuked by the clear simplicity of his style. But he is no exclusive property of Germany. As a complete man, constant, generous, full of honest courage, as a hardy follower of Thought wherever she might lead him, above all, as a confessor of that Truth which is forever revealing itself to the seeker, and is the more loved because never wholly revealable, he is an ennobling possession of mankind. (pp. 342-47)

James Russell Lowell, "Lessing," in his Among My Books, *1870. Reprint by Houghton Mifflin Company, 1898, pp. 291-348.*

BAYARD TAYLOR   (lecture date 1878?)

[*Taylor was an American academic, novelist, poet, journalist, essayist, and travel writer whose most lasting work, a translation (1870-71), in the original meters, of Johann Wolfgang von Goethe's* Faust, *helped to win him the title "laureate of the Gilded Age." In the following excerpt from a lecture given sometime before his death in 1878, Taylor discusses Lessing's passion for truth, his intellectual independence, and his revolutionary role in the development of German drama and criticism.*]

[Lessing's] chief intellectual quality was a passion for truth, so earnest and unswerving, that we cannot help expecting to find it manifested in the events of his life; and we shall not be disappointed. Whatever faults may have been his, he was always candid, honest, honorable and unselfish. He lived at a time when a very little tact and pliancy of nature might have greatly advanced his fortunes—when a little prudent reticence, now and then, would have saved him from many an angry denunciation. But he seems never to have concerned himself with anything beyond his immediate needs. "All that a man wants, is health," he once wrote: "why should I trouble myself about the future? What would be privation to many is a sufficiency to me." . . . This self-reliant spirit, without vanity, only asserting itself when its independence must be maintained, is very rare among men. Lessing understood the character and extent of his own power so well, even as a young man, that all his utterances have a stamp of certainty, which is as far as possible from egotism.

We must bear in mind the fact that, when he began to write, literature was not much else than a collection of lifeless forms; that government still clung to the ideas of the Middle Ages, and that religion had, for the most part, degenerated into rigid doctrine. Lessing's position was that of a rebel, at the start. It was impossible for him to breathe the same atmosphere with the dogmatists of his day, and live. His first volume of poems, chiefly imitations of the amorous lyrics of the ancients, gave the opportunity for an attack upon his moral character. In replying to his father, who seems to have joined in the denunciation, he says: "The cause of their existence is really nothing more than my inclination to attempt all forms of poetry." He then adds: "Am I so very wrong in selecting for my youthful labor something whereon very few of my countrymen have tried their skill? And would it not be foolish in me to discontinue, until I have produced a master-piece?''

Lessing's critical articles, which he began to write during his first residence in Berlin, and especially his *Letters on Literature,* soon made him respected and feared, although they gained him few friends beyond the circle of his personal associates. Industry, combined with a keen intellectual insight, had made him an admirable practical scholar, and few men ever better knew how to manage their resources. His style . . . was somewhat colored by his study of the English language. It is clear, keen and bright, never uncertain or obscure. Like the sword of Saladin it cuts its way through the finest web of speculation. He had neither reverence for names, nor mercy for pretensions, and no mind of looser texture than his own could stand before him. I know of no critical papers in any literature, at once so brilliant and so destructive. They would have had a more immediate and a wider effect, but for the fact that his antagonists represented the general sentiment of the time, which could not be entirely suppressed in them. Yet his principles of criticism were broader than mere defense and counter-attack. To Pastor Klotz, who complains of his "tone" toward him, he answers. "If I were commissioned as a Judge in Art, this would be my scale of tone: gentle and encouraging for the beginners; admiring with doubt, or doubting with admiration, for the masters; positive and repellant for the botchers; scornful for the swaggerers; and as bitter as possible for the intriguers. The Judge in Art, who has but one tone for all, had better have none.'' (pp. 210-12)

[Lessing] marched straight forward, looking neither to the right nor to the left, indifferent what prejudices he shocked, or upon whom he set his feet. Having, as he conceived, the great minds of Greece, Rome and England as his allies in the Past, he was content to stand alone in the Present. His criticism was positive as well as negative: he not only pointed out the prevalent deficiencies in taste and knowledge, but he laid down the law which he felt to have been violated, and substituted the true for the false interpretation.

I do not think that Lessing's biographers have fully recognized the extent of his indebtedness to English authors. It has been remarked that his epigrammatic poems read like stiff translations from the classics: to me they suggest the similar performances of Swift and Herrick. The three plays by which he revolutionized the German stage—*Miss Sara Sampson, Minna von Barnhelm,* and *Emilia Galotti,*—were constructed upon English models. With them a drama of ordinary life was introduced into Germany. They have kept their place to this day, and are, even now, more frequently performed than the plays of Goethe. Although they possess little poetic merit, they are so admirably constructed, with so much regard to the movement of the plot and its cumulative development, that they have scarcely been surpassed by any later dramatic author. Even Goethe declares that it is impossible to estimate their influence on dramatic literature.

The *Laocoon,* although a piece of positive criticism, seems to have been negatively inspired by an English book which has long been forgotten. Joseph Spense, whose ''Anecdotes'' of Pope and others still survives, published in 1747 a work entitled, ''Polymetis,''—a comparison of the poetry and the art of the ancients, in which he took the ground that they illustrate each other—in other words, that they represent the same events. Lessing, whose interest in classic art had been greatly stimulated by the labors of Winckelmann, was led to examine the subject—to contrast ancient art with ancient literature, and ascertain whether indeed they were only different modes of presenting the same subject, as Spense asserted, or whether each had its own separate and peculiar sphere of existence. The description of the fate of Laocoon and his sons, in Virgil, and the famous group of sculpture, mentioned by Pliny . . . , furnished him with a text, and gave the title to his work; but from this starting-point he rises to the investigation of the nature of Poetry and Art, as methods of expression, and the laws which govern them. Where Gottsched and his school furnished patterns of versification, by which men should be able to write mechanical poetry, Lessing revealed the intellectual law, without which all verse is but a lifeless jingle, dreary to the ears of men, and prohibited by the gods. (pp. 213-15)

[In *Laocoon,* Lessing shows] that a mere copy of a natural object, no matter how admirably made, does not constitute painting, and that mere description does not constitute poetry. In both cases the higher element of beauty is necessary, and this element can only exist under certain conditions. For instance, Poetry may express continuous action, but Art can only express suspended action. Poetry may represent the successive phases of passion, Art only a single phase at a time. The agents of form and color assist the representation, in one case; the agency of sound in the other. (pp. 215-16)

[Lessing's] careful and delicate dissection of the principles of Art and Literature, has a greater charm for the German than

Marble sculpture of Laocoön by Agesander, Polydorus, and Athenodorus, completed circa 100 A.D. and today on display in the Vatican. Archivio Fotografico Gallerie e Musei Vaticano.

for the English mind. But without considering Lessing's critical genius, we cannot properly appreciate his power and value. He was forced into this field of activity, and his capacities were sharpened by constant exercise, yet it was his true work after all. The critical and the creative faculties never entirely harmonize in the same brain. The critic detects, by observation and analysis, what the creative genius possesses by a special, splendid instinct. It is therefore possible for an author, commencing an important work, to know beforehand *too well* how it should be done. His intellectual insight may be so clear, so sure and so finely exercised, that nothing is left for the imagination. Instead of following his feeling, knowing that many a bright surprise, many an unexpected illumination of thought will come to help him on the way, he is chilled by the critical faculty, which constantly looks over his shoulder and meddles with his freedom. The evidence of this is nowhere more apparent than in Lessing's poems and plays. With all their excellent qualities, they are almost wanting in that warm, imaginative element which welds thought and passion and speech into one inseparable body. It is remarkable that his style, which is so sustained, so dignified and flexible in his critical papers, should seem slightly hard and mechanical in his verse. His most ambitious work, **Nathan the Wise,** has passages where the blank verse is strong and rhythmical, but it has also passages the effect of which is not different from that of prose. The one thing, which we can all feel better than describe, was wanting, to make him a truly great creative author; but had he possessed it, he would probably have done less service to the world. Just the man that he was, was demanded by the age in which he lived.

It appears from his correspondence and the testimony of his friends, that he wrote a drama entitled **Faust,** the manuscript of which was lost by the publisher to whom it was sent. He never attempted to rewrite it. From the small fragment which remains, and some account of the design of the whole which has been preserved, this work was undoubtedly more poetic and imaginative than any of his other dramatic poems. It coincided with Goethe's great work only in one particular—that the soul of Faust is not lost, and Mephistopheles loses his wager. His mind was not only fruitful, but very rapid in its operation, and only the smallest portion of his literary plans was carried into effect. (pp. 216-18)

Lessing's career . . . might be compared to a pure, keen blast of mountain wind, let loose upon a company of enervated persons, dozing in an atmosphere of exhausted ingredients and stale perfumes. It was a breath of life, but it made them shriek and shudder. When they tried to close the window upon him, he smashed the panes; and then, with the irreverence of all free, natural forces, he began to blow the powder from their wigs and the wigs from their heads. There is something comically pitiful in the impotent wrath with which they attempted to suppress him. (pp. 230-31)

[As a] creative intellect, the highest rank cannot be awarded to Lessing; while, as a revolutionary power, as a shaping and organizing force, he has scarcely his equal in history. He was a Reformer, in the truest sense of the word, and bore himself through life with the same independence, the same dignity, the same simple reliance on truth, as Luther at Worms. Notwithstanding the ephemeral nature of many of his controversies, the greater part of them may still be read with profit; for the truth that is in them belongs to no time or country. While some of his contemporaries—Klopstock and Wieland, for example—are gradually losing their prominence in German literature, the

place which Lessing fills is becoming larger and more important. In one of his early letters to his father, he says: "If I could become the German Molière, I should gain an immortal name." He did more than this: he became the German Lessing! (pp. 232-33)

Bayard Taylor, "Lessing," in his Studies in German Literature, G. P. Putnam's Sons, 1879, pp. 200-33.

WILLIAM LYON PHELPS (essay date 1889)

[*An American critic and educator, Phelps was for over forty years a lecturer on English literature at Yale. His early study* The Beginnings of the English Romantic Movement *(1893) is still considered an important work, and his* Essays on Russian Novelists *(1911) was one of the first influential studies in English of the Russian realists. In the following excerpt from his study of Lessing's place in the history of the German drama, Phelps extols his subject's combination of aesthetic, critical, and dramatic talents.*]

Up to the middle of the eighteenth century, German literature was slavishly imitative. . . . The literary autocrat of the time, Gottsched, was a fair example of the prevailing tendencies of thought. This man, who looked upon originality with horror, who styled Shakspere a barbarian, and claimed that one must follow French rules to produce a work of genius, was worshiped as the literary oracle. No matter upon what subject he chose to open his lips, the cry resounded everywhere, "A Daniel! a second Daniel come to judgment!" Truly it was the dark hour before the dawn.

Even while the harsh clamor of Gottsched and his idolaters was at its height, a new figure stepped out on the stage. Lessing has been called the Luther of German literature. As the great Protestant released men from the bondage of forms and ceremonies, so Lessing, by rebelling against the tyranny of the French rules of art, showed his countrymen both by precept and by practice what a national drama should be. The criticisms of poetry and painting in the **Laokoon** and the dramatic theories expounded and developed in the **Hamburgische Dramaturgie,** opened up endless vistas of thought and imagination, and roused to life all the sleeping energies of the German mind. These books made epochs. The **Laokoon** revealed the beauty of the Greek art and literature in their simple grandeur; and the **Dramaturgie** struck off forever the degrading shackles with which the French had bound poetry and the drama. These books prepared the way for that great burst of splendor, which includes not simply the best, but the only German literature that is well known outside of the Fatherland.

It is not easy to exaggerate the difficulties with which Lessing had to contend. As Mr. Lowell says, "He began his career at a period when we cannot say that German literature was at its lowest ebb, only because there had not yet been any flood-tide." [see excerpt dated 1867]. Lessing saw that before any change for the better could be introduced, the worship of the French must be abandoned. But Gottsched and his shallow school were regarded as the Supreme Court of literature. It is true that Lessing was not the first to attack that autocrat. The so-called Swiss school had made a fierce onslaught on him; but their zeal vastly exceeded their knowledge, and their own theories were carried to absurd excesses. Lessing had to combat the *consensus* of the men of letters. But there were other obstacles of a wholly different nature which cast a dark shadow over a life that was otherwise so bright and cheerful. Lessing's life was a constant struggle with poverty. The king could have removed this difficulty and saved Germany from a lasting disgrace. But Frederick, who professed to be the friend of the literary man as ardently as modern politicians profess to be the friend of the workingman, was strangely blind to the great literary movement going on before his eyes. He saw no political energy in German literature. The French and Italian theatres at Berlin were handsomely supported by the crown; the German theatre was a booth on the public street. The king was an enthusiast in French literature; he added no small number of wretched French verses to the large stock already in existence; he worshiped Voltaire even while he hated him; but for the literature and men of letters of his own country, Frederick had nothing but contempt.

Lessing, however, combined the fiery zeal of the reformer with the deep insight of the scholarly critic. He seems to have seen clearly the possibilities of the future. He never wavered in his purpose to aid the development. Added to his natural wisdom and keenness of vision, his knowledge of the literature and art of the ancients was remarkably profound. With the rich storehouse of Greek literature at his full command, he determined to lay a foundation for the German classical movement. He recognized what no man of his time had seen, that the French, who claimed to be in the direct line of the Aristotelian succession, were really out of harmony with the spirit of the great master. The French, in their ambition to follow the rules of Aristotle, had forgotten that the body was more than the raiment. They abhorred Shakspere as the Greeks and Romans abhorred the barbarians. It enraged them to think that the blood and thunder plays of that ruffian should be compared with the tragedies of Racine and Corneille. But Lessing was convinced not only that Shakspere was greater than the French dramatists, but that he was in spirit a truer follower of Aristotle. To Lessing belongs the honor of making Shakspere a familiar name in Germany. Weisse had translated some of Shakspere's plays; and later Wieland made some translations, and Augustus Schlegel in his Vienna lectures brought out the beauties of the great Englishman; but Lessing introduced Shakspere to the popular heart. Gottsched declared that the way to produce a work of genius was to follow iron-clad rules. Lessing studied what genius had done, to discover the principles of its success. He wrote one sentence that gives a key to all his critical work. "Much would in theory appear unanswerable, if the achievements of genius had not proved the contrary."

Lessing determined to make his countrymen understand that the literature of Germany was at the lowest possible standard and would remain there so long as it blindly followed French dictation. By regarding the French tragedy as the summit of artistic achievement, the way to a knowledge and appreciation of Shakspere was hopelessly closed; so that the Germans were struggling to have a literature without the aid of the influence most necessary. Lessing showed that there could be a great German literature; and he showed it in two ways. He proved it in theory by his unanswerable criticisms, and he proved it in practice by composing two master-pieces of dramatic construction, *Minna von Barnhelm* and *Emilia Galotti*.

Minna von Barnhelm was the first German comedy of any importance and ranks to-day as the best one in the language. It is Lessing's greatest play. It has none of that weakness which is so manifest in all of his other dramas. The characters move and speak like beings of flesh and blood. The construction of the play and the development of the plot are almost perfection. The scenes succeed each other in logical order, and the unity of the piece as a work of art—the only unity worth anything—

is sustained throughout. Its humor is irresistible, but is like its author in being robust rather than delicate and subtle. The comedy is almost flawless and ranks on a par with the classic English comedies of Sheridan and Goldsmith. Lessing's experiences in Saxony during the Seven Years' War gave him abundance of material for *Minna* and the play came just at the time to awaken popular enthusiasm.

Emilia Galotti is a tragedy full of native power and that rises in some scenes to a high pitch of dramatic intensity, as in the dialogue between Claudia and Marinelli where the words are repeated again and again with cumulative effect. . . . Like *Minna*, the play is a master-piece of construction, but it is not so great as a tragedy as the other is in the comic field. The character of the heroine is not consistent; and the gravest dramatic fault is committed by there being no sufficient cause to bring about the climax. Yet with all its defects, the play bears on it the stamp of genius, and still holds a place on the German stage. It revolutionized the German tragedy, and by indicating correct methods of dramatic composition, it became an inspiration for the production of greater plays in the future. For the first time, the German people found themselves in possession of a great tragedy. . . . (pp. 198-202)

But Lessing was not a creative genius of the first order. His dramatic pieces all smell of the lamp. His plays are constructed rather than created. They exhibit too plainly the evidences of hard study and careful workmanship. How totally different, for example, is *Emilia Galotti* from *Macbeth*! The former is constructed with almost painful exactness: the tragic effects are studied. *Macbeth* reads as if it had sprung into existence in its present form: as if the play had been composed in a "literary frenzy," in a transport of imaginative passion. Lessing's other dramas are by no means ideal ones. In *Miss Sara Sampson* he showed that the playwright need not confine himself to court scenes and noble personages; an opinion which it is needless to say was common at the time. This play was at one period widely popular in Germany; but it is too close an imitation of the English drama of that time; it is characterized by the English tendency to cheap moralizing and it is lachrymose enough to suit the most sentimental; it is also artificial, and often drags in interest, in some places becoming positively dull. The character Marwood is evidently from the original Millwood in the English play *George Barnwell*: a play that once had a fabulous reputation, but which one reads nowadays with a smile; it is one of those intolerable plays that are written with a distinct ethical purpose and which are made up of moral platitudes and melo-dramatic situations.

The chief reason why Lessing's dramas are so unsatisfactory, is because he was no poet. Many of his admirers would make him one, but the effort is vain. His nature was of too logical a cast and too strongly marked by shrewd common sense, to vibrate sympathetically to poetic inspiration. The phases of human nature reflected in his plays we recognize instantly as true pictures; but there are great elements of character he never reflects at all. He strikes the chords with a firm and true touch, but he does not sound the deepest notes of human experience. In his hatred of obscurity, he failed to appreciate the power of mystery. If his characters are represented as sad, there is always a distinct reason given: if they appear as passionate, there is always an evident cause for their passion. Lessing's plays make no attempt to probe into the mysteries of life. A nameless melancholy, a heart-consuming yet vague passion, such as is portrayed in [Johann Wolfgang von Goethe's] *Faust*, was beyond the range of Lessing's dramatic power.

But Lessing the critic is another man than Lessing the play-wright. The latter arouses our admiration, but rarely our enthusiasm: the former keeps us in perpetual surprise by the penetration of his thought and the charm of his style. The world has seen many better dramas than Lessing's best; but few men have had that peculiar combination of talents which made him so great a critic. May we not explain the inferiority of his creative ability in the same manner in which he explained Shakspere's mediocrity as an actor? . . . [Perhaps Lessing's] reflections on the playwrights' art were the more profound, because he had so much less genius for it than for dramatic criticism. In logical battles, he marshals his arguments with all the skill of an experienced general. He uses the same plan that the great Theban introduced in military tactics: he selects a weak point in the array of the antagonist, and by concentrating the mass of his strength at that place, the whole line of his opponent appears in confusion and disorder. His armies of arguments succeed each other with cumulative force, all bristling with the keen and polished weapons of his wit and satire.

The *Laokoon,* in which Lessing showed that the laws governing poetry and painting are not identical, was the work which revealed its author's critical genius to Germany. In the course of his reasoning, he brought out the beauty of the Greek literature and its superiority over the Latin. Men turned once more to Homer and Sophokles; and in the light of Lessing's genius, read the great poets as if for the first time. The effect produced on German poetry was incalculable. Descriptive poetry had been the most common and the most generally admired; it scarcely survived the *Laokoon.*

But the *Hamburgische Dramaturgie*—the dramatic papers written for the Hamburg theater—is the most important critical work of Lessing's. . . . (pp. 202-04)

Lessing began these papers with criticisms of the acting as well as of the plays; but after some visits from irate actresses, he felt compelled to abandon this part of his task. There were two great ends in view in Lessing's masterly criticisms in the *Dramaturgie.* He meant to destroy utterly the supremacy of the French drama and to show that their boasted rules were not, as they had claimed, the rules of the ancients; and in the second place, to build up the German stage by expounding the true Greek standards. He was eminently fitted for his task. His learning and command over it were phenomenal, and surprised his contemporaries beyond measure; his dramatic experience had been wide and varied; and the critical bent of his mind had been trained to perfection by his studies in literature and in the history and theory of aesthetics.

His attack on the French theater was fierce and unsparing. The general worship of the French provoked Lessing to the highest degree; but owing to the constitution of his mind, it must have acted as an inspiration. No man ever enjoyed a controversy more keenly than Lessing. The temptation to indulge in that luxury was something he was rarely able to resist. The great literary Frenchman of the time was a constant target for Lessing's shafts of wit. To-day we rarely think of Voltaire as a playwright; but among Lessing's contemporaries his dramas were exalted and extolled beyond measure. To an acute and hostile critic they present many vulnerable points of attack, and Lessing riddled them without mercy. His famous comparison between the Ghost in *Hamlet* and the Ghost in *Semiramis* was a master stroke of criticism, and by itself was enough to ruin the reputation of Voltaire's play. The genius displayed in the comedies of Molière, Lessing fully recognized and gave it its due. Upon Corneille, however, he made many vigorous

attacks. He proved that stickler for artistic rules to be a truant from Aristotle. Lessing accepted the Greek theory that the aim of tragedy is to excite pity (Mitleid) and fear (Schauder); and he showed that the fear is not for others, but for ourselves. The French had substituted *terror* for both of these emotions; and Corneille had so far misinterpreted Aristotle and misunderstood his theory of the drama as to imagine that either of these emotions by itself was sufficient foundation for a tragedy.

Lessing's destructive criticism of the French was as effective as he could have dared to hope; it utterly destroyed Gallic influence on the German stage. Schlegel, in his Vienna lectures, made a passing allusion which shows how completely the work had been done. He said "When the *Dramaturgie* was published, we Germans had scarcely any but French tragedies upon our stages, and the extravagant predilection for them as classical models had not then been combated. At present the national taste has declared itself so decidedly against them, that we have nothing to fear of an illusion in that quarter" [see excerpt dated 1808]. This was spoken in 1808.

But the essential aim of Lessing's criticisms was not to tear down but to build up; it was well worth while to clear away false notions of the drama; but the task was chiefly valuable only that a new superstructure might be built on the right foundation. Lessing's work was not half done when he had pointed out the mistakes of the French; he then developed his own theories of dramatic art, based on a liberal interpretation of Aristotle. In his discussions of the three unities, he exhibited his great common sense as well as his profound learning. The unities had been a stumbling block to the French. . . . Lessing maintained that Aristotle never intended to lay down hard and fast lines for the unities of time and place. They were observed in the Greek dramas, owing to the presence of the chorus, which could not be well conceived to appear at times far apart or in distant places: but that he meant to lay down an absolute *dictum* for all time to come, Lessing declared was absurd. The only unity necessarily required in every dramatic composition is the Unity of Action: which means simply the logical unity of the piece; the scenes must succeed each other in logical order, and every event must be accounted for. Lessing's own dramas are as good examples as can be found of the Unity of Action. By clearing up this subject, he began a broad and true foundation for the German theater.

Lessing's discussion of the great question, Should there be an ethical purpose in the drama? shows how profoundly philosophical was his conception of tragic art. Few who seriously reflect on the subject will maintain to-day that a tragedy ought to teach a direct moral lesson; but in Lessing's time contemporary thought gave unhesitatingly an affirmative answer to the question. The moral tacked on at the end of the tragedies was regarded as the *raison d' etre* of the whole play. Voltaire boasted that in his *Semiramis* horrible deeds were punished in extraordinary ways. Lessing proved such an idea to be a fundamental error. He argued that the effect was far more powerful if crime and punishment were bound together in the ordinary chain of events. This view of the working of natural law in the drama is exactly in harmony with the modern spirit. (pp. 205-08)

Lessing's idea of the relation between the drama and historical truth was far ahead of the prevailing conception of the time; it fairly staggered the German literary public. Many had expressed the opinion that the poet must strictly follow history in his representation of events. Lessing showed that there was no reasonable ground for such an idea; the dramatist must be faithful to history in his portrayal of the characters, otherwise there would be no assignable reason for their having the names given them. But as regards minor matters, the poet may alter details to suit the plot, so long as they are consistent and have an appearance of truth. . . . Lessing also combated the general notion that one aim of the drama was to preserve the memory of great men; showing the narrowness of such a conception, and its cramping effect on the production of great plays. He concluded this subject by remarking that poetic truth is of more importance than historical truth in giving us a knowledge of human nature; in the works of the great masters of tragedy we see reflected more clearly than anywhere else the character of man.

Lessing's influence on English literature has not been very noticeable. It was through the *Dramaturgie* that he began to impress literary Europe, but he was scarcely known in England before 1830. His influence on the English drama is of no visible proportions, mainly because there has been no great dramatic movement in English literature since the time in which Lessing wrote. . . . But the English speaking people ought to feel a special interest in studying the life and works of Lessing: he was greatly influenced by English models; and his criticisms of Shakspere are certainly not the least valuable part of his writings.

Lessing's literary style is like the man; straight-forward, virile, combative, at times sarcastic, yet always betraying great depths of sympathy. Every line he wrote has the ring of sincerity. In a letter to his father, he said: "If I write at all, it is not possible for me to write otherwise than just as I think and feel." These noble words are the echo of his life. To Lessing the pursuit of truth was not a duty, it was a passion. Narrowness and intolerance were hateful to him. He loved truth for its own sake, and it made his blood boil to see truth distorted and used to advertise false ideas. He had that freedom from prejudice which characterizes every great critic. But he was preëminently a man of strong convictions. (pp. 208-09)

> *William Lyon Phelps, "Lessing and the German Drama," in* The New Englander and Yale Review, *Vol. XV, No. CCXXXIV, September, 1889, pp. 198-209.*

T. W. ROLLESTON (essay date 1889)

[*Rolleston was an Irish poet and literary scholar. In the following excerpt, he discusses at length four of Lessing's most important works.*]

[Lessing] was struck down by a dangerous fever in the summer of 1764, and his convalescence was slow. But this period of stillness and contemplation, in which death had to be contemplated too, laid on his vehement spirit a touch which brought it the delicacy and serenity it had lacked.

> "All changes of temperament," he wrote to Ramler on the 5th of August, "are, I think, connected with operations that take place in our animal organization. The serious epoch of my life is approaching; I am beginning to be a man, and flatter myself that in the heat of this fever I have raved out the last remnant of my youthful follies."

A fortnight later, he wrote to the same friend that he still finds some difficulty in settling to his work again. "A sorry life! when one is up, and yet vegetates; it is looked upon as healthy without being so. Before my illness I was working with such

a spirit and energy as I have rarely known. I cannot recall it again, try how I will."

The work on which he had been so pleasantly engaged before his illness, and which he wrote mostly in the little summerhouse of his garden, was *Minna von Barnhelm.* This noble play was the direct outcome of his life in Breslau; the story it contains had been, in substance, enacted under his own eyes in the inn "Zum Goldenen Gans." A Prussian officer, Major von Tellheim, for whose character Kleist furnished several traits, has been dismissed at the close of the Seven Years' War, under the imputation of having attempted a fraud on the Prussian War Treasury. The charge was based on an act of generosity towards some Saxon townspeople from whom he had been required to levy, in cash, a cruel war-contribution. He had advanced, from his own means, the sum which he could not bring himself to wring from their necessities, taking their bills in exchange; and those bills, which the Prussian War Office should have seen honoured, were looked on there as merely a bribe to Tellheim for having exacted less than he could have done. Tellheim, a man of an almost morbid sense of honour, resolves, while the investigation he has challenged is pending, to have no communication with a wealthy Saxon lady, Minna von Barnhelm, to whom he had become betrothed during the war, and whose interest in him was first awakened by the very act of generosity towards her countrymen for which he is now suffering. Suspecting how the case stands, she seeks him out in Berlin, finds him sunk in want and dejection, and endeavours to remove the scruples which forbid him to link his stained career with hers. But he is unmoved until she tells him that her flight to him has caused her to be disinherited and disowned, and that she is alone and helpless unless he will protect her. Tellheim's instant revulsion of feeling is now exhibited with exquisite skill, and his endeavours to meet the problems thus forced upon him awaken both our love and our laughter. At this point arrives a letter from the king, who has been investigating Tellheim's case. It admits the justice of his claims, which the Treasury has orders to honour, and with a flattering acknowledgment of his past services, reinstates him in his rank in the Prussian army. It is now Minna's turn to punish him, to his astonishment and dismay, by imitating the petty punctilio which had made him reject her when the worldly advantages of the union had seemed to be all on his side. At last the arrival of the uncle, by whom Minna had fictitiously represented herself to be disowned, puts an end to his distress. This graceful story is worked out through a number of episodes ingeniously and naturally contrived to keep the interest in action and character alive. The construction of the play is almost faultless, and the minor characters—Tellheim's stubbornly faithful soldier-servant, the mean and inquisitive landlord, Minna's vivacious maid, and the rest, are most happily drawn; the types indeed conventional, but the presentation of them full of originality and humour. The manner, too, in which Frederick is introduced—a majestic impersonation of justice, never appearing in the play, but felt in it throughout as a supreme and beneficent influence—forms a noble expression of Lessing's reverence for his great king.

Minna von Barnhelm was a literary phenomenon of great significance in its day. It was the Rossbach of German literature—the death-blow of French prestige and influence in that sphere. Lessing himself had rarely ventured hitherto to give German names to the persons in his comedies—so fundamentally unfit for artistic purposes did Germans consider the realities that lay nearest to them. Now for Orontes, Lisettes, Theophans, Damons, we have Tellheim, Werner, Franziska, Minna—we can hardly conceive the state of things in which this was a portent, but such it was. The army had never appeared on the stage before, except as represented by some cowardly braggart: on it, too, Lessing laid his ennobling hand. The Franco-German drama of the *Gottschedianer* was a purely artificial and foreign product. It had refinement, elevation, wit; but it had absolutely no connection with the life of the German people. But *Minna* was German through and through—events, characters, manners, sentiments; and on all these was shed that ideal light which the popular and native literature of Germany had theretofore so deeply lacked. Nor is the interest of the play purely literary. The enormous service which the wars of Frederick had rendered towards the solidifying of German national sentiment had been largely annulled by the intense animosity between Saxony and Prussia which had unavoidably arisen in their progress. In Lessing's reconciling drama—the work of one who was Saxon by birth and Prussian by conviction—the grace and spirit of Saxony vanquish the perverse, if honourable, obstinacy of Prussia, and national enmities are lost in individual affections. Never surely did a citizen of one country desert it for another, and a hostile one, with such advantage to both.

All that was effected in *Minna* might, of course, have been conceived by any one, and the times were full of such ideas. But to present them with a power that compelled attention, and dissolved prejudice, was work for a Lessing. Frederick the Great, one laments to find, never could be persuaded to read the greatest German drama of his day; but it was soon read and acted throughout all his dominions and beyond them, and the day when it will cease to be so is not at hand yet. It is true that it contains no profound study of human nature—that even on their own plane of interest the characters impress us rather as manufactures than as creations—that the touches which suggest that they have a life outside of the action of the drama are wanting. But if manufacture, they are the manufacture of a most skilful craftsman, and the play remains a striking proof of how very nearly the results of poetic genius may be attained by a high critical intelligence backed by a moral character of true nobility and refinement. The atmosphere of the play is as wholesome as we can find in literature, and it is written with a genial, sunny power, which tells that it was the fruit of cheerful and hopeful days.

Not only Lessing's best creative, but also (in the sphere of *belles lettres*) his best critical work was mainly produced in Breslau. He had been greatly occupied with antiquarian studies, and especially with the theories advanced by Spence, Count Caylus, and others, as to the relation between the plastic arts and poetry as illustrated in antiquity. The prevailing opinion was that the excellence of a poem was in direct proportion to the number of subjects it afforded for pictorial representation, and that each art found its highest expression in imitating the effects of the other. Nothing could be more contrary to Lessing's general principles of art, and he began to set down his ideas on the subject in his usual way—defining, examining, and confuting the views of various authors in succession, and so advancing towards truth by a method which has all the charm of a dramatic action. While thus engaged, an epoch-making book was published, Winckelmann's *History of Ancient Art*—a work reckoned the primary cause of the movement which soon doubled and trebled the hours given to Greek in all the classical schools of Germany, and made that language what it is now—the basis of her higher culture. Lessing read it with profound delight; but found that Winckelmann had advanced what he considered a false theory as to the period of the execution of the famous Laocoon group. Moreover, in a previous

work of Winckelmann's, the same group had been criticized, in connection with the account of the incident given by Virgil, on the assumption that the two arts are fundamentally one in their limits and capacities.

Taking, then, Winckelmann on the Laocoon as his point of departure—a wise choice, for anything he could write on Winckelmann just then was sure of an attentive hearing—he proceeded to develop his views on the general relation of the plastic and literary arts. Lessing shows that the material of the poet is Time, of the artist, Space—the latter represents objects, the former operations, or objects through operations, even as Homer describes the shield of Achilles by telling us how it was made. Then, from the special nature of the material in which it works, Lessing proceeds to deduce in much detail the true conditions and aims of each art. Music, too, and even dancing, were to have been treated in subsequent parts, whereof only some notes and fragments exist; so that the whole work would have offered a complete science of æsthetics.

The first part, that which alone was fully carried out by Lessing, is chiefly concerned with the vital distinctions which exist between poetry and the pictorial arts in their treatment of visible objects or actions. Virgil represents Laocoon as screaming with anguish in the coils of the serpents. But does the sculptured Laocoon scream? Not at all; the only sound which his lips can utter is a deep, suppressed groan. Winckelmann appears to reckon this difference to the credit of the sculptor—the latter conceiving his subject in a more heroic and dignified light than the poet. Lessing, of course, has no difficulty in showing that the loudest and most unrestrained expressions of grief or pain were not thought, in antiquity, to be inconsistent with the loftiest heroism. But yet the difference is there—and is it to be set down to mere chance? By no means. The plastic artist can treat only a single instant in all the life of Laocoon—shall he select and eternalize one in which the features must be so distorted by the wide opening of the mouth as to make every spectator turn away his eyes in disgust? The end of every art is pleasure; the plastic arts can gain this end through the representation of beautiful form, and of that alone; for every ugly thing becomes unendurable when rendered permanent in painting or sculpture. But the poet, on the other hand, is not confined to the representation of the beautiful. Nothing compels him to concentrate his picture in a single instant. He can relate from beginning to end the details of every action of which he treats. He can bring it before us in all its successive changes; and each change, which would cost the artist a separate work, costs him but a single touch. Even though one of these touches, regarded in itself alone, should displease the imagination of the hearer, yet we have been prepared for it by what went before, or the effect is softened by what follows; we cannot isolate it, and in its proper place and connection it may be of the utmost artistic value. Virgil's Laocoon screams, but this screaming Laocoon is the very man whom we have known and loved as the wise patriot, the affectionate father. We refer his *clamores horrendi*, not to his character, but to his unendurable suffering. This suffering is all we hear in his screams, and by these alone could the poet make us realize it.

Again, Poetry and the visual arts each aim at the production of an illusion in the mind of the hearer or spectator. Poetry does this by means of arbitrary signs to which a certain meaning is conventionally attached—viz, letters and words. But Art effects the same end by *natural* signs—signs which really imitate the thing intended to be signified. Let Art, then, recognize its own sphere and abide in it! Its business is to represent the visible by the visible; not, after the fashion of the allegoristic painters, to use line and colour as a sort of handwriting for the conveyance of other things than those which they can directly represent. And Poetry, too—let it remember that if its arbitrary signs are to create illusion, (as they can do by means of rhythm, metaphor, and the skilful handling of language,) they must not be used to give the impression of any object by describing in succession all its parts, by endeavouring to give the effect of Space through the medium of Time. We can see a statue at a glance, but we cannot read at a glance a detailed description of a beautiful face and form; we have forgotten the beginning before we have reached the end, and no total impression remains on the mind. The business of Poetry is action; if it would show us what a thing is like, let it tell us what it *does*. Homer brings the idea of a beautiful woman more vividly before us by telling us how the old men swore, as Helen passed them, that she was worth all the wars that had been waged for her sake, than Ariosto does in his forty lines of minute description of all Alcina's charms.

Not all of Lessing's conclusions have been established. His knowledge of literature, ancient and modern, was vast, and he wielded it with the ease of perfect mastery. But his knowledge of art was far from being equally complete. The museum at Dresden, which contains much that is interesting but little that is great, was the most important collection of antique sculpture that he had seen. The Laocoon he knew only through engravings, and a plaster cast of the head of the principal figure. Painting had never interested him much; he doubted whether the discovery of oil-painting was an advantage to art—he doubted, indeed, whether colour of any kind could compensate for the loss of the greater freedom and spirit which he found in un-coloured drawings. It is not surprising, then, that he should define the object of art too narrowly as the representation of beautiful form. Beauty consists, he asserted, in the harmony of parts—ideal beauty is form deprived of all that mars this harmony. This ideal is most nearly realized in the human body; this, then, is the true subject for the artist. Portraiture has a certain place in art—for a good portrait is not a mere imitation of an individual face, it is the ideal of that individual face. But "the painter of landscapes and flowers" is told that genius has no part in his work—Lessing could not see how one could make an ideal landscape, and where there is no ideal there is no art.

Lessing's efforts, therefore, to point out its true province to art are much less successful than those in which he does the same office for literature. The artist's object is really not other or narrower than the poet's. It is to represent *life*—life in its widest sense, moral or physical, human, animal, or elemental—so far as it can be directly represented by form or colour. Directly represented—this is a sound limitation of Lessing's; and, of course, the fact that the artist has to deal with visual appearances, not scientific realities, and the necessity he is under of choosing but a single instant to portray, will suggest other limitations which only bad taste will violate. But why should the representation of what is ugly or detestable be more strictly forbidden to the artist than to the poet? Both are forbidden to isolate and dwell upon any manifestation of the forces, organic or moral, which make for corruption and death. But both may represent these forces in due contrast and subordination to those which oppose them; and, as a matter of fact, the great schools of art in all lands and ages have taken this liberty without hesitation. Beauty has never been their aim; it has followed them unsought. It will always follow every faithful effort to represent the life of Nature, and can no more be

exhaustively defined as proportion in form than as harmony of colour.

But whatever may be said against the soundness of this or that conclusion of Lessing's, the effect of the *Laocoon* was stimulating and illuminating in the highest degree, and it had the immediate and salutary effect of putting an end to the vapid descriptive poetry with which the Swiss school was flooding Germany. (pp. 99-109)

[In] April, 1767, we find [Lessing] established in Hamburg. On the 22nd the National Theatre was opened, and on the 1st day of May appeared the first number of the famous periodical known as the *Hamburgische Dramaturgie*. (p. 117)

For two years the *Hamburgische Dramaturgie* continued to appear, and in its hundred numbers Lessing's whole theory of the drama was unfolded in the very manner which suited him best—through the criticism of concrete examples of the art with which he dealt. There was no sort of orderly sequence in the work, taken as a whole; it simply kept pace with the performances of the theatre. But it tried each drama in accordance with fixed and coherent principles, well thought out in Lessing's mind before he began to write. His central objects were to exhibit the true theory of the drama as fixed by Aristotle—to show how the French school, in its supposed rigid adherence to Greek canons, had utterly misapprehended and misapplied them—to hold up Shakspere, who knew nothing of these canons, as the true heir of the greatness of the Greeks, and to inspire the German drama with a bold and native spirit, which should give it a place in its own right beside those of Greece and England. The Greek drama had been supposed to obey those unities of time and place, the slavish adherence to which had led to so many absurdities on the French stage. Lessing shows that it is simply the existence of the chorus in the Greek drama which prescribes these unities: if the action has to be witnessed throughout by a body of persons who cannot be supposed to go to any great distance from their own homes, or to assemble on more than one occasion, it is clear that it must transact itself in one day and on one spot. Abolish the chorus, and where is the necessity for those unities which the French, proud of wearing as fetters the laws which with the Greeks arose from an inward necessity, endeavoured to force upon Europe as fundamental laws of the drama? Even the Greeks, Lessing might have remarked, did not observe these laws where the inward necessity ceased to exist. In the *Eumenides* of Æschylus, the chorus of Furies is represented as chasing Orestes about from place to place, the action lasting over several days, and the scene shifting from Delphi to Athens. The constraint of the unities of time and place was however, he observes, so turned to account by the genius of the Greeks that they won by it far oftener than they lost. It led them of necessity to intensify passion, to banish all digression and accident, and thus to guard the one true and essential unity which the drama is everywhere bound to observe—the unity of action.

The drama, Lessing considered, can go no step outside the laws laid down by Aristotle without going wrong. What then are these laws? That of the unity of action is the chief—the fable must be coherent, its parts duly subordinated, and each making for an end common to all. Again, characters in the drama must be types, not individuals—the spectator loses sympathy if he feels that the action is influenced by idiosyncrasies. Neither a perfectly innocent nor a perfectly evil character must be made the victim of a tragic fate—in the one case the moral sense is wounded, in the other the sympathetic emotions, which it is the motive of tragedy to excite, are not awakened. Lessing considers at great length, in dealing with Weisse's play of Richard III., the famous passage in which Aristotle has laid it down as the aim of Tragedy to "effect, by pity and fear, the purifying of such passions." He brought to bear on this obscure passage a most fruitful principle of interpretation. Aristotle, he argued, must everywhere be interpreted by himself—let us not suppose that we can be sure of his meaning in the Poetics until we have searched for light upon it from the Rhetoric and the Ethics. In the first place Corneille, and other writers, had erred in translating the word φόβος, Fear, as if it meant Terror (Schrecken). The latter is a passion, rather of the nerves than of the spirit, into which we may be surprised by the spectacle of some atrocious savagery or wickedness. But Fear, φόβος, is elsewhere stated by Aristotle to be felt only in witnessing the calamities of men of the same order as ourselves. And, again, Aristotle declares that a true tragic fable should inspire φόβος by the mere narration, without any spectacle at all. It is clear, then, that by φόβος Aristotle meant to denote a feeling which has more of the nature of sympathy with the sufferer than of terror at the tragic deed. And it is easy to see to what extravagances of revolting conception Corneille's false rendering of the words of Aristotle must give rise. It did, in fact, give rise to them in the works of Corneille himself, and for this reason Lessing denies him the title of the Great, and proposes to substitute that of the Monstrous or the Gigantesque.

Again, pity and fear are to effect the purifying—of what? Of all the passions of man, of his whole emotional nature, says Corneille. We are to be taught by tragic examples to shun excessive or evil passions. But this is not what Aristotle says. Pity and fear are to purify passions akin to themselves. And what is the meaning of this purification? It is something which must be effected, not by a didactic example, but by a moral influence. According to Aristotle, virtue lies in a mean between two extremes. The κάθαρσις he speaks of means the transformation of the untrained passions of pity and fear into virtuous dispositions. And this is plainly effected when he who feels too little of these emotions is made to feel more, and he who feels too much is made to feel less. It may be added that it is also a purifying of the passions when they are rightly directed; when we are led to pity what is truly pitiable, to fear what it truly behoves us to fear.

Lessing agrees with the popular view so far as it attributes an ethical sense, that of purification, *Reinigung,* to κάθαρσις. But this is not the only sense it may have. It may mean the *purging away,* not of unwholesome elements *from* the passions, but of the very passions themselves. The dramatist is first to excite them in the mind of the spectator, then to tranquillize and subdue them. In this view Aristotle would be regarded as describing simply the effect of the drama on the feelings of the spectator while he sat in the theatre—not any permanent influence on his moral character. And for this view there is a great deal to be said. It is admirably illustrated by the greatest and most complete tragic work which has reached us from antiquity—the *Oresteia* of Æschylus. Never was a dramatic action more filled with motives of pity and fear, crime breeding crime, and vengeance vengeance while innocence and righteousness seem hopelessly entangled in the fatal sequence. Yet at the close of the trilogy we see the deluge of guilt and woe gradually sink away, the sun breaks out again, the firm, habitable land of a sound social order where men can live and work in peace begins to appear, and the Furies, mysterious and hideous instruments of divine wrath, become the protecting deities of a redeemed world. And there are even subtler ways in which the same end may be reached. The conclusion of a

drama may be as calamitous as it is possible to conceive, and yet the emotions of pity and fear may be counterbalanced by others which arise in the course of the tragic action. What can be more calamitous than the fate of the Antigone of Sophocles, of the Cordelia of Shakspere? Yet Cordelia and Antigone were true to themselves, to their own beautiful natures. In this lies a spiritual victory which subdues our sense of their visible overthrow.

This view of Aristotle's meaning, which is substantially Goethe's, did not occur to Lessing. If it had done so he would probably have considered it, and with justice, a less natural interpretation of Aristotle's language than his own. But it is certainly a possible one, and one which expresses admirably the actual character of the greatest works of the ancient and modern drama.

Even at the date of the *Hamburgische Dramaturgie* Lessing had to complain of the rise of a school which, because he had exploded the French rules of dramatic art, thought it might be as lawless and capricious as it pleased. No greater mistake could have been made from Lessing's point of view. Genius may disregard existing laws, if it perceives a higher end which may be thus attained. But we shall question it rigorously as to whether it has any such end; we shall demand that, in disobeying laws heretofore approved, it shall embody and suggest deeper ones. A series of vividly conceived situations is not necessarily a drama; and herein lies the condemnation of such plays as "Götz von Berlichingen," which, on its publication some four years afterwards, Lessing seriously thought of attacking as a typical example of the errors of the new school.

It would be impossible within our limits to give anything like an adequate account of the wonderful body of criticisms collected in the *Hamburgische Dramaturgie.* Let us be content, then, with having briefly indicated something of their spirit, and proceed with our narrative. (pp. 118-28)

On the 11th of August, 1778, Lessing wrote to his brother Karl:—

> Many years ago I sketched out a drama whose subject has a kind of analogy with these present controversies, which I little dreamt of then. If you and Moses [Mendelssohn] think well of it, I shall have the thing printed by subscription, and you can print and distribute the enclosed announcement as soon as possible.

The announcement informs the public that, as Lessing has been compelled to "desist from a work which he has not carried on with that pious cunning with which alone it can be carried on successfully," he has been led by chance to take up an old dramatic attempt, and give it the last finishing touches. (p. 179)

It was natural that the announcement of a new drama by the author who had given the German stage its first great comedy, and its first great tragedy, should excite much interest. And of course this interest was heightened by the suspicion that *Nathan the Wise* would be in some sense a continuation of that religious polemic by which Germany had been so deeply stirred. (pp. 179-80)

The reader will hardly expect to find a great work of art in a drama avowedly produced as an episode in a theological controversy. Nor probably has *Nathan* had many readers who will agree with Düntzer's assertion that, were it not for Lessing's own declarations, no one would suspect the piece to be written with any polemical purpose. The propagandist character of the drama, ethical or speculative, is stamped on every page of it. How could it be otherwise with a work of which its author wrote, that he would be content "if it taught one reader in a thousand to doubt the evidence and universality of his religion?" Lessing, indeed, does himself injustice in this utterance, for although his drama is certainly and recognizably a "Tendenzstück," it is written in no spirit of doubt, nor is it such a spirit that it could tend to nourish in its readers. Rather is it calculated to appease the pain of doubts which may have already arisen, by pointing to unsuspected possibilities of a wider and nobler belief. The insolence and intolerance of the orthodoxy of Lessing's day are indeed portrayed with a polemical emphasis in the character of the Patriarch; but the drama contains worthier representatives of Christianity than this ecclesiastic, and the famous parable of the Three Rings goes rather to show how well a man may serve God in any religion, than how little he can place his faith in one.

But, unquestionably, one of the means by which Lessing in this play tries to combat intolerance and folly, is the weaning of men's minds from the contemplation of earthly things in the light of theological assumptions. The evil attending this attitude of mind is exhibited in different forms, as it makes itself manifest in different types of character. We perceive it in Recha as a useless and aimless enthusiasm; in the Templar, as a cold spiritual pride; in the Patriarch, as a furious bigotry which has killed every sentiment of charity and rectitude. (pp. 180-82)

[The play] is full of wise and weighty *sententiæ*, and the style has nothing of the laconic energy of Lessing's prose dramas; without being exactly diffuse, it has an Oriental tranquillity and leisure well suited to the subject and the scene. But as a drama of action—and that is equivalent to saying, as a *drama*—the piece has many and obvious faults. Except for the wise, humane, calm and yet impassioned nature of the Jew, and the quaint originality and independence of his friend the Dervish, its personages have really neither convictions nor character. The young Templar who comes to Palestine to fight for the Holy Sepulchre while disbelieving, apparently, in the Divinity of Christ; who is prejudiced enough to hold aloof from the family of the Jew whose daughter he has rescued, and philosophic enough to be attracted by him when he finds him to be merely a Deist who goes to the synagogue because his fathers did; who is enraged at the idea that this enlightened and admirable Jew has brought up a Christian infant in his own ideas; and who flings his own Order and cause to the winds and enters Mussulman service, simply because Saladin has spared his life—there is certainly no more impossible figure in dramatic literature. One feels that he only holds together at all by virtue of the fiery temper which he carries with him into all his contradictions. And so dominant is the ethical and philosophical interest in the play, that Lessing has observed none of those rules in the construction of the plot which he insisted upon so forcibly in the *Hamburgische Dramaturgie*. Once the Templar has been won to visit Nathan, there is absolutely no point in the play to which the action tends, no dramatic *nodus* to be unloosed; for the revelation of the Templar's kinship to Saladin and Recha has a purely ethical, not a dramatic significance. The progress of the Templar's love affair with Recha does indeed excite a certain interest the *first* time we witness it. But the plot of a good play should please us as much when we know the end as when we do not; and who can watch with satisfaction the episodes in a love-tale in which he knows that the lovers will turn out to be brother and sister? Lessing was more concerned to show us that it was his own kin from whom the Templar's religious prejudices were severing him, than to provide his drama with an artistically satisfying *dénouement*.

Lessing himself should have taught us better than to call *Nathan* a good drama; but a bad drama may be a noble poem, and as such we shall not easily cease to love it. (pp. 188-89)

> *T. W. Rolleston, in his* Life of Gotthold Ephraim Lessing, *Walter Scott, 1889, 218 p.*

ROBERT WALLER DEERING   (essay date 1902)

[*Deering was an American essayist, academic, and translator who had a special interest in the works of Johann Wolfgang von Goethe and Johann Christoph Friedrich von Schiller. In the following excerpt from his study of* Nathan the Wise, *he suggests what may have prompted Lessing to write this "book for all men and all time."*]

No student of German literature, however modest his aspirations, can afford to pass by Lessing. He is one of Germany's greatest thinkers and teachers, one of the greatest moral and intellectual benefactors of his age and people. He ranks with Luther as one of the great reformers: the one reformed German religion, the other German literature and criticism. Lessing compels our regard, morever, not merely because he was a pioneer, but because he has a power and influence all his own; he was "in advance of his age" in a sense which does not apply to many.

Born of sturdy, clear-headed, intellectual stock, blessed with a vigorous, eager mind, and sound, far-seeing judgment, equipped with learning and culture truly remarkable, ruled by the highest standards of life and character and by a spirit as sweet and gentle as it was brave, inspired by passionate love of truth and unflinching courage in the pursuit of it, endowed with keen perception of the faults and weaknesses of his age, master of a classic style, whose every word is charged with meaning, and of forceful reasoning, whose logic is irresistible, he took and still maintains a most commanding position in the world of German thought and letters.

Today Lessing's opinions are honored perhaps more than those of any other German author, and one often hears that "to go back to Lessing is to advance." It is likely that he has set more people to thinking than any other German writer. Next to his clear-headedness and large-heartedness, his dominant trait is, perhaps, his genuineness and his love of the truth; he is a fearless defender of truth established, and no less a tireless leader in the search for truth yet undiscovered. "If God," he says, "held all truth in His right hand, and in His left nothing but the ever-restless impulse for truth, though with the condition of ever erring, and should say to me 'Choose,' I would humbly fall at His feet and say: 'Father, give me the left; pure truth is for Thee alone.'" The saying is characteristic, for his life was spent in this cause. His other strongest trait is his sweet-tempered cheerfulness, his poise, balance, self-control—call it what we will—which is astonishing when we remember the continued privation, distress, and disappointment which filled his life. (p. 519)

Among Lessing's works his *Nathan the Wise* deserves especial attention, first because, in its beautiful lesson of unselfish humanity, in its noble ideals of religious life and character, it stands unique in literature. No other book but the Bible has treated these great problems of religion and of life, of the relation of man to man and of man to his God, with such power and beauty. It is a book for all men and all time.

Again, it is his greatest work—in a sense his life work, and at the same time one of the most striking examples of intellectual heredity on record. The earliest ancestor we can find was known for his liberal views; the poet's grandfather is remembered for a notable work on *Toleration in Religion*; his father was an able defender of the Reformation and its religious liberty. Lessing himself, as a boy of twenty, takes up this theme in one of his earliest plays, *The Jews*; later it appears again in his *Vindications*; while in *Nathan,* the ripest fruit of his maturest years, it is still the burden of his thought. Lessing and Nathan are twin spirits, inwardly, at least, so alike that who knows the one knows the other. Nowhere else does the singularly strong and beautiful character of the author find such eloquent expression; nowhere else does he urge with such skill and power the great principles of religious liberty and unselfish humanity for which he stands.

Lessing calls *Nathan* the son of my old age, whom polemics helped to bring into the world.'' His reference is to the famous theological controversy which gave rise to the play. As custodian of the ducal library in Wolfenbüttel, Lessing had published valuable contributions to the history of philosophy and religion; among these, and under the general title of *Wolfenbüttel Fragments,* he had edited several rather radical essays on theological questions written by Professor Reimarus of Hamburg. Though he disclaimed the authorship of them and even agreement with them, these papers soon involved him in bitter controversy. Put on his mettle, he expressed his views in several pamphlets, in which Lessing shows himself a broad scholar, a profound thinker, a passionate lover of truth, and the devoted champion of the freedom of thought and conscience. His enemies were worsted and took cowardly refuge behind the authorities, who were induced to forbid his futher writing on theological questions—on the ground that he ''antagonized the principal doctrines of the sacred writings of Christianity.'' Nothing daunted, he determined ''to mount his old pulpit, the stage, to see if they would let him preach undisturbed from there.'' Taking up the unfinished sketch of an old play laid aside years before, he made it into a ''sermon'' such as has no rival save the Sermon on the Mount. With it his plan was ''to play a better joke on the theologians than with ten 'Fragments' more.'' This sermon-drama was *Nathan the Wise.* It is a strange revenge—an olive branch of love and peace to those who were expecting (and deserving) a lash of scorpions. Lessing is a changed man; he is no longer the ''Hotspur of criticism,'' who fights for the love of fight and out of hatred of error. Deep sorrow has fallen upon him; he has lost his wife, his baby, and with them his happiness; he is again alone and more lonely than ever before in all his lonely life; his health is rapidly failing. Though outwardly calm, his heart is broken; he has paid dear for his one short year of happiness, and feels ''tempted to curse the day when he even *wished* to be as happy as other people.'' It is the awful calmness of madness. Yet with superb control he is ''too proud to acknowledge himself unhappy . . . only set the teeth and let the boat drift at the mercy of winds and waves; enough that I will not upset it myself.'' His loneliness has brought him calm and peace at last. Out of the darkness of this bitter grief has come this play so full of sweetness and light. His dominant passion is now no longer criticism of human error, but compassion upon human blindness, sympathy with human weakness. It is the operating surgeon, firm—even stern—but kind, who now deftly wields the knife for the relief of the suffering body.

Lessing's theological quarrel had raised the question: ''What is the essence of religion?'' The character of Nathan is the answer: Faith in God and in the creed of the fathers, whatever that may be, exemplified in a life of loving service and unselfish humanity. ''For the letter killeth, but the spirit giveth life.''

The religion of *Nathan* is also the creed of its author. With him: ''Well-doing is the main thing; belief is only secondary.'' ''It does not concern one's conscience how useful one is, but how useful one *would* be.'' ''It is not agreement in opinions, but agreement in virtuous actions, that renders the world virtuous and happy.'' And what he believed, he lived. In his poverty and disappointment he carried out that cheerful philosophy which teaches us to thank God for the chastening of sorrow, as for the blessing of happiness—for ''as the gold is tried by fire, so the heart is tried by pain.''

For this play, which deals exclusively with religious types, Lessing was most happy in his choice of the time and place of the action. The scene is laid in Jerusalem: the ''holy city'' of the ''chosen people,'' the *Jews,* memorable for the life and death of Christ, the cradle of *Christianity,* now become the residence of the Sultan and the seat of *Mohammedan* government. All the world pressed together there—the East, the West; the Cross and the Crescent floated over Christian, Moslem, Jew, and all the rest. One need only look about and choose. Nor is the time less fitting. It is the reign of the liberal, generous Saladin, the Third Crusade, when the world was full of sectional hate, when bigotry waged war in the name of religion, when sword and simitar ran red with blood under the shadow of the Holy Sepulcher, the tomb of the Prince of Peace! What a time for the portrayal of true toleration, the common brotherhood of man, the pure unselfish love of humanity! (pp. 520-22)

The objection is often heard the Lessing is very unfair in making the Jew and the Mohammedan so good and noble, while his Christian characters are so mean and selfish or wicked. The objection falls, however, when we see the real purpose of the play. It is not a comparison of religions, but of men, not of creeds, to decide which is best, but of different types of human character, to show that men are good or bad independent of their faith. Lessing is not defending Judaism *as such*, but showing that, in spite of prejudice against it, it *can* produce such men as Nathan; he is not attacking Christianity, but the bigotry and meanness of some Christians; showing that it *does* sometimes produce such men as the Patriarch. The play advocates the *spirit* of the religion Christ taught, as against the letter of the so-called Christian creed. Written for Christians it is a rebuke of the *abuses* of Christianity, not of criticism of that religion itself; if it had been written for Jews, the hero would have been a Christian.

Having used Boccaccio's story of the three rings as the soul of his play, Lessing must keep the Jewish hero of that story for the hero of the play.

The greatest reason lies deeper. The Jews have been from time immemorial, ''the chosen people of God'' and, as such, their traditions would naturally lead to narrowness, to national pride, and religious arrogance; in reaching the high plane of broad humanity and tolerance described by the play, the Jew is the one who has most to overcome. He is thus the most heroic— and Lessing but justly recognizes his heroism.

Times have changed since 1780, but principles never change, though men may. The great truths of this play, the noble ideals it sets forth still live, and as long as human nature remains what it is, we shall need to heed its lesson. (p. 528)

Robert Waller Deering, ''Lessing's 'Nathan the Wise','' in The Chautauquan, *Vol. XXXIX, No. 5, February, 1902, pp. 519-28.*

GEORGE SAINTSBURY (essay date 1904)

[Saintsbury has been called the most influential English literary historian and critic of the late nineteenth and early twentieth centuries. His studies of French literature, particularly A History of the French Novel *(1917-19), have established him as a leading authority on such writers as Guy de Maupassant and Honoré de Balzac. Saintsbury adhered to two distinct sets of critical standards: one for the novel and the other for poetry and drama. As a critic of novels, he maintained that "the novel has nothing to do with any beliefs, with any convictions, with any thoughts in the strict sense, except as mere garnishings. Its substance must always be life not thought, conduct not belief, the passions not the intellect, manners and morals not creeds and theories. . . . The novel is . . . mainly and firstly a criticism of life." As a critic of poetry and drama, Saintsbury was a radical formalist who frequently asserted that subject is of little importance, and that "the so-called 'formal' part is of the essence." René Wellek has praised Saintsbury's critical qualities: his "enormous reading, the almost universal scope of his subject matter, the zest and zeal of his exposition," and "the audacity with which he handles the most ambitious and unattempted arguments." In the following excerpt, Saintsbury describes Lessing's critical achievements, particularly as they are reflected in* Laocoon *and* Hamburg Dramaturgy.*]

[That Lessing] was a great critic nobody can deny: but it is perhaps desirable to warn those who come to him knowing something of literary criticism already, and expecting great things in it from him, that they should not raise their expectations too high, and that they should thoroughly master certain preliminary facts. The most important of these is that Lessing's interests were not, as the interests of very great critics almost invariably have been, either wholly literary, or literary first of all, or, as in Aristotle's case, as literary as possible. As it was said of Clarissa that "there is always something that she prefers to the truth," so there is nearly always something that Lessing prefers to literature, constantly as he was occupied with books. Now it is the theatre; now it is art—especially art viewed from the side of archaeology; now it is classical scholarship of the minuter kind; now philosophy or theology; now it is morals; not unfrequently it is more, or fewer, or all of these things together, which engage his attention while literature is left out in the cold.

The most curious instance of his moral preoccupation (which, as the commonest and that with which we are most familiar, we may get rid of first) has reference to Marmontel's *conte* of *Soliman the Second*. Lessing rather liked Marmontel, who had been civil to **Miss Sara Sampson,** I think, and whom he somewhere couples with Diderot, thereby showing that he at any rate was able to distinguish in the author of the *Eléments de Littérature* something very different from a *perruque* ["a prejudiced old fogy"]. He admits "the wit, the knowledge of the world, the elegance, the grace" of this "excellent and delightful" tale. But he is fearfully disturbed at its morality. The Sultan, it seems, is "a satiated libertine"; (but would not Rymer be for once justified in urging this as "a character worn by them in all ages of the world" in which there were Sultans?) Roxelane is "a baggage which gets its way." (Undoubtedly: but do not baggages as a rule get theirs?) Lessing, however, cannot away with "the thing," as he calls the owner of the *petit nez retroussé* ["upturned little nose"]. What a wretched part is the great Soliman made to play! He and Roxelane "belong neither to the actual world, nor to a world in which cause and effect follow a different order, but to the general effect of good." "The Turk only knows sensual love" (Rymer! Rymer!). Lessing is afraid that the *lune rousse* ["April moon"]

will rise for Soliman on the very morrow of his wedding: and that he will see in Roxelane "nothing but her impudence and the *nez retroussé.*" (Now as these were the very things that captivated him, it might rather seem that all would be well.) In Soliman the instructive is lacking. "We ought to despise both him and Roxelane; or rather one (which one?) ought to disgust and the other to anger us," though, or perhaps more particularly, *because* "they are painted in the most seductive colours." (pp. 33-5)

In the first place, all this good moral indignation simply explodes through the touch-hole. The tale is pure satire on the *actual* weakness of man and triumph of woman—and this actuality who dare deny? If Lessing does not think both Soliman and Roxelane natural, so much the worse for Lessing. In the second place, neither is in the least degree held up for our admiration, though the skill of the artist may deserve that admiration in almost the highest degree. We may, if we like, pronounce Soliman a weak man and rather immoral ruler, and suspect Roxelane (as he suspected her himself) of being very little better than she should be. But not only does the critic waste his powder in the direction in which he actually fires; he loses the opportunity of bringing down excellent game. He lets slip altogether . . . the chance of arguing that most important and interesting critical question of the attraction of the irregular, the unexpected, the capricious, the teasing. He might have got "instruction" to his heart's content, for us and for himself, out of this shocking story of the great Sultan and the *petit nez retroussé*. Surely it were better done thus to profit by the curves of Roxelene's countenance than to read us a dull sermon on her want of moral rectitude? But Lessing does not think so—master though he be, at least according to German notions, of that very irony which should have kept him right.

His merely dramatic and his merely artistic preoccupations deserve less severe treatment, because it cannot be said that they lead him wrong or even astray, except from our special point of view. But from that special point of view they *do* lead him astray: at least in the sense that he becomes sometimes unimportant to us. In the whole of the **Laocoön,** reserving a point to be returned to later, I remember only one passage of any length which is really literary, and that is the famous and not undeserved, but somewhat insufficiently worked out, censure of Ariosto's description of Alcina. Here Lessing does show what a critic he is by his triumphant demonstration that the carefully accumulated strokes which would in the sister art go towards making, if they would not completely make, a most attractive *picture,* produce very little definite effect as a *passage.* (pp. 35-6)

The objection indeed which may be most justly taken to [Lessing's] dramatic and artistic preoccupations is that they too often directly prevent him in this way from doing what he might have done. The **Dramaturgie** is to the student of properly literary criticism a mixture of irritation and delight—a parallel to Coleridge's conversation, in which "glorious" literary "islets" constantly loom through the dramatic haze, and then get engulfed again. How admirable in principle that comparison of Voltaire's and of Shakespeare's ghosts! Yet how we sigh for concrete illustrations from the actual *words.* . . . (p. 37)

The defence of Thomas Corneille's *Comte d'Essex* against Voltaire's unhistorical history is very good; but then it is so unnecessary! and in the longest criticisms of all, those given to the greater Corneille's *Rodogune* and to Maffei's and Voltaire's *Merope* . . . , the entanglements of the preoccupations reach, for a literary critic, the exasperating.

The truth is that in reading the *Dramaturgie* one cannot help remembering Carlyle's capital complaint of Voltaire that "to him the Universe was one larger patrimony of St Peter from which it were good and pleasant to chase the Pope," and regretting that Lessing should have thought it necessary to substitute Voltaire himself for the Holy Father. It was inevitable perhaps and necessary for the time: but the result is tedious. And unfortunately this Gallophobia in general, this Cornelio-phobia and Voltairiophobia in particular, affects, and very unfavourably affects, those rectifications and reconstructions of Aristotle which have given the *Dramaturgie* its great reputation. With all his talent, all his freshness, Lessing is to a very great extent merely varying the Addisonian error—and indeed, as with all these early German critics, Addison himself had too great an influence on him. As Addison had wasted his powers on showing that Milton, whom the pseudo-Aristotelians had decried, was very Aristotelian, or at least Homeric, after all, so Lessing devotes a most unnecessary amount of energy to showing that the pseudo-Aristotelians themselves were not Aristotelian at all. It was true; it was in a sense well worth doing; but there was so much else to do! There is a famous passage at the beginning of No. 7 which itself really annihilates the whole proceeding, and laughs "boundary lines of criticism" out of court. Nor is Lessing's aberration a mere accidental one. It comes from the fact that he had not cleared up his own mind on some important parts of the question. He says, for instance, in his criticism of *Rodogune* (No. 31, beginning), "The revenge of an ambitious woman should never resemble that of a jealous one." *Æternum vulnus* ["Everlasting misfortune"]! What is "*the* revenge of *an* ambitious woman?" "*the* revenge of *a* jealous one?" Show me the revenge of your jealous Amaryllis, the revenge of your ambitious Neæra; and *then* I will tell you whether they are right or not.

The fact is, that on what we may call the other side of his virtue—to call it the defect of his quality would be rather to beg the question—he is, after all, a preceptist with some difference. Not merely is he an unflinching and almost "right-or-wrong" Aristotelian, but from genuine agreement of taste and judgment he still criticises almost wholly by Kinds. It is *the* drama, *the* epic, *the* fable, *the* lyric, *the* epigram that he makes for, across or sometimes almost outside of the actual examples of their classes. And here, too, we find that the more poetical divisions and the more poetical aspects of these and others have no very special appeal to him. He belittles Lyric altogether; if he is particularly fond of the Fable in the special sense, it is because it also has a "fable" in the general, it is an imitation of life, a criticism of it. His attempt to prove that Horace had no looking-glasses in his bedroom is a pleasant pendant to his indignation with Roxalana's *minois chiffonné* ["pretty but irregular features"]; and though there is a great deal to be said for Martial, Lessing is bribed to adopt the *vita proba* ["estimable life"] view rather by the Roman poet's intense *vivacity* than by his literary merit.

Yet this, once more, is but "the other side of a virtue." The best authorities agree that to Lessing may be assigned absolutely the return to, if not the very initiation of, a direct, scholarly, intelligent, *literary* study of the ancients themselves. As far as the Greek Theatre itself is concerned, Brumoy had anticipated him: far too little justice has often been done to the work of this modest and solid scholar. But Brumoy's outlook was wanting in range. Lessing had in his mind, as well as Latin and Greek, English, French and German always, Italian, even Spanish to some extent. And he read the Latin and the Greek in themselves—and with all due apparatus of technical

scholarship considering his time. He was as far from the twice- and thrice-garbled sciolism of the average French, and even English, critic of the late seventeenth and earlier eighteenth century, as from the arid pedantry of the Dutch and German scholars of the same date. To him, more perhaps than to any one else, it is due that modern criticism has not followed, more than it has done, the mere foolishness of the "modern" advocates in the Quarrel—that it has fortified itself with those sound and solid studies which antiquity alone can supply. For once more let it be said that if, from the pure critical point of view, Ancient without Modern is a stumbling-block, Modern without Ancient is foolishness utter and irremediable.

Perhaps Lessing's greatest glory is that he has given answer to the despairing question which his master quoted in the Ethics. "If the water chokes, what must one drink on the top of it?" "More and purer water" is that answer, of course: and Lessing scoured the clogged and stagnant channels of Neo-Classicism by recurrence to the original fount. Of course he was not himself absolutely original. He owed something to Heinsius, in that most remarkable tractate to which we did justice in its place, among the more distant moderns, to Dacier, pedant as he is, to Brumoy, to Hurd among the nearer. But more than to any of them he devoted himself to the real text of the *Poetics,* interpreted by a combination of scholarship and mother-wit. To this day he has to be consulted upon the *cruces* of Fable and Character, of Unity, of knotting and unknotting, of *katharsis*. That he has said no final word on them matters nothing: final words are not to be said on things of opinion and probability

Until God's great *Venite* change the song.

But on these and not a few other matters he reorganised the whole method and the whole tenor of the inquiry. And so he not only earns his own place in the story, but half unintentionally establishes, or helps us to establish, the great truth that the whole *is* a story, a history, a chain of opinion and comment on opinion, now going more, now less, right, but to be kept as a chain. (pp. 37-41)

It is curious that Lessing, so sensitive and receptive to ancient and later modern influences, is almost as proof against mediæval and (in his own language) early modern as Gottsched himself. His low estimate of Lyric seems to come partly from the fact that Aristotle had slighted it, or at least passed it over, partly from the fact that in relation to Germany he is not thinking of her ballads and lays, not even of the extravagances of the seventeenth century, but of the tame Anacreontic of Hagedorn, Gleim, and Company. Even his study of Shakespeare has not set him right in this respect. (p. 41)

The greatest places of the *Dramaturgie* are those at the close of No. 95, and the penultimate passage of all. In the former, after a long discussion of the Aristotelian commentaries of Hurd and Dacier, he refashions his master's famous dictum in other matter, that "accuracy must not be expected." He is not, he says, "obliged to solve all the problems he raises." His thoughts may seem desultory, or even contradictory: but it does not matter if they supply others with the germ of individual thought. He would but scatter "*fermenta cognitionis*" ["random thoughts"]. In the other, he proceeds still farther, though still perhaps without a clear idea how far the path itself will lead. Germans, he says (I shorten somewhat here), had imitated the French because the French were believed to be your only followers of the ancients. Then English plays came in, an entirely different style of drama was revealed, and the Germans concluded that the aim of tragedy could be fulfilled without the

French rules—that the rules were wrong. And then they went on to object to rules altogether as mere genius-hampering pedantry. ''In short, we had very nearly thrown away in wantonness all past experience, insisting that the poet shall in every instance discover the whole art for himself.'' Lessing has endeavoured ''to arrest this secondary fermentation,'' and that is all. (p. 42)

The gift of critical expression [Lessing] most certainly had in a very high degree. His exposition is masterly: though he is constantly . . . leading the discussion aside from concrete to abstract, and from particular to general points, he is scarcely ever obscure, confused, or vague. His language is precise, without being technical or jargonish. He has something of the German lack of urbanity, but he often has a felicity of expression that is French rather than German, with depth and humour which are far more German than French. Never has one of the tricks of the critical pedant—common to the kind in our day as in his—been so happily described as in the opening of *Wie die Alten den Tod gebildeten:* ''Herr Klotz always thinks he is at my heels. But when I look back at his yelp, I see him lost in a cloud of dust quite astray from the road I have trodden.'' The unlucky distraction of his later years to theological or antitheological squabbling may—nay, must—have lost us much. But as it is, he never fails for long together to give those *fermenta cognitionis* of which he speaks. He is always ''for thoughts'': that fecundity, as a result of the critical congress . . . , is everywhere present in him. (pp. 47-8)

George Saintsbury, ''The Rally of Germany—Lessing,'' in his A History of Criticism and Literary Taste in Europe from the Earliest Texts to the Present Day: Modern Criticism, Vol. III, *William Blackwood and Sons,* 1904, pp. 11-52.

JOHN MIDDLETON MURRY (essay date 1929)

[*Murry is recognized as one of the most significant English critics and editors of the twentieth century. Anticipating later scholarly opinion, he championed the writings of Marcel Proust, James Joyce, Paul Valéry, D. H. Lawrence, and the poetry of Thomas Hardy through his positions as the editor of the* Athenaeum *and as a longtime contributor to the* Times Literary Supplement *and other periodicals. Murry's critical works are noted for their unusually impassioned tone and startling discoveries; such biographically centered critical studies as* Keats and Shakespeare: A Study of Keats' Poetic Life from 1816-1820 *(1925) and* Son of Woman: The Story of D. H. Lawrence *(1931) contain esoteric, controversial conclusions that have angered scholars who favor more traditional approaches. Nevertheless, Murry is cited for his* perspicuity, clarity, and supportive argumentation. His early exposition on literary appreciation, The Problem of Style *(1922), is widely esteemed as an informed guidebook for both critics and readers to employ when considering not only the style of a literary work, but also its theme and viewpoint. In it Murry espouses a theoretical premise that underlies all his criticism: that in order to fully evaluate a writer's achievement the critic must search for crucial passages that effectively ''crystallize'' the writer's innermost impressions and convictions regarding life. In the following excerpt from an article first published in 1929, Murry extols Lessing's critical and theological works, surveys his dramatic writings as expressions of his critical principles, and attempts to isolate the distinctive qualities of his mind.*]

[Lessing] was solid. Between him and common reality there was a force of mutual attraction like gravity. He reminds one, in some essentials of Dr. Johnson. He might have refuted Berkeley by kicking a stone; and the sweat that ran down his face while he sat at the faro table has a sort of kinship with the knotted veins of Johnson's forehead when he sat down to one of his voracious meals. They had their feet not of clay, but on it; they were great men of letters, but we remember them as great men.

That is, if we remember Lessing at all. Even the *Laokoon* seems to be out of fashion nowadays, and to have becme demoded like the piece of statuary from which it arose. We suspect that Mr. Irving Babbitt's *New Laokoon* is more familiar to the present generation than Lessing's old one. His discoveries have become commonplaces, his boundaries are landmarks. So also have Aristotle's to whom, nevertheless, we pay lip-homage. But not to Lessing. Yet he was, of all the critics since Aristotle, the most truly Aristotelian; if Aristotle deserves our homage, as he surely does, so does Lessing—and in one sense even more than Aristotle himself, for he first showed the world how to see Aristotle as a master of method, not a mine of maxims. Since it is not an easy lesson to learn, we need not wonder that criticism has not greatly profited by his example. To use Aristotle's method one needs to be almost an Aristotle—and Lessing was.

He was, in short, a very great critic. Probably the greatest literary critic we have had in Europe—not in virtue of the *Laokoon,* though that is possibly his masterpiece, but in virtue of his qualities which are to be discovered everywhere in his work—in his *Dramaturgie,* and in those *Kleine Schriften* which Coleridge (to one's surprise) declared he read every year as a model of critical prose—and are so finely manifest in the *Laokoon.* The chief of these qualities are two. One, which we expect naturally from so great a disciple of Aristotle, is a passion for clear distinction that never loses sight of the particulars to be distinguished. Drama and Art never become abstract for Lessing; they are always these dramas—and he seems to know all of them—and these works of art—and he seems to know a prodigious number even of them. He never talks by hearsay. The second quality is one which we do not naturally expect from a great disciple of Aristotle, not because it is not in Aristotle—it is in him abundantly—but because it is not obvious in the Artistotle expurgated by orthodoxy who is usually put forward for admiration to-day. It is a sense of the genetic and organic in things, and in the mind which strives to master them . . . ; an attitude not at all to be confused with what is vaguely called the evolutionary outlook, or at least not to be equated with any facile version of Darwinism, but an instinctive or intuitive aversion from absolutes—a feeling that truth is as much a quality of the minds that seek it as of the things wherein they find it. The search is as important as the discovery, the method as the matter. 'The manner in which one has come to a matter is as valuable', Lessing wrote in the *Kleine Schriften,* 'and even as instructive as the matter itself.' And it was this sense of a dynamic governing the motions of the mind which made him so masterly an interpreter of Aristotle. He had, what Aristotle had, a mind so naturally comprehensive that it could, so to speak, begin anywhere; he was aware that approaches to the truth are many, and that all statements of it have an element of approximation. He held that it is by our power to hold various approximations together in a single act of apprehension that we show our capacity for truth. In this spirit he interpreted Aristotle, not in accordance with the demands of an impossible and unnatural clarity, but by himself; he did not regard the Poetics as an inviolable Scripture, but sought to learn how to understand them by studying the Rhetoric and the Ethics. It was the mind not the maxims of the master that fascinated him. He might have said of him what he said of Shakespeare, that he 'demands to be studied, not to be plundered'. But the mind and the maxims of Aristotle were not to be separated; they were interdependent. (pp. 141-44)

[In a passage in the *Dramaturgie,* Lessing] speaks not so much of the opposite as the superior of the dogmatic mind. The dogmatic mind reveres principles without understanding them; its opposite rejects principles without understanding them. Lessing was never, like the mere anarchist, afraid of dogma; he only insisted on understanding it, so that it was for him no longer dogma. This quality of mind is strikingly displayed in the *Laokoon.* To the casual glance, which is all he gets to-day, he appears to be reverential to classical authority. The matter in which his argument moves is wholly classical. It is only when we have begun to wrestle with the substance of his book that we discern that he is moving amongst the writers of antiquity as a man amongst men, discriminating, deciding values, accepting this as true, rejecting that as false, allowing nothing that he does not understand. 'We read fine things,' said Keats, 'but we do not understand them till we have gone the same steps as the author.' Lessing's ratification of classical values by his own experience is of this kind. He reanimates, and is reanimated by, the mind of antiquity.

That is why the *Laokoon* is a living book. The breath of life is in its style—swift, clear, colloquial, pungent—the style of a real experience, cutting easily and with a laugh through the tangled confusions of pedantic criticism. Virgil's Laocoon wears his priestly robe; the figure in the statue is naked. Why, asked the critics, this offence against the decorum? Because, they said, statuary cannot imitate drapery. 'The old artist might have laughed at the objection, but I know not what they would have said to this manner of answering it.' Then from his silver bow, Lessing lets fly his real shaft:

> In poetry a robe is no robe. It conceals nothing. Our imagination sees through it in every part. Whether Virgil's Laocoon be clothed or not, the agony in every fiber of his body is equally visible.

How obvious! Yet no one had thought of it before. Nor even to-day is it by any means as obvious to criticism as it was to Lessing, that the application of the words 'imagery' and 'picture' to a work of literature is almost wholly a metaphor.

> A picture in poetry is not necessarily one that can be transferred to canvas. But every touch, or combination of touches, by means of which the poet brings his subject so vividly before us that we are more conscious of the subject than of his words, is picturesque and makes what we call a picture; that is, it produces that degree of illusiion which a painted picture is peculiarly qualified to excite, and which we in fact most frequently and naturally experience in the contemplation of the painted canvas....

That is, or it should be, one of the great commonplaces of literary criticism; even in translation it shows the easy vigour of Lessing's prose. Reading it, one can hardly believe that 'Ut pictura poesis' [the concept that the act of the painter is akin to that of the poet] had reigned unchallenged for a century before it, or that it would have been possible after it for the confusion to lift its head again.

Lessing wrote plays. *Minna von Barnhelm* and *Nathan der Weise* have become classics of the German theatre. But he knew the real nature of his own eminence. He was, first and foremost and all his life long, a critic. Even *Minna von Barnhelm* was written rather to show the nugatory German drama how it might advance to some contact with reality than from autonomous impulse; and *Nathan der Weise* was deliberate

propaganda for the cause which in his later life he had most deeply at heart. (pp. 144-46)

Criticism, as Lessing understood and practised it, was comprehensive and conscious of itself. It therefore passed continually into history, into philosophy and into religion. Yet he was, for most of his life, an ill-paid journeyman of letters; a journalist he would be called to-day, though it is difficult to conceive how a mind so universal would find expression under modern conditions of journalism. His fighting prose might be popular, but his seriousness and profundity would not. One can imagine well enough the general applause at some of his sallies. It had been written: Nobody will deny that the German theatre owes much of its improvement to Professor Gottsched. 'I am that Nobody,' says Lessing. 'I deny it entirely.' There seems nothing more to say.

But Lessing had another fling at Gottsched in the then new pages of the *Vossische Zeitung,* where he inserted this brief review of Gottsched's poems:

> The outside is so excellent that we hope it will do the bookseller's shop great credit, and we wish it will long do so. To give an adequate idea of the inside is beyond our powers. These poems cost 2 thalers, 4 groschen. Two thalers pay for the absurd, and four groschen about cover the useful.

It would be cruel, had it not been so just and so necessary. The dilettante professors who composed cultivated Germany when Lessing entered the arena had to be smitten hip and thigh if a genuine German culture was to have room to grow. Lessing the journalist made fun of them, Lessing the scholar confuted them; and though a professorship was his only hope of security, he refused to join their ranks. The sheer strength of the man who thus, practically single-handed, cleared the path for German literature was prodigious. He created a public and imposed himself upon it; instead of the professor of a university, he made himself the teacher of Germany. 'What would you?' he replied to his friends who remonstrated with him for turning to hack translation, when the outbreak of the Seven Years War brought him once more to hardship. 'My writings are the productions of a man who is an author partly by inclination, partly by force. I cannot study at my own expense, so I try to do so at the expense of the public.' In this spirit, and by this method, Lessing pursued his task. He conducted his search for truth at the expense, and in the eyes, of the public.

But it was not until he was forty and had obtained the small security of a post as Librarian to the Duke of Brunswick at Wolfenbüttel that his dominant interest could fully reveal itself. This was religion.... [Lessing] was himself rooted in and detached from Christianity. He could understand, experience, and sympathize with religious impulse and religious conviction: it never seemed to him, as it did to the fashionable scepticism of his age, an unintelligible aberration of the human mind. To such an attitude, a heresy was as interesting and as valuable as an orthodoxy, and from his study of the heresies Lessing gained, what subsequent students of Church history have sometimes gained, a passionate hatred of religious intolerance. But he was a wiser man than Voltaire; he never indulged the fancy that the way to extirpate religious intolerance was to extirpate religion. It was to purify religion—and this chiefly by two means; by insisting that the centre of gravity of religion lay not in theology, but in conduct, and by giving religion the courage to look fearlessly at its own history.

By these means he believed he was contributing to a development of Christianity that was inevitable. That the nominally

Christian mind should be made to appreciate that an intolerant Christianty was no Christianity at all was an obvious moral preliminary to a religious or philosophical attitude perhaps not so obvious, but in Lessing's view no less necessary. This was to regard the history of Christianity genetically, and to be ever mindful of the fact that it had been manifested through fallible and imperfect human instruments. Already at Wittenberg, in a rehabilitation of Lemnius, he had applied this humanistic calculus to Luther. . . . Since Luther was but a man, he concluded, there was no reason why Protestantism should remain for ever at the point of enlightenment where Luther had left it.

This early [opinion], with its dangerous or pregnant principle that all history is significant of the Divine purpose, . . . was itself a contribution to the further enlightenment of Protestantism. If that be granted of the past, Lessing was well aware, it must be granted also of the present which knows the past; and all that the human mind can do in the way of realizing the past is a necessary furtherance of the Divine economy. This effort to realize the past is the effort which gives unity to all Lessing's work. It is as manifest in his *Laokoon*, in the recurrent discussion of Aristotle in his *Dramaturgie*, in the archaeological studies of his *Contributions*, as it is in the religious and theological writing which wholly occupied the later years of his life. But to realize the past, for Lessing, was not to rationalize it; hence he was a baffling figure to contemporary rationalists. Reason and rationalism were for him two different things. Reason was nourished by the imaginative apprehension which elicited truth from facts; it was essentially a submission to facts: whereas rationalism was an attempt to tyrannize over them. Thus historical criticism, of which Lessing was virtually the discoverer, was the most appropriate field for the exercise of reason. Of true historical criticism rationalism was incapable, because it denied the validity, and even the existence, of many of the profoundest impulses at work in history. Reason was not afraid of mystery; nor did it demand absolute truth. Its delight was in the search for truth, and in the comprehensiveness with which it was pursued. Again it was at Wittenberg, that is when Lessing was only twenty-two, that he outlined his own ideal, in a criticism of the specialist mind:

> Everything outside his own specialism is small to him, not because it really looks small to him, but because he does not see it at all: it lies entirely outside his vision. His eyes may be as sharp as they please: one quality is wanting to make them really good eyes. They are as immovable on his head, as his head is immovable on his body. Therefore he can see only those objects before which his whole body is planted. He knows nothing of the rapid side-glances so necessary to the survey of a great whole.

No single sentence better than the last could convey the distinctive quality of Lessing's mind, or his conception of the training and the use of reason. (pp. 147-52)

What [Lessing] was cannot be easily defined. But the most memorable of his later works, *Nathan the Wise* and *The Education of the Human Race*, were devoted to making his position unmistakable. The main thesis of *The Education* was that revelation, in the history of the Christian religion, was an anticipation of reason—the means employed by the divine economy for inculcating truths too difficult for the unripe understanding of the race. The religious progress of the race therefore consisted in outgrowing the need of revelation. In more modern language, Lessing held that the great religious intuitions were prophetic of truths to be apprehended by reason.

The final purpose of Christianity was to become unnecessary. With the greater freedom allowed him by the dramatic form, he drove home his point in *Nathan the Wise*. In the play the one genuine Christian is the lay-brother, noble-hearted and simple-minded. The Patriarch is a mere unscrupulous schemer, while the Templar passes beyond Christianity to an apprehension of universal truth, and touches the wisdom of Nathan. The bitter criticism of conventional Christianity comes from a Moslem, Saladin's sister, Sittah. . . . Lessing was . . . a humanist; and being a true humanist he was also perforce a naturalist. (pp. 154-55)

A true humility was inseparable from Lessing's ideal of a religion from which all superstition had been eliminated. He detected—and his eyes were keen—a false humility in the apparent sacrifice of reason made by orthodoxy. True humility lay in the patient submission to Nature, of which man also was a part, and the illumination of reason which attended upon that submission. Religion, which cannot be reconciled with the intelligence, would have no difficulty in reconciliation with reason, for these were one. Lessing's life was a hard one, but it had the beauty which comes of deep inward coherence. He never took the easy way when one more difficult led straighter to the truth he sought. His work is a monument to the validity of his own unshakable conviction that not the possession of truth but the passion, the sincerity, and the tolerance with which it is sought, is the noblest achievement of humanity. (pp. 155-56)

John Middleton Murry, "Gotthold Ephraim Lessing," in his Countries of the Mind: Essays in Literary Criticism, second series, *Oxford University Press, London, 1931, pp. 141-56.*

J. G. ROBERTSON (lecture date 1929)

[*Robertson was a distinguished English scholar of German language and literature. Noted especially for his many books on the life and work of Johann Wolfgang von Goethe, Robertson's other writings include* Schiller after a Century *(1905) and* Lessing's Dramatic Theory: Being an Introduction to & Commentary on His "Hamburgische Dramaturgie" *(1939; see Additional Bibliography). In the following excerpt from a bicentennial lecture on Lessing, Robertson praises his subject for his contributions to the drama and to literary theory.*]

To let the occasion of the two hundredth birthday of Gotthold Ephraim Lessing pass uncommemorated in England would be unjust and ungrateful, for he has always stood in high honour amongst us. He has never, I believe, had detractors here; no one has ever questioned his greatness; he has no qualities of mind or character which, so to speak, go against the grain with us. We cannot accuse him, as we used to accuse Goethe, of an egocentric self-culture; nor can we say that his dramas have been kept off our stage, as Schiller's have been, by a rhetorical idealism little to Anglo-Saxon tastes. We have never in our complacently superior English way said of Lessing: "How very German." On the contrary we have often been moved to reflect on how strangely English, how remarkably French he can be. This is not necessarily a compliment to him, but it does mean that we recognize in him a writer and thinker who rose above the narrower limitations of nationalism. Lessing was, if ever there was one, a "good European"—a good European and a great European in the spacious eighteenth century. (p. 103)

In a survey of Lessing's manifold life and activities, three aspects [would] stand out conspicuously: his contribution to the national drama of his country; his work as a critic and theorist of poetry and the arts; and his battles with the theologians. I place Lessing's work as a dramatist first; for there is, I think, a tendency among his biographers unduly to depreciate its significance, to the greater glory of Lessing the critic.

In a famous and often quoted passage in his *Hamburgische Dramaturgie* Lessing had declared, ''I am neither an actor nor a poet. It is true, people have often done me the honour of declaring me to be the latter. But only because they have not understood me. From the few dramatic attempts which I have made, such generous conclusions ought not to be drawn. My earliest attempts were made in years when one likes to regard pleasure and ease in writing as genius. What in my later works is tolerable, I am confident I owe solely to criticism. I have not in me the living spring which works its way up by its own force, by its own force gushes forth in rich, fresh and pure streams; I have to bring everything out of me by pressure, and, as it were, through pipes. I should be so poor, so cold, so shortsighted, had I not in some degree learned to borrow modestly from the treasures of others, to warm myself at others' fires, to strengthen my eye with the glasses of art.''

Lessing himself had spoken; and the world believed his words and re-echoed them: that Lessing was no poet has been told us again and again in the biographies and literary histories of a century and a half. His shortcomings as a dramatist; his all too calculated and mechanical perfection of plot; his ''dramatic algebra'' and the brilliant antithetic ''Lessingisieren'' of his dialogue; his extensive indebtedness to, not to say pilferings from other dramatists—these are the accusations that have been freely brought against him. But surely with very great injustice. I cannot think that they would ever have been brought with such conviction had not Lessing himself made that fatal admission that he was ''no poet''. It is true, Lessing was no ''naïve'' poet in the sense established by Schiller; his imagination never took the reins into its own hands, freed itself from the schoolmastering of the reason, as it must do in all great poetry. It is true also that he owes many a debt to the dramatic literature of England, France and Italy, with which he had a greater familiarity than any other man of his time. But Lessing was never a plagiarist, not even in those early dramas written in his Leipzig and Berlin days, when he was a disciple of Destouches, Marivaux and Nivelle de la Chaussée; and his dramatic dialogue in his masterpieces need not fear comparison with the best of his century.

With his *Miss Sara Sampson* in 1755 Lessing achieved what might be called without prejudice the doughtiest deed that has ever been done for the national theatre of Germany. For with that play he established on the German stage the English ''tragedy of common life''; and to the tragedy of common life Germany was never subsequently to prove faithless. It is, I believe, the form of drama in which she has made her greatest contributions to the literary treasurehouse of the European theatre, and perhaps her most national form of tragedy. *Miss Sara Sampson* is ostensibly an English play; its scene is in England, and its people are English men and women. These come largely from the English novel, especially from Richardson: there is much of Clarissa in the unhappy Sara. Nor had Lessing forgotten his Congreve, from whom he borrowed the names of most of his characters. But the foundation and inspiration of *Miss Sara Sampson* are to be sought, as an American scholar has recently been showing us, in more obscure English dramatic works, in *The Squire of Alsatia,* by Thomas Shadwell, and the *Caelia* of Charles Johnson. Thus the statement of the literary

histories that Lessing's play was suggested by Lillo's *Merchant of London* is erroneous; there are many English ingredients in it, but none of these was supplied by Lillo. The England, however, in whose debt Lessing stood, was the England of his own time; Lessing had as yet no real grasp of the fact that back in a remoter romantic past lay a vast dramatic poetry in England which dwarfed to insignificance the punier playwrights of his own day. Shakespeare was to Lessing still little more than the primitive barbarian with whom Voltaire had acquainted him.

Lessing's next play was *Minna von Barnhelm,* which saw the light in 1767. That *Minna von Barnhelm* is one of the greatest German comedies no one has ever ventured to question. There is, of course, much in it that is mouldy and old-fashioned now; our twentieth century has difficulty in accepting its lachrymose sentiment, its all too large-hearted effusiveness. But the people of ''Minna'' are living people—these soldiers of the Seven Years' War, this innkeeper; Minna herself, the delightful Franziska, before whom the long procession of clever waitingmaids of French comedy pale to unsubstantial shadows. All these people have red corpuscles in their blood; they live the abiding life of great creations. *Minna von Barnhelm,* like *Miss Sara Sampson,* owes a great debt to us. Here, and for the only time as a practical dramatist, Lessing pays material homage to Shakespeare's art. No English reader can but feel that in Minna and her maid there is a reflection of the grace and charm of our Portia and Nerissa; and the *dénouement* of Lessing's comedy has clearly been planned with that of *The Merchant of Venice* in mind. But Shakespeare represents the lesser of Lessing's indebtedness to English literature. He had now discovered a new English dramatist nearer to his own time, who was to mean more for the real progress of the European drama than the mediocre Lillo, and more than all the brilliant dialecticians of the Restoration comedy—George Farquhar. Farquhar was the first modern dramatist, not merely, as has been said of him, to bring the scent of the hay across the footlights, but also to put on the stage real soldiers, beside whom the Bramarbases of the traditional comedy are but as spouting automata. Farquhar's *Constant Couple,* and still more, his *Beaux' Stratagem,* meant more for *Minna von Barnhelm* than any other model; and the place of Lessing's drama in the literature of the eighteenth century is by the side, not of the great French comedies of the century, but of *The Beaux' Stratagem, She Stoops to Conquer* and *The School for Scandal.* The greatness of *Minna von Barnhelm* has always been recognized, not so frequently the fact that its greatness is of the English kind.

Lessing wrote two other dramatic masterpieces: *Emilia Galotti* and *Nathan der Weise.* With the former of these the German tragedy of common life made a vast stride forward. Here, again, more than one English drama on the theme of the Roman Virginia—for such is *Emilia Galotti*—had stood sponsor; but Lessing rose superior to them all. For he discarded the political theses which the English playwrights had woven into their interpretations of the Roman tragedy, and contented himself with depicting a simple conflict of human emotions. The critics have dwelt on the flaws of Lessing's attempt to modernize the Virginia story, but these flaws were inherent in the theme from the beginning; they have not dwelt sufficiently on the skill and intuition with which he has in very large measure surmounted his difficulties and brought his theme within the sphere of eighteenth-century sympathies; they have not always appreciated the dramatic vigour and strength with which the men and women are depicted, who here play out their fates. *Emilia*

Galotti is, again, one of the foundation-stones of the modern German theatre.

And finally, *Nathan der Weise,* Lessing's swan song, the poetic precipitate of his battle for tolerance and humanity. An older generation condemned *Nathan der Weise* as merely a drama for the closet; but they could not envisage those subsequent developments of the drama in which the bustle of Romantic happenings was more and more to give place to psychological conflicts. In this sense Lessing's last drama has much in it that was before its time. If it has, in spite of this, still remained in large measure excluded from the stage, the reason is that it turns upon a motive which was congenial to the taste of the eighteenth century—as witness Voltaire and Diderot—but is no longer to ours, namely, the discovery that two lovers are brother and sister. Such a disillusioning *dénouement* a post-romantic public could not accept with equanimity; and *Nathan der Weise* has remained unpalatable in the theatre. It is also, admittedly, somewhat artificially constructed to enforce the doctrine which was nearer to Lessing's heart than the fortunes of his characters, clear-cut, interesting and even humorous as they are. *Nathan der Weise* is primarily a sermon on religious tolerance, not a drama of the emotions. Deeply significant is another aspect of Lessing's last dramatic work; here he has turned away from our Shakespeare, for whom he had as a critic broken a lance, and followed that writer among his contemporaries to whom he owed his chief debt—Diderot. Nay, more, he has bent the knee to his arch-enemy Voltaire, and written a drama whose place is with the dramas of the great Frenchman whose life, like Lessing's, was one long battle for the liberation of humanity.

Lessing as a critic requires no eulogy or apology. Did not Macaulay, in the middle of the last century, greet him as the "greatest critic of Europe"? Lessing's eminence as a critic has never been disputed; the trenchant vigour of his judgments, his brilliant style, his keen dialectic fencing, above all, his freedom from the fogs of metaphysical confusion which so often beset the German mind—these qualities have always been recognized. I need not dwell on his masterly estimates of men and books, even of such as lay outside his normal personal sympathy; and the crushing irony with which he wiped out the bunglers of literature. His two greatest critical works are the *Laokoon* and the *Hamburgische Dramaturgie.* The first of these is a milestone in the development of eighteenth-century aesthetic thinking. Building on ideas of Marmontel and Diderot, he, for the first time, differentiated clearly the arts according to their aims and functions: pigeon-holed, as it were, the activities of the imagination. The pity of it is that, instead of giving us a finished treatise, he has left us only a collection of materials for such a treatise. Moreover, the *Laokoon* means something different to us to-day than it did to its own time. Then it was regarded—and rightly regarded—as a protest against excessive inroads of the poet on the province of the painter and sculptor. For us of a post-romantic age this delimitation has lost its force; the modern art of Europe has largely repudiated Lessing's teaching, and sought to associate rather than dissociate the arts. But as a monument of acute aesthetic thinking and classic style the *Laokoon* has not yet grown effete.

Lessing's other great contribution to aesthetic theory, his *Hamburgische Dramaturgie,* was, as we have seen, merely a critical newspaper dealing with the mediocre repertory and hardly less mediocre performances of an actor-ridden theatre, in which an artistic conscience was not conspicuous. But the very poverty of his materials gave Lessing his opportunity; he was forced to discuss general questions because the particular ones were not worth discussing. It has often been said that the pivot round which the *Hamburgische Dramaturgie* turns is the *Poetics* of Aristotle. I do not think so. The central figure of Lessing's treatise is Voltaire; the *Dramaturgie* is one long polemic against Voltaire and all that the pseudo-classicism of France involved; against the hampering limitations of the *tragédie classique* ["classical tragedy"]. It is true Lessing does pin his faith on Aristotle, declaring him as much an enunciator of eternal verities as Euclid himself. But Aristotle is only a means to an end, and that end is the demolition of French Classic tragedy. In his actual interpretation of Aristotle Lessing is not always fortunate; in fact, he is more often wrong than right; and when he is right, as in his attack on the French unities as being contrary to the spirit and teaching of Aristotle, or when he substitutes "fear" for "terror" in the translation of the Aristotelian definition of tragedy, he was no innovator. But even when he expresses views that had been put forward before him, he does so with such vigour and brilliance that they appear as new truths. The virtue of the *Hamburgische Dramaturgie* is not in what it says, but in the way it says it.

To us it has always been a source of pride, and one reason why we have taken Lessing to our hearts, that he boldly maintained that our Shakespeare was, in spirit, a truer Aristotelian than the great poets of France, who plumed themselves on their obedience to Aristotle's laws. We prize Lessing's treatise especially as a monument to the greatness of Shakespeare. But is there not something of a fallacy here? Was Lessing really the whole-hearted admirer of Shakespeare we like to believe he was? If you will gather together all the passages in the *Dramaturgie* where Shakespeare is mentioned, I think you will be surprised to find how very little Lessing has to say about him. The Hamburg theatre gave him, of course, no opportunity of criticizing a Shakespearian play; the time was not yet ripe for Shakespeare to be played in Germany; and I am sure Lessing would have been the last to counsel so hazardous an experiment. Thus Shakespeare is never discussed for himself alone; to be quite honest, he is mostly used merely as a cudgel wherewith to belabour the arch-enemy Voltaire. It was a triumph for Lessing's irony to show that the French poet, compared with the English "drunken savage", was the veriest bungler! It may seem a tribute to Lessing's acumen that he should have proclaimed Shakespeare a more faithful observer of the Aristotelian law than Corneille; but far would it have been from him to maintain, as we might maintain to-day, that Aristotle is a great critic of the drama, because his theory is sufficiently elastic to allow of the admission of Shakespeare. In Lessing's eyes Shakespeare is to be praised because he can be proved to be a classic poet, the "brother of Sophocles". For Lessing is a "classic" critic; he had not a drop in his blood of that romanticism which first found the key to Shakespeare's heart. The quality whereby he towers above the other classic critics of his century lies in the nature of his classicism; he did not take his stand, like Boileau, on the baroque interpretation of the antique initiated by Italy and France, but went back to the eternal sources of classicism in Greece. He adapted the classic dogma to the spirit of his time, and by widening it and ennobling it, destroyed pseudo-classicism. To such a mind Shakespeare's works must necessarily have contained much that was antipathetic; and the best proof of it is that Shakespeare meant, as we have seen, so little for his own dramatic work. Much in the *Hamburgische Dramaturgie* is devoid of interest—other than a historical one—for us to-day; it has long been discarded as a book of study in German schools. But it is a notable monument of eighteenth-century aesthetic thought, the greatest text-book of the theatre of that century.

Much might be said of Lessing's theological controversies, his sanguinary tussles with Pastor Goeze and the champions of Lutheran orthodoxy. But these too, are battles of long ago, and awaken but a faint echo in the twentieth-century mind. What this great rationalist fought for—tolerance, freedom of thought and conscience—has long passed into the common-places of our intellectual and spiritual life. But we must not forget that we are the heirs of that freedom which Lessing and men like him won for us. And the manner of Lessing's fighting must always awaken our admiration for him. He went into battle as a St. George of undaunted courage to fight the dragon, to free the languishing human spirit; and more often than not he fought a lone hand against obscurantism, unclearness, insincerity and hypocrisy. Like most brave fighters, however, he came to love the joy of battle for its own sake; to him, too, might be applied the words he quotes about Aristotle: "Solet quaerere pugnam in suis libris" ["He sought a battle in his books"]. He was not always fair to his adversaries; once his holy wrath was kindled, he was relentless—relentless to his first master Gottsched, relentless to his great exemplar Voltaire, and relentless, albeit with greater justice, to Klotz and Goeze. And he was not always fair to his friends. In his onslaught on the baroque pseudo-classicism, he sometimes forgot that all literature is necessarily built upon conventions that are not, and never can be life, and that of no poet may it be demanded that he should repudiate the particular convention of the age into which he is born; a great art is always possible even within the most artificial of conventions. Lessing was unjust to the great poets of France because he attacked the convention they had perforce to obey, instead of endeavouring to appreciate the art and skill with which they achieved what their age demanded of them and thereby fulfilled their poetic mission. But again, we must measure these things by their ultimate results, and not allow ourselves to be blinded by temporary injustices. Had Lessing been fairer to his enemies, more appreciative of the good side of the doctrines he impugned, he would assuredly not have achieved his great work for the advancement and freedom of the human spirit. That is what matters in the end.

On this, the two hundredth anniversary of his birth, we can still speak of Lessing as a man to whom our whole-hearted admiration and sympathy go out; he was a great dramatist, a wise critic, an honest and honourable man of letters—one of the intellectual giants of his century. (pp. 107-17)

J. G. Robertson, "Gotthold Ephraim Lessing," in his Essays and Addresses on Literature, *1935. Reprint by Books for Libraries Press, 1968, pp. 103-17.*

THOMAS MANN   (lecture date 1929)

[*Mann was a German novelist, short story and novella writer, essayist, and critic who singlehandedly raised the German twentieth-century novel to international stature. As did his contemporaries James Joyce and Marcel Proust, Mann reflected and helped to define the intellectual currents of his age, particularly the belief that European realism was no longer viable in a sophisticated and complex century. This belief, which colors much of his fiction, is the foundation of many of his critical, philosophical, and historical essays, the bulk of which are widely acknowledged to show the same level of originality and creative insight as his fiction. In the following excerpt from a lecture delivered to the Prussian Academy to commemorate the bicen-*

tennial of Lessing's birth, Mann surveys Lessing's literary career, assessing him along the way as an example of a classical "type" that is "the original, the first living embodiment of a form of spirit . . . upon which later manifestations . . . will base themselves."]

It was Lessing's mission, in virtue of his penetrating understanding, to make divisions and distinctions; yet his genius was unifying. "Before him," so runs a contemporary letter with reference to **Minna von Barnhelm,** "no German author succeeded in inspiring with the same enthusiasm nobility and people, learned and laity alike, or in pleasing them so universally." Goethe praised the "completely north-German" national content of the same work, admiring what has since so often been admired, the way in which a specifically north-German product succeeded in delighting the whole of Germany, uniting all Germans in conscious sympathy [see excerpt dated 1811-22]. While **Nathan der Weise,** our great critic's last word as a poet— uttered in accents of the profoundest wisdom, that evoked from its greatest admirer (Goethe once more) the cry: "May the divine sentiments of patience and tolerance there expressed ever remain precious and sacred in the nation's eyes!" a poetic composition which is the last word in benevolence—**Nathan der Weise** stands for unification of a still higher sort: its conscious pedagogic goal is the peace of mutual understanding, the peace of mankind. This same brave spirit, so national in character and achievement, who as a poet led Germany towards unification, while as dramatic critic he rent asunder the authority of the French canon—he it was who called patriotism a "heroic weakness," and declared that nothing was further from his desire than to be praised as a patriot, a man who would forget that he should be a citizen of the world. The Hamburg dramaturge makes merry over the provincialism of certain comedies of manners, whose author would like to "take the pathetic little traditions of the corner where he was born for the customs of the common fatherland," whereas the truth was that nobody cared a jot "how many times in the year, or where, or when, green cabbage is eaten." Thus he sets against the provincial point of view the intellectual conception of a common fatherland—the national, this is, against, or at least above, the sectional. But he is also aware of a point of view wherein the national in its turn appears as the sectional; he expresses it in the wish that "there might be in every state men who are above popular prejudice and know precisely when patriotism ceases to be a virtue." Those are his words—the words of a free man and a genuine. They imply that the intellectual and the humane are only a heightening and extension of the natural and national, and they make plain that the trend to further unification lies inherent in the national idea itself, though all unrecognised by those tribal-minded exclusionists who, in amazing miscomprehension inscribe the latter on their banner and see in it nothing but the slogan of segregation and animosity.

Lessing's national mission was one of clarification by criticism. His was a penetrating and inspired understanding. Nathan's phrase, "we must distinguish," might be set as a motto above his great analytical contributions, the **Laocoön,** the **Hamburger Dramaturgie** and the theological controversies. Definition, limitation, lucid statement were his peculiar joy and gift; they were, to employ once more that singularly pregnant word, his mission. For singularly pregnant it is, that in the conception with its implication of task, function and tool, there is an interplay of the personal and the supra-personal imperative. (pp. 118-21)

Lessing was from the first the founder of a mythical type—mythical because it constantly reappears in the flesh. He is the classical creative intelligence, the patriarch of the writing tribe. Most personally and vividly he represents the ideal productive type, the kind of intellectual whose performance is viewed in some quarters with a jaundiced eye, as mere profane writing, sharply and contemptuously distinguished from the sacred sphere of the afflatus. . . . Lessing's own classic personality is a proof that the combination [in one person, of the trained writer endowed with initiative and the conscious, clear-eyed creative artist] exists. The enthusiasts of simplification underestimate the awkwardness of a distinction which is constantly being blurred and obliterated through the critical factor of language itself. An art whose medium is language will always show a high degree of critical creativeness, for speech is itself a critique of life: it names, it characterises, it passes judgment, in that it creates. There is, of course, such a thing as detachment, objectivity—the "sacred sobriety" of which a certain hymnist speaks. But it must have followed the intoxication, on that being felt as something which needed checking. (pp. 121-22)

The type which we are analysing possesses a self-critical acumen, a modesty and candour which unfortunately play all too easily into the hands of those who would deny its claims to membership in the charmed circle of creative artists. Such a man typically runs to meet adverse criticism, not to forestall it, but because he has an objective eye on his own performance. He it is who always says the best things about himself—not complimentary things, but conveying the truth as he sees it, however black and forbidding. Then the others parrot it after him, seldom to his credit, and rather to be able to use his own words against him: "He said so himself, you know." Lessing's love of truth is essentially radical; he has an ungovernable gift for "hunting out the truth in the very last hole," as he puts it; there would of course be a peculiar zest in the game when self-knowledge was the prize. Some pleasing instances of the thing I mean are to be found in his own creative work; as when Minna says to Tellheim that there is a certain hard, casual way of referring to one's own misfortunes, and Tellheim hastens to answer, "Which at bottom is only boasting and complaining too." Or in *Emilia Galotti,* when Conti the painter speaks of his dissatisfaction with himself as an artist, adding: "And yet I am sometimes quite satisfied with my own lack of self-satisfaction." Lessing, paying homage to the critical spirit, and disowning the complaint that it acts as a wet-blanket to genius, asserts that to it alone he owes all that is tolerable in his work, and that he flatters himself to have won from it something akin to genius. "I am neither actor nor poet," he says. "I do not feel in myself the living spirit that rises by its own power and shoots upward in such streams of richness, freshness and purity. With me everything must come out through pressure and pipes." How they have been quoted against him, the pressure and pipes! But if he was right, not so were the others who quoted him. In Lessing's world, truth is very relative—one gets used to that. It becomes humanised, as it were, the criteria lying less in the matter under dispute than in its defender. Goethe never concurred in these judgments of Lessing about himself. The influence he wielded, Goethe says, in the long run gave the lie to his detractors. Goethe was all for letting the end try the man. But if one cannot wait for the judgment of time, then surely one may cite the pre-eminent qualities of personality, originality, boldness. Genius, one may say, betrays itself in the unexpected, in the sudden coming-to-be of something undreamed-of beforehand. It manifests itself in the possibility of something new of its kind, which could be triumphantly valid only by the power of personality. Genius

in art, then, would be the surprise, the wonder and enchantment, the something dared that seemed quite impossible until it was done. In the light of this definition the old question as to Lessing's rank as an author becomes demonstrably idle. For creations like Minna and Nathan bear precisely this imprint of the new and the surprising, of something risked that became possible only by dint of being done, valid and triumphant only by virtue of the mingled characteristics of shrewdness and naïveté. They may, because they can—and only so. Less vital then they are they could not maintain themselves. And in face of this objective artistry, this disarming intelligence, this cordial good sense rising to the highest pitch of amenity, it would be callous and pedantic to challenge its claim to the title of creative art.

Such was Otto Ludwig's view: he said of **Minna von Barnhelm** that the old indictment must fall, in view of an art that could so swell out a single seedcorn of matter as to make of it a play of inexhaustible interest. And yet it is just this art of "swelling out," of irresistibly, inexplicably enlarging upon, which constitutes another trait of the classic type [Lessing exemplifies]. Invention is not its strong point; but it can invest the detail, and the uttermost detail, with rich and unfailing charm. It has small concern with plot, and lacking talent therein dispenses with all but the minimum required to give backbone to the composition. Its strength lies in the power to give that little effectiveness and beauty: digging it in, building it out, exploiting it, sharpening its lines, accenting its facets, illuminating the obscurest corner of its theme, until what would in another's hand be boresome becomes genuinely entertaining. (pp. 123-26)

The case is the same with [another] . . . trait of the type, the characteristic which we might call its masculinity, or its preoccupation with the masculine. The male suits incomparably better than the female its talent for characterisation. Its men are drawn with more depth, power, certainty. Minna is admittedly far outranked by the melancholy and meticulous Tellheim. To begin with, he is much more masculine than she is feminine—a fact for which old Mendelssohn accounted by saying that Lessing was most successful with those characters which were nearest his own—as, for instance, with Tellheim, Odoardo and the Templar. The last has always been considered the freshest and most vivid characterisation of youth upon the German stage, or any stage. It was Friedrich Schlegel who remarked upon how thoroughly Lessing's characters are Lessingised. It is a mark of the type—we might well call it lyrical subjectivity, and thus derive it from the explicitly and peculiarly poetic!

Again, there is a certain proud economy of output, the opposite to unintelligent productivity. Lessing presents a comedy—*the* comedy: as if to say, "See, this is the way to do it!" His pride, and his critical dignity forbid him to follow it with ten poorer ones; he passes on to another form. Such shrewdness, such self-awareness are surely to be appraised higher than dull, haphazard, uneven performance—surely they rank as artistic gift, and if so, then poetic.

But poetic the medium of our type is not. His language is not poetic. Not in the Orphic sense, not high, not a mystery. There is much justice in the accusation that it is dry, that it wants feeling and acme. It does not mount as high as the sources, the fount and spring of our idiom. It is simply cultured, pithy and shrewd. It demands of itself merely clarity, neatness, precision: *"d'être clair et précis"* ["to be clear and precise"], as Lessing himself puts it. That it does not lack vigour is rather remarkable. On the contrary, it aims at and attains that quality in considerable degree, for it has the gift of appositeness, and of a phrasing that makes it at once discursive and dramatic. If our type set itself one day to compose verse, it will be prosaic, like Nathan's, spoken, not sung; very pleasant to hear, not lacking in rhythm, but without *melos,* having no meltingness; such uninspired verse, indeed, that Friedrich Schlegel could speak of its "disillusioned note." And yet verse of such golden-hearted good sense that unless you have steeled your heart beforehand you yield to it none the less. Marvellous, the power wielded by such dry good sense! (pp. 126-28)

We might go on to cite other weak points in Lessing's armour; they would be just so many traits of the type of which he is the classic example. His sensuous equipment was slight, his demands in this respect amounting almost to indifference—for instance, in the *Laocoön,* in his treatment of antique sculpture, his senses never absolve him from the duty of analysis. And yet this in many ways superannuated investigation into the line of demarcation between painting and poetry contains here and there an *aperçu* that is certainly creatively felt. Take that painful perception of the law that language can only praise, not reproduce beauty; that challenge to the poet to give up description and instead paint for us the satisfaction, the sympathy, the love, the delight that beauty confers—"for thereby," says he "you have painted beauty herself." Possible that this anti-descriptive flight into the lyrical constitutes Lessing's approach to the dramatic. Otherwise, there lies no little irony in the fact that this prosaic, half-acknowledged poet, with his limited powers of imagination, should have chosen as a medium of self-expression precisely that creative art-form which since Aristotle has passed for the highest in every school of æsthetics. And not only chosen it, but vivified it in a way that may fairly be called epoch-making.

Or was it the quality of logic in the drama that attracted Lessing, was it the dialectician in him that made him a dramatist?. . . The tendency to polemic—what he himself called the spitfire irascibility (*Spitzbübin Irascibilität*), the love of controversy for its own sake—runs through all his works. He puts in the pepper and salt, sometimes slyly, sometimes with reckless hand; the passion for seasoning grows upon him apace, until it seems that he finds the merely creative and dramatic very flat by contrast. (pp. 128-29)

[If] anything could bring Lessing's good name as a poet into disrepute with his countrymen it would be his zeal in polemic. Heine has put it most wittily: Lessing, the giant he says, in his rage let fly a few random rocks at certain nonentities—to whom then these rocks served as grave-stones to keep them from being forgotten. Lessing himself was not insensible to the superfluity of honour which he showed to some of his opponents. "I should not like," he wrote of one of his controversies, "to have the value of this enquiry measured by its occasion. That is so despicable that only the way in which I have used it can excuse me for wanting to use it at all." To which he appends a little apologia for polemic which even to-day is entirely pertinent. "Not, indeed," he says, "that I did not regard our modern public as a bit too squeamish with regard to controversy or anything suggesting controversy. It seems to want to forget that it owes to sheer contradiction its enlightenment on many subjects of first importance, and that if human beings had never yet quarrelled over anything in this world neither would they be of one mind over anything to this day."

Scepticism, denial, the tendency to these, not merely form a trait of the classic type which Lessing founded; doubt is its native heath, its religion, the soil in which it lives and flour-ishes. Doubt as belief, scepticism as a positive passion—such is quite genuinely the paradox exhibited by Lessing. It is a paradox of the heart and not of the understanding. . . . Man, he asserts, proves his worth not in the possession or the supposed possession of truth, but in the sheer pains he has taken to come at it. That is to subjectivate the value of truth and almost truth itself. It implies a profound philosophic doubt of the objective, together with a passion for research, as which alone he envisages human morality. For how false it would be to confuse this philosophic doubt with nihilism, with intentional malice! He once said of his *Nathan der Weise:* "It is not at all a satirical piece, such as ends with a burst of mocking laughter. It is an affecting piece, such as I have always written." Instead of satirical he would have said nihilistic, had the word been current in his time. His scepticism is as far from flippancy as is his wit, which is a scorching wit, but not supercilious—a genuine expression of his way of reacting to life. He is witty even in the letter where he describes the birth and death of his little Traugott, written while his wife lay dying. Wittiest of all he is when some display of sanctimonious orthodoxy rouses his wrath and dips his restless pen in gall. He it was who spoke the immortal words: "If God held all the truth in his closed right hand and in his left the single ever-living urge towards truth, though with the proviso that I must forever err, and said to me 'Choose!' I should bow down humbly before his left hand and say, 'Father, give me this. Pure truth is for thee alone!' " Note the fervour of the utterance. These are not the accents of irreligion, but of a religious doubt that approaches a worship of the infinite and a perpetual striving towards it.

But what orthodoxy saw therein was a stiff-necked rejection of revelation. This great Protestant had angered literal Lutheranism to the core; it sought—but in vain—to provoke him in the struggle to a compromising admission of his actual beliefs. It looked a though Lessing fought, not so much in behalf of some truth, or of truth in general, as out of a passion for administering small dagger-thrusts that should rouse his opponents out of their comfortable intellectual and spiritual landlordism. And yet the theological controversy with Hauptpastor Goeze is very far from being a satirical or nihilistic performance. There is no "burst of mocking laughter" about it; it is "touching and kindly, such as I have always written." In its fine-tempered ductability, its calm in the face of provocation, in the brilliance of its sallies, in its high seriousness, it is very probably his best work; I would even say his best creative work. It is easier to see this to-day, now that its theology has ceased to be anything but background and *point d'appui* ["point of support"] for ethical and intellectual generalisations.

"The letter is not the spirit"—this is Lessing's position and his theme. It is a position that out-Luthers Luther, carrying him on beyond the text and the letter; by it he probably meant to suggest the saving of religion and the spirit, since the letter was no longer to be saved. . . . True, in Lessing's glorious controversial writings there comes into play so much irony, so much veiled allusion, so much dialectical virtuosity, so much tactical dissembling, that after all some confusion is inevitable. Even the virtuosity is confusing, as being the product not of callousness, vanity or satiric bent, but of a deep seriousness, passionate and "touching." Was Lessing really seeking to save Christianity, by saying that it had been there before the Scripture and would be when the Scripture was no more? Yet he wrote a twelfth "Anti-Goeze," the *Nathan;* and of it he said that he would be content if it taught one out of a thousand readers to doubt the evidence and the universality of his religion. And if this religion were Christianity—what then? Lessing was more radical than he dared to express; but it was precisely in his ambiguity that he was radical. In order to be a thorn in the side of bigoted Lutheranism he chimed in with the Catholics; on the other hand, he was offensive to rationalists and the enlightenment, and had more sympathy with downright orthodoxy than with the half-way kind watered down with liberalism. Was that perfidy and bad faith? The nation in general never found it so; Lessing has always been considered a pattern of courage and manliness. Only this manliness, this trustworthiness was not of a simple kind, but such as an artist can possess, varied and played upon by his art, not only in the matter of form but likewise in that ultimate passion which is the organic secret of all creation. Precisely when Lessing seemed to stand right, he was standing farther left than anything his age could conceive.

And so when this greatest Protestant between Luther and Nietzsche takes the field against a literal interpretation of the Scriptures and the proselytising romanticism of the Catholic Church seizes on his sallies and turns them to the advantage of the Roman tradition and authority, it is hard to conceive anything more disingenuous. But at least the fact is evidence— the only piece of its kind in Germany—that brains can fight on the side of reaction. (pp. 130-35)

He himself, once so living and present, is now an historical figure; his one-sided—and once so salutary—tendency to rationalism, his doctrine of an abstract virtue, put into the mouth of Nathan, that all too humanly sweeps away the conception of *religio* and will not hear of any inborn and positive faith-content, is to-day no longer quite viable. The enlightenment whose true son and faithful knight Lessing always, despite all temperamental irregularities, remained, is to-day intellectually out of date; it has made way for a fuller-blooded, deeper, more tragic conception of life. All this is undeniable. (p. 137)

This great controversialist of ours did not become nihilistic, did not "leave the field with a burst of mocking laughter." He was kindly. And this his nation, and all the nations, should count it his highest claim to praise. He pondered long and deeply. That he then made play with the conclusions to which he came was not done for the sake of the play. His was a spirit as full of faith, love and hope as any that has lived and taken thought for the lot of man. He, manliest of spirits, had faith in the coming of an age of humanity. Let me end on those words in which he bore witness to his faith, words full of an inward emotion that lifts his usual lively clarity of style to a level but seldom—and then how movingly—attained by him: "Wise Providence, move onward, at thine own unnoted pace. But let me never, because I mark not, despair of thee, even when thy step seems to tend backwards. It is not true, that the shortest line is always the straight one." (p. 138)

Thomas Mann, "Lessing," in his Past Masters and Other Papers, *translated by H. T. Lowe-Porter, Alfred A. Knopf, 1933, pp. 117-38.*

GEORG LUKÁCS (essay date 1936-37)

[Lukács, a Hungarian literary critic and philosopher, was a leading proponent of Marxism. His Marxist ideology was part of a broader system of thought which sought to further the values of rationalism (peace and progress), humanism (socialist politics), and traditionalism (realist literature) over the counter-values of irrationalism (war), totalitarianism (reactionary politics), and modernism (post-realist literature). The subjects of his literary criticism are primarily the nineteenth-century Realists—Honoré de Balzac and Leo Tolstoy—and their twentieth-century counterparts—Maxim Gorky and Thomas Mann. In such major works as Essays ueber Realismus (1948; Studies in European Realism, 1950) and Der historische Roman (1955; The Historical Novel, 1962), Lukács explicated his belief that "unless art can be made creatively consonant with history and human needs, it will always offer a counterworld of escape and marvelous waste." In the following excerpt from The Historical Novel, which was written in 1936-37, Lukács discusses Lessing's concept of the dialectical connection between history and tragedy.]

The dialectical connection between history and tragedy is first grasped as a problem, in however approximate a fashion, in the writings of Lessing. This is his great achievement and to this he owes his special position in the history of aesthetics during the Englightenment. In the writings of Lessing the Enlightenment's new conception of the relationship between drama and history finds its highest formulation. . . . [Lessing's attitude] appears at first to be thoroughly anti-historical, since he views history as a mere "repertory of names". However, a closer analysis shows that it is not quite as simple as this. The essence of Lessing's conception may be summed up as follows: "the poet must hold characters more sacred than facts". Hence he formulates the question as follows: "*How far may the poet stray from historical truth?* In all that does not concern the characters, as far as he likes. He must hold *only the characters sacred* and may be allowed to add only what will strengthen them, show them in their best light; the least essential alteration would eliminate the cause of why they hold these names and not others. And nothing is more offensive than something for which we cannot find a cause."

Lessing thus puts the question, above all, more decisively, openly and honestly than the theorists of French classicism. As a great theorist of the theatre he understands that man must be at the centre of drama, that only a person with whom we can directly and wholeheartedly sympathize throughout the entire compass of his destiny and unique psychology can become the hero of a play. Thus, despite the apparently anti-historical formulation of his question, despite many anti-historical tendencies in his outlook, Lessing already poses the question much more historically. He no longer allows playwrights to devise a "path" which will connect uncomprehended historical facts. He demands that they should approach the figures of the past as whole and indivisible characters, that from among them they should choose as their heroes only such as can be made intelligible to the present throughout the entire range of their destinies. This is a great step forward in the theoretical clarification of the question. Admittedly, historical material is still something accidental for Lessing, since history does not yet appear as a process leading up to the present, since the suitability of historical characters which Lessing demands does not yet depend so necessarily on the inner historical nature of the clash of social forces underlying the collision.

Nevertheless, it cannot be denied that there are other tendencies in Lessing which show a dawning appreciation for these connections. To be sure, they are due more to his deep understanding of the special nature of dramatic form than to a real historical sense. But Lessing is entirely in the right when he resolutely rejects any appeal to historical authenticity or lack of authenticity in the assessment of an historical play. This he does for the sake of the necessities of dramatic form. "That has really happened? so be it: there will be a good reason for it in the eternal infinite connection of all things. In the latter there is wisdom and goodness, which, in the few links which the poet takes out, seem to us blind fate and cruelty. From these few links he should make a whole which is fully rounded, where one thing is fully explained by another, where no difficulty arises as a result of which we become dissatisfied with this one plan and must seek satisfaction outside in the general plan of things . . .'' Lessing thus defends the freedom of the dramatist against the merely factual correctness of historical data in the name of the self-contained totality of drama, with which he links the demand that this totality should be an adequate image of the general laws of the historical process. He demands therefore the freedom to diverge from individual facts in the name of a deeper fidelity to the spirit of the whole. This is already a profound demonstration of the relation of drama to reality.

In his concrete analysis Lessing goes still further. He recognizes that there are many cases where historical reality already provides in a pure form the tragedy which the playwright seeks. In such cases he requires that playwright to surrender himself to the inner dialect of the material and to elicit the laws of its movement with the greatest possible faithfulness. In reproaching late Corneille he concentrates on the latter's inability to recognize the great, tragic course of real history and his having to resort, therefore, to trivial inventions which deform and debase this great line of events already present in reality.

In this spirit Lessing defends the material of Corneille's *Rodogune* against Corneille himself. ''What more does it need . . . to provide the material of a tragedy? With the genius, nothing, with the bungler, everything. Only such events can engage the attention of the genius as are grounded in one another, only chains of causes and effects. To trace the latter back to the former, to weigh the former against the latter, everywhere to exclude chance, to allow everything that occurs to occur in such a way that it could not occur differently: this, this is his task, if he works in the field of history, transforming the useless treasures of the memory into nourishment for the mind.'' The ''wit'' of the French classicists on the other hand was merely interested in analogies, it joined incompatibles and therefore found the most powerful historical subjects unfruitful, so that they had to be supplemented and ''embellished'' with trivial love intrigues.

Already here an extremely deep relationship between the dramatist and the life process is being demanded. What Lessing's theory still lacks is the realization that this life process is already historical in itself. It was left to the classical period of literature and philosophy to understand this theoretically, however much individual formulations still inevitably suffer from the perverseness of philosophic idealism. (pp. 162-64)

> *Georg Lukács, ''Historical Novel and Historical Drama,'' in his* The Historical Novel, *translated by Hannah Mitchell and Stanley Mitchell, Merlin Press, 1962, pp. 89-170.*

MARY M. COLUM (essay date 1937)

[*An Irish-American essayist and literary critic, Colum regularly contributed criticism to* Forum, *the* Saturday Review of Literature, *and other periodicals. In the following excerpt, she describes and interprets Lessing's contribution to the development of modern literature and criticism.*]

Modern criticism as a literary force began in Germany in the middle of the eighteenth century and began with Lessing, who laid the foundation on which all critics since have worked. (p. 18)

Lessing's great interest was drama and controversy, so he wrote dramas, controversy, verse, and criticism; he was the first outstanding German dramatist and one of the greatest of controversialists. (p. 20)

[Lessing] who, in the estimation of the present writer, was the most original and the most originating mind in modern criticism, though not the greatest, . . . aroused a whole nation to literary expression. Through the energy of his ideas and his practice he gave release to minds that without him would either never have found a voice or only piped a feeble note. . . . Not only did his splendid thought light up the way for his own countrymen, his influence spread to all European literature. It is even true to say that not only the seeds of contemporary literary ideas, but the seeds of contemporary technical inventions in writing are to be found in Lessing's criticism, for the most recent developments in technique are an outcrop of his special notion of ''action'' in literary composition.

The two main principles with which his name in criticism is associated are the conception of literature as an expression of national or racial genius, and, secondly, the notion that each of the arts has a boundary beyond which it is best not to pass, and that the highest development of any art takes place inside its own boundary. The conception of literature as an expression of racial or national genius derives from the German philosophy of racism and is valid only to a degree: it does not cover the total range of literature in any country or in any period. However, in the heyday of its popularity it represented a high truth and was potent with inspiration until almost the year before last. . . . (pp. 22-4)

The stressing of this idea, the racial and national idea, was a powerful force in exciting Lessing's readers; it was the first time in literary history that it had been put forward as a doctrine of literary production. And as any idea that has once been powerful may, in suitable soil, again be a source of power, it is worth while considering why it was powerful and why the soil was suitable. For one thing, Lessing put it forward both forcibly and convincingly, both in precept and practice; he was that figure who sometimes appears in literary history, the man with a new idea which, when it is expressed, goes straight to the minds and hearts of his readers as a form of nutriment for which they were longing. (pp. 24-5)

[Lessing] had to cure his countrymen of the contempt for their own language and culture and their mania for quoting the verses and dramas of the French poets, and in particular the poetry of Voltaire, which did not happen to be poetry at all, and his dramas, which did not happen to be dramas at all. When Voltaire arrived in Berlin, Goethe was a babe in arms; Herder, who later was to become Lessing's aide and disciple, was a little boy in petticoats, and Lessing himself was only twenty-two. But though Lessing earlier had, like everybody else, floundered around in imitations of the French, he soon outgrew this immaturity, and with the instinct of a man of genius, he perceived that if he was ever to rouse his countrymen to genuine literary expression, one of the first things to be fought was the influence of Voltaire. . . . Lessing had to fight vigorously . . . , and he was well equipped for the battle: he was learned; he was witty; he was satirical; he could be profound; he could himself illustrate his own critical theories. In controversy he was a master. His literary attacks have been described as lacking in urbanity. But urbanity, which is a virtue in personal quarrels, has, it may be, no more place in a fight for intellectual convictions than it has in a statement of the theory of relativity; urbanity is a necessity in social intercourse, but truth, to quote Lessing himself, is a necessity of the soul.

In the realization of his theory that literature was an expression of national being, one of the first things Lessing had to cope with was the language of the literature he was trying to create. The language according to Frederick should be French, and according to Gottsched might be German, but only the German of savants, a language different from that of every-day life. Lessing, in spite of his passion for the Greeks, was, like Coleridge after him, like all the writers sprung from the blood of the old Teutons, by temperament more akin to the spirit of the Hebrew Bible than to that of the Greeks or Latins, or that of any people working in their tradition. He turned back to Luther's Bible, and to those long-despised sources from which Luther said he got the language that he used for his writing— "the mother in the house, the children in the street, the man in the market-place." The language, literature, and emotions of that other great Teutonic or part-Teutonic people, the English, had been profoundly influenced by the Bible, and Lessing now announced that the German mentality was subject to much the same influences as the English. All literatures influence each other, but a choice of influences had to be made and those chosen which were in accord with the national genius. But the only art the ordinary man among Lessing's fellow countrymen came in contact with was the artificial tragedy made in imitation of Racine and Corneille and staged by strolling players all over the country. (pp. 29-32)

[For] the average person interested in character, literature meant a play, generally a play in verse—when people spoke of literature they generally meant a composition in verse. It was for this reason that when Lessing started his literary reforms he began with the drama: with his versatile mind he was not only able to invent the principles of reform but to carry them into practice. The art the people came in contact with, he said, should reflect the people's life, and so he wrote a play, *Minna von Barnhelm,* that, for the first time in German literary history, brought German life on the stage. The audiences were delighted to see, on the boards, themselves and their problems, their life and their language, the contemporary history of their country. It was the first conscious and deliberate experiment in making literature national expression—an expression of the people. (pp. 32-3)

About the same time that he produced *Minna von Barnhelm,* Lessing published his classic in criticism, *Laocoön.* This is one of those books like, in science, Darwin's *Origin of Species;* in criticism, Taine's *De l'Intelligence;* in psychology, Freud's *Interpretation of Dreams,* which turn men's minds in a new direction. Its subject was the boundary between literature or poetry and the plastic arts; its effect was the overthrowing of the rococo formalism, the conventionalism that had had a strangle hold on literature, and the release of the minds of his countrymen to literary expression. *Laocoön* was not only the first piece of real modern criticism—it was the first extensive piece of criticism since Aristotle. By showing that each art has its laws, its boundary beyond which it is possible to pass, but that each art achieves the best results inside its own boundary, that each art has a special function and that it cannot trespass on the functions of the other arts, he introduced into criticism a wholly new principle. *Laocoön* was not limited to the theme proposed: it was filled with exciting ideas about life, psychology, methods of writing. (p. 34)

In his great attempt to define the boundaries of the arts, to show the limits of expression in each art, Lessing brought into criticism a wholly new principle, and if only this principle were put into general practice it would be a liberation for every art. The picture that tries to tell a story can never be anything but an illustration for a piece of literature; the literary passage that tries to produce the effect of a painting loses its natural verve; the poem that insists on being pure music is neither music nor poetry. Lessing meant the *Laocoön* to be only a first volume, the volume in which he delimited the provinces of poetry and the plastic arts; he had meant to write a second volume which would deal with the relations of music and literature and which would delimit the provinces of these two arts, but he did not get down to it—perhaps through lack of sufficient knowledge or simply through lack of time: he lived only to be fifty-two. The fact is that whereas he delivered a lasting blow to the sort of literature that imitated painting and the sort of painting or sculpture that imitated literature, the notion that poetry can reproduce the effects of music still has a sturdy life in literary cliques. (pp. 35-6)

To return to *Laocoön*: Lessing hung his ideas on the Laocoön in sculpture and the Laocoön in literature: the Laocoön of the Greek sculpture and the Lacoön of Virgil. He developed certain ideas of his predecessor, Winckelmann. It would have been against the laws of plastic beauty to show faces with muscles violently and permanently distorted; therefore, in the group of the sculptor, while we have Laocoön and his children entwined in a death grip by the serpent, in the midst of most frightful sufferings, we see on each face the expression of a soul at rest. This was, Lessing explained, because a statue or a picture can show us only a moment of time, whereas in poetry we have the development of an action. (pp. 36-7)

Without the aid of his younger contemporary, [Johann Gottfried] Herder, it might not have been so easy for Lessing to carry out his idea of literature as national expression. For Herder had what Lessing lacked—the lyrical mind. Lessing was learned, witty, satirical, profound: he could analyze to the depths any type of literature except the lyrical, and this drawback made him somewhat lacking in the comprehension of every kind of poetry. He was never the equal of Herder in understanding the workings of the poetic mind. In spite of his spontaneity, in spite of the fact that he published a book of what he called lyrics, his mind was incapable of lyrical flights. (pp. 37-8)

Lessing, for all his hatred of the rule-makers, had a passion for Aristotle. In spite of his belief in what he called "the inner rule" he thought that absolute canons of art could be arrived at and that the way to reach them was through a study of the Greeks. The rules expounded by Aristotle, he maintained, were as infallible as the elements of Euclid, and when he wished to praise Shakespeare highly he said he was truer to the Aristotelian principles than were the French classical dramatists. (p. 39)

In Lessing, who gave his mind especially to the study of form, we have in germ very many of the most modern developments of literary forms—the abolishing of transitions, the revelation of physical traits of people or landscape or things by showing them in action. After two hundred years, sentences from *Laocoön* are still literary sign-posts taking one away from swamps and jungles. Nothing has been said about emotional extravagance in art better than Lessing's—"In the whole gamut of emotion there is no moment less advantageous than its topmost note." For, as he said, "Beyond the top there is nothing more and nothing is left to arouse the imagination." . . . And who

Eighteenth-century etching of Laocoön, rendered by Jean de Gourmont.

better than Lessing has noted the necessity for the extension of the boundaries of art beyond the notions of the Greeks, to include not only the naturally beautiful but the whole of nature and humanity, of which the beautiful is only a part? For, as he remarked, an ugliness of nature can be transformed into a beauty of art. And how clear and emphatic are his objections to the use of propaganda in art! "I should like the name Works of Art to be reserved for those alone in which the artist could show himself actually as artist. All the rest, in which too evident traces of religious dogma appear, are unworthy of the name. Art here has not wrought on her own account but has been auxiliary to religion." . . . In addition to attacking French neo-classicism Lessing made a study of the Greek text of Aristotle's *Poetics* and gave the interpretation that is now generally accepted. (pp. 44-6)

> *Mary M. Colum, "Modern Literature Begins: The Ideas of Lessing and Herder," in her* From These Roots: The Ideas That Have Made Modern Literature, *1937. Reprint by Columbia University Press, 1944, pp. 18-46.*

FORD MADOX FORD   (essay date 1938)

[*Ford was an English man of letters who played an important role in the development of twentieth-century realistic and modernist literature and art. In 1908, he founded the* English Review, *a periodical generally considered the finest literary journal of its*

day during Ford's brief tenure as editor. Much of the journal's renown was due to Ford's acute editorial perceptiveness in publishing works by such writers as Henry James, T. S. Eliot, H. G. Wells, Thomas Hardy, and Ezra Pound, in addition to his discovery of both D. H. Lawrence and Wyndham Lewis. Another contributor, Joseph Conrad, had earlier collaborated on two novels with Ford. Although these experimental works have received little critical attention, scholars recognize the significance of the collaboration in shaping impressionistic techniques which characterized later, highly regarded works by both authors. Many years after resigning the editorship of the English Review, *Ford established the* Transatlantic Review, *to which James Joyce, Gertrude Stein, and Ernest Hemingway contributed. Among Ford's own writings,* The Good Soldier *(1915) and the tetralogy* Parade's End *(1924-28)—novels concerned with the social, political, and moral decline of Western civilization—are considered masterful examples of the modern psychological novel. In the following excerpt from his popular survey of world literature,* The March of Literature from Confucius' Day to Our Own *(1938), Ford describes the merits and faults of Lessing's critical and dramatic works.*]

[Lessing] is a figure of a double international significance. The influence of his *Laocoön* on the critical world of his day was very great, and, indeed, taking into account the difference of its author's tastes and critical dicta, it may still be said to be regarded as a standard critical work. And, on the other hand, Lessing himself was strongly under English influence. Not only in the *Laocoön* does he speak in terms of relative contempt of Molière and Racine as opposed to Shakespeare, but his first play, *Miss Sara Samson,* a tragedy of common life, was an avowed imitation of the English plays of his date. (p. 533)

Lessing's literary output was enormous and of his nine plays, three can be said still to hold the German stage, *Minna von Barnhelm, Emilia Galeotti* and *Nathan der Weise,* though the last is almost more a dramatic poem for recitation than a stage play and *Emilia Galeotti* is almost too terribly harrowing to be supportable by a modern audience. (p. 534)

The great quality of his plays—even such early and little known ones as *Der Junge Gelehrter*—is their really wonderful stage technique, which he is said to have derived from his study of the English drama of common life, though I am inclined to believe that Shakespeare had on him a greater influence than, say, either Congreve who died five years after, or Wycherley who died nine years before, Lessing's birth.

He was, however, hardly in any sense a poet and his blank verse is excruciating. Indeed, the writer is inclined to believe that his disinclination from Lessing and from German writing in general must have come from the really physical pain inflicted on a boy of fourteen, at the time really mad for the blank verse of Shakespeare or Marlowe or Beaumont and Fletcher, by being forced to read aloud and over and over again passages from *Nathan.* There is a dreadful didactic story of a ring introduced into the body of that "poetic drama" that still comes back to me in half-waking nightmares. (p. 535)

Nevertheless, Lessing the man stands out as a splendid character—as iconoclastic thinker, literary revolutionist and as a proto-martyr tortured through his whole career by the yelps of pedants, bigots and mental dwarfs. He bore, nevertheless, that clamor on top of near-starvation, the tragic loss in fruitless childbirth of a wife whom he had long loved—after a year of marriage. He was accused of atheism because his conscience and inclination would not let him become a parson; of treachery to the fatherland, because the king Frederick the Great and his court were under French influence in all things philosophic and Lessing, considering the French lecherous, preached the discipleship of Shakespeare, Steele and Addison; he was accused of being a gambler, although on a microscopic income he supported his destitute family and collected a great library. Finally, on the appearance of *Nathan der Weise,* he was ostracized and howled down by crowds of minor writers as a Judaeophil. He was universally accused of having received a gift of a thousand ducats from the Jews of Amsterdam as the price of writing the play. The Nazi is not merely a growth of our own day. He supported all the attacks with calmness; he gave always better than he got in controversy, but the attacks that he received over *Nathan* and a final charge of atheism which he triumphantly rebutted by proving that all his religious beliefs were supported in the writings of the early Fathers of the Church overtired him in the last two years of his life and he died worn out. Two years later died Frederick the Great and with him disappeared the last traces of French influence and the teachings of Diderot and Rousseau from the German cultural heavens. (p. 536)

Lessing had not Molière's ineffable sense of the comic, his knowledge of humanity nor yet his command of language; nevertheless, his stage-sense was almost incomparable and *Minna von Barnhelm* is one of the world's best constructed comedies. It is not for nothing that even today in Germany Lessing's comedies are more often played than any of the dramas of Goethe—and that obviously because of a legitimate public demand having nothing to do with patriotism. (pp. 538-39)

Ford Madox Ford, in a chapter in his The March of Literature from Confucius' Day to Our Own, *The Dial Press, 1938, pp. 500-40.*

ALLARDYCE NICOLL   (essay date 1949)

[*Called "one of the masters of dramatic research," Nicoll is best known as a theater historian whose works have proven invaluable to students of the drama. Nicoll's* World Drama from Aeschylus to Anouilh *(1949) is considered one of his most important works; theater critic John Gassner has stated that it was "unquestionably the most thorough [study] of its kind in the English language [and] our best reference book on the world's dramatic literature." Another of his ambitious theater studies is the six-volume* A History of English Drama, 1660-1900 *(1952-59), which has been highly praised for its perceptive commentaries on drama from the Restoration to the close of the nineteenth century. Nicoll was also a popular lecturer on Shakespearean drama and the author of several studies of Shakespeare's works. In addition, he was the longtime editor of* Shakespeare Survey, *an annual publication of Shakespearean scholarship. In the following excerpt from* World Drama from Aeschylus to Anouilh, *Nicoll surveys Lessing's literary career, noting especially the strengths and weaknesses of* Hamburg Dramaturgy, Emilia Galotti, *and* Nathan the Wise.]

In the year 1765 the Hamburg National Theatre was established, destined to become, two years later, the German National Theatre, and with it came a hitherto undreamed-of periodical. Lessing had been appointed *Dramaturg* ["dramatic critic"] to the ambitious young playhouse, and, with the sponsorship of its controllers, he started to issue what is the world's first house-organ, the periodical essays issued collectively in 1769 as the *Hamburgische Dramaturgie.*

These essays were not simply occasional reviews of current productions. Throughout Lessing engaged himself in an endeavour, by means of direct criticism, to inspire young writers to turn to the composition of plays and thus to lay the foundations of a national theatrical art. His aim was at once practical and revolutionary: he ever kept the practical stage in view, and at the same time he ever sought to suggest that the pseudo-classic models favoured by Gottsched were not such as his age required. "The one thing we can never forgive in a tragic poet," he writes, "is coldness: if he arouses our interest it does not matter what he does with the petty mechanical rules." What he searches constantly for is form—organic form springing vitally from a genuine harmony between the subject-matter and the poet's untrammelled inspiration; and in his search he preaches the dual truth that the so-called 'rules' were right and proper for the Greek stage, false and improper for ours, and that, whereas the Greeks properly observed certain restrictions precisely because they were organic developments of their theatre form, the French classic authors were forced, while giving lip-service to the restrictions, to seek for means of circumventing them. By such observations and by the general power of his critical thought Lessing was able not merely to accomplish the negative task of destroying the pseudo-classic cult, but also to provide a firm basis for creative artistry of a new and different kind.

He himself endeavoured to put his own theories into execution in a series of carefully wrought plays, but unfortunately we cannot esteem Lessing the dramatist as highly as we may Lessing the critic. The *Hamburgische Dramaturgie* is worthy almost of being placed alongside Aristotle's *Poetics,* but the dramas—*Miss Sarah Sampson, Minna von Barnhelm, Emilia Galotti,* and *Nathan der Weise* . . . , although all deserving of individual attention, and although vastly superior to anything produced contemporaneously in England, never succeed in capturing that elusive quality from which true greatness springs. All are heavily oppressed by the philosophy of the 'enlightenment' which cast such a spell over the author's mind, and are rather expansions of the sentimental than plays suggestive of a fresh endeavour. *Miss Sarah Sampson,* by the very choice of an English domestic theme and setting, betrays its close association with the bourgeois drama of London, while *Minna von Barnhelm* exploits a sentimental situation such as had already served half a dozen other playwrights of this school. Here the hero, Zellheim, penniless on his discharge from the army, refuses to marry his wealthy love—the heroine who gives her name to the play—and a happy solution is found only when a lost fortune is discovered, and Minna herself, giving out that she has become poor, pretends to refuse him in turn. There is a sense of character in the comedy and a skilful development of the theme, without, however, the creation of anything of first-rate value.

Emilia Galotti has somewhat greater worth. The story is clearly taken from the age-old Roman tale of Virginia, stabbed by her father in order to save her from a tyrant's lascivious embraces; but the girl is now presented as a member of the bourgeoisie, her would-be seducer is a member of the aristocracy, and a new turn is given to the theme when Emilia is shown by no means unmoved by the lover's advances. Although there are scenes here that speak to us far more powerfully than anything in *The London Merchant,* yet this play too savours of the dramatic style that gave birth to Lillo's tragedy.

A similar judgment must be passed on *Nathan der Weise,* the subject of which had seen a faint anticipation in one of this author's juvenile works, a one-act drama called *Die Juden.* . . . Its sincerity of aim is unquestionable. Taking Nathan the Jew as his hero, Lessing shows this man, basing his whole life on such a 'natural religion' as was sought after by Diderot and his companions, infinitely superior in morality and in nobleness of mind to those who base their actions upon established creeds. Nathan is a Jew only in name; in himself he embraces all the virtues and none of the vices inherent in the tenets of Judaism, Christianity, and Mohammedanism. By the romantic device of introducing Rebecca, the supposed daughter of a Christian crusader, who falls in love with a Templar—only to discover that both he and she (brother and sister) are in reality the long-lost children of a kinsman of the Sultan Saladin (who had become a Christian just before his death)—Lessing strives to give concrete dramatic expression to his dissatisfaction with all existing creeds and, at the same time, to his belief that in all the creeds reside some elements of divine wisdom. This argument is further pursued when Nathan presents before Saladin his parable of the rings, a parable designed to demonstrate that the only true religion is that which most benefits humanity. The expression of this concept, however, does not equal the vision, or perhaps it would be more true to say that the vision so cumbersomely preponderates that what ought to excite and arouse us remains uninvested with that theatrical fire we look for in the greatest works of dramatic art.

What Goethe said of Schiller might be applied specifically to Lessing and generally to the entire school of dramatic writing that he inaugurated. ''Philosophy,'' said the poet, ''injured his poetry, because this led him to consider the idea far higher than all nature; indeed, thus to annihilate nature. He believed that what he was able to conceive must happen, whether it were in conformity with nature or not.'' (pp. 414-16)

Allardyce Nicoll, ''The Romantic Theatre,'' in his
World Drama from Aeschylus to Anouilh, *1949. Re-*

print by Harcourt, Brace and Company, 1950? pp. 412-43.

STUART ATKINS   (essay date 1951)

[*Atkins is an American scholar and academic who specializes in eighteenth-century German literature. The author of many books and short studies, his major works are* The Testament of Werther in Poetry and Drama *(1949) and* Goethe's ''Faust'': A Literary Analysis *(1958). In the following excerpt from another work, he discusses the parable of the rings in* Nathan the Wise.]

One obstacle to satisfactory literary criticism is too great learning. Interpretation of the parable of the rings in *Nathan der Weise* has not benefited from the study of Lessing's sources to the degree that exponents of the comparative method have believed, however much light may have been thrown by such study on Lessing's poetic practice. Nor has systematic study of reputable interpretations of the ring parable borne satisfying fruit, if only because the text discussed has been further and further removed from its original context by the very process of analyzing the learned interpretations of others. Indeed, the comparative appeal to analogy, and the historical concern with earlier criticism, have helped establish the false impression that *Nathan der Weise* contains an undramatic speech about 150 lines in length in which the title hero narrates a parable to demonstrate the underlying unity of Judaism, Christianity, and Mohammedanism. As a result, there has evolved a tendency to regard the dramatic poem *Nathan der Weise* as a sort of ring whose only *raison d'être* is to furnish a setting for the precious stone which is the famous parable, or else a tendency to regard the parable of the rings as an independent text properly printed as such in anthologies of German verse. In view of the fact that the creator of *Nathan der Weise* was a skillful and successful dramatist several of whose works—*Nathan* included—still hold the stage, the former tendency cannot be plausibly justified. And the latter tendency uncritically ignores two incontrovertible points: (1) that the ring parable is actually a discontinuous text in a larger dramatic context; (2) that in such a context the ring parable demands to be read as dramatic statement—for instance, as revelation of character in action. The otherwise scrupulous critic who disregards these facts may well come to the conclusion that the ring fable, subjected to the logical analysis which fables must traditionally be able to stand, is a strangely imperfect example of its genre.

To understand the parable of the rings, then, both the occasion of its telling and the larger design of the drama in which it is told must be kept in mind. The occasion is an interview between Nathan and Saladin. At his sister's suggestion, Saladin is to try to trap Nathan in some statement revealing that Nathan is the moral and intellectual inferior of his interrogator; if he succeeds, he will have an excuse to force Nathan to lend him much-needed money. This interview however, is but one of a series of tests or trials which Nathan undergoes in the course of the play. If *Nathan der Weise* were simply a character study and its dramatic form merely incidental, the interest of the interview scenes might lie in how Nathan demonstrates a wisdom so far successfully demonstrated in every crisis with which he has been confronted. But, as we shall see, the full complexity of Nathan's philosophy of life has not been revealed by this point in the play's action, and so the primary interest of this group of scenes is genuinely dramatic: we may properly wonder whether Nathan is to meet this new test triumphantly, whether he will again successfully demonstrate his practical wisdom.—The next section of this essay is devoted to a brief examination of Nathan's character and philosophy in the light of the ideological context of that part of *Nathan der Weise* which precedes his interview with Saladin. The subsequent discussion of the dramatic significance of this interview offers an evaluation of Lessing's drama in terms of aesthetic implications of the parable of the rings.

Nathan clearly represents a high type of civilized man. Reverent in his references to God . . . , he considers the possession of worldly goods less important than that of spiritual qualities (a point well demonstrated by his declaration that he owes the "possession" of Recha to virtue rather than to nature and chance). He so strongly prefers truth to the best-intentioned falsehood, the certain to the hypothetical, that he repudiates the ''Wahn''—belief in angels— . . . ; accordingly he forces himself to use painful means to cure his adopted daughter of the confusion of the humanly real with the supernaturally magical that underlies her delusion of owing her life to an angel. . . . (pp. 259-60)

Nathan's ideas on God and religious experience are obviously especially important if his parable of the rings is not to be misunderstood. He considers the created world a realm of strict causality miraculously sustained by a divine force which works only through the agency of finite phenomena—whether these be simple things . . . or something as complex as man. Moral obligations are to be repaid to the agent of God, man for instance, not to the inaccessible first cause, and the only proper way to express religious emotion is to do good. . . . Indeed religious emotion cultivated simply for its pleasurable values is an unconscious evasion of moral responsibility. The ethical, then, is for Nathan the core of religion, and his repeated emphasis on man . . . suggests that his religion is a form of deistic humanism. . . . (p. 260)

Both the Dervish and the Lay Brother make statements which suggest that the views expressed by Nathan are insufficient to explain the position of man in the universe; the Dervish warns that man cannot play at being God, that man can never reward good and evil satisfactorily, while the Lay Brother will say, as does Nathan later, that man's intentions, not achievements, are what count in the eyes of God. Indeed, the Lay Brother will even observe to Nathan that to be certain of what is good is beyond human powers. Nevertheless, the supreme importance of *human* moral standards is nowhere so strongly insisted upon as in the scene between the Templar and the Lay Brother. Both characters implicitly accept Nathan's humanistic ethical principle that human standards of right and wrong are God's also; both agree that even disinterested acts must satisfy the individual's ethical compulsion. And the Templar assures himself of the rightness of his views by arguing that otherwise God would be contradicting Himself in His creation—a common deistic argument. It is therefore not surprising that in the first scene between Saladin and Sittah Christianity is evaluated only by the ultimate standard of the ''Menschlichkeit'' ['humanness''] of its exponents.

With the scene between Saladin, Sittah, and Al-Hafi, however, the problem of religion ceases to be viewed primarily as one of belief and behavior; from now on the main problem of *Nathan der Weise* is the relationship of historical faiths to each other and to the humanistic religion which has already been textually established as the criterion by which all religions must be evaluated. Saladin, for all his good will towards Christians, automatically thinks of himself as a Moslem when faced with personal poverty. . . . We are . . . insistently reminded that Nathan's universal deistic humanism does not allow of prejudice

even against the Zorastrian clinging to a pre-monotheistic religion. If Nathan's ethical activities extend to members of these four faiths, it is probable that they extend also to those who have fallen back from the higher forms of these faiths into primitive superstition—that they extend to the very people who believe, as Sittah informs Saladin, that Nathan owes his wealth to magic powers. Nathan's soul, then, is open to every virtue and is attuned to the beautiful; his mind is free of every prejudice. It is little wonder that Nathan wins the friendship of the Templar despite the latter's strong anti-Jewish sentiments (which are not racially anti-Semitic . . .). (p. 261)

In the scenes that come shortly before Nathan's first meeting with Saladin—shortly before the telling of the parable of the three rings—the problem of the relationship between historical faith and universal religious truth remains paramount. Recha, apparently repeating a lesson her father has taught her well, reproaches Daja for speaking of the Templar's God as though the Templar possessed him. . . . Her religion, and her father's, is that of reason. . . . She can therefore depreciate the articles of faith for which Christians have heroically died and still be sympathetic toward their sufferings, still admire their deeds. Since her position, like that of her father and teacher, is antitheological (or at least untheological), she finds consolation in the Christian doctrine that . . . imperfect knowledge of God does not prevent submission to His will. Even her questions to the Templar about his visit to Mt. Sinai deliberately recall confessional differences, yet also allow a clearly non-Mosaic allusion to God's omnipresence. . . . (p. 262)

When Nathan is interviewed by Saladin, he is modest without being servile. His attempts to forestall a request for a loan only postpone temporarily the Sultan's fatal question. . . . The very phrasing of the question insists on the distinction between Judaic ''law'' and Christian ''faith,'' on the combination of these two types of religious formalization in Mohammedanism. To Nathan's protest that he is a Jew, Saladin counters that only one of the three religions named can be the true one; he claims that a philosopher's choice of a confession—Nathan is the ''Wise''—is not governed by empirical chance . . . but by rational—we would say a priori—reasons. . . . Saladin also sees that Nathan is puzzled by his request, and realizes that Nathan may be suspicious of the motives behind his question and of Saladin's excuse that he has not had time to think about the matter himself. He allows Nathan a moment to think up an answer while he himself leaves to make sure that Sittah is not eaves-dropping.

Nathan's ensuing soliloquy makes clear that he indeed suspects Saladin's motives for wanting a simple answer to what is really a highly complex question, and Nathan wisely concludes that Saladin probably does not. . . . [Nathan] resolves to try to satisfy Saladin with a ''Märchen'' [''fable'']—that is, he will not give the Sultan a real answer to his question. For Nathan has clearly admitted to himself that he is no longer a Jew in a theological sense (an orthodox ''Stockjude''), and we already know that he is not a Christian or a Moslem but rather some variety of enlightened deist. The parable of the rings must thus be read as an evasive answer to Saladin's original question, as a tale sufficiently entertaining to distract Saladin from the original issue of a priori justification of Nathan's apparent Judaism. It may also contain a statement of Nathan's own faith, but this statement will be only incidental to the distractive function of his parable. Indeed, that at some point Nathan will reveal what he considers the highest religious truth is almost certain from the assurance which Nathan expresses after Saladin's return. . . . (pp. 262-63)

Having obtained permission to tell a [tale] . . . , Nathan begins it only after he has deprecated his narrative abilities and, for the second time during his interview, been censured by Saladin for his modesty. What follows is apparently an "oriental tale" in the best eighteenth-century manner, a *conte philosophique* as it were. We learn of a ring which has . . . hidden power. . . . The provenience of this ring is indefinite . . . , but it is the inheritance of the favorite male heirs of the original owner's family, each of whom in turn becomes head of the family regardless of the principle of primogeniture.—On the basis of what is said up to this point it is only safe to claim that the ring is a symbol of its possessor's human love *for* others, and that its ultimate provenience does not seem to be supernatural.

After a brief question to Saladin, perhaps to verify the effectiveness of his narrative technique and to make sure that Saladin is actually distracted from the original question, Nathan comes to the father who has three equally beloved sons, who promises the ring to each in turn. In order to fulfill his promises, the father has made two duplicates of the original ring, and the artist who has duplicated the original is so successful that when the father dies he presumably does not know which ring he is giving to which son. This familiar folk-tale motif of three sons apparently begins to bore Saladin, who urges Nathan to finish his story quickly. Nathan now makes haste to soothe Saladin by declaring that he has really finished, since what follows will be obvious to him—as indeed the dispute of three heirs is in such stories. He pauses for Saladin to comment on the implications of family dissension, the unidentifiability of the original ring; when Saladin does not rise to the bait, Nathan is forced to draw the analogy from his parable. . . . Saladin is not satisfied that this juridical dilemma is analogous with the problem of choosing between the three religions about which he inquired; warning Nathan not to play with him, he points out that each of the religions in question is visibly different from the other, very unlike the three rings.

Nathan now returns to Saladin's original term, "Gründe," reasons, which he however uses not in an aprioristic sense but in an empirical historical one and then in an empirical psychological one. For he appeals first to the universal fact that organized religions are based on historical tradition, and then to the fact that historical tradition is vouched for only by our response to the love evidenced to us by our families from childhood on. The Sultan is so impressed by this argument—which is an argument *ad hominen* in its appeal to his own sense of family loyalty, to his own filial love—that he gives his tacit affirmation to Nathan's argument. Nathan consequently considers it safe to continue the ring story which he has just declared finished.

The depositions in court are briefly summarized. (pp. 263-64)

The judge realizes that there is not enough evidence in connection with the case before him to allow a decision, and is about to dismiss the pleas when he recalls the true ring's magic powers. He then asks which brother is best beloved of the other two. When it transpires that none is, he concludes that the genuine ring has been lost, that the father concealed the loss by having three imitations made. This Saladin finds "herrlich" ["splendid"], although he has already been told as a fact that only two imitations were made. . . . [At this point, the] ring which Nathan originally implied to be the symbol of the best of three religions has disappeared from the parable. The three religions about which Saladin originally inquired have been reduced to imitations of some truer, more valid faith. The issue of the choice of a religion is left exactly where it was at the

moment when Nathan shifted from aprioristic to empirical grounds. What then has Nathan gained by continuing his parable beyond the moment when Saladin tacitly accepted the empirical argument?

The answer would seem to be that the judge's statement allows Nathan to define his own religion in more general terms than he could use in dramatic situations where he had to deal with such specific issues as Recha's lapse into superstition, Al-Hafi's perfectionism, or the Templar's intolerance of Jewish religious intolerance. . . . [The judge's injunction] not only sums up views which Nathan has himself expressed and which he himself has exemplified; it also subsumes principles which, as we have seen, have been expressed or exemplified by Al-Hafi, the Templar, the Lay Brother, and Recha in such a way that Nathan's rational deism, his natural religion, can almost plausibly be claimed to become the original ring of the parable. That the original ring of the parable is no finite man's religion seems more likely however. . . . It is impossible to escape one's historical origins, and that is no doubt why Nathan's ethical deism so closely resembles Christian ethics. If the judge in Nathan's parable really believes that in a million years there will be a wiser judge than himself, it is only because he accepts in secularized form the premise of man's ultimate perfectibility. The truly wise, like Nathan or Saladin, acknowledge that a completely meaningful interpretation of life is beyond man's powers. (pp. 264-65)

If Nathan has not used his ring symbol consistently, if he has exploited it for purposes of deliberate aesthetic misdirection, he has done so because of the dangerous situation in which he finds himself; if he has not answered Saladin's original question, it is because he cannot honestly do so. Nevertheless, when he has won over his listener, he does gratuitously answer a question which Saladin might have put: "What do you think the true, i.e. ideal, religion to be?" He could not honestly answer Saladin's original question because he is not a Jew at all, because he does not accept its premise that one of the three religions named by Saladin is the ideal religion, and so he has used his parable to raise other questions which he can answer. His method is that of a forum speaker who understands exactly how to reformulate a dangerous or impossible question in a way that allows it to be answered to the satisfaction of his interrogator—an answer received is all that we expect when a question is asked, and it makes little difference to most of us whether it is the answer to the question we have asked or not.

The question which Nathan never answers, however, is the question "Why have you chosen your religion?" It is a question which Nathan's self-contained deistic religion never seems to have been able to answer satisfactorily, and it is a question the answer to which can hardly be said to be found in *Nathan der Weise*. Indeed, the very last words of the ring parable may be regarded as Lessing's own tacit admission that he is aware that this question might properly be raised. For the judge urges the representatives of the three religions with which the parable is concerned (which are not, as we have noted, the only historical religions in *Nathan der Weise*) to transmit the true religious spirit to their descendants; these may again appear at the judgment seat ["in a million years"]. . . . The judge's million years are a period of time beyond human historical comprehension. The religion which he has outlined is not justifiable on an a priori basis by human reason; it is an irrational, or at best empirical, faith no less than any irrational historical religion empirically accepted on faith in our fathers. Accordingly, reason is only another name for moral conscience, is another term

for God's mysterious way.... The only solution to the dilemma which Saladin posed for Nathan is the same as that for
the dilemma with which the judge is faced: to suspend judgment
indefinitely.

Although it may be true that Nathan's religion is presented in
such a light as to seem superior to the other religions mentioned
in *Nathan der Weise*, it is not just to claim that Lessing presents
it as the best and only possible ideal religion. *Nathan der Weise*
was written on the eve of Kant's first *Critique*, at a time when
the Enlightenment had ceased to be blindly optimistic. On the
other hand, the only solution to ideological conflict indeed
seems still to be that which the family intrigue of *Nathan der
Weise* unambiguously symbolizes: a universal family of mankind. If Lessing is perhaps unconsciously uncertain of the validity of deism, perhaps secretly dissatisifed with the self-contained causal realm of nature which seemed the only cosmos
rationally acceptable in the light of Newtonian science, the
self-evident inconsistencies of Nathan's ring fable are but further evidence of Lessing's extraordinary intellectual honesty.
If we are constantly reminded throughout *Nathan der Weise* of
its family intrigue, if there is hardly a larger scene in the play
which does not insistently prepare for the ultimate recognition
scene, that is because the family intrigue is the core of the
dramatic action. As author of *Pope ein Metaphysiker!* and the
Hamburg Dramaturgy, Lessing well knew that drama is character in action, not philosophic statement; it can only present,
as action, life as it is, might be, or should be. *Nathan der
Weise* is utopian drama stating Lessing's honest vision of a
viable way of life for mankind. Understanding tolerance is
recognized as the only practicable solution to conflict by a man
whose life had seen him involved by his passion for truth in
many a fight. And before the writing of *Nathan der Weise*, we
are never allowed to forget, had come the *Anti-Goeze*.

Nathan der Weise, then, is not a family drama constructed
around a parable of three rings. The parable of the rings is
rather a function of the all-important family plot which symbolizes the brotherhood of man, the need of men to tolerate
one another, and one another's ways and ideas, even as they
do within their own families. Without the parable of the rings
Nathan could never demonstrate his right to admission, on the
basis of moral-intellectual friendship, to the family circle of
Saladin's blood relatives. Without the parable Nathan could at
best only receive some material reward for saving Recha's
life—if indeed it were not more plausible for him to be punished
for willful violation of international religious law. It is the
successful telling of the parable that causes Saladin to hold
Nathan's hand from the moment the parable has ended until
the conclusion of the scene of which it is a part. The friendship
that it gains him saves Nathan later from the dangers of temperamental Oriental despotic justice; it allows *Nathan der Weise*
to end as a "Family Reunion" in all happier sense of that
phrase. And if harmonious human relationships are in themselves "good," they can yet also symbolize the harmony of
human and divine will which is both Nathan's working faith
and Lessing's highest religious vision. (pp. 265-67)

> Stuart Atkins, "The Parable of the Rings in Lessing's
> 'Nathan der Weise'," in The Germanic Review, *Vol.*
> *XXVI, No. 4, December, 1951, pp. 259-67.*

JOHN GASSNER (essay date 1954)

[*Gassner, a Hungarian-born American scholar, was a great pro-
moter of American theater, particularly the work of Tennessee*

*Williams and Arthur Miller. He edited numerous collections of
modern drama and wrote two important dramatic surveys,* Masters of the Drama (1940) *and* Theater in Our Times (1954). *In the
following excerpt from the third edition (1954) of the first-named
work, Gassner examines Lessing's literary career, praising the
playwright for his original contributions to critical and dramatic
theory.*]

Lessing ... made the flight of the romantic playwrights possible by destroying the shackles of French classicism and setting the drama a high goal of freedom and liberal idealism.
Although his own stature as a playwright is modest, he is a
major figure in the drama by virtue of his polemic activity and
the example he set to his creative superiors.

The theatre which this son of a clergyman ... knew in his
student days at Leipzig was the spawn of decadent French
drama, a stiff and lifeless exercise in classic heroics and recitation. Even this was, in fact, an improvement, from a *literary*
standpoint, over the long reign of undistinguished farces that
had kept the populace edified with the clownings of Harlequin,
Germanicised as Pickelherring. To such a pass had Germany
come owing to the ravages of the Thirty Years' War. It is true
that native seventeenth-century writers like Gryphius, Rist and
Lohenstein produced historical plays, classic exercises, mo-
ralities, and comedies of a sort. But these were crude affairs
and Germany's literary dictator Gottsched saw only one solution for the low estate of the theatre; namely, to import French
tragedies like Pradon's *Regulus*, adapt other items of the Louis
Quatorze repertory, and launch imitations like his own *Dying
Cato*. (pp. 318-19)

Lessing's battles with the German pontiff of classicism were
at first informal and tentative. It was not as a critic and reformer
of the stage that he sought to shine at first. Instead he dreamed
of becoming a comedian and playwright like Molère; he took
lessons in elocution from an actor and progressed rapidly. Still,
his ambitions as a playwright were aroused as early as 1748
by the success of his first play *The Young Savant*, a satire on
a pretentious student written by Lessing to prove that he could
surpass the French school. Six slight pieces followed this initial
effort without marking any development in content or treatment. But in his twenty-sixth year came *Miss Sara Sampson*
which for all its faults is superior to the models of "bourgeois
tragedy" provided by Diderot and Lillo. This tragedy of a
middle-class heroine was the first modern German drama to
be taken from actual life and to be written in natural dialogue.

Literary criticism, which he enriched with his excellent *Literary
Letters*, took him from the theatre for a time. Then came years
of secretarial work in the service of the governor of Breslau,
General Tauentzien, which removed him entirely from the bat-
tlefront of letters between 1760 and 1765. But in 1766 Lessing
was back in harness with the publication of his brilliant study
Laocoon limiting the fields of poetry and painting; and a year
later he gave the German stage its best comedy for many a
decade, *Minna von Barnhelm*.

If Lessing still harbored the hope of becoming a German Molière, candor compels one to admit that he had far to go. Too
much saccharine went into the composition of the piece, and,
as Brander Matthews has noted, "*Minna* is less comic than
Molière's lighter plays and it is less weighty than Molière's
major masterpieces" [see Additional Bibliography]. Still, Lessing's effort is not entirely negligible. Besides being historically important as one of the earliest plays in any language to
change sets for every act, *Minna* provides an appealing romance in the behavior of the spirited heroine who woos her

lover when his loss of position and lack of means prevent him from taking the initiative. Moreover, the comedy was intended to heal the wounds of the Seven Years' War with its celebration of the hero's humanitarianism. Frederick the Great's officer Tellheim having been ordered to collect a fine from the conquered Thuringians, advanced the sum himself and was dismissed from the service on the suspicion of having compromised with the enemy. Living in extreme poverty, helped only by his faithful comic servant, Tellheim nurses his wounded honor in a tavern. But Minna, the Thuringian girl who learned to love him for his generous behavior toward her people, has no difficulty in finding him and overcoming his scruples. The winning characterization of Tellheim, Minna and their servants produces a pleasant comedy. It has long held the German stage in lieu of something better—which the Germans, who have not been remarkable for their sense of humor, have not supplied with much frequency.

Still plying his dual functions of critic and playwright, Lessing soon repaired to Hamburg to assume the position of "critic of plays and actors" or adviser at the newly founded first German National Theatre. The noble enterprise failed ignominiously. However, the criticisms Lessing wrote for it between April 1767 and November 1768, collected under the title of *Hamburg Dramaturgy (Hamburgische Dramaturgie)*, were epoch-making. With this work he became the second great critic of the drama, if Aristotle is to be denominated the first. He not only demolished the stilted French school in Germany but established the critical basis of the whole romantic revolt by his exaltation of Shakespeare as the king of dramatists and by his insistence upon a dramatist's right to create as he pleased without wearing the fashionable straitjacket of the "unities." His statement that "the only unpardonable fault of a tragic poet is this, that he leaves us cold; if he interests us he may do as he likes with the little mechanical rules" is now one of the commonplaces of dramatic criticism.

Lessing was nearly turned against the theatre by the unfortunate complications that ruined the Hamburg experiment. He was oppressed by debts contracted in connection with it, his health began to fail him, and his wife died in childbirth one year after their marriage. Only his post as librarian to the Duke of Brunswick at Wolfenbüttel made life tolerable for him. Nevertheless his embattled intellect lost none of its resolution. The "Reimarus" controversy which he waged against orthodox theologians was one of the most exciting battles of the "rationalists," and his last two plays *Emilia Galotti* and *Nathan the Wise* were his most ambitious works for the theatre. Both were charged with thunder against the prevailing state of affairs. *Emilia Galotti* . . . pointed to the petty despotisms of Germany, *Nathan the Wise*, published in 1779, while the American colonies were fighting valorously to erect a state that would not discriminate against any creed, celebrated religious tolerance.

In *Emilia Galotti* Lessing adapted the classic story of Virginia, the Roman maiden who was slain by her father when her virtue was threatened by a tyrant. The classic Virginia became the middle-class Emilia (a *bürgerliche Virginia* ["middle-class Virginia"] the author called her), and the Roman deceiver became an Italian princeling. Avoiding melodramatic partisanship, Lessing made Emilia susceptible to the charming but dissolute prince. Only when she realizes the hopelessness of the situation of becoming the despot's mistress, when her fiancé has been assassinated and she has been abducted does Emilia prevail upon her upright father to kill her. There is something forbidding in the theme despite Lessing's careful motivation

of the behavior of the principals, and *Emilia Galotti* is deficient in breadth and sympathy. Nevertheless, this "bourgeois tragedy" is a modern drama, and it was sufficiently relevant to conditions in Germany to strike home. The year of its publication heard the firing of the first gun of the romantic revolt in Goethe's *Goetz von Berlichingen*. But the credit for anticipating the barrage belongs to Lessing who conceived *Emilia Galotti* twelve years earlier.

An even more explicit expression of the eighteenth-century "Enlightenment" is to be found in *Nathan the Wise*. This play is to be regarded as Lessing's last testament not only because he died two years later without leaving another play except a provocative fragment of a projected Faust drama but because it is the most spirited and the noblest of his works. He came to it after having concluded a bitter theological battle in favor of rational religion, and it is even possible that *Nathan* would never have been written if the authorities had not forbidden the publication of further pamphlets on his "Reimarus case." No European play gave such direct and elevated expression to the ideals of religious tolerance.

In Nathan, modeled after his Jewish friend the philosopher and reformer Moses Mendelssohn, Lessing not only challenged racial prejudice by portraying one of the noblest characters in literature but presented an example of a man who lives by "natural religion." He is no more an orthodox Jew than he is a Christian or Mohammedan. In opposition to the strident claims of every religion, which insists that it alone has a monopoly on the true faith, Lessing showed Nathan leading a life of impeccable morality without supporting any creed, even if he retains his forefathers' simply because he was born in it. Nathan is more Christian than the followers of Jesus in the play. Having lost his wife and children in a Crusaders' pogrom, Nathan follows the precepts of Christ by saving and rearing the orphaned Rebecca, the daughter of a Crusader.

The story acquires a romantic twist when Rebecca and the Templar fall in love only to learn that they are brother and sister; they are discovered to be the children of the Sultan Saladin's dead brother, who embraced Christianity before his death. The idealization of Nathan also goes to romantic extremes. But the play borrows its thesis and its essential tone, which is cool and reasoned, from the rationalistic liberalism of Voltaire and the Encyclopaedists. Its high point is the indisputably great speech of Nathan when Saladin tries to trap him into forfeiting his goods by asking him which is the true faith.

Nathan replies with the famous Parable of the Rings, adapted from the *Decameron* and the earlier *Gesta Romanorum*. A father possesses a ring which has the virtue of making its owner beloved of God and man, as well as lord of the household. Since the father loves his three sons (Judaism, Christianity, and Mohammedanism) equally well, he promises the ring to each of them. Being unwilling to disappoint any of his sons, the father therefore has two other identical rings made. Then he bestows "his blessing and his ring on each—and dies." Immediately each son, without knowing that the others also possess a ring, claims priority in the house. A quarrel ensues, and a judge is consulted.

Saladin upbraids Nathan for evading the question, but Nathan replies that the three religions, however disparate they may seem now, "differ not in their foundation." The judge is unable to render a verdict. The possessor of the true ring would have to be beloved by all, which is obviously not the case when the young men are bringing each other to court instead of yielding gladly to one brother. "Who of the three is loved best by his brethren?" the judge asks.

> Does each one love himself alone? You're all
> Deceived deceivers. All your rings are false.
> The real ring, perchance, has disappeared.

His judgment, therefore, is that they give their rings a long trial. He who succeeds in making himself most worthy of love will be the true heir. The religion that does the most good or reaps the greatest harvest of love through the ages by its active humanitarianism will prove to be the true faith. Here is the essence of eighteenth-century liberalism, if not of all liberalism in religious matters. To it, moreover, is added a philosophy of freedom.:

> Your father, possibly, desired to free
> His power from one ring's tyrannous control.
> He loves you all with an impartial love
> And equally, and had no inward wish
> To prove the measure of his love for one
> By pressing heavily upon the rest.

If Lessing's poetic powers had been equal to his material, *Nathan the Wise* would probably have ranked with the great plays of the world, instead of being a comparatively poor one. Still its intellectual fire and impassioned modern idealism crack the cold shell of Lessing's didacticism. For all its faults as a play, *Nathan the Wise* is, next to *Faust*, perhaps the noblest expression of Western idealism. (pp. 319-23)

> John Gassner, "Goethe and the Romantic Spirit,"
> *in his* Masters of the Drama, *third edition, Dover*
> *Publications, Inc., 1954, pp. 317-34.*

RENÉ WELLEK (essay date 1955)

[*Wellek is an Austrian-born American literary critic whose many distinguished works have attracted an international audience. He is perhaps best known for* A History of Modern Criticism: 1750-1950 *(begun 1955), a multivolume study of the literary critics of the last three centuries. Wellek's critical method, as demonstrated in* A History *and outlined in his earlier* Theory of Literature *(with Austin Warren, 1949), is to describe, analyze, and evaluate a work in terms of its inherent problems and its author's solutions to them. In the following excerpt from* A History, *Wellek applies this method to Lessing's critical works, focusing especially on his subject's conception of tragedy in* Laocoon *and* Hamburg Dramaturgy.]

Gotthold Ephraim Lessing . . . has an enormous reputation as a literary critic, but a clear account of the reasons for his prominence in a history of European criticism is hard to find. There is no difficulty in accounting for his importance in the development of German literature, and Germans have constantly stressed his historical merits. He was, after all, the first great man of letters Germany produced in modern times: he has been called the founder of modern German literature and its liberator (i.e. the liberator from the dominance of French neoclassicism as represented by the mediocre Gottsched). Lessing certainly was a dramatist of considerable power, though hardly of enduring greatness. He was also a theologian and semiphilosopher who, especially in his last writings, formulated an important version of the optimistic philosophy of the Enlightenment, with surprising touches of mysticism and what the 18th century called "enthusiasm," in his *Education of the Human Race.* He was also a classical philologist and an archaeologist of great erudition, though this phase of his work is inevitably obsolete today. He was, besides, an aesthetician

who, in the *Laokoon,* speculated importantly on the limits of the arts and the differences between poetry and painting. And finally he was a literary theorist and critic. All these varied activities are held together by the power of an obviously straightforward honest personality and an individual style of wonderful clarity and sobriety which is a joy to meet in reading German. Lessing's criticism is frequently encumbered by a heavy ballast of classical learning, and is sometimes marred by the demands of an existence absorbed in literary journalism and thus in the necessity of writing on ephemeral topics of the day and also by the acerbities and brutalities of contemporary polemical manners. But on occasions, and they are luckily not rare, he rises above these handicaps, suddenly breaking into a striking simile or a dignified assertion of his superiority to the times and his opponents. "Why do I detain myself with these chatterers? I will go my way and persist regardless of what the grasshoppers chirp by the roadside. Even a step aside to crush them is too much honor. The end of their summer is not long to await."

Thus it is not easy to isolate Lessing's literary criticism from his manifold activities and its permanent value from its merely historical merit. (pp. 151-52)

It is true that we get in Lessing little practical literary criticism of important authors. There is a good deal of minute discussion of specific plays in the *Hamburgische Dramaturgie,* but, with very few exceptions, even those who are widely read have not and would not care to read the plays in question. The only exceptions are the plays of Voltaire and one play (*Rodogune*) by Corneille, and even they have few admirers today. In the *Laokoon* there is detailed criticism of Homer and Sophocles which is still of interest, and there are the scattered passages on Shakespeare, which are, however, quite disappointing if we judge them as criticism of Shakespeare. They merely echo the passage in Dryden on Shakespeare as the "poet of nature": Lessing had translated Dryden's *Essay of Dramatic Poesy* for one of his early collections, *Theatralische Bibliothek.* The famous 17th *Literaturbrief* (February 16, 1759) attacks Gottsched's introduction of a Frenchified theater into Germany with the claim that "we Germans rather fall in with the taste of the English than of the French"; prints the fragment of a scene from a supposedly ancient German tragedy of *Faust;* and advances the claim, astonishing for the time and place, that "Shakespeare is a much greater tragic poet than Corneille, though Corneille knew the ancients very well and Shakespeare scarcely at all." Corneille rivals the ancients in "mechanical contrivance" (*mechanische Einrichtung*), but Shakespeare in the "essential" (*das Wesentliche*). But beyond the statement that Shakespeare's plays have more power over our passions than any others except Sophocles' *Oedipus,* no reason is given for the superiority of the former, and even in the *Hamburgische Dramaturgie* no plays of Shakespeare are discussed. Lessing seems to have known *King Lear, Richard III, Othello, Hamlet,* and *Romeo and Juliet,* but he never goes beyond saying that *Othello* is "the most complete text book of this sad madness, jealousy" and that *Romeo and Juliet* is "the only tragedy in which Love itself has collaborated," whatever that may mean. The only more specific criticism of Shakespeare in Lessing is the comparison he makes between the ghost in Voltaire's *Semiramis* and the ghost in *Hamlet,* and this is rather a discussion of poetic belief than practical criticism, and in its praise of the effect of the ghost it is derivative of Addison rather than an independent discussion. The praise of Shakespeare is mostly in rhetorical hyperboles, as in the famous passage where Lessing denies that it is possible to commit plagiarism on Shakespeare. "What has been said of Homer, that it would be easier to deprive Hercules of his club [i.e. by Donatus in *Vita Vergilii*] than him of a verse, can be as truly said of Shakespeare. There is an impress upon the least of his beauties which at once exclaims to all the world: I am Shakespeare's—and woe to the foreign beauty which has the self-confidence to place itself beside it." (pp. 152-53)

Lessing's criticism of English prose is not extensive or important. Like so many of his contemporaries, he thought very highly of Richardson, while he disparaged Smollett's *Roderick Random* as being far below Lesage. There is a review highly praising Johnson's *Rambler* without, however, mentioning his name. We must not forget that Lessing translated such books as Francis Hutcheson's *System of Moral Philosophy* (1756) and William Law's *Serious Call* (1756), and that he had a wide acquaintance with English critical and aesthetic literature. A study of his dramas reveals many English sources in the comedies (Farquhar) and bourgeois tragedies (Lillo), though the source hunting has obviously been overdone. But there is little literary criticism in the strict sense.

It would be easy to show this with respect to the other literatures too. It seems significant that Lessing, though he devoted much of his efforts to an attack on French drama, wrote no real discussion of either Racine or Molière. The references to Molière are quite unimportant, and when, in the *Hamburgische Dramaturgie*, Lessing has an opportunity to discuss *L'École des femmes* he merely repeated some information from a French source. He seems to have preferred Destouches (of whom he compiled a *Life* early in his career) and Marivaux, and they certainly are the models of his own early comedies. He admired Diderot as a critic and playwright, but there is no extended discussion of the plays. Corneille and Voltaire draw Lessing's whole fire. (pp. 154-55)

We expect more of Lessing's literary criticism of classical writers, but are hardly rewarded, though there are frequent discussions of philological points and many references. Lessing obviously admired Homer beyond any other author and uses him in the *Laokoon* as a constant illustration of what poetry can and should do: how he describes Helen by her effect on the old men, how he singles out one trait in an object by a single adjective, how he builds up an elaborate description like that of the shield of Achilles by telling of its manufacture. The praise of Homer is always generous, and the consideration, though never directed at the totality of either the *Iliad* or the *Odyssey,* is certainly literary in its attention to descriptive technique. The discussion of Greek tragedy is, however, disappointing as such. Aeschylus is hardly mentioned, and then Lessing commits the gross error of referring to the poet's *Perserinnen*, a confusion of the sex of the chorus which seems derived from D'Aubignac. Sophocles fares somewhat better: Lessing compiled a very learned *Life of Sophocles,* which has, however, no critical content; in the *Laokoon* he uses *Philoctetes* and the *Trachinians* as illustrations for the treatment of bodily pain in drama. The *Hamburgische Dramaturgie* contains, in different contexts, speculations on some of the lost plays of Euripides and on the reasons why Aristotle called him "the most tragic of all the tragedians." But there is no extensive discussion of Greek tragedy. As for comedy, Aristophanes is totally ignored, if we disregard the passage in which Lessing objects to the view that Aristophanes drew the caricature of an individual in the Socrates of the *Clouds.* Roman comedy obviously interested him more: we have from him a fine analysis of Terence's *Adelphi,* especially of the intrigue and the main

character, Demea. Among Lessing's early writings is a *Life of Plautus,* a translation of his *Captivi* and a discussion of its merits which has some critical interest. There is plenty of other evidence to show his wide acquaintance with classical antiquity and its literature: a defense of Horace against charges of immorality; a condemnation of Seneca as an ancestor of Corneille. But there is not much that could be called literary discussion.

Most of Lessing's literary criticism, of course, concerns German literature, and much of it is now of no interest except to specialists. (pp. 156-57)

[Mostly] Lessing wrote about his immediate elders or his contemporaries. He is implacable in his condemnation of Gottsched. Surveying the contemporary German stage, he criticizes many minor authors whose very names are forgotten. This was part of his duty as the Hamburg *Dramaturge*. He constantly attacked the young Wieland both for his shoddy didactic poems and for his imitative dramas, though later he defended Wieland's translation of Shakespeare and called *Agathon* the "work of the century." He admired Klopstock, mainly as a master of diction and verse, though he recognized his lack of epic talent and the dangers of his pietistic sentimentality.

Lessing did not live long enough to see the new Storm and Stress movement as a unity. His opinions of his younger contemporaries were either barely crystallized or not recorded. (p. 157)

[The] individual critical pronouncements of Lessing do not add up to a corpus of sensitive evaluation or close discussion of great works. But it is impossible to overrate his importance in the raising of the general level of German criticism. Negatively his attack on the French classical tragedy must have meant a great deal; and positively his recommendation of Shakespeare was important for the time, though he had precursors such as Gerstenberg even in Germany. There were, besides, traces in Lessing even of interest in folk poetry: in *Briefe die neueste Literatur betreffend* (No. 33) he praises a Lapland song and a Latvian *dainos* (a kind of elegy) for their "native spirit and charming simplicity," concluding that "poets are born under any climate, and vivid sentiments are not the privilege of civilized nations." This opinion is all the more striking since Lessing obviously cared little for lyrical poetry: his interests were in the drama, the epic, and such semididactic genres as the fable and the epigram. On these last Lessing wrote learned theoretical and historical dissertations full of overly ingenious distinctions and subdivisions.

If Lessing had left us only a body of special pronouncements and criticisms of plays forgotten in many cases, he would have merely a historical importance: only historians of German literature would make the effort to read his dissections of German and French plays, even though they are always done with great shrewdness and dialectical power. But Lessing is, of course, far more than just a practical critic. He is a theorist of literature, on the borderline of aesthetics. He cannot be relegated to general philosophical aesthetics with Kant: there are hardly any general speculations on beauty or taste as such in Lessing. Rather he takes up very concrete problems of literary theory, and even those not in any systematic fashion. The *Laokoon* was originally to bear the name of *Hermaea*, and it is described as "collectanea for a book." The *Hamburgische Dramaturgie* by its very plan lent itself to casual discussion, and when Lessing got involved in an abstract problem like that of generality he could break off and say: "I here remind my readers that these sheets are to contain anything rather than a dramatic system. I am therefore not bound to resolve all the difficulties I raise. My thoughts may seem less and less connected, may even seem to contradict themselves. What matter? If only they are thoughts amid which may be found food for independent thinking. I only want here to scatter *fermenta cognitionis* ["random thoughts"]." But in spite of this lack of system we get close discussions of several problems: in the *Laokoon* of the relations between poetry and painting, in the *Hamburgische Dramaturgie* of the function of tragedy, the meaning of pity and fear, purgation, problems which Lessing had discussed years before in an extensive correspondence with Mendelssohn and Nicolai. Besides, in these writings and even scattered through the letters there are many pronouncements on basic problems of 18th-century criticism: on the rules, on genius, on the nature of poetry. Thus something like a picture of Lessing's literary theory can be pieced together. (pp. 158-59)

One must acknowledge the high importance of Lessing's central problem [in *Laokoon, oder über die Grenzen der Malerei und Poesie*]: the differences and limits of the arts. It is impossible to agree with Croce, who refuses to recognize any classification of the arts, putting artistic creation purely in the mental act of the artist, which is assumed to be unaffected by the medium. Lessing himself in *Emilia Galotti* seems to endorse the view that "Raphael would have been the greatest genius among painters, even if he had unfortunately been born without hands." But Lessing's whole theory runs counter to this view: it can even be said that he seems uninterested in or vague about the question: what is the common element in all the arts? Lessing's main distinction between the arts of space and time, though debatable, is basically sound. His objections to static descriptions in literature were not only salutary in their time, but, if properly qualified, are applicable even today: most of us skip the formal descriptions in the novels of Scott or Balzac. Lessing is certainly putting his finger on the issue when he points to the difficulty of our forming a whole from an accumulation of traits, and he is also right in opposing the stress on visualization in literature, which in the 18th century was favored by the current interpretation of the term "imagination" as practically identical with visual imagination. Literature does not evoke sensuous images, or if it does, does so only incidentally, occasionally, and intermittently. Even in the depiction of a fictional character the writer need not suggest visual images at all. We can scarcely visualize most of Dostoevsky's or Henry James's characters, while we know their states of mind, their motivations, evaluations, attitudes, and desires very completely. Lessing stresses characterization by the single trait, by the one Homeric epithet, the method which is substantially that of Tolstoy or Thomas Mann.

Lessing formulates his view best in one of the notes for the continuation of the *Laokoon*. "I assert that only that can be the aim of an art to which it is uniquely and alone fitted, and not that which the other arts can do just as well or even better. I find a simile in Plutarch which illustrates this very well. A person, he says, who tries to chop wood with a key and open a door with an axe, not only spoils both tools, but deprives himself of the use of both tools." Purity of effect is what we sympathize with if we dislike literary painting, program music, poetic architecture, and similar mixtures of the arts. Yet Lessing's conception of what is peculiarly literary will not strike us as convincing. It is, in effect, the view that drama is the highest and the central genre of literature. (pp. 163-64)

[The] *Laokoon* is only part of Lessing's critical work. The theory of tragedy and the interpretation of Aristotle expounded

Drawing of the younger son in the classic Laocoön grouping, by Peter Paul Rubens.

in the later sections of the *Hamburgische Dramaturgie* were almost equally influential. . . . In the *Laokoon* Lessing gives the example of the Roman gladiator who had to suffer silently, because if he had excited compassion the games would have been stopped. The existence of these gladiatorial games proves to Lessing that the Romans could not have had true tragedy. Senecan tragic heroes are nothing but pugilists (*Klopffechter*) on buskins.

The *Hamburgische Dramaturgie* resumes this argument but fortunately goes far beyond it. The reason that the *Dramaturgie* is in many ways a disappointing book may be understood in terms of its genesis. (p. 167)

[The] *Dramaturgie* must be judged as originally designed for day-by-day reviewing of plays on whose selection Lessing had no influence. This alone explains the choice of Corneille's *Rodogune* and the emphasis on Voltaire. They were produced and Racine was not. This explains the attention to French and German plays now totally forgotten; it also explains the general polemical undercurrent against the French drama, from whose fetters Lessing wants the Germans to be freed. The arguments against the French stage are not merely nationalistic. . . . They are based on a different conception of the nature of tragedy and a different interpretation of Aristotle (which undoubtedly is nearer the meaning of the text than Corneille's). What is new and surprising in Germany, and has led to the error of identifying Lessing simply with neoclassicism, is his stress on Aristotle as the master. (pp. 168-69)

[In the **Dramaturgie**] the question of the effect of tragedy, of purgation through pity and fear, is tied in with the question of the structure of tragedy. Lessing has now discovered that it is impossible to define the tragic effect as mere pity or compassion. He interprets the crucial passage in Aristotle to mean "pity with fear" in a situation where fear is a necessary concomitant of pity. The fear is not terror, but fear which "arises for us from our similarity with the suffering person . . . the fear that we ourselves could become this object of pity"; we must pity the hero if the hero is "of the same wheat and chaff," is "one of us" and thus is not above or below common humanity. (pp. 171-72)

[It] is not possible to dismiss Lessing's theory of tragedy as simple didacticism or even as reducible to the balancing of pity and fear which he interprets as "purgation." Tragedy achieves all this because it creates a world analogous to the real one. . . . Tragedy, it appears, is . . . a justification of God, a theodicy, a world inherently ethical, just as God's created cosmos is good even though we may not see the ultimate goodness of any individual evil. . . . Drama . . . shows us the world rational, transparent to the ethical will, subservient to it. There must be no innocent suffering on the stage because reason and religion should have convinced us that the very idea of human beings as wretched because of no guilt of their own is "as false as it is blasphemous." Tragedy has the high function of revealing the order of the universe. Lessing, with the optimism of the 18th century and its peculiar kind of belief in a benevolent God and His universe, dissolves the conception of tragedy: in his tragedy there can be no free will, no conflict between man and God or fate or the universe.

Lessing's conception of tragedy is a deeply ethical one. It agrees with Butcher's later interpretation of Aristotle, according to which "the dramatic action must be so significant, and its meaning capable of such extension, that through it we can discern the higher laws which rule the world." But unfortunately Lessing betrays the limitations of his temper and his time in his conception of these higher laws. His is the 18th-century universe of a benevolent God, a benevolent Nature, and a basically good man. Tragedy is deprived of its connection with sacrifice, with the grandly heroic, the marvelous and divine, the *mysterium tremendum* ["tremendous mystery"] and is reduced to an object lesson in humanitarianism. Lessing's emphasis on the coherence and wholeness of the world of drama, its inner probability, actually justifies any art which is psychologically true and consistent, which is a fully motivated portrayal of life even though it be not tragic or even dramatic at all. The hero is reduced in stature: he cannot be either a martyr or a criminal; he must be a middling man, whose guilt is only an understandable failure, a mistake committed under mitigating circumstances of strain or ignorance. His pathos is that of mere suffering. The auditor is conceived as a virtuoso of pity, a man who has to exercise his humanity and train it in virtuous habits, not a man who is to be either shaken up and torn by tragedy or healed to Stoic endurance and indifference. Thus Lessing illustrates the . . . failure of his age to grasp the nature of art. . . . [He] prepares the conception of literature underlying the psychological and social realism of the 19th century. (pp. 173-75)

> *René Wellek, "Lessing and His Precursors," in his*
> A History of Modern Criticism, 1750-1950: The Later
> Eighteenth Century, *Yale University Press, 1955, pp. 144-75.*

E. H. GOMBRICH (lecture date 1957)

[*Gombrich is a distinguished Austrian-born English academic and scholar who concentrates his studies on the psychology of pictorial art. In addition to his seminal studies* Art and Illusion: A Study in the Psychology of Pictorial Representation *(1960) and* In Search of Cultural History *(1969), he is the author of* Lessing *(1957), an important contribution to Lessing studies. In the following excerpt from the 1957 British Academy "Lecture on a Master Mind," Gombrich surveys Lessing's career as a dramatist, critic, and student of religions.*]

In literary history Lessing is cast in the role of Moses who led his people out of French servitude towards the promised land of *Deutsche Klassik*, which he still saw from afar; the Lawgiver who struck with his rod against the barren rock and lo, it flowed in abundance. But Lessing himself did not believe in miracles. He knew that if the German literary desert was to bloom, water had to be pumped and pumped from somewhere. His quarrel . . . was with those who looked to France for the life-giving tradition. Already in the seventeenth/*Literaturbrief* of 1759 he had championed Shakespeare against Corneille. All Europe, of course, looked to England at the time, as the land of enlightenment, freedom, and sentiment. But in Germany, which was still almost a literary vacuum, the effect of Lessing's words of power was incalculable. Indeed, if the greatness of a master mind could ever be gauged by his influence alone, I could prove Lessing's claim from my own experience. For in German-speaking countries Shakespeare belongs to the intellectual universe called *Bildung*, French classical drama does not. Most of us were taught at school that French tragedies are frigid and contrived and only of interest to specialists.

How Lessing would have enjoyed campaigning against such a prejudice! For if there is one key to his rich and complex mind, it is his persistent non-conformism. Throughout his life he acted like the Freethinker in one of his earliest plays: 'If my opinions were to become too general, I should be the first to abandon them for the opposite view. . . . I cannot believe that truth can ever be common; as little, indeed, as that there could ever be daylight on the whole globe at one and the same time.' (p. 134)

Both in tone and intention Lessing's writings are always a challenge, part of a dramatic dialogue with a real or imagined opponent. He never writes with Olympic calm. He wants to provoke argument. In the company of friends, we are told, Lessing would take some accepted opinion and assert the opposite, improvising reasons as he went along. . . . In his handling of language for argument Lessing displayed a master mind in that precise meaning of the term in which we speak of a master in chess. I think and hope he might have spared my ears for this assertion.

For Lessing enjoyed this mastery, and this exhilaration at the power which language gave him is unmistakable in every line he wrote. Ideas he may have borrowed. This love of the game was his from the start. There is no greater mystery in life than that hallmark of personality which gives to the tone of a writer's voice its unmistakable ring. With Lessing this tone is present in the first letter we have from his hand, written at the age of fourteen, at Christmas 1743. Of course it is polemical. (pp. 135-36)

Lessing always liked to play with pieces rich in associations, and, . . . he thought nothing of borrowing them in all modesty from other people's treasures. In recent years this habit of his has increasingly become a stumbling-block to those who want to assess and appreciate his master mind. For the more research progresses, the more do we realize that Lessing 'thought in quotations'. But the fact is, I believe, he was not interested in the knowledge and ideas of the past for their own sake. He repudiated the title of scholar with almost the same vehemence with which he had refused the title of genius. . . . (p. 137)

The narrow specialist who only collected facts and had his head so tightly screwed on that he could not look right or left was for him a figure of fun, but his real wrath was reserved for the adulterator of knowledge, the sloppy scholar who made it impossible to play an honest game. In a way Nicolai was quite right that Lessing indulged in the antiquarian studies, so beloved of the eighteenth century, only as a pastime and to confirm his conviction, not very flattering to us, that the majority of those erudites were charlatans. But so ardent is Lessing's love of integrity and so high his standards that some of these polemics, notably the *Briefe antiquarischen Inhalts* . . . , are among his most enthralling and most readable works. They find their fitting conclusion in that gem of archaeological exegesis which has always been acclaimed as one of Lessing's masterpieces, the little treatise on *The image of death in ancient art* written to correct poor Klotz.

In England, of course, it is the *Laocoon,* that grand contest between art and literature, which is by far the best known of Lessing's writings. The idea of such a comparison was very much in the air. Diderot, in his *Letter on the Deaf and Dumb* which Lessing had reviewed with enthusiasm, had expressed the hope that a critic would take the problem on. It has been shown [elsewhere] how much the artfully artless presentation of the *Laocoon* owes to [Diderot], and it fits in well with this orientation that he even planned, at one time, to write it in French, since the German language had as yet not been shaped or even created for this type of discussion. It is the measure of Lessing's greatness that he did not succumb to this temptation, that he did take upon himself the trouble of shaping and creating his pieces himself. But the tournament is played by a European team. The first round is against Winckelmann, the German, the second against Spence, the Englishman, the third against the Comte de Caylus, the Frenchman. It is important to keep the dramatic character of the *Laocoon* in mind, because it explains, though it does not always excuse, certain simplifications with which Lessing presents his opponents' views. Their works are held up as examples of a confusion between the means of poetry and of painting, but if you take the trouble to read these authors you will be inclined to acquit them of this particular charge. (pp. 138-39)

It has often been said that Lessing did not know very much about art. I am afraid the truth may be even more embarrassing to an historian of art who has been charged with the task of celebrating Lessing: he had not much use for art. There is a telling aside in one of his writings against 'superfluous engravings in books,' which 'not only fail to assist the reader's imagination but tie it down and thereby mislead it'. He did not mind Ovid being illustrated for the amusement of the public, but let the painters keep their hand from his beloved Homer.

The more one reads the *Laocoon,* the stronger becomes the impression that it is not so much a book about as against the visual arts: 'If Painting is really Poetry's sister', Lessing remarks in it, 'let her at least not be a jealous sister.'

Why this hostility? Can it really have been Lessing's concern with the Horatian tag *ut pictura poesis* ["as in painting, so in poetry"] in the sense that he was bored, like most of us, with long descriptive passages? I do not think so; in fact I believe there is a strong argument against this accepted interpretation. For, discussing the critics of the *Laocoon* three years after its publication, Lessing writes to Nicolai: 'Not one of them, not even Herder, has the faintest idea what I am driving at.'

I am sure we can only grasp this idea if we look at the *Laocoon* in the context of Lessing's work and time. There is one brief but relevant passage in his *Treatise on the Fable,* in which the painter is already put in his place. The test of a good fable, Lessing declares, is that it can not be illustrated. With one fell blow he destroys the combination of picture and moral which was the essence of the emblem book and had enjoyed such a vogue since the Renaissance. . . . Lessing breaks with this tradition. To him a fable condenses not a truth but an argument which he compares to the demonstrations of science. (pp. 140-41)

In one of the notes for the *Laocoon* Lessing expresses the suspicion that it was the ideal of beauty in the visual arts which gave rise to the ideal of moral perfection in poetry—the ideal, of course, of Corneille. Lessing's *Laocoon* opens with a quotation of the very passage from Winckelmann's pamphlet which Mendelssohn had quoted against him, for it was here that Winckelmann commended what he thought was the admirable restraint of *Laocoon,* who does not shout but controls his pain. 'Laocoon suffers', he says, 'but he suffers like the Philoctetes of Sophocles; his agony touches our very soul, but we would wish to be able to bear agony as this great man does.'

What better opening could Lessing hope for than this absurd half-sentence about Sophocles? Philoctetes notoriously shows his suffering. And why not? Everything that is Stoic is undramatic, *untheatralisch.* Self-control may arouse admiration, but admiration is a cold emotion which excludes all warmth of passion.

The polemical reference must be obvious to anyone familiar with Lessing's writings on the drama. It is against Corneille and his ideal of nobility resulting in admiration. That, I submit, is what Lessing was 'really driving at', and why the *Laocoon* had to be written. (pp. 143-44)

In the *Laocoon* Lessing erects a high fence along the frontiers between art and literature to confine the fashion of neo-classicism within the taste for the visual arts, where indeed it remained unchallenged till Fuseli discovered the pictorial equivalent to Shakespeare in the rude sublimities of Rembrandt. Lessing never mentioned Rembrandt and would hardly have approved of him. He was quite satisfied with Laocoon remaining silent in cold marble as long as Philoctetes was allowed to roar on the stage till the French puppets were blown into the wings.

Seen in this light, the *Laocoon* continues the work of the seventeenth *Literaturbrief,* or rather it secures its gains against an unexpected threat from the flank which might indeed have swayed the course of German literature. Two years later, in the *Hamburgische Dramaturgie,* Lessing proceeded to the attack. Forced by external circumstances, he changed from a reviewer who concerns himself with the expression of the passions in acting to a critic who argues with increasing acerbity against Corneille and Voltaire. Ostensibly the argument turns round the somewhat barren problem as to whether the French had understood Aristotle's definition of tragedy correctly, or whether Shakespeare did not more truly conform to the demands of the oracle. But why is this definition of Aristotle pushed around on the chessboard? Because it speaks of arousing and purging the passions, and Lessing is concerned once more with preventing any interpretation which would limit the stirring experience of fear and pity and the profound therapeutic effects of vicarious agony.

I doubt whether such persistent and skilful advocacy can be explained solely in terms of the history of ideas which makes Lessing himself only the puppet of impersonal forces. True, these forces worked on him, but he also worked on them, and we shall not get nearer to the core of this extraordinary mind unless we ask what it was that made him, the master of reasoning, into the champion of passion. (pp. 144-45)

What was this passion and this anxiety [reflected in his occasional violent emotion]? I do not want to inflict a psychological jargon on you, which I could not handle with competence, but I do not think we should go far wrong if we called it aggression. Lessing called it the bile, which amounts to the same thing. (pp. 145-46)

It accounts, I believe, both for his strength and his occasional weakness as a playwright. For in his plays . . . passion is often transmuted into dialectics, which threatens to disintegrate the conflict. In the fragment *Henzi* the hero does not clash with tyrannical authority but with his fellow conspirators who want to proscribe a venerable city father. In *Miss Sarah Sampson* the melodramatic action turns largely on the guilt feelings of the fallen heroine who craves for punishment from her all-forgiving father. The play, of course, ranks high in the annals of German literature for its middle-class milieu and its emotional tone, but I cannot help feeling that in this only instance where Lessing wanted to open the floodgates of emotionalism his dialogue sounds contrived. He has to borrow passion from other people's treasures—I am told, from Richardson's sentimental best sellers. There is little doubt, I think, that the original plan of *Emilia Galotti,* Lessing's most virile play, was conceived as a corrective against this overdose of borrowed emotion. It is the story of Virginia but with a difference. For once more it is the daughter who persuades her father to kill her rather than to expose her to the temptations of her princely pursuer, not, mark you, because she fears violence but because she fears her own hot blood. Strangely enough, a similar tragedy of love for the oppressor underlies even the brittle surface of Lessing's most popular comedy, *Minna von Barnhelm.* It was one of the first plays I saw, but I confess that I never understood its well-concealed plot, which is too often represented as a glorification of the Prussian army. . . . What turns the tragedy into a comedy is mainly that it is the girl who woos and the hero whose sense of honour forbids him to yield. But for a comedy the protagonists show perhaps too much control, too much nobility. When Lessing attacked the stoic ideal in the *Laocoon* he was again turning his criticism against the strongest trend in his own character.

For Lessing . . . could only let himself go in intellectual argument. His anacreontic lyrics are conventional, and even his biting epigrams, beautifully turned as they are, usually borrow their shafts from other people's armoury. His most characteristic creations, I am afraid, lie buried in the rare complete editions of his works; he called them *Rettungen,* rehabilitations, where he takes up with immense learning the case of some obscure figure from the past whose name had been unjustly blackened by official historians. He had discovered, as he remarks with fine self-irony, that 'among scholars the gift to brook contradiction is altogether a gift confined to the dead'. But he also took great care not to take unfair advantage of that discovery: 'Those whom everybody attacks will be safe from

me', he once wrote. He preferred to select his culprits among the great authorities such as Martin Luther, who had maligned the humanist Lemnius without real provocation. It is true, he had been repaid in worse coin, but was it not time history apportioned the blame between the two correctly?

It is fitting that Lessing's greatest works of his last years arose out of these activities as an advocate before the Court of Truth. . . . These [works] included such publications as the *Enquiry into the Age of Oil Painting* or on the *Hirsau Stained Glass Windows,* which would suffice to give stature to a specialist. The theatre had lost all interest. It bored and disgusted him. 'If I need entertainment I shall rather arrange a little comedy with the theologians.'

It was not to be the mocking comedy of the kind so frequent in the libertine eighteenth century. Lessing was no scoffer like Voltaire. On the contrary. Such scoffing always drove him into opposition. He had a profound respect for the great religious thinkers of the past who had grounded their theological system on faith. What he disliked was the well-meaning liberalism of enlightened Christians who wanted to have it both ways and pretended to prove the verities of religion in the light of reason. This Lessing would not have. Once more he insisted on a dividing line, *eine Scheidewand* ["a barrier"]. Trespassers should be prosecuted. Rational Christians were merely irrational philosophers.

He first puzzled his enlightened friends with a number of publications in which he contrasted the consistency of orthodox beliefs with the fashionable compromisers. Only then did he trail his coat properly by publishing the famous *Fragmente eines Ungenannten* which he considered an uncompromising and therefore consistent presentation of the rationalist case against miracles and the gospel story. An early admirer of Pierre Bayle and a Pyrrhonist at heart, Lessing was convinced that historical testimony was as much beyond the reach of rational proof as were the articles of faith. He even expected the orthodox faction to thank him for this clarification. But Hauptpastor Goeze jumped into the fray, holding the Lutheran Bible aloft and insisting on submission to the letter. Lessing found himself involved in the wrong battle, and his exasperation explains perhaps the violence of his language. (pp. 149-52)

In one of his latest philosophical drafts Lessing discusses the perfectibility of man and his inability to possess the whole truth in terms of Newtonian science which hark back to the *Laocoon* problem.

The soul of man has an infinite capacity for ideas, but being finite it can only obtain them step by step, in an infinite sequence of time. The order in which we absorb these ideas is determined by the five senses. But once more we find sight deposed from its Platonic throne. The eye is the organ responsive to light waves, but may we not one day develop senses for electricity or magnetism which will reveal new beauties and new aspects of reality?

I believe these slightly abstruse excursions into 'science fiction' may throw light even on Lessing's most heatedly discussed treatise, *The Education of the Human Race,* and the links between his religious and his aesthetic convictions. Revelation, it claims, can only unfold in time. There are many strands which went into elaboration of this philosophy, but the most important, I think, is the ancient doctrine of accommodation, according to which Revelation had to translate the ineffable truth into the symbolic language of the Scriptures. In early notes to the *Laocoon* Lessing refers to the oriental imagery of the Old Testament and remarks drily that in northern countries the Holy Ghost would have used different images. As with nations, so with ages. As mankind grows up and reason advances, truth appears in less poetic garb and revelation takes on new forms. But by its very nature it can never show us the whole. It must always remain provisional at any moment of time, and to claim any of its manifestations, any of its images, as the whole and absolute truth is to misunderstand God's ways with man.

What we can know of God is the moral law that concerns our emotions and actions in this life. The injunction of St. John to his congregation to love each other, therefore, deserves the epithet 'divine' more truly than the much admired Platonic opening of St. John's Gospel, beautiful as it may be.

It was in this conviction that he embarked on *Nathan the Wise*. His polemics . . . had been banned, and he decided to try whether he could still preach from his old pulpit. It is characteristic of Lessing that scarcely ten years after his campaign against Voltaire's plays he adopted the method and message of the great preacher against *le fanatisme* ["fanaticism"]. Jealousy had blossomed into emulation.

Nathan with its operatic plot is, of course, constructed round the fable of the three rings from Boccaccio. I hope you will not accuse me of overplaying my hand if I suggest that it is a story of jealousy resolved. The precious heirloom which the father is always to hand on to his favourite son suddenly appears in three identical versions in the hands of the three rival brothers. In Lessing's adaptation the genuine ring was to have the secret power to make agreeable to God and man whoever wore it in that confidence. They go to court and Lessing's judge dismisses the case for lack of evidence. . . . Whereupon the sultan rushes towards the sage, grasps his hand, and exclaims: 'I who am dust, am nothing? God!'

I have always found this exclamation the most moving moment in the play. The sage has gently humbled the great sultan and reminded him of the human condition. Nathan, whose wife and seven sons have been burnt to death in a pogrom and who yet submitted to God's will and adopted a Christian child, has the right to preach against the presumption of human beings who commit their crimes in the name of truth.

But just as in *Minna*, the tragedy is behind us. There is a resigned serenity in the blank verse of Nathan which heralds the classic age of German literature. Lessing thought that the play was more the fruit of polemics than of genius. But with his attention diverted from the abstract problems of the dramatist's art, the spring within him began to flow of its own accord and sometimes gushed forth in real and therefore untranslatable poetry. Take the first line of the Templar's monologue:

> Hier hüalt das Opfertier ermüdet still.

I wonder if there is any line in German drama more irrationally moving than this comparison of the harassed mind with the tired animal on the way to the altar. It is hardly fanciful to read in it something of the terrible lassitude which often overcame Lessing in his last years of solitude, since his wife had died in childbirth after a short year of marriage. He died at the age of 52.

It was not only his outward fate which made Lessing's last years tragic. It was that inevitable compulsion to oppose the tide of fashion which made him impatient of the movement of Storm and Stress and that cult of genius and passion he had

done so much to promote. Who could have predicted that the author of the seventeenth *Literaturbrief* would be scathing about Goethe's *Werther* and the turbulent *Goetz von Berlichingen*? 'The devil will get my *Faust* in the end', he said about his long projected play, 'and I shall get Goethe's'. He did not live to see that Goethe as a real genius was to accept his call to discipline, was even to stage Voltaire's *Mahomet* in Weimar, much to Schiller's bewilderment and finally to marry Faust to Helena. If it could be shown that the gadfly of Lessing's criticism had its share in driving Goethe from the mists of the Brocken towards Winckelmann's Hellas, this paradoxical feat would be the fitting conclusion to the lifework of a truly Socratic spirit.

I do not think that a master mind need necessarily have a message for this age. Lessing, of course, belongs with all his fibres to the great eighteenth century. But just because he was so thoroughly of his time, his dedicated life refutes those insidious voices who like to tell the writer today that the only way out of the Ivory Tower leads through what they call 'commitment' to a creed, party, or faction. Lessing was always engaged, but never committed. Indeed he wrote:

> I hate all people who want to found sects from the bottom of my heart. Because it is not error, but sectarian error, nay, even sectarian truth which is the misfortune of mankind; or would be, if truth ever wanted to found a sect.

(pp. 153-56)

> *E. H. Gombrich, "Lecture on a Master Mind: Lessing," in* Proceedings of the British Academy, *Vol. XLIII, 1957, pp. 133-56.*

J. B. PRIESTLEY   (essay date 1960)

[*A highly prolific English man of letters, Priestly was the author of numerous popular novels that depict the world of everyday, middle-class England. In this respect, he has often been likened to Charles Dickens, a critical comparison Priestley disliked. His most notable critical work is* Literature and Western Man *(1960), a survey of Western literature from the invention of movable type through the mid-twentieth century. In the following excerpt from this work, he discusses the dramatic and critical works of Lessing, "one of the most triumphant, as well as one of the most appealing, figures of the age."*]

[Gotthold Ephraim Lessing is] one of the most attractive and influential figures in German literature. With him the characteristically German process of criticism preceding creation takes place in one mind. Apart from some very early work, obviously imitated from French comedy, his major contributions to the theatre represent the triumphant conclusion of some equally creative (in their influence) critical research and speculation. His most famous piece of criticism, *Laokoön*, though important as an early and widely successful example of that type of critical aesthetics to which the Germans are still devoted, is in fact inferior to the best of his dramatic criticism, which appeared originally in a weekly journal associated with the Hamburg National Theatre. Earlier, as a youth in Berlin, Lessing had met and admired Voltaire, but this did not prevent him from revealing the absurdities and aridities of Voltaire's tragedies or even those of Corneille, the gulf there was between French and Greek tragedy, and the immense superiority of Shakespeare. He did not altogether understand Shakespeare and he still depended too much upon Aristotle, but this age cannot show us any better dramatic criticism than Lessing's. It cleared the way, as the way had to be cleared, for Schiller and Goethe and the other dramatists of the next age. But Lessing did more than this . . . : he provided his criticism with its own examples. His bourgeois tragedy *Miss Sara Sampson,* which had an English setting, is not a good play; too much reading and not enough life went into it; but it took tragedy off its classical stilts. In *Minna von Barnhelm* he created genuine comedy out of the German life he knew—an immense step forward. His Italian tragedy, *Emilia Galotti,* rises to an improbable climax—unless one believes that girls ask their fathers to kill them when they feel they cannot resist seductive but unscrupulous princes—but its tight and effective construction made it a good model for future German dramatists. Finally, in his last years, he wrote *Nathan the Wise,* a play in blank verse and—though Lessing was not really a poetic dramatist—his masterpiece. He was at this time librarian to the Duke of Brunswick, and he had published some extracts from the posthumous work of a liberal theologian called Reimarus. He was attacked by an orthodox pastor, Goeze, as an enemy of religion, and replied in a series of pamphlets, *Anti-Goeze,* defending the new biblical criticism and taking a more or less pragmatic view of religion. An official decree forbade any further publication of these pamphlets, so Lessing decided to write a play on a religious theme, hoping that, as he said, "they will at least let me preach on undisturbed in my old pulpit, the theatre." Adapting the story of the three rings in Boccaccio, using a romantic medieval background and making the action simple theatrically but deeply symbolic, Lessing was able to give dramatic expression to all that during these last years he had thought and felt about religion. The wise Jew, Nathan, can bring together, as members of one family, Mohammedans and Christians. What is expressed here is neither the vaguely deistic rationalism of the age nor the inflexible dogmatism of the Lutherans or any other Church. Of the three rings the genuine one has the magic power to bring its wearer the love of God and man, so long as it is worn with faith in this magic power. All religions that ennoble men's relations with one another are partially true, none is exclusively and finally true, and man has still a long way to go. All this reveals an attitude of mind, pragmatic and evolutionary, that is familiar enough now, though by no means common, especially during recent years when we have seen more and more fanatics of atheistic materialism glaring at more and more fanatics of dogma and fundamentalism. It was certainly not familiar in 1779, when as much wisdom as men had heard for a long time now arrived in blank verse for the German Theatre. Two years later, after publishing *The Education of the Human Race,* in which he elaborates his evolutionary view of religion, Lessing died. He had always been poor; he had had to sell the fine library he had collected; he lost both wife and child after less than two years of marriage; his last years were darkened by ill-health, over-work, quarrels with the orthodox; but the essential spirit of the man, nobly serving a mind both critical and creative, vigorous and wide-ranging, liberal and deeply humane, appears to ride so high above poverty, misunderstanding and loneliness, that he seems one of the most triumphant, as well as one of the most appealing, figures of the age. He gave Germany a Theatre of her own, a sound body of criticism, an example of liberal thought without extravagance. He showed the eighteenth century the German mind and temperament at their best. (pp. 79-81)

> *J. B. Priestley, "The Drama," in his* Literature and Western Man, *Harper & Brothers, 1960, pp. 62-81.*

H. B. GARLAND (essay date 1962)

[In the following excerpt, Garland examines the sources, tone, plots, and characters of Lessing's two major experimental dramas, Miss Sara Sampson *and* Philotas.*]*

The English origin of [*Miss Sara Sampson*] is evident not only in the form but in the setting and characters also. Lessing had in fact an English model in mind, *The London Merchant* of George Lillo (1731), which had obtained some considerable fame in Germany. Lessing's characters purport to be typical English men and women of the upper middle classes. They certainly bear a strong resemblance to the characters of the contemporary novels of Richardson, which were presumed in Germany to give an accurate image of life in England. The spectators recognized the world of these popular novels on the stage and this doubtless contributed to some extent to its success.

The theme of the tragedy is an elopement. Mellefont and Sara, the escaping couple, have arrived at an inn. Mellefont, however, defers the marriage ceremony in spite of Sara's pleadings. Meanwhile his former mistress, Marwood, secures an interview with Sara and poisons her. Sara's father arrives, all forgiveness, in time to witness her death. Mellefont then stabs himself over the corpse and the tragedy ends.

By a great effort Lessing has concentrated the events of the play so that the unities of time and place are almost completely observed. The scene opens in the inn very early in the morning, so that the characters, by being up and about betimes, will have some reasonable chance of getting through the various incidents within the limits of one day. And this is certainly accomplished without any striking improbability. The unity of place is another matter. For Lessing's purpose, it was necessary that Sara's father, Sir William Sampson, should arrive and be ready to forgive her before Mellefont's interview with Marwood. But Lessing further wishes to show him to the audience and yet to keep him separated from Sara, for had they met, the play would at once have been at an end and there would have been no tragedy. If he had not felt constrained to avoid changes of scene as far as possible, Lessing could have shown him at first in a neighbouring town, a few miles off. However, the unity of place was still valid for him and consequently the spectator is baffled by the strange scruple which prevents Sir William for hours on end, while residing in the same inn, from hastening into an adjoining room to be reunited with his beloved Sara. In the *Hamburg Dramaturgy* Lessing quotes a remark that characters of tragedies often die of nothing but 'the fifth act'; Sara and Sir William are kept apart by the 'first act', for no separation, no play. Lessing has sought to diminish this improbability by stressing the father's desire to obtain his daughter's forgiveness for his earlier lack of sympathy before he approaches her, but this device has only the effect of rendering Sir William's character less plausible.

None of the characters of *Miss Sara Sampson* is constructed on the grand scale usually associated with tragedy. This is, of course, a natural feature of 'domestic tragedy' which must have as its setting the humdrum middle-class home, and which takes as its sphere the restricted and sentimental emotional life of such an environment. The anonymous Elizabethan play, *Arden of Feversham,* had provided that grandeur could be achieved in a petty environment by the presentation of monstrous crime. The eighteenth century, however, was too cramped by a strict code of morality, by a narrow rationalistic outlook and by an enervating regard for mental as well as physical comfort, to suffer any murder among middle-class characters on the stage, unless it were considerably diluted with sentimental tears and flavoured with a large dose of the tender passion. Lessing himself was constantly agitating against this limitation of the dramatist's sphere, which he attributed principally to the influence of French taste, though it is beyond question that its root lay much deeper in the German middle classes themselves.

Be that as it may, he has here created a typical sentimental heroine. Sara's most salient qualities are that she is kind and virtuous. Her virtue is for Lessing one of the great problems of the play. He found it necessary to lay heavy stress upon it, for she is placed in a very compromising situation, so that only a perpetual emphasis of her fundamental virtue could make her acceptable as a tragic heroine to a public with a very strict view of sexual morality. He certainly achieved his end for the audiences of his time, but at a heavy cost. He engaged their sympathies at the price of Sara's credibility as a character; as she appears in the play, her original slip is quite unexplained and at variance with her character. This exaggeration of Sara's sexual virtue was a concession to the taste of the time and its prejudices. Now that these have passed away, the one-sided portrayal of her character can only alienate the modern reader. Sara suffers from a further defect which is characteristic of Lessing and which arises from his inability to create really living persons. She is too intellectually constructed. As with so many of Lessing's characters one feels that she has always thought carefully of what she intends to say before she opens her mouth. Her long speeches follow a logical order. Even the few exclamations she makes are marred by similes which could only be the product of reflection; one of the worst instances of this occurs in the final scene, when the dying Sara exclaims as she catches sight of her father: 'Is it a quickening apparition sent from Heaven, like the angel which came to strengthen the strong?' Yet in spite of lapses such as this Sara does at the end rise to some measure of strength through her calm resignation and composure in the hour of death. Nor must we overlook the charge of affectation and self-indulgent masochism which the servant Waitwell, for all his devotion and kindness of heart, directs at her. Lessing is conscious that his heroine is not faultless and employs such 'internal' criticism to maintain proportion and balance.

The character of Mellefont also presented Lessing with a problem which he was only able to solve in part. As the choice of the excellent Sara he must be made more than a mere plausible and attractive seducer. He must have more worthy qualities, a goodness of heart and an innate moral sense, if Sara's moral perception is not to be at fault. And yet at the same time he *is* a seducer, for all the responsibility for Sara's lapse must fall on him. And thirdly, he is weak, vacillating and vain, and it is these qualities which cause his own and Sara's destruction. His wavering inconstancy is most manifest in the second act, whilst his weak fear of a permanent union appears in the fourth where it even draws a rebuke from his servant, Norton. Marwood's chance of poisoning Sara is the result of his conceited wish to hear his own admiration of Sara's looks confirmed from the mouth of his former mistress. Lastly, he is never honest and straightforward with Sara, conceals the fact that he has a child by Marwood, lies to her about his reasons for postponing the wedding and even presents Marwood under an assumed name, so that at the moment he is in league with his old love against the new, yet all the time without the slightest awareness that he is being most unfair to Sara. To redeem such a despicable character convincingly was beyond Lessing's power. Mellefont shows up favourably only in his remorse after Sara's illness and death, and there are after all few who would not feel remorse in such circumstances. For the rest, Lessing depends on the statements and attitudes of the other persons to Mellefont. We have therefore to take the favourable aspects of his character on trust from the remarks of Sara and Sir William, a most unsatisfactory device. Lessing has in fact only succeeded in portraying Mellefont as the weak evil-doer, the

philanderer brought to book, leaving Sara's affection for him and her fall almost unexplained.

The most successful of the principal characters is Marwood. She is stronger and more resolute and so a more interesting personality than the passive Sara. Ten years later Lessing himself conceded that the virtuous character had serious disadvantages in literature, since it tended to be passive and to be overshadowed by the more active imperfect character and this is in fact what occurred in *Miss Sara Sampson.* Marwood, though angry and jealous, is a most calculating woman, fully conscious of her aims and, as long as she remains calm, an ideal figure for Lessing's logical presentation of character. He fails with her, too, when passion should get the better of intelligence and in her most unreal monologues. He is at his best with Marwood in the scene where she reveals her true identity to the terrified Sara.

The remaining characters cannot be said to be anything more than types. Sir William is the kind, considerate, sentimental father; Waitwell, the faithful servant. Neither is really individualized. Betty and Norton, the servants of Sara and Mellefont respectively, do not exist in their own right, but fulfil the functions of the confidant in French tragedy, enabling the principals to talk of their state of mind without having recourse to the unnatural soliloquy. In Norton, however, there is a trace of life, first in his compassion for Sara and secondly in his affirmation of the common people's unspoiled and genuine reaction to emotion. . . . (pp. 114-19)

I have made much of the faults of this play, which are indeed such as to render the work unplayable to-day and very nearly unreadable, and yet there is something to be said on the credit side, even from a strictly artistic standpoint. There are several effective scenes, notably the second interview of Sara with Marwood and Mellefont's wavering at his first interview with Marwood, followed by his resolute return. Psychologically this is also the most convincing part of the play. The moment he leaves Marwood and has time for reflection, his better self reasserts itself and he returns to her full of an anger which, though actually directed at her, is subconsciously concerned with his own weakness.

Miss Sara Sampson has, apart from all aesthetic considerations, a very profound historical significance. The eighteenth century had been an age of imitation of French drama in Germany up to this point. Lessing, not content with polemical writings against the French influence in the theatre and in favour of the English drama, now took the decisive step of actually writing and publishing a play in the English manner. *Miss Sara Sampson* is therefore an essay in practical criticism of the first importance. And not only does its success mark a vital phase in the replacement of French taste by English, more congenial to the German cast of mind; it is also a step toward the reaffirmation of the rights of the heart, of the emotional aspect of man, so grievously neglected by the prosaic rationalism of the first half of the century. And lastly, in opening the stage to a realistic presentation of contemporary men and women, it laid the foundation for what has ever since been one of the principle forms of tragedy; for the drama of the Naturalists of the late nineteenth and early twentieth century is a development of the 'domestic tragedy' which Lessing first acclimatized on the German stage with *Miss Sara Sampson.* (pp. 119-20)

In spite of the success of *Miss Sara Sampson,* Lessing had no intention of devoting himself to writing for the theatre as his principal field of activity. His work during the next few years was largely critical and his researches into the drama of the Greeks and Romans . . . were pushed a stage further and his attention began to concentrate itself upon Sophocles. This interest expressed itself in the usual way with Lessing—critical works (e.g., 17 *Literaturbrief, Life of Sophocles*) and in addition a practical attempt to open this new field for the German stage. The play resulting from this effort, *Philotas*, was preceded by a fragment not without interest, on a very similar theme, entitled *Kleonnis*. If the treatment and setting of these plays have their origin in Lessing's Greek studies, their spirit arises from current events. The Seven Years War was now in progress and Lessing, though Saxon-born, was a Prussian patriot. But Lessing's ardour is always tempered with reason and in *Philotas* he abstains from any reference to current events and simply presents the patriotic character in its highest form.

The theme of both the plays is identical. A prince goes forth for his first campaign, at a moment when his father, incapacitated by wounds, cannot accompany him. He is made prisoner (the *Kleonnis* fragment ceases just before this point, but it is obvious that it would have followed the same course as *Philotas*), discovers that the son of the king, whose prisoner he is, has likewise been captured, and thereupon kills himself, so that his own father may be able to exact a full ransom for his prisoner and thereby end the war successfully. In *Kleonnis* the action is viewed from the position of the father, awaiting news of his son. Lessing doubtless realized that this would allow insufficient action and would give no opportunity of portraying the struggle in his son. Accordingly in *Philotas* he begins the action after the prince (Philotas himself) has been captured and sets the play in the camp of his captor.

As might be expected, the emotions and sentiments actuating the characters are martial ones. Patriotism, honour and love of glory dominate the mind of Philotas, together with shame at the stain which captivity brings to his honour. Of all these sentiments, the patriotism is intended by Lessing to be the predominating one. Nevertheless there is another factor which deprives the patriotic motive of some of its force, and this is the filial piety of Philotas. As his father is the only representative of the state in the play, Philotas' sacrifice may be regarded as an act of filial devotion rather than of patriotism. Lessing does his best to counter this difficulty by making Philotas stress above all the political prestige and glory of his father. Philotas is ruthless in his devotion to father and hence to fatherland, as may be seen in the ruse by which he obtains from his captors the sword with which he intends to kill himself. Lessing, by his approval of characters of Philotas, gives his support to the view that any breach of faith is justified if it furthers the interests of one's country, a belief which has characterized many German statesmen from Frederick the Great to Hitler. That it should occur in so just and reasonable a person as Lessing indicates how deeply this extreme patriotism is rooted in the German mind.

Although he makes no attempt to imitate the formal details of Greek tragedy, Lessing has sought to reproduce its general effect. Plot and development are extremely simple. The action begins within an hour of its final catastrophe. The details of the previous events are gradually revealed both to the persons of the play and to the spectators somewhat after the manner in which the revelation takes place in *Oedipus*. There are only four characters and the action is continuous, without division of acts. No concession is made to the demand for a 'love-interest', created by French taste and then current in Germany. No woman in fact appears. In this attempt at a Greek play,

Lessing had come very near creating a new form for contemporary drama. If he could have taken the further step of combining the modern setting and characters of *Miss Sara Sampson* with the simplicity and progressive exposition of *Philotas*, he would have come very near to creating the dramatic form of Ibsen a hundred years before its actual appearance.

The weakness of the play, as so often with Lessing, is its dramatic speech, which is here subjected to an exceptionally severe test by the numerous long monologues. Short speeches, first by one character then another, do something to conceal the ratiocination which pervades Lessing's dialogue and prevents it from coming to life, and the presence of several characters obliges the author to pay some heed to the characterization of their speech, so that they may be adequately differentiated. But in *Philotas* these factors were not involved and consequently the speech is similar in tone for all the characters and is far too logically constructed, as will appear from this sample of Philotas' deliberations on the problem of his suicide:

> But I? I, the seed, the bud of a man, do I know how to die? It is not only man in his maturity, who must know how to die. The youth too, and the boy must know how to, or if not, he knows nothing. He who has lived ten years, has had ten years in which to learn how to die, and what one cannot learn in ten years, cannot be learned in twenty, thirty or more.

The real reason for such defective dialogue in Lessing is that, not being a creative writer, he lacks the gift of getting into the skin of his characters; they are not a part of himself, they are ideas of his; thus *Philotas* is simply the product of a very noble idea of Lessing. And though Lessing's characters speak and act plausibly they do not convince us that they are living, because Lessing has not *felt* himself the emotions of which they speak, he only lets them say what he *thinks* such a character would say in such circumstances. Though *Philotas* was written in prose it is of interest to note that the earlier fragment, *Kleonnis*, was in blank verse; this was Lessing's first experiment with this metre. (pp. 122-25)

> *H. B. Garland, in his* Lessing: The Founder of Modern German Literature, *second edition, St. Martin's Press, 1962, 202 p.*

E. ALLEN McCORMICK (essay date 1971)

[*McCormick is an American academic and scholar who concentrates his studies on German literature, chiefly of the eighteenth and nineteenth centuries. Among his several books is the important* Theodor Storm's Novellen: Essays on Literary Technique (1964). *In the following excerpt from another work, he describes Lessing's legacy to German literature, noting the close relationship between Lessing's dramatic and critical works.*]

Lessing's criticism defies meaningful generalization. He never developed an aesthetic system: of his three major critical undertakings two are collections, a series of unordered notes for a book (''Collectanea'') and scattered ''Fermenta cognitionis'' [''random thoughts''], to use his own words. Furthermore, one is a periodical, to which some of Lessing's friends contributed, another remained a torso, and the third represents accounts of day-to-day theatrical performances intermingled with, and gradually changing to, serious dramatic criticism that is often abstract and primarily concerned with theoretical principles. (p. 109)

Several major concerns emerge from Lessing's critical writings as a whole. First, his concern with the German theater, both in terms of acting and stagecraft and the plays themselves; then, his abiding interest in the theory of literature; and lastly, his insistence on direct, concrete criticism of literary works. Permeating all these is his conviction that the larger, moral view of literature is paramount. Not in the rather limited sense of Gottsched's moralizing but in the deeply ethical one of seeing in literature a humanizing force, which springs from an informed tolerance. In this conviction Lessing is less direct than two of his greatest successors: Herder with his goal of humanism or Schiller with his stress on the harmonious development of man's potential, but the faith in *humanitas* ["humanity"] is nonetheless everywhere present in his work.

The modernity of his stand as a critic is expressed most clearly in the 105th letter of his *Letters Concerning Contemporary Literature:*

> I have always believed it to be the duty of the critic, whenever he undertakes to judge a work, to limit himself solely to this work; to give no thought to the author in doing so; to disregard the question of whether the author has not written other books, worse or better ones; and to tell us forthrightly what opinion we can reasonably form of him solely from this work.

Lessing is not rejecting biography; his *Life of Sophocles* would alone disprove that. He is simply expressing—at a surprisingly early period in the history of German criticism—what has today become an overworked truism: the private life of a writer is often ill-used when made to supply explanations of a particular work. As Lessing puts it in the 17th literary letter:

> Of what concern to us is the private life of an author? I have no use for deriving elucidations of a work from the author's life.

The *Hamburg Dramaturgy,* somewhat less known and certainly less read than the *Laocoön,* shows Lessing in his best light as a critic. Though there is a good deal of ephemeral writing in the 104 pieces comprising the *Dramaturgy,* both his theory and practice of criticism emerge in it in exemplary form. Since Lessing wrote this work in his capacity as critic-consultant to the newly created "national" theater in Hamburg and much of his duty lay in reviewing the performances of plays, he focuses almost exclusively on questions of drama: what is its nature, what rules govern it, how is it to be performed, what is tragedy? Proceeding from concrete examples, usually the performance of a mediocre play the evening before, he turns straightway to these questions, confronts Aristotle, draws comparisons, offers occasional line-by-line analysis, and ultimately produces a simple but effective view of the literary form he had long considered the high-point of literature.

The picture that emerges from these dramaturgical pieces, i.e., the view we get of Lessing the critic, is that of a faithful but by no means blind Aristotelian. He sets himself the task of examining the contemporary stage, primarily in France since that is where most neoclassicists looked in Lessing's and of course Gottsched's time, and of measuring its achievement against Aristotle's rules which he finds infallible. Lessing saw it as his duty to arrest what he calls this fermentation of taste, caused, so he felt, by the delusion of regularity of the French stage. According to him no nation had so misunderstood the rules as the French. Corneille himself, after fifty years of dramatic production, "ought" to have sat down and studied Aristotle more diligently *before* undertaking his commentary to the *Poetics:*

He appears to have done this only in so far as the mechanical rules of dramatic art were concerned. He left essential points disregarded and when he found at the end that he had sinned against Aristotle, which nevertheless he had not wished to do, he endeavored to absolve himself by means of explanations and caused his pretended master to say things which he never thought. (No. 75)

The intent of statements like the foregoing seems to imply a return to Aristotle; and Lessing points out at least once that this philosopher must be studied thoroughly. Yet he is also fully aware of the achievement of the English, and in admonishing the Germans not to throw away all rules in favor of genius he clearly has Shakespeare in mind. Lessing has relatively little to say about Shakespeare directly, but he has him serve on occasion as the model one should study in pursuit of moderation, of the middle way between tradition and genius. Study Shakespeare, he urges, do not plunder him.

In the *Hamburg Dramaturgy* Lessing investigates tragedy and comedy, analyzes the Aristotelian concepts of pity and fear and their supposed misinterpretation by the French, and inquires into the dramatic art and aesthetic phenomenon of illusion. Furthermore, the book offers several insights which pertain to literature specifically. In a discussion of Lope de Vega and mixed forms (tragi-comedy and comi-tragic drama) he digresses long enough to make an acute statement on the principle of selectivity in art:

> The purpose of art is to save us . . . abstraction in the realm of the beautiful, and to render the fixing of our attention easy to us. All in nature that we might wish to abstract in our thoughts from an object or a combination of various objects, be it in time or in place, art really abstracts for us, and accords us this object or this combination of various objects as purely and tersely as the sensations they are to provoke allow. (No. 70)

(pp. 110-12)

His speculations and observations—made, it is worth repeating, in no systematic way—cannot be reduced to a simple formula. Still, it is relatively easy to discern one of Lessing's key convictions about literature: the essence of poetry is action; it presents us with inner perfection which arises from great passions in their freedom of movement. It is an insight won from Aristotle but modified and blended with Lessing's concept of truth as embodied in the natural order and recreated in the work of art as structure or form. It pervades his criticism and recurs in such unexpected places as the detailed review of a minor play or its performance. One such play, *Richard III,* by a now forgotten dramatist named Weiss, occasioned lengthy discussions of Aristotle, Corneille, Dacier's commentary on Aristotle, and literally dozens of other matters. And just when it appears that Lessing has forgotten his example and task, he returns to it by criticism of the most practical sort:

> Now if not one of the personages in Richard possesses the necessary qualities which they ought to have were this work a real tragedy, how has it nevertheless come to be considered an interesting play by our public? . . . If it occupies the spectators, if it amuses them what more do we want? Must they needs be amused and occupied according to the rules of Aristotle? (No. 79)

Lessing is here a devil's advocate, a role he often plays in his attempt to anticipate and dispose of all opposition. He now proceeds to supply his own answers:

Even if Richard is no tragedy, it remains a dramatic poem, even it if lacks the beauties of tragedy it may yet have other beauties: poetical expressions, metaphors, tirades, bold sentiments, the spirited dialogue, fortunate situations for the actor to display the whole compass of his voice, the whole strength of his pantomimic art, etc. (No. 79)

No better example could be given of Lessing's peculiar gift: to remain at, or return to, the most practical level of criticism, even to reviewing, while insisting constantly on calling our attention to the larger theoretical issues. (pp. 113-14)

As subtitle *Laocoön* bears the promising line "On the Limits of Painting and Poetry." Since the time of Martin Opitz, critics had generally equated the two arts, so far at least as their aims and achievements were concerned. Such writers as Simonides (poetry is a speaking picture and painting a mute poem) and Horace (*ut pictura poesis* ["as in painting, so in poetry"]) had established a tradition in which clear lines of demarcation were almost totally erased. Lessing now attempts to restore poetry to its proper place among the arts. His *Laocoön,* he explains, is written to counteract poor criticism and false taste, both of which have led to a mania for description in poetry and for allegory in painting (Preface).

Taking as his starting point a reference made by the classical archeologist and art critic Johann Joachim Winckelmann in his *Thoughts on the Imitation of Greek Works in Painting and Sculpture* (1755) to the figure of Laocoön as he appears in Greek sculpture and in Virgil's *Aeneid*, Lessing proceeds to demonstrate that the differences in artistic presentation of the suffering Trojan priest are due to inherent differences in the two arts, viz., in their means of representation. The poet has Laocoön cry out since a scream is consonant with a noble spirit and since poetry, moreover, may depict the ugly as well as the beautiful. The plastic arts, on the other hand, see beauty as their highest law. And so the Greek artist was forced to soften the priest's scream to a sigh—as all violent emotions must be so reduced in the visual arts—in order to obey this supreme law. The plastic arts, says Lessing, must by virtue of their material limitations confine themselves to one single moment, not necessarily one of greatest emotional intensity but one that enables the observer to grasp the true significance (theme or symbolic intent) of a work of art. There is nothing to compel the poet to compress his picture into a single moment:

He may, if he so chooses, take up each action at its origin and pursue it through all possible variations to its end.

The prolonged cries of a statue would be revolting, while in narration a scream (which we do not *see* in all its ugliness) is transitory and hence quite endurable:

Virgil's Laocoön cries out, but this screaming Laocoön is the same man whom we already know and love as a prudent patriot and loving father. We do not relate his cries to his character, but solely to his unbearable suffering. (Chap. 4)

The second half of the essay attempts to draw general conclusions from these differences. Painting is a spatial art; hence, objects existing in space (figures and colors that coexist) are the subject of painting. Objects that follow one another (articulated sounds in time) are called actions, and these accordingly are the subjects of poetry. Concerning time in relation to the two arts, Lessing says that

painting can use only a single moment of an action in its coexisting compositions and must therefore choose the one which is most suggestive and from which the preceding and succeeding actions are most easily comprehensible.

Similarly, poetry in its progressive imitations can use only one single property of a body. It must therefore choose that one which awakens the most vivid image of the body, looked at from the point of view under which poetry can best use it. (Chap. 16)

Homer demonstrates the truth of these propositions. He represents nothing but progressive actions, depicting objects with a single trait only when they contribute toward these actions. Juno's chariot or Achilles' shield are not described ready-made but as they are formed before our eyes. Enumerative description is wrong, Lessing declares, for this is to attempt to transfer the coexisting objects of nature to the consecutive quality of words.

Much of what Lessing says in the *Laocoön* has been reduced to aesthetic commonplaces by later generations. In the eighteenth century, however, it was, as Goethe put it, a ray of light breaking through dark clouds [see excerpt dated 1811-22].

The *Laocoön* and the *Hamburg Dramaturgy* are chiefly responsible for Lessing's enduring place in criticism. His other major critical effort, the *Literary Letters,* were a joint venture of Lessing, Mendelssohn, and Friedrich Nicolai. Because they came first in the chronology of Lessing's criticism, they must be considered important for having prepared the way for the more substantial later works. The fifty-four letters (about two-thirds of the entire enterprise) which Lessing contributed to the periodical deal mostly with contemporaries or immediate predecessors. Wieland's works come in for lengthy discussion, translations from various literatures are judged, Klopstock is admired and English literature defended as being more faithfully Aristotelian than were Corneille and Racine.

The seventeenth literary letter contains Lessing's spirited attack on Gottsched's "Frenchifying" theater reform. He argues that Gottsched ought to have seen from Germany's older dramatic works that German taste was closer to English than to French. Lessing is convinced that if only Shakespeare's major plays had been translated it would have been more advantageous for the German stage. For Shakespeare is a much greater tragedian than Corneille despite the fact that the Frenchman knew the ancients and Shakespeare did not. As proof that old German dramas were closer to the English Lessing provides the reader with a scene from his *Doctor Faust.*

Any attempt to assess the place and importance of this *Faust* fragment in Lessing's critical and poetic work must remain at the level of speculation. There is too little to go on; we have only the scene from the *Literary Letters,* a prose sketch, and a few references to two versions Lessing worked on intermittently between 1755 and 1767. Beyond pricking our curiosity, however, the bare bones of a Faust drama by Lessing have strong implications for his creation and use of a literary work as an exercise in practical criticism. We recall the admission Lessing makes in the *Hamburg Dramaturgy* that he has practiced dramatic writing so as to be able to have his say as critic.

Shortly after moving from Leipzig to Berlin, Lessing began his first serious critical work, the *Beiträge zur Historie und Aufnahme des Theaters (Contributions to the History and Improvement of the Theater)*, in collaboration with his friend Christlob Mylius. In this quarterly, which lasted for only four issues, Lessing hoped to open Germany's eyes to a theater on a genuinely European scale. The attention that had been paid to the French theater had led to a degree of monotony on the German stage which could only be relieved by attention to the plays of Italy, Spain, Holland, and classical Greece and Rome. Special emphasis was to be placed on English and Spanish drama.

Two other early writings, *The Latest from the Realm of Wit* and the *Kritische Briefe* (25 "Critical Letters," written in 1753), may be seen as sequels to the *Contributions* and as illustrations of Lessing's rapidly maturing critical powers. The first of these contains the detailed commentary on Klopstock's *Messiah*, the attack on Gottsched for his failure to appreciate genius (reference to both has been made), and a number of moralizing stories. The *Critical Letters* are noteworthy for the early example they offer of Lessing's rehabilitations or vindications of unjustly treated or neglected predecessors. (pp. 114-17)

Another vindication *Rettungen des Horaz (Rehabilitations of Horace)* shows the same sense of fairmindedness, of the need to uncover the truth and present it conscientiously and thoroughly, which is indeed the *movens* ["purpose"] of most if not all his polemical writings also. The details of his quarrels with several contemporaries—notably Pastors Lange and Goeze, and Professor Klotz—need not concern us here; but we should not fail to take note of Lessing's keen awareness of professional standards and the constructive ends towards which satire, irony, invective, aggressiveness verging on bullying—there are few such weapons that he failed to use—are turned. But to say that the ends—exposure of ignorance, superficiality, dishonesty, or simply poor scholarship—justify the means is not to suggest that Lessing ever descended to personal levels of attack. His was exclusively an intellectual anger, and the thought of personal or moral defamation was abhorrent to him. (pp. 117-18)

No small part of Lessing's greatness lies in having recognized in himself certain limitations which, in the context of literary criticism and for German literature as a whole, have had as deep and lasting a significance as the very best of his critical efforts. He was obviously aware that his early plays were primarily extensions of his critical efforts; they were written to inspire other playwrights and show them what a German repertoire could contain. They are not profound. *The Free-Thinker* borrows its idea and much of the plot from a French play; *The Jews* is quite openly propagandistic, and *The Treasure* is a rather bald imitation of Plautus' comedies. (p. 118)

With the production in Hamburg of Lillo's *Merchant of London* in 1754, and exactly two years later Lessing's *Miss Sara Sampson*, middle-class tragedy was successfully established on the German stage. In borrowing "foreign treasures" Lessing produced a work not completely satisfactory artistically, to be sure, but the effect of this first domestic tragedy on German literature more than offsets this. By extending his criticism from precept to practice he gave actual demonstration of the correctness of his theories: not French but English drama, not French but English taste, not meter but natural prose dialogue, and not heroic and noble but everyday characters—these are Lessing's innovations.

Even his failures were later turned to successes. The national theme which he found in *Faust* but could not express artistically is brilliantly realized in *Minna von Barnhelm*, and the spirit of tolerance and humanity, coupled with a desire for moral betterment, is evident in *Nathan the Wise*, some of the fables, and *Emilia Galotti*. With the publication and performance of *Minna von Barnhelm*, Lessing's importance shifts from that of a critic to that of the father of the modern German theater. The play,

one of the few excellent comedies written in German, captures the atmosphere of Prussia after the Seven Years' War in a sequence of vivid scenes and above all creates several unforgettable characters. The fast-moving action which revolves around a potentially tragic conflict is resolved by Minna whose love conquers all obstacles and cures Tellheim of the hubris of his excessive pride.

In *Emilia Galotti* Lessing created a play of almost perfect symmetrical construction which moves inexorably toward the final disaster. Emilia's tragic death on her wedding day seems the result of several psychologically well motivated circumstances: the weakness and immorality of the Prince who desires her and orders her abduction, the rage of his former mistress, the plotting of his evil adviser, the stern morality of Emilia's father, and finally her own decision. Basically, however, the tragedy reveals that man's relation to man has become impossible because truth has vanished from life. Emilia finds herself in a world without compassion or equity. The prince, the highest judge in this world, is evil. And Odoardo, despairing in his effort to find justice on earth, sacrifices his daughter and can only hope for a judgment after life. Thus Emilia is defeated by forces beyond her control. The play's final scenes breathe the air of death.

Nathan the Wise, structured around the parable of the ring, is a magnificent testimony to Lessing's humanitarian ideals. In the parable three sons appear before a judge, each claiming that their father had secretly bequeathed him a magical ring which made its possessor beloved of God and men. They learn from the wise judge that only their actions can prove the authenticity of their ring's qualities. The highly successful "dramatic poem" actually established blank verse as the meter most commonly used by German playwrights. *Nathan* presents a picture of a world in which man finally conquers his instincts, listens to reason, tolerates other beliefs, and loves his brother. Thus it introduces themes which Lessing emphasized again in his essay *On the Education of the Human Race*, themes which become also a challenge for Goethe and Schiller.

All in all, it would therefore be wrong to isolate Lessing's literary criticism from his varied activites as playwright, fabulist, and moralist-theologian. . . . [His legacy to German literature is] inseparable from criticism and drama alike. As reformer, critic, playwright, and man, he firmly established the tradition Germany needed and made possible the literary climate from which Storm and Stress and Classicism were to grow. (pp. 120-22)

E. Allen McCormick, "The Eighteenth Century: Foundation and Development of Literary Criticism," in The Challenge of German Literature, *edited by Horst S. Daemmrich and Diether H. Haenicke, Wayne State University Press, 1971, pp. 100-42.*

GERTRUD MANDER (essay date 1975)

[Mander is a German-born scholar, editor, and translator whose interests include the performing and fine arts, literature, and criticism. The author of several studies of the drama, she is perhaps best known for her works in German, George Bernard Shaw *(1965),* Shakespeares Zeitgenossen: Von Marlowe bis Massinger *(1966), and* Jean-Baptiste Molière *(1967;* Molière, *1973). In the following excerpt from a later work, she discusses Lessing's theoretical and practical contributions to the German theater's social and aesthetic reform, noting his use of classical models and his concern with the meaning and function of art.]*

Every German schoolchild is taught that Gotthold Ephraim Lessing . . . was the founder of the German theatre. This is of course one of the terrible simplifications of the personality-centred textbook approach. For how on earth could one man, however determined and talented, undertake alone a task like that, which would have involved theorizing and organizing as well as making the actual product? What the statement suggests is that Lessing—critic as well as playwright and a theoretician who himself tried out the viability of his theories—is *the* big and recognizable figure in a landscape swarming with smaller figures. He clarified and put into words a powerful trend of the time and articulated guidelines, found classifications, issued admonitions and passed judgment, where others merely fumbled and groped for the right words or acted in more practical ways by building theatres, forming acting troupes, and setting up academies. (p. 131)

Lessing was a truly 18th-century figure, a man completely of his time, yet with a vision and a will that reached far into the future. It is fashionable to call him a revolutionary since his aims for the theatre, the writer, and the actor expressed the ambitions of the rising and mutinous educated middle classes in Germany which, at the time, were in silent or defiant opposition to their feudalist and despotic rulers. And yet Lessing, the learned, Classics-trained scholar, is in a way almost as model-dominated and rule-obsessed as his enemy Johann Christoph Gottsched (1700-66), because to him the classical writers represent the absolute standard against which all contemporary ideas and products have to be measured. They are the repositories of the truth—Truth is Lessing's most important concept, often teamed with Nature against Beauty, Art or Manners. However, he did not want the artist and writer to follow the Ancients blindly or mechanically, but to find truly national and contemporary interpretations and equivalents. (p. 14)

Lessing's lively and restless temperament and independent, inquiring mind was eminently well suited to the task of formulating a practicable theory of the theatre and of putting the theory to the test by writing plays. Apart from occasional lapses into antiquarianism and philosophical casuistry, his thinking and writing style combined lucidity and passion, common sense and directness, wit and simplicity, a combination (normally considered un-German) that was made possible at this juncture in German cultural history by the prevailing enlightenment in attitudes and ideals, particularly the belief in reason. Lessing's suggestions for the social and aesthetic reform of the ailing, provincial German theatre—only one of the many causes he took up in the course of his relatively short life—are based on this reasonableness that is attuned to simplicity and to an emphasis on essentials. The rationalist Lessing fights on two fronts—against the pedants (like Gottsched) and against the enthusiasts (the writers of tearful plays and nature poems). He assumes (or rather calls for) a similar reasoning and thinking attitude in the makers and the consumers of theatre—the actor and the spectator. In questions of form and style the rational approach is evident, too. There is a strong interest in classification (of genres, but also of possible subjects as in comedy or of gestures in acting, and Lessing even thought of devising a system of punctuation to ease the task of the actor).

This leads to his important 'Grenzziehungen'—his clear structural distinctions between the functions and the possibilities of different artistic media, of which the theatre, as the most complex and multi-faceted, is assigned the most important and immediate social and educative role. Where Molière—whose ideas and predilections come closest to Lessing's, particularly

as regards comedy—always stressed the entertainment aspect of his craft, Lessing, the son of a Lutheran pastor, the ex-theology student and fervent disciple of the Classics, introduces a moral and social dimension into the discussion on functions. It is an eminently bourgeois approach. And of course it is again mainly French in origin, derived from the Encyclopaedist Diderot and from the classical French comedy. (pp. 14-15)

[Nothing] was further from Lessing's orderly and objective mind than to recommend an absolute disregard for rules and unities. He wanted to expose the courtly theatre of the French with its grand artificiality and mechanical structure as a misunderstanding of Aristotle's dicta on the theatre. What he saw, through slightly biased eyes, was a schematized, stylized, abstract kind of theatre that stressed superficial rules of style and structure at the expense of truth and nature. Being a polemicist with a quick and dialectic turn of mind, Lessing drew his contrasts deliberately and not without exaggerations. Shakespeare is to be his paragon, as a truly popular dramatist, like the Greeks, who employed reasonable rather than strict forms. Yet he is not held up as a model to be followed blindly and slavishly. Lessing insisted that Shakespeare would have to be modified for the Germans, and this advice was put into practice by the first German Shakespeare producer and actor, Friedrich Schröder, in Hamburg, when he played Shakespeare's tragedies with happy endings. (pp. 15-16)

[Lessing's] conception of dramatic character as natural, i.e. true to life, his insistence on the realistic against the artificial and mechanical, on the use of personal and actual experience and contemporary subjects, etc. . . . has never been doubted or refuted. His searching inquiry into the meaning and function of art, particularly that of the theatre, started a debate in Germany that has never come to rest, a debate for (or, in the case of Brecht, against) Aristotle's definition of the theatre as a public institution with social and educative functions apart from its role as entertainment.

In this sense Lessing's aesthetic theories amounted to a national event. The vast influence he exerted on most German writers coming after him proves that he had set something in motion of genuine social significance. (p. 18)

Though Lessing's restless mind ranged over a wide field of subjects in the fashion of the time, which would have called him a philosopher rather than a critic, he is remembered mostly for his theories on the theatre and for his plays. The former determined the shape of German playwriting to come, the latter gloriously exemplified the former, proved their validity and still belong to the basic repertoire of contemporary German theatre because of the freshness, profound psychology, and realism of their characters and their political and humanitarian messages, which are forever topical. (pp. 18-19)

[The very first products of Lessing's] avid theatre going were plays—first the comedy **Der junge Gelehrte (The Young Scholar)** that was . . . written very much in the taste of the time. Another, later in Berlin, followed (**Die Juden, The Jews**), and many fragments and projects of plays some of which never materialized, while others took years before they were finished. The most interesting project of the Berlin years, when Lessing had become a journalist and editor of magazines and books, was the idea of writing up a political *cause célèbre* of the day: the arrest, torture, and execution of the outspoken Swiss journalist Samuel Henzi and his friends by a despotic, oligarchic government in Berne, a plan that got no further than one and a half acts, stiffly written (and in Alexandrines, a metre Lessing would soon replace with blank verse). Yet the dramatic fragment constitutes a landmark in the theatre in that it dares—in 1749—to project a contemporary subject and a bourgeois hero straight on to the stage, and in the form of tragedy, a genre which so far, according to a convention derived from Aristotle, had been reserved for the sufferings of the great. If finished, this would have been the first documentary play in history. The idea alone is of momentous importance: Lessing has seen clearly that the theatre can and should be a political instrument, that it must be a platform in the cities from which the writer educates the public socially and politically.

His next political play, **Minna von Barnhelm,** completed after the Seven Years' War, is a comedy and uses invented characters. Yet the events of the day—or rather of yesterday, since the play is set in the war—are sensed in every word, and its contemporary immediacy seems to have been overwhelmingly felt. Even now it has a liveliness and authenticity of atmosphere and mood which are rare in the theatre. What the public made of it is a different matter. Unlike **Samuel Henzi,** which seems to have been an unequivocal plea for freedom of expression and condemnation of the arbitrary methods of government by the princes of the day, **Minna von Barnhelm** managed to be different things to different people. This most famous of German comedies was taken by most contemporaries to be a pro-Prussian patriotic play—even by young Goethe, who welcomed it enthusiastically as 'truly contemporary, a true product of the Seven Years' War which drew the whole nation's attention to the significant public events.'

There is certainly much more to it than that, though it might seem enough in view of what was offered by other theatrical fare. For instance, it contains a lot of hidden criticism of a political scene in which an omnipotent monarch arbitrarily decides the fate of his subjects—including one Herr Lessing whom he never forgave an unintended offence against M. Voltaire and who is thus considered unworthy of the post of court librarian, although influential people warmly recommend him; an unknown Frenchman is preferred. The comedy is muted, as in Molière's *Le Misanthrope.* It is full of serious social or personal matter and agonising soul-searchings. Lessing's Protestant heritage makes itself strongly felt. It is an aspect of this and of all his works that makes for their continuing interest. The dramatic character is not a type (as in classical and much classicist comedy). Nor is it an embodiment of superhuman emotion (as in French tragedy). It is, according to a definition in the later work *Hamburgische Dramaturgie,* strongly individualized and possesses an 'inner probability' by acting 'not according to the book but as in real life'. Samuel Henzi *was* a real-life character in the historical sense, Minna and Tellheim, Franziska and Werner *are experienced* as real-life people such as only Molière or Shakespeare had put on the stage before.

The play grew out of a five-year stint as secretary to a Prussian General, von Tauentzien, in occupied Breslau. This was Lessing's most prosperous time financially, and he not only collected his thoughts for the major work on aesthetics *Laokoon* (a study on the varying representational techniques of the different media, precursor of the less academic and antiquarian *Hamburgische Dramaturgie*) but also observed life in the centre of the political stage. The fact is that Lessing, who has the reputation of being a bookworm, a man of theories, of general definitions, and systematic thought, was always guided by concrete personal experience. His plays are drawn as much from his observation of contemporary life and human nature as from thinking about the sayings of the immortal Aristotle, and they

are carefully tailored to the practical requirements and possibilities of the stage. (pp. 19-21)

[Much later, Lessing wrote] another political play, this time a bourgeois tragedy. In *Emilia Galótti* a classical subject is set in an Italian court and made to carry Lessing's own melancholy experience of princely government. It is tragic because it portrays the bourgeois citizens' total dependence on their sovereign's whims. Short of revolution there is only murder or suicide for the bourgeois of honour and integrity who has been wronged by his prince—the prince in the play attempts to seduce Galotti's virtuous and virginal daughter Emilia. The spirit of impotence and of defiance felt by the bourgeoisie at the time is given eloquent expression, though the play is perhaps a little sentimental to our taste. There is none of the detached, stylized grandeur and horror of French tragedy, but a direct appeal to the pity and fear of a spectator who tomorrow might be in a similar plight himself. Lessing realized his ideal of bourgeois tragedy as against the courtly tragedy of the French in the sense in which he explained it in his *Hamburgische Dramaturgie:* 'The names of princes and heroes will give nothing but pomp and majesty to a play but they do not produce emotion. The misfortunes of people whose circumstances resemble our own most closely will naturally touch us most profoundly, and if we pity kings it is because they are human beings and not because they are kings. Even though their rank makes their mishaps more important, it does not make them more interesting. Whole nations may be involved in them, and yet our sympathy needs an individual object and a nation is far too abstract a concept for our emotions to get engaged.' After seeing the play, Herder, a great friend and admirer of Lessing's, called for a theatre 'where works of this kind would be shown once a week', to make the citizen more aware and teach him to think about his situation.

This is true to the thinking of Lessing, in which the much-debated concept of catharsis is for the first time taken to mean an affect produced in the spectator and is not merely related to the passions presented on the stage. Lessing's definition was that catharsis amounted to a transformation of these passions into virtuous actions on the part of the audience: 'from the purified passions comes the power of thinking, the healing power of art, whereby reason and virtue are seen to be identical'. Goethe called the play 'a decisive step forward towards the indignant moral opposition against tyrannical despotism'. And yet the Austrian emperor refused to be moved and commented cheerfully: 'Never in my life have I laughed as much in a tragedy.' Which only goes to prove Lessing's point about the unbridgeable gap between the ruler and the ruled, and about the arrogant insensitivity and unreasonableness of the aristocracy and royalty of the time.

Small though his actual output as a playwright may have been, Lessing showed himself in his plays as a masterly political analyst and dialectician, a careful and shrewd craftsman, and a very interesting psychologist. His characters, measured as they are against the high enlightenment standards of virtue, are by no means simple or one-dimensional. The virtuous are always struggling and are always intensely vulnerable. The vicious are shown to be trapped tragically in their class, their upbringing or the political system, and the happy endings of **Minna** and **Nathan der Weise (Nathan the Wise)**—Lessing's last play in which he preaches universal tolerance in religious and racial matters—are narrow escapes and ideal philosophical solutions. (pp. 21-3)

[For all his emphasis] on realism, Lessing was putting forward not a simple doctrine of endorsing reality, but rather an outline for the future; and he was for ever aware of a threat—both constitutional and social—to man's rationality and goodness. That he managed to stick to his belief in the educability of man, in his ability to act reasonably and to exercise tolerance is a remarkable feat, considering the treatment he got in an unfree age as an upright freethinker and as a dependent on patrons and princes. If anyone ever lived what he preached, it was Lessing, who defined the true dramatic character as a character who never acts without intention and thus teaches the spectator to think. Like his Faust, he was motivated by one powerful drive—the search for truth and knowledge. (p. 23)

The most intriguing aspect of his personality and his influence lies in the interaction of theory and practice. These are the two equally important expressions of one mind, there is no lecturing in the plays, no special pleading in the theorizing. The plays were written to set an example, no doubt, an example of the bourgeois drama, the bourgeois comedy, the bourgeois tragedy, yet they were also the spontaneous expressions of a born dramatic writer. The theories are usually triggered by an occasion: a book or ideas put forward by somebody else, the lucky chance of being offered a platform from which to make himself heard (in Berlin the *Letters Concerning Modern Literature,* in Hamburg the *Hamburgische Dramaturgie*) or personal and spiritual experiences (as the religious polemics which occupied the last years of his life and culminated in the 'dramatic poem' *Nathan der Weise*). His argumentative, witty mind excelled in dialogue. When not writing dialogue for the stage he writes in the form of letters or as if talking to an imaginary partner in a conversation, an opponent in a debate. Thus, weighing the pros and cons, if only as a method of argument, as a stratagem, like Socrates, he arrives at his conclusions, carrying the reader with him as no abstract learned discourse or dogmatic manifesto will ever do.

The most important work, apart from the plays, is the *Hamburgische Dramaturgie.* It is the product of a dismal failure—an attempt at setting up—in 1767—a subsidized, national theatre by a group of enterprising Hamburg businessmen—and it is again an illustration of the way in which Lessing managed to coin gold out of the most unpromising, untoward circumstances. (pp. 23-4)

[The Hamburg project] seemed to be the perfect answer at last to Lessing's demands for a truly bourgeois, truly indigenous German theatre. Yet the narrow-mindedness and petty rivalries of the benefactors and the indifference of the audience killed the project after little more than a year. As Lessing had put it in 1760: 'We have no theatre, we have no actors, we have no spectators. The Frenchman at least has a stage, the German has hardly a hut.' Yet this new tombstone on the rough road to a viable German theatre is different from all the earlier ones in that it planted an idea which was to persist for years and even centuries to come: the idea of the serious national theatre supported by an educated audience and subsidized by an impartial body, a scene of real action, an arena of topical ideas, a focusing point for true theatrical talent. (p. 25)

To return to the *Hamburgische Dramaturgie,* the only enduring product of the fated and unfortunate project in Hamburg. . . . There would not be another treatise on the theatre as profound and influential in Germany until Brecht. However much the plays of Goethe, Schiller, Kleist, or Grillparzer—to name only the great classical dramatists—might deviate from the findings and precepts of Lessing, they are all products of a total ab-

sorption of his ideas in the cultural climate of the time. No German play worth its salt would again strive to be regular in the French sense or merely entertaining. The 'new' unities of character and plot, defined in terms of truth to nature or 'realism', have not been doubted until the expressionist and the absurdist theatre put out their antirealist and more subjective ideas.

Yet most important and influential of all proved to be Lessing's emphasis on the social function of the theatre, its role in the life of the German nation as a 'moral institution', as first his enemies and then Schiller would define it, as a place where 'the spectator is purified of his passions and made to think' (or changed, as Brecht later had it). To the non-German who expects his theatre primarily to be entertaining, this is probably the most German aspect of Lessing's theatrical gospel. Yet the gaiety and briskness of Lessing's own plays and his blunt insistence on immediacy and interest of plot and character should make the foreign sceptic reconsider his prejudice against the apparent overseriousness of our legendary *praeceptor Germaniae* ["German anticipator"]. Lessing is less dogmatic than Brecht, than Goethe, or Schiller, the three other theoreticians and great creative minds of the German theatre; he is perhaps the wittiest and certainly the most economical and lucid stylist of them all. On stage and on the printed page he never bores—something that cannot be said with honesty of the other illustrious three. Whatever he did was unexpected and dramatic. He set ideas in motion, stirred up hidden troubles, made people think, laugh and feel disturbed. This last is, perhaps, his most valuable and most enduring achievement. (pp. 25-6)

Gertrud Mander, "Lessing and His Heritage," in The German Theatre: A Symposium, *edited by Ronald Hayman, Barnes & Noble Books, 1975, pp. 13-26.*

F. J. LAMPORT   (essay date 1981)

[*In the following excerpt, Lamport assesses Lessing's reputation as the founder of modern German literature.*]

Lessing has been called the founder of modern German literature. The title is deserved, but it needs some qualification. His formidable gifts were, it has often been said, critical and analytic rather than imaginative; and they were in large measure devoted to matters of a more general scholarly or intellectual kind. As a European figure he is principally remembered as a key contributor to those two central activities of the Enlightenment, the revaluation of classical antiquity and the criticism of traditional Christianity: in particular his theological work is of abiding interest, and he is one of the most important figures in the evolution of the philosophy of history. Concerns such as this may well seem far removed from imaginative literature in the usual sense of the term, though he is one of the greatest masters of German prose, and his critical works, with their relentless probing, their irony, their seizing upon particular issues, and the sharpness of their polemic, often seem more revelatory of Lessing the man and his real response to the world about him than his literary works, where he is concealed by the stylized requirements of particular genres. . . . And within the more purely literary realm his claim to founder's status must still be strictly circumscribed. He played little or no part in the renaissance of lyricism, in practice or in theory; his own verse compositions are bounded almost entirely by the conventions of their time, and his critical remarks on a writer like Klopstock, who was trying to break free of those conventions, often betray an almost complete incomprehension of the latter's attempt to use language in a new and creative way. He played no part in the founding of the modern novel: he seems to have taken no cognizance of Gellert's work in this field, and though he does pay Wieland's *Agathon* an unsolicited compliment in his *Hamburgische Dramaturgie* . . . , it is in fact a rather left-handed one. . . . Regrettably, he does not seem to have had any real feeling for, or interest in, the imaginative possibilities of narrative prose. It is in the drama that his literary pre-eminence lies; here, however, it is unchallengeable.

After a fairly conventional start and some experimentations whose intrinsic success seems doubtful, he produced three mature masterpieces, *Minna von Barnhelm, Emilia Galotti,* and *Nathan der Weise,* which set a standard for modern German drama in three forms: comedy, tragedy, and the modern drama of ideas to which the traditional generic labels are no longer applicable. Here too his achievement is European rather than merely German. For a while in the decades following his death the 'classical' evolution of Goethe and Schiller produced in Germany the last belated flowering of verse drama in the Renaissance tradition, Lessing had pointed the way to a drama of contemporary social realism and of critical debate which was to come to the fore in the nineteenth century and to hold sway in our own.

Moreover, Lessing's claim to be considered the founder of modern German literature seems to have a great deal to do with his choice of genre. There may be something of the chicken and the egg here, in that the success of Lessing's own plays and the intense application of his critical intelligence to the nature and purpose of dramatic art themselves contributed in no small measure to the prestige of the drama in German literature. Yet there is more to it than that. The examples of Elizabethan England the 'grand siècle' in France suggest that the dramatic form is in some way particularly suited to the expression of a newly emergent national culture; Gottsched seems to have perceived as much, though without speculating upon the reasons. . . . [One of the reasons] which we may suggest here has to do with the ability of the dramatist to adapt traditional *forms* for the expression of new *content,* new attitudes or new sensibilities. It is noteworthy that Klopstock and Wieland, the pioneers of the new lyricism and of the novel, are both in many ways more consciously innovatory writers than Lessing. In the terms of one of the most fundamental and wide-ranging in its implications of the literary controversies of post-Renaissance Europe, he was an 'ancient' rather than a 'modern': though his practical dramatic activity is experimental and exploratory, in theory he seems to regard himself primarily as a restorer and purifier of tradition. . . . [In 1759, he attacked] Gottsched for destroying the German theatre and trying to re-create it from scratch, rather than *reforming* it as he should have done. In the *Hamburgische Dramaturgie* ten years later he effectively condemns European (at all events, continental European) drama since the Renaissance as an aberration, and urges a return to the standards of the Greeks. Klopstock and Wieland were confidently forward-looking; but today it is they who seem old-fashioned, the real birth of modern German poetry and the modern German novel having to wait for Goethe, while Lessing appears as the first of the moderns. (pp. 9-12)

Too often one hears it said that Lessing's plays were written to illustrate or exemplify various aspects of his dramatic theory. In fact the relationship between them is complex and often contradictory. The early comedies show the young dramatist trying out the basic tools of his craft, largely if not entirely within already established patterns. Lessing's interest in the more advanced developments of the contemporary theatre is reflected in *Miss Sara Sampson,* which one can thus call a piece of practical dramatic criticism. It is an experiment in 'bürgerliches Trauerspiel' [''bourgeois tragedy''], which is not to say that it was written in illustration of a theory of that genre: indeed, as we shall see, in this case theory follows practice rather than the other way about. *Minna von Barnhelm,* completed before the inception of the *Hamburgische Dramaturgie* and unaccompanied by a theory of comedy such as the *Dramaturgie* was to elaborate for tragedy, seems a work altogether more independent of theoretical considerations, written, one is tempted to believe, to express Lessing's view of the post-war situation and of contemporary German society; in fact . . . , it is at least as much a work intended as a model of a particular dramatic genre—practical criticism again, though here practice neither precedes nor follows theory but, largely, replaces it. *Emilia Galotti* is often thought to be a model tragedy written according to the precepts of the *Hamburgische Dramaturgie.* There is much truth in this view, even if those precepts are never systematically formulated but have to be inferred from a variety of scattered pronouncements; at the same time, what is most interesting, and most valuable, about *Emilia Galotti* arises from the conflict between the requirements of an exemplary form, defined in the *Dramaturgie* in an uncompromisingly conservative or traditional sense, and the vividly contemporary content, the very untraditional sensibilities, and (some would say) the very progressive 'message' of the work. The play offers a remarkable test case for theories on the controversial topic of literary 'intention', for what Lessing was trying to *do* and what his play *means* seem to be different things.

In all these plays we are aware of the direction of Lessing's critical intelligence towards dramatic and theatrical possibilities: the plays and the theoretical pronouncements together make up the picture of Lessing's engagement with the drama, its traditions and its received forms, and its potentialities as an instrument of cultural revival. *Nathan der Weise* stands apart. Alone of Lessing's mature dramas it was written because Lessing had a particular message to convey, rather than because he wanted, whether by way of experiment or of exemplification, to write a particular kind of play. The form is here determined by the content, rather than the other way about, and the critical intelligence is directed not primarily at the cultural potential of the drama in general, but at the real-life issues with which this particular play is concerned and, secondarily, at the potential of the theatre as a 'pulpit' for conveying a specific message—in direct contradiction to some of the most subtle of Lessing's earlier theorizing. Even the choice of the dramatic medium seems to have been made for purely external and fortuitous reasons, Lessing having been forcibly prevented from conveying his message in the medium of critical prose which had seemed in those last years the most congenial to him. And the particular form is one which transcends the traditional genre-boundaries to which, again, Lessing the dramatic theorist had appeared to be so firmly committed. It is no worse a play for this—it is indeed, in my view, Lessing's greatest: the personal urgency of its thematic content brings us closer to Lessing the man than any of his other dramatic works, and in the freedom of its form the practical innovator is no longer compromised by the theoretical conservative. But this in turn means that from the point of view of form, and of the history of Lessing's engagement with dramatic form, it is of unique interest, completing our picture from a new and unexpected perspective. (pp. 12-13)

F. J. Lamport, in his Lessing and the Drama, *Oxford at the Clarendon Press, Oxford, 1981, 247 p.*

ADDITIONAL BIBLIOGRAPHY

Allison, Henry E. *Lessing and the Enlightenment: His Philosophy of Religion and Its Relation to Eighteenth-Century Thought.* Ann Arbor: University of Michigan Press, 1966, 216 p.
Full-length study of Lessing's philosophy of religion, approaching Lessing as one of the most significant religious thinkers of his age.

Angress, Ruth K. "'Dreams that were more than dreams' in Lessing's *Nathan.*" *Lessing Yearbook* III (1971): 108-27.
Explores the interaction of "two clusters of ideas" in *Nathan the Wise:* man's intuition as it complements his reason, and the role of family bonds in shaping the characters' fate.

Barth, Karl. "Lessing." In his *Protestant Thought from Rousseau to Ritschl,* pp. 118-49. New York: Harper and Row, 1959.
Studies Lessing's contribution to Protestant theology, focusing on his criticism of dogma and church history.

Batley, E. M. "Lessing's Dramatic Technique as a Catalyst of the Enlightenment." *German Life and Letters* XXXIII, No. 1 (October 1979): 9-23.
Historical survey of the social impact and aesthetic intentions of Lessing's dramas and criticism.

Behler, Diana I. "Nietzsche and Lessing: Kindred Thoughts." *Nietzsche-Studien* 8 (1979): 157-81.
Compares Lessing's and Nietzsche's ideas about theology, especially their shared dedication to the search for truth.

Borden, Charles E. "The Original Model for Lessing's *Der Junge Gelehrte.*" *University of California Publications in Modern Philology* 36, No. 3 (1952): 113-27.
Studies Lessing's indebtedness to Johann Elias Schlegel's critical and dramatic works, naming Schlegel's *Hermann* and *Der geschäfftige Mussiggänger* as Lessing's models for *Der junge Gelehrte.*

Brodsky, Claudia. "Lessing and the Drama of the Theory of Tragedy." *MLN* 98, No. 3 (April 1983): 426-53.
Interprets the tragic intention of *Emilia Galotti,* comparing its tone, plot, form, and characterization with that of *Minna von Barnhelm* and *Philotas.*

Brown, F. Andrew. *Gotthold Ephraim Lessing.* New York: Twayne, 1971, 205 p.
Overview of Lessing's life and works.

Chadwick, Henry. Introduction to *Lessing's Theological Writings,* by Gotthold Ephraim Lessing, edited by Henry Chadwick, pp. 9-49. Stanford: Stanford University Press, 1957.
Comprehensive survey of Lessing's theological writings.

Coleridge, Samuel Taylor. Notebook entry on Gotthold Ephraim Lessing. In his *The Notebooks of Samuel Taylor Coleridge, Volume I, Part I (1794-1804),* edited by Kathleen Coburn, entry 377. Bollingen Series L. New York: Pantheon, 1957.
Contains Coleridge's textual notes and original comments on Lessing's life and career as portrayed by Johann Friedrich Schink in *Characteristik Gotthold Ephraim Lessing* (1795).

Daemmrich, Horst S. "The Incest Motif in Lessing's *Nathan der Weise* and Schiller's *Braut von Messina.*" *Germanic Review* XLII, No. 3 (May 1967): 184-96.
Compares Lessing's and Schiller's treatment of incest, suggesting that Lessing's handling of this subject in *Nathan the Wise* is perplexing, boring, and unconvincing.

Dunkle, Harvey I. "Lessing's *Die Juden*: An Original Experiment." *Monatshefte* XLIX, No. 6 (November 1957): 323-29.
Revaluation of *Die Juden,* arguing that anti-Semitic critics found Lessing's Jew overidealized because they refused to believe any Jew could be respectable.

Dvoretzky, Edward. *The Enigma of "Emilia Galotti."* The Hague: Martinus Nijhoff, 1963, 126 p.
Surveys German, Swiss, and Austrian reactions to *Emilia Galotti,* from the eighteenth to the twentieth century.

Faljole, Edward S., S. J. "Lessing's Retrieval of Lost Truths." *PMLA* LXXIV, No. 1 (March 1959): 52-66.
Detailed study of Lessing's intellectual debt to the Scottish moral philosopher Adam Ferguson, suggesting that Lessing's interior conflicts led to his awareness of a disharmony between his intellectual convictions and his everyday actions.

Flax, Neil. "From Portrait to *Tableau Vivant:* The Pictures of *Emilia Galotti.*" *Eighteenth-Century Studies* 19, No. 1 (Fall 1985): 39-55.
Probes the semiotics and aesthetics of *Emilia Galotti,* focusing on the Prince and Conti's discussion about painting.

Graham, Ilse Appelbaum. "The Currency of Love: A Reading of Lessing's *Minna von Barnhelm.*" *German Life and Letters* XVIII (1964-65): 270-78.
Examines the theme, plot, language, characterization, and verbal duels of *Minna von Barnhelm.*

———. *Goethe and Lessing: The Wellsprings of Creation.* London: Paul Elk, 1973, 356 p.
Considers Lessing's development as a creative artist, noting the internal and external factors that allowed him to exploit his creative potential to the fullest.

Heidsieck, Arnold. "Adam Smith's Influence on Lessing's View of Man and Society." *Lessing Yearbook* XV (1983): 125-43.
Discusses Lessing's aesthetic of tragedy and its implied ethics, concentrating on Lessing's handling of Adam Smith's theory of sympathy.

Heitner, Robert R. "*Emilia Galotti:* An Indictment of Bourgeois Passivity." *JEGP* LII, No. 4 (October 1953): 480-90.
Approaches *Emilia Galotti* as a "trenchant analysis of society" demanding a "new concept of bourgeois morality."

Heller, Peter. "Lessing: The Virtuoso of Dialectic." In his *Dialectics and Nihilism: Essays on Lessing, Nietzsche, Mann, and Kafka,* pp. 3-68. [Amherst]: University of Massachusetts Press, 1966.
Discusses the principle of dialectic in the style, plot, characterization, and message of *Nathan the Wise.*

Lessing Yearbook I— (1969—).
An annual publication, edited by G. Hillen, issued under the auspices of the Lessing Society of Germany. Each volume contains scholarly articles in English and German on the many facets of Lessing's life and works.

Lukács, Georg. "Lessing's *Minna von Barnhelm.*" *International Social Science Journal* XIX, No. 4 (1967): 570-80.
Close reading of *Minna von Barnhelm,* focusing on the social and moral issues it raises, its language and dialogue, and its philosophical affinities with Wolfgang Amadeus Mozart's music.

Matthews, Brander. *The Principles of Playmaking, and Other Discussions of the Drama.* New York: Scribner, 1919, 306 p.
Contains scattered remarks on Lessing's dramas and criticism, comparing Aristotle and Lessing as history's two foremost dramaturgical theorists.

Maurer, Warren R. "The Interpretation of the Ring Parable in Lessing's *Nathan der Weise.*" *Monatshefte* LIV, No. 2 (February 1962): 49-57.
Studies the dramatic, structural, didactic, and thematic significance of the ring parable in *Nathan the Wise.*

———. "The Naturalist Image of Lessing." *Germanic Review* XLIV, No. 1 (1969): 31-44.
Detailed study of "one of the most interesting periods of critical reaction to Lessing," German Naturalism from about 1880 to 1892.

Metzger, Michael M. *Lessing and the Language of Comedy.* The Hague: Mouton, 1966, 247 p.

Examines the development of Lessing's literary style as reflected in the language of his comedies, chiefly *Minna von Barnhelm, Der Schatz,* and the comic fragments.

Michalson, Gordon E., Jr. *Lessing's "Ugly Ditch": A Study of Theology and History.* University Park: Pennsylvania State University Press, 1985, 158 p.
Examines Lessing's image of the "ugly ditch" in "Über den Beweis des Geistes und der Kraft," showing its historical and religious foundations and describing its influence on Protestant thought.

Nisbet, H. B. "Lessing and the Search for Truth." *Publications of the English Goethe Society* n.s. XLIII (1973): 72-95.
Analyzes the relationship between rational and irrational factors in Lessing's attitude toward knowledge.

Primer, Sylvester. "Lessing's Religious Development with Special Reference to His *Nathan the Wise*." *PMLA* VIII, No. 3 (1893): 335-79.
Investigates Lessing's position on the religious questions of his day, chiefly as revealed in *Nathan the Wise* and *Anti-Goeze.*

Rickels, Laurence A. "Deception, Exchange, and Revenge: Metaphors of Language in *Emilia Galotti*." *Lessing Yearbook* XVI (1984): 37-54.
Introduction to the semiotics of *Emilia Galotti.*

Robertson, J. G. *Lessing's Dramatic Theory: Being an Introduction to & Commentary on His "Hamburgische Dramaturgie."* Cambridge: Cambridge University Press, 1939, 544 p.
Rigorous study of *Hamburg Dramaturgy.* Robertson discusses Lessing's theory of tragedy, noting his success in dethroning the rule-bound artificiality of "classical tragedy" through his cogent discrediting of its rules.

Stamm, Israel S. "Lessing and Religion." *Germanic Review* XLIII, No. 4 (November 1968): 239-57.

Outlines Lessing's views on religion, emphasizing the disparity between the energy of his intellectual work and the small reality he achieved.

Thiemann, Ronald F. "Gotthold Ephraim Lessing: An Enlightened View of Judaism." *Journal of Ecumenical Studies* XVIII, No. 3 (Summer 1981): 401-22.
Investigates Lessing's position on tolerance toward Jews, chiefly as revealed in his theological writings.

Vail, Curtis C. D. *Lessing's Relation to the English Language and Literature.* Columbia University Germanic Studies, edited by Robert Herndon Fife, n.s. vol. 3. New York: Columbia University Press, 1936, 220 p.
Argues that English philosophy and literature profoundly affected Lessing's criticism from 1759 onward. Vail considers *Nathan the Wise* the culmination of the English drama's influence on Lessing, and attributes Lessing's use of blank verse to English models.

———. "Lessing's Attitude toward Storm and Stress." *PMLA* LXV, No. 5 (September 1950): 805-23.
Isolates three stages in Lessing's approach to Storm and Stress, ranging from his near-total approval of its tenets to his unwillingness to regard Storm and Stress as a literary movement.

Wellbery, David E. *Lessing's "Laocoon": Semiotics and Aesthetics in the Age of Reason.* Cambridge: Cambridge University Press, 1984, 275 p.
Studies Lessing's philosophical and aesthetic contributions to the German Enlightenment.

Wessel, Leonard P. *G. E. Lessing's Theology: A Reinterpretation.* The Hague: Mouton, 1977, 283 p.
Examines Lessing's philosophical interpretation of God, revealing inconsistencies in Lessing's theology that suggest he was "caught on the horns of a cognitive crisis."

Niccolò (di Bernardo) Machiavelli

1469-1527

(Also Nicolo, Niccholo, and Nicolas; also Machiavegli, Machiavello, and Machiavel) Italian essayist, dramatist, historian, sketch writer, biographer, dialogist, writer of novellas, and poet.

A Florentine statesman and political theorist, Machiavelli remains one of the most controversial figures of political history. While addressing a wide range of political and historical topics, as well as embracing strictly literary forms, he has come to be identified almost exclusively with his highly controversial manual of state *Il principe* (*The Prince*). This straightforward, pragmatic treatise on political conduct and the application of power has, over the centuries, been variously hailed, denounced, and distorted. Seldom has a single work generated such divergent and fierce commentary from such a wide assortment of writers. Commenting on Machiavelli's colorful critical heritage, T. S. Eliot has remarked that "no great man has been so completely misunderstood."

Machiavelli was born in Florence to an established though not particularly affluent middle-class family whose members had traditionally filled responsible positions in local government. While little of the author's early life has been documented, it is known that as a boy he learned Latin and that he quickly became an assiduous reader of the ancient classics. Among these, he highly prized his copy of Livy's history of the Roman Republic. Machiavelli's first recorded involvement in the volatile Florentine political scene came in 1498, when he helped the political faction that deposed Girolamo Savonarola, then the dominant religious and political figure in Florence. In the same year Machiavelli was appointed to the second chancery of the republic. As chancellor and as secretary to the Ten of of Liberty and Peace, a sensitive government agency dealing chiefly with warfare and foreign affairs, Machiavelli participated both in domestic politics and in diplomatic missions to foreign governments. These posts afforded him innumerable opportunities over the next fourteen years to closely examine the inner workings of government and to meet prominent individuals, among them Cesare Borgia, who furnished the young diplomat with the major profile in leadership for *The Prince*. Machiavelli quickly gained political prominence and influence; by 1502 he was a well-respected assistant to the republican *gonfalonier*, or head of state, Piero Soderini.

In 1512, Spanish forces invaded Italy and the Florentine political climate changed abruptly. The Medici—for centuries the rulers of Florence, but exiled since 1494—seized the opportunity to depose Soderini and replace the republican government with their own autocratic regime. Machiavelli was purged from office, jailed and tortured for his well-known republican sentiments, and finally banished to his country residence in Percussina. Machiavelli spent the enforced retirement writing the small body of political writings that insured his literary immortality. Completed between 1513 and 1517, *Discorsi . . . sopra la prima deca di Tito Livio* (*Discourses upon the First Decade of T. Livius*) and *The Prince* were not published until after Machiavelli's death, in 1531 and 1532 respectively. Around 1518 he turned from discursive prose to drama in *La mandragola* (*Mandragola*); it, like the author's other writings, is firmly predicated on an astute, unsentimental awareness of human

nature as flawed and given to self-centeredness. The play was popular with audiences throughout much of Italy for several years. His next effort, a military treatise published in 1521 and entitled *Libro della arte della guerra* (*The Art of War*), was the only historical or political work published during the author's lifetime. Meanwhile, Machiavelli had made several attempts to gain favor with the Medici (including dedicating *The Prince* to Lorenzo). In 1520 he was appointed official historian of Florence and was subsequently entrusted with minor governmental duties. His prodigious *Istorie fiorentine* (*History of Florence*) carefully dilutes his republican platform with the Medicean bias expected of him. In 1525 Pope Clement VII recognized his achievement with a monetary stipend. Two years later, the Medici were again ousted, and Machiavelli's hopes for advancement under the revived republic were frustrated, for the new government was suspicious of his ties to the Medici. Disheartened by his country's internal strife Machiavelli fell gravely ill and died, a disillusioned man, his dream of an operational republic unrealized.

Critics have found it ironic that the fiercely republican Machiavelli should have written a handbook advising an autocratic leader how best to acquire and maintain power and security. Machiavelli was acutely aware, however, of foreign threats to Italian autonomy and thus deemed it necessary for a strong prince to thwart French and Spanish hegemony. Hence *The Prince*, addressed to the ruling Medici. He believed that a shrewd head of state, exemplified by Borgia, was essential to uniting diffuse elements of self-interest in behalf of joint welfare. Since handbooks of conduct meeting monarchal needs had become immensely popular by the 1400s, the external design of such a volume as *The Prince* was neither startling nor particularly remarkable to Machiavelli's contemporaries. Yet, from its initial appearance, *The Prince* proved no mere manual of protocol nor, for that matter, of even conventional strategy. In its chapters, Machiavelli delineated a typology of sovereignties and the deployment of available forces—military, political, or psychological—to acquire and retain them. *The Prince* is the first political treatise to divorce statecraft from ethics; as Machiavelli wrote: "How one lives is so far removed from how one ought to live that he who abandons what one does for what one ought to do, learns rather his own ruin than his preservation." Adding to his unflinching realism the common Renaissance belief in humanity's capacity for determining its own destiny, Machiavelli posited two fundamentals necessary for effective political leadership: *virtù* and *fortuna*. *Virtù* refers to the prince's own abilities (ideally a combination of leonine force and vulpine cunning); *fortuna* to the unpredictable influence of fortune. In a significant departure from previous political thought, the designs of Providence play no part in Machiavelli's scheme. On issues of leadership hitherto masked by other political theorists in vague diplomatic terms, Machiavelli presented his theses in direct, candid, and often passionate speech, employing easily grasped metaphors and structuring the whole in an aphoristic vein which lends it a compelling authority.

Reaction to *The Prince* was initially—but only briefly—favorable, with Catherine de' Medici said to have enthusiastically included it, among other of Machiavelli's writings, in the educational curriculum of her children. But, within a short time the book fell into widespread disfavor, becoming viewed as a handbook for atheistic tyranny. *The Prince*, and Machiavelli's other writings as well, were placed in the Papal Index of Prohibited Books in 1559. Further scourged toward the close of the sixteenth century in *Discours sur les moyens de bien gouverner et maintenir en paix un royause, ou autre principaute. Contre Nicolas Machiavel, florentin* by Innocenzo Gentillet in France, *The Prince* was held responsible for French political corruption and for widespread contribution to any number of political and moral vices. Gentillet's interpretation of *The Prince* as advocating statecraft by ruthlessness and amoral duplicity was disseminated throughout Britain through the works of such popular, highly influential dramatists as William Shakespeare and Christopher Marlowe. In the Prologue to Marlowe's *The Jew of Malta* (1589?), "Machevil" addresses the audience at length, at one point encapsulating the Elizabethan perception of Machiavelli by saying, "I count religion but a childish toy, / And hold there is no sin but ignorance." Here and in the works of Marlowe's contemporaries, Machiavelli was depicted as an agent of all that Protestant England despised in Catholic, High-Renaissance Italy. Hostile English interpreters so effectively typified Machiavelli as an amalgam of various evils, which they described with the still-used term "Machiavellian," that fact and fabrication still coexist today. Rarely, until the nineteenth century, did mention of *The Prince* elicit other than unfounded and largely unexamined repugnance, much less encourage objective scrutiny of its actual issues. For the most part, as Fredi Chiappelli has aptly summarized: "Centuries had to elapse before the distinction between moral moment and political moment, between technical approach and moralistic generalities, and even between the subject matter of the book and the author's person were finally achieved."

Modern critics, noting these crucial distinctions, have engaged in a prolonged and animated discussion concerning Machiavelli's true intent in *The Prince*. An anomalous seventeenth-century commentator, philosopher Pierre Bayle, found it "strange" that "there are so many people, who believe, that Machiavel teaches princes dangerous politics; for on the contrary princes have taught Machiavel what he has written." Since Bayle's time, further analysis has prompted the most prolonged and animated discussion relating to the work: the true intent of its creator. Was the treatise, as Bayle suggested, a faithful representation of princely conduct which might justifiably incriminate its subjects but not its chronicler? Or had Machiavelli, in his manner of presentation, devised the volume as a vehicle for his own commentary? Still more calculatedly, had the author superseded description in ably providing a legacy for despots? A single conclusion concerning the author's motive has not been drawn, though patterns of conjecture have certainly appeared within Machiavelli's critical heritage. Lord Macaulay, in emphasizing the writer's republican zeal and those privations he suffered in its behalf, has contended that it is "inconceivable that the martyr of freedom should have designedly acted as the apostle of tyranny," and that "the peculiar immorality which has rendered *The Prince* unpopular . . . belonged rather to the age than to the man." Others have echoed this suggestion, examining the work in its historical context: John Addington Symonds has deemed it "simply a handbook of princecraft, as that art was commonly received in Italy, where the principles of public morality had been translated into terms of material aggrandisement, glory, gain, and greatness." Many have urged that Machiavelli intended the treatise as a veiled satiric attack on the methods of Italian tyranny or, by abstruse methods, its converse—a paean to patriotism and sensible government, grounded in a clear-sighted knowledge of the corrupt human condition. According to Harold J. Laski, *The Prince* "is a text-book for the house of Medici set out in the terms their own history would make them appreciate and, so set out, that its author might hope for their realization of his insight into the business of government." While ultimately unable to agree on the underlying purpose of *The Prince*, nearly all critics have nonetheless been persuaded of its masterful composition, even when unwilling to endorse its precepts. Macaulay has affirmed that the "judicious and candid mind of Machiavelli shows itself in his luminous, manly, and polished language." And Francesco De Sanctis has determined that "where he was quite unconscious of form, he was a master of form. Without looking for Italian prose he found it."

For sheer volume and intensity, studies of *The Prince* have far exceeded those directed at Machiavelli's *Discourses*, though the latter work has been acknowledged the more definitive and, further, an essential companion piece to the former. All of the author's subsequent studies treating history, political science, and military theory stem from this voluminous dissertation containing the most original thought of Machiavelli. Less flamboyant than *The Prince* and narrower in its margin for interpretation, the *Discourses* contains Machiavelli's undisguised admiration for ancient governmental forms, and his most eloquent, thoroughly explicated republicanism. Commentators have noted the presence of a gravity and skillful rhetoric that at times punctuate *The Prince* but are in full evidence only in that work's final chapter, a memorable exhortation to the Medicis to resist foreign tyranny. The *Discourses* also presents that methodical extrapolation of political theory from historical documentation which is intermittent in *The Prince*. Max Lerner has observed that "if *The Prince* is great because it gives us the grammar of power for a government, *The Discourses* are great because they give us the philosophy of organic unity not in a government but in a state, and the conditions under which alone a culture can survive."

It has been deemed not at all incongruous that an intellect immersed in historical flow and political impetus should so naturally embrace comedy as well. For Machiavelli regarded comedy exactly as he conceived history: an interplay of forces leading unavoidably to a given result. And in his comedy *Mandragola*, Machiavelli wrought the single imaginative work for which he is widely known. De Sanctis has remarked that "under the frivolous surface [of *Mandragola*] are hidden the profoundest complexities of the inner life, and the action is propelled by spiritual forces as inevitable as fate. It is enough to know the characters to guess the end." The drama's scenario concerns Callimaco's desire to bed Lucrezia, the beautiful young wife of a doddering fool, Nicia, who is obsessed with begetting a son. Masquerading as a doctor, Callimaco advises Nicia to administer a potion of mandrake to Lucrezia to render her fertile, but also warns that the drug will have fatal implications for the first man to have intercourse with her. He slyly suggests to Nicio that a dupe be found for this purpose. Persuaded by her confessor, a knavish cleric, to comply with her husband's wishes, the virtuous Lucrezia at last allows Callimaco into her bed, where he has no difficulty convincing her to accept him as her lover on a more permanent basis. Tales of this sort—replete with transparent devices, mistaken identities, and cynical, often anticlerical overtones—were already commonplace throughout Europe by the Middle Ages, though critics have remarked that Machiavelli lent freshness to even this hackneyed material. Sydney Anglo has commended his "clear, crisp repartee" and ability "to nudge our ribs at improprieties and double-meanings," despite characterization that is "rudimentary, haphazard, and inconsistent, with even protagonists going through their motions like automata." Macaulay, on the other hand, has applauded the play's "correct and vigorous delineation of human nature."

A decided influence on the philosophies of Thomas Hobbes and Sir Francis Bacon and on the thought of such modern political theorists as Vilfredo Pareto, Gaetano Mosca, Georges Sorel, and Robert Michels, Machiavelli has been called the founder of empirical political science, primarily on the strength of the *Discourses* and *The Prince*. Taken in historical perspective, it is understandable that *The Prince* should have dwarfed Machiavelli's other works. For with this slim treatise the author confronted the ramifications of power when its procurement and exercise were notably peremptory—not only in his own country but throughout Europe as well. Commentators have come to weigh the integrity of Machiavelli's controversial thought against the pressing political conditions which formed it. Some, like Roberto Ridolfi, have endeavored through their studies to dislodge the long-standing perception of Machiavelli as a ruthless character: "In judging Machiavelli one must . . . take account of his anguished despair of virtue and his tragic sense of evil. . . . [On] the basis of sentences taken out of context and of outward appearances he was judged a cold and cynical man, a sneerer at religion and virtue; but in fact there is hardly a page of his writing and certainly no action of life that does not show him to be passionate, generous, ardent and basically religious." "Far from banishing religion or ethics from politics," Peter Bondanella has stated in *European Writers*, "Ma-

chiavelli created a new religion out of politics, with all its fateful implications for modern intellectual history."

PRINCIPAL WORKS

Comedia di Callimaco: E di Lucretia (drama) [first publication] 1518?
   [*Mandragola*, 1927; also published as *The Mandrake Root* in *The Literary Works of Machiavelli*, 1961]
Libro della arte della guerra (treatise) 1521; also published as *Dell' arte della guerra*, 1521
   [*The Arte of Warre*, 1560; also published as *The Art of War*, 1815]
La Clizia (drama) 1525
   [*Clizia* published in *The Literary Works of Machiavelli*, 1961]
Discorsi di Nicolo Machiavelli . . . sopra la prima deca di Tito Livio, a Zanobi Buondelmonte, et a Cosimo Rucellai (treatise) 1531
   [*Machivael's Discourses Upon the First Decade of T. Livius*, 1663]
Historie di Nicolo Machiavegli (history) 1532; also published as *Le istorie fiorentine*, 1843
   [*The Florentine Historie*, 1595; also published as *The History of Florence*, 1761]
†*Il principe di Niccholo Machivello . . . La vita di Castruccio Castracani da Lucca . . . Il modo che tenne il Duca Valentino per ammazar Vitellozo, Oliverotto da Fermo il S. Paolo et il Duca di Gravini Orsini in Senigaglia* (treatise, biography, and essay) 1532
   [*Nicholas Machiavel's Prince. Also, the Life of Castruccio Castracani of Lucca. Also the Meanes Duke Valentine Us'd to Put to Death Vitellozzo Vitelli, Oliverotto of Fermo, Paul, and the Duke of Gravina*, 1640]
Favola: Belfagor arcidiavolo che prese moglie (novella) 1559
   [*The Divell a Married Man; or, The Divell Hath Met with His Match*, 1647; also published as *A Fable: Belfagor, the Devil Who Took a Wife* in *The Literary Works of Machiavelli*, 1961]
Tutte le opere storiche e litterarie di Niccolò Machiavelli (treatises, history, dramas, biography, and poetry) 1929
The Literary Works of Machiavelli (dramas, poetry, and novella) 1961
Machiavelli: The Chief Works and Others. 3 vols. (treatises, history, dramas, biography, and prose) 1965

*With the third edition of 1524, *Comedia di Callimaco . . .* assumed the title of its prologue, *La mandragola*.

†*La vita di Castruccio Castracani . . .* and *Il modo che tenne il Duca Valentino . . .* were appended to and originally appeared in print with the first edition of *Il principe*.

CHRISTOPHER MARLOWE   (play date 1589?)

[*Like his contemporary William Shakespeare, Marlowe was a major English dramatist and poet of the Elizabethan age. He is especially renowned for his plays* Tamburlaine the Great *(1587?)*, The Jew of Malta *(1589?)*, *and* Dr. Faustus *(1588?)*. Considered by some critics a sardonic farce,* The Jew of Malta *focuses on the power of wealth and on the machinations of the character Barnabas, a grasping Jew whose greed and unscrupulousness are attributed to the influence of "Machevil." In the following excerpt* *from the prologue of this drama, Machevil assumes center stage to deliver his dicta—as perceived by Marlowe.*]

> Albeit the world think Machevil is dead,
> Yet was his soul but flown beyond the Alps;
> And now the Guise is dead is come from France,
> To view this land and frolic with his friends.
> To some perhaps my name is odious,
> But such as love me guard me from their tongues;
> And let them know that I am Machevil,
> And weigh not men, and therefore not men's words.
> Admired I am of those that hate me most:
> Though some speak openly against my books,
> Yet will they read me, and thereby attain
> To Peter's chair; and when they cast me off
> Are poisoned by my climbing followers.
> I count religion but a childish toy,
> And hold there is no sin but ignorance.
> Birds of the air will tell of murders past?
> I am ashamed to hear such fooleries!
> Many will talk of title to a crown:
> What right had Caesar to the empery?
> Might first made kings, and laws were then most sure
> When like the Draco's they were writ in blood.
> Hence comes it that a strong-built citadel
> Commands much more than letters can import:
> Which maxima had Phalaris observed,
> He'd never bellowed in a brazen bull
> Of great ones' envy; o' the poor petty wights
> Let me be envied, and not pitied!

                                                        (pp. 62-6)

Christopher Marlowe, in his The Jew of Malta, *edited by N. W. Bawcutt, Manchester University Press, 1978, 207 p.*

RICHARD HARVEY   (essay date 1590)

[*Harvey was an English divine. In the following excerpt from a theological treatise, he lambasts Machiavelli for his godless ethics and damaging influence.*]

Italy, in old times the true mirrour of vertue and manhood, of late yeares hath beene noted, to breed vp infinite Atheists, such as *Casar Borgia* was, that vsing or abusing himselfe in his life to contemne religion, despised it on his deathbed, as *Sanazarius* writeth, or as *Alexander* the first, or as *Leo* the tenth, either of the two as irreligious, as beastly & Neronious as *Nero* himselfe, as the same excellent poet and knight, surnamed *Sincerus* for his honesty, & *Actius* for his industrie, hath written: but of chiefest name those three notable pernitious fellowes, *Pomponatius* a great philosopher, *Aretine* a great courtier or rather courtisan, *the grandsire of all false and martinish courtiership,* and *Machiauel* a great politicke. (pp. 94-5)

Yet *Machiauel* not so ill as *Aretine,* yet *Machiauel* too ill, God knoweth this vnchristian master of policie, raysing vp Nicolaites now of his stampe, as *Nicholas* an Apostata did among the seuen Deacons, is not afraid in a heathenish & tyrannical spirit, of warly art, in the person of *Fabricio,* to accuse the gospel of Christ, and the humilitie of the lamb of God, for the decay of the most flourishing and prosperous estate of the Roman Empire, which fell by the owne idlenes and follie, as himselfe confesseth and as other estates are ouerturned by it, *the mother, and nurce, and wife of all euil, saith my honourable Lord of Essex to his Souldiers, a mother that beareth none but bondemen, a nurce that feedeth none but dulpates, a wife that marieth none but vnthrists.* His discoursiue accusation is in many mens hands, & I would to God the intended effect of the discourse were not in some mens harts: howbeit, the same

is learnedly confuted, not only by a religious french protestant, whose commentaries are extant, written *ex professo,* against *Machiauel* and his antichristian groundes of gouernment, but also by no vile Papist, much named and read among students, I meane *Osorius* in his *Nobilitate Christiana,* where it is notably proued by many worthy, diuine, and humane histories, that christian humilitie and the profession of the lambe of God, is not any hinderance to the right fortitude beseeming the people of God, but rather a very great and principall furtherance of their valiant and inuincible acts, in fighting Gods owne battels, and seeking not their owne glorie, but the kingdome of *Dauid,* the kingdome of Israel, the kingdome of Christ. . . . (pp. 97-8)

And to omit the handling of militar vertues, it is most certaine, that no man is more carefull to doe his dutie, then a christian conscience, no man more harty in doing it, then a christian faith, no man more trusty, then christian charity, no man more conscionable, more faithfull, more charitable then a true christian man: and that secretary of hell, not only of Florence is forced to confesse in some places [in the discourses] vpon *Livy* and elswhere, but most emphatically in his proeme to *L. Philip Strozza,* by vehement and zealous interrogation; *In whom ought there to be more feare of God, then in a warriour, which euery day committing himselfe to infinite perils, hath most neede of his helpe?* A right Italian sentence, a notable word, a fit preserue against the other venims which this Spider gathered out of old philosophers and heathen authors; *for that is the wit and disposition of our reformatiue age, to gather precepts from those things which our forefathers in their learning iudged no better then obiections, and to study those matters for practise, which were first taught them for their safety, by knowing and auoiding them, and to gather common places of mens certaine and supposed errours omitting their vertues and commendations.* But I cannot now stand to debate any such particular point or seuerall branch of Antichristianisme. He is already confuted sufficiently by the generall testimony of all good consciences, and by the vniuersall harty consent of all godly and manly christians, as it may also please God, at his gratious pleasure to worke in many other not yet regenerate, that now account too well of him. Be not deceiued, God is not mocked, for whatsoeuer a man soweth that shall he also reape: for he that soweth to the flesh, shall of the flesh reape corruption, but he that soweth to the spirit, shall of the spirit reape life euerlasting. (pp. 98-9)

Richard Harvey, in an extract from his A Theological Discourse of the Lamb of God and His Enemies, *n.p., 1590, pp. 93-9.*

FRANCIS BACON   (essay date 1612)

[*Bacon was a prominent English philosopher, scientist, and essayist whose major literary contribution is his widely acclaimed collection* Essays, *first published in 1597 and revised and expanded in later editions. In the following excerpt from an essay first published in the 1612 edition, he questions Machiavelli's perception of custom.*]

Men's thoughts are much according to their inclination; their discourse and speeches according to their learning and infused opinions; but their deeds are after as they have been accustomed. And therefore, as Machiavel well noteth (though in an evil-favored instance), there is no trusting to the force of nature nor to the bravery of words, except it be corroborate by custom. His instance is, that for the achieving of a desperate conspiracy, a man should not rest upon the fierceness of any man's nature, or his resolute undertakings; but take such an one as hath had his hands formerly in blood. But Machiavel knew not of a Friar Clement, nor a Ravillac, nor a Jaureguy, nor a Baltazar Gerard; yet his rule holdeth still that nature, nor the engagement of words, are not so forcible as custom. (p. 123)

> *Francis Bacon, "Of Custom and Education," in his* The Essays of Francis Bacon, *edited by Clark Sutherland Northup, Houghton Mifflin Company, 1908, pp. 123-25.*

PIERRE BAYLE (essay date 1702)

[*Bayle was a French philosopher and critic whose liberal Protestantism in an age of religious dissent and persecution compelled him to spend much of his life in exile. Although the author of numerous works, it is his* Dictionnaire historique et critique *(1697; rev. ed., 1702;* The Dictionary Historical and Critical of Mr. Peter Bayle, *1710) upon which his reputation rests. Composed of brief, pithy biographical articles that frequently excluded major figures to address obscure names, the* Dictionary *contains Bayle's unabashed opinions and reflects his fundamental skepticism on all issues. The* Dictionary *was influential, particularly in France, in shaping subsequent encyclopedic studies. The French critic Ferdinand Brunetière has avowed that to "forget Bayle or to suppress him is to mutilate and falsify the whole history of ideas in the eighteenth century." In the following excerpt from the translation of the second edition of his* Dictionary, *Bayle mitigates the censure leveled at Machiavelli.*]

[In *The Prince,* the] author's maxims are very pernicious; the world is so persuaded of it, that Machiavelism, and the art of reigning tyrannically, are terms of the same import. . . . It is strange there are so many people, who believe, that Machiavel teaches princes dangerous politics; for on the contrary princes have taught Machiavel what he has written. It is the study of the world, and the observation of the transactions in it, and not a fanciful closet meditation, that have been Machiavel's masters. Let his books be burned, answered, translated, and commented, it will all be one with respect to government. By an unhappy and fatal necessity, Politics set themselves above Morality. . . . [The] same maxims are found in History, as in this author's *Prince*. There we see them put in practice, they are only here advised. It is perhaps upon this foundation, that men of sense judge, that it were to be wished no histories were written. This does not excuse Machiavel: he advances maxims which he does not blame; but a good Historian, who relates the practice of these maxims, condemns it. This makes a great difference between this Florentine's book and History; and yet it is certain, that, by accident, the reading of History is very apt to produce the same effect, as the reading of Machiavel. (p. 12)

> *Pierre Bayle, "Machiavel," in his* The Dictionary Historical and Critical of Mr. Peter Bayle: M-R, *Vol. IV, edited by Des Maizeaux, second edition, J. J. and P. Knapton and others, 1737, pp. 10-17.*

FREDERICK OF PRUSSIA (essay date 1740)

[*Frederick II (also known as Frederick the Great), was king of Prussia from 1740 to 1786. Through his policies of military action—leading to acquisition of territory—abroad and "enlightened despotism" in domestic affairs, he elevated Prussia to the status of a major European power. Also a man of letters, Frederick expressed fervent sentiments in his* Antimachiavel: Examen du "Prince" de Machiavel, avec des notes historiques et politiques *(1740;* The Refutation of Machiavelli's "Prince"; *or, Anti-*

machiavel, 1767) that contrast sharply with the actual policies he practiced after his accession to the throne. In the following excerpt from that work, Frederick castigates Machiavelli's political theory.]

The fifteenth century was like the childhood of the arts and sciences. Lorenzo de Medici revived them in Italy through his protection, but they were still feeble in the time of Machiavelli, as if recovered from a long illness. Philosophy and the geometric spirit had made little or no progress, and reasoning was not as consistent as it is in our day. Even the learned were seduced by brilliant appearances. Then, the ghastly glory of conquerors and their striking actions of imposing grandeur were preferred to mildness, equity, clemency, and all the virtues. Now, humanity is preferred to all the qualities of a conqueror. We are no longer demented enough to encourage, through praise, the furious and cruel passions that overturn the world and make innumerable men perish. Everything is submitted to justice, and the valor and military capacity of conquerors is abhorred whenever it is fatal to the human race.

Machiavelli could thus say [in *The Prince* that] in his time that it was natural for man to wish after conquests and that a conqueror could not fail to acquire glory. We answer him today that it is natural for a man to wish to preserve his wealth and to increase it in legitimate ways, but that envy is natural only to bad characters and that the desire for self-aggrandizement through the despoiling of another will not easily come to the mind of an honest man nor to those who want to be esteemed in the world.

The political theory of Machiavelli can only be applicable to one man to the detriment of the entire human race, for what would happen in the world if many ambitious men wanted to become conquerors, if they wanted to seize each other's goods, if, envious of whatever was not theirs, they thought only of invading everything, of destroying everything, and of dispossessing every one? There would be at the end be only one master in the world, who would have collected the succession of all the others and would preserve it only as long as the ambition of a newcomer permitted it. (pp. 39-40)

The error of Machiavelli on the glory of conquerors might be characteristic of his time, but his viciousness assuredly is not. There is nothing more awful than certain means he proposes for preserving one's conquests: on careful scrutiny, there is not a single one that is reasonable or just. "One must," says this monster, "extinguish the race of the princes who reigned before your conquest." Can anyone read such precepts without shuddering with horror and indignation? This is trampling underfoot all that is holy and sacred in the world; this is overthrowing of all laws the one that men must respect the most; this is opening to interest the path of all violences and crimes; this is approving murder, treason, assassination, and everything that is most detestable in the world. How can magistrates have permitted Machiavelli to publish his abominable political theory? And how can the world have tolerated this infamous scoundrel who overthrows all right of possession and security, everything that men hold most sacred, the laws most august, and humanity most inviolable? Since an ambitious person has violently seized the states of a prince, shall he have the right to have him assassinated, poisoned? But this same conqueror thereby introduces a practice into the world which can turn only to his own confusion. Another, more able and more ambitious than he will punish him in kind, invade his states, and make him perish as unjustly as his predecessor. What a wave of crimes, what cruelties, what barbarities would afflict humanity! Such a monarchy would be an empire of wolves, of which a tiger like Machiavelli merits to be the legislator. If there were nothing but crime in the world, it would destroy the human race. There is no security for men without virtue. (p. 41)

Frederick of Prussia, in his The Refutation of Machiavelli's ''Prince''; or, Anti-Machiavel, *translated by Paul Sonnino, Ohio University Press, 1981, 174 p.*

LORD BOLINGBROKE (essay date 1749)

[Henry St. John, created first Viscount Bolingbroke in 1712, was an English philosopher and Tory statesman. In the latter role, he headed the British delegation that successfully negotiated the Treaty of utrecht with the French in 1713, which ended the War of Spanish Succession. In political philosophy, Bolingbroke believed in a democratic form of Toryism which anticipated British Conservative polity of the next century. He wrote several important works of political theory, notably The Idea of a Patriot King: *a work written in 1738, pirated by his friend Alexander Pope in 1740, and printed in the authorized edition in 1749. In the following excerpt from this work, Bolingbroke comments unfavorably upon Machiavelli's* Discourses.]

Machiavel is an author who should have great authority with the persons likely to oppose me. He proposes to princes the amplification of their power, the extent of their dominion, and the subjection of their people, as the sole objects of their policy. He devises and recommends all means that tend to these purposes, without the consideration of any duty owing to God or man, or any regard to the morality or immorality of actions. Yet even he declares the affectation of virtue to be useful to princes: he is so far on my side in the present question. The only difference between us is, I would have the virtue real: he requires no more than the appearance of it.

In the tenth chapter of the first book of *Discourses,* he appears convinced, such is the force of truth, but how consistently with himself let others determine, that the supreme glory of a prince accrues to him who establishes good government and a free constitution; and that a prince, ambitious of fame, must wish to come into possession of a disordered and corrupted state, not to finish the wicked work that others have begun, and to complete the ruin, but to stop the progress of the first, and to prevent the last. He thinks this not only the true way to fame, but to security and quiet; as the contrary leads, for here is no third way, and a prince must make his option between these two, not only to infamy, but to danger and to perpetual disquietude. He represents those who might establish a commonwealth or a legal monarchy, and who choose to improve the opportunity of establishing tyranny, that is, monarchy without any rule of law, as men who are deceived by false notions of good, and false appearances of glory, and who are in effect blind to their true interest in every respect. . . . He touches another advantage which patriot princes reap: and in that he contradicts flatly the main point on which his half-taught scholars insist. He denies that such princes diminish their power by circumscribing it: and affirms, with truth on his side, that Timoleon, and others of the same character whom he had cited, possessed as great authority in their country, with every other advantage besides, as Dionysius or Phalaris had acquired, with the loss of all those advantages. Thus far Machiavel reasons justly; but he takes in only a part of his subject, and confines himself to those motives that should determine a wise prince to maintain liberty, because it is his interest to do so. He rises no higher than the consideration of mere interest, of fame, of

security, of quiet, and of power, all personal to the prince: and by such motives alone even his favorite Borgia might have been determined to affect the virtues of a patriot prince; more than which this great doctor in political knowledge would not have required of him. But he is far from going up to that motive which should above all determine a good prince to hold this conduct, because it is his duty to do so; a duty that he owes to God by one law, and to his people by another. (pp. 389-90)

Machiavel has treated, in the discourses before cited, this question, ''whether, when the people are grown corrupt, a free government can be maintained, if they enjoy it; or established, if they enjoy it not?'' And upon the whole matter he concludes for the difficulty, or rather the impossibility, of succeeding in either case. It will be worth while to observe his way of reasoning. He asserts very truly, and proves by the example of the Roman commonwealth, that those orders which are proper to maintain liberty, whilst a people remain uncorrupt, become improper and hurtful to liberty, when a people is grown corrupt. To remedy this abuse, new laws alone will not be sufficient. These orders, therefore, must be changed, according to him, and the constitution must be adapted to the depraved manners of the people. He shows, that such a change in the orders, and constituent parts of the government, is impracticable, whether the attempt be made by gentle and slow, or by violent and precipitate measures: and from thence he concludes, that a free commonwealth can neither be maintained by a corrupt people, nor be established among them. But he adds, that ''if this can possibly be done, it must be done by drawing the constitution to the monarchical form of government,'' ''acciochè quelli huomini i quali dalle leggi non possono essere corretti, fussero da una podestá, in qualche modo, frenati.'' ''That a corrupt people, whom law cannot correct, may be restrained and corrected by a kingly power.'' Here is the hinge on which the whole turns. (p. 395)

Lord Bolingbroke, ''The Idea of a Patriot King,'' in his The Works of Lord Bolingbroke, Vol. II, *Carey and Hart, 1841, pp. 376-429.*

JEAN JACQUES ROUSSEAU (essay date 1762)

[Rousseau was a French philosopher and man of letters who has often been called ''the father of Romanticism'' because of his influence on William Wordsworth and Percy Bysshe Shelley in England and Johann von Schiller and Immanuel Kant in Germany. Though he was by no means a literary critic in the strict sense, his ideas of individual freedom, of the supremacy of emotion over reason, of the goodness of the primitive human being as opposed to the civilized one, and of the benefits of ''natural'' education permeate late eighteenth- and much of nineteenth-century literature. His seminal work of political philosophy, Du contrat social; ou, Principes du droit politique *(1762;* A Treatise on the Social Compact; or, The Principles of Politic Law, *1764), outlines a relationship between government and governed whereby the former acts in the service of the collective will of the latter. In the following excerpt from this work, Rousseau discusses Machiavelli as a champion of republicanism.]*

Kings desire to be absolute, and men are always crying out to them from afar that the best means of being so is to get themselves loved by their people. This precept is all very well, and even in some respects very true. Unfortunately, it will always be derided at court. The power which comes of a people's love is no doubt the greatest; but it is precarious and conditional, and princes will never rest content with it. The best kings desire to be in a position to be wicked, if they please, without forfeiting their mastery: political sermonisers may tell them to their hearts' content that, the people's strength being their own, their first interest is that the people should be prosperous, numerous and formidable; they are well aware that this is untrue. Their first personal interest is that the people should be weak, wretched, and unable to resist them. I admit that, provided the subjects remained always in submission, the prince's interest would indeed be that it should be powerful, in order that its power, being his own, might make him formidable to his neighbours; but, this interest being merely secondary and subordinate, and strength being incompatible with submission, princes naturally give the preference always to the principle that is more to their immediate advantage. This is what Samuel put strongly before the Hebrews, and what Macchiavelli has clearly shown. He professed to teach kings; but it was the people he really taught. His *Prince* is the book of Republicans. [In a footnote Rousseau adds: "Macchiavelli was a proper man and a good citizen; but, being attached to the court of the Medici, he could not help veiling his love of liberty in the midst of his country's oppression. The choice of his detestable hero, Cæsar Borgia, clearly enough shows his hidden aim; and the contradiction between the teaching of the *Prince* and that of the *Discourses on Livy* and the *History of Florence* shows that this profound political thinker has so far been studied only by superficial or corrupt readers. The Court of Rome sternly prohibited his book. I can well believe it; for it is that Court it most clearly portrays."] (pp. 62-3)

> *Jean Jacques Rousseau, "Monarchy," in his* The Social Contract & Discourses, *J. M. Dent & Sons, Ltd., 1913, pp. 61-6.*

LORD MACAULAY　(essay date 1827)

[*Thomas Babington Macaulay was a distinguished historian, essayist, and politician of mid-nineteenth-century England. For many years he was a major contributor of erudite, highly opinionated articles to the* Edinburgh Review. *Besides these essays, collected in* Critical and Historical Essays *(1843), his most enduring work is his five-volume* History of England from the Accession of James II *(1849-61), which, despite censure of its strong bias toward the Whig political party, is esteemed for its consummate rhetorical and narrative prose. According to Richard Tobias, Macaulay was a writer who "feared sentiment and preferred distance, objectivity, dispassionate vision. Yet withal, he was a brilliant writer who . . . is still capable of moving a reader by sheer verbal excitement." In the following excerpt from an essay originally published in the* Edinburgh Review *in 1827, Macaulay discusses the ambiguities of Machiavelli's character and surveys his major works.*]

It is indeed scarcely possible for any person, not well acquainted with the history and literature of Italy, to read without horror and amazement the celebrated treatise which has brought so much obloquy on the name of Machiavelli. Such a display of wickedness, naked yet not ashamed, such cool, judicious, scientific atrocity, seemed rather to belong to a fiend than to the most depraved of men. Principles which the most hardened ruffian would scarcely hint to his most trusted accomplice, or avow, without the disguise of some palliating sophism, even to his own mind, are professed without the slightest circumlocution, and assumed as the fundamental axioms of all political science.

It is not strange that ordinary readers should regard the author of such a book [*The Prince*] as the most depraved and shameless of human beings. Wise men, however, have always been inclined to look with great suspicion on the angels and dæmons of the multitude: and in the present instance, several circumstances have led even superficial observers to question the justice of the vulgar decision. It is notorious that Machiavelli was, through life, a zealous republican. In the same year in which he composed his manual of King-craft, he suffered imprisonment and torture in the cause of public liberty. It seems inconceivable that the martyr of freedom should have designedly acted as the apostle of tyranny. Several eminent writers have, therefore, endeavoured to detect in this unfortunate performance some concealed meaning, more consistent with the character and conduct of the author than that which appears at the first glance.

One hypothesis is that Machiavelli intended to practise on the young Lorenzo de Medici a fraud similar to that which Sunderland is said to have employed against our James the Second, and that he urged his pupil to violent and perfidious measures, as the surest means of accelerating the moment of deliverance and revenge. Another supposition which Lord Bacon seems to countenance, is that the treatise was merely a piece of grave irony, intended to warn nations against the arts of ambitious men. It would be easy to show that neither of these solutions is consistent with many passages in *The Prince* itself. But the most decisive refutation is that which is furnished by the other works of Machiavelli. In all the writings which he gave to the public, and in all those which the research of editors has, in the course of three centuries, discovered, in his Comedies, designed for the entertainment of the multitude, in his *Comments on Livy*, intended for the perusal of the most enthusiastic patriots of Florence, in his *History*, inscribed to one of the most amiable and estimable of the Popes, in his public dispatches, in his private memoranda, the same obliquity of moral principle for which *The Prince* is so severely censured is more or less discernible. We doubt whether it would be possible to find, in all the many volumes of his compositions, a single expression indicating that dissimulation and treachery had ever struck him as discreditable.

After this, it may seem ridiculous to say that we are acquainted with few writings which exhibit so much elevation of sentiment, so pure and warm a zeal for the public good, or so just a view of the duties and rights of citizens, as those of Machiavelli. Yet so it is. And even from *The Prince* itself we could select many passages in support of this remark. To a reader of our age and country this inconsistency is, at first, perfectly bewildering. The whole man seems to be an enigma, a grotesque assemblage of incongruous qualities, selfishness and generosity, cruelty and benevolence, craft and simplicity, abject villany and romantic heroism. One sentence is such as a veteran diplomatist would scarcely write in cipher for the direction of his most confidential spy; the next seems to be extracted from a theme composed by an ardent schoolboy on the death of Leonidas. An act of dexterous perfidy, and an act of patriotic self-devotion, call forth the same kind and the same degree of respectful admiration. The moral sensibility of the writer seems at once to be morbidly obtuse and morbidly acute. Two characters altogether dissimilar are united in him. They are not merely joined, but interwoven. They are the warp and the woof of his mind; and their combination, like that of the variegated threads in shot silk, gives to the whole texture a glancing and everchanging appearance. The explanation might have been easy, if he had been a very weak or a very affected man. But he was evidently neither the one nor the other. His works prove, beyond all contradiction, that his understanding was strong, his taste pure, and his sense of the ridiculous exquisitely keen. (pp. 268-71)

Every age and every nation has certain characteristic vices, which prevail almost universally, which scarcely any person scruples to avow, and which even rigid moralists but faintly censure. Succeeding generations change the fashion of their morals, with the fashion of their hats and their coaches; take some other kind of wickedness under their patronage, and wonder at the depravity of their ancestors. Nor is this all. Posterity, that high court of appeal which is never tired of eulogising its own justice and discernment, acts on such occasions like a Roman dictator after a general mutiny. Finding the delinquents too numerous to be all punished, it selects some of them at hazard, to bear the whole penalty of an offence in which they are not more deeply implicated than those who escape. Whether decimation be a convenient mode of military execution, we know not; but we solemnly protest against the introduction of such a principle into the philosophy of history.

In the present instance, the lot has fallen on Machiavelli, a man whose public conduct was upright and honourable, whose views of morality, where they differed from those of the persons around him, seemed to have differed for the better, and whose only fault was, that, having adopted some of the maxims then generally received, he arranged them more luminously, and expressed them more forcibly, than any other writer.

Having now, we hope, in some degree cleared the personal character of Machiavelli, we come to the consideration of his works. As a poet he is not entitled to a high place; but his comedies deserve attention.

The *Mandragola,* in particular, is superior to the best of Goldoni, and inferior only to the best of Molière. It is the work of a man who, if he had devoted himself to the drama, would probably have attained the highest eminence, and produced a permanent and salutary effect on the national taste. This we infer, not so much from the degree, as from the kind of its excellence. There are compositions which indicate still greater talent, and which are perused with still greater delight, from which we should have drawn very different conclusions. Books quite worthless are quite harmless. The sure sign of the general decline of an art is the frequent occurrence, not of deformity, but of misplaced beauty. In general, Tragedy is corrupted by eloquence, and Comedy by wit. (pp. 292-94)

[In] the *Mandragola,* Machiavelli has proved that he completely understood the nature of the dramatic art, and possessed talents which would have enabled him to excel in it. By the correct and vigorous delineation of human nature, it produces interest without a pleasing or skilful plot, and laughter without the least ambition of wit. The lover, not a very delicate or generous lover, and his adviser the parasite, are drawn with spirit. The hypocritical confessor is an admirable portrait. He is, if we mistake not, the original of Father Dominic, the best comic character of Dryden. But old Nicias is the glory of the piece. We cannot call to mind any thing that resembles him. The follies which Molière ridicules are those of affectation, not those of fatuity. Coxcombs and pedants, not absolute simpletons, are his game. Shakspeare has indeed a vast assortment of fools; but the precise species of which we speak is not, if we remember right, to be found there. Shallow is a fool. But his animal spirits supply, to a certain degree, the place of cleverness. His talk is to that of Sir John what soda water is to champagne. It has the effervescence though not the body or the flavour. Slender and Sir Andrew Aguecheek are fools, troubled with an uneasy consciousness of their folly, which, in the latter produces meekness and docility, and in the former, awkwardness, obstinacy, and confusion. Cloten is an arrogant

fool, Osric a foppish fool, Ajax a savage fool; but Nicias is, as Thersites says of Patroclus, a fool positive. His mind is occupied by no strong feeling; it takes every character, and retains none; its aspect is diversified, not by passions, but by faint and transitory semblances of passion, a mock joy, a mock fear, a mock love, a mock pride, which chase each other like shadows over its surface, and vanish as soon as they appear. He is just idiot enough to be an object, not of pity or horror, but of ridicule. He bears some resemblance to poor Calandrino, whose mishaps, as recounted by Boccaccio, have made all Europe merry for more than four centuries. He perhaps resembles still more closely Simon da Villa, to whom Bruno and Buffalmacco promised the love of the Countess Civillari. Nicias is, like Simon, of a learned profession; and the dignity with which he wears the doctoral fur, renders his absurdities infinitely more grotesque. The old Tuscan is the very language for such a being. Its peculiar simplicity gives even to the most forcible reasoning and the most brilliant wit an infantine air, generally delightful, but to a foreign reader sometimes a little ludicrous. Heroes and statesmen seem to lisp when they use it. It becomes Nicias incomparably, and renders all his silliness infinitely more silly.

We may add, that the verses with which the *Mandragola* is interspersed, appear to us to be the most spirited and correct of all that Machiavelli has written in metre. He seems to have entertained the same opinion; for he has introduced some of them in other places. The contemporaries of the author were not blind to the merits of this striking piece. It was acted at Florence with the greatest success. Leo the Tenth was among its admirers, and by his order it was represented at Rome.

The *Clizia* is an imitation of the *Casina* of Plautus, which is itself an imitation of the lost κληρουμξνοι of Diphilus. Plautus was, unquestionably, one of the best Latin writers; but the *Casina* is by no means one of his best plays; nor is it one which offers great facilities to an imitator. The story is as alien from modern habits of life, as the manner in which it is developed from the modern fashion of composition. The lover remains in the country and the heroine in her chamber during the whole action, leaving their fate to be decided by a foolish father, a cunning mother, and two knavish servants. Machiavelli has executed his task with judgment and taste. He has accommodated the plot to a different state of society, and has very dexterously connected it with the history of his own times. The relation of the trick put on the doting old lover is exquisitely humorous. It is far superior to the corresponding passage in the Latin comedy, and scarcely yields to the account which Falstaff gives of his ducking. (pp. 296-98)

The little novel of *Belphegor* is pleasantly conceived, and pleasantly told. But the extravagance of the satire in some measure injures its effect. Machiavelli was unhappily married; and his wish to avenge his own cause and that of his brethren in misfortune, carried him beyond even the license of fiction. Jonson seems to have combined some hints taken from this tale, with others from Boccaccio, in the plot of *The Devil is an Ass,* a play which, though not the most highly finished of his compositions, is perhaps that which exhibits the strongest proofs of genius. (p. 299)

The Prince traces the progress of an ambitious man, the *Discourses* the progress of an ambitious people. The same principles on which, in the former work, the elevation of an individual is explained, are applied in the latter, to the longer duration and more complex interest of a society. To a modern statesman the form of the *Discourses* may appear to be puerile.

In truth Livy is not an historian on whom implicit reliance can be placed, even in cases where he must have possessed considerable means of information. And the first Decade, to which Machiavelli has confined himelf, is scarcely entitled to more credit than our *Chronicle of British Kings* who reigned before the Roman invasion. But the commentator is indebted to Livy for little more than a few texts which he might as easily have extracted from the Vulgate or the Decameron. The whole train of thought is original.

On the peculiar immorality which has rendered *The Prince* unpopular, and which is almost equally discernible in the *Discourses,* we have already given our opinion at length. We have attempted to show that it belonged rather to the age than to the man, that it was a partial taint, and by no means implied general depravity. We cannot however deny that it is a great blemish, and that it considerably diminishes the pleasure which, in other respects, those works must afford to every intelligent mind.

It is, indeed, impossible to conceive a more healthful and vigorous constitution of the understanding than that which these works indicate. The qualities of the active and the contemplative statesman appear to have been blended in the mind of the writer into a rare and exquisite harmony. His skill in the details of business had not been acquired at the expense of his general powers. It had not rendered his mind less comprehensive; but it had served to correct his speculations, and to impart to them that vivid and practical character which so widely distinguishes them from the vague theories of most political philosophers.

Every man who has seen the world knows that nothing is so useless as a general maxim. If it be very moral and very true, it may serve for a copy to a charity-boy. If, like those of Rochefoucault, it be sparkling and whimsical, it may make an excellent motto for an essay. But few indeed of the many wise apophthegms which have been uttered, from the time of the Seven Sages of Greece to that of Poor Richard, have prevented a single foolish action. We give the highest and the most peculiar praise to the precepts of Machiavelli when we say that they may frequently be of real use in regulating conduct, not so much because they are more just or more profound than those which might be culled from other authors, as because they can be more readily applied to the problems of real life.

There are errors in these works. But they are errors which a writer, situated like Machiavelli, could scarcely avoid. They arise, for the most part, from a single defect which appears to us to pervade his whole system. In his political scheme, the means had been more deeply considered than the ends. The great principle, that societies and laws exist only for the purpose of increasing the sum of private happiness, is not recognised with sufficient clearness. The good of the body, distinct from the good of the members, and sometimes hardly compatible with the good of the members, seems to be the object which he proposes to himself. Of all political fallacies, this has perhaps had the widest and the most mischievous operation. (pp. 309-11)

Nothing is more remarkable in the political treatises of Machiavelli than the fairness of mind which they indicate. It appears where the author is in the wrong, almost as strongly as where he is in the right. He never advances a false opinion because it is new or splendid, because he can clothe it in a happy phrase, or defend it by an ingenious sophism. His errors are at once explained by a reference to the circumstances in which he was placed. They evidently were not sought out; they

lay in his way, and could scarcely be avoided. Such mistakes must necessarily be committed by early speculators in every science.

In this respect it is amusing to compare *The Prince* and the *Discourses* with the *Spirit of Laws.* Montesquieu enjoys, perhaps, a wider celebrity than any political writer of modern Europe. Something he doubtless owes to his merit, but much more to his fortune. He had the good luck of a Valentine. He caught the eye of the French nation, at the moment when it was waking from the long sleep of political and religious bigotry; and, in consequence, he became a favourite. The English, at that time, considered a Frenchman who talked about constitutional checks and fundamental laws as a prodigy not less astonishing than the learned pig or the musical infant. Specious but shallow, studious of effect, indifferent to truth, eager to build a system, but careless of collecting those materials out of which alone a sound and durable system can be built, the lively President constructed theories as rapidly and as slightly as card-houses, no sooner projected than completed, no sooner completed than blown away, no sooner blown away than forgotten. Machiavelli errs only because his experience, acquired in a very peculiar state of society, could not always enable him to calculate the effect of institutions differing from those of which he had observed the operation. Montesquieu errs, because he has a fine thing to say, and is resolved to say it. If the phænomena which lie before him will not suit his purpose, all history must be ransacked. If nothing established by authentic testimony can be racked or chipped to suit his Procrustean hypothesis, he puts up with some monstrous fable about Siam, or Bantam, or Japan, told by writers compared with whom Lucian and Gulliver were veracious, liars by a double right, as travellers and as Jesuits.

Propriety of thought, and propriety of diction, are commonly found together. Obscurity and affectation are the two greatest faults of style. Obscurity of expression generally springs from confusion of ideas; and the same wish to dazzle at any cost which produces affectation in the manner of a writer, is likely to produce sophistry in his reasonings. The judicious and candid mind of Machiavelli shows itself in his luminous, manly, and polished language. The style of Montesquieu, on the other hand, indicates in every page a lively and ingenious, but an unsound mind. Every trick of expression, from the mysterious conciseness of an oracle to the flippancy of a Parisian coxcomb, is employed to disguise the fallacy of some positions, and the triteness of others. Absurdities are brightened into epigrams; truisms are darkened into enigmas. It is with difficulty that the strongest eye can sustain the glare with which some parts are illuminated, or penetrate the shade in which others are concealed. (pp. 313-15)

The historical works of Machiavelli still remain to be considered. The life of Castruccio Castracani will occupy us for a very short time, and would scarcely have demanded our notice, had it not attracted a much greater share of public attention than it deserves. Few books, indeed, could be more interesting than a careful and judicious account, from such a pen, of the illustrious Prince of Lucca, the most eminent of those Italian chiefs, who like Pisistratus and Gelon, acquired a power felt rather than seen, and resting, not on law or on prescription, but on the public favour and on their great personal qualities. Such a work would exhibit to us the real nature of that species of sovereignty, so singular and so often misunderstood, which the Greeks denominated tyranny, and which, modified in some degree by the feudal system, reappeared in the commonwealths of Lombardy and Tuscany. But this little composition of Machiavelli is in no sense a history. It has no pretensions to fidelity. It is a trifle, and not a very successful trifle. It is scarcely more authentic than the novel of **Belphegor,** and is very much duller.

The last great work of this illustrious man was the history of his native city. It was written by command of the Pope, who, as chief of the house of Medici, was at that time sovereign of Florence. The characters of Cosmo, of Piero, and of Lorenzo, are, however, treated with a freedom and impartiality equally honourable to the writer and to the patron. The miseries and humiliations of dependence, the bread which is more bitter than every other food, the stairs which are more painful than every other ascent, had not broken the spirit of Machiavelli. The most corrupting post in a corrupting profession had not depraved the generous heart of Clement.

The **History** does not appear to be the fruit of much industry or research. It is unquestionably inaccurate. But it is elegant, lively, and picturesque, beyond any other in the Italian language. The reader, we believe, carries away from it a more vivid and a more faithful impression of the national character and manners than from more correct accounts. The truth is, that the book belongs rather to ancient than to modern literature. It is in the style, not of Davila and Clarendon, but of Herodotus and Tacitus. The classical histories may almost be called romances founded in fact. The relation is, no doubt, in all its principal points, strictly true. But the numerous little incidents which heighten the interest, the words, the gestures, the looks, are evidently furnished by the imagination of the author. The fashion of later times is different. A more exact narrative is given by the writer. It may be doubted whether more exact notions are conveyed to the reader. The best portraits are perhaps those in which there is a slight mixture of caricature, and we are not certain, that the best histories are not those in which a little of the exaggeration of fictitious narrative is judiciously employed. Something is lost in accuracy; but much is gained in effect. The fainter lines are neglected; but the great characteristic features are imprinted on the mind for ever. (pp. 317-18)

> Lord Macaulay, "Machiavelli," in his Critical, Historical and Miscellaneous Essays, *Sheldon and Company, 1862, pp. 267-320.*

FRANCESCO DE SANCTIS   (essay date 1870)

[*A nineteenth-century Italian literary critic and educator, De Sanctis is regarded as a critical innovator whose work provided the basis for modern Italian literary criticism. Fusing the existing critical criterion of "form" with the additional criterion of "idea," De Sanctis created an aesthetic approach to literature in which the critic considers a work of art in and of itself, rather than how it relates to such factors as biography and history. It has been suggested that De Sanctis's work,* Storia della letteratura italiana *(1870;* History of Italian Literature, *1931), in its attempt to provide a historical perspective of Italian literature, insolubly conflicts with the author's critical method of appraising works of literature apart from circumstances. Be that as it may, the* History *remains an influential, very highly regarded work of criticism. In the following excerpt from that study, De Sanctis reviews the principles fundamental to Machiavelli's literary and philosophical writings.*]

[Machiavelli's] **Decennali,** a dry chronicle of the "labours of Italy in ten years," his eight *capitoli* ["chapters"] of the **"Asino d' oro,"** in which he satirizes the degenerate Florentine citizens under the names of animals, his other *capitoli* on

L' occasione ("Opportunity"), on **Fortuna,** on **Ingratitudine,** on *"Ambizione,"* his carnival-songs, and some of his *stanze* or serenades or sonnets or canzoni, are literary works typical of that time; some are a mixture of license and bantering while others are allegorical and sententious, but all of them are arid. His verse is rather like prose; the colouring is sober, often inadequate, and the images are few and ordinary. And yet, in this dull and unfortunate beginning there are fragments that announce a new being, an unusual depth of judgment and observation. There is little imagination, but a great deal of mind. There is the critic, not the poet—not the man in his state of spontaneity who composes and muses, like Ludovico Ariosto. Instead there is the man who observes even when he is suffering, and ponders his own fate and the fate of the universe with philosophical quiet; his poetry is like talking. . . . (p. 536)

And even in prose Machiavelli had literary pretensions in keeping with the taste of that day. At times he is affected and Boccaccian, as in his sermons to the confraternities, in his description of the plague, and in the speeches he puts into the mouths of his historical personages. (p. 537)

But in *Il principe,* in the *Discorsi,* in his letters, in his **Relazioni,** in his **Dialoghi** on the art of war, and in his **Storie** Machiavelli writes as the words come to him, completely absorbed in the thing he is saying, and with the air of a man who thinks it beneath his gravity to go running after words and periods. And here, where he was quite unconscious of form, he was a master of form. Without looking for Italian prose he found it. (pp. 537-38)

There is a little book by Machiavelli that has been translated into every language—*Il principe, The Prince*—and which has put the rest of his works into the background. The author has been judged by this book alone, and the book itself has been judged not by its logical and scientific value, but by its moral value. And the world has declared this book to be the code of tyranny, based on the greatest of all turpitudes, that the end justifies the means and that a deed is magnified by its success. And the world has christened this doctrine "Machiavellism." Many and ingenious apologies have been made for this book, crediting the author with this or that more or less praiseworthy intention. So the discussion has become limited, and Machiavelli himself has been made smaller by it. But this manner of criticism is only pedantry. On the other hand, it is equally trivial to make the greatness of this man depend solely on his Utopia for Italy, which today has come true. So we propose in these pages to reconstruct the image of Machiavelli as a whole, and to look in that whole image for the foundations of his greatness.

Niccolò Machiavelli above everything else is the clear and serious consciousness of all that movement which stretched spontaneously from Petrarch and Boccaccio down to the second half of the *Cinquecento.* In Machiavelli are the true beginnings of prose, in a word, the consciousness and reflection of life. Machiavelli was himself that movement, was of it and took part in it, shared in its passions and its tendencies. But when the movement ceased to be action and he was reduced to a solitary life, musing on the works of Livy and Tacitus, he had the strength to stand outside of his society and to turn to it and ask it, "What are you? Where are you going?" (pp. 539-40)

Country to Machiavelli was a god, higher even than morality, and higher than law. Just as the ascetics saw the individual as absorbed into the Godhead, and just as the Inquisitors burned heretics in the name of God, so for one's country everything was lawful—actions that in private life would be crimes, when done for the sake of country became magnanimous. This right of country above every other right was commonly known as "reasons of state," or "public welfare." God had come out of Heaven and descended to the earth, and had changed His name to "Fatherland" but was no less terrible. Country was supreme, its will and interests were *suprema lex;* the individual was absorbed as before into the collective being. And when this collective being became absorbed in its turn into the will of a single person or of the few, there was servitude. Liberty meant the participation, in some degree, of all the citizens in public affairs. The rights of man did not enter as yet into the code of freedom. Man was not as yet an autonomous being, an end in himself: he was the instrument of his country, or what was even worse, of the state. "State" was the term that applied to governments in general, even to despotic governments depending on the will of a single person; but "fatherland" or "country" was the place where each man took his part, whether large or small, in public affairs, and where all obeyed and all commanded—in fact, the thing that was called a "republic." When a single person commanded and the rest obeyed, it was called a "princedom." But whether republic, princedom, country, or state, the conception was always the same: the individual absorbed into society, or as they called it then, "the omnipotence of the state."

Machiavelli puts these ideas forward not as things discovered or analyzed for the first time by himself, but as things accepted by long tradition and backed by classical culture. They have the spirit of ancient Rome in them. Rome was the exemplar of glory and liberty, to which every one turned as to a magnet; and not only was Rome the exemplar in art and letters, but also in government. (pp. 547-48)

The basis of life on this earth being the fatherland, Machiavelli could not possibly be expected to care for the cloistral virtues of humility and patience, the virtues "by which Heaven itself was disarmed and the world made effeminate," and which rendered men "more prone to suffer injuries than to avenge them." *"Agere et pati fortia romanum est"*—"To do and to suffer greatly is Roman." The Catholic religion, if badly interpreted, is inclined to make a man more ready to suffer than to do, and Machiavelli blames ascetic and contemplative education for the feebleness of body and soul that prevent the Italians from chasing the foreign invader from their country and regaining their freedom and independence. "Virtue" he takes in the Roman sense, meaning strength, energy, the quality that fits a man for great undertakings and sacrifices. Italians are not lacking in this virtue, indeed in single encounters they are often victorious; but they are lacking in training and in discipline, or, as he puts it himself, in the "good systems and good arms" that render nations valiant and free. (p. 549)

He believed that if he could once renew the good systems and the old habits of ancient Rome he could bring back Roman greatness to Italy, and could retemper the metal of her soul. In many of his suggestions and maxims we feel the wisdom of the ancients; it was ancient Rome that gave him his lofty inspirations and that kind of moral elevation which runs through his writings. At times he seems like an ancient Roman himself, wrapped in his toga, so grave he is; but if we look at him again more closely we shall see that he is really the bourgeois of the Renaissance, with the little equivocal laugh of those times. Savonarola had been an echo of the Middle Ages, an apostle or prophet in the manner of Dante; but Machiavelli, in spite of his Roman toga, is the real modern bourgeois, not standing on any pedestal, but speaking simply and naturally, an equal with his equals. With the ironical turn of mind of the Renaissance he has the traits of modern times very clearly indicated. (p. 552)

[Machiavelli's] prose is free from everything that is ethical and abstract. He looks at the world from the lofty height of a superior intellect, and his motto is *Nil admirari*. He neither wonders nor gets impassioned, because he understands. And he spends no time in demonstrating or describing, because he sees and touches. He goes direct to the thing itself, and never indulges in periphrases or circumlocutions, or amplifications, or argumentations, or fine phrases, or figures, or periods, or ornamentation: to him these are only obstacles that delay the vision. And then, having taken the shortest and therefore the straightest path, he keeps his mind on it—and ours too. What he gives us is a limited and rapid series of propositions and facts, with all the middle ideas and all the accidents and all the episodes suppressed. He runs through it quickly, with the air of a Roman praetor who *non curat de minimus;* of a man whose mind is concerned with grave affairs, who has neither the time nor the wish to look around him. That rapid style of his, that habit of condensation, is not the result of art, as is sometimes the case with Tacitus and always with Davanzati, but is due to a natural clearness of vision. Middle ideas are for mediocre minds, to help them to arrive laboriously at conclusions; Machiavelli has no need of them, nor yet of the usual padding and painting of empty spaces, which indolent brains are so fond of: his prose is woven of definite thoughts. It is true that his simplicity is sometimes very like carelessness and his sobriety now and then is meagreness, but these are only the defects of his qualities. The people who dig in that divine prose for Latinisms, loose ends, slips of the pen, and similar negligences, and when they find them blow out their cheeks like pedagogues, need not be considered, for they are nothing but pedants. (pp. 556-57)

Here man is all in all; we only meet with the writer in so far as he is a man. Machiavelli seems almost to ignore that an art of writing exists. Now and then he has a try at it and proves himself to be a master of it; he too can be a literato when he chooses. But the man in him is everything. What he writes is the direct product of his brain. It comes to us warm and breathing, often condensed into a single word. For here is a man who thinks and feels, destroys and creates, and observes and reflects, with a mind unceasingly active and present. What he cares for is the thing, not the colouring, and yet the thing comes out of his brain with its own impressions, its natural colouring, crossed at times with irony, with melancholy, with indignation, with dignity, but more often just the bare thing itself in its plastic clearness. His prose is clear and rounded like a piece of marble, but marble with veins in it. The grand manner of Dante is in it. (p. 558)

This prose of Machiavelli, so dry, so terse, and so precise, composed so entirely of thought and definite matter, shows an intellect already mature, emancipated from all the elements of ethics, poetry, and mysticism, and become the regulator of the world: logic, the force of things, the modern Fate. Fate, in effect, is the inner meaning of the world, as Machiavelli conceives it. The world, no matter how it came to be so, is now what it is; an attrition of forces, human and natural, and with laws of its own. And the thing we call "fate" is logic, and nothing else; it is the necessary outcome of all these forces, appetites, instincts, passions, opinions, imaginations, and self-interests; and it is governed and propelled by a higher force than itself—by the human spirit, the thought and the intellect of man. Dante's God is Love, the force uniting intellect and act, and the result is wisdom. "We must love," says Dante. "We must understand," says Machiavelli. The soul of the Dantesque world is the heart; the soul of Machiavelli's world is the brain. The one is essentially mystical and ethical, the other is essentially human and logical. Virtue has changed its meaning; it is no longer a moral feeling, but is strength and energy, the fibre of the soul. For instance, Cesare Borgia is virtuous, for the reason that he possesses the force of soul to act in accordance with logic; in other words, having accepted the end, he accepts the means to it. The soul of Machiavelli's world being the brain, the prose he gives us is entirely and solely brain. (p. 559)

In the *Discorsi* we get a life more vivid, more awake intellectually; the intellect here has a way of breaking loose from the facts, coming back to them, however, for breath and inspiration. The facts are only the fixed point of the book, its pivot, and the author gets through them quickly, like one who narrates what every one knows already, and who is in a hurry to move on. But when he has finished with the facts and begins to discourse, we notice that the facts have given him life; his intellect seems to rise from them invigorated, freshly inspired, surprised and happy at the same time. And we feel his satisfaction in working his intellect, his pleasure in his own originality, in that special way, entirely his own, of saying things that are only paradoxes to ordinary people. His thoughts are marshalled like soldiers; nothing from the outer world can come into their ranks to disturb them. He has none of that agitation from the heat of production which we find at times even in the greatest writers; his intellect is young and fresh, quiet in its own strength, and mistrustful of everything that is not itself. So in Machiavelli there are no digressions, no images, no efforts to create an effect, no comparisons, no vicious circles; each idea leads in turn to another idea, creating a series of disciplined thoughts, mobile and productive, each linked to the others by inflexible logic, and analyzed with a degree of vigour that is remarkable. It is all so clear, so simple, that it seems superficial—and yet is profound.

The *Discorsi* are based on the conception that "few men can bring themselves to be absolutely good or absolutely bad," therefore they are wanting in the logical temper, are wanting in "virtue"; they have weak wishes but not will; they are weakened by imaginations and by fears and hopes, and by vain cogitations and superstitions; they are chary of committing themselves, choose the middle ways, and run after appearances. In the spirit of man there abides an insatiable appetite, a never-ceasing stimulus that keeps it everlastingly in movement and creates the progress of history. So man is forever restless, and he rises from one ambition only to follow a new one, defends himself and attacks, and the more he has the more he wants; and so the aims of man are never-ending, and the means to attain them confused and uncertain.

The same remarks apply to man as a collective being, as a family or a class. At bottom there are only two classes in society—the upper class and the lower class, the rich and the poor—and history is only the eternal war between him who has and him who has not, and political systems are the means for balancing the classes. But political systems are only "free" when they are based on equality, so that a country which has its "gentlemen," or a privileged class, can never be free.

It is clear that no political science or art would be possible that did not take as its basis a knowledge of the material it had to handle; so the *Discorsi* are in great part made of social portraits, whether of the lower classes or the people, or of the nobles or gentlemen, or of princes, or else of Frenchmen, Germans, or Spaniards, of individuals or of nations. These portraits show a wonderful subtlety in their observations and are very distinctly presented. The thing that stands out from them is character; in other words, the forces that move individuals and peoples and classes to act in this way or in that; and his remarks on these things are the results of his own personal experience, so are fresh and alive even today.

As human desires are never-ceasing and as the strength to attain them is weak and wavering, it is evident that the means are not in proportion to the ends; this and nothing else is the cause of all the oscillations and disorders of history. So the basis of political science, or the art of leading or governing men, is precision of aim and strength of means. In the union of these lies the energy of the intellect which makes individuals and nations great. For the world is governed by logic.

Machiavelli's *The Prince* is this merciless logic applied. He does not blame those princes who by fraud or by force have wrested liberty from peoples. As they have already seized the state, he shows them how best they can keep it. He is not thinking here of the defence of country—except in so far as the prince in providing for himself is providing for the state: public interest is the prince's own interest. He cannot give liberty to his subjects, but he can give them good laws that will protect their honour, their lives, and their property. He should aim at winning the favour and graces of the people, curbing the gentlemen and the turbulent characters. Let him govern his subjects not by murdering them but by studying them and understanding them, "not being deceived by them, but deceiving them." In regard to appearances he must have the best possible; if he does not wish to be religious, or good, or merciful, or a protector of the arts, or a patron of men of brains, let him at least appear so.

This logical point of view, which preponderates in history, is the thing that gives to Machiavelli's exposition its special quality of intellectual calm, forceful and assured, the calm of a man who knows and who wills. A man's heart grows bigger as his brain grows bigger, and the more he knows the more he will dare. But if the temper of his soul be weak, his mind will be confused. A weak man does not know what he wants, is swayed by his imagination and passions, and is pulled this way and that, like the common herd. The prince need never be afraid that his subjects will see through his schemes, for men are simple by nature and easy to deceive. The finest weapon a prince can have is fear, therefore he must aim at being feared more than at being loved. And above everything else he must avoid being odious or contemptible.

Any one who reads the treatise *De regimine principum* of Egidio Colonna will find in it a magnificent ethical world without any connection with life as it is. But any one who reads Machiavelli's *Il principe* will find in it a cruel, logical world, founded on the study of life and of man. Man, like Nature, is subject to immutable laws—not moral laws, but logical laws. The thing a man ought to ask himself is not whether his actions are good or beautiful, but whether they are reasonable or logical, whether his means are consistent with his end. The world is governed not merely by force as force, but by the force of intellect. Italy was no longer capable of giving us a divine and ethical world, so gave us a logical world instead. The only thing that was still alive in her was intellect.

Machiavelli's world is the world of intellect freed from the passions and the imagination.

And this is the lofty point of view from which Machiavelli should be judged. What he advocates is seriousness of intellect, or in other words, precision of aim, and the strength of soul to steer unswervingly for that aim without looking to the right or to the left or allowing one's attention to be turned aside by secondary or extraneous considerations. His ideal virtue is clearness of intellect: a mind untroubled by the supernatural or the fantastic or the sentimental. And his hero is the person who is able to govern man and Nature and use them for his ends. An end may be praiseworthy or blameworthy, and if it deserves blame Machiavelli is the first to raise his voice and protest against it in the name of the human race. (pp. 560-64)

[The] Italy that Machiavelli dreamed of was an independent autonomous nation; and as every one who was not Italian was a foreigner, a "barbarian," an "ultamontane," the savior invoked by Machiavelli had necessarily to be an Italian. Any one who wishes to trace the progress of the Italian spirit from Dante to Machiavelli should compare Dante's *De monarchia,* so very mystical and scholastic, with *Il principe,* so entirely modern in form and conception. Machiavelli's idea proved to be only a Utopia, like Dante's. And we of today can easily see the reason for it. The masses of the people in Italy were still in darkness, unillumined by the smallest ray of education, so that "country," "liberty," "Italy," "good discipline," "good weapons," were only words to them. The upper, the cultured, classes had retired into private life, passing their time in idyllic and literary idlenesses; they were cosmopolitans—people without a country, who were only excited by the general interests of culture and art. The Italy of the literati, fawning and fawned upon, had lost her freedom, though she seemed to be barely conscious of it. At first the foreigners had frightened her with their ferocious acts and habits; and then they had conquered her by cajoling her, bowing down to her, and doing honour to her learning. For a long time the Italians continued to boast of themselves, through the mouths of their poets, as the lords and masters of the universe, and to recall their hereditary glories. There was certainly hatred for the foreigner, and a wish to chase him out. But the wish was only a wish; not a single attempt was made to put it into effect. Even with Machiavelli the wish was no more than an idea; he never, so far as we know, made a serious effort to bring it about, beyond the writing of a magnificent *capitolo* in a poetical and rhetorical language different from his ordinary style, a poem that bears witness rather to the aspirations of a noble heart than to the calm conviction of a politician. These were illusions. He saw Italy a little through his wishes for her. But it is only to his honour as a citizen that he had these illusions. His glory as a thinker is the fact that he based his Utopia on true and permanent elements of modern society and of Italy, which were destined to develop in the future, and he pointed the way for other generations. The illusions of the present became the truth of the future.

And after all, there is nothing strange, if we stop to think of it, in the fact that Machiavelli had illusions, in spite of his sagacity and all his experience of the world. There was a great deal of the poet in his nature. (pp. 570-71)

Machiavelli has a good deal of Dante in him—if we can picture a Dante born after Lorenzo and fed on the spirit of Boccaccio, who makes fun of the *Divine Comedy* and looks for his comedy in the world here below. In his Utopia he reveals an exaltation of soul, a poetical, divining spirit. He calls on his prince to raise his banner and cry, "Out with the barbarians!" like Julius. . . . In his soul was a lovely image of a moral and civilized world and a virtuous, disciplined people, an image from ancient Rome, which made him eloquent when he praised and eloquent when he blamed. But his dream was too unlike reality, and he himself was too unlike that Roman type, and in many ways too like his contemporaries. So the real muse of Machiavelli is not enthusiasm, but irony. His mocking air, joined with his shrewdness of observation, leave no doubt that he was a man of the Renaissance. (pp. 572-73)

In spite of his reverent wording it is not very difficult to surprise on his lips that ironical twist which we find in his contemporaries. His portraits of people are famous for their originality and liveliness. Of Frenchmen and Spaniards he writes:

> Frenchmen are very prone to rob people of their money, but afterwards are ready to spend all they have taken on the very person they have robbed. The Spaniards are of a different turn; if they rob you of anything you need never expect to see the least part of it again.

From this deep and original talent of observation, this ironical turn of mind, was born the *Mandragola*: his illusions and disillusions alike end in this burst of laughter. (p. 573)

Machiavelli conceived comedy in the same way that he conceived history: he saw it as the result of an interplay of forces, each with its own nature, that must lead inevitably to a given result. So the interest of his play is centred in the study of the characters and in their development. (p. 576)

The interest of the play is centred entirely in Nicia, in the stupid husband—so stupid indeed that he becomes the unconscious instrument of the lover, whom he conducts in person to the conjugal bed. While the minor characters are drawn with extreme restraint, the author concentrates his comic spirit in Nicia, and puts him into all the situations most calculated to show him off. With all his stupidity he has the airs of very great wisdom, and behaves with so much assurance that the comedy is heightened. And Ligurio not only tricks him but makes fun of him, and keeps the candle held to his face to show him clearly to the audience. For power of comedy and originality of thought the closing scenes of this play have rarely been equalled in any theatre, ancient or modern. (p. 578)

The most interesting character is Fra Timoteo, a precursor of Tartuffe: less artificial, indeed completely natural. He traffics in the Church and the Madonna and Purgatory, but people have ceased to believe in these things and his receipts are small. So he sharpens his wits. (p. 579)

He mumbles paternosters and *Ave Marias,* and does the usual things of his trade and speaks its jargon with the indifferent, mechanical ease of habit. When Ligurio comes to him and offers him a large sum of money in return for procuring an abortion, he says: "In the name of God, it shall be done as you wish; for the sake of God and charity everything should be done. . . . Hand me over that money, that I may begin to do some good with it." And he often talks to himself, and makes his examination of conscience, and gives himself absolution, always, of course, when it is likely to put something into his pocket. . . . (p. 580)

Things such as these were arousing indignation in Germany, and provoking the Reformation. But in Italy people laughed at them. And the first to laugh was the pope. When an evil is spread like this through a whole country and has become so ordinary a thing that people only laugh at it, then it is gangrene, and incurable.

Everybody laughed. But their laughter was only buffoonery, a pastime. The laugh of Machiavelli is different; it has something sad and serious in it that goes beyond the borderline of caricature and harms his work artistically. It is clear that he is not in touch with Timoteo, does not pose him as he does Nicia, does not get fun out of him, but keeps away from him, almost with disgust. Timoteo is a dry, vulgar, and stupid creature, with no wit or imagination; he is not sufficiently idealized; his colours are too crude, too cynical. And the style, so naked and natural, is more like discourse than dialogue. We feel the poet less than the critic, we feel the great observer and portraitist.

And this is precisely the reason that the **Mandragola** has had its day. It is too much a part of that society in all that it had of most real, most peculiar to itself. Those feelings and impressions which inspired it no longer exist. The depravity of the priests and their terrible influence on women and on families strikes us as a horrible subject: we of today could never, never make a comedy of it. Machiavelli himself, who put so much drollery into his picture of Nicia, loses his good nature and charm when he comes to Timoteo, and is more like a dissecting surgeon cutting the flesh and laying bare the nerves and tendons. In his imagination there is neither laughter nor indignation at sight of Timoteo, but only that frightening coldness with which he painted the prince or the soldier of fortune or the gentleman. They seem like queer animals, and he a curious observer who is analyzing and describing them, almost making a study of them, without any emotions or impressions.

For this very reason the **Mandragola** is the basis of a whole new literature. It is a lively and vivacious world, with variety, swiftness, curiosity; it seems like a world governed by chance. But under the frivolous surface are hidden the profoundest complexities of the inner life, and the action is propelled by spiritual forces as inevitable as fate. It is enough to know the characters to guess the end. The world is a consequence and its premises are in the spirit or the character, in the forces that move it. Whoever can calculate these forces will win. Chance, the supernatural, the marvellous, are all discredited, and are replaced by character. So Machiavelli the artist is the same, after all, as Machiavelli the politician, and Machiavelli the historian. (pp. 581-82)

Of every writer we may say that a part of him dies. And Machiavelli has his dead part like the others: the part that has given him his sad notoriety. It is the grossest part of him, not vital, but only his dross. Yet people have thought it so vital that they have called it ''Machiavellism.'' Even today, when a foreigner wants to pay a compliment to Italy, he calls it ''the country of Dante and Savonarola,'' but keeps quiet about Machiavelli. And even we Italians are afraid to call ourselves ''sons of Machiavelli''; between us and the great man is the barrier of ''Machiavellism.'' It is only a word, but a word hallowed by time, a word that speaks to the imagination, and frightens us like an ogre.

What has happened with Machiavelli is the same thing that happened with Petrarch. The thing called ''Petrarchism'' is a by-product, but his imitators took it to be the whole of him. And ''Machiavellism'' is a by-product, secondary or relative to Machiavelli's teaching, and the absolute and permanent part has been forgotten. Machiavelli has come down to us conventionalized, seen from one side only, and moreover from the

least interesting side. It is time that some one should reinstate him in his completeness. (p. 583)

As a writer not only is he profound, but he is lovable, for between the lines of his political transactions we are always able to see his real leanings: anti-papal, anti-feudal, anti-imperial, civilized, modern, democratic. And even when he is completely absorbed in his aim, and is putting forward certain means, we often find him interrupting himself and protesting against them, as though he were almost asking us to forgive him. He seems to be saying: ''Remember, I am living in corrupt times; it is not my fault if the means are what they are, and if the world is what it is.'' (p. 585)

Francesco De Sanctis, ''Machiavelli,'' in his History of Italian Literature, *Vol. II, translated by Joan Redfern, Harcourt Brace Jovanovich, 1931, pp. 535-97.*

JOHN ADDINGTON SYMONDS   (essay date 1880)

[*Symonds was an English poet, historian, and critic who wrote extensively on Greek and Italian history and culture; he also made several highly praised translations of Greek poetry and the literature of the Italian Renaissance. In the following excerpt from the revised edition (1880) of his* Renaissance in Italy: The Age of the Despots, *he examines Machiavelli's writings, particularly* The Prince, *as natural reflections of their nation and age.*]

In some respects Dante, Machiavelli, and Michael Angelo Buonarroti may be said to have been the three greatest intellects produced by Florence. Dante, in exile and in opposition, would hold no sort of traffic with her citizens. Michael Angelo, after the siege, worked at the Medici tombs for Pope Clement, as a makepeace offering for the fortification of Samminiato; while Machiavelli entreats to be put *to roll a stone by these Signori Medici*, if only he may so escape from poverty and dulness. Michael Angelo, we must remember, owed a debt of gratitude as an artist to the Medici for his education in the gardens of Lorenzo. Moreover, the quatrain which he wrote for his statue of the Night justifies us in regarding that chapel as the cenotaph designed by him for murdered Liberty. Machiavelli owed nothing to the Medici, who had disgraced and tortured him, and whom he had opposed in all his public action during fifteen years. Yet what was the gift with which he came before them as a suppliant, crawling to the footstool of their throne? A treatise *De Principatibus*; in other words, the celebrated **Principe**; which, misread it as Machiavelli's apologists may choose to do, or explain it as the rational historian is bound to do, yet carries venom in its pages. (pp. 251-52)

With regard to the circumstances under which the **Prince** was composed, enough has already been said. Machiavelli's selfish purpose in putting it forth seems to my mind apparent. He wanted employment: he despaired of the Republic: he strove to furnish the princes in power with a convincing proof of his capacity for great affairs. Yet it must not on this account be concluded that the **Principe** was merely a cheap bid for office. On the contrary, it contained the most mature and the most splendid of Machiavelli's thoughts, accumulated through his long years of public service; and, strange as it may seem, it embodied the dream of a philosophical patriot for the restitution of liberty to Italy. Florence, indeed, was lost. 'These Signori Medici' were in power. But could not even they be employed to purge the sacred soil of Italy from the Barbarians?

If we can pretend to sound the depths of Machiavelli's mind at this distance of time, we may conjecture that he had come to believe the free cities too corrupt for independence. The only chance Italy had of holding her own against the great powers of Europe was by union under a prince. At the same time the Utopia of this union, with which he closes the *Principe,* could only be realised by such a combination as would either neutralise the power of the Church, or else gain the Pope for an ally by motives of interest. Now at the period of the dedication of the *Principe* to Lorenzo de' Medici, Leo X. was striving to found a principality in the States of the Church. In 1516 he created his nephew Duke of Urbino, and it was thought that this was but a prelude to still further greatness. Florence in combination with Rome might do much for Italy. Leo meanwhile was still young, and his participation in the most ambitious schemes was to be expected. Thus the moment was propitious for suggesting to Lorenzo that he should put himself at the head of an Italian kingdom, which, by its union beneath the strong will of a single prince, might suffice to cope with nations more potent in numbers and in arms. The *Principe* was therefore dedicated in good faith to the Medici, and the note on which it closes was not false. Machiavelli hoped that what Cesare Borgia had but just failed in accomplishing, Lorenzo de' Medici, with the assistance of a younger Pope than Alexander, a firmer basis to his princedom in Florence, and a grasp upon the States of the Church made sure by the policy of Julius II., might effect. Whether so good a judge of character as Machiavelli expected really much from Lorenzo may be doubted.

These circumstances make the morality of the book the more remarkable. To teach political science denuded of commonplace hypocrisies was a worthy object. But while seeking to lay bare the springs of action, and to separate statecraft from morals, Machiavelli found himself impelled to recognise a system of inverted ethics. The abrupt division of the two realms, ethical and political, which he attempted, was monstrous; and he ended by substituting inhumanity for human nature. Unable to escape the logic which links morality of some sort with conduct, he gave his adhesion to the false code of contemporary practice. He believed that the right way to attain a result so splendid as the liberation of Italy was to proceed by force, craft, bad faith, and all the petty arts of a political adventurer. The public ethics of his day had sunk to this low level. Success by means of plain dealing was impossible. The game of statecraft could only be carried on by guile and violence. Even the clear genius of Machiavelli had been obscured by the muddy medium of intrigue in which he had been working all his life. Even his keen insight was dazzled by the false splendour of the adventurer Cesare Borgia.

To have formulated the ethics of the *Principe* is not diabolical. There is no inventive superfluity of naughtiness in the treatise. It is simply a handbook of princecraft, as that art was commonly received in Italy, where the principles of public morality had been translated into terms of material aggrandisement, glory, gain, and greatness. No one thought of judging men by their motives but by their practice; they were not regarded as moral but as political beings, responsible, that is to say, to no law but the obligation of success. Crimes which we regard as horrible were then commended as magnanimous, if it could be shown that they were prompted by a firm will and had for their object a deliberate end. . . . No: the *Principe* was not inconsistent with the general tone of Italian morality; and Machiavelli cannot be fairly taxed with the discovery of a new infernal method. The conception of politics as a bare art of means to ends had grown up in his mind by the study of Italian history and social customs. His idealisation of Cesare Borgia and his romance of *Castruccio* were the first products of the theory he had formed by observation of the world he lived in. The *Prin-*

cipe revealed it fully organised. But to have presented such an essay in good faith to the Despots of his native city, at that particular moment in his own career, and under the pressure of trivial distress, is a real blot upon his memory.

We learn from Varchi that Machiavelli was execrated in Florence for his *Principe,* the poor thinking it would teach the Medici to take away their honour, the rich regarding it as an attack upon their wealth, and both discerning in it a death-blow to freedom. Machiavelli can scarcely have calculated upon this evil opinion, which followed him to the grave: for though he showed some hesitation in his letter to Vettori about the propriety of presenting the essay to the Medici, this was only grounded on the fear lest a rival should get the credit of his labours. Again, he uttered no syllable about its being intended for a trap to catch the Medici, and commit them to unpardonable crimes. We may therefore conclude that this explanation of the purpose of the *Principe* (which, strange to say, has approved itself to even recent critics) was promulgated either by himself or by his friends, as an afterthought, when he saw that the work had missed its mark, and at the time when he was trying to suppress the MS. (pp. 253-58)

Having set forth in the *Principe* the method of gaining or maintaining sovereign power, he shows in the *Discorsi* what institutions are necessary to preserve the body politic in a condition of vigorous activity. We may therefore regard the *Discorsi* as in some sense a continuation of the *Principe.* But the wisdom of the scientific politician is no longer placed at the disposal of a sovereign. He addresses himself to all the members of a State who are concerned in its prosperity. Machiavelli's enemies have therefore been able to insinuate that, after teaching tyranny in one pamphlet, he expounded the principles of opposition to a tyrant in the other, shifting his sails as the wind veered. The truth here also lies in the critical and scientific quality of Machiavelli's method. He was content to lecture either to princes or to burghers upon politics, as an art which he had taken great pains to study, while his interest in the demonstration of principles rendered him in a measure indifferent to their application. In fact, to use the pithy words of Macaulay, 'the *Prince* traces the progress of an ambitious man, the *Discourses* the progress of an ambitious people. The same principles on which, in the former work, the elevation of an individual is explained, are applied in the latter to the longer duration and more complex interest of a society' [see excerpt dated 1827]. (p. 259)

[The *Art of War*] forms a supplement to the *Principe* and the *Discorsi.* Both in his analysis of the successful tyrant and in his description of the powerful commonwealth he had insisted on the prime necessity of warfare, conducted by the people and their rulers in person. The military organisation of a great kingdom is here developed in a separate essay, and Machiavelli's favourite scheme for nationalising the militia of Italy is systematically expounded. Giovio's flippant objection, that the philosopher could not in practice manœuvre a single company, is no real criticism on the merit of his theory. (pp. 259-60)

[The *Istorie fiorentine,* a] masterpiece of literary art, though it may be open to the charges of inaccuracy and superficiality, marks an epoch in the development of modern historiography. It must be remembered that it preceded the great work of Guicciardini by some years, and that before the date of its appearance the annalists of Italy had been content with records of events, personal impressions, and critiques of particular periods. Machiavelli was the first to contemplate the life of a nation in its continuity, to trace the operation of political forces through successive generations, to contrast the action of individuals with the evolution of causes over which they had but little control, and to bring the salient features of the national biography into relief by the suppression of comparatively unimportant details. By thus applying the philosophical method to history, Machiavelli enriched the science of humanity with a new department. There is something in his view of national existence beyond the reach of even the profoundest of the classical historians. His style is adequate to the matter of his work. Never were clear and definite thoughts expressed with greater precision in language of more masculine vigour. We are irresistibly compelled, while characterising this style, to think of the spare sinews of a trained gladiator. Though Machiavelli was a poet, he indulges in no ornaments of rhetoric. His images, rare and carefully chosen, seem necessary to the thoughts they illustrate. Though a philosopher, he never wanders into speculation. Facts and experience are so thoroughly compacted with reflection in his mind, that his widest generalisations have the substance of realities. The element of unreality, if such there be, is due to a misconception of human nature. Machiavelli seems to have only studied men in masses, or as political instruments, never as feeling and thinking personalities. (pp. 261-62)

After what has been already said about the circumstances under which Machiavelli composed the *Principe,* we are justified in regarding it as a sincere expression of his political philosophy. The intellect of its author was eminently analytical and positive; he knew well how to confine himself within the strictest limits of the subject he had chosen. In the *Principe* it was not his purpose to write a treatise of morality, but to set forth with scientific accuracy the arts which he considered necessary to the success of an absolute ruler. We may therefore accept this essay as the most profound and lucid exposition of the principles by which Italian statesmen were guided in the sixteenth century. That Machiavellism existed before Machiavelli has now become a truism. Gian Galeazzo Visconti, Louis XI. of France, Ferdinand the Catholic, the Papal Curia, and the Venetian Council had systematically pursued the policy laid down in the chapters of the *Prince.* But it is no less true that Machiavelli was the first in modern times to formulate a theory of government in which the interests of the ruler are alone regarded, which assumes a separation between statecraft and morality, which recognises force and fraud among the legitimate means of attaining high political ends, which makes success alone the test of conduct, and which presupposes the corruption, venality, and baseness of mankind at large. It was this which aroused the animosity of Europe against Machiavelli, as soon as the *Prince* attained wide circulation. Nations accustomed to the Monarchical rather than the Despotic form of government resented the systematic exposition of an art of tyranny which had long been practised among the Italians. The people of the North, whose moral fibre was still vigorous, and who retained their respect for established religion, could not tolerate the cynicism with which Machiavelli analysed his subject from the merely intellectual point of view. His name became a byword. 'Am I Machiavel?' says the Host in the *Merry Wives of Windsor.* Marlowe makes the ghost of the great Florentine speak prologue to the *Jew of Malta* thus—

> I count religion but a childish toy,
> And hold there is no sin but ignorance.
>   [see excerpt dated 1589?]

When the Counter-Reformation had begun in Italy, and desperate efforts were being made to check the speculative freedom of the Renaissance, the *Principe* was condemned by the Inquisition. Meanwhile it was whispered that the Spanish princes, and the sons of Catherine de' Medici upon the throne of France, conned its pages just as a manual of toxicology might be studied by a Marquise de Brinvilliers. Machiavelli became the scapegoat of great political crimes; and during the religious wars of the sixteenth century there were not wanting fanatics who ascribed such acts of atrocity as the Massacre of S. Bartholomew to his venomous influence. Yet this book was really nothing more or less than a critical compendium of facts respecting Italy, a highly condensed abstract of political experience. In it as in a mirror we may study the lineaments of the Italian Despot who by adventure or by heritage succeeded to the conduct of a kingdom. At the same time the political principles here established are those which guided the deliberations of the Venetian Council and the Papal Court, no less than the actions of a Sforza or a Borgia upon the path to power. It is therefore a document of the very highest value for the illustration of the Italian conscience in relation to political morality. (pp. 263-65)

Hegel, in his *Philosophy of History,* has recorded a judgment of Machiavelli's treatise in relation to the political conditions of Italy at the end of the mediæval period, which might be quoted as the most complete apology for the author to make. 'This book,' he says,

> has often been cast aside with horror as containing maxims of the most revolting tyranny; yet it was Machiavelli's high sense of the necessity of constituting a state which caused him to lay down the principles on which alone states could be formed under the circumstances. The isolated lords and lordships had to be entirely suppressed; and though our idea of Freedom is incompatible with the means which he proposes both as the only available and also as wholly justifiable—including, as these do, the most reckless violence, all kinds of deception, murder, and the like—yet we must confess that the Despots who had to be subdued were assailable in no other way, inasmuch as indomitable lawlessness and perfect depravity were thoroughly engrained in them.

Yet after the book has been shut and the apology has been weighed, we cannot but pause and ask ourselves this question: Which was the truer patriot—Machiavelli, systematising the political vices and corruptions of his time in a philosophical essay, and calling on the Despot to whom it was dedicated to liberate Italy; or Savonarola, denouncing sin and enforcing repentance—Machiavelli, who taught as precepts of pure wisdom those very principles of public immorality which lay at the root of Italy's disunion and weakness; or Savonarola, who insisted that without a moral reformation no liberty was possible? . . . Meanwhile, it is not too much to affirm that, with diplomatists like Machiavelli, and with princes like those whom he has idealised, Italy could not be free. Hypocrisy, treachery, dissimulation, cruelty are the vices of the selfish and the enslaved. Yet Machiavelli was led by his study of the past and by his experience of the present to defend these vices, as the necessary qualities of the prince whom he would fain have chosen for the saviour of his country. It is legitimate to excuse him on the ground that the Italians of his age had not conceived a philosophy of right which should include duties as well as privileges, and which should guard the interests of the governed no less than those of the governor. It is true that the feudal conception of Monarchy, so well apprehended by him in the fourth chapter of the *Principe,* had nowhere been realised in Italy, and that therefore the right solution of the political problem seemed to lie in setting force against force, and fraud against fraud, for a sublime purpose. It may also be urged with justice that the historians and speculators of antiquity, esteemed beyond their value by the students of the sixteenth century, confirmed him in his application of a positive philosophy to statecraft. The success which attended the violence and dissimulation of the Romans, as described by Livy, induced him to inculcate the principles on which they acted. The scientific method followed by Aristotle in the *Politics* encouraged him in the adoption of a similar analysis; while the close parallel between ancient Greece and mediæval Italy was sufficient to create a conviction that the wisdom of the old world would be precisely applicable to the conditions of the new. These, however, are exculpations of the man, rather than justifications of his theory. The theory was false and vicious. And the fact remains that the man, impregnated by the bad morality of the period in which he lived, was incapable of ascending above it to the truth, was impotent with all his acumen to read the deepest lessons of past and present history, and in spite of his acknowledged patriotism succeeded only in adding his conscious and unconscious testimony to the corruption of the country that he loved. The broad common-sense, the mental soundness, the humane instinct and the sympathy with nature, which give fertility and wholeness to the political philosophy of men like Burke, are absent in Machiavelli. In spite of its vigour, his system implies an inversion of the ruling laws of health in the body politic. In spite of its logical cogency, it is inconclusive by reason of defective premises. Incomparable as an essay in pathological anatomy, it throws no light upon the working of a normal social organism, and has at no time been used with profit even by the ambitious and unscrupulous. (pp. 288-90)

> John Addington Symonds, *"The Florentine Historians"* and *" 'The Prince' of Machiavelli,"* in his Renaissance in Italy: The Age of the Despots, *revised edition, Smith, Elder, & Co., 1904, pp. 194-262, 263-90.*

LORD ACTON (essay date 1891)

[*John Emerich Edward Dalberg-Acton was an English historian and a Liberal member of Parliament. Most of his works, of which* Lectures on Modern History *(1906) and* The History of Freedom *(1907) are representative, are aimed at proving the conscious struggle for power to be a primal motivating force. Acton coined the famous dictum, "Power tends to corrupt and absolute power corrupts absolutely." In the following excerpt, he upholds Machiavelli's importance in the world of contemporary politics.*]

When Machiavelli declared that extraordinary objects cannot be accomplished under ordinary rules, he recorded the experience of his own epoch, but also foretold the secret of men since born. He illustrates not only the generation which taught him, but the generations which he taught; and has no less in common with the men who had his precepts before them than with the Viscontis, Borgias, and Baglionis who were the masters he observed. He represents more than the spirit of his country and his age. Knowledge, civilisation, and morality have increased; but three centuries have borne enduring witness to his political veracity. (p. xix)

[Machiavelli] is the earliest conscious and articulate exponent of certain living forces in the present world. Religion, progressive enlightenment, the perpetual vigilance of public opinion, have not reduced his empire, or disproved the justice of his conception of mankind. He obtains a new lease of authority from causes that are still prevailing, and from doctrines that are apparent in politics, philosophy and science. Without spar-

ing censure, or employing for comparison the grosser symptoms of the age, we find him near our common level, and perceive that he is not a vanishing type, but a constant and contemporary influence. Where it is impossible to praise, to defend, or to excuse, the burden of blame may yet be lightened by adjustment and distribution, and he is more rationally intelligible when illustrated by lights falling not only from the century he wrote in, but from our own, which has seen the course of its history twenty-five times diverted by actual or attempted crime. (p. xl)

> Lord Acton, in an introduction to Il Principe *by Nic-colò Machiavelli, edited by L. Arthur Burd, Oxford at the Clarendon Press, Oxford, 1891, pp. xix-xl.*

PASQUALE VILLARI (essay date 1892)

[*Villari was an Italian educator, historian, and biographer. In the following excerpt from his two-volume life of Machiavelli, he surveys several of Machiavelli's minor poems and essays and comments on his novella,* Belfagor.]

Machiavelli employed his leisure hours in writing several minor works in verse and prose, of which it is now time to speak. As to the few poems he produced, his verses are easy, often satirical and pungently vivacious, but they have too much resemblance to prose. Energetic expressions, profound and well-directed thoughts may frequently be found in them; but they are always philosophic maxims and considerations reminding us of the *Prince* and the *Discourses,* without force of imagery, originality of exposition, or any quality, in short, that is essential to genuine poetry. Nevertheless, these verses often enable us to understand their author's mental condition, and thereby assist us to a clearer conception of the history of his intellect.

The "**Golden Ass**" is the commencement of a poem in *terza rima,* upon which the author was engaged in 1517, as is shown by a letter addressed by him to Lodovico Alamanni in the same year, proving that he considered this to be a work of much importance. Yet, after writing eight very short chapters, he laid it aside, having lost all impulse or desire to continue a narrative devoid of plot, or passion, and without charm. The title is borrowed from Apuleius and Lucian, the theme from Plutarch's dialogue, "The Grasshopper," from which Gelli also derived his "Circe." Here and there, too, we perceive a certain tendency to imitate the *Divina Commedia,* but the substance of it is, or is intended to be, a satire on the Florentines of Machiavelli's own day. (pp. 383-84)

Other minor poems now follow in the *Opere*; first the short "**Capitolo dell' Occasione,**" addressed to Filippo dei Nerli, formerly thought to be imitated from a Greek epigram in the "Anthologia Planudea," but which is instead almost a literal rendering of the version of the same by Ausonias in epigram xii. Of greater length is the "**Capitolo di Fortuna,**" addressed to Giovan Battista Soderini. With much clearness, spontaneity, and some felicitous imagery, Machiavelli once more preaches his ideas upon Fortune. The only happy man is he that can attach himself to the wheels upon which Fortune turns; but as their movement is perpetually changing, even this is not enough. Hence we ought to be ready to leap from wheel to wheel, but the hidden virtue that rules us will not allow us to do so: we cannot change our person, neither can we our nature. Often, accordingly, the higher we have mounted, the lower do we fall, and it is then that Fortune shows the extent of her power. . . . (p. 386)

This "**Capitolo,**" undoubtedly one of the best, is followed by another, "**Della Ingratitudine,**" addressed to Giovanni Folchi. The latter is far more hastily written, but has several noteworthy allusions to the author's misfortunes. Torn by the fangs of others' envy, so Machiavelli begins, my unhappiness would be greatly increased were not the Muses responsive to the strings of my lyre. I know that I am no true poet, yet still hope to glean a few laurel branches in the path that is bestrewn with them. . . .

He refers to Greek and Roman history, Aristides, Scipio, and Cæsar, before touching upon his own times, in which he finds princes to be even more ungrateful than the masses, and instances the great Captain Consalvo who has earned his sovereign's distrust in reward for his defeat of the French—*in premio delle galliche sconfitte.*

This allusion proves the "**Capitolo**" to have been written no later than 1515. (p. 387)

In the "**Capitolo dell' Ambizione,**" addressed to Luigi Guicciardini, he again falls back upon politico-philosophic considerations. It must have been composed soon after its predecessor, for it frequently alludes, as to matters of recent date, to the fraternal struggle of the Petrucci in Sienna, which broke out in the year 1516. (p. 388)

There is little worth remark in the *terzine* of the "**Capitolo Pastorale,**" or the "**Serenade**" in octave verse. The subject of the former leaves no opening either for satire or philosophic reflection; its merits should be purely poetical, and therefore Machiavelli's pen moves more languidly. The octaves are sufficiently easy, but compared with those of Poliziano and Ariosto, can command but scanty admiration. He also composed six "Canti Carnascialeschi" ["Songs Sung in Carnival Time"] in different metres. Several of these are dashing and natural, but that is all. They lack the freshness and vivacity of description so often found in those of Lorenzo dei Medici, the creator of this style of poem. Consequently, their abundant grossness is nothing but sheer indecency. In the first of the series, the "**Canto dei Diavoli,**" fiends come leaping down upon the earth, and declaring themselves the authors of all evil and all good, urge mankind to follow their lead. In the second, the "**Canto d'amanti disperati e di donne,**" lovers bemoan the tortures suffered by them in vain for love upon earth, and declare that they are positively happier in Hell; the women are disposed to take pity on them, but it is now too late, the hour of love is past, and they conclude, therefore, by warning maidens not to be too coy, lest they should suffer vain remorse for their wasted hours. The third, entitled "**Canto degli Spiriti beati,**" is a lament on the ills by which mankind is afflicted, especially in Italy. (p. 389)

From these verses it will be seen, how even amid the fun and indecency of the "Canti Carnascialeschi," Machiavelli finds room for his usual reflections, his persistent thought of the Italian fatherland, and of ancient valour. The "**Canto degli uomini che vendono le pine,**" and the "**Canto de' ciurmadori,**" have a nearer resemblance than the rest to genuine Carnival songs. They are followed by a very short canzonet, two octaves and a sonnet. The canzonet, beginning with the words: *Se avessi l'arco e l'ale,* is believed by several modern critics to be an imitation of a Greek epigram in the "Anthologia Palatina"; but, besides the difficulty of proving that there is any patent imitation, the only codex containing the Anthologia of Cefala, that is of Palatino, was made known by Salmasio some time after the death of Machiavelli. The two octaves and

the sonnet have not much value, and treat of love, like [another] sonnet printed in [a] letter dated 31st of January, 1515. (p. 390)

Now coming to the literary compositions in prose, we will accord the first place to the "**Dialogo sulla lingua,**" a discussion upon the question whether the written language of Dante, Petrarca, and Boccaccio should be styled Italian or Florentine. The reasons adduced by Polidori for his doubts whether this "**Dialogue**" were really by Machiavelli, do not appear to us of any value. . . . Although it certainly shows a certain stiffness and classicality unusual to Machiavelli, it contains nothing to justify the doubts so often mooted as to the authorship of the "**Dialogue.**" Its differences of form are not only easily to be explained by the different nature of so erudite and literary a theme, but are few in number, and may also be met with in the *Discourses,* the *Prince,* and the *Histories.* The rest of the work is not wanting in the usual vivacity, graphic power, and spontaneity. And on examining its substance, we find comparisons, observations, and thoughts of so much acuteness and originality, and so peculiarly of the Machiavellian stamp, that all doubt is necessarily dispelled.

For this "**Dialogo sulla lingua**" opens with the fresh enunciation, in a somewhat grandiloquent style, of the sentiment seldom wanting in any work of Niccolò Machiavelli, whether great or small, namely, that our chief duty is claimed by our native land, to which we all owe our entire being. He then goes on to say that he has been impelled to write "by the question frequently raised during the past days, whether the idiom employed by the Florentine poets and prose writers should be named Italian, Tuscan, or Florentine. . . ." (pp. 391-92)

[He] concludes by saying that in order to write well we must understand all the properties of the language, and to understand these must study their sources, since otherwise we have a composition in which one part is out of harmony with the other. "Poetry passed from Provence to Sicily, thence to Tuscany, and more especially to Florence, because there the most suitable language was to be found. And now that the language is formed, Ferrarese, Neapolitans, Venetians, are found to write well and to have very apt powers of expression, the which could never have come about had not the great Florentine writers first taught them how to forget the native barbarism, in which they were plunged by reason of their familiar dialect. It must, therefore, be concluded that Italy has no court or common language, because that to which this name has been applied is founded upon the Florentine tongue, to which as to an original source it is necessary to revert; and accordingly even our adversaries, without they be truly stubborn, must acknowledge the tongue to be Florentine."

When we consider the condition of philological science among the Italian scholars of that time; when we consider the praise lavished even in our own day upon Leonardo Aretino, merely because he had asserted the existence of a spoken Latin different from the written tongue; and when we remember that Machiavelli was neither a learned man nor a philologist, we must allow that his observations afford additional proofs of his intellectual powers. To assert that the special characteristics of a language do not consist in the greater or lesser number of words which it may have in common with other tongues; but consist in the verb, the only part of speech that really changes in the Italian language which has conjugations but no declensions, is equal to asserting that the special character of a language depends upon its grammar. Now this is the identical idea upon which Frederic Schlegel laid the foundation of comparative philology in 1808. And although it has hitherto escaped notice, the "**Dialogo sulla lingua**" clearly proves that this idea was first divined by Machiavelli three centuries before.

It is true that in explaining his theories, he frequently says: *certain persons hold* (*vogliono alcum*). This might lead to the supposition that he had borrowed his fundamental idea from others. But it should first be remembered that Machiavelli . . . confessed that he found it expedient to make use of this or a like expression, whenever he had to proclaim some very new or daring theory or reflection of his own, the better to attract his readers' attention. Besides, not only, so far as we know, is there no trace, even of the remotest kind, of this idea to be found among the scholars of his time, but almost to the present day it has always been combated in Italy, where the general tendency of philology has been to maintain the contrary doctrine, that the distinctive character of a language is to be sought in its vocabulary. Machiavelli not only started from the opposite principle, but proved it to be his own, by deducing from it very just consequences which were both novel and startling at that day. Certainly the times were not then ripe, nor could he be possessed of the requisite knowledge, for the promotion of the great revolution in science that has only become possible in our own age. Yet even from his secondary observations, and the applications he makes of his idea, it is plain that he had the fullest appreciation of its fecundity and worth. The importance he assigned to accent; his confutation of the hypothesis advanced by Dante, of a court language composed of many dialects, on the ground that it would be a patchwork language with no life in it; his explanation of the mode in which the Florentine speech, while accepting many words belonging to other dialects, assimilated, and made them its own, by subjecting them to its own desinences and special grammatical forms; all this, presented as the logical consequence of his first fundamental idea, is reasoned out in a manner reminding us of the method of a modern philologist. And this furnishes additional proof that, whenever it is a question of discovering the substantial characteristics of social, moral, or intellectual phenomena, and of determining their laws, the genius of Machiavelli is always displayed in its fullest might, and that his vision is not only far-reaching, but piercing deep below the surface of things. (pp. 394-96)

[*Novella di Belfagor arcidiavolo*] has neither much plot, nor much character-painting, and may be described as a witty conceit and pleasantry of the kind often found among our Italian *novelle*. When Pluto noticed that all who arrived in Hell agreed in complaints against their wives, to whom they attributed their perdition, he assembled his counsellors, and it was decided to investigate the truth of the matter. For this purpose the arch-fiend Belphagor was despatched to earth in human shape, with one hundred thousand ducats in his pocket, to seek himself a wife. . . . [In the end, Belphagor] scampered back to Hell at the top of his speed, and ever after testified to the perils and tribulations of the married state.

Some writers have pretended that Machiavelli designed this pleasant fable as an allusion to the sufferings inflicted upon him by his wife Marietta; but all the best-known facts and most authentic documents clearly prove the falsity of this assertion. Marietta, as we have seen, was a good wife to him, and her husband deserved more reproof from her, than she from him. (pp. 399-401)

We need only record the titles of a few other short compositions, of little or no importance. The "**Capitoli per una bizzarra compagnia**" is merely a laughable trifle. The "**Allocuzione fatta da un magistrato nell' ingresso dell' ufficio**" (a magistrate's inaugural address on taking office) consists only of a few general remarks on justice, with regard to the public welfare, together with a long extract from the *Divina Commedia* on the same subject. It reads like a roughly sketched beginning to some literary exercise. There is little more to be said of the "**Discorso Morale**," which seems to have been written for recital at some meeting of one of the religious confraternities abounding in Florence at that time, and treats with much unction, and a certain tinge of veiled irony, of the duties and advantages of charity to our neighbours and obedience to the Almighty. It has no further claim upon our attention. (p. 402)

> *Pasquale Villari, in his* The Life and Times of Niccolò Machiavelli, Vol. II, *translated by Linda Villari, 1892. Reprint by Greenwood Press, 1968, 597 p.*

JOHN MORLEY   (lecture date 1897)

[*John Morley, created first Viscount Morley of Blackburn in 1908, was an English editor, essayist, and politician. He edited the distinguished "English Men of Letters" series, to which he contributed the volume* Edmund Burke *(1879). Influenced by the political thought of his friend John Stuart Mill, Morley was liberal and utilitarian in his views, which were reflected in the journals he edited for many years, the* Fortnightly Review *and the* Pall Mall Gazette. *In addition to his critical biography of Burke, he wrote accomplished lives of Denis Diderot, W. E. Gladstone, and Jean Jacques Rousseau, among others. In the following excerpt from the text of a lecture originally delivered in 1897, Morley discourses at length upon Machiavelli's principles and intent in his most noted works, as well as the Florentine's importance in political history.*]

Machiavelli's merit in the history of political literature is his method. We may smile at the uncritical simplicity with which he discusses Romulus and Remus, Moses, Cyrus, and Theseus, as if they were all astute politicians of Florentine faction. He recalls the orator in the French Constituent Assembly who proposed to send to Crete for an authentic copy of the laws of Minos. But he withdrew politics from scholasticism, and based their consideration upon observation and experience. It is quite true that he does not classify his problems; he does not place them in their proper subordination to one another; he often brings together facts that are not of the same order and do not support the same conclusion. Nothing, again, is easier than to find contradictions in Machiavelli. He was a man of the world reflecting over the things that he had seen in public life; more systematic than observers like Retz or Commynes—whom good critics call the French Machiavelli—but not systematic as Hobbes is. Human things have many sides and many aspects, and an observant man of the world does not confine himself to one way of looking at them, from fear of being thought inconsistent. To put on the blinkers of system was alien to his nature and his object. Contradictions were inevitable, but the general texture of his thought is close enough.

Machiavelli was not the first of his countrymen to write down thoughts on the problems of the time, though it has been observed that he is the first writer, still celebrated, 'who discussed grave questions in modern language' (Mackintosh). Apart from Dante and Petrarch, various less famous men had theorised about affairs of state. Guicciardini, the contemporary and friend of Machiavelli, like him a man of public business and of the world, composed observations on government, of which Cavour said that they showed a better comprehension of affairs than did the author of the *Prince* and the *Discourses*. But then the latter had the better talent of writing. One most competent Italian critic [Francesco De Sanctis] calls his prose 'divine,' and a foreigner has perhaps no right to differ; only what word is then left for the really great writers, who to intellectual strength add moral grandeur? Napoleon hated a general who made mental pictures of what he saw, instead of looking at the thing clearly as through a field-glass. Machiavelli's is the style of the field-glass. 'I want to write something,' he said, 'that may be useful to the understanding man; it seems better for me to go behind to the real truth of things, rather than to a fancy picture.' Every sentence represents a thought or a thing. He is never open to the reproach thrown by Aristotle at Plato: 'This is to talk poetic metaphor.' As has been said much less truly of Montesquieu, reflection is not broken by monuments and landscapes. He has the highest of all the virtues that prose-writing can possess—save the half-dozen cases in literature of genius with unconquerable wings,—he is simple, unaffected, direct, vivid, and rational. He possesses that truest of all forms of irony, which consists in literal statement, and of which you are not sure whether it is irony or *naïveté*. He disentangles his thought from the fact so skilfully and so clean, that it looks almost obvious. Nobody has ever surpassed him in the power of throwing pregnant vigour into a single concentrated word. Of some pages it has been well said that they are written with the point of a stiletto. He uses few of our loud easy words of praise and blame, he is not often sorry or glad, he does not smile and he does not scold, he is seldom indignant and he is never surprised. He has not even our mastering human infirmity of trying to persuade. His business is that of the clinical lecturer, explaining the nature of the malady, the proper treatment, the chances of recovery. He strips away the flowing garments of convention and commonplace; closes his will against sympathy and feeling; ignores pity as an irrelevance, just as the operating surgeon does. In the phrase about Fontenelle, he shows as good a heart as can be made out of brains. What concerns Machiavelli, the Italian critic truly says, 'is not a thing being reasonable, or moral, or beautiful, but that it is.' Yet at the bottom of all the confused clamour against him, people knew what they meant, and their instinct was not unsound. Mankind, and well they know it, are far too profoundly concerned in right and wrong, in mercy and cruelty, in justice and oppression, to favour a teacher who, even for a scientific purpose of his own, forgets the awful difference. Commonplace, after all, is exactly what contains the truths that are indispensable.

Like most of those who take a pride in seeing human nature as it is, Machiavelli only saw half of it. We must remember the atmosphere of craft, suspicion, fraud, violence, in which he had moved, with Borgias, Medici, Pope Julius, Maximilian, Louis XII., and the reckless factions of Florence. His estimate was low. Mankind, he says, are more prone to evil than to good. We may say this of them generally, that they are ungrateful, fickle, deceivers, greedy of gain, runaways before peril. While you serve them, they are all yours—lives, goods, children—so long as no danger is at hand: when the hour of need draws nigh, they turn their backs. They are readier to seek revenge for wrong, than to prove gratitude for service: as Tacitus says of people who lived in Italy long ages before, readier to pay back injury than kindness. Men never do anything good, unless they are driven; and where they have their choice, and can use what licence they will, all is filled with disorder and confusion. They are taken in by appearances. They follow the event. They easily become corrupted. Their will is weak. They know not how to be either thoroughly good or

thoroughly bad; they vacillate between; they take middle paths, the worst of all. Men are a little breed.

All this is not satire, it is not misanthropy; it is the student of the art of government, thinking over the material with which he has to deal. These judgments of Machiavelli have none of the wrath of Juvenal, none of the impious truculence of Swift. They cut deeper into simple reality than polished oracles from the moralists of the boudoir. They have not the bitterness that hides in the laugh of Molière, nor the chagrin and disdain with which Pascal broods over unhappy man and his dark lot. Least of all are they the voice of the preacher calling sinners to repentance. The tale is only a rather grim record, from inspection, of the foundations on which the rulers of states must do their best to build.

Goethe's maxim that, if you would improve a man, it is no bad thing to let him suppose that you already think him that which you would have him to be, would have seemed to Machiavelli as foolish for his purpose as if you were to furnish an architect with clay, and bid him to treat it as if it were iron. He will suffer no abstraction to interrupt positive observation. Man is what he is, and so he needs to be bitted and bridled with laws, and now and again to be treated to a stiff dose of *'medicine forti,'* in the shape of fire, bullet, axe, halter, and dungeon. At any rate, Machiavelli does not leave human nature out, and this is one secret of his hold. It is not with pale opinion that he argues, it is passions and interests in all the flush of action. It is, in truth, in every case,—Burke, Rousseau, Tocqueville, Hobbes, Bentham, Mill, and the rest—always the moralist who interests men most within the publicist. Machiavelli was assuredly a moralist, though of a peculiar sort, and this is what makes him, as he has been well called, a contemporary of every age and a citizen of all countries.

To the question whether the world grows better or worse, Machiavelli gave an answer that startles an age like ours, subsisting on its faith in progress. The world, he says, neither grows better nor worse; it is always the same. Human fortunes are never still; they are every moment either going up or sinking down. Yet among all nations and states, the same desires, the same humours prevail; they are what they always were. Men are for travelling on the beaten track. Diligently study bygone things, and in every State you will be able to discover the things to come. All the things that have been, may be again. Just as the modern physicist tells us that neither physical nor chemical transformation changes the mass nor the weight of any quantity of matter, so Machiavelli judged the good and evil in the world to be ever identical. (pp. 17-23)

In our age, when we think of the chequered course of human time, of the shocks of irreconcilable civilisation, of war, trade, faction, revolution, empire, laws, creeds, sects, we look for a clue to the vast maze of historic and pre-historic fact. Machiavelli seeks no clue to his distribution of good and evil. He seeks no moral interpretation for the mysterious scroll. We obey laws that we do not know, but cannot resist. We can only make an effort to seize events as they whirl by; to extort from them a maxim, a precept, or a principle, that may serve our immediate turn. Fortune, he says,—that is, Providence, or else Circumstance, or the Stars,—is mistress of more than half we do. What is her deep secret, he shows no curiosity to fathom. He contents himself with a maxim for the practical man—that it is better to be adventurous than cautious, for Fortune is a woman, and to master her, she must be boldly handled.

Whatever force or law may control this shifting distribution of imperial destinies, nothing, said Machiavelli, could prevent any native of Italy or of Greece, unless the Greek had turned Turk, or the Italian Transalpine, from blaming his own time and praising the glories of time past. 'What,' he cries, 'can redeem an age from the extremity of misery, shame, reproach, where there is no regard to religion, to laws, to arms, where all is tainted and tarnished with every foulness. And these vices are all the more hateful, as they most abound in those who sit in the judgment-seat, are men's masters, and seek men's reverence. I, at all events,' he concludes, with a glow that almost recalls the moving close of the *Agricola,* 'shall make bold to say how I regard old times and new, so that the minds of the young who shall read these writings of mine, may shun the new examples and follow old. For it is the duty of a good man, at least to strive that he may teach to others those sound lessons which the spite of time or fortune hath hindered him from executing, so that many having learned them, some better loved by heaven may one day have power to apply them.'

What were the lessons? They were in fact only one, that the central secret of the ruin and distraction of Italy was weakness of will, want of fortitude, force, and resolution. The abstract question of the best form of government—perhaps the most barren of all the topics that have ever occupied speculative minds—was with Machiavelli strictly secondary. He saw small despotic states harried by their petty tyrants, he saw republics worn out by faction and hate. Machiavelli himself had faith in free republics as the highest type of government; but whether you have republic or tyranny matters less, he seems to say, than that the governing power should be strong in the force of its own arms, intelligent, concentrated, resolute. We might say of him that he is for half his time engaged in examining the fitness of means to other people's ends, himself neutral. But then, as nature used to be held to abhor a vacuum, so the impatience of man is loth to tolerate neutrality. He has been charged with inconsistency, because in the *Prince* he lays down the conditions on which an absolute ruler, rising to power by force of genius backed by circumstance, may maintain that power with safety to himself and most advantage to his subjects; while in the *Discourses* he examines the rules that enable a self-governing State to retain its freedom. The cardinal precepts are the same. In either case, the saving principle is one: self-sufficiency, military strength, force, flexibility, address,—above all, no half-measures. In either case, the preservation of the State is equally the one end, reason of State equally the one adequate test and justification of the means. The *Prince* deals with one problem, the *Discourses* with the other, but the spring of Machiavelli's political inspirations is the same, to whatever type of rule they are applied—the secular State supreme; self-interest and self-regard avowed as the single principles of State action; material force the master key to civil policy. Clear intelligence backed by unsparing will, unflinching energy, remorseless vigour, the brain to plan and the hand to strike—here is the salvation of States, whether monarchies or republics. The spirit of humility and resignation that Christianity had brought into the world, he contemns and repudiates. That whole scheme of the Middle Ages in which invisible powers rule all our mortal affairs, he dismisses. Calculation, courage, fit means for resolute ends, human force,—only these can rebuild a world in ruins.

Some will deem it inconsistent, that with so few illusions about the weaknesses of human nature, yet he should have been so firm, in what figures in current democracy as trust in the people. Like Aristotle, he held the many to be in the long-run the best judges; but, unlike Goethe, who said that the public is always in a state of self-delusion about details though scarcely ever about broad truths, Machiavelli declared that the public may go wrong about generalities, while as to particulars they are usually right. The people are less ungrateful than a prince, and where they are ungrateful, it is from less dishonourable motive. The multitude is wiser and more constant than a prince. Furious and uncontrolled multitudes go wrong, but then so do furious and uncontrolled princes. Both err, when not held back by fear of consequences. The people are fickle and thankless, but so are princes. 'As for prudence and stability, I say that a people is more prudent, more stable, and of better judgment than a prince.' Never let a prince, he said—and perhaps we might say, never let a parliament—complain of the faults of a people under his rule, for they are due either to his own negligence, or else to his own example, and if you consider a people given to robbery and outrages against law, you will generally find that they only copy their masters. Above all and in any case the ruler, whether hereditary or an usurper, can have no safety unless he founds himself on popular favour and goodwill. This he repeats a hundred times. 'Better far than any number of fortresses, is not to be hated by your people.'

It is then to the free Roman commonwealth that Machiavelli would turn his countrymen. In that strong respect for law, that devotion to country, that unquailing courage, that energy of purpose, which has been truly called the essence of free Rome, he found the pattern that he wanted. Modern Germans, for good reasons of their own, have taken to praise him, but Machiavelli has nothing to do with that most brilliant of German scholars, who idolises Julius Cæsar, then despatches Cato as a pedant and Cicero as a coxcomb. You will hardly find in Machiavelli a good word for any destroyer of a free government. Let nobody, he says, be cheated by the glory of Cæsar. Historians have been spoiled by his success, and by the duration of the empire that continued his name. If you will only follow the history of the empire, then will you soon know, with a vengeance, what is the debt of Rome, Italy, and the world, to Cæsar. (pp. 23-8)

It may be true, as Danton said, that 'twere better to be a poor fisherman than to meddle with the government of men. Yet nations and men find themselves inexorably confronted by the practical question. Government they must find. Given a corrupt, a divided, a distracted community, how are you to restore it? The last chapter of the *Prince* is an eloquent appeal to the representative of the House of Medici to heal the bruises and bind up the wounds of his torn and enslaved country. The view has been taken that this last chapter has nothing to do with the fundamental ideas of the book; that its glow is incompatible with the iron harshness of all that has gone before; that it was an afterthought, dictated partly by Machiavelli's personal hopes, and then picked up later by his defenders as whitewashing guilty maxims by ascribing them to large and lofty purpose. The balance of argument seems on the whole to lean this way, and Machiavelli for five-and-twenty chapters was thinking of new princes generally, and not of a great Italian deliverer. Yet he was not a man cast in a single mould. It may be that on reviewing his chapters, his heart became suddenly alive to their frigidity, and that the closing words flowed from the deeps of what was undoubtedly sincere and urgent feeling.

However this may be, whether the whole case of Italy, or the special case of any new prince, was in his contemplation, the quality of the man required is drawn in four chapters (xv.-xviii.) with piercing eye and a hand that does not flinch. The ruler's business is to save the State. He cannot practise all virtues, first because he is not very likely to possess them, and next because, where so many people are bad, he would not be a match for the world if he were perfectly good. Still he should be on his guard against all vices, so far as possible; he should scrupulously abstain from every vice that might endanger his government. There are two ways of carrying on the fight—one by laws, the other by force. The first is the proper and peculiar distinction of man; the second is the mark of the brute. As the first is not always enough, you must sometimes resort to the second. You must be both lion and fox, and the man who is only lion cannot be wise. A wise prince neither can, nor ought to, keep his word, when to keep his word would injure either himself or the State, or when the reasons that made him give a promise have passed away. If men were all good, a maxim like this would be bad; but as men are inclined to evil, and would not all keep faith with you, why should you keep faith with them? *Nostra cattività, la lor*—our badness, their badness. There are some good qualities that the new ruler need not have; yet he should seem to have them. It is well to appear merciful, faithful, religious, and it is well to be so. Religion is the most necessary of all for a prince to seek credit for. But the new prince should know how to change to the contrary of all these things, when they are in the way of the public good. For it is frequently necessary for the upholding of the State—and here is the sentence that has done so much to damn its writer—to go to work against faith, against charity, against humanity, against religion. It is not possible for a new prince to observe all the rules for which men are reckoned good.

The property of his subjects he will most carefully leave alone; a man will sooner forgive the slaying of his father than the confiscation of his patrimony. He should try to have a character for mercy, but this should never be allowed to prevent severity on just occasion. He must bear in mind the good saying reported in Livy, that many people know better how to keep themselves from doing wrong, than how to correct the wrong-doing of others. Never ought he to let excess of trust make him careless, nor excess of distrust to make him intolerable. He would be lucky if he could make himself both loved and feared; but if circumstance should force a choice, then of the two he had better be feared. To be feared is not the same as to be hated, and the two things to be most diligently avoided of all are hatred on the one hand, and contempt on the other. (pp. 29-32)

Times have come and gone since Machiavelli wrote down his deep truths, but in the great cycles of human change he can have no place among the strong thinkers, the orators, the writers, who have elevated the conception of the State, have humanised the methods and maxims of government, have raised citizenship to be 'a partnership in every virtue and in all perfection.' He turned to the past, just as scholars, architects, sculptors, turned to it; but the idea of reconstructing a society that had once been saturated with the great ruling conceptions of the thirteenth century—as seen and symbolised in Dante, for example—by trying to awaken the social energy of ancient Rome, was just as much of an anachronism as Julian the Apostate. 'Our religion,' said Machiavelli of Christianity, 'has glorified men of humble and meditative life, and not men of action. It has planted the chief good in lowliness and contempt of mundane things; paganism placed it in highmindedness, in bodily force, in all the other things that make men strong. If our religion calls for strength in us, it is for strength to suffer rather than to do. This seems to have rendered the world weak.' This 'discarding the presuppositions of Christianity,' as it has been well described, marks with exactitude the place of Machiavelli in the development of modern European thought. The

Prince—the most direct, concentrated, and unflinching contribution ever made to the secularisation of politics—brings into a full light, never before shed upon it, the awful manicheism of human history, the fierce and unending collision of type, ideal, standard, and endeavour.

Machiavelli has been supposed to put aside the question of right and wrong, just as the political economist or the analytical jurist used to do. Truly has it been said that the practical value of all sciences founded on abstractions, depends on the relative importance of the elements rejected and the elements retained in the process of abstraction. The view that he rejected moral elements of government for a scientific purpose and as a hypothetical postulate, seems highly doubtful. Is he not more intelligible, if we take him as following up the divorce of politics from theology, by a divorce from ethics also? He was laying down certain maxims of government as an art; the end of that art is the security and permanence of the ruling power; and the fundamental principle from which he silently started, without shadow of doubt or misgiving as to its soundness, was that the application of moral standards to this business, is as little to the point as it would be in the navigation of a ship.

The effect was fatal even for his own purpose, for what he put aside, whether for the sake of argument or because he thought them in substance irrelevant, were nothing less than the living forces by which societies subsist and governments are strong. (pp. 49-51)

The sixteenth century in Italy in some respects resembles the eighteenth in France. In both, old faiths were assailed and new lamps were kindled. But the eighteenth century was a time of belief in the better elements of mankind. An illusion, you may say. Was it a worse illusion than disbelief in mankind? Machiavelli and his school saw only cunning, jealousy, perfidy, ingratitude, dupery; and yet on such a foundation as this they dreamed that they could build. What idealist or doctrinaire ever fell into a stranger error? Surrounded by the ruins of Italian nationality, says a writer of genius, 'Machiavelli organises the abstract theory of the country with all the energy of the Committee of Public Safety, supported on the passion of twenty-five millions of Frenchmen. He carries in him the genius of the Convention. His theories strike like acts' (Quinet). Yet after all has been said, energy as an abstract theory is no better than a bubble.

'The age of Machiavel,' it has been said, 'was something like ours, in being one of religious eclipse, attended by failure of the traditional foundation of morality. A domination of self-interest without regard for moral restriction was the result' (Goldwin Smith). We may hope to escape this capital disaster. Yet it is true to say that Machiavelli represents certain living forces in our actual world; that Science, with its survival of the fittest, unconsciously lends him illegitimate aid; that 'he is not a vanishing type, but a constant and contemporary influence' (Acton) [see excerpt dated 1891]. This is because energy, force, will, violence, still keep alive in the world their resistance to the control of justice and conscience, humanity and right. In so far as he represents one side in that unending struggle, and suggests one set of considerations about it, he retains a place in the literature of modern political systems and of Western morals. (pp. 53-4)

John Morley, ''Machiavelli,'' in his Critical Miscellanies, *Vol. IV,* The Macmillan Company, 1908, *pp. 1-54.*

[W. D. HOWELLS]   (essay date 1905)

[*Howells was the chief progenitor of American realism and an influential American literary critic during the late nineteenth and early twentieth centuries. Although he wrote nearly three dozen novels, few of them are read today. Despite his eclipse, however, he stands as one of the major literary figures of his era; having successfully weaned American literature from the sentimental romanticism of its infancy, he earned the popular sobriquet "the Dean of American Letters." In the following excerpt, Howells attempts to synthesize disparate viewpoints of Machiavelli.*]

What Machiavelli beheld round him in Italy was a civic disorder in which there was oppression without statecraft, and revolt without patriotism. When a miscreant like Borgia appeared upon the scene and reduced both tyrants and rebels to an apparent quiescence, he might very well seem to such a dreamer the savior of society whom a certain sort of dreamers are always looking for. Machiavelli was no less honest when he honored the diabolical force of Cæsar Borgia than Carlyle was when at different times he extolled the strong man who destroys liberty in creating order. But Carlyle has only just ceased to be mistaken for a reformer, while it is still Machiavelli's hard fate to be so trammelled in his material that his name stands for whatever is most malevolent and perfidious in human nature. (p. 803)

[Machiavelli] was not only an upright man in private life, a good son, husband and father, but an admirable citizen, a faithful Catholic, and a zealous servant of the Republic, uncorrupted if not incorruptible. He ardently desired the good, not only of Florence, but of all Italy, and he believed that Italian unity was such a supreme good that every other good might be provisionally foregone for its sake. He admired Borgia because his wicked work seemed to make for unity as well as tranquillity, but he admired the Swiss republicans no less than the Italian despot, because he believed that he saw reflected in their personal valor and public spirit the antique virtue of the Romans as he had misread it out of Dante. But he was not, like Dante, an imperialist. He did not look forward to the reconstruction of the Italy they both loved in a state bearing the image and superscription of Cæsar; his patriotism harked back to republican Rome, which his fancy rehabilitated in the likeness of the Swiss federation, and in this ideal of a strong, impersonal commonwealth, demanding and commanding every private sacrifice for the general good, he saw the vision of a potential if not an eventual Italian republic. (pp. 803-04)

There is something very modern in such a Machiavelli; and in his willingness to difference private from public morality we recognize traits of contemporary citizenship, contemporary statesmanship which we find blended with too many amiable qualities to be visited with an indiscriminate condemnation. In fact, it might be said that Machiavelli simply defined and registered the principles which had governed republics as well as princes in all times, and precipitated the emotions if not the motives held in solution from the beginning in every patriotic breast. (p. 804)

It was the misfortune of Machiavelli, as well as other philosophic observers of his time, that he fell a prey to the glamour of force, and imagined a final good from provisional evil. His delusion was so complete that, good man and good Catholic as he was, he censured Christianity for embodying the spirit of Christ, or, as Mr. Dyer says [in his book *Machiavelli and the Modern State* (1904),] "he argues that Christianity, with its life beyond, takes away men's fierceness," and he praised rather the pagan rites, which with what he calls their "bloody

and ferociuous sacrifice" of animals, "infected the spectators of it with the power of inspiring terror." (p. 805)

Machiavelli, then, worshipping the ideal of a state become finally virtuous, no matter what means it has used to become sovereign, could very well be a modern patriot of familiar type: the sort of patriot who always sees in his country's aggrandizement a justification of her policy; and he would hardly find himself at odds with the methods of material development. It is one of the effects of the tendency to unite endeavor in the industrial world that both labor and capital have become incorporated and depersonalized. The union and the trust may have rendered each other inevitable, but in their fatal existence the sense of individual responsibility is lost. The acts of the several persons who compose them have become official acts, for which no one holds himself finally accountable to the eternal justice. Their members fancy that in this official quality they have juggled away the moral consequence of their deeds. But in reality they have only multiplied it in the ratio of their number; for there is morally no such thing as a corporate or official entity; whatever is done by all is done by each, so far as each is privy to the deed. This is what faith clearly sees, the faith that is based upon the assurance of a divinity ruling in the affairs of humanity.

But this faith may be lost not only through evil doing, but through the admiration of evil doing. Is this faith worth keeping? Is its mystical insight valuable to mankind? It seems almost blasphemous to ask such questions, in view of what religion has always claimed and still claims. Yet the actions of men in every guise in which they would escape the sense of individual accountability have constantly denied the pretensions of religion in the matter. So far as these actions are the test of the fact there has never been any such faith in the world, except with a comparatively few fanatics and martyrs. In Machiavelli's time the part of religion was taken by Savonarola, but Machiavelli, who could not believe that the meek would or should inherit the earth, had at the best an ironical smile for Savonarola. In our own time comes a man who simply declares that Christ was in earnest, and the ironical smile of Machiavelli would be the least among the scorns put upon Tolstoy.

This does not mean that Machiavelli was supremely wicked when as a patriot he prized the strenuousness of Borgia above the righteousness of Savonarola; still less does it mean that those who deride Tolstoy are much worse than the people of Sodom and Gomorrah. It means no more than that by the long tacit or practical denial of Christianity in the economical and political affairs of men, faith has lapsed or is lapsing in the witnesses of worldly success, who necessarily become the worshippers of success when they see it nowhere accountable for its means. Industrial organization through both the union and the trust denies the personal conscience, to and from which faith exists, yet the corporate action of these, if evil, brings a measure of reproach to each of their members. Public opinion, founded upon faith, censures them severally in censuring them collectively; but there is apparently no public opinion which is more sovereign than the national collectivity. Patriotism, therefore, is the thing most to be questioned and dreaded, because it cannot, in the minds of its idolators, commit any errors or crimes; whatever it does is transmuted by the doing into wisdom and virtue. It has but one duty: success. In this view, which we should be the last to insist upon, it may be said that Machiavelli, with his worship of force that was to ultimate in virtue, through whatever means it would, was simply a man in advance of his time. He has suffered, as all the prophets have suffered, for anticipating his epoch. If now the world in realizing the patriotic ideals of antiquity has rounded the cycle back to paganism, Machiavelli would be quite at home in it. The worst that could happen him would be that he might be accused of not being a very original thinker, and people would wonder why he had ever been so much talked of. He would seem a rather belated Carlyle. (p. 806)

[W. D. Howells], "Editor's Easy Chair," in Harper's Monthly Magazine, *Vol. CX, No. 659, April, 1905, pp. 803-06.*

BENITO MUSSOLINI (essay date 1924)

[*Mussolini, widely referred to as Il Duce (The Chief) during his twenty-year reign as dictator of Italy, was also a journalist and author. During his early career he wrote for several Italian newspapers while vociferously promoting socialist causes. Twice imprisoned for his revolutionary activities, Mussolini was a nationally known figure by the time he was elected director of the socialist party in 1912 and became editor of its newspaper,* Avanti! *In 1914 he left* Avanti! *to start his own newspaper, the* Popolo d'Italia. *Ousted from the socialist party the following year, he organized the Fascio di Combattimento four years later, marking the beginning of fascism in Italy. Mussolini was elected to the Italian Parliament in 1921, officially established the national Fascist party, and was quickly granted dictatorial powers. A tumultuous political career did not preclude his publishing several books, mainly of an autobiographical nature. In the following excerpt from an essay published shortly after his rise to power, he appraises Machiavelli's relevance to the contemporary era.*]

The question is this: After an interval of four centuries, how much of the *Prince* is still of vital significance to-day? Are the teachings of Machiavelli of practical utility in governing a modern State? Was the value of the political system presented in the *Prince* confined to the time when the book was written, and therefore necessarily limited and transitory, or does it remain of universal and contemporary application—particularly contemporary application? My thesis is designed to answer these questions. I affirm that the teaching of Machiavelli is valid to-day after the lapse of four centuries because, even though the external aspects of our life have changed radically, those changes do not imply fundamental modifications in the mind and character of individuals and peoples.

If politics is the art of governing men—that is, of guiding, utilizing and evoking their passions, their egoisms, their interests, to serve general ends that almost always transcend the life of the individual because they project themselves into the future—if politics is that, there is no doubt that the fundamental element of this art is man himself. It is from man that we must set out. What are men in the political system of Machiavelli? What does Machiavelli think of men? Is he an optimist or a pessimist? In saying 'men' should we restrict the definition to the Italians whom Machiavelli knew and studied as his contemporaries, or should we embrace in that term all men, irrespective of time and place—in other words, 'under the aspect of eternity'?

It seems to me that, before proceeding to an analytical examination of Machiavelli's system of politics as it is summarized for us in the *Prince,* we must first establish exactly what Machiavelli's conception of men in general, and perhaps of Italians in particular, actually was. Now even a superficial reading of the *Prince* at once makes evident Machiavelli's bitter pessimism in respect to human nature. Like all those who have had broad and constant relations with their kind, Machiavelli despises men, and loves to present them to us—as I shall point out immediately by my citations—under their most negative and deceitful aspects.

Men, according to Machiavelli, are evil, more attached to material possessions than to their own kin, ever ready to change their sentiments and their convictions. (pp. 420-21)

Turning now to human selfishness, I find the following statement in his miscellaneous papers: 'Men complain more of losing a fortune than of losing a brother or a father, for we forget our grief over a death but never over a loss of property. The reason is obvious. Everyone knows that if there is a change of government it will not restore his brother to life, but it may restore a lost estate.' And in the third chapter of his *Discourses*: 'As all those who have written of political affairs have pointed out, and as all history shows by numerous examples, a man who founds a republic and drafts the laws that govern it must assume that all men are evil and prone to indulge their evil impulses whenever they are free to do so. Men never guide their conduct by ideal motives, but by necessity. But wherever liberty abounds and license is possible, a country is at once filled with confusion and disorder.'

I might multiply similar quotations, but it is not necessary. The citations I have made are sufficient to prove that Machiavelli's low opinion of men is not accidental and occasional, but fundamental in his philosophy of life. It recurs in all his works; it represents the fixed conviction of an experienced and disillusioned mind. We must keep in view this initial and essential fact if we are to follow intelligently the successive development of Machiavelli's thought.

It is equally obvious that Machiavelli, in forming this opinion of men, was considering not merely the men of his own time—the Florentines, the Tuscans, the Italian cavaliers, of the fifteenth and sixteenth centuries—but men without distinction of time and space. Time has passed, but if I may express an opinion of my contemporaries, I cannot extenuate in any respect Machiavelli's judgment. I might perhaps even increase its severity. Machiavelli did not delude himself, and did not delude the Prince. The antithesis between the Prince and the people, between the State and the individual, is vital in Machiavelli's political thinking. What has been called the utilitarianism, the pragmatism, the cynicism of Machiavelli, is the logical consequence of this initial position. The word 'Prince' should be understood to mean the State. In Machiavelli's mind the Prince is the State. While individuals, impelled by their selfish interests, tend toward what I might call social atomism, the State represents organization and limitation. The individual seeks continually to evade restraint. His impulse is to disobey laws, not to pay taxes, not to fight for his country. Rare are the men—the heroes and the saints—who are willing to sacrifice their ego on the altar of the common weal. All others are, *in posse*, in constant rebellion against the State.

The revolutions of the seventeenth and eighteenth centuries sought to remove this conflict, which is basic in all social organization, by making the powers of government proceed from the free will of the people. Thereby they added merely one more fiction, one more illusion, to the existing stock. (pp. 421-22)

No such thing as a government by contract ever existed, exists to-day, or will probably ever exist in the future. Long before I wrote an article which later became famous, "Force and Consent," Machiavelli said in the *Prince*:—

From this it results that all armed prophets have been victorious and all unarmed prophets have been vanquished, because the mind of the people is fickle, and it is easy to persuade them that a thing is right, but exceedingly difficult to keep them steadfast in that conviction. This is why it is necessary to be constantly prepared so that when they no longer assent they may be compelled to assent by force. Moses, Cyrus, Theseus, Romulus, would not have been able to enforce their constitutions for any length of time if they had been disarmed.

(pp. 422-23)

Benito Mussolini, "Prelude to Machiavelli," in The Living Age, *Vol. CCCXXIII, No. 4194, November 22, 1924, pp. 420-23.*

BENEDETTO CROCE   (essay date 1925)

[*Croce was an Italian philosopher, historian, editor, and literary critic whose writings span the first half of the twentieth century. He founded and edited the literary and political journal* Le critica, *whose independence, objectivity, and strong stand against fascism earned him the respect of his contemporaries. According to Croce, the only proper form of literary history is the* caratteristica, *or critical characterization, of the poetic personality and work of a single artist; its goal is to examine the unity of the author's intention, its expression in the creative work, and the reader's response. In the following excerpt from an essay originally published in 1925, he discusses the ambiguities of Machiavelli's thought, then compares Machiavelli's politics with those of Domingo De Vico.*]

Machiavelli yearns for an unattainable society of good and pure men; and he fancies it is to be found in the distant past. In the meantime he prefers the less civilized peoples to the more civilized, the people of Germany and the mountaineers of Switzerland to the Italians, the French and the Spanish (then at the height of their glory), who are the "corruption of the world." It is his feeling, and he expresses it with a shudder, that whoever reads of the horrors which history relates to us "will undoubtedly, if he is born of man, be frightened by every imitation of the evil times and will be kindled by a great desire to follow the good times." In the face of such evident signs of a stern and sorrowful moral conscience, it is amazing that there has been so much idle talk about Machiavelli's immorality; but the common people term as moral only moralistic unctuosity and bigoted hypocrisy. The lack of this bitter pessimism distinguishes Guicciardini from Machiavelli. The former feels only a sort of contempt toward men in whom he finds so "little goodness," and he settles down peacefully in this disesteemed world, aiming only at the advantage of his own "personal being." If he had not had to serve the Medici popes because of this "personal being" of his, he would have loved "Martin Luther more than himself," because he would have hoped that the rebel friar might undo the ecclesiastic state and destroy the "wicked tyranny of the priests." Guicciardini's man is different in temperament from Machiavelli's man.

It is important to observe that Machiavelli is as though divided in spirit and mind with respect to the politics whose autonomy he has discovered. At times it seems to him a sad necessity to have to soil his hands by dealing with ugly people, and at times it seems to him a sublime art to found and support that great institution which is the State. Fairly frequently he speaks of the State in a religious tone, as when he recalls the saying that one must be prepared for the sake of the State to lose not only one's reputation, but also the salvation of one's own soul; or

as when he looks back, with ill-hidden envy, at the pagan religion, which exalted, as the highest good, honor in this world, extoling human glory, and praising greatness of spirit, strength of body, and all the virtues which make man powerful; whereas the Christian religion, by showing the truth and the real way to the world beyond, despises this world, and praises abjection, setting contemplative men above the others, and endurance above action. Is politics diabolical or divine? Machiavelli imagines it in the guise of the Centaur, described by poets as a very beautiful creature, part man part beast, and he describes his prince as half man and half beast. In order that there may be no doubt as to the integrity of the human self of this creature, he casts even the subtleties of the mind, such as craftiness, into the animal self, recommending that it be part fox and part lion, because the lion does not defend himself against traps and the fox does not defend himself against wolves. One would be acting as a novice in the art of ruling if he wished "always to carry on as a lion." The art and science of politics, of pure politics, brought to maturity by the Italians, were to him a source of pride. For this reason he answered Cardinal de Rohan, who used to tell him that the Italians knew nothing about war, by saying that "the French knew nothing about the State."

The continuation of Machiavelli's thought must not be sought among the Machiavellians, who continue this political casuistry and body of maxims and write about the "*raison d'état*," frequently mixing moralistic trivialities with these maxims. Nor must it be sought among the anti-Machiavellians, who proclaim the fusion and identification of politics with morality and conceive States founded on pure dictates of goodness and justice. Nor must it be sought among the eclectics, who put in juxtaposition theories of morality and theories of politics, and who take the edge from contrasts and make them empirical, instead of solving them, and who change them to misfortunes and inconveniences which happen in life but have the character of accidental things. The continuation of Machiavelli's thought must be sought in those who made an effort to classify the concept of "prudence," of "shrewdness" and, in short, of "political virtue," without confusing it with the concept of "moral virtue" and, too, without in the least denying the latter. (One of these was Zuccolo, a seventeenth century writer.) And it must be sought in some powerful spirits who, beyond the shrewdness and sagacity of the individual, as analyzed by Machiavelli, asserted the divine work of Province. Such a person was Tommaso Campanella. But Machiavelli's true and worthy successor, the powerful intellect who gathered and gave strength both to these scattered suggestions of criticisms and to the immortal thought of the Florentine secretary, was another Italian, Vico. In truth, the whole philosophy of politics in its central idea is symbolized in two Italians. Vico is not kind to Machiavelli, yet is full of his spirit which he tries to clarify and purify by integrating Machiavelli's concept of politics and of history, by settling his theoretical difficulties and by brightening his pessimism.

For Vico, politics, force, the creative energy of States, becomes a phase of the human spirit and of the life of society, an eternal phase, the phase of certainty, which is followed eternally, through dialectic development, by the phase of truth, of reason fully explained, of justice and of morality, or ethics. The symbol of the Centaur now appears inadequate: what once seemed to be the animal part of man is found to be a human part too, the first form of the will and of action, the premise of all others. Humanity does not spring forth without passion, without force, without authority. Strong men are the best, and from the harsh rule of strong men come the civilized and refined societies which form a contrast to that rule and which, nevertheless, would not exist without that generous barbarity. And from time to time they must renew this strength by reverting to that barbarity. So Machiavelli used to say that the States must from time to time be called back to their principles, thus generalizing the maxim, professed by Florentine partisans, that every five years it was fitting "to seize again the State," that is "to cause men the same terror and fear which they had caused in seizing the State." Thus, if Machiavelli becomes religious in dealing with the art of the State, Vico does not hesitate to speak of the "divinity of force." Like Machiavelli, who used to find "the mountaineers in whom there is no civilization" more pliant to the touch of the politician's hand—because "a sculptor will more easily make a beautiful statue from a rough piece of marble than from a piece badly roughhewn by others,"—Vico, too, approved of a more vigorous vitality in the barbarous peoples, thanks to which they are better able to create new States. On the other hand, still according to Vico, civilized and corrupt peoples cannot be reformed; statues that are badly cast and spoiled must be thrown into the furnace and smelted all over again. Brutality and treachery, unavoidable in politics and recognized and recommended by Machiavelli, even though he felt a moral disgust for them, are explained by Vico as a part of the drama of humanity, which is in a perpetual state of creation and recreation. They are viewed in their double aspect of real good and apparent evil, that is, good that takes on the appearance of evil for the sake of the higher good, which indeed springs up from its very heart. In this way bitterness is replaced by the consideration of rational necessity and by the feeling of trust in Providence, which governs human affairs.

Such is the unconscious similarity of Machiavelli to Vico and the unlooked for Machiavellianism of Vico, not expressly formulated in their pages, but as we obtain it both from their scattered concepts, and from their judgments and biases, their likes and dislikes. It reveals itself to the expert eye of those who have followed the development of thought and life after Machiavelli and Vico and who, therefore, understand those things at which Machiavelli and Vico aimed ever better than they themselves could. (pp. 60-7)

> *Benedetto Croce, "Concerning the History of the Philosophy of Politics: Machiavelli and Vico—Politics and Ethics," in his* Politics and Morals, *translated by Salvatore J. Castiglione, Philosophical Library, 1945, pp. 58-67.*

WYNDHAM LEWIS (essay date 1927)

[*Lewis was an English novelist who, with T. S. Eliot, Ezra Pound, and T. E. Hulme, was instrumental in establishing the anti-Romantic movement in literature during the first decades of the twentieth century. He was also a leader of the vorticist movement. Vorticism is related to imagism in poetry and to cubism in painting; its adherents sought the total impersonality of art, achieved by fragmenting and reordering the elements of experience into a new and more meaningful synthesis. Pound and Lewis established the short-lived but now-famous periodical* Blast: The Review of the Great English Vortex *to give the movement a voice and a rallying point. Lewis's savage, satiric fiction has been compared to the work of Jonathan Swift and Alexander Pope. His best-known novel,* The Apes of God *(1930), is a long and aggressive satire on the cultural life of England in the 1920s. Lewis was of the political right: believing that artists were neglected and unappreciated in a democracy and that a strong, authoritarian rule would favor the intellectual elite, he was, for a time, a fascist*

sympathizer and Hitlerite. (In the late 1930s, however, he recanted his more extreme political beliefs.) In the following excerpt Lewis discusses the historical importance of Machiavelli's philosophy.]

The master figure of elizabethan drama is Machiavelli. He was only known through the french of Gentillet, if that: but he was the great character of supreme intrigue that, however taken, was at the back of every tudor mind. Elizabethan drama—"the first terror-stricken meeting of the England of Elizabeth with the Italy of the late renaissance"—was more terrified of Machiavelli than of anybody. The Borgias, Sforzas, Baglionis, Malatestas, Riartes were of far more importance to the elizabethan dramatists than any of their own eminent countrymen. Familiarity bred contempt in the long run. But during its flourishing period the english stage went constantly to the schoolmaster of manslaughter, Machiavelli—and his political paradigms chosen in conformity with his Borgia worship—for its thrills. (p. 64)

Mr Edward Meyer has catalogued three hundred and ninety-five references to Machiavelli in elizabethan literature. As to his influence in England, Dr Grosart wrote:

> I have suggested to the biographer of the renowned Machiavelli (Professor Villari of Florence) that an odd chapter might be written on the *scare* his name was for long in England: so much so that he came to be regarded as an incarnation of the Evil One himself.

If three hundred and ninety-five direct references can be found to Machiavelli in elizabethan literature, it is everywhere steeped in his philosophy and what his philosophy represented. Webster, Massinger, Ford, Marston, Tourneur, Middleton are all indebted to him so heavily that either in the form of revulsion or delight they could be called the children of Machiavelli. *The Unnatural Combat, Women beware Woman, Antonio and Mellida, The Insatiate Countess, The Changeling, The Revenger's Tragedy,* etc., would not have existed in the form in which they did without the showmanship and propagandist zeal of Machiavelli. (pp. 65-6)

But in the long run the English got over their fright, and "saw through Machiavelli"—"Machiavel, thou art an ass!" (*The Distracted State*) dates from 1641. The English were getting cleverer. It may be that, having suitably diluted his creed for British use, and absorbed him, this "seeing through" would ensue. In *Volpone* (iv. 1) Jonson ridicules the popular scare. Chapman in *All Fooles* ridicules the popular conception of Machiavelli. But while it lasted the rage and counter-rage was immense: and it became a component of all subsequent english psychology, just as the *italian* infatuation has never disappeared.

But Machiavelli, "the bible of the queen-mother" (Catherine de' Medici), the bugbear of the elizabethan stage, was at the same time the great formative influence, at once philosophic and political, throughout Europe; although it was only in England that he found a herd of poets to echo and advertise him. His influence must have been far more potent than that of Nietzsche. His bold ideas, falling on the sensitive and superstitious minds of the people only just out of the dusk of the Middle Ages, full of satanic fancies, had everywhere the greatest repercussion. In 1557 the jesuits burned his works, and the Inquisition decreed their complete destruction. The Council of Trent confirmed the edict of the Inquisition. (pp. 68-9)

How the diabolical honesty of Nicolò Machiavelli should have shocked the world at large, and earned him an almost infamous notoriety, is easy to understand. Every organized duplicity felt itself unmasked by one of its own servants. It is doubly easy to see how in England the ungentlemanly frankness of this logician should have been regarded as a first-class scandal. Here was a political philosopher, trained in a small-scale imperialistic school amongst the little factious states of Italy, giving away the whole position of the ruler, and revealing even the very nature of all authority. The meaning of all political conquest, and the character of the people engaged in it, transpired with a startling simplicity in the pages of this pedant of crude "power." With Darwin's *Origin of Species,* [*The Prince*] is a book that forces civilization to face about and confront the grinning shadow of its Past, and acknowledge the terrible nature of its true destiny. In his cold handbook of the *True Politic Method of Enslavement and Expropriation* the real meaning of life by conquest and management, and almost the real meaning in a further analysis of life itself, was shown with that convincing simplicity, in a tone of engaging harmlessness, reminding you of Defoe's style of narration when a cutpurse is speaking. (p. 76)

The strange honesty that characterizes Machiavelli reminds you of a similar honesty often found in the Jew; it would be called a childlike honesty. The german imperialist philosophers of the late nineteenth century also displayed this to most people startling predilection for truth—for calling war murder, with no feeling for decency in the composition of their military textbooks—which made them such sensational reading; they developed such a way of publicly and gratuitously confessing to the necessity of violence and fraud. Western opinion at the time was genuinely scandalized; in America it caused an even deeper indignation, and this clumsy truthfulness resulted in military defeat. As war it was good but as diplomacy it was bad. It was substituting Machiavelli for Cesare Borgia: the philosophy for the fact: the pedantry and exposition for the action. Nietzsche as an expounder of "aristocratic" dogma, with his childlike enthusiasm, suffered from a similar tendency to put the cart before the horse.

To be what Hotspur called a "king of smiles," and to go about well provided with every deadly drug, was essential, Nicolò Machiavelli was never tired of impressing on prospective princes (especially new ones) if *power* was what was wanted. To have *power*—that is to say to become, not by right but by force, the mechanical destiny of other people—you must train your personality with a superhuman severity. You must be as slippery as the eel and as daring as the cat. (pp. 80-1)

The prince, according to Machiavelli, should adopt the animals inevitably reigning in his human composition with some care: and of all possible combinations a compound of the fox and of the lion is proved by experience to be the best. We are half beasts—that we must always remember. The apologue of the centaur Chiron, for instance, is designed to show "that, as they (the greek princes) had for a teacher one who was half beast and half man, so it is necessary for a prince to know how to make use of both natures, and to understand that one without the other is not durable." (p. 83)

It is not my intention here to consider in any detail the doctrine of Machiavelli: but enough must be said about it to make the nature of its influence understood. And first of all it must again be insisted on that in everything the renaissance Italians were first and foremost men of science; and that their political, military and artistic life was a constant experimentation. The façade of their art is probably not so deep and permanent as it has looked to us in the past. It is very thin in places, compared

with the productions of eastern art, having behind them a long matured, undisturbed tradition, all of one piece. The political science of Machiavelli was the first strictly *scientific* doctrine produced in Europe, the result of an inductive psychological method. It was the first political system to refuse to admit anything that it could not directly observe. It was the first to finally break with universalism of theological thought: the first expression of the new nationalist thought, responding to the new conditions of the centralized, differentiated states of Europe, forming outside the imperial system.

It was then, first, scientific or experimental (for that was the specific character of the italian genius of the renaissance). Secondly, it was nationalist—it envisaged conditions released from the notion of a universal control (as that of the Roman Empire or the Roman Church). And there was a third factor peculiar to the archæological mind of the renaissance, and this at first appears to contradict the second characteristic: it was *roman* in spirit, and looked to Rome—but to the Rome of antiquity—for its inspiration.

As Villari points out at great length, there was an important way in which Machiavelli differed from his contemporary Guicciardini: that was that although in a sense as strictly based on direct observation and what roughly can be called psychology as the other, he was besides that a great generalizer; and when he looked to Rome (as Tacitus had looked to the virtuous german tribes of his fancy) almost a political apriorist. He will say, for instance, dogmatically: "It is a general rule"; or: "It should be regarded as a general rule"; whereas Guicciardini would not indulge in any general affirmation of that sort. He is actually trying to found (although ostensibly only from observation) a *system*. Guicciardini is merely providing, by means of a mass of psychological observations, a possible political education for a class of administrators, never generalized or developed into laws. (pp. 90-1)

Serving sometimes one element in the *mixed* government of the contemporary paradigm, sometimes another, the question is often asked what Machiavelli's or Guicciardini's true feeling on the subject of prince, oligarch or people was. As to the third—the people—there is no room for doubt. . . . The second, and middle, category—that of the aristocrat, of the *ottimati*—is not liked by Machiavelli, but is, on the other hand, favoured by Guicciardini. The favourite of Machiavelli is evidently the *individual hero*. It is to the prince that his roman soul gives all the intelligent passion of its predilection. Whatever, in the unfolding of his perfect system, Machiavelli may eventually arrive at, superseding the prince with *ottimati* and delivering them in their turn up to the revolutionary fury of the populace, it is the phase in which the prince is called upon to perform his difficult, lonely work of initiation that interests him most. The *ottimati* are, after all, representatives of the people—they are in the first place the representatives of the Many delegated to encompass and check the heroic power of the One. So he does not like the *ottimati*, the policemen of his prince. He even perhaps prefers the populace.

Though it is perfectly true that in the *Discorsi* Machiavelli completes his structure of mixed government, going through the three phases that he regards as ordained invariably to succeed each other in one form or another, it is certain that it is not solicitude for the personal liberty of the mass of the citizens of any state that caused him in his retirement to write these wonderful books. It is the hero, the prince, that roused him to this action. (pp. 92-3)

In the days of Voltaire and of Frederick the Great conditions had, of course, changed very much. The military art, invented by the free captain of the renaissance, and the political art of Machiavelli, had long been practised everywhere. The less direct, less philosophic, North European had got used to the new point of view; people were thoroughly hardened, and these first manuals of the modern world were already archaic. The earnest philosophic children of the renaissance, and the scientific, disillusioned attitude they had inaugurated, were commonplaces. So the *naïveté* of these first discoverers was regarded as embarrassing. Machiavelli was already in the nature of an *enfant terrible*. Such a statement as his *Prince* was already a feature of the infancy of the scientific outlook: it was the *theory* only, which for long had been perfected and developed in practice. But it is the only clear theoretic statement we have. And from that point of view it is as valuable as ever, historically and philosophically. (p. 106)

We have in *The Prince* the best ABC of power ever compiled with a view especially to obtaining political and despotic power: the steps that you must take as a *sine qua non* of success and subjugation. And it is accompanied with an accurate general description of the creatures that it will be your privilege to subjugate. And *what then?* Well, you will ride about on an immense white horse like the young d'Annunzio, or an elephant: you will live in a palace the size of an elephant, you will have more slaves than anybody else: or if not that, *What?* But, of course, the end is a pretence, success even is a fiction, since nothing accomplished and terminated is worth considering. It is not the end, it is the doing it, that is the reward of these as of all other activities. The excitement of murdering ten of your most malicious friends, or six who fatigue you most with their stupidity, drowning them all in one bath, plunging them all into one well or pit, cementing them all up into one wall; all the contriving and bustling, the breathless, coloured life, the fierce danger, the satisfaction in deceiving as Alexander VI. was able to do, and so on: that is the object of this at first sight strange life. (pp. 107-08)

> *Wyndham Lewis, "Machiavelli," in his* The Lion and the Fox: The Rôle of the Hero in the Plays of Shakespeare, *1927. Reprint by Methuen & Co. Ltd., 1955, pp. 59-114.*

T. S. ELIOT (essay date 1927)

[*Perhaps the most influential poet and critic to write in the English language during the first half of the twentieth century, Eliot is closely identified with many of the qualities denoted by the term* modernism: *experimentation, formal complexity, artistic and intellectual eclecticism, and a classicist's view of the artist working at an emotional distance from his or her creation. He introduced a number of terms and concepts that strongly affected critical thought in his lifetime, among them the idea that poets must be conscious of the living tradition of literature in order for their work to have artistic and spiritual validity. In general, Eliot upheld values of traditionalism and discipline, and in 1928 he annexed Christian theology to his overall conservative worldview. Of his criticism, he stated: "It is a by-product of my private poetry-workshop: or a prolongation of the thinking that went into the formation of my verse." In the following excerpt from an essay originally published in the* Times Literary Supplement *in 1927, Eliot characterizes Machiavelli as a highly influential but "completely misunderstood" figure.*]

'Because this is to be asserted in general of men, that they are ungrateful, fickle, false, cowards, covetous, and as long as you succeed they are yours entirely.' This sentence, and similar sentences torn from their context, have rankled and worried the minds of men for four hundred years: the words of a retired, inoffensive, quiet Florentine patriot occupied in chopping trees and conversing with peasants on his meagre estate. Machiavelli has been the torment of Jesuits and Calvinists, the idol of Napoleons and Nietzsches, a stock figure for Elizabethan drama, and the exemplar of a Mussolini or a Lenin. Machiavelli has been called a cynic; but there could be no stronger inspiration to 'cynicism' than the history of Machiavelli's reputation. No history could illustrate better than that of the reputation of Machiavelli the triviality and the irrelevance of influence. His message has been falsified by persistent romanticism ever since his death. To the humbug of every century Machiavelli has contributed. And yet no great man has been so completely misunderstood. He is always placed a little askew. He does not belong with Aristotle, or with Dante, in political theory; he attempted something different. He does not belong with Napoleon, and still less with Nietzsche. His statements lend themselves to any modern theory of the State, but they belong with none.

On the occasion of Niccolo Machiavelli's anniversary, we should concern ourselves not so much with the history of his influence—which is merely the history of the various ways in which he has been misunderstood—as with the nature of his thought and the reasons why it should have had such influence.

'So that in the first place I put for a general inclination of all mankind a perpetual and restless desire of power after power, that ceaseth only in death.' Such words of Hobbes seem at first to be uttered in the same tone as those quoted from Machiavelli; and the two names have often been brought together; but the spirit and purpose of Hobbes and of Machiavelli are wholly different. *The Prince* is often taken in the same sense as *Leviathan*. But Machiavelli is not only not a philosopher of politics in the sense of Aristotle and Dante, he is still less a philosopher in the sense of Hobbes. He has the lucidity of Aristotle and the patriotism of Dante, but with Hobbes he has little in common. Machiavelli is wholly *devoted*—to his task of his own place and time; yet by surrendering himself to the cause of his particular State, and to the greater cause of the united Italy which he desired, he arrives at a far greater impersonality and detachment than Hobbes. Hobbes is not passionately moved by the spectacle of national disaster; he is interested in his own theory; and we can see his theory as partly an outcome of the weaknesses and distortions of his own temperament. In the statements of Hobbes about human nature there is often an over-emphasis, a touch of spleen arising probably from some perception of the weakness and failure of his own life and character. This over-emphasis, so common in a certain type of philosopher since Hobbes's time, may be rightly associated with cynicism. For true cynicism is a fault of the temperament of the observer, not a conclusion arising naturally out of the contemplation of the object; it is quite the reverse of 'facing facts'. In Machiavelli there is no cynicism whatever. No spot of the weaknesses and failures of his own life and character mars the clear glass of his vision. In detail, no doubt, where the meaning of words suffer a slight alteration, we feel a conscious irony; but his total view was unimpaired by any such emotional colour. Such a view of life as Machiavelli's implies a state of the soul which may be called a state of innocence. A view like Hobbes's is slightly theatrical and almost sentimental. The impersonality and innocence of Machiavelli is so rare that it may well be the clue to both his perpetual influence over men and the perpetual distortion which he suffers in the minds of men less pure than himself. (pp. 39-41)

Machiavelli's attitude towards religion and towards the religion of his country has often been the object of misunderstanding. His attitude is that of a statesman, and is as noble as that of any statesman, *qua* statesman. In fact, it could be no other than it is. He is opposed neither to religion nor to the Catholic Church. He saw quite clearly, as he could hardly have avoided seeing, the corruption of the Church and the baseness of the eminent ecclesiastics with whom he had to do. And in the **Mandragora,** his brilliant comedy, he makes excellent fun of the more petty corruptions of the priesthood. He saw, on the one hand, the extent to which the Church and the powerful individual nobles of the Church had contributed to the dissension and desolation of his country. But he maintained steadily that an established Church was of the greatest value to a State. (pp. 43-4)

No account of Machiavelli's views can be more than fragmentary. For though he is constructive he is not a system builder; and his thoughts can be repeated but not summarized. It is perhaps a character of his amazing exactness of vision and statement that he should have no 'system'; for a system almost inevitably requires slight distortions and omissions, and Machiavelli would distort and omit nothing. But what is more curious is that no account or recapitulation of his thought seems to give any clue either to his greatness or to his great and grotesque reputation. When we first read him we receive the impression neither of a great soul nor of a dæmoniac intellect; but merely of a modest and honest observer setting down matters of fact and comments so true as to be platitudinous. Only after slow absorption and the repeated contrasts which strike the mind between such honesty and the common deceptions, dishonesties, and tergiversations of the human mind in general does his unique greatness reach us. (pp. 46-7)

The passionate nationalism of Machiavelli was hardly likely to be understood in his own time; least of all by his compatriots. But the honesty of his mind is such as is hardly understood at any time. From the first his writings seem to have fascinated and terrified Europe. From the fascination people could not escape; from the terror they escaped by turning him into a myth of terror. Even in Italy, as Charbonnel shows in *La pensée italienne au XVI siècle,* his thought was immediately distorted. Popes and princes seem to have taken from his books what they wanted, but not what Machiavelli wanted to convey. But as his work penetrated farther abroad the greater became the distortion. In France, and especially among the Huguenots, it aroused the most violent rejoinders. He was treated as hardly more than a clever sycophant giving tips to tyrants on the best ways of oppressing their subjects. In France not only religious partisans but the *politiques*—notably Jean Bodin—fell foul of him. Bodin could not get over Machiavelli's praise of Cæsar Borgia in **The Prince**; although, to anyone who reads the book without prejudice, it should be quite clear in what respects and with what reservations Machiavelli bestows his praise. In England Thomas Cromwell and others admired his work, though it is quite unlikely that they understood him better. But the general impression of Machiavelli in England was due to French influence, to the translation of the *Contre-Machiavel* of Gentillet. At every remove Machiavelli suffered. The civilization of France was in some respects below that of Italy, and the civilization of England had certainly not caught up with the civilization of France. You have only to compare the development of prose style in the three languages. Machiavelli is a master of prose style of any age; his prose is *mature*. There is nothing comparable in France until Montaigne, and Montaigne is not a *classique* for French criticism. And there is nothing

comparable in England till Hobbes and Clarendon. But by that time, when the civilization of the three countries was much on a level, there is some deterioration everywhere. Montaigne is inferior to Machiavelli, and Hobbes is inferior to Montaigne. The dramatization of Machiavelli in England has been catalogued by Edward Meyer in his *Machiavelli and the Elizabethan Drama* [see Additional Bibliography], and recently discussed more philosophically by Mr. Wyndham Lewis in his extremely interesting study of Shakespeare, *The Lion and the Fox* [see excerpt dated 1927]. The figure of Richard III is the testimony of the impression made by Machiavelli, and the falsity of this impression.

We have therefore to inquire what there is about Machiavelli to impress the mind of Europe so prodigiously and so curiously, and why the European mind felt it necessary to deform his doctrine so absurdly. There are certainly contributing causes. The reputation of Italy as the home of fantastic, wanton and diabolical crime filled the French, and still more the English, imagination as they are now filled by the glories of Chicago or Los Angeles, and predisposed imagination toward the creation of a mythical representative for this criminality. But still more the growth of Protestantism—and France, as well as England, was then largely a Protestant country—created a disposition against a man who accepted in his own fashion the orthodox view of original sin. Calvin, whose view of humanity was far more extreme, and certainly more false, than that of Machiavelli, was never treated to such opprobrium; but when the inevitable reaction against Calvinism came out of Calvinism, and from Geneva, in the doctrine of Rousseau, that too was hostile to Machiavelli. For Machiavelli is a doctor of the mean, and the mean is always insupportable to partisans of the extreme. A fanatic can be tolerated. The failure of a fanaticism such as Savonarola's ensures its toleration by posterity, and even approving patronage. But Machiavelli was no fanatic; he merely told the truth about humanity. The world of human motives which he depicts is true, that is to say, it is humanity without the addition of superhuman Grace. It is therefore tolerable only to persons who have also a definite religious belief; to the effort of the last three centuries to supply religious belief by belief in Humanity the creed of Machiavelli is insupportable. Lord Morley voices the usual modern hostile admiration of Machiavelli when he intimates that Machiavelli saw very clearly what he did see, but that he saw only half of the truth about human nature. What Machiavelli did not see about human nature is the myth of human goodness which for liberal thought replaces the belief in Divine Grace.

It is easy to admire Machiavelli in a sentimental way. It is only one of the sentimental and histrionic poses of human nature—and human nature is incorrigibly histrionic—to pose as a 'realist', a person of 'no nonsense', to admire the 'brutal frankness' or the 'cynicism' of Machiavelli. This is a form of self-satisfaction and self-deception, which merely propagates the Jew of Malta-Nietzsche myth of Machiavelli. In Elizabethan England the reputation of Machiavelli was merely manipulated unconsciously to feed the perpetually recurring tendency to Manichæan heresy: the desire for a devil to worship. The heretical impulses remain fairly constant; they recur in the Satan of Milton and the Cain of Byron. But with these indulgences of human frailties Machiavelli has no traffic. He had none of the instinct to pose; and therefore human beings, in order to accept him at all, had to make him into a dramatic figure. His reputation is the history of the attempt of humanity to protect itself, by secreting a coating of falsehood, against any statement of the truth.

It has been said, in a tone of reproach, that Machiavelli makes no attempt 'to persuade'. Certainly he was no prophet. For he was concerned first of all with truth, not with persuasion, which is one reason why his prose is great prose, not only of Italian but a model of style for any language. He is a partial Aristotle of politics. But he is partial not because his vision is distorted or his judgment biased, or because of any lack of moral interest, but because of his sole passion for the unity, peace, and prosperity of his country. What makes him a great writer, and for ever a solitary figure, is the purity and single-mindedness of his passion. No one was ever less 'Machiavellian' than Machiavelli. Only the pure in heart can blow the gaff on human nature as Machiavelli has done. The cynic can never do it; for the cynic is always impure and sentimental. But it is easy to understand why Machiavelli was not himself a successful politician. For one thing, he had no capacity for self-deception or self-dramatization. The recipe *dors ton sommeil de brute* is applied in many forms, of which Calvin and Rousseau give two variations; but the utility of Machiavelli is his perpetual summons to examination of the weakness and impurity of the soul. We are not likely to forget his political lessons, but his examination of conscience may be too easily overlooked. (pp. 47-52)

> *T. S. Eliot, "Niccolo Machiavelli," in his* For Lancelot Andrewes: Essays on Style and Order, *1928. Reprint by Faber & Faber, 1970, pp. 39-52.*

HAROLD J. LASKI   (essay date 1930)

[*A controversial figure with strongly held Marxist views, Laski was a noted English political scientist and author who, as a popular lecturer and teacher, maintained a large following of students throughout his career. In addition, he was an outspoken and active participant in the British Labour Party, advocating labor reforms that were in line with his socialist thought. While lecturing at several universities in the United States, he became an astute observer of the American social and political scene, as reflected in his works* The American Presidency *(1940),* American Democracy *(1948), and* Reflections on the Constitution *(1951). In an assessment of Laski, Edmund Wilson stated that he was "not only a well-equipped scholar and an able political thinker but a fighter for unpopular ideals whose career as a whole is an example of singularly disinterested devotion." In the following excerpt, Laski relates the relevance of Machiavelli's philosophy to both his own time and the present.*]

No thinker has so suffered at the hands of his interpreters as Machiavelli. Most generally, it has been assumed that he made a Moloch of success; and, regardless either of his assumptions or of his environment, such critics have set themselves to show that, despite him, honesty can be made to pay. Or it has been urged that he was a great satirist, and that his book is a veiled attack, the more keenly made because of its disguise, upon the methods of the Italian tyrant; by revealing, it is said, the logic of remorseless tyranny, Machiavelli demonstrated its final wickedness. Or, once more, it has been argued that the doctrines he seemed to preach are, in fact, the simple truth about human nature in politics; and we are bidden, as Catherine de' Medici is said to have enjoined upon her children, to instruct ourselves by reading *surtout des traictz de cet athée Machiavel* ["above all the treatises of that atheist Machiavelli"]. Another school prefers the theory of Machiavelli the patriot; and we are thus urged to regard him as the far-sighted precursor of Mazzini and Cavour. Two things, at least, are certain. To understand Machiavelli we must regard him essentially as an Italian of the sixteenth century; and, further, we must read the

Prince, not as a summary of his creed, but as a fragment of a larger whole, of which, for instance, the far more profound *Discourses* are at least of equal significance. In this ample context, there emerges a Machiavelli essentially human, even if less simple than most critics would make him. The complexity is important; for Machiavelli was a great man, and, save in the sphere of religion, great men have rarely the character of simplicity.

Machiavelli, indeed, is peculiarly unintelligible save in the context of the feverish and decadent brilliance of Italy at the end of the fifteenth century. A man of ambition, an ardent lover of his country, bitten, like most of that hard-living and passionate generation, with the hunger for power and fame, he differs mainly from the mass of his contemporaries in his capacity to digest the experience he encountered. Nor must we fail to emphasize the degree in which he was of his age. Like it, he sought to specialize in universality. The diplomat is the administrator; the historian is also the strategist; the political philosopher wrote poetry which, without distinction, is at least not contemptible, and one comedy which competent judges have declared at least equal to Goldoni and hardly inferior to the best of Congreve.

To exhaust the potentialities of human nature, to dare all by experiencing all, was the keynote of the time. A new world had come into being. The old landmarks had been swept away; religion had ceased, at least for ambitious men, to be a canon of conduct, and had become an instrument of control. Birth counted less than capacity as the avenue to position. Status had vanished before the subtle brain and the iron will of the new men. Careers like those of the Medici and the Sforza had shown the immense opportunities laid open to men careless of tradition and willing to make all things new. This febrile spaciousness was true not merely of Italy alone. Machiavelli saw it there, indeed, at its most intense degree; but he might have experienced it also in Spain and France, in Germany and England. Few statesmen of the sixteenth century, pope or emperor, secretary of state or Reformation leader, but accounted means little in comparison with mighty ends. What Machiavelli did was to write with dexterity especially skillful the philosophy of the experience he had known and felt more intimately than most. The men whom he had intimately known were the Iagos and Othellos, the Macbeths and Iachimos, of life; it is not then astonishing that his conclusions should have been built upon his sense of their habits as these worked in the environment most suited to their expression. To the hunter who sets out for the jungle, it is useless to offer a text-book on the ways of the domestic animal.

Machiavelli, in fact, wrote a grammar of power for the use of sixteenth-century Italy. Building upon the world about him, he explained, with a pungency and incisiveness which only Bacon and Hobbes can claim to equal, the way in which alone, as he knew contemporary Italy, the state could be made strong and enduring. He did not inquire whether it was right to attain position in that way; nor did he suggest that other and better ways did not exist. He sought, the evidence seems to show, two essential things: first, the rules which govern the individual's ability to realize his will in a world where such realization was, without regard to its moral substance, the highest ambition recognized by men; and, second, how, in a world of fraud and force and passion, to keep what one has gained. He made entire abstraction of moral argument for obvious reasons. In the world about him, in any case, they had no place; and, moreover, by making power the highest good, he was *a priori*, ruling out the discussion of moral argument in the accepted sense of the term. He asked himself how, in a world where Cesare Borgia could be ardently admired, the rules which govern the attainment of power are to be formulated; and he set them down as he found them.

Let it be added that there is evidence and to spare that Machiavelli was alive to the extraordinary nature of the conditions he was discussing. The *Prince* is not a code of conduct for every-day life; it is a text-book for the house of Medici set out in the terms their own history would make them appreciate and, so set out, that its author might hope for their realization of his insight into the business of government. Like every heart-sick exile, Machiavelli sought the terms of compromise with the power by which he had been defeated. No one, indeed, can seriously read the *Prince* without seeing that, for Machiavelli himself, it was partial, and incomplete as an expression of his total outlook. It is the essay of an advocate who will not, of set purpose, go beyond the facts of his brief. The Medici seek to know how they may perpetuate their power. The *Prince* is at once an effort to enlighten them and a self-contributed testimonial to its author's quality.

But it must be read in the context of the *Discourses*; and it then becomes obvious how much a *livre de circonstance* it is. For if the *Discourses* have any lessons, they teach the nobility of republican Rome, the worth of democracy, the viciousness of Cæsarism. No ruler, says Machiavelli, can ever hope for safety, save as he builds upon the favor of the people. Popular affection is stronger than fortresses—it is always an evil thing to destroy a free government. It is bad not to provide against extra-legal action by constitutional forms. It is never virtuous to betray one's friends or to kill one's fellow-citizens. A people is always more grateful and less avaricious than a prince. Power is poisonous only where it is usurped; for where it is given by the free suffrage of a commonwealth it is rarely exercised without responsibility. Most of the evils from which a people suffers are traceable to faults in its governors. Treaties enforced by the sword lack that consent which is the essence of obligation. These are not the maxims of Machiavellianism as that term is usually understood. And they enforce the point that, at heart, Machiavelli was always loyal to the Florentine Republic as to that greater Italy beyond of which he permitted himself to dream. Utopia is inscribed upon his map; and for all the brave show of *Realpolitik* we catch his glance straying with a sense of longing in its direction.

Behind all this, doubtless, there is a low view of men, and a firm disbelief in the idea, or even possibility of progress. For Machiavelli, history shows no eternal laws; its events are the outcome of capricious fortune, and change occurs as the relentless men bend institutions to their will. The lesson, then, is clear. If you would be master of your fate, you must not shrink from what the events demand. Choose kindness, charity, justice, if in them are the seeds of success. But show, above all, resolution, the inflexible determination which makes obstacles opportunities, the hypocrisy of the fox, and the courage of the lion. These are the qualities that bring the leader to his goal. For when Machiavelli emphasizes the evil nature of men, when, too, he insists upon the cyclic character of history, what he has in mind is that those who are destined to lead in politics are, for the most part, evil men, driven by their fate to seek authority. It is the pervasive atmosphere of all he wrote that government, even at its best, is a grim business. He seems to add that, grim as it is, government there must be; and he sought to depict, within the range of his special experience, the con-

ditions of its maintenance in the sort of world amid which he moved.

It would be easy to show that Machiavelli's underlying assumptions about men are as unwarranted and inadequate as those Rousseau made in an opposite direction. Theories which build upon the over-simple faith that men are either wholly good or wholly bad are bound to result in a distorted political philosophy. The facts are more complex; and it is only as we take account of their formidable intricacy that we are likely to arrive at adequate canons of conduct. All that Machiavelli said is doubtless true of a world composed wholly of men such as those he chiefly knew; and, amid kindred historic surroundings, his insistence that means will count as little in comparison with ends has been verified again and again in the subsequent generations. But any reader of his book will be convinced that, its over-simple psychology apart, it has two great flaws from which permanent error was bound to result.

It fails, in the first place, to relate effect to cause. By its exaltation of Fortune as the master-clue to historic change, it abandons altogether the prospect of a political philosophy. . . . (pp. 239-47)

Machiavelli, in the second place, enormously exaggerated the importance of the individual. It is, of course, true that the contribution of a great man to his age may recognizably alter its character and direction; but an age is not his creature as much as his opportunity. Cromwell was possible in an England torn by civil war; but in the England of the eighteenth century he might well have been no more than a satisfied follower of Walpole. . . . (p. 248)

What, indeed, is most striking in the *Prince* is less its cynical disregard of the normal standards conduct, than the accuracy with which it depicted the necessary conditions of political controversy in any situation where there is no general appreciation of right and wrong. Let men feel injustice passionately, and there is no injustice passionately, and there is no injustice they will not perpetrate in the endeavor to remedy the original grievance. Make possible the existence of dubious roads to power or fortune, and men will, despite all possible consequence, travel along those roads so long as they have confidence that danger is remote. Give men the conviction that they hold the truth which is the price of salvation, and they will torture and imprison their dearest friends in the assured belief that they act for the sake of those friends. To criticize Machiavelli for having said these things with a clarity so admirable is to miss completely the lesson they imply.

Indeed, it would not be unfair to argue that, in the history of Machiavellian criticism, the intensity of invective that has been leveled against him is a measure of the obloquy the critic himself should bear. It is merely ironical that the sixteenth-century papacy should have placed his book upon the Index, and when the Jesuits burned him in effigy at Ingoldstadt, they were, in truth, only revealing their self-reproach at the source from which their technique was drawn. Frederick the Great's reputation is not only built upon a total misunderstanding of Machiavelli, but it reads as mere hypocrisy from the author of the Partition of Poland. The criticism of Machiavelli, indeed, has curiously adjusted itself to the mood of European politics. Where it has been theological in texture, it is Machiavelli's conception of religion as an instrument of state that has been the chief target of attack. Where, as in the century and a half before the French Revolution, political institutions have drifted toward absolutism, Machiavelli has been attacked as the man who devised the instruments of tyranny. Each party in conflict has always used his name as a stone to throw at its rival; and "Hudibras" Butler merely identified Machiavelli with the Devil as a summary of the critical tendencies of the preceding century.

Our business is to disregard such easy invective. We must rather seek to remember less the degree to which Machiavelli is himself a "constant and contemporary influence," than the degree to which the doctrines he so magistrally summarized are the enduring basis of political action. "He is," wrote Lord Acton, "the earliest conscious and articulate exponent of certain living forces in the present world" [see excerpt dated 1891]. Wherever men feel passionately that their end is so great that it is useless to count the cost, there will be found, consciously or unconsciously, a disciple of Machiavelli.... (pp. 249-51)

The temptation, of course, is to throw up one's hands and to insist that man and reason are strangers to one another. Life is a jungle, and the habits of the jungle alone insure survival. Men are a mean and little breed; and force and fear only can keep them to the straight path. So Machiavelli judged; so, also, the greatest of his English disciples, Thomas Hobbes. And it is possible, as Lord Acton and a score of other historians have shown, to compile a formidable list of eminent men whose judgment upon the lesson of history is similar in substance.... (p. 252)

The true answer to Machiavelli's plea is not a simple one. In part, indeed, the answer is one that can be rendered in his own terms. Much of the evidence he considered he seriously misjudged. He wrote of Savonarola that the prophet without arms is doomed to destruction, and in the next generation Calvin arose to confound his maxim.... (pp. 253-54)

That is not to say that force and fraud have not won their victories. To act upon a disbelief in the possibilities of human good has, only too often, brought immense reward. Against its underlying view, we are at least entitled to argue two things. We can say, firstly, that its antithesis is not less true; belief that human nature can be trusted has, at least as often, brought a great reward to its adherents. We can, in the second place, argue with historic justice on our side, that the doctrine of means as the slave of ends is, in its Machiavellian form, incomplete and inadequate. For it is the sober lesson of the record that the means enter into the end and transform it. The Jesuits served a great ideal, but the way in which they served it made the end itself meaningless to them. That imperialist school which sought to confer the blessings of Western civilization on Africa and the ancient East, were the protagonists of a high cause; but the Congo showed that men who are careless in their instruments soon come to disregard their original purpose. The roots of loyalty are ultimately moral in character; and over any lengthy period men can be won to the service of others only in porportion as the purpose they are asked to follow is a high one. Seven centuries of force did not win affection of Ireland for Great Britain; Austria even yet drains the cup she had prepared for Italian consumption. Power, in brief, is never long accorded to minds incapable of great purposes and prepared to achieve them by means correspondingly generous. For a leader cannot count upon followers whose support is a matter of purchase. In the final assessment, his supporters will always act upon the motives he assumes them to possess.

Another aspect of this problem is important. For the most part, even in the internal aspect of the state, the will that Machiavelli considers is one that does not seek the consent of those upon whom it is to be imposed. Fragile though it is, modern constitutionalism has shown that there exists at least a wide prospect of achieving this result. Where a whole people participates in political life, where the sense of interest in the political drama is widely diffused, and the education to understand it as wide as the interest, most Machiavellian axioms are, *a priori* at a discount. It is doubtless true, as Sir Henry Maine once argued, that the pathology of party conflict is as susceptible now as in other realms and ages to the analysis Machiavelli made: certainly, the "boss" of an American state or city has recognizable kinship with the *condottiere* ["captain"] of sixteenth-century Italy. Parties will attain power by fraud and deliberate deceit; but what is important in the modern democratic state is the fact that they cannot hope by those means to retain power for long. Government by discussion engenders a capacity for self-regeneration to which no other system, however powerful in appearance, can pretend. It is, of course, vital that the discussion shall be free; and it is not less urgent that men should be prepared to abide by its results. Yet the history of Europe and America since the middle of the eighteenth century does suggest a growing sensitiveness to the infliction of unnecessary pain which sets ever higher standards in national conduct and national legislation. We move, it may be, at a snail's pace, and upon an irregular front; but it would be sheer blindness in the face of the facts to deny that we move.... (pp. 254-57)

We live in a period in which, as in the sixteenth and eighteenth centuries, the main occupation of thinkers is the dissection and discarding of the traditions we have inherited. Men are conscious of an intense *malaise*, and, along with it, there goes a volume of scientific discovery which makes the problem of social understanding of peculiarly high importance. We are escaping from a materialistic philosophy which closed the eyes of men to the possibilities of conscious coöperation. We know that the environment can be profoundly modified by ourselves. It can be modified along the most varied lines of which the gospel, as Machiavelli taught it, is peculiarly arresting and prominent. In a sense it is the easiest alternative to choose, since it appeals to the most obvious prejudices of men and demands, less than any other, the duty of arduous reflection. But it is a gospel of death. And it is the more disastrous because it is offered to us in a period of unstable equilibrium. It invites support from all who have an interest in disorder; it tends to persuade all who are weary of the struggle against injustice. It tempts the holders of power by suggesting to them that an onslaught upon their competitors may give them the assurance of enduring authority.

In fact, as Machiavelli himself saw, it offers no prospect save that of perpetuating all the evils it seeks to destroy. It offers a momentary advantage in exchange for the prospect of a certain renewal of war. It sharpens in men all that is most inimical to the forces that have exercised a civilizing influence in history. It is the more important to reject it in an age of crisis because, as a rule, periods such as our own, when traditions, ideals, standards, are thrown into the melting-pot, are the creative epochs of history. We seem, both in the sciences and in the arts, to tremble on the verge of great discoveries. We need the passionate denial of maxims that make for conflict if we are to reap the advantages they seem to presage. (pp. 262-63)

Harold J. Laski, "Machiavelli and the Present Time,"
in his The Dangers of Obedience & Other Essays,
Harper & Bothers Publishers, 1930, pp. 238-63.

H. BUTTERFIELD (essay date 1940)

[*Sir Herbert Butterfield was an English educator and historian who is renowned for such works as* Christianity and History *(1949) and* The Whig Interpretation of History *(1951). In the following excerpt from his book* The Statecraft of Machiavelli *(1940), he describes Machiavelli's purpose as a political writer and contrasts his political views with those of his contemporary, Francesco Guicciardini.*]

In studying a writer like Machiavelli it is difficult to avoid seeing the man through the work of a long line of commentators, and imputing to him the theories which have been adduced at later times in order to expand or explain his thought. Nothing more greatly affects our interpretation of a book like *The Prince* or the *Discourses* than the expectations that we bring to the reading of it. We are easily induced to intercept the author's meaning by translating it into categories of our own, and if we have been led to focus our attention upon the wrong points we can easily convince ourselves that we have seen what we went to see. If we judge his work by the things which, though they are present, are merely incidental to its main design, or if we feel at liberty to impute to Machiavelli theories which to us are natural implications of statements that he made—though the author himself did not see the implications, or in any case did not feel it necessary to point them out—we are in a position to impose upon Machiavelli many of our own assumptions, conscious or unconscious, and we shall be greatly tempted to endow him with our modern mentality. It is important, therefore, that we should interpret Machiavelli in the light of his own aims and avowed intentions, seeking to know what his books signified to himself, and what precise changes he wished to make in the thought or the practice of his own day; and we are likely to confuse the issues if we even turn aside to discuss his place in history, or set out to examine his importance to the present day, and let our appreciation of his work be governed by this estimate. It is essential to discover where lay the peculiar genius of the man, and to find out what in real life was his dominating passion; and in particular to keep in mind the declared intention, rather than the historical consequences, of his political thought.

The purpose of Machiavelli's teaching has been often stated, though one might say that it has not always been kept in mind. Villari has said with truth that "the real aim of his researches and his science was the demonstration of precepts relating to political action." The essence of his teaching was the promotion of a more scientific statecraft and he made it clear that he wrote his books in order to produce an actual change in the practice of his day. He had a low opinion of the manner in which policy was conducted by his Italian contemporaries. He criticized particularly the princes who were ruling in Italy—and in western Europe—at the time. Since he had a very high opinion of his own capacity and knowledge his was a discontent that would feed upon itself during his compulsory exile from political life. And his contempt for the statecraft of his generation was justified in his eyes by the wretched condition of Italy. Many of the disasters which the world had been content to attribute to misfortune he looked upon as the result of improvidence and misrule. (pp. 15-17)

Though it was his view that human beings can co-operate with fortune but not resist her—"can follow the order of her designs but can never hope to defeat them altogether"—it was the repeated claim of Machiavelli, and it was one of his arguments on behalf of his science of statecraft, that a certain region of historical event which contemporaries were content to accept as the province of chance, could be brought under human control by systematic and self-conscious statesmanship. He protested against the view that men cannot change events; he complained of those people who "allow things to be governed by chance"; fortune, he said,

> shows her power where no resistance has been organized against her, and directs her attack upon those places where no embankments or barriers have been made to hold her back.

He asserted that unwise princes were "exposed to sudden revolutions of fortune." He claimed in one place that "those who carefully follow [these maxims] will find that they have much less need for the assistance of fortune than others who fail to do so." He showed that those new princes who "owed less to fortune were more successful in maintaining their power"; and that the "most excellent" of them "owed nothing to chance save their opportunity." (pp. 17-18)

It should be noted that Machiavelli's intention was not the study or the creation of that particular science which we to-day call political science; and it is important that we should come to his work as historians, not as theorists who hanker after synthesis. The science which he is regarded as having invented has indeed no point save in its detail. It was always a particular policy or expedient that he was commending for adoption by the practical statesman; or it was an element conditioning political action that he was subjecting to analysis. His teaching is a collection of concrete maxims—warnings and injunctions in regard to certain points of policy, rules of conduct for specified emergencies, and expositions of tactical moves. He gives us the principles to observe if we wish to retain a foreign conquest or to found a new state that is intended for aggrandizement; the conduct to pursue when our neighbours are at war, or when a subject is becoming dangerous, or when institutions are to be altered; the ruses to be employed when besieging a city, or dealing with conspirators, or handling a refractory people.

That this science of statecraft existed as a collection of maxims in Machiavelli's own mind can be seen by a collation of his various writings. In his official correspondence and in his private letters, when he was commenting on the past in his historical writing or trying to prophesy what a certain monarch would do in the future—whenever he had to apply a criterion to events or wished to pass judgment upon political action—Machiavelli would continually draw upon these maxims which seem to have existed in his mind as a basis of reference. The same maxims recur in *The Prince*, the *Discourses*, the *History of Florence*, and the private letters; the statecraft in all these writings is continuous and the exposition is of the same texture throughout; our judgement of Machiavelli and his science is independent of that special pleading which is so often done on behalf of *The Prince*.

It has been said that the first dawnings of this science of statecraft "were visible in the epistles and reports of ambassadors and statesmen." Through Machiavelli the concrete political discussions of a diplomatic dispatch or a ministerial paper were turned into the accumulated wisdom of the printed book and organized into a new science. He himself had written these ambassadorial reports and secretarial papers when he was in the service of the republic of Florence. When he lost his official position, even when he was removed from authentic sources of information, he remained at heart—what he so desired to become again in reality—a professional adviser on political questions and one whose skill was the admiration of his friends. . . . In this way the new science of statecraft developed out of ministerial correspondence, and sprang more or less directly from the practical world; and Machiavelli did not invent statecraft itself, and was not the first to put concrete political advice into writing; he is important because during his exile he accumulated it into a book. We must not say, therefore, that he took hold of political theory and transported it from speculative realms to a region of empirical observation. The subject of his labour was the science of statecraft, and, as we shall see, he made this science more theoretical than before, attaching it to certain dogmas that belonged to the schools. For along with the practical politician there was in Machiavelli something of the doctrinaire. The acutest of his contemporary critics, Guicciardini, objected to his work precisely on this score.

Machiavelli was original most of all in his claim that statecraft could be erected into a permanent science. One of his biographers has noted that he continually asserts: ''and this must be held as a general rule.'' Guicciardini, who was a younger contemporary, always maintained that in politics no general rule holds good. He denied that practical wisdom could be embodied in a book and asserted that long experience and native discretion were the essential guides to political action. . . . [Machiavelli] differed from Guicciardini in a certain rigidity and dogmatism. He presses his theses with urgency, says that the surest way to ruin a state is to contravene a certain principle, and announces that everything is easy if only this or that rule is obeyed. Sometimes he gives extravagant promises of success to those princes who will follow the precepts he has set down. It would seem that any prince who follows these maxims must succeed as Philip of Macedon had done. He can write: ''It is vain therefore to think of ever retrieving Italian arms by any method save such as I have described''; or he can claim: ''Whoever pursues this method in a city that is besieged will find it easy to defend the place.'' And when he says that above all things a prince ought to avoid incurring the general hatred of his subjects, he can add in a manner that is not unusual with him: ''and how he is to do this I have explained in another place.'' (pp. 19-23)

[Some] defect in Machiavelli produced a certain lack of subtlety in his feeling for the interplay of historical events. Student of chance and change, of all the processes of time, he yet had an imperfect sense of their perpetual mobility. Guicciardini would assert that it was wrong for a man to argue, as many do: ''Either this will happen or that other thing will happen, and if this happens I will act in this way but if the other thing happens I will do this other way.'' He would speak of other factors intervening, further complications that no man could predict. He was intensely aware of the combination of chances which might arise to cheat our attempts at prophecy and to deflect our purposes. On shifting sands like these no science of statecraft could find a hold. Machiavelli did not overlook the place of fortune in the affairs of men—indeed he had reason to complain of it too often in the vicissitudes of his own career—but as we have seen he was inclined to emphasize the view that men could insure themselves against the caprice of time and chance. He does in fact argue, if this happens, you must act in this way, but if the other thing happens you must do this other way; and his zeal in the discussion of alternative cases only helps to give the impression that he is providing for all eventualities. It is not strange therefore that even when Guicciardini and Machiavelli are in general agreement on a certain point of policy—as in the case of the thesis that it is wrong to remain neutral when neighbours are at war—it is Machiavelli

who persistently presses the maxim in an absolute form; while Guicciardini makes reservations and allows for the unforeseeable nature of circumstances. So Machiavelli was able to create a science of politics in the sense of a body of rules upon which governments should act and should absolutely rely. Guicciardini on the contrary makes policy a perpetual course of improvization. He represents the view that government is not a science but an art. (pp. 24-5)

> *H. Butterfield, in his* The Statecraft of Machiavelli, *1940. Reprint by G. Bell and Sons Ltd., 1960, 167 p.*

HUNTINGTON CAIRNS, ALLEN TATE, AND MARK VAN DOREN (conversation date 1941)

[*An American lawyer and literary critic, Cairns is the author of* Law and the Social Sciences *(1935) and* Legal Philosophy from Plato to Hegel *(1949). Tate, a prominent American man of letters, is associated with the two critical movements of the Agrarians and the New Critics. Van Doren, perhaps best known as a poet, was also a respected critic. His criticism is aimed at the general reader, rather than the scholar or specialist, and is noted for its lively perception and wide interest. In the following excerpt from a radio broadcast aired in 1941, the critics address ambiguities in the axioms proposed in* The Prince.]

Cairns: Machiavelli's little book [*The Prince*]—it is less than a hundred pages—is so explicit and pointed with anecdotes that it has sent chills along our spines for four centuries. The strong state maintains order and is best for everyone in the long run. Therefore there should be no sentimentality or non-sense about it. That is his thesis. He describes how orderly states in the past have been built and maintained, how weak states have been built and why they disintegrated. He has been denounced as infamous because he argued that the value obtained through unity and order was worth any price. He asserts that the powerful and stable state is founded on the love and respect of the people for their ruler and on a strong army to protect them from other states. This, he says, is the highest good, the morality to which all other morality is secondary. I think that much that is explicit in Machiavelli is implied in Aristotle's *Politics*, exactly as Aristotle made explicit much that was only implied by Plato.

Mr. Tate, do you agree with Machiavelli's thesis that a strong and stable state based on the love and respect of the people is the highest good to be attained in any community? This may seem a bit obvious.

Tate: Yes, Mr. Cairns, I do agree. But don't you think that we ought to point out first of all that Machiavelli is not the cynic that he has been made out to be, that he is interested in something like Aristotle's Commonwealth, or certainly the political virtues that come from such a state?

Cairns: Mr. Van Doren, do you think that Machiavelli's state is Aristotle's ideal state, or do you agree with Mr. Tate that it is comparable to Aristotle's idea of a commonwealth?

Van Doren: Machiavelli is interested in what Aristotle calls the commonwealth, yes, although he spends precious little time talking about it in this particular book. He assumes its existence and its importance, but his concern is not with the defense of it or with an analysis of it.

Tate: But don't you believe that Machiavelli is quite Aristotelian in another sense, that perhaps one reason why he doesn't discuss the commonwealth very much is that, like Aristotle, he is interested in observing what is actually around him—the Italian city-states of his time?

Van Doren: I should say that there is no conflict between him and either Aristotle or Plato. You remember, I was insisting that there was not too much conflict between Aristotle and Plato. That is to say, Machiavelli is grounded upon the same vision of society, except that the actual area which he cultivates here is rather small.

Cairns: Don't you agree that they both have the same ideal conception, namely, one man ruling for the good of all? Isn't that the basis both of Machiavelli and Aristotle?

Tate: I think it is, Mr. Cairns. Machiavelli is not so much interested in classifying the different kinds of states and their theoretical possibilities as Aristotle. It must have appeared to Machiavelli that the most recurrent type of state was a state ruled by a prince. Then the problem arose: How could you rule the state well, and did a prince's personal virtue mean that he would also have political virtue, or vice versa? (pp. 21-2)

Cairns: I wonder, Mr. Tate, if you agree with the point that Aristotle and Machiavelli both make, that the morals or the virtue of the ruler must be different from the morals or virtues of the ordinary citizen.

Tate: Mr. Cairns, I believe that neither Aristotle nor Machiavelli is conclusive on that point. Machiavelli is inclined to believe that the ruler's personal virtue has very little to do with it. That is, a virtuous fool would make a worse ruler than a knavish intelligent man.

Van Doren: Yes. He has nothing but contempt for the virtuous fool, if you mean by that a man who does not know the world.

Tate: And doesn't know how men actually behave.

Van Doren: Probably his greatest respect would be for the man who knew the world and was virtuous.

Cairns: But he does insist that the virtues that we admire in the ordinary man, such as good faith and square dealing, must not be present in the ruler, that the ruler is beyond such virtues, because the stability of the state and the good of all are the objects of the ruler and they are not the objects of the ordinary citizen. (pp. 23-4)

Cairns: As I read *The Prince,* it appears that Machiavelli's principal aim is to tell the prince what he must do if he wants a strong government. He does not attempt to answer the question: Is it good for the ruler to do this or are these methods bad? He merely says that if the ruler wants to accomplish such and such an objective, then he must do these things.

Van Doren: Stability perhaps is the first virtue of a government.

Tate: Gentlemen, there's a point I'd like to raise right there, as to the nature of Machiavelli's advice to the prince. How are we to understand this advice? If Machiavelli is not chiefly interested in sheer power, as Hobbes later on was, are we to understand him as being a little ironical in the advice he gives the prince? He says you can do these things in order to get power. If you go beyond certain extremes you will lose power. Was he thinking of it primarily in terms of power or not? It seems to me it's just a convention, perhaps a sort of literary convention in which he is addressing his patron, the prince, but what he is actually interested in is the good life, a state in which people could live the good life.

Cairns: I can't agree with that. I look upon this book as a textbook for a prince. For example, Machiavelli tells the prince: "When you have conquered a people who are accustomed to live at liberty under their own laws, there are three ways to hold them. The first is to despoil them. The second is to go there and live in person. The third is to allow them to live under their own laws, taking tribute of them and creating within the country a government composed of a few who will keep it friendly to you."

Tate: That is certainly very true. I agree with you, Mr. Cairns, about the practical phase of his observations.

Cairns: I don't see any satire in it.

Tate: No, I don't mean there was satire. He had to convey his ideas in terms that would flatter the prince—the terms of power. His own views had to be inserted slyly, ironically. The powerful and stable commonwealth or something like that is the thing desired by Machiavelli.

Cairns: I think that is his aim, but he says, "You must do these things this way if you want to achieve the stable state." Now some of those things are bad morally. At least we regard them as bad.

Tate: Yes, but do you think he is exhorting the prince to do these things for their own sake, or is he merely saying that power is a means to an end and that the prince will conduct himself along these lines inevitably?

Van Doren: There is a very nice line, apparently, that one would have to draw between a cruel prince whom he seems to respect, Cesare Borgia, and two cruel princes whom he did not respect. Both of them, all three of them, for that matter, fair, but he respects Cesare more than he does the two others, in spite of the fact that all three are cruel. And that fine line of distinction, it seems to me, is a line drawn along Cesare's general purpose, which was not purely his own aggrandizement but the peace of his state.

Cairns: Don't you agree that he is really in the position of an engineer? He says if you want to put a bridge across this stream you can do it this way or this way or this way?

Tate: Yes, but I think at the same time he has some conception of the purpose of the bridges.

Van Doren: And, I should say, of your reason for wanting to cross the bridge.

Cairns: No, he's an engineer. He doesn't say whether the bridge is good or bad to put across the stream. He merely says if you want a bridge, build it this way; whether it is good or bad is for somebody else to determine.

Van Doren: If you want to keep in power, this is the way to do it. Is that what you mean?

Cairns: Yes.

Van Doren: But by the very subtlety of the problem as he presents it, it seems to me, he betrays that he has a vision of what government might be. After all, he isn't giving just a few simple rules. It is a very wise man, actually, who keeps his power. (pp. 24-6)

Cairns: [Machiavelli] makes two points in discussing the virtues of the fox—among many others he makes these two explicitly—that it is necessary for the ruler to have virtues which are dangerous. He must appear to have them, but not have them actually. That is, his subjects must think that the prince keeps his word when in fact he doesn't. He also makes the point that the prince must never keep faith if it is harmful to the state. Do you agree with Machiavelli that this is necessary?

Tate: American history itself would show that they have been. Some of our very greatest statesmen have had to do that.

Van Doren: Have had to go back on their word; have had to break a plank in their platform, for instance.

Tate: Yes, Abraham Lincoln is a beautiful example of that.

Van Doren: Woodrow Wilson would be another.

Tate: And George Washington a third.

Van Doren: And although the question may be discussed for a long time whether they should have done so, it would finally be answered in the light of the further question whether the state had benefited.

Cairns: Do you think Machiavelli is deducing these qualities of the ruler from a position merely of cold observation or was he himself personally a scoundrel?

Van Doren: Certainly not a scoundrel, I should say. He was a very interesting, humane person, and very learned. He wrote, of course, many books besides this one.

Cairns: He says that the ruler must not be despised, and in order to avoid being despised he must avoid appearing feminine, frivolous, irresolute and timid. On the other hand, he had to cultivate the qualities of the lion—fortitude, decision, gravity and spirit.

Van Doren: He knew the truth of the commonplace that there is never respect without fear, some form of fear. (p. 29)

Cairns: Would you say that *The Prince*, like Aristotle's book on politics, is a handbook for statesmen?

Van Doren: Yes. I should say a handbook for statesmen which has not been very well read.

Cairns: You wouldn't say, as Rousseau said, that *The Prince* is merely satire? You would say that Machiavelli is in earnest.

Tate: I think he is in earnest. What I was saying a while ago about possible irony in *The Prince* doesn't mean that it is at all satirical. I think that he started with actual observation.

Van Doren: He certainly is not cynical. Or at least it is a vulgar error always to confound cynicism with realism. There can be a very great deal of difference.

Cairns: Do you regard him as an Italian patriot?

Van Doren: Yes, surely. His last chapter, if no other, would make that clear.

Cairns: I was going to ask if you felt that the last chapter was an afterthought. In that chapter he pleads for Italy to free herself from the barbarians. The barbarians, I take it, being the French.

Van Doren: The French chiefly. The Northern nations.

Cairns: You don't say that that is an afterthought?

Van Doren: I shouldn't think so. It seems to me it might come very easily under the head of a prince's obligation to preserve his commonwealth. (pp. 30-1)

> Huntington Cairns, Allen Tate, and Mark Van Doren, ''Niccolo Machiavelli, 'The Prince','' in their Invitation to Learning, *1941. Reprint by The New Home Library, 1942, pp. 19-32.*

JAMES BURNHAM (essay date 1943)

[*Burnham was a highly respected American social and political theorist. He founded the leftist periodical* Symposium (1931-35) *and later, during the 1940s, served as an editor of the* Partisan Review. *A longtime Marxist, he broke with Marxism in 1939 and spent the next two years writing what proved an influential analysis of governmental bureaucracy,* The Managerial Revolution (1941). *This work and his later* Suicide of the West (1965) *are considered his best works. From 1955 until shortly before his death in 1987, Burnham served in an editorial and advisory capacity with the conservative periodical* National Review. *In the following excerpt from* The Machiavellians (1943), *he discusses a number of Machiavelli's views and concepts.*]

There have been many critical discussions about Machiavelli's supposed views on ''human nature.'' Some defend him, but he is usually charged with a libel upon mankind, with having a perverted, shocking, and detestable notion of what human beings are like. These discussion, however, are beside the point. Machiavelli has no views on human nature; or, at any rate, none is presented in his writings. Machiavelli is neither a psychologist nor a moral philosopher, but a political scientist.

It is clear from a study of Machiavelli that what he is trying to analyze is not ''man'' but ''political man,'' in somewhat the same way that Adam Smith analyzed ''economic man.'' Adam Smith did not suppose for a moment—though he, too, is often enough misunderstood—that he was exhaustively describing human nature when he said that economic man seeks a profit, that, when a man operates in the capitalist market, he seeks the greatest possible economic profit. Of course Adam Smith realized that men, in the course of their many and so various activities, are motivated by many other aims than the search for profit. But he was not interested in human nature as a whole. Man's nature was relevant to his studies only insofar as man functioned economically, in the market. Adam Smith was abstracting from human nature, and introducing the conception of an ''economic agent,'' which he believed, with some justice, would aid him in formulating the laws of economics. (p. 49)

Similarly with Machiavelli. He is interested in man in relation to political phenomena—that is, to the struggle for power; in man as he functions politically, not in man as he behaves toward his friends or family or god. It does not refute Machiavelli to point out that men do not always act as he says they act. He knows this. But many sides of man's nature he believes to be irrelevant to political behavior. If he is wrong, he is wrong because of a false theory of politics, not because of a false idea of man. (p. 50)

From studying the facts of politics, then, Machiavelli reached certain conclusions, not about man but about ''political man.''

First, he implies everywhere a rather sharp distinction between two types of political man: a ''ruler-type,'' we might call one, and a ''ruled-type,'' the other. The first type would include not merely those who at any moment occupy leading positions in society, but those also who aspire to such positions or who might so aspire if opportunity offered; the second consists of those who neither lead nor are capable of becoming leaders. The second is the great majority. There is a certain arbitrariness in any such distinction as this, and obviously the exact line between the two groups is hazy. Nevertheless, it is clear that Machiavelli—and all those, moreover, who write in the tradition of Machiavelli—thinks that the distinction reflects a basic fact of political life, that active political struggle is confined for the most part to a small minority of men, that the majority is and remains, whatever else happens, the ruled.

The outstanding characteristic of the majority is, then, its political passivity. Unless driven by the most extreme provocation on the part of the rulers or by rare and exceptional circumstance, the ruled are not interested in power. They want a small minimum of security, and a chance to live their own lives and manage their own small affairs. (p. 51)

When Machiavelli concludes that no man is perfectly good or bad, he is not making a primarily moral judgment. He means, more generally, that all men make mistakes at least sometimes, that there are no super-men, that no man is always intelligent and judicious, that even the stupid have occasional moments of brilliance, that men are not always consistent, that they are variable and variously motivated. Obvious as such reflections may seem, they are easily forgotten in the realm of political action, which is alone in question. The tendency, in political judgments, is toward black and white: the leader, or the proletariat, or the people, or the party, or the great captain is always right; the bosses or the crowd or the government, always wrong. From such reasoning flow not a few shocks and dismays at turns of events that might readily have been anticipated.

The ruled majority, changeable, weak, short-sighted, selfish, is not at all, for Machiavelli, the black to the rulers' white. Indeed, for him, the ruler-type is even less constant, less loyal, and on many occasions less intelligent. (pp. 54-5)

In understanding Machiavelli, there are confusions that may result from his use of certain words.

In *The Prince*, Machiavelli divides all governments, with respect to their form, into "monarchies" (principalities) and "commonwealths" (republics). A monarchy means a government where sovereignty rests, formally, in a single man; a commonwealth means a government where sovereignty rests, formally, in more than one man. A commonwealth, therefore, need not be "democratic" in any usual sense; nor a monarchy, tyrannical.

At the beginning of the *Discourses on Livy,* Machiavelli distinguishes three kinds of government: monarchy, aristocracy, and democracy. Through this distinction, which is taken from Aristotle, he is referring not only to differences in governmental form, but also to differing social relations in the state. In particular, by the terms "aristocracy" and "democracy" he is taking account of the relative power of "nobility" and "people."

When Machiavelli discusses the nobility and the people, he has in mind the distinction between "patricians" and "plebs" in Rome, and between the feudal nobility and the burghers in the Italian cities. Originally, in Rome, the patricians were the heads of the families belonging to the ancient tribes. Their class included, in a subordinate status, the rest of their families, their clients, servants, slaves, and so on. At first, the patricians alone were eligible to the senate and the consulship.

The class of the "plebs," or "people," was sub-divided primarily according to wealth. Its articulate and politically active members, who gradually won citizenship in Rome, the creation of the office of tribune, and eligibility to the senate and consulship, were for a long time only a small minority of the entire plebs—just as the patricians proper, who were the descendants of the early family heads in the eldest male line, were only a minority of the entire patrician class. In speaking of the "people," therefore, in connection with Rome, the reference is not to

everyone, or even to "the masses" in an indiscriminate sense, but ordinarily to the upper stratum of the plebs.

Analogously in the case of the Italian cities. "People" meant in the first instance the burghers and the leading members of the guilds. These were opposed to the class of the nobility, dominated by the heads of the noble houses. In the course of time, the class of "people" expanded. It became necessary to distinguish between the richer burghers and chiefs of the major guilds *(popolo grasso),* and the lesser people *(popolo minuto),* whom Machiavelli sometimes calls "people of the meaner sort." But when Machiavelli wants to refer to the lower strata of "the masses," to the apprentices and workmen and those not regularly employed, he ordinarily calls them, not "people," but "rabble," or sometimes "multitude."

There are two important consequences of this terminology: The form of government—monarchy or commonwealth—is independent of the social ascendancy or subordination of the "people," since the people could set up a monarchy or tyranny as well as a commonwealth, and the nobility could rule through a republic or commonwealth, as it did during much of the history of Rome, in Venice, and typically in a long period of the history of the ancient cities. Second, the distinction between "ruler-type" and "ruled-type" is also independent: specifically, both types are to be found among the "people" as well as in other classes.

The ruler-type, then, is not distinguished by Machiavelli from the ruled by any moral standard, nor by intelligence or consistency, nor by any capacity to avoid mistakes. There are, however, certain common characteristics that mark the rulers and potential rulers, and divide them from the majority that is fated always to be ruled.

In the first place, the ruler-type has what Machiavelli calls *virtù,* what is so improperly translated as "virtue." *Virtù* is a word, in Machiavelli's language, that has no English equivalent. It includes in its meaning part of what we refer to as "ambition," "drive," "spirit" in the sense of Plato's Øυρός, the "will to power." Those who are capable of rule are above all those who want to rule. They drive themselves as well as others; they have that quality which makes them keep going, endure amid difficulties, persist against dangers. (pp. 55-8)

The ruler-type has, usually, strength, especially martial strength. War and fighting are the great training ground of rule, Machiavelli believes, and power is secure only on the basis of force.

Even more universal a quality of the ruler-type, however, is fraud. Machiavelli's writings contain numerous discussions of the indispensable role of fraud in political affairs, ranging from analyses of deceptions and stratagems in war to the breaking of treaties to the varied types of fraud met with daily in civil life. In the *Discourses,* Book II, Chapter 13, he generalizes "that from mean to great fortune, people rise rather by fraud, than by force." (p. 58)

The combination of force and fraud is picturesquely referred to in the famous passages of *The Prince* which describe the successful ruler as both Lion and Fox. (p. 59)

> Seeing, therefore, it is of such importance to a Prince
> to take upon him the nature and disposition of a beast,
> of all the whole flock, he ought to imitate the Lion
> and the Fox; for the Lion is in danger of toils and
> snares, and the Fox of the Wolf: so that he must be
> a Fox to find out the snares, and a Lion to fright

away the Wolves, but they who keep wholly to the
Lion, have no true notion of themselves. . . .

Finally, political man of the ruler-type is skilled at adapting
himself to the times. In passage after passage, Machiavelli
returns to this essential ability: neither cruelty nor humaneness,
neither rashness nor caution, neither liberality nor avarice avails
in the struggle for power unless the times are suited. (p. 60)

Machiavelli does not have a systematically worked out theory
of history. The many generalizations which he states are for
the most part limited, dealing with some special phase of political action, and a list of them would be a summary of most
of his writings. There are, however, in addition to those that
I have already analyzed, a few wider principles of great influence in the later development of Machiavellism.

I. Political life, according to Machiavelli, is never static, but
in continual change. There is no way of avoiding this change.
Any idea of a perfect state, or even of a reasonably good state,
much short of perfection, that could last indefinitely, is an
illusion.

The process of change is repetitive, and roughly cyclical. That
is to say, the pattern of change occurs again and again in history
(so that, by studying the past, we learn also about the present
and future); and this pattern comprises a more or less recognizable cycle. A good, flourishing, prosperous state becomes
corrupt, evil, degenerate; from the corrupt, evil state again
arises one that is strong and flourishing. The degeneration can,
perhaps, be delayed; but Machiavelli has no confidence that it
could be avoided. The very virtues of the good state contain
the seeds of its own destruction. The strong and flourishing
state is feared by all neighbors, and is therefore left in peace.
War and the ways of force are neglected. The peace and prosperity breed idleness, luxury, and license; these, political corruption, tyranny, and weakness. The state is overcome by the
force of uncorrupted neighbors, or itself enters a new cycle,
where hard days and arms purge the corruption, and bring a
new strength, a new virtue and prosperity. But once again, the
degeneration sets in. (pp. 62-3)

2. The recurring pattern of change expresses the more or less
permanent core of human nature as it functions politically. The
instability of all governments and political forms follows in
part from the limitless human appetite for power. (p. 63)

3. Machiavelli assigns a major function in political affairs to
what he calls ''Fortune.'' Sometimes he seems almost to per-
sonify Fortune, and, in the manner that lingered on through
the Middle Ages from ancient times, to write about her as a
goddess. He discusses Fortune not merely in occasional references, but in a number of lengthy passages scattered throughout his works.

From these passages it becomes clear what Machiavelli means
by ''Fortune.'' Fortune is all those causes of historical change
that are beyond the deliberate, rational control of men. In the
case both of individuals and of states, Machiavelli believes that
those causes are many, often primary, and in the long run
probably dominant. He does not altogether exclude from history the influence of deliberate human control, but he reduces
it to a strictly limited range. (p. 64)

This conception of Fortune fits in closely with the idea, which
we have already noted, that the ruler-type of political man is
one who knows how to accommodate to the times. Fortune
cannot be overcome, but advantage may be taken of her. (p. 65)

Beyond such accommodation (''opportunism,'' we might nowadays call it), men and states will make the most of fortune
when they display *virtù*, when they are firm, bold, quick in
decision, not irresolute, cowardly, and timid. . . .

4. Machiavelli believes that religion is essential to the well-
being of a state. In discussing religion, as in discussing human
nature, Machiavelli confines himself to political function. He
is not engaged in theological dispute, nor inquiring whether
religion, or some particular religion, is true or false, but trying
to estimate the role that religious belief and ritual perform in
politics. He is analyzing, we might say in a general sense,
''myth,'' and myth he finds to be politically indispensable.
(p. 66)

5. We have already seen that Machiavelli's chief immediate
practical goal was the national unification of Italy. In the review
of his descriptive conclusions about the nature of political activity, no reference has been made to any more general goals
or ideals to which Machiavelli adhered. I return now to this
problem of goal, in order to answer the question: What kind
of government did Machiavelli think best?

Machiavelli's writings, taken in their entirety, leave no doubt
about the answer. Machiavelli thinks that the best kind of
government is a republic, what he called a ''commonwealth.''
Not only does he prefer a republican government; other things
being equal, he considers a republic stronger, more enduring,
wiser and more flexible than any form of monarchy. This
opinion is above all clarified by Machiavelli's most important
work, the *Discourses on Livy,* but it is at least implicit in
everything that he wrote. When, in his Letter to Zenobius, he
replies to the accusation that in all his writings he ''insinuates''
his ''great affection to the Democratical Government,'' he
accepts frankly the justice of the accusation. . . . (pp. 67-8)

Nor does this preference for a republic contradict his conclusion
that the leadership of a prince was required for the national
unification of Italy. If a republic is the best form of government,
it does not follow that a republic is possible at every moment
and for all things. Machiavelli's preferences are always disciplined by the truth. The truth here, as he correctly saw it,
was that Italy could not then be unified except, in the initial
stages at least, through a prince.

But in preferring a republican form of government, Machiavelli
paints no utopia. He states the defects of his ideals as honestly
as their virtues. It is true, moreover, that he does not attach
quite the ultimate importance to the choice of form of government that would be attributed to that choice by utopians who
believe that all human problems can be solved if only their
own private ideal can be realized. There is no way, Machiavelli
believes, to solve all or even most human problems.

Beyond and superior to his preference among the forms of
government, Machiavelli projects his ideal of ''liberty.'' For
any given group of people, ''liberty,'' as Machiavelli uses the
word, means: independence—that is, no external subjection to
another group; and, internally, a government by law, not by
the arbitrary will of any individual men, princes or commoners.
(pp. 68-9)

As protectors of liberty, Machiavelli has no confidence in
individual men as such; driven by unlimited ambition, deceiving even themselves, they are always corrupted by power. But
individuals can, to some extent at least and for a while, be
disciplined within the established framework of wise laws. A
great deal of the *Discourses* is a commentary on this problem.

In chapter after chapter, Machiavelli insists that if liberty is to be preserved: no person and no magistrate may be permitted to be above the law; there must be legal means for any citizen to bring accusations against any other citizen or any official; terms of office must be short, and must never, no matter what the inconvenience, be lengthened; punishment must be firm and impartial; the ambitions of citizens must never be allowed to build up private power, but must be directed into public channels.

Machiavelli is not so naïve as to imagine that the law can support itself. The law is founded upon force, but the force in turn will destroy the law unless it also is bridled; but force can be bridled only by opposing force. Sociologically, therefore, the foundation of liberty is a balancing of forces, what Machiavelli calls a "mixed" government. Since Machiavelli is neither a propagandist nor an apologist, since he is not the demagogue of any party or sect or group, he knows and says how hypocritical are the calls for a "unity" that is a mask for the suppression of all opposition, how fatally lying or wrong are all beliefs that liberty is the peculiar attribute of any single individual or group—prince or democrat, nobles or people or "multitude." Only out of the continuing clash of opposing groups can liberty flow. (pp. 69-70)

Liberty, then—not the rhetorical liberty of an impossible and misconceived utopia, but such concrete liberty as is, when they are fortunate, within the grasp of real men, with their real limitations—is the dominant ideal of Machiavelli, and his final norm of judgment. Tyranny is liberty's opposite, and no man has been a clearer foe of tyranny. No man clearer, and few more eloquent. (p. 71)

Men are fond of believing that, even though they may for a while be mistaken, yet in the long run they do suitable honor, if not to the persons then at least to the memories, of those who have brought some measure of truth and enlightenment to the world. We may burn an occasional Bruno, imprison a Galileo, denounce a Darwin, exile an Einstein; but time, we imagine, restores judgment, and a new generation recognizes the brave captains of the mind who have dared to advance through the dark barriers of ignorance, superstition, and illusion. Machiavelli was so plainly one of these. His weapons, his methods—the methods of truth and science—he shared with Galileo and Darwin and Einstein; and he fought in a field of much greater concern to mankind. He tried to tell us not about stars or atoms, but about ourselves and our own common life. If his detailed conclusions were sometimes wrong, his own method, as the method of science always does, provides the way to correct them. He would be the first to insist on changing any of his views that were refuted by the evidence.

Though this is so, Machiavelli's name does not rank in this noble company. In the common opinion of men, his name itself has become a term of reproach and dishonor. He is thought of as Marlowe, not so long after his death, has him speak of himself in the prologue of *The Jew of Malta*:

> To some perhaps my name is odious,
> But such as love me guard me from their tongues;
> And let them know that I am Machiavel,
> And weigh not men, and therefore not men's words.
> Admired I am of those that hate me most.
> Though some speak openly against my books,
> Yet they will read me, and thereby attain
> To Peter's chair: and when they cast me off,
> Are poisoned by my climbing followers.
> I count religion but a childish toy,
> And hold there is no sin but ignorance.

> Birds of the air will tell of murders past!
> I am ashamed to hear such fooleries.
> Many will talk of title to a crown:
> What right had Caesar to the empery?
> Might first made kings, and laws were then most sure
> When like the Draco's they were writ in blood.

Why should this be? If our reference is to the views that Machiavelli in fact held, that he stated plainly, openly and clearly in his writings, there is in the common opinion no truth at all. We face here what can hardly be, after all these centuries, a mere accident of misunderstanding. There must be some substantial reason why Machiavelli is so consistently distorted.

It might be argued that there have indeed been oppressors and tyrants who learned from Machiavelli how to act more effectively in the furtherance of their designs, and that this justifies the common judgment of his views. It is true that he has taught tyrants, from almost his own days—Thomas Cromwell, for example, the low-born Chancellor whom Henry VIII brought in to replace Thomas More when More refused to make his conscience a tool of his master's interests, was said to have a copy of Machiavelli always in his pocket; and in our own time Mussolini wrote a college thesis on Machiavelli. But knowledge has a disturbing neutrality in this respect. We do not blame the research analyst who has solved the chemical mysteries of a poison because a murderer made use of his treatise, nor a student of the nature of alloys because a safe is cracked with the help of his formulas, nor chemists and physical scientists because bombs explode when they drop on Warsaw or Chungking. Perhaps we should do so; perhaps, as the story in *Genesis* almost suggests, all knowledge is evil. But the mere fact that the knowledge made explicit by Machiavelli has been put to bad uses, which is a potential fate of all knowledge, cannot explain why he is singled out for infamy.

It may be remarked that the harsh opinion of Machiavelli has been more widespread in England and the United States than in the nations of Continental Europe. This is no doubt natural, because the distinguishing quality of Anglo-Saxon politics has always been hypocrisy, and hypocrisy must always be at pains to shy away from the truth. It is also the case that judgments of Machiavelli are usually based upon acquaintance with *The Prince* alone, an essay which, though plain enough, can be honestly misinterpreted when read out of the context of the rest of his writings. However, something more fundamental than these minor difficulties is at stake.

We are, I think, and not only from the fate of Machiavelli's reputation, forced to conclude that men do not really want to know about themselves. When we allow ourselves to be taken in by reasoning after the manner of Dante, we find it easy to believe such remarks as Aristotle made at the beginning of his *Metaphysics*: "All men naturally desire knowledge"; and to imagine that it is self-evident that knowledge will always be welcomed. But if we examine not what follows from some abstract metaphysical principle but how men behave, some doubts arise. Even in the case of the physical world, knowledge must often hammer long at the door. Where they are themselves the subject-matter, men still keep the door resolutely shut. It may even be that they are right in this resistance. Perhaps the full disclosure of what we really are and how we act is too violent a medicine.

In any case, whatever may be the desires of most men, it is most certainly against the interests of the powerful that the truth should be known about political behavior. If the political truths stated or approximated by Machiavelli were widely known by men, the success of tyranny and all the other forms of oppressive political rule would become much less likely. A deeper freedom would be possible in society than Machiavelli himself believed attainable. If men generally understood as much of the mechanism of rule and privilege as Machiavelli understood, they would no longer be deceived into accepting that rule and privilege, and they would know what steps to take to overcome them.

Therefore the powerful and their spokesmen—all the "official" thinkers, the lawyers and philosophers and preachers and demagogues and moralists and editors—must defame Machiavelli. Machiavelli says that rulers lie and break faith: this proves, they say, that he libels human nature. Machiavelli says that ambitious men struggle for power: he is apologizing for the opposition, the enemy, and trying to confuse you about us, who wish to lead you for your own good and welfare. Machiavelli says that you must keep strict watch over officials and subordinate them to the law: he is encouraging subversion and the loss of national unity. Machiavelli says that no man with power is to be trusted: you see that his aim is to smash all your faith and ideals.

Small wonder that the powerful—in public—denounce Machiavelli. The powerful have long practice and much skill in sizing up their opponents. They can recognize an enemy who will never compromise, even when that enemy is so abstract as a body of ideas. (pp. 74-7)

> *James Burnham, "Machiavelli: The Science of Power," in his* The Machiavellians: Defenders of Freedom, *The John Day Company, Inc., 1943, pp. 29-80.*

BERTRAND RUSSELL (essay date 1945)

[*A respected and prolific author, Russell was an English philosopher and mathematician known for his support of humanistic concerns. Two of his early works,* Principles of Mathematics *(1903) and* Principia Mathematica *(1910-13), written with Alfred North Whitehead, are considered classics of mathematical logic. His philosophical approach to all his endeavors discounts idealism or emotionalism and asserts a progressive application of his "logical atomism," a process whereby individual facts are logically analyzed. Russell's humanistic beliefs often centered around support of unorthodox social concerns, including free love, undisciplined education, and the eradication of nuclear weapons. Regarding Russell, biographer Alan Wood states: "He started by asking questions about mathematics and religion and philosophy, and went on to question accepted ideas about war and politics and sex and education, setting the minds of men on the march, so that the world could never be quite the same as if he had not lived." In recognition of his contributions in a number of literary genres, Russell was awarded the Nobel Prize in literature in 1950. In the following excerpt, he synopsizes Machiavelli's political platform.*]

The Renaissance, though it produced no important theoretical philosopher, produced one man of supreme eminence in *political* philosophy, Niccolò Machiavelli. It is the custom to be shocked by him, and he certainly is sometimes shocking. But many other men would be equally so if they were equally free from humbug. His political philosophy is scientific and empirical, based upon his own experience of affairs, concerned to set forth the means to assigned ends, regardless of the question whether the ends are to be considered good or bad. When, on occasion, he allows himself to mention the ends that he desires, they are such as we can all applaud. Much of the conventional obloquy that attaches to his name is due to the

indignation of hypocrites who hate the frank avowal of evil-doing. There remains, it is true, a good deal that genuinely demands criticism, but in this he is an expression of his age. (p. 504)

The Prince is concerned to discover, from history and from contemporary events, how principalities are won, how they are held, and how they are lost. Fifteenth-century Italy afforded a multitude of examples, both great and small. Few rulers were legitimate; even the popes, in many cases, secured election by corrupt means. The rules for achieving success were not quite the same as they became when times grew more settled, for no one was shocked by cruelties and treacheries which would have disqualified a man in the eighteenth or the nineteenth century. Perhaps our age, again, can better appreciate Machiavelli, for some of the most notable successes of our time have been achieved by methods as base as any employed in Renaissance Italy. He would have applauded, as an artistic connoisseur in statecraft, Hitler's Reichstag fire, his purge of the party in 1934, and his breach of faith after Munich. (p. 505)

The Prince is very explicit in repudiating received morality where the conduct of rulers is concerned. A ruler will perish if he is always good; he must be as cunning as a fox and as fierce as a lion. (p. 507)

The tone of the *Discourses,* which are nominally a commentary on Livy, is very different. There are whole chapters which seem almost as if they had been written by Montesquieu; most of the book could have been read with approval by an eighteenth-century liberal. The doctrine of checks and balances is set forth explicitly. Princes, nobles, and people should all have a part in the Constitution; "then these three powers will keep each other reciprocally in check." (p. 508)

The love of "liberty," and the theory of checks and balances, came to the Renaissance from antiquity, and to modern times largely from the Renaissance, though also directly from antiquity. This aspect of Machiavelli is at least as important as the more famous "immoral" doctrines of *The Prince.*

It is to be noted that Machiavelli never bases any political argument on Christian or biblical grounds. Medieval writers had a conception of "legitimate" power, which was that of the Pope and the Emperor, or derived from them. Northern writers, even so late as Locke, argue as to what happened in the Garden of Eden, and think that they can thence derive proofs that certain kinds of power are "legitimate." In Machiavelli there is no such conception. Power is for those who have the skill to seize it in a free competition. His preference for popular government is not derived from any idea of "rights," but from the observation that popular governments are less cruel, unscrupulous, and inconstant than tyrannies.

Let us try to make a synthesis (which Machiavelli himself did not make) of the "moral" and "immoral" parts of his doctrine. In what follows, I am expressing not my own opinions, but opinions which are explicitly or implicitly his.

There are certain political goods, of which three are specially important: national independence, security, and a well-ordered constitution. The best constitution is one which apportions legal rights among prince, nobles, and people in proportion to their real power, for under such a constitution successful revolutions are difficult and therefore stability is possible; but for considerations of stability, it would be wise to give more power to the people. So far as regards ends.

But there is also, in politics, the question of means. It is futile to pursue a political purpose by methods that are bound to fail; if the end is held good, we must choose means adequate to its achievement. The question of means can be treated in a purely scientific manner, without regard to the goodness or badness of the ends. "Success" means the achievement of your purpose, whatever it may be. If there is a science of success, it can be studied just as well in the successes of the wicked as in those of the good—indeed better, since the examples of successful sinners are more numerous than those of successful saints. But the science, once established, will be just as useful to the saint as to the sinner. For the saint, if he concerns himself with politics, must wish, just as the sinner does, to achieve success.

The question is ultimately one of power. To achieve a political end, power, of one kind or another, is necessary. This plain fact is concealed by slogans, such as "right will prevail" or "the triumph of evil is short-lived." If the side that you think right prevails, that is because it has superior power. It is true that power, often, depends upon opinion, and opinion upon propaganda; it is true, also, that it is an advantage in propaganda to seem more virtuous than your adversary, and that one way of seeming virtuous is to be virtuous. For this reason, it may sometimes happen that victory goes to the side which has the most of what the general public considers to be virtue. We must concede to Machiavelli that this was an important element in the growing power of the Church during the eleventh, twelfth, and thirteenth centuries, as well as in the success of the Reformation in the sixteenth century. But there are important limitations. In the first place, those who have seized power can, by controlling propaganda, cause their party to appear virtuous; no one, for example, could mention the sins of Alexander VI in a New York or Boston public school. In the second place, there are chaotic periods during which obvious knavery frequently succeeds; the period of Machiavelli was one of them. In such times, there tends to be a rapidly growing cynicism, which makes men forgive anything provided it pays. Even in such times, as Machiavelli himself says, it is desirable to present an appearance of virtue before the ignorant public.

This question can be carried a step further. Machiavelli is of opinion that civilized men are almost certain to be unscrupulous egoists. If a man wished nowadays to establish a republic, he says, he would find it easier with mountaineers than with the men of a large city, since the latter would be already corrupted. If a man is an unscrupulous egoist, his wisest line of conduct will depend upon the population with which he has to operate. The Renaissance Church shocked everybody, but it was only north of the Alps that it shocked people enough to produce the Reformation. At the time when Luther began his revolt, the revenue of the papacy was probably larger than it would have been if Alexander VI and Julius II had been more virtuous, and if this is true, it is so because of the cynicism of Renaissance Italy. It follows that politicans will behave better when they depend upon a virtuous population than when they depend upon one which is indifferent to moral considerations; they will also behave better in a community in which their crimes, if any, can be made widely known, than in one in which there is a strict censorship under their control. A certain amount can, of course, always be achieved by hypocrisy, but the amount can be much diminished by suitable institutions.

Machiavelli's political thinking, like that of most of the ancients, is in one respect somewhat shallow. He is occupied with great law givers, such as Lycurgus and Solon, who are supposed to create a community all in one piece, with little regard to what has gone before. The conception of a community as an organic growth, which the statesmen can only affect to a limited extent, is in the main modern, and has been greatly strengthened by the theory of evolution. This conception is not to be found in Machiavelli any more than in Plato.

It might, however, be maintained that the evolutionary view of society, though true in the past, is no longer applicable, but must, for the present and the future, be replaced by a much more mechanistic view. In Russia and Germany new societies have been created, in much the same way as the mythical Lycurgus was supposed to have created the Spartan polity. The ancient law giver was a benevolent myth; the modern law giver is a terrifying reality. The world has become more like that of Machiavelli than it was, and the modern man who hopes to refute his philosophy must think more deeply than seemed necessary in the nineteenth century. (pp. 509-11)

> Bertrand Russell, "Modern Philosophy: Machiavelli," in his A History of Western Philosophy, and Its Connection with Political and Social Circumstances from the Earliest Times to the Present Day, *Simon & Schuster, 1945, pp. 504-11.*

MAX LERNER (essay date 1950)

[*A Russian-born American political scientist, educator, and social commentator, Lerner served as editor of the* Nation *from 1936 to 1939 and has worked as a columnist for the* New York Post *since 1949. His numerous writings include the popular* It Is Later Than You Think *(1938), a study of contemporary politics, and what he considers his most ambitious work,* America as a Civilization: Life and Thought in the United States Today *(1957). Of his political philosophy, Lerner states: "My political convictions are on the left, although I belong to no party. I feel that my energies must lie with the movement toward a democratic socialism." In the following excerpt, Lerner measures the contribution of* The Prince *to literature and political thought and briefly compares it with* Discourses.]

What gives *The Prince* its greatness? It is not a great formal treatise on politics. It is bare of any genuine insights into social organization as the basis of politics. It has very little passion in it—so little that, because the final chapter crackles and glows with Machiavelli's fervor for the unification of Italy, some commentators have suggested that it is not an organic part of the book but was added as an afterthought. It has been pretty well proved, moreover, by recent scholarship that Machiavelli's little pamphlet on princes is not even original in form. It is part of a whole traditional literature on princes that stretches back to the Middle Ages. The structure of the book, its division into chapters and even some of the chapter headings follow the conventional form of what has been called the mirror-of-princes literature: the discussion of how to rule conquered territory, what advisers a prince should rely on, how he should conduct himself among the intrigues of diplomacy, whether he should depend mainly on fortified castles or entrenched camps in warfare.

But the intellectual spirit that pervades the book is quite another matter. Here we are in the presence of something little short of a revolution in political thinking. The humanists who had written books about princes had written in the idealistic and scholastic medieval tradition; they were ridden by theology and metaphysics. Machiavelli rejected metaphysics, theology, idealism. The whole drift of his work is toward a political realism, unknown to the formal writing of his time.

Title page and beginning of the first chapter of The Prince *(1532).*

I say unknown to the *formal writing*. That does not mean it was unknown to his time. Machiavelli was expressing the realism that characterized the actual politics and the popular ethos of his time. (pp. xxx-xxxi)

He was able, using the traditional humanist literary forms, to pour into them a realistic political spirit which his age was acting on but which had never before been so well expressed in political thought. He had the daring to turn against the whole idealistic preoccupation of the humanists. He had the clear-eyed capacity to distinguish between man as he ought to be and man as he actually is—between the ideal form of institutions and the pragmatic conditions under which they operate.

But if we have come close to his greatness here, we have not wholly succeeded in ensnaring it. There have been other men who have expressed the consciousness of their period. They have in very few instances achieved the highest rank in the history of ideas. And while those who content themselves with seeing Machiavelli thus in the context of his time may succeed thereby in countering the charges made against him of being a sort of anti-Christ who had created a new immorality, they do not thereby get at the roots of his greatness.

To take a further step in our analysis, we must see that Machiavelli, while he expressed the ethical consciousness of his

time, was also a good deal ahead of his time in other respects. He lived in a period when economic growth had gone so far as to burst the bounds of existing political forms. (pp. xxxii-xxxiii)

Machiavelli only dimly foresaw nationalism, but he very clearly expressed . . . the realistic use of power from the center, the methods by which unity could be achieved.

Therein lies the importance of *The Prince* in the subsequent history of the Western world. Machiavelli wrote a grammar of power, not only for the sixteenth century, but for the ages that have followed. Read *The Prince* today and you will be struck by the detonations which its sentences set off in the corridors of our experiences with present-day rulers. Machiavelli seen only in his historical context does become intelligible; but his greatness does not emerge until we see that when he wrote his grammar of power he came close to setting down the imperatives by which men govern and are governed in political communities, whatever the epoch and whatever the governmental structure.

The Prince has become, for better or worse, a symbol of a whole body of literature and a whole approach to politics. Just as in literature and art we must always face, under whatever names, the polar conflict of classic and romantic, so in the history of political thinking we have always to face the polar conflict between the ethical and the ruthlessly realistic. *The Prince* is part of the world's polemical literature because it places itself squarely in the ranks of realism. It brushes aside, with an impatience in which Machiavelli scarcely cares to conceal his disdain, the tender-mindedness of reformers and idealists. (p. xxxiv)

Very few who talk of *The Prince* have ever read more than a few sentences in it. But fewer still have read the work of Machiavelli which, without having the same *éclat* in history as *The Prince,* is nevertheless the saner, the more rounded, the more comprehensive work. I refer to *The Discourses.* (p. xxxv)

Scholarship has not done well by *The Discourses*. The scholars pay lip service to it as the larger frame of reference within which *The Prince* can be understood. Yet having done so, they go on to talk of *The Prince*. Its structure is difficult and fragmentary. Precepts drawn from Livy form the chapter heads. There are whole sections that might easily be cut out to improve the book. A good editor today, receiving such a manuscript, would probably ask the author to cut it down to one-third and pull it together a bit. Yet once read, *The Discourses* stay in your mind as an impressive intellectual experience. And once read, whatever impression you have formed of Machiavelli through reading *The Prince* is rather drastically changed. (p. xxxvi)

[*The Discourses*] has a catholicity and vastness of resource which will make it yield different discoveries for every reader and on every reading.

This is not the place to discuss the themes I have mentioned. I want only to say that if *The Prince* is great because of its intensity, *The Discourses* are great because of their variety; if *The Prince* is great because it is polemical, *The Discourses* are great because they have balance; and if *The Prince* is great because it gives us the grammar of power for a government, *The Discourses* are great because they give us the philosophy of organic unity not in a government but in a state, and the conditions under which alone a culture can survive. (pp. xxxvii-xxxviii)

Max Lerner, in an introduction to The Prince and
The Discourses *by Niccolò Machiavelli, The Modern
Library, 1950, pp. xxv-xlvi.*

ERIC VOEGELIN   (essay date 1951)

[*An educator, author, and a leading twentieth-century political
philosopher, Voegelin emigrated in 1938 from Germany to the
United States, where he taught at Harvard University, Bennington
College, and other principal academic institutions. Voegelin is
best known for his* Order and History *(1956-74), a multivolume
study of the problem of order in human existence, which was left
unfinished at the time of his death. In the following excerpt from
an earlier study, he moves from a general discussion of Machiavelli's thought to focus on the importance of Machiavelli's* Life
of Castruccio Castracani.]

The name of Niccolò Machiavelli . . . , to the public at large,
still lies in the shadow of moralistic condemnation. The anti-
Machiavellian propaganda of the Counter-Reformation concentrated on the principles of political craftsmanship, developed in the *Prince,* as its target; and, apart from a narrower
circle of historians, Machiavelli has ever since remained the
author of the famous work, while the morality of his advice
to rulers has remained the great issue of evaluation. It is hardly
necessary to say that such preoccupations with moralistic propaganda cannot form the basis for a critical analysis of Machiavelli's ideas. All we can retain from the caricature is the
consciousness that something extraordinary has occurred, a
severe break with the traditions of treating political questions,
the consciousness that with the author of the *Prince* we are on
the threshold of a new, "modern" era. Even this element of
the caricature, however, needs qualification. The furious concentration on the evil book has created the illusion that its
author was a solitary figure, something like a moral freak.
That, of course, is not so. There is nothing solitary or enigmatic
about Machiavelli. His ideas, like everybody's, have a solid
pre-history stretching over generations; and they were shared
in his time by others. (p. 142)

A good deal of what conventionally is considered as enigmatic,
or unusual, or idiosyncratic, or immortal in his work, loses
this character as soon as we are not compelled to attribute these
elements to Machiavelli himself but can understand them as
part of the intellectual climate in which his ideas were formed.

The experience of crushing power . . . sharpened awareness of
the fact that an existential force beyond good and evil manifests
itself in the order of a polity. The stronger force will break the
weaker existence, no matter how high its rank in the realm of
civilized values. The response to this experience, however,
was not a naturalistic nihilism that would deny the meaning of
power and order. The weaker order, while physically crushed,
still is a meaningful human order and not a natural phenomenon; and the stronger order, while physically crushing, is not
a natural catastrophe, but the force of organized human existence. The stronger existence, while crushing the weaker order,
establishes itself as the power that maintains a new human
order. The humanist historians responded to the experience by
heightening the human existence which destroys and creates
order into a mythical image. . . . The *virtù* of the conquering
prince became the source of order; and since the Christian,
transcendental order of existence had become a dead letter for
the Italian thinkers of the fifteenth century, the *virtù ordinata*
of the prince, the only ordering force experienced as real,
acquired human-divine, heroic proportions.

This is the situation of Machiavelli. The misery of Italy was
not a fate to be accepted; on the contrary, the depth of political
humiliation was a challenge to a man of semi-divine, heroic
qualities to eject the barbarians, a challenge to restore the order
of Italy through his *virtù* that would overcome the adverse
fortuna—just as often in the past a hero had risen from private
insignificance to become the founder of a people and its order.
The evocation of the mythical hero is at the center of Machiavelli's work in the same sense that the evocation of the
philosopher-king is at the center of Plato's work. Machiavelli
has created a myth; this fact must be the basis of interpretation
if we wish to avoid the misunderstanding of his theory of
politics as the shallow insight that foul means are frequently
more helpful than fair ones in acquiring political power. The
elaboration of the theory in the *Discorsi* and the *Principe* presupposes the myth of the hero. Sketches of a heroic life were
even embedded in the *Prince,* such as the life of Cesare Borgia
(Chapter 7) and Agathocles (Chapter 8), but they were qualified
as imperfect types. The myth itself was fully and consciously
unfolded only in the *Vita di Castruccio Castracani.*

The *Vita* is ostensibly a biography of Castruccio Castracani
(1281-1328), successively lord, imperial vicar and duke of
Lucca. In truth, however, Machiavelli used the well-known
facts of Castruccio's life most cavalierly—selecting some,
omitting others, and inventing a good deal—for creating the
image of an Italian hero who through his *virtù* became the
founder of a great state *(stato)*, frustrated in his enterprise only
by *fortuna,* cutting off his life in the middle of its course and
thus ending the ascent toward the glory promised by so many
happy successes. The creation was conscious. In the dedication
to his friends Machiavelli reflected that, amazingly, those who
have worked great things in this world are frequently of obscure
origin. Fortune seems to persecute them in every way. At their
birth they are surrendered to wild beasts; or their parentage is
so humble that they must pose as sons of Zeus or some other
God. Examples of this kind are well known to everybody.
Fortune, so it seems, wants to show to the world that she, and
not *prudenza,* makes men great; and, therefore, she begins the
shaping of a man's life at a time when there can be no doubt
that prudence has no share in it. The life of Castruccio is of
this kind; and it should be recalled to the memory of men
because it is most instructive *(grandissimo esembla)* for the
operation both of *virtù* and *fortuna.* The irony of the reflection
introduces the *Vita,* as a conscious play, with the serious purpose of creating a *grandissimo esembla* of the forces which
shape the life of the hero.

The *Vita* itself follows the pattern of the myth of the hero. . . .
The consciousness of the construction appears most clearly
when describing . . . the sequences of scenes. The main phases
of the *Vita* are the following: (1) an infant of unknown birth
is found in the garden by the sister of Antonio Castracani, a
clergyman; (2) Castracani adopts the boy and tries to bring him
up in the ideals of his estate and to educate him as a future
priest; (3) at the age of fourteen, the boy asserts himself, abandons the theological books and turns to the art of arms; (4) he
surpasses all his comrades in these exercises; (5) he acquires
a kind of royal leadership over the other boys, and commands
their confidence and loyalty; (6) the discovery: the boy is observed in his games with his fellows by Francesco Guinigi, a
nobleman; (7) Guinigi persuades the clergyman to entrust the
future of the boy to him; (8) at the age of eighteen, Castruccio
embarks on his career as a military and political leader, with
momentous success in expanding the domain of Lucca; (9) in
the midst of these most promising enterprises, *Fortuna* cuts

short his life; Castruccio dies from a fever, resulting from exposure to a miasmal evening wind after a victorious battle.

The story combines the story of the Moses and Cyrus type with circumstances which Machiavelli wanted to see in his Italian, national hero. The deviations from history he permitted himself are most illuminating. The historical Castruccio was not at all an *esposito* ["foundling child"] but belonged to one of the Ghibelline families of Lucca. Moreover, he was married and left children—a point which Machiavelli omitted; for he wanted a hero who would do his work of political salvation and then, conveniently without family attachments, would leave the state to join the people. The fact that the historical Castruccio was an imperial vicar and duke is again judiciously suppressed; for these honors would not look too good in the savior who liberates Italy from the barbarians, including the Emperor. In the description of the political and military career, on the other hand, we find various data on Castruccio's organization of infantry and cavalry, as well as on his battle tactics, which happen to coincide with Machiavelli's own ideas for military reform. And considerable stress is laid on the circumspection with which Castruccio indulges in treacheries and the thorough slaughter of his enemies—rather on the model of Cesare Borgia's day of Sinigaglia.

The story of Castruccio's life closes with a summarizing picture of his character:

> He was dear to his friends and terrible to his enemies; just to his subjects and faithless toward foreigners; he never tried to conquer by force when he could conquer by fraud; for he used to say that through victory, and not through the method of victory, you acquire fame. Nobody was ever more audacious in approaching dangers, and nobody more skilful in extracting himself from them. He used to say that man should try everything and not shy away; and that God loves strong men, for, as anyone may see, he always castigates the powerless by means of the powerful.

The closing remark of this characterization is of special interest because it introduces the element of the *ira Dei* ["wrath of God"] . . . , the victorious prince becomes the *ultor peccatorum* ["avenger of sin"]. Neither in the **Principe**, nor in the **Discorsi** has Machiavelli become so explicit in according to power and *virtù* the meaning of a providential order of politics. (pp. 164-68)

> Eric Voegelin, "Machiavelli's 'Prince': Background and Formation," in The Review of Politics, Vol. 13, No. 2, April, 1951, pp. 142-68.

ERIC BENTLEY (essay date 1953)

[*Bentley is considered one of the most erudite and innovative critics of the modern theater. He was responsible for introducing Bertolt Brecht, Luigi Pirandello, and other European playwrights to America through his studies, translations, and stage adaptations of their plays. In his first important critical study,* The Playwright as Thinker *(1946), Bentley distinguished between "art" and "commodity" in the American theater, asserting that focus on the financial success of a play often leads to neglect of the dramatist. Some critics consider this approach an attempt to compensate for his unwillingness to accept drama as a form of popular entertainment. Bentley's* The Life of Drama *(1964) is a comprehensive study of the development of dramatic form, specifically examining aspects of melodrama, farce, comedy, tragedy, and tragicomedy. His most recent critical works include anthologies of reviews written during his years as drama critic (1952-56) for the* New Republic, *and* The Brecht Commentaries: 1943-80 *(1981).*

In the following excerpt from an essay originally published in the New Republic *in 1953, Bentley discusses* Mandragola.]

The action of [**Mandragola**] consists simply in the accomplishing of adultery. How will our "hero" get into the (married) "heroine's" bed? The husband believes his wife to be sterile, but is persuaded she will become fertile if she partakes of the magic herb mandragola. Yet the first man she sleeps with after doing so will die. The husband must kidnap some lusty young fellow, thrust him into his wife's bed, and discard him. The truth, of course, is that the wife is not sterile, the herb is not magical, and the man is not "some lusty young fellow" but the same person who told the husband about mandragola and who at the end of the play is rewarded for his counsel by the present of a key to the married couple's house: namely, our hero. Not that he was clever enough to hatch the whole plot himself. His contribution is, not brains, but money, and he pays it out to three accomplices: an idea man to draft the plan of campaign and convince the husband, and a couple of moralists to win the cooperation of the wife. Who better for this last function than—her mother and her confessor? The cutting edge of Machiavelli's irony was never sharper than in the confessor's use of Catholic sophistry to justify adultery; Roman farce is transfigured to great drama by a fantastic intellect, an intellectual fantasy.

The crowning event of the plot is the crowning irony of the play: not merely that the hero arrives in the heroine's bed but that he is pushed into it by her husband, not merely that the heroine has a lover but that she has never seen him before he enters her bed, that she is fully reconciled to the situation and, after the first union, determined to perpetuate it. (pp. 116-17)

Mandragola is a masterpiece . . . [belonging] to a school of drama that we do ill to forget. In what probably remains the best essay on Machiavelli in English, Macaulay said that "tragedy is corrupted by eloquence and comedy by wit" and that **Mandragola** is a prime instance of uncorrupted comedy—a comedy in which character is defined, not by clever or graceful talk, but by plot [see excerpt dated 1827]. In short Macaulay uses Machiavelli as a stick to beat Congreve and Sheridan with—today we might be tempted to beat Wilde and Giraudoux with. Whether or no it is fair to describe these four as corrupt, it is certainly salutary to look back at the classic—and could we not say realistic?—comedy of the Italian Renaissance, at Calmo, at Ruzzante, and, above all, at Machiavelli.

Many of the things that Machiavelli does well, Molière, it is true, does better. . . . [The] "diabolical" rhythm of farce is a fine instrument for the "diabolical" mind of Machiavelli. What distinguishes Machiavelli from Molière is a certain fanaticism.

Sheer fanaticism, to be sure, would never yield comedy. We know from **The Prince** that Machiavelli pretends to be the polar opposite of a fanatic—a cynic. Yet (a) he is fanatical in his advocacy of cynicism and (b) his cynicism is contradicted, modified, or transformed by certain ideal allegiances, notably patriotism; and his patriotism is part of a profound and revolutionary humanism.

More important than these *isms* is the spirit of Machiavelli. A clerical government, given a certain sophistication, might tolerate his cynicism and, given a certain liberalism, might tolerate his ideals; what it could never be happy with, unless it were positively stupid, is his restless and questing spirit. I should not wish to deny that his mind was full of ambiguities. Yet I should place him not with second-rate logicians but with first-rate poet-philosophers like Voltaire and Nietzsche—one might almost say: like Swift. In the realm of pure thought, ambiguity may be simply a fault, the fault of indecision or inconsistency. In the realm of the imagination, ambiguities, though not good in themselves, may be put to work. In *Mandragola* they function as comic tensions. The complexity of Machiavelli's personality is in this play, even though, under the control of his genius, complexity takes the form of an unexampled simplicity. (pp. 117-18)

Eric Bentley, "From Leo X to Pius XII," in his *The Dramatic Event: An American Chronicle, Horizon Press,* 1954, pp. 115-18.

GARRETT MATTINGLY (essay date 1958)

[*Mattingly was an American historian and educator whose special interest was Europe in the sixteenth century and whose most successful work,* The Defeat of the Spanish Armada *(1959), was not only praised by other historians for its impeccable scholarship but was also widely read by the public as a captivating narrative. In the following excerpt, he proposes that* The Prince *be interpreted as a satire.*]

The notion that this little book [*The Prince*] was meant as a serious, scientific treatise on government contradicts everything we know about Machiavelli's life, about his writings, and about the history of his time.

In the first place, this proposition asks us to believe that Niccolò Machiavelli deliberately wrote a handbook meant to help a tyrant rule the once free people of Florence. (pp. 483-84)

He has left proof of his devotion in the record of his activities and in the state papers in which he spun endless schemes for the defense and aggrandizement of the republic, and constantly preached the same to his superiors. One characteristic quotation is irresistible. The subject is an increase in the defense budget that Machiavelli's masters were reluctant to vote. He reminds them with mounting impatience that only strong states are respected by their neighbors and that their neglect of military strength in the recent past has cost them dear, and he ends with anything but detached calm: "Other people learn from the perils of their neighbors, you will not even learn from your own, nor trust yourselves, nor recognize the time you are losing and have lost. I tell you fortune will not alter the sentence it has pronounced unless you alter your behavior. Heaven will not and cannot preserve those bent on their own ruin. But I cannot believe it will come to this, seeing that you are free Florentines and have your liberty in your own hands. In the end I believe you will have the same regard for your freedom that men always have who are born free and desire to live free."

Only a man who cared deeply for the independence of his city would use language like this to his employers. But Machiavelli gave an even more impressive proof of his disinterested patriotism. After fourteen years in high office, in a place where the opportunities for dipping into the public purse and into the pockets of his compatriots and of those foreigners he did business with were practically unlimited (among other duties he acted as paymaster-general of the army), Machiavelli retired from public life as poor as when he had entered it. Later he was to refer to this record with pride, but also with a kind of rueful astonishment; and, indeed, if this was not a unique feat in his day, it was a very rare one. (pp. 484-85)

Machiavelli emerged from prison in mid-March, 1513. Most people believe that *The Prince* was finished by December. I

suppose it is possible to imagine that a man who has seen his country enslaved, his life's work wrecked and his own career with it, and has, for good measure, been tortured within an inch of his life should thereupon go home and write a book intended to teach his enemies the proper way to maintain themselves, writing all the time, remember, with the passionless objectivity of a scientist in a laboratory. It must be possible to imagine such behavior, because Machiavelli scholars do imagine it and accept it without a visible tremor. But it is a little difficult for the ordinary mind to compass.

The difficulty is increased by the fact that this acceptance of tyranny seems to have been a passing phase. Throughout the rest of his life Machiavelli wrote as a republican and moved mainly in republican circles. (p. 485)

The notion that *The Prince* is what it pretends to be, a scientific manual for tyrants, has to contend not only against Machiavelli's life but against his writings, as, of course, everyone who wants to use *The Prince* as a centerpiece in an exposition of Machiavelli's political thought has recognized. Ever since Herder, the standard explanation has been that in the corrupt conditions of sixteenth-century Italy only a prince could create a strong state capable of expansion. The trouble with this is that it was chiefly because they widened their boundaries that Machiavelli preferred republics. In the *Discorsi* he wrote, "We know by experience that states have never signally increased either in territory or in riches except under a free government. The cause is not far to seek, since it is the well-being not of individuals but of the community which makes the state great, and without question this universal well-being is nowhere secured save in a republic. . . . Popular rule is always better than the rule of princes." This is not just a casual remark. It is the main theme of the *Discorsi* and the basic assumption of all but one of Machiavelli's writings, as it was the basic assumption of his political career.

There is another way in which *The Prince* is a puzzling anomaly. In practically everything else Machiavelli wrote, he displayed the sensitivity and tact of the developed literary temperament. He was delicately aware of the tastes and probable reactions of his public. No one could have written that magnificent satiric soliloquy of Fra Timotheo in *Mandragola,* for instance, who had not an instinctive feeling for the response of an audience. But the effect of the publication of *The Prince* on the first several generations of its readers in Italy (outside of Florence) and in the rest of Europe was shock. It horrified, repelled and fascinated like a Medusa's head. A large part of the shock was caused, of course, by the cynical immorality of some of the proposals, but instead of appeasing revulsion and insinuating his new proposals as delicately as possible, Machiavelli seems to delight in intensifying the shock and deliberately employing devices to heighten it. Of these not the least effective is the way *The Prince* imitates, almost parodies, one of the best known and most respected literary forms of the three preceding centuries, the handbook of advice to princes. This literary type was enormously popular. Its exemplars ran into the hundreds of titles of which a few, like St. Thomas' *De Regno* and Erasmus' *Institutio principis christiani* are not quite unknown today. In some ways, Machiavelli's little treatise was just like all the other "Mirrors of Princes"; in other ways it was a diabolical burlesque of all of them, like a political Black Mass.

The shock was intensified again because Machiavelli deliberately addressed himself primarily to princes who have newly acquired their principalities and do not owe them either to inheritance or to the free choice of their countrymen. The short and ugly word for this kind of prince is "tyrant." Machiavelli never quite uses the word except in illustrations from classical antiquity, but he seems to delight in dancing all around it until even the dullest of his readers could not mistake his meaning. Opinions about the relative merits of republics and monarchies varied during the Renaissance, depending mainly upon where one lived, but about tyrants there was only one opinion. Cristoforo Landino, Lorenzo the Magnificent's teacher and client, stated the usual view in his commentary on Dante, written when Niccolò Machiavelli was a child. When he came to comment on Brutus and Cassius in the lowest circle of hell, Landino wrote: "Surely it was extraordinary cruelty to inflict such severe punishment on those who faced death to deliver their country from slavery, a deed for which, if they had been Christians, they would have merited the most honored seats in the highest heaven. If we consult the laws of any well-constituted republic, we shall find them to decree no greater reward to anyone than to the man who kills the tyrant." So said the Italian Renaissance with almost unanimous voice. If Machiavelli's friends were meant to read the manuscript of *The Prince* and if they took it at face value—an objective study of how to be a successful tyrant offered as advice to a member of the species—they can hardly have failed to be deeply shocked. And if the manuscript was meant for the eye of young Giuliano de Medici alone, he can hardly have been pleased to find it blandly assumed that he was one of a class of whom his father's tutor had written that the highest duty of a good citizen was to kill them.

The literary fame of *The Prince* is due, precisely, to its shocking quality, so if the book was seriously meant as a scientific manual, it owes its literary reputation to an artistic blunder. (pp. 486-87)

Perhaps nobody should be rash enough today to call *The Prince* a satire, not in the teeth of all the learned opinion to the contrary. But when one comes to think of it, what excellent sense the idea makes! However you define "satire"—and I understand that critics are still without a thoroughly satisfactory definition—it must include the intention to denounce, expose or deride someone or something, and it is to be distinguished from mere didactic condemnation and invective (when it can be distinguished at all) by the employment of such devices as irony, sarcasm and ridicule. It need not be provocative of laughter; I doubt whether many people ever laughed or even smiled at the adventures of Gulliver among the Yahoos. And though satire admits of, and in fact always employs, exaggeration and overemphasis, the author, to be effective, must not appear to be, and in fact need not be, conscious that this is so. When Dryden wrote, "The rest to some faint meaning make pretense / But Shadwell never deviates into sense," he may have been conscious of some overstatement, but he was conveying his considered criticism of Shadwell's poetry. And when Pope called "Lord Fanny" "this painted child of dirt that stinks and strings," the language may be violent, but who can doubt that this is how Pope felt? Indeed the satirist seems to put forth his greatest powers chiefly when goaded by anger, hatred and savage indignation. If Machiavelli wrote *The Prince* out of the fullness of these emotions rather than out of the dispassionate curiosity of the scientist or out of a base willingness to toady to the destroyers of his country's liberty, then one can understand why the sentences crack like a whip, why the words bite and burn like acid, and why the whole style has a density and impact unique among his writings.

To read *The Prince* as satire not only clears up puzzles and resolves contradictions; it gives a new dimension and meaning to passages unremarkable before. Take the place in the dedication that runs "just as those who paint landscapes must seat themselves below in the plains to see the mountains, and high in the mountains to see the plains, so to understand the nature of the people one must be a prince, and to understand the nature of a prince, one must be one of the people." In the usual view, this is a mere rhetorical flourish, but the irony, once sought, is easy to discover, for Machiavelli, in fact, takes both positions. The people can only see the prince as, by nature and necessity, false, cruel, mean and hypocritical. The prince, from his lofty but precarious perch, dare not see the people as other than they are described in Chapter Seventeen: "ungrateful, fickle, treacherous, cowardly and greedy. As long as you succeed they are yours entirely. They will offer you their blood, property, lives and children when you do not need them. When you do need them, they will turn against you." Probably Machiavelli really believed that this, or something like it, happened to the human nature of a tyrant and his subjects. But the view, like its expression, is something less than objective and dispassionate, and the only lesson it has for princes would seem to be: "Run for your life!"

Considering the brevity of the book, the number of times its princely reader is reminded, as in the passage just quoted, that his people will overthrow him at last is quite remarkable. Cities ruled in the past by princes easily accustom themselves to a change of masters, Machiavelli says in Chapter Five, but "in republics there is more vitality, greater hatred and more desire for vengeance. They cannot forget their lost liberty, so that the safest way is to destroy them—or to live there." He does not say what makes that safe. And most notably, with savage irony, "the duke [Borgia] was so able and laid such firm foundations . . . that the Romagna [after Alexander VI's death] waited for him more than a month." This is as much as to put Leo X's brother on notice that without papal support he can expect short shrift. If the Romagna, accustomed to tryanny, waited only a month before it rose in revolt, how long will Florence wait? Tactlessness like this is unintelligible unless it is deliberate, unless these are not pedantic blunders but sarcastic ironies, taunts flung at the Medici, incitements to the Florentines.

Only in a satire can one understand the choice of Cesare Borgia as the model prince. The common people of Tuscany could not have had what they could expect of a prince's rule made clearer than by the example of this bloodstained buffoon whose vices, crimes and follies had been the scandal of Italy, and the conduct of whose brutal, undisciplined troops had so infuriated the Tuscans that when another band of them crossed their frontier, the peasants fell upon them and tore them to pieces. The Florentine aristocrats on whom Giovanni and cousin Giulio were relying to bridge the transition to despotism would have shared the people's revulsion to Cesare, and they may have been rendered somewhat more thoughtful by the logic of the assumption that nobles were more dangerous to a tyrant than commoners and should be dealt with as Cesare had dealt with the petty lords of the Romagna. Moreover, they could scarcely have avoided noticing the advice to use some faithful servant to terrorize the rest, and then to sacrifice him to escape the obloquy of his conduct, as Cesare had sacrificed Captain Ramiro. As for the gentle, mild-mannered, indolent Giuliano de Medici himself, he was the last man to be attracted by the notion of imitating the Borgia. He wanted no more than to occupy the same social position in Florence that his magnificent father had held, and not even that if it was too much trouble.

Besides, in the days of the family's misfortunes, Giuliano had found shelter and hospitality at the court of Guidobaldo de Montrefeltre. Giuliano lived at Urbino for many years (there is a rather charming picture of him there in Castiglione's *Il Cortegiano*), and all his life he cherished deep gratitude and a strong affection for Duke Guidobaldo. He must have felt, then, a special loathing for the foreign ruffian who had betrayed and plundered his patron, and Machiavelli must have known that he did. Only a wish to draw the most odious comparison possible, only a compulsion to wound and insult, could have lead Machiavelli to select the Borgia as the prime exemplar in his ''Mirror of Princes.''

There is one last famous passage that reads differently if we accept **The Prince** as satire. On any other hypothesis, the final exhortation to free Italy from the barbarians sounds at best like empty rhetoric, at worst like calculating but stupid flattery. Who could really believe that the lazy, insipid Giuliano or his petty, vicious successor were the liberators Italy awaited? But if we have heard the mordant irony and sarcasm of the preceding chapters and detected the overtones of hated and despair, then this last chapter will be charged with an irony turned inward, the bitter mockery of misdirected optimism. For before the Florentine republic had been gored to death by Spanish pikes, Machiavelli had believed, as he was to believe again, that a free Florentine republic could play the liberator's role. Perhaps, since he was all his life a passionate idealist, blind to reality when his desires were strong, Machiavelli may not have given up that wild hope even when he wrote **The Prince**. (pp. 489-91)

> *Garrett Mattingly, ''Machiavelli's 'Prince': Political Science or Political Satire?'' in* The American Scholar, *Vol. 27, No. 4, Autumn, 1958, pp. 482-91.*

LEO STRAUSS   (essay date 1958)

[*Strauss emigrated from Germany to the United States in 1938, where he taught political science at a number of leading institutions, among them the University of Chicago. A well-known scholar, he was noted for his lucid and insightful interpretations of classical political theories. The* New York Times *observed that ''Strauss is credited with keeping the study of the political classics alive and for showing students that thinkers such as Plato, Machiavelli, and Hobbes were relevant to present-day political dilemmas.'' In the following excerpt from his critically significant full-length study,* Thoughts on Machiavelli *(1958), Strauss defends the traditional interpretation of Machiavelli as ''a teacher of evil.'' This assessment is refuted by Dante Germino (see Additional Bibliography).*]

We shall not shock anyone, we shall merely expose ourselves to good-natured or at any rate harmless ridicule, if we profess ourselves inclined to the old-fashioned and simple opinion according to which Machiavelli was a teacher of evil. Indeed, what other description would fit a man who teaches lessons like these: princes ought to exterminate the families of rulers whose territory they wish to possess securely; princes ought to murder their opponents rather than to confiscate their property since those who have been robbed, but not those who are dead, can think of revenge; men forget the murder of their fathers sooner than the loss of their patrimony; true liberality consists in being stingy with one's own property and in being generous with what belongs to others; not virtue but the prudent use of virtue and vice leads to happiness; injuries ought all to be done together so that, being tasted less, they will hurt less, while benefits ought to be conferred little by little, so that they will

be felt more strongly; a victorious general who fears that his prince might not reward him properly, may punish him for his anticipated ingratitude by raising the flag of rebellion; if one has to choose between inflicting severe injuries and inflicting light injuries, one ought to inflict severe injuries; one ought not to say to someone whom one wants to kill ''Give me your gun, I want to kill you with it,'' but merely, ''Give me your gun,'' for once you have the gun in your hand, you can satisfy your desire. If it is true that only an evil man will stoop to teach maxims of public and private gangsterism, we are forced to say that Machiavelli was an evil man.

Machiavelli was indeed not the first man to express opinions like those mentioned. Such opinions belong to a way of political thinking and political acting which is as old as political society itself. But Machiavelli is the only philosopher who has lent the weight of his name to any way of political thinking and political acting which is as old as political society itself, so much so that his name is commonly used for designating such a way. He is notorious as the classic of the evil way of political thinking and political acting. Callicles and Thrasymachus, who set forth the evil doctrine behind closed doors, are Platonic characters, and the Athenian ambassadors, who state the same doctrine on the island of Melos in the absence of the common people, are Thucydidean characters. Machiavelli proclaims openly and triumphantly a corrupting doctrine which ancient writers had taught covertly or with all signs of repugnance. He says in his own name shocking things which ancient writers had said through the mouths of their characters. Machiavelli alone has dared to utter the evil doctrine in a book and in his own name.

Yet however true the old-fashioned and simple verdict may be, it is not exhaustive. Its deficiency justifies to some extent the more sophisticated views which are set forth by the learned of our age. Machiavelli, we are told, was so far from being an evil teacher of evil that he was a passionate patriot or a scientific student of society or both. But one may wonder whether the up-to-date scholars do not err much more grievously than the old-fashioned and simple, or whether what escapes the up-to-date scholars is not much more important than what escapes the simple and the old-fashioned, although it may be true that the one thing needful which is ignored by the sophisticated is inadequately articulated and therefore misinterpreted by the men of noble simplicity. It would not be the only case in which ''a little philosophy'' generates prodigious errors to which the unphilosophic multitude is immune.

It is misleading to describe the thinker Machiavelli as a patriot. He is a patriot of a particular kind: he is more concerned with the salvation of his fatherland than with the salvation of his soul. His patriotism therefore presupposes a comprehensive reflection regarding the status of the fatherland on the one hand and of the soul on the other. This comprehensive reflection, and not patriotism, is the core of Machiavelli's thought. This comprehensive reflection, and not his patriotism, established his fame and made him the teacher of many men in all countries. The substance of his thought is not Florentine, or even Italian, but universal. It concerns, and it is meant to concern, all thinking men regardless of time and place. To speak of Machiavelli as a scientist is at least as misleading as to speak of him as a patriot. The scientific student of society is unwilling or unable to pass ''value-judgments,'' but Machiavelli's works abound with ''value-judgments.'' His study of society is normative.

But even if we were forced to grant that Machiavelli was essentially a patriot or a scientist, we would not be forced to deny that he was a teacher of evil. Patriotism as Machiavelli understood it is collective selfishness. The indifference to the distinction between right and wrong which springs from devotion to one's country is less repulsive than the indifference to that distinction which springs from exclusive preoccupation with one's own ease or glory. But precisely for this reason it is more seductive and therefore more dangerous. Patriotism is a kind of love of one's own. Love of one's own is inferior to love of what is both one's own and good. Love of one's own tends therefore to become concerned with one's own being good or complying with the demands of right. To justify Machiavelli's terrible counsels by having recourse to his patriotism, means to see the virtues of that patriotism while being blind to that which is higher than patriotism, or to that which both hallows and limits patriotism. In referring to Machiavelli's patriotism one does not dispose of a mere semblance of evil; one merely obscures something truly evil.

As regards the "scientific" approach to society which many of its adherents trace to Machiavelli, it emerges through the abstraction from the moral distinctions by which we take our bearings as citizens and as men. The indispensable condition of "scientific" analysis is then moral obtuseness. That obtuseness is not identical with depravity, but it is bound to strengthen the forces of depravity. In the case of lesser men, one can safely trace such obtuseness to the absence of certain intellectual virtues. This charitable explanation could not be tolerated in the case of Machiavelli, who was too thoughtful not to know what he was doing and too generous not to admit it to his reasonable friends.

We do not hesitate to assert, as very many have asserted before us, . . . that Machiavelli's teaching is immoral and irreligious. We are familiar with the evidence which scholars adduce in support of the contrary assertion; but we question their interpretation of the evidence. To say nothing of certain other considerations, it seems to us that the scholars in question are too easily satisfied. They are satisfied that Machiavelli was a friend of religion because he stressed the useful and the indispensable character of religion. They do not pay any attention to the fact that his praise of religion is only the reverse side of what one might provisionally call his complete indifference to the truth of religion. This is not surprising since they themselves are likely to understand by religion nothing other than a significant sector of society, if not an attractive or at any rate innocuous piece of folklore, to say nothing of those sincerely religious people who are gratified by any apparent benefit conferred upon religion. They misinterpret Machiavelli's judgment concerning religion, and likewise his judgment concerning morality, because they are pupils of Machiavelli. Their seemingly open-minded study of Machiavelli's thought is based on the dogmatic acceptance of his principles. They do not see the evil character of his thought because they are the heirs of the Machiavellian tradition; because they, or the forgotten teachers of their teachers, have been corrupted by Machiavelli.

One cannot see the true character of Machiavelli's thought unless one frees himself from Machiavelli's influence. For all practical purposes this means that one cannot see the true character of Machiavelli's thought unless one recovers for himself and in himself the pre-modern heritage of the western world, both Biblical and classical. To do justice to Machiavelli requires one to look forward from a pre-modern point of view toward an altogether unexpected and surprising Machiavelli

who is new and strange, rather than to look backward from today toward a Machiavelli who has become old and our own, and therewith almost good. This procedure is required even for a purely historical understanding. Machiavelli did know pre-modern thought: it was before him. He could not have known the thought of the present time, which emerged as it were behind his back.

We thus regard the simple opinion about Machiavelli as indeed decisively superior to the prevailing sophisticated views, though still insufficient. Even if, and precisely if we are forced to grant that his teaching is diabolical and he himself a devil, we are forced to remember the profound theological truth that the devil is a fallen angel. To recognize the diabolical character of Machiavelli's thought would mean to recognize in it a perverted nobility of a very high order. That nobility was discerned by Marlowe, as he ascribed to Machiavelli the words "I hold there is no sin but ignorance." Marlowe's judgment is borne out by what Machiavelli himself, in the Epistles Dedicatory to his two great books, indicates regarding his most precious possession. We are in sympathy with the simple opinion about Machiavelli, not only because it is wholesome, but above all because a failure to take that opinion seriously prevents one from doing justice to what is truly admirable in Machiavelli: the intrepidity of his thought, the grandeur of his vision, and the graceful subtlety of his speech. Not the contempt for the simple opinion, nor the disregard of it, but the considerate ascent from it leads to the core of Machiavelli's thought. There is no surer protection against the understanding of anything than taking for granted or otherwise despising the obvious and the surface. The problem inherent in the surface of things, and only in the surface of things, is the heart of things. (pp. 9-13)

The United States of America may be said to be the only country in the world which was founded in explicit opposition to Machiavellian principles. According to Machiavelli, the founder of the most renowned commonwealth of the world was a fratricide: the foundation of political greatness is necessarily laid in crime. If we can believe Thomas Paine, all governments of the Old World have an origin of this description; their origin was conquest and tyranny. But "the Independence of America [was] accompanied by a Revolution in the principles and practice of Governments": the foundation of the United States was laid in freedom and justice. "Government founded on a moral theory, on a system of universal peace, on the indefeasible hereditary Rights of Man, is now revolving from west to east by a stronger impulse than the Government of the sword revolved from east to west." This judgment is far from being obsolete. While freedom is no longer a preserve of the United States, the United States is now the bulwark of freedom. And contemporary tyranny has its roots in Machiavelli's thought, in the Machiavellian principle that the good end justifies every means. At least to the extent that the American reality is inseparable from the American aspiration, one cannot understand Americanism without understanding Machiavellianism which is its opposite.

But we cannot conceal from ourselves the fact that the problem is more complex than it appears in the presentation by Paine and his followers. Machiavelli would argue that America owes her greatness not only to her habitual adherence to the principles of freedom and justice, but also to her occasional deviation from them. He would not hesitate to suggest a mischievous interpretation of the Louisiana Purchase and of the fate of the Red Indians. He would conclude that facts like these are an additional proof for his contention that there cannot be a great and glorious society without the equivalent of the murder of Remus by his brother Romulus. This complication makes it all the more necessary that we should try to reach an adequate understanding of the fundamental issue raised by Machiavelli.

We may seem to have assumed that Machiavelli is the classic exponent of one of the two fundamental alternatives of political thought. We did assume that there are fundamental alternatives, alternatives which are permanent or coeval with man. This assumption is frequently denied today. Many of our contemporaries are of the opinion that there are no permanent problems and hence no permanent alternatives. They would argue that precisely Machiavelli's teaching offers ample proof for their denial of the existence of permanent problems: Machiavelli's problem is a novel problem; it is fundamentally different from the problem with which earlier political philosophy was concerned. This argument, properly elaborated, has some weight. But stated baldly, it proves merely that the permanent problems are not as easily accessible as some people believe, or that not all political philosophers face the permanent problems. (pp. 13-14)

> *Leo Strauss, in his* Thoughts on Machiavelli, *1958. Reprint by The University of Chicago Press, 1978, 348 p.*

CONOR CRUISE O'BRIEN   (lecture date 1969)

[A politician, historian, and critic, O'Brien served as the Irish representative to the United Nations from 1955 to 1961 and has since held positions in the Irish government and in academia. He has written numerous studies of Irish history, of the United Nations, and of modern politics, and his works are often praised for their iconoclasm as well as their insight. Although O'Brien has concentrated primarily on political and historical matters, his literary opinions are also highly esteemed, and he has written important studies of Catholic writers and the influence of politics on literature. In the following excerpt from a 1969 lecture, he considers Machiavelli's purposes in writing The Prince.*]*

It was *The Prince* above all [the works of Machiavelli] that captured the imagination of men and of rulers, and in *The Prince* what held the attention was the emphasis on the need for the ruler to know how to use deception and cruelty. There was a recklessness, calculated or not, in the candour of his language. Had he consistently put 'diplomacy' or 'subtlety' in place of 'deception' and 'severity' or 'firmness' in place of 'cruelty', and been a little less free with his examples, rulers would have understood him quite as well, and probably esteemed him more. And it was, after all, for rulers that he wrote. Or was it? Certainly, at one level, *The Prince*—composed, of course, after the fall of the Florentine Republic and Machiavelli's loss of his job as Secretary to the Republic—is a sort of prospectus, or self-advertisement, bringing the brilliance, experience, expertise and flexibility of the jobless Machiavelli to the attention of the new masters of Florence. It conveyed a point which needed, for that purpose, to be conveyed: that the former Secretary, under the Republic, was not bigoted in his attachment to any one form of government, and could be a useful servant to a despot.

Yet, if considered only in this light, *The Prince* is not a flattering reflection of the cleverness of a man wishing to advertise his cleverness. Something of the dry tone, the insider's nod-as-good-as-a-wink style of his friend Guicciardini, or, alternatively, something like the ponderous and ostentatious scientific armour worn by his cautious and ungrateful emulator, Hobbes, might well have recommended him, for judgment or

learning, to those in power in Florence and in Rome. Instead he offers them this all-too-readable book, which is both too short and far too long; this alarming squib, with its frequent loud bangs, and its fierce light in all the wrong places. And all this praise of Cesare Borgia! Not only did Cesare Borgia belong to a most unpopular category—that of *dead* tyrants—but he was remembered, not only for his cruelty and bad faith, but for his failure, or rather his spectacular ruin. Men remembered him, abject and on his knees before his enemies, cursing his own dead father in an attempt to avoid his responsibilities. Who needed him, and who needed to be known as the employer of a man who was known to have praised him? Yet, here is Machiavelli, like a peddler, thrusting on one in public this open trayful of the dirty tricks of this extinct villain!

It was as if in our own day someone should seek to win the favour of President Nixon by writing a treatise in praise of the late Al Capone. If the President genuinely abhorred the gangster then he would also abhor the gangster's eulogist. But, if on the other hand, he secretly recognized that the activities and the necessities of presidents and gangsters have more in common than meets the eye, then he would be all the more resolute in excluding from his presence anyone who insisted on declaring that this was the case, and even that a wise president must, at times, behave like a gangster. Furthermore a prince or president would do well to shun Machiavelli, on Machiavelli's own advice. Machiavelli repeatedly reminds princes of the importance of preserving an appearance of piety. Nothing could be more upsetting to a prince, bent on preserving an appearance of piety, than the presence at his side of a person known to hold the opinion that the aspect of piety which it is expedient for a prince to preserve is its *appearance*.

Altogether a self-defeating piece of work, in so far as its object was to restore its author to favour. (pp. 17-19)

Everyone hated him, because of a book he had written in the hope of restoring his credit and fortunes! It is a singular outcome for the enterprise of a very clever man, and nobody, so far as I know, ever contested the cleverness of Machiavelli. Clever people, it is said, are especially liable to do silly things. It is a maxim consoling to the stupid, who however are not so stupid as not to be on the watch for the silly things that clever people do, say and—especially—write. Machiavelli, with his masterpiece of indiscretion, left himself wide open. In terms of the career he sought to resume, *The Prince,* is a self-inflicted and fatal wound. It is so because it is not single-minded, not subjected to the limitations of one narrow purpose, not written to please Lorenzo while offending as few other people as possible, in short not, in the vulgar sense, in the least Machiavellian.

Three main general purposes or wishes have been discerned in *The Prince:* a radical one, a patriotic one, and a scientific one. These I now propose to discuss.

The view of Machiavelli as essentially a left-wing figure goes back a long way. The English republican, James Harrington, and to a lesser degree other seventeenth-century republicans, knew their Machiavelli, and liked to quote in particular those passages from the *Discourses* which express a theoretical preference for popular and republican government. More generally, he could be praised, as he was by Gabriel Naudé, for having 'uttered in public the secrets of rulers, the occult frauds and wickedness of state officials, and all those things that in a country's administration should be kept hidden'. Rousseau interpreted *The Prince* as a warning: 'He pretended to instruct kings, instead he taught the people a magnificent lesson. *The*

Prince is a book for republicans.' Karl Marx admired Machiavelli, and in our own time the intellectual leader of Italian communism, Antonio Gramsci, praised him highly in a work composed in the Fascist prison where Gramsci died. (pp. 20-1)

The thesis of Gramsci's *The Modern Prince* is vulnerable at many points—and Prezzolini makes it seem more vulnerable still by picking out the weakest and most extreme bits, thereby doing serious injustice to Gramsci's rich and complex essay. Yet Gramsci is, I believe, closer to the essential truth than Prezzolini, for whom Machiavelli is an aristocrat, a man of 'the few'. It is true that Machiavelli's pessimistic view of man seems to place him philosophically in what is in the main a conservative tradition of thought. Thus he won the approval of T. S. Eliot, who wrote in an essay in *For Lancelot Andrewes*: 'Machiavelli was no fanatic; he merely told the truth about humanity . . . Lord Morley intimates that Machiavelli saw only half of the truth about human nature. What Machiavelli did not see about human nature is the myth of human goodness which for liberal thought replaces divine grace' [see excerpt dated 1927].

Yet, however acceptable Machiavelli's view of human nature may in theory be to a conservative mind—and however grateful Eliot may have been for a supple Florentine stick with which to administer a passing whack to a nineteenth-century liberal— I believe that Machiavelli, and the Machiavelli of *The Prince* in particular, is profoundly uncongenial to practising conservatives in active politics, and irreconcilable to the interests which they seek to protect. This is not because of anything that he may have consciously intended, but because of what he was. The fellow was what the French call a vulgarizer, indeed a vulgar person who wrote—by preference in the vulgar tongue—the sort of thing that should not be left around for the servants to see. He was, in the language of a distinguished White Russian lady, 'not out of the top commode'. In Italian terms, the ex-Secretary brought the language of the Palazzo right out into the Piazza, where it should have no place. Gramsci is surely right in saying that the people—'those who do not know'—*necessarily* have more to learn from Machiavelli than princes have. Where Burke, in the true conservative tradition, would cloak the origins of the state with 'a politic well-wrought veil', and have us 'approach to the faults of the state as to the wounds of a father with pious awe and trembling solicitude', Machiavelli, who seems to have been incapable by nature of experiencing anything resembling awe, simply tears away the veil, or bandage. Rousseau, Marx and Gramsci were perhaps more consistent with the general pattern of their thinking in expressing admiration for Machiavelli than Eliot was. Nietzsche was an enthusiastic Machiavellian, but Nietzsche was not a conservative. He was a reactionary revolutionary. (pp. 22-4)

Machiavelli's patriotism has sometimes been discounted. The famous 'Exhortation to Liberate Italy from the Barbarians' which concludes *The Prince* is sometimes treated as an irrelevance, or excrescence, especially by those who are at pains to emphasize the scientific character of Machiavelli's writing. Today the idea of patriotism, or nationalism, tends to make people uncomfortable or depressed because of our knowledge of what its uninhibited expression has brought and could bring. We feel more at home with the universal, conceptually if not in reality: 'parochial' is a term of abuse, often rather freely used, as when the Chinese are accused of being parochial. It is, I think, this anti-parochial bias—or this honourable and salutary aspiration to transcend nationalism—that tends to blind some commentators on Machiavelli—by no means all—to the

rather obvious fact that the drive behind Machiavelli's political writings is a patriotic one: the burning wish to liberate Italy from the barbarians. This was clearly seen by Eliot—'patriotic passion is the motor of his mind'—but resistance to this conception is stronger today than it was forty years ago. (p. 25)

The grand defence and justification of Machiavelli has always been, and remains, the fact that he founded the scientific study of politics. Others had talked about politics as it ought to be. Machiavelli cleared the cant away, and tried to 'tell it like it was'. He simply told the truth about how power works. If you don't like the heat keep out of the torture-chamber. This theme has often been eloquently developed, and needs no further emphasis. I believe it to be mainly true, but subject to more qualifications than it usually gets. The fact that the initial impetus is not scientific but patriotic does not invalidate the scientific character of the work itself: that point is well covered in Eliot's essay. But the patriotic intent does imply that, where the author has found something which he believes to be true, he will also wish to persuade the reader that it is true: the unscientific temptation to pile on a bit enters here. Machiavelli's wish that his own boss, the Gonfalonier of Florence, Pier Soderini, had a bit more devil in him may well have impelled him to glorify by contrast the banditries of Borgia. There was some romanticism there also. Machiavelli, as Guicciardini rather sourly observed, had an excessive taste 'for violent and extraordinary remedies'. He also wished to shine: one of the objects of *The Prince* was to attract attention, and one of the ways of attracting attention is to shock. It did not turn out to be a good idea, in terms of political rehabilitation but, in terms of literary immortality, it did. It would be wrong to assume, as Ridolfi tends to do, that Machiavelli was indifferent to literary fame, and that his *sole* passion was for active politics. He writes too well for that.

These considerations by no means negate the well-founded claim that Machiavelli is the father of political science. On the contrary they reinforce this: he was a funny kind of father, for a funny kind of science. (pp. 28-9)

What fascinates in Machiavelli is not scientific method but the resourceful and surprising energy of intelligence, and joy in the exercise of intelligence. Sometimes, admittedly, it appears a somewhat primitive joy in the *advantage* which intelligence confers—that pleasure in the idea of pulling the wool over the eyes of the stupid, which is so evident in Machiavelli's comedy, *Mandragola*. But it goes further than that. Even the patriotism of this Florentine is a patriotism of intelligence. The enemy is the barbarian invader, brute force, *furore* against *virtù*. The order which is imagined, passionately desired, and to be encompassed at all costs is a triumph of intelligence, through intelligence and the courage of intelligence; the courage to look steadily at the block and the bloody knife, and try to think steadily through what they mean. This is also revolutionary: the most intelligent of conservatives, Edmund Burke, does not set this kind of value on intelligence: rather he deliberately discounts it, bidding us value prejudice and habit as against it.

We do not care about the victory of Florence, or about revolution in sixteenth-century Italy, much less about a new Roman Empire. It is the imagined order, of which these things were supposed embodiments, that concerns us permanently, and now most pressingly: the victory of imaginative intelligence over brute matter, including the brute matter of our own destructive passions—through the harnessing of these destructive passions themselves—into an order under the control of intelligence. The sixteenth-century Italian gave expression to the passionate need for that victory. Our own age, in the shadow of the apocalypse, knows that victory as the alternative to the disappearance of the species. But where he could still think in local terms, we are required to think in universal terms, not for utopian reasons, but because of the necessities of our situation. 'Pent-up fury' can now no longer be safely exported anywhere. We need to live with it. For that, we have need of the courage, the creative imagination, and the candour which Machiavelli so dazzlingly exemplified. But the point is approaching where we can no longer afford his little bag of tricks. (pp. 30-1)

> Conor Cruise O'Brien, "The Ferocious Wisdom of Machiavelli," in his The Suspecting Glance, Faber & Faber Limited, 1972, pp. 15-31.

MERA J. FLAUMENHAFT (essay date 1978)

[*Flaumenhaft is an American essayist, translator, and educator whose literal translation of* Mandragola *(1981) is considered both scholarly and readable. In the following excerpt, she details Machiavelli's manipulation of the play's audience.*]

In October, 1525, Niccolò Machiavelli wrote to his friend Francesco Guicciardini to explain some difficult passages in the *Mandragola,* passages which had brought Guicciardini great "distress of mind." In this letter, Machiavelli playfully clarifies a colloquial expression by commenting on a mysterious sonnet by a modern writer, Burchiello. Machiavelli says he believes that a person who considers the sonnet well "may continue to stir up our times." He also refers to an ancient authority: "as Titus Livius says in his second decade . . ."— although he is aware that the second decade of Livy's Roman history is not extant. Perhaps his parody of a scholarly analysis of the "light material" (Prologue) of *Mandragola* should caution those who wish to read the play seriously as well as lightly: one must never forget that it is a staged comedy, "a thing to break one's jaws with laughter" (Prologue).

But since Machiavelli has the distinction of being both an eminent playwright and an outstanding thinker apart from his plays, seriously amused readers should ask how the comedies and the political books are related. The letter to Guicciardini, which seems to mock scholarly commentary, should stand as a check against the *distortions* of scholarship. Nevertheless, it should not discourage exploration of the sources, subject, and intent of Machiavelli's most famous and most original play. Indeed, the letter may even direct our attention to some of the central meanings of *Mandragola.* (p. 33)

In form, *Mandragola* resembles ancient Roman comedy. But its plot is to be found in ancient Roman history, the very history Machiavelli claims as his subject in *Discourses on the First Ten Books of Titus Livius,* and which he jokingly connects with *Mandragola* in the letter to Guicciardini quoted above. (p. 37)

Machiavelli tacitly comments on Livy's version of Lucretia— both in his play and in his account of the episode in the *Discourses.* In the latter, he omits all of the passionate outrage found in Livy, and also present in Ovid's account and in Boccaccio's *De Claris Mulieribus.* There is no anger about the violation of a grave Roman matron's honor. Contrary to Machiavelli's later statement, the rape of Lucretia was not even the major cause of the fall of the Roman tyrant. It simply provided the first occasion for Romans to react decisively to continued deprivation of their liberties. . . . In shifting the emphasis, Machiavelli says seriously in the political treatise what

the play depicts comically: chastity like the other moral virtues, is a matter of political prudence, to be judged according to the situation. (p. 44)

Machiavelli's writings openly teach the use of virtue and vice in clever alternation; no deed is ruled out. His play celebrates adultery, and the *Discourses* approve of worse crimes in some circumstances. The founding of Rome, made possibly by fratricide, also required the rapes of Rhea and the Sabine women. Machiavelli does not mention these rapes but one can asume he could justify them if necessary. (p. 45)

Leaving Machiavelli's view of chastity, as seen through his version of the Lucretia story, we turn to a famous Christian commentary on the incident. In *The City of God*, Saint Augustine, upholding the value of chastity, exonerates Lucretia from any blame for having been overcome by Tarquin. Like the authors of the many medieval exempla based on her story, Augustine asserts that a woman's most precious possession is her sexual purity. He recognizes that Lucretia was chaste in intention and was violated against her will. But he does fault her for her characteristic pagan attachment to worldly honor. Christian women, similarly violated, would suffer patiently and would neither postpone nor pursue death to preserve their reputations. . . . Machiavelli's Lucrezia begins as a Christian version of Livy's idealized Roman matron. She abandons the chastity of her forbear, but shares her pagan concern for honor. She lives to enjoy continued sexual infidelities with an untroubled conscience, but is careful to preserve her reputation, that is, the *appearance* of honor, as well. While both imitating and revising the Roman example, Machiavelli thoroughly rejects the Christian view.

Paul and Augustine preach the moral virtue of chastity because powerful sexual attractions, and even marriage, distract the Christian's attention from his primary concern with God and the eternal afterlife. If, to avoid worse distractions, one must marry, the marriage must be chaste. In a theology whose central notion is Love, deviation and failure are aptly described as fornication and adultery. The great Christian poets whom Machiavelli's contemporaries revered depict love for a woman as an image of the divine love to which man's soul aspires. Dante's Beatrice is unattainable except in the life hereafter, and even there she is a temporary stop on the way to a Love which no longer desires. This Christian view, reinforced with Renaissance Platonism, emerges as the ideal courtly love in *The Book of the Courtier.* The formulation is given after strict injunctions to faithfulness of wives to husbands, no matter how badly matched two partners are, and after rejections of deceit in courtship. . . . Machiavelli's remedy is a direct attack on the views which come together in *The Courtier.* Boldly, he introduces Callimaco as an outstanding example of "courtesy [*gentilezza*]." But the object of Callimaco's love is only a beautiful and virtuous woman. There is no indication that she represents anything more than that; he never speaks of her as the embodiment of a perfect ideal. Concentrating on the "things of the world," Machiavelli abandons the quest for the City of God to speak about cities of men as they are, not as they ought to be. He follows Boccaccio's example in another "new" genre, and exalts the natural and present pleasures of sex. He recognizes that most men must abide by sexual regulations as a means to avoid th related evils of striving and strife. Thus, the Romans were wise to forbid mere mortals to indulge in the philanderings of Jupiter, and Moses' Decalogue prudently included a prohibition against adultery. But Machiavelli's play shows that, if one can indulge one's sexual desires secretly and with impunity, and even satisfy the desires of others in doing so, there is nothing inherently wrong with lust: purity is not a prime value for men or women (pp. 45-7)

Under the guise of Christian piety [Timoteo, in **Mandragola,**] teaches the road to hell. But in Machiavelli's play neither the Frate's flock nor the Florentine audience to whom this road is shown is counselled to avoid it. In fact, like many of Machiavelli's other works, the play does not seriously dwell on the existence of hell—or of sin, conscience, or immortal souls. Timoteo's traditional Christian authority is depicted as serving private and profane aims contrary to traditional Christian beliefs. He is initially described as an "ill-living friar [*frate mal vissuto*]"; an audience would expect him to resemble the hypocritical friars so often condemned in Renaissance literature. But as the play progresses, the "ends" of his participation in the conspiracy are repeatedly referred to as *"beni."* The good is now synonymous with the advantageous. By redefining "the good," Machiavelli's play rejects the Christian notion that "an evil man out of his evil treasure" will always bring forth evil. (p. 48)

Here, as elsewhere, Machiavelli indicates that the virtues, as taught by Christianity, appeal to and cultivate the feminine in human nature. To Machiavelli, those like the friars, who might be said to have "made themselves eunuchs for the sake of the kingdom of heaven," are no different from women. Christian virtue thrives on peace and indoors activities, and teaches brotherhood and submissive obedience to authority. The strife that arises in modern times, like that mentioned in the play between Christians and Turks, or between Florence and France over Papal alliances, is between conflicting religious parties. It may be especially fierce and bloody, but it is carried out in the name at least of future peace and love. Machiavelli sees these aims as unattainable and regards attempts to achieve them as likely to produce even worse disorders than the pre-Christian world endured. In place of this effeminate, even impotent, humane notion of human virtue and the evils it gives rise to, Machiavelli would substitute the vigorous *"antica virtù"* that he admires in the Romans. He would like to see this *virtù*— with all the implications of virility in its Latin root—born anew in his city. This renaissance would be accompanied by an ardent love of liberty and independence, and by the ability to defend oneself and one's domain. In this renewal, the virtues taught by religion and treasured by the common people, especially women, would or would not be employed by strong men, according to their aims and circumstances. (pp. 48-9)

Timoteo, too, combines worldy *virtù* with Christianity. We *know* that his miracles are man-made. Like *mandragola,* they are contrived by astute men to manipulate beliefs, and thus events, as they desire. Just as Callimaco's "remedy" works only because Nicia has "faith" in him, the Frate's miracles work because of his ability to inspire belief, faith, and trust. The connection between the success of "miracles" and the ability of the people involved is nicely presented in **Clizia.** At one point, Sofronia's credulous husband refers to the characters of **Mandragola** and to Timoteo's success when he prayed that Lucrezia might have a child. Sofronia, who prays for a miracle on her own behalf and then manipulates her husband's beliefs to insure that it occurs, knows how the Frate works miracles. Like other prudent and competent people in Machiavelli's works, he relies only on himself. (p. 50)

From his first appearance, to the last scene of the play, Timoteo is depicted in the act of receiving money. The Frate's desire for private wealth is not emphasized, for reasons discussed

below, but the likely abuse of the responsibility to collect money for others is evident to Machiavelli, who repeatedly refers to the prominent place of greed in human nature. He is deeply critical of teachings and institutions which do little to mitigate the evils of human nature while ineffectively exhorting men to purify themselves in anticipation of an afterlife. The Frate's position shows what Machiavelli sees as a tension between prescriptions of otherworldliness and poverty on the one hand, and the injunction to minister to one's flock on the other. He also thinks that "love of money" need not be the "root of all evils." The Frate's aim is clearly money, but in this play its use is not specified. Timoteo's continuing personal "good" depends on the "good" of his parishioners, and so he aims at a Machiavellian arrangement of mutual self-interest: some of the money *will* be used to maintain belief by acts of charity. Thus Machiavelli suggests that Timoteo's "love of money" may result in some "goods,"—though not in Paul's sense— as well as evils. The same would be even more true of unfettered political leaders in uncorrupt states. While avoiding the amassing of private fortunes and the concomitant growth of faction, luxury, and indolence, a prudent leader *can* guide his state to glory and power by the judicious management of money and men's love for it. (pp. 53-4)

Those who believe that Machiavelli was a believing Christian will question the identification of Timoteo with his creator. Such readers might protest that the distortions of religion by a stage character are not Machiavelli's and that the author is attacking only institutional corruption and not the principles of the religion itself. They might remind us that thoughtful readers of dramatic dialogue always assume that no character is speaking for the author; relaxing this assumption would be like attributing to Molière the casuistic blasphemies of Tartuffe, something Molière goes to great lengths to deny in his defensive and moralistc preface to that play. But, as we have seen, Machiavelli is curiously unassertive about the conventional moral lessons to be drawn from this play. He does not claim—because he cannot—as Molière does, that he has removed all that might confuse good with evil. (p. 55)

Like the Platonic Socrates and like Saint Paul, Machiavelli is, in his political writings, self-conscious and explicit about his relationship to the young. His aim is to substitute his teachings of "new modes and orders" for the teachings of earlier writers. **The Prince** and the **Discourses** are written treatises. Although they differ in form, magnitude and emphasis, they are alike in that they are books with public subjects which are addressed to readers who will study them privately. (p. 56)

Mandragola differs from the treatises in being a publicly presented work with a private subject. The hostile Prologue, as Guicciardini suggested, says more about the author than about his audience, and cannot be considered a dedication. But the identity of this audience is of the utmost importance in understanding Machiavelli's intent. Insofar as **Mandragola** has the same aim as the political writings, it too is addressed to the young, to those who are not yet fully formed. Machiavelli's audience is composed of young gentlemen, like Buondelmonte and Rucellai of the **Discourses,** who frequented the social and cultural gatherings in the courts and great houses of Italian cities. In Urbino they participated in soirées of the sort depicted in Castiglione's *Courtier;* in Florence they gathered for discussions with Marsilio Ficino in the court of Lorenzo de' Medici or, more recently with Machiavelli himself in the Rucellai gardens. And they attended productions of Roman and contemporary plays like those patronized by the Duke of Ferrara, or presented at various celebrations, like the wedding of Lucrezia Borgia.

Mandragola is not intended directly to reach the public at large. But the particular coterie to whom the play is addressed is one whose attitudes and future actions will have the greatest effect on the wider community. For these elite young gentlemen are the future princes, or in the right circumstances, the future republican leaders of Italy. The circumstances under which Machiavelli wrote make all his writings ''political'' events. What he says must always be considered in the context of what he *could* say. It is thus necessary to pay the utmost attention to the sources to whom he attributes his teachings, that is, to the dramatic ''characters'' in his political books. The genre of *Mandragola* makes it the most public of his attempts to teach the young. It also permits Machiavelli to say everything, for in a drama, the author himself says nothing.

Machiavelli's concern with the young is especially evident in *The Art of War,* which should be considered with *Mandragola.* Like the play, it is a dialogue in which the author never speaks. These two ''dramatic'' works are vehicles for the same principles Machiavelli sets forth in the political books, but their forms make these teachings more palatable, and hence, more publishable. In the lightest and in the gravest pursuits the core of Machiavelli's teachings about justice is commonly acknowledged: all's fair in love and war. In the political books, not published during the author's lifetime, we learn that the true prince is as self-serving as a lover and as ruthless as a military *capitano.*

The Art of War is a technical handbook; its comments on Christianity, justice, and leadership are absorbed as the reader pores over military strategems. The dialogue is clearly concerned with the young. Old Fabrizio Colonna converses in the Rucellai gardens with elite young men who will learn from him to revive ancient military practices. Like Machiavelli, Fabrizio won't live to see the enterprise through. The youngest questioner wishes to see the imagined army in action. Fabrizio's exchanges with him seem to parody Socrates' discussions with other young men about an imagined city: Fabrizio's projections are realizable.

The Art of War, like *Mandragola,* makes clear that love is an activity inferior to war. Cosimo Rucellai wrote love poems until Fortune would lead him to ''higher activities.'' The form of the dialogue seems to parallel that of Boccaccio's *Decameron:* in a ravaged and suffering Italy worthy young people retire to a garden for conversation, taking turns at ''absolute power.'' Machiavelli's version replaces the theme of love with that of war. There are no women in the Rucellai gardens, and the consolations of love are replaced by the remedy of military *virtù.* (pp. 56-8)

Readers of the *Discourses* know that Machiavelli thought carefully about what might now be called the ''psychology'' of conspiracies. Readers of *Mandragola* have recognized, in the remarks of Callimaco, Ligurio, and Timoteo, key maxims of Machiavelli's teachings about conspiracy. The early acts of the play depict the formation of the conspiracy as new members are added. In comedy Machiavelli employs an appropriate vehicle for his teachings because comedy often works by effecting a ''conspiracy'' outside the play, as well as within it. Bergson's suggestion that laughter functions as a ''social gesture,'' assumes that members of an audience in a theatre feel a common bond as they identify with some characters on stage and laugh at others: ''laughter always implies a kind of secret free-masonry,

or even complicity with other laughers.'' The nature of the conspiracies which a playwright establishes (1) among the characters, (2) among the spectators, and (3) between the spectators and the characters on stage, is responsible for whether the play will have a conservative or subversive effect on the morality of those spectators. (pp. 60-1)

The tendency to be ''drawn into'' the play is especially strong in intrigue comedies because the spectator is so often invited to identify with a successful *group*, rather than with an outstanding but isolated and doomed individual, as in tragedy. This suggests that comedy is capable of both greater social and moral ''affirmation'' (the spectator vicariously participates in the *group* reconciliation and celebration of accepted values), *and* greater ''subversion'' (the spectator identifies with a *group* that successfuly celebrates its rejection of those values).

Returning now to the play itself, we can see that Machiavelli's views about human nature and politics are responsible for his revisions of the conventional conspiracy plot. These revisions are, in turn, responsible for differences in audience response, and, thus, for the Machiavellian subversion. This is evident in his depiction of the intriguers and their success, and his depiction of the duped—the objects of the intrigue—as well.

In his comic intriguers, Machiavelli makes attractive what would ordinarily be condemned as immoral. Callimaco is young, handsome, vigorous, and intelligent. Macaulay's objections to the comedies of Wycherly and Congreve is apt here, since the writers for the English Restoration stage sometimes used—or abused—some of the same comic elements as Machiavelli. Referring especially to their subversive attitudes towards ''conjugal fidelity,'' Macaulay argues that ''. . . morality is deeply interested in this, that what is immoral shall not be presented to the imagination of the young and susceptible in constant connection with what is attractive.'' ''Conservative'' comedies often present an attractive young hero who embraces immoral schemes to satisfy immoral desires. But, as I shall suggest below, in these comedies our potential sympathy for such actions and passions gradually undergoes a metamorphosis. For example, either the hero's (and our sympathetic) initial fancy or lust is discredited by laughter or punishment, or it is controlled and transformed into a more spiritual and a legally sanctioned love. Neither of these things happens in *Mandragola.*

Machiavelli's conspirators defy a distinction often made in comedies between ''well- or ill-intentioned'' rogues. They most resemble the sympathetic schemers of a plot like that of *Cassina / Clizia.* However, in *Mandragola,* the young dupers are not the rightful opponents of a would-be usurper, but, as I have suggested, the usurpers themselves. Thus, like Volpone and Mosca in Jonson's play, they are underminers of morality. The merging of the two intrigue plots described above and exemplified here by *Cassina* and *Volpone,* leads the audience to approve of Machiavelli's attractive conspirators. There is no conventional ''poetic justice'' in *Mandragola.* According to Machiavelli, justice is not a primary consideration, except insofar as it too might contribute to success. Machiavelli's rogues are eminently successful and thus are never exposed and punished. Their success, as I have suggested, depends on their benefiting others. Thus, although the conspirators are subverters of morality, they are not conventionally vicious, that is, ill-intentioned. If comedy supports morality by making us angry at (or at least contemptuous of) the right things—by sharpening our sense of justice—Machiavelli's comedy deliberately undermines morality. We experience nothing like our desire to see the tripping up of such arch-deceivers as Molière's

Tartuffe, Jonson's Volpone and Mosca, or even more sympathetic deviants like Malvolio or Falstaff. Nor do we feel our initial relish for the intrigue turn to contempt, as we do for Boccaccio's comic (though unstaged) Frate Alberto. The conspiracy succeeds completely and there is no suggestion, like those found repeatedly in Jonson's didactic comedies, that the partners will defeat themselves. (pp. 61-3)

Machiavelli's view of human nature is responsible for differences in our attitudes towards the conventionally *deceived* characters, as well as towards their deceivers. In most "conservative" comedies the former are either virtuous and unjustly abused innocents, or vicious and justly abused rogues. In *Volpone* the victims with whom we sympathize are superhuman personifications named Bonario and Celia. Similar characters often appear in plays whose authors emphasize their moral purpose. Even *The Country Wife* has its Alithea and Harcourt, hardly superhuman, but clearly exemplary by the end of the play. *Mandragola* strikingly lacks characters like these who, however pallid and weak they appear next to Jonson's and Wycherly's able rogues, invite allegiance because they stand for an uncorrupt morality. *Mandragola,* as Robert Heilman remarks, "is sometimes called a satire, but it is hard to see it as such, for it includes no dramatic assertion of an alternative standard which would invite criticism of the mode of life depicted." Once again, the absence of such characters is not surprising in a play by a writer who rejects the traditional exhortations to imitate the superhuman as a standard for human beings. Machiavelli also omits—and in this he resembles Jonson—any characters who are virtuous but also intelligent and witty. Once more this suggests that intelligence means knowing how to be both moral and immoral, depending on the circumstances. (pp. 64-5)

Messer Nicia and Jonson's Corvino both arrange for their wives' adultery and their own cuckolding. But the naturalistic characterization and almost affectionate tone of Machiavelli's play reveal a radical difference between the two comedies. Corvino is depicted as vicious and evil, while Nicia is shown only to be simple and lax; Corvino is punished by the Scrutineo, while Messer Nicia not only escapes notice of the Eight, but is peculiarly rewarded. . . . Lowering our moral expectations or standards makes us judge only in terms of *virtù.* In stage comedy, as in life, it is difficult to feel righteously hostile or vindictive towards people who lack ability. Justice does not require the punishment of stupidity and Machiavelli mutes Nicia's moral shortcomings. Thus, we only laugh at Nicia's simplicity. If ability and aptness to succeed are all that matter, we will support the conspiracy of the able. (pp. 65-6)

There are still other ways in which Machiavelli encourages the acquiescence of the audience in his "new case." In addition to amplifying our complicity in the plot and removing all suggestions that its values are temporary fictions, Machiavelli prepares us to accept his premises by offering more shocking notions in order to get us to accept less shocking ones. We, like Timoteo, are tested by the proposed abortion plan which is then withdrawn. *Mandragola* is substituted for the abortion medicine and, like the Frate, we abandon abortion and accept adultery. However, one might wonder whether, once chastity, conjugal fidelity, honesty, and the other virtues which Machiavelli turns to matters of prudential judgment elsewhere, are reduced to mere "fables," one shouldn't accept the practical arguments Ligurio makes in favor of abortion as well. Given the principles of action and "conscience" articulated in the play, one also wonders whether any but a prudential ar-

gument would stand up against *really* killing a vagrant lute player if this would further the purpose of the conspirators. If the power of *mandragola* were not a fiction, and Callimaco and many others would benefit from one unfortunate sacrifice, Machiavelli's play might seem to sanction such a murder.

But *Mandragola* is effective precisely because it only implies the most unseemly consequences of the action. When the Machiavellian principles are put forth in *The Prince,* readers are shocked and repelled. But comedy, by convention, is permitted to treat the most serious matters lightly. Comedy laughs at everything, and the audience laughs too. The same immoral teachings, now exhibited in the private, as well as the public, realm are less shocking. But, as Machiavelli says in **"Discourse about Our Language,"** the concealed serious lessons of comedy are tasted only after the laughter in the theatre has stopped. In *Mandragola* these new lessons are "underneath" the ancient comic form and come into focus when viewed alongside the ancient historic subject. Machiavelli does well not to call attention, in this play, to the conventional didactic purpose of comedy, because what he has to teach is far from conventional; it is truly "a new case born in this city." In the Prologue, the alienated author says that he hopes "you will be tricked [*ingannate*]" as Lucrezia was. This seems to apply to the ladies in the audience. But by the end we all have been taken in, and by taking us into the plot, the author insures that we have been taken in by his teachings. Machiavelli, the formidable *capitano* in a new campaign against the old teachings, is an articulate "preacher" of the *"verità effettuale'* ["effectual truth"]. As the most eloquent "seducer" in his comedy *Mandragola,* he administers a remedy for the illness of the "present age." (pp. 69-70)

> *Mera J. Flaumenhaft, "The Comic Remedy: Machiavelli's 'Mandragola',"* in Interpretation: A Journal of Political Philosophy, *Vol. 7, No. 2, May, 1978, pp. 33-74.*

SILVIA RUFFO-FIORE   (essay date 1982)

[*In the following excerpt, Ruffo-Fiore presents an overview of Machiavelli's writings.*]

The Art of War was not intended as a technical treatise on how to wage war, but was designed to reform the corrupted civic and military life by stimulating men's wills to initiate change. Machiavelli invokes Roman antiquity in order to teach men and to spur them to achievement. The use of this paradigm, like the elegant expression, latinized phrases and other elements of humanist rhetoric, functions as a meaningful literary device in reforming the real world. The idealized conventional portrayal of ancient, as well as contemporary, princes, republics, and generals is intended to influence the remolding of Italian political and military life. The significance of rhetoric's role in politics and warfare resides in the ethical foundations and educative goals which motivate its use in the renewal of civic aspirations. Both rhetoric and military training were viewed as political instruments, and as such any analysis of Machiavelli's **The Art of War** must consider how his military ideas drew from politics and rhetoric, and how rhetorical methods are used in military analysis. Therefore, while in **The Art of War** Machiavelli eloquently aspires toward a renewal of political autonomy and liberty by a return to Roman military practices, an aspiration consonant with the Florentine humanist tradition, he also presents a pragmatic and technical assessment of the interrelationships of military and political efficacy based upon the direct experience of facts and theoretical reflection on events. In attempting to characterize *The Art of War,* it would be as simplistically misleading to conclude that military considerations are analyzed detached from all other social factors, as it would be to say that in *The Prince* politics is treated as an autonomous activity. The imaginative dimension of Machiavelli's vision of war, as in his vision of politics, helps to explain the fictionalized, caricatured battles, historical anachronism and distortion, and prophetic didacticism.

The preface to *The Art of War* brilliantly portrays this complex synthesis both in its style and thematic content. Machiavelli addresses Lorenzo with the problem of how many have viewed civilian life as being different from military life. In elegantly balanced sentences using compound verbs and typical "either-or" constructions, Machiavelli first outlines the opposing view, why civilian and military life are different, and then defends their complementary nature and at times identity based on a careful examination of ancient ways. To demonstrate that good customs in a well-ordered state must be protected by the military, Machiavelli resorts to the analogy of how the rooms of a splendid, kingly palace ornamented with gems and gold would deteriorate if a roof did not protect them from the rain. In preparing for his point that the low opinion of soldiering results from the corrupt divergence from ancient military custom, Machiavelli employs a series of rhetorical questions emphasizing how lawgivers and military men have recognized the civic responsibility and loyalty which a disciplined military life inculcates. His belief in the possibility of reform founded on a return to ancient forms and methods of excellence derives from his experience and reading, knowledge he does not wish to waste in idleness. (pp. 83-4)

Book I begins by praising the now dead Cosimo Rucellai as a good friend, dedicated citizen, and skillful poet. Although the work focuses on Fabrizio as the main expositor of military principles, Machiavelli's praise of Cosimo establishes a positive attitude toward the character who will function as Fabrizio's principal questioner in Book I. Dramatically, the scene is set for the entire work, the Orti Gardens just after a banquet. The participants, including Zanobi Buondelmonti, Battista della Palla, Luigi Alamanni, Cosimo, and Fabrizio, retire from the summer heat to the shade of some tall trees. Fabrizio questions his host on the names of these trees, Cosimo answering that the modern unfamiliarity with their names is not strange or uncommon, although the ancients would have known their names. This remark provides Fabrizio's lead into the subject of the excellence of the ancients. . . . Realizing how effective a written work can be if it possesses an oral character, Machiavelli announces that he will shift from the narrative style, in which speakers are identified each time with awkward tags, to the straightforward dramatic form, as in a play. By removing himself as an authoritative spokesman, Machiavelli achieves the dramatist's aesthetic distance and allows Fabrizio, a celebrated, heroic *condottiero* ["captain"], to express views which undercut the system he represented and from which he had benefited. The main rhetorical device is the Socratic dialogue, well suited for the humanist propensity to discover the truth about matters open to debate, offering different alternatives or points of view, and not subject to concrete, irrefutable proof. (p. 85)

The rest of Book I deals with the citizen's militia, as opposed to professional or mercenary soldiers, as a solution to Italian military decadence, with the function of the militia in a well-ordered state in peacetime and war, and with the physical and moral criteria for recruitment.

Book II focuses on equipment, training, and battle drills. It compares Greek, Roman, and modern weapons, noting the resemblance between the battle effectiveness of the Greek spear and Swiss pikes. By pointing out their relative defects, Fabrizio demonstrates the superiority of his ideal militia equipped primarily in the manner of the Roman legion. Fabrizio is often inexact about details and telescopes his citation of authorities without distinguishing various historical periods. (pp. 86-7)

The ancients possessed more *virtù* because their republican institutions nurtured the development of many virtuous men, as seen in Europe which had more republics than monarchies, in contrast to Africa and Asia where no republics and only a few monarchies existed. Republics, like Rome, lived under threat of invasion and tyranny; therefore, they promoted military defense out of necessity which in turn generated *virtù.* War can be a positive force preventing foreign incursion and internal apathy. It is difficult to revive good order and discipline once abolished, and the Christian religion, unlike Roman paganism, contributed to this breakdown by promoting values inconsistent with military *virtù.* States often chose to live an indolent life, free from confrontation, struggle, or inconvenience, relying on *fortuna,* rather than contending with it for superiority.

Book III examines in detail the battle actions of an ideal army, demonstrating attack and artillery methods. Luigi Alamanni now becomes Fabrizio's interlocutor. Fabrizio's description of tactics, training, combat, weapons, and organization in this model battle synthesizes the best of ancient and contemporary methods and concretizes the theoretical discussion in the previous books. Machiavelli's contribution to the literature of warfare is partially evident in three specific ways in this remarkable Book: in the adaptation of the Roman legion, in the role of the decisive battle, and in the function of the artillery. (pp. 87-8)

Machiavelli's second contribution is the vivid description of the imaginary battle, which deviates from Vegetius and other sources. As a high point in Machiavelli's reiteration of his persuasive aims and in his emphasis on the role of the decisive confrontation in winning a war, the battle occupies the rhetorical and ideological core of Book III and of the entire work. The two previous books treated the recruitment and training of men to prepare them for military action, and the topics of the subsequent four books deal with marching formations, encampment, and fortifications. The battle description skillfully intertwines dramatic, emotional statements functioning as stirring battle calls, with exceptionally visual and auditory effects heightened by directive tags such as "You see," and "Observe." It is described from the point of view of a strategically positioned observer witnessing the scene from a distance, an experience both Fabrizio and Machiavelli undoubtedly had. Yet while mainly narrative in form, it previews the dramatic skill of the play in the way Machiavelli sustains the effect of actual involvement in the events. The battle is an idealized painting of a military landscape portraying the best tactics known from ancient and contemporary example in their almost mechanistic perfection without any limiting practical considerations. The success on the audience of these rhetorical and persuasive methods is evident in Luigi's responses before and after the description. "Truly, Sir, I imagine this army in such a way that I actually see it and I burn with desire to behold it in action," Luigi excitedly comments. After the description, he responds dumbfounded, "You have won this battle with so much speed that I am completely astonished and so bewildered that I do not believe I could explain it well if any doubt did remain in my mind.'' Fabrizio's intention was to expound on those battle methods which had proved militarily effective, but more importantly to inspire his audience, for the most part nonprofessionals, inexpert in military matters, with the desire to take up arms.

Despite the criticism Machiavelli has received for his apparent deemphasis of the artillery, it is here that he makes his third major contribution in the literature of warfare. The discussion of firearms is initiated by Luigi's inquiry as to why Fabrizio permitted the artillery to shoot only once and retreat quickly. The basis of his argument is the same as that regarding the debilitating effect of Christianity on military *virtù*. Machiavelli focuses on the human factor in war, on the soldiers' intelligence, initiative, and courage, their mental and moral excellence, resolve, and heroism. The attitude toward the artillery, like that toward Christianity, is not one of inherent rejection, but rather of qualified reassessment. Both had reduced the ability to practice *virtù* and undermined the resolute mental state required of the good citizen and dedicated soldier. Machiavelli's attitude toward the artillery and toward Christianity stresses how religious fervor and intelligent use of firearms could enhance and intensify civic and military *virtù*, not replace it. Moreover, his opinion of the artillery is determined by the primitive stage of its development at that time and by its usual ineffectiveness in the open field where hand-to-hand combat prevailed. Despite its drawbacks, Machiavelli acknowledged its demoralizing effects and destructive offensive power which he thought could be countered by the rapidity of a determined infantry and vigorous cavalry. The mechanisms of technological warfare are always viewed, then, within a humanistic context which accounts for the parameters of practical warfare in those times, and Machiavelli does not theoretically speculate on the future of firearms. Machiavelli's military, as well as his political, theories are based on the universality of historical experience and on the psychological consistency of human nature in any age, rather than on isolated, specialized, scientific or technological factors relegated to uninvolved technicians. He succeeded in presenting a nonliterary topic with the rationality and theoretical consistency of the scientist, while allowing war to remain an art which challenged the total creative and cultural capacities of a man and a state.

While Book III describes the military application of the aggressive methods of the lion, Book IV defines the deceptive methods of the fox. With Zanobi as the questioner, it discusses the disposition of the army, the selection of opportune battle sites, the exemplary tactics of Hannibal and Scipio, the strategies of encirclement, surprise, confusion, and how to make use of victory and defeat. The analysis of tactical planning before and after the battle and of the principles of effective military leadership concludes by showing the leader's role in preserving morale through oratory and religion. As examples from past and present history show, an eloquent general can inspire his men in the face of death with the enthusiasm and will to overcome superior military strategy and weaponry.

In Book V Fabrizio , with Zanobi still the questioner, discusses methods of crossing enemy territory, proposing that the army be disposed in the form of a square. He describes methods to counter attacks made from the rear, flanks, or from two or more sides. He demonstrates the necessity of exact maps of enemy territory and the importance of guides and reconnaissance techniques in avoiding ambushes, in fording rivers, in safe marching, in pursuit and escape. He advises on the disbursement of supplies and provisions and on the disposition of booty and pay.

Book VI proposes a new design for the encampment of the model army in the form of a square having wide streets and open spaces. The camp plan, utilizing ancient practices, is invariable wherever it is set up and is like a movable city. (pp. 88-91)

Book VII culminates both Machiavelli's original contributions to the technical side of the art of war and the work's rhetorical intention. A little more than one-half of the book deals with the techniques of besieging and defending cities, explaining how walls, moats, ditches, forts, castles, mining, bastions, and other devices assist or obstruct in a battle for a city. Machiavelli's ideas on fortifications against the artillery, anticipating the proposals he would write a few years later in collaboration with Pietro Navarro on this subject, derive from his direct experience in the Pisa campaigns and at Prato. They reflect how the practical dimension of war coalesces with man's creative capacities in overcoming brute power. (p. 91)

A synthesis of dialectical dialogue between past history and present experience on the one hand, and of an adherence to a traditional literary form on the other characterizes Machiavelli's approach to the study of history as well as his ideas on political and military matters. His two ''historical'' pieces, *The Life of Castruccio Castracani* and *The History of Florence*, reflect the assimilation of his early political and diplomatic experiences both foreign and domestic, his reading of classical models such as Xenophon's *Cyropaedia,* and his humanistic awareness of how his writings related to the well-established genre of rhetorical history. Modern scholars accustomed to the criteria of factual, unbiased, historical accuracy have often rejected Machiavelli's ''untruthful'' approach to history in *The Life* and *The History of Florence,* viewing these works either as compromises of his historical integrity in favor of artistic inspiration, or as written exclusively to patronize the ''court'' favor of the Medici, from whom Machiavelli was supposedly seeking employment after his 1513 dismissal from office. On the other hand, critics of Renaissance humanist historiography have not hesitated to reproach Machiavelli for generally falling short in the practice of that fashionable art, especially when compared to his paradigmatic predecessors.

The Life of Castruccio has suffered from a similarly confusing plurality of critical opinions. Guarino calls it a ''fictionalized biography,'' Prezzolini a ''historical romance''; Ridolfi cannot decide if it is a political or a literary work, at one point saying that Machiavelli superimposed politics and poetry on history. Turri deems it a political romance, Hale ''an historical fantasy,'' Russo a military story, and Voegelin ''a mythical image'' [see excerpt dated 1951].

It is unfortunate that critics should be so preoccupied with classifying Machiavelli's works rather than discovering the various forces and influences which contributed to that distinctively attractive quality in his writing. Although categorization can and is a useful tool in attempting to understand the cultural achievements of any age, the Renaissance period, and Machiavelli's work, are better understood when approached from the point of view of synthesis. His theory and practice of history is an amalgamation of various elements rather than a reproduction or a repudiation of any single one. In assessing his contribution to the development of historical writing, it is more useful to trace the relationship between humanist rhetorical historiography as a theory, tradition, and actual practice and Machiavelli's foreign and domestic political experiences in shaping his method, ideas, and tone in *The Life* and *The History of Florence.* (pp. 96-7)

Several qualities distinguish Machiavelli's view of history. He saw past history in terms of its relevance to the present, often seeming only to consider history as either Roman or modern. In interpreting and evaluating past events and figures, he deduces a perpetual repetitiveness in the historical process which the events of contemporary history verify. The repetitiveness is not identical in quality, since he also documents examples of unrelenting corruption which demonstrate a steady degeneration from the historical pinnacle achieved by Rome. The study of history is useful not only because of its cyclical nature, but also because its spiral decline demonstrates the immutability of man's evilness, the eternally self-interested motives behind human action, and the inevitable decline in man's ability to cope with the human situation. These private ambitions, egoism, and quest for power result from a lack of *virtù* in the life cycle of a state as well as in individual men. In *The Prince* and the *Discourses* Machiavelli presents this same vision of history, but the focus is on how history demonstrates rules and methods of action as *exempla* assuring success to the leaders, while in *The History of Florence* he presents a broad vision of the evolutionary repetitiveness of history and how this repetitiveness reveals recurring patterns. His cyclical-spiral theory of history saves itself from complete cynicism and pessimism by the notion of the possibility of ascent and renewal through the emergence of a political redeemer, another point of contact between *The History* and *The Prince*, where this notion receives its fullest development. The great historical figures which appear in these two works are portrayed as eternal symbols of political action, as paradigms of an immutable historical law, as universally recognizable actors in an apocalyptic drama. (pp. 99-100)

[*The Life of Castruccio*] opens with a statement on how great men often come from a low birth, being abandoned by their parents and exposed to wild beasts. The afflictions of *fortuna* show themselves early in the lives of excellent heroes. Imitating and combining elements from the stories of Moses, and Romulus, and Cyrus, Machiavelli then recounts how Castruccio was found by a widow, Lady Dianora, the sister of Antonio Castracani, a priest. The couple decide to adopt the baby and name him Castruccio. The story tells how the couple hoped the child would follow the priestly vocation, but at age fourteen the boy, already showing a strong individualism, ". . . laid his church books aside and began to cultivate arms." He is then transferred to the house of General Francesco Guinigi, where he trains as a soldier. Guinigi later dies, leaving to Castruccio the custody of his son and the administration of his estate. Although Castruccio had gained everyone's friendship, this increased status caused envy in the people. The narrative recounts Castruccio's encounter with Uguccione della Faggiuola d'Arezzo, tyrant of Pisa. The story emphasizes Castruccio's superior knowledge of military tactics as responsible for his defeat of the Guelfs. Uguccione, for whom Castruccio worked, becomes jealous because Castruccio had taken away his sovereignty, and has him arrested. The Pisans revolt and Uguccione is forced to release Castruccio, who then organizes his supporters and attacks Uguccione. The latter flees and finally dies in Lombardy. Through the use of exemplarism the remainder of the story similarly surveys Castruccio's life by demonstrating how his character, his military expertise, and political maneuvering are revealed in various successful attempts to expand Luccan territory and power. His character portrays many of the qualities Machiavelli had cited in *The Prince* as essential to the successful leader. But as so often occurs with great men, *fortuna* frustrates his quest for ultimate success; at the age of forty-four he became severely ill with a fever resulting from exposure to a wind after a victorious battle and died. His deathbed oration and the long list of sayings Machiavelli attributes to him at the end of the work summarize many of Machiavelli's military and political ideas.

Machiavelli's account of Castruccio obviously cannot be called an accurate historical rendering, as, for example, might be argued for Niccolò Tegrimi's factual biography of Castruccio. Tegrimi presents verifiable facts in his study of the evil effects of tyranny and reveals his sympathy for republicanism, while Machiavelli selects, omits, invents, and exaggerates in the mythographic creation of an artistic, idealized, and imaginary portrait of a legendary hero who might have been the restorer of Italy. Castruccio becomes a mythical prototype for the ideal Renaissance prince whose brilliant *virtù* operates as an ordering force in the chaotic political and military situation. His image and preserved memory is instructive to those in Machiavelli's contemporary Italian and Florentine scene. Although Machiavelli may have only intended to provide his Orti friends with an enticing sample of his abilities to write a history of Florence (Machiavelli does deal with Castruccio later in *The History of Florence,* II), the suggestive implications of his work extend beyond this immediate purpose to interesting points of relationship with his other writings, and even further to a more modern pertinence. (pp. 101-02)

The structure of *The History* is as follows: Book I deals with the general events from the fall of the Roman Empire to 1434 focusing on the theme of decline and corruption; Book II traces the specific internal history of Florence from its origins to the plague of 1348 and the expulsion of the Duke of Athens; Book III, ending in the year 1414 with the death of King Ladislas of Naples and, considered the most distinguished of the whole work, treats the destructive factions and internal struggles in Florence by contrasting them with the constructive, vitalizing role factions played in Roman civil life; Book IV continues the emphasis on Florentine internal affairs up to 1434 when Cosimo dei Medici returned from Exile; Books V, VI, and VII interconnect foreign and domestic affairs in their treatment of the Medici rule in Florence to 1462 and general conditions in Italy and Europe, while Book VIII focuses on Florence under Lorenzo il Magnifico from the Pazzi conspiracy to Lorenzo's death in 1492. In imitation of classical models each of the books opens with an introductory chapter which announces the content of the book and presents general reflections. (p. 103)

Although the *Mandragola* is perhaps the most original play of the Italian Renaissance, it relates to classical and contemporary dramatic sources and traditions, a comparative study of which reveals Machiavelli's innovation and ways in which subsequent dramatists, Continental and English (Shakespeare not excluded), would build on the road he paved. During the fifteenth century a tradition of Latin comedy developed in Italy receiving impetus from the humanist revival of the ancient texts of Plautus and Terence. The discovery of classical texts and early critical commentaries, such as that by the fourth-century Donatus, along with the increased study, editing, translation, and circulation of printed editions resulted in the development of what came to be known as *commedia erudita* ("learned comedy") in the sixteenth century. Its name derived from its erudite recollection of the Latin comic structures of Plautus and Terence, its composition by the humanist *letterati,* and its frequent performance before such literary court circles as Urbino, Ferrara, and Rome. These plays, of which Cardinal Bernardo Dovizi da Bibbiena's (1470-1520) *Calandria* (an adaptation of Plautus' *Menaechimi*) is the most influential, were lively, spontaneous, and satiric representations of the social life of the times. Often they ironically juxtaposed learned, aristocratic views with more simple, popular elements. Basically they imitated classical form, assimilating and adapting classical themes and character types to contemporary and local concerns.

Mandragola imitates classical structure in its simple, direct, unilinear plot organization (*protasis, epitasis,* and *catastrophe,* with *paraskene,* or transition scenes) and its observance of the unities of place and time even before they were formally authenticated in Renaissance critical theory. Yet the play is more remarkable in how it deviates from classical models. Written in Florentine idiomatic prose, it mirrors a localized setting and texture as well as the unique Florentine attitudes and temperament. The language and gestures that might have accompanied it imprint a memorable picture of Renaissance Florentine customs. Machiavelli's insertion of *intermedi*—songs between the acts—also deviates from classical structure, while his thematic exploration of marriage as a sacrament and social institution reflects a new attitude on appropriate dramatic subjects. Finally, in noting Machiavelli's debt to or divergence from traditions, we need to mention that in its cynical characterization, its prose tale narrative form, and in its emphasis on trickery and sensuality, *La mandragola* reverts to Boccaccio's *Decameron.* (pp. 110-11)

In several ways *Clizia* is superior to the *Mandragola.* Its picture of daily urban Florentine life, its markets, pharmacies, househelp, bourgeois values, etc., is more genuine, vivid, and complete, its dialogue imbued with a more subtle sense of the ironic and unknowingly self-revealing. The roles are developed through longer speeches and more extensive exchanges between characters. It boasts several memorable scenes which embody major themes and contribute to its unique effect, as the throwing of lots and Nicomaco's simultaneously cosmic and pathetic account of how he was deceived.

Machiavelli's psychological penetration is revealed in the multileveled moral and ethical implications of *Clizia's* themes. The play's rich texture of themes is expressed by means of an interwoven network of similes and metaphors. While the *Mandragola* uses native Florentine dialect for its unique comic effect, *Clizia* synthesizes that dialect with a variety of poetic imagery giving the play its quality of a true *commedia erudita.* (p. 119)

While the plays have sometimes been studied as dramatic literature with a value and integrity of their own, the most common approach by those who even bother to discuss Machiavelli's poetry is as a tool in interpreting his political writing. A study of the Machiavelli canon affirms how he used his literary skill and imagination for political statement. The literary dimension permeates and illuminates all his writings, and his inspiration came as much from Ovid, Dante, and Petrarch as it did from Livy and Polybius, as is evident from his December 13, 1513, letter to Vettori and from the many allusions to these writers throughout his works. Yet when one turns to his verse after an intense study of his political and historical writings, there is an undeniable disappointment. Machiavelli's poetry is the poetry of political idea and statement rather than the poetry of transcendental vision. Although it possesses the same imaginative scope, universal quality, and verbal power of his prose writings, it lacks the fiery passion, musical rhythm, and inspired visionary odysseys that are associated with Romantic conceptions of poetry. Tusiani has rightly noted that Machiavelli's poetry is different from much of that of his age; however, it may be in this difference that distinguishes his

poetic originality. Just as Machiavelli forged new ground in political writing, so his poetry seems to anticipate and to have more in common with the age of Dryden or Pope when emotion and suggestion were subordinated to reason and statement in poetry and when history and politics were often the primary subjects of memorable poetical treatments. (pp. 120-21)

Silvia Ruffo-Fiore, in her Niccolò Machiavelli, *Twayne Publishers, 1982, 179 p.*

HANNA FENICHEL PITKIN   (essay date 1984)

[*In the following excerpt, Pitkin examines several of Machiavelli's works from the standpoint that although Machiavelli's "themes are political and public, . . . the imagery in which they are expressed is often personal and sexual."*]

Though his explicit concerns are overwhelmingly political and public, Machiavelli's writings show a persistent preoccupation with manhood. What matters for both security and glory, for both individuals and states, is autonomy; and autonomy constantly refers back to psychic and personal concerns. Beginning with the obvious, Machiavelli's most characteristic, central, and frequently invoked concept is that of *virtù,* a term by no means regularly translatable by "virtue," and certainly not equivalent to virtue in the Christian sense. Though it can sometimes mean virtue, *virtù* tends mostly to connote energy, effectiveness, virtuosity. Burckhardt described it as "a union of force and ability, something that can be summed up by force alone, if by force one means human, not mechanical force: will, and therefore force of ability." The word derives from the Latin *virtus,* and thus from *vir,* which means "man." *Virtù* is thus manliness, those qualities found in a "real man." Furthermore, if *virtù* is Machiavelli's favorite quality, *effeminato* (effeminate) is one of his most frequent and scathing epithets. Nothing is more contemptible or more dangerous for a man than to be like a woman or, for that matter, a baby or an animal—that is, passive and dependent.

The themes are political and public, yet the imagery in which they are expressed is often personal and sexual. Political, military, and sexual achievement are somehow merged. Political power and military conquest are eroticized, and eros is treated as a matter of conquest and domination. In Machiavelli's plays, love is discussed in the military and political terms of attack and defense, the rousing of troops, and the mastery of states. The city is a woman and the citizens are her lovers. Commentators often see Italy, in the famous last chapter of *The Prince,* as a woman "beaten, despoiled, lacerated, devastated, subject to every sort of barbarous cruelty and arrogance," who will welcome a rescuing prince as "her redeemer," but also as her lover, "with what gratitude, with what tears!" And of course fortune is explicitly called "a woman," favoring the young, bold, and manly, to be confronted with whatever *virtù* a man can muster.

But what does being a man really mean, and how does one go about it? Machiavelli's writings are deeply divided on these questions, presenting conflicting images of manly autonomy. I shall begin by delineating two such images, one founded mainly in his own political experience, the other in his reading and fantasy about the ancient world: "the fox" and "the forefathers."

At the outset of both of his most important political works, Machiavelli ascribes his knowledge to two sources: "lengthy experience with recent matters" and "continual reading of ancient ones.'' To begin with the former and the vision of manliness to which it gives rise, what can be learned from experience depends of course on the nature of that experience (just as what can be learned from reading depends on the works read). (pp. 25-6)

Within this world, one can discern an ideal that becomes centrally (though not, as will emerge, exclusively) formative of Machiavelli's understanding of politics and autonomy. The ideal is of a manliness aiming not toward the actual, overt rewards of power, but rather toward indirect gratifications: the pleasures of identification with great men, the secret pride of being smarter than they and able to manipulate them.

One way to make that ideal of manliness accessible is through an examination of Machiavelli's greatest play (and the only one that is entirely original), *Mandragola*. It is a bawdy comedy, whose young hero, Callimaco, has lost his heart to the beautiful Lucretia. Unfortunately, she is already married to a foolish and aged lawyer, Nicia. But Callimaco's friend, Ligurio, invents a plot to help him win Lucretia. The marriage is childless, and Nicia desperately wants a son and heir. Ligurio convinces him that his wife will conceive if she drinks a potion of mandrake root, but that the first man to sleep with her after she drinks it will surely die. So Nicia is tricked into letting Callimaco sleep with Lucretia after she drinks the potion. The plot is successful, Lucretia falls in love with Callimaco, and the lovers agree to continue their illicit relationship, and to marry after old Nicia dies. It is a sordid story, without a single really admirable character; yet in the end everyone is, in a sense, better off. Nicia will have an heir, Callimaco and Lucretia have each other. As Ligurio says, contemplating his plan unfolding, ''I believe that good is what does good to the largest number, and with which the highest number are pleased.''

If one were to select one character in this play with whom Machiavelli might best be identified, the choice seems clear enough. It is not, despite the possible pun on his name, Nicia, nor, as one might conventionally suppose, the hero Callimaco. Instead, it is Ligurio, the author of the plot. Ligurio is an erstwhile ''marriage broker'' who has fallen on hard times and taken to ''begging suppers and dinners''; he has become ''a parasite, the darling of Malice.'' Not only are both Ligurio and Machiavelli authors of the play's plot, and both of them negotiators and go-betweens, but the play's prologue stresses the parallel by identifying the playwright as a man now constrained to ''play the servant to such as can wear a better cloak than he,'' writing comedies only because he ''has been cut off from showing other powers with other deeds.'' Like Ligurio, he is on intimate terms with malice, which was ''his earliest art''; he is an expert at ''how to find fault'' and ''does not stand in awe of anybody'' in the Italian-speaking world.

The suggestion that *Mandragola* in some ways parallels *The Prince*—with Machiavelli as counselor in the latter resembling Ligurio in the former—has been made repeatedly by Machiavelli scholars. Like Ligurio, Machiavelli seeks to manipulate the prince into seizing power—for both the prince's glory and the good of Italy. If we were to succeed, the prince would get the actual power just as Callimaco gets the girl: poor despoiled Lady Italy as she appears in the last chapter of *The Prince*, eager to receive him so that on her he may father a new state and perpetuate his name. Machiavelli himself is pimp to the union, rearranging present disorder and conflicting desires in a way that leaves all concerned better off; the real credit should be his.

The point, however, is not establishing the parallel between Ligurio and his creator, so much as exploring its meaning and what it can teach about their shared role or character. One might, for instance, pose this naive question: why would someone creating a fantasy imagine himself in a subordinate role rather than that of the hero who gets the girl? At the close of her night with the hero, Lucretia tells him that she loves him, having been tricked into doing what she would never otherwise have consented to do—tricked by ''your cleverness, my husband's stupidity, my mother's folly, and my confessor's rascality.'' But it was not Callimaco's cleverness that won him access to his lady; actually he isn't very bright. Ligurio is the clever one who deserves the credit, and thus the lady's love. Why, then, does he not take her for himself? Why is he content to serve Callimaco?

Or, to put the question in a different way, instead of calling Callimaco the hero, should one not say the play is thoroughly problematic with respect to heroism? Callimaco gets the material reward, and gets the credit in the heroine's eyes, but Ligurio deserves the credit and receives it in the eyes of the audience. Yet Machiavelli also mocks and abuses Ligurio in the play, calling him a parasite and a glutton. It would not be difficult to read *Mandragola* as an Oedipal tale, like a hundred other bedroom farces in which a foolish old husband is cuckolded. The old man is bested by the young man, his wife becomes the young man's lover. In this vein, one might even suggest that the real point of the young man's victory is symbolic rather than physical—the conquest not of Lucretia but of her husband. Such a reading finds support in the fact that the old man is, like the playwright's own father, a lawyer. But is it not remarkable that in Machiavelli's Oedipal tale it takes *two* young men to do the job? It is as if the hero of this play were split into a matched pair, two halves of a hero, each incomplete without the other: the clever but somehow sexless adviser, agent of the victory, and the physically virile but rather dull advisee. Indeed, Ligurio tells Callimaco that they are (figuratively) of one blood, twins. Is such splitting the price paid for an Oedipal victory in Machiavelli's world?

Perhaps such speculations seem irrelevant and excessively psychological. The more precise question of why Ligurio might be content to serve Callimaco instead of furthering his own cause is addressed explicitly within the play. (pp. 29-32)

Despite the disparaging things said in *Mandragola* about Ligurio, he represents a character type, a pattern of skill and achievement that is familiar and much admired in Machiavelli's world. It is a pattern characteristic of Machiavelli himself in important ways, though never exhausting his aims and ideals as a man. To make this suggestion more plausible, we might tentatively revive the old cliché of national character, as it is treated, for instance, in John Clarke Adams and Paulo Barile's *The Government of Republican Italy*. Opening, as many such texts do, with sections on the Italian land and people, it then lists as one of the ''main characteristics of the Mediterranean culture . . . an inordinate desire to be a *'furbo'* coupled with an obsessive fear of being *'fesso.'''* *Furbo* is described as ''an untranslatable word,'' characterizing Renard the Fox in medieval French stories and Jeha in Arab tales, and meaning something like ''skill in employing ruses that are usually, but not necessarily, dishonest.'' In such a culture, everybody wants to be outstandingly *furbo,* and a man may be scrupulously moral in his relations with family and friends, yet take pride in his ability to cheat someone outside his intimate circle or, better still, to defraud an organization or public agency. . . .

Even small trickery can be a source of pride if it is done with particular skill or against a worthy opponent. "A *furbo* often gets more satisfaction out of taking an unfair advantage in a single business deal than from making an honest profit in a series of deals with the same man."

The counterpart of the desire to be *furbo* is the fear—perfectly reasonable in a society where each is trying to outfox the others—of being a *fesso:* the person whom the *furbo* cheats, someone whose lack of character or ability condemns him to be a victim. The fear of being *fesso*, the textbook adds, "leads to an inordinate amount of mutual suspicion and naturally makes amicable or honest relations . . . exceptional" outside of the immediate family. (pp. 32-3)

Call him the fox, then, after Renard—this *furbo* who runs the show from behind the scenes through his cleverness; who never himself wins the girl or the glory but takes his pleasure in the secret knowledge of his own surpassing foxiness; and whose pride and skill lie in the ability to deceive without being deceived. Cynic and doubter, nobody's fool, inside dopester, master of maneuver, the fox struggles to survive and even to do good in a world where no one can be trusted. The metaphor of the fox is not central in Machiavelli's writing, though it does appear occasionally. . . . [In] *The Prince,* the fox appears in the famous passage asserting that a successful prince must know how to fight corrupt men with the weapons of corruption, to fight animals like an animal when necessary. Since a prince must sometimes

> play the animal well, he chooses among the beasts the fox and the lion, because the lion does not protect himself from traps; the fox does not protect himself from the wolves. The prince must be a fox, therefore, to recognize the traps and a lion to frighten the wolves.

Despite this unequivocal recommendation, much of the rest of the book suggests that Machiavelli intends not for the prince to be a fox himself but for him to employ a foxy counselor (Machiavelli himself is available). The fox is the clever one without overt power or glory. He remains inconspicuous. (p. 34)

The fox prides himself on his ability to see the unsavory truth and on the courage to tell it. But he also prides himself on his ability to dissemble. Is there a conflict here? Perhaps not if he is employed as a diplomat for a government of his choice and in a city he loves, for then the world is divided between friends and (potential) enemies. The diplomat must convey *la verita effettuale* ["the actual truth"] to his superiors and deceive enemies abroad. In modern terms, one might say that diplomacy can provide a relatively stable level of gratification for a fox's conflicting psychological needs, which makes possible a "partially sublimated discharge" of drives and impulses and allows a "corresponding reduction in the warding-off activities of the ego." That is, when employed as a diplomat for a government he supports, a fox can both unmask and dissemble, know when to do each, and achieve both personal satisfaction and external rewards. And so it may have been for Machiavelli: through his diligence and skill, he supported his dependents and served both the Florentine Republic and his friend and leader. (pp. 38-9)

The fox is an underling, and it is characteristic of underlings both to despise and to glorify their masters. They are likely to resent their subordination to "such as can wear a better cloak," and to entertain fantasies of revenge or of displacing the master; but they may also derive gratification from their association with "so great a master," or at least from fantasies of serving some imaginary great master. To be an underling means to endure continual frustration and deprivation, and thus to have continual reason for envy and resentment. The resentment born of frustrated ambition is what makes Ligurio "the darling of Malice," and no doubt it is also what makes "the author" of *Mandragola* so skilled at "finding fault," his "earliest art." But underlings cannot afford too much of such angry feelings, or at least they must learn to contain and disguise them through self-control, and through the safe and indirect devices of humor and wit, paradox and ambiguity.

The device of humor and "playing the fool" can be particularly useful here, as a safe and even rewarding outlet for malice. For the fool, as everyone knows, is exempt from the usual rules of decorum and courtesy; he is not a serious competitor and therefore can say what is forbidden to others: the fool may insult the king and be praised for his wit to boot. Indeed, the court fool's special license is traditionally symbolized by the jester's cap, whose jagged points figure an inverted crown. Machiavelli himself was noted among his friends as a jokester and raconteur, and his writings frequently display a mordant, satirical wit. Commentators often have difficulty deciding when Machiavelli is being serious and when satirical. He himself comments in a letter to a friend by quoting Petrarch: "If sometimes I laugh or sing, I do it because I have just this one way for expressing my anxious sorrow."

Playing the fool, moreover, can lead to better things; it can be a prudent form of self-concealment while one awaits the right time for revenge or even for an open seizure of power. Thus the jester can not only express his anger indirectly in the present, but can also comfort himself with fantasies of later, more direct expressions. (pp. 42-3)

Themes and fantasies of inversion, or reversing convention or established authority, are pervasive in Machiavelli's work, both in its substantive content and in its style. Again and again he takes up an established form, a conventional assumption, a familiar doctrine, only to reverse it. *The Prince* inverts the moralistic outlook of the medieval "mirror of princes" literature it culminates, teaching the opposite of conventional moral precepts: that apparent kindness can turn out to be cruel, that apparent stinginess in a prince amounts to liberality, that the conventional keeping of faith can be a betrayal of public trust. The passage about the lion and the fox already cited appears to be a similar reversal of a passage in Cicero. More generally, Machiavelli often makes use of Christian themes for his own secular or anti-Christian purposes, speaking of "redemption," "rebirth," "sin," all in transmuted form. (p. 43)

The inversion of conventional hierarchies or established rule is also a familiar theme in many of Machiavelli's literary works. In *Belfagor* one finds a kingdom of devils, in [*The Golden Ass*] a kingdom of women ruled by a woman, and in *Mandragola* Ligurio calls Lucretia "fit to rule a kingdom." The rules Machiavelli draws up for a hypothetical "pleasure company" are direct reversals of conventional fashion and manners: no member may tell the truth or speak well of another; the minority is to win in any vote; whoever reveals a secret must do so again within two days or incur "the penalty of always having to do everything backwards.". . . Even more significant, though less obvious, is the role of imitation and inversion in Machiavelli's literary style; he often prefers adapting or reversing in inherited form to following it or creating a new one. Besides *The Prince*, there is his play *Clizia,* essentially a translation of a play by Plautus, though its prologue explicitly reverses the announced theme of the ancient play. *The Art of War* derives its form from Ciceronian dialogue, its content from ancient writers on warfare like Vegetius, yet with a new twist. [*The Golden Ass*] owes its form to Apuleius and Plutarch, and many of its lines play off of Dante. *Mandragola* is probably an inversion of an incident central to Livy's history of Rome. And of course the ***Discourses on Livy*** themselves take the form of a commentary on an ancient authority, though Machiavelli often uses Livy to prove his own, somewhat different doctrines. It is a thoroughly foxy way of both disguising and presenting the self, promoting its goals from behind another ostensible authority; simultaneously serving and assaulting authority, identifying with the master's power and prestige while scheming to manipulate and use him for one's own purposes. The fox may wish to overthrow authority, but it may never come to that, for he adapts for survival in his situation. Whether or not Machiavelli sometimes imagined himself as Cesare Borgia or Brutus, in his life and in his writing he remained an underling, a go-between who transmitted the ideas and adopted the forms of others for his own purposes—an intellectual Ligurio, as it were.

And yet Machiavelli the playwright speaks of Ligurio with contempt. But of course he often speaks of himself with contempt as well, and of those associated with him, those concerning whom he might want to say "we": we Florentines, we Italians, we modern men. "The present age in every way is degenerate," he says, over and over; the Italians have become the "scorn of the world.". . . I and my kind—we are poor, ambitious, cowardly. Perhaps it is only an objective assessment in a list that is, after all, flattering to hardly any European nation. But perhaps it is also a scornful self-assessment by a fox in a world of foxes; as Hale has suggested, Machiavelli's letters indicate "some core of reserve, some disappointment or self-disgust."

If a person, an action, or a pattern of character seems contemptible, that implies the existence of some standard against which it has been measured and found wanting. By what standard might Machiavelli have judged his best skill, his pride and delight, as also a source of shame, a sign of degeneracy or a lack of manhood? That standard is found in Machiavelli's second great source of knowledge, his reading, and particularly his reading in ancient works. (pp. 44-5)

Returning to *Mandragola*, one can now see that Machiavelli has there created a circumscribed world—a world of foxes and their prey, of *furbi* and *fessi*, a world devoid of *virtù*. For that reason, it is a mistake simply to identify *Mandragola* with ***The Prince*** and both with the whole of Machiavelli's teachings, as some commentators do. . . . Social relations in the play are "in essence . . . exploitative." But a world devoid of *virtù* cannot be the political world of Machiavelli's theorizing. He may well have been a fox, but he was not merely a fox. Indeed, the play's prologue says explicitly that the present age is "degenerate" by comparison with "ancient worth [*virtù*]." And it is surely not pure coincidence that the play's heroine, Lucretia, bears the same name as an ancient lady central to the establishment of the Roman Republic, as described by Livy.

The ancient Lucretia, a virtuous wife, kills herself after being raped by one of the sons of the Roman king. Brutus, who had been playing the fool, waiting for his opportunity, uses the occasion to arouse popular indignation against the monarchy, overthrow it, and establish a republic. In both Livy's account and Machiavelli's *Mandragola*, a virtuous wife is sexually conquered. In both, the man who takes her has first heard of her while abroad, in a conversation in which men have boasted competitively about the merits of their women. In both tales,

old and formally legitimate authorities that are substantively inadequate are displaced by new, younger, and better ones. Yet nothing could be more different than the two sexual conquests, the two overthrowings of authority, the "virtues" of the ancient and modern world. In *Mandragola*, the violated wife does not kill herself but happily adapts to an adulterous life; is it for that sensible flexibility that Machiavelli (through Ligurio) calls her "wise" and "fit to rule a kingdom"? A fox would surely mock at a conception of virtue that brings a woman to suicide simply because she has been raped under the threat of death and because her husband's effort to absolve her of blame have failed. Yet the ancient rape of Lucretia led to the transformation of a social world, the birth of a republic of true *virtù*. The modern comic version leads only to the birth of a child, in a world that remains as corrupt as before. Though the cuckolded husband tells Lucretia after her adulterous night that "it's exactly as though you were born a second time," one knows that no regeneration—either Christian or classical—has taken place. *Mandragola* is not a recapitulation of the tale of Lucretia and Brutus in ancient Rome, but a satire on or an inversion of it.

Once again it is ancient Rome that supplies the standard by which modern times and modern people are measured and found wanting. Rome was the culture that invented the concept of *virtus* and best exemplified its pursuit. It was the very model of masculinity and autonomy. As a state, Rome kept itself strong, independent, and healthy; it grew and prospered among states and won its battles. And the Roman citizenry exemplified *virtù* as well, being courageous and public-spirited, and serving in a citizen militia that was sufficiently disciplined and effective to protect their collective autonomy. Here was an uncorrupted community of real men, competent to take care of themselves without being dependent on anyone else, sharing in a fraternal, participatory civic life that made them self-governing. Nor was their public-spiritedness a spineless, deferential uniformity; in their domestic politics, as in their relations abroad, they were strong and manly: fighters. Political conflict—that "fighting by laws" of which only true men are capable—was what made and kept Rome free, healthy, and honorable.

In this respect, Rome stands in marked contrast to modern Florence, where all is weakness and cowardice, privatization and corruption. There is plenty of domestic political conflict, but it is factional, divisive, destructive of power and manliness; it is fighting in the manner of beasts. A world of foxes and their victims is incapable of true manliness or virtuous citizenship, for its members cannot trust each other and cannot genuinely subscribe to any standards or ideals. They are essentially *privatized*—that is, absorbed in their immediate and direct relationships, unable to perceive the larger whole, incapable of sustaining a public, political life. For a public life depends on a living structure of relationships among citizens, relationships that extend beyond the personal and face-to-face to the impersonal, large-scale, and remote. (pp. 46-8)

It will help to recall the special significance that ancient Rome had for Machiavelli's time, and the distinctive character of ancient Roman society, since both are intimately bound up with paternity. The Romans, after all, were not an ideal that Renaissance Italians picked arbitrarily from the catalogue of past greatness. For Machiavelli and his audience, the Romans were literally forefathers. Where Florence stood, the Roman state had once ruled; the ancestors of the men of Florence had been Roman citizens. Rome had founded Florence. To be sure, the questions of exactly who founded Florence, when it was founded, and what relationship the city had to Rome in ancient times are a central and revealing problem for Machiavelli. But the ambiguities and problems arise within an imagery of fathers and children, not as an alternative to this imagery. (p. 49)

All of the qualities of character central to the Roman table of virtues had to do with this original, sacred patriarchal founding and its transmission: *pietas,* which we call piety, but which to the Romans meant reverence for the past and proper submission to ancestors; *gravitas,* the ability to bear the sacred weight of the past, like armor, with courage and self-mastery; *dignitas,* a manner worthy of one's task and station; *constantia,* to guarantee that one never strays or wavers from the ancient path. All of these together make up Roman *virtus:* that quality of stern, serious, strong-minded, courageous manliness that despises pleasure and playfulness, cleaving to duty and strenuous effort. With their strongly patriarchal households and ancestor-oriented religion, this society of soldiers, builders, lawyers, and administrators proves the very model of significant (fore)fatherhood. Often on the verge of being pompous but never frivolous, perhaps stolid but never petty, they were always a little larger than life. Add to this Roman self-conception the Renaissance glorification of all things ancient, and one begins to see how Rome and the ancients might serve as an alternative model of manhood that puts the fox to shame. By comparison with a forefather, a fox is impotent and contemptible; a forefather need not stoop to the weapons of a fox, for he can put his imprint on the world openly and directly.

Yet the model of the forefather is not really a single, coherent image but is deeply divided into two visions of manhood, as much in conflict with each other as with the image of the fox. On the one hand, there is a singular forefather as founder, whose potent generativity transforms beasts into men; on the other hand, there are the forefathers of Roman republican citizenship, the members of a self-governing community who fight by laws. The images differ as much as paternity differs from fraternity, as uniqueness differs from mutuality, as unanimity differs from conflict. (pp. 50-1)

The seemingly exclusively masculine world of Machiavelli's political writings, where men contend in the arena of history, is actually dominated or at least continually threatened from behind the scenes by dimly perceived, haunting feminine figures of overwhelming power. The contest among the men turns out to be, in crucial ways, their shared struggle against that power. The feminine constitutes "the other" for Machiavelli, opposed to manhood and autonomy in all their senses: to maleness, to adulthood, to humaneness, and to politics. (p. 109)

[At] the same time as they are contemptible, foolish, and weak, women also somehow possess mysterious and dangerous powers; they constitute a threat to men, both personally and politically. Looking particularly at Machiavelli's fiction, one might say that these mysterious and dangerous powers seem to be of two distinct kinds, the one corresponding to young or unmarried women or daughters, the other to older women, wives, mothers, matrons. Often the two types of women appear in linked pairs: daughter and mother, servant and queen, or beautiful virgin who is transformed into shrewish wife.

The young women or daughters are, almost without exception, depicted as sex objects, in the proper sense of that term: they are beautiful, desirable as possessions, potentially sources of the greatest pleasure for men. They are somehow simultaneously both virginal or chaste and passionate or potentially capable of sexual abandon. But they are passive, and themselves scarcely persons at all. They have no desires or plans of their own, initiate no deliberate action, are not significant agents in the world. They are objects of the men's desire, conquest, or possession. As desirable objects, however, they do have great "power" of a sort to move and hold men; without meaning to or actually doing anything, they are the central force that makes the plot more forward. Their power is like the power of gold; or, as the priest says in *Mandragola,* "he who deals with them gets profit and vexation together. But it's a fact that there's no honey without flies."

Lucretia, the "heroine" of *Mandragola,* is not totally devoid of personality or characterizations, yet what we learn about her is inconsistent and puzzling. On the one hand, she is the paragon of virtue and chastity and must be so for purposes of the plot, both to make her desirable and to make her inaccessible. Thus her "beauty and manners" are so exemplary that men who hear of her are "spellbound"; she is a "cautious and good" woman, "very chaste and a complete stranger to love dealings." She kneels praying for hours at night and has already successfully defended her virtue against the advances of lecherous friars. Her character is so pure and steadfast that no servant in her house would dare to plot against her or take bribes; her husband is certain she would never consent to any illicit scheme. Indeed, when she hears of Ligurio's plan she objects strenuously to the "sin" and "shame" of it, as well as to the idea of taking an innocent man's life. In short, she is, as Ligurio says, "virtuous, courteous, and fit to rule a kingdom." Yet this paragon of virtue not only turns out to be so malleable in the hands of her foolish husband, wicked mother, and a corrupt priest that she agrees to commit an obvious sin (which may still be within the bounds of credulity) but is transformed after one night with her lover into a resolute and competent adultress who, without any pang of conscience, knows just how to arrange things so that she and her lover may continue to cuckold her husband as long as he lives. As the characterization of a real person, a person in her own right, this is hard to accept. As an account of an object of desire and action whose contradictory characteristics make the plot move forward, however, it makes fairly obvious sense.

This somewhat inconsistent image of the romantic heroine is not, of course, unique to Machiavelli; it is, indeed, a stock image for many comedies. Yet Machiavelli's ambiguity about Lucretia runs deeper than the convention. There is the question, already raised, of her relationship to the ancient, historical Lucretia, suggesting that *Mandragola* plays out as farce, in relation to family life, what Livy relates as heroic tragedy in relation to ancient Roman political life. The modern Lucretia is a paragon of virtue, yet easily corrupted; the ancient one, though she knows that "only my body has been violated. My heart is innocent," nevertheless kills herself as a public example and insists on taking her "punishment." (pp. 110-12)

Hanna Fenichel Pitkin, in her Fortune Is a Woman: Gender and Politics in the Thought of Niccolò Machiavelli, *University of California Press, 1984, 354 p.*

ADDITIONAL BIBLIOGRAPHY

Adams, Robert M. "Machiavelli Now and Here: An Essay for the First World." *The American Scholar* 44, No. 3 (Summer 1975): 365-81.

  Briefly summarizes past reactions to Machiavelli's ideals and determines their validity and significance.

Adeney, Douglas. "Machiavelli and Political Morals." In *Political Thinkers,* edited by David Muschamp, pp. 51-65. London: Macmillan, 1986.
Surveys Machiavelli's major political writings.

Anglo, Sydney. *Machiavelli: A Dissection.* London: Victor Gollancz, 1969, 300 p.
Learned, insightful study of Machiavelli's works.

Aron, Raymond. "Machiavelli and Marx." In his *Politics and History: Selected Essays,* edited and translated by Miriam Bernheim Conant, pp. 87-101. New York: Free Press, 1978.
Characterizes contrasting ways in which Machiavelli and Karl Marx envisioned history and politics.

Borgese, G. A. "Political Creeds and Machiavellian Heresy." *The American Scholar* 9, No. 1 (Winter 1939-40): 31-50.
Examines Machiavelli's tenets within a context of previous and subsequent political philosophies.

Chabod, Federico. *"The Prince"* and "Machiavelli's Method and Style." In his *Machiavelli & the Renaissance,* translated by David Moore, pp. 30-125, pp. 126-48. Cambridge: Harvard University Press, 1960.
Considers *The Prince* within the flow of European and Italian history. Chabod also expounds on Machiavelli's characteristic approaches to his material.

Colish, Marcia L. "Cicero's *De officiis* and Machiavelli's *Prince. The Sixteenth Century Journal* XI, No. 4 (1978): 81-93.
Draws parallels between *The Prince* and Cicero's *De officiis.*

D'Andrea, Antonio. "Machiavelli, Satan, and the Gospel." *Yearbook of Italian Studies* (1971): 156-77.
Claims that in Calvinist orthodoxy lies the origin of the common perception of Machiavelli's alliance with evil.

Feinberg, Barbara Silberdick. "Creativity and the Political Community: The Role of the Law-Giver in the Thought of Plato, Machiavelli and Rousseau." *Western Political Quarterly* XXIII, No. 3 (September 1970): 471-84.
Compares the legislator's function within the societies envisioned by Machiavelli, Plato, and Jean Jacques Rousseau.

Filler, Louis. "Machiavelli for the Millions: Some Notes on Power Structures." In *American Dreams, American Nightmares,* edited by David Madden, pp. 28-44. Carbondale: Southern Illinois University Press, 1970.
Affirms that the "challenge of Machiavelli's best-known principles survived the turbulent events of his era, and reach directly into our own times and affect our own judgments."

Fleisher, Martin, ed. *Machiavelli and the Nature of Political Thought.* New York: Atheneum, 1972, 307 p.
Seven essays on various aspects of Machiavelli's thought, by such essayists as J. G. A. Pocock, Brayton Polka, and Harvey C. Mansfield, Jr.

Friedrich, Carl J. "Machiavelli and Hobbes—Theorists of Political Power." In his *An Introduction to Political Theory: Twelve Lectures at Harvard,* pp. 133-49. New York: Harper & Row, 1967.
Compares the political attitudes of Machiavelli and Thomas Hobbes.

Germino, Dante. "Second Thoughts on Leo Strauss's Machiavelli." *The Journal of Politics* 28, No. 4 (November 1966): 794-817.
Objects to Strauss's conclusion that Machiavelli was essentially evil [see excerpt dated 1958]. Germino suggests that Machiavelli's ambiguities and inconsistencies were not deliberately deceptive but "the result of an authentic inability to make up his mind on some of the great issues of ethics and political theory."

Harbison, E. Harris. "The Intellectual as Social Reformer: Machiavelli and Thomas More." *The Rice Institute Pamphlet* XLIV, No. 3 (October 1957): 1-46.
Contrasts the political experiences and concepts of Machiavelli and Sir Thomas More.

Hexter, J. H. "The Predatory and the Utopian Vision: Machiavelli and More. The Loom of Language and the Fabric of Imperatives: The Case of *Il principe* and *Utopia.*" In his *The Vision of Politics on the Eve of the Reformation: More, Machiavelli, and Seyssel,* pp. 179-203. New York: Basic Books, 1973.
Examines the power of rhetoric in *The Prince* and More's *Utopia.*

Kraft, Joseph. "Truth and Poetry in Machiavelli." *The Journal of Modern History* XXIII, No. 2 (June 1951): 109-21.
Refutes the scientific framework ascribed to Machiavelli's thought.

Major, J. Russell. "The Renaissance Monarchy as Seen by Erasmus, More, Seyssel, and Machiavelli." In *Action and Conviction in Early Modern Europe: Essays in Memory of E. H. Harbison,* edited by Theodore K. Rabb and Jerrold E. Seigel, pp. 17-31. Princeton: Princeton University Press, 1969.
Discusses the chief differences between Machiavelli, More, Desiderius Erasmus, and Claude de Seyssel in their interpretations of monarchal rule.

Mansfield, Harvey C., Jr. *Machiavelli's New Modes and Orders: A Study of the "Discourses on Livy."* Ithaca: Cornell University Press, 1979, 460 p.
Close reading of the *Discourses.*

Maritain, Jacques. "The End of Machiavellianism." In his *The Social and Political Philosophy of Jacques Maritain,* edited by Joseph W. Evans and Leo R. Ward, pp. 292-325. New York: Charles Scribner's Sons, 1955.
Informed condemnation of Machiavelli's thought and influence.

Meyer, Edward. *Machiavelli and the Elizabethan Drama.* 1897. Reprint. New York: Burt Franklin, n.d., 180 p.
Chronicles the demonization of Machiavelli's name and ideas in many works of Elizabethan literature.

Norton, Paul. "Machiavelli and the Modes of Terrorism." *Modern Age* 29, No. 4 (Fall 1985): 304-13.
Affirms that Machiavelli's comments on cruelty, fraud, and conspiracy are fundamental to modern terrorism.

O'Brien, Conor Cruise. "What Exhortation?" *Irish University Review* 1, No. 1 (Autumn 1970): 48-61.
Relates Machiavelli's campaign for Italian self-determination to current issues.

Petre, M. D. "Machiavelli and Modern Statecraft." *The Edinburgh Review* CCXXVI, No. 461 (July 1917): 93-112.
Finds in his subject's ethics "first of all Machiavellianism in the most cold-blooded and inhuman sense of the word; but afterwards the germ and promise of a state-craft inspired by more human and spiritual ideals."

Pocock, J. G. A. "The Medicean Restoration: Machiavelli's *Il Principe*" and "Rome and Venice: Machiavelli's *Discorsi* and *Arte della Guerra.*" In his *The Machiavellian Moment: Florentine Political Thought and the Atlantic Republican Tradition,* pp. 156-82, pp. 183-218. Princeton: Princeton University Press, 1975.
Analyzes three of Machiavelli's principal works in humanistic terms and in relation to medieval and Renaissance political thought.

Praz, Mario. *Machiavelli and the Elizabethans.* n.p., 1928, 49 p.
Focuses on particular interpretations of Machiavellian evil as evidenced in the works of William Shakespeare, Christopher Marlowe, and other Elizabethan writers.

Prezzolini, Giusseppe. "The Kernel of Machiavelli." *National Review* X, No. 13 (8 April 1961): 215-17.
Restates and defends Machiavelli's principles.

————. *Machiavelli.* New York: Noonday Press, 1967, 372 p.
Critical work "based on the concept that Machiavelli's thought cannot be adequately understood solely through a study of his works." Prezzolini contends: "The power of Machiavelli's thought is found in Machiavellianism," that is, in the writings Machiavelli has inspired through the centuries.

Priestley, J. B. "The Italian Scene and Machiavelli." In his *Literature and Western Man,* pp. 10-17. New York: Harper & Brothers, 1960.
    Places Machiavelli spiritually in the Counter-Reformation rather than the Renaissance.

Raab, Felix. *The English Face of Machiavelli: A Changing Interpretation, 1500-1700.* London: Routledge & Kegan Paul, 1964, 306 p.
    Surveys the reception in England of Machiavelli's ideals, from the Tudor age to the Restoration. Raab includes the specific reactions of such prominent individuals as Thomas Hobbes and James Harrington.

Ridolfi, Roberto. *The Life of Niccolò Machiavelli.* Chicago: University of Chicago Press, 1963, 337 p.
    Noncritical biography detailing Machiavelli's life and career.

Rousseau, G. S. "The *Discorsi* of Machiavelli: History and Theory." *Cahiers d'histoire mondaile* IX, No. 1 (1965): 143-61.
    Expósition of the political assumptions upon which Machiavelli's *Discourses* is predicated.

Trevor-Roper, H. R. "Niccolò Machiavelli." In his *Men and Events: Historical Essays,* pp. 61-6. New York: Harper & Brothers, 1957.
    Traces the elements of controversy engendered by Machiavelli's political opinions.

"The Last of Machiavelli?" *The Unpopular Review* XI, No. 21 (January 1919): 56-68.
    Anonymous discussion of the resemblance between Machiavelli's doctrines and some policies of the Kaiser's Imperial German government.

Whitfield, J[ohn] H[umphreys]. *Discourses on Machiavelli.* Cambridge, England: W. Heffer & Sons, 1969, 243 p.
    Critical overview of Machiavelli's canon.

————. Foreword to *Il principe,* by Niccolò Machiavelli, pp. v-xxix. Wakefield, England: S. R. Publishers, 1969.
    Outlines salient points in *The Prince*.

Michel (Eyquem) de Montaigne

1533-1592

French essayist, diarist, and translator.

The inventor of the essay form as a literary genre, Montaigne raised introspection to the level of art in his monumental work *Les essais* (*The Essays*). The French "essai" means an experiment, test, or attempt, and such was Montaigne's intention in his series of essays: to attempt to understand himself and, by extension, the human condition in a series of introspective "experiments." In so doing, Montaigne extended his questioning to the very limits of human knowledge, for throughout *The Essays* runs the thread of thoughtful skepticism that is the trademark of its author, who took for his motto the words "Que sçay-je?" ("What do I know?").

Montaigne was born Michel Eyquem in the district of Périgord in the Gascony region of France. Although his forebears had long been bourgeois traders, in 1477 his great-grandfather had purchased the château of Montaigne along with the right to add the noble title "de Montaigne" to the family name. (Michel was the first to do so.) Little is known of Montaigne's Protestant mother, who is given only cursory mention in *The Essays*. It is his staunchly Catholic father, Pierre Eyquem, who figures prominently in the work and who exerted the greatest influence on the author's early childhood. Pierre Eyquem's innovative child-rearing techniques included sending his son to spend his infancy with peasant godparents so that he might develop a sense of attachment to the lower classes, and insuring that Michel's native language was Latin rather than French by requiring that the entire Eyquem household speak only Latin to the boy until he reached the age of six. At this time Montaigne was sent to the Collège de Guyenne in Bordeaux, where he spent seven years. The particulars of his activities after he left the school are unclear, but it is thought that he studied law, probably in Toulouse. In 1557 Montaigne became a councillor in the parliament of Bordeaux, acquitting his duties competently though unenthusiastically. Here he met and befriended fellow councillor Étienne de La Boétie, the subject of one of Montaigne's most famous and moving essays, "De l'amitié" ("Of Friendship"). La Boétie's death in 1563 was a great shock and a deep sorrow to his friend. A few years later Montaigne married Françoise de La Chassaigne; their marriage (apparently an arranged match) was amicable if not passionate.

Until his middle years, Montaigne was only slightly involved in the literary world: he had arranged the publication of some of La Boétie's writings and his translation of Raimond Sebond's *Theologia naturalis*. Only in 1571 did his literary career begin in earnest. Leaving his law career and retiring to the Montaigne estate (of which he was now lord, his father having died a few years before), Montaigne began the task that occupied him for the remainder of his life: writing *The Essays*. Following the work's first publication in 1580, Montaigne, who was an enthusiastic traveler, embarked on an extensive journey through France, Italy, Switzerland, and Germany, recording his observations and experiences in his *Journal de voyage* (*The Journal of Montaigne's Travels*), which, unlike *The Essays*, was not written for publication. While still traveling, Montaigne was elected mayor of Bordeaux, a position he accepted for two two-year terms. In the last years of his life Montaigne contracted another important friendship, this

one with Marie de Jars de Gournay, whom he met on a trip to Paris in 1588 and whom he called his "fille d'alliance" ("adopted daughter"); it was she who edited and published the posthumous edition of *The Essays*. Suffering from quinsy, Montaigne died at his château at the age of fifty-nine.

The length and complexity of *The Essays* have baffled critical attempts to categorize the work satisfactorily, for in it form and content, subject and style, are so closely interwoven and interdependent that it is difficult to focus on any single aspect of *The Essays* apart from the whole. Hence, a knowledge of the formal arrangement and publication data of *The Essays* is essential to an understanding of the work in its entirety, as Montaigne's method mirrored his purpose. *The Essays* consists of three books of 107 chapters (Montaigne's use of the term "essay" referred to his method and intent, not to his individual chapters), which range in length from a few paragraphs to over a hundred pages, and which treat myriad subjects from the trivial to the profound—Montaigne's attitude toward radishes as well as his feelings about God. Montaigne never considered his essays "finished." Books I and II, first published in 1580, were revised for republication two years later and again for the 1588 edition, which included a third book. The process of revision continued, and the posthumous edition of the three books incorporates Montaigne's further annotations and marginalia.

Attempts to assign some sort of structural, thematic, or stylistic unity to *The Essays,* both within individual essays and among them, have usually proved difficult. The mercurial nature of *The Essays* resists generalities; the only observation that may be made with any certainty is that, despite some exceptions, the essays tend to become longer, less imitative, and more personal as the work progresses. A random selection of essay titles—"Des coches" ("Of Coaches"), "Sur des vers de Virgile" ("On Some Verses of Virgil"), "De la cruauté" ("Of Cruelty")—reveals the remarkable diversity within *The Essays.* The issue of unity is further clouded by the frequent disparity between essay title and essay content: Montaigne's ostensible subject may be completely overshadowed by another topic, either related or unrelated; or the stated subject may serve as but a springboard for Montaigne's real concern; or Montaigne's stated intention may have no discernable relation to the actual essay content at all. In many cases identifying an essay's true subject proves to be extremely challenging, as even among those essays that do correspond to their titles, an orderly progression of thought or clear connection of idea is rare. Similarly, the plethora of subject matter has daunted critical efforts to discover formal or thematic unity among the essays as a whole. While recurring themes and preoccupations have been noted—among them, the dichotomies of mutability and stability and of the public and private realms; the limits of human reason and knowledge—such recurrences fall short of providing a logical, cohesive structure to *The Essays.* Even a chronological unity is sometimes invalid or suspect, as Montaigne published some of the essays in a different order from that in which he wrote them. Montaigne himself said that there is no formal arrangement or imposed order to his book. While it is conceded that *The Essays* possesses no formal unity (at least insofar as that term is commonly employed in literary criticism), yet most critics contend that the work displays an "organic" unity achieved through Montaigne's portrayal of his own personality and its development. This striking aspect of *The Essays* is best summed up by the author himself, who wrote: "Je suis moy-mesmes la matière de mon livre" ("I am myself the subject of my book"). Commentators therefore find no fault with *The Essays'* lack of formal coherence, agreeing that the author's communication of the evolving essence of himself, if it be honest and natural, must preclude the usual strictures of art. As Edward Dowden expressed it: "When Montaigne wanders from his professed theme, why should we quarrel with him? He never wanders from himself, and from humanity which is his true theme."

The truth of Montaigne's claim that he himself is the subject of his book is proved throughout *The Essays.* "For Montaigne," Lewis Thomas commented, "the nearest and most engrossing item in all of Nature is Montaigne." Although decidedly autobiographical, *The Essays* cannot be described as a diary or journal, for Montaigne wrote not a chronological recitation of his deeds but rather recorded his thoughts, ruminations, and impressions, a procedure George Saintsbury called one of "meditative egotism." Montaigne sought to understand himself, the essential Montaigne who existed within his ever-changing thoughts, habits, and emotions. Nearly all critics have found Montaigne's preoccupation with self charming and engrossing (the one notable exception to this assessment, Blaise Pascal, complained that Montaigne "told too many tales and talked too much about himself"); in general, Montaigne's egoism is considered his book's greatest asset.

Commentators assert that beyond Montaigne's egoism lies a higher purpose; believing as he did that he, as one man, man-ifested within himself the quintessential humanity common to all people, Montaigne held that in seeking to understand his individual self, he was examining the universal traits of humanity. This belief is reflected in the style and substance of *The Essays.* As the spontaneous and random record of a man's beliefs and impressions as they occur and as they develop, *The Essays* has been described as an experiment in becoming rather than being. This evolutionary aspect of the work is both reflected in and augmented by the style Montaigne employed. The essays are discursive and digressive: Montaigne's approach is informal, meandering, as he moved from one subject to another, following a train of thought or chasing an association of ideas. This relaxed style, spiced with the idiom and dialect of his native Gascony, is conducive to the general atmosphere of *The Essays,* which scholars call one of friendly intimacy. Approximating as they do a genial conversational style—one which is, in J. B. Priestley's words, "as easy and flexible and racy as good talk"—the essays have been applauded for their simplicity of speech and directness of sentiment. Though often circuitous in route, they are forthcoming in honesty; indeed, Montaigne's experiment as an introspective essayist required sincerity, and critics believe he achieved it. Wrote Montaigne in his preface, "C'est un livre de bonne foy" ("This is a sincere book"), and with this assessment commentators concur. Montaigne's rambling, intimate style and unpretentious manner foster a sense of camaraderie between writer and reader that largely accounts for the work's success. Montaigne, it is said, is ordinary, and while such a criticism might be derogatory when applied to another author, with regard to Montaigne it is high praise. Readers of Montaigne cite a sense of recognition in reading *The Essays,* a feeling of connection and a realization of kinship with the author. As André Gide noted, "the human being he discovers—and uncovers—is so genuine, so true, that in him every reader of the *Essais* recognizes himself." "I am a man, and nothing human is alien to me," wrote Montaigne, and critics respond that as this is so, so nothing in *The Essays* is alien to humanity, and so Montaigne's self-exploration transcends his individuality to encompass all of humanity. According to Charles Augustin Sainte-Beuve: "There is something of Montaigne in every one of us." This accounts for the high esteem accorded the essays—an esteem that a mere introspective journal would be unlikely to command.

Neither Montaigne's position as spokesman for ordinary humanity nor his disarming homeliness precludes intellectualism in *The Essays.* On the contrary, as Montaigne's exploration of self embraced an exploration of the human condition, so *The Essays* is replete with its author's philosophical, political, and social concerns. A few critics disagree on this point, denying Montaigne status as a serious thinker, among them G. L. Strachey, who declared that Montaigne's mind "was devoid both of the method and of the force necessary for the pursuit and discovery of really significant intellectual truths." However, most commentators concur that Montaigne's philosophical speculations, while not amounting to a doctrine of systematic thought, nevertheless exist and are important. Attempts have been made to categorize Montaigne's philosophical thought as it evolved throughout the essays. Perhaps the most thorough research done in this area has been undertaken by Pierre Villey, a prominent Montaigne scholar whose many critical studies of the essayist have unfortunately not to date been translated into English. In his *Les sources et l'evolution des Essais de Montaigne* (1908), Villey argued that Montaigne's philosophy evolved from stoicism in the first book, to skepticism in the second, to a reliance on nature and an increasing epicureanism in the third book. While Villey's categories are still considered useful indicators of the main thrust of thought in *The Essays*, his sequential analysis is no longer accepted as entirely valid, as recent critics have discovered that while these elements of philosophical thought are decidedly present in the work, their pattern is not so easily determined. It appears that Montaigne tested and explored philosophy as he tested and explored himself. Classical and contemporary quotations are liberally sprinkled throughout *The Essays*, testifying to Montaigne's wide range of knowledge, and scholars have traced in his work the influence of a wide array of thinkers, including Socrates, Seneca, Aristotle, Plutarch, and the Stoics. But by far the most consistent and omnipresent element of Montaigne's thought is his Pyrronism, or radical skepticism, expressed in his motto, "Que sçay-je?" Montaigne brought his scepticism to bear on nearly every topic that concerned him. As Francis Thompson described it: "He proves—*i.e.*, tests—all things. His criticism is a dissolving acid. But when it comes to deciding what is finally true, he prefers to play with a number of possibilities, and leave the reader to decide."

Because of Montaigne's omnipresent skepticism, critics frequently debate the nature of the principles he actually embraced, particularly concerning politics and religion, for these were important subjects in his time: sixteenth-century France was wracked by religious wars between the government-sanctioned Catholics and the Protestant reformers known as Huguenots. Critics have characterized Montaigne as a political conservative for his desire to preserve the status quo, even where repressive, and as a liberal for his tolerance and open-mindedness. He has been considered a devoutly orthodox Catholic, a humanist, or even, according to Sainte-Beuve, one who evidences "consistent paganism." This confusion is exemplified by the fact that although in Montaigne's lifetime *The Essays* was virtually untouched by the rigid papal censorship that then prevailed, in the early eighteenth century the work was listed in the Papal Index of Prohibited Books. Perhaps there can be no definitive conclusions concerning such questions, for in a real sense, the very exercise of writing *The Essays* constitutes an attempt to understand and define the limits of human knowledge, as Montaigne sought to discover in himself and in his contact with the world what he could know and how he could know it.

Ultimately, many conclude, it is not Montaigne's answers that matter, but his questions; not his precise philosophy, but his method of exploring it; not the conclusions he drew but the self-examination he essayed. "These essays," wrote Virginia Woolf, "are an attempt to communicate a soul." That attempt has attracted and retained appreciative readers from the sixteenth century to the twentieth. Traces of Montaigne's influence have been cited in countless thinkers and writers—among them, René Descartes, Friedrich Nietzsche, William Shakespeare, and the long tradition of the great English essayists. The enduring appeal of Montaigne's *Essays* lies in its questioning introspection and the intimacy created between author and reader, an intimacy which Ralph Waldo Emerson felt in reading the book and described thus: "It seemed to me as if I had myself written the book, in some former life, so sincerely it spoke to my thought and experience."

PRINCIPAL WORKS

La théologie naturelle . . . [translator] (essay) 1569
Les essais de Messire Michel Seigneur de Montaigne (essays) 1580; revised editions, 1582, 1588, 1595
 [*The Essayes; or, Morall, Politike, and Millitarie Discourses of Lo: Michaell de Montaigne*, 1603; also published as *The Essays of Michael Seigneur de Montaigne*, 1685-86]

Journal de voyage de Michel de Montaigne en Italie par la Suisse et l'Allemagne en 1580 et 1581 (travel journal) 1774
 [*The Journal of Montaigne's Travels*, 1903]
The Complete Works of Montaigne (essays, travel journal, and letters) 1957

MICHEL DE MONTAIGNE (essay date 1580-95)

[*The following excerpt is a pastiche of Montaigne's comments, sprinkled throughout* The Essays, *on his work's design and method. The superscript letters in the text indicate which edition of* The Essays *first included that section: A = 1580; B = 1588; C = 1595.*]

[A]This book was written in good faith, reader. It warns you from the outset that in it I have set myself no goal but a domestic and private one. I have had no thought of serving either you or my own glory. My powers are inadequate for such a purpose. I have dedicated it to the private convenience of my relatives and friends, so that when they have lost me (as soon they must), they may recover here some features of my habits and temperament, and by this means keep the knowledge they have had of me more complete and alive.

If I had written to seek the world's favor, I should have bedecked myself better, and should present myself in a studied posture. I want to be seen here in my simple, natural, ordinary fashion, without straining or artifice; for it is myself that I portray. My defects will here be read to the life, and also my natural form, as far as respect for the public has allowed. Had I been placed among those nations which are said to live still in the sweet freedom of nature's first laws, I assure you I should very gladly have portrayed myself here entire and wholly naked.

Thus, reader, I am myself the matter of my book; you would be unreasonable to spend your leisure on so frivolous and vain a subject. (p. 2)

[A]Judgment is a tool to use on all subjects, and comes in everywhere. Therefore in the tests ["essais," in Montaigne's original French] that I make of it here, I use every sort of occasion. If it is a subject I do not understand at all, even on that I essay my judgment, sounding the ford from a good distance; and then, finding it too deep for my height, I stick to the bank. And this acknowledgment that I cannot cross over is a token of its action, indeed one of those it is most proud of. Sometimes in a vain and nonexistent subject I try to see if it will find the wherewithal to give it body, prop it up, and support it. Sometimes I lead it to a noble and well-worn subject in which it has nothing original to discover, the road being so beaten that it can walk only in others' footsteps. There it plays its part by choosing the way that seems best to it, and of a thousand paths it says that this one or that was the most wisely chosen.

I take the first subject that chance offers. They are all equally good to me. And I never plan to develop them completely. [C]For I do not see the whole of anything; nor do those who promise to show it to us. Of a hundred members and faces that each thing has, I take one, sometimes only to lick it, sometimes to brush the surface, sometimes to pinch it to the bone. I give it a stab, not as wide but as deep as I know how. And most often I like to take them from some unaccustomed point of view. I would venture to treat some matter thoroughly, if I knew myself less well. Scattering a word here, there another, samples separated from their context, dispersed, without a plan and without a promise, I am not bound to make something of them or to adhere to them myself without varying when I please and giving myself up to doubt and uncertainty and my ruling quality, which is ignorance. (p. 219)

Now as Pliny says, each man is a good education to himself, provided he has the capacity to spy on himself from close up. What I write here is not my teaching, but my study; it is not a lesson for others, but for me.

CAnd yet it should not be held against me if I publish what I write. What is useful to me may also by accident be useful to another. Moreover, I am not spoiling anything, I am using only what is mine. And if I play the fool, it is at my expense and without harm to anyone. For it is a folly that will die with me, and will have no consequences. We have heard of only two or three ancients who opened up this road, and even of them we cannot say whether their manner in the least resembled mine, since we know only their names. No one since has followed their lead. It is a thorny undertaking, and more so than it seems, to follow a movement so wandering as that of our mind, to penetrate the opaque depths of its innermost folds, to pick out and immobilize the innumerable flutterings that agitate it. And it is a new and extraordinary amusement, which withdraws us from the ordinary occupations of the world, yes, even from those most recommended.

It is many years now that I have had only myself as object of my thoughts, that I have been examining and studying only myself; and if I study anything else, it is in order promptly to apply it to myself, or rather within myself. And it does not seem to me that I am making a mistake if—as is done in the other sciences, which are incomparably less useful—I impart what I have learned in this one, though I am hardly satisfied with the progress I have made in it. There is no description equal in difficulty, or certainly in usefulness, to the description of oneself. Even so one must spruce up, even so one must present oneself in an orderly arrangement, if one would go out in public. Now, I am constantly adorning myself, for I am constantly describing myself. (pp. 272-73)

My trade and my art is living. He who forbids me to speak about it according to my sense, experience, and practice, let him order the architect to speak of buildings not according to himself but according to his neighbor; according to another man's knowledge, not according to his own. If it is vainglory for a man himself to publish his own merits, why doesn't Cicero proclaim the eloquence of Hortensius, Hortensius that of Cicero?

Perhaps they mean that I should testify about myself by works and deeds, not by bare words. What I chiefly portray is my cogitations, a shapeless subject that does not lend itself to expression in actions. It is all I can do to couch my thoughts in this airy medium of words. Some of the wisest and most devout men have lived avoiding all noticeable actions. My actions would tell more about fortune than about me. They bear witness to their own part, not to mine, unless it be by conjecture and without certainty: they are samples which display only details. I expose myself entire: my portrait is a cadaver on which the veins, the muscles, and the tendons appear at a glance, each part in its place. One part of what I was produced by a cough, another by a pallor or a palpitation of the heart—in any case dubiously. It is not my deeds that I write down; it is myself, it is my essence. (p. 274)

CI know well that very few people will frown at the license of my writings who do not have more to frown at in the license of their thoughts. I conform well to their hearts, but I offend their eyes. It is a well-ordered humor that criticizes Plato's writings and glides over his supposed relations with Phaedo, Dion, Stella, and Archeanassa. *Let us not be ashamed to say what we are not ashamed to think* [author unknown]. (pp. 641-42)

BFurthermore, I have ordered myself to dare to say all that I dare to do, and I dislike even thoughts that are unpublishable. The worst of my actions and conditions does not seem to me so ugly as the cowardice of not daring to avow it. Everyone is discreet in confession; people should be so in action. Boldness in sinning is somewhat compensated and bridled by boldness in confessing. CWhoever would oblige himself to tell all, would oblige himself not to do anything about which we are constrained to keep silent. God grant that this excessive license of mine may encourage our men to attain freedom, rising above these cowardly and hypocritical virtues born of our imperfections; that at the expense of my immoderation I may draw them on to the point of reason. A man must see his vice and study it to tell about it. Those who hide it from others ordinarily hide it from themselves. And they do not consider it covered up enough if they themselves see it; they withdraw and disguise it from their own conscience. (p. 642)

BIn honor of the Huguenots, who condemn our private and auricular confession, I confess myself in public, religiously and purely. Saint Augustine, Origen, and Hippocrates have published the errors of their opinions; I, besides, those of my conduct. I am hungry to make myself known, and I care not to how many, provided it be truly. Or to put it better, I am hungry for nothing, but I have a mortal fear of being taken to be other than I am by those who come to know my name. (p. 643)

BReader, let this essay of myself run on, and this third extension of the other parts of my painting. I add, but I do not correct. First, because when a man has mortgaged his work to the world, it seems to me that he has no further right to it. Let him speak better elsewhere, if he can, and not adulterate the work he has sold. From such people nothing should be bought until after their death. Let them think carefully before publishing. Who is hurrying them?

CMy book is always one. Except that at each new edition, so that the buyer may not come off completely empty-handed, I allow myself to add, since it is only an ill-fitted patchwork, some extra ornaments. These are only overweights, which do not condemn the original form, but give some special value to each of the subsequent ones, by a bit of ambitious subtlety. Thence, however, it will easily happen that some transposition of chronology may slip in, for my stories take their place according to their timeliness, not always according to their age.

BSecond, because, as far as I am concerned, I fear to lose by the change: my understanding does not always go forward, it goes backward too. I distrust my thoughts hardly any less for being second or third than for being first, or for being present than for being past. We often correct ourselves as stupidly as we correct others. CMy first edition was in the year 1580. Since then I have grown older by a long stretch of time; but certainly I have not grown an inch wiser. Myself now and myself a while ago are indeed two; but when better, I simply cannot say. It would be fine to be old if we traveled only toward improvement. It is a drunkard's motion, staggering, dizzy, wobbling, or that of reeds that the wind stirs haphazadly as it pleases. (p. 736)

ᴮThe favor of the public has given me a little more boldness than I expected; but what I fear most is to surfeit my readers: I would rather irritate them than weary them, as a learned man of my time has done. Praise is always pleasing, from whomever and for whatever reason it may come; yet to enjoy it properly, we must be informed of the cause of it. Even imperfections have a way of recommending themselves. Vulgar and popular esteem is seldom happy in its choice; and in my time I am much mistaken if the worst writings are not those which have gotten the best share of the wind of public favor. Certainly I give thanks to those good people who deign to take my feeble efforts in good part.

There is no place where the faults of workmanship are so apparent as in material which has nothing in itself to recommend it. Do not blame me, reader, for those that slip in here through the caprice or inadvertency of others: each hand, each workman, contributes his own. I do not concern myself with spelling, and simply order them to follow the old style; or with punctuation; I am inexpert in both. When they wholly shatter the sense, I am not much troubled about it, for at least they relieve me of responsibility; but when they substitute a false meaning, as they do so often, and twist me to their view, they ruin me. However, when the thought is not up to my strength, a fair-minded man should reject it as not mine. Anyone who knows how little I like to work, how much I am formed in my own way, will easily believe that I would rather write as many more essays again than subject myself to going over these again for such childish correction. (pp. 736-37)

ᶜAmusing notion: many things that I would not want to tell anyone, I tell the public; and for my most secret knowledge and thoughts I send my most faithful friends to a bookseller's shop. (p.750)

It is the inattentive reader who loses my subject, not I. Some word about it will always be found off in a corner, which will not fail to be sufficient, though it takes little room. ᴮI seek out change indiscriminately and tumultuously. ᶜMy style and my mind alike go roaming. (p. 761)

ᴮI want the matter to make its own divisions. It shows well enough where it changes, where it concludes, where it begins, where it resumes, without my interlacing it with words, with links and seams introduced for the benefit of weak or heedless ears, and without writing glosses on myself. Who is there that would not rather not be read than be read sleepily or in passing? ᶜ*Nothing is so useful that it can be of value when taken on the run* [Seneca]. If to take up books were to take them in, and if to see them were to consider them, and to run through them were to grasp them, I should be wrong to make myself out quite as ignorant as I say I am.

ᴮSince I cannot arrest the attention of the reader by weight, it is all to the good if I chance to arrest it by my embroilment. "True, but he will afterward repent of having wasted his time over it." That may be, but still he will have wasted his time over it. And then there are natures like that, in whom understanding breeds disdain, who will think the better of me because they will not know what I mean. They will conclude that my meaning is profound from its obscurity, which, to speak in all earnest, I hate very strongly, and I would avoid it if I could avoid myself. Aristotle somewhere boasts of affecting it: blameworthy affectation!

ᶜBecause such frequent breaks into chapters as I used at the beginning seemed to me to disrupt and dissolve attention before it was aroused, making it disdain to settle and collect for so little, I have begun making them longer, requiring fixed purpose and assigned leisure. In such an occupation, if you will not give a man a single hour, you will not give him anything. And you do nothing for a man for whom you do nothing except while doing something else. Besides, perhaps I have some personal obligation to speak only by halves, to speak confusedly, to speak discordantly. (pp. 761-62)

ᴮ[Someone] might say of me that [in quoting others so often] I have here only made a bunch of other people's flowers, having furnished nothing of my own but the thread to tie them. Indeed I have yielded to public opinion in carrying these borrowed ornaments about on me. But I do not intend that they should cover and hide me; that is the opposite of my design, I who wish to make a show only of what is my own, and of what is naturally my own; and if I had taken my own advice I would at all hazards have spoken absolutely all alone. ᶜI load myself with these borrowings more and more heavily every day beyond my intention and my original form, following the fancy of the age and the exhortation of others. If it is unbecoming to me, as I believe it is, no matter; it may be useful to someone else. (p. 808)

ᴮIf I had wanted to speak from knowledge, I would have spoken earlier. I would have written at a time nearer to my studies, when I had more wit and memory, and would have trusted myself more to the vigor of that age than of this one, if I had wanted to make a profession of writing. ᶜMoreover, one gracious favor that fortune perhaps offered me by the mediation of this work would then have come in a more propitious season. ᴮTwo of my acquaintances, great men in this ability, have in my opinion lost by half for having refused to publish at forty in order to wait until sixty. Maturity, like youth, has its defects, and worse ones. And old age is as unsuited to this sort of work as to all others. Whoever puts his decrepitude into print plays the fool, if he hopes to squeeze out of it humors that do not smell of ungraciousness, dreaminess, and drowsiness. Our mind grows constipated and sluggish as it grows old.

I speak ignorance pompously and opulently, and speak knowledge meagerly and piteously, ᶜthe latter secondarily and accidentally, the former expressly and principally. And there is nothing I treat specifically except nothing, and no knowledge except that of the lack of knowledge. ᴮI have chosen the time when my life, which I have to portray, lies all before my eyes; what is left is more related to death. And even of my death, if I should find it garrulous, as others do, I would willingly give an account to the public on my way out. (p. 809)

> *Michel de Montaigne, in his* The Complete Essays of Montaigne, *translated by Donald M. Frame, Stanford University Press, 1958, 883 p.*

SAMUEL DANYEL   (poem date 1603)

[Danyel (or Daniel, as the name is usually given) was an English poet and composer of court masques who is best known for his sonnet sequence Delia *(1592). The following poem is addressed to Danyel's brother-in-law John Florio and included in Florio's 1603 translation of* The Essays. *Danyel enthusiastically welcomes this first English rendering of Montaigne.]*

> Bookes the amasse of humors, swolne with ease,
> The Griefe of peace, the maladie of rest,
> So stuffe the world, falne into this disease,
> As it receives more then it can digest:

And doe so overcharge, as they confound,
The apetite of skill with idle store:
There being no end of words, nor any bound
Set to conceipt, the *Ocean* without shore.
　　As if man labo'rd with himselfe to be
As infinite in words, as in intents,
And drawe his manifold incertaintie
In en'ry figure, passion represents;
That these innumerable visages,
And strange shapes of opinions and disourse
Shadowed in leaves, may be the witnesses
Rather of our defects, then of our force.
And this proud frame of our presumption,
This *Babel* of our skill, this *Towre* of wit,
Seemes only checkt with the confusion
Of our mistakings, that dissolueth it.
And well may make us of our knowledge doubt,
Seeing what uncertainties we build upon,
To be as weake within booke as without;
Or els that truth hath other shapes then one.
　　But yet although we labor with this store.
And with the presse of writings seeme opprest,
And have too many bookes, yet want we more,
Feeling great dearth and scarsenesse of the best;
Which cast in choiser shapes have bin produc'd,
To give the best proportions to the minde
Of our confusion, and have introduc'd
The likeliest images frailtie can finde.
And wherein most the skill-desiring soule
Takes her delight, the best of all delight,
And where her motions evenest come to rowle
About this doubtfull *center of the right.*
　　Which to discouer this great Potentate,
This Prince *Montaigne* (if he be not more)
Hath more adventur'd of his owne estate
Then ever man did of himselfe before:
And hath made such bolde sallies out upon
Custome, the mightie tyrant of the earth,
In whose *Seraglio* of subjection
We all seeme bred-up, from our tender birth;
As I admire his powres, and out of love,
Here at his gate do stand, and glad I stand
So neere to him whom I do so much love,
T'applaude his happie setling in our land:
And safe transpassage by his studious care
Who both of him and us doth merit much,
Having as sumptuously, as he is rare
Plac'd him in the best lodging of our speach.
And made him now as free, as if borne here,
And as well ours as theirs, who may be proud
That he is theirs, though he be everywhere
To have the franchise of his worth allow'd.
　　It be'ing the portion of a happie Pen,
Not to b'invassal'd to one Monarchie,
But dwell with all the better world of men
Whose spirits are all of one communitie.
Whom neither *Ocean,* Desarts, Rockes nor Sands
Can keepe from th'intertraffique of the minde,
But that it vents her treasure in all lands,
And doth a most secure commercement finde.
　　Wrap *Excellencie* up never so much,
In Hierogliphicques, Ciphers, Caracters,
And let her speake never so strange a speach,
Her *Genius* yet finds apt discipherers:
And never was she borne to dye obscure,
But guided by the Starres of her owne grace,
Makes her owne fortune, and is ever sure
In mans best hold, to hold the strongest place.
　　And let the *Critic* say the worst he can,
He cannot say but that *Montaigne* yet,
Yeeldes most rich pieces and extracts of man;
Though in a troubled frame confus'dly set.

Which yet h'is blest that he hath ever seene,
And therefore as a guest in gratefulnesse,
For the great good the house yeelds him within
Might spare to taxe th'vnapt convayances.
But this breath hurts not, for both worke and frame,
Whilst England English speakes, is of that store
And that choyse stuffe, as that without the same
The richest librarie can be but poore.
And they unblest who letters do professe
And have him not: whose owne fate beates their want
With more sound blowes, then *Alcibiades*
Did his Pedante that did *Homer* want.

(pp. i-ii)

Samuel Danyel, "To My Deere Friend M. John Florio, Concerning His Translation of Montaigne," in The Essays by Michel de Montaigne, *translated by John Florio, The Scolar Press Limited, 1969, pp. i-ii.*

BLAISE PASCAL　(essay date 1662?)

[*Pascal was a French theologian and mathematician who is remembered primarily for his masterly work of moral philosophy,* Lettres écrites par Louis de Montalte à un provincial *(1656-57), commonly referred to as* Les provinciales. *Pascal's other important work, a projected apology for the Christian religion, remained unfinished at the time of his death in 1662. Known as the* Pensées *(1844), the work consists of a fragmented series of thoughts and reflections. In the following excerpt from the* Pensées, *Pascal records his unfavorable impression of Montaigne.*]

To speak of those who have dealt with self-knowledge; of Charron's divisions which depress and bore; of Montaigne's confusion; how he was aware of his want of method, which he tried to avoid by skipping from topic to topic; how he sought to be in the fashion.

The folly of trying to paint his own portrait! And that not by the way, and against his own principles—we all make mistakes—but on principle, and of set and primary purpose. For to talk nonsense by chance and out of weakness is a common failing, but to do so deliberately is intolerable. . . . (p. 17)

Montaigne's faults are grievous. Wanton expressions; this is all wrong, whatever Mademoiselle Gournay may say. Credulous, men without eyes. Ignorant, squaring the circle, another greater world. His sentiments on suicide. On death. He induces indifference to salvation, without fear and without repentance. His book was not written to teach piety, so he was not bound to attempt that; but one is always bound not to turn men away from piety. One may excuse his rather loose and voluptuous sentiments on certain occasions . . . , but one cannot excuse his wholly heathen sentiments concerning death; for we must say goodbye to piety if we have no desire for at least a Christian death. Now throughout his book he thinks only of a soft and easy death.

The good in Montaigne is difficult to acquire. The bad—apart from immorality—could have been quickly cured if he had been informed that he told too many tales and talked too much about himself. (p. 365)

Blaise Pascal, in his Pensées, *translated by H. F. Stewart, Pantheon Books, 1950, 543 p.*

VOLTAIRE　(letter date 1733)

[*A French philosopher and man of letters, Voltaire was a major figure of the eighteenth-century European Enlightenment, a move-*

ment in which reason and empiricism markedly superseded re-
liance on prescription, faith, and authority. As a man of diverse
and intense interests, Voltaire wrote prolifically on many subjects
and in a variety of genres, always asserting the absolute primacy
of personal liberty—be it intellectual, social, religious, or polit-
ical. Consequently, he opposed religious traditions and political
organizations that he believed thwarted or curtailed individual
freedom. Voltaire's most valuable contribution to literature is
usually considered his invention of the philosophical conte, *or*
tale, in which the story is a vehicle for an ethical or philosophical
message; the most famous of these contes *is the highly regarded*
Candide *(1759). The following excerpt is from one of a series of*
letters originally published in England as Letters concerning the
English Nation *by M. de Voltaire (1733). In this letter, Voltaire*
transcribes selections from Blaise Pascal's Pensées, *and then*
responds with his own commentary. Here, he refutes Pascal's
negative remarks about Montaigne (see excerpt dated 1662?).]

I am sending you the critical remarks I have been making for
some time on the *Pensées* of M. Pascal. Don't compare me in
this matter with Hezekiah, who wanted to burn all the books
of Solomon. I respect the genius and the eloquence of Pascal,
but the more I respect them the more I am persuaded that he
would himself have corrected many of these *Pensées*, which
he had jotted down on paper for further examination later. It
is while admiring his genius that I challenge some of his ideas. . . .

I have chosen with care some thoughts of Pascal and put the
rejoinders after them. It is for you to judge whether I am right
or wrong. (p. 120)

Montaigne's defects are great. He is full of lewd and improper
words. This is thoroughly bad. His sentiments about suicide
and death are horrible.

Montaigne is speaking as a philosopher, not as a Christian,
and he is stating the pros and cons of suicide. Philosophically
speaking, what harm does a man do society by leaving it when
he is of no further use to it? An old man who suffers unbearable
agonies with the stone is told: "If you don't have it cut out
you will die, if you do you may dodder on, dribble and drag
about for another year, a burden to yourself and everybody
else." I presume that the old man decides to cease being a
burden to anybody: that is roughly the case Montaigne sets
out. (pp. 135-36)

What a foolish project of Montaigne to portray himself! And
to do so not by the way and against his own principles, for all
of us fall short sometimes, but acting according to his principles
and with a prime and main design. For saying silly things by
chance or weakness is an ordinary complaint, but to say them
deliberately cannot be tolerated, and especially such things as
those.

What a delightful design Montaigne had to portray himself
without artifice as he did! For he has portrayed human nature
itself. And what a paltry project of Nicole, Malebranche and
Pascal, to belittle Montaigne! (p. 139)

> Voltaire, *"On the 'Pensés' of Pascal," in his* Letters
> on England, *translated by Leonard Tancock, Penguin*
> *Books, 1980, pp. 120-45.*

THOMAS CARLYLE   (essay date 1830)

[*A noted nineteenth-century essayist, historian, critic, and social*
commentator, Carlyle was a central figure of the Victorian age
in England. In his writings, Carlyle advocated a Christian work
ethic and stressed the importance of order, piety, and spiritual
fulfilment. Known to his contemporaries as the "Sage of Chel-

sea," Carlyle exerted a powerful moral influence in an era of
rapidly shifting values. In the following excerpt from an essay
originally published in 1830, Carlyle tempers his praise of Mon-
taigne with censure of the one quality of the essayist he finds
disturbing.]

In this singular production [the ***Essays***], Montaigne completely
fulfils the promise of "painting himself in his natural and
simple mood, without study or artifice." And though Scaliger
might perhaps reasonably ask, "What matters it whether Montaigne liked white wine or claret?"—a modern reader will not
easily cavil at the patient and good-natured, though exuberant
egotism, which brings back to our view "the form and pressure" of a time long past. The habits and humours, the mode
of acting and thinking which characterised a Gascon gentleman
in the sixteenth century, cannot fail to amuse an inquirer of
the nineteenth; while the faithful delineation of human feelings
in all their strength and weakness, will serve as a mirror to
every mind capable of self examination. But if details, otherwise frivolous, are pardoned, because of the antique charm
which is about them, no excuse or even apology of a satisfactory kind, can be devised for the gross indelicacy which frequently deforms these ***Essays;*** and as Montaigne, by an abundant store of bold ideas, and a deep insight into the principles
of our common nature, deserves to be ranked high among the
great men of his own original age, he also deserves the bad
pre-eminence, in love at once of coarseness and obscenity.

The desultory, careless mode, in which the materials of the
Essays are arranged, indicates a feature in the author's character
to which his style has likewise a resemblance. With him, more
than with any other, words may be called the garment of thought;
the expression is frequently moulded to fit the idea, never the
idea to fit the expression. The negligence, and occasional obscurity of his manner, are more than compensated by the warmth
of an imagination, bestowing on his language a nervousness,
and often a picturesque beauty, which we should in vain seek
elsewhere.

From the perusal of those ***Essays,*** it is natural to infer, that the
author must have studied men, not only in the closet but the
world. . . . After the first publication of his ***Essays*** he did not
long continue stationary. . . . [He] left home in 1581, and,
attended by several of his friends, traversed Lorraine, Switzerland, Bavaria, and Italy. . . . [The critic adds in a footnote:
"About fifty years ago, a manuscript account of this journey
was accidentally found in the chateau which Montaigne inhabited. Being ascertained to be his composition, it was published in 1774. But neither the curiosity attached to everything
which bears the name of Montaigne, nor the learned notes of
M. Querlon, are sufficient to make us relish the insignificant
and often disgusting contents of a work that seems never to
have been at all intended for meeting general inspection."]
(pp. 66-7)

The character of Montaigne is amply delineated in his ***Essays***.
On contemplating this picture, we are surprised to find the
principles of a stoic incongrously mingled with the practice of
an epicure; and the *pillow of doubt,* upon which during the
flow of health he professed to repose, exchanged in sickness
for the opiates of superstition. But notwithstanding these inconsistencies, it is impossible to avoid admiring the continued
benignity and pensive gaiety which distinguished his temper.
(pp. 68-9)

> *Thomas Carlyle, "Montaigne," in his* Critical and
> Miscellaneous Essays, *Vol. V,* Charles Scribner's
> Sons, *1901, pp. 65-9.*

CHARLES AUGUSTIN SAINTE-BEUVE (essay date 1842)

[*Sainte-Beuve, one of the most important French critics of the nineteenth century, was widely revered for his erudition and his judicious appraisals of literature. Because he believed that a work of literature is inseparable from the person who wrote it, his critical writings focus to a great degree on the life, psychology, and historical milieu of an author. This perspective gave his method a definite psychological bent and led to his tendency to classify writers into what he called "familles d'esprits," or "families of the mind." In the opinion of many twentieth-century critics and scholars, Sainte-Beuve was primarily a historian of manners, a psychologist, and a moralist. In the words of René Wellek, he "should be described as the greatest representative of the historical spirit in France. . . . True historicism is not simply a recognition of historical conditioning, but a recognition of individuality along with and even through historical change. Sainte-Beuve recognizes both things, and at his best he preserves the delicate balance needed to save himself from relativism or over-emphasis on external conditions." In the following excerpt from an essay originally published in 1842, Sainte-Beuve admiringly discusses the philosophy and style of* The Essays *and examines Blaise Pascal's assessment of the work and its author (see excerpt dated 1662?).*]

Over the past two centuries a great deal has been written about Montaigne. Authors as important and brilliant as Pascal have spoken their minds [see excerpt dated 1662?], and yet there is one point that, in my opinion, has not been stressed enough. Namely, that Montaigne does not give us a philosophical system, is not primarily the Pyrrhonian skeptic—Montaigne is the very embodiment of nature.

He is nature in all her purity, yet civilized; nature in her broadest, most typical expressions as well as in her most individual moods, not excluding her aberrations. All of nature untouched by grace. (p. 13)

The more I reflect about Montaigne, the more I am convinced that he was the natural man par excellence.

Let me dwell on this point, if I may. The phrase is so often and so vaguely used, I should like to analyze it more carefully and to develop its fuller implications.

There is something of Montaigne in every one of us. Every one of our inclinations, moods, and passions—every one of our diversions, amusements, and flights of fancy upon which Christianity has made no mark—all such states of mind deserve to be called "Montaigne" states of mind. To accept the "naturalness" of our lives, for all the operations of what is called "divine grace"—a sort of unreflective nakedness into which we relapse when following our natural inclinations, as though the soul had never been redeemed—to accept this "Tahiti" of the soul is also to accept Montaigne's empire, the realm in which he lived and wrote. We ought not to be surprised that Pascal had such difficulty disposing of Montaigne. The problem Montaigne poses is not one of philosophy but that of nature itself, of the individual self: he poses a philosophical problem only in the sense that he represents nature in all its purity.

Pascal inveighed against Montaigne, studying him closely so as to condemn him more sternly—and with a vehemence such as only the true believer may permit himself (and then only on the condition that the end justifies such means). And yet, in order to gain full understanding of Montaigne and of the "indulgence of so many intelligent persons" who "have failed to realize how dangerous he is" (as Arnauld complains in his *Art de penser*), we must consider Montaigne's thought in its original, informal, loose expression. The tidiness of Pascal's indictment is a barrier to grasping Montaigne as a whole. The fact is, all things considered, three-quarters of Montaigne does not essentially differ from what we find in a number of other writers: but those others do not arouse criticism, because they speak without malicious intent. Had M. de Saci read Montaigne before talking to Pascal about him—M. de Saci who made it his rule to follow the will of God at every moment . . .—he would have said something like this to Pascal:

"This author to whom you ascribe so much intelligence and whose ideas you erect into a system, does not rely upon arguments to all that extent. What appeals to the reader is present in most men, including those who call themselves Christians, but who live as if the Cross had never been. When I am walking in the countryside—when, perhaps, I have retired there in my old age, taking my ease, free of responsibility, with nobody to think of but myself—where then is my Christianity? When I look at a lovely flower, admire a shaft of sunlight, or lie down on a patch of greensward to take a little nap, there to dream of who knows what fantastic things, wholly caught up in concerns of this world, forgetting all else—where then is my Christianity? When I read, as I like to do, of unusual manners and customs in books of travel, and meet the Devil in a hundred guises, now as a naked cannibal, now as an Italian fop, not caring so much that he is the Devil but only whether he is interesting—where then is my Christianity? And when I sit down to Montaigne in moments of leisure, with nothing more in my mind than reading Montaigne—where then is my Christianity?"

That is enough about what I call "three-quarters of Montaigne." Now we must address ourselves to the rest, his attitude toward religion, which Pascal and the recluses of Port-Royal condemned so harshly. They did not misrepresent him. Montaigne is, indeed, naïve, and we do not underestimate the naïve, casual, easygoing aspect of his thought. However, there is also in him a background of conscious intention, which gives a special sense to the whole. The hostility and fear which Montaigne has aroused in religious men comes from their realization that his portrayal of nature conceals a consistent paganism. He almost always treats religion as a thing apart, as something much too respectable to be discussed—but this does not prevent him from discussing it constantly. He is against translating and reading the Scriptures—a point on which, as on many others, he prefers the Catholic Church to the Reformers. Politically, such an attitude was not unwise, but there is more to it. He also says that the use of the "sacred and divine songs" (i.e., the Psalms) ought to be restricted to the priesthood. Being himself but a layman, a mere writer of imagination, he would not presume so far as to recite the Psalms. For him, a simple Lord's Prayer is quite enough, he tells us. Such is his way of inspiring respect for religion! Where Voltaire said, "These things are sacred, *because* no one will touch them"—he was speaking of canticles by Lefranc de Pompignan—Montaigne in effect says, "These things are sacred, *therefore* no one should touch them." The higher the portals of the Temple, the less risk we run of knocking our heads against them as we go in or out. He knows very well that so extreme a point of view was out of date in his own day. That he would have been perfectly happy in certain countries where, apart from the obligatory observances, one does as one likes, where you can be a cardinal and a man of the world at the same time—this is clear from the general tenor of his book. I know that he made a proper Christian death—Gassendi and La Rochefoucauld also received the sacraments. It is not for me to judge his sincerity at such an awesome moment, but his book is there for all to read, and my judgment is of it.

Many a chapter—that on Prayers and Orisons, and that on Repenting, for example—would be as revelatory, on close analysis, as the **"Apology of Raymond Sebond."** In such chapters, we find sentences that are moderate and unobjectionable from the religious point of view, but they are not enough to modify the general tone. In fact, we never know quite where we are with men of this ilk—with Bayle any more than with Montaigne. We might say of them what Pascal said of Opinion, that it is the more fraudulent for not being consistently so.

Pascal also said: "One saying of David, or of Moses, for instance that 'God will circumcise the heart,' enables us to judge of their spirit. If all their other expression were ambiguous, and left us in doubt whether they were philosophers or Christians, one saying of this kind would in fact determine all the rest. From that point on, ambiguity no longer exists." The very opposite is true of Montaigne: if some passages state his thought, others conceal it. He is betrayed by random remarks that are like flashes of lightning illuminating a whole landscape. Montaigne's "dirty" passages are especially revealing, when he addresses himself to the most intimate aspects of human life. He really enjoys tearing away the poor rags with which we cover our baser nature—and it is then that we glimpse him as he truly is under the high spirits, the eloquence, and the gentility. He sets out to humiliate us in such passages (try listening to them read aloud). Unlike Pascal's, his tone is never one of grief at our natural condition, but one of malicious delight: he fairly rubs his hands with self-satisfaction.

Montaigne's longest, most vigorous, and most important chapter is the one titled **"An Apology of Raymond Sebond."** This is the heart of the *Essais;* everything about it is purposeful, and the calculated tortuous sentences which say the opposite of what the author really thinks nonetheless convey it. Studying it closely, we find that his so-called Pyrrhonism rings hollow: for all his restless rambling Montaigne knows where he is going. Out of this **"Apology"** I can imagine assembling a chapter that might be headed "Montaigne's Dogmatism." Where Spinoza's form is geometrical, Montaigne's is skeptical, but the essence of his doctrine seems to me unmistakable. (pp. 15-19)

To humor his father (who was more of an enthusiast for the new learning than himself learned) the youthful Montaigne had translated a Latin book by the fifteenth-century Spanish author, Raymond de Sebond. Titled *Theologia naturalis,* it demonstrated the existence of God and the truth of the Christian religion on the basis of rational arguments, drawn as far as possible from observation of nature. (pp. 19-20)

Montaigne's French version of *Theologia naturalis* was published in 1569, in compliance with a wish expressed by his father on his deathbed—the older Montaigne had been charmed and consoled by this book. It was criticized on two counts. Some (the Catholic party) said that the attempt to give revelation and faith a foundation in reason was opening a door that should remain closed. Others maintained that Sebond's arguments were weak and failed to make their point. It was ostensibly to answer both types of objection that Montaigne wrote this chapter of the *Essais.*

He addresses himself first to his religious critics, treating them with conspicuous respect. He says that he cannot blame those who, because of their "zeal of piety," are afraid to let reason be used in support of religion. But while he is well aware that the knowledge of God can be attained only by extraordinary supernatural means, he "fears" that we could not "enjoy" it unless we had access to it "not only by discourse, but also by humane means." For, he says, if we could grasp Godhead "through the interposition of a lively faith," surely we would not find so many contradictions and inconsistencies between Christian words and Christian deeds. Citing one instance after another, he goes on maliciously to demonstrate the inadequacy of precisely these "humane means," that is, without the intervention of divine grace. What is he driving at? It is obvious that from this point on he is no longer concerned with Raymond de Sebond. He had translated the latter's book to please his father; now, on the pretext of defending that author, he is pursuing another aim altogether. If he is not actually refuting Sebond, he is using him as a pretext for carrying on a very broad and "probing" discussion of religion. His tone of respect for all who would place faith above reason makes him seem to be on their side. With the greatest humility he confines his defense of Sebond to the observation that the latter's method, though very crude and limited, might have a certain practical value for bringing certain persons back to the faith. And he cites one such instance: he knew a man who had actually been influenced by Sebond's arguments. As he puts it, "Faith, giving as it were a tincture and lustre unto Sebond's arguments makes them the more firme and solid."

However, when he addresses himself to those of his critics who were not inspired by "zeal of piety" and who found Sebond's arguments weak and inconclusive, his tone changes. Now he is as outspoken as one could wish. "Such fellowes must somewhat more roughly be handled," he says, "for they are more dangerous and more malicious than the first." In fact, it is he who becomes more dangerous and more malicious at this point. For what does he do? To refute the second type of objectors, he proceeds to outdo them at their own game on a tone of high indignation. What he says, in effect, is: Of course, I am well aware that poor Sebond's arguments are weak and don't prove much. Yet, madmen that you are, proud wretches (he is taking up the cudgels in defense of the Godhead they would defame)—tell me, how can there be any arguments capable of proving anything in such matters? Cannot every one of them be countered with an argument equally—that is to say, just as little—convincing? Thereupon, as though carried away by his own self-righteousness, he embarks on a long discussion, in the course of which he enumerates ad infinitum every possible cause of errors and ineffectuality to which the human reason is prone when unsupported by religious beliefs. Once this chapter has been properly understood, we realize that Montaigne is from beginning to end playing a part. Only a reader determined to be deceived could be taken in by it. For Montaigne, Sebond serves the same function the Manichaeans were to serve for Bayle.

To begin with, Montaigne tries to show that man "alone without other help," without the grace and knowledge of God, is but a miserable and wretched creature. "Who hath perswaded him that this admirable moving of heavens vaults; that the eternal light of these lamps so fiercely rowling over his head; that the horror-moving and continuall motion of this infinite vaste Ocean, were established, and continue for so many ages for his commodite and service?" In such connections, Montaigne does not seem to notice that he is actually refuting the same Raymond de Sebond whose apology he claims to be undertaking. The latter had argued in favor of final causes, and had defended the idea that the universe is made for man. To chastise such human presumptuousness, he studies each animal in turn—the swallow, the dog, the falcon, the elephant, the ox, the magpie, the spider—each of whom has his own instincts, his own language, his own way of life, his own talents, his own reasoning power, his own capacity of loyalty, even his own (in the case of the elephant) kind of religious worship. Consequently, they are all our "fellow bretheren and compeers." This is the opposite pole from Descartes, who viewed animals as automatons, and whose ideas on that score influenced Pascal and Port-Royal. Pascal, the inventor of the adding machine, had no difficulty thinking of animals as pure automatons. In this connection, there is a much-quoted passage: "Touching strength, there is no Creature in the world open to so many wrongs and injuries as a man: He need not a Whale, an Elephant, nor a Crocodile, nor any such other wilde beast, of which one alone is of power to defeat a great number of men: seely lice are able to make Sulla give over his Dictatorship: The heart and life of a mighty and triumphant Emperor, is but the breakfast of a seely little worme."

Pascal imitated and rediscovered Montaigne's words when he attributed the death of Cromwell, the modern Sulla, to "one little grain of sand." He was also indebted to Montaigne when he said: "Man is but a reed, the most feeble thing in nature; but he is a thinking reed. The entire universe need not arm itself to crush him. A vapor, a drop of water suffices to kill him. But if the universe were to crush him, man would still be more noble than that which killed him, because he knows that he dies and the advantage which the universe has over him; the universe knows nothing of this."

It has been said that Montaigne's thought has been incorporated and completed in Pascal. When the latter employs coarse language calling attention to man's baser nature, we feel that he speaks in all sincerity, and that his purpose is to lift man above the mire in which he finds himself; when he speaks of the miseries of the human condition, we are sure that he really wants to put an end to them. Montaigne, for his part, seems always to be gloating. Nonetheless, there are several passages in the **"Apology"** where Montaigne rises to real heights of sincerity and eloquence: "This manyheaded, divers-armed, and furiously raging monster [an army] is man; wretched weake and miserable man: whom if you consider well, what is he, but a crawling, and ever-moving Ants-neast? . . . A gust of contrarie winds, the croking of a flight of Ravens, the false pase of a Horse, the casual flight of an Eagle, a dreame, a sodaine voyce, a false signe, a mornings mist, an evening fogge, are enough to overthrow, sufficient to overwhelme and able to pull him to the ground. Let the Sunne but shine hot on his face, he faints and swelters with heat: Cast but a little dust in his eyes, as do the Bees mentioned by our Poet, all our ensignes, all our legions, yea great Pompey himselfe in the forefront of them is overthrown and put to rout."

When Pascal treated this subject, he could at best equal, not surpass, such passages.

After this humbling comparison between mankind and the animals, Montaigne addresses himself to each of the philosophical schools in turn, beginning with Thales. Making the most of their disagreements, he puts himself to great trouble, summoning up every resource of learning, to pit the arguments of each school against those of the other schools, so as to confute them all. Having accomplished this, he is at pains not to be misunderstood, and he warns Queen Marguerite and his other readers that the tactic he has employed, rejecting reason so as to deprive his adversary of its aid, is a "desperate" tactic, and one to be resorted to but rarely.

At the very moment he utters his warning, however, and we might think he will not go on in this vein, he abandons the philosophers' changing systems and attacks all human faculties in so far as they might be supposed to be means of getting at the truth. Having doubted of reason, now he doubts of the senses, and we read: "It is not onely fevers, drinkes and great accidents, that overwhelme our judgement: The least thing in the world will turne it topsieturvie." This and the passage that follows directly anticipate Pascal's saying: "The mind of this sovereign judge of the world is not so independent that it is not liable to be disturbed by the first din about it."

As we trace the development of Montaigne's thought in this part of the *Essais,* we are continually reminded of Pascal. The latter's *Pensées* could be described as a profounder version or revision of the apology of Sebond. Pascal repeats many of Montaigne's sayings on the vanity, weakness, and contradictoriness of mankind. In doing so, however, he makes the sign of the Cross over Montaigne's words, and what is more striking than their obvious similarities (which Pascal would certainly have acknowledged in publication) is their difference in tone. Where Montaigne was simply employing a novel intellectual tactic, Pascal has a serious purpose. Where the former abandons himself to every passing current, the latter knows where he is going and works hard with the oars. The one is distracted, even entranced with his own shipwreck, while the other clings to the bit of driftwood with whose help he still can, by indomitable effort, reach the distant shore, his homeland in eternity. The feebleness, the wretchedness, the nullity of human life: this is their common refrain. But while Montaigne finds amusement in the spectacle, and sneers at man's kinship with the animals, Pascal counsels courage and prayer. To him, man, however wretched, is an exiled monarch, of the noblest lineage, and it behooves him to regain his rightful place.

We have said enough about this Apology, which is very long, and which concludes with a pompous quotation from Plutarch. God alone *IS*, we are suddenly told, and aside from God, who is eternal, necessary, and immutable, all things are transitory and in flux. Montaigne's intention in quoting this religious-passage from Plutarch is highly suspicious. If we scrutinize it carefully, taking into account where Montaigne inserts it, and in the light of the chapter as a whole, we must conclude that the ideas it expresses are Spinozist and pantheistic. By elevating God above created things, including mankind, Montaigne denies the notion of a provident and personal God. We are now in possession of a key that enables us to pass from conjecture to certainty, to assess Montaigne's intentions both stated and unstated.

His playfulness and casualness are purely superficial. Montaigne, in the **"Apology"** as well as throughout the *Essais,* is a kind of sorcerer, an evil genius who takes us by the hand, and who, guiding us through the labyrinth of opinion, tells us at every step, just when we think we know where we stand, "All this is false or at least dubious; don't give your trust so readily; don't pay too much attention to this or that in the hope it can serve as a landmark. All you can trust is the light I go by; nothing else matters. This light is enough." And after he has led you far afield, got you thoroughly disoriented and exhausted from being led down so many garden paths—just then he blows out the light and leaves you utterly in the dark. You may hear a little snicker from your guide.

To what conclusion does Montaigne lead? Universal doubt? But if so—if this is his final conclusion, what a vastly significant conclusion it is! When we stand there, finally having lost our way in utter darkness, it is Spinoza whom we are to call upon. The world is to be grasped as a great, gloomy, endless universe moving silent and unknown under skies perpetually gray. A bit of life appears now and again for a brief span, only to flicker out and die like an insect in a swamp. Such is the supreme answer a number of men have given, sometimes in the form of mathematical demonstration, sometimes in the form of Pyrrhonian argument. Montaigne's charm and good humor serve merely to screen off the spectacle of the abyss or, as he would put it, to prettify the tomb.

One of the great reasons for Montaigne's popularity—indeed, the one and only explanation for it—is his magical style. Style, in the exalted degree to which Montaigne possessed it, suffices to absolve any writer in the eyes of posterity. The disorderliness of his argument, his inconsistencies, licentiousness, and lapses of taste—all are covered over most attractively, plausibly, and pleasantly. We can never admire him enough. Style is the golden scepter which, in the last analysis, holds sway over the kingdom of this world.

Perhaps more than any other man, Montaigne had the gift of pleasing expression; his style is one continuous metaphor, sustained and renewed at every step. He always presents ideas in the form of images, varying them and yet keeping them clear and striking. Only the slightest interval separates one from another—the reader is given but a moment to prepare for the transition. Any one of his pages is a luxuriant, untamed field bursting with rustling plants and fragrant flowers, buzzing insects, and gurgling brooks. His is no integral conception, no ordered large-scale structure. He did not put himself to so much trouble. To him, inventiveness in detail and unflagging brilliance of expression sufficed. He understood this very well: "I have no other Sergeant of band to marshall my rapsodies, than fortune."

In Montaigne, idea and image are one and the same thing. . . . There is no real link between image and image; one merely succeeds the other: like a sure-footed Basque, he jumps from rock to rock. (pp. 20-6)

In respect of style, Montaigne is like Ovid and Ariosto. The rhapsodic felicity of the successive images, however varied, is an unbroken stream. The thread of his thought is never lost amid the continual metamorphoses.

Shakespeare and Molière, geniuses with the gift of creating unified wholes, could with ease endow characters with life. Montaigne's imagination, on the other hand, operates within individual sentences and in the articulations of the ideas. The result is just as alive, and, viewed closely, just as marvelously poetic. Every detail, every stage in the development of the thought, takes shape and wakes to life as though of itself, and is sufficient unto itself. The result is a whole new world most agreeable to dwell in. This very personal style—I shall not weary of repeating—is an important characteristic of Montaigne. Pascal, who takes little joy in his own style and keeps firm control of it, did not make enough of this characteristic of Montaigne's. Montaigne uses the expression *"avoir le boutehors aisé,"* meaning to have what we would call "the gift of the gab"; actually, with him language is the *boute-en-train*—the life and soul of the party. (p. 27)

Charles Augustin Sainte-Beuve, "Montaigne," in his Selected Essays, *edited by Francis Steegmuller, translated by Norbert Guterman, Doubleday & Company, Inc., 1963, pp. 13-28.*

Frontispiece of the first edition of The Essays *(1580), bearing Montaigne's handwritten corrections.*

RALPH WALDO EMERSON   (essay date 1850)

[*An American essayist and poet, Emerson was one of the most influential figures of the nineteenth century. As a founder of the transcendental movement and the shaper of a distinctly American philosophy embracing optimism, individuality, and mysticism, Emerson stressed the recognition of God Immanent: the presence of ongoing creation and revelation by a god apparent in all things, who exists within everyone. Also crucial to Emerson's thought is the related Eastern concept of the essential unity of all thoughts, persons, and things in the divine whole, and an emphasis on individualism and the quest of each person to break free from the troubles and trappings of the illusory world in order to discover and learn to trust the godliness of the inner Self. In the following excerpt from an essay originally published in 1850, Emerson expresses his delight in both the content and style of* The Essays.]

A single odd volume of Cotton's translation of the *Essays* remained to me from my father's library, when a boy. It lay long neglected, until, after many years, when I was newly escaped from college, I read the book, and procured the remaining volumes. I remember the delight and wonder in which I lived with it. It seemed to me as if I had myself written the book, in some former life, so sincerely it spoke to my thought and experience. (p. 155)

Montaigne is the frankest and honestest of all writers. His French freedom runs into grossness; but he has anticipated all censure by the bounty of his own confessions. In his times, books were written to one sex only, and almost all were written in Latin; so that in a humorist a certain nakedness of statement was permitted, which our manners, of a literature addressed equally to both sexes, do not allow. But though a biblical plainness coupled with a most uncanonical levity may shut his pages to many sensitive readers, yet the offence is superficial. He parades it: he makes the most of it: nobody can think or say worse of him than he does. He pretends to most of the vices; and, if there be any virtue in him, he says, it got in by stealth. There is no man, in his opinion, who has not deserved hanging five or six times; and he pretends no exception in his own behalf. "Five or six as ridiculous stories," too, he says, "can be told of me, as of any man living." But, with all this really superfluous frankness, the opinion of an invincible probity grows into every reader's mind. "When I the most strictly and religiously confess myself, I find that the best virtue I have has in it some tincture of vice; and I, who am as sincere and perfect a lover of virtue of that stamp as any other whatever, am afraid that Plato, in his purest virtue, if he had listened and laid his ear close to himself, would have heard some jarring sound of human mixture; but faint and remote and only to be perceived by himself."

Here is an impatience and fastidiousness at color or pretence of any kind. He has been in courts so long as to have conceived a furious disgust at appearances; he will indulge himself with a little cursing and swearing; he will talk with sailors and gipsies, use flash and street ballads; he has stayed in-doors till he is deadly sick; he will to the open air, though it rain bullets. He has seen too much of gentlemen of the long robe, until he wishes for cannibals; and is so nervous, by factitious life, that he thinks the more barbarous man is, the better he is. He likes his saddle. You may read theology, and grammar, and metaphysics elsewhere. Whatever you get here shall smack of the earth and of real life, sweet, or smart, or stinging. He makes no hesitation to entertain you with the records of his disease, and his journey to Italy is quite full of that matter. He took and kept this position of equilibrium. Over his name he drew an emblematic pair of scales, and wrote *Que sçais je?* under it. As I look at his effigy opposite the title-page, I seem to hear him say, "You may play old Poz, if you will; you may rail and exaggerate,—I stand here for truth, and will not, for all the states and churches and revenues and personal reputations of Europe, overstate the dry fact, as I see it; I will rather mumble and prose about what I certainly know,—my house and barns; my father, my wife and my tenants; my old lean bald pate; my knives and forks; what meats I eat and what drinks I prefer, and a hundred straws just as ridiculous,—than I will write, with a fine crow-quill, a fine romance. I like gray days, and autumn and winter weather. I am gray and autumnal myself, and think an undress and old shoes that do not pinch my feet, and old friends who do not constrain me, and plain topics where I do not need to strain myself and pump my brains, the most suitable. Our condition as men is risky and ticklish enough. One cannot be sure of himself and his fortune an hour, but he may be whisked off into some pitiable or ridiculous plight. Why should I vapor and play the philosopher, instead of ballasting, the best I can, this dancing balloon? So, at least, I live within compass, keep myself ready for action, and can shoot the gulf at last with decency. If there be any thing farcical in such a life, the blame is not mine: let it lie at fate's and nature's door."

The *Essays,* therefore, are an entertaining soliloquy on every random topic that comes into his head; treating every thing without ceremony, yet with masculine sense. There have been men with deeper insight; but, one would say, never a man with such abundance of thoughts: he is never dull, never insincere, and has the genius to make the reader care for all that he cares for.

The sincerity and marrow of the man reaches to his sentences. I know not anywhere the book that seems less written. It is the language of conversation transferred to a book. Cut these words, and they would bleed; they are vascular and alive. One has the same pleasure in it that he feels in listening to the necessary speech of men about their work, when any unusual circumstance gives monetary importance to the dialogue. For blacksmiths and teamsters do not trip in their speech; it is a shower of bullets. It is Cambridge men who correct themselves and begin again at every half sentence, and, moreover, will pun, and refine too much, and swerve from the matter to the expression. Montaigne talks with shrewdness, knows the world and books and himself, and uses the positive degree; never shrieks, or protests, or prays: no weakness, no convulsion, no superlative: does not wish to jump out of his skin, or play any antics, or annihilate space or time, but is stout and solid; tastes every moment of the day; likes pain because it makes him feel himself and realize things; as we pinch ourselves to know that we are awake. He keeps the plain; he rarely mounts or sinks; likes to feel solid ground and the stones underneath. His writing has no enthusiasms, no aspiration; contented, self-respecting and keeping the middle of the road. There is but one exception,—in his love for Socrates. In speaking of him, for once his cheek flushes and his style rises to passion. (pp. 157-61)

> *Ralph Waldo Emerson, "Montaigne; or, The Skeptic," in his* Emerson's Complete Works: Representative Men, Seven Lectures, Vol. 4, Houghton Mifflin and Company, *1883, pp. 141-77.*

T. A. TROLLOPE (essay date 1871)

[*Trollope was an English man of letters. He spent much of his life in Italy, and his books—among them* A Decade of Italian Women *(1859) and* A Peep Behind the Scenes at Rome *(1877)—reflect his interest in Italian history and culture. In the following excerpt, he speculates on the reasons for Montaigne's enduring popularity.*]

Of all the thousands of writers of the sixteenth, seventeenth, and eighteenth centuries, whose names and works are recorded in the history of literature, a few scores of names only have become household words among the men of this nineteenth century. And, considering all the calls on the attention and time of the present generation made by its own literature, the continued existence of any past name among us as a generally known and household word must be held to imply no small degree of eminence and merit. But of this small band of survivors—of these few scores of names which still are on the tongues of all men—a very much smaller and more select band is that which is composed of the old writers who are still really read.

And of this very select and small company Michel de Montaigne is one. (p. 352)

What is it that has enabled Montaigne to float still a strong swimmer beneath the glimpses of the moon, he alone of all his French contemporaries, while black oblivion has engulfed, or all but engulfed, all those others?

In seeking a reply to this question, we may begin by observing that Michel de Montaigne, besides belonging, as has been said, to the small band of survivors whose works are still really read after the lapse of three centuries, is in a special and very notable manner one of that little and privileged knot of writers of whom succeeding generations love to speak and think as of a personal acquaintance and friend. The names of the genial compeers of that immortal round table, where the peaked beard of Montaigne wags above the board between his admiring juniors, Burton and Sir Thomas Brown, might be enumerated within a very moderate compass. But they will readily occur to the reader, who will have no difficulty in recognising the type of writers of whom we are speaking. They are the men whom the world affects to call by some pet name, who are always spoken of with more of the familiarity of affection than of the formality of respect, and who are never mentioned without the addition of some kindly epithet, which adheres to them as closely as the Homeric "Swift-of-foot" does to Achilles. They are "old John" this, "rare Ben" that, "quaint Tom" t'other. Montaigne owns fellowship with all these worthies.

And this is a mark characteristic of all the company, and of our kindly Michel as much as of any one of them—that the world loves, remembers, and prizes them, not so much for what they have said, as for their manner of saying it. "Le style, c'est l'homme" ["The style is the man"], says the French critic. And the dictum is especially true of the writers belonging to the class of whom we are speaking. They have so put themselves and their own individuality into their writings that the reader feels, not as if he were gathering information through the medium of paper and print (which, excellent as the invention is, stands like a very undiaphanous screen between one human soul and another), but as if he were listening to the chat of a very delightful companion. Hence the airs of intimacy which the world of readers assumes in speaking of these men.

And it is to be observed further, that these facts explain not only the popularity of such writers, but the causes of the permanency of that popularity also. With the exception of chroniclers, from whose pages historians have perhaps not yet succeeded in wringing the last drop of truth that may be got from them, what book of two hundred—ay, or of one hundred years old—can ever be opened for the sake of the matter it has to impart to us? It is all *connu, connu* ["known, known"]! The world has got on too far ahead. But for the manner of the writer—the "style," which is the man! This is the charm which is in its nature immortal.

And to the present writer such reflections seem to be entirely applicable to our well-loved Michel de Montaigne. No doubt there are many men, lovers of old books, and in some cases lovers of old times, who would exclaim against such a notion as a heresy of the most detestable kind, conclusive as to the self-sufficient ignorance of the utterer of it. They will assert that lessons of wisdom for the conduct of life of the most practically valuable kind are yet to be learned from the old Gascon philosopher. They will maintain that specially as a master in the science of mankind he is still supreme. They will assure you that he who would sound and understand the human heart and its weaknesses, he who would school his own against them, he who would learn to practise a philosophy of life profound in its wisdom, because of the largest in its humanity, can do no better than "turn over with a daily, turn over with a nightly hand" the pages of Montaigne.

But to the present writer this seems to be an illusion the cause of which it is not difficult to imagine. The student who would feed his mind with all the good things enumerated in the preceding paragraph, can, it is submitted, do better than go to Montaigne for them. Not that nothing of the sort is to be found in his pages. That is far, very far, from being the case. But let a moralist, full fed with the current literature and speculations of the present day, go to Montaigne's pages to seek the philosophy to be found in them, totally regardless of all the charms of the great writer's style, wholly uninterested by the *naïveté* of the self-revelations he is so liberal of, careless of the historico-social speculations called forth by the fact that such a man should have so thought and so written at such a time and under such circumstances, and he will hardly need a more irresistible proof of the reality of the world's progress. Such a seeker would find the maxims of wisdom very trite, the speculations very jejune, the morality very superficial, the world-knowledge very shallow. But then such a seeker, such a reader, never does look into Montaigne's book. The men who read Montaigne are those who look for and are competent to find all those other charms which we have been supposing our student moralist to neglect. And, as has been said, it is not difficult to imagine the nature of the illusion, which predisposes such men to find in the subject matter of the old philosopher's writings all those valuable things which have been above rehearsed. There is the prestige of antiquity, which adds the authority of venerability to cathedratic precepts. There is the charm of style, which, specially heightened and flavoured by the racy quaintness of an old-world diction, has the effect of adding new point and weight to dicta, which have since been said to far greater effect, because said in connection with a wider science, and based on far more extended generalizations. There is also, contributing to the same result, a feeling which, however little men may be conscious of its operation, is probably hardly ever altogether absent from the mental attitude, with which we contemplate the operation of the minds of men of long-passed generations. It is a pleasurable feeling arising from the recognition of a similarity to our modes of thinking and reasoning in beings divided from us by vast spaces of time. "Nay, sir," said Dr. Johnson of the dancing dogs, "the creature, it is true, dances ill, but the wonder is that it should do it at all!" And it may perhaps be said, without intending any of the disrespect to those who have gone before us that the implied analogy might seem to involve, that a complacent though not self-conscious feeling of a somewhat similar kind mingles with the half-surprised recognition of modes of thought that we know as our own, in those who, as we cannot help perceiving, are to us ever as children.

If, however, the student of morals and of man, who is conversant with the present aspects of those studies and with the best modern literature in which those aspects are presented, cannot be counselled to turn to the pages of Montaigne with the hope of finding much that will be suggestive or useful to him, very different advice may be offered to the purely literary *dilettante*. French critics are never weary of enlarging on the very special and individual beauties of the style of the old Gascon philosopher, and the alluring charm of his manner. (pp. 352-55)

In fact, there are few writers—perhaps it would be more correct to say that there is not one—to whom the French tongue is more deeply indebted for the improvement of the language into the polished instrument which modern writers find ready to their hand. He was indeed a greater benefactor in this kind than he would have been if he had been a less lawless, wilful, and audacious writer than he was. He had no models, and he owned subjection to no rules. He wrote precisely as it pleased his own fancy; he compelled his pen to follow his thoughts, and he let the latter wander as they would. No phrase, no metaphor, no similitude, was rejected by him if it served well and truly for the forcible expression of his thought; and he hesitated not to coin new words whenever he wanted them and could find them. Many of the terms thus imported into the language by him have permanently remained to enrich it; and many more have been rejected by the modern masters of the language which, as Le Clerc admits, might have been advantageously retained. Words now so common and accepted as "gratitude," "diversion," "enfantillage," "enjoué," are cited by Le Clerc as among a very much greater number which the language owes to Montaigne. Among others, which the same critic cites as words found in the *Essays,* but which are not now extant in modern French, several have, at all events, become perfectly naturalized on our side of the Channel, as "condiment," "equanimite," "improvidence," "inanite," "magnifier," "procerite," &c. (pp. 355-56)

To return, however, for one word more respecting that quality of "quaintness" and simplicity which imparts so much of the charm which modern readers find in many old writers, and very notably in Montaigne. It is to be remembered that much illusion is produced by considering this to arise from qualities inherent in the writer. It is produced, in most cases, simply by the distance of time which separates the writer from the reader. The "simplicity," which delights us, is due to the fact that men's thoughts two or three hundred years ago were not laden, complicated, and diversified by all the wealth of speculation and knowledge which have since been added to the human stock. And the "quaintness" is simply the result of the difference of time, and the comparatively unformed condition of the language those writers had to use. Had the same men written in our own day, they would not have written "quaintly." In the remarks of children a similarly amusing simplicity and quaintness may often be observed. And a few generations hence the writers, who would be the last that we should think of crediting or taxing with quaintness, will be found as quaint as we find the writings of Montaigne.

There are, however, qualities very intrinsically the special properties of the man, which have been very influential in making the style and manner of Montaigne's writings what they are. His immensely strong feeling of personality is the principal of these. Hardly any writer ever made so great and constant use of the capital *I,* and certainly none ever has been so entirely pardoned by his readers for the abuse of it. In fact, the main subject of the *Essays* is Michel de Montaigne himself; and in more than one passage he pretty well tells us that such is the case, and that he intends such to be the case. But one of the merits which may most readily cause the egoism of a writer to be forgiven by his reader, Montaigne had to perfection—sincerity in self-portraiture. . . . In fact, it is this continual reference to and miniature painting of himself that produces that sense of acquaintanceship and companionship between the writer and the reader, which is perhaps the principal source of the universally admitted attractiveness of Montaigne's writings, and one of the most marked features of that *manner* which has been declared to be the real merit, for the sake of which a few hours of our sorely-occupied time may yet be bestowed on them.

But it was hinted at the opening of this paper that there is one other point of view, equally distinct from any value, which the *Essays* may be supposed still to possess as moral teaching, from which they may be considered with great interest. And this is their value as documents in the history of social progress—especially, of course, of French social progress. (pp. 357-58)

Of course the causes of the evils, which were rending the body of French society in twain during the reigns of the last Valois kings, and were normally preparing a due crop of always increasing evils to follow, were manifold. But it would not probably be far from the truth to assert that the worst, most prominent, most hopeless, and most radical of these causes was the absence of toleration; and the absolute incapacity of *all* the men of the time to conceive the idea that tolerance was a good, a desirable, or a possible thing. Now, Montaigne was the most tolerant of men. Toleration of the opinions, and even to a great degree of the conduct, of others, is the key-stone of his philosophy and the key-note of his writings. It is in this respect that he was so remarkably in advance of his age, and truly the degree of the advance may besaid to have been infinite. (p. 359)

Now, Montaigne was above all else a sceptic. Scepticism upon every sort of subject that can occupy the human mind made the very substratum of his mental constitution, and was habitually cultivated by him in all his speculations and philosophizings. The general outcome of these was expressed in the well-known motto which he took to himself as setting forth the sum of his thoughts and experiences, "QUE SAIS-JE?" He had come to the conclusion that "there is nothing certain save uncertainty." "The persuasion of certitude," he tells us in another place, "is a sure mark of folly and of extreme incertitude." "Is it not better," he asks again, "to remain in suspense than to fall into so many errors which human phantasy has produced?" Fontenelle, towards the end of his life, declared himself to be dismayed at the certitude he saw around him on all sides. On which Le Clerc remarks that the saying is profound, and is worth a whole page of history. Truly he might have said that it was worth very many volumes. (p. 360)

It is impossible to read his *Essays* without perceiving very clearly that he doubted respecting many things, assured certainty regarding which is essential to the faithful Christian. (p. 361)

It must not be imagined, however, that Montaigne was by any means a professed unbeliever. Very far from it. He died in the act of raising himself painfully in his bed to join his hands in prayerful veneration of the elevation of the host, in the course of the service being performed in his sick chamber. Nor at any period of his life did he express disbelief in any fact or doctrine that the Catholic Church required him to believe. But Montaigne was as inconsistent in this respect as very many other men are. He would fain have been not sceptical in the matter of religion. But his nature was too strong for him. His whole intellect was sceptical. He received no opinion on any subject without proceeding at once to ascertain for himself what was to be said on the other side of the question. If you had proposed to him the controversy between the little-endians and the big-endians he would have made an excellent defence on either side, and then have left the matter with his favourite *que sais-je?* (pp. 361-62)

> T. A. Trollope, "Michel de Montaigne," in The Saint
> Pauls Magazine, *Vol. VIII, April, 1871, pp. 352-63.*

REV. W. LUCAS COLLINS   (essay date 1879)

[*An English clergyman, biographer, and essayist, Collins edited the 20-volume series "Ancient Classics for English Readers" (1870-76) and wrote critical biographies of such figures as Livy, Samuel Butler, and Montaigne. In the following excerpt from his study of Montaigne, he surveys and discusses what he considers the preeminent works among* The Essays.]

In any attempt to give, within the compass of a few pages, an idea of the spirit and character of the *Essays* of Montaigne, it is well to bear in mind, as a warning, what their author himself lays down in his celebrated essay on the **"Art of Conversation"**—that "every abridgment of a good book is a foolish abridgment." The only defence of such an attempt in the present case is, that Montaigne can scarcely be said to have written "a book" at all, and himself disclaims any such intention. We feel, as we read him, that we are in charming company; but he is rather the companion for an hour's delightful gossip, to which we return with fresh appetite from time to time, than the author to whose work we devote ourselves, from the first page to the last, with a continuous interest and attention. He is "the handbook for gentlemen in their leisure hours," says Huet: we can take him up and lay him down as we will. Nothing is more characteristic of his essays than their desultoriness. And this is intentional and conscious on the part of their author. (p. 102)

The very titles of his chapters often seem as though they had been adopted purposely to show on how slender a thread of that kind he could hang page after page of amusing discourse. The chapters **"On Cripples"** and **"On Coaches"** contain very little to satisfy the curious inquirer upon either subject: the essay **"On Vanity"** consists chiefly (perhaps not so very inappropriately) of the personal history of the Essayist himself. These titles, he confesses, "do not always comprehend the whole matter" (indeed very seldom); "they often denote it by some mark only": and he is somewhat unreasonable in expecting his readers to follow him through all that curious chain of thought of which many of the connecting links existed only in the mind of the writer. . . . But he not only treats in the same essay of half-a-dozen different things,—he returns sometimes again and again to the same subject in portions of different essays; detached fragments from his writings can hardly be more fragmentary reading then the *Essays* themselves: and in some cases it might be possible to piece together, out of their pages, scattered thoughts on the same subject which would present in appearance a more connected train of ideas than one of the longer essays as they stand. (pp. 103-04)

Let us begin here with the essay **"On the Education of Children,"** thrown into the form of a letter to the author's friend and country-neighbour Diana de Foix, Countess of Garson, who was at that time expecting to give birth to a son and heir. Here, as in other cases, the writer talks of many things besides education; but what he does say on the subject is pertinent and sensible. (p. 105)

He ranks a scientific and technical education far below that which we call (and, as he would contend, justly) a liberal one. And, as we might readily foresee, his idea of the root of a liberal education is the study of moral philosophy:—

> It seems to me that the first teaching with which we ought to imbue his mind should be that which is to regulate his morals and his feelings; which shall teach him to know himself, and to know how to live well and to die well. Amongst the liberal arts, let us begin with that which makes us free; they all serve, no doubt, in their degree, to the ordering and employment of our life, as everything else does also, in some sort: but let us make choice of that which serves to that end directly and professedly. 'Tis great foolishness to teach our children the knowledge of the stars and the motions of the eighth sphere before we teach them the knowledge of themselves.

And after insisting upon it that children are never too young to learn at least the elements of this knowledge, and that the lessons of moral philosophy are not more difficult for the youthful student than the subtleties of logic or the problems of geometry—"things by which our lives can never be mended"—he adds these striking words:—

> To our young scholar, his closet or the garden, his table and his bed, solitude or company, morning and evening,—all hours shall be alike, all places shall serve him for study: for philosophy, which, as being that which moulds our judgments and our characters, will be his principal lesson, has the privilege of mingling itself with everything.

He is to be early taught also to form an independent judgment, and to take nothing on trust. In fact, Montaigne would have his young gentleman something of a Pyrrhonist, like himself. . . . (pp. 111-12)

To conclude these extracts from an essay which will repay thorough and careful reading, and from which later writers (notably Rousseau in his *Emile*) have drawn largely, let us take the "short method" in which the author would deal with a wilful and hopeless pupil:

> If the pupil should turn out to be of such a contrary disposition, that he loves better to listen to a foolish story than to the narrative of some interesting travel, or to a rational discussion; that at the sound of a drum that stirs the youthful ardour of his companions he will turn to follow another that calls to their tricks a troop of mountebanks; if in his heart he does not find it more pleasant and delightful to return covered with dust and glory from the field of battle, than from the tennis-court or the games in which he has carried off the prize;—I can find no other remedy for such a case but that he be bound apprentice to a pastry-cook in some respectable town, were he the son of a duke.

In the copy which the author left with corrections in his own handwriting, the method recommended is shorter and sharper still: "That his tutor strangle him in good time, *if he can do so without witnesses:* or otherwise put him apprentice." M. Naigeon has thus printed the passage in his edition of 1802.

No one can fail to recognise, in the principles of education sketched out in this essay, the essential points of the training of a gentleman in the true sense of the word. If some of the suggestions should seem to the wisdom of our nineteenth century trite and commonplace, let us bear in mind that they were put on paper three hundred years ago. How many steps have we made in advance since their date, in real education? and how many even of these have been made within the present century? Had English education, a hundred years ago, approached in principle or practice to anything like the ideal of Montaigne?

One grave omission will be remarked. Not a word is breathed of any religious principle or duty to be inculcated,—any religious foundation on which morality is to rest. In the great issues of life, philosophy is to be the only guide. As to anything higher than that, Montaigne is silent, because he has nothing to teach. If the intelligent pupil should question him on that great subject, he could only answer in the words of his motto, *"Que sais-je?"*

The essay which has generally been considered as the author's masterpiece is that on **"The Art of Conversation,"** which was one of his last written, and stands eighth in the Third Book. Pascal has called it "incomparable," and his judgment of Montaigne is, to say the least, not partial. The chapter is discursive, like nearly all the rest: if it teaches the art of conversation at all, it is by the example of how a good talker may handle, with a light and sparkling touch, a dozen subjects strung together by the very slenderest thread of connection. But it is not really what we call "conversation" which he here discusses, though in that art we may be sure that Montaigne was a proficient. The essay is rather the laying down of certain rules and principles on which an intellectual argument or discussion (which Montaigne declares he loved) should be conducted, in order to secure at once free expression of opinion and command of temper—to show how gentlemen may dispute without thinking it necessary to quarrel. (pp. 113-15)

It is the pleasure of finding himself matched with a skilful and vigorous opponent, a master of his art, and who always fights fair, that Montaigne appreciates, and which, in his view, alone makes argument a valuable intellectual exercise. The question as to which opponent has the best of it is little to the purpose, provided the bout be well and fairly fought on both sides. He knew well enough, as we all know, that men are very rarely convinced by argument, and are not much nearer the truth after it than before.

> The excitement and the chase of our quarry is the true sportsman's part: we are not to be excused if we follow it clumsily and against the rules of the field. To fail to catch our game is quite another matter; for we are born to make the quest of truth,—to possess it belongs to a higher power. The world is but a tilting-school of inquiry: it is not who shall carry off the ring, but who shall run the best career. He may play the fool who asserts what is true, as well as he that asserts what is false; for we are here treating not of the matter but the manner of an argument.

He had some experience of those pompous and arrogant gentlemen who consider that their wealth, or rank, or reputation supply them with sufficient and material arguments in support of any assertion or opinion they may be pleased to make,—who say to society in general—

> I am Sir Oracle,
> And when I ope my lips, let no dog bark.

He would not have cared to argue with Sydney Smith's "country gentlemen, who talk in a landed manner." Against such throwing of social weight into the scales of discussion he vigorously protests. . . . (pp. 118-19)

He sees the enormous advantage which rank and position give, not only in the estimate which society will form of a man's abilities, but in the very facility which it gives him of putting forth his best with ease and confidence, with the assurance of its being appreciated. . . . On the other hand, [Montaigne] does not care to argue with fools. If you try to set them right, either they are obstinate, or they say, "That was exactly what I meant, only I did not know how to express it."

> As for assertions made ordinarily, in the course of conversation, I never set myself to refute them either by word or sign, however false or absurd they may be.

It would save considerable waste of words and disturbing of tempers in daily society, if we were more ready to adopt in this respect the self-denying ordinance of Montaigne.

It has been seen that, in his views on education, Montaigne looks upon philosophy as the master-science. But philosophy as he finds it, even amongst his favourite Greeks and Romans, is very far from satisfying him. The leaders of ancient thought, he finds, do but contradict each other. No two sects—and he has learnt from Varro that there are no less than two hundred and eighty-eight—agree among themselves what is the "sov-

ereign good," or wherein lies the essential distinction between vice and virtue. His own school of thought and belief (he does not tell us so in actual words, but it is written on almost every page of the Essays, as well as on the rafters of his library) is that of Pyrrho—"whose profession is to oscillate, to doubt, to inquire, to feel sure of nothing, to make one's self responsible for nothing." This is, in his eyes, the essence of human wisdom; and he seems to insinuate that even Socrates and Plato were Pyrrhonists at heart. But the philosophy which he really values, and which he would fain both teach and learn, is practical; and it is that which can teach us how to meet death. This forms the subject of one of his best and most serious essays— **"That to study philosophy is to learn to die."** He takes his text from Cicero, who again does but translate from the *Phædo* of Plato. The proposition laid down at the outset of the essay might seem, at first sight, strangely chosen to prove his conclusion—"Let philosophers say what they will, the final end we all have in view, even in virtue itself, is pleasure." The pleasure which the Stoic takes in being strong enough to resist the pleasures of sense is only pleasure of a higher kind. And they are wrong, he argues, who assert that the quest of virtue is indeed difficult and disagreeable, but that virtue when attained is pleasant: who *does* attain it?

> They are wrong; seeing that of all the pleasures we know, the pursuit itself is pleasant. The attempt must needs have a savour of the quality of that to which it is directed; for it is a component part of the result, and of the same essential nature. The happiness and blessedness which shines in virtue illumines all its avenues and approaches, from the first entrance to the last inner-gate.

Seldom, even in the writings of graver philosophers, has a noble conception been clothed in language so brief and picturesque.

The highest blessing that virtue can confer upon us, the author contends, is the contempt of death. If philosophy teaches us to despise poverty, or pain, or sorrow, it is well. But some men's lives such accidents touch but little; and at the worst, from all of them death will relieve us. It is death only which comes inevitably to all men. If we tremble at it, "how can we advance a single step in life without an ague-fit?" he asks. "The remedy of the vulgar is not to think about it at all;" "most people cross themselves at the very word, as though it were the name of the Devil."

He rambles off to string together a score of instances of sudden or unexpected death, ancient and modern (reminding the reader here, as in many other places, of Burton's style in his *Anatomy*), to illustrate the commonplace that death has no respect of ages or persons. Then he proposes to himself and to his readers a remedy against the fear of death quite contrary to the habit of the vulgar.

> Let us disarm him of his strangeness: let us converse with him, grow familiar with him; let us have nothing so often in our thoughts as death, let us continually represent him to our imagination under all possible shapes: at the stumbling of a horse, at the fall of a tile, at the prick of a pin, let us straightway think— 'Well! supposing it had been death itself!' and thereupon encourage and fortify ourselves against it. In our feasts and revels, let there evermore occur to us, as a refrain, the thought of our condition; and never let us be so far carried away by pleasure, but that it cross our recollection from time to time in how many ways this very enjoyment lays us open to death, and with how many snares it threatens us.

For his own part, he declares that, but for thus accustoming himself to the thought, he should live in perpetual terror: "Never man was so distrustful of his life, yet never was man so indifferent as to its duration." (pp. 120-24)

As to anything beyond death, Montaigne is silent. There comes no voice for him out of the cloud, and there is no cry of inquiry on his part. "The deadest deaths are the best"—that is the sum of his feelings, so far as he expresses them. He would have his last moments calm: but whether it is the calmness of the Stoic, the Materialist, or the Christian, cannot be with certainty gathered from any word of his. (pp. 129-30)

The most cursory perusal of these *Essays* will convince us that in many things the writer was before his age. We have seen his general tolerance of religious and political opinions, his hated of cruelty in all shapes, his sympathies with the poor. We might trace, perhaps, in his pages the first rise, or at least the first unreserved expression, of ideas utterly foreign to the spirit of the sixteenth century, which have since won their way into modern legislation and practice. He saw clearly what seems to us now the most obvious truism, that judicial torture was "a trial of patience rather than of truth; for why should pain make a man confess a fact, rather than make him assert what is not the fact?" The practical result in many cases was that "the man whom the judge remits to the torture in order that he may not be made to die innocent, is made to die both innocent and tortured." The cogent arguments he uses against the horrible cruelties perpetrated under cover of the law, sound to us in these days as commonplace; but they were political and religious heresies when he dared to print them. It was not until more than two hundred years afterwards that the judicial question was finally abolished in France: it lingered in England until near the middle of the seventeenth century, and was in use long after in the dungeons of the Holy Inquisition. He is bold enough to follow Plato, and to insist that all punishment is for correction, not for revenge, that we do not correct the man we hang, but correct others through him. The principle is sufficiently familiar to modern legislators: but it had been too much forgotten in the long interval between Plato and Montaigne. Nay, he would even go further than our modern legislation has yet ventured, though many steps have been taken in that direction; for he seems to have held that capital punishment was altogether a mistake,—that the worst use you could put a man to was to hang him. He had remarked, long before the existence of Vagrant Acts and Mendicity Societies, that begging was a profession—a profession that had its charms as well as its profits—not a misfortune; and that the professional mendicant was, as we have found him, quite irreclaimable. He has lost the little belief he once had in sorcery and witchcraft. . . . He "would rather prescribe hellebore than hemlock" in cases of reputed witchcraft; and in all such cases "it is surely setting an extraordinary value on one's own conjectures to have a poor creature roasted alive for them." Yet it was near a hundred years afterwards that such a judge as Hale declared his belief in the guilt of two poor wretches, against whom Sir Thomas Browne was a witness; and it was so late as 1712 that the last "witches" were judicially murdered in England.

Our modern divorce-courts, whose effect upon public morals is yet a disputed question, would have commended themselves to Montaigne's deliberate judgment. He did not believe in the principle that the recognised indissolubility of marriage will lead both parties to make the best of it.

> We have thought to tie the marriage-knot more firmly
> by taking away all means of dissolving it; but the tie

of the will and the affections is relaxed and loosened, the tighter that of obligation is drawn. On the other hand, what kept marriage honourable and sacred at Rome so long was the liberty given to those who would to dissolve it. They took the more care of their wives, the more risk there was of losing them; and with the full liberty of divorce, they passed above five hundred years before any availed themselves of it.

Valerius Maximus is his authority for this rather questionable statement. But the purity of domestic lfe in the early ages of Rome is frequently the regretful theme of her poets: our modern civilisation has reproduced the morals of the Empire, not of the Republic.

Some of the reforms which suggested themselves to his busy mind have not yet found favour with legislators. But many readers will see a good deal of force in his idea that the State should exercise more control over the power of the individual to dispose of his property by will, and that the best will is, after all, that which leaves the ordinary law of succession to take its course. . . . He has no patience with those churlish testators who

> Die, and endow a college or a cat;

and speaks with well-deserved abhorrence of the capricious selfishness of wealthy relatives, "who play with their wills as they would with apples or rods, to reward or chastise every turn of conduct in those who profess an interest in them. A will is a thing of too lasting consequence and too serious importance to be thus brought out for review at every turn."

He has an opinion, too, which bears upon the competitive examinations which have been the hoddy of modern reformers,—an opinion to which the more rational section of the public are gradually coming round:—

> Some of our parliaments, when they are about to admit officers, examine them in knowledge only; others add to this a trial of their sense, by referring to them the judgment of some legal case. The latter seem to me to adopt by far the better method; and though both these qualifications are necessary, and it is requisite that both should be found in the candidates, yet most certainly that of knowledge is less indispensable than that of judgment: the last may possibly make shift without the first, but the first without the last, never.

In his essay "On Sumptuary Laws" he points out, with his usual good sense, the futility of all such restrictions. He saw that they rather tended to encourage the taste for what they were meant to prohibit. (pp. 144-48)

The antipathy which he had conceived (or at least chose to profess) against law and lawyers, in spite of his own connection with the profession . . . breaks out from time to time in the *Essays*. It has been sometimes ascribed to a kind of affectation in the man: as he rails against pedantry and the display of learning, in order to prove that he is not a scholar but a gentleman, all the while that he is quoting from one Latin or Greek author after another in a fashion which his enemies might well have called pedantic, so, they would say, he attacks the law because he would have us understand that his profession is rather the sword than the gown, which he has only worn by accident. It is possible that there may be something of this. But he had even a greater natural antipathy to another of the learned professions—that of medicine. He has given vent to this feeling in a chapter bearing the not very appropriate title,

"On the Resemblance of Children to their Fathers." He there introduces one of his many good stories,—the history of a village called Lahontan, of which he was patron, which had long been a kind of "Happy Valley," independent of the surrounding world, and free from its vices and troubles, until in an evil hour one ambitious native brought up a son as a notary, and another married his daughter to a physician. From that time all their peace and happiness was gone. The lawyer set them all at logger-heads; the physician taught them the names of diseases, and the use of drugs.

> They swear it was only from that time forth they began to feel that the night-air made their heads bad, that to drink when they were hot made them ill, that the autumn winds were more dangerous than the spring; that since the invention of this art of medicine, they found themselves overwhelmed with a legion of maladies they had never known before, they felt a general failure of their ancient vigour, and their lives were cut shorter by half.
>
> (pp. 149-50)

He thought his hatred of physicians and their drugs must be hereditary: neither his father, grandfather, nor great-grandfather had ever consulted a physician, and he himself had a thorough contempt for them. (p. 151)

Old age is regarded from no very favourable point of view. He has none of the smooth things to say of it which are so popular, so commonplace, and so generally untrue. He does not believe that we grow wiser or better as we grow old. He does not look forward to it with any pleasure, nor, what is rarer, will he pretend to do so. (p. 155)

He speaks of himself at forty as having entered the avenue of old age,—when "what he shall be from that time forth will be but a half-existence, and no longer his whole self": though he thinks that men should perhaps "not be dismissed to the fireside till they are fifty-five or sixty." What would he have thought of our modern statesmen who show no signs of senility at threescore years and ten? On the other hand, he believes the mental powers "are as adult at twenty as ever they are likely to be, and that they then show all that they can do"—a fact which is surely contrary to experience. More grand deeds, he finds, are done before thirty than after that age; and he instances Hannibal and Scipio, and here he is perhaps nearer to the truth. (p. 157)

Montaigne is, in many points, a conservative both politically and socially.

> To my thinking, in public affairs there is no system so bad, provided it be of long standing and firmly established, that is not better than change and alteration. Our manners are very corrupt, and have a marvellous tendency to grow worse; amongst our laws and usages there are many which are barbarous and monstrous; nevertheless, by reason of the difficulty of putting ourselves into a better condition, and the risk of meddling with things, if I could put anything under the wheel to stop it where it is, I would do it with all my heart. The worst evil I find in our state is its instability; and that our laws, no more than our clothes, can take any settled shape. It is very easy to accuse a government of imperfection, for all things human are full of it; it is very easy to beget in any people a contempt for ancient ordinances: no man ever yet attempted it but he succeeded. But to set up a better constitution in place of that which has been destroyed,—very many have foundered who have undertaken it.

> The best and most excellent government is that under which a nation has maintained itself. . . . Nothing presses so hard on a state as innovation: change alone gives shape to injustice and tyranny. When a portion of the fabric is out of order, it should be propped: we may prevent the decay and corruption natural to all things from carrying us too far from our foundations and principles; but to undertake the reconstruction of such a vast fabric, and to change the foundations of such a great building, is for those only to take in hand who efface in order to cleanse, who would reform particular defects by a universal confusion, and cure diseases by death. The world is by no means apt at mending itself: it is so impatient of any pressure, that it thinks only of cutting itself clear, no matter at what price. We see by a thousand examples that it generally cures itself to its cost.

It was this conservative spirit which made him regard the Protestant reformers with no very favourable eye. Their principles were subversive of the established order to things: and that order, whether in Church or State, he was stout in upholding. (pp. 161-63)

> *Rev. W. Lucas Collins, in his* Montaigne, *William Blackwood and Sons, 1879, 192 p.*

FRANCIS THOMPSON   (essay date 1898)

[*Thompson was one of the most important poets of the Catholic Revival in nineteenth-century English literature. Often compared to the seventeenth-century metaphysical poets, especially Richard Crashaw, he is best known for his poem "The Hound of Heaven," published in his collection* Poems *(1893), which displays Thompson's characteristic themes of spiritual struggle, redemption, and transcendent love. Like other writers of the fin de siècle period, Thompson wrote poetry and prose noted for rich verbal effects. In the following excerpt from an essay originally published in the* Academy *in 1898, Thompson discusses Montaigne's personal style and philosophy and comments on their relation to William Shakespeare's Hamlet.*]

Montaigne is a patriarch, the father of a great people. From him are descended all they upon the face of the earth that write essays; from him all they that combine a bold garrulity with the . . . first personal pronoun. He invented the essay, both name and thing. Nor have any talked about themselves with more applause to more crowded European houses. Rousseau, indeed, is more read; but the fame of the *Confessions* is marvellously allied to infamy. And, then, Montaigne had a century or two the start of him with readers. Montaigne's book founded no social revolution; but its intellectual influence throughout Europe, down to the eighteenth century, was immense. To name its mightiest disciple, Shakespeare drew on it frequently for his philosophy, and was evidently a profound student of it. Nay, in the close of this article we shall bring forward a still grander claim. It would be difficult to say by what great English writer of the sixteenth or seventeenth century he was not quoted, down to Butler in *Hudibras*. Mr. Lowndes says of him that, with all his popularity among his contemporaries, he did not interpret his age. But in every age there are two currents to be distinguished—the surface-current and the undercurrent. Montaigne belonged to the under-current. The greatest writers usually belong to the under-current; for the under-stream represents what an age produces, the surface-stream merely what it develops. The leaf does not fall from the bough till it has prepared the germ of the future leaf; an age does not end till it has prepared and enunciated the ideas which are to govern the succeeding age. This is its real contribution to the progress of thought, and this is the work of its writers who belong to the under-current. On the other hand, the ideas which govern it are the legacy of the preceding age, which it merely popularises. Montaigne's ideas are those with which his epoch was in travail; he was part of his age as truly as the child in the womb is part of the mother. In effect, Mr. Lowndes acknowledges this. He fails only to perceive that Montaigne was not exceptional in his position, and that every age has two classes of representative writers—"representative" in two distinct ways. (pp. 408-09)

[Montaigne was] the most delightful, shrewd, compact of rambling essayists; the most popular writer that ever professed the creed of systematic selfishness. He did not so much lack method—he was indifferent to it; he was, in truth, much too lazy, too self-indulgent, to trouble himself with system. An hour's reading, he declared, was a great stretch for him. The sagacious givers of advice to young men who warn them against vagrant reading would have found a frightful example in Montaigne. He wrote as he read, and he travelled as he wrote. When he was journeying through Germany and Italy to Rome, his chief end was not to reach his end. The longer he could delay on the way, the better he was pleased.

> "When the complaint was made" (says his amanuensis) "that he often conducted the party by devious and contrary ways—often getting back close to the place he had started from—he replied that, for his part, he had no other destination than the place where he chanced to be; and that he could not go wrong, or out of his way, having no other end in view than to reside in new localities."

This might stand for an excellent description of the methodical absence of method in the essays. It is decidedly the right way to see countries, the Cook's tourist method being the way to overlook them. And every reader of the essays entirely agrees that when he most goes astray he "then does most go right."

But this writer, so sauntering and *insouciant* in method, is direct, quick, pregnant in style. Excursive in method means generally diffuse in style; but Montaigne is all point, vividness, picturesqueness. He loved directness in others—a good deal, we suspect, because of his constitutional aversion to taking trouble. He objected to Cicero, the eloquently diffuse, though Cicero was the idol of Montaigne's age; he admired Seneca the sententious, Plutarch the full of matter. "Meatiness" he loved in others, and "meaty" he was himself. If he wanders, he never leads you through dry places. This is the more remarkable because it is so total a breaking away from the spirit of his time. To write not only in the vernacular, but in the spirit of the vernacular, was a new departure for that age of imitative classicism. . . . (pp. 409-10)

Montaigne's chief reputation with us is that of a picturesque and gossiping observer of life; and upon this, indeed, he chiefly prided himself. But he was also a philosopher, and observed life with the *parti-pris* of a philosopher. He was the forerunner of the sceptical and *laisser-aller* philosophy which afterwards gained such power. Not of strong affections (he seems never really to have been in love), averse from practical affairs, cursed with irresolution, yet gifted with a keen analysis of human nature, sceptical philosophy was his natural refuge. He belonged to the cross-benches of the human mind. We cannot but agree with Pascal, against Mr. Lowndes, that Montaigne's philosophy was an ignoble thing in its application to practical life. It is a skilful blend of whatever is selfish in the Stoic with whatever is self-gratifying in the Epicurean. It enforces the

Christian counsel of detachment, but deletes the one thing which makes that detachment noble. Detachment from the affections of the world becomes purest selfishness, unless it be to attach oneself to the affections of the other world. Yet this is Montaigne's rule of life:

> One must have wife, children, possessions, and above all health, if one can, but not hold to these things so that one's happiness depends upon them. . . . One must disavow these overstrong obligations, and love indeed this or that, *but espouse nothing save oneself.*

The italics are ours. This is the higher selfishness with a vengeance! . . . We once heard a gentleman of the "bounder" persuasion expatiate on the perfect life of another gentleman of the "bounder" persuasion whose house ran with drink, but who never got drunk. This, he affirmed, was the true art of life—to manipulate your drinks so that you stopped short of intoxication. It seems to us that this gentleman was an unconscious, but rigidly logical disciple of Montaigne. If Montaigne had placed the *summum bonum* in whiskey and soda, to this complexion he must logically have come.

On the theoretical side he played with great effect the Pyrrhonic juggle of balancing *pros* and *cons* till they killed each other, and was an adept in sitting between two stools without coming to the ground. Of this Kilkenny cat philosophy he was the modern founder, and, did he live now, would be an agnostic. Yet his book is not odious, like the productions of most sceptical egotists; it is saved by the geniality of his scepticism. He is better than his creed; takes keen interest in humanity while professing to consider it a very poor affair; and shows himself a good and kindly neighbour, a warm friend. And so they last for ever, these shrewd, strolling, zig-zag, fascinating, personal essays; with their racy, original, pregnant style, like the architecure of an old French town; professing an inhuman creed in the most human and humane way; shaking the head over that sad dog Man, and finding nothing in the world so well worth writing or meditating about.

We said that we had one claim on behalf of Montaigne which we reserved to the last. This is it. We do in conscience believe not only that he furnished Shakespeare with philosophy, but that he actually suggested the whole conception of *Hamlet*. Hamlet, that is to say, was suggested to Shakespeare by Montaigne's description of himself. He found portrayed in the *Essays* a man who was an onlooker upon life, a constitutional speculator upon men and human affairs, addicted to an indecisive philosophising which examined everything, analysed everything, but decided nothing; a man averse to action, and unfit for affairs (for so Montaigne pictures himself); cursed, moreover, with a disabling *irresolution.*

> He was incapable (so Mr. Lowndes summarises Montaigne's confession) of taking part in a dubious enterprise because he saw always the reasons on both sides—so that he reserved his judgment until occasion forced his hand, and then, he confesses candidly, he mostly flung reason to the wind, and followed the lead of circumstance and chance.

That is a perfect description of Hamlet. So he hesitates, "seeing the reasons on both sides"; so, when his hand is forced, following the lead of circumstance and chance, he kills Polonius, and, finally (by a mere sudden thought), kills the king. To take such a character as that sketched by Montaigne, to place it in a situation which clamoured for action, and then to work out the inevitably resulting tragedy—that was the idea which dawned on Shakespeare, if we are right. Viewed in this light, it becomes most natural that *Hamlet* is full of Montaigne philosophy, and that we should encounter a direct quotation from Montaigne: "For there is nothing either good or ill, but thinking makes it so." Montaigne has a whole essay on the theme, *That the taste of good things and ill depends in great measure upon the opinion we have of them*—a maxim which he in his turn borrowed from Epictetus. That Hamlet is younger than the Montaigne of the essays, that he differs in many subordinate details of character, does not defeat our thesis. Shakespeare was too good a dramatist not to make such divergences from his model for the sake of dramatic requirements. We think the theory has at any rate something to say for itself. (pp. 410-13)

Francis Thompson, "Montaigne," in his Literary Criticisms: Newly Discovered and Collected, *edited by Rev. Terence L. Connolly, S. J., E. P. Dutton and Company Inc., 1948, pp. 407-13.*

EDWARD DOWDEN (essay date 1905)

[*An Irish educator and man of letters, Dowden was primarily a Shakespearean scholar, editing many of the dramatist's plays and numbering among his several critical studies* Shakspere, His Mind and Art *(1875). Also a biographer of some note, Dowden believed that criticism of a literary work must be allied with an understanding of the personality and biographical circumstances of the author. In the following excerpt from an essay originally published in 1905, Dowden appraises Montaigne's method and talent.*]

The *Essays* themselves give various accounts of the motives which brought them into being, and probably in each account there is a fragment of the entire truth. In his retirement there were times when Montaigne suffered from the tedium of solitude; a "melancholic humour", very much out of accord with his natural complexion, threatened to lay hold upon him; he needed some occupation to banish his ennui, and he took up his pen and found that he was happily astir. But to write was not only a stimulus; it was also a control. A rich soil that lies idle produces all manner of troublesome weeds; so it is with the mind, which if not occupied and restrained runs into every kind of extravagances in the vague field of the imagination. Whe he retired to his own house, he tells us, intending, as far as might be, to pass in repose the short remainder of his life, he supposed that he could do himself no better service than to let his mind entertain itself, as it should please, in entire idleness. He hoped that years had tamed his spirit, and brought it within the bounds of reason. But it proved otherwise. Like a horse broken loose from the rider, his mind flung up its heels and started on an extravagant career. "It gives birth to so many chimeras and fantastic monsters, one upon another, without order or design, that to contemplate at my ease their ineptitude and strangeness I have begun to set them down in a roll, hoping with time to make my mind ashamed of itself." There was never any very acute shame in Montaigne's contemplation of his chimeras, for he did not aspire to be an angel or a Cato; he was only, he would reflect, a specimen of the average human being, with certain advantages arising from the fact that he recognised his monsters as fantastic; and it was not his business to play the weeping philosopher of humanity, when it was more agreeable and perhaps more effective to smile. But, in truth, he did not at first take himself for the central subject of his study. On whatever matter happened to interest him he made the trial of his judgment, and every matter proved fertile; a fly would serve as well as a philosopher or an envoy of state. To be started on a train of meditation was all that he required—"I take the first argument that fortune offers me; they are all

equally good for me; I never design to treat them in their totality, for I never see the whole of anything, nor do those see it who promise to show it to us. Of a hundred members and faces which each thing has, I take one, sometimes to touch it only lightly or to graze the surface, and sometimes to pinch it to the bone; I give a stab not as wide but as deep as I can, and in general I love to seize things by some unwonted lustre." The judgment was an instrument which had always its uses. If the subject was one which he did not understand, he used his judgment to sound the depth of the ford, and finding it too deep for one of his stature, he kept to the bank. If the subject was frivolous, the judgment was an instrument which might give it substance and support. If the subject was a noble one, already trodden and trampled into a thousand paths, the judgment had still its opportunity in discovering the best of all those paths.

The master faculty worked in mysterious ways; not always deliberately; often spontaneously, oracularly, suddenly, carrying one away, persuading or dissuading, speaking with authority, not balancing and weighing, as the judgment ordinarily does, but presenting itself like some unexpected fiat of the will. What else but this was the demon of Socrates? And have we not, each of us, our demon? Montaigne's best thoughts came to him when he seemed to seek them least; and, to his grief, they often vanished as quickly—gifts of the gods, but snatched away by some invisible harpies. Such thoughts offered themselves as he lay in bed, or sat at table, or on horseback—especially on horseback, for the stir in the blood somehow set his mind astir and made it quick and apprehensive. But if they were not captured and secured on the moment, only a vain image remained with him, like the shadow of a lost dream which haunts us after waking.

The subjects which set him thinking as he rode through the country or sat in his library might be remote from Michel de Montaigne; yet somehow Michel de Montaigne almost always consciously or unconsciously played his part in the meditation. Even on a wholly detached theme it was his own judgment which was defining itself. He could not think or write like a pedant whose wisdom lies all on his shelves and not in his own consciousness, his own experience. Good and evil, he held, reside not so much in things themselves as in our opinion of things, the way we regard them, the way we deal with them; and therefore if he sought for wisdom and knowledge, he must to a great extent seek it in himself, in the form imposed on things by his own mind, in his opinions, in his feelings, in his habits of living, even in his trivial peculiarities, for these might have some significance which he did not wholly comprehend, and more might be implied by them than appeared upon the surface. Thus, without at first entertaining such a design, he was drawing, pencil-stroke by pencil-stroke, a portrait of himself. The features of a man began to look out upon him from the drawing-board, and the features were his own. A new motive and a new pleasure entered into Montaigne's work; he would complete by a multitude of touches seemingly casual yet nicely calculated, this work of art, and it should remain as a memorial of him with his friends. A foolish project! Pascal afterwards pronounced it [see excerpt dated 1662?]; a foolish project to occupy one's self with this hateful thing, the *ego*. But Montaigne, with easier wisdom, maintained that if he was playing the fool, at least it was at his own expense; his folly would die with him and would create no train of evil consequences. And he did not, in truth, regard the project as foolish. The attainment of self-knowlege was no fool's task, but an arduous undertaking for those who would be wise. . . . If Montaigne's way of self-study were to be dignified with the name of a method,—a word inappropriate enough with such a writer— we should have to describe it as the method of observation, the empirical, or—shall we say?—the experimental method. He started with no *a priori* assumptions, theological or philosophical; he did not systematise his results; he made no attempt even to unify the record of his thoughts and feelings under any theoretical conception of himself; he was content to set down an observation here and another observation there; if the Montaigne of to-day differed from the Montaigne of yesterday, he recorded the present and immediate fact; he differed from himself as much as from other men; he was one of a diverse and undulant species. Yet an ideal conception of himself gradually formed itself in his mind; a unity in multiplicity gradually became apparent; and there was a certain artistic pleasure in giving salience to those traits which served best to illustrate and expound this, his own ideal of Montaigne. And why should he not speak of himself? The rule to be silent with respect to one's self is only a bridle for calves! Neither the saints, who speak of themselves so loftily, nor the philosophers, nor the theologians tolerate such a curb.

Montaigne was not a saint; nor did he claim for himself the title of philosopher. He professed himself no more than the average man. And precisely for this reason he had the better right to be communicative about himself; through his representation of an average man—neither a saint nor a beast—he was really exhibiting humanity itself; "each man carries in his own person the entire form of the condition of the race". He offered himself to the world, if the world chose to take him so, as a specimen of the genus *homo,* as one of themselves. . . . All the worth of his book lay in the fact that it was "a book of good faith". And yet the other thought, that in painting himself he was painting the human creature, and not merely an individual, was always in the "back-shop" of Montaigne's mind. He could not construct a foursquare body of philosophy; he was not a system-maker or system-monger; yet one thing he might give as his gift to the world—some scattered notes on that curious creature, man, as seen in the example which lay nearest to his observations; as seen in himself.

As he proceeded with his task, which was also his recreation, he began to perceive that his book was reacting upon his character. He did not form his book more than his book was forming him. After all, the portrait had in it something of an ideal. He was sometimes hasty and intemperate, but here he was giving pledges to reasonableness and moderation. He was often tempted to exclaim "All or nothing", but here he pleaded for the wisdom of the mean, the *"juste milieu"*. He sometimes wearily gave over the search for truth, and despaired of any certitude, but here he declared that the world is a school of inquisition; to enter it is not the great point, but to run the fairest course; the chase is our business, our game; we are inexcusable if we conduct the chase carelessly and ill; to fail in capturing the game is another matter; we were born to pursue the quest for truth; to possess it belongs to a higher power. Thus the *Essays* became to their author in some measure a rule of conduct; or, if not a rule, for he loved to live in the freedom of the present moment, at least an impulse and a guide. Montaigne had become through them in some degree the director of his own conscience, his own Seneca, and also his own gentle and encouraging counsellor and companion, his more intimate Plutarch. (pp. 230-38)

To render some service to others—this was assuredly one of the motives which impelled and sustained Montaigne in his delightful labours, egoist though he sometimes professed himself. Did he exhibit his own faults or defects? Well, this might be of use as a warning to others. Did he point to the infirmities of the intellect of man? This should touch at once the dogmatists who would forever moor in some oozy haven the voyaging spirit of man, and those wild speculators who would subvert the old order of society for the sake of a theory. He could not dazzle men with a vision of great hope, as Rabelais had done; then it was the morning, and now the noon hung heavy and clouds had overcast the heavens. But he might do what perhaps was needed by his time—he could plead for sanity. The future of his country depended on the presence in it of a group— possibly an enlarging group—of men who were sane, who could play the part of reconcilers between the madness of extremes, who were not blinded by authority or by custom, who were universal questioners, who were pliable to the touch of reality, who dared to doubt as well as to believe, who took, as he did, the balance for their emblem, and who could pause to weigh things before they applied themsevles to action. Of zeal and passion there was enough; there was too much. It were better for France if men were less zealous if only they were more sane.

Trenchant critic of the vices and errors of his own time as Montaigne was, he did not declaim in the manner of a preacher. His tone was that of conversation: "I speak to paper as I do to the first person I meet." But what a conversation it is! how rich in ideas! how vivid and opalescent in expression! . . . No one felt more than he that the right word, the word which lives with a strong corporeal life, springs from intensity of vision; that style, as we call it, is simply the body of thought, and that nothing proper to us is either wholly corporeal or incorporeal. If his *Essays* were praised, it ought not to be for their language, nor yet precisely for their matter, but for the form impressed upon the matter by his mind, of which spiritual form the language was only the inevitable consequence. And therefore he was in the highest degree curious and scrupulous about the language which he would not wish to see praised by any one apart from the spiritual form. . . . Yet there is no appearance of curiosity, of painful research; there is not a touch of preciosity in his style. "May I use no words," he writes, "but those which are current in the Paris markets." His utterance seems to be, and no doubt in great part it was, in the highest degree spontaneous, as if he caught his prey at the first bound. Its characteristic, at its best, lies in the union of strength with ease. To the imagination it is a perpetual feast, with its litheness of movement, its iridescence, its ideas incarnated in metaphors, metaphors often homely yet each a fresh surprise; always original, always his own. And out of this admirably pedestrian prose rises now and again a lyric cry (all the more poignant and penetrating because to be a poet is not the writer's trade); now a cry of indignation, now a cry of pity, now the cry of memory or of desire. And sometimes the page is one of a superb rhetoric. . . . (pp. 239-43)

The essays are, as is natural, of very unequal merit. Some are mere notes on subjects which have little or no relation to life and character. If the essays appropriated by the servant-man, who thought he had obtained a treasure in his master's manuscripts, were of a kind like unto that on **"Thumbs"** or that on **"Posting,"** we can bear our loss with equanimity. Although a fly might be enough to set Montaigne's mind in motion, he is at his best only when he deals with some serious matter of human life or some of the great powers or the infirmities of human nature. We cannot, indeed, found our anticipations respecting the interest of an essay on the title at its head. That on "**Coaches**" contains a majestic description of the pomps of ancient Rome and an eloquent denunciation of the perfidies of the conquerors of the New World; when it is time to utter the words, "Return we to our coaches," the essay is ended, and only the reverberation of its lofty music lives in our memory. The Essayist's career has been somewhat extravagantly run on horseback, and at the close it is the King of Peru, and not we, whose carriage stops the way. When Montaigne wanders from his professed theme, why should we quarrel with him? He never wanders from himself, and from humanity which is his true theme. . . . He does not care to link matter with matter by formal connections, and supposes that there may be as much continuity in a rivulet as in a chain. Such an apology for his leaps and "gambades" means that Montaigne in his *Essays* does not write treatises, nor deliver speeches, but converses with himself and his readers. The unity which each posseses is not that of formal arrangement but the unity of a mind at play with us and with itself. We come to his book not to exhaust a subject, but to hold converse with a friend. (pp. 246-48)

Edward Dowden, in his Michel de Montaigne, *J. B. Lippincott Company, 1905, 383 p.*

GEORGE SAINTSBURY (essay date 1910-11)

[Saintsbury has been called the most influential English literary historian and critic of the late nineteenth and early twentieth centuries. His studies of French literature, particularly A History of the French Novel *(1917-19), have established him as a leading authority on such writers as Guy de Maupassant and Honoré de Balzac. Saintsbury adhered to two distinct sets of critical standards: one for the novel and the other for poetry and drama. As a critic of novels, he maintained that "the novel has nothing to do with any beliefs, with any convictions, with any thoughts in the strict sense, except as mere garnishings. Its substance must always be life not thought, conduct not belief, the passions not the intellect, manners and morals not creeds and theories. . . . The novel is . . . mainly and firstly a criticism of life." As a critic of poetry and drama, Saintsbury was a radical formalist who frequently asserted that subject is of little importance and that "the so-called 'formal' part is of the essence." René Wellek has praised Saintsbury's critical qualities: his "enormous reading, the almost universal scope of his subject matter, the zest and zeal of his exposition," and "the audacity with which he handles the most ambitious and unattempted arguments." In the following excerpt from an essay originally published in 1910 or 1911, Saintsbury comments on the form, style, and matter of* The Essays.]*

[Montaigne's *Essays* is] a book which has hardly been second in influence to any of the modern world.

This influence is almost equally remarkable in point of matter and in point of form. The latter aspect may be taken first. Montaigne is one of the few great writers who have not only perfected but have also invented a literary kind. The essay as he gave it had no forerunner in modern literature and no direct ancestor in the literature of classical times. It has been suggested that the form which the essays assumed was in a way accidental, and this of itself precludes the idea of a definite model, even if such a model could be found. Beginning with the throwing together of a few stray thoughts and quotations linked by a community of subject, the author by degrees acquires more and more certainty of hand, until he produces such masterpieces of apparent desultoriness and real unity as the essay "**Sur des vers de Virgile.**" In matter of style and language Montaigne's position is equally important, but the ways which led him to it are more clearly traceable. His favourite author was beyond all doubt Plutarch, and his own explicit confession

Château de Montaigne, the author's ancestral estate. From Montaigne: A Biography, *by Donald M. Frame. North Point Press, 1984. Copyright © 1965 by Donald M. Frame.*

makes it undeniable that Plutarch's translator, Jacques Amyot, was his master in point of vocabulary and (so far as he took any lessons in it) of style. Montaigne, however, followed with the perfect independence that characterized him. He was a contemporary of Ronsard, and his first essays were published when the innovations of the Pléiade had fully established themselves. He adopted them to a great extent, but with much discrimination, and he used his own judgment in latinizing when he pleased. In the same way he retained archaic and provincial words with a good deal of freedom, but by no means to excess. In the arrangement, as in the selection, of his language he is equally original. He has not the excessive classicism of style which mars even the fine prose of Jean Calvin, and which makes that of some of Calvin's followers intolerably stiff. As a rule he is careless of definitely rhythmical cadence, though his sentences are always pleasant to the ear. But the principal characteristic of Montaigne's prose style is its remarkable ease and flexibility. A few years after Montaigne's death a great revolution, as is generally known, passed over French. The criticism of Malherbe, followed by the establishment of the Academy, the minute grammatical censures of Claude Favre Vaugelas, and the severe literary censorship of Boileau, turned French in less than three-quarters of a century from one of the freest languages in Europe to one of the most restricted. During this revolution only two writers of older date held their ground, and those two were Rabelais and Montaigne—Montaigne being of his nature more generally readable than Rabelais. All the great prose writers of France could not fail to be influenced by the racy phrase, the quaint and picturesque vocabulary, and the unconstrained constructions of Montaigne.

It would be impossible, however, for the stoutest defender of the importance of form in literature to assign the chief part in Montaigne's influence to style. It is the method, or rather the manner of thinking, of which that style is the garment, which has in reality exercised influence on the world. Like all the greatest writers except Shakespeare, Montaigne thoroughly and completely exhibits the intellectual and moral complexion of his own time. When he reached manhood the French Renaissance was at high water, and the turn of the tide was beginning. Rabelais, who died when Montaigne was still in early manhood, exhibits the earlier and rising spirit, though he needs to be completed on the poetical side. With Montaigne begins the age of disenchantment. By the time at least when he began to meditate his essays in the retirement of his country house it was tolerably certain that no golden age was about to return. As the earlier Renaissance had specially occupied itself with the practical business and pleasures of life, so the later Renaissance specially mused on the vanity of this business and these pleasures. The predisposing circumstances which affected Montaigne were thus likely to incline him to scepticism, to ethical musings on the vanity of life and the like. But to all this there had to be added the peculiarity of his own temperament. This was a decidedly complicated one, and neglect of it has led some readers to adopt a more positive idea of Montaigne's scepticism than is fully justified by all the facts. The attitude which he assumed was no doubt ephectic and critical chiefly. In the **"Apologie de Raymund Sabunde,"** he has apparently amused himself with gathering together, in the shape of quotations as well as of reflections, all that can be said against certainty in aesthetics as well as in dogmatics. It is even said by some who have examined the original . . . that the text and alterations show a progressively freethinking attitude, side by side with a growing tendency to conceal it by ambiguity and innuendo. But until all the documents are accessible this must remain doubtful. The general tenor of the essays is in complete contrast with this sceptical attitude, at least in its more decided form, and it is worth notice that the motto *Que scai-je?* does not appear on the title-page till after the writer's death. Montaigne is far too much occupied about all sorts of the minutest details of human life to make it for a moment admissible that he regarded that life as a whole but as smoke and vapour. And it is almost certainly wrong, though M. Brunetière may have given countenance and currency to the idea, to regard his philosophy as in the main intended as a succour against the fear of death. The reason of the misapprehension of him which is current is due very mainly to the fact that he was eminently a humorist. Perhaps the only actual parallel to Montaigne in literature is Lamb. There are differences between them, arising naturally enough from differences of temperament and experience; but both agree in their attitude—an attitude which is sceptical without being negative and humorous without being satiric. There is hardly any writer in whom the human comedy is treated with such completeness as it is in Montaigne. There is discernible in his essays no attempt to map out a complete plan, and then to fill up its outlines. But in the desultory and haphazard fashion which distinguishes him there are few parts of life on which he does not touch, if only to show the eternal contrast and antithesis which dominate it. The exceptions are chiefly to be found in the higher and more poetical strains of feeling to which the humorist temperament lends itself with reluctance and distrust, though it by no means excludes them. The positiveness of the French disposition is already noticeable in Rabelais; it becomes more noticeable still in Montaigne. He is always charming, but he is rarely inspiring, except in a very few passages where the sense of vanity and nothingness possesses him with unusual strength. As a general rule, an agreeable grotesque of the affairs of life (a grotesque which never loses hold of good taste sufficiently to be called burlesque) occupies him. There is a kind of anticipation of the scientific spirit in the careful zeal with which he picks up odd aspects of mankind and comments upon them as he places them in his museum. Such a temperament is most pleasantly shown when it is least personal. A dozen generations of men have rejoiced in the gentle irony with which Montaigne handles the *ludicrum humani saeculi* ["show of the human race"], in the quaint felicity of his selection of examples, and in the real though sometimes fantastic wisdom of his comment on his selections. (pp. 32-5)

George Saintsbury, "Montaigne," in his French Literature and Its Masters, *edited by Huntington Cairns, Alfred A. Knopf, 1946, pp. 27-38.*

G. L. STRACHEY (essay date 1912)

[*Strachey is best known as a biographer whose iconoclastic reexaminations of historical figures revolutionized the course of modern biographical writing. He conceived a type of biography that integrated established facts, speculative psychological interpretations, and imaginative recreations of his subjects' thoughts and actions which resulted in lively, perceptive, and above all "human" biographical portraits. In his major biographies,* Eminent Victorians *(1918),* Queen Victoria *(1921), and* Elizabeth and Essex: A Tragic History *(1928), Strachey disclosed previously overlooked complexities of personality in some of the most prominent and revered figures of English history. Like his biographies, Strachey's literary criticism is considered incisive and interestingly written. Although he wrote on a wide variety of topics, his discussions of French literature are particularly insightful. In the following excerpt, Strachey professes admiration for Montaigne as a writer but denies him profundity as a philosopher.*]

[In the *Essays* of Montaigne] the spirit of the Renaissance, which had filled the pages of Rabelais with such a superabundant energy, appears in a quieter and more cultivated form. The first fine rapture was over; and the impulsive ardours of creative thought were replaced by the calm serenity of criticism and reflection. Montaigne has none of the coarseness, none of the rollicking fun, none of the exuberant optimism, of Rabelais; he is a refined gentleman, who wishes to charm rather than to electrify, who writes in the quiet, easy tone of familiar conversation, who smiles, who broods, and who doubts. The form of the detached essay, which he was the first to use, precisely suited his habit of thought. In that loose shape—admitting of the most indefinite structure, and of any variety of length, from three pages to three hundred—he could say all that he wished to say, in his own desultory, inconsecutive, and unelaborate manner. His book flows on like a prattling brook, winding through pleasant meadows. Everywhere the fruits of wide reading are manifest, and numberless Latin quotations strew his pages. He touches on every side of life—from the slightest and most superficial topics of literature or manners to the profoundest questions that beset humanity; and always with the same tact and happiness, the same wealth of learned illustration, the same engaging grace.

The *Essays* are concerned fundamentally with two subjects only. First, they illustrate in every variety of way Montaigne's general philosophy of life. That philosophy was an absolutely sceptical one. Amid the mass of conflicting opinions, amid the furious oppositions of creeds, amid the flat contradictions of loudly asseverated dogmas, Montaigne held a middle course of calm neutrality. *Que sçais-je?* was his constant motto; and his *Essays* are a collection of numberless variations on this one dominating theme. The **"Apologie de Raimond Sebond,"** the largest and the most elaborate of them, contains an immense and searching review of the errors, the incoherences, and the ignorance of humanity, from which Montaigne draws his inevitable conclusion of universal doubt. Whatever the purely philosophical value of this doctrine may be, its importance as an influence in practical life was very good. If no opinion had any certainty whatever, then it followed that persecution for the sake of opinion was simply a wicked folly. Montaigne thus stands out as one of the earliest of the opponents of fanaticism and the apostles of toleration in the history of European thought.

The other subject treated of in the *Essays,* with an equal persistence and an equal wealth of illustration, is Montaigne himself. The least reticent of writers, he furnishes his readers with every conceivable piece of information concerning his history, his character, his appearance, his health, his habits, and his tastes. Here lies the peculiar charm of his book—the endless garrulity of its confidences, which, with their combined humour, suavity, and irresponsibility, bring one right into the intimate presence of a fascinating man.

For this reason, doubtless, no writer has ever been so gushed over as Montaigne; and no writer, we may be sure, would be so horrified as he at such a treatment. Indeed, the adulation of his worshippers has perhaps somewhat obscured the real position that he fills in literature. It is impossible to deny that, both as a writer and as a thinker, he has faults—and grave ones. His style, with all its delightful abundance, its inimitable ease, and its pleasant flavour of antiquity, yet lacks form; he did not possess the supreme mastery of language which alone can lead to the creation of great works of literary art. His scepticism is not important as a contribution to philosophical thought, for his mind was devoid both of the method and of the force necessary for the pursuit and discovery of really significant intellectual truths. To claim for him such titles of distinction is to overshoot the mark, and to distract attention from his true eminence. Montaigne was neither a great artist nor a great philosopher; he was not *great* at all. He was a charming, admirable human being, with the most engaging gift for conversing endlessly and confidentially through the medium of the printed page ever possessed by any man before or after him. Even in his self-revelations he is not profound. How superficial, how insignificant his rambling ingenuous outspokenness appears beside the tremendous introspections of Rousseau! He was probably a better man than Rousseau; he was certainly a more delightful one; but he was far less interesting. It was in the gentle, personal, everyday things of life that his nature triumphed. Here and there in his *Essays,* this simple goodness wells up clear and pure; and in the wonderful pages on Friendship, one sees, in all its charm and all its sweetness, that beautiful humanity which is the inward essence of Montaigne. (pp. 37-41)

> G. L. Strachey, *"The Renaissance,"* in his Landmarks in French Literature, *Henry Holt and Company, 1912, pp. 26-41.*

VIRGINIA WOOLF   (essay date 1924)

[*Woolf is considered one of the most prominent literary figures of twentieth-century English literature. Like her contemporary James Joyce, with whom she is often compared, Woolf is remembered as one of the most innovative of the stream of consciousness novelists. Concerned primarily with depicting the life of the mind, she revolted against traditional narrative techniques and developed her own highly individualized style. Woolf's works, noted for their subjective explorations of characters' inner lives and their delicate poetic quality, have had a lasting effect on the art of the novel. Also a discerning and influential critic and essayist, Woolf began writing reviews for the* Times Literary Supplement *at an early age. Her critical essays, which cover almost the entire range of English literature, contain some of her finest prose and are praised for their insight. Along with Lytton Strachey, Roger Fry, Clive Bell, and others, Woolf and her husband Leonard formed the literary coterie known as the "Bloomsbury Group." In the following excerpt from an essay originally published in the* Times Literary Supplement *in 1924, Woolf attempts to capture the essence of Montaigne's writing.*]

Once at Bar-le-Duc Montaigne saw a portrait which René, King of Sicily, had painted of himself, and asked, "Why is it not, in like manner, lawful for everyone to draw himself with a pen, as he did with a crayon?" Off-hand one might reply, Not only is it lawful, but nothing could be easier. Other people may evade us, but our own features are almost too familiar. Let us begin. And then, when we attempt the task, the pen falls from our fingers; it is a matter of profound, mysterious, and overwhelming difficulty.

After all, in the whole of literature, how many people have succeeded in drawing themselves with a pen? Only Montaigne and Pepys and Rousseau perhaps. The *Religio Medici* is a coloured glass through which darkly one sees racing stars and a strange and turbulent soul. A bright polished mirror reflects the face of Boswell peeping between other people's shoulders in the famous biography. But this talking of oneself, following one's own vagaries, giving the whole map, weight, colour, and circumference of the soul in its confusion, its variety, its imperfection—this art belonged to one man only: to Montaigne. As the centuries go by, there is always a crowd before that picture, gazing into its depths, seeing their own faces reflected in it, seeing more the longer they look, never being able to say quite what it is that they see. (p. 18)

To tell the truth about oneself, to discover oneself near at hand, is not easy. . . . There is, in the first place, the difficulty of expression. We all indulge in the strange, pleasant process called thinking, but when it comes to saying, even to someone opposite, what we think, then how little we are able to convey! The phantom is through the mind and out of the window before we can lay salt on its tail, or slowly sinking and returning to the profound darkness which it has lit up momentarily with a wandering light. Face, voice, and accent eke out our words and impress their feebleness with character in speech. But the pen is a rigid instrument; it can say very little; it has all kinds of habits and ceremonies of its own. It is dictatorial too: it is always making ordinary men into prophets, and changing the natural stumbling trip of human speech into the solemn and stately march of pens. It is for this reason that Montaigne stands out from the legions of the dead with such irrepressible vivacity. We can never doubt for an instant that his book was himself. He refused to teach; he refused to preach; he kept on saying that he was just like other people. All his effort was to write himself down, to communicate, to tell the truth, and that is a "rugged road, more so than it seems."

For beyond the difficulty of communicating oneself, there is the supreme difficulty of being oneself. This soul, or life within us, by no means agrees with the life outside us. If one has the courage to ask her what she thinks, she is always saying the very opposite to what other people say. (pp. 18-19)

Really she is the strangest creature in the world, far from heroic, variable as a weathercock, "bashful, insolent; chaste, lustful; prating, silent; laborious, delicate; ingenious, heavy; melancholic, pleasant; lying, true; knowing, ignorant; liberal, covetous, and prodigal"—in short, so complex, so indefinite, corresponding so little to the version which does duty for her in public, that a man might spend his life merely in trying to run her to earth. The pleasure of the pursuit more than rewards one for any damage that it may inflict upon one's worldly prospects. The man who is aware of himself is henceforward independent; and he is never bored, and life is only too short, and he is steeped through and through with a profound yet temperate happiness. He alone lives, while other people, slaves of ceremony, let life slip past them in a kind of dream. Once conform, once do what other people do because they do it, and a lethargy steals over all the finer nerves and faculties of the soul. She becomes all outer show and inward emptiness; dull, callous, and indifferent.

Surely then, if we ask this great master of the art of life to tell us his secret, he will advise us to withdraw to the inner room of our tower and there turn the pages of books, pursue fancy after fancy as they chase each other up the chimney, and leave the government of the world to others. Retirement and contemplation—these must be the main elements of his prescription. But no; Montaigne is by no means explicit. It is impossible to extract a plain answer from that subtle, half-smiling, half-melancholy man, with the heavy-lidded eyes and the dreamy, quizzical expression. . . . He had always mixed with clever men, and his father had a positive veneration for them, but he had observed that, though they have their fine moments, their rhapsodies, their visions, the cleverest tremble on the verge of folly. Observe yourself: one moment you are exalted; the next a broken glass puts your nerves on edge. All extremes are dangerous. It is best to keep in the middle of the road, in the common ruts, however muddy. In writing choose the common words; avoid rhapsody and eloquence—yet, it is true, poetry is delicious; the best prose is that which is most full of poetry.

It appears, then, that we are to aim at a democratic simplicity. We may enjoy our room in the tower, with the painted walls and the commodious bookcases, but down in the garden there is a man digging who buried his father this morning, and it is he and his like who live the real life and speak the real language. There is certainly an element of truth in that. Things are said very finely at the lower end of the table. There are perhaps more of the qualities that matter among the ignorant than among the learned. But again, what a vile thing the rabble is! ''the mother of ignorance, injustice, and inconstancy. Is it reasonable that the life of a wise man should depend upon the judgment of fools?'' Their minds are weak, soft and without power of resistance. They must be told what it is expedient for them to know. It is not for them to face facts as they are. The truth can only be known by the well-born soul—''l'âme bien née.'' Who, then, are these well-born souls, whom we would imitate if only Montaigne would enlighten us more precisely?

But no. ''Je n'enseigne poinct; je raconte'' [''I do not instruct; I relate'']. After all, how could he explain other people's souls when he could say nothing ''entirely simply and solidly, without confusion or mixture, in one word,'' about his own, when indeed it became daily more and more in the dark to him? One quality or principle there is perhaps—that one must not lay down rules. The souls whom one would wish to resemble, like Étienne de La Boétie, for example, are always the supplest. ''C'est estre, mais ce n'est pas vivre, que de se tenir attaché et obligé par necessité a un seul train'' [''It is to be, but not to live, to hold oneself bound and obliged of necessity to only one course'']. The laws are mere conventions, utterly unable to keep touch with the vast variety and turmoil of human impulses; habits and customs are a convenience devised for the support of timid natures who dare not allow their souls free play. But we, who have a private life and hold it infinitely the dearest of our possessions, suspect nothing so much as an attitude. Directly we begin to protest, to attitudinize, to lay down laws, we perish. We are living for others, not for ourselves. We must respect those who sacrifice themselves in the public service, load them with honours, and pity them for allowing, as they must, the inevitable compromise; but for ourselves let us fly fame, honour, and all offices that put us under an obligation to others. Let us simmer over our incalculable cauldron, our enthralling confusion, our hotch-potch of impulses, our perpetual miracle—for the soul throws up wonders every second. Movement and change are the essence of our being; rigidity is death; conformity is death: let us say what comes into our heads, repeat ourselves, contradict ourselves, fling out the wildest nonsense, and follow the most fantastic fancies without caring what the world does or thinks or says. For nothing matters except life; and, of course, order.

This freedom, then, which is the essence of our being, has to be controlled. But it is difficult to see what power we are to invoke to help us, since every restraint of private opinion or public law has been derided, and Montaigne never ceases to pour scorn upon the misery, the weakness, the vanity of human nature. Perhaps, then, it will be well to turn to religion to guide us? ''Perhaps'' is one of his favourite expressions: ''Perhaps'' and ''I think'' and all those words which qualify the rash assumptions of human ignorance. Such words help one to muffle up opinions which it would be highly impolitic to speak outright. For one does not say everything; there are some things which at present it is advisable only to hint. One writes for a very few people, who understand. Certainly, seek the Divine guidance by all means, but meanwhile there is, for those who live a private life, another monitor, an invisible censor within . . . , whose blame is much more to be dreaded than any other because he knows the truth; nor is there anything sweeter than the chime of his approval. This is the judge to whom we must submit; this is the censor who will help us to achieve that order which is the grace of a well-born soul. . . . But he will act by his own light; by some internal balance will achieve that precarious and everchanging poise which, while it controls, in no way impedes the soul's freedom to explore and experiment. Without other guide, and without precedent, undoubtedly it is far more difficult to live well the private life than the public. It is an art which each must learn separately, though there are, perhaps, two or three men, like Homer, Alexander the Great, and Epaminondas among the ancients, and Etienne de La Boétie among the moderns, whose example may help us. But it is an art; and the very material in which it works is variable and complex and infinitely mysterious—human nature. To human nature we must keep close. ''. . . il faut vivre entre les vivants'' [''We must live among the living'']. We must dread any eccentricity or refinement which cuts us off from our fellow-beings. Blessed are those who chat easily with their neighbours about their sport or their buildings or their quarrels, and honestly enjoy the talk of carpenters and gardeners. To communicate is our chief business; society and friendship our chief delights; and reading, not to acquire knowledge, not to earn a living, but to extend our intercourse beyond our own time and province. Such wonders there are in the world; halcyons and undiscovered lands, men with dogs' heads and eyes in their chests, and laws and customs, it may well be, far superior to our own. Possibly we are asleep in this world; possibly there is some other which is apparent to beings with a sense which we now lack.

Here then, in spite of all contradictions and all qualifications, is something definite. These essays are an attempt to communicate a soul. On this point at least he is explicit. It is not fame that he wants; it is not that men shall quote him in years to come; he is setting up no statue in the market-place; he wishes only to communicate his soul. Communication is health; communication is truth; communication is happiness. To share is our duty; to go down boldly and bring to light those hidden thoughts which are the most diseased; to conceal nothing; to pretend nothing; if we are ignorant to say so; if we love our friends to let them know it. (pp. 20-4)

There are people who, when they travel, wrap themselves up, "se défendans de la contagion d'un air incogneu" ["defending themselves from the contagion of an unfamiliar air"] in silence and suspicion. When they dine, they must have the same food they get at home. Every sight and custom is bad unless it resembles those of their own village. They travel only to return. That is entirely the wrong way to set about it. We should start without any fixed idea where we are going to spend the night, or when we propose to come back; the journey is everything. Most necessary of all, but rarest good fortune, we should try to find before we start some man of our own sort who will go with us and to whom we can say the first thing that comes into our heads. For pleasure has no relish unless we share it. As for the risks—that we may catch cold or get a headache—it is always worth while to risk a little illness for the sake of plea-sure."Le plaisir est des principales espèces du profit" ["Plea-sure is one of the chief kinds of profit"]. Besides if we do what we like, we always do what is good for us. Doctors and wise men may object, but let us leave doctors and wise men to their own dismal philosophy. For ourselves, who are ordi-nary men and women, let us return thanks to Nature for her bounty by using every one of the senses she has given us; vary our state as much as possible; turn now this side, now that, to the warmth, and relish to the full before the sun goes down the kisses of youth and the echoes of a beautiful voice singing Catullus. Every season is likeable, and wet days and fine, red wine and white, company and solitude. Even sleep, that de-plorable curtailment of the joy of life, can be full of dreams; and the most common actions—a walk, a talk, solitude in one's own orchard—can be enhanced and lit up by the association of the mind. Beauty is everywhere, and beauty is only two fingers' breadth from goodness. So, in the name of health and sanity, let us not dwell on the end of the journey. Let death come upon us planting our cabbages, or on horseback, or let us steal away to some cottage and there let strangers close our eyes, for a servant sobbing or the touch of a hand would break us down. Best of all, let death find us at our usual occupations, among girls and good fellows who make no protests, no lam-entations; let him find us "parmy les jeux, les festins, faceties, entretiens communs et populaires, et la musique, et des vers amoureux" ["among games, feasts, jests, general and popular conversation, music, and love poetry"]. But enough of death; it is life that matters.

It is life that emerges more and more clearly as these essays reach not their end, but their suspension in full career. It is life that becomes more and more absorbing as death draws near, one's self, one's soul, every fact of existence: that one wears silk stockings summer and winter; puts water in one's wine; has one's hair cut after dinner; must have glass to drink from; has never worn spectacles; has a loud voice; carries a switch in one's hand; bites one's tongue; fidgets with one's feet; is apt to scratch one's ears; likes meat to be high; rubs one's teeth with a napkin (thank God, they are good!); must have curtains to one's bed; and, what is rather curious, began by liking radishes, then disliked them, and now likes them again. No fact is too little to let it slip through one's fingers, and besides the interest of facts themselves there is the strange power we have of changing facts by the force of the imagi-nation. Observe how the soul is always casting her own lights and shadows; makes the substantial hollow and the frail sub-stantial; fills broad daylight with dreams; is as much excited by phantoms as by reality; and in the moment of death sports

with a trifle. Observe, too, her duplicity, her complexity. She hears of a friend's loss and sympathizes, and yet has a bitter-sweet malicious pleasure in the sorrows of others. She believes; at the same time she does not believe. Observe her extraor-dinary susceptibility to impressions, especially in youth. A rich man steals because his father kept him short of money as a boy. This wall one builds not for oneself, but because one's father loved building. In short, the soul is all laced about with nerves and sympathies which affect her every action, and yet, even now in 1580, no one has any clear knowledge—such cowards we are, such lovers of the smooth conventional ways— how she works or what she is except that of all things she is the most mysterious, and one's self the greatest monster and miracle in the world. ". . . plus je me hante et connois, plus ma difformité m'estonne, moins je m'entens en moy" ["the more I associate with and know myself, the more my hide-ousness astonishes me, the less I understand myself"]. Ob-serve, observe perpetually, and, so long as ink and paper ex-ist . . . , Montaigne will write.

But there remains one final question which, if we could make him look up from his enthralling occupation, we should like to put to this great master of the art of life. In these extraor-dinary volumes of short and broken, long and learned, logical and contradictory statements, we have heard the very pulse and rhythm of the soul, beating day after day, year after year, through a veil which, as time goes on, fines itself almost to transparency. Here is someone who succeeded in the hazardous enterprise of living; who served his country and lived retired; was landlord, husband, father; entertained kings, loved women, and mused for hours alone over old books. By means of per-petual experiment and observation of the subtlest he achieved at last a miraculous adjustment of all these wayward parts that constitute the human soul. He laid hold of the beauty of the world with all his fingers. He achieved happiness. If he had had to live again, he said, he would have lived the same life over. But, as we watch with absorbed interest the enthralling spectacle of a soul living openly beneath our eyes, the question frames itself, Is pleasure the end of all? Whence this over-whelming interest in the nature of the soul? Why this over-mastering desire to communicate with others? Is the beauty of this world enough, or is there, elsewhere, some explanation of the mystery? To this what answer can there be? There is none. There is only one more question: "Que scais-je?" (pp. 24-6)

> *Virginia Woolf, "Montaigne," in her* Collected Es-says, *Vol. III,* Harcourt Brace Jovanovich, 1967, *pp. 18-26.*

J. M. ROBERTSON   (essay date 1927)

[*Robertson was a Scottish statesman, journalist, and writer who served as editor of the London papers the* National Reformer, *the* Free Review, *and the* National Observer. *A Liberal Member of Parliament, Robertson wrote several defenses of free thought, most notably* A History of Free Thought in the Nineteenth Century *(1929), but is primarily remembered for his many critical studies of William Shakespeare. In the following excerpt, he discusses the special qualities of Montaigne's work that make it "enduring literature."*]

Montaigne has won and kept the ear of the world by reason, largely, of having never planned to gain it. Having as little vocation for systematic thinking or teaching as for the arts of poetry and drama and fiction, he sought none of those fields. He never even strove to cultivate the "literary" style of his time. Happily nourished on the Latin classics, he found in them practically all the artistic literature he wanted, though he read Italian poetry for his pleasure. What he began to write was not literature. What he came to write was literature of a new and enduring kind. (p. xix)

In the **"Apology for Raymond Sebond"** he can be seen as it were giving out, under cover of orthodoxy, his own reaction, in his first years of retreat, against all the dogmatism of his age. It appears to have been written at intervals round 1576, when he had a medal struck with his effigy and the inscription *Que sçay je?* "What know I?" Portions cannot be of earlier date than 1578. The result is a treatise in which credulity and incredulity, faith in tradition and derision of common belief, insistence on scientific doubt and disparagement of all science, oddly alternate. But the total effect is a discrediting of the normal religious certitudes. That ethics are matters of custom; that creeds are matters of place of birth; that Moslem faith is the twin of Christian faith; that religious zeal turns men into savages; that wars are matters of mere nationality or of mere partisanship; that men in the mass are for ever ignorantly sure of what they know nothing about, and childishly heedless of how they risk life and well-being for vain causes—such is the burden of Montaigne's "sceptical" polemic, addressed to a generation that had brought France nigh to both moral and material ruin by stress of the certitudes in question.

It is forcing an open door to retort that Montaigne, parading universal "doubt," was no consistent sceptic. Of course he was not, as he expressly avows; though for a time he sought to be, sawing at the bough on which he sat. For a time, perhaps, he had little confidence in any abstract moral proposition; and, living in an age whose "science" had its hinder parts embedded in delusion, he was always dubious about science, new and old. When certitude spelt havoc, such a rebounding spirit as his might touch the state of universal uncertainty which some of his earlier essays profess. But his large and sane understanding and his searching thought soon brought him to steady moral bearings. When he had re-made his philosophy of life for himself, he was full of hearty certitudes, moral, educational, political, and literary. The certitudes he distrusted and deprecated were mainly those which made men anti-moral, disloyal, internecine, barbarian, decivilized. That these things were bad, he never doubted. A sceptic in the strict theoretic sense, indeed, a doubter of all things, a consistent "Pyrrhonist," never existed, as Montaigne himself observes. Pyrrho at his start evoked the challenging and unanswerable question whether he doubted that he doubted; and Montaigne's polemic was but a shrewd yet artless strategy to turn fierce believers into sobered doubters on one side, by showing them that the enduring certitudes lay with the vital pieties of human relationship, which were being utterly lost in the desperate maintenance of the other sort.

It is not to be pretended that he was all along clear and consistent in his thought. His dialectic often outgoes his own conviction, and clashes flatly with his profession of faith. And though it may be argued, as by his latest and most accomplished editor, the veteran Dr. Armaingaud, that some of his self-contradictions are deliberate and strategic, some are not so describable. Just as he at times contradicts himself, within a page, on concrete matters, through sheer change of mood or stress of argument, he varies in his philosophic positions. Few men of his day, indeed, passed their intuitions and their prepossessions so energetically through the alembic of thought; but to the last he exhibits some that have not undergone the

process. He shaped his philosophy as he went along, expressing himself differently at different times, constantly avowing, even in excess of the fact, that he was "undulating and diverse" in his thinking. This was at once his security and half the secret of his influence. Had he been the confident framer of a new system of precise doctrine, he would have aroused hot hostility where in his own way he disarmed it. His congenital conservatism, making him dubious about Copernicanism and many other "upsetting" notions, gave him a footing with many who might easily have been alienated by any large show of faith in "new-fangled" doctrines. His flouting of innovation won him their ear for his counsels against dogmatism. The outcome was that on the wasting fever of French fanaticism Montaigne sprinkled cool reason. . . . (pp. xxxvi-xxxviii)

To note the evolution is to realize at once the sagacity and the efficacy of Montaigne's literary course. He has been on the one hand censured for circuitous tactics, and on the other praised for pioneering hardihood. Both views have their measure of justification. Montaigne's tactic was the only one that in his day could have to any important extent carried his point. He was, in fact, playing with fire, and could succeed only by protesting that he was but playing. Yet he writes at times with an astonishing temerity; and not least audaciously when he humorously hints that he means more than he says. It is to be suspected, on the other hand, that the tissue of trivialities which he spins in the closing essay was inserted by way of giving an air of slightness to the whole, as well as of covering the mordancy of some sayings in that very essay. How dangerous it was to do the same work in a systematic and dead-serious fashion was seen in the decade after his death, when his friend and disciple, the churchman Charron, put into his treatise *Of Wisdom,* in close order, the gist of Montaigne's teaching, unwittingly bringing out the contradictions in startling relief. The disciple was execrated and persecuted where the master had gone scot-free. (pp. xxxviii-xxxix)

If we turn aside from the course of State life to that of philosophic thought, we see the influence of Montaigne at work in another fashion. The reconsideration of faith and dogma had of course begun long before him: the very treatise of Raymond Sebond was a reaction against it in the previous century; and such writings as those of Bonaventure des Périers were partly co-operant with those of Montaigne in his own day. But the **"Apology for Raymond Sebond,"** and the recurrent pressure of the same course of thought in Montaigne's later essays, constituted the most effective impulse of the kind that had yet arisen. The covert humour of Montaigne outdid the humorism of Des Périers. The once famous treatise of Sanchez (1581) *Quod Nihil Scitur,* 'That Nothing is to be Known,' is thoroughly sceptical; but to read it is to listen to the click of logical castanets, and to turn away unmoved. Montaigne's impact is vital. It is accordingly a warrantable statement that Montaigne is the spiritual father of Descartes, as Descartes in turn was the spiritual father of Spinoza. This does not seem to have been fully realized in Descartes' own day, by reason of the complete contrast between his grave methodic ways and the gaily unmethodic fashion of Montaigne, as well as of the conflict of their views on reason in animals; but in retrospect it seems clear enough. And the fact that Montaigne was not soon recognized as a philosophic force is the decisive proof of the completeness with which he had achieved his practical end, the undermining of active fanaticism, the lowering of men's blood pressures, the change of mood which put peace and progress in place of wholly destructive strife. (pp. xxxix-xi)

His quiet success was the outcome of three factors, his manifold matter, his unmethodical method, and his unmannered manner. His serious counsel was the febrifuge that most men needed. But it was blended with a vast variety of expatiation on a hundred topics of human interest, the talk of a widely read and widely interested man, chatting with his fellows as having no axe to grind, but merely delivering himself of most of the thoughts and comments on life that came to him in the chances of his discursive reading and his daily experience. No such mass of diversely interesting discourse had been put forth by any modern before the appearance of the expanded edition of the *Essays* in 1588.

It was indeed no small range of fascinating talk that won for Montaigne the ear of his countrymen in an age in which such serious counsels as his were by so many viewed askance. They were won by a quite novel vivacity of discussion of life in all its aspects, in which the perilous thoughts passed in the crowd of others. And he whose main service to his age was to calm passions that are now obsolescent is just as readable in ours by force of his vividness, his variety, his reality. In the age of Sidney he spontaneously acted on Sidney's counsel to the English rhymers. He looked in his heart and wrote.

Hence the *Essays* differed vitally from the most famous work of previous publicists, such as Petrarch and Erasmus and Lipsius, in respect of a new simplicity and spontaneity, a disregard of all academic artifice, alike in style and in structure. And this course was not taken for lack of literary instinct, but because of an instinct freshly alive. No man knew better than Montaigne the force of style at its best. In one essay, of equivocal inspiration, he breaks away in a truly well-inspired excursus on the potency of the right choice of words as made by the old masters of the art—the cry of a reader who from youth up had been progressively bored by the arts of the schooled virtuosi in prose and verse.

Montaigne's main literary secret is the resort to the mood of animated conversation for his driving force; the fit method of one who never planned an essay as it came to be finished, and who to the last was capable of inserting new blocks of matter in old discourses, with small concern for the sequence of the paragraphs. As against the essayists of the desk, he is the essayist of the armchair. He does not conceal his secret. "The style I like," he writes "is one that is simple and unaffected, the same in writing as on the tongue; a succulent and nervous style, terse and packed; not so much elegant and trimmed as vehement and brusque." In his case, the style was truly the man. In reading many serious authors of that and previous centuries we have a sense as of listening to falsetto, or to the "intoning" of the pulpit. In Montaigne we get always the living voice. And thus he adds to the effect of his utterance that of urgent personality, which is one of the vitalizing forces of literature. When matter and manner thus coalesce . . . , there results an impact on the reader's whole perceptive faculties such as no writer on education before or since has surpassed, even though the doctrine be classic.

Launched at last on the enterprise of expressing his "me" in as many of its facets as he was concerned to expose—and they were many, though not all—he utters himself with the stress and vivacity which, as he tells us, belonged to his conversation. He confesses to a vehement exuberance of asseveration in his talk, a characteristic still notable in Frenchmen of the south, whether gifted or ungifted as writers. To be direct, straightforward, keeping insistently to the point, he tells us, was his habit in talking to the great. He has paid his readers the com-

pliment of talking to them in the same fashion; though with a breadth and range of discourse, and at times of impropriety, beyond the normal limits of spoken converse.

That conforms spontaneously to his character. Rhetoric he recognizes as the stock-in-trade of the conventional thinker and the professional demagogue. At the outset, despite his appreciation of skilled style, he places Cicero, the master of rhetoric, lower than Seneca, the man specially concerned for conduct; and Seneca, finally, he ranks below Plutarch (so pleasantly translated for him by Amyot), the writer who is so sure of his principles that he is content to let them be carried on the stream either of biography or essay, with a minimum of scholastic argumentation. Plutarch's essays, if any, are Montaigne's models after he has settled down to his work as an essayist.

But no essayist of any age has talked about himself and everything else with such radiant energy as fills his page after he has got into his stride. (pp. xli-xliii)

It is this living utterance, and this unlimited interest in everything human, that gives him his hold on all the generations since his time. In his quite different way, he conveys that sense of universality of outlook that we find in Shakespeare, and call Shakespearian. The two minds are alike cosmopolitan, open-eyed on all sides, responsive to all human concerns, cognizant of the sins of the great and the virtues of the poor, and of the littleness and the absurdities of all. (p. xliv)

Three elements, broadly speaking, go to the making of enduring literature, the factors of style (in the widest sense), of impact of personality, and of vital purport. In Montaigne these are all at work in a high degree; the second, perhaps, in the highest; but the first in a degree not before attained in post-classic prose. And so, whatever we may think of him and his doctrine, he is a permanent figure in the world of books. (p. 1)

> *J. M. Robertson, in an introduction to* The Essays of Montaigne, Vol. I, *translated by E. J. Trechmann, Oxford University Press, London, 1927, pp. xix-l.*

T. S. ELIOT   (essay date 1931)

[*Perhaps the most influential poet and critic to write in the English language during the first half of the twentieth century, Eliot is closely identified with many of the qualities denoted by the term Modernism: experimentation, formal complexity, artistic and intellectual eclecticism, and a classicist's view of the artist working at an emotional distance from his or her creation. He introduced a number of terms and concepts that strongly affected critical thought in his lifetime, among them the idea that poets must be conscious of the living tradition of literature in order for their work to have artistic and spiritual validity. In general, Eliot upheld values of traditionalism and discipline, and in 1928 he annexed Christian theology to his overall conservative worldview. Of his criticism, he stated: "It is a by-product of my private poetry-workshop: or a prolongation of the thinking that went into the formation of my verse." In the following excerpt from an essay originally published in 1931, Eliot discusses the influence of Montaigne on Blaise Pascal, despite the latter's avowed disapproval of the essayist (see excerpt dated 1662?).*]

[The] great adversary against whom Pascal set himself, from the time of his first conversations with M. de Saci at Port-Royal, was Montaigne. One cannot destroy Pascal, certainly; but of all authors Montaigne is one of the least destructible. You could as well dissipate a fog by flinging hand-grenades into it. For Montaigne is a fog, a gas, a fluid, insidious element. He does not reason, he insinuates, charms, and influences; or if he reasons, you must be prepared for his having some other design upon you than to convince you by his argument. It is hardly too much to say that Montaigne is the most essential author to know, if we would understand the course of French thought during the last three hundred years. In every way, the influence of Montaigne was repugnant to the men of Port-Royal. Pascal studied him with the intention of demolishing him. Yet, in the *Pensées,* at the very end of his life, we find passage after passage, and the slighter they are the more significant, almost "lifted" out of Montaigne, down to a figure of speech or a word. The parallels are most often with the long essay of Montaigne called **"Apologie de Raymond Sébond"**— an astonishing piece of writing upon which Shakespeare also probably drew in *Hamlet.* Indeed, by the time a man knew Montaigne well enough to attack him, he would already be thoroughly infected by him.

It would, however, be grossly unfair to Pascal, to Montaigne, and indeed to French literature, to leave the matter at that. It is no diminution of Pascal, but only an aggrandizement of Montaigne. Had Montaigne been an ordinary life-sized sceptic, a small man like Renan, or even like the greatest sceptic of all, Voltaire, this "influence" would be to the discredit of Pascal; but if Montaigne had been no more than Voltaire, he could not have affected Pascal at all. The picture of Montaigne which offers itself first to our eyes, that of the original and independent solitary "personality," absorbed in amused analysis of himself, is deceptive. Montaigne's is no *limited* Pyrrhonism, like that of Voltaire, Renan, or France. He exists, so to speak, on a plan of numerous concentric circles, the most apparent of which is the small inmost circle, a personal puckish scepticism which can be easily aped if not imitated. But what makes Montaigne a very great figure is that he succeeded, God knows how—for Montaigne very likely did not know that he had done it—it is not the sort of thing that men *can* observe about themselves, for it is essentially bigger than the individual's consciousness—he succeeded in giving expression to the scepticism of *every* human being. For every man who thinks and lives by thought must have his own scepticism, that which stops at the question, that which ends in denial, or that which leads to faith and which is somehow integrated into the faith which transcends it. And Pascal, as the type of one kind of religious believer, which is highly passionate and ardent, but passionate only through a powerful and regulated intellect, is in the first sections of his unfinished Apology for Christianity facing unflinchingly the demon of doubt which is inseparable from the spirit of belief.

There is accordingly something quite different from an influence which would prove Pascal's weakness; there is a real affinity between his doubt and that of Montaigne; and through the common kinship with Montaigne Pascal is related to the noble and distinguished line of French moralists, from La Rochefoucauld down. (pp. 155-59)

> *T. S. Eliot, "'The Pensées' of Pascal," in his* Essays: Ancient and Modern, *Harcourt, Brace Jovanovich, 1936, pp. 142-68.*

JOHN COWPER POWYS　(essay date 1938)

[*Powys was a remarkably prolific English novelist, poet, and essayist whose work reveals his interests in myths, cosmic fantasies, and the elemental forces of nature. Noted for the self-revelatory tendency of much of his work, Powys is the author of* Autobiography *(1934), which is, in Mark Van Doren's words, "completely and frankly about himself." In the following excerpt,*

Powys offers a general discussion of Montaigne and his work in explaining what the essayist means to him.]

It is of a peculiar interest to me as an elderly man to note exactly how I react to Montaigne now that, numbering the years of my life, I have managed to outlive the years of the great essayist.

I think he is, for all his gallant praise of youth as the heyday of our intellect, a writer peculiarly and especially adapted to old age. (p. 146)

Certainly it seems to me that his work grows in interest the older *he* grows.

And how curious it is the way each great book of the world has its own special history with us, the successive stages of our own private life running parallel to our reactions to this particular mirror of the general life!

My own first acquaintance with Montaigne goes back to that profoundly subtle picture of the man and his ideas introduced by Walter Pater into the pages of *Gaston de Latour.*

But as I read him now, after this lapse of years, I feel as if I were encountering quite a different Montaigne from that image of him which so kindled the imagination of young Gaston.

The Montaigne who arrests me now arrests me no more as a universal sceptic whose second thoughts, turning to the homely wisdom of the piety of the generations, subtly undermine his first, and by means of scepticism extract the sting of scepticism, and by doubting dull the edge of doubt.

He arrests me now as one whose chief wisdom has to do rather with the art of life and with the art of integrating one's essential personality than with any final conclusions of philosophic thought, whether sceptical or otherwise.

The secret I get from him now, as I brood over his words and seek to catch the dominant element in the floating solution of his drifting ruminations, is of far greater day-by-day value to me at my present age than the precise reasons why he could or could not accept the Athanasian Creed. (pp. 146-47)

I suppose the idea that most English-speaking book-lovers have of Montaigne, unless they themselves possess an edition of Cotton's splendid translation, is that of the self-portrait of a magnanimous egoist, whose shrewd, kindly, earth-bound views upon our wrestling with the world are casually set down with an epicurean lavishness.

But if such a book-lover whom the accidents and chances of life have hitherto debarred from actually reading the essays in Cotton's translation *does* get hold of a copy, or even of an odd volume or two, and bringing it home with that peculiar thrill of pleasurable anticipation so beautifully described by Charles Lamb, *does* begin seriously to read it, I am prepared to wager he will suffer a grievous disappointment.

For in place of what he has been led to expect by such deep Montaigne-experts as Walter Pater, or my own brother Llewelyn, whose whole tone of writing, even to his use of that Montaignesque expression "the instinct of a well-descended spirit," is riddled with his influence, what our novice will stumble upon, unless he opens at the essay entitled **"Of Presumption,"** or **"Of Repentance,"** or **"Of Vanity,"** or **"Of Experience,"** will be page after page of historic anecdotes and of quotations from classical writers.

Of course the use of quotation *can* become a fantastical and artful adjunct to the living style of an author, as we note in *The Anatomy of Melancholy* and in the *Essays of Elia,* but Montaigne uses *his* quotations to quite other than stylistic effect. He uses them purely and simply for the curious and to his own mind fascinating nature of their contents.

Now to any intelligence resembling Montaigne's, with a passion for the classical authors, especially the Latin ones, and a mania for curious and monstrous human happenings wherever and whenever occurring, every page of the *Essays* must be full of salt and tang; but I profoundly suspect that Pascal and Walter Pater, both of whom saturated themselves in Montaigne's *philosophy,* were wont to skim over at great speed the bulk of these anecdotes!

Voltaire probably read every one of them with infinite relish; and so I dare say did Anatole France; but I have an inkling that William Hazlitt, our own egoistical essayist, was as wont to skip in following the great Gascon's circumambulatory strolls round his circular book-shelf as shamelessly as I do myself.

However! Even if there does not yet exist a version of the *Essays* shorn of the anecdotes, and I suppose most Montaigne-lovers would scorn such a pimping concession, it is not, after all, so very difficult to turn over the pages till we come to some pungent opinion of his own that will pull us up short.

And as to the quarrel I have now with that incomparable summary of Montaigne's philosophy in *Gaston de Latour,* I only feel that it makes him a little too deliberate and purposeful in his particular kind of scepticism. Judging from the general drift of his work, and putting one inconsistency against another, it seems to me that there was much less of calculated metaphysic and much more of temperamental conservatism in those fluctuating *after-thoughts* of his, about which Walter Pater, assimilating, as we all will in such cases, Montaigne's attitude to his own, makes such an elaborate coil.

What a difference just a little shift of emphasis in these delicate psychological matters can make!

What Pater's young Gaston got from his host's epicurean discourse in that tower-library looking over the Perigord orchards was a system of thought far more deliberately rounded-off than what I at least am able to find.

And though I do dodge on my road, even as Bunyan's Christian might dodge a number of circus-caravans, all these classical fables and gossiping scandals, I cannot be persuaded that I lose the essence of his wisdom by this avoidance. (pp. 148-50)

Let the word be frankly spoken—Montaigne's wisdom is not a metaphysical wisdom or a wisdom concerned with what, in Nietzsche's phrase, we call "First and Last Things." It is a practical, moral wisdom, primarily concerned, as was that of Confucius, with the conduct of life rather than with its purpose or its remote cause.

The conduct of life and pre-eminently of his own personal life is the subject-matter of the *Essays;* and like Socrates whom he cannot praise too highly, and who, Greek though he was, was evidently dearer to him than any other classical thinker, his grand starting-point—and not only starting-point, for he is never weary of returning to it—is self-knowledge, the everlasting analysing of himself and his moods.

But even here we must advance cautiously and shrewdly in our estimate of Montaigne's everlasting preoccupation with himself. He takes advantage of the attitude of Socrates, both

in regard to his oracle's "Know thyself," and in regard to his "I know nothing," but the longer you read the *Essays* the clearer it becomes that this ceaseless absorption in himself was a profound psychological, or if you are averse to such a tendency you can even use the word *pathological,* peculiarity of his whole nervous organization.

With what a gusto of life-deep relief, a relief that is spiritual, physical, and mental, does he speak of these felicitous escapes from his duties to others, from his duties to his country, from his duties to posterity, as he sinks back into himself!

It must be remembered he was a man of an extremely responsible conscience in all these things; but when he returns to himself in reaction from them it is as if he returned to the embraces of an adored lover.

Over and over again he celebrates these sinkings back into himself, making it clear from the variety of his descriptions of these self-orgies that they were an indulgence in a physical, mental, and spiritual narcissism so well constituted, so integral, so balanced, that, as a human phenomenon, it must be very rare.

For there wasn't a trace of vanity in the narcissism of Montaigne. He loved his old "grizzled face" not because it was handsome but simply because it was *his.* (pp. 151-52)

It is indeed hard to overrate the moral and philosophical importance of the particular kind of egoism advocated by Montaigne.

It is "*the Ego and its Own*" of Max Stirner; only in Montaigne's case this superindividualism is mitigated by his reverence for the laws of his country, by his love of the old traditions, by his hatred of innovation, and by his profound distrust of the insane logic of that dangerous tyrant, the human reason. His scepticism takes refuge from its own corrosive undermining of all philosophical theories in a deep instinctive piety, according to the dictates of which he prefers to keep God and "His Holy Word" well out of reach of the wild antics of the human intellect. (pp. 157-58)

[But,] though Montaigne's scepticism, by its undermining of the pride of reason, landed him on the bed-rock of old-fashioned faith, he apparently found nothing in this basic faith to conflict with his cult of self-realization. To shut himself up "like a tortoise in his shell" in the study of himself and in the enjoyment of himself was the supreme aim and purpose of his life.

His nature was so luckily constituted that no agitations of conscience, no qualms of superstitious fear, no spiritual wrestlings ever troubled his serene happiness, when once, retired within that shell of which his library-tower was the outward symbol, he caresses the most fleeting of his sensations and ideas as if they had been so many soft-furred pets.

He dared in fact, in the midst of that ferocious struggle between Catholics and Protestants, to give himself up to the sensuous deliciousness of a lifelong series of egocentric contemplations, stroking himself, tickling himself, stretching himself, making love to himself, while murder and fanaticism and treachery and massacre tore at his country's bowels. (pp. 158-59)

[The] *Essays* were the expression of his real life all the while, and not only the expression; for, as he says, this constant painting of his own portrait compelled him *to live up to* the lineaments he painted, while to the very last he was always adding some new and yet more revealing touch to the picture.

It would be possible, I suppose, to put forward a claim that Montaigne's constant expressions of faith in a God whose ways are not our ways and indeed are altogether beyond the soundings of our presumptuous, private judgment, was a crafty sop to Cerberus. But the longer I read the *Essays* the more strongly it comes over me that this faith in something "eternal in the Heavens," something unaffected by the tossings and "rollings" of human reason, was the thing that saved him from a sense of futility, and enabled him to present such a shrewd, earthy, solid front to this confused world.

It is not in regard to God but in regard to human custom that his feeling varies according to his mood; and in the endless examples he loves to give us of the grotesque and monstrous nature of custom he hesitates not to indicate his own corrective to that instinctive preference for old ways over new ways into which his ingrained conservatism led him.

In his opinion all the dictates of our conscience come from this too-human and often preposterous adherence to custom, and not at all from any categorical imperative in nature; but just at the point where we nihilistic moderns would for this very reason be tempted to relax our moral harness Montaigne invariably pulls himself up, and by some allusion to "God and His Holy Word" brings back his toppling and shaky conscience to its true foundation, a foundation entirely outside the shifty phenomena of time and space. (pp. 159-60)

There have been few famous writers, and still fewer men of the great world, who have had, and been at pains to express, such a loathing of cruelty. Montaigne seems to have felt as much repulsion at seeing animals suffer, even in the normal processes of what we call "sport," as any sympathetic person of our own day; and in the education of children he would have us cease once and for all our curst attempts to cudgel them into learning and virtue. He goes out of his way to reprobate the burnings and torturings of his time and no more vigorous protest has ever been raised by a great European writer against persecution for matters of opinion. Thorough Frenchman as he was and great devotee of Paris "the glory of France and one of the most noble ornaments of the world," Montaigne may be regarded as among the founders of a magnanimous internationalism. (p. 161)

I have wondered, considering what a family of bookworms my own family is, which of all the great profane works of the world would lend itself best to be made into our secular family Bible; and I am tempted to think that Montaigne's *Essays* might be this book. (p. 162)

When one turns the calm gaze of what might be called humanity's unsanctified *common sense* upon the world spread out before us to-day, with its bombings and shootings and murderous "ideologies" and its ferocious hatred of all unregimented, unhypnotized free souls, it begins to appear as if Montaigne's sensuous-psychic *love of himself* and obstinate concern with himself were quite possibly going to prove the chief oracular word for the next great psychological reaction.

Dante put this self-centered type of person in hell, along with a group of Montaignesque angels, who were neither "for God" nor "for the enemies of God" but *were for themselves;* and the great Erasmus would have suffered the same doom, and so most certainly would Walt Whitman, who refused to "take off his hat" to any spiritual authority or to find any sweeter flesh "than stuck to his own bones."

But the whole issue, raised thus boldly by Montaigne, goes deeper and further than almost any other human problem; and in estimating exactly to what this self-love, about which he makes such a clatter, really amounts, we must remember that egoism *à la* Montaigne is prepared to give to others all the privileges it claims for itself. His father brought him up to be able to rough it with working people and to rate all his advantage of wealth and birth as a mere accident of chance. He needed no one to teach him to be hostile to every sort of cruelty, hostile, above all, to the exercise of violence and torture where private opinions, whether religious or moral or political, were concerned.

That he was so opposed to innovation did not mean that he was blind to the unfairness of old customs; it only meant that he saw so many innovators become tyrants and so many innovations do more harm than good, that it seemed to him that the path of prudence, both in religion and politics, was "to let sleeping dogs lie."

Against this if you jerk the hands of time's clock forward a little and imagine Montaigne, with his shrewd merchant-squire sympathies, confronted by a starving people, a frivolous aristocracy, and so extremely different a king from Henri Quatre, is it not likely that even *his* rooted conservatism would have moved in its socket?

But the point for us now is not what he would have done in another age but what he did in his own; and *that* was to trim his sails to the wind, to cut his coat to his cloth, and though not exactly to run with the hare and hunt with the hounds, at least to keep his doors so wide open that if the hunt came in at the front the hare could slip out at the back. And all the while to "loafe and invite his soul," to stroke, pet, fondle, caress, and hug his identity, first for himself and then, in the *Essays,* for all of us who come after so that if we belong to that "middle region" not too stupid and not too subtle our laudable and righteous egoism can get the comfort and support it needs.

For myself, who had managed in my skimble-skamble way to hug and cherish myself even before I read Montaigne—for Nature hesitates not to give us all a push in this direction—I think this whole question of the individual against state, society, government, religion, is of the most sharp and stinging importance. My own private feeling, if under the aegis of a Mayor of Bordeaux I can gather up enough courage to express it, is that of all our political and economic theories the anarchist one is the one that eventually will prevail.

If our descendants have any libraries left, circular or otherwise, from which to collect anecdotes of our day and age, surely there will be, as they study the murderousness of our present national spirit, a reversion to Montaigne's self-centred cult.

Will not that remote and happy age feel that in the wise selfishness of the individual rather than in the ferocious and fanatical unselfishness of the public-spirited, the will of Heaven is revealed? (pp. 168-70)

For myself, for all my love of our secular family Bible, I note very clearly down at the bottom of my heart an irradicable tendency to admire Don Quixote, even though he never did any one any good, a good deal more than I admire Montaigne who has done us all so much good.

Now why is this? What we really need to help us clear up this nice point—perhaps the most delicate point in the whole of life's casuistry—is some tremendous modern Socrates, who would have the tolerance and the intelligence to analyse to the very bottom this inarticulate preference which we feel, at least which I feel, for the glow experienced when we read *Don Quixote* over the glow experienced when we fortify ourselves in our wise and humble egoism by reading the *Essays*!

But then Don Quixote is himself, as was Jesus Christ, the most reckless of anarchists. When he set the galley-slaves free he was certainly on the opposite side from all religions and all governments; and it is difficult to imagine how a community of tolerant Montaignes contemplating the world from their libraries could uphold the freedom of the soul without the help of a few desperate knights-errant. Or, alas! even *with* their help, unless some of them were shrewder in their valour than the Knight of the Rueful Countenance. (pp. 171-72)

What we get from Montaigne is really a series of hints, and they are as shrewd as any to be found in the whole history of human culture, as to the way to use this precious margin of our existence wherein we live to ourselves and enjoy our classics and our classical histories, our philosophers and our philosophizing, so as to be fuller, happier, riper, wiser, and more tolerant human beings.

His grand ''open secret''—and it is a secret revealed to most of us only after the most troublesome mental disturbances and miseries—is the importance of starting ''from the ground up'' and never losing touch with the ground. The spiritual trick of lying back upon our ignorance, of accepting our limitations, of taking mentally, as well as physically, ''the lower seats in the synagogue,'' of ceasing to ''lie awake in the night'' repining about our sins, of creating a life-illusion of ourselves that shall follow the curves of all our weaknesses as the tide follows the hollows of its estuaries, is a trick not easily acquired.

Still harder is it to us to overcome that undue pressure of the race-conscience which makes us afraid of hugging ourselves to ourselves, in all our deformity, against the background of the cosmos, lest the jealousy of the gods smite us with a thunderbolt.

Every living creature has a divine right, as Goethe says, to those special and peculiar pleasures, uninjurious to its fellows, which its unique temperament *must* have, if it is to bear up under the common burden with any spontaneous resilience; and if for us the greatest of such pleasures is to make a cult of the half-mental, half-physical sensations that solitude invites, even as the windrow between sea and sand invites the gulls, the reading of Montaigne will certainly assist in keeping clear from conscientious invasion that narrow strip of spiritual independence which, just because it is free to all, can be made more entirely our own than anything else in the world. (pp. 172-73)

> *John Cowper Powys, ''Montaigne,'' in his* Enjoyment of Literature, *Simon and Schuster, 1938, pp. 146-73.*

JOHN MIDDLETON MURRY (essay date 1938)

[*Murry is recognized as one of the most significant English critics and editors of the twentieth century. Anticipating later scholarly opinion, he championed the writings of Marcel Proust, James Joyce, Paul Valéry, D. H. Lawrence, and Thomas Hardy through his position as the editor of the* Athenaeum *and as a longtime contributor to the* Times Literary Supplement *and other periodicals. Like his magazine essays, Murry's book-length critical works are noted for their unusually impassioned tone and startling discoveries; such biographically centered critical studies as* Keats and Shakespeare: A Study of Keats' Poetic Life from 1816-1820*

(1925) and Son of Woman: The Story of D. H. Lawrence *(1931) contain esoteric, controversial conclusions that have angered scholars who favor more traditional approaches. Nevertheless, Murry is cited for his perspicuity, clarity, and supportive argumentation. His early exposition on literary appreciation,* The Problem of Style *(1922), is widely admired as an informed guidebook for both critics and readers to use when considering not only the style of a literary work, but its theme and viewpoint as well. In it Murry espouses this theoretical premise that underlies all his criticism: in order to evaluate fully a writer's achievement the critic must search for crucial passages that effectively ''crystallize'' the writer's innermost impressions and convictions regarding life. In the following excerpt, Murry highlights several remarkable aspects of Montaigne's philosophy, emphasizing the essayist's consciousness of individualism.*]

No other equally great writer in the world's history makes so slight an initial demand upon us when he seeks our complicity in re-entering existence, as Montaigne. He is like a gift of nature: a sunshiny day. We have nothing to do but to bask in it and him. There is nothing to pay, nothing to wrestle with, nothing to be endured. The path to enjoyment, and to the essential Montaigne, seems to lie open on every page. ''The bees plunder the flowers,'' he says, ''here a little, and there a little; but afterward they make honey of them which is all their own: it is not thyme, or marjoram, any more.'' That is the perfect figure for the kind and quality of delight which Montaigne distilled. His honey is neither thyme nor marjoram any more, it is honey. But it is honey which always faintly reminds us of where it was gathered, and has so many subtle tones of flavor that we can never forget how widely ranging was the creature who made it. And not in books alone.

That easy approach, that natural familiarity, that sense of belonging to the family which Montaigne bestows upon his reader, is not fortuitous. When gradually it has begun to dawn upon us that Montaigne is not merely a friendly man but a great one, indeed a Colossus, we begin to realize at the same moment that he has grown into a giant almost by accident—or rather by that necessity of nature which always wears the appearance of accident. He starts, so to speak, where everybody started; he is compiling another enormous commonplace book; he is gathering the truth, as so many had gathered it before him. Slowly we become conscious that the emphasis has shifted; he is doing something different, or rather—such is the massive and impersonal force of his accumulation—something different

A view of Montaigne's library in the Château de Montaigne. From Montaigne: A Biography, *by Donald M. Frame. North Point Press, 1984. Copyright © 1965 by Donald M. Frame.*

is being done through him. The Man is not exploring the Truth, but the Truth is exploring Man. In creating a book, he had created himself. He knew it. "I have not made my book any more than my book has made me." And in responding to his book, we have been witnesses, accomplices, collaborators almost, in the work of a demiurge—the creation of the first conscious individual man.

Not the least mark of Montaigne's peculiar greatness is that nothing he tells us directly about himself cannot be corroborated, and given amplitude and richness from the body of his work. . . .

> I have not studied at all in order to make a book, but I have studied to some extent because I had made one, if it be any kind of studying to skim over and catch, by the head or the feet, now one author and now another, with a view not to form my opinions but to assist those long since formed, to second them, and to be of service to them.

A thousand subtle gradations, differences, distinctions in his experience had thus been recognized, and by being thus recognized had been in some sense created. The quotations were not merely his own, they were himself. And this again in no perfunctory or vaguely metaphorical meaning. The Montaigne of whom these quotations were part was a man who grew, and who never ceased to grow; and the quotations were part of that growth. (pp. 49-50)

[By Montaigne's] effort to know himself entirely, he had lifted himself above the flux of circumstance. He was under no illusion that he did know himself entirely: that was impossible. Like Socrates, he was as ignorant as other men save in his knowledge of his own ignorance: but, being Montaigne, he gives the famous saying a turn of his own. "Je me tiens de la commune sorte, sauf en ce que je m'en tiens"; "I am an ordinary man, except that I know it." The lingering trace of Socratic intellectualism departs. Montaigne, to himself, is simply a man, who knows it.

But the process and achievement of that knowing—how great it was! And he makes it so easy for us to forget that it was great. The Montaigne we meet is already mature. The storm and stress are over. He has already learned the secret; he is a man, who knows it. The manner of his coming to a knowledge so simple and so rare has been all his own. It seems familiar enough. "Moi, qui m'espie de plus prez, qui ay les yeulx incessament tendus sur moy" ["I, who see myself the closest, who have my eyes incessantly turned on myself"]. An Amiel, surely, might claim to be as perfect in the art of self-examination? So it seems; but only seems. For Montaigne's method has been to find himself in the men of old time. He has been guarded by a prophylactic against egoism. From the beginning his discovery had been, not how much and how strange there was in him, but how much of what was in him had been in other men. He was looking for the truth, searching out all that in the experience of the ancients had been ratified by his own, establishing how completely he had been anticipated—in all, except the occupation. And the exception is the essence of Montaigne. To the extraordinary essay in which he describes the sensations of his nearly fatal accident, he subsequently added pages which perhaps more directly than any others convey the sensation of this conquistador of the human personality—"silent, upon a peak in Darien."

> We hear but of two or three ancients who have traveled this road, and yet we cannot say it was at all in this manner, since we know nothing of them except

their names. No one since has rushed into their path. It is a thorny undertaking, and more so than it seems, to follow a movement so wayward as that of the mind, to penetrate the opaque depths of its innermost folds, to pick out and arrest so many of its little breathlike stirrings. It is a new and extraordinary occupation, that withdraws us from the ordinary employments of the world, ay, from those most in repute.

But this was, as it were, the unexpected and residual quintessence in Montaigne's alembic after a process of self-discovery through self-cancellation. So little of himself was indeed his own, he found, that there was nothing left but "the corner in his soul" where he could rest in the recognition that he belonged to the common sort. In his own inimitable way, following his own natural bent, having for his native bias that passion for the total truth which he regarded as the one basic human virtue, Montaigne had undergone an arduous spiritual discipline before the composition of the *Essais* began. He was already capable of looking upon himself dispassionately as an object. He had had a glimpse of Montaigne *sub specie aeternitatis;* irresistibly he followed the gleam, and organized it into a vision.

He had discovered a profound philosophy, and in his book we watch him taking complete possession of it, or it of him. As his book grows so does he. Degree by degree, trait by trait, he comes under the lucid scrutiny of his own increasing awareness. What is happening he knows well, far better than most of those who have sought to expound his philosophy. The philosophy of a man, who understands by the word "philosophy" the seeking of wisdom, is always elusive to those for whom the word means a systematic doctrine. They look down upon Montaigne as an amateur; they do not notice that he is smiling at them as professionals. . . . He must be taking the name of philosopher in vain.

But not at all. He is serious while he smiles; he is serious because he smiles. He is establishing, *à bon escient* ["wittingly"], a solid and unsuspected claim to have climbed to the very pinnacle of philosphy, to have become a man so imbued and pervaded with awareness that he can put reason in its own subordinate place without having to invoke the aid of faith, if by faith is meant something different in nature from experience. He is become a man, who knows he is only a man, and is content; because the knowledge is of such a kind that it fills him with happiness. And that, for Montaigne, is the end of all philosophy, if philosophy would but know it. . . . Philosophy for him is the pursuitt of perfect consciousness, which when achieved returns, by virtue of its own perfection, to be the finer life of the body. Then there is no division any more. The total man is, as it were, redeemed and purified by the imaginative spirit, so that he is made whole and made one, not with an enforced but with a natural unity. And this unity of the man, being a natural unity, is not a uniformity; it is compact of variety and animated by conflict.

> Such discourses are, in my opinion, infinitely true, and reasonable: but we are, I know not how, double in our selves, so that what we believe, we disbelieve, and cannot rid ourselves of what we condemn.

Once more, it is not the utterance of an easy skepticism; it is the self-knowledge of a great man who knows that "without contraries there is no progression," and that here can be no finality in the growth of a man indeed. Those who seek finality can have it at a price: they must eradicate some part of their humanity. To Montaigne that was sacrilege. To let die an appetite was one thing, to mortify it quite another; and to him they were as different as life and death. Not to conceal oneself from oneself, not to hide one's secret shames by violence, but to look serenely upon them, was the way of life. It was also the way of truth.

The doctrine is not an easy one, nor is it easy to be a Montaigne. Many have found that to their cost, who, charmed by his transparency, have sought to emulate him. They have proved to be as wide of the mark on one side as have been on the other those austere interpreters who have believed that Montaigne taught men "to follow nature," which seems to them an easy and dangerous doctrine. Perhaps it is; but Montaigne did not teach it. His doctrine is not dangerous, and is very difficult. It is that, if you have a nature like Montaigne's, you were best to follow it, because you will not be able to do otherwise. The essential requisite, for a nature to be like Montaigne's, is that it should possess, and be possessed by, a fundamental generosity of soul. With that to start with, you will meet Montaigne somewhere; because from that beginning the conclusion is inevitable. Finally, one is a man and knows it, and that is to have become a man.

> A generous heart must not disown its own thoughts;
> it desires that its inward parts be seen; everything in
> it is good, or at least, everything is human.

Nothing more simple, nothing more difficult. In that transparent dictum is unambitiously expressed what philosophers have meant by passing beyond good and evil, what mystics have meant by passing beyond creatures, what Blake meant by declaring that "Art could not exist except by naked beauty display'd." Montaigne's *Essais* are, precisely, art in this high sense. "If I had lived among those nations which are reported still to live under the sweet liberty of the original laws of nature, I assure you that I would very willingly have painted myself entire and naked," *tout entier et tout nu.*

Montaigne is the standing confutation of all that is excessive and inhuman in Pascal. By his mere being he dissolves the menace of the judgment: "le *moi* est toujours haïssable"; "the *Self* is always hateful." Not that Montaigne would deny it, exactly: but he has something more to tell us than that, something wiser and therefore less distinctly formulable. It is that the Self is lovable, if a man can bring himself to love it. What the Self becomes depends on how we behave toward it. It can be lovable, because it can be loved; but it can be loved only by the not-Self. In his early manhood Montaigne knew the secret of love. Self-obliteration came to him naturally in his friendship with Étienne de la Boétie. "If I should be pressed to say why I loved him, I feel that that cannot be expressed." And afterward he added the immortal phrase: "Except by saying, because it was he, because it was I." The very pulse of human love beats in those words. To have felt it is to have known that life is blessed: for love is the vision of the incomparable, the nonpareil, and the vision is seen only in self-forgetfulness.

To have turned his power of self-forgetfulness upon himself—this was Montaigne's triumph. He looked upon the Self with the eyes of the not-Self. And the history of that singular achievement is written at large in his book; indeed, the *Essais* are the embodied process of that achievement. Montaigne knew that also better than posterity has known it. His book is one long and infinitely various act of self-discovery, self-objectification, made possible only by self-forgetfulness. (pp. 54-8)

[Compare him] with the later masters of self-revelation, with Rousseau of the *Confessions,* with Châteaubriand of the *Memoires d'Outretombe.* The difference is not of degree, but of kind. In Rousseau and Châteaubriand we are interested; we read avidly all that they have to say; nevertheless, at the end, with Pascal at our elbow sternly demanding our final judgment, we are forced to confess that "the Self is always hateful." But with Montaigne it is quite different. Where Rousseau and Châteaubriand blench before the sentence of Port Royal, Montaigne stands secure and invulnerable, as though he had been refined in the fire, and all the dross purged away. Because he defends nothing, conceals nothing, he has nothing to defend or conceal. He is proof against all the acids of modern analysis; he had applied a radical skepticism, not to others, but to himself.

As the features of such a man—head and shoulders above his great age, with only Shakespeare for his peer—began to define themselves to Montaigne's consciousness, it was impossible that he should not see the significance of his instinctive enterprise. His book stood then before him as a work to be completed "with all his faith and all his force." He dedicated himself to it, and his sense of the spiritual significance of his "attempts" is conveyed in his suggestion that his book is a new and more veracious form of the practice of Christian confession, as though it were a solitary and unprecedented effort to bring religion into the stream of life. "I hold that it requires wisdom to make an estimate of oneself, whether it be high or low, impartially, and conscientiousness to publish it." Yet such was the unerring natural genius of the man that not even the strong determination which speaks in such phrases could corrupt his own spontaneity. Returning home to his work after a year and a half of travel, he said:

> Meanwhile, I do not correct my first imaginations
> by second ones; yes, it happens that I correct a word,
> but to vary it, not to take it away. I wish to represent
> the progress of my humors, and desire each piece to
> be seen as it was born. I should like to have begun
> earlier, and be able to recognize the process of my
> mutations.

Beneath the apparent carelessness is the scruple of the new completely conscious man. Montaigne, who knows what he is doing, knows also the dangers of such knowledge. He must be faithful to his own growth. He must not prune, he must not trim, above all he must not suppress what he had written. It had come from him spontaneously, "naturally, as the leaves to a tree"; therefore it had its place in the final pattern. The scruple did not prevent him from making his language more vivid and nervous, and saying more exactly what he had meant to say. That would have been a fanaticism. As artist, and as man, Montaigne knew when not to be bound by his own rules. Since his style had always been one in which "les choses surmontent," in which things "showed their back above the element they lived in," it was his duty to let them rise still sharper and clearer if he could. But in the essential substance there must be no change. He felt not merely that right and proper reverence for his own past which is the privilege of men who know their own integrity, but also the peculiar obligation of his own great work.

Indeed, the *Essais* are wonderful—a book of destiny, that had to be. "A man's life of any worth," said Keats, "is a continual allegory"; and the obvious and exoteric side of the allegory of Montaigne may be found in the history of the word which his book launched into European currency—the word "essays." How startling and mysterious is the contrast between the sense of the urge and heave of creation which the word awakens as the title of Montaigne's book, and its meager and finical connotation today! . . . The *Essais* and the plays of

Shakespeare complement one another. They are personal obverse and impersonal reverse of a single medal that imperishably commemorates the inward spirit of the high Renaissance in Europe. It is, in my eyes, far from an accident that in *The Tempest* Shakespeare turns to Montaigne for help in his great and final argument for forgiveness. In that halcyon moment it was as though in Montaigne and Shakespeare, nature had come to her own in man once more, and inspired him, as she must in her perfection, with a new kind of reverence for man.

> Nativity, once in the main of light,
> Crawls to maturity, wherewith being crowned,
> Crooked eclipses 'gainst his glory fight,
> And Time that gave doth now the gift confound.

But the conscious Individual who emerges in Montaigne's *Essais* was saved from eclipse by his own spiritual humility. That is the fragrance which preserved this great man from corruption. Beside him we feel that even Pascal was proud, and for very lack of humility was driven desperately to redress the balance by humiliating himself and man. But, alas, in this man of a second nature, who takes shape as concrete individual in Montaigne, and as imaginative creation in the works of Shakespeare, the religious impulse takes forms which are too generous for the age in which they live. They, like Hamlet, are beyond revenge; they cannot be fanatical. They are too aware of the individual for that.

They saw too far and too wide. Conscience makes cowards of them; they could not be men of action. Yet the man of action is necessary if the crust of custom is to be upheaved. Yet what conceivable action could express the universal tolerance which blossoms out of their recognition and realization of the Individual? Tolerance, it seems, can only suffer; its activity is passivity.

Hamlet's question is real. It is the one real question for humanity, henceforward.

> Whether 'tis nobler in the mind to suffer
> The slings and arrows of outrageous fortune,
> Or to take arms against a sea of troubles,
> And by opposing, end them?

Cromwell will have no doubt about taking arms; and he will be able to take arms for tolerance and for the individual, because he does not see too much or too far. He believes in a God of Vengeance still. Shakespeare and Montaigne cannot. Yet Cromwell's God of Vengeance is divided against himself; he calls for vengeance only on those who will not abandon vengeance. He is the authentic God of the Bible, revered as a work of total inspiration. What comes after the Bible? The gospel of Christ? Or the gospel of Man? But these are the same gospel—the gospel of the Divine Humanity. In another three hundred years it will be not a dream of the individual, but a necessity of the world, if it is to escape catastrophe.

Of that universal church of Christ, Montaigne is a forerunner. He liberates the individual that the individual may know his limitations; he makes man free in order that man may surrender his freedom, knowing that he must. He rediscovers—in a new world of freedom and responsibility—"the misery and grandeur of man." (pp. 59-62)

John Middleton Murry, "The Birth of the Individual," in his Heroes of Thought, *Julian Messner, Inc., 1938, pp. 49-62.*

ANDRÉ GIDE   (essay date 1939)

[Many critics regard Gide as one of the most influential thinkers and writers of twentieth-century France. In his fiction, as well as his criticism, Gide stressed autobiographical honesty, unity of subject and style, modern experimental techniques, and sincere confrontation of moral issues. In the following excerpt, Gide defines what he considers Montaigne's quintessential quality before treating specifics of the author's thought and writing.]

Montaigne is the author of a single book—the **Essays**. But in this one book, written without preconceived plan, without method, as events or his reading chanced to suggest, he claims to give us his whole self. (p. 1)

The success of the **Essays** would be inexplicable but for the author's extraordinary personality. What did he bring the world then that was so new? Self-knowledge—and all other knowledge seemed to him uncertain; but the human being he discovers—and uncovers—is so genuine, so true, that in him every reader of the **Essays** recognizes himself.

In every historical period an attempt is made to cover over this real self with a conventional figure of humanity. Montaigne pushes aside this mask in order to get at what is essential; if he succeeds it is thanks to assiduous effort and singular perspicacity; it is by opposing convention, established beliefs, conformism, with a spirit of criticism that is constantly on the alert, easy and at the same time tense, playful, amused at everything, smiling, indulgent yet uncompromising, for its object is to know and not to moralize. (p. 3)

The importance of an author lies not only in his personal value but also and greatly in the opportuneness of his message. There are some whose message is only of historical importance and finds no echo among us today. In past times, it may have stirred men's conscience, fed their enthusiasms, aroused revolutions; we have no ears for it now. Great authors are not only those whose work answers to the needs of one country and one period, but those who provide us with a food which is able to satisfy the different hungers of various nationalities and successive generations. "A heedy reader," says Montaigne, "shall often discover in other men's compositions perfections farre different from the Author's meaning, and such as haply he never dreamed of, and illustrateth them with richer senses and more excellent constructions." Is he himself such an author and will he be able to answer such new questions as the "heedy reader" may wish to put to him? I take leave to hope so.

In our time and in all countries whatsoever, constructive minds are in particular request; the authors who are most admired are those who offer us a carefully composed system, a method for solving the agonizing political, social, and moral problems which are tormenting almost all peoples and every one of us individually. Montaigne, it is true, brings us no method (how could a method that might have been valid at his time be practicable in ours?), no philosophical or social system. No mind could be less ordered than his. He lets it free to play and run wild as it pleases. And even his perpetual doubt which made Emerson consider him as the most perfect representative of skepticism (that is to say of antidogmatism, of the spirit of enquiry and investigation) [see excerpt dated 1850] may be compared, it has been said, to those purgative medicines which the patient ejects together with the stuff of which they rid him. So that some people have seen in his *"Que sçais-je?"* at once the highest mark of his wisdom and of his teaching. Not that it satisfies me. It is not their skepticism that pleases me in the

Essays, nor is that the lesson I draw from them. A "heedy reader" will find in Montaigne more and better than doubts and questions.

To Pilate's cruel question which re-echoes down the ages, Montaigne seems to have assumed, though in a quite human and profane manner, and in a very different sense, Christ's divine answer: "*I am the truth.*" That is to say he thinks he can know nothing *truly* but himself. This is what makes him talk so much about himself; for the knowledge of self seems to him indeed as important as any other. "The mask," he says, "must as well be taken from things as from men." He paints himself in order to unmask himself. And as the mask belongs much more to the country and the period than to the man himself, it is above all by the mask that people differ, so that in the being that is really unmasked, it is easy to recognize our own likeness.

He even comes to think that the portrait he paints of himself may be more generally interesting in proportion as it is more peculiar to himself; and it is by reason of this profound truth that we do in effect take so great an interest in his portrait; for "every man beareth the whole stamp of human condition." And more than this: Montaigne is convinced that, "as Pindarus said, to be sincerely true is the beginning of a great virtue." These admirable words which Montaigne borrowed from Plutarch, who himself took them from Pindar, I adopt as my own; I should like to inscribe them in the forefront of the *Essays,* for there above all lies the important lesson I draw from them.

And yet Montaigne does not seem to have himself at first grasped the boldness and reach of this resolve of his to admit only the truth about himself and to paint himself as nature made him. This accounts for a certain early hesitation in his drawing, for his attempt to find shelter in the thick undergrowths of history, for his piling up of quotations and examples—authorizations, I was tempted to say—for his endless gropings. His interest in himself is at first vague and confused, with no very clear idea as to what is important, and with a suspicion that perhaps the things that are most negligible in appearance and the most commonly disdained may in reality be just those that are most worthy of attention. Everything in himself is an object of curiosity, amusement, and astonishment: "I have seen no such monster or more expresse wonder in this world than myself. With time and custom a man doth acquaint and enure himself to all strangeness; but the more I frequent and know myself, the more my deformitie astonieth and the less I understand myself." And how delightful it is to hear him talking like this of his "deformitie," when what we like about him is precisely what enables us to recognize him as one of ourselves—just an ordinary man.

It is only when he gets to the third and last book of the *Essays* (which does not figure in the first edition) that Montaigne, in full possession, not of himself (he will never be that—no one can be) but of his subject, ceases to grope his way; he knows what he wants to say, what he must say, and he says it admirably, with a grace, a playfulness, a felicity and ingenuity of expression that are incomparable. "Others," he says (speaking of moralists), "fashion man, I relate him." And a few lines further on and more subtly, "I describe not the essence but the passage." (The Germans would say the "*werden.*" For Montaigne is constantly preoccupied by the perpetual flux of all things, and in these words he points to the non-stability of human personality which never *is,* but only conscious of itself in the evanescent moment of *becoming.* And as all other certainties break down around him, this one at least grows

greater and stronger, that on this subject, at any rate—the subject of himself—he is "the cunningest man alive" and that "never man waded further into his subject, nor arrived more exactly and fully to the end he proposed unto himself" for which he has "neede of naught but faithfulnesse"; and he immediately adds "which is therein as sincere and pure as may be found."

I think the great pleasure we take in Montaigne's *Essays* comes from the great pleasure he took in writing them, a pleasure we feel, so to speak, in every sentence. Of all the chapters that compose the three books of the *Essays,* one alone is distinctly tedious; it is by far the longest and the only one he wrote with application, care, and a concern for composition. This is the **"Apology of Raymond Sebond."** . . . This chapter is the first that Montaigne wrote. It is one of the most celebrated and oftenest quoted, for Montaigne's mind, by nature so rambling and unorderly, here strives to develop a sort of doctrine and give apparent consistency to his inconsistent skepticism. But just because he is keeping his mind on the lead, it loses almost all its grace, the exquisite charm of its indolent progress; he is directing it, we feel, towards an object, and we are never enchanted as we are later on when he allows it to venture tentatively down untraced paths and gather all the casually encountered flowers that grow by the wayside. No works, I should like here to remark, are more naturally perfect and beautiful than those which the author has most delighted in writing, those in which difficulty and effort are least apparent. In art, *seriousness* is of no avail; the surest of guides is enjoyment. In all, or almost all, the other writings which go to make up the different chapters of the *Essays,* Montaigne's thought remains as it were in the fluid state, so uncertain, so changing, and even contradictory, that the most diverse interpretations of it were subsequently given. Some writers as, for instance, Pascal and Kant, attempt to see in him a Christian; others, like Emerson, an exemplar of skepticism; others a precursor of Voltaire. Sainte-Beuve went so far as to look upon the *Essays* as a sort of preparation, an antechamber to Spinoza's *Ethics.* But Sainte-Beuve seems to me nearest the truth when he says: "With an appearance of making himself out peculiar, of reducing himself to a bundle of odd manias, he has touched each one of us in his most secret part, and while portraying himself with careless, patient and incessantly repeated strokes, he has cunningly painted the majority of mankind, and all the more successfully as he has the more minutely dissected his single self—'wavering and diverse' as he says. Each one of us finds a morsel of his own property in Montaigne."

I consider it a mark of great strength in Montaigne that he succeeded in accepting his own inconsistencies and contradictions. At the beginning of the second book of the *Essays* the following sentence strikes the alarm: "Those which exercise themselves in controuling human actions, find no such difficulty in any one part as to piece them together and bring them to one same lustre; for they commonly contradict one another so strangely, as it seemeth impossible they should be parcels of one warehouse." Not one of the great specialists of the human heart, be his name Shakespeare, Cervantes, or Racine, has failed to have at any rate fleeting glimpses of the inconsequence of human beings. . . . It seems to me that Montaigne . . . saw more than mere 'inconstancy'; I think that it is precisely under cover of this word that the real question lies hidden, and that it was not until much later that Dostoievsky, and then Proust, attacked it, so that some people say, "What is at issue here is the very conception of man on which we are now living," a conception which Freud and some others are now in process of breaking down. Perhaps the most surprising thing about Montaigne, the thing that touches us most directly, is those few, sudden lights he casts unexpectedly, and as it were involuntarily, upon the uncertain frontiers of human personality and upon the instability of the ego. (pp. 4-11)

There is nothing Montaigne dislikes more than a personality—or rather an impersonality—obtained artificially, laboriously, contentiously, in accordance with morals, propriety, custom, and what he likens to prejudices. It is as though the true self which all this hampers, hides, or distorts, keeps in his eyes a sort of mystic value, and as if he were expecting from it some surprising kind of revelation. I understand, of course, how easy it is here to play upon words and to see in Montaigne's teaching nothing but a counsel to abandon oneself to nature, to follow one's instincts blindly, and even to grant precedence to the vilest, which always seem the sincerest, that is, the most natural, those which, by their very density and thickness are invariably to be found at the bottom of the recipient, even when the noblest passions have shaken it. But I believe this would be a very wrong interpretation of Montaigne who, though he concedes a large allowance, too large perhaps, to the instincts we have in common with animals, knows how to take off from them in order to rise, and never allows himself to be their slave or their victim.

It is natural that with such ideas, Montaigne should feel very little inclined to repentance and contrition. . . . Every time Montaigne speaks of Christianity it is with the strangest (sometimes one might almost say with the most malicious) impertinence. He often treats of religion, never of Christ. Not once does he refer to His words; one might almost doubt whether he had ever read the Gospels—or rather, one cannot doubt that he never read them seriously. As for the respect he shows Catholicism, there undoubtedly enters into it a large amount of prudence. (We must remember that the great massacre of Protestants throughout the whole kingdom of France on the eve of St. Bartholomew took place in 1572.) (pp. 15-16)

In order still further to protect his book, he felt impelled to insert further passages of a very reassuring nature, in which he is hardly recognizable, into those very parts of the *Essays* which are most likely to arouse alarm in the hearts of sincere Christians: "This only end of another life, blessedly immortal, doth rightly merit we should abandon the pleasures and commodities of this our life." This passage (which for that matter was left in manuscript and only published after his death) and other similar ones seem to have been stuck into his book like so many lightning-conductors, or better still, like labels of lemonade or ginger-ale fixed upon bottles of whiskey when a régime has gone dry. And in fact a few lines after the lightning-conductor come the words: "We must tooth and naile retain the use of this life's pleasures, which our years snatch from us one after another."

This passage of the first edition, which the added lines attempt in vain to disguise, shows the true Montaigne, that "sworne enemy to all falsifications"; and I should be indignant at this cautious recantation, if I did not think that it had perhaps been necessary in order to get his wares safely through to us. Sainte-Beuve says of him very justly: "He may have appeared a very good Catholic except for not having been a Christian." . . . What he likes about Catholicism, what he admires and praises, is its order and ancientness. . . . There is no need to look for any other explanation of his ignorance of the Gospels and his hatred of Protestant reformers. He wishes to keep the Church's religion—France's religion—as it is, not because he thinks it the only good one but because he thinks it would be bad to change it.

In the same way we feel throughout Montaigne's life and writings a constant love of order and moderation, care for the public good, a refusal to let his own personal interest prevail over the interest of all. But he believes that the honesty of his own judgment and the preservation of that honesty are more valuable than any other considerations and should be set above them. "I would rather let all affairs go to wracke than to force my faith and conscience for their availe." And I prefer to believe in the sincerity of this statement rather than ask myself whether he is not bragging a little; for it is as important nowadays that such words should be listened to as it was important in Montaigne's troubled times that there should be men to keep the integrity of their conscience and maintain their independence and autonomy above the herd instincts of submission and cowardly acceptance. (pp. 17-19)

In his drift away from Christianity, it is to Goethe that Montaigne draws near by anticipation. "As for me who love life and cultivate it, such as it hath pleased God to grant it us . . . Nature is a gentle guide, yet not more gentle than prudent and just." Goethe would no doubt gladly have endorsed these sentences which are almost the last of the *Essays*. This is the final flowering of Montaigne's wisdom. Not a word of it is useless. How very careful he is to add the idea of prudence, justice, and culture to his declaration of the love of life!

What Montaigne teaches us especially is what was called at a much later date, *liberalism*, and I think that it is the wisest lesson that can be drawn from him at the present time when political or religious convictions are so miserably dividing all men and opposing them to each other. "In the present intestine trouble of our State my interest hath not made me forget neither the commendable qualities of our adversaries, nor the reproachful of those I have followed." (pp. 23-4)

This rare and extraordinary propensity, of which he often speaks, towards listening to, and even espousing, other people's opinions, to the point of letting them prevail over his own, prevented him from venturing very far along the road that was afterwards to be Nietzsche's. He is held back by a natural prudence from which, as from a safeguard, he is very loth to depart. He shrinks from desert places and regions where the air is too rarefied. But a restless curiosity spurs him on. . . . (p. 24)

If I am accused of having sharpened Montaigne's ideas to excess, my answer is that numbers of his commentators have busied themselves with blunting them. I have merely removed their wrappings and disengaged them from the wadding that sometimes chokes the *Essays* and prevents their shafts from reaching us. The great preoccupation of pedagogues, when they are faced with authors of some boldness who yet are classics, is to render them inoffensive; and I often wonder that the work of years should so naturally contribute to this. After a little it seems as though the edge of new thoughts gets worn away, and on the other hand, from growing in some sort accustomed to them, we are able to handle them without fear of injury.

Montaigne, during his travels in Italy, is often surprised to see the loftiest monuments of ancient Rome half buried in a mass of fallen litter. Their summits have been the first to crumble and it is their own fragments that strew the earth around them and gradually raise its level. If, in our day, they do not seem to tower so high above us, it is also because we do not stand so far below them. (pp. 26-7)

André Gide, "Presenting Montaigne," translated by Dorothy Bussy, in The Living Thoughts of Montaigne *by Michel de Montaigne, edited by André Gide, Longmans, Green and Co., 1939, pp. 1-27.*

DONALD M. FRAME (essay date 1955)

[*Frame is an American educator and author whose critical studies of Montaigne are supplemented by his translation of* The Essays *and his biography of the essayist (see Additional Bibliography). In the following excerpt from an exhaustive analysis of the chronological development of Montaigne's thought, Frame presents the culmination of the essayist's philosophy of human nature and purpose.*]

[In Book Three of the *Essays,*] Montaigne's mind, though not closed, is now fully formed.

Still skeptical in temper and turn of mind, he is yet very sure of many things. Foremost of these is the value of his plan of self-study and self-portrayal. More and more he writes about himself, aware that he will never know all the answers but also that he knows this subject of his better than any other writer ever knew his own. And now he sees the resemblance between men that makes knowledge of self mean knowledge of mankind. Now he sees man as a social being, not merely as an individual. Now he speaks his mind positively about the two matters that are closest to his heart and that fill the final essays—human nature and human conduct. (p. 140)

What is man's nature? How therefore should he live? These are the questions that Montaigne asks himself throughout his final essays. And since proper living depends on our nature, the first question to answer is what we are.

In the early essays Montaigne often seems to question whether there is such a thing as human nature. He sees little but chaos and inconsistency in the individual, little but diversity in the race. His sense of differences in man and men is one of his vitalizing contributions to human psychology; but it makes any generalization virtually impossible.

At the end of his life, however, he finds unity both within each man and in mankind. (pp. 141-42)

Montaigne still sees more difference than resemblance in mankind, but now he sees both: though our faces, he says, are different enough to tell us apart, they are enough alike to tell us from the animals. He finds that his long self-study has made him a good judge of others, often better able than they to explain their conduct to them. Evidently, his observations have general validity. "I set forth a humble and inglorious life," he writes; "that does not matter. You can tie up all moral philosophy with a common and private life just as well as with a life of richer stuff: each man bears the entire form of man's estate."

Montaigne's sense of kinship and solidarity now extends, more seriously and less paradoxically than in the early essays, to many large groups: the people of the New World, foreigners in general, the populace of Bordeaux, freaks, and women. Now he senses, and fully shares, a broad strain of common humanity.

For Montaigne, the basic fact of man's nature is that he is made up of body and soul. And his basic deduction is that these two are equal parts. (pp. 142-43)

The body as Montaigne sees it is simple, earthy, solid, sane, slow to change. It appears to be entirely subject to nature, in which it is fortunate; for nature makes even pain contribute by contrast to its pleasure and places its greatest pleasures in the satisfaction of its needs. The body can sometimes even help the soul by giving it stability.

The soul is very complex and infinitely powerful for our good or ill. Centrifugal, erratic, never at rest, it is always trying to improve on nature and succeeds only in making us miserable. Properly directed, however, it can do wonders.

Its parts or functions are not always clear. The mind (*esprit*) sometimes represents the entire soul, sometimes its knowing and reasoning function. The imagination is the most flighty part of the soul, undiscerning between truth and falsehood, often needing consolation from the mind. Reason (*raison*) has at least two distinct meanings or aspects for Montaigne—that of *reasoning*, which is rash, plausible, and dangerously irresponsible, and that of *reasonableness*, which is excellent. Understanding (*entendement*) and judgment, which are virtually synonymous, test new appearances by comparing them with present and past evidence and then assign them the appropriate degree of truth or falsehood, good or evil. Judgment is the master quality, of which conscience appears to be one function. Where judgment rules the soul harmoniously, all will be well; where it does not, mind and soul are dangerous even to their possessor.

Located within us, the soul, or mind, has no direct contact with externals. It receives the reports of the senses on the impacts that objects make on them and tries to find the truth from these reports. In this it has no assurance of success, since it accepts things always in its own fashion. But this same arbitrariness gives it infinite power for our happiness. (pp. 143-44)

Since the soul deceives the senses even as it is deceived by them, it may exercise its power through pleasant delusion. No matter; the point is that it has the power:

> The body has, except for a little more or less, only one gait and one bent. It [the soul] is diversifiable into all sorts of forms and adapts to itself, and to its condition, whatever this may be, the feelings of the body and all other accidents. Therefore we must study and investigate it, and awaken in it its all-powerful forces. There is neither reason, nor prescription, nor force which has power against its inclination and its choice. Of so many thousands of biases that the soul has at its disposal, let us give it one suitable for our repose and preservation, and we are not only safe from all injury but even gratified and tickled, if it seems good to it, by injuries and evils.
>
> It makes its profit from everything indiscriminately. Error, dreams serve it usefully as a lawful means to place us in security and contentment.

All this, of course, is vanity: the senses gullible, the soul deceptive and irresponsible, the body decadent from youth, disobedient to the soul and rivaling it in importance. This is a far cry from the usual bright Renaissance picture of man as the little universe, the microcosm.

Moreover, vice comes as naturally to us as vanity. Ambition, jealousy, envy, vengefulness, superstition, despair, cruelty—the seeds of these are inborn, and to destroy them would be to destroy the fundamental conditions of our life. However, we also have it in us to recognize vice and control it. To know it is to hate it; repentance follows it as the night the day. Thus although vice is important, vanity remains the keynote: "I do not think there is as much unhappiness in us as vanity. . . . We are not so much full of evil as of inanity."

Vanity is not a new idea to the author of the **"Apology for Raymond Sebond."** He merely argues it now better and of-tener, making it a theme of most of the essays of Book Three.

It is man's wisdom, not man's follies, he writes in **"Three Kinds of Association,"** that makes him laugh. Is there anything except us in nature, he asks in **"Diversion,"** that feeds on inanity and is controlled by it? **Some Verses of Virgil"** treats the vanity of our physical makeup. The whole world revolves about the urge for copulation, which we call love; yet no other action so comically reveals us as the plaything of the gods. **"Husbanding Your Will"** shows mostly vanity in public affairs and the motives that drive us into them; **"Cripples,"** our love of the vanity of speculation and dispute; **"Physiognomy,"** the vanity of artificial reason and knowledge, which do us more harm than good as defenses against the fear of pain and death. Finally, **"Experience"** finds vanity in our very essence: "I who boast of embracing the pleasures of life so assiduously and so particularly, find in them, when I look at them thus minutely, virtually nothing but wind. But what then? We are all wind. And even the wind, more wisely than we, loves itself for making a noise and moving about, and contents itself with its own functions, without wishing for stability and solidity, qualities that do not belong to it."

Vanity is the heart as well as the title of Chapter 9. (pp. 145-47)

Our essence, then, is vanity. But the equation works both ways. Vanity is our essence; and we are fools if we despise our essence. Montaigne had attacked this malady of self-disdain earlier, and now, in the chapter on vanity itself, he returns even harder to the attack.

To be sure, we must recognize our vanity, our great limitations. We are very physical, very variable, often comical, something less than omniscient. To ignore this is to invite arrogance, presumption, and self-disdain, dangerous faults but easily cur-able. But at the same time we must recognize our possibilities, which are richly adequate for living. The little learning that we need to live at ease is in us; and if we cannot find it by ourselves, Socrates will teach us how. His greatest service was precisely that of showing all that human nature can do by itself. We may not even need his help if we look within us as Mon-taigne does, and try to become authorities not on Cicero but on ourselves. "In the experience I have of myself," Montaigne writes, "I find enough to make me wise, if I were a good scholar." The best cure for our vanity, indeed for all our errors—anger, inconstancy, ignorance, bad judgment, and all the rest—is not to read about them in books but to see them, truly and steadily, in ourselves. It is not really at our own expense, as he had written earlier, that we become wise in this way; it is only at the expense of our self-conceit. "Let us only listen: we tell ourselves all we most need."

These are the main facts of human nature for Montaigne. Our limitations are great, but our resources for living well are greater. If we look into ourselves, we shall find them.

In all man's limitations and all his resources Montaigne finds tremendous possibilities for happiness or unhappiness, for good or evil, for wisdom or folly. These pairs of opposites are closely related. Happiness produces neither goodness nor wisdom, though it is favorable to them; goodness produces happiness but not wisdom; wisdom produces both goodness and happiness and depends on neither. Thus wisdom is basic. The surest way to seek goodness and happiness is through wisdom.

Perhaps, indeed, it is the only way. Only a miraculous inter-vention of God, Montaigne believes, can make radical changes in our intellect or morals. By ourselves we cannot force our "ruling pattern" or extirpate our vices. However, we can con-trol these by a wise use of our virtues. The essence of a good education is not to impose on us "right" ways of thinking and acting but to train our judgment to make us wise, and therefore good, with a wisdom and a goodness that is our own. We should "know how to do all things and like to do only the good." Only such free choice has moral meaning.

Wisdom, for Montaigne, consists entirely in knowing how to live. This involves four things: knowing ourselves, accepting ourselves and our life, learning what to expect of ourselves, and learning our duty to ourselves and others. Here the basic element, on which all the others depend, is self-knowledge. Ethics must be firmly rooted in psychology: what we should be, in what we are. Acceptance is equally necessary. For unless we accept as well as know ourselves, with our strengths and our weaknesses, we will expect too much or too little of our-selves, and in either case fall short of our best possible moral effectiveness. And unless we accept life with its joy and its pain, we will fall into the vice of sourness and ingratitude.

The last two parts of wisdom guide us in our main responsibility here on earth, namely our conduct. To do what is fitting and best we must first know what is fitting and best. To know this for ourselves alone is not easy; to know it for others as well is still harder. But the challenge is as rewarding as it is difficult.

For Montaigne this is the only way to seek real goodness. As long as there is inner strife, we cannot be entirely good, and we fall short of the ideal. Judgment, the voice of wisdom in us, must rule within; but it rules by persuasion, so that our whole selves join in our action. Only a soul in harmony with itself can be wholly good. Integration is a condition of integrity.

The most difficult thing is to know what we owe to ourselves and to others. Montaigne's final conviction of this is a measure of his growth. In the early years of his retirement . . . , he had called it the greatest thing in the world to know how to belong to oneself. Now his sense of solidarity makes him reject this ideal as one-sided and incomplete. The problem is to belong to oneself and to the human race as well. (pp. 147-50)

No longer will complete withdrawal do for Montaigne: "He who lives not at all with respect to others (*à autruy*)," he now writes, "hardly lives with respect to himself (*à soy*)." But the opposite is equally foolish and unnatural: "Just as anyone who should forget to live a good and saintly life, and think he was quit of his duty by guiding and training others to do so, would be a fool; even so he who abandons healthy and gay living of his own to serve others therewith, takes, to my taste, a bad and unnatural course."

The ideal balance lies in proper self-possession, which means lending but not giving ourselves to others. (pp. 151-52)

Proper self-possession in general lies in a delicate balance of conflicting duties. It would be fairer and better for man, Mon-taigne believes, if he consciously included himself in applying the golden rule. His argument rests not on hedonism but on justice. Excessive self-devotion defeats itself; but excessive self-abnegation, however admirable (like that of Montaigne's father as mayor), is also unjust. The true point of justice, Montaigne believes, is to contribute all fitting duties and ser-vices to society, but with the aim of applying our experience to our own lives. We owe friendship not only to others but also to ourselves: not a false friendship that drives us to frantic pursuit of false goods such as glory, learning, riches; nor an overindulgent one that breaks down our character as the ivy does the wall it clings to; but "a salutary and well-regulated friendship, useful and pleasant alike." The true point of this friendship is difficult to find but all-important, a secret mystery of the temple of Pallas. "He knows its duties and practices them . . . has attained the summit of human wisdom and of our happiness." (p. 152)

Since our *raison d'être* is our conduct, private life is our proper function and domain. To live it well is the greatest masterpiece of all. (p. 153)

In order to perform this masterpiece, we must recognize and accept ourselves as children of nature. From the **"Apology"** and **"Cannibals"** to **"Physiognomy,"** Montaigne continues to insist on this point. We belong in nature, but we will not admit it. In our reckless attempts to improve on her by art, we have lost her track; we have changed her into all sorts of forms, as perfumers do with oil, so that we no longer recognize her in ourselves and must seek her in simple people or animals. We have been fools to abandon a guide who led us so happily and so surely.

Nature helps us in every way. She uses our inconstancy to divert our grief; gives us better laws than our own, since she knows her business better than we do; makes pain serve pleasure, and our needs pleasant to satisfy; teaches us how to die, and in fact all we need to know to be content. She is a sweet guide, but no more sweet than prudent and just; we cannot fail if we follow her, and the more simply we follow her the better.

Artificiality is our undoing. Foolishly we take its glister for gold. Sometimes—and her Montaigne speaks from personal experience—we let it spoil our lives. We beset ourselves with all sorts of fears, like that of death, which may not even be natural; we give ourselves more trouble in preparing for death than we would in dying; we make death the goal of life instead of merely the end. For all her grateful children nature takes care of these things better than ever we can and on a moment's notice.

From the refusal to accept ourselves as children of nature comes presumption and its offspring, the wildest of our maladies, self-disdain. Because we think of ourselves as above and apart from the order of creation, we cut our obligations to fit a higher being than ourselves, and so order ourselves to be necessarily at fault. We like to think that the higher our aim, the higher will be our attainment. But Montaigne disagrees, like Socrates, whose motto, "According as one can," he often borrows. Our nature, he finds, simply does not work that way: constant failure, however inevitable, makes us give up trying, either through discouragement or through too easy acceptance of the inevitable. There is the danger also that it will make us actually worse; for our normal impulse to cover up perhaps a minor vice will add to it the ugly vice of hypocrisy. "Between ourselves," Montaigne writes, "these are two things that I have always observed to be in singular accord: supercelestial thoughts and subterranean conduct. . . . They want to get out of themselves and escape from the man (*eschapper à l'homme*). That is madness: instead of changing into angels, they change into beasts; instead of raising themselves, they lower themselves."

In Montaigne's eyes this is perhaps our greatest folly: to want to escape from man's condition. It is not natural but purely manmade, a product of our erratic mind. We would be wiser, happier, and better, he insists, to accept ourselves as we are,

to let our conscience be content with itself not as the conscience of an angel or of a horse but as the conscience of a man. Self-knowledge is the road to acceptance: "We seek other conditions because we do not understand the use of our own, and go outside of ourselves because we do not know what it is like inside." (pp. 154-55)

Montaigne is often at odds with himself—verbally at least—on the question of self-improvement. It is no wonder that his moral countenance has appeared to different readers as anything from earnest reformer to complacent hedonist. Often it is his love of sally and paradox, humor and irony, that leads him into inconsistency of statement; but there are other reasons, too. In respect to himself, frankness makes him say that he has sought to be better, and perhaps in some measure succeeded; but frankness and modesty make him regard this measure as small. Moreover, he considers self-acceptance bad in excess but good in moderation: in excess the enemy of self-improvement, in moderation the condition of it. Since most people put all the emphasis on self-improvement, Montaigne usually stresses his lack of it. "I have not corrected, like Socrates," he writes, "my natural dispositions by force of reason. . . . I let myself go as I have come, I combat nothing." What virtue he has, he calls a sort of accidental innocence.

Yet even in this same context, while saying that he has restricted his vices too little, he admits that since they aid and abet one another, he has kept them apart and confined, as isolated and simple as he could. Such statements seem more candid than the others and closer to the center of his thought. Without boorish conceit he could not claim much more than

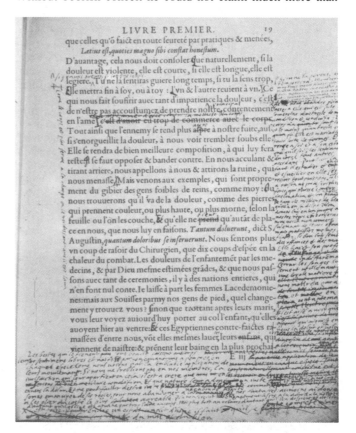

A page from The Essays *(1580), with Montaigne's handwritten corrections.*

he does when he says that he has put all his efforts into forming his life. And still more revealing is a later comparison of himself with the stoics: "What they did by virtue, I train myself to do by disposition (*complexion*)."

The somewhat surprising use of the term *complexion* (as something trained and acquired) is a result of Montaigne's conception of the mechanics of self-improvement. It is through habit, he finds, that wisdom works to produce goodness. Habit is all-important, all-powerful; a second nature, as Aristotle says, and no less strong than the first. Virtue can work by fits and starts, and in that way we can do almost anything. But what we really are we are constantly, by habit. One of the reasons why Montaigne sets Socrates so high is that by habit he had made his goodness a second nature. When Montaigne trains himself to do well by disposition, he is following what he considers the best way to be good and the only way to be really and wholly good.

For we can improve on nature, good and strong as she is. Our native state seems to be a sort of balance of conflicting elements: the vices on the one hand, and on the other hand conscience and repentance. As we grow, either side may prevail, or neither. Education can do much but not everything; we may control, but we cannot extirpate, our natural propensities. Reason will normally tell us to follow nature, but not always; when it does not, it is reason we must follow.

Montaigne's main hope of human betterment lies in an inborn seed of universal reason. Although he is sincerely religious, the Protestant experience and the religious wars apparently make him feel that religion has failed as a moral stimulus, presumably because it has not allowed enough for human limitations. (pp. 156-58)

Just as Montaigne rejects nature as the arbiter of our morals, so he rejects religion as their base. He dislikes its constraint, its self-seeking motivation by fear and hope. He not only accepts us as neither horses nor angels, he does not want us to be anything but men. He seems to feel that in giving us reason to help us rise above mere nature, God has put us quite on our own to be fully ourselves.

In the early essays, doubtful of our ability to become good, Montaigne had mainly urged us to be natural. Now he still urges that, but most of all he wants us to be human.

Our vices, for example, he regards as natural but not human. Most of those that he hates worst—disdainful treatment of social inferiors; contempt for the body and its rights; eagerness to make others sad by our misery; lying, disloyalty, mob violence, torture, cruelty—he clearly connects, by statement or suggestion, with inhumanity.

Meanwhile his highest praise for ideas, actions, or men is to call them human. (pp. 158-59)

To be natural and yet naturally to surpass the rest of nature; to accept ourselves and yet by the means God has given us to improve ourselves: this for Montaigne is to be truly human. (p. 159)

> *Donald M. Frame, in his* Montaigne's Discovery of Man: The Humanization of a Humanist, *Columbia University Press, 1955, 202 p.*

ABRAHAM C. KELLER (essay date 1957)

[*An American professor of French, Keller is particularly interested in the literature and thought of the French Renaissance. In the following excerpt, he outlines a theory to reconcile Montaigne's seemingly inconsistent political liberalism and conservatism.*]

Swift once said, speaking of profundity, that "it is with writers as with wells—a person with good eyes may see to the bottom of the deepest, provided any water be there: and often, when there is nothing in the world at the bottom besides dryness and dirt, though it be but a yard and a half underground, it shall pass, however, for wondrous deep, upon no wiser a reason than because it is wondrous dark." Happily for the world at large, scholars usually see to it that in the well of literature nothing shall remain hidden in darkness.

There are, certainly, many ways of looking into the well, and more than one, it is to be hoped, can yield the observer the determination he seeks. Negatively, it may be said that consistency, though often highly esteemed for various valid reasons, has no positive correlation with profundity. There is no reason why a writer should agree today with what he said yesterday. Indeed, if we believe Montaigne, who is the subject of this study, just the opposite should be true, for a man who is vital, who is active and thoughtful, should grow in understanding and maturity, and as he grows, his ideas should change also. Faithful to this notion, Montaigne made himself the world's master of contradiction, cavalierly affirming as true or good what previously he had condemned, and unashamedly allowing his publishers to print statements and even whole essays which in new essays he expressly attacked. (p. 408)

But beneath Montaigne's contradictions—it has always been assumed by lovers of the *Essays*—lies a fidelity to principle which is more meaningful and more appealing than mere literary consistency. The very fact, for example, that, as new editions of the *Essays* appeared, Montaigne refrained from deleting statements with which he no longer agreed shows his solid attachment to the principle of self-portraiture—for how should we know a man if we do not follow his growth? When Montaigne totally reversed his judgment of Alexander the Great, or his estimate of the worth of the common people, or his ideas on death, was he being inconsistent? "I may perhaps contradict myself," he will answer us, "but the truth I do not contradict." Usually, indeed, we can see Montaigne trying hard to clarify his ideas, striving for nothing so much as to be true to himself, and in those cases the apparent inconsistencies usually dissolve in the light of biography and simple chronology.

Some contradictions, however, are not so easily disposed of. One of the most stubborn of these, which it will be the purpose of this paper to elucidate, concerns Montaigne's social and political views. To say that one side of Montaigne was "liberal" and the other "conservative" seems unsatisfactory to many, because neither those terms nor the line-ups which they evoke in our minds were the same in the sixteenth century as they were later to become. The terms do, however, suggest the two complexes of ideas which we find in the *Essays*. One Montaigne implores us to tolerate and respect other people's ways, to keep our minds open—for who can say what is best?—the other tells us that nothing in a state is as harmful as change or variation. The first Montaigne believes in constant flux, the second in the most extreme rigidity. The one will openly criticize laws as foolish or obsolete, the second will be revolted at the idea of altering them. (p. 409)

The Montaigne who is the independent thinker and the tolerant world-citizen has, of the two, been the more appealing to nearly every generation of readers. Indeed, the name Montaigne has become almost synonymous with the denial of finality in ideas, the spirit of free examination, and the intense individualism which characterize much of modern thought, and it is not surprising that some critics have tended to regard this as the true Montaigne. Others, while loving the free Montaigne, have tended to picture him as preoccupied with political stability to such a point that he would allow individual freedom of conscience to operate only if and when it does not threaten the social order.

However the case may be, and whichever of the two Montaignes one may choose to emphasize, the existence of these two sides of his thought has always been recognized. (p. 410)

Certain aspects of Montaigne—his tolerance, open-mindedness, and devotion to the untrammelled development of individuals and peoples—represent the most advanced thinking of his time, and for this Montaigne has always been properly praised. What has never been made fully clear, even by Montaigne's bitterest critics and detractors, is the retrograde quality of his conservatism, in which his obscurantism is in reality more signal than his enlightenment is elsewhere. It may be well to clarify this point before proceeding to examine on what common ground Montaigne's two divergent attitudes rested. The reader of these remarks might well object that it is misleading to characterize Montaigne's conservatism as extreme without reference to his contemporaries, merely because he urged men to follow the order of the world without inquiry, or because he said that, if he could, he would gladly put a peg under the wheel of history and stop it where it was. We, it is true, might not share these sentiments, but the question is whether they were unusually conservative in Montaigne's own time. The answer is that they were. . . . In the closing decades of the sixteenth century, the various writers in Montaigne's intellectual class who may be regarded as conservatives all had reservations with regard to the ruler's authority. (pp. 411-12)

If, now, instead of reading Montaigne's contemporaries, we cast a glance backward at the political thought of the middle ages, Montaigne's ideas appear even more benighted. He took no account of the traditional restraints on rulers, restraints which every political writer of the middle ages in some measure formulated and which even the theoreticians of absolute monarchy in the sixteenth century felt obliged to maintain, at least in theory. (p. 412)

That there was a conflict between his independent and his submissive attitudes was, of course, as clear to Montaigne himself as to any of his commentators. A writer as perceptive and self-conscious as Montaigne was could hardly tell us, first to accept nothing on authority or trust, and then to follow every law and custom without question, without being aware of a serious contradiction. The problem, indeed, was considerable, for Montaigne was more and more committed, as time went on, to a Follow-Nature doctrine according to which each individual must seek to discover his true self and then remain faithful to it. Will a man not be violating this natural self by submitting to laws or customs which run counter to it? Montaigne solved his problem, and assured a faithfulness to nature, by resorting to an interesting pair of ideas. The first was that a law or custom is itself an expression of nature and as such deserves to be obeyed in the same way as an individual's own nature. But, the reader may ask, in the event of a conflict between the individual and society (a conflict which Montaigne never tried to gloss over or deny), can a man be faithful to both? He can, Montaigne answered, by considering the second of these two ideas: that the individual's inner life is what really counts. Giving external obedience to society (and society asks

no more) permits the individual to preserve his true feelings intact, and this is what is morally important. (p. 413)

To many men since Montaigne's time—as well as to some in his own day and before—this barrier which Montaigne set up between thoughts and acts has not appeared honest or conscientious. (p. 414)

The point here, however, has been not to criticize Montaigne's solution but to state it and to indicate that Montaigne consciously erected a wall between the areas of submission and independence. In his own case, the ground was very different on the two sides of the wall, and scholars have worked long and hard to explain how a common proprietorship was possible. The most popular explanations for integrating the independent, freedom-loving Montaigne and the conventional, obedient Montaigne have been based on two main points . . . : his skepticism and his experience of the religious wars. As so often happened in Montaigne's case, each of these influences worked in both directions. Thus, his skepticism, which caused him to doubt that there were many absolutes in the world, kept him safely away from dogmatism and gave him what is sometimes admired as the openest mind in all Western literature. Since we can never know for certain what is right, said Montaigne, let us not kill men who disagree with us: with the passage of time and the accumulation of knowledge, our thinking may be utterly changed. But in politics Montaigne applied his skepticism exclusively to those who sought reform or revolution: Since nothing is certainly true or sound or final, since it is impossible to know that this or that reform will benefit the nation, why trouble ourselves to make the change? Thus the same skepticism which led him to be tolerant and sympathetic vis-à-vis the mores of strange or barbarous peoples, the skepticism, indeed, which led him to deny the whole concept of barbarism (which to him seemed simply to be that which is unfamiliar)—this same skepticism led him in his own country, to justify the status quo in a most rigid manner.

The importance of the civil wars, which racked the French body politic from the early 1560's to the end of the century, has always been seriously recognized by students of Montaigne and historians of French literature who have probed the formation of Montaigne's thought, being often regarded as the principal source of his political conservatism. The anarchy resulting from the civil wars alarmed Montaigne and caused him, as it did many other men, to prefer the status quo, with all its faults, to a new state for which the price was so high. (pp. 414-16)

It is, then, in the opinion of scholars, Montaigne's skepticism and his experience of the French civil wars that held the two sides of his thought together. But both of these factors are essentially negative, and to that extent unsatisfying as a unifying force in a thinker as positive as Montaigne. Moreover, the one deals with mere reaction to events, the other is limited to epistemology, and it is a question whether such narrow explanations should be allowed to account almost totally for such significant parts of Montaigne's thought. It would be much more satisfying, and more interesting, to find the unifying force in some broad philosophical notion which has to do with Montaigne's view of the world. Is there, we may ask, any metaphysical view with which both of the thought complexes that have been distinguished in this paper can be associated, and associated in such a manner as to appear basic to both?

We shall now examine in turn these two complexes of ideas in order to discover whether any such philosophical groundwork appears. Mere statements which tell us, either on the one side, Think for yourself, Accept nothing as final, or, on the other side, Never make changes, will not interest us as much as passages where Montaigne seems to be presenting some philosophical explanation for those ideas, whether on the side of tolerance, open-mindedness, and "liberalism," or of rigidity and conservatism. We shall examine the liberal side first.

On this side one of the best statements, probably, is that which comes near the end of the **"Apologie de Raimond Sebond,"** where he gives us reasons for his beliefs:

> If Nature encloses within the bounds of her ordinary progress, along with all other things, the beliefs, judgments, and opinions of men; if they have their cycle, their season, their birth, their death, like cabbages; if the heavens more and roll them about at their pleasure, what magisterial and permanent authority can we attribute to them? If we see by palpable experience that the form of our being depends on the air, on the climate, and on the soil on which we are born, and not only our complexion, our stature, the mixture of our humours, and our countenance, but even the faculties of our soul, . . . so that, just as fruits and animals are born unlike, so men too are born more or less warlike, just, temperate, and docile; here given to wine, elsewhere to theft or lechery; here inclined to superstition, there to unbelief; here to liberty, there to servitude, capable of one science or one art; dull or clever, obedient or rebellious, good or bad, according as the place where they are situated inclines them, and they assume a new disposition if their location is changed, like trees. . . . If we see now one art flourishing or one belief, now another, through some celestial influence; a certain age producing certain kinds of nature and giving to the human race such and such a bent; the minds of men lusty, now meagre, like our fields: what becomes of all those fine prerogatives on which we flatter ourselves? Seeing that a wise man may be mistaken, and a hundred men, and many nations, nay, since human nature itself, according to our view, has for many ages been mistaken in this or that, what assurance have we that she at any time ceases to be mistaken, and that it is not mistaken in this particular century?

What has always been emphasized in this passage and others like it is Montaigne's skepticism—for does he not say at the end that there is no sure and final knowledge, and did he not say, just preceding this passage [in the 1580 edition], that one should not get too excited about the Copernican cosmography, because it may eventually go the way of the Ptolemaic? This, certainly, is true, and the passage is justly regarded as an expression of Montaigne's skepticism. But much more important is the reason for that skepticism. Disbelief in the certainty of knowledge rests, in most cases, on a demonstration of the imperfection of man's apparatus to receive and interpret the phenomena of nature, and Montaigne—above all in this **"Apologie de Raimond Sebond"**—presented such a demonstration in an admirable and thorough-going manner. But in this passage he presents an added obstacle: variety. There are so many kinds of beings and of men, so many opinions, humors, and intelligences, that even the wisest of men would be unable to come to any valid conclusions. Nature is simply too vast to permit dogmatism. (pp. 417-18)

Nature in Montaigne's *Essays* is rich, so rich that for Montaigne it is a mistake to seek any kind of singleness or uniformity. . . .

Speaking elsewhere of ways of life . . . , Montaigne writes: "I believe in and conceive a thousand contrary ways of living; and, reversing the common practice, more easily admit difference than resemblance among us. I am as ready as anyone would like to excuse another from possessing my own inclinations and principles, and I consider him simply in himself, without reference to others, fitting him according to his own model." There is no indication here of any single right way of life, but only of a plurality of right ways. (p. 419)

[With] these ideas we find ourselves, of course, thick in the philosophy of optimism. [Arthur O.] Lovejoy, in his now standard book, *The Great Chain of Being,* examined the history of the two principal components of the optimistic philosophy (without, fortunately, assigning Montaigne much importance). About these two components and about optimism in general it may be well to say a word before proceeding, since Montaigne has never, to my knowledge, been discussed from the standpoint of philosophical optimism. He has only been called an optimist or pessimist in the more popular sense—and here a reader may have his choice, for in some ways Montaigne's outlook was gloomy, in other ways cheerful.

Philosophical optimism is not the same as the optimism of popular speech, which is a kind of sanguinity or cheerfulness, or ability to see the bright side of things. In philosophy, optimism is, in Webster's words, "the opinion or doctrine that everything in nature is ordered for the best; or that the order of things in the universe is adapted to produce the most good." To believe that everything is *ordered for the best* does not necessarily imply a belief that it *is good*. Leibniz, the chief theoretician of modern optimistic philosophy, would have us imagine a hypothetical moment at which God is about to create the world. In surveying the types of world which it is possible for Him to create, He will, naturally, being Perfection itself, choose the best. He could not do otherwise. But any resemblance between this "best of all possible worlds" and a world which men might consider "good" would, in the very nature of things, be sheer coincidence. The reason for this is that men lack the vision of the whole; what may appear unfortunate on the scale of human existence in reality forms part of a large pattern which ensures the functioning of the world in the best possible manner. Man's "good" and God's "best" have thus very little in common, and philosophical optimists have not, in spite of Voltaire's satire, been distinguished by any belief that things in the world, especially on earth, are good. (pp. 422-23)

The two closely related ideas which formed the mainstay of the optimistic philosophy were the "great chain of being" and the "plenitude of nature." According to these ideas, creation is spread over a vast "chain" (something called a ladder or scale), with a creature at each link (or rung). . . . Man is somewhere between the extremes, his precise position varying from writer to writer, with creatures stretching away beyond his vision in either direction. God in his goodness left no link of the chain unoccupied. Nor—transferring the application of the idea slightly—is there any heavenly body that does not contain beings (whether animate or inanimate), all of which have their assigned places in the chain of being.

We have had so far, an indication of Montaigne's adherence to these ideas in relation to his "liberal" ideas. The full importance of optimism as his philosophical base will now appear if we examine its connection with the conservative side of his thinking.

Chain-of-being and plenitude-of-nature reasoning, used as justification for the status quo, is familiar to us in eighteenth-century contexts. We know that Pope's "Whatever is, is right" philosophy, when applied by himself and others to society, led to a preaching of resignation and became an apologia for the social ills which accompanied the industrial revolution. The philosophy of optimism could neatly explain away any particular evil on the ground that there was a general good which that evil subserved. Thus the optimists, as much as they might be personally disturbed by evil, were philosophically unruffled, for their doctrine embraced evil as a necessary part of the whole, so necessary that without it the good itself would be impossible.

The extent to which Montaigne was prepared, a century and a half before Pope, to use the optimistic philosophy as a rationalization for evil of every kind may appear from the following quotation. The case will be particularly clear if it is remembered, among other things, that Montaigne had a special hatred and horror of cruelty, as he explains in detail elsewhere.

> Our structure, both public and private, is full of imperfection. But there is nothing useless in Nature, not even uselessness itself. Nothing has insinuated itself into this universe that has not an appropriate place in it. Our being is cemented with sickly qualities: ambition, jealousy, envy, revenge, superstition, despair, dwell in us with so natural a possession that we recognize their reflections even in beasts. Nay, cruelty too, so unnatural a vice; for even in the midst of compassion we feel within us I know not what bitter-sweet pricking of malicious pleasure in seeing others suffer; even children feel it. . . . Whoever should remove from men the seeds of these qualities would destroy the fundamental conditions of our life. Likewise, in every government there are necessary offices that are not only abject, but even vicious. Vices have their place in it, and are useful for making the seams in our union, as poisons are useful for the preservation of our health.

Montaigne then goes on to explain that, though a certain amount of vice is necessary in a state, not every individual need feel obliged to participate in it; the great chain of being will undoubtedly provide men of every needed character, including those who are fit for treachery or murder.

Here, as at many other points, the zeal with which students of Montaigne have approached their author has led to over-indulgence and even misinterpretation. The common explanation of the foregoing sentences is that Montaigne was a "realist": knowing that politics was a dirty business, he took cognizance of that fact, but with remorse and under protest. Much as he would have liked to inject ethics into politics, he ended by separating the two, because—somewhat like Machiavelli—he understood the realities. The gloomy political statements in Montaigne, as in Machiavelli, thus represent not the situation as those writers would have liked to see it, but the stern political truths of their century. (pp. 423-25)

This interpretation takes no account of Montaigne's rationalization of political vice, and without rationalization we have no Montaigne; for him things had to be philosophically satisfying. His acceptance of "Machiavellism" was "realistic" enough, it is true; but in addition, by virtue of his belief in the optimistic chain-of-being philosophy, he was able to integrate political vice into an overall philosophical pattern which justified vice on grounds much more profound than political realism. Montaigne believed that evils have their life and lim-

its. . . . It is for these optimistic reasons, which are well summarized in the phrase "What is, is right," that Montaigne held that "the best and most excellent government for every nation is that under which it has subsisted." The fact that a government or an institution has endured is sufficient reason to preserve it.

What makes this discussion relatively simple and the conclusion almost incontrovertible is that Montaigne has supplied all the clues. In neither the general nor the particular respects is it necessary to speculate about Montaigne's adherence to the optimistic philosophy and its importance to his conservatism. One of the most effective evidences of his general adherence to the theory has not yet been adduced. It may be well to look at it and then at a last direct application in a political context. In the essay, **"Du Repentir,"** it appears that Montaigne's whole objection to repentance hinges on the fact that repentance, in seeking to undo things which result from a person's constitution, gives too little respect to the individual's natural bent. In that essay Montaigne makes the following general comment:

> With respect to any business, when once it is over, I have little regret, however it may have turned out. For this idea relieves me of worry, that the thing had to happen just so. It is seen to be a part of the great stream of the universe and of the chain of Stoical causes. Your imagination cannot by wish or thought disturb one tittle without overturning the whole order of things, both past and future.

(pp. 425-26)

There can be little doubt that it is this approach to the world which lies at the bottom of Montaigne's political conservatism. Montaigne himself makes the transfer to politics when he writes that a government is like a structure of which no single piece may be disturbed without danger to the whole. . . . To disturb one of the links in the chain of being, or one of the "divers pieces" in the structure, can only cause disaster. To disturb the status quo in politics, considering that a government with its institutions and traditions is a complex affair with each link or piece responding to a particular need of society; to Christianize the Turks, whose religion and mores grew up over a long period of time in response to many factors in their environment and their history; or to interfere with the free development of an individual, whose actions and inclinations represent a multitude of deep personal inpulses—any of these would do violence to Nature. Nature has provided instances of every possible creature, and every conceivable characteristic. They all deserve to be respected because they are necessary to the proper functioning of the world.

It may be asked whether it is the intention of this paper to classify Montaigne as an optimist, whether optimism was his philosophy, and whether now the disscussions of Montaigne's ideas can safely cease. The answer is that to call Montaigne an optimist does not tell everything about him. A man may be an optimist and a materialist, or an optimist and an idealist, just as he may be an American and a Catholic or an American and a Jew. Montaigne was an optimist and many other things at the same time. Nor is any claim made here that Montaigne's attachment to the optimistic philosophy provides the whole explanation even of his liberalism and conservatism. His skepticism and his experience living through many years of civil war each led him simultaneously in both directions, and those influences have been justly emphasized in studies of Montaigne, as have many other elements of his observation and experience, both physical and spiritual, which it has not been within the scope of this paper to recapitulate. What has been added is one new point of view which may help tie together some of the diverse elements of Montaigne's thought, for, no matter how contradictory a man's statements or ideas, they must nevertheless have, underneath, some firm foundation in the form of a unified system of values or outlook on the world. In Montaigne's case, it is suggested, that foundation, at least insofar as the ideas examined here are concerned, was provided by the doctrine of philosophical optimism. (pp. 426-28)

> Abraham C. Keller, *"Optimism in the Essays of Montaigne,"* in Studies in Philology, *Vol. LIV, No. 3, July, 1957, pp. 408-28.*

ALDOUS HUXLEY   (essay date 1959)

[*Known primarily for his dystopian novel* Brave New World (1932), *Huxley was an English novelist of ideas. The grandson of noted Darwinist T. H. Huxley and the brother of scientist Julian Huxley, he was interested in many fields of knowledge, and daring conceptions of science, philosophy, and religion are woven throughout his fiction. Continually searching for an escape from the ambivalence of modern life, Huxley sought a sense of spiritual renewal and a clarification of his artistic vision through the use of hallucinogenic drugs, an experience explored in one of his best-known later works,* The Doors of Perception *(1954). In the following excerpt from a consideration of the nature of the essay, Huxley admires Montaigne's treatment of the genre.*]

"I am a man and alive," wrote D. H. Lawrence. "For this reason I am a novelist. And, being a novelist, I consider myself superior to the saint, the scientist, the philosopher, and the poet, who are all great masters of different bits of man alive, but never get the whole hog.... Only in the novel are *all* things given full play."

What is true of the novel is only a little less true of the essay. For, like the novel, the essay is a literary device for saying almost everything about almost anything. By tradition, almost by definition, the essay is a short piece, and it is therefore impossible to give all things full play within the limits of a single essay. But a collection of essays can cover almost as much ground, and cover it almost as thoroughly as can a long novel. Montaigne's Third Book is the equivalent, very nearly, of a good slice of the *Comédie Humaine.*

Essays belong to a literary species whose extreme variability can be studied most effectively within a three-poled frame of reference. There is the pole of the personal and the autobiographical; there is the pole of the objective, the factual, the concrete-particular; and there is the pole of the abstract-universal. Most essayists are at home and at their best in the neighborhood of only one of the essay's three poles, or at the most only in the neighborhood of two of them. There are the predominantly personal essayists, who write fragments of reflective autobiography and who look at the world through the keyhole of anecdote and description. There are the predominantly objective essayists who do not speak directly of themselves, but turn their attention outward to some literary or scientific or political theme. Their art consists in setting forth, passing judgment upon, and drawing general conclusions from, the relevant data. In a third group we find those essayists who do their work in the world of high abstractions, who never condescend to be personal and who hardly deign to take notice of the particular facts, from which their generalizations were originally drawn. Each kind of essay has its special merits and defects. (pp. v-vi)

The most richly satisfying essays are those which make the best not of one, not of two, but of all the three worlds in which it is possible for the essay to exist. Freely, effortlessly, thought and feeling move in these consummate works of art, hither and thither between the essay's three poles—from the personal to the universal, from the abstract back to the concrete, from the objective datum to the inner experience.

The perfection of any artistic form is rarely achieved by its first inventor. To this rule Montaigne is the great and marvelous exception. By the time he had written his way into the Third Book, he had reached the limits of his newly discovered art. "What are these essays," he had asked at the beginning of his career, "but grotesque bodies pieced together of different members, without any definite shape, without any order, coherence, or proportion, except they be accidental." But a few years later the patchwork grotesques had turned into living organisms, into multiform hybrids like those beautiful monsters of the old mythologies, the mermaids, the manheaded bulls with wings, the centaurs, the Anubises, the seraphim—impossibilities compounded of incompatibles, but compounded from within, by a process akin to growth, so that the human trunk seems to spring quite naturally from between the horse's shoulders, the fish modulates into the full-breasted Siren as easily and inevitably as a musical theme modulates from one key to another. Free association artistically controlled—this is the paradoxical secret of Montaigne's best essays. One damned thing after another—but in a sequence that in some almost miraculous way develops a central theme and relates it to the rest of human experience. And how beautifully Montaigne combines the generalization with the anecdote, the homily with the autobiographical reminiscence! How skilfully he makes use of the concrete particular, the *chose vue* ["thing seen"], to express some universal truth, and to express it more powerfully and penetratingly than it can be expressed by even the most oracular of the dealers in generalities! Here, for example, is what a great oracle, Dr. Johnson, has to say about the human situation and the uses of adversity. "Affliction is inseparable from our present state; it adheres to all the inhabitants of this world, in different proportions indeed, but with an allotment which seems very little regulated by our own conduct. It has been the boast of some swelling moralists that every man's fortune was in his own power, that prudence supplied the place of all other divinities, and that happiness is the unfailing consequence of virtue. But, surely, the quiver of Omnipotence is stored with arrows, against which the shield of human virtue, however adamantine it has been boasted, is held up in vain; we do not always suffer by our crimes, we are not always protected by our innocence.... Nothing confers so much ability to resist the temptations that perpetually surround us, as an habitual consideration of the shortness of life, and the uncertainty of those pleasures that solicit our pursuit; and this consideration can be inculcated only by affliction." This is altogether admirable; but there are other and, I would say, better ways of approaching the subject. *"J'ay veu en mon temps cent artisans, cent laboureurs, plus sages et plus heureux que des Recteurs de l'Universite."* (I have seen in my time hundreds of artisans and laborers, wiser and happier than university presidents.) Again, "Look at poor working people sitting on the ground with drooping heads after their day's toil. They know neither Aristotle nor Cato, neither example nor precept; and yet from them Nature draws effects of constancy and patience purer and more unconquerable than any of those we study so curiously in the schools." Add to one touch of nature one touch of irony, and you have a comment on life more profound, in spite of its casualness, its seeming levity, than the most eloquent rumblings of the oracles. "It is not our follies that make me laugh,'' says Montaigne, ''it is our sapiences.'' And why should our sapiences provoke a wise man to laughter? Among other reasons, because the professional sages tend to express themselves in a language of highest abstraction and widest generality—a language that, for all its gnomic solemnity is apt, in a tight corner, to reveal itself as ludicrously inappropriate to the facts of life as it is really and tragically lived. (pp. vii-viii)

> *Aldous Huxley, in a preface to his* Collected Essays, *Harper & Brothers Publishers, 1959, pp. v-ix.*

J. B. PRIESTLEY (essay date 1960)

[*An English man of letters, Priestley was the author of numerous popular novels that depict the world of everyday, middle-class England. In this respect, he has often been likened to Charles Dickens. His most notable critical work is* Literature and Western Man *(1960), a survey of Western literature from the invention of movable type through the mid-twentieth century. In the following excerpt from this work, Priestley praises Montaigne's innovation and discusses his importance to the sixteenth century and beyond.*]

Certain places at certain times seem to men, perhaps in very different places and long afterwards, to possess a magical quality, capturing and holding the imagination. This is true of the Italy of the early Renaissance; it is equally true of France during most of the sixteenth century. We cannot have travelled southwest from Paris without returning in thought, almost as if we shared a dream with men long dead, to the French Renaissance. (p. 18)

[Though] no two writers could seem more strikingly different than Rabelais and Montaigne, both emerge from the Renaissance in France, one expressing the earlier and wilder phase of it, the other the later and graver phase. . . .

Both authors were notable originals, and their influence, direct and indirect, can hardly be over-estimated. (p. 19)

Montaigne, the scholarly country gentleman meditating in his tower among his books, is a very different figure from Rabelais, born fifty years before him and representing an earlier and wilder phase of the Renaissance in France. Their literary manners are even more widely different than their backgrounds and modes of life. It is the difference between a town fair in full swing and a lecture delivered to the local Philosophical Society, between its largest tavern at closing time and mid-afternoon in the quiet room of the municipal library. Nevertheless, both men move along the same broad middle road; they share a common dislike of pedants, intellectual bullies, bigots and fanatics; they are not irreligious but deeply sceptical about the claims of the theologians; they are humanists under God. Their popularity was equally great, but it is Montaigne who has had the wider influence. Out of what began, in the rather tedious fashion of the time, as a mixture of classical quotations and brief comments on them, there emerged the famous essays, gaining both in length and depth with each volume. And with these Montaigne performed a triple act of original creation: he fashioned a prose style that appears to be as easy and flexible and racy as good talk, a style that could serve as a model for many generations of French prose writers; he created a literary form, the personal essay, that has been since used, more or less as he originally used it, by innumerable good authors not only in French but in other literatures, notably English; and finally, and most important of all, as he developed this essay form he came more and more to take his own character, his own habits, idiosyncrasies, preferences, prejudices, hopes and

fears, as his chief subject-matter, turning his attention inward, into consciousness itself and towards the mysterious depths of the unconscious, first setting sail on what has become since a vast expedition of discovery. This Périgord gentleman in his tower, smilingly referring to some fad or whimsy, is the ancestor in literature of Proust, desperately disengaging the last shred of motive, three-and-a-half centuries later, in his cork-lined room.

Men had written about themselves before Montaigne. But they had presented themselves for a purpose outside self-discovery, to make a confession, to prove something; and what they had revealed had not been a true self but a faked image, a mask, a *persona*. Amused, tolerant, neither well-pleased nor angry with himself, Montaigne the observer regards and considers Montaigne the observed as he might look at a pear ripening on the wall or the summer's crop of hay. This had not been done by anybody before him, and, although long after his time elaborate self-analysis would be widely attempted, it has rarely been done as he did it, perhaps never in his prevailing spirit, by all the introspective writers since his time. For Montaigne, for all his scepticism and his dubious queries about death, felt himself to be more securely placed than these later writers did. He did not stare at himself until he saw nothing but a skeleton at the edge of the abyss. This man he had to live with, whose foibles and likings and doubts he describes with such frankness and charm, was nourished and refreshed by Nature, and consoled, for all that was relative and impermanent in this life, by his constant thought of God's eternity. He did not know, nor want to know, too much about either; what he knew was the man lodged between them, above the green grass and beneath the blue dome. His scepticism, lightly ironical, was broadly based, as we may see in his longest essay, **"An Apologie of Raymond Sebond"** (the spelling here is Florio's in his English translation, which, incidentally, Shakespeare must have read); but if it slyly mocked the bigots and the warring sects, turned sharply away from the torture chambers and the reek of burning flesh, it kept its hold upon this earth and refused to darken the sky. Montaigne's own acceptance of orthodoxy is that of a man who falls in with the custom of the country; his conservatism has in it nothing cynical, nothing aggressive; his distrust of the abstract, the high-flown, the intellect on stilts, iron dogmatism, everything that tries to break the human scale, has warmth and heart behind it, a feeling for what is real and alive, for what can be seen and touched. Heroes and saints, martyrs and mystics, may be made of other stuff, but so too are all the life-haters, the black oppressors of the human race. And in this moment of our history, we are in no position to despise that smaller, but smiling and sun-lit, world of Montaigne.

The chronicles of his time, the age seen as history, repel us; the very air seems stifling, murky with dark fanaticism, intrigue, murder and civil war. It is only in literature, around these little essays in self-knowledge, that the sun seems to shine and the air to have some sweetness. But then the essayist does not claim to know too much outside himself; God is a mystery and not a fellow-conspirator in the power-plot; the universe still escapes the limits of the human mind, and does not obligingly dwindle to suit a sect; there is so much that cannot be known, that exactitude, logic, consistency, must be sacrificed, with some loss of force and pride, to humility and good sense, which can at least enjoy what God appears to have provided. All this there is in Montaigne, and in all those who have travelled, then and since, that broad road with him. But there is something that can begin to be known, as he proved to his and our profit, something much closer and more comprehensible than the doctrine of the Trinity or the world plan of the Absolute, and that is—the mind, the inner world, that shapes and colours both character and action. No wonder that Montaigne was free from the raging and murderous fanaticism of his time. He had taken a peep into the kitchen where that hell-broth was being stirred. Not for him, with his self-knowledge, the consciousness that claims too much, the rising tide of doubt in the unconscious, the barriers hastily raised against this tide, the savage repression of all feeling of uncertainty, the over-compensation bursting into the world as intolerant dogmatism, violence and cruelty. This, the shadow-side of the brilliant Renaissance, darkened the sixteenth century; and if now, four hundred years later, we imagine we are in clear daylight at last, we had better look at the nearest newspaper or switch on the television set. We may feel, not unreasonably if we are thinking in terms of literary form, manner, style, that we have outgrown, left far behind, the gigantic and uproarious buffooneries of Rabelais, the quaint, modest self-revelations of Montaigne; but what lies and lives at the very centre of their thought and feeling, the truly religious good sense to which Rabelais returns after his wildest sallies, the double recognition of the human scale and the surrounding mystery that accompanies Montaigne's self-knowledge, all of this is even more salutary and precious to us now than it was to Renaissance France. Perhaps we are dimly aware of it, are quickened by the spirit of these great Frenchmen, as we stare across the meadows and the water at the châteux of the Loire, order an *Omelette Gargamelle* at the old inn at Chinon, or descend the thirsty limestone hills of the Dordogne in search of the local wine. (pp. 22-5)

> J. B. Priestley, "France: Rabelais and Montaigne," in his Literature and Western Man, *Harper & Brothers, 1960, pp. 18-25.*

FRIEDA S. BROWN (essay date 1963)

[*Brown is an American professor of French who has written extensively on André Gide and Montaigne. In the following excerpt, she clarifies the liberal/conservative dichotomy of Montaigne's religious and political beliefs.*]

The religious and political conservatism of Montaigne must be understood in the context of the turbulent situation that prevailed in sixteenth-century France.... (p. 94)

Montaigne was temperamentally and intellectually opposed to "nouvelletés" ["novelties, changes"]. The civil wars had demonstrated conclusively, in his opinion, that the desire for inordinate reform was productive only of violence and cruelty, which he had detested ever since childhood, and that it had brought inordinate harm to France. From an intellectual point of view, his awareness of the weaknesses of human reason and his knowledge of the myriad religious and political opinions professed throughout the world made him a vigorous opponent of Protestant exegetical presumption. He could not rationally conceive of the intrinsic superiority of any one philosophy.

On the other hand, he did not attack the religious beliefs of the Huguenots. Religion to him was a matter of conscience, and obedience to conscience was the principle on which Montaigne's entire life, both public and private, was based. His constant appeals to the *réformés* ["reformers"] to return to the fold were rooted not in theological but in civic reasons. An attack on the Catholic Church constituted for him an attack on the monarchy, for he viewed the State as an organic structure which would surely be overturned if any of its important mem-

bers were destroyed. In his eyes, the only possibility for peace and harmony lay in the indissoluble unity of Church and State. Given the tragic experiences of sixteenth-century France and his conviction that reason was impotent to cope either with the matter of faith or the complexities of social organization, he had concluded that the most rational course was obedience to established laws and customs.

The *Essais* attest repeatedly to the fact that their author was not primarily concerned with religious belief but with human betterment and moral improvement. Since he may not have reached the ultimate conviction that Christianity had found the solution to these problems, he established a rule of conduct divorced from religion and religious constraints and depended rather on rational principles and self-knowledge. This, however, does not preclude his profound faith in Catholicism, which is explicit throughout his writings. The Catholic religion was the only thing he never doubted, for he had placed it outside the realm of reason, and as a permanent result of his radical skepticism with regard to the efficacy of reason in religious matters, his faith remained permanently secure.

Montaigne's ultimate position was the resultant of irresistible forces, social and intellectual, that determined his political and religious attitudes throughout his life. He believed that the Christian religion and the laws of conscience commanded obedience to authority, and this belief was profoundly corroborated not only by the strain of skepticism that in certain respects never entirely abandoned him, but perhaps even more by what he had personally witnessed of the unspeakable disorders resulting from the politico-religious wars. He therefore adhered and urged adherence to the institutions and traditions of France. If many of its laws were unjust and even barbaric, it was not the right of the citizen to revolt against them. Revolution, as had amply been demonstrated, bred destruction, not progress. Human reason was too weak to guarantee that a proposed reform would necessarily be better in practice than its predecessor.

Social change, however, was neither undesirable nor impossible to Montaigne, and there is good evidence to support the belief that during a long public career, while never deviating from the conservative path which his conscience had marked out, he attempted to implement many of the liberal ideas so often and earnestly expressed in the *Essais*. For this reason and to the extent that the *Essais* are frequently a plea for religious tolerance, humanity and respect for the rights of the individual, we cannot agree with the position taken by numerous scholars to the effect that Montaigne was liberal only in thought and conservative in action.

To place his liberalism and conservatism in irreconcilable opposition is an oversimplification of the seeming paradox between the two positions as they apply to Montaigne. Far from being in contradiction with each other, Montaigne's conservatism and liberalism were necessarily complementary attitudes growing from the single Socratic principle of the self-realization of the individual in his political, religious and ethical relationships. For him, peace and order in society, in so far as they could be attained without the sacrifices of personal autonomy and integrity, created the indispensable conditions for the achievement of the self-realization of the individual, and with it, of human dignity and liberty. (pp. 94-6)

> Frieda S. Brown, in her Religious and Political Conservatism in the 'Essais' of Montaigne, *Librairie Droz, 1963, 109 p.*

PHILIP P. HALLIE (essay date 1966)

[*Hallie is an American educator and philosopher. In the following excerpt, he addresses the issues of unity and language in* The Essays.]

The most acute twentieth-century Analytic philosophers share with Montaigne an unshakable confidence in the power of language. The modern apologists for science and the sixteenth-century Sceptical Humanist agree that this power can help bring about our troubles as readily as it can help bring about our happiness. They believe that this power can help disintegrate minds and societies, and it can help integrate them into durably progressive, peaceful structures. They do not believe that there is some deep chasm between men's minds, across which we cry to each other in vain. Especially Wittgenstein and Montaigne try in many ways to show how language is embedded in observable action, how indeed it is a kind of action. Wittgenstein calls languages *"Lebensformen"*—"ways of life." (p. 94)

Those who underestimate the power of language sometimes think of it as a set of cookie-cutters that are imposed from the outside on the dough that is our mental life. It is as if this mental life has all the ingredients in the right combination before the cookie-cutter descends upon it, and all the cookie-cutter does is give this stuff shape and commercial salability. Perhaps such an external relationship between words and thoughts was what Thomas Gray had in mind when he wrote of "mute, inglorious Miltons" who had all the thoughts and feelings of genius, but simply could not find in their little towns the right language.

But for Montaigne clarity and order in thought and clarity and order in language are one and the same thing. If anybody tells him that he has a head full of many splendid ideas but lacks the eloquence to express them, his answer is brief: "That is all bluff." The mute Miltons may have yearnings, glimmerings of some sort, but "whoever has a vivid and clear idea in his mind will express it, if necessary in Bergamask dialect, or, if he is dumb, by signs." "Splendid ideas" are for him through-and-through expressible, communicable; this expressibility, this communicability, is part of their vividness, their clarity, their force, the way the shape of a hand is part of the hand. (p. 95)

In the important essay **"Of Giving the Lie"** [Montaigne] tells us that this book is "consubstantial with its author, concerned only with myself, part of my flesh." In that same essay he assures us that a few times in this book he has lashed out at the public for their sake (and the [**"Apology for Raymond Sebond"**] is an obvious instance of this). But, he asks, "If no one reads me, have I wasted my time . . .?" And the answer he gives is a firm No. He sat down to write his essays in order to give clarity, order, and stability to his own thoughts; he wrote to give himself a firm shape: "In molding a cast upon myself, I have had to form and solidify myself in order to bring out my shape, and the model under the mold has become firmer and has achieved sharper form in the process."

It is of very great importance in understanding Montaigne that we see what is at issue here. He is saying that though language can *communicate* our thoughts to the public, its basic function for him is *expressive*. He had his essays published; but his primary act, not only chronologically primary, but of primary importance to him, was one of keeping the bits and pieces of his mental life from being squandered in that profligate wind, time. He wrote to give a healthful lucidity and order to his mind. And since words do have a deep involvement with the

mind of their user, he could hope for success. If others did not read him or if they chose to misunderstand him, he had still set out to put his mental house in order. Like any other animal, he is trying to find his well-being, and like a Humanistic animal he finds it in using words to shape his life. (p. 96)

Now what, more exactly, was the language of the *Essays* designed to do? Certainly it was not designed to prove something about precise, "original essences" which are supposed to be objectively discoverable beneath our gross awareness of things. The essays were written . . . to notice, order, and record his own thoughts and feelings about various subjects. At the same time they would make these thoughts and feelings communicable to others. And this communicative function could be performed easily, given Montaigne's doctrine of language: the same words that express to yourself the shape of your mind can, if you so wish, be published. For Montaigne, metaphysical solitude is a daydream. Knowing yourself and getting yourself known are two sides of the same mold: the rule or prescription of language makes both possible. If you want to be known, write well, take your writings to a good printer, and get them distributed broadly.

Fortunately for anyone trying to understand Montaigne's use of language, Montaigne, like any Humanist, was very curious about language in general and about his own use of language. As a matter of fact, he is the best authority we have on the subject of his own way of writing. And so, in our effort to see more clearly what he wanted language to do, let us look at the way he used the key word *essai*. He used it very carefully, very self-consciously, and he used it in a very revealing way. What *was* the *essai* supposed to express and communicate? (pp. 97-8)

Consider some possible translations of the word *essai*. The word "trial" is sometimes used to translate it, but this word does not plainly convey the tentative nature of an *essai*, at least as Montaigne uses the French word. A trial is final, though the judgment of the judge or jurors is, except in the highest courts, subject to revision; we think of trials by ordeal or by fire, or trials of strength as having something of finality about them; and even in court-trials the "judgment" of the court is, on that level at least, final, other things being equal. The word "test" has connotations of finality as well, plus an air of precision in many of its uses. The word "experiment" has its difficulties too, but is useful, implying as it does tentative searching, and often searching not for one particular result, but for any or all the capacities or powers of the object we are experimenting with. To experiment with an acid, for example, would be to investigate its behavior under a variety of circumstances, under different temperatures, in various containers. Here, as in Montaigne's essays, we are interested in these external circumstances mainly insofar as they tell us something about the stuff that we are experimenting with: in this case, Montaigne's mind.

But the word "experiment" reminds us of systematically varied factors in a laboratory; its connotations of precise, even quantitative analysis make it a misleading term to apply to our Humanist's writings. We can say in general that an essay resembles a trial, a test, and an experiment insofar as these words refer to an active exploration of the powers something has.

A good working translation for his word *essayer* is a phrase that carries with its swinging sound, some idea of trial, test, or experimenting without having enough detailed meaning in modern English to be misleading; the phrase is the English verb "to essay" or the noun-form usually adopted by translators, "essay." What Montaigne is "essaying" is his own capacities or powers; he is making his "judgment" act or react in order to give comprehensible shape to its powers. He is doing new things with it in order to display its inherent limitations and peculiarities, but he is doing all this in an unsystematic, inconclusive way, taking whatever subject comes along, because the subject is not the main thing he is looking for. Montaigne had a "greedy appetite for new and unknown things," not only because he enjoyed diversity but because diversity brought out the properties of his judgment more fully. Essays are the form self-knowledge takes in a shifting world.

By displaying in use the groping, changing judgment of the same man, all the essays of Montaigne, and notably the major ones, exhibit a tension between change and stability, between diversity and unity, between spontaneity and control. Aside from a unity of purpose or subject matter, there are various dominant metaphors that unify many of them; the most complex and omnipresent of these is the image of conflict or change. (Consider the **"Apology"** and **"Of Repentance."**) But it takes experience and a rather keen eye for ideas and metaphors to see at an early reading the unity of many of Montaigne's essays. In part this is so because Montaigne deliberately avoided putting in connective words or phrases. . . . He wants each chunk to be a whole entity.

The *Essays* do not give what their titles promise; digressions often drown any principal idea; there is often only a physical proximity of groups of words with each other. He wants to arrest the attention of the reader and to keep him awake: "Who is there that would not rather not be read than be read sleepily or in passing? *Nothing is so useful that it can be of value when taken on the run.*" (Seneca.)

But getting or maintaining attention is not the main reason for the sometimes baffling variety of ideas an incidents and metaphors that he shoots in our faces in most of his longer and many of his shorter essays. Communication for Montaigne, especially the communication between man and man, involved an *empathic* or sympathetic awareness of the movement of a mind. Montaigne's pen moved the way his mind moved, often jumpily, sometimes logically and coherently, and he wanted the reader's mind to move just that way. He wanted the reader (himself, or somebody else) to think his way for a little while, and in doing so to get a direct acquaintance with that way. He did not want the reader to understand him only in an objective way; he wanted the reader to get the feel of the way his mind moved, and thereby to understand him without categories, without any claims to objectivity or precision—by direct acquaintance. He wanted the reader to get from the essays not *"la science"* ["objective knowledge"] of Montaigne, but as he put it in the Preface, *"la connoissance"* ["acquaintance, understanding"]; familiarity with him. This is the way he "knew" Etienne de la Boétie, the best friend he ever had; this is the way he wanted to be "known" by those of his readers who would give him their attention; this is the way he wanted to know himself.

He wanted many of his sentences to be understood alone, not as part of an argument, but as the direct, immediate expression of insights or feelings. Each such remark, each epigram, has its own kind of obviousness and therefore its own kind of appeal to his "judgment." . . . If each moment reveals us, or at least if certain moments can reveal us for what we are, so can each sentence or each phrase, if it is well molded and if it is carefully set off from the surrounding text so it jumps out at you. Self-

contained *sententiae* ["opinions"], individual judgments, are at least as important—each on its own—as the conclusion the whole essay is trying to substantiate. Montaigne insists that we respect the autonomy of the moment, the distinctness of the individual phrase. For him such moments, such sentences, do not readily blend into wholes. Each is an organism: it contains within itself its own best excuse for being.

A man is not a logical unity; he is a set of individual moments spread out in the time between his birth and death. And if you would understand him you must see him in these terms. Montaigne believed that any man's most trivial actions reveal him. Do you want to know Alexander the Great? Watch the way he plays chess or the way he talks and drinks at table. Is every sinew of his soul strained? Or is he detached? And watch his reaction when he wins or loses. Watch these moments closely, and you get a deep insight into this man. In such moments, his habits and temperament appear plainly. And to construct airtight logical arguments on paper is to hide—not reveal—the variety and disparateness of these moments. . . . A tightly knit argument is a stiff mask over the face of the man who offers it. And Montaigne is not presenting a mold of the face that men artificially prepare to meet the faces that they meet. He is presenting a mold of his personality, down to its guts.

Finally, the reader of the *Essays* who spends much time looking for a single conclusion or "point" in every essay will miss a great deal and will often get very little for his pains. In **"Of Some Verses of Virgil,"** for example, he will come up with a very thin generalization or he will get quite befuddled looking for an informative one. He will not enjoy a tree in that amorphous forest. You fail to read Montaigne well if you always look for an important unifying idea and try to explain away his individual *aperçus*. To spend much time looking beneath the surface for abstract unities is in some instances to miss the palpable substance of the *Essays*.

They are intended to give you an acquaintance with someone who loves "the poetic gait, by leaps and gambols. . . . Lord, what beauty there is in these lusty sallies and this variation, and more so the more casual and accidental." For an accident is a mixture of circumstances, and a mixture named Michel is what he is portraying. . . . [The] universe for Montaigne—and this includes his mind—is full of changes, uncertainties. . . . (pp. 100-03)

The essays are iconic; and what they portray is a shifting part of a shifting world. His pen must move the way his feet move in this world. He is portraying a particular living man, not a neatly articulated, anonymous skeleton.

And yet, Montaigne *is* often out for bigger game than separate little maxims or reactions to maxims and stories. A man can have a direction, and an essay can have a *"bout d'un poil,"* a bit of hair to hold it together. The wildest poetry sometimes needs some pressure, some discipline, in order for it to come forth strongly, as does air; an essay can have a burden to carry, a ford to probe, a quotation to turn around and examine. Montaigne himself tends to get sluggish and muddled when he has no sense of direction. He is fully aware of the difference between spontaneity and wildness, change and chaos, diversity and utter disorder. And many of his essays communicate that awareness with their bit of hair.

Sometimes the title points out the shape or direction of an essay; at other times the title refers only to an unimportant occasion that happened to give rise to the essay (see **"Of Some Verses of Virgil,"** in the Third Book). Sometimes an essay acquires what unity it has by a rich interplay between a dominant idea (like the idea of vanity s ignorance of one's limitations in **"Of Vanity"**) and a large, overarching metaphor (like that of traveling in that same essay). But whether it be the title, an idea loosely related to the title, a metaphor, a quotation, or more than one, the ideas in a given essay may "follow one another, but sometimes it is from a distance, and look at each other, but with a sidelong glance." Montaigne is not simply careless, though he is usually free from overrestrictive plans.

Before turning to more special aspects of Montaigne's style, it would be useful to make one more point. . . . The *opposition* between a unified essay and a disunified one can be misleading. There are many sorts of order, many sorts of unity: there is the kind of unity and orderliness a whole essay can have, and there is the kind of orderliness an individual epigram or insight can have. Looked at from the point of view of the whole essay, Montaigne's writings can often be described as "disorderly"; but if we look at each epigram we often find a single, lucid view of the whole world or of a given subject. What looks like disorder when one thinks of the essay as a whole becomes a set of separately revealing perspectives, each of which unifies its "subject." Montaigne said: "Each man bears the entire form of man's condition." Many of his separate epigrams do this; they are microcosms, revealing the world or some subject ordered in a little space. They are judgments "of universal scope," though they occupy a small space and may not fit into the other judgments of a given essay. (pp. 104-05)

[There] are two ways Montaigne used his judgment to give order to his mental life: through each individual epigram, and through a total essay made up of more or less loosely unified epigrams. He spoke in a moment, and he spoke in a more or less unified sequence of moments. And so in an important but loose sense of the word "order," epigrams as well as unified essays expressed the "order," the clarity and unity, of his judgment.

When Montaigne is in Paris he speaks like a Parisian, not like the Gascon he is. When he was young and wrote Latin verse, each new production "clearly revealed the poet I had last been reading." (p. 105)

Montaigne does not try to destroy this tendency in himself, though he may shake it up a bit and weaken its hold on him. After all, he is not trying to reform man; he is trying to portray one, imitativeness and all. But Montaigne has other traits that have rendered his imitativeness harmless. One of them is his lack of memory. For instance, he tells us at the end of **"A Consideration upon Cicero"** that he simply forgets the steps of ceremony, the oft-repeated words and phrases that people use around him. Such fluent, rote language simply cannot come out of his mouth; he neither remembers them nor feels the desire to do so.

And this brings us to another trait that more than counterbalances his imitativeness: he has a way of talking, a way of acting, whether in Paris, Bordeaux, or his own castle, that is "of a form all my own," despite any tendencies to superficial imitation. When somebody is entering his castle or leaving it he is as barren of courtly language as a stump. A person entering his castle or approaching him in the streets of Paris can read his feelings right off, not through a haze of empty phrases. His manner, no matter where he is, is "disorderly, abrupt, individual." He stands at his door, or anywhere, not with the old, empty words on his lips, but with his own feelings in his heart. And he has a deep confidence that they will simply shine forth and be seen in their individuality, in their immediacy.

What happens when such a man is standing at the door of his home saying good-bye to someone he cares for deeply, but is unable to bow with a flourish or offer those fashionable, courtly long promises of eternal servitude and respect? What does he do to express his feelings when he can neither remember nor want to remember the monkey-tricks? He uses what he has, these eyes, these lips, this head, his own everyday words, with his own felt warmth residing in them. With these he speaks to his friend in a language not worn thin of meaning by mindless repetition, not impersonal by virtue of having been said carelessly by so many different persons, but a language intimately his own and abundantly clear to anybody interested in understanding it.

And what has he done with his face and with the language of everyday speech that has invested them with his own individual, personal meaning? Has he twisted that language or that face into shapes absolutely new, absolutely unheard of, and thereby individual? Hardly. On the contrary, he has used the same sorts of expression that men customarily use in such circumstances, and he is speaking plain, very unspectacular French. But what has happened to create *his* "style"? He has slightly varied, he has slightly altered, that face and that colloquial speech, stretched them and added to them. Perhaps he gives a little sigh; perhaps he withholds one and simply looks with a warmth deeper than gesture at the person he is addressing. Perhaps he utters a playful threat or a promise that both parties know will be kept. He has bent, by just a little, but enough, the shape of his face, the shape of his language, so that they fit the shape of his soul at that moment and so that the person he is addressing sees and knows this.

It is Montaigne's contention that the same sort of bending, the same sort of stretching, is what we do with language in our writing when we struggle to give it more weight, more penetration, more power to say something faithfully, fully, and freshly. It would not be wise to do so by making an ass of oneself with wild grimaces or unheard-of speech: Montaigne would not give language fresh "unaccustomed movements," as he puts it, by abandoning ordinary speech in favor of radical innovation. Such innovation expresses and communicates only the asininity and self-consciousness of the innovator, and not the richness or individuality of his thought and feeling. (pp. 105-07)

But Montaigne tells us of another way he uses to make his language more expressive of what he is, and this way indicates his esteem for laconic action:

> There is nothing that might not be done with our jargon of hunting and war, which is a generous soil to borrow from. And forms of speech, like plants, improve and grow stronger by being transplanted.

He had used this metaphor of transplanting at the beginning of the essay **"Of Books,"** in the Second Book, when talking about what he got from Latin and Greek authors. There he had discussed the fact that he wanted to "confound" these quotations with his own words and thoughts, so that if you wanted to criticize Plutarch you would have to give him "a fillip on my nose," so closely would the plant and the new soil—Montaigne—be involved with each other. And the same holds in regard to transplanting the language of "hunting and war." He would make that language part of himself by changing it.

Montaigne always admired what he once described as language that is *"sec, bref, signifiant"* ["spare, brief, meaningful."] . . . You will find, especially in the first Book of the Essays, but also elsewhere, many signs of Montaigne's admiration for action without verbosity, honor without long explanations, vigor, healthful out-of-door living, all those things that he associated with the military life and with hunting. The essay **"Of Cannibals"** is a good example of this. Despite his refusal to hunt and his hatred of fractricidal war, he saw in war and hunting, and in the language they used, many important virtues. Soldiers and hunters use a language whose metaphors and phrases are embedded in action, in suddenness, in a kind of heavy, male impetuosity. (pp. 108-09)

An essay is for Montaigne usually a set of pictures of actions like a walk, a climb, or a probing. (p. 111)

Language as it appears on the printed page is a stable thing; it is not life, nor is it an image of life. It is only the movements and the shapes that the human mind experiences when confronted with that stable thing that makes it possible for piles of still, black ink on hard, white paper to become life or to become like life. Montaigne felt all this very strongly, and he used all his powers to embody in ink on paper the movements, sometimes patterned, sometimes random, of his mind. Control and spontaneity, pattern and variety, were the two kinds of naturalness he had found in antiquity as well as in his own mental life. He would express them both, using kinesthetic metaphors, the language of war and hunting, sudden changes of direction in his ideas, and broad, unifying ideas. His was a way of thinking and feeling somewhere between "sleepy idleness" and "painful busyness," though closer to the latter because he was a physically active man. Montaigne said in his essay **"Of Presumption,"** "I do not have my tools catalogued and arranged; and I know about them only after doing something." If we would know him, if we would become acquainted with him as he is displayed in these essays of his mind, we should not try to make of him an "imaginary republic" whose powers are all labeled and precisely related to each other; we should let our thoughts move with his in their patterns and in their self-contained, individual patternlessness and then look back *"après l'effect,"* after the metaphors, after the sharp breaks between ideas, and after all the other expressive elements of his "style" have done their work. We should look back with the awareness that though we cannot catalogue all the powers he has exhibited in action, we are acquainted with them, the way a person becomes acquainted and intimate with another person in the progress of a friendship. There is much that one can say *"en proposition"* ["as a proposition"] about Montaigne after one has read his essays, and there is much that Montaigne has said about his way of living, much that he has explicitly laid out *"en proposition,"* after he has seen himself in action and read his own words. But his judgment can be fully understood, at least the way Montaigne wanted us to understand it, only *"après l'effect,"* only after we have participated in the pace of his own thinking. And even then we shall not be able to give a precise, neat map of his soul, for it is not, it seems, a neat soul "at bottom" or anywhere else. It is a changing thing, only broadly describable, and it is as important to get to know it by acquaintance as it is by description. "Friendship" and "acquaintance" are deeply related terms in the thought of Montaigne; *"l'amitié"* and *"la connoissance,"* involve knowledge *"après l'effect,"* in action and after action.

In short, Montaigne *shows* us what he is and what he is not at least as much as he *tells* us *about* his judgment. With images

of action, with mental jumps and zigzag motions, he shows us the abruptness, the mobility, the male, active force of his judgment. And he also shows us in the plainness of his vocabulary the respect he has for the "rule or prescription" of ordinary usage, of day-to-day life. He shows us both his unique self and what he feels to be the human condition in general. His essays are to a great extent iconic, as their Preface tells us: they portray a man (with both of these last words emphasized—a particular one, and man in general); they reveal him directly, not merely through abstract categories. They are essays of his mind, not merely descriptions of it. There are plenty of descriptions of his way of thinking in the *Essays,* but you read the *Essays* poorly if you do not see how much Montaigne's style reveals the man, how much Montaigne's way of talking reveals his mind. In the [essay] you are now reading, I am primarily describing that mind; in *his* book he is presenting it more directly.

I do not mean to say that there is a sharp final distinction between showing and describing; but there is a useful distinction. When Montaigne tells the reader to notice his manner as well as his matter, his style as well as his subject matter, he is being most fully himself. He is a Humanist profoundly aware of the deep relationship between one's language and one's life. . . . What the *Essays* boil down to is this: here is a certain man, impulsive within limits; he is one man, but also he is deeply involved, intermixed, with society and nature. This is what his language shows us; this is what his language also tells us. (pp. 111-13)

Philip P. Hallie, in his The Scar of Montaigne: An Essay in Personal Philosophy, *Wesleyan University Press, 1966, 204 p.*

ZOE SAMARAS (essay date 1970)

[*In the following excerpt from a full-length study of style in* The Essays, *Samaras adumbrates the characteristics of Montaigne's technique.*]

[It is possible to reach] certain conclusions concerning Montaigne's style. Irony and humor are its predominant characteristics. Incongruities in imagery, contrast of different styles, mimicry, surprising juxtaposition of words, and play on words are Montaigne's means of expressing his ironic or comic view of human life. Irony is essential, for without it there can be no lucidity and no authentic self-portrayal. Montaigne's irony also shows his interest in his readers: he considers them capable of understanding him, of distinguishing between his serious and playful tones. He treats them as his equals.

Naturalness of speech is the outcome of his free sentence construction, clichés, and the playful tone. They create a style reflecting a friendly conversation, which the author carries on with himself and his reader. He depicts himself without artificiality, for he is a man who follows his nature.

A lack of artificiality, however, need not mean a lack of art. Montaigne's artistic talent is evident in his manipulation of words, in his mimetic style, especially in his avoidance of artificiality itself. His knowledge of rhetorical devices he displays when he deals with traditional topics, like man's fear of death and pain, and the attempts of the human mind to penetrate divine secrets. He uses his knowledge of traditional art to parody art, to show its limitations.

Since Montaigne was not a writer or a philosopher in the accepted sense of the terms but a man, his style is concrete and

Caricature of Montaigne by David Levine. Reprinted with permission from The New York Review of Books. *Copyright © 1965 Nyrev, Inc.*

precise. He accumulates personifications and metaphors to give a physical aspect to his style, a body to his portrait, and to make it not a painting but a living copy of himself.

His images, sentence construction, and word groups are characterized by movement and force, for he is in constant search for answers and this movement is reflected in the syntax of his sentence. He faces the world without fear, and his strength and fearlessness create a dynamic effect in his style.

Being aware of the natural restrictions of his mind, he professes doubt on all matters that transcend his abilities. But he maintains a dogmatic attitude when he studies dogmatic philosophers, and displays his certainty when he discusses questions to which his experience can supply an answer. Both facets are the fruits of his self-study, for he has learned to accept his limitations and to trust his experience.

Montaigne's style is both expressive and mimetic of his thought. He provides ample proof of his artistic talent in his surprising combination of words and his imitative sentence structure. Most of his stylistic devices create a conversational style and contribute to the authenticity of the portrait. This illustrates Montaigne's principle of words that mirror acts rather than substitute for them. It explains his title *Essais,* for his writings are an experience, an act. If we gather his writings as fruits of wisdom, it is because we see in them an authentic portrayal of the artist and the man. (pp. 150-52)

> *Zoe Samaras, in his* The Comic Element of Montaigne's Style, *Editions A.-G. Nizet, 1970, 252 p.*

R. A. SAYCE (essay date 1972)

[*Sayce is an English educator and scholar specializing in French literature. In the following excerpt, he explores Montaigne's attitude toward external reality.*]

In spite of his introspection Montaigne, like Gautier, was a man for whom the external world existed. . . . [The] two sides are almost inseparable: the world outside him is refracted through himself, offering perpetual occasion for judgement and observation (and for observation of his own reactions to it); the study of the self is constantly enriched by the absorption of what he has observed. The mind cannot move in a void, it must have something to work on. . . . (p. 74)

The basis of appreciation of the external world is of course the senses. Their reliability and mode of operation present serious problems to Montaigne, as to all philosophers, but for the moment what matters is his own sensory range, his sensibility, sensuousness, sensuality. The pure pleasures of the imagination, he says, are no doubt the highest, but he does not pretend to rise to them: for him they are always mixed. . . . [He has a] voluptuous interest in material objects, their shape, consistency, taste, smell. . . . A whole essay, though short, **"Des senteurs,"** is devoted to the sense of smell, to the way, for example, in which scents cling to his moustaches, or actually affect his mood. This quite exceptional intensity of reaction to sense impressions, his sensual-aesthetic approach to life, are fundamentally poetic, or at least part of what may be called the poet's equipment. . . . (pp. 74-5)

With keen sense perception goes, naturally and almost inevitably, a keen response to beauty in all its manifestations. . . . His feeling for natural beauty, scarcely equalled in his time, at least in prose writing (Shakespeare . . . offers the obvious parallel), emerges mainly in the *Journal du voyage.* The reason for this seems clear enough: natural description is only incidentally relevant in the *Essais,* in the *Journal* it is the spontaneous outcome of each day's new experience. Wherever he goes, especially in the Alps and the Apennines, he is likely to give brief but unconventional and extraordinarily felt notations of the surrounding landscape. (p. 75)

Nature, of course, means more than mountains, and in dealing with any philosophical or poetic writer (and Montaigne is both) we will probably have to take account of his cosmology, the idea he has of the universe. Here a familiar difficulty presents itself in a more acute form: Montaigne's cosmology is to a large extent a reflection of the extraordinarily varied speculations of Greek antiquity (with some admixture of modern science). What appear to be intuitions of astonishing boldness and prescience can often be traced to Greek sources, and where no source is known we may still suspect the same origin. Since what matters to us is his view of reality as a whole rather than where he got it from, it will be best, except incidentally, to leave aside the question of sources and try to see how the world appeared to him.

It must be admitted that his cosmology, mainly contained in the [**"Apologie de Raymond Sebond"**] is basically of the old-fashioned kind. The earth is literally at the bottom . . . , with the moon above it and, higher still, serene spheres in which incorruptible celestial bodies move in stately measure. He believes in the four elements (an important component of Sabunde's argument), but of course no other coherent theory had yet been advanced.

On the other hand, his insatiable intellectual curiosity leads him to advance (if only sceptically, as evidence of the diversity and uncertainty of human science) many theories which do not accord with this simple Aristotelian scheme. Thus he admits the possibility that the earth moves round the sun, citing Cleanthes and Nicetas but also Copernicus. . . . (pp. 78-9)

Of particular interest, in view of the later history of the idea, are his references to the plurality of worlds. It is true that he makes fun of those who imagine mountains and valleys (and human colonies) on the moon, or think that the earth is a luminous star. For these fantasies about the moon he quotes Anaxagoras, Plato, and Plutarch, and in spite of his scepticism he thus marks a link with Wilkins, Cyrano de Bergerac, and other literary precursors of space travel. More seriously, he quotes Lucretius, Plato, Democritus, and Epicurus to show the probability of other worlds exactly similar to ours (or very different), since nothing in the universe is unique nor can God's power be limited. Though he is in no way original here, he continues Cornelius Agrippa and he anticipates Fontenelle and some of the speculations of modern cosmology. (pp. 79-80)

Montaigne contrasts Ptolemy's clear and definite view of the world with the uncertainty of his own time. . . . His attitude is perhaps summed up in:

> *(b)* Si nous voyons autant du monde comme nous n'en voyons pas, nous apercevrions, comme il est à croire, une perpetuele *(c)* multiplication et *(b)* vicissitude de formes.

> [If we saw as much of the world as we do not see, we would perceived, it is likely, a perpetual multiplication and vicissitude of forms.]

But this universe is not only infinite in variety, it is also unified (and here . . . we may perceive a connection between the structure of Montaigne's world-picture and the structure of his work). . . . Contradictions give life to each other and so create harmony rather than disrupt it. In the same way, just as in economic affairs profit for one can only be achieved at the expense of others, so in the physical world one thing can only grow at the expense of another. Everything is interdependent and coherent.

Having seen how Montaigne looks at the universe, we can now ask what he conceives to be man's place in it. It is in some ways a Pascalian vision (as Thibaudet has . . . observed), and of course Pascal was directly inspired by it. An individual, even a kingdom, is a minute speck in comparison with the vastness of nature. . . . (pp. 80-1)

So far we have considered mainly the world in the sense of cosmos, but Montaigne is naturally much more concerned with this earth, with what he sees around him, at home or on his journeys, and with the greater world which he knows from hearsay or more fully (if not always accurately) from the works of the sixteenth-century cosmographers and travellers as well a the historians. Among European countries Italy is, as might be expected, the one which is most familiar to him and which appears most often in the *Essais.* Apart from anecdotes (like the execution of Catena), observations of detail are introduced in passing for illustration or analogy, like the Italian use of umbrellas or parasols or the comparison of Indian untouchables giving warning of their approach to Venetian gondoliers shouting at corners (a remarkably vivid example of Montaigne's capacity for precise notation and his use of it to explain the unknown in terms of the known). Some of these details (and many besides) are to be found in the *Journal du voyage*; perhaps more typical of the *Essais* are the general reflections they inspire. Thus **"Sur des vers de Virgile"** includes a sketch of Italian *mores* and character: there are a greater number of beautiful women than in France (contradicted by the *Journal*) but in supreme beauties the two countries are about equal; the same is true of mental characteristics—brutality (probably in the sense of stupidity) is incomparably rarer in Italy, but the num-

ber of truly elevated characters is not dissimilar; bravery is universal among the French but the highest examples are to be found in Italy; marriage for Italian women is constraint and servitude. If we are prepared to admit the possibility of generalising about national characters at all, we must be struck by the shrewdness of these judgements, still partly valid. His journey had left him with a very good impression of the Germans and the Swiss, notable for their honesty and truthfulness. As always, he looks for the tell-tale differences of customs which confirm his relativism, as when he compares German stoves with French fires and remarks that it makes a German ill to sleep on a mattress, an Italian on a feather bed, or a Frenchman without fire and curtains. (pp. 82-3)

However, the main weight of his observation naturally bears on France, of which he had most direct experience, and here the breadth of the picture, the handling of narrative in anecdote, and the vivacity of detail reveals gifts akin to those of the novelist, if less sustained (this is not, of course, peculiar to him, since before the development of the modern realistic novel a number of writers naturally anticipate its methods even though using other forms). Such glimpses of everyday life, being scattered through the *Essais,* cannot easily be systematised, but they may be illustrated. So we find numerous references to dress and manners (usually disapproving), like the new fashion of farthingales or the older one of codpieces, the false teeth and padded thighs of women (used as an analogy for the pretences of science), the characteristically French custom of kissing as the normal greeting between the sexes. . . . Often such rapid perceptions are built up into scenes or pictures: there are those who use their wills like apples to reward and punish the heirs who please or displease them (a typical scene from a comedy, or novel) or, still more vivid, and worth quoting in full to show how Montaigne seizes reality, the picture of the soldier and the scholar:

> Celuy que tu vois grimpant contremont les ruines de ce mur, furieux et hors de soy, en bute de tant de harquebuzades; et cet autre, tout cicatricé, transi et pasle de faim, deliberé de crever plutost que de luy ouvrir la porte, pense tu qu'ils y soyent pour eux? . . . Cettuy-ci, tout pituiteux, chassieux et crasseux, que tu vois sortir apres minuit d'un estude, penses tu qu'il cherche parmy les livres comme il se rendra plus homme de bien, plus content et plus sage? Nulles nouvelles. Il y mourra, ou il apprendra à la posterité la mesure des vers de Plaute et la vraye orthographe d'un mot latin. . . .

> [The man you see climbing atop the ruins of that wall, frenzied and beside himself, a mark for so many harquebus shots; and that other, all scarred, pale and faint with hunger, determined to die rather than open the gates to him—do you think they are there for their own sake? . . . This fellow, all dirty, with running nose and eyes, whom you see coming out of his study after midnight, do you think he is a seeking among his books how to make himself a better, happier, and wise man? No such news. He is going to teach posterity the meter of Plautus' verses and spelling of a Latin word, or die in the attempt.]

The apostrophe to the reader ('tu vois'), the soldiers' arquebus-shots and scars, the scholar's catarrh and bleary eyes, the range and diversity of the vocabulary from the learned *pituiteux* to the vigorous, though not yet popular, *crever,* all this produces an impression of outstanding visual power. But, as usual in these cases, the picture is not offered for its own sake, it illustrates an argument (here the folly of doing things for glory or for posterity rather than for the good of one's own soul). And, again as usual, the tone is humorous. All sorts of incongruity come into play: not only the obvious ones of disproportion between the effort and the result or the contrasts of vocabulary, but the subtle unexpectedness of the identity shown to exist between the soldier's violent fury and the scholar's peaceful and secluded labours (both prepared to sacrifice their lives for their absurd projects). It is to be noted that this remarkably finished example of Montaigne's descriptive technique is already in the 1580 edition. The same is true of the well-known deathbed scene at the end of **"Que philosopher, c'est apprendre à mourir"**: the weeping women and the pallid servants, the darkened room and the candles, the doctors and preachers crowding at the bedside, combine to create an atmosphere of solemnity and horror as well as a vivid pictorial (and auditory) representation of the way death came to a sixteenth-century nobleman. It will be seen that, though the tone is normally humorous, Montaigne is equally successful with serious and tragic subjects. The parallel with the novel is, however, closest when Montaigne goes beyond the picture to introduce a narrative element, that is in his sustained anecdotes. We need not take too seriously the story of Marie-Germain, the girl who took a great leap and found that she was a boy (reproduced almost verbatim from the *Journal de voyage*) or that of the gentleman whose only interest in life was the movement of his bowels. But when we come to the dean of Saint-Hilaire at Poitiers, who stayed in his room, never emerging, for twenty-two years, or the exceptionally brilliant story (especially in the Bordeaux Copy editions) of the old man (identified with Montaigne's friend the Marquis de Trans) gulled by his family and servants so as to be in complete ignorance of the affairs he thought he was managing, we have a premonition of the world of Balzac. To exact observation of manners and skill in handling narrative Montaigne joins the keenest sense for oddity of character.

What has been said is sufficient to show something of the social range of his observation. From kings and courtiers (of whom he disapproves, though he sometimes speaks as if he were one of them), through the humanists, soldiers, lawyers and physicians who appear frequently, to the peasants of Pèrigord or the beggar at his door, he furnishes a fairly complete view of contemporary French society (there is, however, little reference to the commercial classes). Apart from the familiar hymn of praise to Paris (he is French only through it, he says, perhaps with some exaggeration), the city is often mentioned: thus he regrets that he will not live to see the completion of the Pont-Neuf. But country life is, as we should expect, much more extensively treated. (pp. 83-6)

It will be readily seen that what we have been discussing is in fact the part played by experience in the book. We have here, needless to say, one of the central strands in Montaigne's thought, emerging in the final essay (**"De l'experience"**) as perhaps the most important strand of all. So far we have considered it in relation to the observing self, as the raw material of judgement and self-exploration, and as the sheer enjoyment of the multiplicity of the world. . . . [We] must notice that as his horizon widens beyond the confines of Europe, although some of these connections persist, the element of personal experience naturally gives way to the purely bookish. Yet this would not quite be a true conclusion either. Although for his remarks on exotic countries, which are very numerous, he must inevitably rely on the reports of others (and sometimes very fanciful reports), his interpretation of them is illuminated and controlled by his

observation of the familiar: his experience of the remote remains in a way a lived experience.

The passages dealing with America (especially in **"Des cannibales"** and **"Des coches"**) are the most famous, the most original, and the most important for an understanding of Montaigne, but references to eastern countries are much more frequent (though individually less extensive). (p. 88)

But if references to Asia (especially Turkey) are more numerous, those to the New World have a much greater impact on the reader and much deeper consequences for Montaigne's thought. . . . [The] 1580 preface includes a prominent reference to 'those nations who are said still to live under the sweet liberty of the first laws of nature', and are thus accorded a place among the leading themes of the book as they appeared to the author at the moment of first publication. (p. 90)

The consequences of the preoccupation with America are pervasive and far-reaching: for the moment we are concerned with it simply as evidence of this grasp of external reality. Passing allusions are found in many essays, but detailed discussion is concentrated in three: the **"Apologie"** (to some extent), **"Des cannibales,"** and **"Des coches."** The description of the life, customs and beliefs of the Brazilians in **"Des cannibales"** is precise, so far as one can judge accurate, and at the same time most lively. It matters little that Montaigne still believes that America touches the East Indies or is separated from them only by a narrow strait. What does matter is the vividness of his picture, both physical and moral, and the way it is arranged so as to place the indigenous inhabitants in the most favourable light, which is what distinguishes him from most of his printed sources like Thevet and Lèry. Thevet's style, for example, is very flat and dull in comparison, but the real point is his lack of sympathy and understanding, the qualities which create the beauty and poetry of Montaigne. (pp. 92-3)

However, this outline of Montaigne's view of America would hardly be adequate if we did not at least hint, anticipating later developments, at the persistent argument which underlies it, the equality of mankind, even the superiority of unspoiled natural man as found in America to the Christian and 'civilised' nations of Europe. (p. 93)

No theme could be more central to his purpose.

Looking back now on his view of the world as a whole, familiar or exotic, we can see that the *Essais* constitute not only a self-portrait but a kind of general anthropology. The **"Apologie"** and **"De la coustume"** in particular (but only to a greater degree than the other essays) are full of observations of the most diverse human customs, traditions, and institutions, not, in spite of appearances, assembled at random but chosen for their pertinence to the same pervasive theme. As usual these observations are based partly on personal experience, partly on the reports of others. Thus to the description of the simple and untarnished existence of the American Indians can be joined that of the isolated community of Lahontan in the foothills of the Pyrenees, whose idyllic happiness was undisturbed by lawyers and doctors; but, as with the Indians, ruin followed when these agents of civilisation gained admittance. Direct observation on his home ground (he was patron of the living of Lahontan) produces the same results as the indirect accounts of America. It might almost be said, allowing for the difference of time and scientific temper, that there is something of Frazer in the way he pieces his various reports together. But of course these reservations are capital. Together with the exact observation of local *mores* or the careful way in which he collects and checks the evidence of travellers to America goes a readiness to accept any story which serves his turn, ancient or modern (and . . . in the case of history he does not always seem aware of the distinction), countries which have a dog as king, where men have eyes and a mouth in their chest or change into wolves and mares and back again. **"De la coustume"** especially is an extraordinary mixture of the true and the fantastic: a long list puts side by side, all treated alike, genuine customs such as exogamy or female circumcision and fables such as the country of the Amazons. In spite of so many excursions into fantasy, he undoubtedly has an anthropologist's eye. (pp. 94-5)

Still, he would not be himself if he did not feel the need to explain his attitude to truth and falsehood in these matters. . . . One argument is that nothing can be imagined so fantastic that it will not correspond to some real practice somewhere. . . . Though this is not the attitude of a scientific anthropologist, it is hard to gainsay him. We are here . . . very close to Aristotle's view of poetic as opposed to historical truth, and also to the *vraisemblance* of seventeenth-century classical theory, though Montaigne, as we should expect, puts it in a less abstract and simpler way.

Beyond the fairly detached concern with anthropology, whether scientific or poetic, lies something else, where a still stronger moral sense comes into play. This is his cosmopolitanism, most sharply reflected in the *Journal du voyage* and the parts of the *Essais* inspired by his travels. (pp. 95-6)

[Montaigne's cosmopolitanism means] a total acceptance of the diversity of human life, a refusal to be bound by prejudices of time and place. Not only every country, he says, but every city and every profession has its own manners. This diversity is indeed part of the pleasure of travelling. . . . But pleasure points to a deeper lesson, the absurdity of judging by parochial standards, which finds its positive expressions in the declaration:

> Non parce que Socrates l'a dict, mais parce qu'en verité c'est mon humeur, et à l'avanture non sans quelque excez, j'estime tous les hommes mes compatriotes, et embrasse un Polonois comme un François, postposant cette lyaison nationale à l'universelle et commune.

> [Not because Socrates said it, but because it is really my feeling, and perhaps excessively so, I consider all men my compatriots, and embrace a Pole as I do a Frenchman, setting this national bond after the universal and common one.]

We have here not only a noble profession of faith in humanity but an anticipation of one of the dominant lines of thought in the seventeenth and eighteenth centuries. (pp. 97-8)

[We] see the difficulty of compartmentalizing Montaigne. However much we try to concentrate on a single aspect of his complex literary personality (here his rendering of external reality), we find that it has necessary implications for the whole of his thought (here leading to the diversity of life, to relativism, and ultimately to liberalism). (p. 98)

> *R. A. Sayce, in his* The Essays of Montaigne: A Critical Exploration, *Weidenfeld and Nicolson, 1972, 356 p.*

MARCEL TETEL   (essay date 1974)

[*A French-born American educator and author, Tetel is particularly interested in Renaissance studies. In the following excerpt, he examines the evolutionary nature of* The Essays *through a discussion of the work's ambiguities, paradoxes, and evidence of introspection.*]

When a major critic writes a major study on a major writer, such an endeavor can rejuvenate the subject it deals with, but at the same time it frequently also locks this subject into a critical position for a long time to come, though on the positive side it offers a challenge to future critics. Such has been the effect of Pierre Villey's *Les Sources et l'évolution des Essais de Montaigne*. Villey established that Montaigne's thought evolved through three stages: Stoicism marks the first book; skepticism the second book; naturalism (follow nature) and the goodness of man the third book, while epicureanism pervades all three books. The first question the reader may ask himself is how there can be a conscious and authentic evolution from the first to the second book when many essays in both parts were composed around the same period of time, and Montaigne himself chose to arrange some of his essays more according to thematic patterns than chronologically.

Without a doubt these three positions occur in the respective three books; what remains problematic is whether they occupy such a dominating role as to warrant the notion of an evolution. What troubles the reader again is that Montaigne's mind does not function along the lines of fixed patterns that dominate it for extended periods of time. In other words, the very genre of the essay—weighing, experiment, tryout—does not allow one stance to override another. Of course, in the first book the stoic viewpoint is very clearly and explicitly discernible:

> Here very eloquently and fully is that state of the Stoic sage:
> The mind remains unmoved, the tears all useless flow.
>   Virgil
> > The peripatetic sage does not exempt himself from
> > perturbations, but he moderates them. . . .

The key word here, summing up Montaigne's thinking process, is "Peripatetic" which suggests a circular motion in accord with the exploratory spirit of the essays, and not a linear one more concordant with the concept of evolution. Not adopting any ism may be a wiser device for singling out the highlights of the first book. . . . The lack of a label confers flexibility, and this kind of synthesis remains relative to others and in a global existential perspective.

The second book most readily falls prey to an overriding synthesis because one essay, **"Apology of Raymond Sebond,"** quite centrally situated, dominates the whole book by virtue of constituting more than one-third of it. In this essay Montaigne develops the insufficiency of reason, judgment, and the senses as means to attain knowledge. The result is the renowned "What do I know?" and submission to God. The skepticism inherent in this essay pervades, of course, the entire second book, but it echoes equally strong and convincing notes of the first book, notes that are echoed in the third book as well, because Montaigne's temper is basically skeptic; his questioning mind remains suspended, and he never tires of inquiring. There is a difference of surface stress, of the number of pages devoted explicitly and theoretically to doubt, but the very method of the essay common to all three books results from a skeptical point of departure and arrival.

No one can object to the assertion that following nature and a belief in the natural goodness of man play an important role in the third book. But one may question a critical opinion advocating that Montaigne evolves to this position with the advent of the last book, as Villey proclaimed. To counter this viewpoint, it suffices to take one of the early essays in the first book, **"That to Philosophize is to Learn to Die."** Here Montaigne wants to relegate to obsolescence man's fear of death and substitute the scorn of death for the scorn of life. All are equal before death, for which we must be ready at any moment. If death spares us until old age, then the sunset years bring a gradually disintegrating body and ease us into the final step. Furthermore, on the threshold of death a man must shed all paraphernalia—the hysterical, mourning relatives, the seemingly concerned preachers and doctors: "We must strip the mask from things as well as from persons; when it is off, we shall find beneath only that same death which a valet or a mere chambermaid passed through not long ago without fear", because "Such are the good counsels of our mother Nature." In the final analysis, Montaigne advocates a simple, natural, and quiet death, one that has become an integral but not an obsessive part of life; of course this ultimate position holds for a death that occurs at home or in old age, not on the field of battle. In the third book Montaigne will take an identical stance.

The fact remains that the concept of evolution is endemic to the *Essays;* only the type of evolution may be questioned. (pp. 20-2)

Ultimately, the concept of evolution, on a thematic level at least, depends on whether or not Montaigne offers a synthesis of his thought; if there is no synthesis, then the resulting suspension of judgment denies any possibility of evolution because a constant state of ambiguity does not allow for a thematic curve. Under these circumstances, even the notion of duration, the arching span of time during which the *Essays* was composed, cannot substantiate a thematic evolution. Since the general consensus of opinion now holds that the *Essays* defies synthesis, the belief in a thematic evolution of Montaigne's thought is accorded less and less of critical favor.

Because Montaigne wants to omit no valid viewpoint, he creates an ambiguity in his essays; indeed, the reader is at a loss to choose the validity of one opinion over another. The thorough dissection of an argument inevitably produces conflicting meanings, since one is always reversed by another. In the maze of opinions, to give one a privileged position over another, to consider one a conclusion or a definitive stance above another, is to fall into a trap and not discern much tongue-in-cheek aimed at purposely disconcerting the reader. If one of the aims of the *Essays* is to form Montaigne's and our judgment, as is unanimously acknowledged, then this goal cannot be achieved by accepting absolutes or choosing stances, but by weighing arguments—that is, ambivalence and ambiguity.

A close examination of an essay will provide the concrete means of illustrating a typical case of ambiguity. **"A Custom of the Island of Cea"** deals with the question of suicide. It is composed of a series of examples and anecdotes offering arguments for and against suicide. The overwhelming bulk of arguments favors it under some circumstance, such as suffering from some illnesses (long mental ones or kidney stones) and inevitable loss of honor or virtue, usually by force. Montaigne even offers the stoics' argument that suicide allows man to remain free and choose, if need be, a "reasonable exit." On the other hand, one of the fewer arguments against suicide states that man is not free to dispose of his life, God's gift to him. The last sentence of the essay, significantly enough a post-1588 addition, indicates that Montaigne remains consistent between his early and late positions, on the surface at least: "Unendurable pain and fear of a worse death seem to me the most excusable motives for suicide."

The title of the essay, however, unsettles the underpinning of the synthesis suggested by this consistency. Why does Montaigne call his essay **"A Custom of the Island Cea"** and choose thereby to focus on a specific example over others? To further stress its importance, not only is it the longest example in the essay, but it occurs at the end of the essay, where its unsettling and destructive effect on what precedes it will be felt more acutely. On that island, "a woman of great authority" who "had spent ninety years in a very happy state of mind and body" decides that the time has come to dispose of her life. She wants all to witness it and proceeds to describe the progress of the poison through her body and takes pleasure in her ability to watch herself die. Although Montaigne has assured the reader previously that a life is long enough wherever it stops, does he not offer here a projection of the death he would like to have—a death that in fact rejects suicide, since it occurs at age ninety and looks back to a long and useful life? In theory, then, Montaigne advocates suicide under certain circumstances, but in practice he denies it and even leads up to rejecting it by implication. In the last analysis he refuses to take a categorical stance on this issue, and many another because "Only the fools are certain and assured."

On occasion Montaigne contrives the end of an essay in such a way as to deliberately pull the rug from under his feet, and thereby contributes to an ambiguity of subject matter. One instance of this technique occurs at the end of the well-known essay **"Of Cannibals."** Here Montaigne praises the notion of the noble savage and questions the concept of civilization as Western man understands it. He focuses on the cyclical nature of civilization and the superiority of a natural way of life unencumbered by materialism. However, unwilling to find himself out on a limb, he makes one last remark that clouds his earlier perhaps idealistic outlook: "All this is not too bad—but what's the use? They don't wear breeches." It is as if Montaigne built a larger and taller argumentative castle in order to watch it fall, with some glee, from a greater height. He can accept fully neither the noble savage's innocence nor Western man's often corrupt and false well-being; he perceives the good and the bad of both sides.

Because Montaigne endeavors to show both sides of an argument, or more often its multifaceted complexity, he is constantly confronted with antithesis. He does not flee it, but on the contrary, seeks it out, for it expresses what he reads, experiences, and sees all about him. Of course, what he reads or experiences may conflict with what he sees, or what he sees may contradict his reading, but the convergence of these antitheses provides the impetus to search further, to try again and again, with no hope of arriving at conclusive answers: "My conceptions and my judgment move only by groping, staggering, stumbling, and blundering; and when I have gone ahead as far as I can, still I am not at all satisfied: I can still see country beyond, but with a dim and clouded vision, so that I cannot clearly distinguish it."

The presentation of antithetical patterns of thought does not necessarily reflect belief in a universe hopelessly fragmented and of irreconcilable views. In Montaigne's mind opposites coexist, reinforce each other, and actually harmonize into a composite flexible whole. At the same time, one finds in the *Essays* a series of opposites: a love of life and a detachment from it, hedonism and heroism, an acceptance of the principle of becoming and an aspiration toward constancy and serenity, the eventual failure of thought before the vastness of knowledge, or an intellectual humility, and yet a limitless pride and conviction of the hegemony of thought (a variant of the Pascalian reed), virtue emanating both from spontaneous and rational sources and inherent to our nature, the dichotomy of the artful and the natural, the conscious and the subconscious. I cite only a few. On a smaller scale, the reader will often encounter antithesis on the paragraph level. Here Montaigne will start the argument along one line of thought and will surreptitiously lead the reader to the opposite viewpoint without realizing it, until he finds himself on the other side of the argument and often equally convinced of both. The use of the antithesis mystifies the reader and toys with him; black and white fuse into a grey zone. It may produce surprise, but more important, one consequence of Montaigne's antinomism or dualism is that it is unwise to make any statement about him without immediately stating the contrary.

The paradox is the most intensive form of antithesis because the weighing process disappears; instead, the result turns out to be the opposite of the avowed purpose of the argument. It constitutes a challenge to thought and appeals therefore to the humanistic mind. The Renaissance relishes the paradox, because this device reflects the infinity and inscrutability of knowledge constantly faced by the humanist. At the same time, paradox becomes one of the few reliable means of arriving at a perplexing and elusive truth. Thus Montaigne likes to take the counterpoint of an argument. In discussing education, he pictures himself unworthy of tackling such a subject matter; this kind of reasoning is one of his favorite ploys to draw the reader to his side. He creates a hesitant, unpresumptuous persona for himself, to attack and sometimes praise presumption. He devotes a whole essay to repentance, and in it advocates nonrepentance. His treatise on friendship sees the complete transformation of this concept into that of love, and conjugal love in his eyes becomes friendship. Desires, passions, anger, fright form the very core for opposite themes such as moderation, ataraxy (complete spiritual quietude), sleep, death, reconciliation. Neither moderation nor excess are ever exempt from incertitude and inquietude; therefore the questioning, the essay, continues. The oscillation persists: "Wisdom has its excesses, and has no less need of moderation than does folly." The paradox, then, is to be seen as a positive device, because the need to surprise that it supplies is less important than the apparent negation of the accepted ordinary in order to explore and reevaluate.

When Montaigne decides to take a stance, he does so temporarily in a single matter and for a single moment. The paradoxes derive from a dialectical process inherent to the *Essays,* namely, from the relationship, the movement between his readings and his experiences, between his ideas and other people's, the perpetual dialogue within himself, between him and his book, between the past, the present, and himself. This constant interchange, what Montaigne calls the pouring out and the filling, remains at a loose equilibrium and culminates in the last essay, **"Of Experience",** which combines reading and experience, the past and the present, into an entity based as well on the interdependence of these elements. Again the presence of a paradoxical and dialectical thinking process effects and may even negate the concept of an evolution. (pp. 23-7)

The one explicitly pervading element in the *Essays* is the self and its study by Montaigne. Since this self-observation lasted about twenty years, it can be assumed that the "I" underwent some changes. On the most obvious plane, it evolved from a middle-aged man to an old one; consequently, the last essays do exhibit a dominant preoccupation with old age and a decaying body, yet one of the early essays, **"Of Age",** written when Montaigne was in his late thirties, already reflects and projects a latent obsession with the question. In a more subtle vein, the self moves from a "diverse and undulating" being in the first essays, the very condition leading to the act of writing, toward a formed and fixed being, but one who still seeks for self-definition. In other words, Montaigne tries out stability just as he had tried out and parried with vacillation earlier. In the process, he moves from being a mere borrower to becoming a proprietor of the past, of his sources, and of himself, as he proceeds to an unattainable future. What matters to the "I" is the present, the only temporal phase that can be ordered, created, and lived. Given this premise, the self feels the oppression and limitations of time from which its consciousness emerges. This awareness makes the self live time and thereby conquer it, the purpose of the *Essays.* From the beginning to the end of his writings, Montaigne points to the supremacy of living, the existence of the self, and the integration of the self with his environment and with the *Essays.* (pp. 33-4)

Although this self-scrutiny becomes more and more introspective, the body as whole is at the same time agent and instrument. Indeed, Montaigne takes pleasure in rolling himself within himself like a twirling ball, for it is through this action that he defines himself, not so much through the amount or nature of the space explored as through the energy expended in the exploration of the self. This energy alternates between an active and a passive self, between initiating and sustaining; even in the latter role the object is to remain a free agent, to be able to resist if the choice so warrants it. The involvement with oneself operates on the same bilevel as the involvement with the outside world.

As the essays progress and old age sets in, Montaigne exhibits more and more intimate details about himself. The wines and dishes he likes or does not like; those he used to enjoy and can no longer have now. The loss of a tooth, his bowel movement, his kidney stones, matters with which he becomes more and more obsessed. These personal preoccupations, less frequent in the first essays than in the last, do mark a movement of the *Essays* toward an interior physiological level that functions in the light of living in harmony with oneself: "The most beautiful lives, to my mind, are those that conform to the common human pattern, with order, but without miracle and without eccentricity." Shifts here and there of details do not alter the main thrust of the essays: the analysis of the self.

On the surface it appears that the essays evolve from an impersonal to a personal level, from the outside world, being in function of the inner self, toward a fusion of the outside and personal worlds in function of the inner self, but this kind of evolution does not take into account the all-pervading consubstantiality throughout the three books. Yet a perceptible movement toward a narrower and narrower self who at the same time claims world citizenship and universality remains one of the more evident and plausible—indeed, paradoxical—evolutions. The individual looking at the outside world becomes the prototype looking inside of himself. The more Montaigne wraps himself up with himself, the more aware he becomes of his universality; convolution produces nakedness and unveils a "ruling pattern", the growing inner core that resists mutation but profits from experiences and essaying because, in spite of appearances, man carries on "all in one piece." (pp. 34-5)

Marcel Tetel, in his Montaigne, *Twayne Publishers, Inc., 1974, 138 p.*

RICHARD L. REGOSIN (essay date 1977)

[Regosin is an American educator and author. In the following excerpt, he determines the extent to which The Essays *is a pure "mimetic" reflection of its author through an analysis of Montaigne's treatment of the nature/art dichotomy.]*

In that process of self-reflection which is the heart of his portrait, Montaigne considers his writing as he does his other activities. Self-study demands that his theme turn in on itself, that the observer be observed. . . . The purpose of the enterprise, the nature of the procedure, considerations of style and of language all occupy his attention, making it difficult for the critic to discuss anything that the essayist has not already treated himself. As a result, Montaigne has become the most influential commentator on the *Essais*. We have been inclined to accept his point of view, to feel that his intimacy with the work allows privileged insight; the essayist's insistence on his truthfulness and sincerity has led us to make his observations and judgments our own.

Nowhere is Montaigne's word taken more readily than in his assertion of originality, his claim that unlike other writers he is one and indivisible with his book. . . . [The] essayist insists on the unity of man and book, the coincidence of life and writings. The metaphor of the self-portrait—evoking the popular vogue of realistic portraiture in sixteenth-century France—seems to confirm the representational, mirror quality of the *Essais*. Without art or artifice, Montaigne maintains, he seeks to depict himself in his simple, natural, and ordinary fashion.

Taking this lead, readers have tended to treat the *Essais* as personal document, as source of both social and intellectual biography, of the writer's life and times and his ideas and attitudes. And the man depicted in the work—his chronology, his actions and opinions—and the historical context in which he resides do seem to correspond to much of what we know of the existential Montaigne and of the contemporary scene. At the same time, there exist a number of discrepancies between the historical and textual Montaigne that suggest a distinction between man and writer and move the *Essais* closer to the domain of art. . . . The essayist's depreciation of his writing, his reasoning power, and his memory, the military face of this most unmartial jurist suggest that something other than mimetic fidelity alone determines the portrait of the *Essais*. (pp. 7-8)

The discussion of art in the *Essais* has to wend its way carefully through the implications both pejorative and positive of Montaigne's varied use of the word. Generally speaking, the subject arises as the negative term in the couple *nature-art,* a favorite antithesis that spreads out to inform a wide range of familiar Montaignian oppositions . . . : ignorance-knowledge; the primitive-the cultured; philosophy-the way of nature; conscience-law; conversational style-rhetoric and oratory. When Montaigne speaks of art, he implies an obscuring veil that the working of speculative reason, pride, the desire to know or to impress casts over a kind of essential form or way of being inherent in things. Human constructs and artifacts also becloud "true nature," seen in temporal and spatial terms as a remove closer to the "real" point of man's origin (in this lies the basis of Montaigne's primitivism). They disguise and distort the fact of nature considered the vivifying force of the universe and the supreme good. In each case what is inherent has been subordinated to what is external, what is real to what is artificial, manmade. Something original, something essential, something at the very heart of being human appears to get lost. . . . And it gets lost to art.

Art meets with poor treatment since it represents contrivance that smothers the source of virtue, truth, knowledge, pleasure. . . . The effort to escape the misery of his condition through art only plunges man deeper into it. . . . Human art is not the outgrowth of freedom or the sign of dignity; it signals man's alienation from his rightful and proper place in the universal scheme of things. Nature as *maratre* ["unkind mother"] is a perverse myth engendered by human pride to valorize the achievement of its art.

In that continuing movement of the *Essais* which is recovery as well as discovery, Montaigne seeks to reestablish what he senses as lost: his grasp of the self enjoyed in the perfect friendship, his image held by La Boétie before his death—that stability and wholeness represented by their union. The preference for nature, the desire to penetrate the false way she has been painted, to seek out her true path beneath the artificial tracks that cover her—whether what is meant by nature is the animating force of the universe or the way things "are"—manifest the same effort at recuperation. In the essays the quest for self-knowledge and the pursuit of nature and the natural are merely differing faces of the same dialectic. (pp. 227-29)

To suggest that the natural equals the good in every circumstance, and that art is always bad, however, is to oversimplify their relationship. In **"De l'affection des peres aux enfans"** Montaigne takes a view of reason different from that dictated by the framework of the [**"Apologie de Raimond Sebond"**] to see in it man's distinct, and privileged, faculty. . . . The tendency to subordinate nature to reason and judgment, or perhaps to being them together to attain a higher form of human behavior, increases through the *Essais*. Montaigne appears willing to treat nature more equivocally, to allow . . . that man not slavishly submit to it but rather use his reason either to override it or enhance its impulse by adding the consent of judgment, freely practiced. In **"De la cruauté"** he suggests that virtue achieved by reason overcoming temptation stands higher than natural goodness or innocence even though he has to place God and Socrates beyond all consideration. When Montaigne reaffirms the imperative "know thyself" at the end of **"De la vanité,"** he recognizes the demand that man overcome his natural inclination to preoccupation elsewhere. . . . Benevolent nature, it appears, protecting man from the disconcerting view of his own inadequacy, must be overcome if man is to seek himself as he is. The visualist metaphors that dominate the close of the essay underscore the place of reason and judgment in the quest for self-knowledge.

Montaigne allows himself the same latitude as he deals with art, for although it remains firmly anchored in opposition to nature, there are occasions when, like things intellectual, it functions positively. (pp. 229-30)

The potential of art to play a meaningful positive role in human life looms distinctly in the *Essais,* particularly in the last book, as if to suggest that the obscurities, disguises, and distortions it produces derive from perverse practice and excess. Nowhere is the notion of proper employ more evident than in **"De l'art de conferer."** . . . Here *art* is a skill acquired, attitudes and postures assumed in order to reach a higher level of human conduct. The way of discussion becomes a means to the way of living, both because usage and custom form part of the man and because discussion, essays, and life blend in a common activity. Montaigne pinpoints the tension between the proper and improper use of this art, as aware of the danger of verbal encounter as of its promise. . . . The theme of ineptitude implies that the problem is less art than its use. (pp. 230-31)

Montaigne's characteristic attitudes on life are generally lumped together in what is often called his "art of living." Drawn for the most part from the Third Book and based on the interplay of nature, custom, reason, judgment, and the watchful eye, this "art" represents his efforts to come to grips with pain and discomfort (both bodily and spiritual) and to heighten the enjoyment of pleasure and the physical experience of life. The quotation from Manilius which opens **"De l'experience"** indeed suggests that experience can lead to an art of living if one heeds its examples:

> Per varios usus artem experientia fecit:
> Exemplo monstrante viam
> [Experience, by example led
> By varied trials art has bred.]

In a general way, our discussion bears on this rather broad sense of *art*. At the same time, we must take into account the varied and precise dimensions of *art* in the *Essais*, for, as we have seen, the concept is not unequivocal. For all of its made-up and managed qualities, art is indivisibly related to nature and truth. Or perhaps we should say because of those qualities, for it is art as literature that becomes the means to life. . . . Rather than deny or subordinate the notion that the *Essais* are *art,* or literature, we begin to understand that only in that role do they bear a meaningful relation to life. Art and life, the made-up and the real, are bound together as one.

Montaigne's familiar leit-motif of the world as a theater functions at multiple levels to express his views on existence and human behavior. In characteristic baroque metaphor, he imagines life lived as roles played on a stage, but here the role and reality are confused, indeed the two as indistinguishable give rise to deep feelings of instability, of fragmentation, of the illusory nature of life. While this perspective finds expression in countless works of the late-sixteenth and seventeenth centuries—one thinks of Shakespeare, Cervantes, Corneille—these common baroque elements are the basis of Montaigne's personal vision. (pp. 232-33)

But the world as a stage is more than the backdrop for the partial, disoriented self, for Montaigne links the idea of roles to the problem of authenticity. In the constant tension between inside and outside, between private self and public persona, man seeks continuously to suggest that he is as he appears. Position, status, eloquence in speech and elegance in manner disguise what lies beneath, always threatening to stick to the skin, as in the case of the orator whose counterfeit melancholy became real. Montaigne aims at the discrepancy between the parts played and the real, essential dimension of being. He strives to peel back the mask, to uncover the sham of illusion, to breakthrough artifice and superficies to disclose substance. (p. 233)

Social man assumes postures and puts on airs in the public arena, but Montaigne implies that life as a stage is not exclusively a function of the outside world. However much the mask is to be regarded with suspicion, the playing of roles itself remains an inextricable part of human existence. In the early essays on death the "real" moment at man's inevitable end concludes life's play and illusion, but it too is a role, albeit an authentic one. . . . It is not that the play ends so that life (or death . . .) can take over; rather, the play that is pretense—*masque,* as Montaigne says—gives way to the real play. Lucretius would separate life as play from reality:

> Nam verae voces tum demum pectore ab imo
> Ejiciuntur, et eripitur persona, manet res.
> [At last true words surge up from deep within our breast,
> The mask is snatched away, reality is left.]

Montaigne uses the vocabulary of drama to describe that reality. Death is still the last act of the comedy, its final confrontation the last scene. The play has become authentic, real, we said earlier in an apparent paradox, but if life is a play, one's own role can be counterfeited or faced up to. Masks may be worn in that play within the play of life, roles changed at will until death forces man to play himself.

Life is theater and the self a role at the point where illusion and reality converge and intermingle. . . . The emphasis is less on masks, worn consciously or unconsciously, and rather on the broader implications of the metaphor of the play, on the idea that man even plays at being himself. . . . [In] the *Essais* Montaigne refers to his own life as comedy, a function of his modest role, consistent with his tendency to deprecate his activities and achievements, and to articulate the low style he finds appropriate to his subject.

Comedy, theater, laughter imply audience as Montaigne looks out from his physical and psychological remove at the spectacle of life about him. Whether at home in his tower or away on a voyage, the essayist is always the outsider—that is, he stands as a spectator apart from the world. His purpose is study, and what he hopes to gain is wisdom and virtue. Montaigne articulates this lesson in **"De l'institution des endfans"**, although he is content to leave literal theater as mere diversion for the people. On the ideal level at which the essay is written, and with the analogy of essaying constantly in the background, the outside world serves as a book where the student learns how to do, as a school where he learns of others, but most importantly as a mirror where the individual learns about himself. . . . (pp. 234-35)

The observer of the world is most profoundly the observer of the self; the metaphor of theater and its roles touches all aspects of human life. . . . Montaigne plays the parts both of actor and spectator to his own action and, as in the case of public spectacle, he seeks to learn, to know about himself, and to acquire wisdom and virtue. In the world of the *Essais* those who err do so because they deny the necessity, or the validity, or the practice of this play of the self. The failure to look, or to see, results in arrogance, in the tendency to take oneself too seriously as absolute term, to assume that one's role is always authentic. Without separation, without distance, the self cannot locate and know itself, cannot distinguish borrowed roles from real. However paradoxical it may appear, the dichotomy of the self, its fragmentation, is a condition necessary to wholeness and authenticity. Truth resides in the interaction of spectator and actor.

The discussion of art, theater, and roles leads back to its source in the *Essais* as literature and in the relation of literature to life. We have seen Montaigne purposely blur the distinctions in his juxtapositions of art and nature and in the metaphor of life as a play. In **"De la vanité"** he judges ideas in the same mode Horace used to describe the poet's aim: "Je ne me soucie pas tant de les avoir vigoureuses et doctes, comme je me soucie de les avoir aisées et commodes à la vie: elles sont assez vrayes et saines si elles sont utiles et aggreables" ["I don't care so much to have them vigorous and learned, as I do to have them comfortable and convenient to life: they are true and sane insofar as they are useful and agreeable"]. As he does throughout the essays (and particularly in the Third Book), Montaigne reduces the general to the particular, substituting criteria relevant to the individual (useful and pleasing) for universal considerations (truth and soundness). The Horatian *utile* and *dulce* ["useful and pleasant"] apply to elements of life as if it were a work of art. . . . Truth derives from a view of life that can only be called artistic.

Literary criteria also apply to the *Essais* themselves. . . . Claiming to be absolutely faithful to the original accounts of his stories, the essayist introduces the notion of verisimilitude, of things possible. In terms reminiscent of Aristotle, Montaigne suggests that in the area of human behavior and motives, the potential, that which might have happened, is more useful, more informative and, one senses, more true than that which has happened. At this point, he digresses to wonder out loud how historians can pretend to describe what "really" was, given the unreliability of witnesses, the difficulty of discerning intentions. Against the conjecture of history masquerading as reality Montaigne sets the possibility of literature as a way to truth.

The implications of this view that art provides the means to truth, and, in a deeper sense, to life, are multiple. The dialectic of the quest for self-knowledge rests on the premise that seeing oneself involves projecting an image, in Montaigne's case a construct, a counterpart in words whose motion can be charted, whose ideas and activities considered and judged. The dominant vision is artistic, one might even say poetic, as the *Essais* penetrate the superficies of historical reality to consider most profoundly human experience and the essayist's own. The military bearing of the imagined self, his ideal union with La Boétie, his lack of memory and of science and his situation in the Third Book as an old man good only for musing about himself, are aspects of the personal presentation whose textual significance transcends biographical import. The utopianism of friendship, death proceeding from life in the cycle of nature, the voyage that is life, the ideal of the past, Montaigne's primitivism, these are all elements of the world in which that projected self seeks meaning that would be called literary. The purpose is not to build up an imaginary structure for its own sake, nor to make a fiction that expressly distorts and misleads. The *Essais* are a construct from beginning to end, but they aim at all points to contact life.

The roles Montaigne plays in the *Essais,* the various postures and perspectives he assumes in the diverse contexts of different essays, function at this convergence. We no longer have to confine ourselves to an evolutionary reading of the work in biographical terms, considering the change from Stoic through the crisis of skepticism to a kind of Epicurean humanism as a personal journey, for positions taken and argued have a deeper significance. Any subject matter, and the view taken of it, sets the mind in motion to reveal the quality of its judgment. A point of view is not inevitably a matter of conviction but of trial (or tryout) and exercise. Montaigne can slip into the skin of the Stoic, skeptic, or Epicurean as he can argue both sides of a question or be the devil's advocate to point up paradox (as in **"De la phisionomie"**). Whether he plays the confident teacher in **"De l'institution des enfans"** (in spite of his initial protestation to the contrary) or assumes the humble posture of **"De la praesumption"**, the exteriorization provides the opportunity for stocktaking. His area of concern is always himself. . . . (pp. 236-39)

The projected image of the self and the construct that is the essayist's vision of the world most meaningfully represent Montaigne's "art" of living. In this endless movement back and forth between life and literature, the distinctions are blurred: indeed, as we have seen, the two are one, for in Montaigne's case writing is living.

Two sides of a single act. The writer as artist, as *facteur* ["maker"], comes into the truth of things by conferring shape, arrangement. . . . By "making" the book, Montaigne "invents" the man.

If we look at the other side of the act, the living, we find coincidental movement. In **"Du repentir"** Montaigne disclaims any intention of instructing the world or of trying to form Man, or even of remaking himself since he is already fashioned. And yet his whole activity involves instructing, amending, and reforming himself; not refashioning from scratch, but taking on a shape consistent with his nature and the larger scheme of things. We watch Montaigne continually attempting to introduce this kind of unity between his personal substance and its form. . . . (pp. 240-41)

Thematically and formally, the mode is circular and self-enclosed. The tendency to view the *Essais* as linear and open-ended remains valid as the reader uncovers traces of evolution—Stoic to skeptic to Epicurean humanism; the effort to recover the lost utopia—and acknowledges the unending quest for self-knowledge. But we recognize as well that the work opens out to close back upon itself. The writer is his own reader. . . . And in parallel postures, both the self as its own best friend and the book as another self stand face to face; the man makes the book as the book makes the man. As if the *Essais* were enclosed in sets of mirrors, self-reflecting images express the essential circularity of the Montaignian dialectic: the internal focus of the "self-seeker," the movement out from and back to the self describing the secular conversion and the play of infinite regress, the writer observing himself observing, and so on. (p. 242)

Montaigne turns to writing not to accomplish unadulterated mimetic transfer of experience, for to do so would reproduce the conditions of his point of departure. While he seeks to remain true to the nature of things as they are, the *Essais* demand transformation to allow form, accessibility, meaning. They work toward Montaigne's goals—self-portraiture, self-knowledge—precisely because they are other than, or more than, the raw material of experience. . . . By making the artifact and claiming for it substance as a self-sufficient entity, the origin and end of its meaning, Montaigne brings about a kind of incarnation. And because the body created is his own, he stands by analogy with God as his own maker. Not a creator *ex nihilo*, which is the exclusive province of Divinity but as one who, like the writer-inventer, fashions pre-existent matter to come into the true nature of things. Montaigne never doubts the existence of that self he seeks to know; he is, after all, a Christian. At the same time he alone is the source of its discovery, of its uncovering through that process of exteriorization which is the writing of the *Essais.* (pp. 243-44)

Richard L. Regosin, in his The Matter of My Book: Montaigne's 'Essais' as the Book of the Self, *University of California Press, 1977, 275 p.*

JEAN STAROBINSKI   (essay date 1982)

[*Starobinski is a Swiss author whose study of Montaigne (originally published in French in 1982) was awarded the Prix européen de l'essai by the Veillon Foundation of Lausanne. In the following excerpt from this work, he closely examines Montaigne's discussion of sexuality in "On Some Verses of Virgil," noting how the essayist related the subject to art and to artifice.*]

"On some verses of Virgil" is the place where Montaigne most fully develops his thinking on the subject of the "relation to others,'' since love, which is the central theme of this essay, is (along with friendship through ''far beneath it'') the quintessential such relation. . . . His starting point is his relation to himself. Movement is introduced by way of a series of inversions: old age brings a surfeit of such qualities as fullness, gravity, weightiness, temperance, dryness, cold, etc., and each of these calls to mind its opposite. The suffering body is an inescapable inconvenience that must be counterbalanced by ''moderation'' and self-control:

> (B) It does not leave me a single hour, sleeping or waking, unoccupied with instruction about death, patience, and penitence. I defend myself against temperance as I once did against sensual pleasure; for it pulls me too far back, even to the point of insensibility. *Now I want to be master of myself in every direction.* Wisdom had its excesses, and has no less need of moderation than does folly.

Montaigne's motives are plainly of two kinds. He is guided, first of all, by the medical (and moral) principle according to which an excess of one quality can be counteracted by administering a dose of its opposite: cold is compensated by heat, severity by gaiety, and ''wisdom'' itself by ''folly,'' in order to arrive at a proper ''temperament.'' In addition, he is concerned lest he fall under the sway of one of his ''parts'' (in this case the body), which has come to exercise undue dominance over the rest. To be truly and freely in possession of oneself, one must take care to indulge nothing in excess, not even ''wisdom,'' paradoxical as that may seem. This is why Montaigne says that I ''deliberately let myself go a bit to license.'' By this he means simply that he occasionally lets his mind dwell on ''youthful wanton thoughts'' and ''remembrance of my past youth.'' Faced with the ''stormy and cloudy sky''—i.e., with death—Montaigne indulges his memory for the sake of diversion: ''As long as my eyes can discern that lovely season now expired, I turn them in that direction at intervals. If youth is escaping from my blood and my veins, at least I want not to uproot the picture of it from my memory.'' Yet another example of the diversion recommended in the previous chapter, this return to the past is a ''ruse,'' a remedy taken ''in a dream'': ''a feeble struggle, that of art against nature.'' All the movement on this page has its source within Montaigne: he calls upon his own thoughts, images, and memories for aid. Only an addition made in 1595 invokes the authority of Plato in support of another method, which calls for turning one's attention to the outside world: ''Plato orders men to attend the exercises, dances, and games of youth, *in order to rejoice in others* at the suppleness and beauty of body that is no longer in themselves.'' But this is advice gleaned from reading, not a remedy envisioned by Montaigne himself.

The compensations of the imagination, in which awakened images of the past enable the mind to ''feed on its own substance'' (to borrow the words of Rousseau, who resigned himself to this kind of pleasure), may be seductive but can never mask the absence of real pleasures. The caprices of ''fancy'' are never more than a pale substitute. Nothing surpasses genuine pleasure. ''Even the slightest occasions of pleasure that I can come upon, I seize. . . . My philosophy is in action, in natural and present practice, little in fancy. Would I might take pleasure in playing at cobnut or with top.'' Montaigne would like to find in the present moment the antidote to the ''grave subjects [that] grieve us.'' He would like to banish weighty concerns in favor of light amusements, games concerned with slight and unimportant matters. Now the very thought of face-to-face confrontation in a game, the desire for carefree amusement, awakens the hope of a meeting, the wish for a relationship with another person. . . . (pp. 185-86)

Thus it is association with others in friendship and conversation (a subject treated a short while before in the essay **''Of three kinds of association with others''**) to which Montaigne turns first. Though this may be a desire destined to remain unrequited, it is clear why the thought of another *person* or *company* (so much more effective as remedies than anything the lonely imagination has to offer) brings to an aging sick old man the hope of amusement that he needs. For what has he to hope from a private conversation with himself? Very little, to judge by the following sentence: ''Though I tickle myself, I can scarcely wring a poor laugh out of this wretched body any more.'' Given the tight ''bond'' between mind and body, it is impossible for the mind ''to rescue itself from old age'' when the body's health is failing. The beautiful image of the mistletoe growing green and flourishing ''on a dead tree'' expresses a wish that cannot be fulfilled. The mind ''has such a tight brotherly bond with the body that it abandons me at every turn to follow the body in its need. I take it aside and flatter it, I work on it, all for nothing.'' The mind is not an independent partner in conversation. The participation of others is therefore indispensable to anyone who wants to escape the lugubriousness of old age and disease. ''I love a *gay and sociable* wisdom'': gaiety and sociability go together, and they require ''communication.''

Rather than ''furnish essays in flesh and bone'' to ''persons or good company'' that would somehow have to be found, Montaigne settles for the association with his contemporaries established through his book. No sooner does he mention this relationship, however, than he describes it in terms of opposition: his attitude, which is to ''dare to say all that I dare to do,'' is the exception that proves the rule. Other people, obedient to the ''laws of ceremony,'' are unwilling to go so far toward establishing complete and tranquil equality between *saying* and *doing*. In a time of insincerity Montaigne is alone in confessing himself with total candor. . . . This is one of many places where Montaigne is concerned to show how different he is from his contemporaries (to whom he refers as *ils, on, les autres*), whose paths are opposite to his own. But even as he directs this scolding polemic against his contemporaries, he is fixing and specifying his own project as a writer, his desire to make himself known for what he is (unlike ''those who have a false opinion of themselves'' and ''can feed on false approbations''). We have seen him, on many occasions, resign himself to take his distance, to stand aloof in this way, but only in order to show himself as he really is, to *represent* his true being in the most exact manner possible. ''A man must see his vice and study it to tell about it. . . . *It is only for a waking man to tell his dream* [Seneca].'' At this point Montaigne narrows the focus of his remarks in a most singular manner: he addresses himself to ''the ladies'' and expresses the hope that (because of the nature of the theme he is about to take up) he will be read in a place more intimate than the ''parlor'':

> (B) I am annoyed that my essays serve the ladies only as a public article of furniture, an article for the parlor. This chapter will put me in the boudoir. I like their society when it is somewhat private; when public it is without favor or savor.

Having turned his attention to his own youth, Montaigne found that he was not satisfied to dwell in memory alone. He imagined a ''company'' that suited him, that he would gladly ''run'' to join were he invited to do so. Yet his only real resource is his book of essays; with this he will entice his female reader into the intimacy of the boudoir. The offer of something to read is a symbolic seduction: it is the form of association that comes closest to love. With the statement of his theme—"the sexual act" [*l'action génitale*]—and the statement that he himself is consubstantial with his work, Montaigne crosses into forbidden territory. As soon as his book crosses the threshold of the boudoir, where his reader is in the habit of being alone with her most intimate secrets, he begins to caress the body of another. There is nothing illicit about such intimacy, since it coincides with *separation* of the most radical kind: the preparation for death. At no other time, perhaps, does Montaigne establish such a close relationship between opposites as when he pens the following lines, which immediately follow those cited above: "(B) In farewells we exaggerate the warmth of our affection toward the things we are leaving. I am taking my last leave of the world's pastimes; here are our last embraces. But let us come to my theme."

It is Thanatos that liberates Eros and gives him voice. Thus this chapter of the *Essays* presents itself as the harbinger of death as well as love. Because he is bidding life farewell, Montaigne feels he has the right to speak of what used to fuel life's fires (already he shifts to the imperfect tense). It is a final flame that will catch fire in this chapter, nearly every paragraph of which has its image of heat, intended to ward off the cold that threatens to break in at any moment. Embraces remembered (or still vaguely hoped for) are "our last accolades." Thus there is no frivolity in this portrait set against a background of death. It is possible to discuss the most intimate bonds of the flesh when all bonds are about to come undone. Here the workings of Montaigne's dialectic are plain to see: imminent loss confers an infinite value upon that which can still be articulated and possessed; at the same time death makes it legitimate to take every liberty with language so as to uncover even the secretest of thoughts.

Language itself is the first item of concern. Once again, the problem is the disparity between *saying* and *doing*. The first thing that Montaigne has to say about sexuality is that we are not allowed to talk about it. Hence there is, at first sight, a very close connection between love and words. But this connection is a paradoxical one, because the less one talks about sexual matters, the more one thinks about them. . . . (pp. 187-89)

In the case of sexuality, the mask we wear consists in our not saying anything about it, in our not giving it a name. But what is the essence of this hidden reality, which in any case is no secret from anyone? The reader will soon see that Montaigne suggests at least two answers to this question: first, sexuality is repressed speech, and second, its heat burns only briefly. Let us start by considering the first of these two answers: love is a hidden language whose words are imprinted "in each and every one of us." It is given to the Muses and to the most sublime poetry to express its full force. Only literature can give body to the imagination and represent the fictional component that is an essential part of love's value. This explains why Montaigne invokes the name of Virgil in the very title of his essay—an allusive title but in fact related to a central theme of the piece:

> (B) Whoever takes away from the Muses their amorous fancies will rob them of the best subject they have and the noblest matter of their work. And whoever makes Love lose the communication and service of poetry will disarm him of his best weapons. . . . Dried out and weighed down as I am, I still feel some tepid remains of that past ardor. . . . But from what I un-

derstand of it, the powers and worth of this god are more alive and animated in the painting of poetry than in their own reality,

> And verses have their fingers to excite.
> —Juvenal

Poetry reproduces an indefinable mood that is more amorous than love itself. Venus is not so beautiful all naked alive and panting, as she is here in Virgil:

> The goddess ceased to speak, and snowy arms outflung
> Around him flattering, soft fondling as she clung.

This admirable erotic passage from Virgil is not only literature, it is also a conversation of husband and wife ("the goddess ceased to speak . . . he spoke"). The body's burning heat and ensuing languor are mixed in with a *conversation*. The images of ardor are interpolated between the poetic representation of an exchange of words between husband and wife and an evocation of the thunderbolt that rends and illuminates as it descends from heaven. The flame of love that passes through the body of the goddess is portrayed as both the consequence of a linguistic act and as something resembling a natural phenomenon. If, as Juvenal says in a line cited earlier by Montaigne, verses have fingers, the reason is that words made flesh can penetrate the body, and this "painting" of love can surpass "love itself." Earlier Montaigne seemed critical of the prohibitions that prevent us from "chastising" the "sexual act" except "roundaboutly and figuratively." Now, however, he expresses his preference for what the "painting of poetry" has to tell us about love. What is more, after adding to the passage from Virgil (which depicts the loves of Venus and Vulcan) a fine passage from Lucretius concerning the loves of Venus and Mars, he praises both authors for not saying all that might be said about the act of love. This painting that he ranks higher than the reality of love itself owes its superiority to what remains hidden, to what entices the imagination without violating the disguise that love cannot do without. The ellipsis *shows* more than it conceals. . . . The power of love poetry to surpass love itself and to produce, as does the verse of Lucretius and Virgil, "an indefinable mood more amorous than love itself," is linked to the *reserve* that contrives to give us a fuller image of Venus by keeping her veiled, by not saying all that might be said about her. The language of love, which Montaigne accuses his contemporaries of concealing beneath a facade of hypocritical prudishness, turns out to derive its power from the fact that it is itself a language that *conceals* and that uses the heightening power of chiaroscuro to capture the imagination. In love our feelings are so full that they need an object whose final secret seems to elude our grasp. Montaigne sees this language, which arouses love by feigning reticence, as having the virtue of "presence." He discovers in it not only the presence of thought but also the presence of the body: the words in true poetry are not mere "conceits" or "verbal tricks." When he "ruminates" upon the syllables of Lucretius or Virgil, he feels that "their language is *all full and copious with a natural and constant vigor*. They are all epigram, not only the tail but the head, stomach, and feet. . . . This painting is the result not so much of manual dexterity as of having *the object more vividly imprinted in the soul*." This is also the case with Horace, who "sees more clearly and deeply into the *thing*." In the amorous scenes of Virgil and Lucretius, even though these deal with mythical subjects, "the sense illuminates and brings out the words, which are no longer wind, but flesh and bond. The words mean more than they say." If Montaigne is right, the power of *incarnation* and sexualization that language has is indistinguishable from the *excess* of meaning that surrounds each word like an aura and thus bridges the gap that Montaigne believes generally separates the word (mere "wind" that it is) from the thing. (**"Of glory"** begins: "There is the name and the thing.")

Montaigne, whose work is in so many ways comparable to mannerist art, is critical of poetry that cultivates "mannerism," in its primary sense of "manual dexterity"; of such poetry only the wind remains. Against poets who rely on "conceits" and epigrammatic "tails" he protests: "If I were of the profession, I would naturalize art as much as they artify nature." But so much art is needed to give life to amorous conversation! The poetry that best expresses love is that whose words are invested with meaning ("the sense that illuminates and brings out the words"), that which makes itself "flesh and bone" by *meaning* more than it actually *says,* that which adds to physical love something more, the veil that transfigures the reality. The same transformation that enables words to mean more than they say also enables love that is attended by the Muses to transcend the very "essence" of love. Now, as we saw a moment ago, this addition is, paradoxically, the result of an impediment (the veil or mask or detour) that *culture* places between our desire and the *natural* satisfaction that is its goal. This accounts for the praise—rather surprising in any enemy of deception—that Montaigne here bestows on fraud and illusion, which he sees as stratagems of modesty or coquetry that keep hope in a state of breathlessness: "Let us teach the ladies to make the most of themselves, to respect themselves, to beguile and fool us." The duration of desire (and the pleasure associated with it) is increased by delay of the final conquest. . . . We must proceed in love as in a labyrinth. Love must be enhanced if it is to transcend the disappointing brevity of physical pleasure: therein lies the need for poetic *discourse,* for a tour through the galleries of the metaphorical palace.

Montaigne prefers his love with a dash of fiction because he knows all too well what the "act" is worth when reduced to its simple physical reality. All that survives is the temporary, but constantly renewed, heat of passion. In a passage of the **"Apology for Raymond Sebond"** Montaigne seems to foreshadow the theory proposed by Freud in *Beyond the Pleasure Principle,* that desire seeks only to quell some "pain," to be "assuaged" and "set at rest":

> (A) For that very tickling and sting that is found in certain pleasures and seems to raise us above simple health and absence of pain, that active, stirring, and somehow or other burning and biting voluptuousness, even that itself points only to freedom from pain as its goal. The appetite that sweeps us away into intercourse with women seeks only to drive out the pain that ardent and furious desire brings us, and asks only to assuage it and to be set at rest and exempted from this fever.

But the pursuit of rest is ever restless. "There is no passion more pressing than this." Through a sequence that Montaigne's sentence seeks to imitate, love can never settle permanently for one object: "It is contrary to the nature of love if it is not violent and contrary to the nature of violence if it is constant." Even in its physical aspect it is a "frantic desire for what flees from us." Unlike the beasts, however, man is not concerned solely with physical satisfaction; a component of imagination always enters into his pleasure: "It is not simply a bodily passion. . . . It still lives after satiety; no constant satisfaction or end can be prescribed to it, for it always goes beyond its possession." Of course, knowledge of love's excesses requires no familiarity with books and poets. If Montaigne attributes

insatiable sexual appetites to women, it is not so much out of misogyny as out of desire to emphasize the contrast between the chastity imposed upon woman and the reality of the desire that torments them just as much as it torments men: "There is not a word, not an example, not a trick that they do not know better than our books: it is a teaching that is born in their veins. . . . The whole movement of the world resolves itself into and leads to this coupling. It is a matter infused throughout, it is a center to which all things look." Ubiquitous and irresistible, sexuality, as soon as one takes away the share of "fancy" and the value attached by culture, can be seen to be nothing more than a natural function, an "insipid pleasure." The exaltation of love in Neo-platonic thought (known to Montaigne through Marsilio Ficino, Bembo, Leon Ebreo, and Equicola) requires the corrective of medical knowledge, which ever since antiquity had held, as in the writings of Hippocrates and Galen, that love is simply one form of "evacuation" among others: "Now then, *leaving books aside* and speaking more materially and simply, I find after all that love is nothing else but the thirst for sexual enjoyment in a desired object, and Venus nothing else but the pleasure of discharging our vessels—a pleasure which becomes vicious either by immoderation or by indiscretion." What a gap between love reduced to its material expression and the exalted image of it presented in books! What are we to think of that gap? To begin with, we must agree with Plato, who held that physical pleasure is a humiliating affliction that reduces us to the level of the beasts:

> (B) I believe that (C) what Plato says is true, that (B) man is the plaything of the gods . . . and that it was in mockery that nature left us the most confused of our actions to be the most common, in order thereby to make us all equal and to put on the same level the fools and the wise, and us and the beasts. . . . Truly it is a mark not only of our original corruption but also of our inanity and deformity.

But this reference to Plato and to the Christian dogma of the Fall makes only a brief appearance, in the midst of a denigrating commentary. What can be reduced to nature soon finds full justification in nature itself. The reader of the **"Apology for Raymond Sebond"** knows full well that the behavior of animals sometimes reveals a wisdom deeper than man's: what puts us on the same level as the beasts therefore does not degrade us. Montaigne's text continues, particularly in its later additions, in the form of a plea on behalf of the physical aspects of love:

> (B) On the one hand Nature pushes us on to it, having attached to this desire the most noble, useful, and pleasant of all her operations; and on the other hand she lets us accuse and shun it as shameless and indecent, blush at it, and recommend abstinence. (C) Are we not brutes to call brutish the operation that makes us? . . . we regard our being as vice.

Since Montaigne has previously located what is best in love in the words of the poets—in the *verses* of Virgil and Lucretius—his assent here to the physicality of sexual life might lead us to believe that he has now accommodated himself to the coexistence of opposites, to the persistence of antinomy. But as we continue our reading, we find that it is the acceptance of physical pleasure in its materiality and universality that brings Montaigne back to the "verses of these two poets" and that leads him on to develop his praise of imagination, reserve, and the seduction ritual, the importance of which we have already seen. For physical pleasure, reduced simply to what the body experiences, is brief and fleeting. In making this point, Montaigne slips in a personal confidence:

(B) I don't know who it was in ancient times who wanted his throat as long as a crane's neck so as to relish longer what he swallowed. That wish is more appropriate in this quick and precipitate pleasure, especially for such natures as mine, for I have the failing of being too sudden. In order to arrest its *flight* and prolong it in preambles, everything among them serves as a favor and a recompense: a glance, a bow, a word, a sign. . . . This is a passion that with *very little solid essence* mixes in much more vanity and feverish dreams: it should be satisfied and act accordingly.

This is the route that leads to rehabilitation of appearances. The reader will recall that this chapter, like so many others, begins with a critique of dissimulation: silence surrounds matters of love, which no one dares to name. Still, in the hands of those who use it most effectively, the language of love preserves some shadows and slips a gossamer veil back over things. Shall we snatch away this veil and accept love as nature has made it? Certainly. But desire, with its "very little solid essence," is fugitive and hard to seize; and if its essence eludes us, our faulty grasp is this time not to blame, for insubstantiality is indeed the reality of physical pleasure. Whoever wants to "halts its flight" must call upon vanity, "deception," "gradation," and that "languor in dispensation" with which the ladies grant their "favors." Accordingly, Montaigne, even though he is an enemy of appearances, does not hesitate to advise women to use duplicity, to accept their lovers even as they play out the comedy of chastity: "So I counsel them abstinence, as I do to us; but if this generation is too hostile to it, at least discretion and modesty. . . . If she will not keep her conscience clear, let her keep her name clear; if the substance is not worth much, let *the appearance be preserved.*" To be sure, the appearance that Montaigne here approves is deliberate appearance, shorn of naïvete, appearance that dupes no one: a lady's name, worthless though it is, is nevertheless worthy of protection. (pp. 190-96)

Jean Starobinski, in his Montaigne in Motion, *translated by Arthur Goldhammer, The University of Chicago Press, 1985, pp. 185-213.*

MARK HALL (essay date 1984)

[*In the following excerpt, Hall examines* The Journal of Montaigne's Travels *as "a rare and raw portrait of a great man in his most human form."*]

[Michel de Montaigne's *Travel Journal*] was not written to edify the fireside reader, inspire the adventurous, or educate the provincials back home. It is in fact not an intentionally written work; rather, it is a splendid accident of literary history.

The *Journal* . . . was written by two men. The chronicle begins in the hand of Montaigne's unnamed secretary, who . . . is under the direction of his employer. For more than half the book we are treated to his anonymous and clever observations of M. Montaigne's journey. This abruptly changes when Montaigne's first person informs us: "Having dismissed one of my men who was doing this fine job, and seeing it so far advanced, whatever trouble it may be to me, I must continue it myself." He does so in Italian, then later he changes to French, his native language.

This complexity gives the work both its distinctive and appealing qualities, as well as its disconcerting and tiresome moments. There are delightful anecdotes, abundant in the sec-

retary's portion, and asphyxiating details of the costs of everything, interesting only to those of us with an intimate understanding of the economics of the Reformation era. There are sections of great intellectual force and others of rambling, useless moaning.

While reading the latter part of the work in Montaigne's words, we are given nauseating and tedious details of the poor man's discomfort. His unrelenting pain spills onto the pages with the frenzy of a man possessed. It is this same suffering, however, that brings him to his rational Stoicism, his insightful perspective on the human condition. "And in the meantime," he writes, "it will be wise to accept joyously the good that it pleases God to send us. There is no other medicine, no other rule of science, for avoiding the ills, whatever they may be and however great, that beseige men from all sides and at every hour, than to make up our minds to suffer them humanly, or to end them courageously and promptly."

Montaigne is the true thinker. His literate secretary cannot match the quality of his master. Still, this unknown writer offers us more insight into the compulsiveness of his boss and the compellingness of the countryside.

We know from the secretary that Montaigne endured extreme conditions in his urinary and bowel functions. In fact, the trip is being taken in large part to allow Montaigne to take a "cure" through the baths and waters of France, Switzerland, Germany, and Italy. We also witness the abandon at which the great essayist throws himself into the cure. If one bath calls for drinking "seven pounds of water" every morning, so be it. If another demands that a man sit in sulphur-smelling water for eight hours, Montaigne would comply. To relieve his agony, Montaigne would go to the greatest of lengths.

The secretary is at his best, however, when he relates the stories told to him by the local population. From him we learn of the sexual ambiguity of some 16th-century peasant girls. Having just entered Vitry-le-Francois early on in the journey, the travellers have just missed the execution of a girl who "was hanged for using illicit devices to supply her defect in sex." We can infer, then, that pretending to be a man in Montaigne's sexist society was a capital offense. Compounding this "crime" was the fact that "for four or five months" the girl had been married to another young woman from Vitry "to her satisfaction, so they say." Had the girl renounced her behavior, the locals would have probably spared her life. But she refused and so died by the hangman's rope.

Neither Montaigne nor his ghost writer are prudes. The story is related without any moral condemnation for the girl or the people who put her to death. To these travellers, sex seems to be a normal and pleasurable part of man's meagre lot in life. Montaigne says, "the greatest pleasure is derived . . . to see the ladies at the windows . . . who show themselves how they tantalize our eyes as they do," as he recalls his walks through the Italian cities. Sex, like his health, was a part of life. It existed in all manner and form. It was a subject as fascinating as any other, no more, no less.

The book, lively and anecdotal as it is, was not intended for publication and suffers from lack of focus. There are passages that serve no purpose other than as a release for Montaigne's continual and horrible pain. *Travel Journal* is a rare and raw portrait of a great man in his most human form. (pp. 23, 26)

Mark Hall, "The Unintentional Book: Michel de Montaigne's 'Travel Journal,'" in San Francisco Review of Books, *Spring, 1984, pp. 23, 26.*

ELAINE LIMBRICK   (essay date 1984)

[In the following excerpt, Limbrick elucidates Montaigne's theological position in "Apology for Raimond Sebond."]

> . . . for the paradox is the source of the thinker's passion, and the thinker without a paradox is like a lover without feeling: a paltry mediocrity.
>
> S. Kierkegaard, *Philosophical Fragments*

Kierkegaard's words are deeply relevant to Montaigne's **"Apologie de Raimond Sebond,"** the longest, the most controversial and the most complex of the *Essais*. In considering the **"Apologie"** as a series of paradoxes, reflecting both the philosophical and literary trends of the day, we may be able to arrive at a more just appreciation of this seminal chapter in the *Essais* and of its philosophical heritage.

We are told by Montaigne himself that his father asked him to translate from the Latin the *Book of Creatures, or Natural Theology* of the fifteenth century theologian Raymond Sibiude who was professor of medicine, of philosophy, and of theology at the University of Toulouse. Although, as the title of Montaigne's essay would seem to indicate, it purports to be an apology, a defence of Sebond, the title **"Apologie"** is paradoxical for it is, in fact, an attack upon the basic premises of natural theology. By natural theology we understand the attempt to demonstrate rationally the existence of God. Christian philosophers, following in the footsteps of St. Thomas Aquinas, had tried to bridge the gap between faith and reason by constructing a theology based on pure reason, God being the absolute norm of perfection and the highest principle of being. However, this rational theology, strongly influenced by Aristotle, was replaced in the writings of the Nominalists and the mystics by an "affective theology," Augustinian in origin, and in which the role of faith, not intellect, was of prime importance. We hope to show in this brief study that the conflict between reason and faith, faith and doubt in the **"Apologie de Raimond Sebond"** is largely due to this scholastic inheritance. . . . (p. 75)

Just as St. Anselm's famous *Monologion* is an example of a meditation upon the rationality of faith, so the **"Apologie de Raimond Sebond"** is an example of a meditation upon the irrationality of faith. Both are soliloquies which introduce us to a mind which searches while reasoning, while disputing with itself in the Socratic manner. Rosalie Colie in her book *Paradoxia Epidemica* has called the **"Apologie"** "a complicated piece of paradoxy: it denies its expressed aim, since it does not defend but destroys the position Sebond held; it calls into question, for good and all, the Renaissance praise of man, of human dignity, and of human reason, thus running strikingly counter to 'received opinion.'" We agree entirely with this summary of the major themes in the **"Aoplogie"** and view the essay as an attempt to come to terms with both a theological and philosophical problem, summed up in Kirkegaard's statement that "The supreme paradox of all thought is the attempt to discover something that thought cannot think." In other words, Montaigne was trying to reconcile the existence of God with the demands of natural reason. In order to continue to believe he had to deny the validity of a natural theology such as the one propounded by Sebond. This meant denying also the humanist belief which the words of the Greek sophist Protagoras so aptly summarize: "man is the measure of all things, of things which are that they are, and of what is not, that it is not." Montaigne's conclusion was to be that of Plato and St. Augustine: God is the measure of all things. Since God, however, for Montaigne, is the Unknown, he found himself in the

same metaphysical dilemma as Kierkegaard later. "The paradoxical passion of the Reason thus comes repeatedly into collision with this Unknown, which does indeed exist, but is unknown, and in so far does not exist. The Reason cannot advance beyond this point, and yet it cannot refrain in its paradoxicalness from arriving at this limit and occupying itself therewith."

This metaphysical crotchet, as Kierkegaard calls it, lies at the heart of the sceptic's dilemma: in order to believe he must suspend reason. . . . In essence this is the central pivot of the **"Apologie de Raimond Sebond."** . . . (p. 76)

The major paradox of the **"Apologie"** is that scepticism leads to faith, for Pyrrhonian scepticism allows man to become "a white sheet prepared to take from the finger of God what form soever it shall please him to imprint therein." Although Montaigne praises Sebond's intention in wishing "by humane and naturall reasons, to establish and verifie all the articles of Christian religion against Atheists," he quickly notes the first charge to be laid against such a rational theology: "that Christians wrong themselves much, in that they ground their beleefe upon humane reasons, which is conceived but by faith, and by a particular inspiration of God." At first Montaigne says this shows excessive zeal of piety but then goes on himself to declare: "It is faith onely, which lively and assuredly embraceth the high mysteries of our Religion." (p. 77)

The first paradox, or series of paradoxes, that Montaigne employs in combatting the enemies of the faith is that "all our wisdome is but folly before God; that of all vanities, man is the greatest; that man who presumeth of his knowledge, doth not yet know what knowledge is: and that man, who is nothing, if he but thinke to be something, seduceth and deceiveth himself?" These quotations from the Bible seem to destroy man's pride in his intellectual powers and thereby his essential dignity and place in the scale of being. (p. 79)

Montaigne's chastisement of man's presumption, since he is "Of all creatures . . . the most miserable and fraile, and therewithall the proudest and disdainfullest" leads him naturally into the consideration of another paradox, the superority of beasts over man. Nature has denied man the natural sufficiency of brute beasts "So that their brutish stupidity doth in all commodities exceed, whatsoever our divine intelligence can effect." The next forty pages or so of the **"Apologie"** expound the doctrine of theriophily and most of Montaigne's examples are taken wholesale from Plutarch's treatise on the cleverness of animals. George Boas in his fascinating study, *The happy beast in French thought of the seventeenth century,* was one of the first to point out that Montaigne's love of paradox made him apparently defend the back to nature movement. (pp. 79-80)

The last paradox we wish to consider in the **"Apologie"** is the paradox of a "learned ignorance." The doctrine of "learned ignorance," although Socratic in origin, and this is a major theme in the *Essais* as a whole, became incorporated into Christian mystical thought chiefly through the writings of St. Augustine, the Neoplatonists and mediaeval mystics. Dionysius the Areopagite is the patriarch of this particular movement of thought and his mysterious theology was based on the paradox of God = Being = Non-Being. Consequently the attributes of God are arrived at by the path of negation. Montaigne became acquainted with these ideas upon reading the works of Nicolas of Cusa, and, in particular, the *De docta ignorantia*. The Infinite, Cusa concludes, is unknown to us and all the names we give to God bear no relation to His nature so that a negative theology would seem the necessary corrective. Faith above all is the necessary condition for seeing God. In his *Apologia Doctae Ignorantiae* Cusa assimilates learned ignorance with mystical theology. He maintains a series of paradoxes on the nature of God: he is both Maximum and Minimum, exists necessarily because in Him non-being coincides with being, and because to say that God does not exist is to affirm at the same time His existence. All of these ideas we find in the **"Apologie"** and also in Montaigne's borrowings from St. Augustine, who inspired Cusa's title. (p. 80)

The concept of God which emerges from the **"Apologie"** is one which emphasizes the incomprehensibility and inaccessibility of God. Montaigne, like many of his contemporaries, prefers to think of God in abstract terms and approves of the Athenians dedicating their temple to the "Unknown God" and finds that Pythagoras' definition is even nearer the truth, for God was nothing else "but the extreme endeavour of our imagination toward perfection, every one amplifying the Idea thereof according to his capacitie." Indeed, it would seem that Montaigne, like St. Augustine before him, assimilates the Christian God with the Platonic God. The final pages of the **"Apologie"** are extremely ambiguous, for Montaigne quotes mainly from Plutarch's treatise *The E at Delphi*, as well as from the *Timaeus* and *Theaetetus* of Plato. He concludes "that only God is, not according to any measure of time, but according to an immoveable and immutable eternity, not measured by time, nor subject to any declination, before whom nothing is, nor nothing shall be after, nor more new or more recent, but one really being: which by one onely Now or Present, filleth the Ever and there is nothing that truly is but he alone." The Platonic definition of God as "that which is, which is" becomes merged with the definition given to Moses in Exodus of "He who is." Doubt must give way to faith and this depends upon God's grace. (p. 81)

> Elaine Limbrick, *"The Paradox of Faith and Doubt in Montaigne's 'Apologie de Raimond Sebond',"* in Wascana Review, *Vol. 9, No. 1, Spring, 1984, pp. 75-84.*

ADDITIONAL BIBLIOGRAPHY

Beaujour, Michel. "Speculum, Method, and Self-Portrayal: Some Epistemological Problems." In *Mimesis: From Mirror to Method, Augustine to Descartes,* edited by John D. Lyons and Stephen G. Nichols, Jr., pp. 188-96. Hanover, N.H.: University Press of New England, 1982.
> Examination of *The Essays* within the context of the Aristotelian "rhetorical-logical" literary form.

Boase, Alan M. *The Fortunes of Montaigne: A History of the "Essays" in France, 1580-1669.* London: Metheun & Co., 1935, 462 p.
> Exhaustive examination of the influence of *The Essays* on "the development of Humanism as opposed to orthodox Christianity."

Bowen, Barbara C. "Montaigne and the Art of Bluff." In her *The Age of Bluff: Paradox and Ambiguity in Rabelais and Montaigne,* pp. 103-61. Urbana: University of Illinois Press, 1972.
> Argues that *The Essays* is "composed of deliberate untruth, ambiguity, irony, paradox, and contradictions."

Burke, Peter. *Montaigne.* New York: Hill and Wang, 1981, 81 p.
> Contains brief treatments of various aspects of Montaigne's work, including his humanism, his skepticism, and his aesthetics.

Cairns, Huntington; Tate, Allen; and Van Doren, Mark. "Michel Eyquem de Montaigne, *Essays.*" In their *Invitation to Learning,* pp. 68-81. New York: New Home Library, 1941.
> Transcript of a radio broadcast. The critics, joined by guest Marvin Lowenthal, offer general conversation concerning Montaigne.

Chambers, Frank M. "Pascal's Montaigne." *PMLA* LXV, No. 5 (September 1950): 790-804.
> Attempts to reconcile Blaise Pascal's "double attitude" toward Montaigne, concluding that for all Pascal's avowed dislike of his predecessor, "Montaigne served Pascal somewhat as Virgil served Dante in the *Divine Comedy.*"

Compayré, Gabriel. *Montaigne and Education of the Judgment.* Translated by J. E. Mansion, 1908. Reprint. New York: Burt Franklin, 1971, 139 p.
> Study of Montaigne concentrating on the progressive theories of education outlined in *The Essays.*

Connolly, Cyril. "Montaigne." In his *Previous Convictions,* pp. 124-27. London: Hamish Hamilton, 1963.
> General remarks on *The Essays.*

De Lutri, Joseph R. "Montaigne on the Noble Savage: A Shift in Perspective." *The French Review* XLIX, No. 2 (December 1975): 206-11.
> Considers how Montaigne's attitude toward the concept of the noble savage varies in "Of Cannibals" and "Of Coaches." De Lutri contends that the difference constitutes a "quasi-evolutionary statement."

Doucette, Clarice M. "Discovery and Celebration of Self in Montaigne and Whitman." *Walt Whitman Review* 27, No. 2 (June 1981): 62-70.
> Notes similarities between Montaigne's and Walt Whitman's conceptions of the self and its place in art.

Frame, Donald M. *Montaigne: A Biography.* San Francisco: North Point Press, 1984, 408 p.
> Reprint of Frame's 1965 standard biography of Montaigne. Frame states that his intention is "to make this a scholarly and readable biography; scholarly in presenting the evidence . . . ; readable in making the scholarly apparatus unobtrusive."

Gosse, Edmund. "Montaigne." In his *Leaves and Fruit,* pp. 11-20. London: William Heinemann, 1927.
> Favorable general observations about Montaigne.

Gray, Floyd. "The Unity of Montaigne in the *Essais.*" *Modern Language Quarterly* XXII (1961): 79-86.
> Examines Montaigne's personal evolution in thought as it relates to the development of *The Essays.*

Greenberg, Mitchell. "Montaigne at the Crossroads: Textual Conundrums in the *Essais.*" In his *Detours of Desire: Readings in the French Baroque,* pp. 41-59. Columbus: Ohio State University Press, 1984.
> Psychological interpretation of *The Essays.* Greenberg contends that Montaigne "is driven to writing in order to reproduce and capture the echo of masculine presence, and this writing in return becomes for him an act of potency. The echo Montaigne hears in his writing is always attached to, is the trace of, the Father."

Grimsley, Ronald. "Kierkegaard and Montaigne." In his *Søren Kierkegaard and French Literature: Eight Comparative Studies,* pp. 64-72. Cardiff: University of Wales Press, 1966.
> Traces Montaigne's influence on the thought of Søren Kierkegaard.

Heck, Francis S. "Montaigne's Conservatism and Liberalism: A Paradox?" *The Romanic Review* LXVI, No. 3 (May 1975): 165-71.
> Addresses the question of contradictions between Montaigne's political affiliation and his political beliefs.

Holyoake, S. John. "How to Read Montaigne." *Kentucky Romance Quarterly* XIX, No. 3 (1972): 337-45.
> Proposes explanations for inconsistencies in Montaigne's ideas. Holyoake cites and defines four main reasons for Montaigne's inconsistency: impressibility, fascination with ideas, irresolution, and auto-suggestion.

Insdorf, Cecile. *Montaigne and Feminism*. Chapel Hill: North Carolina Studies in the Romance Languages and Literatures, 1977, 102 p.

Studies of Montaigne's attitude toward women. The book includes a historical overview of the role of women as well as biographical elements illuminating Montaigne's personal relationships with women.

Keller, Abraham C. "Montaigne on the Dignity of Man." *PMLA* LXXII, No. 1 (March, 1957): 43-54.

Examines Montaigne's conception of the innate worth of humanity, comparing the essayist's views with contemporary Renaissance thought.

Kellerman, Frederick. "The *Essais* and Socrates." *Symposium* X, No. 1 (Spring 1956): 204-16.

Indicates the importance of Montaigne's references to Socrates in *The Essays*.

Le Charité, Raymond C., ed. *O un Amy! Essays on Montaigne in Honor of Donald M. Frame*. Lexington, Ky.: French Forum, 1977, 341 p.

Collection of essays on Montaigne in French and English. Among the contributions are R. A. Sayce's appraisal of *The Journal of Montaigne's Travels* and Philip P. Hallie's discussion of "Of Cruelty."

Lehrmann, Charles C. "Toward the Formation of the Classical Spirit: Montaigne." In his *The Jewish Element in French Literature*, translated by George Klin, pp. 69-75. Rutherford, N.J.: Fairleigh Dickinson University Press, 1971.

Briefly traces the influences of Jewish thought and tradition on Montaigne's philosophy.

MacCarthy, Desmond. "The Essays of Montaigne." In his *Experience*, pp. 3-8. 1935. Reprint. New York: Books for Libraries Press, 1968.

General study of *The Essays*.

Marchand, Ernest. "Montaigne and the Cult of Ignorance." *The Romanic Review* XXXVI, No. 4 (December 1945): 275-82.

Includes comments on Montaigne's thoughts on education and intellectualism.

McKinley, Mary B. "The *City of God* and the City of Man: Limits of Language in Montaigne's 'Apologie'." *The Romanic Review* LXXI, No. 2 (March 1980): 122-40.

Compares "The Apology for Raymond Sebond" with Augustine's *The City of God* in an examination of Montaigne's articulation of divinity. McKinley concludes that "Montaigne in the *Essais* renounces the Augustinian aspiration to the divine realm of silence and affirms the secular world of words."

Norton, Glyn P. *Montaigne and the Introspective Mind*. The Hague: Mouton, 1975, 219 p.

Comprehensive study of Montaigne's literary introspection.

Ornstein, Robert. "Donne, Montaigne, and Natural Law." *The Journal of English and Germanic Philology* LV, No. 2 (April 1956): 213-29.

Chronicles the development of the concept of a natural ethical law, to ascertain how and to what extent the views of Montaigne and John Donne conformed to this philosophical tradition.

Paulson, Michael G. "Montaigne and Corneille: Creators of the French Cinna." *North Dakota Quarterly* 46, No. 2 (Spring 1978): 38-46.

Notes similarities between Pierre Corneille's *Cinna ou la Clémence d'Auguste* and Montaigne's essay "By Diverse Means We Arrive at the Same End," recognizing the source of both as Seneca's *De clementia*, but maintaining that "Corneille consciously borrowed . . . from Montaigne's essay . . . [and] adapted it to the seventeenth-century stage requirements."

Saintsbury, George. "Montaigne and Florio." In his *Last Vintage: Essays and Papers*, edited by John W. Oliver, Arthur Melville Clark, and Augustus Muir, pp. 128-35. London: Methuen & Co. 1950.

Reprint of an 1892 essay. Saintsbury assesses John Florio's 1603 translation of *The Essays* and concludes with remarks on Montaigne's writing.

Scodel, Joshua. "The Affirmation of Paradox: A Reading of Montaigne's 'De la Phisionomie'." *Yale French Studies* No. 64 (1983): 209-37.

Close reading of the essay, which Scodel characterizes as "Montaigne's acceptance of the paradoxes inherent in the human condition."

Screech, M. A. *Montaigne and Melancholy: The Wisdom of the "Essays."* Selinsgrove, Pa.: Susquehanna University Press, 1984, 194 p.

Consideration of melancholy and its effect on Montaigne.

Sherman, Stuart. "An American Version of Montaigne." In his *The Main Stream*, pp. 226-39. New York: Charles Scribner's Sons, 1927.

Favorable assessment of Montaigne in which Sherman surveys several of "Saint Michel's" individual essays.

Stevens, Linton C. "The Meaning of 'Philosophie' in the *Essais* of Montaigne." *Studies in Philology* LXII, (1965): 147-54.

Explains what Montaigne intended by the word "philosophie" in *The Essays*. Stevens compares Montaigne's concept of the term with its customary usage during the Renaissance, concluding that while Montaigne used the word in several ways, his use of it is, "for the most part, firmly rooted in classical tradition."

Stone, Donald, Jr. "Montaigne Reads Montaigne." *Modern Language Review* 80, No. 4 (October 1985): 802-09.

Makes extensive use of the evidence of textual revision to explicate "Of Cruelty" in terms of a "tripartite hierarchy of reason, nature, and virtue."

Taylor, George Coffin. *Shakespeare's Debt to Montaigne*. New York: Phaeton Press, 1968, 66 p.

Exhaustive study of Montaigne's influence on William Shakespeare. To prove his contention that the dramatist was "profoundly and extensively influenced by Montaigne, definitely influenced in regard to vocabulary, phrases, short and long passages, and after a fashion, influenced also in thought" by Montaigne, Taylor juxtaposes excerpts from Shakespeare's plays with passages from *The Essays*.

Vacca, Carlo. "A Modern Inquiry into the Educational Ideas of Montaigne." *The Modern Language Journal* XXXIX, No. 6 (October 1955): 314-16.

Enumerates points of contact between Montaigne's thoughts on education and modern educational theory.

Hallgrímur Pétursson

1614-1674

(Also transliterated as Hallgrim; also Pjetursson) Icelandic hymn writer and poet.

Pétursson is acclaimed for his vital legacy of spiritual verse, which remains unsurpassed in his nation. His masterpiece is *Fimmtíu passíusálmar* (*Passion Hymns*), a collection of fifty devotional lyric poems derived from the story of Christ's Passion. This work—which Sigurbjörn Einarsson has called "a pinnacle among the heights of the Christian literature of the world"—is so engrained in Icelandic Lutheran-Christian life that Pétursson's name is synonymous with sacred poetry and traditional hymnology in his native country. He is also respected, but much less known, for his secular poems, which include elegies, light verse, and *rímur* (Old Icelandic ballad cycles).

Pétursson was born in 1614 into a poor Lutheran family. Scholars are uncertain of his birthplace but know that he received his early education at Holár. For unknown reasons (it is posited that he was expelled from school for misbehavior), Pétursson left his homeland for Denmark at a young age, becoming a blacksmith's apprentice in Copenhagen. There he was purportedly discovered by fellow Icelander Brynjólfur Sveinsson, who, sensing the boy's potential, arranged for him to study theology at Frúar Skóli, a noted Copenhagen school. Pétursson remained there from 1632 until 1636 or 1637, when he was enlisted as a religious tutor to a group of recently freed Icelanders returning home via Copenhagen after being held captive for ten years by Algerian pirates. Falling in love with one of the former captives, Gudrídur Símonardóttir, Pétursson abandoned his studies to return with her to Iceland, where they married. For the next seven years, Pétursson lived in near poverty, supporting himself and his growing family through menial jobs and fishing. In 1644, he was again aided by his former benefactor Sveinsson, now a prominent bishop, who ordained him as pastor of the parish of Hvalsnes. Thereafter, Pétursson gradually rose in prominence, particularly after his assumption of parish duties at Saurbær in Hvalfjördur in 1651. It was here that he composed his *Passion Hymns,* a work joyously welcomed by the late-Reformation Icelandic congregations upon its publication in 1666. Afflicted with leprosy during the last years of his life, Pétursson died at age sixty: honored as a preacher and revered as a poet.

Over sixty editions of *Passion Hymns* have appeared since 1666, attesting to the enduring importance of Pétursson's work to the Icelandic religious community. As C. Venn Pilcher wrote in 1913: "He raised, as it were, a mighty crucifix of song over Iceland, and thither, for nearly two centuries and a half, the weary and the heavy laden have turned their eyes. He sang the theme of the ages, and his song has become immortal." Based partially on the German writer Martin Möller's *Soliloquia de passione Jesu Christi* (1587), *Passion Hymns* traces Christ's last days from his entrance into the Garden of Gethsemane to his crucifixion and entombment. The Rev. Jakob Jónsson has pointed out that each hymn resembles a sermon in form. Prefaced by a paraphrase of biblical text, each then expands the given theme in a meditative interpretation or prayerful paean containing moral and social implications for the individual believer; for, as critics have remarked, Pétursson sought to link Christ's Passion to the individual's intimate, personal experience of life and faith. Although the religious message of *Passion Hymns* is overtly didactic—"irritatingly" so, according to Pilcher—prevailing critical opinion holds that the work transcends this flaw, distinguished as the hymns are by eloquence, simplicity, emotional sincerity, and intensity.

Pétursson's other poetry—comprised of additional hymns on a wide variety of subjects as well as burlesques of Icelandic commonplaces, a number of epitaphs and elegies, and accomplished *rímur*—is less discussed but nonetheless esteemed for its metrical and linguistic skill. The hymn "Alt eins og blómstrid eina" ("Just Like the Tender Flower") is a classic of Icelandic Lutheran services. When, in an earthier vein, Pétursson focused his pen on everyday events, he produced what critics deem some of the best satirical, humorous, and occasional poems of the time.

Pétursson's reputation is firmly grounded, however, on his creation of spiritual hymns that still speak to the hearts of Icelanders. Although he remains obscure in world literature, Pétursson has had, as virtually all scholars of his work emphasize, a remarkable impact on his countrymen: *Passion Hymns* is a fixed component of Icelandic worship, language, and culture. The hymns are used as prayers and still frequently sung, particularly during Lent, and certain phrases have become Icelandic proverbial expressions. Einarsson has contended that the dominion of *Passion Hymns* in Icelandic religious culture is so great that Pétursson "has been the companion of every child of Iceland, from the cradle to the grave, for three centuries. His contribution to the religious life of the nation and its spiritual endurance in the hard days gone by can never be fully estimated."

PRINCIPAL WORKS

Fimmtíu passíusálmar (hymns) 1666
  [*Translations from the Hymns of Hallgrim Petursson* published in *The Passion-Hymns of Iceland: Being Translations from the Passion-Hymns of Hallgrim Petursson and from the Hymns of the Modern Icelandic Hymn Book* (partial translation), 1913; also published as *Icelandic Meditations on the Passion: Being Selections from the Passion-Hymns of Hallgrim Petursson Translated from the Icelandic and Arranged as a Series of Meditations for Each Day of the Month* (partial translation), 1923; and *Hymns of the Passion: Meditations on the Passion of Christ,* 1966]
Sálmar og kvæði. 2 vols. (hymns and poetry) 1887-90
Hallgrímur Pétursson. 2 vols. (hymns, poetry, and *rímur*) 1947

FREDERIK WINKEL HORN (essay date 1884)

[*In the following excerpt, Horn praises Pétursson's works, particularly his* Passion Hymns.]

[There arose during] the seventeenth century two men whose lives and works had a radical influence on the religious development and opinions of the Icelanders. One of them was the preacher and psalmist Hallgrim Pjetursson. . . . Though he is neither as voluminous nor inclined to soar on as lofty a poetic pinion as his great contemporary psalmists in Denmark and Sweden, still his works are of great value since they give the clearest revelations we have in a northern tongue of the spirit of the Reformation. This is particularly true of his fifty psalms [in *Passion Hymns*] which have the passion story for their theme, and which have in so remarkable a degree won the hearts of the Icelandic people that they have become one of the first necessities of every household. Thirty editions of this work have appeared. With fervent emotion the poet grasps in each part of the passion story its significance to the life of every Christian in relation to God, and his psalms are clothed in clear and stately language with phrases and figures here and there of startling originality and beauty. No less important was the preacher Jon Thorkelsson Vidalin (died 1720), whose works still rank very high and are much read by the people. His postil (family book of sermons), especially, can be found everywhere both among the rich and among the poor. In profound comprehension of the Bible, and in a faculty of reproducing its passages in such a manner that they illustrate and explain one another and thus touch the heart, in force of language and boldness of thought, and in deep insight into the conditions and wants of the human soul, these sermons of Vidalin are surpassed by few religious works. Pjetursson and Vidalin were followed by a long line of talented psalmists and preachers. The former made valuable contributions to the Icelandic psalm book, which is a splendid collection of Christian hymns, while the various religious views of the successive epochs are fully and uniquely recorded in a series of postils. (pp. 76-7)

In few countries in the whole world is the talent for poetry in the true sense of the word so universal as in Iceland, and nowhere else is the true poet so highly honored by his people as here. (p. 88)

A catalogue of modern Icelandic poets would embrace everybody who in any way has been conspicous in Iceland. On the one hand it is true that Iceland has not a single poet who has made poetry the chief avocation of his life, but on the other hand all the literary men of that island have also been poets. The psalmist Hallgrim Pjetursson . . . and the lyric poet Stefan Olafsson (1620-1688) must be considered the fathers of modern Icelandic poetry. . . . [The former is] one of the greatest psalmists that ever lived, and that not only in Iceland. . . . (p. 89)

Frederik Winkel Horn, "Modern Icelandic Literature," in his History of the Literature of the Scandinavian North from the Most Ancient Times to the Present, *translated by Ramus B. Anderson, revised edition, S. C. Griggs and Company, 1884, pp. 74-90.*

C. VENN PILCHER (essay date 1913)

[*In the following excerpt from the introduction to his English translation of a selection of Pétursson's work, Pilcher describes what he considers the character and greatness of* Passion Hymns.]

Nearly two hundred and fifty years ago, in a lonely Icelandic farm-house a leper lay dying. Outside the doors of the cottage Nature was lavish in her gifts of beauty. To the west the waters of the Whalefirth widened towards the Greenland Sea and the sunset. To the east they narrowed into a girdle of hill and fell, forming a land-locked bay, scene of exploits told in one of the Sagas of long ago. But within the cottage all was bare and comfortless. The membrane of the primitive window rattled in the autumn wind, while on the wooden locker-bed, built into the wall of the house, amidst the heart-breaking squalor of his disease, the leper lay dying. But look! his lips are moving, and, as we listen, we hear him pour forth in his beautiful language a hymn bright with the deathless hope of Christ's Gospel, glad with the assurance of a speedy release from the bondage of corruption into the glorious liberty of the children of God. It was the man's swan-song. Not long afterwards, by the quiet hand of death, he gained his heart's desire.

Such must have been, as in imagination we reconstruct the scene from the knowledge at our disposal, the passing of Hallgrim Petursson, the sacred singer of Iceland. It was a notable example of the victory of the spirit over the flesh, of the triumph of the Christian in his hour of deepest physical need. Small wonder that this was the man who out of his poverty left to his countrymen one of the most precious legacies which they have ever received—those *Passion-Hymns,* which Iceland hearts will cherish, as a poet of their own has said, "as long as the sun shines upon the cold Jokull." (pp. 3-4)

The *Passion-Hymns* are fifty in number. They tell the story of Christ's sufferings from the moment when the Master sang the Pascal Hymn with His disciples in the Upper Room until the military watch was set and the seal made fast upon His tomb. Each hymn consists, as a rule, of from fifteen to twenty stanzas. The poet begins by paraphrasing the biblical narrative of that incident in the Passion Story with which he is about to deal. He thus accomplishes what is achieved in Oratorio by the recitative. He then passes on to meditation, exhortation, prayer or praise. The hymns were written to be sung, generally speaking, to German chorales of the sixteenth century. With these tunes of stately dignity they naturally blend. To sing them to lighter modern airs would jar on the ear as a kind of sacrilege. In fact, to fully appreciate the hymns, it is necessary to hear them sung to these slow and majestic melodies from the times of Luther, which give free play and scope to the beauty of the Icelandic vowel sounds.

In former days it was the custom in the scattered farm-houses of Iceland to sing the *Passion-Hymns* through during Lent. This custom is still to some extent observed, as, for instance, in the chief Icelandic Church in Winnipeg. Nor can a better preparation for Good Friday, the "Long Fast Day," as it is called by the Icelanders, be well imagined. The practice however is not as universal as it was, partly owing to the indifference which pervades so much of the modern world, and partly through the prevalence of views in recent years, which, as an Icelandic clergyman has pointed out, "must make the *Passion-Hymns* of Hallgrim Petursson die upon the lips." It is however still true to say that this singer of the Cross is the outstanding poet of his people. His hymns have been called "The flower of all Icelandic poetry." He is still sung and quoted with reverence and with affection. He holds his position, we might almost say, as the Shakespeare or the Milton of his native land.

If we seek for the reasons for the spell which the *Passion-Hymns* have cast over the heart of Iceland for nearly two centuries and a half, we shall not have to look far for an answer. It is true that the range of thought is not wide, that the style is sometimes almost irritatingly didactic, and that the charm of colouring from nature through metaphor or simile is conspicuous only by its absence. The *Passion-Hymns* possess, however, one mighty secret. In exquisite Icelandic the poet dwells upon the benefits procured for sinful man by Christ's Passion. He isolates (and surely we may forgive him for doing so) each particular suffering which the Redeemer underwent, and shows the gain wrought for man thereby. Was Christ left alone in His hour of need? It was that we might never be forsaken. Was Christ clothed in a robe of mockery? It was that we might be arrayed in a robe of glory. Was Christ hounded to death with the cry of "Crucify Him?" It was that heaven and earth might over us call "peace." Were Christ's feet pierced? It was that the sins of our wayward feet might be forgiven. Was Christ's side, as Adam's, opened? It was that His Bride, the Church, in that healing stream of Water and of Blood, might be born. The Passion of Christ is the adoring poet's theme. Now in homely teaching, now in pathetic prayer, now in rapturous praise, he "placards" Christ Crucified before his countrymen. He raised, as it were, a mighty crucifix of song over Iceland, and thither, for nearly two centuries and a half, the weary and the heavy laden have turned their eyes. He sang the theme of the ages, and his song has become immortal.

Matthías Jochumsson, the leading poet of modern Iceland, has written a beautiful ode to commemorate the bicentenary of Hallgrim Petursson's death. He therein speaks of him as "the David of this land of Jokulls." He calls him a light "who lightened two centuries." He tells us that from the time when the child first says his prayers at his mother's knee, until the day when as an old man he turns him to his last sleep, it is Hallgrim's hymns which have power to soothe and to heal. And when Matthías Jochumsson is describing in another poem the passing of Gudbrand Vigfusson, the great Icelander of Oxford, he pictures him lying with the *Havamal* [a gnomic poem composed of Odin's sayings] at his head, *Heimskringla* [a classic Old Norse saga] at his breast, but the ***Passion-Hymns*** at his heart. That is their secret. The ***Passion-Hymns*** have spoken to the heart of Iceland. (pp. 9-12)

> C. Venn Pilcher, "Introduction: Hallgrim Petursson," in The Passion-Hymns of Iceland, *edited and translated by C. Venn Pilcher, Robert Scott, 1913, pp. 3-12.*

W. A. CRAIGIE   (essay date 1925)

[*In the following excerpt, Craigie affirms Pétursson's role as a preeminent religious poet of Iceland.*]

[Hallgrímur Pétursson] was essentially a religious poet, gifted with the power of expressing intense devotional feeling in warm and eloquent language. His fifty ***Passíusálmar,*** hymns on the Passion of Christ, are on such a level that they have been called 'the flower of Icelandic poetry ancient and modern'—an estimate which can only be fully understood by taking them as a whole and by realizing what they have meant to Iceland for more than two centuries and a half; during that time they have been printed in no less than forty-five editions. For as long a time the usual hymn sung at Icelandic funerals has been his **"Alt eins og blómstrið eina."** In comparison with these the secular poetry of Hallgrímur is of less note, though in itself of no small merit. Skill in the handling of metre, and rich knowledge of the poetic vocabulary, is clearly shown in such pieces as his **"Aldarháttur,"** in which the good old times are contrasted with the inferior present. (p. 335)

> W. A. Craigie, "The Poetry of Iceland: Introduction," *in* The Oxford Book of Scandinavian Verse: XVIIth Century—XXth Century, *edited by Sir Edmund Gosse and W. A. Craigie, Oxford at the Clarendon Press, Oxford, 1925, pp. 333-40.*

RICHARD BECK   (essay date 1938)

[*In the following excerpt, Beck notes Pétursson's achievement as both hymn writer and secular poet.*]

Two poets from the seventeenth century have a permanent place in Icelandic literature: the hymnologist Hallgrímur Pétursson . . . , who towers high above his contemporary writers of sacred songs, and Stefán Ólafsson (1620-88), also a clergyman, who was a very popular lyric poet, writing both on religious and secular subjects, but at his best in his satirical and humorous pieces. With his hymns on the Passion of Christ, *Passíu-sálmar,* Pétursson takes his place among the great Lutheran hymnwriters of other lands. Profound and sincere religious feeling here expresses itself in simple, though eloquent, language. Generation after generation of Icelanders have sung these hymns and commited them to memory, and their influence on the religious and moral life in Iceland is far beyond estimation. This becomes clear when attention is called to the fact that no less than forty-eight editions of them have been printed to date (1666-1929). Pétursson's memorable funeral hymn, **"Alt eins og blómstrid eina"** (**"Even As a Little Flower"**), is to this day generally sung at Icelandic funerals. He also wrote secular poetry of great merit, often characterized by rare metrical skill. (pp. 250-51)

> Richard Beck, "Icelandic Literature," *in* The History of the Scandinavian Literatures, *edited by Frederika Blankner, 1938. Reprint by Kennikat Press, Inc., 1966, pp. 233-90.*

STEFÁN EINARSSON   (essay date 1957)

[*In the following excerpt, Einarsson surveys Pétursson's work, focusing on the satire of his secular poems and the spirituality of his devotional hymns.*]

[Hallgrímur Pétursson is] the greatest [Icelandic] poet of the seventeenth century and one of the greatest religious poets that Iceland has fostered. . . . (p. 196)

Not counting the three *rímur* cycles of Hallgrímur, in which he showed great mastery of form, his secular poetry does not amount to one fourth of his voluminous production, and even so it was often permeated by his religiosity. But though he took a dark view of the world in general, we often find him yielding to a mellower and merrier mood. His praise of good food, beer, and tobacco was mockingly fulsome, his descriptions of rustic activities, like mowing hay or winding a "leg" of yarn, were extravagant burlesques. His thumbnail sketches of farmlands and neighbors were much gentler in their humor than similar poems by his colleague, Stefán Ólafsson. His satire could be sharp. In **"Aldarháttur"** (**"Ways of the Present World"**), it was humanistic and pagan, comparing the Golden Age of the Icelandic Commonwealth, with its military virtues and heroic deeds, to the present. Its leonine hexameter evoked the Renaissance spirit, its rich diction the skaldic style. Not only did Hallgrímur employ skaldic style and meters, but he was also considered, by scholars like Brynjólfur Sveinsson and Þormóður Torfason, one of the authorities of his age on Old Icelandic poetry. In some of his Christian didactic poems there are touches of *Hávamál.*

But chiefly Hallgrímur's satire was of the Christian kind, contrasting this evil world, ever worsening, and the brilliant picture of the happy world to come—for those who are not destined to go to the darker world after death. Naturally, there is much that was conventional in these descriptions, but one must not forget that Hallgrímur's was a dark age of poverty and depression with the poor either sunk in slothfulness or prone to boisterous ribaldry (like Hallgrímur's neighbors at Hvalsnes), while the rich were given to ostentation, pride and graft. Hallgrímur himself, though learned and not badly off, always identified himself with the poor common people. His censure of falseness, guile, bribery, and mockery has an authentic ring.

If Hallgrímur's satire fell short of Bjarni skáldi's fulminations, it was because of Hallgrímur's more positive nature, nowhere as evident as in his wise Christian counsel to young and old, timeless and classic in its simplicity and directness. Apart from his **"Heilræðavísur"** (**"Good Counsel"**) still on the lips of most Icelandic children, he composed a long row of hymns on related subjects. Otherwise his hymns dealt with the inconstancy and fickleness of this world and death; some were seasonal (New Year, summer, winter), others occasional (bridals, table, travel hymns) or prayers. His Bible hymns, like those of Einar Sigurðsson, were purely didactic. He also wrote some epitaphs and deeply-felt elegies and memorial poems, notably the beautiful and sensitive ones on his young daughter, Steinunn.

Hallgrímur's depth of spiritual feeling culminated in his *Passion Hymns* (*Passíusálmar*). They were based on Martin Möller's *Soliloquia de Passione Jesu Christi* (1587), a famous German work of meditation and edification which became very popular in Iceland in Arngrímur the Learned's translation (1599). The *Soliloquia* represented a return, among the writers of prayer books in Germany, to the medieval mysticism of Augustin and Bernhard. The form of addressing the meditations to one's soul was adopted by Hallgrímur as was also the mechanism of quoting a bit of text, expounding it, and pondering on it in the course of each meditation or hymn. The story opens in hymn one with the Lord's entering the Garden of Gethsemane; it closes in hymn fifty with the guards posted by Pilate to watch the grave. And all along the thorny road Hallgrímur is ready with his Christian allegory and symbolism not only to point morals and draw consolation from the dread aspect of the crucified Lord, but also to submerge himself in Christ's Passion—indeed, to such an extent that it is often difficult to distinguish the suffering of the author from that which he so poignantly portrays. And he has done much more. He has made Christ a living symbol of suffering humanity—the suffering humans of the seventeenth century—whose only hope of escape from a cruel world as well as from a wrathful and righteous God was Christ's redemption, Christ's cross, hope of the heavenly Zion.

Closely related to the *Passion Hymns* was the great meditation **"Um dauðans óvíssan tíma"** (**"On the Uncertain Hour of Death"**). And as the *Passion Hymns*—printed for the first time at Hólar in 1666 and for the sixtieth time in Reykjavík in 1947—became the favorite "God's Word" of generation after generation of Icelanders, so Hallgrímur's powerful dirge has been intoned over the ashes of most of his countrymen from its first appearance in 1660 up to the present day. (pp. 197-99)

> *Stefán Einarsson, "Secular Poetry, 1550-1750," in his* A History of Icelandic Literature, *The Johns Hopkins Press, 1957, pp. 185-205.*

SIGURBJÖRN EINARSSON   (essay date 1966)

[*In the following excerpt, Einarsson describes the profound appeal of* Passion Hymns *in Iceland.*]

Although the external circumstances of the [Icelandic] people at this time were hard in the extreme, and getting harder, the 17th century was a period of considerable literary activity. Foreign theological works were translated and interpreted and there was a great deal of poetic composition. Most of the output, both in prose and verse, was of an occasional nature and never rose to such a level as to become an enduring part of the nation's literary heritage. However, out of this extensive undergrowth that sprang up and has since largely withered away, there grew a single tree, nourished by the surrounding vegetation and endued with an eternal vitality; one work emerged which, in its own sphere, is a pinnacle among the heights of the Christian literature of the world: the *Hymns of the Passion* of Hallgrímur Pétursson.

The author composed much else besides his fifty *Passion Hymns,* and among these other compositions are to be found some of the best poems in the Icelandic language. But his fame and popularity are based on this single work. Here is a book that became loved by his fellow countrymen to a degree unequalled by any, before or since. And it is open to question whether any teacher in the history of Christianity ever exercised a stronger or more enduring influence over a whole nation for centuries on end than this Icelandic poet-priest has, for the past three hundred years, over his fellow-countrymen. (pp. xi-xii)

What is the secret of the popularity of the *Hymns of the Passion?*

It is never easy to give a satisfactory answer as to what constitutes a great work of art. Still less can one define the way in which the Spirit of God breathes into human words the life that gives them 'the power of salvation' (Rom. I, 16). The common people of Iceland have never asked, nor could they have answered, the question why they have taken these poems so closely to their hearts. They have submitted to their inexplicable enchantment, finding in them consolation and strength. They have learned them spontaneously, the child turning to them for its first words of prayer; in times of temptation, and in the battle of life with its trials and tribulations their lines have sprung to the lips; in the last conflict they have served best to strengthen and console, and were unfailingly used when loved ones were laid to their final rest. The *Hymns of the Passion* were sung or read during Lent in every Icelandic home: one hymn each evening. Today they are broadcast throughout Lent on the radio. Thus Hallgrimur has been the companion of every child of Iceland, from the cradle to the grave, for three centuries. His contribution to the religious life of the nation and its spiritual endurance in the hard days gone by can never be fully estimated.

From a formal point of view, the *Hymns of the Passion* are an unquestionable work of genius. Their author has a perfect mastery of the tongue and chooses his words with an infallible sensitivity, while in his interpretation of the subject-matter he combines profound insight, wisdom, and simplicity. The sacred story comes alive for us today. From its incidents are drawn lessons that are relevant to the diverse events of daily life. Rebuke and admonition meet their mark with unerring accuracy, thanks to the precision of language and argument. A wide knowledge of human nature goes hand in hand with a deep reverence for his Saviour and a close, unqualified personal union with Him. Naturally the author preaches according to the religious lights of his time. But the temporal and ephemeral does not cast a shadow on the eternal message of good tidings which he offers: the word of the cross; Christ, the power of God and the wisdom of God (I. Cor. I. 24). Hallgrimur understood man and knew his Master. Thus was he able to become the evangelist and shepherd of souls he has been to his people, leading generations by the hand into the holiest mysteries of the faith. (pp. xvii-xix)

Sigurbjörn Einarsson, in an introduction to Hymns of the Passion: Meditations on the Passion of Christ *by Hallgrímur Pétursson, translated by Arthur Charles Gook, Hallgrims Church, 1966, pp. ix-xxi.*

REV. JAKOB JÓNSSON (essay date 1972)

[In the following excerpt, Jónsson discusses the religious intent and expression of Pétursson's poetry and describes his continuing influence in Iceland.]

Hallgrímur Pétursson's poetry was not only religious, but also secular. All his literary production shows the marks of great poetic skill, knowledge of language and history, and good musical taste. The masterpiece of all his poetry is, however, the cycle of fifty [*Passion Hymns*], telling the Passion story from the Bible from beginning to end. The hymns are not written as congregational hymns for the purpose of being sung in ordinary church services. The poet mostly uses the first and second person singular. The individual rather than a large congregation is meditating over the events of the Bible. On the other hand, the construction of every hymn is very much like a sermon, where the Biblical text is first repeated and then expounded and interpreted. Besides the Bible itself, the literary tools which the author used are mainly *Harmonia evengelica* by Johann Gerhard and *Soliloquia de Passione Jesu Christi* by Martin Möller. In his use of this and other theological and devotional literature he is, however, quite independent. He is also in many ways different from his contemporary colleagues in the field of religious poetry. Most authors of Biblical hymns during the period of Lutheran orthodoxy were satisfied with repetition of the Biblical subject matter, but Hallgrímur Pétursson is more personal and reveals his own intimate feelings with great sincerity. He is never sentimental. Quite often he makes use of similes which are derived from old typological and allegorical vocabulary of the medieval theology. Expressions like "The heart of Jesus is the window through which we will see into the heavens" are not only poetical symbols, but show some relationship with Catholic mysticism. This mysticism does not diminish the dramatic tension of the Passion story, which from beginning to end is a battle between good and evil, the divine and the demonic. Even if Hallgrímur's theory of the atonement is of the orthodox type, the so-called "classical" theory seems to be very near to his thinking. He finds in Christ's Passion the victory over the evil powers of the world, and his faith in the love of God in spite of devil, sin and death is the strongest theme of the whole cycle of hymns. Perhaps the most admirable and the most interesting characteristic of the work is the "actualization", the poet's method of making the subject matter actual for his own days and practically for all future generations. He makes his readers contemporary with the people of the Passion story, and at the same time he brings the events of the story into the life of his own times. The reader of the hymns is himself taking part in everything that happens.

He will see himself both as Peter, Caiphas, Judas, etc. The moral teaching of the hymns is first of all the "imitatio Christi",

the obedience to his words and likeness to his life and behaviour. The sins that the poet finds it most difficult to bear with are falsehood and hypocrisy. As a true humourist he hates scoffing, especially the ridiculing of the poor and weak. On the whole, the paradox of the Passion is expressed in the "divine irony" that every step that leads towards the "victory" of the enemies is actually a step towards the true victory of Christ.

Besides the *Passion Hymns,* the hymn "about the uncertain time of death", **"Allt eins og blómstrid eina"**, has become the typical example of Hallgrímur Pétursson's religious poetry. The final conclusion of that hymn is the welcoming of death, which has through the victory of Christ become an angel sent by God instead of being the "mower who cuts all flowers alike".

In 1974, on 27th October, it will be exactly three centuries since the death of Hallgrímur Pétursson. He died at the farm Ferstikla in Hvalfjördur at the home of his son. During three centuries he has been one of the spiritual guides of his nation. Sayings from his hymns are used as proverbs, so that people quote him quite often without thinking of the source. The first things parents teach their children when they teach them to pray, are verses from Hallgrímur Pétursson's hymns, and the last verse that is sung at any Icelandic funeral is taken from his above-mentioned burial hymn. In the old days it was traditional in Icelandic homes to sing one passion hymn every evening during Lent, but now you will hear on Reykjavik Radio one hymn every evening, read by clergymen or laymen, sometimes by outstanding literary scholars. Where there are special Passion services during Lent, no other songs are used. Icelandic composers and musicians have shown their interest in the hymns, both by collecting old musical tunes that have been used in the past, and by composing new ones. Hallgrímur Pétursson is consequently still active in the devotional life of the Icelandic people. (p. 48)

Rev. Jakob Jónsson, "Hallgrímur Pétursson: Pious Poet Who Inspired the Soul of a Nation," in Atlantica & Iceland Review, *Vol. 10, No. 3, 1972, pp. 46-50.*

ADDITIONAL BIBLIOGRAPHY

Green, W. C. "From Hallgrim Petursson." In *Translations from the Icelandic: Being Select Passages Introductory to Icelandic Literature,* edited and translated by W. C. Green, pp. 227-50. London: Chatto & Windus, 1924.

> Brief introduction to Pétursson followed by annotated selections from his work.

Halmundsson, Hallberg. "Hallgrímur Pétursson (1616-74)." In *An Anthology of Scandinavian Literature from the Viking Period to the Twentieth Century,* edited by Hallberg Hallmundsson, pp. 213-17. New York: Collier Books and Macmillan Co., 1965.

> Biographical sketch of Pétursson as "the most outstanding hymnist Iceland has produced." The sketch is followed by translations of Pétursson's final hymn in *Passion Hymns* and the funeral song "Just Like the Tender Flower."

Mary (Griffith) Pix

1666-1709

English dramatist, novelist, and poet.

Pix was a prolific English dramatist and one of the first women to write for the English stage. Through her plays she helped effect the transition from the licentiousness associated with the Restoration playhouse to the sentimentalism typical of much eighteenth-century drama. Pix composed in an age when female dramatists were practically unknown. She is therefore considered a pioneer of sorts—a woman who, against all odds and risking ridicule, defied tradition and made a literary life for herself. That she succeeded is alone considered noteworthy, but that she did so with distinction has accorded her a small but important place in the history of the English drama.

Little is known about Pix's life and literary career; no contemporary biography has been found, and even the sparse statistical records—the only source of information besides the scattered remarks of acquaintances—are not deemed completely reliable. She was born in 1666 at Nettlebed, Oxfordshire, the daughter of Roger Griffith, the local vicar. She married George Pix, a merchant tailor, in 1684, probably at St. Saviour's, Benet Fink, London. The couple had one child, who died in 1690. It is not known what became of George Pix. A few scholars have speculated that he died early, forcing the financially distressed Mrs. Pix into a writing career, but there is no strong evidence of this. Others claim he lived for many years into his marriage, providing his wife a comfortable existence. In 1696 Pix burst upon the London literary scene with three works: a novel, *The Inhumane Cardinal;* a tragedy, *Ibrahim, the Thirteenth Emperour of the Turks;* and a farce, *The Spanish Wives.* The next year she left the Theatre Royal in Drury Lane, where her first two plays were performed, to write for the rival company in Lincoln's Inn Fields. Soon she was cultivating friendships among the London literati, becoming particularly close to the dramatist William Congreve and the two women, Cathrine Trotter and Mary Delariviere Manley, who were lampooned alongside her in an anonymous satrical drama entitled *The Female Wits; or, The Triumvirate of Poets at Rehearsal* (1696). (In this work Pix appears as Mrs. Wellfed, one ''that represents a fat Female Author, a good sociable well-natur'd Companion, that will not suffer Martyrdom rather than take off three Bumpers in a Hand.'' That Pix was tremendously fat and physically unattractive is affirmed in numerous accounts and parodies of the time.) Congreve supported her during the most trying incident of her career, a battle with the actor/writer/manager George Powell waged publicly during the 1697-98 season. Pix, it appears, had submitted a comedy, *The Deceiver Deceived,* to Powell at Drury Lane before leaving for Lincoln's Inn Fields. Powell rejected the work but evidently did not return the manuscript. Shortly thereafter Drury Lane produced *The Imposture Defeated; or, A Trick to Cheat the Devil,* ''by George Powell.'' The play was manifestly stolen from Pix's manuscript: one of Powell's two plots was in every respect identical with Pix's, even to the main character's name. Pix's reputation was never in serious doubt, but the incident caused her much pain, especially after Powell alleged in the preface of the first printing of *The Imposture Defeated* that both he and Pix had independently made use of a third source, an unspecified novel, for their plots. Powell probably also had the last word, lampooning Pix in an anonymous dialogue widely attributed to him, *Animadversions on Mr. Congreve's Late Answer to Mr. Collier* (1698). In spite of the bad feelings left by the plagiarism affair, Pix continued to write until at least 1706, although after 1699 she signed her name to only one of the seven remaining plays believed to be by her, *The Double Distress.* Shortly after her death in 1709—the end of a literary career that apparently lasted a mere ten years—the *London Gazette* and the *Daily Post Boy* announced a performance of Susanna Centlivre's new drama *The Busy Body* ''for the benefit of the Family of Mrs. Mary Pix, deceas'd.'' Like so much about Pix, exactly who constituted her remaining family is a mystery—just one of many information gaps which show how little is really known about this leading female dramatist.

With the exception of her novel and a few scattered poems, Pix's literary canon is limited to the drama. Altogether she wrote twelve or thirteen plays—the exact number is uncertain because some were published anonymously—on subjects ranging from life at the Russian court to cuckoldry. All were produced on the London stage, most were reasonably successful, running for at least four or five nights—a good showing at the time—and some enjoyed revivals. For the most part, Pix's plays are grounded in the diverse dramatic elements of her time: an era of theatrical transition in which, in her role as dramatist, she was herself instrumental. Some of her tragedies adhere closely to the so-called ''blood and thunder'' tradition of late-Restoration heroic tragedy. An example of this is *Ibrahim, the Thirteenth Emperour of the Turks,* which is set at the sultan's palace in Constantinople, involves unrestrained passion and vengeful carnage, and ends with the deaths of most of the principals. Yet while most of Pix's tragedies are historical and designed to illustrate the snares of violence and passion, some, critics note, move away from the heroic convention, modifying its emphasis on epic characters and grandiose action in a way that prefigures the pathetic and domestic tragedy associated with the eighteenth century. Mixing English history with domestic romance, another tragedy, *Queen Catharine; or, The Ruines of Love*—considered by Herbert Carter the best drama written by a woman during the Restoration—focuses on Edward IV's love for Henry V's widow; the play thus ''reduces the Wars of the Roses to a quarrel over thwarted love,'' according to Nancy Cotton. Further from the established tradition are *The Double Distress* and *The Czar of Muscovy,* two ''tragedies'' with happy endings. Moreover, Pix abandoned the heroic verse common to Restoration tragedy in favor of blank verse and, in the case of *The Czar of Muscovy,* prose. One tragedy, *The False Friend,* is notable as Pix's only tragedy with an explicitly stated moral intent. This drama, which breaks decisively from the kind of exotic sexuality explored in *Ibrahim,* appears to be Pix's concession to Jeremy Collier, who in *A Short View of the Immorality and Profaneness of the English Stage, Together with the Sense of Antiquity upon This Argument* (1698) launched a devastating and influential attack on what he considered the rampant licentiousness of the Restoration theater.

Moral didacticism is especially common in the comedies, with frequent foreshadowings of the coming vogue of sentimentalism, too. Yet Pix's moral purpose, exemplified by her gradual abandonment of tragic plots emphasizing violence, betrayal, and bloody death, is hardly unadulterated here, for the comedies retain many stock Restoration features, including emphasis on bawdy wit and sexual intrigue. In fact, modern critics of the comedies, like those of the tragedies, have stressed the importance of Pix's having composed in an age of theatrical transition, citing her juxtaposition of Restoration rakes and paragons of virtue, of the Restoration ethos of rakishness and coquetry and the sentimental ideals of fidelity and virtuous love. According to Cotton, "Pix's attempt to write both hard and soft comedy at the same time is characteristic of playwrights at the turn of the century under pressure for stage reform." As a result, many of the comedies are a "popular combination of smuttiness and sentiment"—a phrase Edna L. Steeves used to describe the plays. Another example of such a comedy is *The Spanish Wives,* which is replete with pimping, abduction, and seduction and has an improbable plot contrived solely for satiric and comedic purposes. Like most of Pix's comedies, *The Spanish Wives* is generally acknowledged superior to her tragedies; in spite of its stock theme of cuckoldry the play is deemed highly original. Recent scholars have isolated another noteworthy feature of Pix's plays: incipient feminism. Many of her dramas, including *The Spanish Wives* and *The Deceiver Deceived,* involve forced marriage and tyrannical husbands. Critics note that Pix's insistence in these works on a woman's right to choose in romance, as well as her right to freedom and trust within marriage, evidence a recurring sympathetic concern with feminine issues.

Pix's two principal nondramatic works are *The Inhumane Cardinal* and *Violenta; or, The Rewards of Virtue.* Until recently believed lost, the first work has of course been scarcely commented upon, but readers agree this novel suffers badly from faulty plot construction, crudely amateurish characterization, and a discordant blending of sentiment and soporific. Nevertheless, it is important insofar as the narrative—a tale of a lecherous Roman Catholic cardinal who deceives a virgin, seduces and impregnates her, and then has her poisoned—foreshadows concerns of Pix's early tragedies, namely intrigue, duplicity, and copious bloodshed. Commentators note that the author's handling of these matters improved greatly in the wake of this, her apprentice piece. Decidedly different in tone and intent, *Violenta* is a verse adaptation of the eighth book of the second day of Boccaccio's *Decameron.* The poem is one of Pix's latest works and, accordingly, a paean to virtue. It tells of a nobleman's forced separation from his children and their eventual reunion, the latter made possible only by a succession of selfless acts by each of them. With *Violenta* Pix's career effected its final transition, having moved from the sinister tone of her novel, through the general gradual lightening of dramatic plots, and culminating in the rewarding of virtue in *Violenta*—a favorite theme for Pix during the two remaining years of her career.

"At the very least she was workmanlike and knowledgeable in her craft. At her best, she wrote some excellent comedies, and for that she deserves more than the obscurity to which she has fallen." So wrote Paula Louise Barbour in her 1975 doctoral dissertation on Pix. Until the publication of *The Innocent Mistress* in a collection in 1981, only one of Pix's plays had gone beyond a first edition. But in her lifetime Pix was well enough known to be both frequently lampooned for being a female dramatist and approached seriously and soberly by the critical community. Judgments varied, but overall she was rated a competent, often amusing writer, and the runs her plays enjoyed testify to their popularity with the public. Yet Pix's

early works were not without detractors. Richard Steele, for example, in a 1711 Collier-like attack on "bawdry" in the theater, cited *Ibrahim* as an example. In the outcry against perceived immorality the literary qualities of Pix's plays were sometimes ignored, and it was not until late in her career, when she had apparently more closely heeded the strictures of Collier and his followers, that Pix found herself essentially free from hostile criticism. But as quickly as she achieved success, so with equal swiftness did her works tumble into obscurity. After her death Pix was nearly forgotten: her dramas, especially the early brooding ones, fell out of fashion as early-eighteenth-century audiences demanded good cheer and sentiment at the playhouse; her novel became virtually unobtainable; and her poetry—much of it published anonymously and therefore never of much use for promoting Pix's name—lost whatever appeal it once had as readers embraced a new crop of versifiers. With the exception of a few scattered comments, Pix's reputation consequently languished until well into the twentieth century, when Myra Reynolds offered the first modern evaluation of Pix's canon. Since then interest has increased steadily: Pix's plays have been closely studied in several essays; her novel has been pored over by critics who consider its generic features ahead of the time; and Robert Adams Day has studied the poetry—at least all that is known to be by Pix—for evidence of the author's frame of mind at different points in her career. Today Pix's literary works are considered important documents for the study of the place of women in English literary history, and such commentators as Cotton and Constance Clark acknowledge the value of many of the plays as entertainment alone. Her dramatic works and novel recently restored to print, Pix is now, in remote posterity and in company with other female writers of her age, gradually regaining the prominence she once knew.

Pix wrote plays at a time when dramatic composition was a markedly male domain, and she was successful enough to see twelve or thirteen works produced. No other woman of the age achieved anything like this in the theater, and even the nearest contenders—Trotter, Manley, and, somewhat later, Centlivre—hardly matched Pix in both range and prolificness. Pix built a landmark career in literature, helping pave the way for later female writers and usher in the so-called Augustan Age of English letters. For after Pix's death a host of women entered the literary mainstream, and, as her dramas demonstrate, in her brief career she helped effect the transition from mores commonly labeled "Restoration" to "Augustan" ones. Her reputation may be said to have come full circle: once famous but then forgotten, she is today deemed a notable figure in English literary history.

*PRINCIPAL WORKS

The Inhumane Cardinal; or, Innocence Betrayed (novel) 1696
Ibrahim, the Thirteenth Emperour of the Turks (drama) 1696
The Spanish Wives (drama) 1696
The Innocent Mistress (drama) 1697
The Deceiver Deceived (drama) 1697; also produced as *The French Beau,* 1699
Queen Catharine; or, The Ruines of Love (drama) 1698
The False Friend; or, The Fate of Disobedience (drama) 1699
**The Beau Defeated; or, The Lucky Younger Brother* (drama) 1700
The Double Distress (drama) 1701
**The Czar of Muscovy* (drama) 1701

The Different Widows; or, Intrigue all-a-Mode (drama) 1703
Violenta; or, The Rewards of Virtue, Turn'd from Boccace into Verse (poetry) 1704
*Zelmane; or, The Corinthian Queen (drama) 1704
*The Conquest of Spain (drama) 1705
*The Adventures in Madrid (drama) 1706
The Plays of Mary Pix and Catharine Trotter, Vol. I: *Mary Pix* (dramas) 1982

*Many of Pix's dramas were published anonymously, making the establishment of a canon problematic. Unasterisked dramas listed here are known to be by Pix, either by the appearance of her name on the title page or by a signed dedication. Asterisked dramas are generally accepted to be by Pix, but in some cases are not universally acknowledged to be so.

THE FEMALE WITS   (play date 1696)

[*The following excerpt is from* The Female Wits; or, The Triumvirate of Poets at Rehearsal, *a satire performed at the Theatre Royal in Drury Lane in 1696 but not published until 1704. The drama appeared anonymously, the only clue to authorship being the presence of "Written by Mr. W. M." on the title page. Scholars have speculated on the identity of "W. M.": he may have been Joe Haynes, a celebrated comic actor, or his friend William Mann, or neither (or both) of these men; what is clear is that the author (or authors) knew the Drury Lane company intimately and had a close knowledge of the three female authors lampooned in the play, Pix, Catharine Trotter, and Mary Delariviere Manley. Here, in two excerpts from Act I, Pix appears as Mrs. Wellfed, one who, according to the dramatis personae, "represents a fat Female Author, a good sociable well-natur'd Companion, that will not suffer Martyrdom rather than take off three Bumpers in a Hand"; Manley appears as Marsilia; and Trotter, as Calista. The minor characters are Patience, Marsilia's maid, and Mr. Praiseall, a "conceited, cowardly Coxcomb."*]

MARSILIA. My Service to you Madam, I think you drink in a Morning.

MRS. WELLFED. Yes, else I had never come to this bigness, Madam, to the encreasing that inexhausted spring of Poetry; that it may swell, o'erflow, and bless the barren land.

MARSILIA. Incomparable, I protest!

PATIENCE. Madam *Calista* to wait upon your Ladyship.

MARSILIA. Do you know her Child?

MRS. WELLFED. No.

MARSILIA. Oh! 'Tis the vainest, proudest, senseless Thing, she pretends to Grammar, writes in Mood and Figure; does every thing methodically.———Poor Creature! She shews me her Works first; I always commend 'em, with a Design she shou'd expose 'em, and the Town be so kind to laugh her out of her Follies.

MRS. WELLFED. That's hard in a Friend.

MARSILIA. But 'tis very usual.———Dunce! Why do you let her stay so long? (*Exit* Patience. *Re-enter with* Calista.) My best *Calista!* The charming'st Nymph of all *Apollo's* Train, let me Embrace thee!

MRS. WELLFED. (*Aside*) So, I suppose my Reception was preceeded like this.

MARSILIA. Pray know this Lady, she is a Sister of ours.

CALISTA. (*Aside*) She's big enough to be the Mother of the Muses. Madam, your Servant.

MRS. WELLFED. Madam, yours.

MARSILIA. Now here's the Female Triumvirate; methinks 'twou'd be but civil of the Men to lay down their Pens for one Year, and let us divert the Town; but if we shou'd, they'd certainly be asham'd ever to take 'em up again.

(pp. 4-5)

• • • • •

PATIENCE. Madam, your Chair Men are come.

MARSILIA. Let them wait, they are paid for't.

PATIENCE. (*Aside*) Not yet to my Knowledge, what ever they be after the third Day; there's a long Bill I'm sure.

MARSILIA. How do you think to go Mrs. *Wellfed?* Shall *Patience* call you another Chair?

MRS. WELLFED. I have no Inclination to break poor Mens Backs; I thank you, Madam, I'll go a Foot.

CALISTA. A Foot!

MRS. WELLFED. Ay, a Foot, 'tis not far, 'twill make me leaner. Your Servant Ladies. (*Exit*)

MARSILIA. Your Servant.

PRAISEALL. A bouncing Dame! But she has done some things well enough.

MARSILIA. Fye, Mr. *Praiseall!* That you shou'd wrong your Judgment thus! Don't do it, because you think her my Friend: I profess, I can't forbear saying, her Heroicks want Beautiful Uniformity as much as her Person, and her Comedies are as void of Jests as her Conversation.

PRAISEALL. I submit to your Ladyship.

(p. 11)

W. M., in his The Female Wits, *1704. Reprint by William Andrews Clark Memorial Library, 1967, 67 p.*

GEORGE POWELL?   (poem date 1698)

[*An English essayist, dramatist, and actor, Powell is chiefly known through contemporary accounts of his literary quarrels. He acted in* The Female Wits, *a satire directed against Pix and other literary women (see excerpt dated 1696), and the following year was accused by Pix of plagiarizing her play* The Deceiver Deceived. *Many critics believe that Powell is the author of the anonymously published* Animadversions on Mr. Congreve's Late Answer to Mr. Collier *(1698), a diatribe against alleged immoralities of the English stage. In the following excerpt from this work, the critic presents contemptuous verse characterizations of Pix and a contemporary playwright, Catharine Trotter.*]

[O] could I write like the two Female things
With *Muse Pen-feather'd,* guiltless yet of Wings;
And yet, it strives to Fly, and thinks it Sings.
Just like the Dames themselves, who slant in Town,
And flutter loosely, but to tumble down.
The last that writ, of these presuming two,
(For that [**Queen Catharine**] is no Play 'tis true)
And yet to Spell is more than she can do,
Told a High Princess, she from Men had torn
Those *Bays,* which they had long engross'd and worn.

But when she offers at our Sex thus Fair,
With four fine Copies to her Play,—O rare!
If she feels manhood shoot—'tis I know where.
Let them scrawl on, and Loll, and Wish at ease,
(A Feather oft does Woman's Fancy please.)
Till by their Muse (more jilt than they) accurst,
We know (if possible) which writes the worst.
Beneath these Pictures, sure there needs no name,
Nor will I give what they ne'er got in Fame.

> *George Powell? "To the Ingenious Mr. ——.," in*
> Animadversions on Mr. Congreve's Late Answer to
> Mr. Collier, *1698. Reprint by Garland Publishing,
> Inc., 1972, 88 p.*

MARY PIX?   (poem date 1698)

[*In the following prologue to* Queen Catharine; or, The Ruines of
Love, *the critic—believed to be Pix but cited by Charles Dibdin
(see excerpt dated 1797-1800) as the dramatist Catharine Trotter—describes how a woman dramatist will treat the heroic subject
of the play.*]

'Tis grown so hard a Task to please the Town,
We scarce can tell what Prologue will go down:
But right or wrong a Prologue must be writ,
A dull one sometimes may divert the Pit,
Substantial dullness does as well as wit.

Queen Catharine

OR, THE

Ruines of Love.

A

TRAGEDY,

As it is Acted at the

New THEATRE in *Little-Lincolns-Inn-Field*

BY

His MAJESTY's Servants

Written by Mrs. *Pix*.

LONDON,

Printed for *William Turner*, at the *White Horse* without,
and *Richard Baſſet*, at the *Mitre* within, *Temple-Bar*.
M DC XCVIII.

Title page of the tragedy Queen Catharine *(1698).*

For if you laugh, what matter whence the mirth,
Whether from plenty of the Wit, or dearth?
A heavy *English* Tale to day, we show
As e'er was told by *Hollingshead* or *Stow*,
Shakespear did oft his Countries worthies chuse,
Nor did they by his pen their Lustre lose.
Hero's revive thro' him, and *Hotspur's* rage,
Doubly adorns and animates the Stage:
But how shall Woman after him succeed,
And what excuse can her presumption plead.
Who with enervate voice dares wake the mighty dead;
    To please your martial men she must despair,
    And therefore Courts the favour of the fair:
    From huffing Hero's she hopes no relief,
    But trusts in *Catharine's* Love, and *Isabella's* grief.

> *Mary Pix? in a prologue to "Queen Catharine or,
> the Ruines of Love: A Tragedy," in* The Plays of
> Mary Pix and Catharine Trotter, Vol. I: Mary Pix,
> *edited by Edna L. Steeves, Garland Publishing, Inc.,
> 1982.*

[CHARLES GILDON]   (essay date 1699)

[*An English critic, Gildon abridged and updated Gerard Langbaine's 1691 investigation of the London stage,* The Lives and
Characters of the English Dramatick Poets, *giving special attention to the rising dramatists of the 1690s. In the following excerpt
from Gildon's 1699 revision of this work, he briefly describes and
comments on Pix's plays.*]

[In] this Poetick Age, when all Sexes and Degrees venture on
the Sock or Buskins, [Mrs. Mary Pix] has boldly given us an
Essay of her Talent in both, and not without Success, tho' with
little Profit to her self.

Ibrahim, the Thirteenth Emperor of the Turks, a Tragedy, acted
at the Theatre Royal, 1696. 4*to.* and dedicated to *Richard
Minchal,* of *Burton,* Esq; This Play, if it want the Harmony
of Numbers, and the Sublimity of Expression, has yet a Quality, that at least ballances that Defect, I mean the Passions; for
the Distress of *Morena* never fail'd to bring Tears into the Eyes
of the Audience; which few Plays, if any since *Otway's,* have
done; and yet, which is the true End of Tragedy. She informs
us, that by mistake it was called **Ibrahim the Thirteenth,** when
it should have been called, *Ibrahim the Twelfth,* the Story you
may find in Sir *Paul Ricaut's Continuation of the Turkish
History.*

The Innocent Mistress, a Comedy, acted at the Theatre in *Little
Lincolns-Inn-Fields,* by his Majesty's Servants, 1697. 4*to.* The
Prologue and Epilogue writ by Mr. *Motteux.* This is a diverting
Play, and met with good Success, tho' acted in the hot Season
of the Year, our Poetress has endeavoured to imitate the Eas-
iness and Way of the Author of *Vertue in Danger,* and *The
Provok'd Wife.* She has borrowed some Incidents from other
Plays; as Mrs. *Beauclair's* carrying of Mrs. *Flywife* from Sir
Francis Wildlove, from the *Vertuous Wife* doing the same to
her Husband's *Mistress.* Then the Scene in the *Park* betwixt
Sir *Francis* and her in her *Mask,* is a kind of Copy in young
Bellair, and *Harriots* in Sir *Fopling.* Miss *Peggy* seems a Copy
of Miss *Hoyden,* and *Chattal* is of several of the parts written
of late for Mr. *Dogget.* But notwithstanding these Imitations,
which ever have been allowed in Poets, the Play has its peculiar
Merit; and as a Lady carried the Prize of Poetry in *France* this
Year, so in Justice, they are like to do in *England;* tho' indeed
we use them more barbarously, and defraud them both of their
Fame and Profit.

The Spanish Wives, a Farce, acted at the Theatre in *Dorset-Gardens,* by his Majesty's Servants, 1696. and dedicated to the Honourable Collonel *Tipping,* of *Whitfield.* This Farce had the good Fortune to please, and it must be own'd, there are two or three pleasant Turns in it. (pp. 111-12)

This Prolifick Lady has again gratified the Town with a Play, call'd **The Deceiver Deceiv'd,** a Comedy, as 'tis now acted by his Majesty's Servants, at the Theatre in *Little Lincolns-Inn-Fields, 4to.* 1698. and dedicated to Sir *Robert Marsham,* Knight and Baronet. This Play and *The Impostor Cheated,* are on the same Bottom, built on a little printed Story of the same Subject. I think the Scene where the Blind Man's Wife make's Love before his Face, is better manag'd in Mr. *Powel*'s Play, than here, tho' in general, this is the better Play. (p. 178)

> [*Charles Gildon*], "Mrs. Mary Pix," in Momus Triumphans; or, the Plagiaries of the English Stage and The Lives and Characters of the English Dramatick Poets *by Gerard Langbaine, Garland Publishing, Inc., 1973, pp. 111-12, 178.*

MARY PIX? (poem date 1699)

[*In the following prologue to* The False Friend; or, The Fate of Disobedience, *apparently written by Pix, the author states the moral purpose of the play and asks the audience to be kind to the female dramatist.*]

Amongst Reformers of this Vitious Age,
Who think it Duty to Refine the Stage:
A Woman, to Contribute, does Intend,
In Hopes a Moral Play your Lives will Mend.
Matters of State, she'l not pretend to Teach;
Or Treat of War, or things above her Reach:
Nor Scourge your Folly's, with keen *Satyrs* Rage;
But try if good Example will Engage.
For Precepts oft do fail from *Vice* to win,
And Punishments but harden you in Sin.
Therefore (*Male Judges*) She prescribes no Rules,
And knows 'tis vain to make Wise Men of Fools.
Lest all those Wholesom Laws that she can give,
You'd think too much below you to receive.
———That part then of the Reformation,
Which she believes the fittest for her Station;
Is, to shew *Man* the surest way to Charm:
And all those Virtues, *Women* most Adorn.

First then,———No *Beau* can e're Succesful prove,
Narcissus like, who's with himself in Love.
No wretched *Miser* must e're hope to find,
With Chest's Lok'd up, a Friend 'mongst Woman kind.
No *Drunkard, Fool, Debauchee,* or one that Swears,
Can Win a Woman, or beguile her Fears;
But he that's *Honest, Generous,* and *Brave,*
That's *Wise* and *Constant,* may his Wishes have.

But Hold, I'de forgot———
You must not be *Ill natur'd* and *Unkind,*
Moroseness Suits not with their Tender Minds.
They are all soft, as is the Down of *Doves,*
As Innocent and Harmless are their Loves;
And those Misfortunes which on *Men* do fall,
To their False Selves they Chiefly owe 'em all.
Did *Men* Reform, all *Women* wou'd do well:
In *Virtue,* as in *Beauty* they'd Excell.
But while each strive the other to Betray,
Both are to *Fears* and *Jealosie's* a Prey.

Let not *Ill-nature* then Reign here to Night,
Nor think you shew most Wit, when most you Spite;
But Strive the Beauties of the *Play* to find,
The Modest *Scenes,* and Nicest *Actions* mind,
Then to your *Selves,* and *Authress* you'l be kind.

(pp. 1-2)

> *Mary Pix? in a prologue to "The False Friend; or, The Fate of Disobedience," in* The Plays of Mary Pix and Catharine Trotter, Vol. I: Mary Pix, *edited by Edna L. Steeves, Garland Publishing, Inc., 1982.*

A REPRESENTATION OF THE IMPIETY & IMMORALITY OF THE ENGLISH STAGE (essay date 1704)

[*In the following excerpt from the anonymous* Representation of the Impiety & Immorality of the English Stage, *the critic accuses Pix of immorality and profanity in* The False Friend *and* The Different Widows, *quoting examples. The page numbers given in the excerpt refer to the first printings of the dramatic texts.*]

The various Methods that have been used for Preventing the outragious and insufferable Disorders of the STAGE, having been in a great measure defeated: It is thought proper, under our present Calamity, and before the approaching FAST, to collect some of the *Prophane and Immoral Expressions* out of several late PLAYS, and to put them together in a little Compass, that the Nation may thereby be more convinced of the *Impiety of the Stage,* the Guilt of such as frequent it, and the Necessity of putting a Stop thereto, either by a total Suppression of the *Play-Houses,* as was done in the Reign of Queen *Elizabeth,* or by a Suspension for some considerable time, after the Example of other Nations. . . . (pp. 3-4)

[In] Easter-Term, 1701, *the* Players *of one House were Indicted at the* King's-Bench-Bar, *before the Right Honourable the Lord Chief Justice* Holt, *for using these following Expressions, and were thereof Convicted.* (p. 7)

In the Comedy call'd,
The False Friend, 1702.

Pag. 7. 'Pox take ye.' *Pag.* 12. 'The Devil fetch me, *&c.*'

Pag. 22. 'Heaven's Blessing must needs fall upon so dutiful a Son; but I don't know how its Judgments may deal with so indifferent a Lover.'

Pag. 28. 'Say that 'tis true, you are married to another, and that a———'Twou'd be a Sin to think of any Body but your Husband, and that———You are of a timorous Nature, and afraid of being damn'd.'

'How have I lov'd, to Heaven I appeal; but Heaven does now permit that Love no more.'

'Why does it then permit us Life and Thought? Are we deceiv'd in its Omnipotence? Is it reduc'd to find its Pleasure in its Creature's Pain?'

Pag. 33. '*Leonora*'s Charms turn Vice to Virtue, Treason into Truth; Nature, who has made her the Supream Object of our Desires must needs have design'd her the Regulator of our Morals.'

'There he goes I'faith; he seem'd as if he had a Qualm just now; but he never goes without a Dram of Conscience-water about him to set Matters right again.'

Pag. 43. 'Speak, or by all the Flame and Fire of Hell eternal; speak, or thou art dead.' (pp. 11-12)

In the *Different Widows*.

Pag. 1. 'Damn'd Lies, by *Jupiter* and *Juno,* and the rest of the Heathen Gods and Goddesses; for I remember I paid two Guinea's for swearing Christian Oaths last Night.'

Pag. 2. 'Pox take him.' *Pag. 24.* 'Ye immortal Gods, who the Devil am I?'

Pag. 61. 'May the Devil, Curses, Plagues and Disappointments light upon you.' (p. 14)

> *An excerpt from* A Representation of the Impiety & Immorality of the English Stage (1704) *and* Some Thoughts Concerning the Stage (1704), *The Augustan Reprint Society, 1947, pp. 3-14.*

RICHARD STEELE (essay date 1711)

[*An Irish-born English politician, dramatist, and essayist, Steele is best known for his journalistic enterprises. Among the periodicals he founded and edited are the* Tatler *and the* Spectator, *the former a thrice-weekly review which ran from April 1709 until January 1711, the latter a highly popular and influential daily created in partnership with Joseph Addison. Commentators note that Steele was ever conscious of moral issues in his essays, having, in addition to amusement and diversion, the ethical improvement of the reader as a goal. In the following excerpt from a 1711* Spectator *essay censuring immorality in the theater, Steele singles out* Ibrahim *for criticism.*]

[No one] ever writ Bawdry for any other Reason but Dearth of Invention. When the Author cannot strike out of himself any more of that which he has superior to those who make up the Bulk of his Audience, his natural Recourse is to that which he has in common with them; and a Description which gratifies a sensual Appetite will please, when the Author has nothing about him to delight a refined Imagination. It is to such a Poverty we must impute . . . Sentences in Plays . . . , which are commonly termed Luscious Expressions.

This Expedient, to supply the Deficiencies of Wit, has been used, more or less, by most of the Authors who have succeeded on the Stage. . . . (p. 154)

It lifts an heavy, empty Sentence, when there is added to it a lascivious Gesture of Body; and when it is too low to be raised even by that, a flat Meaning is enlivened by making it a double one. Writers, who want *Genius,* never fail of keeping this Secret in reserve, to create a Laugh, or raise a Clap. I, who know nothing of Women but from seeing Plays, can give great guesses at the whole Structure of the fair Sex, by being innocently placed in the Pit, and insulted by the Petticoats of their Dancers; the Advantages of whose pretty Persons are a great help to a dull Play. When a Poet flags in writing Lusciously, a pretty Girl can move Lasciviously, and have the same good Consequence for the Author. Dull Poets in this Case use their Audiences, as dull Parasites do their Patrons; when they cannot longer divert them with their Wit or Humour, they bait their Ears with something which is agreeable to their Temper, though below their Understanding. *Apicius* cannot resist being pleased, if you give him an Account of a delicious Meal: or *Clodius,* if you describe a wanton Beauty: Tho' at the same time, if you do not awake those Inclinations in them, no Men are better Judges of what is just and delicate in Conversation. But, as I have before observed, it is easier to talk to the Man, than to the Man of Sense.

It is remarkable, that the writers of least Learning are best skill'd in the luscious Way. The Poetesses of the Age have

done Wonders in this kind; and we are obliged to the Lady who writ **Ibrahim,** for introducing a preparatory Scene to the very Action, when the Emperor throws his Handkerchief as a Signal for his Mistress to follow him into the most retired Part of the Seraglio. It must be confessed his *Turkish* Majesty went off with a good Air, but, methought, we made but a sad Figure who waited without. This Ingenious Gentlewoman, in this piece of Bawdry, refined upon an Author of the same Sex [Aphra Behn], who, in the *Rover,* makes a Country Squire strip to his Holland Drawers. For *Blunt* is disappointed, and the Emperor is understood to go on to the utmost. (pp. 154-55)

> *Richard Steele, "No. 51," in* The Spectator: Addison & Steele and Others, Vol. 1, *edited by Gregory Smith, J. M. Dent & Sons Ltd., 1961, pp. 153-56.*

GILES JACOB (essay date 1719)

[*Jacob was an English man of letters who is best remembered as a painstaking compiler of literary facts. Also an authority on legal matters, he was jeered thus by Alexander Pope in* The Dunciad *(1728): "Jacob, the Scourge of Grammar, mark with awe, / Nor less revere him, Blunderbuss of Law." In the following excerpt from a work originally published in 1719, he comments briefly on the seven plays by Pix known to him, adding his opinion of* The Inhumane Cardinal.]

This Gentlewoman [Mary Pix] was the daughter of Mr. *Griffith,* an eminent Clergyman, born at *Nettlebed* in *Oxfordshire,* and by her Mother's Side was descended from a very considerable Family, that of the *Wallis's.* She has given us Seven Plays, *viz.*

I. *The Spanish Wives*; a Farce of three Acts, acted at the Theatre in *Dorset-Garden,* 1696, with Applause. Dedicated to the Honourable Sir *Thomas Tipping.* For the Plot, see the Novel of the *Pilgrim.*

II. *Ibrahim the XII* (by her Mistake call'd the XIII) *Emperor of the Turks*; a Tragedy, acted at the Theatre Royal, 1696. Dedicated to *Richard Minchal,* Esq; This play has not the Harmony of Numbers, nor a Sublimity of Expresion; but the Distress of *Morena* is very moving. The Story is to be found in Sir *Paul Ricaut's* Continuation of the *Turkish History.*

III. *The Innocent Mistress*; a Comedy, acted at the Theatre in *Little Lincolns-Inn-Fields,* by his Majesty's Servants, 1697. This Play met with very good Success, tho' acted in the Summer Season. She has borrow'd some Incidents from other Plays, particularly Sir *Fopling Flutter.*

IV. *Queen Catharine, or The Ruines of Love*; a Tragedy, acted at the Theatre in *Little Lincolns-Inn-Fields,* 1698. Dedicated to the Honourable Mrs. *Cook* of *Norfolk.* For the Plot, consult *Baker, Speed, Stow,* &c. in the Lives of *Edward* IV, and *Henry* VI.

V. *The Deceiver Deceiv'd*; a Comedy, likewise acted at the Theatre in *Little Lincolns-Inn-Fields,* 1698. Dedicated to Sir *Robert Masham.*

VI. *The Czar of Muscovy*; a Tragedy, acted at the Theatre Royal in *Drury-Lane.*

VII. *The Double Distress*; a Tragedy. Besides these Plays, she writ a very ingenious Novel, call'd, *The Inhuman Cardinal.* Dedicated to the Princess *Anne* of *Denmark.* (pp. 203-04)

> *Giles Jacob, "Mrs. Mary Pix," in his* The Poetical Register; or, the Lives and Characters of All the

English Poets, Vol. I, *1723. Reprint by Gregg International Publishers Limited, 1969, pp. 203-04.*

[CHARLES] DIBDIN   (essay date 1797-1800)

[*Dibdin was an English essayist, dramatist, critic, and songwriter whose literary career was colored by a hodgepodge of tremendous successes, huge failures, and much infighting among his colleagues. He is best remembered for his sea songs and* A Complete History of the English Stage *(1797-1800), the latter a hastily written, comprehensive survey that has been criticized for poor attention to detail. In the following excerpt from this work, he sarcastically dismisses Pix's dramatic canon.*]

Mrs. PIX, Mrs. MANLEY, and Mrs. TROTTER, alias COCKBURNE, made up a triumvirate of Lady wits who enjoyed a great deal of the admiration of the namby pamby critics, and the indifference, and sometimes the ridicule of those whom heaven had vouchsafed to endow with taste and judgement.

Mrs. PIX wrote nine dramatic pieces. The first a farce, 1696, was called The *Spanish Wives*. It is entirely borrowed, and, after a few nights, was returned to the owner. *Ibrahim the Twelfth,* same year, is a tragedy, and the warmest advocate that I can find for it only allows that it is not contemptible. The *Innocent Mistress,* a comedy, 1697, borrowed from Sir GEORGE ETHERIDGE's *Man of Mode,* is much inferior to the original, and therefore very soon got out of fashion. The *Deceiver Deceived,* a comedy, 1698, was helped forward by DUFFREY and MOTTEAUX, but ineffectually, for it had no success. *Queen Catherine,* a tragedy, same year, reigned a very short time; for, in spight of the assistance of all the triumvirate, and particularly a prologue [see the poem by Mary Pix? dated 1698] from Mrs. TROTTER, she abdicated her throne in about four nights.

The *False Friend,* a tragedy, 1699, has not found a single advocate among all the panegyrists of Mrs. PIX, therefore we may naturally suppose it played her false as well as others. The *Czar of Muscovy,* 1701. Here Mrs. PIX was determined to do the thing at once and introduce PETER the Great upon the English stage. The emperor, however, though at that time he was playing a conspicuous part on the theatre of the world, was scurvily handled, and forced, in spight of all his former victories, to a precipitate retreat. The *Double Distress,* a tragedy, was as scurvily treated as the *Czar Peter,* and in the same year. Mrs. PIX went as far as *Persepolis* for her plot; but, whether she lost in it her way back again, or in whatever manner she managed to convey it to her audience, for I believe she had but one, it was the universal opinion that she had been wool-gathering.

With the *Conquest of Spain* we shall take leave of Mrs. PIX, of which play we have as few particulars as of the rest. Indeed it should seem as if all her productions had been foisted on the public through the medium of connexions; and, just as we have frequently seen in the productions of lady writings, they became a sort of fashion of the ephemeron kind, but were too slight to be permanent. (pp. 342-45)

[*Charles*] *Dibdin, "Southern, Mrs. Pix, Mrs. Manley, Mrs. Cockburne, Lord Landsdowne, Dennis, Oldmixon, Motteaux, and Gildon," in* A Complete History of the English Stage, Vol. IV, N.p. *1797-1800, pp. 329-60.*

JOHN GENEST   (essay date 1832)

[*Genest is recognized as one of the first serious students of the English drama. His ten-volume masterwork,* Some Account of the English Stage from the Restoration in 1660 to 1830 *(1832), is admired for its accuracy and comprehensiveness, and, though Genest was often severe in his judgments, commentators agree that his criticism is usually balanced and fair. In the following excerpt from* Some Account, *he unfavorably evaluates two of Pix's plays,* The Double Distress *and* The Czar of Muscovy.]

Double Distress. . . . .—this is a poor [Tragedy] by Mrs. Pix—it is written partly in rhyme and partly in blank verse—Mrs. Pix should have stuck to Comedy, and not have meddled with Tragedy.

Czar of Muscovy. . . . .—this is an indifferent [Tragedy]—it is attributed to Mrs. Pix—almost the whole of it is written in prose—it appears from the Prologue that it came out in Lent—the Editor of the B. D. sometimes makes his remarks on a play without having read it—of this we have here a flagrant instance—he says—"this [Tragedy] is founded on some of the incidents of the then recent history of the great Czar Peter"—in fact there is not one single syllable about the Czar Peter. . . . (pp. 240-41)

John Genest, "L. I. F. 1701," in his Some Account of the English Stage from the Restoration in 1660 to 1830, Vol. II, *1832. Reprint by Burt Franklin, 1964, pp. 240-48.*

[JOHN] DORAN   (essay date 1863)

[*Doran was an English essayist, critic, and travel writer who wrote widely on the history of the theater. In the following excerpt, he offers a generally favorable overview of Pix's dramatic works.*]

Fat Mrs. Pix enjoyed a certain sort of vogue from 1696 to 1709. She came from Oxfordshire, was the daughter of a clergyman, was married to a Mr. Pix, and was a woman of genius, and much flesh. She wrote eleven plays, but not one of them has survived to our time. Her comedies are, however, full of life; her tragedies more than brimful of loyalty; later dramatists have not disdained to pick up some of Mrs. Pix's forgotten incidents; and, indeed, contemporary play-wrights stole her playful lightning, if not her thunder; her plots were not ill-conceived, but they were carried out by inexpressive language, some of her tragedies being in level prose, and some, mixtures of rhyme and blank verse. She herself occasionally remodelled an old play, but did not improve it; while, when she trusted to herself, at least in a farcical sort of comedy, she was bustling and humorous. (pp. 166-67)

[*John*] *Doran, "The Dramatic Authoresses," in his* "Their Majesties' Servants": Annals of the English Stage from Thomas Betterton to Edmund Kean, Actors—Authors—Audiences, Vol. I, *1863. Reprint by W. J. Widdleton, Publisher, 1865, pp. 163-68.*

EDMUND GOSSE   (essay date 1896)

[*Gosse was a distinguished English literary historian, critic, and biographer who wrote extensively on seventeenth- and eighteenth-century English literature. In the following excerpt from the Pix entry (first published in 1896) in* Dictionary of National Biography, *he comments briefly on Pix's principal dramas and considers the author's achievement as a playwright.*]

[Mrs. Mary Pix] devoted herself to dramatic authorship with more activity than had been shown before her time by any woman except Mrs. Afra Behn. . . . In 1697 she produced at Little Lincoln's Inn Fields, and then published, a comedy of *The Innocent Mistress.* This play, which was very successful, shows the influence of Congreve upon the author, and is the most readable of her productions. The prologue and epilogue were written by Peter Anthony Motteux. . . . It was followed the next year by *The Deceiver Deceived,* a comedy which failed, and which involved the poetess in a quarrel. She accused George Powell . . . the actor, of having seen the manuscript of her play, and of having stolen from it in his *Imposture Defeated.* On 8 Sept. 1698 an anonymous "Letter to Mr. Congreve" was published in the interests of Powell, from which it would seem that Congreve had by this time taken Mary Pix under his protection, with Mrs. Trotter, and was to be seen 'very gravely with his hat over his eyes . . . together with the two she-things called Poetesses.'. . . Her next play was a tragedy of *Queen Catharine,* brought out at Lincoln's Inn, and published in 1698. Mrs. Trotter wrote the epilogue. In her own prologue Mary Pix pays a warm tribute to Shakespeare [see poem dated 1698]. *The False Friend* followed, at the same house, in 1699; the title of this comedy was borrowed three years later by Vanbrugh.

Hitherto Mary Pix had been careful to put her name on her title-pages or dedications; but the comedy of *The Beau Defeated*—undated, but published in 1700—though anonymous, is certainly hers. In 1701 she produced a tragedy of *The Double Distress.* Two more plays have been attributed to Mary Pix by Downes [in his *Roscius Anglicanus* (1708).] One of these is *The Conquest of Spain,* an adaptation from Rowley's *All's lost by Lust,* which was brought out at the Queen's theatre in the Haymarket, ran for six nights, and was printed anonymously in 1705. . . . Finally, the comedy of the *Adventures in Madrid* was acted at the same house with Mrs. Bracegirdle in the cast, and printed anonymously and without date. . . .

The style of Mrs. Pix confirms the statements of her contemporaries that though, as she says in the dedication of the *Spanish Wives,* she had had an inclination to poetry from childhood, she was without learning of any sort. She is described as 'foolish and open-hearted,' and as being 'big enough to be the Mother of the Muses' [see excerpt dated 1696]. Her fatness and her love of good wine were matters of notoriety. Her comedies, though coarse, are far more decent than those of Mrs. Behn, and her comic bustle of dialogue is sometimes entertaining. Her tragedies are intolerable. She had not the most superficial idea of the way in which blank verse should be written, pompous prose, broken irregularly into lengths, being her ideal of versification. (p. 1275)

> Edmund Gosse, "Pix," in Dictionary of National Biography: Owens—Pockrich, Vol. XV, *edited by Sidney Lee, The Macmillan Company, 1909, pp. 1274-76.*

MYRA REYNOLDS   (essay date 1920)

[*Reynolds was an American scholar who wrote widely on English literature. In the following excerpt, she negatively assesses heroic traits in Pix's tragedies.*]

[Mrs. Pix] was thirty when she brought out her first play. During the ensuing ten years she put on the stage five tragedies, one comedy, and possibly other plays not under her name. Her tragedies, though written in blank verse, yet belong to the heroic *genre,* and their chief interest lies in the fact that they

represent that *genre* in its dying throes. In Mrs. Pix's tragedies the heroic play of Dryden's day could look upon its enfeebled and distorted image. We have the war background, the remoteness of time and place, the historical source with free alterations of persons and events, that mark the heroic drama. The type characters are the same. The heroine is unapproachable in beauty, unassailable in virtue. The hero, godlike in personal prowess, the idol of the army, framed by nature to be the darling joy of womankind, cares for glory only that he may lay it at the feet of his beloved. Blest by her he will leave unenvied monarchs to "fight for this Dunghil Earth." This noble pair, joined by indissoluble vows or by a secret marriage, are subjected by the plot to the machinations of the beautiful wicked woman in whose heart has sprung into being a passion for the hero, and to the arrogant demands of the tyrant who claims the heroine as his prey. The result is disaster and the last act is a holocaust. Fights, murders, and suicides carry off all the important *dramatis personae.* Disguises, mistaken identity, the ravings of sudden madness, ghosts, and secret documents, determine the events of the play. Passion is torn into exclamatory tatters from the first scene to the last. We have rant and bluster and tortured similes, until taste, good sense, and correct English suffer the same fate as the chief characters. The description of Mrs. Pix as "a fat female author," appropriately called "Mrs. Wellfed" [see excerpt dated 1696], would prepare us for something more placid than the chaos into which she leads us.

The one possible explanation of Mrs. Pix's acceptance year after year by the audiences of Drury Lane and Lincoln's Inn Fields is that the business of her plays never lags. They are short, full of action and surprising turns. An event is never delayed by a disquisition. They also gave excellent opportunity for scenic effects of palaces, prisons, and camps. (pp. 132-33)

> Myra Reynolds, in an excerpt from her The Learned Lady in England: 1650-1760, *Houghton Mifflin Company, 1920, pp. 132-33.*

ALLARDYCE NICOLL   (essay date 1925)

[*Called "one of the masters of dramatic research," Nicoll is best known as a theater historian whose works have proven invaluable to students of the drama. His* World Drama from Aeschylus to Anouilh *(1949) is considered a masterpiece; theater critic John Gassner, for example, described it as "unquestionably the most thorough [study] of its kind in the English language [and] our best reference book on the world's dramatic literature," and other critics have cited Nicoll's highly original and perceptive commentary here and elsewhere. In the following excerpt from a work first published in 1925 under a different title, Nicoll argues that Pix's tragedies are notable as early manifestations of developments that took place in the English drama during the first half of the eighteenth century.*]

[The] typical form of eighteenth century tragic drama, to which has been given the name of Augustan, was an amalgam of diverse forces—pseudo-classicism influencing it externally, pathos entering in to colour certain scenes and characters, Shakespearian style directing occasionally dialogue and theme, and heroics flickering luridly if spasmodically over the whole production. Quite naturally, this type presents no very decided and characteristic elements; it is to be regarded as a blundering attempt on the part of men who knew not what they desired to furnish actable plays for the theatre. They could give nothing definite to the stage; their plays are amorphous, chaotic in plot and undistinguished in character-drawing, yet such as they are they form the typical dramatic productions of the period.

Mrs Pix, possibly, is the first to call for attention. Her tragi-comedy, *The False Friend, Or, The Fate of Disobedience,* after her two tragedies, her farce and her two comedies of 1696-8, appeared at Lincoln's Inn Fields in the spring of 1699. This play, which seems to have been almost universally neglected by those who have written of her works, is symptomatic of her later efforts. Already she had tried heroics in *Ibrahim* and in *Queen Catherine*; now she attempted an essay in a slightly domestic theme with a "moral" plot. The play is not valuable unless when considered in relation to her other works. From this date (1699) to 1705 Mrs Pix furnished the stage with three tragedies, all presenting mixed characteristics of classicism, heroics and pathos. *The Double Distress* came out at Lincoln's Inn Fields about March 1701, an unsuccessful production. Interesting in it are the many passages in rimed verse. *The Czar of Muscovy* was produced at the same theatre a few months later. It is more classical than any of her other dramas, although in this tragedy of Dmitri the Pretender there are many features of a sentimental cast. Particularly noticeable are the touches of nature love, such as Marina's moralisations in v. iii.; "How happy is the humble Cottager, who never knows the Madness of Ambition?" is a sentence premonitory of many sentimentalisings in the years to come. Mrs Pix' last serious drama was *The Conquest of Spain,* a play founded on Rowley's *All's Lost by Lust.* There are elements of romantic treatment in it; there are features of the heroic tragedy; there is the loyalty adored by the Stuart writers; there are the same touches of nature love. Even from this necessarily brief account, it will be evident that Mrs Pix gave nothing new to the theatre. Her plays have interest solely because they provide early examples of that union of the separate dramatic forces which was to dominate tragedy for well over fifty years. (pp. 96-7)

Allardyce Nicoll, "Tragedy," in his A History of English Drama, 1660-1900: Early Eighteenth Century Drama, Vol. II, third edition, Cambridge at the University Press, 1952, pp. 51-114.

JAMES M. EDMUNDS (essay date 1933)

[*In the following essay, Edmunds points to sentimental elements in* The Spanish Wives *as signs of "a definite break" with Restoration drama.*]

The Spanish Wives by Mary Griffith Pix, presented at Dorset Garden about September 1696, represents in spite of its date a definite break with the Restoration tradition, a break which in some respects is almost as definite as that of its predecessor of a few months, *Love's Last Shift.* Yet it seems to have been overlooked by most commentators on the sentimental comedy. Allardyce Nicoll says of it **"The Spanish Wives . . .** moves in a purely Restoration atmosphere, is set in Barcelona and deals mainly with the Governor, (a merry old Lord), who gives his wife, but not successfully for himself, more liberties than appear to have been usual in contemporary Spain" [see Additional Bibliography].

Like so many other plays of its period, this one deals with the problem of marriage. What is the proper method to control a wife? How can the husband insure himself against becoming a cuckold? There are two treatments of the problem in this

play. The first concerns the Governor and his Lady. The Governor sums up his method in one of his many songs:

> Give but a Woman her Freedom still,
> Then she'll never act what's ill:
> 'Tis crossing her, makes her have the Will.

Needless to say, the Governor is unsuccessful. He preserves his honor, but discovers the weakness of his wife. Even in this typically Restoration situation there is some evidence of a weakly sentimental treatment; the wife is excused because her lover is a paragon of lovers, the only one of his kind. Once separated from him, the wife is sure she will never again overstep the bounds of modesty; the husband believes her, and all is forgiven.

If it were true that the main plot is concerned with the Governor, there would be justification for the statement of Nicoll quoted above; but by page count, the amount of space devoted to the Governor plot and to the linkages between that plot and the other constitutes much less than half the play. The Governor and his Lady form the background against which the more interesting and more dramatic Marquess of Moncada–Elenora–Count Camillus plot is worked out. A noble Roman lady is married to a jealous Spanish lord against her will. She had earlier been betrothed to the Count Camillus, but financial settlements had led her relatives to marry her to the Spaniard. Her only care is to escape from the Spaniard and join her lover, provided of course, that her marriage can be annulled and the Count will maintain his purpose to marry her.

Mrs. Pix makes lengthy preparation for the excusing of Elenora's action. She presents her sad case to the audience in the opening of Act Two:

> I am a thing accurs'd by cruel Guardians,
> For my Parents dy'd when I was young; they wou'd not else
> Sure have fore'd me, condemn'd to an old jealous
> Madman. . . . I saw his Follies and his Humors, and I begg'd,
> Like a poor Slave, who views the Rack before him, . . .
> All in vain; they were inexorable . . . so may just Heaven
> Prove to them in their greatest need!

The audience, though knowing the play is not serious, is led to fear with her that she must "remove from *Barcellona* to Wilds and unfrequented Desarts, impenetrable Castles, and all the melancholy Mischiefs spritely Youth can fear." Even before Elenora's speech, Mrs. Pix prepares for the forgiveness of the lovers through one of the Count's speeches. Early in Act One he says:

> You know there's Justice in my Cause. . . .
> *Elenora* was, by Contract, mine, at *Rome;*
> Before this old Marquess had her. And cou'd I agen
> Recover her: I don't question but to get Leave of his Holiness
> For a Divorce, and marry her my self.

The Count's attitude is not that of the Restoration rake. Mrs. Pix further shows her hero in a new light when she has him reprove the Colonel, the lover of the Governor's wife, for his evil ways:

> *Camillus.* Ah Colonel! our Cases are very different,. . . You hunt but for Enjoyment, the huddl'd Raptures of a few tumultuous moments:. . . But I am in quest of Virgin-Beauty, made mine by Holy Vows; constrain'd by Fiends, instead of Friends, to break the sacred Contract, and follow the *Capricio* of a mad Old Man. . . . Virgin did I call her?. . . By Heaven, I dare believe she is one, at least her Mind is such;. . . and were she in my power, I'd soon convince the World of the Justice of my Cause.

263

This is not a secret intrigue, something to keep from the eyes of the world, but something of which to be proud.

Even the Friar, aid to Count Camillus, the most thoroughly Restoration character in the play, recognizes that his master is not in the existing tradition:

> By St. *Dominick,* well said, old Boy: I'll stick to thee. I hate these whining Romantick Lovers. Nor wou'd I have trudg'd to *Barcellona,* had I thought the Count only fix'd on *Honora,*. . . Psha, I can get it out, Honourable Love.

At the first meeting of Elenora and the Count Camillus, after the abduction, the Count runs to her. She says, "I can say only this: I love ye . . ." to which he replies:

> And not descending Angels, with all their Heavenly Tunes, cou'd Charm like that dear sound!. . . safe in a Monastery thou shalt remain, till the Dispute is ended. And then . . . Oh! thou blest Charmer . . . then all my Sufferings shall be liberally paid; and longing Love Revel in Feasts of unutterable Delight.

Later, when the Governor arrives, Camillus again mentions the monastery. Elenora agrees: "I freely submit, and will retire to what Monastery you appoint. I hope my future Conduct will satisfie the World of my Innocency." Camillus replies, "And mine, of my Faith and Constancy." Certainly these are not the sentiments of a Restoration lover. Nor is the Count's speech, "I'm glad on't . . . in your Age you never will repent an uncommitted Sin," spoken to the Colonel, when that character says that he is entirely reformed, Restoration in tone.

Perhaps the atmosphere of the play is Restoration, for the servants are typical, intriguing, Restoration servants, not above serving two masters at the same time; the story of the Governor and his Lady is not sufficiently different to be worthy of note; and the Colonel is a true Restoration rake. But the larger portion of the play is based upon the Elenora–Camillus plot, and neither of these characters belongs to the time in which they were portrayed.

Bernbaum defines sentimental comedy in part by saying that it shows characters "contending against distresses but finally rewarded by morally deserved happiness." The Elenora–Camillus plot fulfills at least this much of the definition. Elenora, as presented in her speech at the opening of Act Two, quoted above, is a heroine worthy of Richard Cumberland. Alone, orphaned, in the care of unscrupulous relatives, forced to break her betrothal vows and marry an ogre who is interested only in the marriage settlement, Elenora would have found favor with a Cumberland audience. We are expected to sympathize with her and to rejoice in the eventual overcoming of the obstacles put in her way to happiness. (pp. 94-7)

> *James M. Edmunds, "An Example of Early Senti-mentalism," in* Modern Language Notes, *Vol. XLVIII, No. 2, February, 1933, pp. 94-7.*

ROBERT ADAMS DAY (essay date 1980)

[*Day is an American scholar of English literature. In the following excerpt, he attempts to account for the failure of Pix and her female contemporaries to be adequately recognized for their intellects and their works.*]

Among the mournful cypresses metaphorically laid on the tomb of the English Poet Laureate John Dryden in 1700 was a tasteful folio pamphlet entitled *The Nine Muses,* containing laments allegedly by these deities, each in a meter and with themes appropriate to its author. The verses were by aspiring women poets, of whom most were, and must remain, anonymous; but three are identified as "Mrs. Pix, Mrs. Manley, and Mrs. Trotter." Each had had a play produced in the season of 1695-96, and they had been bound together in caricature, pilloried in a play called *The Female Wits* [see excerpt dated 1696], produced at Drury Lane in October 1696. Together with Mrs. Aphra Behn, who had died but a few years earlier, in 1689, they were among the most prominent of the few women writers in seventeenth-century England.

Although these four British Muses possessed no small measure of literary talent, and though each wrote in several genres enough to fill two or more stout volumes, none of them was able to attain or at any rate to maintain the combination of a comfortable living, a respectable status in society, fame, or a general recognition of merit in literary circles, even if not with the general public. Why did our British Muses fare so ill? For fare ill they did.

After admirably competing with male playwrights through the 1670s, Aphra Behn seems to have spent the 1680s in poverty, grinding out at a frantic rate short novels, translations from the French, and occasional poems for the few pounds a dedication might bring. Her posthumous reputation, until she was rescued in the early years of this century by the eccentric scholar Montague Summers, was for nothing more than shocking obscenity, or at very least improper eroticism. Mrs. Mary Pix, for ten years a writer of farces, serious plays, and an almost unknown novel, seems to have met derision with equanimity and had some modest success; but her plays were ignored after 1706. Mrs. Catherine Trotter, author at fourteen of a remarkable little novel and at seventeen of a successful tragedy, *Agnes de Castro,* wrote four other plays with rather less success, some poems, and treatises which we shall consider presently. But after 1708, when she married an impecunious and high-minded clergyman, she was, says her biographer [Thomas Birch in *The Works of Mrs. Catherine Cockburn* (1751)], "entirely diverted from her studies for many years, by attending upon the duties of a wife and mother, and by the ordinary cares of an increasing family, and the additional ones arising from the reduced circumstances of her husband." A political journalist and pamphleteer, Mrs. Delariviere Manley wrote five plays and at least six works of fiction. Yet she seems to have been more than glad to forsake politics for love in 1714, both in her writings, as she avers, and in life; heavily in debt and perhaps suffering from phlebitis, she was for her last ten years the mistress of Alderman John Barber, a prosperous printer, and remained silent except for a single play, some stories, and a novel which was published posthumously. Thus the Muses of King William's London, after shining briefly, were ignominiously extinguished, dying poor and obscure. Was their neglect merited, or not? Let me complicate the question by considering four facts: they wrote plays, they wrote novels, they were socially in the same rather unusual category, and they were intellectuals. The last fact first.

If our four Muses had done no more than produce a few trivial comedies, we might dismiss them with the rule *de minimis non curat lex* ["the law does not regard trifles"]: why *should* they deserve anything more than the corner of a footnote? But three of them (and Mary Pix, the exception, is an instructive exception, to whom we shall return) would rate on anybody's scale as intellectuals. Mrs. Trotter . . . was almost certainly the author, at the astonishing age of fourteen, of a technically excellent novella, *Olinda's Adventures,* which had the distinction, virtually unique at the time, of appearing in France as *Les amours d'une belle angloise;* she learned French, Latin, and logic with little or no assistance; she wrote two comedies that earned the flattering attention of the playwright William Congreve, with whom her platonic friendship became well known; she wrote and published philosophical treatises, one in defense of Locke's *Essay Concerning Human Understanding* against an anonymous attacker in the so-called "Locke-Stillingfleet controversy" of 1697, resulting in a letter from Locke which was more than merely a polite compliment. Leibniz was told about her, as was the cultivated Queen of Prussia, who referred to her as "the Scots Sappho."

Mrs. Behn wrote as her first essay in fiction a technically astonishing epistolary novel, *Love Letters Between a Nobleman and his Sister,* and her stories *Oroonoko* and *The Fair Jilt* still figure regularly in anthologies. She acquired sufficient knowledge of French to publish several book-length translations: not of frivolous fiction, but of Rochefoucauld (entitled *Seneca Unmasq'd*); of Fontenelle's *Dialogues on the Plurality of Worlds* and his translation of a history of pagan oracles, and of a work of Cowley on botany. In her preface to Fontenelle she made pronouncements on the theory and practice of translation which, though less clearly expressed, are not notably inferior to Dryden's, and some brief though rather amazing comments, concerning what would later be called the Higher Criticism of Scripture. Mrs. Manley (if we except her five plays, dramatic attempts which were technically innovative, and even if we except her scandal-chronicles *Queen Zarah, The New Atlantis,* and *Memoirs of a Certain Island*) generated sufficient intellectual voltage to receive high if qualified compliments from Swift in the *Journal to Stella,* and the higher compliment of relinquishing into her hands the editorship of his political journal *The Examiner* in 1711. She wrote at least seven *Examiners,* and five or six political pamphlets praised by Swift, so that without exaggeration we may call her Swift's collaborator in an enterprise that he saw as having a weighty and serious political purpose. A biographer holds that "in open competition with the best minds, she held her own and emerged with a creditable record," and that Swift, arguably the best mind of Queen Anne's day, "treated her simply as a fellow writer." Some of her critical remarks in the preface to *Queen Zarah* have been hailed by modern critics as of great innovative significance.

Now let us briefly consider the first, second, and third points mentioned earlier. Authors of eighteen (Behn), twelve (Pix), five, and five plays respectively, they were not mere dabblers in drama; and though Catherine Trotter and Mary Pix wrote but one novel each, Mrs. Behn's collected fiction would fill two good-sized modern volumes and Mrs. Manley's three. They were not "one-book novelists." The last point is a double one: they were all of gentle, though not of aristocratic birth; and they were all, for their day, socially unmoored—that is, adrift. Mrs. Manley, daughter of Sir Roger Manley, a Royalist military governor and man of letters, was the survivor of a disastrous marriage to a cousin in adolescence. Mrs. Trotter, daughter of a naval captain and distantly related to the eminent Burnet family, was living in genteel poverty with her widowed mother, while Mrs. Behn was probably of gentle or conjecturally of illegitimately noble birth. Mrs. Pix, child of a country clergyman, was married to a merchant tailor, and she was notoriously fond of the table and the bottle.

So much for the lives: now for the documents. The authors of *The Nine Muses* are identified only by initials, and the dedicatory preface is written by the bookseller, Richard Bassett. It is pretty clear that he solicited the poems himself, to turn an honest penny; but he refrains from taking whatever advantage he might gain by naming names, he harps at length on the modesty of the fair sex, and he rather irrelevantly, it would seem (since the ladies are unknown), refers to their supposed beauty, seeming to feel that a plain or ugly female wit is shoddy goods indeed. Of our ladies Mrs. Manley is Melpomene, the Tragick Muse; Mrs. Pix Clio, the Historick Muse; and Mrs. Trotter Calliope, the Heroick Muse. All three write their elegies in iambic pentameter couplets, with an occasional triplet; they dwell respectively on Dryden's tragedies, public poems, and Vergilian translations; and except for Mrs. Trotter, who takes a witty swipe or two at such third-rate poetic translators of epic as Blackmore, Hobbes, Chapman, and Ogilby, their verses are as bad as verses can be. *The Nine Muses* is worthless in itself, but for our purposes three facts are salient and will be reverted to. The form is old, sanctioned, respectable—the garland of elegies for a deceased worthy. The mode is classical—the elegy, replete with Great Pan, nymphs, genii, and deities. And the authors are women, modestly veiled.

Our second document is also very bad indeed. The modern editor concludes, however, that the author's animus is principally against two disquieting facts—that *The Royal Mischief* (and other recent plays by, and to a certain extent for, women) had been rather more successful than he liked, and that Mrs. Manley's heroine, supremely wicked and lustful, had out-ranted the heroines of heroic tragedy (she has an unprecedented *six* tirades to deliver) in a way that the audience liked too much for competing male playwrights' peace of mind. For something of a phenomenon had marked the theater seasons of 1695 and 1696; no less than seven plays by women had appeared—Mrs. Pix's tragedy **Ibrahim** and her comedy **The Spanish Wives,** Mrs. Manley's comedy *The Lost Lover* as well as *The Royal Mischief,* Mrs. Behn's posthumously produced comedy *The Younger Brother,* Mrs. Trotter's very popular tragedy *Agnes de Castro,* and a comedy entitled *She Ventures and He Wins* by a lady who called herself "Ariadne." *The Royal Mischief* and its sister plays were no worse than much of the trash that London was applauding in the 1690s. Mrs. Manley says bitterly and not unjustly of herself in her romanticized autobiography, *The Adventures of Rivella,* "if she had been a man, she had been without fault," and concludes tartly and probably with reference to her detention and interrogation by the secretaries of state over *The New Atalantis* in 1709, "politicks is not the business of a woman." We could multiply examples, but a few more, with reference to Mrs. Behn and of particular significance, will suffice. Her first plays, *The Forc'd Marriage* and *The Amorous Prince,* appeared with only passing reference—the pronoun "she"—to the author's sex, but in her third, *The Dutch Lover* (1673), an epistle to the reader reveals it with wry humility in a discourse where irritation clearly struggles with caution. But she makes the significant and protective statement, "Plays have no great room for that which is men's great advantage over women, *that is learning.*" However, regardless of what critics might think of her, the public went assiduously to see her plays throughout the 1670s. But in 1683, when she had turned to other kinds of writing, Dryden issued a translation of Ovid's *Heroides* by several hands, the epistle of Oenone to Paris being from her pen. Dryden said gallantly in the introduction, "I was desir'd to say that the author, who is of the Fair Sex . . . understood not Latine. But if she does not, I am afraid she has given us occasion to be ashamed who do." But the poet Matthew Prior lost his temper. In his *Satyr* *on the Modern Translators*, the lady is vituperatively skewered as

> our blind translatress *Behn*,
> The Female Wit, who next convicted stands,
> Not for abusing *Ovid's* verse, but *Sand's:*
> She might have learn'd from the ill-borrow'd Grace,
> (Which little helps the ruine of her Face)
> That Wit, like Beauty, triumphs o're the Heart,
> When more of Nature's seen, and less of Art:
> Nor strive in *Ovid's* letters to have shown,
> As much of skill, as lewdness in her own:
> Then let her from the next inconstant Lover,
> Take a new Copy for a second *Rover,*
> Describe the cunning of a jilting Whore,
> From the ill Arts her self has us'd before;
> Then let her write, but Paraphrase no more.

No holds barred. If a woman writer was the victim, the "slovenly butchering" of which Dryden spoke was the preferred method in satire. In the context of the times, the playwright, unless buttressed by rank and position or an eminent patron, was not taken seriously—he lived in a no man's land beneath consideration, socially and intellectually. In Dr. Johnson's words, "We, that live to please, must please to live;" and with the much-derided exception of *Ben* Jonson's *Works*, the haphazard textual and publishing history of Elizabethan and seventeenth-century plays gives ample supporting evidence for this statement. But Jonson is likewise important as an example: he, unlike Shakespeare, publicly plumed himself on his classical learning, and wrote comedies and tragedies ostentatiously modeled on the classics: unlike Shakespeare, he was, he hoped, the successor of Terence and Plautus, and therefore wrote *Works—opera—*not "stage-plays."

Anthropologist Mary Douglas has investigated traditional systems of taboo and concepts of dirt or pollution. She sums up her conclusions (which she applies not only to the taboos of African tribesmen, but to Hebrew dietary laws and many analogous cultural systems): "We avoid anomalous animals because in defying the categories of our universe they arouse deep feelings of disquiet." The three most important characteristics of taboo systems are extreme rigidity, simple criteria based on grossly inadequate observation, and enormous emotional power. It may seem anomalous to speak of taboo and pollution in connection with the arts, but the classical theory of genres and of literature, given at least lip-service by all in 1700, is very much to the point.

Heroic poetry, classical comedy and tragedy, history, oratory, the elegy and epistle, and satire, make up a sacred system: drama not imitative of the classics, and prose fiction, are taboo, because they were nonexistent or anomalous when the categories developed and froze. The Ancients-and-Moderns controversies in late seventeenth-century England and France are relevant here; and even that pioneering critical document, the *Traité sur les romans* of the learned Bishop Huet of Avranches (1673) spends most of its time on the novel of antiquity and on prose fiction as a variant of the heroic poem. Three or four taboo-systems operate here—that of clean and unclean literature, that of public behaviour for men and for women, that of clean and unclean literary persons, and that of classical education and higher knowledge—reserved, like the fat of beasts, for the priestly class, though Levites might partake with caution and in the fear of God. Such an anthropological view has been applied to education by Walter Ong, who aptly compares classical education, with its required mastery of Latin, to a puberty rite, an initiation, a *rite de passage:* "isolation from the family, the achievement of identity in a totally male group (the school), the learning of a body of relatively abstract tribal lore inaccessible to those outside the group." Including the lower classes (though perhaps not the occasional peasant-poet, made much of by the avant-garde) and all women.

But it would be a distortion to say that at the end of the seventeenth century European prose fiction and popular drama were merely ritually nonexistent, taboo, or unclean and therefore terrifying. Mary Douglas also points our that when "dirt" has been swept aside into its proper place and is undifferentiated, ignored, and therefore above all unclassified, it loses its power: "so long as identity is absent," she says, "rubbish is not dangerous." We now begin to see daylight if we combine literary history with anthropology and bring them to bear on the hierarchical circles of society and art. If clean literature is bounded by the lines laid down in antiquity and if clean literary practitioners are men of position, by definition trained in the classics, clean women cannot of course practice literature for the simple reason that they never did, except for the two ancient Greek monsters Sappho and Corinna; and in the 1890s Eugene Field depicted a Midwestern *arbiter elegantiarum* as saying, "That Sappho was a gamey old girl, you know; she would have been tabooed in Chicago."

> # THE
> # ADVENTURES
> ### IN
> # MADRID.
> ### A
> # COMEDY,
> As it is Acted at the Queens Theatre in the *Hay-Market.*
>
> ## By Her Majesty's Servants.
>
> ---
>
> ### *LONDON:*
> Printed for *William Turner* at the *Angel* at *Lincolns-Inn* Back-Gate, *James Knapton* at the *Crown* in St. *Paul's Church-Yard,* *Bernard Lintot* in *Fleetstreet,* and B. *Bragg* at the *Black Raven* in *Pater-Noster-Row.* Price 1*s.* 6*d.*

Title page of one of Pix's later dramas, a comedy first performed in 1706.

It might be objected that Dryden's famous poem of 1686, "To the Pious Memory of Mrs. Anne Killigrew," which extravagantly celebrates her as a poet and a painter, is an example to the contrary. But it is not, if we consider that Dryden knew which side his bread was buttered on. Mistress Killigrew had been maid of honor to Mary of Modena, Duchess of York and Queen to James II, she was a member of the Killigrew family, favorites of both Charles II and his brother James and proprietors of one of London's two theaters (and Dryden was a playwright); she was sister to an admiral; and most important, she died young, before she had time either to become very sinful or to accomplish very much at either poetry or painting. And her poems were published posthumously.

Of course there were exceptions; these prove the rule. Katherine Philips, "the matchless Orinda," was a gentlewoman born, married to a gentleman of wealth; her poems circulated only in manuscript, and she was furious when they were published by an enterprising bookseller. Elizabeth Elstob, who knew eight languages and published Anglo-Saxon texts and a grammar of that language, got her learning from, and lived with, her learned brother; after his death she become a poverty-stricken schoolteacher and governess. Mme. Dacier was the wife of a learned humanist and the daughter of another. The eccentric Duchess of Newcastle was a duchess; need one say more? Though she was often called "mad," no one said it to her face. Recent studies of Anne Finch, Countess of Winchilsea, make it obvious that she was torn between the desire to write and the fear that she would be condemned for seeming to seek public praise. She adopted the matchless Orinda as her model. Lady Mary Wroth, who published in 1621 a prose romance, *Urania*, containing many Petrarchan sonnets, had to withdraw it from sale and retrieve as many copies as she could when courtiers complained to King James that court scandals were depicted in it. Daughter of Sir Philip Sidney's brother Sir Robert, she had to content herself thereafter, as befitted a lady, with such praise as she might gain from the circulation of her poems in manuscript among the poets of the day and the reprinting of some of them in *The Countess Montgomery's Urania*. All were "clean" women. Mrs. Pix, the remaining anomaly, was not so at all; jolly and comfortable (*and*, after all, married), she never raised her head above the dunghill of fiction and popular drama, where she remained rooting contentedly or at least quietly. Lastly, the dramatic successes of Mmes. Behn, Manley, Pix, and Trotter were short-lived. The reasons were complicated, but one at least is clear: a clean woman, except in the wicked 1670s, now piously scorned, had not yet been a successful playwright. (pp. 61-9)

> *Robert Adams Day, "Muses in the Mud: The Female Wits Anthropologically Considered," in* Women's Studies, *Vol. 7, No. 3, 1980, pp. 61-74.*

NANCY COTTON (essay date 1980)

[*Cotton is an American scholar who has written extensively on early English women dramatists. In the following excerpt, she surveys Pix's literary career, describing and evaluating most of the plays.*]

The 1695-96 theatrical season introduced four new women playwrights. An anonymous "young Lady" wrote *She Ventures and He Wins* under the nom de plume Ariadne. The other newcomers were Catherine Trotter with *Agnes de Castro*, Delariviere Manley with *The Lost Lover* and *The Royal Mischief*, and Mary Pix with *Ibrahim* and *The Spanish Wives*. All these women wrote in emulation of Behn, but each was markedly different from the others. (pp. 81-2)

The third new woman playwright, Mary Griffith Pix (1666-1709), was different in class and background from Manley and Trotter. Her father was a vicar in Oxfordshire, and her mother had good family connections, so we can assume a home of some books and learning. In 1684, at the age of eighteen, Mary Griffith married George Pix, a London merchant tailor about her own age. They had one child, who died in 1690. At the age of thirty, Mary Pix began a career as a writer, an unusual step for the wife of a London merchant. It is possible that George Pix died and that Mary Pix turned to the theater for a livelihood; perhaps the Pix family may have been economically distressed for some other reason. It is also possible that Pix wrote merely to please herself: she says in the dedication to her first comedy, *The Spanish Wives*, that from childhood she had an "Inclination to Poetry." Whatever the reasons for Pix's becoming a professional author, in 1696 she produced a novel, *The Inhuman Cardinal; or, Innocence Betrayed*; a tragedy, *Ibrahim, the Thirteenth Emperor of the Turks*; and a comedy, *The Spanish Wives*.

Ibrahim, a historical tragedy, was produced by the patent company in late spring. The action turns on Sultan Ibrahim's rape of Morena, fiancée of General Amurat. Sheker Para, the sultan's chief mistress, instigates the rape to gain revenge on Amurat for rebuffing her amorous advances. The play ends with the political downfall and death of Ibrahim, and the suicide of Sheker Para. Morena poisons herself in emulation of Roman heroines like Lucrece, and Amurat stabs himself for grief. Although based on historical events, the play is Fletcherian in structure and language; it reads like *Valentinian* with an eastern setting. *Ibrahim* contains some stageworthy scenes, Morena kneels to the sultan and pleads piteously for her honor; she bloodies her hands snatching the sultan's scimitar in a suicide attempt; after the rape, she raves and Amurat rages. A contemporary critic [Charles Gildon; see excerpt dated 1699] gives a fair evaluation: "This Play, if it want the Harmony of Numbers, and the Sublimity of Expression, has yet a Quality, that at least ballances that Defect, I mean the Passions; for the Distress of Morena never fail'd to bring Tears into the Eyes of the Audience; which few Plays, if any since Otway's have done."

Ibrahim was successful not only in 1696 but in later years; it was performed several times in 1704 and revived in 1715. In the dedication Pix modestly credits her success to the fact that the story was true and that the actors "gave it Life . . . each maintain'd their Character beyond my hopes." She adds a preface to correct a mistake: Ibrahim was the twelfth rather than the thirteenth Turkish emperor. This self-conscious accuracy goes along with the humility she expresses, in both dedication and preface, about her sex. A close reading, she says, "will too soon find out the Woman, the imperfect Woman."

That summer Pix asked the town to "Oblige a Woman twice" in her prologue to a three-act comedy, *The Spanish Wives*. A skillful double plot contrasts the situations of two young wives. The first is married to the merry old governor of Barcelona, who "gives his Wife more Liberty than is usual in Spain" (dramatis personae). His policy is vindicated. Although the governor's lady is tempted by the advances of a young English colonel, she is touched by her husband's goodness, repents, and vows fidelity. In contrast, Elenora is kept "under eleven Locks" by her husband, a jealous and avaricious marquess forced on her by cruel guardians. She had previously been contracted to Count Camillus, who, bent on retrieving his bride, successfully intrigues to steal Elenora from her husband and obtain a divorce for her. The marquess is comically contemptible. He regrets the loss of his wife's fortune as much as the loss of her person, crying out distractedly, "My Estate and my Wife" in the manner of Shylock's "My ducats, and my daughter." The governor is also comic, but neither foolish nor contemptible. Continually breaking into snatches of song, he is reminiscent of Old Merrythought in *The Knight of the Burning Pestle*. *The Spanish Wives,* though slight, is a lively and amusing farce. Some of the marital repartee is tellingly human. Music, song, dance, and disguise add to the fun and provide stage spectacle. Not surprisingly, "this Farce had the good Fortune to please"; performances are recorded as late as 1726. Of the plays offered by women in the 1695-96 season, Pix's are the most entertaining and stageworthy. (pp. 88-90)

[In the summer of 1697, Pix] brought out a comedy, *The Innocent Mistress*. . . . The play picks up again the theme of forced marriage used in *The Spanish Wives*. The most important of a number of interwoven plots concerns Sir Charles Beauclair, now master of a large estate, but earlier "Marrid by his Friends, to a Rich ill-favour'd Widow" (dramatis personae). He nobly endures his terrible wife and "instead of making his life easie with jolly *Bona-robas,* dotes on a Platonick Mistress, who never allows him greater favours then to read Plays to her, kiss her hand, and fetch Heart-breaking Sighs at her Feet." This is Bellinda, who fell in love with Sir Charles before she knew he was married. Even though their relationship is strictly platonic, her conscience afflicts her. After a high-flown renunciation scene between the lovers, Lady Beauclair is recognized and reclaimed by her first husband, long thought dead. [According to Charles Gildon] *The Innocent Mistress* was "a diverting Play, and met with good Success, tho' acted in the hot Season of the Year."

Oddly enough, it was "sociable well-natur'd" Mary Pix who a few months later was at the center of an acrimonious dispute between the rival playhouses. In September 1697 George Powell, an actor and sometimes playwright for the patent company, brought out a comedy called *Imposture Defeated; or, A Trick to Cheat the Devil*. Pix protested that the play was a plagiarism. (pp. 111-12)

A comparison of the two plays shows that Powell lifted the main plot outline. In Pix's *Deceiver Deceived,* an avaricious old Venetian senator named Bondi counterfeits blindness in order to avoid the expense of the presidency of Dalmatia. His young wife and his daughter seize the opportunity to wear their richest jewels and clothes, to write love letters, and to entertain their gallants—all under Bondi's very nose. Unable to bear this torture, Bondi fakes a miraculous religious cure. At this point the young lovers are helped by a servant who knows the blindness was a cheat. Under threat of exposure for political and religious fraud, Bondi is forced to dower his daughter so that she can marry her poor but worthy suitor. The young wife, a sympathetic *mal mariée*, was in love with her gallant before she was forced to marry Bondi. She has flirted during her husband's "blindness" but has preserved her honor; she now gives up her gallant with the wistful hope that she may be left a young widow. In Powell's *Imposture Defeated,* Bonde also feigns blindness in order to avoid the expense of the governorship of Dalmatia. Like Bondi, Bonde, when threatened with exposure, gives up his wealth and his daughter to the daughter's suitor. Powell exploits the pretended blindness to better dramatic effect than Pix. Bonde's wife is actually lustful and dishonest, and the revelation of Bonde's pretense comes at the right moment to expose her. This is the natural and expected turn in such a plot—the moment when the "blind" husband can no longer restrain himself and exposes his own dishonesty to catch his wife *in flagrante delicto*. Pix cannot exploit this expectation because she is sentimentalizing the wife; the wife is never going to be *in flagrante delicto*. Bondi's "cure" is oddly flat. (pp. 112-13)

Pix's prologue [to *Queen Catharine; or, The Ruines of Love;* see poem dated 1698] acknowledges the presumption of writing a history play after Shakespeare, and modestly admits the inability of her "enervate voice" to "wake the mighty dead." She will therefore confine herself to the romantic rather than the martial side of history. Accordingly, her heroine is Henry V's widow. Edward IV in his youth fell in love with Catharine but she preferred Owen Tudor. Edward has since done all he could to persecute the queen and her husband, who are the model of a happy couple. The Duke of Gloucester (only perfunctorily characterized, since the audience already knows he will be the villainous Richard III) arranges for Edward to surprise Tudor and Catharine. Tudor is killed, the queen goes half-mad with grief, and Lord Dacres predicts that their children will produce a noble race of princes. In the subplot, Gloucester's schemes prevent a marriage between the Duke of Clarence and Queen Catharine's ward Isabella. This romance has naturally divided Clarence's loyalties in the ongoing civil war. The play reduces the Wars of the Roses to a quarrel over thwarted love.

In 1699 Pix wrote *The False Friend; or, The Fate of Disobedience,* announcing in the prologue her intention of participating in the reform of the stage [see poem dated 1699]. This purpose produced the worst of her plays. She intends to show the error of two young couples who marry secretly without parental consent, but since all are noble and wealthy, it seems likely that the father's consent would eventually have been forthcoming. The real mistake the young lovers make is trusting their false friend Appamia, who secretly loves one of the young men. Her jealous machinations lead to a fatal duel between the two husbands, the poisoning of one wife, and the madness of the other. Appamia, as she is led away to prison, counsels: "Let me for ever / Warn my Sex, and fright 'em from the thoughts of / Black Revenge." The father draws the feeble moral that children should obey their parents "Lest they are punish't such a dismal way."

The next year, in 1700, Pix returned to intrigue comedy and wrote one of her best, *The Beau Defeated; or, The Lucky Younger Brother*. The play is based on Dancourt's *Le Chevalier à la Mode*, and Pix is careful in the dedication to announce that "the Play is partly a Translation from the French," a point she reemphasizes in the prologue and epilogue. *The Beau Defeated* is an amusing play about two wealthy widows. Lady Landsworth, a widow of quality, resolves to marry a man virtuous and witty; he must also be poor and unaware that she is rich. She finds the man by going vizarded to the playhouse. He thinks her a prostitute; she is made to believe that he is a libertine. When the misunderstandings are cleared up, they decide to marry. In an interwoven plot, Mrs. Rich, a merchant's widow, resolves to attain quality. She assumes fashionable affectations and supports a retinue of parasites to instruct her in scandal and gaming. She plans to gain a title by marrying Sir John Roverhead. Her friends expose this beau as a disguised servant, and half-trick, half-persuade her into marrying a country squire, bumpkinish but honest and wealthy. She abandons her class pretensions, and her brother-in-law, Mr. Rich, concludes the play with an encomium of the English merchant.

In 1701 Pix wrote two more tragedies, *The Czar of Muscovy* and *The Double Distress*. Like *Queen Catharine, The Czar of Muscovy* reduces history to amorous intrigue. The impostor Demetrius, successfully installed as the Russian czar, proceeds to a course of tyranny that alienates his former allies and provokes a revolution in which he is slain by the true heir, Zueski. We hear of Demetrius's political tyranny; what is dramatized is his sexual tyranny. At his wedding to Marina he falls in love with Zarrianna, Zueski's fiancée. Demetrius intends to divorce Marina and marry Zarrianna. When both ladies resist dishonor, he determines to rape Zarrianna and murder his wife. In the fifth-act finale, the ladies are rescued by Zueski and Alexander, Marina's former fiancé. The dying Demetrius regrets more than the loss of empire the loss of amorous gratification. This fast-paced prose tragedy reads like a lively acting play. There are spirited scenes of rant for the heroines, threats of rape and speeches of defiance, melting scenes between lovers in transports. Although derivative of Fletcher in content and language, *The Czar of Muscovy* is one of Pix's better tragedies. *The Double Distress* depicts the adventures of two princesses whose love affairs are snarled by the wars between the Persians and the Medes. The plot, with its mistaken identities and suggested incest, is a variant of Beaumont and Fletcher's *A King and No King;* Pix uses the name Tygranes to call attention to the borrowing. The only information about the fate of the play is Pix's comment in the dedication: "The Success answered my Expectation."

Pix's production now slowed. Her next play appeared two years later, in 1703. *The Different Widows; or, Intrigue All-A-Mode* comically contrasts two sisters, Lady Gaylove and Lady Bellmont. The idle and intriguing Lady Gaylove conceals her age by dressing her grown son and daughter in children's clothes and keeping them in total ignorance. Valentine, who wishes to marry the daughter, steals the two and enlightens them as to their age and fortunes. The daughter easily adapts to her new status, but Lady Gaylove's son remains a hopeless booby. Contrasted with her sister is Lady Bellmont, virtuous mother of the witty debauchee Sir James Bellmont. She plans to marry him to the rich and beautiful Angelica, who uses her wit to attract and then reform Sir James. The plot is extremely busy, full of complicated intrigues, disguises, and mistaken identities. Numerous subplots involve characters whose assignations end laughably with the parties hiding in closets, under couches, in chests, and under beds.

Mary Pix finished her career as a playwright with a tragedy and a comedy—*The Conquest of Spain* (1705) and *The Adventures in Madrid* (1706)—very similar to the first two plays she wrote. As *Ibrahim* had been a variant on Fletcher's *Valentinian,* so *The Conquest of Spain* is a variant on his *Loyal Subject.* Rhoderique, lascivious king of Spain, persuades the obsessively loyal general Julianus to come from retirement to fight against the Moors. The king rapes Julianus's daughter, Jacinta, but she escapes to the battlefield to tell her father. Julianus is too loyal to take revenge against the king, but Jacinta's fiancé Theomantius leads a revolution, making the Moors his allies. When the king is defeated, the Moors reveal their true purpose as allies was to conquer Spain. Meanwhile, the king has been shamed into repentance by Julianus's noble behavior, but too late. Jacinta is fatally wounded traveling through the war zone, and Theomantius falls on his sword. *The Adventures in Madrid,* like *The Spanish Wives,* is a sentimentalized intrigue comedy. Gaylove and Bellmour, two English gentlemen staying at the ambassador's house in Madrid, strike up an intrigue with two ladies in the neighboring house of old Gomez. The ladies—

Laura and Gomez's wife Clarinda—are able to play amusing and flirtatious tricks on the gallants because they know of a secret passage to the ambassador's house and also because a woman friend persuades Gomez to hire her as a servant by disguising as a eunuch. In typically Pix fashion, the seemingly erring wife is actually virtuous. As the action unfolds, we learn that Gomez's estate really belongs to his nephew, Don Phillip; Gomez had his nephew abducted by assassins, and, thinking him dead, seized the estate and forced his niece to pass as his wife by threatening her with death. Don Phillip rescues his sister and has Gomez arrested by the Inquisitor General. The young couples are happily united at the curtain.

By the end of her theatrical career, Pix had written twelve plays—six tragedies and six comedies—more than any previous woman except Aphra Behn. Pix continued the Fletcherian tradition in tragedy; three of her tragedies are imitations of Fletcher with little added to revivify old plots. Her tragedies point forward in the increasing prominence given to the heroine and to the fatal accidents to love. Her one overt attempt at stage reform, *The False Friend,* was a muddle of melodrama and moralizing. The theaters probably continued to produce these plays because Pix had a knack for alternating scenes of rant with melting love scenes in which a mighty hero languishes at his lady's feet. However silly such scenes seem on the page, they act well, and audiences continued to like them. *The Czar of Muscovy* is important in a formal element that looks forward to the future. While the medium of her other tragedies was inflated prose lined out in print as blank verse, *The Czar of Muscovy* was printed in prose.

Pix's best works are her comedies, lively intrigue plays full of stage business, bustle, and surprises. The dialogue is usually flat, but the action never flags. The comedies contain pleasant songs, some by Pix, some by Motteux, and these, set to music by Purcell or Eccles, were published separately or in contemporary anthologies. Her encomium of the English merchant in *The Beau Defeated* suggests Lillo and the bourgeois drama of the next generation. Forced or unhappy marriages appear frequently in the comedies; they are prominent in *The Spanish Wives, The Deceiver Deceived, The Innocent Mistress,* and *The Adventures in Madrid.* Pix uses the forced marriage as a plot device, but unlike Behn, does not crusade against it in strong thematic statements. Pix's treatment of the unhappily married person is sentimentalized. Either the *mal mariée* is rescued and married more satisfactorily, as in *The Spanish Wives* and *The Adventures in Madrid* (this also happens in a tragedy, *The Czar of Muscovy*); or, as in *The Deceiver Deceived* and *The Innocent Mistress,* the seemingly errant wife or husband is really virtuous. Pix's use of sentimentalized characters in intrigue actions causes oddities of plotting. Generally her comedies show the changing temper of the times in that there is less emphasis on cuckoldry and more on virtuous love. Pix's attempt to write both hard and soft comedy at the same time is characteristic of playwrights at the turn of the century under pressure for stage reform.

Mary Pix achieved some modest recognition. The dedicatees of her plays are first gentlemen, then baronets, then a countess, a viscount, and a duchess. *The Conquest of Spain* was the first new play acted at Vanbrugh's theater in the Haymarket. She had no illusions, however, about her talents. Her prologues, epilogues, and dedications always speak humbly of her efforts; they are "worthless trifles" (Dedication, *Deceiver Deceived*). Her insistent modesty may have been due partly to her fear of attack as a woman playwright. Certainly the only two times she was publicly abused were because of her sex. Had she been the only new woman playwright of the 1695-96 season, her existence alone would not have provoked *The Female Wits* [see excerpt dated 1696]. Similarly, George Powell probably stole from her play because she looked a likely victim, one whose sex as well as social class made her seem too insignificant to protest. Except for these two occasions, her public and personal life was inconspicuous. She worked quietly for ten years as a minor, although professional, playwright of modest abilities. (pp. 115-21)

> Nancy Cotton,"*The Female Wits: Catherine Trotter, Delariviere Manley, Mary Pix,*" in her Women Playwrights in England, c. 1363-1750, *Bucknell University Press, 1980, pp. 81-121.*

EDNA L. STEEVES (essay date 1982)

[*Steeves is an American scholar who specializes in eighteenth-century English and French literature, John Milton's works, and the history of feminism. In the following excerpt from her introduction to the 1982 facsimile reprint of Pix's plays, she examines Pix's dramatic works as evidence of contemporary literary taste and considers them as early manifestations of feminism.*]

My theme is a petticoat author who succeeded in getting her plays produced on the London stage by the best-known theatrical company of the time—no mean achievement for a woman. An examination of Mary Pix's dramatic works makes it possible to evaluate and understand—perhaps even to enjoy—the minor but in no sense negligible drama popular in her day. For drama, more than any other form of art, must cater to the taste of its audience, and Mrs. Pix knew what her audience liked. Her strengths as a playwright lay in her keen nose for a thriller; in her ability to create characters whose motives she can keenly analyze; in her knack for dialogue—fast-paced and often witty in her comedies, theatrical and in the high rant style in her tragedies; and in her eye and ear for stage effects.

The decade in which Mrs. Pix's plays appeared, between 1696 and 1706, witnessed significant changes in the London theatrical world, and her plays mirror these changes. In the days of the Merry Monarch, the London playhouse was largely an aristocratic one, the audience comprised chiefly of royalty and nobility. A leisured society, it demanded wit and polish and was not in the least squeamish. The advent of ladies in the audience, on the stage, and as playwrights became an increasingly influential factor. Allardyce Nicoll notes that between December 1695 and December 1696 five new plays written by women appeared on the stage: two by Mary Delariviere Manley, two by Mary Pix, one by Catharine Trotter. Heroic tragedy and licentious comedy were the preferred types of entertainment. Though the two seem miles apart, both equally pleased the audience, and the same dramatist produced both types. High heroics alternated easily with the gayest and smuttiest comedy.

Although in Dryden's heyday the heroic play employed heroic rhyme as its medium, by the closing years of the century rhyme is seldom used. Heroic sentiment, rather than heroic rhyme, is the essential; love and honor, the subject. Blank verse has been substituted for rhyme. Yet some of the characteristics remain: still popular are the spectacular scenes of blood and thunder; the stock characters of an exaggerated sort; and the rant and rave style of the tragic actor. Nevertheless, the pathetic tragedy and the she-tragedy, both steeped in pathos and sentiment and employing blank verse as their medium, gain increasing popularity with audiences by the closing years of the century.

Comedy also witnessed changes. The hard-nosed, brutal amorality of Wycherley softens to a more sentimental, romantic tone in Steele and Cibber. By the eighteenth century comedy surpasses tragedy in popularity, and the variety of comedy is striking: the comedy of manners and the comedy of intrigue continue on the boards, but sentimental comedy and romantic comedy are on the rise. Farce, especially farces with a Spanish setting, appear frequently.

Significant changes also occurred in the playhouses and the acting companies in the later years of the Restoration. When the United Company, which had operated since November 1682, broke up early in 1695 with the secession of Betterton and sixteen of the best-known actors and actresses, London audiences benefited from the intense rivalry between the two houses, the Theatre Royal in Drury Lane and the New Theatre in Lincoln's Inn Fields. At the same time, the lord chamberlain's office called for a stricter licensing of plays on moral grounds. On January 24, 1696, the lord chamberlain issued a new order that all plays must be fully licensed; and on June 4, 1697, the master of the revels was ordered to correct all obscenities and scandalous matters in stage plays that might offend against God and good manners. Collier's attack upon the stage, then, merely pointed to what was already in the air. The new audiences reflected an upper-middle-class morality stricter than that of the aristocratic audiences of the time of Charles II. Well before the turn of the century, the trend toward sentimentalism was on the increase, all but banishing the sparkling wit of the earlier comedy and altering the tragic to the pathetic. The new century evidenced significant changes in the composition of the audience, which in turn affected the nature of the theatre itself, the acting companies, and the plays written for the stage. As is usual in the theatre, plays continued to be written for particular actors and actresses. One practice appears to have remained constant: that of saucy young actresses dressed in male attire romping about the stage.

Produced between 1696 and 1706, Mary Pix's plays illustrate many of these changes of taste in the theatrical audience. In her best-known tragedy, *Ibrahim,* she combines lust, horror, and bloodshed with some effective scenes of pathos. The heroine, Morena, about to be raped by the sultan, attempts to kill herself with the sultan's scimitar. Drawing the scimitar through her hands, she faints and suffers rape. After the rape, she returns to her father's house with her hair hanging down and her clothing in disarray (all stock symbols of ravishment), poisons herself, and dies a lingering death in her lover's arms. Her grief-stricken lover stabs himself; the villainess, who has engineered the rape, stabs herself; the sultan and the eunuch who has abetted the rape are killed by the hero's loyal friend, who is himself killed in the fray. By the closing scene, practically everyone has suffered a bloody death. Mrs. Pix provides a moving climactic scene for the hero and heroine, full of pathos and sentiment. According to a contemporary dramatic critic [Charles Gildon; see excerpt dated 1699], the role of Morena, played superbly by the great tragic actress of the company, Elizabeth Barry, always brought tears to the eyes of the audience.

Even more in the fashion for pathos is Mrs. Pix's tragedy, *The False Friend.* Two sets of young lovers, having married without the consent of their parents, suffer death as the consequence of their disobedience. Madness, poison, stabbings, and villainies fill the plot, and the play ends in general carnage. Greater emphasis is placed here on the domestic nature of the plot than is typical of the earlier heroic play. The theme is not the conflict between love and honor to one's country but is concerned with the relations between parents and children.

In *The Double Distress* Mrs. Pix attempts a tragedy with a happy ending. After much distress (two heroines doubly distressed), mistaken identity, the machinations of a cruel stepmother, and a marriage consummation arranged in the dark of night to avoid incest, everyone is happy in the end.

Mrs. Pix eschews heroic rhyme in her tragedies, employing blank verse instead. Indeed, in *The Czar of Muscovy* she uses prose, a medium which in the eighteenth century gradually supplanted heroic rhyme.

In other ways, too, Mrs. Pix has her eye on her audience. The fact that audiences expected virginity in their tragic heroines had always created difficulties in dealing with widows or ravished innocents. In *Queen Catharine* Mrs. Pix does not permit the queen, who had been previously married, to consummate her love with Owen Tudor, and the heroine of *The Czar of Muscovy* cannot be united to the hero until her scheming husband has met his well-deserved death.

Mrs. Pix also fashions her plays for the actors and actresses in Betterton's company. Betterton grew up in the tradition of the heroic play, taking the leads in many of the tragedies of Dryden and his contemporaries. Best suited to tragic roles, he was by the 1690's rather old-fashioned in his style of acting, yet still the most distinguished actor of his time. Since Mrs. Pix gave her first two plays to Drury Lane, it was not until 1697 that she offered a play to the company at Lincoln's Inn Fields. In that comedy, *The Innocent Mistress,* Betterton took the lead role. In two of her plays performed at Lincoln's Inn Fields in the 1697-98 season—*The Deceiver Deceived* in November 1697 and *Queen Catharine* in June 1698—Betterton played the leading male role. But in 1698, Betterton was sixty-eight, and he was undertaking fewer new roles and falling back upon the roles he had played successfully for many years in the company's stock repertory. His heavy duties as manager of the company also took their toll on his energies. But the two leading actresses in Betterton's company, Mrs. Barry and Mrs. Bracegirdle, assumed the leading women's roles in every one of Mrs. Pix's plays from 1697 on for which we know the casts. The one exception was *The Czar of Muscovy,* in which Mrs. Barry took the role of the heroine; there was no role in that play for Mrs. Bracegirdle. Each of these famous actresses, paired in so many plays performed at Lincoln's Inn Fields, had her own definite style of acting: Mrs. Barry stormed and ranted through her roles; Mrs. Bracegirdle, softer in voice and manner, suffered her agonies less violently. No dramatist could fail to take into account the distinctive acting styles of these two popular actresses.

Like her tragedies, Mrs. Pix's comedies mirror the taste of her audience. As Robert Hume has pointed out [see Additional Bibliography], the hard view of the older comedy has by the closing years of the century given way to a more humane outlook. Exemplary characters appear side by side with witty and satiric types professing thoroughly amoral attitudes. *The Deceiver Deceived* is a good example of a comedy filled with intrigue, fortune hunters, tricksters, conniving servants, an adulterous wife (who, of course, reforms), witty and sexy scenes, and plenty of smutty dialogue. The popular combination of smuttiness and sentiment can be seen in both Mrs. Pix's tragedies and comedies. Extremely loose and smutty dialogue between young girls and boys occurs in *Ibrahim, The Deceiver*

Deceived, and *The Adventures in Madrid.* The scheming rakes and evil plotters are generally foiled in their designs and poetic justice effected. In *The Spanish Wives,* for example, the tricksters are balked; in *The Innocent Mistress* and *The Different Widows* the rake ends up reformed and married to his intended victim.

The Spanish Wives affords a particularly interesting insight into the changing tastes of audiences. Cibber's *Love's Last Shift* had appeared a few months before *The Spanish Wives.* Mrs. Pix's comedy is much more like the type of sentimental comedy both Cibber and Steele were to produce in the coming century than it is like the typical Restoration comedy. The plot, revolving about the governor of Barcelona and his errant wife, resembles the treatment in countless Restoration comedies dealing with the titillating question: how to prevent your wife from cuckolding you. But the other plot, revolving about the jealous marquess of Moncada, his wife Elenora, and her former fiance and faithful lover, Count Camillus, is a sentimental romance. The servants in the play are the usual witty tricksters; the lover of the governor's wife is the rake type; but Elenora and Count Camillus are true romantics. This comedy, in many respects better typed as a farce, sounds at an early date the note of sentimentalism that sweeps over English comedy with the coming of the eighteenth century.

Even in *Queen Catharine,* where distributive justice does not take place, Mrs. Pix assures her audience that Providence will eventually distribute rewards and punishments properly. History could be blamed for any miscarriage of justice here: in due time the villain, Richard III, would get his just desserts.

Mrs. Pix's plays give evidence of the taste of the audience for scenic effects. *The Double Distress,* for example, has an ornate temple as a scenic backdrop; *Ibrahim* shows the sultan's palace in Constantinople with the army camp outside the city's walls; Ludlow Castle is the scene in *Queen Catharine*; and Persian, Spanish, and Muscovite palaces and castles appear as scenic backgrounds for various of her plays. Elaborate and costly scenery was part of the stock-in-trade of the acting companies and could be used again and again. Flats depicting groves, woods, fields, forests, fountains, ''pleasant prospects,'' temples, castles, palaces, country seats, prisons, fires and conflagrations, seas with sailing ships thereon, in addition to the more ordinary scenes depicting rooms, houses, streets, views of London—all these the audience demanded. Accompanying the trend toward sentimentalism, love of nature strikes a chord occasionally. The heroines of *The Czar of Muscovy* and *The Conquest of Spain* voice longings for the humble cottage life, the feast of nature and the peace of retirement in the country. The attitude seems more pose than actual intention, but it is there.

The popularity of women wearing men's clothes is seen in *The Adventures in Madrid.* As a means of catching the attention of the audience, this device continued in use even after the attempt at the turn of the century to reduce the immorality of the stage. Along with the smutty dialogues and duets introduced into the plays themselves, prologues and epilogues (often specifically advertised) frequently employed a popular young actress, even a child actress, dressed in men's attire, to romp across the stage appealing to the audience for its applause.

The she-prologue was particularly popular. Actresses used coquetry to beg, conjure, or challenge the audience, sometimes even to preach to the audience, but always to be merry and to please. Very young children, aged eight or so, often spoke the prologues and epilogues, especially the latter. Usually such children were billed simply as Boy or Girl and not identified. In *The Deceiver Deceived* and *The Beau Defeated,* young children spoke the epilogues. The very young Miss Cross spoke the prologue to *Ibrahim.* The popular Mrs. Mountfort (later Mrs. Verbruggen) spoke the epilogue to *The Spanish Wives.* The young Miss Porter spoke the prologue to both *Queen Catharine* and *The Different Widows.* "Pray, think no worse of me for my petticoat" is the theme of these young actresses who deliver the prologues and epilogues. It is interesting that playwrights trusted the first and last words to be heard on the stage to women. (pp. xl-xlvii)

In the decade between her first play in 1696 and her last play in 1706, twelve plays written by Mary Pix or attributed to her appeared on the London stage. Seven of those plays, when published, either bore her name on the title page or the dedication to the play bore her signature. These were *Ibrahim,* (1696), *The Spanish Wives* (1696), *The Innocent Mistress* (1697), *The Deceiver Deceived* (1698), *Queen Catharine* (1698), *The False Friend* (1699), and *The Double Distress* (1701). Five plays, performed at Lincoln's Inn Fields between 1700 and 1706, have been generally attributed to her. These are *The Beau Defeated* (1700), *The Czar of Muscovy* (1701), *The Different Widows* (1703), *The Conquest of Spain* (1705), and *The Adventures in Madrid* (1706). In the course of a decade, the writing of a dozen plays and the feat of getting them performed by the best-known acting company of the day would appear to be no small achievement.

What seems perhaps most significant to modern readers about Mary Pix's plays is the feminist views therein. She was a feminist before feminism became trendy. Although not stridently offensive in her feminism, as her contemporary Mrs. Manley could be, she seizes every opportunity to defend women against attacks upon their character and intelligence. And like her near contemporaries, Mrs. Manley and Mrs. Trotter, Mrs. Pix by her success as a playwright served as a model for other women aspiring to write for the stage.

The influence of women on the Restoration stage, not only as actresses but as members of the audience, has been long recognized. Although Aphra Behn had been active as a dramatist from 1670 to her death in 1689, it was only in the last decade of the century that plays by female writers began to appear in sizable numbers. The ladies exercised their influence by direct opposition to plays not meeting their approval. Certainly their presence in the audience tended to tone down the boisterous conduct of the pit. (pp. xlviii-xlix)

Although Mrs. Behn had early been a star to steer by for many women who dared put pen to paper, few women writers were willing to risk putting their names to their works because of the satire leveled at learned women. The number of pen names used and the number of title pages that announced Written by a Young Lady or Written by a Lady of Quality was legion. But by the 1690's, women writers, particularly women writing for the stage, increased rapidly, and these women often courageously declared their identity. Still a certain hesitancy remained, and women often concealed their identity under male pseudonyms. As late as *The Conquest of Spain* (1705), the next to the last of Mrs. Pix's plays, the prologue referred to the author as "he." Most women writers keenly resented the criticism launched at them because they were *women* writers, not bad writers. The prologues and epilogues of the time were rife with pleas begging the indulgence of the audience for the au-

thoress: "Be kind, dear sirs, to the female who wrote this." Prejudice of that sort invited strong feminist reaction.

A few examples sounding feminist overtones taken from the prologues and epilogues of Mrs. Pix's plays are representative of a common attitude. The prologue to *The Innocent Mistress* refers to "our Poetess" who has twice found kind usage from the audience (this was her third play). Verbruggen, who spoke the prologue, begs the audience to continue her good fortune with their applause. The epilogue comments: you judges of wit will scorn to condemn a woman's wit. We have a reformation now, continues the speaker; our audience will applaud dry morals, and nice dames will no longer be offended by a cuckold's wit. City wives and daughters will now throng to us.

The prologue to *The False Friend* [see poem dated 1699] states a conventional enough view. A woman, the speaker announces, is the author of this moral play:

> Matters of State she'll not pretend to Teach;
> Or Treat of War, or things beyond her Reach;
> Nor Scourge your Folly's with keen Satyrs Rage;
> But try if good Example will Engage.

No beau, drunk, debauchee, or swearer will prove successful here, the speaker asserts; only the honest, generous, brave, wise, and constant will succeed in this play. Common enough sentiments these, and to be found in plays written by men as well as by women. But the line which clinches the view as feminist states plainly:

> Did Men Reform, all Women wou'd do well.

Some particularly interesting examples of rather advanced feminist views can be found in *The Spanish Wives.* The old governor of Barcelona allows his brisk young wife much freedom to pursue her own desires. A foppish Englishman sees an opportunity to have an affair wth the governor's lady. She is not immune to his charms, but the generosity and trust of the governor prevent her from cuckolding her husband.

This comedy sets forth in revealing ways various attitudes toward women characteristic of the period. The plot revolves around two very dissimilar marriages, both involving an older husband and a younger wife: the governor and his wife and the marquess of Moncada and his wife. The governor believes that if he gives his wife freedom and trusts her, she will behave; he thinks that if he coops her up, she will cuckold him if only out of revenge. The marquess' view is exactly the opposite: he keeps his wife closely confined. He is considered a rude brute for thus abusing her. "And 'tis thy Doubts, Old Man, not I, torment thee," says his wife. "Our sex," she continues, "like Water, glides along pleasant and useful; but if grasped by a too violent Hand, unseen they slip away, and prove the fruitless Labour vain." The marquess' wife, who had been forced into marriage with him, is freed from her marriage at the close of the play by an annulment, and she can now marry the young nobleman to whom she was contracted before her forced marriage. This humane attitude toward marriage and the view that sentiment and romance are an integral part of marriage indicate a decided change from the treatment of love and marriage in the old Restoration comedy. Arranged marriages, especially forced marriages, seem less acceptable to the improved and improving minds of the ladies in the audience than they were to their mothers and grandmothers. Women playwrights and women on the stage and in the audience influenced these changes.

Often in the plays themselves the plots are constructed to demand the sympathies of the audience for the women characters, in particular the betrayed heroine or the abused wife. The dialogue frequently sounds a feminist note. A few examples must suffice.

In *Ibrahim,* the hero, Amurat, addresses the heroine thus:

> Oh, Morena! My Morena, Now
> Permit me to approach, and swear
> Upon thy snowy bosom, how much
> I love thee, till with warm sighs,
> I've thaw'd thy Virgin Icy Heart,
> And made it burn like mine.

To which the heroine, Morena, replies:

> What Maid can hear, and be unmov'd,
> The Man she loves talk at this charming rate;
> But Oh! I've read, that Men are all by Nature
> False; and this dear pleasing tale of Love,
> To which I listen with such rapture,
> Will hereafter be, perhaps, Word for Word
> Repeated to another.

Never, swears the hero:

> . . . though our Law allows [in Turkey] Plurality of Wives
> And Mistresses, yet I will never practise it;
> May Dishonour wrap my head with shame

IBRAHIM,

THE

Thirteenth Emperour

OF THE

TURKS:

A

TRAGEDY.

As it is Acted

BY HIS

MAJESTIES SERVANTS.

By Mrs *Mary Pix.*

LONDON,

Printed for *John Harding* , at the *Bible* and *Anchor* in *Newport-street,* and *Richard Wilkin,* at the *King's-Head* in St. *Paul's* Church-Yard , 1 6 9 6.

Title page of the first edition of Pix's first "blood and thunder" tragedy.

> Instead of Laurels, may I be beaten
> Through the Army I command, and branded for a Coward,
> When I admit another Love into my Bed or Bosom.

Hold on, replies the heroine, who wants to say something appropriate in answer to this wondrous love. Her answer is, "Yet wou'd I be torn in thousand pieces, rather than break my Plighted Faith."

In *The Innocent Mistress,* Bellinda is talking to the man she loves, Sir Charles Beauclair, whom she mistakenly believes to be married. For the sake of honor, they must give each other up, says Bellinda. Beauclair replies: "'Tis happier far to have sighed for thee than to have enjoyed another." Bellinda says: "Grant it true, but we might have lived till weary grown of one another, till you perhaps might coldly say, I had a mistress. Now to part, when at the mention of each other's name our hearts will rise, our eyes run o'er, 'tis better much than living to indifferency, which time and age would certainly have brought." His reply: "Oh never never; tho' the bauble gaudy beauty die, yet sense and humor still remain—on that I should have doated." A keen analysis of the marriage relationship frequently forms a substantial part of Mrs. Pix's plots and dialogue.

In *The Deceiver Deceived,* Fidelio assures his beloved Ariana that her dowry is not the object of his attentions. Ariana considers his words. "'Tis pretty," she comments, "to hear a young fellow one loves talk thus, but this wont do, Love and Plenty crown the circling Year with Pleasure, but where either's wanting, Content scarce ever appears." This romantic ingenue has a level head on her shoulders.

In *The Beau Defeated,* Lady Landsworth has been married as a very young woman to an old debauchee who has kept her like a nun on his country estate. She made him a good wife, tended his ills, and when he died, inherited his estate. She is still young, has a title, money, and freedom and has come up to town to find herself a second husband, one to her own liking. She confides to Betty, Mrs. Rich's maid: "I am resolv'd to indulge my Inclinations, and rather than not obtain the person I like, invert the Order of nature and pursue tho' he flies. . . . Being once condemn'd to Matrimony without ever asking my consent, now I have the freedom to make my own choice." Betty asks Lady Landsworth what kind of husband she wants. Lady Landsworth says: "He should be Gentle, yet not a Beau; Witty, but no Debauche; susceptible of Love, yet abhorring lew'd Women; Learned, Poetical, Musical, without one Dram of Vanity; in fine, very meritorious, yet very modest; generous to the last degree, and Master of no Estate; mightily in Love with me, and not so much as know I am worth the cloaths I wear." Betty laughs: "To your Romances again Lady fair, 'tis only there you can converse with those heros, this town affords no such." But in the end, Lady Landsworth finds her hero; and they marry and, of course, live happily ever after.

Mrs. Pix allows her feminist views to operate within the context of her plays to the extent she feels such views are acceptable to her audience. Certainly, her views are not those of Mary Wollstonecraft a century later. Like all playwrights hoping for a successful run, she caters to the taste of her audience. Her women characters are on the whole much better constructed, more credible, than her male characters. She thinks and writes like a woman, as one would expect. Although in the short decade when her plays appeared upon the stage there was an increasing number of plays written by women, nevertheless, most playwrights were men. Consequently, the impact of her plays, and the support given by her success to the general history of feminism and women's rights long before those terms took on their modern connotation, is not an insubstantial one. For this, she deserves modest praise. (pp. xlix-liv)

> Edna L. Steeves, in an introduction to The Plays of Mary Pix and Catharine Trotter, Vol. I: Mary Pix, edited by Edna L. Steeves, Garland Publishing, Inc., 1982, pp. xi-liv.

CONSTANCE CLARK (essay date 1986)

[*An American actress, director, playwright, and scholar, Clark is an authority on the early history of English women dramatists. In the following excerpt, she closely examines the themes, plots, and sources of Pix's dramas, commenting as well on the author's major nontheatrical works.*]

Since it has a factual basis, **Ibrahim** can be considered an historical tragedy. It is a "villain tragedy" in that the title character is unrelentingly evil and causes everyone's downfall, including his own. And also in a twofold sense, because of Sheker Para's manipulation of the circumstances which bring on the inevitable catastrophe. It has many of the trappings of Dryden's heroic dramas of the 1670s: the exotic setting, a beautiful heroine obsessed with honor, an idealistic hero of fantastic accomplishment. It also has the sensational elements of Beaumont and Fletcher: titillation, rape, revenge, and violence. In the prologue it is presented as an "Heroick Play."

Can **Ibrahim** be considered a pure tragedy? Critics whose taste is offended by the relatively poor quality of the tragedies of this period, compared to those of the great Elizabethans, would withhold the lofty appellation. But if one uses the yardstick of the components necessary to comprise a tragedy, rather than an argument based on aesthetic quality, a case can be made, one way or the other. If a tragedy can be loosely understood to be a tale about great people who suffer tremendously, and who, as often as not, have a hand in their own destruction, then certainly elements of tragedy are to be found in **Ibrahim**. All the main characters are of the requisite stature, and certainly catastrophe abounds. The question becomes not so much . . . whether it is a tragedy but rather whose tragedy is it? Ibrahim knowingly commits the sacrilegious act which serves as justification for the mutiny of his previously adoring populace. Sheker Para, who enjoyed more freedom than any woman before her time in Turkey, is shamed into suicide. Amurat, the champion of the army, is hopelessly caught in the classic dilemma of conflicting loyalties. He is not at fault for what he suffers. He has not been an agent in the rape of his lover, the deaths of the Sultan, Sheker, his friend Solyman, or Morena. Yet, in the end, when he is made Vizier, and offered the reins of the nation, it is his decision to kill himself for lost love. Finally, Morena, who has suffered the "horrour of horrours," rashly commits suicide at the very moment before her reunion with her beloved. The latter two characters are totally noble in intention, and there is a special poignancy to Morena's mistaken self-sacrifice. It was her plight which moved the audience for which the play was written. A most telling assessment of what they expected of a tragedy is Gildon's critique [see excerpt dated 1699]:

> This play, if it want the Harmony of Numbers, and the Sublimity of Expression, has yet a Quality, that at least balances that Defect. I mean the Passions; for the Distress of Morena never fail'd to bring Tears into the Eyes of the Audience; which few Plays, if any since Otway's have done; . . . which is the true end of Tragedy.

The Spanish Wives, Mrs. Pix's second offering, was a comedy described on its title page as a farce, and in that tradition it was in three acts. (pp. 233-35)

The source of the plot of **The Spanish Wives** is a novel written by Gabriel de Brémond and translated from the French by Peter Belon as *The Pilgrim* in 1680. (p. 236)

Pix selected and juggled the characters and events from Belon's version to serve her own ends in **The Spanish Wives.** Paula Louise Barbour's dissertation [see Additional Bibliography] contains a detailed discussion of the similarities between Pix's play and the original source and her departures from it, pointing out the changes made, not only in adapting the French material to suit the English sensibilities of the audience, but in the structural realignment necessary to adapt a novel's plot into dramatic form. She sums up:

> Mary Pix adapted her characters and their motives to the tastes of an English audience by downplaying the irreverent satire on the Roman Catholic Church, creating native English types, making almost everybody just a little bit more lovable and capable of improvement, and expanding the roles of two of her characters into a major statement about marriage . . . as she multiplied characters and added nuances to characterization, Pix streamlined the original plot.

Pix shares her source with a distinguished colleague. John Dryden also borrowed the comic subplot of his tragicomedy *The Spanish Friar* (1681) from *The Pilgrim*. Barbour suggests that Pix may have read Dryden's play as well as *The Pilgrim*, since, like Dryden, she too made the would-be seducer of an old man's wife a "Colonel." Pix may also have had an opportunity to see Dryden's play. Though she was only sixteen and not known to reside in London in 1681, [Emmet L. Avery's *The London Stage, 1660-1800* (1960-68)] hints at a possible revival of *The Spanish Friar* in the 1693-94 season.

If **The Spanish Wives** owes elements of its plot to a French novel, the theme clearly shows the influence of Aphra Behn. The themes of the evils of forced marriages, true love triumphing over other bonds, the sympathetic treatment of women—even those who were not models of conventional virtue—permeate Behn's works. Her *The False Count* (1681) is also set in Spain, and like **Wives** has an insanely jealous old husband who keeps his wife locked up. In the end he is shamed into giving his wife over to her young lover. A previous contract has been made between the pair, and, as in **Wives,** the mismatch has been consummated, but there is no mention of a legal separation. Owing to the stricter social mores of her time, Pix had to clean up Behn's act, so to speak. She included the sanction of a legally viable precontract, and the resolution of an annulment, plus a cooling-off period in order to reunite her lovers. Again, while in Behn's *Sir Patient Fancy* (1678) Lady Fancy, married to an old fool, has a lover all along, and in the end can openly admit it and live in sin with her husband's resigned consent, Pix's wife is, albeit reluctantly, faithful until she is freed by a morally acceptable deus ex machina, a Papal mandate. However, in **The Spanish Wives,** we not only have a heroine, no longer a virgin, reunited with her true love, but also, in the character of the Governor's Lady, a wife who "would have if she could have" and who is forgiven and reinstated, not punished, when she is discovered. The stuff of potential tragedy is shaped into commendable sentimental comedy. Colley Cibber's *Love's Last Shift*, produced in the same season, has often been heralded as the first "sentimental comedy,'' in that it centered on the reform of a rake and his return to the fold of marriage.

Pix was turning the coin with her female penitent. A discussion of *The Spanish Wives* as sentimental can be found in James M. Edmunds's ''An Example of Early Sentimentalism'' [see essay dated 1933]. Although Edmunds bases his categorization on the Elenora-Camillus plot, sentimentalism may also be seen in the happily resolved ''working marriage'' of the Governor and his Lady.

Allardyce Nicoll sees *The Spanish Wives* as directly in the line of Aphra Behn's comedy of intrigue, while noting the arguments for its having elements of sentimentality presented by Edmunds, and also those against by J. Harrington Smith in *The Gay Couple in Restoration Comedy.* Nicoll sums up [see Additional Bibliography]:

> Intrigue seems, in this age, to have been particularly acceptable to the women writers, Mrs. Pix and Mrs. Manley uniting with Mrs. Behn in presenting dramas of this type with, running through them, threads of sentiment and moralization. *The Spansh Wives,* of the former . . . , mingles Restoration license with touches of sentimentalism. . . .

However many influences, derivations from specific works, or merely applications of the popular formulas of the time Pix shared with the other professional ''hacks '' of the day in the search for a crowd-pleasing recipe, there is one element in *The Spanish Wives* that is not only original but unique. As Barbour has astutely observed, *The Spanish Wives* ''offers an example unparalleled in Restoration Comedy—a young woman contentedly happy with an old husband.''

It was six months after *The Female Wits* [see excerpt dated 1696] that Mary Pix presented her comedy *The Innocent Mistress* at the rival Lincoln's Inn Fields theatre. . . . (pp. 253-56)

The setting is London, with actual places depicted on stage, such as Lockett's, a fashionable restaurant, and Mrs. Bantum's coffee house. The main action concerns Sir Charles and Bellinda, who are trapped in a hopelessly platonic relationship until it turns out that his wife is a bigamist. In the secondary romantic plot, Mrs. Beauclair puts her rake to several tests, including resorting to breeches disguise, finally taming him. Yet another plot has a woman rescued from a forced marriage, a recurring theme of Pix's. (p. 257)

With the two main plots Pix seemed to be going in two directions at once—towards sentimentalism with the high-minded Charles and Bellinda, but counterpointing the ''gay'' Restoration couple. The latter shows the influence of Congreve, who is even complimented in an exchange between them. Mrs. Beauclair chides Sir Francis for his behavior at the theatre: ''Have I not seen you at the play slighting all the bare-faced beauties, hunting up a trollop in a mask with pains and pleasure; nay more for her gaping non-sensical banters, neglecting immortal Dryden's eloquence, or Congreve's unequalled wit.'' The focus of the busy play, however, keeps returning to the platonic couple, whose relationship verges on the cloying. The description of it by the rake Wildlove early in the play sums up what in fact ensues:

> He, notwithstanding the provocation of an ugly, scolding Wife at home, and the temptation of a good Estate, and a handsome Fellow into the bargain, instead of making his life easy with jolly Bonarobas, dotes on a platonic Mistress, who never allows him

greater Favors than to read Plays to her, kiss her Hand, and fetch heart-breaking sighs at her Feet.

Perhaps the ladies in the audience were pleased with this new sort of romantic arrangement where the ''good'' woman had the upper hand for a change, but Beauclair's maundering and Bellinda's agonizing with her conscience come off as mushy and discordant in tone in the setting of an otherwise earthy comedy. Yet Pix's heart was apparently in her statement about two innocent lovers who are rewarded, however implausibly, in a world usually dominated by rakes and coquettes.

The production of *The Deceiver Deceived* in November 1697 was . . . [an] answer to George Powell's plagiarism of Pix's plot in his *The Imposture Defeated.* . . . (pp. 259-60)

The premise of the play is that Bondi, a miserly and jealous old Venetian . . . has feigned blindness in order to avoid the expenses incurred by election to the presidency of Dalmatia. As the play opens he is stewing in his own juices because, assuming he cannot see them, his wife is being courted by a gallant to whom she was formerly engaged, while his daughter is being wooed by the son of a bankrupt. In the end the daughter is allowed to marry her choice, but the wife, though tempted to the brink, remains chaste. Bondi himself reforms: ''I have been a cross, stingy, old captious fellow, but henceforth I'll throw it away with the best of ye.'' Pix also pokes fun at her own profession in making the fop character, whom Bondi would have forced his daughter to marry, a playwright of boundless and groundless conceit. (pp. 260-61)

The main difference between the Pix and Powell treatments is that Powell has Bonde . . . actually catch his wife *in flagrante delicto,* while Pix's wife is sentimentalized in that she stumbles but does not fall. Again in this Pix comedy there are the themes of forced marriage and the tyranny of Latin husbands.

The character of the fop playwright was doubtless a hit back for the satire on her and her sister authoresses in *The Female Wits* the previous season.

Mrs. Pix's next offering, *Queen Catherine; or, The Ruines of Love,* produced at Lincoln's Inn Fields in June 1698, was an admittedly ambitious one. The play presented English historical characters, some of them coinciding with those treated in Shakespeare's history plays. Pix wove domestic romances within historical events. Her dedicatory epistle defends the effort, even as her prologue (apparently the author's words) apologizes for the presumption of following in such illustrious footsteps [see poem dated 1698]. Pix confided to the Honourable Mrs. Cook of Norfolk in her dedication:

> Did not some of the brightest and best of our Sex can boast of incourage attempts of this kind, the snarling critics might prevail and cry down a diversion which they themselves participate though their ill nature makes them grumble at their entertainment.

The prologue, like the content of the play, aimed to win the female audience:

> Shakespeare did oft his Countries worthies chuse,
> Nor did they by his pen their lustre lose.
> Heroes revive thro' him, and Hotspur's rage,
> Doubly adorns and animates the Stage.
> But how shall woman after him succeed,
> And what excuse can her presumption plead.
> Who with enervate voice dares wake the mighty dead;
> To please your martial men she must despair,

And therefore courts the favor of the Fair.
From huffing hero's she hopes no relief,
But trusts in Catherine's Love, and Isabella's grief.

(pp. 261-62)

It is a shame this play has been forgotten and ignored. A rereading might be of interest to Shakespeare scholars, if only because Pix set the play in an historical niche, the time between the actions of Henry VI (part 3) and Richard III. There is interest in her manipulation of the famous characters' historical actions into personal romantic frameworks, but it is hardly, as Carter averred, "in the true tradition of Shakespeare's histories" [see Additional Bibliography]. Pix's characterization of "Gloucester" is directly akin to Shakespeare's, however. He is the agent of evil deeds, busily laying the groundwork for his own accession: "Tho' seas of blood my Title do divide, / Cruel and bold I'll wade the kindred tide."

The False Friend; or, The Fate of Disobedience opened in May 1699. The prologue [see poem dated 1699] advertises its purpose to reform:

> Amongst reformers of this vitious Age,
> Who think it duty to reform the Stage,
> A woman to contribute does intend,
> In hopes a moral play your lives will mend.

This would seem to be in response to Jeremy Collier's *A Short View of the Immorality and Prophaneness of the English Stage* (March 1698), the controversy over which had been raging in the ensuing year, and in which Pix's friend Congreve was one of the major figures. Pix had obviously made the professional choice to join rather than to fight. (pp. 263-64)

The plot concerns the son and daughter of the Viceroy of Sardinia. Emilius has brought his beloved Lovisa back from France without the permission of either of their fathers. His sister Adellaida, though intended by her father for another, has secretly married Don Lopez. The Viceroy orders Emilius to kill Adellaida's husband, who is in fact his own wife's brother. Meanwhile, Appamia, Emilius' forgotten former love, plants a poison draught in Lovisa's chamber, which Emilius inadvertently gives her when she faints. Don Lopez mistakenly wounds each with poison-tipped swords, left by Appamia, who is finally betrayed by an accomplice. Adellaida is left alive, but mad from grief. (p. 265)

Perhaps Mrs. Pix was in thrall to Mrs. Trotter's *The Fatal Friendship* when she offered this play the following season. The moral of the tale just is not convincing. As in Trotter's play, the young lovers' misfortunes are either the result of accidents or the evil deeds of others. Marrying without parental consent was certainly a graver offense then than now, but the natural swing of sympathy toward young lovers and away from tyrannical parents defeats the purpose of the so-called message.

With *The Beau Defeated* (c. March 1700), for the first time Pix went anonymous—even to the point of posing as a male author. . . . The dedication to the Duchess of Bolton is gallantly flattering in regard to the effect of her feminine charms upon the author: "My Charm'd Eyes being lately bless'd with the sight of You, have let into my mind such a Beautiful Idea, that I liv'd in pain till I cou'd express my Admiration," etc. The reason for the established author's using such a screen at this point is a matter for speculation. Was it to avoid the stigma from her recent failure? Was it pressure from the management or players for fear of losing business on account of a play advertised as by a woman? Was the play indeed written by a "Mr. Barker," as Giles Jacob had stated [in *The Poetical*

Register (1719)]? Another possibility is a male collaborator, perhaps the translator of the French source from which the play was adapted, F. C. Dancourt's *Le Chevalier à la Mode* (1687). (pp. 266-67)

The Double Distress opened in March 1701. Pix signed the published version of it. In the dedication, however, she spoke of collaboration: "The Play is not wholly mine, because I thought [wished?] it done and revised by abler Hands, and therefore fitter to lay at your Lordship's feet [Viscount Fitz-Harding]." (p. 269)

More striking than the plot similarities to previous plays is the difference, the variation upon what was, after all, a not uncommon theme in drama. In *The Double Distress* it is the heroine who is first strongly aware of the forbidden passions she feels, and the emphasis is on hers, not her lover's, emotional and moral struggle. It might also be mentioned that Bevil Higgons's *The Generous Conqueror* (1701), for which Pix wrote a commendatory letter . . . , also concerned a nearly fatal triangle resolved when one of the suitors turns out to be the heroine's father. (p. 271)

The Czar of Muscovy, Pix's prose tragedy, opened almost immediately after *The Double Distress.* . . .

The plot harkens back to *Ibrahim* in the situation of an unfit ruler obsessed with an illegitimate lust for a subject. The opening scene juxtaposes festivity with foreboding. (p. 272)

Although, like *The Double Distress,* this play provides a happy ending for the innocent parties, it is distinctly different in tone. The pervading presence of the evil usurper and his death make it more of a villain tragedy than a tragicomedy.

The Different Widows; or, Intrigue à la Mode is aptly named. The comedy, which opened in November 1703, abounds in interwoven intrigues. (p. 273)

[One] of the multiple plots involves Lady Loveman, a wife à la *The Spanish Wives,* who repents in the end and tells the assembled united couples: "Hear me and believe me, I have had my Ramble, and this is the Effect: I hate the Town, despise young Fellows, renounce Intrigues, and am resolved to love nothing but nown Dear as long as I live."

The epilogue gives Collier his due as a successful reforming influence upon the stage. The controversy was still very much alive five years after the appearance of the original attack:

> Long have we suffered and the injur'd Stage
> Laboured beneath the censure of the Age:
> We own our Faults, and pardon crave today,
> When we present to You a modest Play.
> Here no lewd lives offend the chaster ear,
> No jests obscene raise blushes in the Fair;
> This we could wish Collier himself would hear.

(p. 275)

Zelmane; or, The Corinthian Queen, attributed to Pix . . . , opened at Lincoln's Inn Fields in November 1704. The dedication defends the stage against "the snarling zealot" and insists that "an inclination to plays never injured the fortunes of any man," reiterating the main argument against Collier's criticisms. It also gives the information, "The following play was a piece left unfinished by Mr. M_____t." This was probably William Mountfort, the actor/author who was murdered in 1692. (p. 276)

The play was called a tragedy although the villain is killed at the end and the lovers reunited. Zelmane's father had promised both her and his kingdom to Amphialus, general and prince, if he won the war. Amphialus secretly marries Antimore. Zelmane, who is in love with him, forces him to honor her father's pact, but when she finds out about the bigamy, she banishes him and calls for an annulment. In the meantime, Zelmane's step-brother attempts to rape Antimore but is prevented by Amphialus' younger brother, Arcanes, who is in love with Zelmane. After a tremendous victory Amphialus is allowed to return and rejoin his bride. The noble Queen resigns herself and promises to entertain Arcanes's suit. (pp. 276-77)

If this play is indeed an adaptation from a draft of a play written by Mountfort more than a decade before, it is easy to see why the subject matter appealed to Pix. The plot features a heroine of strong passions who is the aggressor in a love affair and, if Pix literally finished it—that is, composed the ending—it can be seen that she took a potential villainess and transformed her into a noble character.

The Conquest of Spain, put up in May of 1705, was the first new play to open at the new Queen's Theatre in the Haymarket. . . . (p. 277)

[In *Some Account of the English Stage from the Restoration in 1660 to 1830* (1832)] John Genest cites the source of *The Conquest of Spain* as William Rowley's *All's Lost by Lust,* printed in 1633. He gives a detailed synopsis of that plot, discussing the similarities and concluding: ''Mrs. Pix is greatly indebted to the old play—she has however materially altered both parts of the plot, and written nearly the whole of the dialogue afresh.'' One of the major changes was the creation of the romantic interest in Theomantius.

The theme of the general's dauntless loyalty is not found in the source play. Nancy Cotton sees this play as a variant on Fletcher's *The Loyal Subject* [see excerpt dated 1980]. . . . (p. 279)

Aside from outside influences, Barbour notes the resemblance not only in plot, but in style, of *The Conquest,* Pix's last tragedy, to *Ibrahim,* her first: ''The play . . . is surprisingly reminiscent of *Ibrahim.* In *The Conquest of Spain* Pix returns to full-fledged blood and thunder tragedy.''

If a return to the blood-and-thunder tragedy can be discussed in *The Conquest of Spain,* with a repetition of some of the situations of her early tragedy, *Ibrahim,* an evolution can be seen in Pix's heroine figure. The piteous Morena drank poison after being raped; Jacinta dashes into the midst of a full-tilt battle in search of an avenger!

Mary Pix's last play was a comedy, *The Adventures in Madrid.* It was presented at the Queen's Theatre in June 1706. (pp. 279-80)

There were four romantic pairings in this three-act intrigue farce set in Spain, which is in many ways similar to Pix's first farce, *The Spanish Wives.* (p. 280)

In *A History of English Drama,* Nicoll uses this play as an example to point out Susanna Centlivre's superiority: ''*Adventures in Madrid* is a three-act piece of no particular merit introducing stock characters of a rather monotonous type. Obviously, Mrs. Pix has here been endeavouring to emulate Mrs. Centlivre, but she lamentably lacks the flair for the theatre which the latter possesses in so marked a degree.'' It seems unlikely that it was a case of an attempt at emulation on Pix's part, since she produced comedy of this type four years before Centlivre made her debut. If Nicoll's value-judgment is correct, then it appears to be a case of the pupil surpassing the teacher.

T H E
Inhumane
CARDINAL,
O R,
Innocence Betray'd.
A
N O V E L.

Written
By a Gentlewoman, for the
Entertainment of the Sex.

L O N D O N,
Printed for *John Harding,* at the
Bible and *Anchor* in *Newport-
ſtreet,* and *Richard Wilkin,* at the
King's-Head in St. *Paul's Church-
Yard,* 1 6 9 6.

Title page of Pix's only novel.

Pix's two major nontheatrical works were a novel, *The Inhumane Cardinal,* published in 1696, the same year as her theatrical debut, and *Violenta,* a verse translation of the eighth book of the second day in Boccaccio's *Decameron,* which came out in 1704.

The Inhumane Cardinal, thought to be lost, has been overlooked in discussions of Pix's works, or mentioned as having existed from the sole evidence of an advertisement for it on the back of *Ibrahim.* (pp. 282-83)

Now that *The Inhumane Cardinal* has been located and republished, it can be studied. There is an interesting handwritten note on the title page signed by Joseph Knight: ''This novel is by Mrs. Pix, the well-known dramatist. It is very uncommon. I have never seen another copy.'' Under the title is the description, ''A Novel written by a Gentlewoman, for the Entertainment of the Sex.'' The dedication was signed ''Mary Pix.''

The story, which follows the seduction of an innocent maiden by a lecherous cardinal, includes two other long tales told to the girl in the process of her wooing. The narratives are augmented by a song, letters, and dialogue.

Pix introduces the novel with: ''All that are conversant in History, must remember the unbecoming sway Donna Olympia held in the Court of Rome during the papacy of Innocent the

Tenth.'' It is related that he was lazy and effeminate, and that she was actually in control of policy. Her particular favorite was the evil and cunning Cardinal Antonio Barbarino. As the story opens he confesses that the reason he has been avoiding her importunities is that he has fallen in love with a young girl, Melora. Olympia sets out to procure her for him. She takes the girl under her wing, telling her that she is saving her for a prince, who was sent a jeweled case for her portrait. Olympia relates a romantic tale, ''The History of Alphonsus and Cordelia.'' Alphonsus was the son of the Duke of Ferrara and Modena. One day, on a lark, he climbed over a garden wall and was surprised to encounter a beautiful young maiden with whom he fell immediately in love. Wishing her to love him for himself, not his exalted position, he married her in disguise. But when on his father's death he had to assume the dukedom, he called her to the court, revealed his true identity, and the two lived happily. Upon the Duke's death, an enemy attacked the young heir's legitimacy, and now he has come to Rome to sue for his rights, which are certain to be granted. It is this young man, Olympia tells Melora, who has seen her and fallen in love with her and compares Melora to Cordelia. Thus she has set the bait. ''A Scene of greatness straight appeared to Melora, and she, with the eye of Fancy, beheld herself seated in a Palace, attended by persons, born above her. . . . Women are generally ambitious and opinionated of their own merit.'' One day the Cardinal is on the other side of the door of Melora's chamber. He hears her singing and bursts in on her. She flees, but he now pursues her with such ardor, pretending to be dying of love, sending her poems, etc., that she begins to weaken. One day when he is entertaining her, knowing that she likes stories, he has his servant Francisco relate the ''true'' history of Emilius and Lovisa.

Young Emilius, second son of the Duke of Parma, returned from war to his father's court. At a ball, he saw Lovisa and fell in love with her. She was an orphan taken in as his mother's ward. A group of young people at the court had formed a ''Friendly Society'' in which they met and read each other's letters aloud. One day Emilius surprised Lovisa trying to conceal a letter. It was from his father betrothing her to another man. When their own love was revealed, the Duke sent Lovisa from the court and betrothed Emilius to another. Just as Lovisa was about to enter a convent, the Duke had relented on his death bed. The lovers were reunited.

Shortly after this, Melora's father finds a letter from the Cardinal. She is able to persuade him that it is someone else's, but the danger of exposure causes Olympia and the Cardinal to press Melora into a secret private ''marriage.'' Pix provided the following description of the wedding night: ''Innumerable were the prayers before they could obtain a full consummation: at length powerful immportunity overcomes; and the Cardinal has sacrific'd to his Lust Nature's Masterpiece.''

After six months, ''His fierce desires begin to cool in that certain cure for love, full enjoyment.'' Lovisa is pregnant. The servant Francisco, whose conscience has been bothering him about the deception tells Melora the truth. When the Cardinal and Olympia discover that she knows, they poison her. In the conclusion Pix explains that because of their power, the two were not immediately punished, but both met miserable deaths: she alone and banished, of the plague, he of various unsavory diseases.

The novel shows the influence of Boccaccio in the device of the telling of tales that tie in to the overall plot. The situation of Olympia pimping for the Cardinal is much like the situation in her play *Ibrahim,* with Sheker Para performing the same function for the Sultan. Pix claims history as the story's source. That source is possibly *The Life of Donna Olympia Maldachini* by Gregorio Leti under the pseudonym ''Abbot Gualdi,'' which had been translated into English in 1667. The account claimed to be an eyewitness report by an ex-priest. The names of Emilius and Lovisa were used later in a play, *The False Friend.* In that instance the young pair who wed against a parent's wishes suffered a tragic fate.

In 1704, *Violenta; or, The Rewards of Virtue,* a verse translation of the eighth novel of the second day from Boccaccio's *The Decameron,* was published by Pix. It was composed in heroic couplets and was doubtless influenced by Dryden's *Fables Ancient and Modern,* brought out just before his death in 1700, a work which included adaptations from Chaucer and Boccaccio.

The novel *Violenta* is based on is titled *The Duke of Angiers* and concerns a wronged duke who flees with his two children and is reduced to beggary in exile. For their safety, he makes them swear not to reveal their true identities. In London, he gives his daughter over to the care of a Lady. In Wales, his son is taken up by a nobleman. He himself ends up in Ireland as a common servant.

Violenta's story is as follows. She grows up to be a beauty, and the only son of the lady falls in love with her. The boy is a model of virtue. Knowing that his parents would oppose his love and think the girl to be of base birth, he conceals it from them. The torment throws him into a violent wasting illness. A young doctor perceives that every time Violenta enters the room the youth's pulse quickens and makes his diagnosis known to the mother. She seeks a remedy in trying to persuade Violenta to become his mistress. The thought of this horrifies her and the young man equally. Finally rather than see him pine and die, the parents consent to their marriage.

In the meantime, the count's son has become president of Wales, and, in the end, the count is restored to all his former honors, and the family is reunited. Thus is virtue rewarded. This embodiment of poetic justice has come full circle from the sinister naturalistic ending of her early novel. (pp. 282-87)

> *Constance Clark, ''Mary Griffith Pix,'' in her* Three Augustan Women Playwrights, *Peter Lang, 1986, pp. 183-287.*

ADDITIONAL BIBLIOGRAPHY

Barbour, Paula Louise. ''A Critical Edition of Mary Pix's *The Spanish Wives* (1696), with Introduction and Notes.'' *Dissertation Abstracts International* 36, No. 12 (June 1976): 8030-A.

    Abstract of the author's 1975 Yale University Ph.D. dissertation, summarizing commentary on the sources, staging, and critical history of *The Spanish Wives.*

Carter, Herbert. ''Three Women Dramatists of the Restoration.'' *The Bookman's Journal* XIII, No. 51 (December 1925): 91-7.

    Contains a mixed evaluation of Pix's dramas, concluding: ''Mrs. Pix had not the slightest turn for poetry and the verse of her tragedies is indescribably bad. The dramatic element, however, is of some value, considerably more than that of Mrs. Manley's plays.''

Clark, Constance. Introduction to *The Inhumane Cardinal* (1696), by Mary Pix, pp. v-xiii. Delmar, N.Y.: Scholars' Facsimiles & Reprints, 1984.

Discusses the origin, plot, and psychology of *The Inhumane Cardinal*.

Hume, Robert D. *The Development of English Drama in the Late Seventeenth Century*, pp. 165ff. Oxford: Oxford University Press, Clarendon Press, 1976.
Scattered brief references to Pix, noting especially her role in the emergence of Augustan drama.

Lock, F. P. "Astraea's 'Vacant Throne': The Successors of Aphra Behn." In *Woman in the 18th Century and Other Essays*, edited by Paul Fritz and Richard Morton, pp. 25-36. Toronto and Sarasota: Hakkert, 1976.
Examines Pix's major dramas, briefly comparing them with the works of Catharine Trotter and Mary Delariviere Manley.

Macqueen-Pope, W. "First Ladies of the Pen." In his *Ladies First: The Story of Woman's Conquest of the British Stage*, pp. 126-42. London: W. H. Allen, 1952.
Notices Pix as a playwright whose plots are well conceived but whose dialogue is weak. The critic adds that Pix may be seen as a "living example that fatness and stupidity do not go together."

Maison, Margaret. "Pope and Two Learned Nymphs." *The Review of English Studies* n.s. XXIX, No. 116 (November 1978): 405-14.
Approaches Pix in connection with the anonymous drama *The Female Wits; or, The Triumvirate of Poets at Rehearsal* (see excerpt dated 1696), commenting on her portrayal in the work.

Morgan, Fidelis. "Mary Pix." In her *The Female Wits: Women Playwrights on the London Stage, 1660-1720*, pp. 44-50. London: Virago, 1981.

Concise overview of Pix's life and works, lamenting her preference for tragedy in the drama.

Nicoll, Allardyce. "Comedy." In his *A History of Restoration Drama, 1660-1700*, 3d ed., pp. 168-267. Cambridge: Cambridge University Press, 1940.
Provides a brief overview of Pix's principal dramas, focusing on the Restoration atmosphere of *The Spanish Wives*, sentimental tone of *The Innocent Mistress*, and overall weakness of *The Deceiver Deceived*.

Smith, John Harrington. "French Sources for Six English Comedies, 1660-1750." *The Journal of English and Germanic Philology* XLVII, No. 4 (October 1948): 390-94.
Contains an account of Florent Carton Dancourt's 1687 drama *Le chevalier à la mode*, said here to be the source of Pix's *Beau Defeated; or, The Lucky Younger Brother*.

Sutherland, James. "Drama (I)." In his *English Literature of the Late Seventeenth Century*, pp. 32-87. Oxford History of English Literature, edited by Bonamy Dobrée and Norman Davis, Vol. VI. New York and Oxford: Oxford University Press, 1969.
Labels Pix one of the "dreary exponents" of late-seventeenth-century tragedy.

Thorn-Drury, G. "An Unrecorded Play-Title." *The Review of English Studies* VI, No. 23 (July 1930): 316-18.
Maintains that because *The Deceiver Deceived* was revived in 1699 under a new title, *The French Beau*, the original 1697 production evidently was not a success.

Nicholas Rowe

1674-1718

English dramatist, editor, poet, and translator.

As one of the most popular tragedians of the eighteenth century, Rowe was instrumental in introducing the so-called domestic tragedy to the English stage. In his best plays—which are, by consensus, *The Fair Penitent* and *The Tragedy of Jane Shore*—he modified the existing Restoration convention of heroic drama through substituting for the usual royal or noble protagonists characters of lower social status and replacing the convention's exotic settings and grandiose, epic-style themes with more ordinary, accessible scenarios and situations. Perhaps most significantly, he chose for his dramatic goal not the inspiration of awe, but the evocation of pathos. Rowe was also the first critical editor of William Shakespeare's dramas, and his labors at that task laid the foundation for modern editorial approaches to Shakespeare's works.

Rowe was born in Little Barford, Bedfordshire. Educated at the private Highgate Free School, he later attended prestigious Westminster School, where he was made a King's Scholar in 1688. At the urging of his father, himself a barrister, Rowe entered the Middle Temple in London in 1691 to study law. He never practiced the legal profession, however, for soon after he was called to the bar his father died, leaving him a legacy of three hundred pounds a year. Thus financially secure, Rowe was free to follow his growing literary inclinations. His first play, *The Ambitious Step-Mother,* was produced in 1700 at Lincoln's Inn Fields in London. The tragedy met with gratifying success, and Rowe had five additional plays produced in London over the next seven years.

A fervent supporter of the then-dominant Whig party, Rowe was appointed to a series of advantageous governmental posts, beginning with his position as secretary to the Duke of Queensberry in 1709. Also in that year appeared Rowe's critical edition of Shakespeare's plays. He published a volume of poetry and had two more plays produced within the next few years. Upon the death of Nahum Tate in 1715, Rowe was honored with his most important appointment, that of Poet Laureate. Ironically, in the three years between his assumption of the laureateship and his death, Rowe wrote little beyond a few obligatory odes for special state occasions and a translation, published posthumously, of Lucan's *Pharsalia*. Despite the doleful nature of much of his work, Rowe the man was of a very different cast: twice married, the friend of such literary notables as Alexander Pope, William Congreve, and Joseph Addison, Rowe was one who, according to his contemporary John Dennis, "loved to be in bed all day for his ease, and to sit up all night for his pleasure." At his death, Rowe was buried in Poets' Corner in Westminster Abbey.

Commentators note that Rowe's plays form a link between the heroic drama of the Restoration and the sentimental drama of the later eighteenth century; his seven blank verse tragedies contain, in varying degrees, elements of both. Like those of the heroic convention, Rowe's plays contain violently emotional characters, passionate, ranting speeches, and extravagant scenes of mayhem and death. Rowe's best plays, however, represent a marked departure from the prevailing tradition in that their characters are not the highborn personages insisted upon by epic-conscious heroic dramatists, but "ordinary,"

middle-class people. Rowe's intent was to create "domestic tragedies" containing dramatic characters with whom his audience could identify. As he promised in his prologue to *The Fair Penitent,* "you shall meet with Sorrows like your own." In this respect and in their melodramatic appeal to the emotions, Rowe's plays foreshadow the sentimental drama. However, critics caution that the tragedies cannot be defined simply as the hybrid products of a transitional era, for Rowe strove to produce a unique tragic effect. At their best, Rowe's dramas evoke not Aristotelian catharsis (the goal of the heroic playwrights), nor the melancholic distress encouraged by the sentimental dramatists, but, instead, a sense of pathos. To achieve this involved nothing less than a change in tragic effect. Traditionally, tragic effect lay in the consequences of a sinful deed; that is, the audience was moved to pity or horror by the frightful results of the commission of a sin. In such plays as *The Fair Penitent* and *Jane Shore,* on the other hand, some of the pity evoked accrues to the sinners themselves. Thus, while Rowe's erring characters suffer their proper comeuppance (thus satisfying the audience's expectation of poetic justice), that audience is yet meant to experience sympathetic compassion for them. Because of this, Rowe's most successful characters are not set in clear-cut molds of virtue or villany as is generally the case in both heroic and sentimental drama.

According to audiences and scholars alike, Rowe's trademark pathetic strain reaches its fullest expression in *The Fair Penitent* and *The Tragedy of Jane Shore,* tragedies which are equally noteworthy for another innovation: these two plays, along with *The Tragedy of Lady Jane Gray,* are dramas with female protagonists—"she-tragedies" as Rowe called them. *The Fair Penitent,* which appropriates much of its plot but little of its structure or themes from Philip Massinger and Nathan Field's *The Fatal Dowry* (1632), recounts the fateful tale of Calista, the title character. Calista is a passionate young woman who, prior to her marriage to a man of her father's choosing, succumbs to the blandishments of her unscrupulous lover, thereby losing her honor. (In the character of Calista's lover, incidentally, Rowe gave to literature the prototype of an enduring—if subsequently stereotyped—character, for his "gay Lothario" presages every heartless but charming rake in literature.) The discovery of Calista's moral lapse precipitates the tragic deaths of most of the play's characters; it is left to the injured husband's loyal friend Horatio, whose own happy marriage is insisted upon throughout the play, to sum up the final lesson concerning the value of constancy and moral rectitude. *The Tragedy of Jane Shore* similarly concerns an adulterous woman, this time the historical mistress, a commoner, of Edward IV. After the king's death, Jane finds herself at the mercy of his brother and successor, Richard III. Betrayed to Richard by a woman who falsely believes that the now chaste and truly repentant Jane is a rival for her lover's affections, the heroine is denied food and shelter by edict of the king, and dies a sorrowful death. (The historical Jane Shore actually survived a good many years longer.) The tragedy of the situation is heightened by the presence of Jane's wronged husband who, in disguise, has shadowed his errant wife throughout the play, attempting, in vain, to succor her.

Melodramatic as *The Fair Penitent* and *Jane Shore* undeniably are, they are considered significant for their treatment of the theme of the "fallen woman." Both protagonists break a fundamental moral and social law; both are punished by death, the inevitable consequence of sin in traditional tragedy. However, although it is never intimated in these plays that Calista and Jane have not indeed committed a grave offense, there is some suggestion that they are as much sinned against as sinning. Both are given speeches—judged rather startling in the eighteenth century—in which they ponder the injustice of woman's lot: Calista bemoans the fact that women just be subservient first to their fathers and then to their husbands, powerless to effect their own choices; Jane complains of the inequity of the sexual double standard, whereby a man who philanders is considered normal, but a woman who strays from the sexual straight and narrow deserves ostracism and worse. Furthermore, as reviewers note, in the case of both women, their injured husbands are willing to forgive them; can the audience do less?

Rowe's other plays are considered generally less innovative, though they too strive for a pathetic tone and effect. The third she-tragedy, *Lady Jane Gray,* differs from the other two both in its return to a high-born character and in the pristine purity of that character. The play is based on the historical Jane Grey (as her name is usually spelled), who, during a time of uncertainty concerning the line of royal succession, was placed on the throne of England for nine days in 1553, only to be forcibly ousted and subsequently executed for treason. The historical Jane Grey was an innocent political pawn; Rowe's dramatic Jane Gray is, as Alfred Jackson has called her, "seraphic." *The Ambitious Step-Mother, Tamerlane, Ulysses,* and *The Royal Convert* also exhibit a closer affinity to the heroic convention, treating as they do figures of high station embroiled in affairs of state. *The Royal Convert,* for example, is a tale

of political intrigue and treachery, while *Tamerlane* is a thinly disguised political allegory celebrating William III of England in the personage of the wise, benevolent Tamerlane, and denouncing Louis XIV of France in the character of the evil Bajazet. Indeed, critics observe that characterization in these more heroic plays tends to be more starkly polarized into absolute good and evil than is the case with *The Fair Penitent* and *Jane Shore,* as the characters are significant less for their individuality than for their status as public figures. Rowe's one attempt at comedy was a farce called *The Biter.* "Biter" was a slang term for one who attempts to deceive another for the simple purpose of making the dupe look foolish; the biter of this play has an easy task with Rowe's central character, a ludicrous Sinophile called Sir Timothy Tallapoy. The play's plot concerns a fairly conventional love intrigue, and the humor arises mainly from jokes at Sir Timothy's expense. Initial reaction to the play is succinctly expressed in a remark made by William Congreve in a letter to a friend dated 9 December 1704: "Rowe writ a foolish farce called the *Biter,* which was damned." Subsequent critical opinion upholds the validity of Congreve's choice of adjective and the justice of *The Biter's* fate.

Rowe's tragedies were without exception enormously popular with their eighteenth-century audience. The most renowned actors and actresses of the day—including Betterton, Elizabeth Barry, and Anne Bracegirdle—performed in the tragedies, to the enhanced reputation of both the plays and the players. Critical dissent was not lacking in the early eighteenth century, however, for in 1715 Charles Gildon objected strenuously to Rowe's art on the grounds that it did not properly accord with classical dramatic criteria. Gildon also took exception to what he deemed the unseemly moral atmosphere of the plays, stating flatly, with regard to *Jane Shore:* "A Whore profess'd, is no Tragic Character." Other early critics were likewise disturbed by moral issues in Rowe's plays, observing that, while evil always receives its due punishment in the last act, virtue does not always escape a similar dire fate, thereby giving rise to complications and ambiguities in what ought to be a clear morally didactic lesson. Lothario of *The Fair Penitent* presented a particularly disconcerting ambiguity; though undoubtedly an immoral cad, he is yet an attractive cad—too attractive, according to early reviewers. As Francis Gentleman warned, Lothario is dangerous "like the snake with a beauteous variegated skin, which lures the unguarded hand to a poisonous touch." Nevertheless, Rowe's tragedies continued to find extraordinary favor with playgoers; indeed, *The Fair Penitent, Jane Shore,* and *Tamerlane* were among the most frequently produced plays of the century. Rowe's fluid blank verse was particularly admired; in the latter part of the eighteenth century Samuel Johnson praised "the elegance of his diction, and the suavity of his verse." Johnson further commented: "He seldom moves either pity or terror, but he often elevates the sentiments; he seldom pierces the breast, but he always delights the ear, and often improves the understanding." While the more heroic plays came to be presented less and less frequently, *The Fair Penitent* and *Jane Shore* were acted and esteemed throughout the eighteenth and well into the nineteenth century. In the last century, August Wilhelm Schlegel expressed much the same thought as had Johnson when he wrote: "Rowe did not possess boldness and vigour, but was not without sweetness and feeling; he could excite the softer emotions."

Since then, though Rowe's plays have all but disappeared from the stage, they are still read and discussed by modern scholars. Twentieth-century criticism has confirmed what eighteenth-century audiences believed: *The Fair Penitent* and *Jane Shore* are Rowe's finest plays. Frank J. Kearful wrote that "they constitute an important development in the history of English drama, for they are the first attempts to fuse the naturalism of domestic tragedy and the patheticism of 'sentimental' tragedy with a new didacticism which is part of the Augustan temper." Annibel Jenkins has found the plays important for another reason, calling them, together with *Lady Jane Gray*, "classics in the long and continuing exploration of woman's place in the public and private segments of our world." The plays qua plays, irrespective of their contributions to literary or social development, have received mixed reviews. Bonamy Dobrée suggested that they are "worth reading for relaxation," thus reiterating the critical judgment first articulated by Johnson: the tragedies are indeed pleasing, but lacking in depth, touching in their pathos, but not deeply moving in their tragedy. Modern critics have attributed this largely to Rowe's failure to take his dramatic innovations far enough. Although it may fairly be said that Rowe was leading the drama in a new direction, toward more natural characters and situations, scholars have warned that it is important not to overemphasize the magnitude of this achievement, as Rowe's plays are not realistic as that term is understood today. Critics add that they frequently exhibit the worst faults of both the heroic and sentimental dramas, most notably the declamatory bombast of the former and the excessive melodrama of the latter. His characters remain, as Sophie Chantal Hart wrote, "little more than vehicles for the expression of a certain type of sentiment and moral reflection, or for the expression of that which the exigencies of a situation demand." Still, Rowe's tragedies continue to please; as Dobrée explained it: "Rowe does not in any way explore life or add anything to our knowledge of the emotions, yet he succeeds in taking us into a sort of coherent, self-consistent fairyland, where the fancy can amuse itself, lulled by sounds that are undeniably sweet." That Rowe's style can be "sweet" has been acknowledged by all critics, though most have added that the quality of his verse is very uneven, ranging from melodic grace to ludicrous bombast. At his best, Rowe can be described, according to Jean H. Hagstrum, as "a master of sweetly harmonious verse and gentle poetical coloring."

Rowe's edition of Shakespeare's plays has long been hailed as a milestone in editoral treatment of that author. While some of Rowe's work has been revised by subsequent editors, much of his editorial policy has become standard procedure: Rowe was the first to provide the plays with lists of dramatis personae, to note act and scene divisions and scene locations, and to add necessary stage directions. Rowe also attempted to clarify obscurities in the text, and on at least one occasion—in *Hamlet*—reinstated an entire missing passage. Rowe included in this work a biography of Shakespeare, in which endeavor he was aided by the noted actor Thomas Betterton, who journeyed to Warwickshire to research Shakespeare's life and times. The result, though a mixture of fact and legend, contains all the biographical data known today. Commentators are not, however, blind to Rowe's editorial faults. His work has frequently been criticized for occasional carelessness and inconsistency. Furthermore, though Rowe claimed to have compared all the extant Folios of the plays before selecting his definitive version, modern critics have observed that Rowe's edition mainly follows the text of the Fourth Folio (1685), perpetuating the errors contained therein. These lapses notwithstanding, *The Works of Mr. William Shakespear* remains an impressive example of early Shakespearian scholarship. Rowe's poetic canon consists largely of panegyrics to contemporary leaders or celebrations of state events, and thus has a decidedly topical cast. Infre-

quently studied, his poetry "can hardly be said to have died," according to W. Forbes Gray, "for it never really lived." Rowe also undertook English translations of ancient Greek and Roman authors; his most notable work in this line is his paraphrastic *Lucan's Pharsalia*.

It is thus as a tragedian that Rowe is principally remembered. He defied convention with his she-tragedies, virtual anomalies in an age of male-dominated drama, and, significantly, achieved considerable success with this defiance. In his attempt to make dramatic characters and situations more accessible to the average audience, he is one of the first and most important writers of domestic tragedies. Finally, through his plays' communication of haunting pathos rather than high tragedy, he created a viable alternative to the Aristotelian concept of cathartic terror and awe as the goal of tragedy. Although Rowe has never been called a great dramatist, his tragedies retain an interest and a meaning; as Vivian De Sola Pinto has said of them: "His plays are a curious mixture of stagy artifice and unreal psychology with touches of genuine pathos and humanity."

PRINCIPAL WORKS

The Ambitious Step-Mother (drama) 1700
Tamerlane (drama) 1701
The Fair Penitent (drama) 1703
The Biter (drama) 1704
Ulysses (drama) 1705
The Royal Convert (drama) 1707
The Works of Mr. William Shakespear. 6 vols. [editor] (dramas) 1709
Poems on Several Occasions (poetry) 1714
The Tragedy of Jane Shore (drama) 1714
The Tragedy of Lady Jane Gray (drama) 1715
Lucan's Pharsalia [translator] (poetry) 1719
The Works of Nicholas Rowe (dramas, poetry, and translations) 1728

A COMPARISON BETWEEN THE TWO STAGES (essay date 1702)

[*The following excerpt is taken from a wide-ranging critical appraisal of the dramatic productions of London's two theaters. Written in the form of "a Dialogue between Ramble and Sullen, two Gentlemen, and Chagrin, a Critick," the work was published anonymously in 1702. Although authorship is often attributed to Charles Gildon (see excerpt dated 1715), the evidence remains inconclusive. Here, as the speakers turn their attention from the Drury Lane Theater to Lincoln's Inn Fields Theater, where many of Rowe's plays were first performed,* Tamerlane *comes under discussion.*]

Ramb. But Gentlemen—Why do we fall foul only on this *Theatre*? Are the Plays so pure in *Lincolns-Inn-fields*, that nothing can be said gainst 'em? (p. 96)

Sull. The Tragedy of **Tamerlane** is put up.

Ramb. That's the same Author's as the [*Ambitious Stepmother*], and truly I think he may stand the first Man in the List of our present Dramatists.

Crit. As I said before, he has excell'd all his Cotemporaries in correctness of Language; but in that I have said the best part of him.

Ramb. I wonder you will talk at that rate; he has many Excellencies besides.

Sull. He has so, tho' *Criticks* ill nature will not suffer him to speak well of any body.

Crit. You're mistaken; I've not so much ill nature as you imagine; nor will I to the best of my knowledge pass an unjust censure on any Man; but 'twere impious to offer it to this Gentleman. Pray send for his Play.

Ramb. 'Tis here; I hug it as *Alexander* did *Homer*, or as *Ben Johnson Horace*, I always carry it about me.

Crit. Pray lets see it: I read it t'other Day very carefully, and made some slight Remarks. (pp. 97-8)

Ramb. Read it over? You need not give your self that trouble, I have it every Word by Heart. (p. 98)

[*Crit.* Because] we all run away with a great Opinion of this Author's Stile and propriety of Words, it may be matter of some curiosity to examine that Truth, and try if he be so infallible as we believe him. Let me direct you to two or three places, not, that I expect to find any thing that wou'd be worth mentioning in any other Poet, but in a Poem so very beautiful as Mr. *Roe*'s the least spots may be seen, as we say freckles are plainest discover'd in the finest Skins. (pp. 98-9)

[Speaking] of the King, he says—*I can hardly run back to his having sav'd his own Country*—that Participle *having* makes the Sentence rough and ungrammatical; it either shews the Author very lazy or very unknowing; when with as little trouble he might have said the same thing another way—as, *I can hardly run back to the safety he gave his own Country*—that Substantive had made it smooth and strenuous.

Ramb. This is as very a trifle as ever *Dryden* and his Club publish'd against the *Empress of Morocco*.

Crit. 'Tis not of much importance truly; but I say out of so correct a Poem as this, 'tis worth our curiosity to pick what we can to shew he's not without fallibility.

Ramb. I shou'd rather think it ungenerous to censure a Man of such approv'd worth for such Trifles.

Crit. I mean him no Injury upon my Word; I honour him as much as you do, but perhaps on better assurances of his Merit; you take up a Friendship for him on account of his Fame, but I have enter'd into his Deserts, and judged him without partiality. (p. 99)

Ramb. Pray go on. What have you more?

Crit. Another blemish in his writings is—he concludes a Sentence with a *Parenthesis*, which is directly wrong: A *Parenthesis* has no Period; it always stands in the middle of the Sentence, and the very Etymology of the Word directs us how to use it.

Ramb. Whereabouts is that?

Crit. 'Tis here, toward the bottom of the second Page of the Dedication: But now I'll turn into the Play.

Moneses says—*hast me to find the place*—Why *me* after *hast*? 'tis an expletive not only unnecessary, but it makes the Line Nonsense. Again, the same—*Tam.* says—*I fear me—thou outgoest*, &c.—there's *me* after *fear*. . . . No manner of Interpretation can make these two Orthographical.

Ramb. They are *Anglicisms*, a common way of speaking.

Cri. A very improper manner it is, nor can it by being an *Anglicism*, be therefore excus'd in Tragedy, not only whose Thoughts, but whose Expressions ought to be Sublime. . . . *The Mind grows rough and loses all her firmness.* Why *her*, Mind is of the masculine Gender; if he had said Soul, *her* had been proper. *Arp.* says . . . *Her mind is come within the Ken of Heav'n. Ken* is too *Scottish* and familiar for Tragedy: *Laggard in the Race.* I hardly believe that to be an *English* word. I will not be too particular: But I can't forbear taking notice how fond he is of *Face of Death, Face of Battle, Face of Danger;* 'tis a good Phrase, but he uses it too often, no less than four times in this Play, which is too much for one *Metaphor. Virgin Youth* is repeated very frequently; *late Posterity* as often, and thrice he introduces the Comparison of the fallen Angels.

Sull. These are over-sights, but hardly worth reckoning.

Crit. I say so too; but you see he is not infallible.

Ramb. I fancy you'l find very few of your Opinion in these Remarks.

Crit. I appeal to all the World if these are not Blemishes: I appeal to the Author himself; not that I oppose 'em to his Merit; I say again, they are not of that force as to come into competition with the rest of his Language; I only hint 'em from the provocation you give me. But to be very sincere with you, I must needs say I do not see that Magnificence either in his *Drama* or in his *Words,* that bears it up to the mighty Reputation it has: The thing is very well, but you must pardon me if I can't conceive so loftily of it as others do. I have read twenty Tragedies that have pleas'd me more, for I never can consent to range it among some of *Shakespear*'s, some of *Dryden*'s, some of *Lee*'s, notwithstanding all his Rants, or some of *Otway*'s, notwithstanding his humility and vulgarity of Expression.

Sull. You must allow something for his Youth and Inexperience.

Crit. And yet for all this I will allow you, that neither his Youth or Inexperience have injur'd him so much, but his Play might claim an elder Author; nor need any of them I have nam'd ha' been asham'd to own it; but still my Friends, you must grant me, there is not that Vivacity, that Spirit, that Fire, which is in *Lee,* or *Dryden,* that Variety which is in *Shakespear,* nor that Power of moving that we feel in *Otway:* I don't read it with that concern either of Terror or Compassion which theirs give me: Upon the Stage it may appear well, but he had some of the best Tragedians in the World to Act it, and who knows not the Advantage a Play receives from their Mouths? Who knows not the effect of *Batterton*'s fine Action? Who is not charm'd with Mrs. *Barry*? What Beauty do they not give every thing they represent? Still don't mistake me Gentlemen; I am not solliciting against the Poet's Merit, but am insinuating t'ee how many an indifferent Play has had good success when these Persons have been concern'd in it. I wou'd as soon as you stand up for this Gentleman's Applause; for indeed, considering the degeneracy of our present Poets, Mr. *Roe* has the fairest Pretence to succeed *Dryden* in *Tragedy* of any of his Brethren, excepting none; and may he prove as I wish him . . . *Spes altera Romæ* ["hope of another Rome"].

Sull. If you have done, give me leave in opposition to those inconsiderable Faults which you have mention'd, to tell you what I think very fine in him.

First, he has describ'd *Bajazet* most exactly as the Histories have left him; a Man of stern invincible Ambition, Rage, Cruelty, Atheism, and an Insensibility to all Impressions of Friendship and Generosity: He has drawn him as if he had liv'd in his Court, and been the intimate of all his Passions: There is not one false Line in the whole Picture. On the other hand, he has describ'd *Tamerlane* as his reverse; that is, he has made him Mild, Tractable, Generous, Humble, Serene, and Compassionate; Brave without Ostentation, without Superstition Religious; that Hero in all Records, is delivered just such a one as he has made him, allowing something for the shadowing and ornaments of Poetry. *Axalla* is a fine Copy of the Soldier and the Lover; *Moness* is a Character of Distress: *Omar* and the *Dervise* are good Descriptions of all Malecontents in the State and Church: *Arpasia* awakes us with her great Spirit, and *Selima* softens us with her Tenderness: Every one in its kind is well, and altogether excellent.

Crit. Very good; then I reply thus . . . That *Tamerlane* with all his Humility, has an allay of vain Glory in several Speeches where he extolls the Vertues of a true Mussel-man, by adducing them all to himself; sundry Lines in his Part wou'd be better from the Mouth of another: Again, the Characters of *Arpasia* and *Selima* are too much a-kin; there's so great a resemblance between them, that with very little alteration they might change Parts; they are both Lovers, and are both belov'd; and their Distress turns with the same Spring; they two and their two Lovers are miserable without variety: *Axalla* loses his Mistress because of her Obedience to *Bajazet* her Father, and *Moness* despairs of his, because she was Marry'd to *Bajazet;* so that both suffer on account of their Mistresses alliance to the same Person, and almost for the same reason.

Again: The Marriage of *Arp.* to *Bajazet* is not well describ'd; she tells *Moness* the Priest pronounc'd the Marriage Rites, but she consented not: How then was it a Marriage? All Religions, Pagan, Mahometan, as well as Christian, require in Wedlock the Consent of both Parties, for if one stands Obstinate, the Rites are stop'd; and to render it still more improbable, the Histories of the *Ottoman* Emperors tell us, that the *Sultan* never Marries her who is in his Power, till by her Assiduities, Artifices and Cunning, and the Desire of being chief *Sultana,* she infatuates him; backing all these with her Charms, to gain the Empire of the Sera'lio, and to domineer over the rest; several Examples prove this, as we may read particularly in the Story of this very *Bajazet*'s Grandson.

Ramb. Are you sure of that?

Cri. I refer you to the *Turkish* History. But to proceed. . . . *Bajazet*'s surprizing the Christian Princes, is [improbable] . . . ; that is, that a Treachery of so fatal a nature, in the centre of *Tamerlane*'s Camp, shou'd be conspir'd, nay perpetrated, without the least noise; that all Parties shou'd so universally agree, even in the Face of their conquering Emperor, in the minute of Leisure and Peace, when the least Eruption might alarm the Camp; when *Tam.* had such assur'd Experience of his Enemy's mischievous Temper. . . . I say, 'tis a little strain'd beyond Policy and Belief.

But that which surprizes me most, is *Tamerlane*'s offering him his Liberty and Empire, on the Condition of his future Friendship, when the very reason of this War arises from *Bajazet*'s Perfidy; this Circumstance, I think, makes *Tamerlane*'s Generosity little better than Frenzy: But the Story in *Ricaut* and *Knolles,* don't say a word like it. I might add to *Arpasia*'s Character, that she pretended Christian Vertue is nice to a folly; she might ha' renounce'd *Baj.* with a good Conscience, and gone back to *Moness* who was first Marry'd to her, which renders the second Marriage null: Or if she grew desperate, to

ha' kill'd her self wou'd have imply'd as little guilt as wishing so impatiently to die, for dying and desiring to die is the same in a religious Sense, and the latter as well as the former, makes her a *Felo de se* ["committer of a felony by self-murder"]. I shall urge no more. . . .

Ramb. You have urged enough in all Conscience; too much indeed, for I can't agree with you that half of what you have said are Faults in him. But pray answer me this . . . don't you think there are many fine Lines in it?

Crit. Yes indeed, I do think there are many fine Thoughts, some shining *Sentences,* and several Reflections very Beautiful.

Ramb. I know some People whjo think the Author had a double Object in view when he writ it; and that most of his Characters are assimulated to some great Persons now living.

Crit. Those People are of a greater Penetration than I, I must confess.

Ramb. Nay, there is a manifest Similitude in *Tamerlane, Bajazet, Axalla,* and *Omar,* to some that we can name; and the Author seems apprehensive of it in the beginning of his Epistle.

Sull. I hardly believe he had any Person in his Eye when he drew the Scheme but his own People, nor in the Writing, but the Actors.

Ramb. Well, let that pass; and if you have nothing more to say, return my Book. (pp. 100-04)

"A Comparison Between the Two Stages," in A Comparison Between the Two Stages: A Late Restoration Book of the Theatre, *edited by Staring B. Wells, Princeton University Press, 1942, pp. 1-110.*

NICHOLAS ROWE   (poem date 1703)

[*The following excerpt is taken from Rowe's prologue, recited by actor Thomas Betterton in the original 1703 performance, to* The Fair Penitent. *Here, Rowe emphasizes his departure from the heroic tragic convention.*]

Long has the Fate of Kings and Empires been
The common Bus'ness of the Tragick Scene,
As if Misfortune made the Throne her Seat,
And none cou'd be unhappy but the Great.
Dearly, 'tis true, each buys the Crown he wears,
And many are the mighty Monarch's Cares:
By foreign Foes and home-bred Factions prest,
Few are the Joys he knows, and short his Hours of Rest.
Stories like these with Wonder we may hear,
But far remote, and in a higher Sphere,
We ne'er can pity what we ne'er can share:
Like distant Battles of the *Pole* and *Swede,*
Which frugal Citizens o'er Coffee read,
Careless for who shall fail or who succeed.
Therefore an humbler Theme our Author chose,
A melancholy Tale of private Woes:
No Princes here lost Royalty bemoan,
But you shall meet with Sorrows like your own;
Here see imperious Love his Vassals treat,
As hardly as Ambition does the Great;
See how succeeding Passions rage by turns,
How fierce the Youth with Joy and Rapture burns,
And how to Death, for Beauty lost, he mourns.

Let no nice Taste the Poet's Art arraign,
If some frail vicious Characters he fain:
Who Writes shou'd still let Nature be his Care,
Mix Shades with Lights, and not paint all things fair,
But shew you Men and Women as they are.

> Nicholas Rowe, "Prologue to 'The Fair Penitent'," in his Three Plays: Tamerlane, The Fair Penitent, Jane Shore, *edited by J. R. Sutherland, The Scholartis Press, 1929, p. 161.*

CHARLES GILDON (essay date 1715)

[*Gildon was an English writer of verse and prose. His critical works—among them,* The Laws of Poetry *(1721)—prove him a vigorous defender of neoclassical literary principles. The following excerpt is taken from Gildon's 1715 critical evaluation of Rowe's tragedies; the criticism is itself written in dramatic form. The dramatis personae include: Mr. Freeman, "a Gentleman of a good Taste and Learning"; Mr. Truewit, "a Man of Wit and Good Taste"; Sir Indolent Easie, "a Man of Wit, but one who is, or seems to be pleas'd with every Thing and every Writer"; and Sawny Dapper, "a young Poet of the Modern stamp, an easy Versifyer." Here, Freeman and Truewit lambast Rowe's dramas.*]

Sir *Ind.* I confess, Gentlemen, that were I to Write my self, I wou'd have a true and just Regard to both Art and Nature; but then I do it, because I find it very agreable to my Humour; I can't please my self without Order, and the Harmony of Parts. But 'foregad if the obtaining these Perfections were troublesom to me, I wou'd not give my self any Concern about it. Perhaps these poor Gentlemen find a difficulty in these Points, perhaps they cannot with all their Application attain them. Wou'd you be so unreasonable to require that of them which they cannot do?

Free. Let them Continue then courteous Readers, and not presume to Scribble, and assume an Air from a false success, to make them greater Coxcombs than they would be without it.

Sir *Ind.* 'Foregad you're too severe, must none but Ciet-Cats have leave to———Scribbling's the Diabetis of the Mind; and when a Man's infected with it, he can't help clapping Pen to Paper, and then what ensues you generally find. Besides, what need they take pains to arrive at Art, when they do their Business without it. What Plays have taken more than those of Mr. BAYS, ev'n from his first Appearance to this day. If his Plays take, what wou'd you have more? And 'forgad I think the **Ambitious Stepmother** is an excellent Tragedy as Tragedies go now. Then here's his **Tamerlane, Ulysses, Fair Penitent,** and last and greatest of All, **Jane Shore.** Who can contend with him? the Ladies admire them, the Lords encourage them, and every one goes to them, what wou'd you have more?

True. One Man of Learning, Art and Understanding, faithfully and sincerely declare his Approbation of any one of them: For I confess we in the Country were wonderfully supriz'd to find that they were so very well receiv'd, without any one Beauty through them all, that we cou'd find from the reading them.

Sir *Ind.* Nay, for the Reading them, I must own I never gave my self the Trouble to do that; I was satisfied with seeing them, and was active to promote the Author's Benefit on their being Acted.

Free. Well faith, Sir *Indolent,* you ought to do some Penance for such a supererogatory Transgression; especially since I know you have been slack enough in encouraging much better Performances, because they did not take so well. *True-wit,* Seat your self on the other side the Knight, whilst I secure him on

this; I am resolv'd to mortify him with our Examination of them all, by which he shall see, what an Incubus he has hugg'd with so much Ardour, under the disguise of Success.

Sir *Ind.* 'Foregad, Gentlemen, I can't bear it, I must be gon, I have Business.

Free. You shall not stir one Foot, Sir *Indolent,* till we have perform'd the Operation—You are Master of so much good Sense, that it is an Act of Humanity to cure you of the only monstrous failing you have. Come, 'tis in vain to struggle; submit patiently, and the Cure will be effected with the less trouble.

Sir *Ind.* Well, 'foregad if it must be so I will be patient; but handle my good Friend with as much tenderness as possible, I beg you.

True. Well, Sir *Indolent,* for your sake, we will not insist on Peccadillo's, we'll pass over his dull Insipidness, and a little heavy Nonsense or so, without any Notice, if that will satisfy you. We will begin with his first *Play,* from whence he deriv'd his Authority, only premising a few necessary Preliminaries; as to the Nature of Tragedy, on which we shall build our Criticisms.

Sir *Ind.* Well, Gentlemen, what you please.

Free. The Antients———

Sir *Ind.* Phoo, What signify the Antients, since they are unknown to our Wits of a Court and Town Education, who can go no farther back into Antiquity, 'foregad, than their Pedigree can shew them. (pp. 9-12)

Free. I do persuade my self that you will allow, that the Perfection of whatever Art we derive from the Antients, is to be judged by the Antients and their Practice, who were the Founders of that Art. (p. 13)

[*True.*] *Tragedy* was the Invention and Product of *Athens,* and . . . the Rules which *Aristotle* has given us, were Receiv'd and Establish'd in that City, they being indeed drawn from the Practice of the best of the *Athenian* Poets before his Time, and exactly agreeable to Reason and Nature.

Sir *Ind.* I can't deny the Fact.

Free. It is pretty Remarkable, that as all the Politer Arts had their Rise from this little Commonwealth, so they all Arriv'd to such a Perfection there, that no other Nation has yet been able to improve them. (p. 14)

Sir *Ind.* The sum of what you aim at Gentlemen, by what you have said, seems to me to imply, that as Tragedy was a Poem invented and made perfect, and adorn'd with all its Rules of arriving at Perfection and Nature by the *Greeks;* if we will call ours by the same Name, and pretend it to be the same Poem, it must be judg'd by the same Rules?

Free. You take us, Sir *Indolent,* perfectly well. . . . (p. 15)

True. From thence we shall only infer, that the Principal Care of the Poet ought to be employ'd in the principal part of the Poem, the *Fable;* and that any Play that is defective grosly in that, must be a detestable *Tragedy;* that next to that, the *Manners* are to be taken Care of, as that they be *Good,* that is, *Well-mark'd, Convenient, Like, Equal,* and *Necessary,* and that the Sentiments be the genuine and natural Result of the Manners, that is, such Thoughts as a Person endow'd with such Manners, under such Passions and such Circumstances, wou'd think; for the Temper of the Person gives different Sentiments of the same Things, and the same Circumstances. It is therefore the Poet's Business to enter into the Nature of the Character he draws, and give such Sentiments, as the Manners of the Dramatic Person require. (p. 16)

Free. I shall only add to what has been said, that the End and Aim of *Tragedy,* is to move Fear or Compassion, or both; and therefore what ever Fable of a Tragedy is not Calculated for this End, is Faulty and not Tragical.

Sir *Ind.* Well, allowing all you have said, for in Reason it appears to me but just; pray proceed to your Business, that I may pass thro' my Torture the sooner.

Free. To that we now come; the **Ambitious Stepmother,** the very Name of the Play is wrong; for Ambition is not properly a Dramatic Passion, it has too much of Sedateness, 'tis too particular, it extends not to the general Life, as Anger, Curiosity, Rashness, Obstinacy, and the like, which render, by Indulgence, the Common or General Life of Man uneasy, and often very Unhappy. But not to stand upon Trifles, where there are more Substantial Errors, let us go to the Plot or Fable. (pp. 17-18)

[*True.* The Plot or Fable] is indeed a strange kind of Medley, and has nothing either Rational or Dramatic in it; it has no *Moral,* or none of any use; and is indeed directed by *Artaban* himself only to his own public Conduct, in which the Audience have not the least Interest or Concern; it moves neither Terror nor Compassion, nor are the Manners any way *necessary* to the end propos'd. Nay, *Mirza*'s Lust had nothing to do with the bringing *Artaban* to the Throne, but must have totally disappointed it, had not *Orchanes,* contrary to the Honour of a Soldier and a Man, villainously forc'd *Amestris* to the dying, prime Minister to be stabb'd; which was highly improbable, if not impossible, that *Orchanes* shou'd do, even for his own Interest, since he might have made better Terms for himself (which cou'd be the only motive of an Action to a Man of his Character) with *Artaxerxes,* than with a dying Villain, who by Consequence cou'd do him no manner of Service.

Free. Mirza is represented as a Cunning Man, but his Conduct with *Amestris,* is the most silly, that an unruly Boy cou'd be guilty of. As his falling in Love at that Juncture, and his design'd Rape, were without any manner of Use to the Catastrophe or the Design of the Play, so was it manag'd like a Fool; his Age and Weakness in the Attempt, discover that he might have delay'd the Execution till all was safe, and nothing cou'd contradict his Will. He tells us it is but Lust mingled with Revenge; and then it was natural for him to defer his salacious Entertainment for a few Hours, when he might have taken a securer way to his Satisfaction, ev'n by the Rules of Common Sense, than by a Struggle with Youth prepossess'd against him by Love and Hatred, the detestation of his Murder of her Lord and her Father. Since the Author was resolv'd to make him a Villain, He shou'd not have made him a Fool too, because he had call'd him a cunning Politic Person. *Orchanes,* or many of his Domestics, who are always diligent in promoting their Lord's Vices for their own Benefit, wou'd have held her, whilst the Impotent Master might have nothing to do but to take his beastly satisfaction of her. From this and a living Prime Minister, the Capt. of the Guards might have assur'd himself of some Reward, which he cou'd not expect from dying *Mirza.* Humane Nature is not so very depraved as to do Villanies only for Villany's sake; so that *Orchanes* had not the least Reason to obey his cruelty in his last Agonies of Life without any Respect, since he did not know but *Artaxerxes* and *Memnon*

had made their Escape, and so he might bepunish'd for a Deed, from which he cou'd expect no manner of Benefit. But indeed *Orchanes* is not punish'd at all, but goes off triumphant in the possession of his Place, for all that we can find to the Contrary.

True. 'Tis plain that the Story of this Play was taken from the Establishing *Solomon* on the Throne of *David,* by *Bathsheba, Nathan* the Prophet, *Zadok* the Priest, &c. And if the Poet had follow'd the Holy History more closely, there wou'd have been no need of those monstrous Characters of *Mirza, Magas,* &c. (pp. 20-3)

Free. Nay, he seems very fond of Rogues. . . . (p. 31)

True. The Queen's first Speech is Monstrous, out of Nature, out of Character, fond of her Adultery in a long calm Sililoquy; nor do we know why she comes in, or why she goes out; But that is a common Fault of our Modern *Playwrights,* especially of Mr. *Bays* the Younger.

Free. The concluding Lines of the first Act are extremely Boyish, when he tells his Mistress, That the Sun shou'd think her Eyes shou'd light the World in his Absence.

True. In the second Act, he talks of *Memnon*'s having recourse to Arms, of which Power we have not the least Word in the first: All that we know is, that he returns from Banishment on a day of Jubilee, when all was Safe and Free. The Queen and *Artaxerxes* call Names very handsomly in the second Act, which is extremely agreeable to their high Station.

Free. Artaxerxes in the third Act, gives a very merry Solution to the Fears of *Amestris,* and tells her, that if she fears Parting, why let them take a Touch together presently; but she is indeed very whymsical to fear the future Falshood of *Artaxerxes,* when he shall be cloy'd with Fruition. But he swares he will Feague her off for it, and that, when a Bed she shall give him Satisfaction.

True. Right—and she is touch'd with this to the quick; for she tells him, asking Pardon of her Modesty, that she is ready, ay marry is the Buxom Jade, ready to dissolve, where she stands, with Pleasure. Oh the Luscious Rogue *Bays.*

Free. A noble Author to be encourag'd by the Ladies of Honour and Chastity. . . . (pp. 31-3)

True. All the Unfortunate Characters are good, and the most Fortunate the worst of the bad, as for *Artaban,* he is for having the Crown that is not his due; but he is for Fighting for it, he wou'd take it by Force, not Fraud. He differs from his Mother, *Mirza,* &c. as a *Highwayman* does from a *Pickpocket,* both are Felons; *Artaban* is the *Highwayman,* and *Artemisa* the *Pickpocket.*

Free. In short, this Murdering so many, shows the Weakness of the Poet's Genius; the Dagger-being at hand to help out every Bungler. And it farther justifies the Reproach thrown on our Country by *Rapin* and some others, That we *Insularies* are delighted with Blood in our Sports, and to our Shame, our Tragic Poets every day confirm it; but none more, than your worthy Friend Mr. *Bays.*

Sir *Ind.* Well, I hope we may have a little Cessation now, and send a Glass about to Good Nature, for you have been sufficiently severe on this Piece of Honest *Bays.*

Free. I hope with Truth and Justice—for where we have said one thing, the Play, under Consideration, afforded Matter for Twenty; but to avoid Tediousness, we have but touch'd upon it. (pp. 35-6)

True. Well, Sir *Indolent*, we will not be so long on any of his other Plays; but this being his first, and that, on which he built all his after Authority, we cou'd not say less than we have, in Justice to the Art. (p. 36)

Free. Well, Sir *Indolent*, giving but a Word or two on *Ulysses*, and the **Fair Penitent**, we will, with as few on **Jane Shore**, dismiss you in Peace.

True. I shall be the more tender of *Ulysses*, because it is by much the best of his, and has a sort of a Face of Tragedy. The Poet indeed has left it without any Moral; he has made *Semanthe* unfortunate without any demerit. He has taken all *Ithaca* for his Scene, which, by as good a Reason, might have been extended to all *Greece*, and so to all *Europe*, nay, indeed, to the whole Earth. He has introduc'd I know not how many Kings with the Manners of Scoundrels or Porters; he has been fond, admiring *Penelope*'s Beauty at Forty odd. He has made *Ulysses* put *Penelope* to an unnecessary and unjust Tryal, not at all conducive to the Plot, nor agreeable to the Wisdom, or Gratitude of his Hero. But these, and a great many more Absurdities of the Design, Conduct, and indeed of the Sentiments and Diction, I will sacrifice to your good Nature; and to the weak Appearance of a Tragedy, which he has in no other of his Performances.

Sir *Ind.* They say 'tis an easie thing to find fault; 'foregad I think it is the hardest thing in Nature; I am sure I should have read and seen *Ulysses*, an hundred Times, before I cou'd have discover'd the third part of the Faults you have produc'd; and yet you wou'd persuade me that you are silent as to the Rest, in Complaisance to me, and the uncommon Merit of the Play.

True. Why, Sir *Indolent*, to satisfy you that I had made a Considerable Sacrifice to you in this, I will give you the Faults of *Ulysses* more at length; nor abridge you of their Number.

Sir *Ind.* Nay, Sir, 'foregad I'd rather thank you for your Complement, than stand the Tryal of the Reality. I pray proceed.

Free. The **Fair Penitent** was built on a much better Play of *Massinger*'s, call'd the *Fatal Dowry*. The Poets are equally guilty of making their Heroine a *Whore;* but the latter Poet has made her more unpardonable and obstinate, and still less worthy of Pity. *Charolois* in *Massinger* resents the Incontinence and Injury to his Bed like a Man of Honour; yet will not punish her till her Father had heard the Cause, and decided it against her; and when the Father's Justice had Condemn'd her, the Husband strikes the Dagger into her Bosome: This makes Nature return to her Father, and his Grief for the untimely loss of his only Child, produces a very noble, and natural Scene. But in Mr. *Bays*, the Husband is a true tame Cuckold, tho' an *Italian*, and is for forgetting all that's past. But the Father is implacable, and will admit of no Compensation; in spight of all the Pleas of Nature, and even the Husband's Indolence in desiring to sit down contented with her as she is: If she had been a Maid it had been better; but since it was, as 'twas, why good Man he wou'd take up with her as he had, *for better or for worse*.

True. To say no more of this *Italian* NIKY, we will only read you a Prologue design'd for this Play, by a Gentleman.... (pp. 56-8)

> Let others toil beneath the Load of Thought,
> Of what is just, what natural, what not;
> They're dull mechanick Things below Regard,
> From such a bold, and such a lucky Bard.

> Uncumber'd with those Fetters, still he'll write,
> Whilst *Ignorance* assures his hoodwink'd Flight.
> He fears no Danger, for he none foresees;
> In happy *Ignorance* secure to please,
> Without those forreign Aids, th' indulgent Town,
> With Heroes and with Language, *All his own*.
> The Hooded Falcon so, in haste let fly,
> Tours swift aloft undaunted to the Sky
> With upright Wing, till lost to human Eye.
>   From Thrones he *sauntring, talking HEROES* chose,
> But for an *active HEROINE* now rakes the Stews;
> And whence he'll fetch the next—*he only knows.*

(pp. 60-1)

[*Free.*] I will say no more of this Play, but what may justly be said of all those with which this Author has yet visited the Town————That Nature, Character, and Design, are wholly unknown to him; that a sort of sonorous numerous Verse, very empty of Sense and Poetry, is what has rais'd him a Name, and that the justest Criticism on this and others, wou'd be, . . . a Spunge dip'd in Ink. (p. 63)

Dap. Mr. *Freeman*, I protest I have a great esteem for you, and I wish you wou'd abate of that Ill-nature you have shown against Mr. *Bays*, and the taking Poets; for you must know that we all take it for Envy.

Free. I am not at all concern'd, what you Gentlemen Writers think of my Good or Ill Nature; but Truth and Art, are what I value before all Men, when they are the Subject of my Discourse, and I shall never sacrifice them to the Success of any Coxcomb in Vogue.

Dap. Why, Sir, you may be a *Critic* still, and not disoblige the Town by condemning what it likes.

Free. As how, Mr. *Dapper*?

Dap. Why I am a *Critic* my self————but then I write always in Praise of what is cry'd up by the Town; by that I oblige the Authors, and get the Reputation of a well natur'd Fellow, free from Envy, Malice, and the like. Have you not seen a *Review of Jane Shore*?

Free. Yes marry have I, Sir; but what of that, honest well-natur'd *Sawny*?

Dap. Why, I my self writ that gentle Piece of Criticism; and I think I have there shown, that I understand Art as well as the severest of you all.

Free. Did you write that wonderful Piece Mr. *Dapper*? I protest I thought that the Bookseller had written it himself. (p. 65-6)

[*Dap.*] Faith I said all I cou'd for him, and I hope some things that will bear the Test.

Free. I shou'd be glad to hear them honest *Sawny* for thy sake, As how?

Dap. Why first, I show that the Characters are Tragical, and then that the Play carries a Moral Instruction; nay, I do pretend to assert, that the Poet's Conduct is of a piece thro' the whole *Drama*.

True. In that you are certainly in the Right, for the Poet's Conduct thro' the whole, must by all Men, that have seen or read the Play, be own'd to be of a piece, that is, every where Faulty; the chief Character, which is *Jane Shore*, is no Tragical Character.

Dap. How, Sir, not Tragical! (pp. 67-8)

True. A Whore profess'd, is no Tragic Character, *Incontinency* in Woman being on the same Level with *Cowardice* in Man; and Mr. *Bays* might as well have brought a Coward for his Hero, as a Whore for his Heroine. (p. 68)

Dap. But, Gentlemen, may not Circumstances make a Vicious Character the Object of Pity? As from the Strength of the Temptation, the natural weakness of the Offender, or the Power and Influence of some other Person in the Commission of the Crime.

Free. No bright Quality can balance a Vice that is Scandalous, as Incontinence in a Woman, and Cowardice in a Man.

True. But *Jane Shore,* had she been Innocent of this Crime, had been no Tragic Character, for her Station of Life was too low; a Shop-keepers Wife of the City never can rise above the Soc; and her having lain with the King and two or three Lords, will never be thought ennobling enough to fit her for the Buskin, since that very Crime renders her entirely incapable of it.

Dap. But then she is Penitent for this Crime, has a due sense of her Guilt, and shows a suitable Compunction for her Offence, which makes her the Object of Mercy, that is, Pity.

True. Penitence may move our Joy, but can never touch our Compassion; and the price of lost Reputation can never be paid, unless that cou'd be restor'd, which never was, nor ever can be.

Dap. But then she wou'd not yield to *Gloster*'s Wicked Design of putting aside the Young King.

Free. It is not sufficient to move our Compassion, that one that has been Guilty of a Scandalous Vice, will not be Guilty of a more Enormous Wickedness.

Dap. 'Tis true she is an Adulteress, but then her fellow offender was a Monarch.

True. As for her fellow offender being a Monarch, that takes not away the Scandal of the Fault, but adds the guilt of Ambition to that of Lust; and here I must observe, that Mr. *Bays* makes *Jane Shore*'s Virtue produce her Misery, and not her Vice. Whereas the ancient Tragic Poets made the Hero's Vices produce their Misfortunes. It was the Obstinacy, Rashness and Curiosity of *Oedipus* that made that discovery which render'd him entirely miserable; but *Jane* is so, because she will not add another Wickedness to her former. (pp. 69-71)

[*Free.* Poor] *Jane* still thinks it Delight to be Wicked———

> No Roses bloom upon my fading Cheeks,
> Nor laughing Graces wanton in my Eyes;
> But haggard Grief, lean-looking sallow Care,
> And piercing Discontent, a rueful Train
> Dwell on my Brow, all hideous and forlorn.

Is this the Language of a Penitent? As such she shou'd rather have describ'd the Beauty of the Mind, the satisfaction of a Converted state, and the Charms of a heavenly Spouse: Whereas all that she says, seems to place her Pain in that her Pleasures are past Recall.

True. *Jane*'s last Speech in the first Act is another proof that she repents not her Adultery; for she complains of the hard Fate of Womankind, that they can't Whore with the same safety to their Reputatious, as Mankind can.

> Mark by what partial Justice we are Judg'd:

partial Justice, by the way, is an extraordinary Epithet, he might as well have said, Mark by what unjust Justice we are Judg'd; but this is a Pecadillo.

> Such is the Fate *unhappy* Women find;
> And such the *Curse* entail'd on Womankind.

Here poor *Jane* thinks it *unhappy,* nay, a *Curse,* that Women have not the Liberty of roving———

> That Man the lawless Libertine may rove,
> Free and unquestion'd through the wilds of Love,
> While Woman, Sense, and Natures easie Fool,

the last Line I take to be absolutely unintelligible.

> If poor weak Woman swerve from Virtue's Rule,
> If strongly Charm'd she leave the *Thorny Way,*

The poor penitent *Jane,* still thinks the Paths of Virtue a thorny Way.

> And in the softer Paths of Pleasure stray,
> Ruin ensues, Reproach and endless Shame,
> And one false step entirely damns her Fame.
> In vain with Tears the Loss she may deplore,
> In vain look back to what she was before,
> She sets like Stars that fall, to rise no more.

Dap. That's wonderfully fine, *She sets like Stars that fall to rise no more.*

THE

TRAGEDY

OF

JANE SHORE.

Written in IMITATION of

Shakespear's Style.

By N. ROWE, Efq;.

――――*Conjux ubi priftinus illi Refpondet Curis.*   Virg.

LONDON:

Printed for BERNARD LINTOTT, at the *Crofs-Keys,* between the *Two Temple-Gates,* in *Fleet-ftreet.*

Title page of the first edition (1714) of one of Rowe's celebrated "she-tragedies."

True. Very fine Nonsense! that is, She sets, like that which does not set at all.

Dap. Mr. *Bays* had made it she sets like falling Stars that rise no more; but he did me the Favour to take my Correction in that Line.

True. I never heard of Stars, that fell, except in the *Revelations*. But is it not strange that Mr. *Bays* shou'd think a Whores Fame irretrievable, and yet imagine she cou'd be a fit Heroine for a Tragedy. (pp. 73-5)

[*Free*.] Fame is dispens'd by the Ignorant; And to what purpose then shou'd a Man of Judgment spend his time to expose himself to the World, when if he meets with Success, he is but on the Level with such a Writer as this, whose Plays have no one quality of the *Drama*, but are a strange Medley of Grotesque Figures that cannot be brought to any Form or Regularity. (p. 87)

> *Charles Gildon, in his* Remarks on Mr. Rowe's "Tragedy of the Lady Jane Gray," and All His Other Plays, *second edition, 1715. Reprint by Garland Publishing, Inc., 1974, 88 p.*

CHARLES BECKINGHAM　(poem date 1719)

[*Soon after Rowe's death there was published* Musarum Lachrymæ; or, Poems to the Memory of Nicholas Rowe, Esq. *In the following excerpt from one of the eulogies contained in the work, Beckingham, an English dramatist and poet, praises various aspects of Rowe's writing.*]

> Is then the Summons true! does partial Fate
> Retract so early what it gave so late?
> Must the Grave chuse?—Must ROWE the Tribute pay,
> And Merit moulder with the common Clay?
>
> 　　　　　　　　　　　　　　　　(p. 13)
>
> Does sacred Heat Prophetick Breasts inspire?
> Burns not the Poet's with an equal Fire?
> From Heav'n a joint Commission can he claim,
> His Soul as large, as sacred is his Name;
> Both universal Benefits design'd,
> Both sent to govern, and to save Mankind;
> T' unveil mysterious Truths to human Sight,
> And set the false bewilder'd Judgment right,
> Instructed great Ideas to impart,
> To warm the Bosom, and enrich the Heart.
>
> 　　　　　　　　　　　　　　　(pp. 14-15)
>
> Here Laurell'd Shade! thy own great Image see;
> To draw the Poet is to picture Thee:
> Th' extensive Thought, the Energy divine,
> The Flame, the Genius, and the Soul was Thine;
> Each various Note declares thy Master-Skill,
> How form'd to write, how worthy to excell.
> To Virtue steddy, to thy Country true,
> We read the Poet, and the Patriot too.
> Does Liberty demand thy loftier Strain?
> We gaze with Wonder on thy *Tamerlane;*
> Thro' every Scene pursue the Godlike Cause;
> And give the Fav'rite Hero full Applause.
> When the shrill Trumpet summons him away,
> The warm'd Spectator shares the bloody Fray;
> In anxious Wishes feels a Soldier's Pride,
> Lifts in the War, and combats on his Side.
> How does he charm, when bounteous in Distress,
> Sedate in Fight, and humble in Success?
> A Victor, yet without a Victor's Mind,
> He Conquers not t'enslave, but free Mankind,

> To distant Times marks out th' unerring Way,
> Learns Kings to Rule, and Subjects to obey;
> Strikes every Bosom with a sacred Awe,
> And shews the happy Age a true NASSAU.
> Of if some lowly Theme the Poet claim,
> Some banish'd Lover, or neglected Dame,
> Love's thousand Passions all his Skill employ,
> The quick alternate Tides of Grief and Joy:
> How well the paints the sad Extremes of Fate!
> How well describes th' unhappy———happy State?
> Each conscious Sinner does his Guilt confess,
> And awful Silence speaks the Bard's Success;
> So well th' expressive Miseries are shown,
> Some tender Breast still makes the Woe its own:
> The Virgin's Cheek the moving Scene approves,
> And artless Sighs betray how well she loves.
> The scornful Nymph condemns her long Disdain,
> And to her Arms invites her injur'd Swain.
>
> 　When some fair Wanton [Jane Shore] mourns her past
> 　　Desires,
> Love's soul Embraces, and unlawful Fires;
> So soft she pleads, the pitying Audience melt,
> And clear the Sinner, tho' they damn the Guilt.
> The Libertine in Love [Lothario] exults a-while
> On violated Charms, and ravish'd Spoil;
> But soon his Triumphs find a timely Date;
> The Villain's Crimes receive the Villain's Fate.
> But why on single Beauties do I dwell,
> When ev'ry finish'd Scene is wrote so well?
> When thy vast Works are in themselves repaid,
> And modest Nature owns thy happier Aid.
> But now the Skill is lost, the Musick o'er,
> And he who charm'd us once, can charm no more.
> Envy at last repents her canker'd Hate,
> And feels her Error in her Loss too late.
> To native Dust now wastes the mortal Frame,
> And nought survives the Poet, but his Fame.
> Brave then in that, or Time, or Envy's Rage,
> And be a LUCAN to a distant Age.
> Yes, sacred Shade, thy Writings shall be read,
> 'Till even Arts are with their Founders dead:
> Whilst Friendship burns within a faithful Breast,
> Thy Name be cherish'd, and thy Worth confest.
> Oblivion is the common Mortal Doom
> But thou shalt Live when Dead, and Flourish in the Tomb.
>
> 　　　　　　　　　　　　　　　(pp. 16-21)

> *Charles Beckingham, "A Poem to the Memory of Nicholas Rowe, Esq.," in* Musarum Lachrymæ; or, Poems to the Memory of Nicholas Rowe, Esq., *edited by Charles Beckingham, 1719. Reprint by University Microfilms International, 1977, pp. 13-21.*

THOMAS NEWCOMB　(poem date 1719)

[*Newcomb was an English poet. In the following excerpt from "An Ode Sacred to the Memory of N. Rowe, Esq.," included in* Musarum Lachrymæ, *he praises the emotive power of Rowe's dramas.*]

> While o'er thy Hearse, with sad Surprize,
> 　And solemn Grief the *Muses* mourn;
> Permit a *Stranger*'s flowing Eyes
> 　To shed their Sorrows round thy Urn.
>
> 　　　　　　　　　　　　　　　(p. 41)
>
> Surprize or Joy alike to yield,
> 　Thy various artful Muse was made;
> To dress the Warrior for the Field,
> 　Or paint the Lover in his Shade.

Now in the eager Chace of Fame,
　　With some brave Chief you upward fly;
Now sink, and teach some *Virgin* Name
　　In softer Numbers how to Die!

Those Forms, which to our wondring Mind
　　Thy Fancy paints, new Glories wear;
While Love and Friendship seem *more* kind,
　　And Beauty's self appears *more* Fair.

Such Force, fair Virtue does impart,
　　By Thee presented to our View;
It moves and melts each stubborn Heart,
　　Her Brightness cannot quite subdue.

While drest in Angels purest Light,
　　Her smiling Image does appear
Pleasing, as Beauty to the Sight,
　　Or Musick to the ravish'd Ear.

Wou'd she once more her Skies forsake,
　　What other Features cou'd she chuse?
What fairer Form the Goddess take
　　To bless Mankind, than from thy Muse?

Transported then with fond Surprize,
　　The lovely Guest we shou'd adore;
And wonder how our partial Eyes
　　Refus'd to own such Grace before!

'Till viewing those deceiving Charms,
　　Each Breast subdue, we all agree,
That Power which thus our Soul disarms,
　　Was not her own, but lent by Thee!

Greatness no more, with all her Train,
　　The virtuous Mind shall now beguile;
By *Thee* instructed to disdain,
　　When Glory calls, the *Syren*'s Smile.

No more Renown and specious Fame,
　　Shall strive Ambition's Rage to hide;
Nor Honour be a treach'rous Name,
　　To shade the Tyrant's guilty Pride.

The Brave and Generous Breast to awe,
　　The Honest Upright Heart to gain;
The Coward's Hand his Sword shall draw,
　　The Courtier's Smiles be try'd in vain.

Against that Dread thy Scenes unfold,
　　To arm our Breasts in vain we try;
Soon as the Tragick Tale is told,
　　We Melt, *We* Languish, and *We* Dye.

The Soul a while her Ground maintains,
　　Each Death resolving to deride;
But when the Captive tells her Pains,
　　That Softness owns, she strove to hide.

To view her Rage direct the Dart,
　　Wakes in our Breast a kind Surprize;
Speaking the Frailty of our Heart,
　　By the soft Streams that fill our Eyes.

Eager our Souls to bring Relief,
　　Swift from their opening Bosom flow,
To sooth the mourning Parents Grief,
　　Or guard the Infant from the Blow.

So lively has each Nymph complain'd,
　　When Fate thy Muse despairing drew;
That tho' we know her Sorrows feign'd,
　　Yet still we weep, and think 'em true.

A while we argue to perswade
　　Our melting Eyes to hide their Woe,
Till to their View the lovely Maid
　　Reveals her Wounds, and bids 'em flow.

Thy artful Voice, with equal Ease,
　　Each diff'rent Passion can employ;
Now give us Pain, but to increase,
　　And from our *Grief* improve our Joy.

Who in your soft deceiving Strains
　　With *those* kind Conquerors agree;
Who threaten first the dreadful Chains,
　　Then set the trembling Captive free.

What Raptures does thy Verse infuse,
　　When Beauty does the Theme inspire!
What Heat transports thy soaring Muse!
　　If Scenes of War thy Bosom Fire!

While for bright Fame, or gay Delight,
　　Each *Hero* you alike prepare,
Lead the fierce Warrior to the Fight,
　　Or the young Lover to the Fair.

Nature astonish'd at thy Art
　　Casts on thy Muse a jealous Eye;
Her Joys unable to impart,
　　Or longer please when thou art by.

The Artist thus, his Skill to grace,
　　Some beauteous breathing Form design'd,
Forsakes the Virgin's Cheek, to trace
　　Features more bright in his own Mind.

Each glowing Charm the Canvass fires,
　　Does with Delight the Nymph surprize,
Who owes that Beauty she admires,
　　More to his Pencil than her Eyes.

What, tho' our Lawrels fairer rise,
　　And from thy Ashes date their Bloom,
We pay too dearly for the Prize,
　　Thus sadly purchas'd by thy Doom.

　　　　　　　　　　　　　　　　(pp. 47-55)

See SHAKESPEAR's Awful Reverend Shade
　　Rising, his Fav'rite to adore!
And binds thy Brows with Lawrel, made
　　By Fame, to shade his own before.

　　　　　　　　　　　　　　　　(p. 57)

Whose Tragick Voice shall next presume
　　To fill our Breasts with sad Despair?
Or trembling for the Lover's Doom,
　　Or anxious for the Dying Fair?

To Tears, whose Sighs her Wrongs confess,
　　Our Eyes with soft Compassion flow;
Teaching thy Virgin's feign'd Distress,
　　To give our Bosom real Woe.

In vain we ask our Reason's Aid,
　　To stop our Tears, or ease our Pain;
To view thy *Fair Repenting Maid*,
　　Each Cheek must swell, each Heart complain.

O! sooth her Anguish! calm her Grief!
　　O! quickly to her Refuge fly!
O! bring the Fainting Fair Relief,
　　Or with her give us Leave to Dye!

Such moving Scenes thy Muse unfolds,
　　Constrain'd its Anguish to declare;
A Savage Heart each Bosom holds,
　　That can attend and not despair.

What Wonders does thy Verse contain,
　　What Magick thro' thy Numbers flows,
Pleas'd with our Grief, we then complain,
　　Then only, when we want our Woes.

No Eye those Sorrows does refuse,
　Thy pensive Maids expiring give;
Scarce more delighted, when Thy Muse
　Suspends their Fate, and bids 'em live.

Strange that our Cheeks shou'd grieve the more
　When you the falling Tear restrain;
And to forbid us to deplore,
　Shou'd only give us greater Pain.

Thus trembling for her Lover's Fate,
　A while the Virgin's Sorrows flow;
Owning, to hear his Sighs abate
　Her Joy, more painful than her Woe.

O, may each Muse with Sorrows meet!
　Soft as thy own, thy Worth declare;
Since nothing but a Voice so sweet,
　Can ever sing a Fame so Fair.

A second Life to thy Great Dead,
　Thy kind Inspiring Numbers Gave;
Had We that Power, the Tears We shed
　Had fell to wet some other Grave.

Thine, like each Fabled Hero's Age,
　Thy self with Virtue didst Inspire;
And acting well on Life's frail Stage,
　Dost with the same Applause retire.

　　　　　　　　　　　　　　　　(pp. 58-62)

Thomas Newcomb, "An Ode Sacred to the Memory of N. Rowe, Esq.," in Musarum Lachrymæ; or, Poems to the Memory of Nicholas Rowe, Esq., *edited by Charles Beckingham, 1719. Reprint by University Microfilms International, 1977, pp. 41-62.*

SAMUEL RICHARDSON　(essay date 1748)

[*Considered the originator of the modern English novel, Richardson is perhaps best known for* Pamela; or, Virtue Rewarded *(1741), in which the heroine successfully resists the sexual advances of her employer and is rewarded by his offer of marriage. He is also credited with introducing to his eighteenth-century audience the first tragic novel,* Clarissa; or, The History of a Young Lady. *Written in epistolary form, Richardson's novels are noted for their detailed psychological exploration of their characters' motives and feelings, as well as their avowed moral didacticism.* Clarissa *concerns the seduction of the virtuous Clarissa Harlowe by the attractive but unscrupulous Lovelace, a character based on Rowe's Lothario of* The Fair Penitent. *The following excerpt from* Clarissa *is taken from a letter to Lovelace from John Belford, in which the latter, describing to his guilty friend Clarissa's pious repentance, compares Clarissa with Rowe's Calista.*]

I have frequently thought, in my attendance on this lady, that if . . . Nic Rowe had had such a character before him, he would have drawn another sort of a penitent than he *has* done, or given his play, which he calls *The Fair Penitent,* a fitter title. Miss Harlowe is a penitent indeed! (p. 118)

The whole story of the other is a pack of damned stuff. Lothario, 'tis true, seems such another wicked, ungenerous varlet as thou knowest who: the author knew how to draw a rake; but not to paint a penitent. Calista is a desiring luscious wench, and her penitence is nothing else but rage, insolence, and scorn. Her passions are all storm and tumult; nothing of the finer passions of the sex, which, if naturally drawn, will distinguish themselves from the masculine passions by a softness that will even shine through rage and despair. Her character is made up of deceit and disguise. She has no virtue; is all pride; and her devil is as much *within* her as *without* her.

How then can the fall of such a one create a proper distress, when all the circumstances of it are considered? For does she not brazen out her crime even after detection? Knowing her own guilt, she calls for Altamont's vengeance on his best friend, as if he had traduced her; yields to marry Altamont, though criminal with another; and actually beds that whining puppy, when she had given up herself body and soul to Lothario; who, nevertheless, refused to marry her.

Her penitence, when begun, she justly styles *the frenzy of her soul;* and, as I said, after having, as long as she could, most audaciously brazened out her crime, and done all the mischief she could do (occasioning the death of Lothario, of her father, and others), she stabs herself.

And can this be an act of penitence?

But, indeed, our poets hardly know how to create a distress without horror, murder, and suicide; and must shock your soul to bring tears from your eyes.

Altamont, indeed, who is an amorous blockhead, a credulous cuckold, and (though painted as a brave fellow and a soldier) a mere Tom Essence, and a quarreller with his best friend, dies like a fool (as we are led to suppose at the conclusion of the play), without either sword or pop-gun, of mere grief and nonsense, for one of the vilest of her sex: but the *fair penitent,* as she is called, perishes by her own hand; and, having no title by her past crimes to *laudable* pity, forfeits all claim to *true* penitence, and, in all probability, to future mercy. (pp. 118-19)

Samuel Richardson, "Belford to Lovelace," in his Clarissa; or, The History of a Young Lady, *Vol. 4, 1748. Reprint by E. P. Dutton & Co. Inc., 1932, pp. 117-20.*

SAMUEL JOHNSON　(essay date 1781)

[*A critic, essayist, and lexicographer, Johnson was the major English literary figure of the second half of the eighteenth century; his criticism strongly influenced the taste of his time while his dictionary helped standardize English spelling. Johnson ascribed to most of the principles of neoclassicism. The neoclassic artists and critics imposed a heretofore unknown order on English literature: using classic literature as their ideal, they stressed the importance of logic, restraint, design, and decorum, and judged literature according to its service to humanity. Philosophically, the neoclassicists believed that human beings were imperfect and denied the possibility of perfection; they distrusted individualism and felt that all should subscribe to a general set of behaviors and beliefs. Similarly, they rejected mystical religious faiths and supported a rational deism; they were suspicious of innovation and invention while revering reason and rules. Mental agility was more favorably judged than were emotions, thus their art was witty, intellectual, and rarely passionate. Didactic literature flourished during the period. Through the influence of neoclassicism, English literature became more polished, more carefully structured, and more concerned with accurate depictions of both nature and human society. Of these various neoclassic tenets, Johnson was particularly concerned with morality and realism. He viewed art as a vehicle for moral or psychological truth and judged the value of a work on its ability to please and instruct. Johnson also believed that art should imitate life, depicting the universal elements of human experience in a manner that could be understood by a general audience. However, Johnson was more liberal regarding rules for order than were other neoclassicists: he contended that the critic or artist should be guided by reason and necessity rather than theoretical dogma. For that reason he rejected the adherence to rigid unities of time and place, promoting unity of action or sentiment as the only absolute necessity. Johnson also demonstrated a feeling for the historic sense*] *of literature by attempting to convey the effects of the various forces of an age upon a writer. Because he held that critics should note the defects of the works they admired, an uncharacteristic practice during his time, Johnson is often best remembered for his witty scathing remarks. Nevertheless, his work is considered judicious and reasonable, the preeminent literary qualities of his era. In the following excerpt from an essay originally published in 1781, Johnson provides a balanced assessment of Rowe's endeavors as dramatist, editor, poet, and translator.]*

At twenty-five [Nicholas Rowe] produced *The Ambitious Stepmother,* which was received with so much favour, that he devoted himself from that time wholly to elegant literature.

His next tragedy was *Tamerlane,* in which, under the name of Tamerlane, he intended to characterize king William, and Lewis the Fourteenth under Bajazet. The virtues of Tamerlane seem to have been arbitrarily assigned him by his poet, for I know not that history gives any other qualities than those which make a conqueror. The fashion however of the time was, to accumulate upon Lewis all that can raise horror and detestation; and whatever good was withheld from him, that it might not be thrown away, was bestowed upon king William.

This was the tragedy which Rowe valued most, and that which probably, by the help of political auxiliaries, excited most applause; but occasional poetry must often content itself with occasional praise. *Tamerlane* has for a long time been acted only once a year, on the night when king William landed. Our quarrel with Lewis has been long over, and it now gratifies neither zeal nor malice to see him painted with aggravated features, like a Saracen upon a sign.

The *Fair Penitent,* his next production, is one of the most pleasing tragedies on the stage, where it still keeps its turns of appearing, and probably will long keep them, for there is scarcely any work of any poet at once so interesting by the fable, and so delightful by the language. The story is domestick, and therefore easily received by the imagination, and assimilated to common life; the diction is exquisitely harmonious, and soft or spritely as occasion requires.

The character of *Lothario* seems to have been expanded by Richardson into *Lovelace,* but he has excelled his original in the moral effect of the fiction. Lothario, with gaiety which cannot be hated, and bravery which cannot be despised, retains too much of the spectator's kindness. It was in the power of Richardson alone to teach us at once esteem and detestation, to make virtuous resentment overpower all the benevolence which wit, elegance, and courage, naturally excite; and to lose at last the hero in the villain.

The fifth act is not equal to the former; the events of the drama are exhausted, and little remains but to talk of what is past. It has been observed, that the title of the play does not sufficiently correspond with the behaviour of Calista, who at last shews no evident signs of repentance, but may be reasonably suspected of feeling pain from detection rather than from guilt, and expresses more shame than sorrow, and more rage than shame.

His next was *Ulysses;* which, with the common fate of mythological stories, is now generally neglected. We have been too early acquainted with the poetical heroes, to expect any pleasure from their revival; to shew them as they have already been shewn, is to disgust by repetition; to give them new qualities or new adventures, is to offend by violating received notions.

The *Royal Convert* seems to have a better claim to longevity. The fable is drawn from an obscure and barbarous age, to which fictions are most easily and properly adapted; for when objects are imperfectly seen, they easily take forms from imagination. The scene lies among our ancestors in our own country, and therefore very easily catches attention. *Rhodogune* is a personage truly tragical, of high spirit and violent passions, great with tempestuous dignity, and wicked with a soul that would have been heroic if it had been virtuous. The motto seems to tell that this play was not successful.

Rowe does not always remember what his characters require. In *Tamerlane* there is some ridiculous mention of the God of Love; and Rhodogune, a savage Saxon, talks of Venus, and the eagle that bears the thunder of Jupiter.

This play discovers its own date, by a prediction of the *Union,* in imitation of Cranmer's prophetick promises to *Henry the Eighth.* The anticipated blessings of union are not very naturally introduced, nor very happily expressed.

He once tried to change his hand. He ventured on a comedy, and produced the *Biter;* with which, though it was unfavourably treated by the audience, he was himself delighted; for he is said to have sat in the house, laughing with great vehemence, whenever he had in his own opinion produced a jest. But finding that he and the publick had no sympathy of mirth, he tried at lighter scenes no more.

After the *Royal Convert* appeared *Jane Shore,* written, as its author professes, *in imitation of Shakespeare's style.* In what he thought himself an imitator of Shakespeare, it is not easy to conceive. The numbers, the diction, the sentiments, and the conduct, every thing in which imitation can consist, are remote in the utmost degree from the manner of Shakespeare; whose dramas it resembles only as it is an English story, and as some of the persons have their names in history. This play, consisting chiefly of domestick scenes and private distress, lays hold upon the heart. The wife is forgiven because she repents, and the husband is honoured because he forgives. This therefore is one of those pieces which we still welcome on the stage. (pp. 390-92)

As his studies necessarily made him acquainted with Shakespeare, and acquaintance produced veneration, he undertook an edition of his works, from which he neither received much praise, nor seems to have expected it; yet, I believe, those who compare it with former copies, will find that he has done more than he promised; and that, without the pomp of notes or boasts of criticism, many passages are happily restored. He prefixed a life of the author, such as tradition then almost expiring could supply, and a preface, which cannot be said to discover much profundity or penetration. He at least contributed to the popularity of his author. (pp. 392-93)

Rowe is chiefly to be considered as a tragick writer and a translator. In his attempt at comedy he failed so ignominiously, that his *Biter* is not inserted in his works; and his occasional poems and short compositions are rarely worthy of either praise or censure; for they seem the casual sports of a mind seeking rather to amuse its leisure than to exercise its powers.

In the construction of his dramas, there is not much art; he is not a nice observer of the Unities. He extends time and varies place as his convenience requires. To vary the place is not, in my opinion, any violation of Nature, if the change be made between the acts; for it is no less easy for the spectator to suppose himself at Athens in the second act, than at Thebes in the first; but to change the scene, as is done by Rowe, in the middle of an act, is to add more acts to the play, since an act is so much of the business as is transacted without interruption. Rowe, by this licence, easily extricates himself from difficulties; as in *Jane Grey,* when we have been terrified with all the dreadful pomp of publick execution, and are wondering how the heroine or the poet will proceed, no sooner has *Jane* pronounced some prophetick rhymes, than—pass and be gone—the scene closes, and *Pembroke* and *Gardiner* are turned out upon the stage.

I know not that there can be found in his plays any deep search into nature, any accurate discriminations of kindred qualities, or nice display of passion in its progress; all is general and undefined. Nor does he much interest or affect the auditor, except in *Jane Shore,* who is always seen and heard with pity. *Alicia* is a character of empty noise, with no resemblance to real sorrow or to natural madness.

Whence, then, has Rowe his reputation? From the reasonableness and propriety of some of his scenes, from the elegance of his diction, and the suavity of his verse. He seldom moves either pity or terror, but he often elevates the sentiments; he seldom pierces the breast, but he always delights the ear, and often improves the understanding.

His translation of the *Golden Verses,* and of the first book of *Quillet's* Poem, have nothing in them remarkable. The *Golden Verses* are tedious.

The version of *Lucan* is one of the greatest productions of English poetry; for there is perhaps none that so completely exhibits the genius and spirit of the original. *Lucan* is distinguished by a kind of dictatorial or philosophic dignity, rather, as Quintilian observes, declamatory than poetical; full of ambitious morality and pointed sentences, comprised in vigorous and animated lines. This character Rowe has very diligently and successfully preserved. His versification, which is such as his contemporaries practised, without any attempt at innovation or improvement, seldom wants either melody or force. His author's sense is sometimes a little diluted by additional infusions, and sometimes weakened by too much expansion. But such faults are to be expected in all translations, from the constraint of measures and dissimilitude of languages. The *Pharsalia* of Rowe deserves more notice than it obtains, and as it is more read will be more esteemed. (pp. 397-98)

> Samuel Johnson, "Rowe," in his Lives of the English Poets, Vol. I, *Oxford University Press, London, 1955-56, pp. 389-98.*

AUGUST WILHELM SCHLEGEL   (essay date 1811)

[*A German man of letters, Schlegel was instrumental in introducing the art of William Shakespeare to Germany through his translation of seventeen Shakespearean plays. He advocated the tenets of German Romanticism in the* Athenäum, *a periodical he cofounded and edited with his brother Friedrich, and in his highly regarded literary criticism. In the following excerpt from an essay originally published in 1811, Schlegel briefly discusses the nature of Rowe's dramatic talent.*]

Tragedy has been often attempted in England in the eighteenth century, but a genius of the first rank has never made his appearance. They laid aside the manner of Dryden, however, and that at least was an improvement. Rowe was an honest admirer of Shakspeare, and his modest reverence for this superior genius was rewarded by a return to nature and truth. The traces of imitation are not to be mistaken: the part of Gloster in *Jane Shore* is even directly borrowed from *Richard the Third.* Rowe did not possess boldness and vigour, but was

not without sweetness and feeling; he could excite the softer emotions, and hence in his *Fair Penitent, Jane Shore,* and *Lady Jane Gray,* he has successfully chosen female heroines and their weaknesses for his subjects. (p. 484)

> August Wilhelm Schlegel, "Closing of the Stage by the Puritans," in his Lectures on Dramatic Art and Literature, *edited by Rev. A. J. W. Morrison, translated by John Black, revised edition, George Bell & Sons, 1902, pp. 475-87.*

THE GENTLEMAN'S MAGAZINE   (essay date 1846)

[*In the following excerpt, the critic transcribes a conversation he held with an unnamed individual and Sir James Macintosh (designated as "M"). Here, in the midst of a general literary discussion, the talk turns to* Jane Shore.]

"English has always suffered," said ——, "when it has been formed upon French. Gibbon's style, noble, is as tiresome as it is vague. And all the wretched tragedies that people sit to hear ranted through, they always appear to me pitiful imitations of the cold forced bombast of France,—Dryden's, and Rowe's, and all that set."

> *M.*   From bard to bard the frigid caution crept,
>   Till declamation soared while passion slept—

is very true of many of Dryden's and Lee's plays, but you must except Rowe—at least *Jane Shore.* Perhaps you never saw Mrs. Siddons act it, but, even read, it is most touching poetry. You must allow Jane Shore her rank among the heroines of the English stage. Alicia's speech to her—

> But let thy fearful doubting heart lie still,
> The saints and angels have thee in their charge,
> And all things shall be well. Think not the good,
> The gentle, deeds of mercy thou hast done.
> Shall die forgotten all: the poor, the pris'ner,
> The fatherless, the friendless, and the widow,
> Who daily own the bounty of thy hand,
> Shall cry to Heav'n and draw a blessing on thee.
> Ev'n man, the merciless insulter man,—
> Man, who rejoices in our sex's weakness,—
> Shall pity thee, and with unwonted goodness
> Forget thy failings, and record thy praise.

If this is not worthy of Shakspere, it is worthy to come next to him; and Jane Shore's own touching appeal to Hastings—

> All tongues, like yours, are licensed to upbraid me,
> Still to repeat my guilt, to urge my infamy,
> And treat me like that abject thing I've been.

"It is very beautiful, I acknowledge," said ———, "but it is all the wrong way—it interests you for vice: now Shakspere never interests you for a bad woman."

"Cleopatra and Cressida for instance," said I.

M. Rowe's Jane Shore I maintain to be perfectly moral; he paints her only in her penitence—in all the horror of remorse—in abject poverty: she is brought before you as the victim of her own guilt, and, if you will compare with Shakspere, I must say that Cleopatra is immoral, and Jane Shore is not. For the Egyptian queen is painted in all the enjoyments of her passion, she is made captivating in the very height of her guilt; and, if one feels for her at the end, it is only as a queen—one is interested, not in her remorse, but in her escape from slavery, and she is not made to suffer as the inevitable consequence of her own vices, she is allowed to make her exit in all the dignity of a royal suicide. Rowe makes you pity the sufferer, but it is pity for, not sympathy with, her crime. (pp. 587-88)

"Extracts from the Portfolio of a Man of the World," in The Gentleman's Magazine, *Vol. XXIV, July, 1845 & June, 1846, pp. 3-17; 582-90.*

SOPHIE CHANTAL HART   (essay date 1907)

[*Hart was an American educator and editor. In the following excerpt, she discusses Rowe as dramatist and as Shakespearean critic, emphasizing his adherence to eighteenth-century critical strictures in the former role and his transcendence of them in the latter.*]

Both *The Fair Penitent* and *Jane Shore* are eighteenth century versions of Elizabethan dramatic methods. Rowe, as we know, planned an edition of Massinger, with the probable intention of doing for him what he did so successfully for Shakespeare. He got no further than taking the plot of *The Fair Penitent* from Massinger and Field's *The Fatal Dowry*. The difference between Massinger's play and Rowe's well illustrates the change in the drama from the sixteenth to the eighteenth century in the greater insistence on regularity of plot; but this regularity of plot seems to be purchased at the cost of vitality of treatment. Both plays have roughly the same characters, the same relationships among them, and the same general course of events, but Rowe greatly simplifies the action by beginning his play at what is the close of Massinger's second act. *The Fatal Dowry* opens with a scene of real dramatic pathos. Young Charalois (Rowe's Altamont), overwhelmed with grief that his father's body must, on account of debts, remain unburied, petitions the judges for clemency. When he sees them first, he is dumb under the stress of his feeling, but finally with deep eloquence recounts the services of his father, who, as Marshal of France, lost life and fortune in defence of the state. When he offers himself, as a last resort, to the creditors for the release of his father's body, the pure filial devotion of the youth is exhibited with sustained power. This "golden precedent in a son" so moves the hearts of the judges that one among them offers the needed money to Charalois and gives him at the same time his daughter's hand in marriage. With the Elizabethan love of spectacle and incident, Massinger introduces the funeral scene of the dead Marshal of France: Charalois, the son, attended by his gaolers, is chief mourner; the old soldiers who fought in the wars receive now from this captive son spurs, scarf, cuirass; and medals as memorials of their great leader. The sympathy of the reader is strongly evoked in this whole scene for Charalois, built as it is around the love of son for father, and the contrast of great, heroic deeds against the pitiless avarice of creditors. Consequently, when misfortune overtakes him through his wife, the reader suffers with him in dread apprehension.

It is hard, on the other hand, to feel anything more than lukewarm interest in Rowe's Altamont, who, when the play opens on his wedding morn, invites the world somewhat pompously to rejoice in a happy bridegroom. We have no particular reason for caring for him, though his friend Horatio, with amiable repetition of what was known perfectly to both of them, recounts the story of Altamont's sacrifice for his father; the mere recounting of it, however, as a piece of information antecedent to the play, robs it of the strong appeal gained in Massinger's version by the actual representation of the incidents. It is strikingly characteristic of the eighteenth century that people should talk about things rather than actually do them on the stage. The practical result in Rowe's play is that only a general regard

for ethics and decency makes the reader feel concerned when Altamont is deceived in his wife. There is a curious reversal in the importance of hero and villain in the two plays. Rowe makes Lothario, the villain, as Dr. Johnson shrewdly observes, occupy too much attention [see excerpt dated 1781]. His seductive charm is exploited with every lavish device of rhetoric, so that his name, since Richardson took him and transformed him into Lovelace, has become the synonym of the gay libertine. By centering so much interest on the betrayer, Rowe makes the husband secondary, and the tragedy loses in dignity thereby. In the case of Calista, the heroine, Rowe has also changed the emphasis. He represents her as yielding to Lothario in a scene of hot, mawkish passion, elaborately recounted for its own sake. Then she marries Altamont. Massinger has saved the situation, in so far as such a situation can be saved, by a different mode of handling and of emphasis. Beaumelle, his heroine, marries in good faith, but through the machinations of an evil serving-woman, in the employ of Young Novall (Rowe's Lothario), she falls from virtue. Massinger makes Young Novall a contemptible dandy who triumphs rather by his cunning than by his personal charm or power of fascination. At the end, however, Beaumelle rises to true tragic dignity in her repentance, and, through her sin, sees her life with a sudden higher understanding of it. Her remorse is so genuine that her death does not merely suggest "an eye for an eye, and a tooth for a tooth."

The Fair Penitent, a title which could well fit Massinger's play, is a misnomer for Rowe's. There is lamentation on Calista's part and a grim acceptance of death for her fault as inevitable and just, but no accent of genuine contrition. (pp. xi-xiii)

To be sure, Calista satisfies poetic justice by her death,—she would not be an eighteenth century heroine otherwise, but the experience does not bring her, as it does to Beaumelle, any inner regeneration. The final death scene in the two plays exhibits the authors characteristically. Rowe makes Calista's father present to her a dagger with stilted comment on the courage

> That dwelt in ancient Latin breasts, when Rome
> Was mistress of the world,

and so incites her to a self-inflicted death. Massinger's scene is more terrible, and yet in every way greater. He shows how the father, who, as a judge, is forced to pronounce doom on his daughter, breaks down utterly with a father's natural anguish, when Charalois, the husband, has executed the sentence. The human quality grips the reader in these last speeches as it never does once in Rowe's ending. . . . (p. xiv)

If Rowe, instead of appropriating the plot of Massinger and Field's play, had studied it in detail, he might have learned some important things in play-writing; he might have learned what flesh and blood characters are; how much more convincing is the homely, robust directness of speech that springs straight from the feelings than the most polished but vapid generalities. It is true he was conditioned by the taste of his age, that our eighteenth century ancestors had an insatiate love for smooth rolling numbers, that distinctness in the conception and handling of character was not so definite a requirement then as now; for even up to our day plays like *The Lady of Lyons*, with no more differentiation of character from the broad type than Rowe's, have flourished. If Rowe shows no habit of concrete observation, no first-hand perception of life, he has invariable elegance of diction, with line upon line of moral sentiment that can be easily quoted, and a pleasant, worldly-wise sophistication of tone. But in spite of fair words and blandness, there is something meretricious in the emphasis.

On the purely technical side, a few points remain to be considered. The play opens with a device for giving antecedent material that is no less crude than the conventional servant dusting a room, and, apropos of nothing, reciting the family history. The discovery of a letter on which the whole plot turns is a poor resort for tragedy. The action of the play is strictly complete in the fourth act, and the fifth act is consequently an ineffective tag, as was pointed out by Rowe's contemporaries the first night it was acted. The appeal to melodramatic accompaniments is marked in the play, particularly at the beginning of the fifth act, where in a room hung with black, Lothario's body on a bier, a skull and cross-bones on the table, Calista sits during a song of some length. Such an assemblage of gruesome objects might well inhibit action, as it does in her case. (pp. xiv-xv)

[Rowe's] plays were written for imposing declamation in accordance with the taste of his day,—a fact which must ever be borne in mind in a final estimate of Rowe's work. His reputation was due primarily to his style and diction, which charmed the ear by its suavity and by its polished vivacity of manner. It is for these reasons that passages from his writings were so generally committed to memory by our ancestors and quoted. His verse always smacks of the Town, and has much of its elegance and ease, its aphoristic wisdom and terseness. To tax it for lack of imaginative beauty, for lack of insight into the deeper issues of life, for its inability to suggest the richer emotional associations that the Elizabethans compacted into their phrasing would be to tax it for qualities which the eighteenth century lays no claim to. Of its kind, with the limitations its kind imposes, it is excellent. It is true beyond cavil, as Dr. Johnson says, ''Rowe seldom pierces the breast, but he always delights the ear.'' (p. xviii)

In making over Massinger's *The Fatal Dowry* into **The Fair Penitent**, Rowe followed the . . . procedure of rejecting in the Elizabethan dramatist the action through which the character attained to life and individuality, and substituting instead pages of descriptive epithets. The French fashion of narrating instead of doing on the stage had taken deep hold on Rowe.

As would be expected of a dramatist in the period when Aristotle's and Bossu's rules held supremacy, Rowe is careful about his plot, which is in **Jane Shore** regular and well articulated. The exposition at the beginning sets forth the situation skilfully, and with good economy. By the end of the first act the reader has a clear indication of the nature of the complication on which the other acts are built: he knows Jane Shore's connection with Edward and her forlorn state since Edward's death; her remorse for her deserted husband; Gloucester's ambition for the kingship and designs against Edward's children; Hastings' support of Edward's heir and less commendable devotion to Jane Shore; Alicia's love for Hastings, which shall make her an instrument of jealous fury when she finds out Hastings' inclination to Jane Shore. Here in a nut-shell is sufficient entanglement of interests to make an excellent plot, and as a piece of play-writing it is a very creditable first act, except for the length of some speeches. The later acts unfold in causal sequence the situations that are bound to arise in such a conflict of purposes. Indeed, on the side of plot-building, Rowe must be acknowledged in this play to be a careful architect. His plots elsewhere, however slender, have the eighteenth century virtue of regularity.

But the best of plots in logical articulation cannot cover thinness of character-drawing. It is in the handling of character that Rowe is most inadequate. His people are little more than vehicles for the expression of a certain type of sentiment and moral reflection, or for the expression of that which the exigencies of a situation demand. There is only one kind of dramatic motif that seems to appeal to Rowe, and this necessarily limits his range of charcters,—the tempting of a virtuous woman by some libertine. There is always, as in **Jane Shore,** the plaintive figure of a woman who resists unwelcome advances, who calls on heaven to defend her purity, upbraids man for his lustful desire, and protests to the unheeding firmament that death is to be preferred to dishonor. Again and again she makes her moan in precisely the same key, in the same declamatory spirit. There is no differentiation in the women, no individual color in the reaction which the temptation brings to each personality. Penelope wards off Eurymachus in **Ulysses,** Amestrius wards off Mirza in **The Ambitious Stepmother,** Calista upbraids Lothario in **The Fair Penitent,** with the same profuse and ringing rhetoric with which Jane Shore addresses Hastings. It is hard, therefore, to feel moved by their agony of distress when it vents itself in outcry against the wrongs which woman in general suffers at the hands of man in general, and breaks under the strain of its own tension. . . . It was this tone of high sentiment that delighted Rowe's contemporaries and won fame for him as a master-hand in the portrayal of women. (pp. xxv-xxvii)

Rowe's failure in the characterization of both men and women, as we view it to-day, is due to his hopeless lack of concreteness. Nowhere are there those little touches that express the very savor of human life, such as abound in Heywood's play [*Edward IV* (1599)]. For instance, when Jane Shore has been proclaimed outcast by Gloucester, Heywood gives a charming picture of her serving-boy Jockie and his companion, ''under colour of playing at bowles,'' breaking bread and cheese to give surreptitiously to her. The homely devotion of the lad and the interplay of feeling in the scene does more to breed in the reader's consciousness a vital sense of Jane Shore's being than any number of Rowe's usual twenty-line speeches. Rowe is so thoroughly imbued with the Restoration conception of a character as expressing one sort of mood only that his people lack the infinite variety of life. Alicia is a case in point. She is all one thing, untempered fury and ranting madness, ''a character of empty noise,'' as Dr. Johnson calls her. Gloucester loses the matchless dash and brilliancy of evil that he has in Shakespeare and is just the dissembling villain. Hastings, who is half bully, half martinet . . . , dwells in rhetorical remoteness. Shore and Belmour are handled with an honesty of sentiment that makes strong dramatic appeal and comes with the force of direct pathos; it is easy to believe that, were their parts well acted, they might be moving and significant. Yet the characters as a group are too florid of speech and too slabsided to grip the reader deeply.

The reader of **Jane Shore** wonders how an editor of Shakespeare could fancy this play bore any resemblance to the work of the great dramatist. (pp. xxvii-xxviii)

[In the] principles of the pseudo-classical creed, Rowe was thoroughly orthodox. A rapid examination of his plays will perhaps reveal more concretely the points in which he is spokesman for the dramatic theory that dominated the eighteenth century. In the matter of poetical justice he is impeccable. Every character who sins in **The Fair Penitent** or in **Jane Shore** or in any of his other plays meets a sure death, and other mildly offending characters are involved in their ruin when they can point the moral more strongly. *The Fair Penitent,* it will be remembered, closes with the death of Altamont, Calista, Sciolto, and Lothario. What more could the most exacting fates demand! Jane Shore in her suffering is surely an edifying lesson to erring wives. In the Prologue to *The Ambitious Stepmother,* Rowe boasts "that what they call poetical justice is, I think, strictly observed," a boast to which he might lay claim for all his dramatic work. In the matter of love-scenes, too, he even outruns the demands of eighteenth century taste. Love-scenes abound in his plays; or rather, he wrests the material of his plot so as to force in love-scenes at any cost. This is inevitable when, as has been previously shown, the rough working theme of all his plays turns on the temptation of a pure woman by a libertine. In the matter of the unities, it must be admitted Rowe lapses from dramatic virtue, but they were an ideal requirement before which even the most fanatic devotee of pseudo-classic rules flinched in actual practice. Again, in the treatment of the principal characters in his plays, Rowe took great pains that they should not be of mean position, though they are not always of exalted rank. In the *Prologue* to *The Fair Penitent* he professes an interest in domestic drama [see excerpt dated 1703], but on analysis it is plain that he is following along the old lines. Indeed it is because Rowe deviates not at all from eighteenth century standards that his popularity was so enormous. Even in *The Fair Penitent,* the characters are of sufficient dignity of station not to clash with the supposedly Aristotelian requirement, though they come dangerously near it. Some of the scurrilous prologue-mongers of his day gravely discuss whether it is fitting a goldsmith's wife should be heroine of a tragedy, but they decide Rowe probably justified Jane Shore by the assumption that the King conferred nobility upon her. In all but *The Fair Penitent,* then, Rowe would be entitled in spirit to the high praise Voltaire gives Addison for his *Cato,* in that no one appeared in it below the rank of a foreign monarch or a patrician. From the observance of this rule of rank in characters, it follows inevitably that Rowe should be faithful to the pseudo-classical tenet excluding comic scenes and low characters from tragedy. Indeed Rowe remarks rather indulgently in his *Life of Shakespeare,* "the way of Trage-comedy was the common mistake of that age." Even in *Jane Shore,* his professed imitation of Shakespeare, he never falters for an instant in the accepted belief of all the critics, "There is no place in tragedy for anything but grave and serious action." In Rowe's fondness for declamation and Senecan rhetoric, in his preference for long speeches describing action or character rather than for action taking place on the stage, Rowe is again carrying out the spirit of the new law. Rowe is thus splendidly typical, point by point, of the pseudo-classical rules. *Jane Shore* becomes suddenly intelligible and significant only by holding these facts in the background of one's estimate. (pp. xxxvi-xxxviii)

[When] Rowe tried to popularize Shakespeare by imitating him, he wrote a play which resembled Shakespeare in one point,— that it drew material from English history, from scenes which Shakespeare had in part developed; in method and handling, in its adherence to the rules and the dramatic motives that governed the stage, it was thoroughly eighteenth century. Yet the instinctive attraction which Shakespeare's work had for Rowe was far deeper than such results as *Jane Shore* . . . would seem to testify. There are rare reminiscent suggestions of Shakespeare's imagery that glow with an alien brightness in eighteenth century formal verse, fragments of lines that startle the reader with a forgotten music, but they unmistakably show reading and familiarity; there are comments scattered through

the *Life of Shakespeare,* that reveal how far Rowe's native understanding of Shakespeare's mood and characters outstripped his capacity of analysis. It was like the spontaneous appeal which beauty of line and spacing in Japanese art might make to a man who had at his command only the language of the classical school in painting; how register and equate the strangeness of the new æsthetic insight? Rowe could not penetrate it in the case of Shakespeare; he vaguely but heartily assented to its power without attempting a synthesis of it with the scheme of things which he knew. Though held in amazement by the fecundity of Shakespeare's genius, he was so limited by the conditions of his age, that in trying to imitate Shakespeare he serves rather to exhibit Shakespeare in pseudo-classical guise. To say this is, however, but to say that he did not anticipate work which was not accomplished for nearly half a century later. (pp. xxxix-xl)

None of Rowe's writings in the opinion of the present editor presents him in so attractive a light as the *Account of the Life of Shakespeare.* It has solid merit in giving most of the facts then known about Shakespeare, and it has in addition a quality of directness, of charm and ease of manner, and justness of feeling that his plays give no warrant for expecting. There is critical acumen of no mean order, though the tone of treatment is avowedly that of the dilettante. After commenting upon the parentage and education of Shakespeare, Rowe is led naturally to the controversy about his knowledge of the "antient poets," and wisely suggests: "Tho' the knowledge of 'em might have made him more correct, yet it is not improbable that the regularity and deference for them, which would have attended that correction, might have restrained some of that fine impetuosity and even bashful extravagance, which we admire in Shakespear." In much the same vein of common sense he desists from criticising Shakespeare's lack of skill in the conduct of the fable in his plays, a lack which he recognizes as both "tedious and ill-natur'd to dilate upon," since "it is not in this province of the drama that the strength and mastery of Shakespeare lay." In the character of judicious editor, he puts stress on those parts which seem noble and worthy of admiration, making concrete reference to individual characters or passages.

The resemblance in general method to Addison's famous *Spectator* papers on Milton [1712] is not more than a coincidence. Both critics consciously exhibit the merits rather than the defects of their respective authors; both show their honest admiration for the great passages; both share in common the striking limitation of the critical vocabulary of the day, which had not devised for itself a sensitive and varied phrasing for registering the finer aesthetic effects. . . . The special merit of Rowe's criticism of the plays lies . . . in his general soundness of taste and concreteness of method; references to character, to individual lines, to incidents in the plays abound. Only a study of the contemporary criticism reveals how unusual this virtue was prior to the *Spectator* papers on Milton. (pp. xlvii-xlix)

The gist of Rowe's criticism of Shakespeare is frank acknowledgment that Shakespeare does not follow "the rules of the Antients"; that his genius is so mighty he can afford to transcend them; but that it is in spite of his failure to conform, not because of it, that he achieves greatness. Rowe typifies the curious mingling of admiration qualified by bewilderment which an elegant age gave to Shakespeare. He did not have a penetrating mind, and though he loved Shakespeare's genius, he had neither the insight nor the daring to imitate Shakespeare's characteristic methods as a dramatist. His is the attitude of the gentleman scholar who loves to pass on his criticisms in literature without ever coming to a close understanding of the elements involved in them. A man of cultivation, polished in diction, ingenious in dramatic construction and moral sentiment, he won the suffrages of the best of his generation and held sway far down into our own. A strong feeling for dramatic situation and an uncommon degree of literary amenity lie at the heart of this success. The reader-to-day cannot fail to be gripped by the deep pathos of some of the scenes, the Racine-like quality of poignant emotion developed to the uttermost limit, monotonous in length, perhaps, except to the true lover of sentiment and rhetoric. Yet in the interpretation of an actor of power, who could re-create the emotion with freshness and vitality of expression, how moving the appeal inherent in the situation. Rowe sometimes shows a master-hand in such scenes, and it is this primarily that accounts for his continued presentation on the English stage for over two centuries. In his own time, his work must have been in agreeable contrast to the heroic plays still in vogue. Though his plays have much of their exaggeration, they follow Shakespeare "at a distance," a long distance, to be sure, in keeping to some sense of fact. Compared with the fustian and inflation and tropical exuberance of such heroic plays as *Almanzor and Almabide; or, The Conquest of Granada by the Spaniards, The Emperor of Morocco,* and *Rival Kings; or, The Loves of Oroondates and Statira,* three of Rowe's tragedies, **Jane Shore, Lady Jane Grey,** and **The Fair Penitent,** might well seem to the early eighteenth century to hark back to the older dramatic tradition.

As an editor, Rowe wrote before the days of textual criticism, publishing Shakespeare's plays, as he would his own, with an appreciative, genial interest. But he did an immensely important work in promoting a better understanding of Shakespeare, in heading the long line of eighteenth century contributors to Shakespeare study. In this double capacity, as first editor and biographer of Shakespeare, Rowe is a significant figure in the Augustan age. As playwright, exhibiting the characteristic mood of that age, exhibiting very completely its dramatic method, he well repays the attention of students of the history of the English drama. (pp. l-li)

> *Sophie Chantal Hart, in an introduction to* The Fair Penitent and Jane Shore *by Nicholas Rowe, edited by Sophie Chantal Hart, D. C. Heath and Co., Publishers, 1907, pp. ix-li.*

W. FORBES GRAY (essay date 1914)

[*Gray was a Scottish author. In the following excerpt, he delineates Rowe's achievements as the first critical editor of Shakespeare's plays.*]

Paradoxical it may appear, but it is none the less true that no one incurred heavier responsibility for the decline in popular favour of Rowe's tragedies than Rowe himself. Their original vogue was not due to the presentation of any profound view of human life, or to masterly delineation of character, or to deftness of literary workmanship, but to the fact that they provided a tawdry sentimentalism which suited the taste of an age that was slowly liberating itself from the sinister influence of low and artificial forms of dramatic art. Once the plays of Shakespeare were presented to the public in their pristine purity, a reaction was bound to set in against the dramatists of the Restoration and Georgian eras.

Rowe, quite unconsciously, was one of the most effective instruments in bringing about this welcome transformation. By

THE

WORKS

OF

Mr. *William Shakespear*;

IN

SIX VOLUMES.

ADORN'D with CUTS.

Revis'd and Corrected, with an Account of the Life and Writings of the Author.

By *N. ROWE*, Efq;

LONDON:

Printed for *Jacob Tonfon*, within *Grays-Inn* Gate, next *Grays-Inn* Lane.   MDCCIX.

Title page of Rowe's edition of Shakespeare's dramas (1709).

publishing the first critical edition of Shakespeare's plays, he gave an impetus to the study of the writings of the prince of dramatists which, in the long run, operated most powerfully and salutarily on the fortunes of the drama of this country. Rowe's predecessors in the Laureateship produced versions of the principal Shakespearian plays, but the text was so corrupt, and so overlaid with the creations of their own poetic fancy, that they did little more than remind a degenerate age that Shakespeare once lived.

Rowe's efforts towards the popularisation of Shakespeare proceeded on constructive lines. It is true that he failed to provide what was essential before all else—a sound text. His six-volume edition of the plays was, unfortunately, based on the Fourth Folio of 1685 with its half-dozen spurious pieces, which he merely transferred from the beginning to the end. Neither the First Folio of 1623 nor any of the pre-existent quartos, with the exception of that of *Romeo and Juliet,* were consulted by him. Consequently, his text was seriously vitiated. But he corrected a number of errors which brought his edition into line with the First Folio. He also smoothed the path of the student by modernising the spelling of Shakespeare's text, and by correcting the grammar and punctuation; while he added enormously to the intelligent performance of the plays by prefixing a list of *dramatis personae* to each drama, by dividing and numbering the acts and scenes on common-sense principles, and by marking the entrances and exits of the characters.

Hardly less important was Rowe's work in elucidating Shakespeare's life-story. The first editor of Shakespeare worthy of the name, he was also the first to make important contributions to his biography. The memoir, which he prefixed to his edition of the great dramatist's works, is of abiding interest and value. . . . (pp. 120-22)

> W. Forbes Gray, "Nicholas Rowe (1715-18)," in his The Poets Laureate of England: Their History and Their Odes, Sir I. Pitman & Sons, Ltd., 1914, pp. 114-30.

J. R. SUTHERLAND (essay date 1929)

[Sutherland is a Scottish educator who served as editor of the Review of English Studies from 1940 to 1947. His critical works include The English Critic (1952) and English Satire (1958). In the following excerpt, Sutherland surveys Rowe's dramatic career.]

The Ambitious Stepmother is quite clearly a first play; it affords evidence of considerable dramatic talent struggling through a clumsy technique, and, as might be expected, it owes a good deal to the work of Rowe's immediate predecessors. The tricks and conventions of the heroic drama are all here—the heroic blasphemy, the apostrophe, the habit of flattering self-description, the air of conscious worth in the heroes, the lengthy simile, the oaths, the conflict between love and honour. Rowe even appropriates some of Dryden's phrases, such as "It wo' not be," and makes them peculiarly his own. Equally marked, however, is the influence upon the young dramatist of 1700 of a drama more distant. Cleone, for instance, in Rowe's first play, is a sort of eighteenth-century Bellario. Her father having occasion to speak of the girl slips easily into the fluent sadness of Beaumont and Fletcher:

> A melancholy Girl;
> Such in her Infancy her Temper was,
> Soft ev'n beyond her Sexes tenderness;
> By nature pitiful, and apt to grieve
> For the mishaps of others, and so make
> The sorrows of the wretched world her own;
> Her Closet and the Gods share all her time,
> Except when (only by some Maid attended)
> She seeks some shady solitary Grove,
> Or by the gentle murmur of some Brook
> Sits sadly listning to a tale of sorrow,
> Till with her tears she swell the narrow stream.

The freshness and flow of this passage are partly natural to Rowe, partly acquired from Elizabethan models. It was the unforced fluency of Rowe's blank verse that was most often remarked upon by his contemporaries when they thought of his plays. Even his severest critics were prepared to allow him some credit here. . . . Unfortunately, at its best, this verse is narrative rather than dramatic; and this fact, in conjunction with a tendency to long speeches of tedious argument or futile lament (which Rowe most probably caught from the French classical drama) slows up his plays considerably. What saves The Ambitious Stepmother is the genuine pathos that runs through the play, particularly in those scenes in which Cleone appears. (pp. 22-3)

There is no lack of telling scenes in this first play; Rowe, indeed, had the dramatist's feeling for the effective situation. He deserved success if only for the construction of his plots, which were generally original and often genuinely dramatic. But just at those points where his opportunity is greatest Rowe frequently breaks down in the most disappointing fashion, and

allows some flat and insufficient remark to ruin a fine situation. (p. 23)

[Rowe's second play] is not essentially different from his first. In Tamerlane we find again the same heroic atmosphere, the gales of sighs, the floods of tears, the tedious agonies of lovers, the pompous slaughter at the close. Bajazet is perhaps the most heroic thing in all Rowe's seven tragedies. There is no lack of conscious worth in Bajazet; and he has at least the attraction, not common to all Rowe's heroes, of knowing precisely what he wants. He is not so much a human character as a storm of passion spending itself and reviving in varying gusts; but there is nothing sentimental about him. He has the bragging manliness of Dryden's heroes; he can be relied upon to avoid any feeble penitence or sickly remorse. On the other hand there is abundance of sentiment in the amours of Moneses and Arpasia. These two unhappy lovers give Rowe his opportunity for melodious lament. The whole tone is effeminate; at times it descends to a sickly doting that throws "a damp on the spirits." The love affair of Axalla is a livelier business, and rather more closely connected with the main action of the play, but it merely duplicates the Arpasia-Moneses situation. As before, passages of conventional rant alternate with others of quieter and more natural feeling. Rowe can be foolish enough. (p. 24)

[Dramatically], Tamerlane has little, apart from the restless energy of Bajazet, to commend it. Tamerlane himself might be removed from the play without serious loss. The appeal of Rowe's second tragedy was local and temporary; and, as Dr Johnson judiciously notes, "occasional poetry must often content itself with occasional praise" [see excerpt dated 1781].

In Tamerlane, then, Rowe had made little advance upon his first tragedy. He had attempted to "thunder after the manner of Dryden" instead of developing that element of pathos which he had introduced so successfully in the person of Cleone. In The Fair Penitent he shifted his focus; and, in making an unfortunate woman the central figure of his third tragedy, he showed again where his real talent lay. (p. 25)

As the first of Rowe's "she-tragedies" The Fair Penitent is a landmark in eighteenth-century drama. But it has an even more important claim upon our attention; it is the first of a long line of domestic tragedies, which Rowe himself aptly describes in the prologue as the "melancholy tale of private woes" [see excerpt dated 1703]. Rowe, indeed, sounds an arresting parley in his prologue which the play itself hardly justifies. It was not until Lillo's George Barnwell that domestic tragedy really returned to its own; but here, as in other directions, Rowe was pointing the way with a cultured if rather tentative gesture. He was no daring innovator. What was new in him was invariably qualified by a timid assent in what was traditional; but that his Fair Penitent gave the tragic drama a new direction there can be no question. Nor can there be any doubt that to the new bourgeois audiences the woes of Calista were more real than the sorrows of Cleopatra. It must be recorded, however, that Rowe advanced with extreme wariness over this new ground. (pp. 27-8)

It is not difficult to account for the popularity of The Fair Penitent in Rowe's day. Sadly unreal as the greater part of the play may sound to modern ears, it must not be forgotten that The Fair Penitent was once "the last new tragedy," an ultra-modern play, whose heroine with due allowance made for the blank verse, spoke and acted in a manner similar to that of the other young females of the day. Rowe, who set out to show his audience "men and women as they are," had none of the conscientious realism of a Crabbe. He did not sing the married state, the humble life, or anything else,

> As truth will paint it, and as bards will not.

Yet he was moving, timidly perhaps but none the less effectively, towards a greater naturalism, a sentiment more real, certainly more democratic, than that which inflated the "blown puffy" plays of the heroic period which had just passed. Not the least among his achievements was the adoption (more particularly, however, in *Jane Shore* that in *The Fair Penitent*) of a language at once simpler and more natural than that which had become conventional to tragedy. From the point of view of character too, *The Fair Penitent* shows an advance upon Rowe's earlier plays. In Calista and Lothario he created a livelier and more spirited pair of characters than any he had yet conceived. Calista was sufficiently animated to reappear as Clarissa Harlowe in Richardson's novel; and Lothario's dashing villainy so impressed his own and a succeeding generation of playgoers that he gave his name to the whole genus of amorous rakes. The cool, gay assurance of Lothario, the entire absence from his character of all sentiment and conscience, make him a welcome figure in a drama of lovesick heroes and weeping heroines. Lothario says fewer senselessly heroic things than most of Rowe's young men; and what he has to say is usually in character. This last point is worth a passing note; for in the tragic drama of the period little effort was expended on differentiating the various characters by what they said and how they spoke. (pp. 29-30)

[*The Biter*] is worse than dull; it is definitely childish. *The Biter*, with its clumsy dramatic tricks, its flat dialogue, its uninspired horseplay, was as far removed as could be from the witty and delicate comedy of his friend Congreve. What induced Rowe, the wit, the intelligent writer of tragedy, the man about town, to write so badly as he does in this play, it is difficult to imagine. . . . The poverty of his comic genius may be seen in his relying upon a stuttering character and one that hiccups to win laughter from an unresponsive audience. To the student of social history *The Biter* is an interesting enough document, for Rowe's characters are drawn from the middle and lower classes; to the dramatic critic Rowe's literary drolling is only an unfortunate episode.

Ulysses, his fourth tragedy, is a dramatic hybrid. Rowe was attempting here to graft the gentler scion of classicism upon the more buoyant stock of Elizabethan drama. In the strict adherence to the unities of time and place, in the attempt to achieve poetic justice, in the set speeches of great length, the influence of French models may be readily traced. But in the two almost independent plots, in the increased number of characters, in the thunder scene when the clouds part to disclose Pallas, in the sound and fury with which the play draws to its close, and in the increased freedom of the verse, there are equally obvious traces of a more robust drama. But Rowe had not the Elizabethan exuberance that could reanimate a Ulysses. He had little of that imaginative sympathy that could breathe new life and vigour into an Antony or a Coriolanus; nor had he that lower gift of impudent familiarity by which a living dramatist has succeeded in imparting a new, if rather impertinent, liveliness to Caesar and Cleopatra. He found his characters dead, and he left them so. The play remains too remote from life to excite any but a literary interest.

The Royal Convert is a belated offspring of the heroic drama. The passionate Hengist and the imperious Rodogune have nothing of the new sentiment; they are spirited survivals of the old school. The play was not a success; and its failure may be attributed mainly to the fact that by the year 1708 a London audience was expecting more than heroic bluster and a hero who is mainly concerned with weighing the outworn claims of love and honour. *The Royal Convert* was set in Saxon England; and this fact enabled Rowe to indulge his patriotic feelings to some extent. It was a healthy instinct that planted English tragedy once more in England, and abandoned oriental courts for the English countryside. Rowe, of course, was not the first in the field; but, as usual, he was early in the field. The most original feature, however, in this old-fashioned play, is the character of Ethelinda, a Christian maiden, who is animated by a not unattractive piety. In the last scene of the play Rowe has moved far indeed from the impious rants of the heroic drama. (pp. 31-2)

In 1714 appeared *Jane Shore,* a tragedy "written in imitation of Shakespear's style." Critics have all along been prone to deny that Rowe's play contains the least trace of Shakespeare. "I have seen a play professedly writ in the style of Shakespeare," wrote Swift, "wherein the resemblance lay in one single line,

> And so good morrow t'ye, good master lieutenant."

But *Jane Shore* is so obviously written in a style unfamiliar to playgoers of the second decade of the eighteenth century, and that style is so clearly pseudo-Shakespearean, that Rowe's claim cannot be disputed. The most casual examination of his play must reveal to any competent critic frequent echoes and parodies of Shakespeare's voice, such as

> The long Train of Frailties Flesh is Heir to.

Most striking of those echoes is the scene in the fourth act where Gloucester gives his order for the death of Hastings.

As might be expected, Rowe relies too much for his Elizabethan atmosphere upon such tags as "Beshrew my heart," and "Soft ye now," and such obsolete words as "resty" and "hilding." Occasionally, too, he permits himself such a phrase as "Avaunt, base groom," which even in his own day must have been the theatrical sort of thing that a cautious writer would shun. But had he confined himself to such obvious appropriations, there would be little interest in his imitation of Shakespeare. His editorial work, however, had left a deeper impress than those casual phrases would indicate. We find him coining words in the free Shakespearean fashion. "Thus to coy it!" cries Hastings when Jane refuses to welcome his advances. Again, he is surely writing in a consciously Shakespearean manner when he makes Alicia say,

> The Fatherless, the Friendless, and the Widow,
> Who daily own the Bounty of thy Hand,
> Shall cry to Heav'n, and pull a Blessing on thee.

The word "pull" would never have occurred to Rowe unless he had been writing, as he thought, in imitation of Shakespeare. We find, that is to say, words wrenched slightly out of their customary usage to fit the needs of the moment. And Rowe catches at times the very rhythm of Shakespeare's blank verse:

> These trickling Drops chase one another still,
> As if the posting Messengers of Grief
> Could overtake the Hours fled far away,
> And make old Time come back.

The tears are Rowe's; the manner, Shakespeare's. That Shakespeare nowhere called a tear "the posting messenger of grief" seems almost an oversight; the phrase has a noble ring. Sometimes in his anxiety to be Shakespearean, Rowe writes as only Shakespeare parodying himself would have written.

> My feelbe Jaws forget their common Office,
> My tasteless Tongue cleaves to the clammy Roof,
> And now a gen'ral Loathing grows upon me.

Rowe, of course, meant to be a little more than himself in this passage; and, in pitching a simple statement into this over-adequate form, he slipped over the edge of a precipice which Shakespeare often walks perilously near. In various other ways Rowe has caught the Shakespearean manner. He takes wing on his timid flights at just those points where Shakespeare mounts so frequently in a sudden glory of expatiation. Confronted with an abrupt doom, Hastings takes stock of the situation in a manner far inferior to Shakespeare's, and yet Shakespearean:

> 'Tis but to die,
> 'Tis but to venture on that common Hazard. . . .

In *Jane Shore,* too, Rowe pours out at times a Shakespearean profusion of metaphor, and he has caught Shakespeare's peculiar trick of cumulative description, where a whole passage mounts in a steady crescendo, and then topples over.

Rowe, in fact, was only bringing to a head in *Jane Shore* certain tendencies that had long been latent. . . . It need not surprise us to find that when Rowe is most Shakespearean he is generally at his best. When Calista shrinks from the prospect of living on from day to day to be reminded continually of her shame—

> Daily to be reproach'd, and have my Misery
> At Morn, at Noon and Night told over to me,
> Lest my Remembrance might grow pitiful,
> And grant a Moment's Interval of Peace—
>
> (*The Fair Penitent*)

it is Rowe writing in imitation of Shakespeare who is capable of transfiguring the simple idea, "Lest I forget," into that proud line,

> Lest my Remembrance might grow pitiful.

Dramatically *Jane Shore* is superior in almost every respect to Rowe's earlier plays. . . . There is, too, a pleasant simplicity in much of the language, a new willingness to rely upon the mere force of the situation. The unity of interest, too, is better maintained in *Jane Shore* than in any of Rowe's other plays.

In *Lady Jane Gray* Rowe repeated the genre, but not the success of *Jane Shore*. . . . Apart from short passages widely scattered, *Lady Jane Gray* is the most tedious and dispiriting of all Rowe's plays. The flow of tears proceeds unhindered. No play could long support such misery, and a heroine so uniformly wretched as Jane soon forfeits our sympathy. *Lady Jane Gray* is a disappointing climax to Rowe's dramatic work. (pp. 33-6)

> *J. R. Sutherland, "Life," in* Three Plays: Tamerlane, The Fair Penitent, Jane Shore *by Nicholas Rowe, edited by J. R. Sutherland, The Scholartis Press, 1929, pp. 1-38.*

ALFRED JACKSON   (essay date 1930)

[*In the following excerpt, Jackson comments on several aspects of* Jane Shore, *"the accepted monument to Rowe's genius."*]

On February 2nd 1714 Rowe's acknowledged masterpiece *Jane Shore* was produced at Drury Lane. . . . Acted repeatedly amid unfailing acclamation, it definitely placed Rowe in the front rank of contemporary dramatists. Its pathetic theme, dealing with the distress of Edward's favourite mistress, appealed strongly to all sections of the audience, and made a happy compromise between French pseudo-classicism and the domestic tale of humble life. It deals with historical facts and historical persons. The idealistic, mythological setting of the heroic drama is discarded in favour of London. (p. 313)

Apart from its historical significance Rowe's tragedy is interesting as being written "In imitation of Shakespeare's Style." . . . Rowe's professed imitation of Shakespeare has been treated with scorn by some critics and, as far as plot is concerned, the play bears little resemblance to *Richard III*. Apart from the character of Gloster and the short scene of Hastings' impeachment which follows Shakespeare closely there is no connection between the two dramas. In Rowe, Jane Shore is the centre of the story, in Shakespeare she makes no actual appearance and is heard of but incidentally. Most of the male figures introduced by Rowe appear also in the earlier play but they are reduced to subordinate positions. Rowe's tragedy, indeed, is more akin to Heywood's *Edward IV* than to *Richard III* although they, too, differ widely in detail. Heywood deals with the whole course of Jane's life from her first encounter with Edward IV to her death; he introduces numerous characters to connect his various incidents, and avoids formal descriptions. Where Rowe narrates he resolves into action, where Rowe paints with a large brush he uses a small. Still, Heywood was not hampered by any French precepts, and had, in his two parts, much more scope than Rowe possessed in his five acts. Detail, and subtle touches therefore, were only to be expected in the larger work. It must be remembered in a comparison of accounts dealing with Jane Shore that identical features were bound to be present. The main aspects of her life were so well known that any representation of her would necessarily follow the usual clear-cut lines. Rowe, following the example of Banks in his historical tragedies, took a suitable tragic character, retained the broad historical outline, and constructed a sentimental drama. Jane Shore's pitiful story was the sole attraction for Rowe; biographical accuracy was of minor importance. . . . Although the restriction of characters and the absence of comedy betray French precept, the tragedy of *Jane Shore* shows indisputable marks of Shakespearian influence. Rowe's earlier methods are modified in accordance with Shakespeare's procedure. The romantic, oriental setting, prominent in his earlier dramas is rejected in favour of real history. The unities of time and place are definitely broken. The noble characters, essential to the pseudo-classical creed, although still present, take second place to a figure of humble life. Rhetorical effusions, it is true, still abound, but they are less declamatory and have a ring of Elizabethan grandeur, especially in the soliloquies. The dialogue, stilted in the *Royal Convert,* is animated and less histrionic, the speeches following the natural development of the characters. In his attempt at unaffected conversation Rowe sometimes introduces expressions as "by my hollidame" and "by St. Paul", but these are sparingly used and have no incongruous effect. Throughout the play there is a sense of simplicity which compares favorably with the laboured workmanship of the heroic plays. The characters do not pose. They do not rant like resuscitated pictures of Kneller. Their language, occasionally florid and ornate, is not overburdened with similes and metaphors and flows harmoniously along.

Rowe naturally could not approach Shakespeare's ingenuity. He could not match the general power of his drama, the beauty of his thought or the force of his characters. In spite of Pope's contention "that it was mighty simple in Rowe to write a play now professedly in Shakespeare's style that is, professedly in the style of a bad age'' he could merely strive after his universality and fecundity. Yet he reflects something of Shakespeare's greatness. His adopting of Shakespeare's characteristics is seen in more than a single line as Pope thought. The well-worn story of Jane Shore is treated with a skill absent in all his other plays. Coming after his labours as a Shakespearian editor, Rowe's advance in dramatic art can only be attributed to his study of the great master.

The major characters of the play are drawn with ability. Although they still express the Restoration conception of one sort of mood, and lack the variety of life, they have yet much vitality. Unlike the puppet-like princes of the *Royal Convert* the men act like human beings. Hastings, half-villain, half-hero, in spite of his resemblance to the moralising philosopher of Rowe's earlier plays, does play an active part. A much more attractive figure than the Hastings of the *True Tragedie* he serves a useful purpose in the development of Jane Shore's character. His soliloquy on death is among the finest passages in the play. . . . Gloster, the most important character in Shakespeare's play, is, in Rowe's drama, given less scope. He does not occupy the stage for long intervals, but gives the usual impression of a rascally, scheming villain. He is the popular type of heartless intriguer so dear to Elizabethan and 18th century audiences. The other male characters, Shore and Bellmour, are drawn with a sympathy which agrees with their station; Shore's part is restricted to a minimum, but, where he appears, he brings a touch of pathos reminiscent of Heywood's counterpart. The smallness of the part allotted to him is amply balanced by the prominence attached to Jane herself. The supreme example of repentant love, she is by far the most effective figure in the drama. From her first appearance with Alicia, till the scene of her death she elicits our compassion. The various phases of her wretched life are depicted with a pathos strongly akin to Otway. Once all-powerful, the influential mistress of a king, she suffers repeated reverses till her final catastrophe. Bereft of husband and protector, she flees to her friend her ''dearest truest, best Alicia'' for comfort, but, instead of help, she meets disaster. Her absolute confidence in Alicia is a excellent example of dramatic irony. Throughout the play Jane is shown no mercy and is made a formidable warning against unchastity. Hastings refuses to believe her penitence and is transformed from a friend to a furious lover; Dumont, her sole defender, is cast into prison; whilst Gloster, unmerciful and despotic, condemns her to the most degrading punishment. . . . At times Jane is made the medium of Rowe's moralising intention. At times, too, her long speeches revert to the declamatory fashion of the heroic drama. Yet on the whole, she moves with the grace and naturalness of a true dramatic figure. With the exception of Calista, the pitiful heroines of Rowe's earliest plays are mere figure-heads compared with her. She is no longer a type but a personality. (pp. 314-20)

Opposite to the pitiful Jane is the contrasted character of Alicia, her rival. Jealous, impetuous and rash, she changes suddenly from an affectionate companion to a scheming antagonist, and finally becomes half-insane. She differs from Jane in every respect. The one is compassionate, lachrymose and sad; the other villainous, raving and mad. Their differing natures, brought out well by the complication of their relations with Hastings are excellently portrayed and their final meeting is of considerable emotional power. By all dramatic critics Alicia was regarded as more than ''a character of mere empty noise'' as Dr. Johnson declared [see excerpt dated 1781], and was rendered almost as powerful as Jane by capable performers.

Rowe's success in characterisation in this play was no doubt due to his progress in constructional skill. The plot is managed with ability and care. The exposition at the beginning is clear, and the main issues are introduced with lucidity. The difficult task of indicating the relations of Jane with Hastings and Alicia, and Gloster's enmity to Hastings is rendered with penetration and economy. Much of the action as was usual in all Rowe's plays is reduced to narrative, but the descriptions (especially Jane's walk of penance) are given with colour and intensity. The acts also unfold in causal sequence, and the exits and entrances are judiciously arranged. The breaking-up of the unities gave Rowe's genius room to expand, and the acquisition of this freedom enabled him to dispense with artificial and improvised stage tricks. There are no dei ex machina [''gods out of machines''; contrived solutions to difficulties in plot]; there are no unnatural scene-drawings; there is no frantic haste to rid the stage of the actors. The plot evolves in a striking succession of events, the concluding scene bringing the logical result. There are in Rowe, however, none of the homely touches which betray the perfect technician. Unlike Heywood, he does not introduce a minor character for the sole purpose of natural effect. His dramatis personae are adequate, and their parts are proportioned according to their importance. In this economy of performers Rowe still keeps to the tenet of the French school. In this play Rowe's ''nightingale descriptions'' show evident signs of Shakespearian influence. The long declamatory speeches, the high-soaring rants, give place to freer and more spontaneous expressions. Rhyme, except in tags is avoided; the metre flows in ''large periods and the rhythms are larger, broader and less obvious.'' The whole atmosphere of the play is one of compassion, and the flowing harmony does much to enhance this effect. With this ''heart-withering'' drama, Rowe was recognised as the supreme portrayer of pitiful woman characters, and the foremost master of pathos. . . . To this day *Jane Shore* remains the accepted monument to Rowe's genius. (pp. 320-23)

> *Alfred Jackson, ''Rowe's Historical Tragedies,'' in* Anglia, *Vol. LIV, 1930, pp. 307-30.*

V. DE SOLA PINTO (essay date 1930)

[*Pinto was an English educator, editor, and poet whose many critical studies include* Sir Charles Sedley, 1639-1701 *(1927) and* The Restoration Court Poets *(1965). In the following excerpt from a review of J. R. Sutherland's edition of three Rowe plays, he succinctly assesses Rowe's importance to dramatic literature.*]

Eighteenth-century tragedies are surely among the mustiest of the denizens of old libraries. (p. 225)

Nicholas Rowe is one of the earliest and best of a bad lot. He is a kind of weakened and watery Otway with a gift for the writing of fluent blank verse, which occasionally almost blunders into poetry. His plays are a curious mixture of stagy artifice and unreal psychology with touches of genuine pathos and humanity. His place in dramatic and in general literary history, however, though small is really significant. He was a minor classic to the men of the eighteenth century, even to such a critic as Johnson [see excerpt dated 1781], who praised him for ''the reasonableness and propriety of his scenes,'' ''the elegance of his diction and the suavity of his verse,'' and declared that ''he always delights the ear, and often improves the understanding.'' There is little doubt that his plays are one of the chief sources of the great stream of eighteenth-century sentimentality, and that his *Lothario,* who like *Mrs. Grundy* has become part of the English language, was the ancestor of

Lovelace and one of the remote progenitors of the Byronic hero-villain. So there is plenty of justification for a scholarly reprint of a selection from his works as an aid to the student of literary history, although, if they depended on their intrinsic merit, it is unlikely that any one would have disturbed their repose. (pp. 225-26)

V. de Sola Pinto, in a review of "Three Plays by Nicholas Rowe: Tamerlane, The Fair Penitent, Jane Shore," in The Review of English Studies, *Vol. VI, No. 22, April, 1930, pp. 225-26.*

BONAMY DOBRÉE (essay date 1959)

[*An English historian and critic, Dobrée distinguished himself both as a leading authority of Restoration drama and as a biographer who sought, through vivid depiction and style, to establish biography as a legitimate creative form. Dobrée is also known for his editing of* The Oxford History of English Literature *and* Writers and Their Work *series. In all his writings, Dobrée's foremost concern was to communicate to the reader his aesthetic response to the work under discussion. In the following excerpt, Dobrée concentrates on Rowe's sentimentalism and on poetic diction in the tragedies.*]

Rowe occupies the foremost place as a writer of tragedy in the first part of [the period from 1700 to 1740]; as closest inheritor of the form he worked in, he is the best of the tragic playwrights of the whole century, which is to make no extravagant claim. To write plays was, it may be imagined, not more than the favourite serious pastime of this apparently not very profound man, whose frivolity scandalized Addison. Nevertheless, his plays are not slapdash; they are well constructed, owing a good deal of their power and readability, and no doubt their stage success, to the arrangement of the acts, and the movement of the emotions within the acts. It is tempting to think that born into an age offering better material to handle, he would have been more important in the history of the drama than he actually is; yet the sentimentality of his diction, his frequent 'Oh!'s, the constantly recurring 'never more' refrain, seem to fit in so pat with the sentiments he dealt with, that it is impossible not to concede that the man superbly fitted the occasion.

Superbly is the right word, for it is difficult to imagine a diction—one which seemed natural to him—which would better bring home the sentiments which were his material; apart from, and perhaps above, construction, his words as [*A Comparison Between the Two Stages*] rightly stated, were his chief merit [see excerpt dated 1702]. . . . [It] was precisely what Rowe called 'poetic coloring' that gave his tragedies their particular flavour. It was not within him to produce a stark final vision; his intention was to offer something which would be charming and soothing to an audience which had its notions as to what constituted the beautiful. His work had to be smooth and gentlemanlike, clothed in neo-classic draperies, with corresponding gestures. As Smollett remarked, it is solid, florid, declamatory. His figures are simplified; strong in their virtue or their vice, with little inner struggle, except against the debilitating effects of love. Only in *The Fair Penitent* is the serenity, or at least the decorous melancholy of his dramas, ruffled by any turbulence or trouble, and in that play we are less aware of poetic beauties.

In *Tamerlane,* his favourite play, the hero is drawn, it would appear, from that perfect, great, and benevolent monarch William III, and the villain, Bajazet, from that compendium of all horrific wickedness Louis XIV: it is replete (no other word will quite fit) with such beauties. The main appeal, of course,

apart from the 'liberty' theme which runs through so much of the Whig writing of the period, is to pity for lovers in distress, but great warriors express themselves in the tones of pastoral poetry. Thus Axalla, towards whom Selima has relented and expressed fears for his safety in battle, answers:

> The murm'ring Gale revives the drooping Flame,
> That at thy Coldness languish'd in my Breast;
> So breathe the gentle Zephyrs on the Spring,
> And waken every Plant, and od'rous Flower,
> Which Winter Frost had blasted, to new Life.

And so it goes on, the good in the play uttering the noblest sentiments in such terms; but the sentiments are not the heroic ones of the older drama so much as those of the Sunday school, while the wicked are purely vicious, without any of the subtlety of the old Machiavells. The odd thing is that it is not boring. Rowe does not in any way explore life or add anything to our knowledge of the emotions, yet he succeeds in taking us into a sort of coherent, self-consistent fairyland, where the fancy can amuse itself, lulled by sounds that are undeniably sweet. Here, if anywhere, a certain peace of the Augustans may be found.

Rowe's attitude to the old heroic values is amusingly dubious. There are echoes of a 'Roman strictness', but ambition has become a passion that pushes man 'beyond the bounds of nature', and love is a softening emotion. Thus Antinous in *Ulysses* remarks:

> Youth by Nature
> Is active, fiery, bold, and great of Soul;
> Love is the Bane of all these noble Qualities,
> The sickly Fit that palls Ambition's Appetite;

While Seofrid in *The Royal Convert* frankly states that love 'or call it by the coarser name, lust', is 'what most we ought to fear'. Rowe was shrewdly aware that what passed for love in the plays of his time did usually deserve the coarser name, and this hardly fitted in with the family virtues he was intent to preach. Thus we feel he is more at home, more actual, when he passes from classical scenes to those of English history; and his later plays, if they lack the tension of *The Fair Penitent,* bear a certain relation to life, and are more fitting vehicles for the sense of domesticity which was to pervade the age. His *Jane Shore,* 'written in imitation of Shakespeare' (Professor Nicoll suggests he meant Banks), and his *Lady Jane Gray,* give an effect of greater freedom, while the verse is easier and more flexible, released to greater degree from the shackles of the couplet. The dialogue in the last play between Guilford and Pembroke, though still a little flowery, is no longer floral; it gives some sense of power, as it does the 'distressed lady' scene in *Jane Shore.* Rowe for all his faults, his weaknesses, his sentimentality, and his occasional absurdities, achieved something which is still worth reading for relaxation. (pp. 246-47)

Bonamy Dobrée, "The Drama," in his English Literature in the Early Eighteenth Century, 1700-1740, *Oxford at the Clarendon Press, Oxford, 1959, pp. 223-56.*

FRANK J. KEÁRFUL (essay date 1966)

[*In the following excerpt, Kearful illuminates Rowe's "bifurcated conception of the emotive and moral functions of tragedy" in a discussion of* The Fair Penitent.]

[In *The Fair Penitent*] Nicholas Rowe eschews even the modified heroics of his earlier plays, *The Ambitious Step-Mother* and *Tamerlane,* and focuses on the pathetic. Accompanying this emphasis, however, is an overt didacticism already anticipated in *Tamerlane,* which differentiates Rowe from his late senventeenth-century predecessors in the pathetic vein, notably Otway, Southerne, and Banks. Even as he could not employ earlier the conventions of heroic drama without qualifying and modifying them, so now in his first essay in "she-tragedy" he does not pursue pathos for its own sake so as to sacrifice judgment for sentiment. In *The Fair Penitent* Rowe strives to create a form of tragedy closer to the experience of his audience than heroic dramaturgy however modified might ever attain; but even as he rejects the bombastic rhetoric of heroic drama, so he also endeavors to transcend the gratuitous emotionalism of late seventeenth-century blank-verse pathetic drama. The function of tragedy in *The Fair Penitent* is not merely to arouse vicarious suffering: it is also to instruct Rowe's audience in the kind of moral knowledge requisite to their own lives.

Rowe's prologue is typically Augustan in its theorizing about tragedy in that it argues from the effect tragedy has upon its audience rather than from any abstract premises [see excerpt dated 1703]. Not what tragedy according to any *a priori* assumptions *is* but what tragedy *does* concerns Rowe. So, while admitting the existence of other literary forms of tragedy, he justifies his own not by an appeal to rules or precedent but by the immediacy of its effect upon the audience. Rowe's predilection for the domestic is, then, part of an aesthetic of naturalism based on a fundamentally rhetorical concern with the most effective way to arouse the desired response in his audience. It is this concern with literature as a means of affecting others which unites as Augustans Rowe and such different writers as Swift and Pope.

In addition to introducing into tragedy a social milieu more nearly resembling that of his audience, Rowe places new emphasis on emotional experience in itself as a source of the tragic. Accordingly, throughout the Prologue recur words like *unhappy, cares, joys, wonder, pity, melancholy, woes, bemoan, sorrows, passions, rapture, mourns.* Tragedy is for Rowe an experience communicated to an audience: not something whch happens, but the human reaction to something which happens, as shared by audience and protagonist. Rowe's central problem in the creation of a new, Augustan tragedy is to enable the audience to maintain a balance between this sympathetic participation in the experience of the characters and that intellectual detachment from them necessary for moral judgment. (pp. 351-52)

In the context of Rowe's earlier dramatic writing what is most remarkable about the language of [*The Fair Penitent*] is its integrity. Almost totally missing are those abrupt changes of poetic style and dramatic appeal which are characteristic of *The Ambitious Step-Mother* and still frequent in *Tamerlane.* In *The Fair Penitent* Rowe achieves a greater consistency of tone and technique, as language becomes the organic image of the action and not merely poetic ornament or rhetorical elaboration upon it. Accordingly, the level of style generally remains within his most effective, "middle" range, self-consciously literary and rhetorical figures being comparatively few.

It is through characterization, however, that the nature of tragedy in *The Fair Penitent* becomes most apparent, particularly in the creation of Lothario, destined to be the prototype of all subsequent "gay Lotharios" and perhaps a direct source for Richardson's Lovelace. Although his counterpart in *The Fatal Dowry,* Novall junior, is a foppish young fool, Lothario himself is a vivid dramatization of a dedicated sensualist. Indeed, to

some moralizing critics, the righteous but doltish Altamont has seemed by comparison scandalously dull. Thus in 1770, Francis Gentleman observed: "Lothario is the most reproachable character our moral author ever drew, and indeed as dangerous a one as we know; like the snake with a beauteous variegated skin, which lures the unguarded hand to a poisonous touch; this licentious gallant gilds his pernicious principles with very delusive qualifications, especially for the fair sex, which cannot be more plainly evinced than by a declaration which has often been made at the representation of this piece, by volatile, unthinking females; who have not scrupled saying, that they would rather be deceived by such a pretty fellow as Lothario, than countenance such a constant passive, insipid creature as Altamont" [see Additional Bibliography]. Similarly, Doctor Johnson, even though he believed "there is scarcely any work of any poet at once so interesting by the fable and so delightful by the language" as *The Fair Penitent,* felt obliged to observe that "Lothario, with gaiety which cannot be hated, and bravery which cannot be despised, retains too much of the spectator's kindness" [see excerpt dated 1781]. Such attacks fail to do justice to the complexity of both Rowe's moral awareness and his conception of the nature of tragedy. Precisely because evil so often is more obviously attractive than goodness is Rowe's characterization appropriate—and moral. Tragedy in *The Fair Penitent* is not merely ethical demonstration after the dictates of Rymer nor emotional excitation after the manner of Lee. It is, rather, an exploration at once sympathetic and critical of the experience of sin.

That *The Fair Penitent* aspires to be more than melodrama is evident in the portrayal of Lothario, who for all his stage villainy is not a stage villain. In Act I Altamont voices doubts over Calista's love, which for the audience are soon confirmed by a conversation between Lothario and his friend Rossano. Lothario pleasurably recalls the night when, "hot with the *Tuscan* Grape, and high in Blood," he "stole unheeded to her Chamber" and seduced the half-willing, half-reluctant Calista. . . . On their next meeting Lothario's "Reason took her turn to reign," while Calista "talk'd of a Priest and Marriage." . . . The seducer's motives are complicated by an apparently sincere claim advanced at the beginning of the dialogue:

> I lik'd her, wou'd have marry'd her,
> But that it pleas'd her Father to refuse me,
> To make this Honourable Fool her Husband.
> For which, if I forget him, may the Shame
> I mean to brand his Name with, stick on mine.

Clearly, Rowe is endeavoring to create something more than a melodrama of unsuspecting virtue assailed by diabolical vice. By injecting issues of property and respectability into the drama, he confronts his audience with the complexity of moral experience and the kinds of moral problems they might in their own lives know.

Rowe's interest in making the tragic action more naturalistic, to "shew you Men and Women as they are," as well as ethically more meaningful to his predominantly middle-class audience can be seen through a comparison of passages more or less parallel in function with certain passages in his earlier plays. (pp. 353-55)

Rowe's success in transforming the theatricalities of heroic drama into the moral substance of domestic tragedy is made manifest by a juxtaposition of Artemisa's rhetorical monologue in *The Ambitious Step-Mother* on her lot as woman with Calista's impassioned complaint on the same theme. Artemisa, in the ranting manner of Dryden's god-aspiring heroes, declaims:

> Ye Diviner Pow'rs!
> By whom 'tis said we are, from whose bright Beings
> Those active Sparks were struck, which move our Clay;
> I feel, and I confess the Etherial Energy,
> That busie restless Principle, whose Appetite
> Is only pleas'd with Greatness like your own:
> Why have you clogg'd it then with this dull Mass,
> And shut it up in Woman? Why debas'd it
> To an inferior part of the Creation?
> Since your own heavenly Hands mistook my Lot,
> 'Tis you have err'd, not I. Could Fate e'er mean
> Me, for a Wife, a Slave to *Tiribassus*!
> To such a thing as he! a Wretch! a Husband!
> Therefore in just Assertion of my self,
> I shook him off, and past those narrow Limits,
> Which Laws contrive in vain for Souls born great.
> There is not, must not be a Bound for Greatness;
> Power gives a Sanction, and makes all things just.

Calista's sentiments may be similar, but her expression of them anticipates Ibsen more than it recalls Dryden:

> How hard is the Condition of our Sex,
> Thro' ev'ry State of Life the Slaves of Man?
> In all the deal delightful Days of Youth,
> A rigid Father dictates to our Wills,
> And deals out Pleasure with a scanty Hand;
> To his, the Tyrant Husband's Reign succeeds;
> Proud with Opinion of superior Reason,
> He holds Domestick Bus'ness and Devotion
> All we are capable to know, and shuts us,
> Like Cloyster'd Ideots, from the World's Acquaintance,
> And all the Joy's of Freedom; wherefore are we
> Born with high Souls, but to assert our selves,
> Shake off this vile Obedience they exact,
> And claim an equal Empire o'er the World?

Whereas in Artemisa's speech the dramatic occasion is seized upon as an opportunity for heroical rodomontade, in Calista's her personal moral predicament is made relevant to the experience and frustrations of the middle-class female members of the audience.

What makes **The Fair Penitent** the very original play it is, is the manner in which Rowe, in accordance with his bifurcated conception of the emotive and moral functions of tragedy, combines its sympathetic and ethical appeals. Unlike, for example, Otway in *The Orphan* (1680), a tragedy of domestic relations also conventionally labeled "pathetic," Rowe is not content to have the ethical significance of the action emerge by dramatic implication. Otway also focuses his audience's attention on a "melancholy Tale of private Woes" and does indeed show the tragic consequences of a lack of trust between individuals, but he does not share Rowe's moralizing habit. He makes a domestic situation the source of his tragedy primarily to make sympathetic participation in the sufferings of his characters more immediate and poignant. Rowe, however, endeavoring to inculcate a moral view of marriage, is as much concerned with the didactic force of the domestic situation itself as with the personal misfortunes of the human beings caught up in it. Because her actions must be placed within a corrective moral framework, Rowe prevents his audience from participating fully in the experience of his heroine; pathos must not cause them for a moment to sympathize with sin, even though they may sympathize with the sinner. In *The Orphan,* moral theme and dramatic action are integrated with less difficulty, for Otway is not intent upon making his tragedy serve as a moral exemplum.

The presence of Horatio and Lavinia within the play allows Rowe to present a moral view of the action, for they function as examples of and spokesmen for marital virtue.... (pp. 356-58)

[Throughout the play] Horatio provides the ethical perspective within which the tragedy occurs. Never does one so sympathize with the major characters or pity them that the moral significance of their actions is lost sight of; in that respect Rowe anticipates Brecht. Taken out of dramatic context, Horatio's and Lavinia's speeches may indeed overemphasize the didactic element within the play; nevertheless, their most explicitly moralistic speeches occur at the ends of acts, each of which is provided with an appropriate moral conclusion. That this similarity is more than structural coincidence is suggested by the fact that Rowe customarily makes his act-closing speeches of unusual importance. In **The Ambitious Step-Mother** and **Tamerlane** they are used regularly as occasions for extended rhetorical or poetic displays, while throughout Rowe's works the use of rhyme to close an act deliberately sets off and draws attention to the speech while giving to the act a certain finality. The same technique, employed for moral emphasis, is even more apparent in the largely prose *London Merchant* (1731) of George Lillo.

Rowe's moral conception of tragedy is also evident in his presentation of Calista. She is, as Horatio and Lavinia point out, a cautionary example for the members of the audience; yet, no less than Lotario, she possesses a genuinely human complexity of moral awareness which raises her tragedy above the level of formulary exemplum. From the beginning of the play her feelings toward Lotario are ambivalent—even as was her first yielding to him—and all the while she realizes her guilt even when pursuing it. It is when others, particularly the righteous Horatio, charge her with sin that she most confirms herself in it. Thus she exclaims before her confidante, Lucilla: "To be a Tale for Fools! Scorn'd by the Women, / And pity'd by the Men! Oh insupportable!" Perhaps the subtlest aspects of Rowe's ethical presentation of Calista is the presumed repentence which justifies the title of the play. Calista never makes of herself an example to the audience—as, for instance, Lillo's George Barnwell does—nor does she ever explicitly confess her guilt. Indeed for many critics she is not repentant at all, the Jacobean horrors of Act V being accounted by them no more than melodramatic sensationalism. Calista's scorn for the artificial means of penitence forced upon her is, in fact, a measure of the depth of her interior realization of the state of her own soul.

The kind of overt moral concern with domestic relations which characterizes **The Fair Penitent** is again a prominent feature in **Jane Shore,** Rowe's other standard anthology-piece. Together they constitute an important development in the history of English drama, for they are the first attempts to fuse the naturalism of domestic tragedy and the patheticism of "sentimental" tragedy with a new didacticism which is part of the Augustan temper. That they in some measure succeeded in making tragedy once again a significant experience for their audiences is suggested by the fact they were among the most frequently performed tragedies of the entire century. If nonetheless one should be inclined to belittle Rowe's achievement, he should reflect that one age's sentiment is another's reality, and that Ibsen, Miller, and Osborne are Rowe's lineal descendants. (pp. 359-60)

Frank J. Kearful, "The Nature of Tragedy in Rowe's 'The Fair Penitent'," in Papers on Language and Literature, *Vol. 2, No. 4, Fall, 1966, pp. 351-60.*

ANNIBEL JENKINS　(essay date 1977)

[*Jenkins is an American educator and author who specializes in eighteenth-century studies. In the following excerpt, she explicates the themes of* Lady Jane Gray.]

Rowe achieves a kind of epic unity in [*Lady Jane Gray*] that he does not match in any other play. Perhaps he loses some of the domestic pathos of *Jane Shore* by centering attention on Lady Jane, but by this concentration on his martyred queen he gains a kind of classic simplicity. We are not distracted by a powerful figure like Gloucester who must impose his own plot, or by passionate ones like Alicia or Hastings who are rivals for the attention that Jane herself should have in the play. *Lady Jane Gray* is a series of vignettes that reveal Lady Jane's tragic story, a story wholly involved with church and state. (p. 121)

However slight the action of *Lady Jane Gray* may be, it is sufficient to carry the themes that make up the major interest of the play. These themes, established in the exposition of the first act, are woven together in such a way that the play becomes a play of themes, not of character or plot, As the play opens, Edward is already beyond human aid; the Duke of Northumberland and the Duke of Suffolk converse with their friend Sir John Gates about the church and the throne. Suffolk is already concerned for his country as he says, "Religion melts in ev'ry holy eye, / All comfortless, and forlorn / She sits on earth, and weeps upon her cross." The years have been short ones since the English church "late from heaps of *Gothic* ruins rose / In her first native simple majesty" and Suffolk very much fears that "again old Rome / Shall spread her banners; and her Monkish host, Pride, ignorance, and rapine shall return." But Suffolk's speech characterizing Mary is not personal; it reminds Rowe's audience of the traits traditionally assigned to Rome.

Northumberland, Suffolk, and Gates pledge to resist "proud presuming Romish Priests," and never to "Bow down before the holy purple tyrants," of Rome. Such declarations are not enough; political action must be swift and vigorous. The scheme to place Lady Jane upon the throne must have wide support, and the aid of the Earl of Pembroke is sought. Pembroke and Guilford are friends; Pembroke calls Guilford "The noblest youth our England has." Their rivalry for Lady Jane has not separated them. And thus their friendship, introduced early in the first act establishes another major theme of the play.

Rowe has made their relationship as exactly Elizabethan as would fit his play. They are noble youths, full of courage, bound by the courtly code of ethics, and skilled in courtesy. Pembroke is filled with passionate pride; Guilford, with ideal loyalty. Their responses to each other and to Lady Jane delineate two Renaissance court portraits. When Guilford first meets Lady Jane, all is fortune and fate; and they talk as if they stood in the woods of Sidney's *Aracdia,* unaware of anyone or anything except their own emotional responses. Pembroke cannot bear defeat; Guilford, the more even-tempered of the two men, is also the more generous. In their first discussion of their rivalry, Pembroke concludes that they must remember "Our friendship and our honour" and that they should contend "as friends and brave men ought, / With openness and justice to each other." (pp. 122-23)

Guilford addresses [Lady Jane] in the same mood of courtly speech as he has used with Pembroke. He compares her to the moon, the "silver regent of the night," and he would have her "sacred beams" help "dispel our horrors / And make us less lament the setting sun." Lady Jane is in a somber mood—she has just left the dying King Edward, and she is full of fear

for the fate of England. But Guilford forgets the dangers to his country; he gazes into Lady Jane's eyes and wonders "how excelling nature / Can give each day new patterns of her skill, / And yet at once surpass 'em." She will have none of his fair speech; she would rather hear "the raven's note"; it strikes her ear more sweetly. She ends the scene and, in fact, the first act with a somber speech suited to her mood of despair. The Elizabethan and Renaissance qualities of the early scenes in the act have made way for the seventeenth-century dirge of death.

It is fitting that the play as Rowe conceived it should be turned frequently to the theme of death. The historical episode of Lady Jane Gray was itself remembered largely in the context of death and the church, for these two topics were as current for Rowe's audience as politics and economics are constant themes for the twentieth century. The significant point in *Lady Jane Gray* is the way in which the two themes are handled. In this play, unlike the earlier ones, we have none of the shrill exaggeration of the charnel scene in *The Fair Penitent* or of the bombastic declarations of *The Ambitious Step-Mother* or, for that matter, the rather platitudinous attitudes found in *Ulysses* and in *The Royal Convert*. It was a fact that Lady Jane Gray had briefly been a queen—made so by her family and their supporters—to insure a Protestant succession. It was natural for her to examine her position, purge her soul, and meditate upon death. Given the vogue for the "grave-yard" literature of the early eighteenth century, Rowe's handling of the theme in *Lady Jane Gray* is dignified, sane, and proper; it befits the kind of matter a Poet Laureate would compose; and it is suitable for dedication to a royal princess.

One of Rowe's real problems in the play is to introduce and develop the theme of love in such a way that it does not detract from the serious contemplation of death and the dangers to England and the church attendant upon the loss of the young king. Lady Jane is young and beautiful, and both Guilford and Pembroke are passionately in love with her, but her response to the palpable hand of death upon her beloved Edward and her almost immediate personal encounter with it allows little time—or place—for a consideration of love or joy with anyone under any circumstances.

In the first scene of the second act, all the principals—Northumberland, Suffolk, Guilford, the Duchess of Suffolk—attempt to reconcile the two topics, death and love. They understand clearly that they must unite the two families—that Lady Jane, the daughter of the Duke of Suffolk, and Guilford, the son of the Duke of Northumberland, must be married to each other to insure the unity of the two families. They also realize that, since the young Edward VI is dying, their hope of having Jane become his queen must be immediately forgotten. They must turn from his death to Jane's future, and they must act quickly. This scene is an especially important one as each of the principal characters in it adds to the delicate reconcilation. . . . Guilford is gracious and proper; the Duchess of Suffolk is equally so. Northumberland, speaking to them both, describes Lady Jane as "All desolate and drown'd in flowing tears, By Edward's bed the pious princess sits"; when Lady Suffolk replies to this remark, the audience is hardly aware that she is establishing the legal basis for their attempt to set aside Princess Mary and to make Lady Jane the queen.

Rowe's handling of this problem of reconciling death and love is delicate and sure. Guilford as Lady Jane's future husband must bring together fate, love, death—for these are all interwoven in the larger themes of loyalty to church and state. He would have her "give one interval to joy," and, when she agrees, his speech is tender and considerate. In a subtle way, he uses the idea of death to plead his own cause as he says,

> . . . our noble parents had decreed,
> And urg'd high reasons which import the state,
> This night to give thee to my faithful arms,
>
> *   *   *
>
> Yet if thou art resolv'd to cross my fate,
> If this my utmost wish shall give thee pain,
> Now rather let the stroke of death fall on me,
> And stretch me out a lifeless corse before thee:
> Let me be swept away with things forgotten,
> Be huddled up in some obscure blind grave,
> Ere thou should'st say my love has made thee wretched,
> Or drop one single tear for Guilford's sake.

Lady Jane's response, "Alas! I have too much of death already," is simple and natural; but it cannot make proper a scene that includes the monstrous and macabre in its unnatural juxtaposition of life and death. As if seeing the inappropriateness of their conversation, Guilford offers to leave the marriage unconsummated until, as he says, "at thy pleasure" she may portion out the blessings. He will go away; he will leave her alone, but Lady Jane would have a companion in her sorrow. Offering him her hand, she says, "Here then I take thee to my heart forever, / The dear companion of my future days; / Whatever Providence allots for each, / Be that the common portion of us both." Their concluding dialogue in this scene is a duet of poetry. Indeed, the whole of the scene might have been written for the opera—it begins in a recitative that quickly sets the future action of the play and then becomes a long lyric composition of love and melancholy sorrow, not yet tragic, but with the promise of becoming so. . . . And after she leaves, Guilford, reviewing their situation, finds little prospect of joy. Even as he says he could "muse away an age in deepest melancholy," Pembroke appears and begins to speak of Edward's death; but he is immediately aware that something of great consequence has occurred since he last saw Guilford. Guilford tries to prepare him for the news; but Pembroke, impatient and hasty, partly guesses it and is so furious about the marriage that, although Guilford would temper the blow, Pembroke calls him a traitor, threatens his life, and denounces their friendship.

Again Rowe has written a scene of passion in which the uncontrolled fury of Pembroke is matched by the reason of Guilford—reason that is the warm, genuine support of the ties of friendship. This confrontation between Pembroke and Guilford is a more believable, if less dramatic, scene than the ones between Hastings and Jane Shore or between Alicia and Hastings in *Jane Shore*. Refusing to fight, Guilford will not profane the sacred grounds of the court "with brawls and outrage"; but Pembroke, who will listen to nothing, declares: " . . . when we meet again, may swift destruction / Rid me of thee, or rid me of myself." Whereupon Pembroke leaves; and Guilford, having lost a friend and made an enemy—all for love—is left alone.

By Act III the situation of the play has been so well established that the themes of church and state may be seriously considered in the context of the action and in the plans made by Northumberland, the Suffolks, and Guilford. Gardiner, the priest of Rome, has long been held prisoner; and Pembroke has just arrived in the Tower, placed there by Northumberland, now head of the Protestant faction. Gardiner's first speech shows his cunning awareness of both the political situation and Pembroke's personal disappointment. Warning Pembroke "to be master of yourself," he reveals that he has learned "yester

ev'ning late, / In spite of all the grief for Edward's death, / Your friends were married.". . . [Gardiner] has still more information; perhaps Pembroke may yet possess the Lady Jane. If the rebellion mounted by Northumberland, Suffolk, and Guilford is thwarted, perhaps Guilford will be slain in the conflict. Pembroke cannot believe in such an eventuality; but he agrees, for his "sweet revenge," to aid in Gardiner's plan to support the Princess Mary.

The scene between Pembroke and Gardiner in the Tower is followed by one between the new-made bride and groom who also talk of love and loyalty. Still lamenting Edward's loss, still concerned with death, Lady Jane feels somehow that grief awaits them at every turn. It is only at this point that she realizes the plan that her husband and her father have made. . . . The whole vast scheme is now fully revealed to Lady Jane; but, before she fully comprehends her position, the lords from the Council enter to hail her as queen of England. They kneel to her in spite of her protestations. When she turns to Guilford and asks him, "Come to my aid, and help to bear this burden / Oh! save me from this sorrow, this misfortune, / Which in the shape of gorgeous greatness comes / To crown, and make a wretch of me forever," he, like the other lords, pledges his sword to her support.

Again the action of the play is suspended and each person speaks in turn of man, of his place in the universal scheme of God, of his duties to his own society, and finally of his relationship to his rulers—his king upon this earth and his supreme ruler, God. All the sentiments of the speeches are commonplaces of eighteenth-century thought, but they gain added interest as such for the critic who sees them interwoven into the dramatic fabric of Rowe's play. They gain, moreover, as the critic realizes that Rowe has united the climax of the action and the complexities of the interwoven themes of the play. Church, state, and private destinies are united.

Lady Jane herself sees the responsibilities of the throne, "to watch, to toil, to take a sacred charge, / To bend each day before high Heav'n." Her mother offers tribute to the English monarchs of the past "who liv'd not for themselves." Suffolk paints a lurid and dramatic picture of what will happen if Rome's Mary should be triumphant. Towns and churches will burn, "Our youth on racks shall stretch their crackling bones," and the land will be filled with "a continu'd peal / Of lamentations, groans, and shrieks." Guilford makes his plea for the liberty of his land and his people. In the final line of the scene—the final line of Act III—Lady Jane, though she knows her doom is inevitable, agrees to do what she can "To save this land from tyranny and *Rome*." (pp. 124-29)

But Lady Jane's acceptance does not close the discussion; the views of the others must be presented. The beginning of the fourth act continues the scene of the preceding one, but the actors are changed. Instead of Lady Jane Gray and her sponsors, Pembroke and Gardiner discuss their view of the situation. Gardiner characterizes Northumberland as "that traitor Duke," and he prays to "holy Becket, the protector / The Champion, and the martyr of our Church" to appear "And cover foul rebellion with confusion." Pembroke has seen Northumberland, armed for battle, issue from the city gate and pass in eerie silence through "a staring ghastly-looking crowd / Unhail'd unbless'd. . . ." Gardiner is certain that Mary and her cause will prevail; but, before the triumph of the Catholic Queen Mary and her Roman priest, Gardiner, the fate of Lady Jane and her Guilford must be played out; and the themes of friendship and love must be finished.

At this point in the action, Guilford comes to rescue Pembroke from his confinement in the Tower. Pembroke is caught between his sworn allegiance to Mary and Guilford's generous action; and where his loyalty lies becomes a nice question—one that again reveals Rowe's use of the traditions of the Renaissance view of such a friendship, a tradition that sees friendship as permanent and binding as love between father and son or between man and woman. Persuaded that Guilford speaks as friend, Pembroke agrees to take his sword and escape; and he declares to Guilford as he does so that all there is of good or excellence in man may be found in the bond of friendship. With this evidence of friendship, the theme is complete; but, when Pembroke offers Guilford and Lady Jane their freedom later in the closing drama of their doom, his friendship is not enough to save them. Pembroke's loyalty to Mary cancelled the loyalty of friendship. The Roman Catholic Church offers mercy only to those who will accept its tenets—the mercy of friendship is not enough to pardon Guilford and Lady Jane.

In developing Lady Jane as a saint and as a martyr, Rowe has simply extended the traditional virtues of the historical Lady Jane. In Act IV, he shows her reading Plato's *Phaedo*. When Guilford tells her that their cause is lost, she reminds him that now is the time "to bid our souls look out." And as saint and martyr, she must be sacrificed without guilt. Perhaps her very guiltlessness, required to complete Rowe's scheme, makes us admire her but not love her.

In the end, their doom comes quickly; Northumberland is taken prisoner, charged with treason; Mary, hailed queen; the Tower taken by her supporters; and Gardiner released. Lady Jane's premonitions begin to be reality. For her, "The gaudy masque, tedious, and nothing meaning, / Is vanish'd all at once," and she kneels in "humble adoration of that mercy" that has saved her from "the vast unequal task." In the last moments before they are parted, Guilford and Lady Jane speak together. Again, as in the earlier parts of the play, they converse in dialogue that is a duet; for each extends and harmonizes the thoughts of the other. And again there is the recital of love and death.

This scene, however, is very much in the manner of pathos—indeed, of sentimentality. Guilford marvels at Lady Jane's cool courage as she faces certain death; she who has wept before has now no tears. Her last two speeches return to the more universal sentiments of Rowe and his audience. She speaks of the "great Creator's never-ceasing hand" and of the even pattern of the cycle of life and death in God's great Providence. . . . (pp. 129-31)

Rowe's invention of the incident of Pembroke's appearance in the final act is a nice touch that serves to add intensity to the pathos of Lady Jane and Guilford's fate. Pembroke has a conditional pardon from Queen Mary, and it is his means of repaying Guilford's magnanimity to him when his life, like Guilford's now, was in danger. (p. 131)

But Gardiner will have no mercy extended to the two royal prisoners. He gives the justification for his views when he defends his judgment that they must be executed for Queen Mary's sake and, even more, for the position of the Roman Catholic Church. Pembroke argues that the church—the Church Universal—offers love and mercy for all when he says "Is not the sacred purpose of our faith / Peace and good-will to man? The hallow'd hand, / Ordain'd to bless, should know no stain of blood.". . . [This] scene must have held interest for Rowe and his audience, however dated it may seem to us.

Having shown Lady Jane as blameless, Rowe must now show her to be a saint. The last two scenes in the play are "set" scenes—pictures without action. The directions for the first of these are significant: "The SCENE draws, and discovers the Lady Jane kneeling, as at her devotion; a light, and a book plac'd on a table before her." In *Jane Shore,* there is no such tableau; indeed, Jane's procession of public penance is related by Bellmour; and, effective as his recital is, it cannot be a substitute for the experience of personal observation. Jane, who kneels in prayer, is dressed in her black robes and has the open Bible before her—quite an effective bit of staging. This portrayal is reinforced by her maid's report that Jane had risen before midnight, dressed herself, knelt, and "fix'd her eye upon the sacred page before her, / Or lifted with her rising hopes to Heav'n." The maid's report is followed by Guilford's even more impassioned words as he sees her already as a saint and as a martyr.

Moreover, as Lady Jane comes forward toward Guilford and the maid, she makes a difficult transition to the real world, saying to Guilford, "Wherefore dost thou come . . . I meant to part without another pang, / And lay my weary head down full of peace." Rowe's task of reintroducing and keeping alive the love elements of this scene is a difficult one. Guilford himself must carry most of the sentiments, for Lady Jane is so completely the saint, has already become so absorbed with death, that she has litle to say of love.

Pembroke arrives dramatically at this point, and the action of the plot is revived for a brief moment. Pembroke offers his pardons, and he and Guilford are reunited. Both Lady Jane and Guilford are saints; he prays that the new queen be blest, for she has spared his wife. Gardiner has had his will, for he returns from the queen to demand of Lady Jane and Guilford that they "Do instantly renounce, abjure your heresy, / And yield obedience to the See of *Rome*." Pembroke refuses to believe the queen to be so merciless, and both Lady Jane and Guilford refuse to disavow their faith. When Gardiner says "Death, or the mass, attend you," Guilford simply says, "'Tis determin'd: / Lead to the scaffold." Guilford is led off by the guards.

Again in a set scene Rowe shows, a scaffold hung with black, with executioners and guards silently waiting. In the face of her executioners Gardiner once more asks Lady Jane to "repent, be wise, and save your precious life," but she again refuses. . . . Lady Jane climbs the scaffold, and the scene closes. Two characters remain on the stage, Gardiner and Pembroke; and Rowe's final message is Pembroke's conclusion to Gardiner—a conclusion worthy of the eighteenth-century compromise:

> . . . Who gave thee to explore
> The secret purposes of Heaven, or taught thee
> To set a bound to mercy unconfin'd?
> But know, thou proud, perversely-judging *Winchester*,
> Howev'r you hard, imperious censures doom,
> And portion out our lot in worlds too come,
> Those, who, with honest hearts, pursue the right,
> And follow faithfully truth's sacred light,
> Tho' suff'ring here, shall from their sorrows cease,
> Rest with the saints, and dwell in endless peace.
>
> (pp. 132-34)

Lady Jane Gray was Rowe's last play. Along with *The Fair Penitent* and *Jane Shore,* it exemplifies the "she-tragedy" that Rowe promoted. He was not the first to explore the pathos of the beautiful woman in adversity and certainly not the only one in his time. Thomas Heywood's *A Woman Killed with Kindness* evokes quite as much pity as *Jane Shore;* Thomas Otway's *The Orphan,* as *Lady Jane Gray.* Like Calista, Belvederia in Otway's *Venice Preserved* is an ambiguous figure, a woman not wholly good—certainly not wholly bad. In fact, all three of Rowe's "she-tragedies" share the interests of other plays familiar to his audience; but the combinations he made in them; the three principal characters he created—Calista, Jane Shore, and Lady Jane Gray; and his sense of the elegance in drama—the formal speech, music, the set scene—that was the vogue of his own first two decades of the eighteenth century— these characteristics make his plays important beyond any single unique contribution he might have made to the history of the drama. In this context, Lady Jane Gray is the ideal; she had, or was given, all the worthwhile things of this world— beauty, love, power. But, faced with death because of her loyalty to church and country, she made the right choices and assumed the proper eighteenth-century attitudes and sentiments. (p. 137)

> *Annibel Jenkins, in her* Nicholas Rowe, *Twayne Publishers, 1977, 167 p.*

J. DOUGLAS CANFIELD (essay date 1977)

[*Canfield is an American educator, author, and scholar of Restoration drama. The following excerpt is taken from his study of all Rowe's tragedies, in which he claims that the plays ultimately "assert eternal Providence." Here, he applies this theory to* The Royal Convert.]

[In *The Royal Convert*] Rowe concentrates on the theme of Christian martyrdom as the extreme trial of the innocent—as the trial of the saint. (p. 77)

As in *Tamerlane,* the motif of *peace* pervades *The Royal Convert* and thus provides an approach to the meaning of the play. Although King Hengist of Kent and the Saxon Princess Rodogune are betrothed as a pledge of alliance among the Saxons against the Britons, each is secretly in love with someone else: he with the British Princess Ethelinda, whom he has kidnapped but who is secretly married to his younger brother Aribert; and she with Aribert himself. Both Hengist and Rodogune lose their *peace of mind* in pursuit of their uncontrollable—and, they discover to their dismay, illicit—desires. As a consequence even the peace of the country is threatened, in the destruction of the alliance and the strife among the Saxons which ensue. Aribert and Ethelinda, on the other hand, despite the shattering of their bridal peace by these raging intruders, find *peace of mind* in their reliance on "The great o'er ruling author of our beings," and they are rewarded for their constancy with a peace on earth in which their ascendance to the throne signifies the crowning of virtue.

Hengist, whose "nature" is described as "warm," "fierce," and "prone to sudden passions," is "curst within" by his lust for Ethelinda . . . and, despite the fact he is a king, lacks "that peace / Which ev'ry slave enjoys." For he must marry Rodogune or endanger his country's peace. . . . And yet to marry Rodogune and lose Ethelinda would be "to reign in hell" and "never know one hour of peace again." Thus, the "medley war within" and "sickness of soul" which he suffers involve a conflict between his private passion and his public responsibility as king, a responsibility that requires him to be the "common victim of the state" and the "nursing father" of his people. Hengist and his cunning minister Seofrid devise a stratagem to save the alliance: Prince Aribert will marry Rodogune

and will become the "pledge of peace." Yet ironically, he to whom Hengist turns for peace becomes the cause of his complete frustration, for Ethelinda turns out to be Aribert's secret bride. Ostensibly because Aribert has broken a solemn childhood vow never to become or to marry a Christian, but really because of jealous rage, Hengist sentences him to death. Hengist's language evinces his lack of peace as he bids "ten thousand thousand horrors" come, for they "fit the present fury" of his "soul.". . . (pp. 79-80)

The subsequent identification of his "inborn tempest" with an external tempest suggests the far-reaching ramifications of Hengist's rage. As the King's soul is disordered, so is his kingdom: at this very moment Rodogune begins to plot the rescue of Aribert and the overthrow of Hengist by her brother and his band of Saxons, and Aribert's faithful lieutenant Oswald escapes to the Britons to enlist their aid in rescuing his master. Furthermore, nature itself seems really headed toward a "general wreck." The restraining bond of "nature" between brothers is overcome as Hengist prepares to carry out his sentence. When he learns that Ethelinda's destination is the Briton's camp, he threatens to "shake / The Island to the centre" to get her back. Nor does the breach of nature stop there. When Hengist demands again the return of Ethelinda, Aribert reproaches him in terms common to Western, and particularly Christian, tragedy:

> Rage, and the violence of lawless passion,
> Have blinded your clear reason; wherefore else
> This frantic wild demand! What! should I yield,
> Give up my love, my wife, my *Ethelinda,*
> To an incestuous brother's dire embrace?

But Hengist contemptuously boasts that he is not awed "with that fantom, incest," "Lawless passion" has perverted reason and nature, and only the arrival of Rodogune and the Saxons frustrates his evil designs.

Since the gods thus refuse him "their better blessings," the defeated King disdains the "worthless crown" he has lost and determines to "rest in sullen peace." The key word "sullen" connotes both apathy and despair and indicates no real peace of mind at all. And when Seofrid in desperation informs him that Ethelinda is to be killed by Rodogune, Hengist's "medley" of warring passions returns. Instead of securing the throne as Seofrid had intended, however, Hengist purposes to let "fighting fools contend in vain" for empire, while he escapes to his castle, where, contemning "idle rules," he will "riot" in incestuous lust with Ethelinda. Ironically, with Seofrid crying, "What know'st thou not the King?", a soldier deals Hengist his mortal wound as he comes in pursuit of his designs. Thus this King who has rejected his public responsibility is himself the victim of the ensuing anarchy. Furthermore, though he does not succeed in his incestuous intent, he rejects the admonition of the "fair teacher" Ethelinda to repent and to "deprecate the wrath divine," concluding, "The Gods and I have done with one another." Remaining to the end "fierce, untam'd, disdainful," he curses the gods and his brother and dies. The implication is that he goes to suffer more than just an internal hell. Such is the reward—"gnashing fiends beneath, and pains eternal"—clearly promised in the play for "man's injustice" and unbounded "passions."

Despite her haughty pride, Rodogune also loses her peace of mind in her passion for Aribert. Her hopes in him of both love and empire are "blasted" by his sudden declaration of his marriage, and "ten thousand racking passions" are released to plague her. Yet she approaches Aribert in his prison to offer him freedom, empire, and herself, for despite his marriage, she can find no rest without him. Expecting to find him similarly distraught at the thought of death, however, she finds him instead patiently resolved, with a "face of triumph, not of mourning." "Has death so little in it?" she asks, utterly piqued. For she cannot comprehend the martyr's resolution. Most of all, she cannot brook his refusal of her offer. The fury of a woman scorned breaks out in storm imagery that recalls Hengist's passion and the threat of internal and external chaos. . . . She surrenders herself to the passion of "revenge" and vows to make Ethelinda the "victim" of her "offended love." (pp. 81-2)

Nevertheless, when she returns to rescue Aribert from Hengist, Rodogune seems to have conquered her passions momentarily and to act with genuine magnanimity, for, "No matter what ensues," she breaks Aribert's "bonds" and bids him forget her and "Fly far away," presumably to Ethelinda. When the recaptured Ethelinda appears in the same room and rushes into Aribert's arms, however, Rodogune's jealous rage explodes, and she exclaims, "Hence, bear her hence. / My peace is lost for ever—but she dies." Rodogune bitterly grants Aribert's wish to die with her and vows to "tear" him from her "remembrance" and "be at ease for ever." But she is unable to free herself from her passion, and as she comes to put them to death, she must struggle to put her heart "at peace." Finally, she is denied the "sullen pleasure" of her rage—one is reminded of the "sullen peace" Hengist seeks—by the arrival of Hengist and the Britons. Though she considers it "vain to rave and curse" her "fortune," she spitefully does curse the race of man and impotently prays that "woman" be allowed to

> Subdue mankind beneath her haughty scorn,
> And smile to see the proud oppressor mourn.

But in so cursing Aribert she rejects his offer of mercy (which itself belies her judgment of man as "proud oppressor") and dooms herself to the total loss of peace concomitant to despair.

Contrasted to the madness of uncontrolled passion which consumes Hengist and Rodogune is the inner peace attained by Aribert and Ethelinda, despite their loss of bridal peace and happiness. In the opening scene of the play Aribert describes to Oswald the joys of his and Ethelinda's love, joys comparable to *"Elysium"* or "the first Paradise, / When nature was not yet deform'd by winter." But their paradise is doomed from the start not to last in a fallen world, a world that *is* "deform'd by winter." Ethelinda has already described to Aribert the Christian vision of the human condition:

> I heard her with an eloquence divine,
> Reason of holy and mysterious truths;
> Of Heav'n's most righteous doom, of man's injustice;
> Of laws to curb the will, and blind the passions;
> Of life, of death, and immortality;
> Of gnashing fiends beneath, and pains eternal;
> Of starry thrones, and endless joys above.

The passage is not just a gratuitous review of Christian doctrine, for its relevance to the entire play is obvious merely from the injustice and unbounded passion we have already observed. Aribert is soon to learn that, given such a world, the only "endless joys" are those "above."

When Hengist asks him to share half the burden of his sorrow, Aribert unhesitatingly offers to bear "all" of it and to be "greatly tried." With Hengist's request that he marry Rodogune, however, Aribert has only begun to be "tried," and yet

he precipitately concludes that he is "lost for ever." Cursing the "Fantastic cruelty of hoodwink'd chance," he yearns for the comfort of his Ethelinda, "that dear one, / That gently us'd to breathe the sounds of peace" on his "tempestuous soul." Ironically, at that moment Seofrid drags in Hengist's captive, Ethelinda herself. The amazed Aribert rashly suggests that they should "resolve to die together" to "Defy the malice" of their "fate" and "preserve the sacred bond" of their marriage "inviolable.". . . He goes into a "rash" and "frantic rage," desperately trying to buy a respite with Seofrid's murder.

Ethelinda's response to her plight is in sharp contrast to Aribert's. As he had offered to bear all of Hengist's sorrow, so she asks to suffer all manner of pains, except the "pollution" of incest. . . . Unlike Aribert, however, Ethelinda does not forget in the first moment of trial this faith and resolution of the martyr. Nor does she, like Aribert, blame her condition on "hoodwink'd chance" or the "malice" of "cruel fate," nor conclude that the "malice" of hell is "more potent" than Heaven. Instead she calls on "gracious Heaven," which till now has defended her chastity, to guard her from hell and "its blackest crime." When Aribert is about to kill Seofrid for their momentary safeties, Ethelinda beseeches him. "Trust 'em to Heaven." Ethelinda is an example, then, not only to the audience (like other saints in martyrologies, in miracle and martyr plays), but also to her *royal convert*. She is an "angel" who instructs him in the "way to everlasting happiness," and the focus of the play is on the development of his trust in Providence. Now in Act II, Ethelinda brings peace to the distracted, doubting soul of Aribert, as she introduces the theodicean argument of the play. She has a vision of angels who "succour truth and innocence below."

> Hell trembles at the sight, and hides its head
> In utmost darkness, while on earth each heart,
> Like mine, is fill'd with peace and joy unutterable.

Such inner peace, what Milton calls a "paradise within," is the result of "hope and never-failing faith" in the "holy pow'r." It enables the Christian to "triumph o'er the world," despite his temporary paradise lost. Aribert is "touch'd with the sacred theme" and sees himself a vision of "the guardian-angels of the good," who "pity what we suffer here below" and make the saintly Ethelinda (and himself) "their common care."

The rest of the play shows Aribert vacillating between trust and distrust in Providence. Finally, condemned to die with Ethelinda for both his love and his faith, very much like Milton's Adam, he plaintively asks if Heaven has "decreed" that "none shall pass the golden gates above, / But those who sorrow here" to purge their "inborn stains away." Ethelinda's theodicean answer combines the traditional metaphor of trial with the traditional concept of the Happy Death. . . . (pp. 82-5)

Aribert still complains. He has not asked for the blessed life but only for "life and *Ethelinda*." Yet, "Heav'n thought that too much," he murmurs. Ethelinda also sorely feels the loss of that much happiness: she has admitted that Aribert's image "intercepts" her "journey to the stars." Yet she answers that since they have been denied their paradise on earth, they should seek

> That wond'rous bliss which Heav'n reserves in store,
> Well to reward us for our losses here;
> That bliss which Heav'n and only Heav'n can give.

That promised bliss—and the inner peace of those who patiently expect it—is immediately juxtaposed to Rodogune's suffering ("still I am doom'd to suffer"), as it has all along been contrasted to the general lack of peace in the world. . . . But now, since Rowe is never content to allow his protagonists the simple trial of merely dying, Aribert is submitted to the severest trial of all. He must watch Ethelinda die first: "And can my eyes endure it!" To Rodogune, then to the "saints and angels," Aribert pleads for Ethelinda, seemingly in vain. In contrast, as she meets her trial "arm'd and equal to the combat" like the true Christian hero, the constant Ethelinda would give Aribert the final lesson of example and "lead" him on "in the triumphant way." . . . In the midst of this triumph of the martyr, Aribert and Ethelinda are saved, strangely enough, by the arrival of the brother who has come bent on their destruction but whose ironic death leaves them King and Queen of Kent and victors over Rodogune and her rebelling Saxons. Thus the play ends in perfect poetic justice, and every indication is that such justice is the work of Providence. The crowning of Aribert and Ethelinda seems a reward for constancy in their trial, and Aribert attributes their final peace on earth to Heaven's influence. . . . The punishment of the wicked, too, implies the Hand of Heaven, for it is remarkably appropriate. Seofrid, who to save his master would sacrifice Aribert, loses his master in rescuing Aribert. Hengist is killed in the pursuit of hell's "blackest crime" (a circumstance considered by the theologians to be an instance of particular Providence), and the chaos he has caused consumes him. In her extreme pride and passion, Rodogune has attempted to take vengeance into her own hands: "The Gods are just at length," she exults to Aribert and Ethelinda as she prepares to murder them, and she appears to be ironically right, for justice is ultimately served and her jealous rage thwarted. All her hopes of love and empire are destroyed as she sullenly banishes herself from the race of man.

Moreover, the play has all along asked Rowe's primary question, whether the gods care. Ethelinda has insisted throughout that they do, but even Aribert at first blames either "hoodwink'd chance" or the "malice" of fate for his loss of paradisal peace. On the other hand, Seofrid at first appears to believe in Providence, for he tells Aribert and Ethelinda, "Whatever Gods there be, their care you are," and he asserts that "the ruling Gods are over all, / And order as they please their world below." When Hengist's intention to rape Ethelinda destroys Seofrid's plan for him to regain the throne, however, Seofrid (like Mirza, Bajazet, and Eurymachus before him) declares the "restless racking care" of statesmen "in vain" and swears allegiance to the "Blind goddess chance.". . . . Rodogune doubts whether there are really gods "who rule o'er love and jealousy," and she blames whatever gods there are for dealing so "unjustly with their creatures" as to deny them pleasures and make them suffer. She seems to see the gods as merely vengeful and otherwise scornful "of the world below," and her final prayer to the "partial goddess" Nature that woman be allowed to "Subdue mankind beneath her haughty scorn" is an indication that she thinks the deities as perverse and spiteful as she. Hengist also sees the Saxon gods as vengeful: he offers Aribert as "a royal victim" to "glut the vengeance of our angry Gods." Furthermore, in Epicurean fashion (which is the pervading fashion of all these comments), he blames "the meddling hand of chance" for causing the chaos in which he finds himself. . . . (pp. 86-8)

But Ethelinda's faith in the "great o'er ruling author of our beings," who "Deals with his creature man in various ways, / Gracious and good in all," is vindicated. Hengist says in Act II that "or love, / Or some divinity, more strong than love, / Forbids my bliss." He appears to be right, for in the next moment Ethelinda maintains that "gracious Heaven" has de-

fended her up to that point from the "pollution" which Hengist's "bliss" would entail. The implication is that "Heaven" continues to defend her throughout the play. Aribert has speculated that "the ruling hand of Heaven," working "thus unseen by second causes," has ordained Seofrid "for its instrument of good," and despite his machinations and his final allegiance to the "Blind goddess chance," Seofrid does appear to have been Heaven's instrument, for it is he who provokes Hengist to rescue Aribert and Ethelinda from Rodogune. Though the outcome is counter to Seofrid's and Hengist's separate designs, it appears to evince the design of Providence.

And so we must conclude, I think, that "the ruling hand of Heaven *is* in it" and "at length *is* gracious" to its faithful (italics mine). Their virtue literally crowned, Aribert and Ethelinda become the monarchs of a new "*Britain*" which "takes its pledge of peace" from their union of Saxon and Briton. "Nor are those pious hopes of peace in vain," prophesies Ethelinda, for that "pledge" will be fulfilled when again "Auspicious Heav'n" shall "smile" and "bless" the "*British* Isle" of Rowe's Queen Anne with the "eternal UNION" of the Union Act of 1707. The inner peace of Aribert and Ethelinda's Christian faith, then, has received an external manifestation in the peace of the land, a manifestation that is emblematic of the ultimate reward of Providence for those who, with the peace of mind of the saint and resolution of the martyr, trust in Its care. Thus the play has portrayed not only "patterns of piety" in the trusting royal couple but also "things celestial" in the care of that Providence, the metaphysical reality which corresponds to their faith. (p. 88)

> *J. Douglas Canfield, in his* Nicholas Rowe and Christian Tragedy, *The University Presses of Florida, 1977, 212 p.*

DEREK COHEN (essay date 1979)

[*In the following excerpt, Cohen compares* The Biter *with Aphra Behn's farce* The Emperor of the Moon (1687).]

It is not widely known that Nicholas Rowe, by some accounts the best tragedian of the eighteenth century, made a sally into the realm of comedy. The incursion was brief and tentative and its result was insufficient to encourage the dramatist to try his hand in the field again. And yet, judged by the comedies of his immediate contemporaries and by its relatively respectable six-day run, [*The Biter*] cannot be regarded as a complete failure. This is not to say that it was a genuine success or that it stands as an unacknowledged masterpiece. Yet the play has merit; certainly it has historical interest. (p. 383)

Sir Timothy Tallapoy is the only well-known character in the play. By no means an inspired or original creation he is, nevertheless, the one character capable of providing a sustained, if shallow, pleasure to an audience. The callous way in which he is treated by the protagonists suggests that Rowe conceived him as hateful as well as humorous. But he is not hateful and does not deserve the wretched humiliation to which he is finally subjected. His humiliation and that of Lady Stale are the worst aspects of *The Biter*. The young people are gratuitously cruel to the older characters who, because so easily manipulated, never really threaten their happiness. The reason for this fault in the play is not far to seek. Rowe has contented himself with wholly second-rate characterization. Clearly, to make the gulling a cause for audience rejoicing—which he seems to have had in mind—Rowe should have made the protagonists more sympathetic and interesting. He should also have made their antagonists more menacing and powerful. Instead, however, his young lovers are boring pretenders to fashion while their opponents are half-witted and basically harmless. The hideously trite first line of *The Biter* (*''Friendly* stays somewhat long, for so passionate a Person as he seems to be. This Laziness in Love looks as if Matrimony had gone before, and the best part of the Bus'ness had been over'') exemplifies the fatuous flatness of the young lovers. Rowe's way of showing that Clerimont is merely posturing and that he is a basically decent young man is to inform us of his recent freely chosen marriage to Mariana. It does not help. All of the young lovers are facetious, dull stereotypes and sympathy for them is impossible.

The Biter's best moments are those in which Sir Timothy and Pinch (the biter) ''engage.'' Otherwise it is conventional and unexciting. A far better and more satisfying farce is Aphra Behn's *The Emperor of the Moon*. This play, first produced with great success in 1687, continued to be performed throughout the eighteenth century, including at least one successful run during the pentad in which *The Biter* was performed. A comparison of the two plays explains why Rowe's play was never a success and demonstrates the influence of *The Emperor of the Moon* on *The Biter*.

The plots of the two farces have much in common. Like *The Biter, The Emperor of the Moon* centres upon the efforts of young lovers to marry in the face of parental and, in one instance, avuncular opposition. Doctor Baliardo stands in the way of the unions of his daughter and niece to Charmante and Cinthio. His opposition stems from a crackbrained infatuation with the society he believes to exist upon the moon and his ambition to marry the two girls to princes from that sphere. The young men, after much cunning and complicated preparation, get Baliardo to accept them as these princes and to bless their unions with his daughter and niece. This done, the disguises are thrown off and the doctor is forced to face reality. The shock of the recognition is salubrious and he is cured of his insanity.

Counterpointing the romantic aspirations of the young men are the farcical endeavours of their servants, Harlequin and Scaramouche, to win the hand of Mopsophil, governess to the young ladies. Because Mopsophil is of Baliardo's household, her admirers have difficulty meeting her. Most of the action of the play hinges upon the ingenuity of the lovers in overcoming the difficulty of meeting.

While the plot of *The Emperor of the Moon* is somewhat simpler than that of *The Biter,* it is more fantastic. It is designed to provide the basis for a number of scenes, actions, and pageants. Rowe was clearly influenced by Behn's farce and seems to have had her chief character in mind when he was creating Sir Timothy. Like Sir Timothy, Baliardo is obsessed with another society than the one in which he participates. Each regards his utopian society as vastly superior to English and ''Italian'' actuality, and close to perfection in wisdom, justice, order, and beauty.

The plots of the two plays differ in the worlds their authors portray. Rowe is strongly influenced by the comedies of manners and strives, in some measure, to recreate their world in his farce. This means that many of the values, standards, and assumptions about those comedies apply to *The Biter*. Rowe's plot is constructed like Restoration comedies with the heroes triumphant and the obstructing characters exposed and humiliated in the end. While Rowe dramatizes some accepted social conventions, Aphra Behn makes extravagant use of the fantastic and incredible. In other words, Rowe attempts to maintain some realism while Behn, with a better understanding of farce, permits wildness of fancy to reign in the zanier world of her play. She is not concerned with social conventions, as Rowe is, and in her play creates her own conventions and standards of behaviour.

By basing her plot on so preposterous a foundation as interplanetary social intercourse Behn opens the way to even wilder and more ridiculous action and activity. (pp. 387-89)

The Biter, on the other hand, is a naturalistic work and does not allow for fantastic occurrences. . . . Its world demands an adherence to the conditions of realism that any Restoration comedy demands. Moreover, Rowe's play, like most Restoration comedies, differentiates between plausibility and likelihood. It and they permit what is improbable in life to occur onstage so long as that improbablity is plausible—however remotely. It is unlikely, for example, that Sir Timothy would sign over his possessions to a man he has never met, but it is possible. In Behn's play the violation even of plausibility is a standard condition. Instead of balking at such impossible actions as the love-poem scene where Harlequin, under the table, pens appropriately rhyming responses to Charmante's lines without being detected, we delight in them. They are charming and funny and conform to the ludicrous circumstances that are commonplace in the world of this play.

Part of Rowe's intention is to satirize elements of his society. The conclusion to his play is an implicit condemnation of the marriage of convenience as the young lovers are shown to triumph over the mercenary ambitions of the older characters. In refusing to permit Angelica to marry Friendly, Sir Timothy is acting antisocially; he is obstructing the normal and proper evolution of society. Aphra Behn shows relative indifference to social questions in *The Emperor of the Moon*, dedicating herself wholly to the business of entertaining her audiences. In refusing permission to marry to the young lovers of that play Baliardo is acting in accordance with his lunatic imaginings, and society, in the larger sense, is irrelevant. At the end of *The Emperor of the Moon* there is a desirable and humane restoration of order as Baliardo is made to perceive his folly and to be grateful for the perception. This farce, which has pleased us through its cheerful and fanciful nonsense, ends cheerfully with a happy future for all clearly implied.

While the note of gaiety is sounded throughout *The Emperor of the Moon*, it is heard only occasionally in *The Biter*. Its tone, pace, and air of frolic and fun mark *The Emperor of the Moon* as a superior work. A major reason for this superiority is the makeup and the function of its characters. Behn, unlike Rowe, is not content to use her young lovers merely as ciphers representing ''right'' attitudes. She makes them lose dignity and participate vigorously in the action. They are not, like Rowe's young lovers, in complete and secure control of the situation. They do not, like Rowe's young lovers, look with detached amusement at the follies and mishaps of others, being themselves capable of follies and subjected to mishaps. They are of the play and are thrust, willy-nilly, into the heat of the action. They cannot escape it as Rowe's do, for it is their play. They are the catalysts of the action. Being desperately in love— something Rowe's young lovers never show signs of—the two young men are prepared to do almost anything, however embarrassing or silly, to be near the women of their hearts. When caught in difficult situations they have to demean themselves by acting ridiculously to avoid being caught. They do not, like

Rowe's protagonists, merely manipulate the action—they are involved in it. (pp. 389-91)

As Aphra Behn's young lovers are put to better use than Rowe's, so her farcical characters, Harlequin and Scaramouche, are superior to Rowe's farce characters who tend to rely on the merest devices for provoking laughter: Scribblescrable for example, is ridiculed for his incurable—and usually unfunny—stutter. The actions in which they are engaged are not merely ridiculous, but are ingenious, witty, and original. Harlequin, for example, thinking himself spurned by Mopsophil, hilariously attempts suicide by tickling himself to death.

Unlike any of Rowe's characters, Scaramouche has a real and ready wit which he puts to excellent use. . . . (p. 391)

Rowe is generally less adept than Behn and includes little ingenuity of dialogue, action, or complication. The scene in which Pinch confronts Sir Timothy, for example, leads too obviously to the moment when a beating becomes dramatically and logically necessary. Rowe's farce is less complex and, finally, less satisfying than Behn's. He fails to deal fully with the problems he tackles. He sees a satirical possibility in the provision of an alternative and better way of life—suggested by Sir Timothy's obsession—but he explores it too tepidly for it to be significant to the play. (p. 392)

It is obvious that one of the conditions of farce anticipated by the audience and deliberately included by the author is a great deal of nonsense. This fact explains one of the difficulties that farce offers the reader who has frequently to come to terms with nonsensical and apparently unrelated matter. *The Biter* and *The Emperor of the Moon* are replete with such matter. In *The Biter* the action bustles along at a fairly consistent pace until one is suddenly and illogically in the presence of a domestic squabble between the Scribblescrabbles which has little or nothing to do with the plot. The same idiosyncrasy is even truer of *The Emperor of the Moon* which relies heavily on extraneous actions for its effects.

This lack of unity gives farce a mosaic effect. It appears finally as a single unit containing many other units which are put together in an occasionally random and disconnected order. To arouse laughter the plot of *The Biter* employs the devices of incongruity, surprise, dramatic irony, mistaken identity, and sheer physical conflict. There is instant antagonism between the obstructing characters instead of the more usual and sinister collusion. There is a ludicrous pursuit of a hot old harridan after a young gallant. There is a drunk scene which relies on surprise, outrage, and physical frolicking for its humour: a nonsensical piece of action, it might, with skillful acting and a great deal of noise and bustle, produce a comical effect. The bruising and humiliation of *The Biter*'s fools is a source of some pleasure. Partly, no doubt, this kind of pleasure arises from the fact that in life fools and knaves do not receive the kinds of deserts their observers and victims wish upon them. Comedy's dream world, with its ubiquitous poetic justice, gives the audience the vicarious pleasure of seeing social oppressors and obstructors justly dealt with. (pp. 392-93)

It is likely that Rowe perceived the likeness of the world of farce to that of heroic tragedy. Both, in varying measure, retreat from reality. In heroic drama the retreat from the real world occurs through selectivity, through the unrealistic—even absurd—emphasizing of some aspects of reality, through touching it up and transforming it into a sort of dream world. The world of farce is one in which gross brutality and physical pain are at once asserted and negated. Real as its pain and violence

may be, by miraculous recoveries from injury and humiliation the audience is assured that they are not really real and accordingly is able to enjoy them. The character of Sir Timothy Tallapoy is perilously close to that of Rowe's tragic hero Tamerlane: it seems deliberately to burlesque the heroic bombast and purple pomp of the kind of tragedy which Rowe himself wrote. Sir Timothy assumes the attitude and demeanour of an oriental dictator. His dress, diction and behaviour are exaggerations of those of heroes like Tamerlane. His plane of existence is merely a comic exaggeration of that of heroic tragedy. We are dramatically reminded in the behaviour of characters like Sir Timothy how tragic virtues of stubbornness, obstinacy, and indifference to popular opinion become, in comedy, the most heinous of follies. That Rowe recognized the closeness of the two worlds is illustrated in his parody, in *The Biter,* of one of his own most famous tragic lines. The scene involves Scribblescrabble and Mrs. Clever who, upon seeing the lawyer's woeful face after he has been humiliated, exclaims, "Is it possible, the gay, the witty, the gallant Mr. Scribblescrabble?" She is echoing Calista who, on the threshold of a terrible death, cries out in anguish over her lover's corpse, "Is this that haughty, gallant, gay Lothario?"

In all of his drama Rowe preferred the relatively simple and the palpably theatrical. As a comic writer he attempted what was then regarded as the least complicated type. His farce reveals a penchant for the obvious and the unsubtle. He tried to elicit laughs from relatively ordinary theatrical tricks by the employment of dramatic and histrionic cliches. Sometimes he was successful, sometimes not. *The Biter* is in places simply juvenile. But it is equally true that in the tragedies—even the most successful—one is occasionally presented with as grave and pretentious nonsense as that of *The Biter.* One suspects that even amongst his admirers the nonsense was perceived but that out of respect for his merits it may have been ignored. For Rowe's merits as dramatist are many. He had an acute sense of the theatre, and usually he had tact. He understood clearly the mood and temper of the people for whom he was writing and how to tailor his plays for them. The emotionality of his tragedies and the hurly-burly of his farce were carefully contrived to suit popular taste. It is a matter of record that he was generally successful. (pp. 393-94)

Derek Cohen, "Nicholas Rowe, Aphra Behn, and the Farcical Muse," in Papers on Language and Literature, *Vol. 15, No. 4, Fall, 1979, pp. 383-95.*

JEAN H. HAGSTRUM (essay date 1980)

[*An American educator and author whose interests include psychology and eighteenth-century and Romantic literature, Hagstrum has written* The Sister Arts *(1958) and* William Blake: Poet-Painter *(1963). In the following excerpt, he discusses the implied moral and societal values of* The Fair Penitent *as they are expressed through the character of Calista.*]

[Rowe's *Fair Penitent*] carried forward into Augustan England the pathos and perhaps also the morbidity of Otway's domestic drama, which influenced it; its Lothario is partly responsible for that magnificent creation, Richardson's Lovelace; and it possesses a few moments pregnant with anticipation of important things to come. Those moments spring from the fine rebelliousness of the title character and the poetically realized pagan mood and Gothic gloom that are made the objective correlative of the heroine's grief at the end.

We begin with the Gothic conclusion. *The Fair Penitent* uses as its epigraph a sentence from Dido's lonely night-time lament to herself, in which she decides on suicide: "Quin morere, ut merita es, ferroque averte dolorem" ["Why not die as you deserve and end your pain with a sword?"]. In deciding to die by her own hand, Dido chooses a way open to a queen and a pagan but . . . not to a Catholic religious. Why does Rowe make suicide the fate of his Italian Calista, the heroine of an English drama whose chief aim was to excite pity in a "melancholy tale of private woes"? [see excerpt dated 1703]. Calista is unhappy partly because she has been unvirtuous but also because, no less than Dido . . . , she is a woman abandoned, even though married and in the midst of society. In fact, marriage means for her primarily separation from the man who ravished her and whom she continues to love even after union with another and worthier man. Marriage, forced on her by her father, makes of her a lonely sufferer with only the recollection of passion and places her in the company of heroines high in state and church, like Dido. . . . The fact that . . . she appears in a literary form requiring a catastropic end denies her the opportunity of dwelling on her passion, whose persistence makes of her a spiritual adulteress. She herself feels deeply stained with an "inbred, deep pollution." The only solution is death, a death her father seems to suggest to her when he calls on her to repossess the ancient Roman spirit.

THE

FAIR PENITENT.

A

TRAGEDY.

As it is Acted at the

NEW THEATRE

IN

Little Lincolns-Inn-Fields.

By Her MAJESTY's SERVANTS.

Written by *N. ROWE*, Efq;

Quin morere, ut merita es, ferroque averte dolorem.
Virg. Æn. Lib. 4.

LONDON,

Printed for *Jacob Tonfon*, within *Grays-Inn Gate* next *Grays-Inn Lane*. 1703.

Title page of the work Rowe called "a melancholy Tale of private Woes."

When his mortal wound in a Genoese fray over the dead body of Lothario is reported to his daughter, she feels even more polluted than before, since she regards herself as the cause. . . . She then stabs herself, but not before her father comes in to forgive her and die.

The most noteworthy aspect of the suicide of the heroine is the ambiguity that attends the state of her soul, which does seem to be at peace as she gazes at her good though unexciting husband. But does she deserve to seem at peace either for the present or the future? Johnson complained that she "shows no evident signs of repentance" and that she "expresses more shame than sorrow, and more rage than shame" [see excerpt dated 1781]. Cibber said she should be called "the Fair Wanton," and Belford in *Clarissa* says that she is "a desiring luscious wench, and her penitence is nothing else but rage, insolence, and scorn" [see excerpt dated 1747-48]. Richardson's reformed rake exaggerates, and though he is right in observing a lack of repentance, we must remember that a truly Christian submission would have aborted suicide. The point I am making is that, though Christian values are present in the play, they are dramatically less powerful than other forces, and that what Calista feels very strongly is not the pull of heavenly bliss but the morbid attraction of death itself. . . . Here death is associated with an illicit passion that marriage does not terminate, a fact that makes its cold embrace doubly welcome. Even the good husband, Altamont, seeing that the heroine is bent on death, joins her in her wish for mortality. Such emotions in act 5 make the Gothic gloom of act 4 anything but gratuitous; these moments are more significant than the conventional and superficial gestures toward distributive justice that disposes of the illicit lovers. The compelling, substructural movement of the play is toward death, not toward justice. Sciolto tries to kill his daughter but is restrained by her husband, who himself longs for death and oblivion. Calista, in a charnel house with the corpse of her lover, Lothario, his deadly wounds displayed, throws aside the book of meditation and pious reform. She is dressed in black, and her hair hangs loose and disordered. The songs being sung are as Gothic as the ambience, with its damp horrors that freeze the blood; they tell stories of midnight phantoms and a fair maiden's imminent death. There is no priest, no confession; only a father who enters with a dagger, which he himself cannot use against her but which he leaves for her. It is all most melancholy—and musical, for Rowe, as has been widely recognized, is a master of sweetly harmonious verse and gentle poetical coloring. In these Gothic scenes he has given us an example of love turning toward death in a society that is beginning to lack the judging and classifying hierarchies of Milton and Dryden and beginning to luxuriate in the morbidities of the tender Otway without very many institutional restraints.

The Gothic ending comes after an even more effective episode in the play, the unrestrained and memorable rebelliousness of Calista. This transcends the somewhat conventional unconventionality of the gay Lothario, providing welcome relief from the cloying, though consciously approved, meekness and pity of Horatio and Lavinia. Horatio, a friend of the bridegroom Altamont, is married to Lavinia, and the married pair is regarded by the heroine's father as his own children. It is Horatio who declares the joys of virtue and who points to his loyal and passive wife as a contrast to the proud and sinful Calista:

Then—to be good is to be happy. Angels
Are happier than mankind, because they are better.
Guilt is the source of sorrow; 'tis the fiend,

The avenging fiend, that follows us behind
With whips and stings; the blest know none of this,
But rest in everlasting peace of mind,
And find the height of all their heav'n is goodness. . . .

Contrast such sentiments with those of Calista, who says,

How hard is the condition of our sex,
Through ev'ry state of life the slaves of man!
In all the dear, delightful days of youth
A rigid father dictates to our wills,
And deals out pleasure with a scanty hand;
To his, the tyrant husband's reign succeeds;
Proud with opinion of superior reason,
He holds domestic business and devotion
All we are capable to know, and shuts us,
Like cloistered idiots, from the world's acquaintance
And all the joys of freedom; wherefore are we
Born with high souls but to assert ourselves,
Shake off this vile obedience they exact,
And claim an equal empire o'er the world?

Her use of the phrase "high souls" throws the mind back to the heroic drama and reminds us of the newer tendencies to locate heroism in a domestic scene, close to the business and bosoms of men. Calista's fine speech rings in our ears, especially after Rowe bows his neck to the yoke of conventional rules and rigors. One suspects that he distrusts them; at least he cannot make his bold and attractive heroine bend to them too easily. He transforms frustrated will into the death wish, which is better than meek submissiveness. It is difficult for a modern to deny that Calista at her moment of fine, perceptive rebelliousness breathes a more attractive spirit than Horatio, who preaches an angelic and sexless kind of postmortem joy. Calista, for all her waywardness, seems somehow closer to the kind of fulfillment that Spenser and Milton sang than does the bland Horatio.

It is difficult to say whether the playwright was aware of what I have called the deep structure and the unconscious values of the play—the welling up of personal rebellion in woman whom society forces into a movement toward death. Almost to the very end the doomed heroine appears to blame her guilt on the fact that she "loved, and was a woman." The reader must surely be chilled by her father's response: "Hadst thou been honest, thou hadst been a cherubin." The fact that many perceptive critics have noted the lack of clear moral value in the play has encouraged us to discover in the strength of the sinners and the weakness of the good some kind of symbolic value. The absence of Christian order presages century-long developments that will substitute instinct for institutions, emotion for conscience and creed. The fear of sexuality by the good and its embrace by the bad, who are given moments of power and persuasiveness, seem to comment on the potential loss of morally directed energy in modern man. It is noteworthy that the good husband anticipates the Man of Feeling and at the same time is weak, timid, listless, possessed of a death wish and called at the very end "a drooping flower." Can it be that the skillul Rowe, so often regarded as merely soothing, tender, and complacent, was more prophetic than he knew and penetrated more deeply into some of the effects of sensibility than we have realized? Did one whose melodious and traditional verse and whose historical plots recalled the golden age of English drama sense a reduction of sensual and imaginative power in modern man? He certainly had no full vision of the withering of the heroic spirit that was to overtake Western culture; but we, from our later vantage point, can see that Prufrock and Lambert Strether are not totally unrelated to Altamont and Horatio. Ibsen's Nora can scarcely be said to grow

out of Calista's moment of proud identification with her oppressed sex. But Rowe has given us a glimpse of what a greater and freer spirit might have done with a female character determined to realize her identity in unconventional sexual behavior. (pp. 117-21)

Jean H. Hagstrum, "Woman in Love: The Abandoned and Passionate Mistress," in his Sex and Sensibility: Ideal and Erotic Love from Milton to Mozart, *The University of Chicago Press, 1980, pp. 100-32.*

JANET E. AIKINS   (essay date 1982)

[*In the following excerpt, Aikins explores* The Fair Penitent *and* Jane Shore *as "works of entrapment."*]

[**The Fair Penitent** and **The Tragedy of Jane Shore** are] best viewed as works of entrapment, for while they please their audiences, they do so in part by frustrating the usual expectations about plot progression in dramatic tragedy.

These plays differ from many others in that they do not offer us a morally determinate, causally connected sequence of events in which characters are responsible for what happens to them so that their external fates take on significance in connection with the judgments we make of the characters themselves. Instead, in **Jane Shore** as in **The Fair Penitent** the gradual revelation of a static character or state of soul is the action of the tragedy. In the process Rowe asks us to accept inconsistencies within the protagonists which in Aristotelian terms would be regarded as failures in characterization. (p. 260)

The Fair Penitent begins where most comedies end, with the formal celebration of the marriage of Altamont to Calista. . . . However, although the play appears to begin as a happy celebration symbolized by the ceremony of marriage, it turns out to be a true festival of woe, ending with a ritual of suffering and penance. Tension between the anticipated joy and the woe that replaces it gives this play its power so that emotional experience is itself the action that causes the audience to progress through the work.

Rowe focuses on Calista's wedding day; thus, the heroine's doom has been sealed before the play has even begun. (p. 264)

The first words we hear from her are those of her letter, read aloud by Horatio and Lothario, in which she styles herself "the lost Calista," signalling that her fate has been sealed. This impression is affirmed in act 2 when we see that she is both painfully aware of her sinfulness in loving Lothario and is yet unable to "turn from the deceiver." She has no possibility of happiness because she possesses only one internal option. All she can do in the course of the play is to attempt to hide "the warring passions and tumultuous thoughts / That rage within thee [her] and deform thy [her] reason." Rather than portraying the process by which this situation came to be, the action centers on the actual "crisis of my [Calista's] fate." The plot consists in her internal experience of suffering during the period between the sealing of her doom and her actual destruction, a phase which in many tragedies would lack interest because no moral issues remain to be resolved. Rowe thereby denies us the expected progression of morally determinant action that is fundamental to Aristotelian tragic plots.

Though Calista does not appear on stage until act 2, we are given descriptions of her in act 1, and they all center on her psychic struggle. First Altamont has a foreboding of trouble, for he says to Sciolto, "Amidst this stream of joy that bears me on,. . . / There is one pain that hangs upon my heart." He then describes the "rising storm of passion" that shook Calista's breast when she consented to marry him, "as if her heart were breaking." Lucilla similarly portrays Calista's melancholy mood, explaining that she herself has "learned to weep" by watching Calista's continual suffering. Lothario elaborately describes the "storm" of "enthusiastic passion" that overtook her when he refused to marry her. All of these characters have observed the intensity of Calista's internal, emotional torment and have been so struck by its force that they feel compelled to portray it with vivid detail to others. Calista's own letter in act 1 tells the "story of her woes," and Horatio, who reads it, finds himself horrified at the very thought of what goes on in Calista's "hot imagination." He states his belief here and elsewhere that her body, which is beautiful, is quite different from the nature of her soul, which he feels is corrupt. In spite of his disapproval, however, by the end of the first act we have received such a full portrait of Calista's tormented inward nature that we begin to sympathize with her, even though she has not yet appeared on stage.

Calista's first spoken words at the start of act 2 give us proof of her psychic torment and that her doom is sealed: "I've gone around through all my thoughts, / But all are indignation, love, or shame, / And my dear peace of mind is lost forever." Here as throughout the play she conveys her suffering by elaborately expressing her desire for a "dismal," "unfrequented," melancholy "retreat" inhabited only by "ill-omened" birds and skeletons of despairing lovers, insisting that her situation is both hopeless and "insupportable." Although these are her very first speeches on stage, already it is clear that she is determined to die rather than face "public loss of honor," and as we shall see, the fulfillment of this decision will lend the play its sense of closure.

This mood of willing acceptance of misery is consistent in Calista throughout the play. For example, when she confronts Lothario in act 4, she tells him that all her "hours of folly and fond delight" are wasted and that her remaining hours "are doomed to weeping, anguish, and repentance." The metaphor of a "storm of passion" which Altamont uses to describe her in act 1 recurs in her own speeches throughout the work and thereby reminds us that we are not experiencing a development or change in Calista herself. Discovery and discussion of her fixed state of mind are the main activities that go on throughout this play, and because Calista does not change we feel a peculiar sense of stasis in the experience. This feeling is ironically mirrored in Altamont's final words at Calista's death, "Cold! Dead and cold! And yet thou art not changed, / But lovely still!" Calista may have died, but because her death is merely the material destruction to which she was doomed and an outcome which she had accepted long before the start of act 1, we as an audience feel that we end where we began.

Some critics have complained that the last act is superfluous because it is all talk and no action. Yet if we accept the exploration of Calista's psychic torment as a major structuring principle of the work, the final scenes are clearly crucial. Her emotional speeches of longing for exile are importantly echoed in act 5 where her state of mind is made manifest by the sensationalism of the charnel house. By actualizing Calista's fancied torture Rowe signals that the end of the play is approaching. Being shut in the tomb fulfills Calista's desire to suffer in a melancholy retreat, replacing her metaphors with a literal counterpart. The final act thereby provides a sense of closure in the play by terminating the pattern that has sustained our interest throughout the action. (pp. 265-67)

The critics correctly point out that the final act consists of little other than discussion of the woes that have been suffered; yet despite the lack of action, act 5 is clearly an important part of this play since it reveals Calista's psychic state in the most vivid, literal way possible. It thereby terminates the progression of mental struggle that replaces morally determinant action in this tragedy. As she is about to die, Sciolto acknowledges that her tears and suffering have sufficiently compensated for her errors:

> Thou hast rashly ventured in a stormy sea,
> Where life, fame, virtue, all were wrecked and lost;
> But sure thou hast borne thy part in all the anguish,
> And smarted with the pain; then rest in peace. . . .

Because she has "borne" sufficient "anguish," real happiness is at last possible for Calista, though it will take the form of death and translation into heaven rather than marriage to Altamont. Enduring adversity, not repentance, is what qualifies her for salvation, and she responds to her father's words by saying, "Peace dawns upon my soul."

In this fuller context we may see more clearly why it is unnecessary to demonstrate that Calista's final expression of pleasure at seeing Altamont is or is not a deathbed repentance. Her admission of error at the end is not a sudden resolution of a moral dilemma but is only one of many such admissions in the play; the expression of love for Altamont occurs only after it is clear that her actual destruction is imminent. Rowe was interested in exploring her psychic struggle involving certain morally contradictory elements, not in writing a drama of proper punishment and reward for moral behavior. The evidence for this view is that he at least partially exonerates Calista both by removing her seduction from the action, thereby muting its effect on the audience, and by suggesting that society itself is responsible for her error.

To verify this second point we have only to turn to Calista's soliloquy, in which she exclaims, "How hard is the condition of our sex, / Through ev'ry state of life the slaves of man!" She complains of the domination of men over women and questions why women are "born with high souls" if they cannot use them to "assert" themselves in the world. Lucilla's frequent remarks criticizing men reinforce this theme. The cause of Calista's difficulty is society's unnatural insistence on women's subordination to men rather than her own moral failure. Her struggle to control her powerful passions and "high soul" while suffering under such "vile obedience" demonstrates her very nobility to the audience. Full repentance or denial of her emotions would constitute for us a denial of the very bases of our sympathy. Certainly we cannot condemn her for being a victim of social convention. At the same time this play does not attempt to criticize society itself. Rowe is interested in examining the condition of a person in a hopeless situation, not in effecting change in the society that renders such a situation hopeless.

Still another stance taken by those who try to find a clear moral in the play is the claim that Horatio and Lavinia provide the ethical norms as "spokesmen for marital virtue" [see excerpt by Frank J. Kearful dated 1966]. In this view Calista ought to have emulated Lavinia, who so faithfully and exclusively loves her husband. When Horatio describes Calista, at the end of act 1, as one of the "fatally fair" who love only variety, Lavinia claims that she herself can love only one man. . . . Ironically, when we encounter Calista in the next scene, we discover that precisely such devotion to a single man, though the wrong one, has been her downfall. She does not suffer from a love of variety, as Horatio suggests and the critics have insisted; she is tormented by the futility of her single, driving passion for Lothario. Her devotion is futile because of Lothario's unfaithfulness and her father's hatred of him; yet in her steadfast love she could not more closely resemble Lavinia than she already does. (pp. 267-69)

Rowe suggsts that Calista's misery was not caused by a flaw or limitation in her inward nature but was at least partly a function of her external circumstances. Her repentence alone would not provide a satisfactory conclusion to the play since she is a victim of more than her own passions. Rather than turning to Horatio's final moralistic words for an expression of the play's meaning, we might more accurately claim that the heroine's life illustrates the truth of the humorous statement in the "Epilogue":

> Italian ladies lead but scurvy lives;
> There's dreadful dealing with eloping wives;
> Thus 'tis because these husbands are obeyed
> By force of laws which for themselves they made.

Calista is a victim of forces over which she has no control.

Such an argument must be made to the objecting critics, including Belford, who claim that Calista is guilty of moral failure. Even so we must recognize that she has sinned and that her constant internal flirtation with evil is partially responsible for the fascination of her character. As we progress through the play and experience more and more of her misery but no new instances of her sinfulness, we are increasingly able to forgive this sinner though we damn her guilt. In a similar fashion Sciolto's sympathy for his daughter grows during the play as his knowledge of the nobility of her soul increases by means of her revealed suffering. Because Sciolto's experience so clearly parallels that of the reader, it is possible to regard him as a tool that Rowe created to help us to deal with the apparent contradictions in the work which have teased audiences and led to such a variety of critical response.

Sciolto himself is subject to psychic torment, for although he is Calista's father, he must also be her judge. . . . Like the reader he is forced to reconcile contradictory elements in his reaction to his daughter's plight and to pity her. Like Sciolto, we recognize that she still passionately and wrongly loves Lothario, yet we still feel sympathy for her. We are asked to forgive the frailty of human nature and exercise a form of humane judgment that resembles the justice of heaven, as described by Calista. She says that "heav'n, who knows our weak, imperfect natures, / How blind with passions and how prone to evil, / Makes not too strict enquiry for offenses." Heaven does not judge by rigid standards of morality but takes into account what Altamont calls our "unequal tempers." The variable emotionalism of men and women is not only forgivable in *The Fair Penitent* but is a necessary part of human nobility, since it is so fundamental to human nature. Horatio may be right that angels are happier because they are better, yet such an alternative does not exist for Calista during the course of the play.

The heroine is not an angel, but she is quite aptly called "the fair penitent." Richardson's Belford was correct that "her devil is as much *within* her as *without* her" [see excerpt dated 1748], for she remains insistently in love with Lothario to the end of the play. Even so, we feel a sympathy for her of the kind we would normally extend only to someone fully repentant of such misplaced emotion. If we remember that the word "fair" means "free from moral stain" as well as "beautiful,"

we must finally recognize that the title of the work is more rather than less misleading than thought by the critics. The clearly paradoxical experience of Calista as an "unblemished penitent" is precisely the response in which she entraps her audience.

Rowe's choice eleven years later to make Jane Shore more truly repentant than Calista perhaps reflects his awareness of the difficulties of the demand for suspension of judgment in the earlier work. Even so, Rowe asks us in the Epilogue to "pity" Jane Shore not because she is innocent or sorry for her sin but because she has "dearly paid the sinful score." He describes Jane as "not quite so good," making her suffering rather than her purity what qualifies her for sympathy. The heroine has sinned by eloping with Edward IV, repented, and been thereby doomed to destruction all before the start of the action, so that just as in *The Fair Penitent* her situation is static. All she can do during the work is to endure misery. (pp. 270-72)

The directive in the "Epilogue"—"Be kind at last, and pity poor Jane Shore"—suggests Rowe's awareness of a need to guide his readers' responses even more carefully than he had done earlier, and Dumont is his primary vehicle for doing so. By using Jane's husband in disguise as Dumont and as an observer of the action, Rowe offers us a figure whose point of view we may partially share. Through him we gradually attain a fuller knowledge of the complexities of Jane's soul. Sciolto's character was the germ of such a figure in *The Fair Penitent*, yet the device is much more explicit in *Jane Shore*. By functioning as a perceiver, Dumont is the creator of the significance of the action for the audience. He knew Jane before she had sinned, and through the first four acts he perceives her "virtue," thereby allowing us to view her as if from an earlier vantage point, when she was still his untainted wife. Although Dumont assists us in understanding more than we otherwise could about Jane, he himself suffers from limitations of vision which we must finally take into account. Here we have clearly moved beyond the usual epistemological boundaries of dramatic tragedy into a world more like that of such novels as *To the Lighthouse* or *Mrs. Dalloway*.

The suggestion that we are in the same position as the observer, Dumont, is conveyed early in act 1, when Bellmour says to him, "How she has lived, you've heard my tale already; / The rest, your own attendance in her family, . . . / And nearer observation best will tell you." Dumont has heard the "tale" of "how she has lived" from Bellmour, and the audience has just heard the sequence of events in her life recounted by Hastings and Gloster at the end of the previous scene. We know what has caused her fall and doomed her to destruction, and like Dumont we are now to learn the remainder of her story from our observation of Jane herself. Together we shall come to know the state of Jane's mind and how she bears her sufferings internally, since nothing further of morally determinant significance will occur.

The sequence of events in the play, including Gloster's attempt to gain power, his tests of Hastings' loyalty, and the collapse of the affair between Alicia and Hastings, provides a sense of progressing action through the work which helps to maintain our interest, although there is no true causal connection among all of the incidents in the sequence. These events are most important, however, as means of revealing Jane's inward nature, and it is that process which constitutes the work's plot. For example, Alicia's suggesting that her friend use her beauty to win favor with Gloster and Hastings' attempts at seduction offer occasions for Jane to reveal the intensity and firmness of her repentance. She repeatedly says, "I detest my wretched self, and curse / My past polluted life." Gloster's test of Jane's loyalty to Edward's sons enables her to explain the cause and justice of her love of Edward, despite her repentance.... Gloster's accusation that she wishes to meddle in affairs of state allows her to indicate that her only concern is to look into her own heart and "weep the sorrows" she finds therein. In none of these instances does Rowe let us experience the event as a true "trial" of Jane, for never do we feel a genuine possibility that the heroine will fail the test. Instead these incidents all help to reveal Jane's nature which we perceive as having reached an unshakable equilibrium.

Alicia's fierce jealousy provides a striking contrast to the calm control that Jane herself exerts over her passions. The contrast is so marked in Hastings' eyes that he says, "Of equal elements / Without one jarring atom, was she formed, / And gentleness and joy make up her being." With what we know of Jane's history we must realize that although she is now externally calm because of her deep repentance, in the past there have indeed been "jarring atoms" within her soul; and to the extent that she still suffers inwardly, they remain. Hastings vividly describes the effects of jealousy as they manifest themselves in Alicia, and his words, as well as Alicia's struggles with her passions during the play, remind us of elements within Jane that must actually have led to her abandonment of her husband, even though she now "disclaims / Strife and her wrangling train." The portrayal of Alicia's fury gives a kind of emotional immediacy to Jane's past but without making her the object of the reader's moral outrage.

Because Hastings is involved in nearly all the incidents throughout the action that affect Jane externally, his character, like Jane's, is strangely contradictory. In one sense we are tempted to view him as the Aristotelian tragic hero of the piece. He is of appropriate stature, and he brings his doom upon himself through his own error. Yet since his error involves the threatened violation of Jane we are compelled to experience it as an evil that cancels his claim to tragic heroism. He is not only Jane's attempted seducer, but Alicia's oppressor, since he gives her true reason to be jealous. Yet later Hastings displays a patriotism and loyalty to Edward's sons which Jane deeply admires, as would the loyal royalists of Rowe's day in whose minds the succession to the English throne was an issue of major concern.... We cannot define Hastings as either a villain or a hero since he variously displays the qualities of both in extreme forms, and Rowe does not hesitate to ask us to accept the consistency of such a character. Although Jane does not display sinful tendencies during the play itself, the fact of her past transgression is crucial to the interest of her nature. Both she and Hastings are characters whose fascination depends on our acceptance of their genuine internal contradictions.

Like Calista's role, Jane's is also a passive one. She takes little aggressive action, but by simply expressing her misery she inflames Alicia's jealousy, Hastings' lust, and Gloster's political antagonism. In each case her honest and undesigning avowal of feeling also wins our sympathy and reminds us that her very virtue has doomed her to destruction. We realize that there is no course of action which Jane can take that is acceptable in terms of her spiritual excellence and that will also allow her to live happily.

Dumont's role clinches this point, though at first his presence would seem to suggest that a reconciliation with him is possible and that his wife might live happily after all. In act 5 when he casts aside his disguise, Bellmour asks him whether he can "resume a husband's name" without letting "the husband / Destroy the generous pity of Dumont." These words force Shore to acknowledge that within him, now that he has resumed his true identity, the torment still rages.... The "generous pity of Dumont" is not the same.

With the help of Dumont, we and Jane's husband Shore have explored the nature and complexities of Jane's character. That experience did not depend upon a linear progression for its logic or upon a sequence of action analogous to the structure of time. Instead it involved our temporarily escaping from time and forgetting the events that have occurred over the years. Like Dumont we have been allowed during the course of the play to "think on all time, backward, like a space / Idle and void, where nothing e'er had being"; we have felt sympathy for Jane while absolving her of the sin she committed as if it had not occurred and have thereby perceived her grandeur and nobility. Yet the experience cannot continue indefinitely. For the play to come to a satisfying end we much reconcile what we know of her inward state with her external situation. Rowe must bring us to feel that death is the only possible solution to her difficulties by causing us again to acknowledge the passage of time and the reality of past error in her life.

He accomplishes this feat in act 5 by forcing us to undergo an experience analogous to that of Dumont when he resumes both his identity as Shore and his memory of the past. By reminding the audience of the "train" of events that preceded Jane's fall, Rowe implies that their conclusion, Jane's actual destruction, is impending.... Along with Shore, we re-experience Jane's initial sin, the fact that "she fled," with a fresh sense of the pain it caused. By this means we are prepared for her destruction. The presence of the mental torment within Shore makes us realize that the possibility of reconciliation with him does not exist. From the very start of the play Jane has been repentant enough to entitle her to forgiveness, yet it is finally beyond the capacity of human beings to sustain the "generous pity of Dumont" in their hearts. Her reward must come in heaven.

Though it is a very crude device, Shore's disguise is a crucial clue that we are to regard Jane Shore from an unusual perspective, as if this play possessed a definable point of view as many narratives do. We are asked to assimilate Jane's past and her present in a way that breaks the usual epistemological boundaries of stage representation. In his role as Dumont, Jane's husband is able to perceive her virtue and to respond with "generous pity"; Rowe uses this same term in the Preface to **The Fair Penitent** to describe what ought to be our proper response to tragedy in general. Dumont thus enriches our understanding of Jane, since we go through an experience analogous to his. When he resumes his identity as Shore he simultaneously remembers Jane's sin and yet forgives her. These acts relieve her suffering but mark his own acknowledgement of her necessary destruction. In this way he prepares us for her death and the end of the action. Coming to know Jane's character has forced us to "think on all time, backward" as Dumont does and to accept both Jane's sinfulness and her nobility as part of her fascinating nature. Rowe entraps us by raising and upsetting the conventional expectations about tragic action. He disturbs us by refusing to provide a time-bound progression of morally determinate events as our guide through these two tragedies. In place of such action he makes the profoundly unsettling demand that we accept the consistency and the grandeur of his unblemished penitent and his flawed paragon. We are to "be kind at last" as we compassionately watch these tortured women suffering in their static fates. (pp. 272-77)

Janet E. Aikins, "To Know Jane Shore, 'Think on All Time, Backward'," in Papers on Language and Literature, *Vol. 18, No. 3, Summer, 1982, pp. 258-77.*

ADDITIONAL BIBLIOGRAPHY

Austin, Wiltshire Stanton, Jr., and Ralph, John. "Nicholas Rowe." In their *Lives of the Poets-Laureate*, pp. 223-38. London: Richard Bentley, 1853.
Anecdotal biographical essay interspersed with occasional critical comments.

Boas, Frederick S. "Nicholas Rowe." In his *An Introduction to Eighteenth-Century Drama: 1700-1780*, pp. 1-31. Oxford: Clarendon Press, 1953.
Introductory survey of Rowe's dramatic career.

Clark, Donald B. "The Source and Characterization of Nicholas Rowe's *Tamerlane*." *Modern Language Notes* LXV, No. 3 (March 1950): 145-52.
Suggests that Richard Knolles's *Historie of the Turkes* (1603) was Rowe's source for *Tamerlane*.

Colvile, K. N. "Shakespeare's First Critical Editor." *The Nineteenth Century and After* LXXXVI, No. DX (August 1919): 266-79.
General survey of Rowe's literary career that concentrates on the tragedies.

Cumberland, Richard. Review of *The Fair Penitent*, by Nicholas Rowe. In *Eighteenth-Century Critical Essays*, Vol. II, edited by Scott Elledge, pp. 948-70. Ithaca, N.Y.: Cornell University Press, 1961.
Reprints a series of essays first published in the *Observer* in 1785. In this insightful and detailed study of *The Fair Penitent*, Cumberland takes the reader step by step through the play, commenting on adroit or awkward plot development, language, and characterization. Cumberland's critique also includes a comparison—largely unfavorable to *The Fair Penitent*—of Rowe's play with its dramatic source, Philip Massinger and Nathan Field's *The Fatal Dowry* (1632).

Dammers, Richard H. "To Teach and to Please: The Literary Achievement of Nicholas Rowe." In *Review*, Vol. 2, edited by James O. Hoge and James L.W. West III, pp. 189-96. Charlottesville: University Press of Virginia, 1980.
Review of Annibel Jenkins's *Nicholas Rowe* and J. Douglas Canfield's *Nicholas Rowe and Christian Tragedy* [see excerpts dated 1977]. Dammers draws upon these and other critical studies of Rowe to illuminate aspects of the tragedies, especially the attitude they reveal toward marriage.

[Gentleman, Francis]. Review of *The Fair Penitent*, by Nicholas Rowe. In his *The Dramatic Censor; or, Critical Companion*, Vol. 1, pp. 256-77. London: J. Bell, 1770.
Plot synopsis of *The Fair Penitent*, including critical comments representative of eighteenth-century views of the play. Gentleman also rates the performances of various actors and actresses—including James Quin and David Garrick—who acted key roles in the play.

Goldstein, Malcolm. "Pathos and Personality in the Tragedies of Nicholas Rowe." In *English Writers of the Eighteenth Century*, edited by John H. Middendorf, pp. 172-85. New York: Columbia University Press, 1971.
Points to a recurring pattern of characterization in Rowe's tragedies. Goldstein claims that all the plays contain antithetical female protagonists who both contrast with and complement each other—the strong-willed, domineering woman and the innocent, naive woman.

Hesse, Alfred W. "Who Was Bit by Rowe's Comedy *The Biter*?" *Philological Quarterly* 62, No. 4 (Fall 1983): 477-85.
Posits that the model for Sir Timothy Tallapoy in *The Biter* was Elihu Yale.

Hopkins, Kenneth. "Nicholas Rowe." In his *The Poets Laureate*, pp. 55-61. London: Bodley Head, 1954.
Brief sketch of Rowe's life and career.

Matlack, Cynthia S. "'Spectatress of the Mischief Which She Made': Tragic Woman Perceived and Perceiver." In *Studies in Eighteenth-Century Culture*, Vol. 6, edited by Ronald C. Rosbottom, pp. 317-30. Madison: University of Wisconsin Press, 1977.
Discussion of the tenets and techniques of pathetic tragedy, centering on the theme of female eroticism in the plays of Rowe and others.

McAleer, John J. "Nicholas Rowe—Matrix of Shakespearean Scholarship." *The Shakespeare Newsletter* XVII, No. 1 (February 1967): 6.
Enumerates and critiques Rowe's achievements as Shakespeare's editor.

Monk, Samuel H. Introduction to *Some Account of the Life of Mr. William Shakespear*, by Nicholas Rowe, pp. 1-11. Los Angeles: Augustan Reprint Society, 1948.
Assesses Rowe's "historic mission" as editor and critic of Shakespeare.

Schwarz, Alfred. "An Example of Eighteenth-Century Pathetic Tragedy: Rowe's *Jane Shore*." *Modern Language Quarterly* XXII, No. 3 (September 1961): 236-47.
Examines *Jane Shore*, emphasizing Rowe's dramatic innovations, particularly insofar as the play "illustrates the transitions . . . from the well-made tragedy after the French and heroic pattern to the frankly pathetic tragedy using chiefly native characters and settings and inviting commiseration and tears."

Thorp, Willard. "A Key to Rowe's *Tamerlane*." *The Journal of English and Germanic Philology* XXXIX, No. 1 (January 1940): 124-27.
Assigns historical identity to the politically allegorized characters of *Tamerlane*.

Whiting, George W. "Rowe's Debt to *Paradise Lost*." *Modern Philology* XXXII, No. 3 (February 1935): 271-79.
Finds resonances of John Milton's *Paradise Lost* in Rowe's plays.

Wyman, Lindley A. "The Tradition of the Formal Meditation in Rowe's *The Fair Penitent*." *Philological Quarterly* XLII, No. 3 (July 1963): 412-16.
Examines the literary connotations of the beginning of the fifth act of *The Fair Penitent*, a melodramatic scene in which Calista enters the dark room where her lover's body lies, to explicate Rowe's themes of meditation and penitence.

Jacopo Sannazaro

1456?-1530

(Also Sannazzaro; also Sannazarius; also wrote under academic name of Actius Syncerus) Italian poet and prose writer.

An influential poet of the Renaissance, Sannazaro is famed for his *Arcadia,* a work of interwoven poetry and prose that both defined and popularized the genre of pastoral romance. Drawing on elements of classical pastoral and traditional Italian vernacular poetry, Sannazaro created in *Arcadia* a sustained pastoral idyll, providing a model for such later pastoral ventures as Edmund Spenser's *The Shepheardes Calender* (1579) and Sir Philip Sidney's own *Arcadia* (1593). In addition, Sannazaro wrote Latin verse, including his ambitious epic of the birth of Christ, *De partu virginis,* noted for its unique blending of Christian and classical themes and styles.

Born in Naples to a moderately wealthy aristocratic family, Sannazaro spent much of his childhood in the country around Salerno, where his family moved after his father's death. Sannazaro returned to the city as a young man, joining the Accademia Antoniana, a society of humanist writers and thinkers led by the poet Giovanni Pontano, and assuming the academic name Actius Syncerus, which he used with pride throughout his life. Also during this time Sannazaro formed a connection with the Aragonese court and in particular with Prince Frederick, who later became king. Although the composition date of Sannazaro's early vernacular work is a matter of conjecture, many scholars surmise that he began *Arcadia* in the early 1480s, perhaps even before his return to Naples; a manuscript dated 1489 proves that *Arcadia* was finished at least through Eclogue 10 (there are twelve in the final version) by this date. In any event, *Arcadia* is a work of Sannazaro's youth, and there is evidence to indicate that in later years the author considered the work mere juvenilia, of lesser importance than his subsequent Latin poetry.

In 1499 King Frederick presented Sannazaro with an estate, Villa Mergellina, overlooking the Bay of Naples; some commentators believe that Sannazaro's residence here may have inspired his *Eclogae piscatoriae (Piscatory Eclogues):* Latin imitations of classical bucolics featuring fishermen instead of the usual shepherds. When in 1501 a volatile political situation forced Frederick into exile in France, Sannazaro accompanied his patron, remaining with him until Frederick's death in 1504. Piqued that a pirated, unfinished edition of *Arcadia* had been published during his absence, Sannazaro issued an authorized version upon his return to Naples, augmented by two additional eclogues and prose chapters as well as an epilogue. For the remainder of his life, Sannazaro lived quietly at his villa, writing and publishing only Latin poetry, which he believed a worthier literary endeavor than his now-famed *Arcadia.*

All of Sannazaro's work, in common with most Italian literature of the Renaissance, is heavily influenced by classical authors, both in matter and in style. Although written in the Italian vernacular, *Arcadia* is a cornucopia of classical elements, as its author freely imitated and borrowed from classical pastoral writers, particularly Vergil and Theocritus. Stylistic emphasis on classical formality and decorum further cement Sannazaro's debts to his predecessors. Also evident in the work, though to a lesser extent, is the influence of such Italian vernacular writers as Petrarch—whose lover of the *Canzoniere* is

figured in Sannazaro's lovesick swains—and Boccaccio, whose *Ameto* (1341-42) appears to have furnished Sannazaro with the idea to alternate poetry and prose. Athough *Arcadia* contains imitations, paraphrases, and even outright translations of classical pastorals, the work yet represents an important innovative departure from its pastoral antecedents. Composed of twelve eclogues connected by narrative prose, *Arcadia* goes beyond the isolated bucolic eclogues of the past to form a sustained pastoral vision. The work is therefore renowned as a model for later pastoral dramas and as the forerunner of the subsequently developed pastoral novel.

Anchored in the literary past yet foreshadowing developments to come, *Arcadia* is, commentators have noted, above all a consciously "literary" creation, based in and furthering a written tradition of rusticity rather than attempting to depict the reality of country life and people. Yet critics have stressed that *Arcadia* does not suffer from its deliberate artificiality; as Charles Sears Baldwin has written: "Though [Sannazaro] weaves throughout from literature, never directly from life, he was artist enough to weave originally." In addition to its overt ties with the pastoral literary tradition, *Arcadia* exhibits a peculiar self-consciousness that many critics have found one of the work's most intriguing aspects. David Kalstone has characterized *Arcadia* as "a paradise for poets," comprising "a self-consciousness and a self-admiration that may disturb the reader's sense of appropriateness at the same time as its rhetoric teases him out of thought.'' The poem, then, defines a pastoral world which is always conscious of its existence purely as a literary creation, purely as poetic pastoral; ''and thus,'' as Ralph Nash has explained, ''Arcadia becomes a country of the mind, a symbol of dedication to poetry.'' Further, the poem's self-consciousness extends to a self-examination of the very genre it exemplifies. The narrator-protagonist of *Arcadia*, Sincero, has come to Arcadia from his native Naples, seeking solace for an unhappy romance. Although at first the rustic world he enters seems idyllic, replete with bountiful natural beauty and exquisite country joys, disturbing elements of immoderate grief and potential social disorder soon arise. *Arcadia*'s narrator and its author share an ambivalence toward this pastoral retreat, which appears alternately admirable for its bucolic simplicity and utopian innocence and objectionable for its naive rusticity and possible underlying corruption. It has been suggested that such contrariety mirrors Sannazaro's greater ambivalence toward his chosen genre: uneasily aware of pastoral's literary inferiority to the heroic epic, Sannazaro evaluated and criticized his romance even as he wrote it. It is such self-conscious literary assessment, occurring within the bounds of the work itself, that many critics believe invests *Arcadia* with a special interest.

Instantly and immensely popular from the time of its first publication, *Arcadia* enjoyed resounding success for centuries. But with the advent of the Romantic movement, with its emphasis on spontaneity, originality, and individual emotion, classical and classically inspired works fell from favor. As a literary artifact, however, representative of a pivotal moment in the evolution of pastoral fiction, *Arcadia* continues to be studied and appreciated.

Sannazaro's Latin works have received comparatively little critical attention. *Piscatory Eclogues* sparked a minor debate in eighteenth-century England over the appropriateness of its subject matter. Most commentators believed the eclogue better suited to the countryside and shepherds than to the sea and fishermen, and judged Sannazaro's efforts accordingly. While subsequent critics ceased to fault the work on these grounds, *Piscatory Eclogues* has been considered of marginal interest only beside Sannazaro's most important Latin work, *De partu virginis*. This poem has been described as an attempt to write a Vergilian epic on a Christian theme: the Annunciation and the birth of Christ. Written in Latin hexameters, the work has suffered censure for what has been perceived as its incongruous merging of classical and Christian motifs. Although Sannazaro's theology is unfailingly orthodox, *De partu virginis* abounds with mythological allusions and pagan deities, rendering the poem vulnerable to charges ranging from poor taste to outright blasphemy. As the nineteenth-century critic Francis Philip Nash phrased it: ''We are sorely tempted to quarrel irreconcilably with Sannazaro's taste and poetic feeling.'' Still, Nash admitted that *De partu virginis* contains some fine poetry, and it is generally agreed that the poem is on the whole an admirable treatment of so ambitious and exalted a subject; in 1877 M. P. Thompson stated flatly: ''The *De partu Virginis* is the most remarkable poem of the Renaissance.''

''The *Arcadia* must have a larger place in literary history than in the hearts of its readers,'' wrote J. H. Whitfield in his *A Short History of Italian Literature* (1960), and indeed *Arcadia* has been studied more as a significant link in the chain of pastoral literature than for its intrinsic merit. This is largely because *Arcadia* is very much a product of its era, adhering to poetic standards which have since lessened in appeal. As

Ralph Nash has noted, Sannazaro's work is indicative of a peculiarly Renaissance poetic: the subordination of originality to classical imitation, together with highly stylized and formal decorum. Nonetheless, Nash has concluded: ''If we read [Sannazaro] with attention, and without prejudice, I think we must answer finally: Yes. This too is poetry.''

PRINCIPAL WORKS

Arcadia   (poetry and prose)   1504
   [*Arcadia* published in *Arcadia & Piscatorial Eclogues*, 1966]
De partu virginis   (poetry)   1526
Eclogae piscatoriae   (poetry)   1526
   [*Piscatory Eclogues* published in *Select Translations from the Works of Sannazarius, H. Grotius, Bapt. Amaltheus, etc.*, 1726]
*Sonetti e Canzoni   (poetry)   1530
Elegiae   (poetry)   1535
The Osiers: A Pastoral   (poetry)   1724
Opere   (poetry and prose)   1952

*This work is commonly known as *Rime*.

DESIDERIUS ERASMUS   (essay date 1528)

[*Erasmus was a Dutch humanist and priest who exerted a tremendous influence on European thought during the Renaissance. Both a classical and a biblical scholar, he combined in his works rationalism, tolerance, and skepticism with an emphasis on personal, keenly felt Christian pietism. Nearly an exact contemporary of Sannazaro, Erasmus shared with the poet a humanistic worldview, which included a reverence for classical Latin authors. However, he deplored the extremes to which this adulation had led a segment of Renaissance scholars known as Ciceronians, who were so excessively devoted to the Roman orator Cicero that they would sanction no contemporary writing that did not directly imitate him. Erasmus wrote his* Dialogus Ciceronianus *(1528; Ciceronianus; or, A Dialogue on the Best Style of Speaking) to satirize such punctilious adherence to one individual's style, for he believed this imitation to be slavish and even morally and theologically reprehensible, as Christian writers, in their efforts to cleave to the style of a pre-Christian author, had perforce to paganize all religious references. In* Ciceronianus, *which Paul Monroe has called "Erasmus' one great contribution to literary criticism," Erasmus employed a dialogic device, pitting the confirmed Ciceronian Nosoponus against Bulephorus, who represents Erasmus's own beliefs. In the following excerpt, Bulephorus counters Nosoponus's praise of* De partu virginis *with criticism of the poem's Latin style and secularism.*]

Nosoponus—[Accius Syncerus] described the birth of the Virgin Mother in a wonderfully clever poem [*De Partu Virginis*] which was applauded beyond measure in the theater at Rome.

Bulephorus—The breviaries (for so they call them today) of Leo and Clement testify abundantly to this. Then a preface was added of Cardinal Aegedius, not to mention others, and it had reason to be pleasing. Indeed I read both books with delight. He wrote eclogues on fishing too. Who would not admire such talent in a noble youth? He must be placed before Pontano because he was not ashamed to write on a sacred theme and because he treated it neither in a sleepy nor in a disagreeable fashion, but he would have deserved more praise if he had treated his sacred subject somewhat more reverently. Indeed Battista Mantuano could excel him. What was the use of his invoking so many times in a sacred poem the Muses and Phoebus? of his painting the Virgin intent upon the verses of the Muses? of introducing Proteus foretelling Christ? and peopling the whole world with nymphs, hamadryads, and neriads? How harsh this verse sounds to Christian ears which, if I mistake not, is spoken to the Virgin Mary: *Tuque adeo spes fida hominum, spes fida Deorum!* [''And you therefore the sure hope of gods and men!''] Of course *Deorum* for the sake of the meter was put in place of *Divorum*. Among so many virtues his frequent elisions count for little, but they mar the smoothness. To be brief: if you should cite this poem as a typical work of a youth studying to write poetry, I should think it good; but if as a poem written by a serious man on the subject of piety, I should far prefer the single hymn of Prudentius, *De Natali Jesu,* to the three little volumes of Accius Syncerus,— so far does this poem fail to suffice for the overthrowing of Goliath as he threatens the church with a sling, or for soothing Saul in his madness with the harp as the preface declares him to do. And I do not know which is more blameworthy for a Christian to handle secular themes in secular language, pretending that he is not a Christian, or in pagan tongue; for the mysteries of Christ ought to be treated in both a scholarly way and reverently. It is not enough to arouse in the reader little temporary feelings of delight; emotions worthy of the Lord must be aroused. And you cannot do this unless you have the subject you are handling thoroughly mastered: for you will not inflame if you yourself are cold; you will not set the reader's mind on fire with the love of celestial things, if you yourself are but lukewarm. If you have at hand either spontaneously or at the cost of no great labor fine phrases and figures to attract the fastidious reader and cause him to linger, I think they ought not to be despised, provided those things which are of chief importance have the first place. Would it be possible for a religious theme to be distasteful to us because it has been clothed in religious language? How can you use religious language if you never take your eyes from Vergil, Horace, and Ovid?—unless, perchance, you approve of those who have described the life of Christ by gathering fragments of Homeric and Vergilian verses from everywhere and sewing them into a patchwork. Surely a painstaking kind of writing,—but have they ever brought tears to the eyes of any? Whom have they moved to pious living? Whom have they recalled from an impure life? And yet not so different is the attempt of those who clothe Christian argument in words, phrases, figures, and rhythms gathered from Cicero. To return, what reward of praise does this rhapsodist gain? This, to be sure, that he has busied himself carefully with Homer and Vergil. What reward of Ciceronianism? That he is applauded only by those who are busied in the same and recognize what has been gathered and whence. This sort of thing certainly furnishes a kind of pleasure, I confess, but to very few and of such a kind that it is easily turned into satiety, and in the end it is nothing more than pleasure. That power of arousing the emotions, without which, in the estimation of Quintilian, there can be no eloquence worthy of admiration, is absolutely lacking. (pp. 118-19)

> *Desiderius Erasmus, in his* Ciceronianus; or, A Dialogue on the Best Style of Speaking, *edited by Paul Monroe, translated by Izora Scott, 1908. Reprint by AMS Press, 1972, 130 p.*

LUDOVICO ARIOSTO   (poem date 1532)

[*Ariosto is considered one of the foremost poets of the Italian Renaissance. His characteristic blend of masterly storytelling, inimitable narrative technique, and graceful linguistic expression is most evident in the work synonymous with his name: the epic romance* Orlando furioso *(1532). In the final canto of this work, Ariosto imagines his epic poem as a ship reaching harbor. Among the poets and scholars gathered to greet the returning poet and his work is Sannazaro, to whom Ariosto pays tribute in the following excerpt.*]

> A burst of joy which quivers on the air,
> Rolling towards me, makes the waves resound.
> I hear the peal of bells, the trumpets' blare,
> Which the loud cheerings of a crowd confound;
> And who these are I now become aware
> Who the approaches to the port surround.
> They all rejoice to see me home at last
> After a voyage over seas so vast.
>
> (p. 636)
>
> I see, conjoined in friendship and in blood,
> Pico and Pio, geniuses sublime.
> The noblest spirits in that multitude
> Revere one of the greatest of our time.
> I never met him but long wished I could,
> And gladly bid him welcome in my rhyme:
> Iacopo Sannazaro, he who lures
> The Muses from the mountains to the shores.
>
> (p. 640)

> *Ludovico Ariosto, ''Canto XLVI,'' in his* Orlando Furioso (The Frenzy of Orlando): A Romantic Epic, Part II, *translated by Barbara Reynolds, Penguin Books, 1977, pp. 636-71.*

THE OSIERS: A PASTORAL   (essay date 1724)

[*In the following excerpt from the anonymous preface to* The Osiers, *a translation of one of Sannazaro's Latin pastorals, the critic comments on* Piscatory Eclogues, *discussing the general inappropriateness of adapting pastoral to a piscatory setting.*]

It would be superfluous to mention the great Success [Sannazarius's] Poem on the *Birth of Christ* met with, or the Noble Reward he received from the R. P. of *Venice,* for his Celebrated Epigram on that City, being what every Man of Letters is well acquainted with; neither shall I say any thing of his *Italian Pastorals* as being foreign to my purpose, so shall confine my self to his *Latin Eclogues,* which being all *Piscatory,* are liable to some Censure: He having in them, chang'd the *Scene* from *Woods and Lawns,* to the barren *Beach* and boundless *Ocean.*

All true Pastorals have something in them so sweet and tender, or so innocently Gay, and agreeable to an un-artful, uncorrupt Country Life, as to raise in us the most delicate, and pleasing Ideas: it is the Innocence and Tranquillity in the Life of Shepherds, the natural Turn, and Sincerity of their Thoughts, and Expressions, and even the Cheapness, as well as Easiness of their Pleasures, that Charm us. There is a certain Indolence, a Desire of Quietness natural to every Man, and as that is inseparable from, and indeed scarce to be found any where, but in a Pastoral Life, we delight to find in that kind of writing, what is so agreeable to our own natural Inclinations. Now could the Scene of this Quiet Life, separated from all Passion, but that best, and sweetest, of Innocent Love, be plac't any where but in the Country among Shepherds, whose Life is the most indolent, and consequently most susceptible of Love: if the Scene could be chang'd with these Advantages, it would be never the worse, tho' there were no *Goats* or *Sheep* introduc't.

This being granted, as I think it fairly may; we shall find *Sannazarius* not blameable meerly for changing the Scene, but for changing it for such a one as fills us with Ideas incoherent with that Serenity and Tranquillity, we are naturaly so desirous of. If the Pastoral Life pleases Us, because it is free from Care, and Trouble, the Laborious and Painfull Life of *Fishermen* must for the same reason raise Ideas in Us, of a Nature far from Pleasing.

Should *Virgil* himself, whose Description of a Storm is so great a Masterpiece, that as Mr *Addison* says, a *Man (of Taste) can scarce read it, without being Seasick;* should *Virgil* himself I say, describe in a Pastoral, *"The Billows breaking against a Rock, that was an habitation only to Sea-Calves, and other frightfull Monsters,"* tho' he did it in the best Verse in the World, it would be so far from soothing our Minds, and raising beautyful Ideas in Us, that we should be shock't at it.

What might induce *Sannazaro* to affect this Inelegancy, is not certain. . . . (pp. 1-3)

One can scarce believe that it was in imitation of *Theocritus,* who has given Us one of that sort. That *Sannazarius* made all his Latin Eclogues *Piscatory;* tho' in his Beauties he has frequently copied him. I am apt to think *Sannazarius* a Man of too polite a Taste, not to distinguish this of *Theocritus* to be none of those, *in which Venus, Cupid, and the Graces are said to have assisted him.*

In his fourth Eclogue, He seems to value himself upon being the first Latin Writer that attempted any thing in this way; which may be imagined a reason why he was so fond of it. (pp. 3-4)

> *"Some Account of Sannazarius and His Piscatory Eclogues,"* in The Osiers: A Pastoral *by Sannazarius, Cambridge University Press, 1724, pp. 1-4.*

[M. P. THOMPSON]   (essay date 1877)

[*In the following excerpt, Thompson praises* De partu virginis *as a successful blend of Christian and mythological symbolism.*]

The *De Partu Virginis* is the most remarkable poem of the Renaissance, and its publication was an event in the literary world. It was everywhere eulogized, and the author was styled the Christian Virgil. (pp. 517-18)

The *De Partu Virginis* is an epic poem, in which the birth of Christ is sung with the harmonious flow, the variety of imagery, and the elevated tone of Virgil. But, strange to say, none of the sacred characters introduced are called by their real names— perhaps because unknown to the Latin muse. Even the names of Jesus and Mary are expressed by Virgilian paraphrases. . . . The author calls upon the inhabitants of heaven (*cœlicolæ*) to reveal to his limited vision the profound secrets of the mystery he is about to sing, and invokes the sacred Aonides as the natural protectresses of virginal purity. (p. 518)

The birth of Christ is related with delicacy and poetic grace. There is a sublime energy worthy of Dante in the lines that speak of the Incarnation, and the astonishment of nature in view of the prodigy. Angels in the air celebrate it by sports and combats in the style of Homer's heroes, with the instruments of the Passion for arms. Other angels, like Demodocus, sing the creation, renovation of nature, the seasons, etc. The Jordan, leaning on its urn, is moved to its depths, and relates to the Naiads gathered about him the wonderful event on its shores. An angel comes to bathe the Child in its waters. A dove hovers above. The water-nymphs bend around in veneration. The Jordan, amazed, stays its current with respect, and recalls the prophecy of old Proteus, that the time would come for it to be visited by One who would raise the glory of the Jordan above the Ganges, the Nile, or the Tiber. After which the river, wrapped in its mantle, wonderfully wrought by the Naiads, returns majestically to its bed.

This is too brief an outline of the splendid crown Sannazzaro has woven for the Blessed Virgin, set with so many antique gems. Many have been shocked at the mingling of paganism and Christianity in this poem, but to us it is as if the waters of the Permessus had been turned into the Jordan. All these pagan deities and profane allusions that sprinkle its pages seem to sing the triumph of Christianity. They are in harmony, too, with the Virgilian region in which the poem was written, as well as with the spirit of the age. There was such a passion for the antiquity and for Greek and Latin authors in the sixteenth century that even religion and art put on a classic air. (pp. 519-20)

Sannazzaro's poem, therefore, is only an expression of the tastes of his age. It may also be considered in harmony with those of the primitive church, which adorned the very walls of the Catacombs with pagan symbols, and blazoned them in the mosaics of their churches. There we find Theseus vanquishing the Minotaur, beside David slaying Goliath. The Jordan is represented as a river-god leaning on an antique urn, his head crowned with aquatic plants and his beard dripping with moisture; Cupids flutter among the vines around the form of the Good Shepherd; and Orpheus is made the emblem of our Saviour.

The *De Partu Virginis* is like one of those beautiful Madonnas so often met with in Italy, not seated in a humble chair at Nazareth, but robed like a queen, occupying a throne covered with mythological subjects and antique devices—an emblem of the church enthroned on the ruins of paganism. (p. 522)

> [*M. P. Thompson*], *"Sannazzaro,"* in The Catholic World, *Vol. 25, No. 148, July, 1877, pp. 511-22.*

JOHN ADDINGTON SYMONDS   (essay date 1877)

[*Symonds was an English poet, historian, and critic who wrote extensively on Greek and Italian history and culture; he also made several highly praised translations of Greek poetry and the literature of the Italian Renaissance. In the following excerpt from a work originally published in 1877, Symonds touches briefly on Sannazaro's minor poetry.*]

What we admire in Sannazzaro's *Arcadia* assumes the form of pure Latinity in his love poems. Their style is penetrated with the feeling for physical beauty, Pagan and untempered by an afterthought of Christianity. Their vigorous and glowing sensuality finds no just analogue except in some Venetian paintings. (pp. 338-39)

Sannazzaro's own elegies on the joys of love and country life, the descriptions of his boyhood at Salerno, the praises of his Villa Mergillina, and his meditations among the ruins of Cumæ, are marked by the same characteristics. Nothing quite so full of sensual enjoyment, so soft, and so voluptuous can be found in the poems of the Florentine and Roman scholars. They deserve study, if only as illustrating the luxurious tone of literature at Naples. It was not by these lighter effusions, however, that Sannazzaro won his fame. The epic on the birth of Christ cost him twenty years of labour; and when it was finished, the learned world of Italy welcomed it as a model of correct and polished writing. At the same time the critics seem to have felt, what cannot fail to strike a modern reader, that the difficulties of treating such a theme in the Virgilian manner, and the patience of the stylist, had rendered it a masterpiece of ingenuity rather than a work of genius. Sannazzaro's epigrams, composed in the spirit of bitterest hostility towards the Borgia fmaily, were not less famous than his epic. Alfonso of Aragon took the poet with him during his campaign against the Papal force in the Abruzzi; and these satires, hastily written in the tent and by the camp-fire, formed the amusement of his officers. From the soldiers of Alfonso they speedily passed, on the lips of courtiers and scholars, through all the cities of Italy; nor is it easy to say how much of Lucrezia Borgia's legend may not be traceable to their brief but envenomed couplets. What had been the scandal of the camp acquired consistency in lines too pungent to be forgotten and too witty to remain unquoted. As a specimen of Sannazzaro's style, the epigram on Venice may here be cited:—

> Viderat Hadriacis Venetam Neptunus in undis
>   Stare urbem, et toto ponere jura mari:
> Nunc mihi Tarpeias quantumvis, Jupiter, arces
>   Objice, et illa tui moenia Martis, ait:
> Si Pelago Tybrim præfers, urbem aspice utramque;
>   Illam homines dices, hanc posuisse deos.

[When Neptune beheld Venice stationed in the Adriatic waters, and giving laws to all the ocean, "Now taunt me, Jupiter, with the Tarpeian rock and those walls of thy son Mars!" he cried. "If thou preferrest Tiber to the sea, look on both cities; thou wilt say the one was built by men, the other by gods."]

(pp. 341-42)

John Addington Symonds, "Latin Poetry," in his The Revival of Learning, *Peter Smith, 1967, pp. 324-71.*

FRANCIS PHILIP NASH   (essay date 1881)

[*Nash was an American professor of Latin language and literature. In the following excerpt, he counterposes the poetic beauties and lapses of* De partu virginis.]

Among all Sannazaro's Italian and Latin poetry I have chosen for examination in this paper what the poet himself considered his greatest work, the poem *De Partu Virginis*; though when we examine it in detail we shall see that it deserved to be, as it has been, the most severely criticised. Indeed, if the poet's fame rested, as he was willing that it should, upon that work alone, we should have to place him far below his present estimation and his real value, which is better judged of from his Italian poems and his exquisite sea-shore idyls. Nevertheless, I have chosen in this paper to devote my attention to an inferior poem, because its peculiarities of thought, figure, and expression make it one of the most typical productions I have met with of the period of transition which followed the close of the Middle Ages, when the thought of Europe was still turbid with the imperfectly combined elements of ancient and modern ideas. It is doubly interesting as one of the last poems, of any considerable length, written in Latin, with the serious hope of a reading public, and also as a remarkable product of the period known as the *Renaissance*. (p. 174)

Some of my readers may have already received an unfavorable impression of this work from the absurd account given of it by William Hone. Hone's was a coarse, ungentle nature, upon which the beauties of poetry were quite thrown away; and he was moreover so much inclined to irreverence and profanity that he was once actually indicted and tried for a profane parody on the Liturgy, and only escaped conviction through the unpopularity of the government of the day. But more: he virtually acknowledges that he never read the poem, which indeed would

be evident enough even without that acknowledgment. It may be therefore safely taken for granted that the judicious reader will not allow the flippant impertinence of Hone to prejudice him against a poem the beauties of which, though marred by great defects, have been commended by the best critics from the time of its publication to our own day. For my part, I shall neither disguise its faults nor exaggerate its merits, but shall give the reader as fair an analysis as I can, and leave him to judge for himself.

The most obvious fault of the poem, the incongruous introduction of heathen mythology into a Christian epic, meets us in the opening lines, where the poet invokes the Muses (as if he really believed in them), for these two remarkable reasons— first, that they are heaven-born, and next, that, as virgins, they must sympathize with the Virgin Mary.

After this invocation the author dashes at once *in medias res.* The Almighty, seeing that all mankind are on the road to perdition, takes high counsel to avert the fate entailed upon them by their first parents' disobedience. He perfects in His Eternal Mind a plan of redemption whereby man's restoration shall come, like his fall, through a woman, and redeemed humanity shall fill in heaven the seats of the fallen angels. This idea is familiar to the reader of Milton, but was much improved by him; for, while Sannazaro seems to represent the Lord as determining the scheme of redemption just before the annunciation, Milton more scripturally represents Him as foreordaining the plan of our salvation before the fall.

In pursuance of the divine purpose, the angel of the Lord is sent to a virgin, who, *though married,* keeps and will ever keep her virginity. The description of his descent upon earth is a fine passage. (pp. 177-78)

The angel finds the Virgin reading, according to her wont, the writings of the sibyls and the prophets. This is another incongruity for which our poet has been blamed; but it is hardly fair to blame in Sannazaro what nobody seems to find fault with in the "Dies Iræ," especially when there are still not a few scholars who look upon Virgil's "Pollio" as a Christian prophecy. If any one objects on the score of improbability, I have nothing to say. The poet, with a happy conceit, makes the simple maid of Galilee, all unconscious of her destined honors, worshipping and "calling her blessed" who should be "the mother of the coming God."

Gabriel announces himself in a paraphrase of St. Luke i:28. Let me say once for all that these paraphrases of Scripture, of which there are several, besides being deformed by errors of doctrine, are the most feeble things in the whole poem, and, like most paraphrases, generally in bad taste. Mary's terror at the angelic salutation is illustrated by a figure which, from its very improbability in our age, takes us back with great vividness to the times, so familiar to the poet and so full of thrilling romance, when corsairs roamed the Mediterranean waters and it was unsafe to linger by the seashore with a strange craft in sight. "Pale and amazed she stood," says the poet, "like a little maid who, while gathering sea-shells on the sands of some small Ægean isle, beholds a peaceful merchantman sailing in toward the shore, and, paralyzed with terror, forgets even to seek safety in flight."

The angel continues paraphrasing St. Luke (vv. 30-33). In Mary's answer Sannazaro departs very seriously from the New Testament story, following apparently the apocryphal gospel of the birth of Mary or a tradition founded upon it. Instead of the simple, wondering, innocent question which St. Luke reports, our poet, influenced no doubt by false mediæval notions of sanctity, makes Mary reply somewhat pertly, that her vow of perpetual virginity, which from her infancy she has jealously kept, is an insuperable objection. Gabriel, however, overcomes her scruples by promising that she shall remain a virgin.

Mary then answers in a paraphrase of St. Luke I:38, after which a sudden light fills the house and the miraculous conception takes place. At the moment of the conception all nature stands astonied: the earth quakes, and it thunders on the left hand from a cloudless sky, according to those familiar classical models which every scholar will recall. The angel then leaves her, and Mary turns her thoughts to that which she has heard from him concerning her cousin Elizabeth.

Here the scene shifts, and we are introduced to the pale dwellings of Hades, where, as might now be expected, we are spared none of the mythological horrors of the place. To the author's mind they appear to be as real as anything else in the poem, and it costs him no effort to present us King David in the midst of all these pagan surroundings. David, "an old man distinguished by his *cithara* and sling," is inspired with prophetic fury, and sings of the birth of the Spoiler of Hell. He tells of the Magi, whom he calls *Æthiopes,* as I have seen them all represented in a very ancient picture; he sings of Simeon, of the slaying of the Innocents, of the flight into Egypt, of Christ's finding in the Temple, and of the touching scenes of the Passion. We find here and there in David's prophecy some fine bits of poetry, and also some offences against good taste which even the very different notions of an earlier age and of another people do not seem to justify. Thus the Virgin is described, at her Son's death, as filling the air "with a mournful howl" (*luctisono ululatu*), a mode of expressing grief which may be natural among an uncultivated or a barbarous people, but is certainly no fit subject for poetry. But here again the poet has been misled by his classical models. (pp. 178-80)

At David's prophecy Hell trembles, dark Cocytus shudders in his caves, Cerberus howls, and Sisyphus forgets to roll the still-returning stone, while the delighted saints applaud the sweet singer of Israel, and bear him away on their shoulders. And so ends the first book.

In the second book we are again brought into the presence of Mary, who, on the departure of her heavenly visitor, arises to go up into the hill-country, that with her own eyes she may behold the miracle of Elizabeth's pregnancy. She is described as setting forth, simply clad, and yet more lovely than the polestar in the frosty night or fair Aurora rising from her bed. Where she treads the flowers spring; the rivers stay their course at her passage; valleys and hills dance with joy; the palm and the pine shoot forth tender branches, and every wind is hushed but Zephyrus.

On Mary's arrival, Elizabeth, shaken with a sudden tumult in her womb at her greeting, breaks forth into that inspired welcome which is so familiar to us from St. Luke's narrative. In reading the vapid paraphrase of this famous passage, and still more that of Mary's answer, that glorious outburst of fervent piety which we know as the "Magnificat," we are sorely tempted to quarrel irreconcilably with Sannazaro's taste and poetic feeling. But it should not be forgotten that his error lies not so much in the manner of paraphrasing as in the attempt to do so at all; and that Sannazaro's original was not that picturesque and exquisitely beautiful language of our English version which makes any paraphrase an impertinence, but the

cold, unpoetic, and unclassical Latin of the Vulgate, for which he as a Latin purist could feel but little respect.

The aged Zacharias, still dumb for his want of faith, follows Mary adoringly with his eyes, and kisses the earth her virgin feet have trod. He points out to her in the Prophets the passages which concern her; and Mary, reading them now in a new light, recognizes herself as the burning bush, the rod of Jesse, and the fleece in Gideon's floor. Too much moved for speech, she can only thank God in silence. With Elizabeth, as in St. Luke's story, Mary remains three months; after which, yearning for her mother's pious discourse, and for her own little cell, now sanctified to her by her heavenly visitation, she returns home, there to await her time, recognizing the divine burden she bears in her immunity from those *longa fastidia* which Virgil's "Pollio," on the contrary, does not spare the mother of the coming child. Leaving her there, the poet now relates how Imperial Augustus, having at last closed the doors of Janus for a lasting peace, wished for a better knowledge of the extent and resources of his empire. Augustus therefore issues his decree that the whole world shall be enrolled; and here the author avails himself of a very fair opportunity to give us a catalogue—somewhat after the manner of Homer's catalogue of the ships—of all the nations enrolled under this census. He displays a knowledge of ancient geography which is remarkable if we consider that in his day there were no books of reference such as would now make the task very easy. He also displays his great command of epithets, which are, for the most part, well chosen; and here and there we find a choice bit of poetic description. Beginning with the far East—Armenia and the sources of the Euphrates and Araxes—he leads us westward through Southern Asia Minor, up along the famous eastern shore of the Ægean, and back again by the Euxine coast; thence through Thrace to Macedon, Thessaly, Greece, Epirus, Illyria, Italy, the Danube, the Rhineland, and so to Gaul and Spain; thence by the northern coast of Africa to Cyrene and Egypt, and finally to Syria.

We must not overlook the poet's art in beginning this catalogue at such a place that it should lead us naturally to the scene upon which the grand event of the epic was to be enacted. We are led from the cradle of mankind, in the wake of that star of empire that has always moved westward, to imperial Rome; thence, in the same course, around the Mediterranean Sea, about which all ancient history revolves, to farthest Spain; and back, by the ruins of the abortive empire of Carthage, to those Eastern lands where human history is to begin a new and greater cycle with the birth of the Saviour of mankind. We cannot dwell long upon the delicate beauties of our author's descriptions, in which it is chiefly remarkable that, instead of borrowing from the ancients, he has thought for himself and ventured on new things; but I may be permitted to give one or two specimens. Here, for example, is a terse and happy description of the Troad:

> Troy, the Sigæan bluff, Priam's ancient reign
> For arms and chiefs once known—*now for their graves.*

And this of Carthage:

> Alas! what fear, what labors laid she once
> On Latium and the fair Laurentian fields!
> A ruin now, a half-forgotten name,
> Prone in her fall, unrecognizable.

(pp. 181-83)

Returning to Syria we find the Virgin, now under the care of her aged protector, on her way to Bethlehem. Joseph, as he goes on this toilsome journey at the bidding of a foreign master, naturally thinks of his own royal ancestry, of whose deeds and glories every place on the way reminds him; and when he comes in sight of Bethlehem he exultingly prophesies that here, in her turn, shall Rome come—proud Rome—to honor the birthplace of a scion of his house, and before the glories of this little spot shall pale the splendors of Crete and Ortygia, though Jove was born in the one and Latona laid down her twofold burden in the other—a familiarity with Grecian mythology that I suspect none of my readers has ever given Joseph credit for.

Bethlehem, which they reach at sunset, is full of strangers, as if a fair were in progress, or as if the people of the surrounding country had taken refuge there from an invading foe. Finding no house-room, the travellers are divinely guided to a cave near the city walls, where they arrive after dark. (pp. 183-84)

We have come now to the grand event of the epic. The poet, impressed with the grandeur of the theme, stops again and again to invoke celestial aid in relating things never before sung, and treading where never poet's foot has trod before. At last he takes courage to enter upon his task. It is the time just before midnight, when all is still, and the weary world reposes. The fire is smouldering, and Joseph, stretched upon the hard rock, sleeps at last. Suddenly a new light shines through the cave from above, and the voice of celestial choirs is heard. The Virgin feels that her time has come, and piously commits herself to the divine protection; and presently, even as the dew gathers in pearls upon the grass though no man has felt one falling drop, so from the Virgin Mother's womb the Divine Child has passed forth, while she remained all unconscious of the painless labor. (pp. 184-85)

Among all the criticisms which have been made of Sannazaro's great work I have not found one that pointed out what, after all, seems to me its most serious fault. The poem . . . is an epic; but of epics there are two distinct varieties. The one, having what I may call a cyclic character, like Homer's *Iliad* or Virgil's *Æneid,* has no natural limit, no point where it is required to stop; the other, which is in its nature dramatic, is naturally limited by what is technically called the catastrophe. The first takes its subject vaguely, as the wrath of Achilles with its consequences, or the deeds and adventures of Æneas: no one can restrict the poet in his treatment of it, and he may spin out the thread of his story as long as he can make it interesting. The second takes for its subject a definite event—the loss of Paradise, the Passion of our Lord, the downfall of Thebes, or the like—and after that event has been described the poem should immediately close. Now, Sannazaro, having announced the Virgin's childbirth as his subject, was bound to stop as soon as that event had been described. He has neglected this rule of art, and having exhausted his subject in the second book has added a third. No wonder that the third book is in every respect inferior to the others.

It opens with a holy convocation of the heavenly Powers at the call of the Almighty. He sits among them clothed in a vast robe, where, on a ground of pure gold set about with priceless emeralds, Nature herself has woven images of all created things. The description of this robe is very elaborate, and recalls that of the shield of Achilles in the *Iliad.* The Almighty addresses the assembled nobility of Heaven in anthropomorphic language, to which we are no longer accustomed in uninspired writings. He reminds the angels of their fidelity when Satan rebelled. For this He has exalted them to great power, and has given them a share in His own operations. They have often witnessed His grief at man's disobedience, and have taken part in punishing mankind with shortness of days and labor un-

ceasing. They shall now hear how mercy hath conquered wrath, and a Virgin hath been miraculously filled with the power of God. Thus it was meet to ally the heavenly Powers with mankind, that they should love each other for the sake of this great mutual pledge; wherefore they are now to undertake the destinies of man. He then sends them to the cave, there to wait upon the Babe and to celebrate His birth and the Peace now established for all ages; the new birth of the world and the great victory over the Serpent.

After this the Father calls Joy from her choral dances—she it is that lights the Thunderer's face when the cloud passes, but earth she seldom visits, preferring to dwell in Heaven, whence she drives away all sighs and tears—and sends her upon earth to announce the Advent. We have here again a fine description of her descent. As she passes through the principal gate of heaven with her joyous escort, the sleepless Hours, that keep the gate, open wide the brazen portals, and she softly descends through the starry spaces, making every light in the heavens more bright at her passing, until she alights by the huts of the shepherds, whom she bids go with gifts of milk and honey to the Queen and newborn King. In St. Luke the shepherds are directed to the city of David, where they are to find the Babe lying in a manger, or perhaps in *the* manger, some well-known place near the inn where there was no room. Our poet's version of the story leaves them without any direction where to go. Nevertheless, they set about obeying the divine commandment. Crowning themselves with evergreens, they search the forest with flaming torches, and are ultimately led to the cave by the braying of the ass. The shepherds are filled with joy. Some of them bring a bay-tree and a palm to plant by the door of the cave; others adorn it with boughs of the olive and the cedar, and with long garlands of myrtle. Joseph comes forth to ask by what revelation they have been guided, and is told that God or His messenger spake to them, and was seen and heard to fly through the night. The shepherds are then admitted to salute the Virgin and Child, when Ægon and Lycidas—Ægon, a rich Numidian landowner, and Lycidas, an humble shepherd, sing a birth-song to the Son of God.

This song of the shepherds follows closely the famous fourth Eclogue of Virgil, the "Pollio." It is interesting as one of the many Christian interpretations of that much-commented poem. . . . After their song the heavenly host holds a review and a mock-battle in the air, closing with various evolutions in which some of the angels brandish the familiar instruments of the Passion, while others sing the praises of the Incarnate God.

Here follows an episode, both pretty and well told, but so absurd in this connection as to baffle description. Jordan, an old river-god, sits in his watery palace surrounded by his eighteen daughters, "all beautiful of mien and clad in white." The crystal urn from which he pours his waters is prophetic, and now shows him a picture of John Baptist baptizing Christ, whereat the waters well forth more abundant and of sweet flavor. The god lifts his horned and weedy head above the waves, and perceives, by all Nature's rejoicing, that God has come down upon earth. "This, then," he exclaims, "is what Proteus (in all things else a liar) truly promised, that one should come who should make me more famous than all the rivers of the earth." He then goes on with Proteus' prophecy, showing how the promised One should be a wonder-worker and a healer of diseases, in which connection the poet gives a complete list of Christ's miracles of healing; how he should come to be baptized in Jordan; how from that day a special blessing should rest upon rivers and all waters; how Christ should choose his companions among lowly fishermen. To these He should give all authority and the power of healing; He should make them custodians of the gates of Heaven and rulers over His people. Besides all this, great miracles should be showed in the waters. Water, blushing at her new honors, should be turned into the liquor of Bacchus; there should be a miraculous draught of fishes, a wonderful quelling of the storm. With two fishes multitudes shall be fed, and Christ Himself shall walk dry-shod upon the waters, while the Nereids swim about Him, while Neptune recognizes his Master, and the sea-gods come worshipping to kiss His feet. Now, says Jordan, the promised day has come. He therefore dons a festal garment, woven for him by the Naiads of murex-dyed water-mosses and embroidered with gold, and so leaves the scene.

The weakness and absurdity of this part of the poem far outweigh its beauties. It is as though, after the pretty *dilettantism* of his Virgilian cento, the poet had found it impossible to renew his inspiration. All this mechanism of heathen deities, which the cultivated pagans themselves did not believe in, they could use nevertheless without any impropriety, because it was, after all, the received theology, and they could not dispense with the supernatural in epic poetry. But the true supernatural element in a Christian epic is that which the Christian religion itself supplies; and such an interweaving as we have here of heathen mythology with a Christian story necessarily gives to the whole epic transaction a color of unreality utterly destructive of all its power over the reader's emotional nature. Milton did far better; for while he now and then alludes to classic mythology, he identifies the heathen gods with the devils of the Christian theology, and thereby invests them with all that truth and reality without which no accessory has any value at all in poetry.

But if the poet's inspiration flagged in this superfluous third book, it certainly revived for a moment at the close of his work. The last verses are so serene, so restful, that I venture to translate them, although I know what they must lose in the process:

> Enough, ye Powers! enough thus far to have sung
> The Birth august. Me now to welcome shades
> Calls loved Posilipo and Neptune's shore,
> The Tritons, Nereus old and Panope,
> And Ephyre, and Melite, and she
> Who (best of all) affords me tranquil ease
> And haunts the Muses love along her rocks,
> Dear Mergilline. There her orange-groves
> Bloom, like a Median paradise, with buds—
> With wealth of buds, whence, gracious nymph, she weaves
> Garlands of leaf unwonted for my brow.
>
> (pp. 186-90)

So ends this remarkable poem. When we consider that in the sixteenth century such a jumble of heathen mythology and doubtful tradition was admired for its deep religious feeling even more than for its genuine literary beauty, so that Peter Gravina, one of the author's contemporaries, could say with general applause that it was of divine inspiration, I think it can be easily judged, even from the rapid analysis to which my space has confined me, what results the Romanism of the Middle Ages had wrought in the religious sentiment of the Western world. Formalism, Phariseeism, and superstition had borne their natural fruit in an age which produced Alexander VI. and Leo X., the one a fiend incarnate and the other an æsthetic unbeliever. The religious sentiment of the cultivated classes must have been something purely conventional and

unreal, when one of their most pious lay representatives could feel and write like Sannazaro, and be praised for it in the almost impious words of Gravina. It is instructive to reflect that all this was the growth of the same soil in which Mariolatry, Hagiolatry, and every form of supestition had been thriving for centuries, until they were now beyond cure, even by the heroic treatment of the Reformation. In such a soil had the unfortunate exaggerations of some of the Fathers grown up into dogmas which stand to this day a solemn warning of the dangers of unbridled rhetoric in the mouth of the preacher of truth.

I hope—although this was not my chief aim—that I have done such justice to the literary merits of the *De Partu* that my reader will be disposed to give it its just place among Christian epics, perhaps the most difficult kind of composition that has ever been attempted. Nevertheless, as I said at the beginning of this paper, Sannazaro's reputation should not rest on this work. It is by his idyls and his Italian poems that he should be judged; and I do not hesitate to say that his best claim to be considered a true poet rests on his originality in transplanting the idyl from the woods and fields to the sea-shore; surpassing in this even Virgil himself, who copied the mechanism and *technique* of Theocritus and the Sicilians in a manner almost servile. To have surpassed the great Mantuan even in one thing is the boast of but very few of those who wear the crown of bays. (pp. 190-91)

> *Francis Philip Nash, "A Famous Religious Epic of the Sixteenth Century," in* The American Church Review, *Vol. XXXIII, No. 1, January, 1881, pp. 173-91.*

THE NATION, NEW YORK (essay date 1915)

[*In the following excerpt from an anonymous review, the critic appraises* Piscatory Eclogues *as a variation of pastoral.*]

Sannazaro's fame to-day rests mainly upon his pastoral romance, *Arcadia,* a work regarded by its author as a youthful indiscretion. His greatest achievement, in the judgment of his contemporaries, was his Virgilian epic on the Nativity, *De Partu Virginis,* a poem which obtained the benediction of two Popes and which is at least a most interesting document in the history of Christian humanism. The *Arcadia* was also surpassed, thought the critics of that day, by the *Piscatory Eclogues.* Here the author justifiably declares himself the inventor of a literary form. The twenty-first idyll of Theocritus, or if not of Theocritus then of some poet notably his peer, deals with the life of fishers, and is redolent with the brine of the sea. It does not, however, establish the piscatory eclogue as a class: it shows rather that the pastorals of Theocritus belong with it in the larger category of the mime. Similar material may be found in the marine dialogues of Lucian and the letters of fishermen in Alciphron, but Sannazaro had the same right as Ovid and Horace in pretending to the establishment of a type. Curiously, with the later invention of sailor-eclogues and vine-dresser eclogues, pastoral poets were all unconsciously returning to the more inclusive type of the realistic mime, whence the bucolic eclogue had sprung.

Various critics have regretted that the invention was ever made. Dr. Johnson [see Additional Bibliography] and his tribe queerly objected that the sea lacks variety and is an unknown and unattractive realm to all but learned readers. Modern critics bring another indictment. Sannazaro serves with the noble army of Virgiliolaters and incurs the inevitable charge of artificiality. His object is to translate pastoral phrases and incidents into terms appropriate for toilers of the sea. Scythes are beaten into tridents, the crook is exchanged for a rod, and the spreading tree becomes a cave on the beach; it is the golden age for the lobster-pot, which had never been exalted to a conventional type before. Instead of Pales and the sylvan deities, Glaucus and the Nereids give to the new conceit the ancient sanction of mythology. The subjects of the new eclogues bespeak their pastoral origin—a lover's lament, an amœbæan contest, a song of incantation. The characters all speak perfect Virgilian. The scenes are described in phrases which, when not found in some ancient poet, are quite what the ancient poet would have used. There is no possible offence against good form. Even when Phyllis mixes seaweed with her bouquet of violets and narcissus, the language somehow shows that this is proper.

Such conventionality, however cleverly managed, would spell the death of the piscatory eclogue, were there not an animating purpose, too. This is Sannazaro's love for every cove and headland on the Bay of Naples. With an imaginative force that takes us back to the creative days of Greek myth, he conjures the indwelling spirits from island and hill, and even from his own villa, where the nymph Mergillina dwells. Of this graceful personification of delightful places endeared to the poet, some traces may be found in Statius, but Pontano and Sannazaro made of it an art and almost a religion. La Cerda, the famous Spanish scholar, rightly maintained that Naples received a greater meed of honor from Sannazaro than from the ancient poet. There is surely nothing in Statius like the sincere and noble panegyric of Naples in the fourth eclogue. Proteus, overheard by two homefaring fishers, sings in the style of Virgil's Silenus, not, however, of cosmic science and primeval myths, but of the glories of the Bay of Naples, its Nereids and Sirens, its Cumæ and Vesuvius, its Virgil and Pontano. This is a theme cosmic enough for Sannazaro, and it makes his poetry enduring. So long as rivers run into the sea and Naples has charm, Sannazaro will find his readers.

> *"Toilers of the Sea,"* in The Nation, *New York, Vol. C, No. 2588, February 4, 1915, p. 145.*

JEFFERSON BUTLER FLETCHER   (essay date 1934)

[*Fletcher was an American educator and author regarded in his time as an authority on Italian Renaissance literature. He is noted for his studies of Dante as well as for his* Literature of the Italian Renaissance *(1934). In the following excerpt from that work, Fletcher considers* Arcadia *in relation to its literary antecedents.*]

Jacopo Sannazaro was destined, and without really intending it, to make the one important contribution of Naples to the Italian revival. (p. 167)

As a young man he composed in the vernacular—besides the *Arcadia*—much verse, some humorous and some Petrarchistic; but his mature writing,—the writing by which he hoped to win enduring fame,—was all in Latin. He himself regarded as his masterpiece an epic in Virgilian style but on a religious subject—*De Partu Virginis,*—to modern taste a rather frigid *antiquing* of the Gospel narrative, but at least more sincere and in better taste than most humanist epics. In it Sannazaro expresses the common aspiration of nearly all Renaissance poets,—to be to his princely patron what Virgil had been to Augustus, or putting it more broadly, to be the Virgil of the new age. . . . Like Edmund Spenser in his *Shepheardes Calendar,* accordingly, Sannazaro followed Virgil's example by first trying his wings in "the low-flying pastoral." Only, as befitted his bayside home, he wrote eclogues of fisher-folk instead of shepherds. His *Eclogae Piscatoriae* had international vogue and influence. (pp. 168-69)

Perhaps the mature Sannazaro still deprecated his *Arcadia* for being in the vulgar tongue. But certainly the term *vulgar* applies to the language of the work neither in its meaning of *inelegant* nor yet of common local usage. . . . [The] Italian of the *Arcadia* is not merely bookish, it was book-made. The severer humanists of the previous generation had scrupulously purged their Latinity, their *eloquentia,* of every word or phrase not sanctioned by Virgil or Cicero. And now Sannazaro, before Bembo, gives assurance that he has never "used anything not to be found in good authors." And so far as Italian was concerned, "good authors" for him meant Boccaccio for prose, Petrarch for verse.

To Boccaccio the *Arcadia* owes also more than language and style. At least, Boccaccio's own pastoral *Ninfale d'Ameto* had similarly—although not indeed with equal balance—mixed prose and verse. And the love-story of Sincero, hero of the book, has been shown to combine into one the two stories of Florio and of Fileno in Boccaccio's *Filocolo.*

Sincero's unhappy tale of love gives dramatic unity to the work. Rebuffed by the lady of his heart, Sincero has come to Arcadia seeking distraction. He has interested himself in the affairs of its pastoral folk,—their love-makings and merry-makings, their contests of song and dance, their rites and ceremonies. Like Childe Harold, he travels to escape from himself, from unhappy memories. But, again like the disguised Byron, he must tell us about himself, and devotes his seventh chapter to a recountal of his amorous misadventure. And in the twelfth and last chapter—that newly added one—he returns to and concludes his personal tale. Oppressed by a premonition of evil, he is anxious to return home to his native land. Rather surprisingly,—for it is the first intimation of anything supernatural or allegorical,—his return-trip is facilitated by the kindly offices of a nymph, who conducts him adventurously by the subterranean channel of her dedicated river. Sincero arrives home—to find his lady love dead. And the book ends mournfully with an elegy of farewell to his shepherd's pipe. (pp. 169-71)

The thread of personal romance in the *Arcadia* serves principally to hang the pictured panels of pastoral life. Also, no doubt, Sincero's woes set the contrast of a note

> Most musical, most melancholy,

against the merry pipings of the care-free shepherds.

Sannazaro is really the first returned traveller to tell of Arcady the Blest. I say *Arcady,* for Sannazaro's land (*very literally*) of milk and honey has little in common but name with the real Arcadia, tract of rugged mountains and ruggeder mountain-folk. Virgil indeed first associated the name with literary pastoral. . . . Polybius in his history of Greece stressed the simple-living and the fondness for song and song-contests of the Arcadians. And in his *Fasti,* Ovid, always given to magnifying the first Golden Age of simplicity and peace, and of springtime perpetual, found its reflection in an imaginary "Arcadia."

But to the making of Sannazaro's Arcady went—besides these hints—the whole paraphernalia of previous pastoral—and yet more that was literary. With punctilious industry Scherillo has picked out in Sannazaro's text bits inserted from the Greek idyllists Theocritus, Moschus, Bion,—from the late Greek romances, especially Longus,—from Roman Virgil, Nemesianus, Calpurnius. Erotic touches are identifiable as from Ovid and Catullus, Claudian, Anacreon, Ausonius, Apuleius, Petrarch. *Prosa* X is an epitome of the *Georgics*. The whole work would appear to be an intricately built-up mosaic of borrowed bits. So far from offending as unoriginal, even plagiaristic, such literary Cosmati-work, so to speak, was especially to the taste of an age delightedly responsive to every reminder of classical antiquity. The same taste liked, analogously, to inset fragments of antique marbles into the walls of its palaces and public monuments.

To veneration of remote Roman ancestors, Renaissance Italians joined that of the near literary masters of the *Trecento*,—of Petrarch and Boccaccio even more than of Dante. There are some echoes of Petrarch in the *Arcadia;* of Boccaccio, as I have said, many. But what particularly pleased Sannazaro's more immediate Renaissance audience—and not in Italy alone— was the intensified echo of Boccaccio's Ciceronian style, his stately and balanced periods and sugared diction. It is Boccaccio indeed at his most urbanely serious. Even when he describes a pastoral merrymaking, Sannazaro himself is never merry. (pp. 171-72)

It will be agreed, I think, that in calling Sannazaro's manner of describing country life "*urbanely* serious" I did not use an incongruous term. The literary pastoral is for the most part at least an *urban,* a citified, conception of country life. (p. 173)

It would be unfair to leave the impression that Sannazaro's praise of nature and the natural is altogether a literary pose.

Title page of the first edition of Sannazaro's Arcadia *(1504).*

Indeed, even supposing he borrowed from other poets of nature all the colours of his landscape, it was a landscape he painted. And he was—for his own time and place—creating a fashion, not following one. Admittedly later, in the full vogue of the pastoral, imitation became too often merest closet-echo without reality. There is no reason to doubt the sincerity of Sannazaro's feeling for nature. Only, it was nature at her very very gentlest and most decorous that he looked to and longed for,—a land of moral holiday from hard reality. . . . There, I think, is the fundamental and quite sincere appeal of the pastoral to the Renaissance. The times were strenuous; and more than one artist of delicate dreams was—like Perugino—a hard-bitten and hard-living man. It is *in principle* the same gospel as Wordsworth's—of "the healing power of nature." Only, we may believe that Wordsworth has painted a truer and more significant nature. (pp. 175-76)

> *Jefferson Butler Fletcher, "Sannazaro," in his* Literature of the Italian Renaissance, *The Macmillan Company, 1934, pp. 165-76.*

THOMAS GREENE (essay date 1963)

[*An American educator and author, Greene is a scholar of Renaissance literature and epic poetry. In the following excerpt, he examines* De partu virginis, *observing the poem's mixing of classical and Christian elements.*]

[Although *De Partu Virginis*] is centered upon the nativity, Sannazaro encircles it with a cluster of other Gospel stories: the annunciation, the visitation of Elizabeth, the adoration of the shepherds, briefer glimpses of the presentation in the temple, the massacre of the innocents, the crucifixion, the harrowing of hell, and more. With this there are ulterior scenes of the poet's invention: evocations of the gleaming halls of heaven, thronged with decorative angels; a descent to limbo where King David prophesies the advent of the Messiah; a pastoral scene dominated by the Jordan, a hoary personification of the river. All of this various material is fitted neatly, even precisely, into the three books which comprise the poem. The architecture indeed is carefully calculated; each of the books is in turn divided roughly into three sections, and the sections tend to counterpoise one another symmetrically. So the descent of Gabriel to the Virgin in Book One, for example, is balanced by the descent of the allegorized Laetitia in Book Three. The workmanship which Ariosto strove to conceal is not paraded here but it is plain enough, less intricate but equally assured.

Of the two descents, Gabriel's is closer to the Virgilian model and perhaps the more interesting for our purposes. The sovereign Ruler of heaven has pondered his design to redeem man from the ancient blot . . . , has summoned the angel, explained his design, and designated the woman worthy to bear his son. Whereupon the angel takes his leave and makes his shattering annunciation. . . . (pp. 145-46)

[The scene's] unfolding follows with fidelity, however great the stylistic distance, the much briefer scene in Luke I:26-38. . . . Sannazaro's only true structural departure is his concluding attempt to describe the conception itself, which the original account leaves discreetly in the shadow.

Thus we have, on the one hand, a scrupulous respect for the Gospel narrative, so far as it goes, and on the other hand, the greatest liberty taken with style, with background, with details from the poet's own imagination. This is the paradox of the scene as it is indeed the paradox of the poem. The angel, who lacks a single distinguishing trait, a single adjective, in the Gospel, acquires a *presence* in the poem, deriving not only from his fuller speeches but from the precise and beautiful description of his descent, the long swan simile, the epithets accorded him . . . , the few strokes suggesting his physical appearance . . . , the scent which he emits, his eloquence . . . , his power over natural forces. . . . The Virgin is not so fully developed, but she too acquires traits not found in Luke: a certain regal majesty (she is called "Regina" and "Diva") and an intellectual curiosity (she is discovered reading, according to an old tradition, prophecies of the Incarnation). The girlish hesitation which the Gospel records is evoked here with more sophisticated art by means of the shell-gatherer simile.

The material which has been added is drawn clearly enough from two principal sources: from Italian painting and from classical poetry. Had the poet never seen a fresco of the Annunciation, one imagines, the episode would lack a part of its freshness, its delicacy, its coolness; the angel might have been made less youthful, less graceful, rather weightier, and more mature. But so deep is the influence of antique Latin poetry that it is impossible to say what the scene would have been without it. One feels it in the language which seeks always control, nobility, clarity, and restraint, and in the imagery, in the reminiscences of Virgil and Ovid and the formality of the similes. Scholars have been able to point to specific passages of the *Aeneid* or Virgil's *Eclogues* which might have inspired a given detail: the swans haunting the Caystros or the scent which accompanies Gabriel. It is obvious that the descent as a whole, in its conception, stems from Mercury's descent to Aeneas. The only other indisputable derivation from a specific passage occurs at the end of the angel's second speech; in the evocation of the child's future power, Sannazaro alludes directly . . . to Jupiter's panegyric of Roman power in Book One of the *Aeneid*. . . . This however is surely the single deliberate *allusion* to a classical text. So steeped in classical imagery was the poet's imagination that he least of all, doubtless, could have specified the provenance of a given detail. Sannazaro was attempting to write a poem which, despite its subject, might have been read without confusion by a patrician of the first century. Thus the omission of the Virgin's name—Mary, and the angel's name—Gabriel, although both are named of course in the Gospel; thus the reference . . . to "Numina"—the gods—in the plural; thus the references to the Zephyrs and to Mount Olympus; thus the vague circumlocution . . . for the Hebrew prophets. The poem is written according to a strict and hampering sense of decorum, a decorum scarcely compatible at first view with any Biblical story whatever.

As a result of its rigid decorum, the style is slightly flattened out by a kind of academicism. Like the bulk of neo-Latin poetry, it has a tendency to stiffen; it becomes less open to the demonic properties of language at the same time that it conserves, mummified as it were, the devices by which classical poets had introduced the demonic. Thus the similes, lovely as they are in themselves, tend to function more as decorations, less as narrative devices which impose subtle colorings of feeling upon their contexts. This is particularly true of the swan simile. (pp. 149-52)

The classical mannerisms we have observed in Sannazaro's Annunciation are less striking than several subsequent anomalies—for example the imitation of Virgil's messianic fourth eclogue placed in the mouths of the Hebrew shepherds at the nativity. The shepherds' names are Lycidas, Tityrus, and Menalca. There is, in fact, scarcely a Biblical proper noun in the whole work; neither Gabriel, nor Mary, nor Joseph, nor Jesus, nor David, nor Elizabeth is named directly once, although all figure in the action. The proper nouns which do appear belong to the incidental figures drawn from mythology: Tethys and Amphitrite, Cerberus and Pluto, the Muses, Apollo and Proteus. The mythological machinery reaches its most bathetic point when the feet of Christ, walking upon the waves and surrounded by Nereids, are kissed by a reverent Neptune!

The classical coloring "dignifies' the Gospel stories, substituting for their bareness and simplicity a more ornate and aristocratic tonality. The epic manner, as understood by the Renaissance, required a certain grandiosity which might have reduced the original stories to absurdity. So Sannazaro's most formidable artistic problem was to raise the level of the material without destroying its essential dramatic qualities. He could not, for example, "dignify" the Virgin so greatly at the outset as to permit our wonder at the angelic visit to fade. She had to remain, to a degree, virginally delicate and girlishly uncertain. But in the Annunciation scene, this problem is complicated by the particular paradox of the situation: the Virgin is apparently inferior to the angel in the scale of being, but as mother of the godhead is worthy of his reverence. The paradox has already been made explicit before the angel's entrance; God the Father has described her as worthy of reigning gloriously in heaven . . . whereas in fact she dwells under a humble roof. . . . The problem for the poet was to make the most of the paradox dramatically without violating either of its aspects. Against all probability Sannazaro brings off the scene masterfully.

It was necessary first to establish the dignity of the two figures. The angel's speed, power, and grace, emerging first from the account, are turned in a sense to the honor of the girl for whom he descends and whom he compliments so graciously. But despite that honor, and despite her deep religious feeling which we perceive immediatley, her dignity is qualified by a human ignorance: filled with awe for the future mother of God, she cannot know that she is herself that mother. Her humanity shows itself more fully in her confusion and fear after the angel's greeting and is intensified by the shell-gatherer simile. At this point the apparent distance between angel and girl is widest, and widened more by the greater powers now attributed to the angel: if she is like a poor frightened girl by the sea's edge, he is like a god who can still the raging sea with a word. Here Sannazaro's perilous balance might have been irretrievably lost. But in fact the simile is brilliantly conceived, with the cool distinctiveness of its language, with the natural grace one intuits in the girl, with the tranquillizing reassurance following the illusory alarm. The Virgin loses no true dignity but gains a gentle delicacy. And the angel's second speech, evoking the vastness of her son's future empire, makes a contrast with her gentleness and rights the balance of greatness in her favor. So it will remain through the rest of the scene.

Thus, in the moments when it touches us, the poem's success involves discreet solutions of very nice artistic problems. The wonder is that the Gospel story is not crushed by the elevated tone and the extrinsic pagan apparatus. Transmuted it certainly is, but not unrecognizably. In his personal life, it appears that Sannazaro retained a devout orthodox faith (despite the superstition and hypocritical skepticism of his contemporaneous Naples) to balance his Humanistic enthusiasm; so analogously his poem communicates a Christian fervor through the welter of classical divinities. It is a *tour de force* which no other age could have produced, depending as it does on both the supplest religiosity and on a Humanistic sense of great spontaneous vitality. Sannazaro brought his Humanistic art, the only art he knew, as an offering to the church and to the Virgin. He could scarcely have modified the nature of his art, and had he tried could only have made an inferior thing. In a curious way he was an erudite *jongleur de Notre Dame.*

Sannazaro's transmutation of the Gospel story is representative in several ways of Italian religious feeling in the early sixteenth century. I have said above that his faith was orthodox, but orthodoxy under Leo X was not the orthodoxy of St. Augustine or St. Francis. And one may speak in this regard not only of orthodoxy in doctrine but in sensibility also. The sensuousness of Renaissance religiosity, its emotional facility, its easy optimism, its ostentation, its pagan eccentricities, its need for pictorial imagery—all find their reflectionin the *De Partu Virginis.* With what half-pagan pleasure in sound and color, what faith in the externals of religious ceremony, is the Virgin's aid invoked at the opening of the poem! . . . The poetic élan swells unbroken throughout the single long sentence, with its opening clarion summons of chariots and trumpets, its suspenseful repetition of ''si'' [''if''] clauses, and its ultimate resolution delayed until the last line and sprung climactically by the twin imperatives. It is a poetry of gleaming surfaces, reflecting the radiance of the central feminine figure, smiling and gracious, wreathed with the pomp of heaven. Something of the concreteness, splendor, joy, and music in Milton's heaven may derive from this brilliant Italian vision.

But the world which this poetry evokes emerges nonetheless as a little emasculated, lacking the vital energy of the finest epics. Thus the swan to which Gabriel is compared does not truly communicate the sensation of quickness, although it is apparently supposed to. You need only think of Homer's cormorant to feel the difference; this bird is comparatively leisurely in its descent to the quiet Caystros. . . . Nature is tamed as man and the world are tamed. The poet conveys an imperial view of things, the view of ecclesiastical imperialism, which softens the violence it would like to subdue. The imperial principle extends even to Sannazaro's heaven, where the Deity appears as a kind of Renaissance prince with angels for courtiers, each angel assigned to his own palace, each palazzo bearing its owner's name and heraldic arms. . . . It is impossible to be offended by this but it is difficult not to be amused. Clearly the Christian tradition has undergone a radical shift of emphasis.

The shift is made explicit in the Pelagian interpretation which Sannazaro placed upon the redemption. In dispatching Gabriel to earth, God has chosen to wipe away all vestiges of original sin and to raise man to the status of the angels. Once the Son's sacrifice has been made, man will regain his rightful place in paradise and the infernal powers will be forever thwarted. . . . The contrast with Milton imposes itself. Nothing is said by the Father of those who will not be saved after the Redemption, although these for Milton will be in a heavy majority. Sannazaro scarcely glances at the harsh theology which requires human sacrifice for Adam's sin, the theology which Milton's God will be at such pains to explain. It is characteristic of Catholicism before the Council of Trent that it place emphasis on the Redemption (not only in Sannazaro but in Mantuan's *Parthenicae,* Vida's *Christias,* and other poems) just as it is characteristic of Puritanism that its greatest, most representative poem dramatize the Fall. Buoyed up by Renaissance individualism, intoxicated by an oversimplified perspective upon antiquity, the church's conception of man never placed him closer to the angels than during these decades. In this it fol-

lowed the philosophy of the fifteenth century. As unlike as the aging Sannazaro was from Pico della Mirandola, one senses in the former's untroubled optimism a pale afterglow of the latter's youthful and magnificent manifesto—the *De Hominis Dignitate.*

A corollary of the Pelagianism is the absence in the poem of a diabolic principle. There are, to be sure, picturesque allusions to Gorgons and Hydras and Chimeras dire in Hades, but the Incarnation represents their total and irrevocable defeat. As a result the poem is ultimately passionless, a pageant rather than a drama. The note of joy, struck first by Gabriel . . . and sustained almost uninterruptedly through the three books, permits no dramatic tension. The poised and regal figure of the Virgin lacks a heroic dimension because her moral distinctiveness is asserted but never dramatized; no moral austerity is demanded of her. . . . Gabriel descends to announce, not to command, and later the personified Laetitia will descend only as a source of refulgent joy. No effort is asked of anyone, and given the exaggerated view of the human condition which animates the poem, no effort has to be asked.

The force which one does feel operating in the poem is the poet's creative, esemplastic will, moving with precision and grace human beings whose personal wills are slight. (pp. 153-59)

Thomas Greene, "Sannazaro: Feigning without Scandal," in his The Descent from Heaven: A Study in Epic Continuity, *Yale University Press, 1963, pp. 144-75.*

RALPH NASH   (essay date 1966)

[*Nash is an American educator and scholar of Renaissance literature. In the following excerpt from the introduciton to his translation of* Arcadia, *he provides a comprehensive overview of the work.*]

The narrative action of *Arcadia* begins with a gathering of shepherds near the summit of Mt. Parthenius, in the springtime. After listening to Eclogue 1, a Petrarchizing complaint from Ergasto, the shepherds return at evening to their cottages.

A few days later the narrator, Sincero, goes forth alone to pasture his sheep. At noontime he encounters the shepherd Montano, who sings a song in company with Uranio, whom Montano came upon and roused from sleep after his own song was already begun. This eclogue is a good example of the mixture in Sannazaro's work of literal and non-literal. Uranio and Montano are imagined as realistic, working shepherds. But their eclogue—which begins at noon and closes at evening with a discussion of whether the two shepherds should return to their companions—is then praised by those very companions, who have heard the entire song (including the awakening of Uranio) and who discuss its literary virtues while walking home by moonlight. The discrepancies, probably clues to the nature of Sannazaro's process of composition, make it clear that coherent realism will not be an object in this book.

On the following day the shepherds celebrate the feast of Pales (April 21) in an episode unusual for two things: it is the only episode situated in a village rather than in the open countryside, and it is the only one in which women actually appear, although even here they are only described, without being given speaking roles. The shepherds and shepherdesses are entertained by the songs of Galicio and of Elpino and Logisto in honor of their mistresses. With the return to the village at nightfall, the first section of *Arcadia* draws to a close.

Up to this point the tone has been relatively lighthearted and uncomplicated. Ergasto is melancholy, but most of the shepherds have been jesting, laughing, sporting, or praising their mistresses. The Arcadian landscape has been one of pleasant plateaus, flower-strewn, moonlit paths, garlanded houses and stables, and what the Elizabethans would call "enamelled meads." The thin narrative has been filled out with elaborately artificial descriptions of places of people or paintings. But in Chapter 5 Opico suggests a change of scene, and with it comes a change of tone.

The stream Erymanthus "hurls itself forth with a mighty and fearful uproar" such as might "breed incalculable fear" in the lonely traveller. This "picturesque" scene, which suggests Sannazaro as a forerunner of the mannerist landscapists, is succeeded by a more conventionally idyllic tableau, but that in turn is interrupted by a confused noise of music and shouting which leads the shepherds to the funeral rites for the cowherd Androgeo. From this point on, the motifs of elegiac pastoral dominate *Arcadia,* while the prose links become more and more a pastiche of deliberate imitations from various sources in the pastoral tradition. The long prose version of the first eclogue of Nemesianus, succeeded by Ergasto's elegy, brings on a despondent mood in Sincero, not much improved by the gloomy satirical reflections of Serrano and Opico in Eclogue 6. In response to the sympathetic inquiries of Carino, whose arrival is the whole business of the sixth chapter, Sincero decides to tell the shepherds his story, and the shift in tone, already begun in Chapter 5, becomes decidedly more pronounced.

First, the narrative impulse grows much stronger as the prose links are given more scope. Sincero's tale involves his whole life-history, with a slight digression on his ancestors, and it evokes a similar life-history from Carino in Chapter 8. After these tales episodic narrative gives place to something like dramatic, as the shepherd company meets the lovelorn Clonico, gives him good counsel, and takes him to the learned Enareto for further advice. This purposive action by the whole company is followed by the deliberate honoring of Massilia's tomb, which is the only episode to present consecutive dialogue and characterization among several characters in a continued action. Even in the dreamlike allegory of the last chapter we encounter more coherent narrative and purposive dialogue than in the first section of *Arcadia.*

The growing concern with coherent narrative is perhaps linked to a second aspect of the shift in tone—that is, the introduction of the autobiographical—in that Sannazaro's appearance as Sincero naturally fosters one kind of unity and sustained interest. But it also produces several ambivalences. Least troublesome is Sannazaro's double identity, as Sincero and as Ergasto (whose mother Massilia seems unmistakably meant for Sannazaro's mother, Tomassa . . . , but whose other appearances hardly need be reconciled with this ad hoc arrangement). More important is the ambivalence in Sincero himself. Proud of his city, his ancestors, and his own status, he is almost contemptuous of "these Arcadian solitudes in which—by your leave I will say it—I can hardly believe that the beasts of the woodlands can dwell with any pleasure, to say nothing of young men nurtured in noble cities." The jarring effect has been widely remarked, and need not be elaborated here. But more important than this concern about social inequalities is the concern with inequalities of genre. Ergasto-Sannazaro exerts himself to rise, "abandoning my rude pastoral style," in order to do honor to his mother in the future with a lofty style formed, in the words of Opico, through "steadfast and studious perseverance." And Carino offers Sincero-Sannazaro not only a shepherd's pipe but also a flattering hope:

> With this I trust that you, if it be not denied you by the fates, in the future will sing in loftier vein the loves of the Fauns and the Nymphs. And even as up to this point you have fruitlessly spent the beginnings of your adolescence among the simple and rustic songs of shepherds, so for the future you will pass your fortunate young manhood among the sounding trumpets of the most famous poets of your century, not without hope of eternal fame.

First *Georgics,* then *Aeneid.* Not for nothing does Sannazaro make room in Chapter 10 for another reed and another trumpet.

What does this mean? It means that with the introduction of Sannazaro-Sincero, and his literary aims, *Arcadia* itself has become self-conscious. The fine passage in Chapter 10, just alluded to, insists as much on the honorable ancestry of pastoral song as does Sincero on his noble family. Yet, in spite of this honorable ancestry, whenever we encounter the contrast between pastoral and heroic, as in the passages quoted above and many besides, we encounter some uneasiness about the hierarchies of literary genre. *Arcadia* not only becomes self-conscious, but conscious of itself as inferior to the heroic. (pp. 12-15)

Presumably the major factor in his evaluation of [the pastoral and heroic] genres was the weight of tradition in favor of tragedy and epic. A further factor, however, may be Sannazaro's view of pastoral as primarily devoted to love. In this he is amply justified by the precedent of Theocritus and Virgil. . . . Sannazaro's whole approach to poetry encourages the reproduction of common topics as commonly treated. But throughout the elegy to Maio we are reminded that Sannazaro inherits a long tradition from both classical and Christian sources, and sharply focused by the poetry of Petrarch, that looks upon love as a weakness, a snare and a delusion. Spiritually, in this tradition, and often physically too, love is a sickness—frequently a sickness unto death. Under such a view, a genre devoted to the celebration of love may be in some danger of becoming a celebration of sickness and death.

Something very like this occurs in the latter six chapters of *Arcadia* . . . as Sannazaro picks up and elaborates the strong elegiac strain that runs through the pastoral tradition. The introduction of Sincero-Sannazaro in Chapter 7 marks yet another difference in the tone of *Arcadia.* In addition to the strengthening narrative impulse and the increased self-consciousness about genre, the subject matter now begins to center on love and death. Sincero's story of a desperate love-sickness that leaves him still pale and enervated, preferring death to such a life, is followed by a sestina in much the same spirit: "Like the nocturnal bird an enemy of the sun / Weary I go among places shadowy and black." Carino's answering narrative is in its latter half a story of yet more desperate sickness and lamentation, to the point of attempted suicide. Its final paragraphs provide a happy ending, with a moral of hope for Sincero, but this point is sadly blunted by the immediate introduction of the lovelorn Clonico, whose name and appearance mark him as mad with love-melancholy, or very near madness. Clonico receives advice from Eugenio on the proper treatment for love, in an eclogue . . . modelled on Theocritus' Idyll 10, without much perception of the comedy in Theocritus.

The cure of Clonico provides a kind of narrative thread through Chapters 9 and 10, which seem arbitrarily divided by an eclogue of slight relevance to the narrative, but much of the material for these chapters is based on a recounting of miscellaneous superstitions out of Pliny. Although the second idyll of Theocritus, and its imitation in Virgil, provided justification for the inclusion of such material, it is rather out of keeping with the earlier portions of the book. As early as Chapter 9, then, and certainly with the "picturesque" ravine, Sannazaro's interest seems to be turning toward the esoteric, the supernatural—that is, toward some ingredients of the Boccaccian mixture of dream and allegory that dominates the final chapter of *Arcadia*. (pp. 19-21)

In spite of shifts and inconsistencies of tone, the work holds together fairly well. Sannazaro's great achievement—the imaginative leap that creates something new, in spite of his technique of imitation—is the perception that Arcadia is a country of the mind. His book is not limited to its Grecian topography, nor to its Sicilian and Mantuan antecedents, nor to Val Chiusa, nor to Florence, nor to Naples. It partakes of all. And yet it is more than an anthology of pastoral motifs.

No doubt it is true that Sannazaro shows something of the instincts of the scholar—at least, of the collector. Shrewdly eclectic, he perceives the relevance of Propertian elegy and Petrarchan canzone. It is the skill of his craft to interweave poetry with prose, ancient with modern, Christian with classical; and it is the mark of his age to dwell on the splendors of variety, to disdain fears of anachronism, and occasionally to attempt too much—as in his extension of the love-charms of Theocritus and Virgil to a rather drear catalogue of folklore from the elder Pliny. This generally skillful eclecticism is not always uniform—the prose links seem capable of accomplishing more than the verse, perhaps because in prose the smoothly cadenced rhetoric can cover all inequalities, perhaps because the verse needed to rely more specifically on those who had shown how Italian verse could be written. But it is almost always there, moving back and forth, altering perspective, illuminating, comparing, reminiscing, and emulating.

In other words, the process of imitation in *Arcadia* is dynamic, and it is focused on combining and blending features common to several different modes of prose and poetry. To that extent Sannazaro goes beyond the compilers of *florilegia* ["anthologies"], and—taking his cue from Virgil's account of the origins of pastoral—arrives at a sense of literary tradition, almost of literary history. It is, moreover, a tradition of praise: praise for one's homeland, praise beyond that for the fecundity of life and the abundance of love. Along with this praise, naturally if not inevitably, goes censure for forwardness in woman, for avarice and envy in man, for complexities marring a premise of perfect simplicity.

And thus Arcadia becomes a country of the mind, a symbol of dedication to poetry, to pleasure, to love, to contemplation. The woods that sweetly echo are idealized, abstracted, classicized: but Naples has its singers too, Sincero has his ambitions in poetry, and the ultimate emphasis falls on the bond between Arcadia and the world of Naples, quite as much as on the gulf between them. . . . Like Petrarch and Boccaccio before him, and perhaps with more self-consciousness, Sannazaro is celebrating and exploring his own commitment to poetry and examining the claims that he and his fellows can make for admission to the company of poets. This is a large sense of "poetic tradition," but it has its own attraction and its own verity.

Arcadia may be taken, then, almost at face value. It is the story of a young man's temporary withdrawal from his normal mil-

ieu, his ardent dedication to poetry, and his return to the world from which he had exiled himself. In that way, a *Bildungsroman*. Except that Sannazaro never really returned from Arcadia. The *Piscatorials* and *De Partu Virginis* carry on in the same mode as *Arcadia,* presenting a poetry of lucid rhetoric, dextrous imitation—above all, of fastidious exclusiveness, both in method and in content. Many years of labor went into the five hundred lines of the *Piscatorials* and the fifteen hundred lines of the brief epic. The single-minded concentration of energies upon relatively limited poems is matched by their exclusion of contemporary events and attitudes. Even when topical allusiveness is completely overt, as in *Piscatorials* 3 and 4, the manner is loftily abstract, firmly founded in a belief that there is a language proper to poetry and a rhythm and idiom proper to that language. If such poetry appeals only to the selected few, that is because not everyone can journey to Arcadia. Sannazaro is writing for trained poets and trained audiences, accustomed to careful perception of minutiae. . . . (pp. 22-5)

No doubt we believe that this approach relies too much on the pleasures of recognition, not enough on the pleasures of discovery. Its virtual exclusion of ethics and politics may seem to us an unnecessary exclusiveness. . . . Certainly all things are calculated, nothing is spontaneous, and hardly a gleam of the comic can be found anywhere. It is a serious, concentrated, aristocratic, and limited kind of poetry. Like other movements away from the imperfect flux and toward contemplation of the eternal and ideal, it is subject to various criticisms centering around our common human perception that life is on the side of the imperfect. But Sannazaro devoted himself honestly and thoroughly to his craft as he conceived it, with enough results that he may make us think again about our own conceptions. In particular, he may perplex the reader who conceives originality (or self-expression) to be the very hallmark of poetry, and the reader who assumes that aesthetic pleasure is a means rather than an end, or that it is an end necessarily subordinate to some other end. Both kinds of readers are often perplexed, to be sure, by other Renaissance and classical authors, but Sannazaro, pushing his method to the extreme, presents the question sharply. If we read him with attention, and without prejudice, I think we must answer finally: Yes. This too is poetry. This too we must accept.(p. 25)

> *Ralph Nash, in an introduction to* Arcadia & Piscatorial Eclogues *by Jacopo Sannazaro, translated by Ralph Nash, Wayne State University Press, 1966, pp. 7-26.*

BARBARA MUJICA (essay date 1979)

[*An American educator, Mujica has written extensively on the development of the European pastoral novel. In the following excerpt, she examines a menace underlying the utopia in* Arcadia.]

The negative elements that characterize the Spanish pastoral novels are present in a muted form in their principal model, Jacopo Sannazaro's *Arcadia*. In Sannazaro's novel, evil is an omnipresent underlying reality, an element common to both man and nature. The very first eclogue of the novel is replete with violent images: two rams joust, while the hypocritical flock praises the winner and ridicules the loser; evil wolves lie waiting to attack innocent flocks abandoned to lazy dogs by unconcerned shepherds; Cupid throws unsuspecting victims into inner turmoil; Procne and Cecropia lament ancient acts of violence. These images reveal the psychological, social, and political realities that pervade the novel in spite of the superficial harmony. Sannazaro, a politically active Neopolitan who went into voluntary exile with King Frederick of Naples when the latter was expelled to France, incorporated his bitterness over the political situation of his homeland into *Arcadia,* and parts of the novel are undoubteldy to be understood as sociopolitical satire.

The second eclogue is likewise full of references to political and social violence represented by frequent mention of wolves and thieves. Like the first one, this eclogue serves to broaden our understanding of the true nature of Arcadia: a conventionalized utopia which corresponds to man's dream of harmony, beauty, and emotional sublimation, but which is nevertheless inseparable from those political, social, and psychological realities with which man lives.

This notion is developed more fully in Chapter 3. Here, the characters are primarily nymphs and satyrs. Playing naked in the fields, the nymphs arouse the desires of the satyrs, who clamor after them only to be disappointed when the nymphs leap into the river and swim away. The episode captures the essence of Arcadia: anonymous imaginary beings exuding sensuality arouse desires never to be satisfied, but rather to be maintained in a state of intensely pleasurable sublimation. The nymphs escape danger, not by following an intellectualized strategy, but by following their natural instincts. They are part of the natural harmony of Arcadia, where violence is always a possibility, but is never actually realized.

Nevertheless, violence remains a potentiality. Although violence never erupts among the characters, it is present in the man-made art forms, that is, in the poetry, paintings, and sculpture. For example, the confrontation between nymphs and satyrs is avoided in the episode just described, but in a later episode there is mention of a coup that has painted on it the kind of violent scene that might have resulted if the nymphs had not escaped: a god kisses a nymph against her will while she struggles to get loose, scratching his nose and pulling his beard.

Yet, among the characters themselves, conflict is meticulously avoided. For example, in the episode in which the various shepherds pass judgment upon Galicio's song, each shepherd praises a different aspect of the song, but none expresses a negative opinion of it. There is no clash among them. Like the different shades of a painting, their different views combine to produce one harmonious whole.

In Chapter 5 there is a rather abrupt change of tone, and, although the atmosphere of general harmony is maintained, the underlying violence present in the first four chapters becomes more pronounced. The mood becomes increasingly melancholy, and elegiac eclogues become more important. The change of atmosphere is reflected in the landscape: the old shepherd Opico leads the other shepherds to a waterfall so terrible that it fills the observers with fear. Not long afterwards, the group chances upon the funeral rites for Androgèo, and Opico and Serrano sing a song in which the former dwells on the prevalence of envy, lack of faith between friends, depraved wills, malice, and greed that exist even in Arcadia.

The introduction of the character Sincero, who also identifies himself as Sannazaro, intensifies the elements of melancholy and violence. Sincero tells of his past happiness in the city of Naples, and the circumstances that prompted him to leave. As Sincero speaks of his past, he becomes increasingly aware of his present dissatisfaction. The victim of the disdain of a young

woman, he contemplates the amorous doves exchanging kisses in the meadow and feels estranged from his surroundings. Through Sincero, the reader becomes conscious of the conflict that exists within the superficial harmony of the Arcadian utopia. Sincero, surrounded by bucolic peacefulness, is unable to divorce himself from his turbulent past and from the outside world.

The pleasurable self-torment that characterizes the love episodes described earlier in the novel now becomes a morbid obsession with death; the poet examines the various means by which one can commit suicide. The oppressive melancholy of later Spanish pastoral novels that some critics have attributed to the Jewish presence in Spain is already evident in the *Arcadia.*

Now Carino and Clonico appear and tell stories that are variants of Sincero's. Like Sincero, Carino was the victim of an unrequited love and fell into a state of intense grief in which he sought death. He turned against his former friends, divorced himself from the Arcadian shepherds, and retired into solitude. Although Carino's situation was rectified when his loved one had a change of heart, the optimism of his tale is dimmed by the arrival of the disconsolate Clonico.

After attending to Clonico, the shepherds join Ergasto, who is mourning for his dead mother Massilia. In the episode involving the games and competitions sponsored by Ergasto in honor of Massilia there prevails once again an atmosphere of underlying potential violence which is never allowed to erupt. For example, a conflict arises when Carino stumbles in a race and either by accident or out of maliciousness trips Logisto. Ofelia, who is in next place, claims the prize is his. The shepherds take sides among the three contenders, and the harmony of Arcadia seems to be momentarily disrupted, but Ergasto resolves the problem by giving each of them a prize. There is another potential conflict in the wrestling match between Selvaggio and Uranio. But once again, violence is avoided when Ergasto agrees to reward both contenders.

Throughout this episode of *Arcadia* there is a tone of muted violence as conflicts come to the verge of eruption but are quickly dissolved by the generosity of one of the shepherds. In the last chapter the precarious harmony of Arcadia is finally shattered as the narrator, overcome by conflicts and sorrows, goes off by himself. The superficial peacefulness of Arcadia has been nothing more than an illusion into which the turmoil of the narrator's inner reality constantly intrudes. Now, overcome by sleep, he dreams he is alone in a solitary place, surrounded by tombs, overwhelmed by fear, unable to flee. It is the dream that reflects Sincero's psychological reality. Everywhere he sees nymphs weeping. There is a sinister, oppressive atmosphere reflecting, possibly, the political situation that forced Sannazaro to leave his native land. Faced with the imminence of his return to Naples, Sincero ardently seeks death. The novel ends on a morbid, desolate note: "... ogni cosa si perde; ogni speranza è mancata; ogni consolazione è morta" ["everything so lost; all hope is unfulfilled; all consolation is extinguished."] ... Sincero is now close to Naples. In the midst of reality, the dream of peace represented by Arcadia must necessarily disappear. (pp. 263-66)

Barbara Mujica, "Antiutopian Elements in the Spanish Pastoral Novel," in Kentucky Romance Quarterly, *Vol. 26, No. 3, 1979, pp. 263-82.*

WILLIAM J. KENNEDY (essay date 1983)

[*An American educator, Kennedy is the author of the only full-length study of Sannazaro written in English. In the following*

excerpt from this work, for which he was awarded the Howard
R. Marraro Prize, he examines Sannazaro's use of the pastoral
mode, comparing Piscatory Eclogues with Vergil's Eclogues.]

[Sannazaro's *Piscatoriae*] fully resist allegorical, anagogical,
tropological readings and at every turn they urge a secular rather
than Christocentric form of interpretation. They adopt the hexameter line of Virgil's *Eclogues,* and much more consistently
than Petrarch's pastorals [*Bucolicum carmen*] they incorporate
the bucolic diaeresis. They carefully alternate dialogue and
monologue, and they closely interweave the Virgilian motifs
of personal, political, and poetic concern. The landscape, or
rather seascape, however, is Sannazaro's own. This striking
innovation in the pastoral mode demonstrates how fully Sannazaro had appropriated its uses for his own purposes.

The collection's early eclogues dramatically integrate the pastoral seascape into the poetic action. **"Piscatoria I"** is a funeral
lament by the fisherman Lycidas on the death of his beloved
Phyllis. Framing it at the beginning and end is a dialogue
between Lycidas and his friend Mycon. There Lycidas takes
his first tentative steps towards confronting Phyllis's death
more honestly than he had done before. He advances from a
general perception of sorrow experienced metonymically in
nature to a specific articulation of her death as its cause. More
dramatically, he advances from an abstract recollection of her
funeral to a particular recollection of the solemn ritual associated with it, and, from attributing sorrow to the community
at large, to attributing it to himself as the most ardent mourner.
The dialogue moves gracefully from the speaker's recognition
of the outer world to his confirmation of the power of his inner
world.

Lycidas answers Mycon's challenge to sing with enthusiasm:
"Immo haec quae cineri nuper properata parabam" ("Yes
indeed I shall begin these hurried verses"), and further asks
his friend to cover her grave with cypress boughs and myrtle
while he sings his song: "Sparge manu et viridi tumulum super
intege myrto" ("Scatter with your hand and cover the grave
mound over with green myrtle"). The forms of the verbs are
important. Lycidas addresses Mycon in the imperative singular,
but Mycon replies in the first person plural: "Afferimus" ("We
are bringing"). In the next line this plural comes to include
more than Lycidas and Mycon when the latter points to yet
another fisherman, the silent Milcon: "Incipe, dum ad solem
Bajanus retia Milcon / Explicat et madidos componit in orbe
rudentes" ("Begin while the Baian Milcon lays out his nets
to the sun and coils in a circle his dripping lines"). Up to now
the reader has assumed the presence of only two characters
within the poem's landscape. The sudden multiplication of
personae, though thoroughly conventional in classical Latin
eclogues, often indicating the presence of silent auditors, reg-
isters a curious effect. In this poem about death and absence,
the new character's unanticipated appearance evokes a wider
community of living beings within earshot of the grieving
speaker, and it implies a still larger community outside of it.
Likewise it expands the range of the speaker's audience inside
the poem. The silent presence of Milcon acts as a foil to the
lamented absence of Phyllis, as a buffer to the apparent solitude
of Lycidas and Mycon, and as a complement to the role of
Mycon as eager audience.

This expanded audience performs an important function as the
theme of the poetic inner world begins to unfold. In the final
lines, after Lycidas has completed his lament, Mycon urges
his friends to repeat the song. Lycidas refuses, partly on the
grounds that he cannot bear the brief of repetition. More sub-

stantial grounds entail Lycidas's commitment to his own poetic
career. He vows one day to inscribe his poetry at the seashore
as palpable and tangible traces in the sand or on cliffs, so that
passing sailors may see the poems: "Quin et veliferis olim
haec spectanda carinis" ("But these too I shall someday inscribe to be seen by the passing ships"). In this form the poems
will become entities existing in their own right apart from their
creator and in the public domain, perceived by various audiences on various horizons, unfolding at different times in human history. His articulation of this vision seals his commitment. Its reward comes in his signature. His name and proof
of authorship, carved in rust on stone, will outlast the ravages
of time and earn him true poetic glory: "Inscribam grandesque
notas ferrugine ducam / Praeteriens quas nauta mari percurrat
ab alto / Et dicat: 'Lycidas, Lycidas haec carmina fecit'" ("I
shall trace in rust great letters which the passing sailor may
scan from the open sea and say: 'Lycidas, Lycidas made these
songs'").

The precedent for this striking topos is in Virgil's "Eclogue
V." There the elder poet Menalcas asks the younger Mopsus
to sing a song. The topic is unimportant, but Mopsus embarks
upon a funeral lament for Daphnis. It so impresses Menalcas
that he acknowledges Mopsus's attainment of maturity, mastery, and skill. Sannazaro's poem, like Virgil's, dramatizes a
young poet's coming of age. The lament for the dead beloved
provides a vehicle for the young poet's performance, but emphasis falls on the poet rather than on the deceased. Milton
would attempt a similar feat in his own pastoral elegy entitled
Lycidas, perhaps not without reference to Sannazaro's poem.

The clearest imitation of Virgil's "Eclogue V" in **"Piscatoria
I"** occurs in the poem's second half. There Sannazaro's speaker
vows to honor his deceased beloved with carefully prepared
rites:

> *Nos tibi, nos liquidis septem pro fluctibus aras*
> *Ponemus septemque tibi de more quotannis*
> *Monstra maris magni vitulos mactabimus hirtos,*
> *Et tibi septenis pendebunt ostrea sertis,*
> *Ostrea muricibus variata albisque lapillis.*

> [Seven altars for you will we raise beside the wet
> sea-waves, and seven rough sea calves, deep-water
> monsters, will we sacrifice to you in yearly ritual,
> and oysters will hang for you in sevenfold wreaths,
> oysters varied with murex and shining pearls.]

In Virgil's eclogue Menalcas proposes a land-bound memorial
to honor Daphnis:

> *Sis bonus o felixque tuis! en quattuor aras:*
> *ecce duas tibi, Daphni, duas altaria Phoebo.*
> *pocula bina novo spumantia lacte quotannis*
> *craterasque duo statuam tibi pinguis olivi.*

> [Be kind and gracious to thine own! Lo here are four
> altars—two, see, for thee, Daphnis; two for Phoebus!
> Two cups foaming with fresh milk, will I year by
> year set up for thee, and two bowls of rich olive oil.]

Sannazaro's appropriation notably secularizes Virgil's altars. . . . Sannazaro does not deify the object of Lycidas's lament. Instead he renders her more concrete as an emblem of
the best in humankind. To her Lycidas will erect seven altars,
signifying her position as the sum and substance of God's six-
day creation and seventh-day rest.

Likewise Sannazaro secularizes the role of the poet. At the end
of **"Piscatoria I"** Lycidas engraves a final song on Phyllis's
tomb for fishermen to read as they prepare their lines: "Interea

tumulo supremum hoc accipe carmen, / Carmen quod, tenui dum nectit arundine linum, / Piscator legat et scopulo suspiret ab alto'' (''Meanwhile receive for your tomb this final song, that, while he ties the line to the slender rod, the fisherman may read, and utter a sigh from the lofty cliff''). In Virgil the corresponding verses inspire Menalcas's address to Mopsus as a ''divine poet'': ''Tale tum carmen nobis, divine poeta, / quale sopor fessis in gramine'' (''Your lay, heavenly bard, is to me even as sleep on the grass is to the weary''). For Badius Ascensius, Virgil's sixteenth-century commentator, the address signifies the poet's likeness to divinity as a creator in his own right. . . . Sannazaro's hexameters, however, base the composition in the concrete reality of everyday human action. The poet engraves his words on Phyllis's seaside tomb while the fisherman ties his lines to a fishing pole. The response that the poet demands is nonetheless analogous to the fisherman's act of tying his lines. It is the act of reading, a binding (*legere*) of lines of verse into varied metrical units, an act that epitomizes the human capacity to construe, understand, and interpret.

The topic of **''Piscatoria II''** is the most artificial and conventional of all pastoral topics, the amorous lament. . . . In it Lycon complains of Galatea's unresponsiveness towards him. He alludes to a misunderstanding between them occasioned by a false rumor of his infidelity to her. To defend himself he balances the rumor, which is one kind of fiction, against another kind of fiction, which is myth, and he fashions his lament as yet a third kind of fiction, the pastoral poem. Fiction therefore plays against fiction on a number of levels, and all of them emphasize the inner world of the poem as an overarching fiction. Its center shifts with the imposition of each new level, and the shifting imparts an elusive beauty to it.

The beauty is hard won. As one result of shifting the ground so often, the poem risks losing its center altogether. The speaker seems conscious of this danger as he iterates the emptiness of the landscape dominating Lycon's lament. Lycon sits wearied in a vacant cave composing his poem throughout the dark night. He complains that his own words are as useless as hollow waves hurled against the cliffs. His audience, Galatea, has denied her hand to him. The cause of her displeasure is the rumor about his relationship with Lyda. To answer the accusation, Lycon can only resort to vain pleading. At the poem's end the speaker underscores the emptiness of his lament. Lycon's discourse is insubstantial; he can only fling his words hopelessly at the deaf wind. And yet the lament carries a strange beauty, a warm glow. The poem ends not with a sense of uselessness but with an image of soft morning light suffusing the sea and sky with rosy brightness. Dawn brings new hope, a promise of continuance, an impulse to take up the burden and try again. For all its negative feeling, the poem has achieved something positive. (pp. 158-63)

By comparison Sannazaro's central model for this poem, Virgil's ''Eclogue II,'' offers a less optimistic conclusion. There Corydon laments that he has rejected all women for the love of a single boy, Alexis, who now ignores him. Corydon invites Alexis to accompany him on the pastoral pipes that Pan has bequeathed them and that the shepherd Damaetas has taught them to use. He hopes that art will cement their relationship, but by the poem's end, when sunset drives the flocks home, he has come to perceive the futility of his imagination. He must now turn to other pursuits. . . . In Sannazaro's poem, on the other hand, the final lines depicting the passage of night and the return of morning metonymically reflect the speaker's recovery. . . . Of course, he recovers only to renew his grief

with the return of night. But the important point is that a resolution does occur, and that the play of fictions within the poetic discourse has brought it about. For all the speaker's amorous irresolution, he has not lost faith in his art.

The poem's Virgilian focus occurs at its climax, when the speaker despairs of escaping Love's power over him. Addressing himself, the speaker questions whether foreign travels and intense labors can help him forget his love:

> *Quid loquor infelix? an non per saxa, per ignes,*
> *Quo me cumque pedes ducent, mens aegra sequetur?*
> *Vitantur venti, pluviae vitantur et aestus,*
> *Non vitatur amor; mecum tumuletur oportet.*

[Unhappy man, what am I saying? Will not my sick mind follow me through rocks, through fires, wherever my feet shall lead me? Winds are avoidable, rains and heats are avoidable, love is not to be avoided; it needs must be buried with me.]

The lines evoke a similar climax in Virgil's ''Eclogue X'' with its famous conclusion that love conquers all:

> *non illum nostri possunt mutare labores,*
> *nec si frigoribus mediis Hebrumque bibamus*
> *Sithoniasque nives hiemis subeamus aquosae,*
> *nec si, cum moriens alta liber aret in ulmo,*
> *Aethiopum versemus ovis sub sidere Cancri.*
> *omnia vincit Amor: et nos cedamus Amori.*

[No toils of ours can change that god, not though in the heart of winter we drink the Hebrus and brave the Thracian snows and wintry sleet, not though, when the bark dies and withers on the lofty elm, we drive to and fro the Aethiopians' sheep beneath the star of Cancer! Love conquers all; let us, too, yield to Love!]

It may not be fanciful to see in Virgil's hexameters a literary self-referentiality that Sannazaro adapts in his own manner. Virgil's Gallus laments his inability to alter Love's will even after the change of seasons when bark, *liber* dies on the trees and shepherds turn, *versemus* their sheep in new directions. Both *liber* and *versare* suggest literary production by evoking the paronomastic book (*liber*) and act of turning metrical verses (*versare*). Likewise Sannazaro's hexameters refer paronomastically to their own literary production, first in the speaker's explicit questioning of his own verbal performance (''quid loquor''), next in his use of literary topoi that link classical Latin conventions to Petrarchan vernacular ones (''per saxas, per ignes''), and finally in his curious evocation of feet (*pedes*) that lead him onwards, suggesting the propulsion of metrical feet that draw the poem towards its conclusion. If in this context Virgil's final line, ''omnia vincit Amor: et nos cedamus Amori,'' implies the complicity of poetic activity in the experience of love, Sannazaro's reworking of it, ''Non vitatur amor; mecum tumuletur oportet,'' seals that complicity. **''Piscatoria III''** extends the topic of literary self-referentiality by dramatizing the effects of absence and separation on three different levels. It moves from the outer world of the speaker's political exile to the inner world of his composing poetry. An initial comparison with its Virgilian model, ''Eclogue VII,'' shows how much Sannazaro emphasizes this movement. Virgil's Meliboeus, searching for a lost goat, encounters Corydon and Thyrsis, whose singing contest he judges. Sannazaro's frame is more elaborate. In it Celadon asks Mopsus to recount what happened when storms forced him and his fishing party to a standstill. Mopsus responds with an account of how they lamented their king's exile, and of how he judged a singing contest between Chromis and Iolas. Celadon's request, Chromis's lament, and the singing contest with Iolas all reflect various forms of discontent. Celadon's is personal, yet friendly; his companions have been detained at a remote harbor for twelve days. Chromis's is initially social and political: his countrymen have sadly followed their king into exile. The singing contest is private and amatory: the singers complain of their beloved's coldness.

Still other forms of discontent mark the poem's witty development. Mopsus is addressing an audience (Celadon) already unsatisfied by an earlier account (Aegon's) of a speech (Chromis's) that has itself retreated into past history. Mopsus moreover implies that Chromis's account itself is flawed. The king's physical separation has left him with only a secondhand report of the journey. Relying upon his memory of this report, "Nam bene si memini, Rhodanum referebat Amilcon" ("For if I remember rightly, Amilcon spoke of the Rhone"), Chromis has reconstructed the king's itinerary in his own words. Celadon is thus receiving Mopsus's account of Amilcon's account at several removes.

Emotionally, however, these words have the power to bridge the distance betweenthe separated parties. The lover's ensuing rhetorical performance, then, becomes a test of language's power to compensate for absence. The lover can remove the barrier between himself and the beloved if his imprecations move her. For that very reason, however, the lover's imprecations impose on him as a speaker a more arduous task than other forms of discourse might impose on their speakers. Because this task promises at least some chance for success, whereas the others do not, there is more to hope for, more to aim for, and ultimately more to lose. The stakes are higher.

The singing contest proceeds in alternating quatrains, with Iolas duplicating each theme that Chromis announces. In it Chromis's attachment to his own beloved loses its linguistic moorings. Her name shifts from Chloris to Hyale, and he will repeat the shift [later]. . . . Nor is the confusion merely verbal. Chromis has in mind not the presence of a real beloved, but rather the idea of a conventional beloved, an idea attached more to words than to things, embodied in fictive language and the inner world of poetry. The reappearance of Chloris's name in the fifth quatrain brings Chromis's discourse full circle, as though the speaker had moved from a real woman to artful convention by citing Hyale and Phoebe, and finally back again. For Iolas, meanwhile, Nisa's continued proximity affords reason enough to stay on the island. Her presence assures a secure haven against the storms of adversity.

Nor are these storms idle imaginings. In this sea-enclosed landscape storms constitute a very real force in the fisherman's lives. The singing contest has led the speaker to assert that landscape's importance. There the beloved's presence or absence makes all the difference between the joy and pain that the speaker feels. In the eclogue's final lines Mopsus reestablishes Celadon's presence by addressing him as his immediate audience. Summarizing his story of the singing contest, Mopsus inserts a participial phrase that confers a final perspective on the action: "Inter se vario memini contendere cantu / Horrida ventosi ridentes murmura ponti" ("I have called to mind how these lads contended between themselves in various song, laughing at the savage rumblings of the windy sea"). *Ridentes* is the key word because it establishes a human and civilized reaction to the pressures of nature. The presence of the sea and its savage rumblings is inevitable. One seeks the presence of another—a lover, a friend, a king—to laugh and face the storm with confidence. (pp. 164-68)

[Sannazaro's *Piscatoriae*] succeed in moving between the outer and inner worlds of the pastoral with an ease reminiscent of the best classical models. Unlike Mantuan's eclogues, which epitomize the didactic, sententious tones of the early renaissance pastoral, these eclogues create an "other" world whose poetic speakers have the leisure to resolve tensions between their outer and inner selves. Unlike contemporary eclogues by Pontano, Castiglione, Vida, and Navagero that established the mode as the premier vehicle for dirge, Sannazaro's eclogues treat the motifs of presence and absence, hope and despair, memory and desire in rich and satisfying ways. Unlike eclogues by Strozzi and Boiardo that appropriate the technical form with minimal feeling for its subtler conventions, Sannazaro's poems achieve a balnce of form and idea where the two are suffused into one. Sannazaro's merit in the *Piscatoriae* was to have realized the topical potentials of the classical pastoral in Latin hexameters of charm and polish. No other collection of Latin eclogues in the Renaissance duplicated them. (pp. 179-80)

William J. Kennedy, in his Jacopo Sannazaro and the Uses of Pastoral, *University Press of New England, 1983, 238 p.*

DAVID QUINT   (essay date 1983)

[*The following excerpt is taken from a detailed and subtle analysis of the tension implicit in Sannazaro's treatment of the pastoral and epic genres of* Arcadia *and* De partu virginis. *Here, Quint summarizes this opposition.*]

[The] opposition of pastoral to epic aptly describes a literary career whose dual achievements are the pastoral "novel," the *Arcadia,* and the *De partu Virginis,* a three-book epic on the subject of the Nativity. The earlier work is written in the *lingua volgare* ["vernacular"]; the second, in high-style Latin hexameters. The Virgilian pattern of this career . . . [is] conventional: more than one Renaissance writer began with the pastoral in order to hone his skills for the more arduous task of epic. But the tension between pastoral and epic continues even within Sannazaro's two major works. The funerary games and the underworld descent in its final two prose sections draw the *Arcadia* toward an "epic" conclusion, while the apparition of the angels to the shepherds of Bethlehem affords the occasion for a pastoral interlude in the third book of the *De partu Virginis.* The question of genre is inseparable from Sannazaro's thematic and poetic concerns. In his fiction, epic and pastoral present conflicting versions of the claims and scope of the literary work. (p. 44)

The reemergence of the epic and pastoral genres in Renaissance literature may be linked to different attitudes toward the authority of the literary text. Pastoral meaning points to the textual structures from which it is exclusively produced; epic meaning claims to derive from a transcendent source outside the text. The turn in Jacopo Sannazaro's career from the *Arcadia* to the *De partu Virginis* reflects a conscious attempt to transcend a self-enclosed, ultimately inauthentic pastoral fiction and to ground the literary text in authorized truth: his epic meditates on nothing less than the Incarnation. Both works thematize the epistemological implications of their poetics with a descent to the source of rivers in imitation of the *Fourth Georgic,* and each emphasizes a different aspect of Virgil's epyllion. The intratextual fiction of the *Arcadia,* acknowledging the inadequacy of its language in the face of history, stresses the poetic failure of Orpheus. The *De partu Virginis,* celebrating in epic verse the fullness of the Word which gives meaning to all history, features the prophetic voice of Proteus. (p. 48)

Sannazaro's literary career, divided between the *Arcadia* and the *De partu Virginis,* fits neatly into an opposition between the ways in which historicist and allegorical modes of reading could define the nature of the Renaissance literary text. The neatness is the more complete because of the extreme positions taken by both works. In the face of history, the *Arcadia* reduces literary meaning to the kind of autonomous system which the pastoral fiction self-consciously declares itself to be. The *De partu Virginis* makes its meaning absolutely dependent upon the Word of God, to the point where the identity of the human writer all but disappears. The alternative ways in which the two works ask that they themselves be read are displayed in the double reading which they offer of Virgil. The *Arcadia* undertakes an imitation which is also a skillful historical reconstruction of the meaning of the *Eclogues* and the *Fourth Georgic;* the *De partu Virginis* allegorizes those works—and, in the figure of Proteus the reluctant pagan *vates,* points to its mode of allegory—in order to produce a Christian meaning from Virgil's poetry.

Partly because of the purity of their respective styles, partly because their subject matter *is* so conventional, the *Arcadia* and the *De partu Virginis* enjoyed a canonical status and immense popularity in the sixteenth century—and a subsequent decline in readership and reputation. They became instant classics because their author tried so little to assert his individual divergence from prevailing classical standards; they now seem brilliantly finished but one-dimensional and rather academic exercises. Such academicism was a common enough pitfall for humanist authors intent upon the imitation of classical models. In the case of Sannazaro, a poet of genuine talent, the charge of empty formalism results from a retreat from history, away from vital human problems which resist conventional explanation. Perhaps when his two major works are read together, as the third book of the *De partu Virginis* suggests they should be, they may question eachother's generic assumptions and gain a measure of human depth and complexity. The contrast between their pastoral and epic aspirations points to Sannazaro's divided attitude toward his vocation, as well as to his awareness of the limits of literary convention itself. (pp. 79-80)

> *David Quint, "Sannazaro: From Orpheus to Proteus," in his* Origin and Originality in Renaissance Literature: Versions of the Source, *Yale University Press, 1983, pp. 43-80.*

ADDITIONAL BIBLIOGRAPHY

Baker, Stewart A. "Sannazaro and Milton's Brief Epic." *Comparative Literature* XX, No. 2 (Spring 1968): 116-32.
> Discusses Sannazaro's techniques in adapting heroic epic to his Christian theme in *De partu virginus* and relates the work to John Milton's *Paradise Regained* (1671).

Baldwin, Charles Sears. "Imitation in Lyric and Pastoral." In his *Renaissance Literary Theory and Practice: Classicism in the Rhetoric and Poetic of Italy, France, and England, 1400-1600,* edited by Donald Lemen Clark, pp. 65-90. Gloucester, Mass.: Peter Smith, 1959.
> Judges Sannazaro's achievement in *Arcadia.* Baldwin concludes: "In 1504 Sannazaro succeeded at the Renaissance task of making literature out of literature."

Fucilla, Joseph G. "Sannazaro's *Arcadia* and Gálvez de Montalvo's *El Pastor de Fílida.*" *Modern Language Notes* LVII (1942): 35-9.
> Perceives echoes of *Arcadia* in Luis Gálvez de Montalvo's *El pastor de fílida* (1582).

[Johnson, Samuel]. *The Rambler,* No. 36 (21 July 1750): 205-10.
> Includes, within a general discussion of pastoral poetry, a consideration of the appropriateness of the piscatory eclogue. Citing Sannazaro's *Piscatory Eclogues* as an example, Johnson concludes that this form of pastoral is unsatisfactory due to the nature of its subject.

Kalstone, David. "The Transformation of Arcadia: Sannazaro and Sir Philip Sidney." *Comparative Literature* XV, No. 3 (Summer 1963): 234-49.
> Evaluates *Arcadia* as a transitional work between Petrarch's sonnets and Sidney's *Arcadia.*

Mujica, Barbara Louise. "The Wizard in the Spanish Pastoral Novel." In *Homenaje a Humberto Piñera: Estudios de literatura, arte e historia,* pp. 179-86. Madrid: Editorial Playor, 1979.
> Contains a short exploration of magic and eroticism in *Arcadia.*

Mustard, Wilfred P. Introduction to *The Piscatory Eclogues of Jacopo Sannazaro,* by Jacopo Sannazaro, edited by Wilfred P. Mustard, pp. 11-53. Baltimore: Johns Hopkins Press, 1914.
> Introduction to an annotated Latin edition of *Piscatory Eclogues.* Mustard discusses the early reputation of the work in Italy and elsewhere and examines the imitations it inspired.

Perry, Thomas Amherst. "Geography as a Structural Element in the Early Pastoral Romances of the Renaissance." In *Proceedings of the 8th Congress of the International Comparative Literature Association,* Vol. 1, edited by Béla Köpeczi and György M. Vajda, pp. 119-25. Stuttgart: Kunst und Wissen, 1980.
> Views *Arcadia* as incorporating three levels of geography: the world of literary pastoral tradition, the world of actual rustic life, and the poet's real homeland.

Piepho, Lee. "The Latin and English Eclogues of Phineas Fletcher: Sannazaro's *Piscatoria* among the Britons." *Studies in Philology* LXXX, No. 1 (1984): 461-72.
> Traces the influence of Sannazaro's *Piscatory Eclogues* upon Englishman Phineas Fletcher's *Piscatorie Eclogues.*

Stillman, Robert E. "Poetry and Justice in Sidney's 'Ye goatherd gods'." *Studies in English Literature* 22, No. 1 (Winter 1982): 39-50.
> Demonstrates Sir Philip Sidney's indebtedness to Sannazaro and to Gaspar Gil Polo for the double sestina "Ye goatherd gods" in his *Arcadia.*

Wilkins, Ernest Hatch. "Neapolitan, Ferrarese, and Other Writers." In his *A History of Italian Literature,* edited by Thomas G. Bergin, pp. 167-76. Cambridge: Harvard University Press, 1974.
> Contains a brief, favorable summary of Sannazaro's literary career.

Carlos de Sigüenza y Góngora

1645-1700

Mexican chronicler, historian, essayist, biographer, and poet.

One of the leading intellectuals of colonial New Spain, Sigüenza was renowned in his own day and remains noteworthy today as a remarkably versatile scholar and man of letters. His writings encompass chronicles of contemporary events, accounts of historical ones, pioneering scientific inquiry, and poetry. His current literary reputation rests primarily on the historically valuable chronicles, particularly *Infortunios que Alonso Ramírez (The Misadventures of Alonso Ramírez),* a factual and entertaining narrative which has been compared to the picaresque novel in form and style. The solid scholarship evident in Sigüenza's chronicles, histories, scientific works and other attainments mark him, critics have noted, as one of the most able and interesting men of his era.

Sigüenza's life was one of intellectual activity and achievement. Born in Mexico City to parents of Spanish and Creole heritage, he was educated by the Jesuits. Although (inexplicably to biographers) he never joined the order, Sigüenza received under the Jesuits' tutelage a thorough education in the humanities and sciences; this training, combined with his great intellectual capabilities, suitably prepared him for his varied and distinguished career. In 1672 he was ordained a lay priest, soon afterwards winning acceptance to the chair of mathematics and astrology at the Royal University of Mexico. During his career Sigüenza was also a proficient cartographer—as Royal Cosmographer he joined an exploratory expedition to the Pensacola Bay area of Florida—and engineer—aiding in the design of new canals in the capital city, among other tasks. As a scholar, he was avidly interested in the aboriginal and colonial history of New Spain, conducting extensive research into early Mexican Indian civilizations as well as writing histories of Spanish exploits in the New World. He became, particularly during the viceroyalty of the Conde de Galve (1688-1693), a court historian, often commissioned to write chronicles of important current events. So great was Sigüenza's reputation during his lifetime that he was reportedly invited to the court of Louis XIV, though he either could not or chose not to go. He died in Mexico City in 1700, donating his extensive library to the Jesuits.

Throughout his life, Sigüenza wrote copiously and indefatigably on the many subjects which interested him, but few of these works were published. In seventeenth-century New Spain the publication of secular works, while not forbidden, was discouraged. Further, publication required a substantial financial outlay to cover the costs of paper and printing; as Sigüenza, for all his myriad endeavors, was not a rich man, few of his works beyond those expressly commissioned (and paid for) by others saw print. Consequently, most of his writings have been lost, though enough remain to testify to his remarkable versatility and range of talent.

The work considered by modern scholars Sigüenza's most significant is *The Misadventures of Alonso Ramírez.* It is also one of the few yet translated into English. This chronicle of the perilous journeys of a Puerto Rican adventurer was related to Sigüenza by Alonso Ramírez himself; reportedly, Sigüenza recorded the narrative in order to help Ramírez secure financial assistance from the viceroy. Scholars have noted that this

chronicle of a boy leaving home to make his fortune and his subsequent vagrant life and adventures on land and sea (including capture by English pirates), shares many qualities with the picaresque narrative: indeed, *Alonso Ramírez* is frequently considered a novel, despite its basis in fact. Julie Greer Johnson has called the work "a striking example of the efficacious intertwining of history with literary technique prevalent in the picaresque genre," adding that "the result of this delicate balance between historical documentation and creative form not only confirms Sigüenza's outstanding ability as an historian but distinguishes him as a gifted storyteller as well."

Sigüenza's *Mercurio volante (The Mercurio Volante,* commonly known in English as "Flying Mercury"), tells of Don Diego de Vargas's 1692 reconquest of the region today known as New Mexico, following an Indian revolt. Based on Vargas's own reports to the viceroy, the work was intended as an official statement of the events of the expedition. Thus, as Irving A. Leonard has emphasized, while *The Mercurio Volante* is "essentially accurate," it is to some extent propagandist in its purposeful portrayal of the reconquest in the most favorable light possible. Besides its historical value, an additional interest adheres to *The Mercurio Volante;* as it was written to disseminate the news of the expedition both at home and abroad, Leonard has designated the work a "primitive example of journalism."

Sigüenza's other chronicles and histories, while attracting less critical notice, are yet deemed interesting for their historical value. Such works as *Glorias de Querétaro* ("Glories of Querétaro"), which records the founding of the Church of the Virgin of Guadalupe in Querétaro, and *Parayso occidental* ("Occidental Paradise"), a history of the Royal Convent of Jesus Mary in Mexico City, together with biographies of some of the convent's more prominent nuns, are considered significant chronicles of the colonial culture of New Spain.

Sigüenza's most important scientific work is his *Libra astronomica* ("Astronomical Libra"), an inquiry into the nature of celestial phenomena. The original impetus for the work was the appearance of a comet in 1680; while the event inspired fear and awe in his contemporaries, it only piqued Sigüenza's scientific interest. He issued a pamphlet, *Manifesto philosophico contra los cometas despojados del imperio que tenian sobre los timidos* ("Philosophical Manifest against Comets Stripped of Their Dominion over the Timid"), in which, while admitting ignorance of the true cause and meaning of comets, he asserted that they were not to be superstitiously feared as omens of evil. Sigüenza's theorizing raised the ire of other astronomers, most notably Italian-born missionary and explorer Father Eusebio Francisco Kino, who responded with *Exposicion astronomica de el cometa* . . . ("Astronomical Exposition"), in which he insisted upon the traditional view of comets as portents of disaster, referring pointedly and insultingly to "dull wits" who thought differently. Stung, Sigüenza replied immediately with *Libra astronomica*, though the book was not published until 1690. Sigüenza infused his work with all the scientific data available to a seventeenth-century scholar in order to refute his opponent's position, utilizing as well evidence from the Bible, support from classical writers, and, occasionally, satirical polemic to prove his point. Naturally, Sigüenza's observations concerning certain celestial phenomena have long since been superseded by subsequent developments in astronomical science; still, critics note that he deserves much credit as the author of one of the earliest and most forceful attempts to liberate astronomy from superstition.

Modern critics have dealt less kindly with Sigüenza's poetry, although it was apparently well received by his contemporaries. Related through his mother to the well-known Spanish poet Luis de Góngora y Argote, whose style was much in vogue at the time, Sigüenza composed poetry which has been described as exhibiting the worst excesses and defects of Gongorism: affected bombast, artificial language, willful obscurity, and convoluted ideas.

It is thus for his prose works that Sigüenza is recognized today as one of the most important figures of colonial Mexico: a superior chronicler, historian, and scientist, he is considered a talented, uniquely multifaceted intellectual. The regrettable loss of much of his research and work notwithstanding, his histories and chronicles proclaim his literary ability, while his devotion to scientific inquiry proves him a dedicated scholar. Leonard has said of Sigüenza that "the diversity of his interests, the high degree of attainment reached in all of them, and his prolific literary activity mark him as one of the greatest scholars of the seventeenth century in the Western Hemisphere—including the English colonies—and a figure whom no true historian of the early cultural history of the New World can properly neglect."

PRINCIPAL WORKS

Primavera indiana, poema sacro-historico, idea de María Santissima de Guadalupe . . . (poetry) 1662

Glorias de Querétaro en la neuva congregacion eclesiastica de María Santissima de Guadalupe . . . (chronicle) 1680
Teatro de virtudes politicas que constituyen a un principe . . . (history) 1680
Manifesto philosophico contra los cometas despojados del imperio que tenian sobre los timidos (pamphlet) 1681
Triumpho parthenico que en glorias de María Santissima immaculadamente concebida . . . [with others] (poetry and chronicle) 1683
Parayso occidental, plantado y cultivado por la liberal benefica mano de los muy Catholicos . . . (history and biography) 1684
Infortunios que Alonso Ramírez natural de la ciudad de S. Juan de Puerto Rico . . . (chronicle) 1690
[*The Misadventures of Alonso Ramírez*, 1962]
*Libra astronomica y philosophica . . . (essay) 1690
Mercurio volante con la noticia de la recuperacion de las provincias del Nuevo México conseguida por D. Diego de Vargas, Zapata, y Luxan Ponce de Leon . . . (chronicle) 1693
[*The Mercurio Volante of Don Carlos de Sigüenza y Góngora; An Account of the First Expedition of Don Diego de Vargas into New Mexico in 1692*, 1932]
†Oriental planeta evangelica epopeya sacro-panegyrica al apostol grande de las Indias S. Francisco Xavier (poetry) 1700
Obras (chronicles, history, and poetry) 1928
Poemas (poetry) 1931

*This work incorporates the earlier *Manifesto philosophico contra los cometas*.

†This work was written in 1668.

IRVING A. LEONARD   (essay date 1929)

[An American historian and critic specializing in Hispanic culture, Leonard is the author of the most comprehensive biographical and critical study of Sigüenza available in English. In the following excerpt from this work, he surveys Sigüenza's writings.]

Don Carlos had too deep-rooted a fondness for writing to permit his various duties, even if they had been more burdensome, to interfere with this favorite pastime. From his student days in Tepotzotlán until the end of his life he was steadily engaged in some form of composition. Even the knowledge that most of his writings would probably never appear in the more permanent printed form did not daunt him though it was ever a source of profound regret to him. This devotion to his pen or, rather, his quill, and his undeniable talent, soon won him recognition and he was called upon to record various public events of importance. One of these, which he was delegated to write even before he became a chaplain in the Hospital del Amor de Dios, was an account of the founding and erection of the church of the Virgin of Guadalupe in the city of Querétaro. This was printed in 1680 under the title of the **Glories of Querétaro.**

It is a sad fact and not, perhaps, a flattering commentary on his times, that the works of Sigüenza of greatest value, at least to the general historian, were in most cases never published. Aside from his **Astronomical Libra,** to be discussed later, scarcely any of his works of genuine erudition came out in book form. (p. 16)

It is not to be deduced from these reflections, however, that the published works of Sigüenza are valueless. On the contrary, they are frequently veritable mines of miscellaneous information. Though his themes are primarily of an ecclesiastical nature (with the exception of the *Astronomical Libra,* of course) his mind was too richly stored and his powers of observation too keenly developed for more or less extraneous facts of interest to be excluded. This is especially true of the *Glories of Querétaro.* His comprehensive knowledge of the history of New Spain and its peoples and his delight in detailed descriptions appear constantly in this comparatively short work of eighty pages which will be briefly summarized.

The desire for a suitable structure in Querétaro in which to do honor to the Virgin of Guadalupe was one of long standing. When a small amount of money had been raised for this purpose the cornerstone was laid on June 1, 1675. The faith—and possibly the ambition—of certain of the local ecclesiastics impelled them to take an optimistic view of the likelihood of completing it. And so, with appropriate ceremonies, the beginning was made. Don Carlos composed the inscription in Latin which, in the manner of the ancients, was engraved upon a bronze plate. This was placed, together with gold and silver medals and coins, in a leaden casket and imbedded in the foundation stone "to be transmitted to posterity as a pleasing symbol of the piety of the builders." The confidence of the founders proved not to be misplaced and five years later the completed structure was dedicated. The bulk of the book is taken up with a description of this event.

The opening chapter is devoted to some interesting facts of the pre-Cortesian history of Querétaro; Don Carlos dilates at length upon the richness of the natural resources and the beautiful surroundings of this favored city. He is unable to resist the opportunity, from time to time, to correct, parenthetically, the statements of earlier historians such as Herrera. The singular means by which the devotion of the Virgin of Guadalupe was introduced into this region are recounted. A royal cédula ["decree"] from the Queen Regent, Doña Mariana of Austria, in 1672, and the generosity of a certain Juan Caballero y Ocio, had brought into existence the church which was being consecrated. The installation of the Holy Sacrament, attended with all the pomp and dignity of so grave an event, took place. This affords Don Carlos an occasion for a tedious, though remarkably detailed, description of the church and its furnishings.

Emerging from this cloud of minutiae we are reminded of the more mundane features of the program of dedication. One more than half suspects that the Mexican humanist takes sly delight in the description of such events as a "máscara" ["masquerade"] of the Indians, the bullfights, and other forms of entertainment so dear to the Spanish and Indian heart alike. (pp. 17-18)

One of the inevitable features of such a program was the "certámen" or poetical joust; no public celebration was complete unless it was crowned by a contest of the muses. The ceremony of awarding the prizes was usually the *piece de résistance* of such a banquet of entertainments. Those with any claims to intellectual prominence—and many without any—made special efforts to shed the luster of their persons on this occasion. The secretary, or master of ceremonies, of the certámen at the dedication of the church in Querétaro was one "of whose qualities I would duly say a great deal," writes Don Carlos, "if the pride which I might take in having been his teacher did not prevent me from doing so." (p. 19)

Don Carlos' satisfaction was increased no doubt by the fact that a "canción" ["song"] which he entered in the poetical

competition received a prize. With exaggerated modesty he attributes this success not to the music of his metrical composition but to the theme of which it treated. It was, in reality, a panegyric of the Viceroy, Payo de Ribera Enríquez. Notwithstanding this diffidence it is to be noted that the poet considered his brain child worthy of the perusal of posterity for he reproduces it in its entirety in the *Glories of Querétaro.*

It is opportune, at this juncture, to discuss our author as a writer of verse. With regret it must be confessed that Don Carlos, who, in many ways rose above his environment and was in advance of his time, succumbed all too completely to the prevailing literary tendencies of his century. (p. 20)

Pompous, affected, and heavily freighted with classical and mythological allusions, strained conceits, and a distorted syntax, the metrical productions of this era are, in general, difficult to decipher as to their meaning if, indeed, they possessed any. As a curious paradox, Mexico's greatest lyric poetess [Sor Juana Inés de la Cruz] lived at this time and produced verse which the historians of Spanish literature gladly include with that of the motherland. But Don Carlos cannot be compared in this respect to his famous contemporary. After reading some of his poems, one shares the opinion of an eminent critic [Marcelino Menéndez y Pelayo] who states [in *Historia de la Poesia Hispano-Americana*]: "He is worth much less as a poet and he is the most lugubrious and obscure of the school [of gongoristic poets]."

The first metrical composition of Don Carlos, of which we have any knowledge, is a sacred, historical poem of the Virgin of Guadalupe, that perennial inspirer of verse, much of it poor, in New Spain. It is entitled *Indian Spring.* It consists of seventy-nine *octavos reales* [eight-line stanzas with eleven syllables to a line] and was written while he was still in the Jesuit college, a youth of seventeen or eighteen. His most ardent biographers are not ecstatic when referring to this work. Eguiara speaks of it [in *Bibliotheca Mexicana*] as a "very youthful poem, indeed, as no one who reads it will deny. . . ." Menéndez y Pelayo, who has nothing but praise for the prose works of Sigüenza, tells us . . . that "some samples [of the *Indian Spring*] may be read . . . which take away any desire to read the rest."

There is another youthful composition of Don Carlos' published posthumously by his nephew, Don Gabriél López de Sigüenza in 1700. Bearing the title *Eastern Evangelical Planeta,* it is a panegyric of the great missionary of the Far East, St. Francis Xavier. Don Gabriél tells us that his uncle composed this poem when he was twenty-three years old (therefore in 1668) and at that time the necessary licenses for its publication were given. In view of his incomplete familiarity with the subject at that time he feared that some of his astrological terms might not be well turned and so withheld it. His nephew might well have done the same though we are grateful for his dedicatory letter giving interesting information about Don Carlos.

Though modern judgments of his poetry may be harsh there is little doubt that in the eyes of his contemporaries he was possessed of marked ability. Ample testimony of this admiration is shown in the frequency with which he was drafted for public ceremonies where literary talents were requisite. Generally these were the certámenes ["contests"] in which the intelligentsia of the capital took delight or, at least, pretended to do so. These were the *raison d'être* of another book of Don Carlos entitled the *Parthian Triumph.*

This volume of one hundred and nineteen pages is a compilation of poems awarded prizes in the contests of 1682 and 1683 together with explanatory material setting forth, in some detail, the motives of the two celebrations. (pp. 20-3)

There is no mistaking the fact that Don Carlos was proud of his verse-writing and he seldom lost an occasion to exercise his muse. It might well be said of him that:

> The more the poet shall be questionable,
> The more unquestionably comes his book!

But in a life so singularly free of blemishes of the cruder sort, we may be tolerant and forgive him for this little *defectillo* ["minor flaw"] which only proves him to be a very "human" being. Let us, then, turn to the consideration of another phase of his character in which a more admirable trait may be discerned. (pp. 27-8)

[Impressive] evidence of the disinterestedness of Don Carlos is found in the case of an impecunious Porto Rican adventurer, Alonso Ramírez. The latter had made a journey around the world through a series of unusual misfortunes and had, at last, returned to Mexico City. The viceroy, thinking that Sigüenza might be interested in such a curious tale, sent the unfortunate man to him. Sigüenza was profoundly moved by the recital of the misadventures of Ramírez and not only wrote a long account of them but personally besought the viceroy to issue a decree to the Inspector of the Royal Treasury, D. Sebastián de Guzmán y Córdoba, a warm friend of Don Carlos, to assist the worn traveler with money. With this request the viceroy complied.

Through this incident we have one of the most readable products of the facile pen of Don Carlos. The ***Misfortunes of Alonso Ramírez,*** published in 1690, was dedicated "in the name of the one who gave me the material to write it" to the Conde de Galve and was designed to enlist his further aid to Ramírez. Thus we have a distinctive piece of writing which, as a narrative of adventure, may possibly be regarded as the forerunner of the Mexican novel. (p. 29)

This somewhat lugubrious account is enlivened toward the end by an incident reminiscent of the picaresque novels of the type of the *Lazarillo de Tormes,* for which the literature of Spain is famous and with which Don Carlos was possibly familiar. In one of the towns of Yucatan an individual, who had been casting longing eyes at Ramírez' slave, approached the master and embraced him most affectionately.

> "Is it possible, my friend and beloved countryman, that my eyes behold you! Oh, how many times have I wept in thinking about you! Who would ever have told me that I should see you in such poverty! Embrace me tightly, dearly beloved, and give thanks to God that I am here!"

Ramírez was skeptical at this effusive greeting and asked the newcomer who he was.

> "What's that!" [he answered me, Ramírez reports] "when in your early years you had no greater friend! That you may recognize that I still am what I used to be, I'll tell you that there are rumors about that you are a spy or some pirate and, as the governor of this province has heard of it, he will have you arrested and, doubtlessly, will put you to torture. Now, I have a little 'pull' with him and he will do anything I ask of him. It will be a good thing to win his good will by presenting him with that Negro, and for this purpose it won't be a bad idea for you to hand him over to me." And it was suggested that the matter be kept secret.

> "I'm not such a fool," Ramírez answered him, "that I do not recognize you to be a big liar and fully able to give lessons to the worst of pirates. Whoever will give 300 reales in pieces of eight, can have this slave and good luck to him!" But the stranger was no longer interested.

(pp. 35-6)

Here we may see Don Carlos at his best as a prose writer and we may hazard a guess as to how great a writer he might have been if circumstances had permitted him to write fiction. The style is simple and unaffected, conspicuous for the lack of ponderous Latin quotations which make so much of his available work so unpalatable to the modern reader. We see the human side of the scholar and his ability to appreciate a good "yarn." For once he separates himself from the dulness and heaviness characteristic of the writing of his time and gives us an interesting little book whose length we can wish were greater. (p. 36)

* * * * *

"On this day a comet was seen toward the East which rose at four o'clock in the morning." In this simple manner was recorded in Mexico City an event which was to distress the ignorant and exercise the best minds on both sides of the Atlantic. This was the "Great Comet of 1680," first seen in Mexico City on November 15 of that year. (p. 58)

Such phenomena were ever a source of dread to the superstitious masses not alone in the viceroyalty of New Spain, but in Europe as well. This particular comet seems to have produced an even greater amount of fear and anxiety than usual and it became widely regarded as a presage of dire calamities and misfortunes. For Sigüenza . . . , such heavenly manifestations were matters for rejoicing since they offered rare opportunities for study. Consequently, with a generous desire to allay these groundless fears and the uneasiness which tormented all classes of Mexican society, Don Carlos brought forth on January 13, 1681, a pamphlet entitled a ***Philosophical Manifest against Comets stripped of their dominion over the timid,*** which he later incorporated in his ***Astronomical Libra.*** (pp. 58-9)

In this ***Manifest*** Sigüenza declared that he did not attempt to ascertain the true significance of these phenomena which, he stated, should be venerated as a work of God; his only purpose was to remove from human hearts the clutch of fear which such astral manifestations invariably imposed. He made reference to the objections of the astrologers and stated in this connection, "I also am an Astrologer and I know very well on which foot Astrology limps and upon what exceedingly weak foundations its structure is reared." This assertion, among others of Sigüenza's, seems to have sounded the "call to arms" to a certain Flemish gentleman then living in exile in Campeche. Feeling, no doubt, that this was an unprovoked attack upon the science which claimed his admiration and allegiance, this individual, Don Martin de la Torre by name, published a pamphlet under the title, a *Christian Manifest in favor of the Comets maintained in their natural significance,* evidently availing himself of many astrological data to demonstrate that comets were, in reality, heavenly indications of coming calamitous events sent by God himself.

Without hesitation Don Carlos replied to this attack with another pamphlet to which, permitting himself to indulge in the poor taste of his time, he gave the ponderous, not to say, thunderous title of the ***Mathematical Bellerophon against the Astrological Chimera of Don Martin de la Torre, etc.*** [Leonard adds in a footnote that "this work of Sigüenza had already disappeared at the time of the publication of *The Astronomical Libra* in 1690.''] In this he discussed comets in a rational manner, touching upon technicalities relating to paralaxes, refractions, the theory of the movements of comets, etc. In the latter part of the *Astronomical Libra* he again adverts to the declarations of Don Martin de la Torre and assails astrology with great vehemence and learning. (pp. 59-60)

[The] most important figure to take up the cudgels in refutation of Sigüenza's contentions was Father Kino [in his *Astronomical Exposition*]. (p. 62)

Despite the fact that nowhere in the book did his opponent refer to him by name (and it is a curious fact that in none of the papers of Kino which have come to light do we see the name of Sigüenza mentioned), the Mexican scholar nevertheless regarded himself as unmistakably the object of Kino's occasionally pointed remarks. "No one knows better where the shoe pinches than the one who wears it and, since I assert that I was the object of his invective, everyone may believe that, without question, it was I." It was not that he objected to anyone differing in opinion regarding comets, the professor continues, but he feels that Father Kino might have done so without resorting to mockery and ridicule. (p. 64)

Moreover, Don Carlos was not the sole proprietor of his own reputation and since that of his country is also involved he cannot, therefore, permit it to be obscured without just cause. Consequently, it becomes a patriotic duty for him to take up his pen in defense of his country as well as himself. Before Heaven, he protests, he is obliged by the Reverend Father Kino to write his *Astronomical Libra* lest those who read Kino's work think that the Spaniards in the Mexican university have merely a "trabajoso juizio" ["dull wit"] serving as a professor of Mathematics.

Thus the writing of one of Sigüenza's most learned books came about. (p. 66)

No attempt will be made here to appraise this work nor to analyze the rebuttals and arguments set forth with such erudition. A few observations of a superficial nature may, however, be permitted in order to indicate the general organization of the book.

After the introductory remarks . . . , the author reproduces his *Philosophical Manifest* around which the polemic had centered. Two paragraphs are then devoted to a summary of Father Kino's *Astronomical Exposition* and the principal fields in which the two combatants are to lock horns are marked out. With an "all hands to work and may Right help the one who has it!" Sigüenza plunges into the matter.

After stating Father Kino's argument against his own contentions that comets are not, in reality, harbingers of evil, he proceeds to support his original assertions with additional data. Thus, point by point, he wrestles with his opponent. As was natural in the forensics of the time, theological considerations played a large part in the discussion, and the authority of the Bible was constantly sought. The classic writers of antiquity were laid under heavy contribution as well as more modern authors. Ponderous Latin citations are called in on nearly every page to witness to certain facts or refute certain assertions. And the whole is spiced with occasional thrusts of a personal nature. These barbed darts are enlivening to the modern investigator for they show the great scholar to be intensely human and subject to the same temptations as the rest of mankind.

Even works of pure literature are utilized for the discomfiture of the "Reverend Father" who had had the temerity to allude to certain "trabajosos juicios" in Mexico. Don Francisco de Quevedo Villegas, "great glory of the Spanish nation," is drafted into service with a satirical poem which closes with an apt punning stanza referring to comets.

At length, having defended his own contentions and refuted Father Kino's statements to his own satisfaction, our worthy professor, now thoroughly warmed up to the subject, feels free to turn his guns directly upon Kino's own propositions set forth in his *Astronomical Exposition*. "It is plain," he writes, "that the Reverend Father will not be surprised at what I seek to do here which is either to enhance the virtues of his *Exposition* in the crucible of my examination or scorn it as dross if," he adds slyly, "by chance, that is what it is." Having thus relieved himself, he proceeds to examine the basis of Father Kino's arguments and succeeds in undermining them in a manner wholly satisfactory and convincing to himself.

Perhaps the good professor is even less averse here to indulging in bits of satire and rarely loses an opportunity to transform certain of Father Kino's phrases which he had found particularly offensive, such as "trabajoso juizio," "the high, the low, the noble and the plebeian, the learned and the unlearned, etc.," into verbal boomerangs. It is evident that he is endeavoring to hold in check his resentment against Father Kino's somewhat scornful manner. Not infrequently he breaks forth in sarcastic allusions to Father Kino's Latin, his knowledge of history, and his apparent duplicity in advising the viceroy in his dedicatory that this comet was of good omen to that high official, while the body of the work is taken up in proving its ill effects on the world in general. Not content with this, Sigüenza even assails the veracity of his opponent in claiming to have made observations in Cádiz. In this manner the Mexican scholar expresses himself fully and with considerable freedom. In closing his diatribe, however, he repeats that this dispute in entirely a personal matter between Father Kino and himself and is in no way connected with that missionary's affiliations. This done he offers his opponent the olive branch.

The remaining pages of the *Astronomical Libra* are devoted chiefly to a discussion of Astrology and are aimed more directly at Don Martin de la Torre. The book closes with facts and figures connected with Sigüenza's observations of the comet made from January 3 to January 20, 1681.

Judgment may be suspended as to the relative merits of the books written by these two learned men, one from the Old and one from the New World. We are not here concerned with the technical and scientific aspects of the debate. The modern investigator will undoubtedly be inclined to sympathize with the main contention of Don Carlos and his honest attempt to free the minds of his time from the shackles of fear and superstition. And we cannot but be amazed at the erudition and industry of this Creole who had never crossed the ocean to Europe and who had never come directly under the influence of that struggle between science and ignorance which was beginning to shake Europe and tear it from its medieval moorings. That he was well read is evident in his *Astronomical Libra* as well as in his other writings which have survived; that his familiarity with his books was great is equally patent; that he was painstaking and thorough can be seen in the careful organization of his book and the well executed diagrams which accompany it. Considering the remoteness of New Spain from Europe and the infrequency of communication, together with his meager pecuniary resources, we can only marvel at his ability to keep abreast of his times and, in some respects, to be in advance of them. (pp. 67-70)

. . . . .

One of the first of Don Carlos' more strictly historical works to be printed was the *Occidental Paradise,* published in 1684. Divided into three books it deals with the history of the Royal Convent of Jesus Mary of Mexico City and the biographies of various nuns who had shed the luster of their ascetic glory upon the institution. It was written at the behest of the Convent, and Mother María Antonia de Santo Domingo had assisted him with data and encouragement in the composition of the first two books whose finished drafts she had read. She had urged him to write the third, recording the extremely holy life of Mother Mariana de la Cruz. The death of Mother María Antonia before the completion of the work had moved Sigüenza to include an account of her exemplary career also in the third part.

Aside from the first chapter sketching the manner in which the pagan Mexicans had consecrated their Vestal Virgins, this volume is of little interest and resembles the many similar writings of the same period. It was, obviously, a conscientious effort on the part of the scholar to write an accurate history based upon the methodical and scientific study of a large number of documents which he had assembled for this purpose. From a modern point of view the work must be regarded as uncritical; naïvely he accepts the miracles reported to have occurred in the lives of his worthy nuns and their virtues he exalts with unstinting praise. He does not indulge in the florid style of writing which he himself confesses using in other places, though the whole is liberally leavened with pious and philosophic observations. In deference to his feminine readers, for whose consumption the book is intended, he forbears cluttering the text with marginal notes. "Since my business is to write a history of women for women, it is plain that I would do wrong in doing so," he declares. And besides, he has serious misgivings regarding the amount of attention given to these annotations even by the more sophisticated masculine mind. (pp. 102-03)

Another product of Sigüenza's pen, somewhat similar in nature, was his *Heroic Piety of Don Fernando Cortés, Marqués del Valle,* published in Mexico City in 1689. This deals with the history of the Hospital of the Immaculate Conception of Our Lady, the oldest institution of its kind in Mexico City and one which had enjoyed the patronage of Cortés. It contains a staunch defense of the great Conquistador as a protector of the Catholic faith, gives some facts about the capital after the Conquest, and rounds out the account, like the *Occidental Paradise,* with some incidents of doubtful verisimilitude taking place within the Hospital, and an over-enthusiastic biography of a pious printer.

More interesting are the few writings of contemporary history which are extant. These show how well informed the learned professor was on public matters connected with the realm; his intimate association with the viceroy and his councillors enabled him to be cognizant of the events which were transpiring throughout New Spain and elsewhere and to have access to important documents bearing upon these affairs. The fame of his learning, his knowledge of practical matters, and his skilful wielding of his pen brought about his appointment for especial commissions. Among other things he was designated as a sort of official historian.

MERCURIO VOLANTE CON LA NOTICIA de la recuperacion de las PROVINCIAS DEL NVEVO MEXICO CONSEGVIDA Por D. DIEGO DE VARGAS, ZAPATA, YLUXAN PONZE DE LEON, Governador y Capitan General de aquel Reyno. ESCRIVIOLA Por especial orden de el Excelentissimo Señor CONDE DE GALVE VIRREY, GOVERNADOR, Y CAPITAN GENERAL DE LA NUEVA-ESPAñA, &c. DON CARLOS DE SIGVENZA, Y GONGORA, Cosmographo mayor de su Magestad en estos Reynos, y Cathedratico Iubilado de Mathematicas en la Academia Mexicana. Con licencia en Mexico: EN LA IMPRENTA DE ANTUERPIA de los Herederos de la Viuda de Bernardo Calderon, año de 1693.

Title page of Mercurio Volante *(1693).*

Possibly one of the most straightforward, simple, but forceful works of this sort which he wrote was the *Trophy of Spanish Justice,* printed in 1691. It concerns itself chiefly with a Spanish expedition sent to the Island of Santo Domingo on the Windward Fleet. A resounding defeat was administered to the French settlements there which were the rendezvous of the fierce pirates so continuously infesting the Caribbean region, and seriously hampering if not threatening Spanish sovereignty in that basin. The news of this success brought such rejoicing to the capital that a thanksgiving service was celebrated and Don Carlos was delegated to write the account.

The *Trophy of Spanish Justice* is a little book of thirteen short chapters, the first eleven of which are devoted to a circumstantial relation of the expedition from its start at Vera Cruz, its decisive victory at Guarico of which chapter 7 affords a spirited description, and its triumphant return to San Juan Ulúa (Vera Cruz) in March, 1691. It is Don Carlos in one of his happiest veins; it affords a vivid and moving recital of the events of this exciting campaign with an entire absence of the artificial note which is frequently struck in his prose as well as his poetry. (pp. 104-06)

No doubt Don Carlos took an especial interest in the northern frontier of New Spain particularly the region known as New Mexico; here an uncle of his, that hardy fighter and one-time governor-general who became conspicuous in the reconquest of that province from the rebellious Indians, Don Domingo Jironza Petrís Cruzate y Góngora, spent much of his time. Possibly this blood relationship with a prominent frontiersman was an added reason for commissioning the trusted professor in the Royal University to write an account of this splendid achievement which redounded so much to the credit of the viceroy. At any rate the somewhat inappropriate title of the **Flying Mercury** was attached by Sigüenza to a narrative record of the re-acquisition of "Nuevo México." More fortunate than most of the work of Don Carlos this has come down to us in printed form though copies of it are exceedingly rare. It is a brief account of some thirty-seven pages detailing the important incidents connected with the reduction of the seditious Indians on the upper Rio Grande. (pp. 107-08)

• • • • •

The study of the life and works of Don Carlos de Sigüenza y Góngora suggests certain analogies with the early humanists of the Italian Renaissance. Despite the fact that he lived in one of the most important and the most advanced of Spain's possessions in the New World, this son of seventeenth-century Mexico found himself in an atmosphere which was essentially medieval. The society of the capital as in the provinces was in many respects feudalistic; the venerable University with which he was associated during the most active years of his career was an interesting and curious survival of European medievalism particularly in the matter of its government and curriculum. The "Athens of the New World," as the city proudly termed itself, was far removed from the centers of learning in Europe and was only slightly touched by the currents of thought which were beginning to circulate there. Indeed, the men of learning of the viceroyalty were almost wholly dedicated to the study and to the perpetuation of a doctrinal theology which, elsewhere, was gradually becoming obsolete.

The seventeenth century in New Spain gave rise to some literature, to be sure, but this was almost entirely in the form of religious guides, the chronicles of missionaries, theological tracts, and an almost uninterrupted flood of gongoristic poetry, unutterably dull and tedious for the most part with its cloying artificiality and inanity. This relatively slight literary activity was cultivated by an infinitesimally small and select group of intellectuals, standing like a tiny edifice upon a vast foundation composed of an ignorant and hopeless native population.

Into this unpropitious environment was born a man who, like the great humanists of fourteenth and fifteenth-century Italy, was to make all human knowledge his province. As in the case of most of the conspicuous figures in the rebirth of learning in Europe, there had been forerunners of this enlightened spirit and they had, in some measure, lighted the way. But it remained for this man, Don Carlos de Sigüenza y Góngora, to lift the torch higher than his predecessors and to illumine many nooks and crannies formerly enshrouded in obscurity. Not contented with the knowledge of his contemporaries, his curious mind peeped into dark corners and ferreted out new facts. (pp. 182-83)

A just estimate of him as a man of letters presents numerous difficulties not the least of which is the disappearance of much of his work. If he should not be remembered for his poetry, a great deal of his prose writing and particularly his achievements in the field of history may well claim our consideration and respect. The loss of so much of this precious material is a source of profound regret.

It is equally difficult to appraise him properly as a scientist. From the few extant writings in this connection it is only possible to speculate on the position he might have held had his genius been placed in the more congenial atmosphere of contemporary Europe or had he accepted the invitation of Louis XIV to come to his Court. If it cannot be said that he extended human knowledge in the field of mathematics, astronomy, and kindred sciences, he showed far more understanding and enlightenment on these subjects than did the vast majority of his contemporaries on either side of the Atlantic. What *can* be stated with confidence is that the diversity of his interests, the high degree of attainment reached in all of them, and his prolific literary activity mark him as one of the greatest scholars of the seventeenth century in the Western Hemisphere—including the English colonies—and a figure whom no true historian of the early cultural history of the New World can properly neglect. (pp. 184-85)

> *Irving A. Leonard, in his* Don Carlos de Sigüenza y Góngora: A Mexican Savant of the Seventeenth Century, *1929. Reprint by Kraus Reprint Co., 1974, 287 p.*

JULIE GREER JOHNSON   (essay date 1981)

[*In the following excerpt, Johnson examines the picaresque elements of* Alonso Ramírez, *noting particularly the relationship between this work and Mateo Alemán's picaresque novel,* Guzmán de Alfarache *(1599-1604).*]

On hearing the touching story of Alonso Ramírez, Sigüenza y Góngora quickly recognized the opportunity to capture effectively a moment in Spanish colonial history and he did so with the flare of a good writer. His account of an innocent boy who leaves home to make his own way in the world emulates one of the most popular forms of Spanish literature, the picaresque novel. In essence, this innovative prose fiction reflects the life and times of one who remains on the periphery of society but who displays a dauntless determination to survive and an instinctive drive to overcome his present circumstances and better his lot.

Alonso's personal nature and his haphazard endeavors which were reminiscent of the life of the *pícaro,* especially that of Alemán's Guzmán de Alfarache, inspired Sigüenza to write the **Infortunios.** Although the author's finished composition is basically an historical account, it is a striking example of the efficacious intertwining of history with literary technique prevalent in the picaresque genre. The result of this delicate balance between historical documentation and creative form not only confirms Sigüenza's outstanding ability as an historian but distinguishes him as a gifted storyteller as well. The novelistic perspective which he employs enhances immeasurably the interest of this historical document and contributes substantially to its commendable stature as a literary work. Conclusive evidence linking Sigüenza's work to picaresque literature in general, and to Alemán's masterpiece in particular, may be found throughout his exciting account and may readily be seen in its main character, setting, structure, and style.

According to Sigüenza y Góngora's portrayal, Alonso Ramírez, like such Spanish literary models as Lazarillo, Pablos, and Guzmán, is an anti-hero. He is a common boy vested with average abilities whose stalwart resolution to survive and courageous endurance to face the challenges of his daily life are unquestionably admirable and ultimately noteworthy. (pp. 60-1)

Just as the appearance of the *pícaro* in sixteenth- and seventeenth-century Spanish literature reflects the declining and decadent social and economic conditions of the country, so the *Infortunios de Alonso Ramírez* betrays a similar plight in the Spanish Indies. With skill and understanding, Sigüenza undertakes to portray accurately the turbulent years of a great empire which compose the colorful and lively backdrop for his protagonist's tale of woe. Although he focuses mainly upon the seamy side of life, a dominant feature of works written in the picaresque vein, by revealing some of the ugly aspects of existence in the colonies, he uses this particular perspective to dispel existing myths concerning Spain's wealth and power. It is by probing extensively the fascinating historical setting that Sigüenza scrutinizes several aspects of social, economic, and political importance and exposes the discrepancy between appearances and reality. . . .

A glorious era in Spanish history was coming to an inevitable close. Although Sigüenza gives little detailed information concerning the colonial economy, poverty looms everywhere in his narrative, and starvation constantly threatens the young Ramírez. (p. 62)

While revealing surprising weaknesses in the Spanish imperial structure, Sigüenza also unmasks the bold and repugnant nature of Spain's rivals. Because of the infamous Black Legend maliciously propagated by Spain's enemies, European public opinion had branded it as the cruelest, most unprincipled nation in the world. This false impression, as well, is shattered by Sigüenza who continually narrates the heinous crimes of Spain's adversaries. One episode in which he recounts a cannibalistic celebration among Alonso's captors is an especially good example of this, and scenes of murder, torture, robbery, and destruction of property which dominate the narration of the protagonist's captivity add elements of fear and suspense to his story. (pp. 62-3)

Infortunios de Alonso Ramírez, like the classic representatives of the picaresque genre, *Lazarillo de tormes, Guzmán de Alfarache,* and *El Buscón,* is a loosely constructed account presented in autobiographical form. After an introductory statement of purpose, the protagonist embarks upon a chronological narrative of the events of his childhood, adolescence, and manhood. The unity of these separate entities is provided by the presence of the protagonist himself, and the composition of the work is deliberately left open, ostensibly to continue the main character's adventures at some future date.

While the structure of Sigüenza's account bears a certain resemblance to the Spanish picaresque works produced during the Golden Age, its numerous parallels with one in particular, *Guzmán de Alfarache,* are quite striking. These points of comparison may be found not only in some of the specific details of the lives of the two protagonists but in the duplication of select episodes as well.

Both Guzmán and Alonso preface a recapitulation of their respective adventures by divulging their family backgrounds and by alluding to the unpropitious circumstances of their departures from home. Poverty is a crucial factor in their decisions, and the two boys strike out on their own determined not only to survive but to encounter a better life as well. . . .

The early upbringing and environment of these two juveniles bore a profound stigma for them, and as a result they sought to be rid of their all too familiar surroundings and escape to another country. Alonso naïvely contemplates the opportunities that await him in New Spain, and Guzmán seeks to elude parental opprobrium by traveling to Italy. The two undertake sea voyages, and both become the servants of captains to secure their passage. (p. 63)

In their quest for economic self-sufficiency, both youths travel widely and enter into the service of numerous masters. For seven years after leaving Puerto Rico and before departing for the Orient, Alonso's wanderings take him throughout the Viceroyalty of New Spain. During his meandering from Puebla de los Angeles to Mexico City and down to Guatemala, he is retained by at least six employers and at various times works as a carpenter, a page, a muleteer, a traveling salesman, an apprentice to an architect, and an aid to a gentleman named Cristóbal Medina.

Throughout the travels of these two young protagonists, hunger is an important motivating force in their lives. In fact, as they journey from place to place, their immediate necessities seem to eclipse any recognition of the beauty of their environs. However, on one occasion, in each case, the overwhelming magnificence of a major cultural center, one in the New World, the other in Europe, receives their unending praise. On entering Mexico City, Alonso is awed and elated to find that the widely circulating rumors of its greatness are not unfounded, and Guzmán experiences the same sensations during his stay in Florence and expresses almost identical impressions of that great city.

After being out in the world for some time, both Alonso and Guzmán decide to marry. While the nature of their conjugal relationships is entirely different, their marriages are terminated abruptly by the death of their spouses after only a brief period of matrimony.

As both individuals find themselves down on their luck, Alonso reviews his situation carefully and sentences himself to be banished to the Philippines. Guzmán, on the other hand, accused and convicted of committing a crime, receives a very real sentence and is condemned to the galleys for life. While Alonso's self-imposed exile does not mean immediate confinement, it does eventually lead to his seizure by English corsairs. During the time that both Alonso and Guzmán, now men, spend as prisoners, they are both held captive on sailing vessels. Throughout their respective voyages, each protagonist experiences physical restraints of one sort or another, is betrayed by friends, and becomes involved in mutinies. As a result of their knowledge of these conspiracies on shipboard, both Alonso and Guzmán divulge the names of the participants as well as their plans to the proper authorities. This affirmation of loyalty, together with their previously established associations with certain officers in charge, earns them their freedom.

With the announcement of a pardon for Guzmán, Part II of Alemán's work comes to a close; however, for Alonso, set adrift in the Caribbean Sea, the series of tribulations is not yet over. From this point until his arrival back in the capital, he goes on to relate additional encounters and ordeals which are surprisingly reminiscent of earlier occurrences in the *Guzmán.* Here, however, the correlations is merely suggestive rather than explicit.

As is characteristic of human nature, it is a time of crisis that elicits a reaffirmation of faith, and both protagonists ascribe their very survival on several occasions to divine protection. The news of the release of Alonso and his companions is hailed by them with thankfulness and jubilation. Alonso, himself, attributes his personal salvation to his undying devotion to the Patron Saint of Mexico, as a small memento of hers was a source of great consolation to him. After surviving a devastating storm on his way home from Italy, Guzmán makes a solemn pledge to the Holy Matriarch of Seville whose timely intervention, he believes, delivered him from the throes of destruction.

While both instances represent isolated religious acts, respect and reverence for the divine is a constant factor in both the *Infortunios* and the *Guzmán*. The two protagonists are portrayed attending masses, both claim to have witnessed miracles, and both implore God or the Virgin to aid them with considerable frequency. (pp. 64-5)

Although similarities between these two works are numerous, Sigüenza's manner of presentation of these common elements is quite different.

Unlike the works of the picaresque genre previously mentioned, the *Infortunios de Alonso Ramírez* is the documentary record of historical fact. Its content, therefore, by its very nature, requires the clear, concise exposition that Sigüenza has accorded it to maintain the accuracy of his report. However, his intimate view of his protagonist's life and his informal manner of expression reflect the youthful vantage point from which he narrates his brief account and exude a human warmth designed to appeal to the sensitivity of his readers as well as to entertain them. Although the Baroque influence is visible in several passages, the general precision and clarity of Sigüenza's narration, together with the inclusion of scientific data, portend the writings characteristic of the Enlightenment in Spanish America.

Sigüenza's enthralling adventure story of an errant Puerto Rican youth serves as excellent testimony to his well-deserved reputation for being one of the best prose writers of the colonial period and provides a vital link between Spanish literary tradition and early Spanish American literature. While the extent of Sigüenza's knowledge of the entire gamut of picaresque writings remains undetermined, it is evident that he was well acquainted with *Guzmán de Alfarache* and that it influenced him to some degree in his literary rendering of the events of Alonso's life as well as the formulation of his personality. Sigüenza's clever adaptation of certain picaresque elements for his historical presentation proves the effectiveness of such a combination and serves as a forerunner of Spanish America's first novel and totally picaresque work, *Periquillo Sarniento* by José Joaquín Fernández de Lizardi, published over a century after Sigüenza's pioneering creation. (pp. 65-6)

> Julie Greer Johnson, "Picaresque Elements in Carlos Sigüenza y Góngora's 'Los Infortunios de Alonso Ramírez'," in Hispania, Vol. 67, No. 1, March, 1981, pp. 60-7.

J. S. CUMMINS and **ALAN SOONS** (essay date 1984)

[*In the following excerpt from the introduction to their edition of* Alonso Ramírez, *Cummins and Soons comment on Sigüenza's contribution to narrative composition, explain the plan of the work, and consider its historical accuracy.*]

There has been some discussion of the nature of [*Infortunios que Alonso Ramírez*]: whether it is fact or fiction, a chronicle or a novel, or whether it is typical of that fusion of the two which nowadays is known as 'faction'. Our conclusion is that the framework of the narrative is true, but that Sigüenza y Góngora probably added some details of his own.

The pirates who captured Ramírez are unknown to us, except for the few he names, such as Captains Bell and Donkin. They have left no account of their adventures and so it fell to Sigüenza to record the story, as seen through Ramírez's eyes. Yet Ramírez might easily have been captured by the pirates with whom the celebrated William Dampier sailed for many years. (p. 5)

Had that happened, Ramírez would now be known to us, not in Sigüenza's *Infortunios,* but in that classic of English travel literature, Dampier's *New Voyage around the World* (1697), arguably the greatest seafaring narrative in English. (p. 6)

Sigüenza vivifies the *Infortunios* by bringing a pattern and unity to the account given him by a presumably illiterate Alonso Ramírez, an account of scattered occurrences in his life before 1690. So far is this true that Ramírez might appear to be a figment of the author's imagination created for literary and apologetic ends. In the matter of style, Sigüenza attempts to mix learned prose, using a somewhat latinised and recherché vocabulary, and that of a realism with 'pathetic' resonances. The principal intention is for the piece to serve as a kind of *hoja de servicios* (record of services rendered) for the Viceroy's attention, and additionally as a document of Sigüenza's talents for publicity directed at a readership whose religiosity he was well acquainted with.

The work is organised into seven chapters, with a certain symmetrical plan: chapters II and III, and chapters VI and VII contain the episodes of adventure and misfortune, while chapters I and V are so to speak introductory to the others, establishing a state of mind in the reader for what is to come. Chapter IV and the Prologue (which may be viewed as the last portion of the text to be composed) are, in conformity with this symmetrical plan, the sections which look back and moralise. There is a mythic dimension to be perceived throughout the work, in that the trials endured at sea by Ramírez are presented as almost salutary and as an occasion for the demonstration of his faith in the Virgin of Guadalupe. The pirates who capture Ramírez are made by Sigüenza to represent metaphysical evil, and in this he follows classical authors who made the comparison with the pirate (Cicero, *Philippic XIII;* Seneca, *De beneficiis;* St. Augustine, *City of God*) the most telling of all in their invectives against tyrants. These English pirates are even presented as active cannibals at Pulicondón, and here we may surmise a literary exaggeration. The contemporary filibuster Raveneau de Lussan explains, however, that at the time of his voyages in the Pacific between 1684 and 1688 the Spanish priests ashore 'disliked them so cordially that they assured women who had never seen filibusters that . . . we ate women and little children'. . . . The strange manifestations of Protestant piety and of shipboard parliamentarianism on the part of the pirates probably added to the abhorrence the Mexican readers were intended to feel. Again, that same public would be supposed to feel greater sympathy for Ramírez as a passive bearer of tribulation than for any courage he might have shown and acted upon. The ingrained habit of admiring patience in the lives of some of the saints would be appealed to by Sigüenza, as well as their shared veneration of the Virgin of Guadalupe.

The second portion of the story takes Ramírez to Yucatán, where he encounters, besides actual privations in a virtual desert, a society almost alien to charity, and typified by corrupt civil and military authorities. We have left the ambient of mythical evil, to enter that of mere malice. The pirates had some sense of degree, were what they seemed to be, and were, even, occasionally better than they seemed to be; but in Yucatán everyone apart from a few priests is an untrustworthy cheat. The Confidence Man whom Ramírez encounters there symbolizes this world of swindlers, from Don Ceferino de Castro downwards. So Sigüenza can maintain that only the Viceroy can show Ramírez the benevolence he deserves as a sufferer for his patriotism and his faith.

Ramírez sells his slave-companion later on, just as Robinson Crusoe (1719) was to sell Xury, who had saved him from the Moors, to the Portuguese. This curious attitude towards other races is exemplified on another occasion with respect to the Indians whom Ramírez encounters. He is persuaded by the first European he meets that it is permissible to capture and despoil them, even as he himself had been captured and despoiled. It is, after all, for the good of their souls, since their capture leads to their being converted. To have considered the feelings of captured Indians to be similar to his own when *he* was a captive is perhaps too much to ask of a simple believer.

In general, *Infortunios* stands up well as a historically accurate account; the accuracy of its details, especially the dating of episodes, can be confirmed by other records. (pp. 15-17)

On the other hand, as has been said, no certain trace is yet found of the English pirates, Bell and Donkin, into whose hands he fell. And it must be admitted that some of the speeches attributed to them seem highly improbable as recorded, e.g. that allegedly made by Donkin near the opening of chapter IV. That has clearly been embroidered by Sigüenza. And what does seem to be entirely Sigüenza's contribution to the work is the addition of precise geographical, navigational, and cosmographical information. This is not necessarily due to professional pedantry, but to his perception of a need to instruct his public, not least in their realisation of Spanish military unpreparedness in many regions. (p. 18)

[*Infortunios*] is an example in Spanish of a well-represented genre of the latter years of the seventeenth century. In the work there is a fusion of two types within the genre: that of travel and shipwreck, and that of captivity and deliverance. In any of these works, in various European languages, the shipwrecked traveller, or the captive of corsairs or pirates, tends to show a remarkable courage and an equanimity founded on his beliefs. It is for this reason that the narratives can be presented as morally uplifting: the reader also is invited to reassess

himself spiritually after his vicarious experience of captivity and disaster.

In his *aprobación* (the certificate that the work was fit to be printed) the diocesan censor, Francisco de Ayerra de Santa María, compares Ramírez's narrative to an embryo. It must originally have been a labyrinth of incident, which found in Sigüenza y Góngora the reworker it deserved, and it became what we have, a kind of thesis-novel equipped with animation, decorum and regularisation by means of *discursos* ["philosophical discourses"]. The religious content may be either Ramírez's or Sigüenza's. Indeed it is intended to play its part in sustaining the text as a strategy for making supplication to the Viceroy of New Spain. (p. 20)

> *J. S. Cummins and Alan Soons, in an introduction to* Infortunios que Alonso Ramírez, natural de la ciudad de San Juan de Puerto Rico, padeció *by Carlos de Sigüenza y Góngora, edited by J. S. Cummins and Alan Soons, Tamesis Texts Ltd., 1984, pp. 5-21*

ADDITIONAL BIBLIOGRAPHY

Cummins, James S. "The Philippines Glimpsed in the First Latin-American 'Novel'." *Philippine Studies* 26 (1978): 91-101.
    Capsulizes *Alonso Ramírez*, examining the chronicle as it relates to the history of the Philippines.

——. "*Infortunios de Alonso Ramírez:* 'A Just History of Fact'?" *Bulletin of Hispanic Studies* LXI, No. 3 (July 1984): 295-303.
    Recapitulates Alonso Ramírez's adventures as they were recounted by Sigüenza, verifying the tale's historical accuracy with other document sources, where available.

Leonard, Irving Albert. Introduction to *The Mercurio Volante of Don Carlos Sigüenza y Góngora: An Account of the First Expedition of Don Diego de Vargas into New Mexico in 1692,* by Carlos de Sigüenza y Góngora, translated by Irving Albert Leonard, pp. 13-47. Los Angeles: Quivira Society, 1932.
    Provides background information for *The Mercurio Volante* under various headings: the rise of journalism in New Spain, a brief biography of Sigüenza, political and social conditions of New Spain at the time of Vargas's expedition, and the motives of Vargas and his superiors for undertaking the reconquest of New Mexico.

Catharine Trotter (Cockburn)

1679-1749

(Also Catherine; also Trother; also Cockburne) English dramatist, essayist, novelist, and poet.

Trotter was one of the first female dramatists to compose for the English stage and a philosophical writer. As a dramatist she was instrumental in promoting moral reform in the Restoration playhouse, while as a philosopher she probed the nature of knowledge, tackled moral and religious issues, and asked fundamental questions about how human beings should best live their lives. She was also a novelist, one whose single prose narrative, *Olinda's Adventures; or, The Amours of a Young Lady,* helped inaugurate the novel as an English literary form. Working in an age when women authors were highly unusual and often the butt of ridicule, she triumphed over convention and built a long career in literature, thereby helping open the door to the host of female authors that came after her.

The first biography of Trotter appeared in 1751, two years after her death, and, as it was written under the guidance of Trotter herself, is considered highly reliable. She was born in London in 1679, the daughter of David Trotter, a respected Scots commander in the Royal Navy, and Sarah Ballenden, a close but impoverished relative of the prominent Scottish families of Maitland and Drummond. Trotter's father died when she was five years old, leaving the family in financial chaos. Apparently eager to offset the cultural disadvantages caused by her family's poverty, Trotter began cultivating literary connections at age fourteen, sending verses to Bevil Higgons, a young man of letters. Within months she anonymously released *Olinda's Adventures,* an epistolary novel today widely acknowledged as an astonishing achievement for a writer in her early teens. In December 1695, Trotter's first drama, the tragedy *Agnes de Castro,* was produced with great success at the Theatre Royal in Drury Lane. Though only sixteen, the author (who released the work anonymously but whose identity was soon discovered) was honored by Mary Delariviere Manley, a leading female novelist and dramatist, with a commendatory poem written especially for the first publication of the text. Before a year had passed, Trotter was closely acquainted with London's foremost writers, was beginning to attract offers of patronage, and, in a dubious compliment, had been pilloried, along with Manley and another woman dramatist, Mary Pix, in a popular anonymous satirical play, *The Female Wits: or, The Triumvirate of Poets at Rehearsal* (1696). *Agnes de Castro* was followed during the next eleven years by other plays, each successful to some degree: *Fatal Friendship, Love at a Loss; or, Most Votes Carry It* (Trotter's only comedy), *The Unhappy Penitent,* and *The Revolution of Sweden.* Each of these productions furthered Trotter's reputation, some even attracting commendations from such luminaries as William Congreve and William Wycherley. But just as her dramatic career was advancing steadily, Trotter turned her attention to philosophy, issuing in 1702 her anonymous *A Defence of the "Essay of Human Understanding,"* a highly favorable critique of John Locke's theory of knowledge.

From this point onward Trotter's literary interests were chiefly philosophical, though her final drama, *The Revolution of Sweden,* had yet to be produced. Trotter allied herself closely with intellectuals in the Church of England, particularly Bishop Gil-

bert Burnet, who, as sometime philosophical mentor and spiritual guide, deeply influenced her mature life. In 1707 she published *A Discourse concerning a Guide in Controversies, in Two Letters,* in which she explained her reconversion into the established church—she had early in life become a Roman Catholic—and declared her orthodoxy. Around this time she also became romantically involved with Patrick Cockburn, a candidate for ordination, and married him in 1708. For the next few years the two lived comfortably, Cockburn rising in the church, Trotter forsaking literary affairs in order to raise a family. Upon the accession of George I, however, Cockburn was deprived of a church living by his refusal to take the compulsory oath of allegiance. Not until 1726 did he reconcile to the oath, ending years of financial hardship for his family. In the same year Trotter returned to philosophical study, issuing another treatise on Locke, *A Letter to Dr. Holdsworth.* It was also at this time that she apparently sought favor from poet and critic Alexander Pope, flattering him in letters infused with appeals for recognition, but Pope seems to have ignored Trotter's supplications. During the next two decades she wrote occasionally on philosophical subjects, but her efforts were hampered by poor health and failing eyesight. She died at age seventy, outliving her husband by only a few months.

Trotter's writings are characterized as much by variety as by a strong sense of mission, chiefly a morally didactic one. Her first major work, *Olinda's Adventures,* later proved an anomaly in her canon: it is her only novel, and its subject, a young lady's growth into womanhood, was never taken up again. Commentators consider the work partly autobiographical. In eight brief letters the narrator relates the frustrations of adolescent love, strongly upholding conventional morality while evidencing a sharp sense of humor and a keen self-awareness. The novel is not considered a great work, yet critics agree it employs many features then barely embryonic in the novel form, including a subplot, careful motivation behind events, and a cast of nonaristocratic characters living in ordinary circumstances. Trotter's first drama, the historical tragedy *Agnes de Castro* (modeled on the same story that Aphra Behn employed in her 1688 novel *Agnes de Castro; or, The Force of Generous Love*), is thoroughly aristocratic in setting, plot, and dramatis personae. The play treats the psychological dilemmas of lovers at the Portuguese court, especially those of the title character, a deeply moral woman who must choose between the pains of virtue and the pleasures of carnal lust. Like Olinda, she opts for the former, enforcing the lesson that proved ubiquitous in Trotter's imaginative works: the preeminence of noble righteousness in ethical matters. Trotter's next drama, *Fatal Friendship*, is set in France and also treats romantic love, this time among members of the minor aristocracy. It is a markedly didactic drama and may in fact have been written to protest the rampant licentiousness of the late-seventeenth-century English theater—a licentiousness ruthlessly attacked by Jeremy Collier in *A Short View of the Immorality and Profaneness of the English Stage, Together with the Sense of Antiquity upon This Argument* (1698), which was published almost simultaneously with *Fatal Friendship*. Contemporary critics, at least, detected a reforming spirit beneath the action, and it is clear that Trotter's desire to promote virtue was well established by this time. The comedy *Love at a Loss* followed *Fatal Friendship* in 1700. The play consists of three plot lines and involves the romantic dilemmas of three young women. Again, the lesson of the play is a pointedly moral one: "What certain hazards do poor Women run! / They hear, believe, they taste, and are undone. . . . / And hands, and seals, and Oaths cannot secure / A Mind like Man's unfaithful and impure." Trotter returned to tragedy in her two final dramas, *The Unhappy Penitent* and *The Revolution of Sweden*. Both are based on historical incidents, and both conclude with moral statements. Like Trotter's other dramas, they are shaped by a desire to reaffirm the merits of virtuous behavior, but critics have found them stiff and unconvincing. (Even Trotter herself faulted *The Unhappy Penitent*, stating in the dedication of the work that the subject, "the misfortune of Lovers," was an insufficient plot motive.) Nevertheless, *The Revolution of Sweden* is considered an important early feminist statement, having, as it does, female characters who know enough not to trust the promises of men, embody intellectual and physical strength, and live almost completely without the support of peers, male or female.

Trotter's philosophical essays—the only type of work she wrote after age twenty-six—have been scrutinized less than her dramas, but they are an important component of her oeuvre and, most critics believe, competent exercises in a challenging field of thought. Her chief philosophical inquiry is *A Defence of the "Essay of Human Understanding,"* a defence of John Locke's *Essay concerning Human Understanding* (1690) written in response to attacks that appeared during the late 1690s. Locke himself was deeply impressed by Trotter's mastery of his theory of knowledge and called the work "the greatest honour my *Essay* could have procured me." But if contemporary readers shared Locke's enthusiasm, they left little record of it: with the exception of a few scattered comments, the work was virtually ignored. Trotter also wrote extensively on religious and moral philosophy, principally in *A Discourse concerning a Guide in Controversies* and *Remarks upon Some Writers in the Controversy concerning the Foundation of Moral Duty and Moral Obligation*. The former is a discussion of denominational Christianity prompted by Trotter's leaving the Roman Catholic Church, the latter a close study of current opinion concerning human conduct and values. Neither work, however, attracted much attention in the critical press or learned reviews, and it is likely both had little reputation outside a small circle of philosophers and Trotter's personal friends. Trotter's most successful philosophical work was also her last: *Remarks upon the Principles and Reasonings of Dr. Rutherforth's "Essay on the Nature and Obligations of Virtue."* This confutation of Thomas Rutherforth's criticisms of Samuel Clarke's metaphysics, "finished," according to Trotter's biographer Thomas Birch, with "a spirit, elegance and perspicuity equal, if not superior, to all her former writings," sold well and apparently led Trotter to authorize a collected edition of her works—an edition that appeared in 1751 and gave pride of place not to Trotter's dramas but to her philosophy. (Indeed, only one play—*Fatal Friendship*—was included in the collection.)

"So little mark did poor Mrs. Cockburn make on her younger contemporaries that she disappeared forthwith from literary history." So wrote Edmund Gosse in his 1919 study of Trotter, adding: "The champion of Locke and Clarke, the correspondent of Leibnitz and Pope, the friend of Congreve, the patroness of Farquhar, she seems to have slipped between two ages and to have lost her hold on time." In life Trotter stood tall among contemporaries, often in spite of invective hurled at her because she sought a place in what was chiefly the domain of men. Congreve, for example, admired her as a dramatist, and Locke accorded her high respect. Still, even by the middle of her career Trotter was moving toward obscurity, and, as new female writers emerged and other dramatists and philosophers supplanted her in currency, the bold relief in which she once stood turned shallow. By 1800 Trotter was but a name in historical chronicles of the drama, and a dim one at that. The few critics who deigned to discuss her generally did so briefly and condescendingly. Not until Gosse's time did favorable interest reawaken. Since then, concern for her works has increased appreciably, principally in line with the developing study of the place of women in English literary history. During the past half century or so Trotter has gradually regained some of the eminence she enjoyed in early life, reemerging as a dramatist whose plays remain compelling, even if more for the picture they offer of late Restoration life than as pure entertainment. Trotter is recognized today as a writer who could hold her own in a literary world dominated by men. And, commentators add, she accomplished this in a manner practically unique, for the apparent impetus of her career, a zeal for moral reform, firmly grounded her literary work with much didactic teaching—teaching which, seen in perspective, helped pave the way for much of the literature that followed.

In his 1751 biography of Trotter, Birch considered the value of studying the author's life and works: "Posterity at least will be solicitous to know, to whom they will owe the most demonstrative and perspicuous reasonings, upon subjects of eternal importance; and her own sex is intitled to the fullest information about one, who has done such honour to them, and raised our ideas of their intellectual powers." For the most part, twentieth-century commentators have echoed Birch's conclusion, noting that Trotter affords a precious glimpse of the role of women in the literary affairs of the age and a window on the larger scene of English intellectual life. Trotter helped bring about the moral regeneration of the English drama, participated actively in the philosophical and intellectual debates of the era, wrote a novel that anticipated major developments in the genre, and contributed to the controversy concerning the respective merits of the Anglican and Roman Catholic communions. Most of all, she did these things with notable success and against difficult odds—a fact well supported by contemporary appraisals of her works. Writing in 1696 in commendation of Manley's play *The Royal Mischief*, Trotter praised the woman and her work in words that may be applied with equal justice to her own achievement: "Th' Attempt was brave, how happy your success / The Men with shame, our Sex with Pride confess. . . ."

PRINCIPAL WORKS

Olinda's Adventures; or, The Amours of a Young Lady, in Letters of Love, Gallantry, and Several Occasions (novel) 1693; published in *Letters of Love and Gallantry and Several Other Subjects, All Written by Ladies*
Agnes de Castro (drama) 1695
Fatal Friendship (drama) 1698
**Love at a Loss; or, Most Votes Carry It* (drama) 1700
The Unhappy Penitent (drama) 1701
A Defence of the "Essay of Human Understanding" (essay) 1702
The Revolution of Sweden (drama) 1706
A Discourse concerning a Guide in Controversies, in Two Letters (essay) 1707
A Letter to Dr. Holdsworth (essay) 1726
Remarks upon Some Writers in the Controversy concerning the Foundation of Moral Duty and Moral Obligation (essay) 1743; published in journal *The History of the Works of the Learned*
Remarks upon the Principles and Reasonings of Dr. Rutherforth's "Essay on the Nature and Obligations of Virtue," in Vindication of the Contrary Principles and Reasonings Inforced in the Writings of the Late Dr. Samuel Clarke (essay) 1747
†*The Works of Mrs. Catharine Cockburn: Theological, Moral, Dramatic, and Poetical.* 2 vols. (essays, drama, poetry, and correspondence) 1751
The Plays of Mary Pix and Catharine Trotter, Vol. II: *Catharine Trotter* (dramas) 1982

*This work was revised as *The Honourable Deceivers; or, All Right at the Last*, but it is not known to have been produced and is believed lost.

†This work contains *A Vindication of Mr. Locke's Christian Principles from the Injurious Imputations of Dr. Holdsworth*, written in 1724.

WILLIAM WYCHERLEY (poem date 1695)

[*Wycherley was one of the foremost dramatists of the Restoration. His plays, which combine irreverent social satire with complex verbal wit, are recognized as lasting celebrations of the hedonistic cynicism of the London aristocracy. His acknowledged masterpiece,* The Country-Wife *(1675), exemplifies all that is considered best about his writings: it is highly indecent but vastly entertaining, mercilessly satirizes hypocrisy and social folly, and mirrors the sophisticated urbanity of the age. In the following prologue* of Agnes de Castro, *written at Trotter's request and spoken on stage by a woman, Wycherley asks the audience to think kindly of the female author and to give her drama the attention due a male dramatist.*]

> Ladies and Gallants, you we hope to find,
> To her, who brings you now together, kind;
> That you, will to your pleasing her consent,
> Not out of your own Nicety prevent,
> But to spight her, your own divertisement;
> And will not your Displeasure to her show,
> Who your scorn Ventures, but to pleasure you,
> Nay, her own pleasure, does for yours, forego;
> And like the Pregnant of her Sex, to gain,
> But for your pleasure, more Disgrace, and Pain,
> Who, but because she'd do you, a good Turn,
> Unask'd, unsu'd to, may become your scorn;
> But you; the Men of Honour, or of Wit,
> To set yours to a Woman can't think fit,
> And Ladies; as necessitous of Fame,
> Ne'er raise your Credit, by another's shame,
> Censuring others, to 'scape others blame;
> And Gallants, as y'are Men of Honour, you,
> Will ne'er speak ill, of her you do not know;
> The more she strives, to give you Pleasure too,
> Which is most often, (as we Women find,)
> The sole cause, you prove to us, but less kind;
> As well-bred *Beaux's* with Noise too, ne'er thinks fit,
> To silence on the Stage, as in the Pit,
> Another's Sense, to hide your want of Wit;
> But Beaux's and Wits, I pray be silent now,
> And hear without Noise, nay with Patience too,
> Our Female Wit, if you'd have her, hear you;
> Especially, since your own talking does,
> Your Pleasure interupt, your Sense Expose,
> Whilst Silence, good Sense, and good Breeding shows;
> And each Man's manners, Honour, Wit appear,
> More, as he's less a Woman's Censurer,
> Then Censures, which wou'd spoil your sport forbear:
> Think not the Ladies Wit, or Honour less,
> Because she seeks those who have less to please;
> Let not her aim, to please the Publick now,
> Design'd her Credit, but your Scandal grow,
> Make not her proffer'd favour, her Disgrace,
> Nay, though it shou'd not please th'Intention praise,
> 'Tis merit only, to desire to please;
> Then be not, as Poor Women often find,
> Less kind to her, but as she's more inclin'd,
> At venture of her Fame, to please Mankind.

William Wycherley, in a prologue in The Plays of Mary Pix and Catharine Trotter: Catharine Trotter, *Vol. II, edited by Edna L. Steeves, Garland Publishing, Inc., 1982.*

CATHARINE TROTTER (essay date 1696)

[*In the following excerpt from the dedication of* Agnes de Castro, *prefaced to the first printing of the play in 1696 and addressed to Charles, Earl of Dorset and Middlesex, Trotter reflects on the composition of this, her first dramatic production.*]

This little Off-spring of my early Muse [*Agnes de Castro*] was first Submitted to Your Lordship's Judgment, Whether it shou'd be Stifled in the Birth, or Preserv'd to try its Fortune in the world; and since 'tis from Your Sentence it has ventur'd thus far, it now Claims a sort of Title to Your Lordships Protection, which it cou'd not have the least pretence to from its own Merit; But 'tis Your Lordships Character to Encourage all great Attempts, though Unsuccessful: This was indeed a Bold one for a Woman at my Years, but I wou'd not offer my little

Experience, as a reason to be Pardon'd for not acquitting my self well, (for I think the Incapacity of producing any thing better, a very ill Excuse for exposing a Foolish Thing) if the same inconsidering Youth might not excuse the rashness of the Undertaking; and I shall be much less Pardonable, if the next I bring upon the Stage has not a better Title to the Favour of the Town. This seems to promise another attempt, which shou'd not be expected from one who Conceals her Name, to shun that of Poetress.

> *Catharine Trotter, "To the Right Honourable Charles," in* The Plays of Mary Pix and Catharine Trotter: Catharine Trotter, Vol. II, *edited by Edna L. Steeves, Garland Publishing, Inc., 1982.*

MARY DELARIVIERE MANLEY   (poem date 1696)

[*Manley is best remembered for* The New Atalantis, *a series of self-contained novels published between 1707 and 1710 which introduced the roman à clef, already popular in France, to eighteenth-century England. In these works, as well as her other "scandalous chronicles," she revealed the political and sexual vices of prominent members of the Whig party during the reign of Queen Anne. Manley was also the first woman journalist in England: she edited the* Female Tatler, *worked with Jonathan Swift on the* Examiner, *and succeeded Swift as editor of that publication. One of the triumvirate of women authors pilloried in the anonymous drama* The Female Wits (*see Additional Bibliography*), *she was closely allied with the two other leading women dramatists of the day, Trotter and Mary Pix. In the following commentary poem added to the first printing of* Agnes de Castro, *she praises Trotter for demonstrating what a woman writer is able to accomplish. Manley later satirized Trotter in one of her scandalous chronicles,* The Adventures of Rivella (1714), *accusing her fellow dramatist of cunning and deceit (see Additional Bibliography).*]

> *Orinda,* and the Fair *Astrea* gone,
> Not one was found to fill the Vacant Throne:
> Aspiring Man had quite regain'd the Sway,
> Again had Taught us humbly to Obey;
> Till you (Natures third start, in favour of our Kind)
> With stronger Arms, their Empire have disjoyn'd,
> And snatch a Lawrel which they thought their Prize,
> Thus Conqu'ror, with your Wit, as with your Eyes.
> Fired by the bold Example, I would try
> To turn our Sexes weaker Destiny.
> O! How I long in the Poetick Race,
> To loose the Reins, and give their Glory Chase;
> For thus Encourag'd, and thus led by you,
> Methinks we might more Crowns than theirs Subduc.

> *Mary Delariviere Manley, "To the Author of 'Agnes de Castro'," in* The Plays of Mary Pix and Catharine Trotter: Catharine Trotter, Vol. II, *edited by Edna L. Steeves, Garland Publishing, Inc., 1982.*

[JOHN HUGHES]   (poem date 1698)

[*An English poet, dramatist, and historian, Hughes is chiefly known for* The Siege of Damascus, *a highly successful play produced at Drury Lane in 1720. In the following commendatory poem, published anonymously as a preface to Trotter's* Fatal Friendship *but attributed to Hughes by Thomas Birch in the biographical introduction to* The Works of Mrs. Catharine Cockburn: Theological, Moral, Dramatic, and Poetical *(1751), he salutes*

Trotter's triumph in the masculine arena of literature and praises her as a moral dramatist.]

> As when *Camilla* once, a Warlike Dame
> In bloody Battles won immortal Fame;
> Forsook her Female Arts, and chose to bear
> The pondrous Shield, and heave the massy Spear,
> Superiour to her Sex; so swift she flew
> Around the Field, and such vast Numbers slew,
> That Friends and Foes alike surpriz'd behold
> The brave *Virago* desperately Bold,
> And thought her *Pallas* in a human Mold.
> Such is our Wonder, matchless Maid! to see
> The Tragick Laurel thus deserv'd by thee.
>   Yet greater Praise is yours; *Camilla* shines
> For ever bright in *Virgil's* Sacred Lines,
> You in your own;—where to the World's last Date
> You shall survive, and Triumph over Fate;
> Nor need you to anothers Bounty owe
> For what your self can on your self bestow
> So Monarchs in full Health were wont to rear
> At their own charge, their future Sepulchre.
>   Who thy Perfections fully wou'd commend
> Must think how others do their Hours mispend,
> In Trifling Visits, Pride, Impertinence
> Dress, Dancing, and Discourse quite void of Sence.
> To twirl a Fan, to please some foolish Beau,
> And sing an empty Song the most they know,
> In Body weak, more Impotent of mind—
> Thus some have represented Woman-kind;
> But you your Sexes Champion are come forth
> To fight their Quarrel, and assert their Worth.
> Our *Salique* Law of Wit you have destroy'd,
> Establish'd Female Claim, and Triumph'd o'er our Pride;
> While We look on, and with repining Eyes
> Behold you bearing off so rich a Prize,
> Spright of Ill-Nature we're compell'd t' approve
> Such dazling Worth, and spright of Envy love.
>   Nor is this all th' applause that is your Due;
> You Stand the first of Stage-Reformers too.
> No Vicious Stains pollute your moral Scene;
> Chast are your Thoughts, and your Expression clean.
> Strains such as yours the strictest Test will bear:
> Sing boldly then! nor busy Censure fear;
> Your *Virgin* Voice offends no *Virgin* Ear.
> Proceed, in Tragick Numbers to disclose
> Strange Turns of Fate, and unexpected Woes!
> Reward and punish; awfully dispence
> Heav'ns Judgments, and declare a Providence!
> Nor let the Comick Muse your Labours share;
> 'Tis Meaness after this the Sock to wear.
> Tho' that too merit Praise, 'tis nobler Toil
> T' extort a Tear, than to provoke a Smile.
> What Hand that can design a History
> Wou'd Copy Low-Land Boors at Snick a Snee?
>   Accept this Tribute Madam! and excuse
> The hasty Raptures of a Stranger-Muse.

(pp. ix-x)

> [*John Hughes*], *"To the Ingenious Author, on Her Tragedy, Call'd "Fatal Friendship'," in* The Plays of Mary Pix and Catharine Trotter: Catharine Trotter, Vol. II, *edited by Edna L. Steeves, Garland Publishing, Inc., 1982.*

GEORGE POWELL?   (poem date 1698)

[*Powell was an English essayist, dramatist, and actor who is chiefly known through contemporary accounts of his literary quarrels. In 1696 he acted in the anonymous play* The Female Wits (*see Additional Bibliography*), *a satire directed against Trotter and other literary women of the day. Powell is widely believed,*

*though not universally acknowledged, the author of the anony-
mously published* Animadversions on Mr. Congreve's Late Answer to Mr. Collier *(1698), a diatribe against alleged immoralities
of the English stage. In the following excerpt from this work, the
critic presents verse characterizations of Trotter and a contemporary playwright, Mary Pix. The play mentioned in the seventh
line of the excerpt is Pix's* Queen Catharine; or, The Ruines of
Love *(1698). The reference to the "High Princess" in line nine
probably alludes to the dedication of* Fatal Friendship, *"To Her
Royal Highness the Princess."*]

[O] could I write like the two Female things
With *Muse Pen-feather'd,* guiltless yet of Wings;
And yet, it strives to Fly, and thinks it Sings.
Just like the Dames themselves, who slant in Town,
And flutter loosely, but to tumble down.
The last that writ, of these presuming two,
(For that *Queen Ca—ne* is no Play 'tis true)
And yet to Spell is more than she can do,
Told a High Princess, she from Men had torn
Those *Bays,* which they had long engross'd and worn.
But when she offers at our Sex thus Fair,
With four fine Copies to her Play,—O rare!
If she feels Manhood shoot—'tis I know where.
Let them scrawl on, and Loll, and Wish at ease,
(A Feather oft does Woman's Fancy please.)
Till by their Muse (more jilt than they) accurst,
We know (if possible) which writes the worst.
Beneath these Pictures, sure there needs no name,
Nor will I give what they ne'er got in Fame.

(pp. iv-v)

George Powell? "To the Ingenious Mr. ——," in
Animadversions on Mr. Congreve's Late Answer to
Mr. Collier, *1698. Reprint by Garland Publishing,
Inc., 1972, pp. iii-v.*

[CHARLES GILDON] (essay date 1699)

[*An English critic, Gildon abridged and updated Gerard Langbaine's 1691 study of the London stage,* The Lives and Characters
of the English Dramatick Poets, *giving special attention to the
rising dramatists of the 1690s. In the following excerpt from
Gildon's 1699 revision of this work, he compliments Trotter's
philosophical abilities and favorably reviews the two plays yet
written by her,* Agnes de Castro *and* Fatal Friendship.]

This Lady, [Mrs. Catharine Trotter], by her Parents, is of
Scotch Extraction, tho' born and bred in *England;* admirable
for two things rarely found together, *Wit and Beauty;* and with
these a *Penetration* very uncommon in the Sex. She discovers
in her Conversation, a *Fineness* and *Nicety* of *Reasoning* on
the highest *Metaphysical Subjects;* nor is she less entertaining
on the more Gay and Conversible. She has already given us
two Plays, which challenge our Admiration, we like the first,
but are transported with the last; there is the Chastity of her
Person, and the Tenderness of her Mind in both; the Passions
are natural and moving, the stile just and familiar, and adapted
to the subject; if there be not the Sublime, 'tis because there
was no room for it, not because she had not Fire and Genius
enough to write it. What I say will be secur'd from the Imputation of Flattery, by what she has writ; and 'tis the Brevity
I have propos'd my self in this Undertaking, that confines me
to this little, and obliges me to proceed to her Plays.

Agnes de Castro, a Tragedy, acted at the Theatre Royal, and
dedicated to the Right Honourable *Charles,* Earl of *Dorset* and
Middlesex, &. This Play met with good Success. 'Tis built on
a Novel of the same Title, written Originally in *French,* by a
French Lady, and translated into *English* by Mrs. *Behn.*

Fatal Friendship, a Tragedy, as it is acted at the new Theatre
in *Little Lincolns-Inn-Fields,* 1698, and dedicated to her Royal
Highness the Princess of *Denmark.* I need say nothing of this
Play, the Town has prevented my Approbation; and I can only
add, that I think it deserv'd the Applause it met with, which
every Play that has the Advantage of being Clapt, cannot get
from the severer and abler Judges.

[*Charles Gildon*], *"Mrs. Catharine Trother," in*
Momus Triumphans; or, The Plagiaries of the English Stage *and* The Lives and Characters of the English Dramatick Poets *by Gerard Langbaine, Garland Publishing, Inc., 1973, p. 179.*

SARAH PIERSE (poem date 1701)

[*Practically unknown to biographers and historians, Piers (as her
name is commonly spelled) was one of Trotter's closest friends
and may have helped her financially in her writing career. In the
following poem, composed specially for the first printing of* The
Unhappy Penitent *and addressed to "the excellent Mrs. Catherine
Trotter," she warmly praises Trotter's character and talent.*]

As when *Aurora's* graceful Blushes chear,
With gentle beams, the glimering Hemisphere,
Faint are her glances, and her feeble fire,
Compels no saucy Critick to retire;
Her weak efforts small Victory can boast,
And her slight Charms but warm us at the most.
  Thus like the Morning Star *Orinda* rose
A Champion for her Sex, and wisely chose,
Conscious of Female weakness, humble wais
T' insinuate for applause, nor storm the Bays.
Next gay *Astrea* briskly won the Prize,
Yet left a spacious room to Criticise.
  But when bright *Phœbus* gilds the Orb around,
And from *Olympus* strikes the distant ground,
With rays of glory, whose refulgent light,
Dazle the shallow Opticks of our fight,
By the strong force of excellence alone
The mighty Deity erects his Throne,
And by sublimer faculties is known.
  Like him bright Maid thy great Perfections shine,
As awful, as resplendent, as divine;
Like him thy Soul in its Cœlestial frame,
Darts forth as pure, as vigorous a flame;
And in the full *Meridian* you fit,
With Sov'raign pow'r of Beauty, and of Wit;
And as the dimmer Tapers of the Skies,
Vail when the more transcendent God does rise,
So those precedent Lamps withdrew their light
Timely to do thy wond'rous Genius right.
Mirtle and Bays about thy Temples twine,
Plac'd by *Apollo,* and the Sacred Nine,
And ev'ry Grace, and ev'ry vertue's thine.
By thy judicious Rules the Hero learns
To vanquish Fate, and weild his Conq'ring Arms,
The bashful Virgin to defend her heart,
The prudent Wife to scorn dishonest Art,
The Friend sincerity; temp'rance the Youth,
The Lover Chastity, and Statesman Truth.
Within thy bosom all these Treasures dwell,
Nor can we judge in which you most excell.
So perfect even Envy you controul
Minerva and *Diana* guard your Soul.

*Sarah Pierse, "To the Excellent Mrs. Catherine
Trotter," in* The Plays of Mary Pix and Catharine
Trotter: Catharine Trotter, Vol. II, *edited by Edna
L. Steeves, Garland Publishing, Inc., 1982.*

E[LIZABETH] BURNET   **(letter date 1702)**

[*Burnet was the third wife of Gilbert Burnet, a bishop and historian who is best remembered for his studies of the English Reformation. An author in her own right and, like her husband, one of Trotter's closest friends, she is chiefly known for her prayers and devotional essays. In the following excerpt from a letter written shortly after the anonymous publication of Trotter's* Defence of the "Essay of Human Understanding," *she thanks Trotter for sending her a copy of the book, praising its style and fair-minded arguments.*]

Madam,

If I have not more hastily returned my thanks for the valuable present you sent me [*A Defence of the "Essay of Human Understanding"*], it has been, in part, out of a desire to send you better judgments than my own for its approbation and praise. The Bishop, Mr. *Norris,* and some others, no ill judges of such a performance, have, with great readiness, professed themselves extremely pleased: and it is not without difficulty some can believe, that any one, not bred to science, and logic in particular, could be capable of so close and clear reasoning. I am no fit judge of this, nor of the certainty of all the proofs, which are things so nice, as to make me suspect my capacity to determine about them; so can only say, I am satisfied and pleased. But that can be no confirmation, were you doubtful; but what I cannot but observe and commend, is, that the whole is written short and clear, without affectation of wit or eloquence, needless reflections on your adversary, or making him ore in the wrong than he is; rather bringing him nearer, than driving him farther from truth; taking his words in as good a sense, as they would bear, in which I heartily with the searchers after truth would imitate you. If they did, I am persuaded, there would be both more light, as well as more charity in the world, than at present, while such destructive methods to both are taken,can be expected. I confess I cannot but repeat what I ever think, and have generally found, so sure a mark of a good judgment, modesty, and freedom from affectation, which is alone a beauty, but when accompanied with other excellencies, makes them much more valuable, and the want of them makes wit and knowledge itself disagreeable. I heartily wish you may improve to the best uses such excellent talents, that nothing may obscure their lustre, but that you may be delivered from *every error.* (pp. xvii-xviii)

> *E[lizabeth] Burnet, in a letter to Mrs. Trotter on June 19, 1702, in* The Works of Mrs. Catharine Cockburn: Theological, Moral, Dramatic, and Poetical, *Vol. I., edited by Thomas Birch, J. and P. Knapton, 1751, pp. xvii-xviii.*

JOHN LOCKE   **(letter date 1702)**

[*Locke was an English rationalist philosopher whose numerous and varied works dominated English thought in the first half of the eighteenth century, extending the author's influence to America, France, and beyond. His monumental* Essay concerning Human Understanding *(1690), written to discover "the original, certainty and extent of human knowledge," furnished basic premises concerning such matters as empiricism, language, and personal identity. Though not without its detractors—the work was violently attacked in some quarters upon publication and remains controversial—the* Essay *is today recognized as one of the greatest works of world philosophy. In the following excerpt from a letter prompted by Trotter's anonymous publication of* A Defence of the "Essay of Human Understanding," *Locke responds warmly to Trotter's favorable appraisal of his work, adding his apology*

for "transgressing" her apparent desire to remain anonymous by seeking out her identity.]

Madam,

There was nothing more public, than the obligation I received from you, nor any thing more concealed, than the person I was obliged to. This is a generosity above the strain of this groveling age, and like that of superior spirits, who assist without shewing themselves. I used my best endeavours to draw from you, by your Bookseller, the confession of your name, the want whereof made me, that I could, whilst you kept yourself under that reserve, no more address myself directly to you with good manners, than I could without rudeness have pulled off your mask by force, in a place where you were resolved to conceal yourself. Had not this been so, the bearer hereof had not the first time have come to you, without a letter from me, to acknowledge the favour you had done me. You not affording me an opportunity for that, I designed to make you some small acknowledgement, in a way, that chance had opened to me, without your consent. But this gentleman transgressed my order in two main points of it. The one was, in delaying it so long: The other was, in naming me to you, and talking of matters, which he had no commission from me to mention. What he deserves from you for it, must be left to your mercy. For I cannot in earnest be angry with him for procuring me, without any guilt of mine, an opportunity to own you for my protectress, which is the greatest honour my *Essay* could have procured me. Give me leave therefore to assure you, that as the rest of the world take notice of the strength and clearness of your reasoning [in *A Defence of the "Essay of Human Understanding"*], so I cannot but be extremely sensible, that it was employed in my defence. You have herein not only vanquished my adversary, but reduced me also absolutely under your power, and left no desires more strong in me, than those of meeting with some opportunity, to assure you, with what respect and submission I am, Madam, Your most humble, and most obedient servant. . . . (pp. 730-31)

> *John Locke, in a letter to Catharine Trotter on December 30, 1702, in his* The Correspondence of John Locke: Letters Nos. 2665-3286, *Vol. 7, edited by E. S. DeBeer, Oxford at the Clarendon Press, Oxford, 1982, pp. 730-31.*

WILLIAM CONGREVE   **(letter date 1703)**

[*Universally acknowledged the greatest comic dramatist of the Restoration, Congreve is best known for the unflagging wit with which he infused a repertoire of plays still widely performed and read today. His skillful representations of human behavior in society—effected primarily through the brilliant banter of his characters in such celebrated plays as* Love for Love *(1695) and* The Way of the World *(1700)—have established his prominence within an age which considered intelligent and imaginative wit of premier importance. It is not known when Congreve met Trotter, but it is likely they were friendly, possibly even courting, by 1696 or 1697. In the following excerpt from a 1703 letter to her, he offers suggestions on how she might improve a draft of* The Revolution of Sweden.]

Madam,

I had sooner acknowledged the favour of your letter, together with the agreeable entertainment of the scheme you were pleased to send with it, if I had not been unavoidably engaged in business. But at this time I can hardly complain of a great cold, which has confined me, and given me an opportunity to obey your commands. I think the design [of *The Revolution of Sweden*] in general very great and noble; the conduct of it very artful, if not too full of business, which may either run into length or obscurity; but both those, as you write, you have skill enough to avoid. You are the best judge, whether those of your own sex will approve as much of the heroic virtue of *Constantia* and *Christina,* as if they had been engaged in some *belle passion:* for my part, I like them better as they are. In the second act, I would have that noise, which generally attends so much fighting on the stage, provided against; for those frequent alarms and excursions do too much disturb an audience. The difficulty in the third act is as well solved by you as possible; and certainly you can never be too careful not to offend probability, in supposing a man not to discover his own wife.

In the fourth act, it does not seem to me to be clear enough, how *Constantia* comes to be made free, and to return to *Gustavus;* the third act intimating so strongly, why we might expect to have her continued in the viceroy's power. This act is full of business; and intricacy, in the fourth act, must by all means be avoided.

The last act will have many harangues in it, which are dangerous in a catastrophe, if long, and not of the last importance. To conclude, I approve extremely of your killing *Fredage* and *Beron.* Poetical justice requires him; and for her you may easily drop a word, to intimate her delivering of *Gustavus* to have proceeded from some spark of love, which afterwards she may repent of, and her character remain as perfect as nature need require. One thing would have a very beautiful effect in the catastrophe, if it were possible to manage it thro' the play; and that is to have the audience kept in ignorance, as long as the husband (which sure they may as well be) who *Fredage* really is, till her death.

You see, Madam, I am as free as you command me to be; and yet by objections are none but such, as you may provide against, even while you are writing the dialogue.

I wish you the success, which you can wish, and that, I think, will hardly be so much as you deserve, in whatever you undertake. (pp. 212-13)

> *William Congreve, in a letter to Catharine Trotter on November 2, 1703, in his* Letters & Documents, *edited by John C. Hodges, Macmillan & Co. Ltd., 1964, pp. 212-13.*

CATHARINE TROTTER (essay date 1706)

[*In the following preface written for the first printing of* The Revolution of Sweden, *Trotter responds to criticism prompted by the initial performances of the play.*]

I am willing to believe that the distaste of Plays which the Town is fall'n into, (tho' encreas'd since some care has been taken to Reform them) was at first produc'd by the just Complaints that have been Publickly made on the Abuses of the Stage, which might incline the Ladies especially, to seek in Musick, fine scenes and Dancing, a Diversion that wou'd at least be harmless.

But however, an Amusement of three Hours, that can be no way profitable, may be Innocent in an Audience. I cannot but think an Author wou'd very ill employ the much longer time, and greater application he must use, in contriving an Entertainment for no other end but to divert, and cou'd never allow

my self to think of any Subject that cou'd not serve either to incite some useful Virtue, or check some dangerous Passion. With this design I thought writing for the Stage, a Work not unworthy those who wou'd not trifle their time away, and had so fix'd my Mind on contributing my part towards reforming the Corruptions of it, that no doubt I have too little consider'd the present tast of the Town; I shou'd not have wholly neglected those Ornaments, which all are now fond of, since the end of Tragedy is to profit the Audience by Pleasing, and every Body will be pleas'd their own way.

Whether my turning this Play [*The Revolution of Sweden*] into the World thus undress'd, be the chief defect of it, must be left to the Reader's Judgment, to whom I shall be allow'd to appeal, at least, from two sorts of Judges who have pass'd their Censure on it; those who have never seen any part of it, and those who, tho' present at it, minded very little of it. Some of the first of these have absolutely determin'd, that no body of good Sense, can think it a tolerable Play; a Sentence they are most concern'd in, who were pleas'd to give it their Applause in the Representation, but it needs not be pleaded against, those who pass it sufficiently exposing themselves, by condemning a thing, which they own they know nothing of. From the other sort, I have met with some turns of Raillery, which had no Foundation, but mistakes from an intire Ignorance of what had pass'd before, or was to follow, what they were pleas'd to be Witty upon; of which I need only give the Reader one for a Tast. Some finding that *Arwide* has set his Hand to a Paper, in which there are Articles that he knows nothing of, conclude that he sign'd a Treaty with his Enemy, without ever reading it, and on this wise Contrivance of their own Imagination, laugh at a *Woman's Plot,* when the least attention to the conclusion of the Play, must have satisfy'd them that the deceit was a little more artfully laid.

'Tis confess'd it would be very unreasonable to desire, that every one who comes to a Play, shou'd be attentive at it; those who find in the Audience a better Entertainment, must be allow'd to turn their Eyes and Thoughts from the Stage; but then 'tis no more than equitable to expect, that they should not judge at all, of what they have not leisure to mind.

What objections I have heard from the less rash, or at least more attentive Criticks, are not very considerable; some who had read the History, expected to find all the remarkable Passages of it in the Play, and particularly hop'd to see *Gustavus* labouring in the Mines, not knowing, or not considering the Rules of the *Drama,* that Tragedy is confin'd to represent only such incidents as immediately conduce to the effecting the one great Action it proposes, all which must be suppos'd to happen in a small space of Time: And the Action I had chose, being the Election of *Gustavus* to the Throne, upon the entire Deliverance of his Country; it must have been very absurd, to have represented him at the beginning of the Play in such an unhopeful condition, when the *Danes* were in full Power, and not one Man had ventur'd to appear against them. But those who know the History, will find, that to give them as much of it as cou'd be in so narrow a compass, I have us'd the Poetick License in bringing several Incidents and Places, much nearer together, than in reality they were, as far as probability wou'd allow.

Another piece of Criticism I have heard, is, that I have made *Christina* speak an Hour after she is dead: As to the time, I shall not stand upon giving 'em three quarters of an Hour, it being every whit as absurd to make her speak one Minute after she is dead, as a whole Hour; and for her speaking after she has been in a Swoon, and *suppos'd* dead,——an Hour, if they will have it so, as there is nothing in that, but what has very frequently happen'd, the Jest will, notwithstanding, be intirely lost.

The only Remark I have met with besides is, that the Senators are very basty Judges, in giving, and revoking, their Sentence; to which I shall answer, that Proceedings of that nature, being very little entertaining on the Stage. I endeavour'd to make it as short as Reason and the Matter would bear; and if my Criticks will dispense with me from using the Forms of *Westminster-Hall,* I believe they will find that the Evidence appears sufficiently full, and clear, to condemn any Man; and that the whole force of it is afterwards taken off, by the farther Declaration of one, whose Sincerity they had no cause to doubt of. But how far their proceedings are justify'd by Reason, and Equity, where Forms cannot be observ'd, is submitted to the Judgment of every Reader, who is not merry enough to sacrifice Truth, and good Nature to his Jest. (pp. vi-vii)

> *Catharine Trotter, in a preface in* The Plays of Mary Pix and Catharine Trotter: Catharine Trotter, *Vol. II, edited by Edna L. Steeves, Garland Publishing, Inc., 1982.*

GILBERT BURNET   (essay date 1707)

[*Burnet was an English bishop and historian who wrote on the English Reformation and composed a sparkling eye-witness account of contemporary life,* The History of My Own Times *(published posthumously, 1724-34). He was a close friend of Trotter and probably was influential in her return to the Church of England. In the following excerpt from his 1707 preface to her* Discourse concerning a Guide in Controversies, *he describes the origin of the work and praises the argument as considered and reasoned.*]

The ingenious author of these papers [*A Discourse concerning a Guide in Controversies*] being not easily prevailed with to permit the publication of them, I am not at liberty to inform the reader any farther, than that they were writ by one, who had been many years of the church of *Rome,* but having been for some time dissatisfied with several doctrines and practices in that church, had resolv'd to examine, with great care, the grounds of that authority, on which they were received, by consulting the best books on that subject on both sides, and by advising with men of the best judgments of both communions: And that these papers were the result of those free and impartial enquiries, designed only to impart the Author's thoughts to a friend, without any intention of making them public.

But falling into the hands of some very good judges, as well divines as others, the publishing of them was very much desired, both for the strength and clearness of the reasoning, and for the shortness of them; many readers being encouraged to seek for information in pieces of this size, who have neither the mind nor the leisure to go through large volumes.

They are, I think, writ with that judgment, and withal with that plainness, that they may be at all times useful to those of our own communion, that want to be fortified against the bold pretences to infallibility to the church of *Rome;* and will, I hope, help to open the eyes of such of the *Romish Communion,* as are persuaded, that those, who deny that infallibility, take away all certainty of the Christian religion, or of the authority of the Scriptures; the grounds of those pretences being the chief subject of these letters. (pp. 3-4)

I need say no more concerning the author, or the performance. I pray God it may have the good effect, to excite all sorts of persons, of what persuasion soever, seriously and impartially to enquire into the grounds and reasons of their religion, as this author has done: for it is not only the most rational method for finding out truth, but what is indispensably required of us by revelation; where we are enjoined *to prove all things,* in order to the *holding fast that which is good.* (p. 4)

> *Gilbert Burnet, in a preface to "A Discourse concerning a Guide in Controversies," in* The Works of Mrs. Catharine Cockburn: Theological, Moral, Dramatic, and Poetical, *Vol. I, J. and P. Knapton, 1751, pp. 3-4.*

GILES JACOB   (essay date 1719)

[*Jacob was an English man of letters who is best remembered as a painstaking compiler of literary facts. Also an authority on legal matters, he was jeered thus by Alexander Pope in* The Dunciad *(1728): "Jacob, the Scourge of Grammar, mark with awe, / Nor less revere him, Blunderbuss of Law." In the following excerpt, he comments briefly on Trotter's five dramas, adding his favorable opinion of her principal philosophical work yet published,* A Defence of the "Essay of Human Understanding."]

This Gentlewoman [Mrs. Catharine Trother] was descended of *Scots* Parents, but born and bred in *England.* She has writ Five Plays, wherein the Passions are well describ'd, and the Diction is just and familiar.

I. *Agnes de Castro*; a Tragedy, acted at the Theatre Royal, 1696. Dedicated to the Right Honourable *Charles* Earl of *Dorset* and Middlesex. This Play met with very good Success. 'Tis built on a *French* Novel of the same Title, translated into *English* by Mrs. *Behn.*

II. *Fatal Friendship*; a Tragedy, acted at the Theatre in *Lincolns-Inn-Fields,* 1698. Dedicated to her Royal Highness the Princess *Anne* of *Denmark.* This Play was acted with very great Applause.

III. *The Unhappy Penitent*; a Tragedy, acted at the Theatre Royal.

IV. *Love at a Loss, or Most Votes carry it*; a Comedy, acted at the Theatre Royal.

V. *The Revolution of Sweden*; a Tragedy, acted at the Theatre Royal. Mrs. *Trother* was very much inclin'd to Philosophical Studies, and has written a very pretty small Piece in Defense of Mr. LOCKE's *Essay concerning Human Understanding* [*A Defence of the "Essay of Human Understanding"*]. Some time after the writing of her last Play, she was, by the late Bishop of *Salisbury,* converted from the *Romish* Persuasion, and was, by his Lordship's Recommendation, married to a Clergyman.

> *Giles Jacob, "Mrs. Catharine Trother," in his* The Poetical Register: or, The Lives and Characters of the English Dramatic Poets, *Vol. I, 1719. Reprint by Garland Publishing, Inc., 1970, p. 260.*

ALEXANDER POPE   (poem date 1732-34)

[*Pope has been called the greatest English poet of his time and one of the most important in world literature. As a critic and satirical commentator, he wrote works that epitomize neoclassical thought. While Pope's works are recognized as models of restraint, clarity, and order, his special greatness lies in his cultivation of style and wit, rather than sublimity and pathos—an inclination that influenced his criticism of other writers. It is not known if Pope knew Trotter personally, but it is likely that by the mid-1730s she had written to him seeking friendship and approval of her works. If Pope responded favorably, no record of this appears to survive, and most commentators believe he chose to ignore her advances. In the following excerpt from a poem written sometime between 1732 and 1734, Pope's satirical dig at ''Rufa''— identified by some critics as Trotter—was prompted by Trotter's reputation among her contemporaries as a loose woman. (The allegation is largely dismissed by modern scholars.) ''Sappho'' has been identified as Lady Mary Wortley Montagu.]*

> Rufa, whose eye quick-glancing o'er the Park,
> Attracts each light gay meteor of a Spark,
> Agrees as ill with Rufa studying Locke,
> As Sappho's diamonds with her dirty smock,
> Or Sappho at her toilet's greazy task,
> With Sappho fragrant at an ev'ning Mask:
> So morning Insects that in muck begun,
> Sine, buzz, and fly-blow in the setting-sun.

(pp. 50-2)

Alexander Pope, ''Epistle II (To a Lady),'' in his Epistles to Several Persons (Moral Essays), *edited by F. W. Bateson, second edition, Methuen & Co. Ltd., 1961, pp. 39-74.*

WILLIAM WARBURTON   (essay date 1747)

[Warburton was an English prelate, critic, editor, and theological controversialist who edited Shakespeare's plays, prepared a comprehensively annotated edition of Alexander Pope's works, and wrote numerous philosophical and apologetic commentaries. He is best remembered as the author of The Divine Legation of Moses *(1738-41), a lengthy, rambling treatise written to demonstrate the reasonableness and necessity of Christianity. In the following excerpt from his 1747 preface to Trotter's* Remarks upon the Principles and Reasonings of Dr. Rutherforth's ''Essay on the Nature and Obligations of Virtue,'' *he praises Trotter's confutation of Rutherforth's criticism of Samuel Clarke's metaphysics.]*

The author of the *Divine Legation* [William Warburton] had observed, that God, in order to secure the practice of moral virtue, had been graciously pleased to bestow on man an instinctive approbation of right, and abhorrence of wrong; to which some philosophers have given the name of the *moral sense:* That God had further established a real, essential difference in the qualities of human actions, whereby some are seen to be fit and right, and others wrong and unfit. But, as this author thought, that *obligation* without an obliger, and an *obliger* without agency, were mere jargon, he therefore had recourse to a superior *will,* as the proper and real ground of *moral obligation.* For tho' *instinct felt* a difference in actions; and *reason discovered* that difference to be founded in the nature of things; yet it was *will* only, that could make *compliance* with such difference to be our *duty;* whereby that, which was, before, a *fitness,* now became a *virtue.* On these *three principles,* therefore, he supposed the whole edifice of practical morality to be erected. He observed further, that this admirable provision for the support of virtue had been, in great measure, defeated by its pretended advocates; who, in their eternal squabbles about the true foundation of morality, and the obligations to its practice, had sacrilegiously untwisted this threefold chord, and each (whether he placed it *falsely,* in the moral sense or essential differences; or *truly,* in the will of God) running away with the part he esteemed the strongest, had affixed *that* to the throne of Heaven, as the golden chain, which is to draw all unto it.

Since the making these observations, the writer here confuted [Thomas Rutherforth] hath afforded one of the most notable examples of the folly there condemned. He seemed indeed to aim at placing the foundation of morality rightly, in the *will of God:* but then he would not so much as allow the other principles to be even a *rule,* to direct us in the knowledge, and, consequently, in the observance of that will. And see, the mischiefs of separating what the divine wisdom had united; for, to support the extravagance of his scheme, he was forced to intrench himself in a vile and abject selfishness; by which he hath not only degraded human nature, and defiled moral virtue, but hath even slipped beside his own professed foundation, the *will of God;* by which miscarriage he hath fallen, before he was aware, into the most impious, as well as most absurd system, that ever entered into the head of a professed religionist; as may be seen by a perusal of the following sheets.

But his answerer [Catharine Trotter], the author of them, proceeds with much greater discretion; as intent only on the advancement of truth and piety. This writer, though placing the foundation of moral virtue (I think, wrongly) in the *eternal relations* of things; yet allows the other principles all their efficacy; and so sagely secures the interests of practical morality. And by this means, seconded by a fine genius and infinite superiority in reasoning, hath given so thorough a confutation of this exclusive, exterminating system, as is rarely to be met with in controversies on these subjects. Indeed, there was little or nothing in the work confuted, but sophistical wrangling, and disingenuous tergiversation; embarrassed by an understanding more than ordinarily condensed with the frigid subtilty of school moonshine. To make amends for this, you have, in the confutation, all the clearness of expression, the strength of reason, the precision of logic, and attachment to truth, which make books of this nature really useful to the common cause of virtue and religion. (pp. 3-5)

William Warburton, in a preface to ''Remarks upon the Principles and Reasonings of Dr. Rutherforth's 'Essay on the Nature and Obligations of Virtue','' in The Works of Mrs. Catharine Cockburn: Theological, Moral, Dramatic, and Poetical, Vol. II, *J. and P. Knapton, 1751, pp. 3-5.*

THOMAS BIRCH   (essay date 1751)

[Birch was an eminent English historian and biographer whose meticulous works are considered invaluable to students of English history. He was not, however, universally respected by his contemporaries. ''Who would give a rush for Dr. Birch's correspondence?'' Horace Walpole once asked, describing him as ''a worthy good-natured soul, full of industry and activity, and running about like a young setting-dog in quest of anything new or old, and with no parts, taste, or judgment.'' Birch is believed to have met Trotter late in her life, and it is certain that she helped him prepare the first collection of her writings, The Works of Mrs. Catharine Cockburn: Theological, Moral, Dramatic, and Poetical *(1751). In the following excerpt from his biographical introduction to this work, Birch describes Trotter's character and advises her readers to bear in mind the special circumstances in which her works were produced.]*

There is observable in mankind a natural and almost universal curiosity, concerning the persons of those, from whose writings they have received entertainment or instruction. And the gratification of this desire is attended with a very considerable use, as the history and characters of the writers generally tend to cast a light upon their works, and heighten our relish for them. It is therefore a justice due to the public, as well as to the memory of our author [Mrs. Catharine Cockburn], to premise some account of so extraordinary a person. Posterity at least will be solicitous to know, to whom they will owe the most demonstrative and perspicuous reasonings, upon subjects of eternal importance; and her own sex is intitled to the fullest information about one, who has done such honour to them, and raised our ideas of their intellectual powers, by an example of the greatest extent of understanding and correctness of judgment, united to all the vivacity of imagination. Antiquity indeed boasted of its *female philosophers*. . . . But our own age and country may, without injustice or vanity, oppose to those illustrious ladies the defender of *Locke* and *Clarke;* who, with a genius equal to the most eminent of them, had the superior advantage of cultivating it in the only effectual method of improvement, the study of a real philosophy, and a theology truly worthy of human nature, and its all-perfect author. (pp. i-ii)

Mrs. *Cockburn* was no less celebrated for her beauty in her younger days, than for her genius and accomplishments. She was indeed small of stature, but had a remarkable liveliness in her eye, and delicacy of complexion, which continued to her death. Her private character rendered her extremely amiable to those, who intimately knew her. Her conversation was always innocent, useful, and agreeable, without the least affectation of being thought a wit, and attended with a remarkable modesty and diffidence of herself, and a constant endeavour to adapt her discourse to her company. She was happy in an uncommon evenness and chearfulness of temper. Her disposition was generous and benevolent; and ready upon all occasions to forgive injuries, and bear them, as well as misfortunes, without interrupting her own ease, or that of others, with complaints or reproaches. The pressures of a very contracted fortune were supported by her with calmness and in silence; nor did she ever attempt to improve it among those great personages, to whom she was known, by importunities, to which the best minds are most averse, and which her approved merit and established reputation should have rendered unnecessary. (pp. xlvi-xlvii)

The collection [of her works] now exhibited to the world is so incontestable a proof of the superiority of our author's genius, as in a manner supersedes every thing, that can be said upon that head. But her abilities as a writer, and the merit of her works, will not have full justice done them, without a due attention to the peculiar circumstances, in which they were produced; her early youth, when she wrote some; her very advanced age, and ill state of health, when she drew up others; the uneasy situation of her fortune, during the whole course of her life; and an interval of near twenty years, in the vigor of it, spent in the cares of a family, without the least leisure for reading or contemplation: After which, with a mind so long diverted and encumbered, resuming her studies, she instantly recovered its intire powers, and in the hours of relaxation from her domestic employments pursued, to their utmost limits, some of the deepest inquiries, of which the human mind is capable. (p. xlviii)

> *Thomas Birch, "The Life of Mrs. Catharine Cockburn," in* The Works of Mrs. Catharine Cockburn: Theological, Moral, Dramatic, and Poetical, Vol. I, *edited by Thomas Birch, J. and P. Knapton, 1751, pp. i-xlviii.*

JOHN DUNCOMBE   (poem date 1754)

[*Duncombe was a minor eighteenth-century English poet, essayist, and critic who is best remembered for* The Feminiad (1754),

an epic-style moral poem in praise of women writers. In the following excerpt from this work, he records Trotter's fame as a "Philosopher, Divine, and Poet join'd."]

> But say, what Matron now walks musing forth
> From the bleak mountains of her native North?
> While round her brows two sisters of the nine
> Poetic wreaths with philosophic twine!
> Hail, COCKBURN, hail! ev'n now from Reasons's bow'rs
> Thy Locke delighted culls the choicest flow'rs
> To deck, his great successful champion's head,
> And Clarke expects thee in the laurel shade.
> Tho' long, to dark, oblivious want a prey,
> Thy aged worth past unperceiv'd away,
> Yet Scotland now shall ever boast thy fame,
> While England mourns thy undistinguish'd name,
> And views with wonder, in a female mind,
> Philosopher, Divine, and Poet join'd!
>
> (pp. 13-14)

> *John Duncombe, in his* The Feminiad: A Poem, *1754. Reprint by William Andrews Clark Memorial Library, 1981, 31 p.*

CHARLES DIBDIN   (essay date 1800)

[*Dibdin was an English essayist, dramatist, critic, and songwriter whose literary career was colored by a hodgepodge of tremendous successes, huge failures, and much infighting among his colleagues. He is best remembered for his sea songs and* A Complete History of the English Stage (1797-1800), *the latter a hastily written, comprehensive survey that has been criticized for poor attention to detail. In the following excerpt from this work, he finds little to praise in Trotter's dramatic canon.*]

Mrs. PIX, Mrs. MANLEY, and Mrs. TROTTER, alias COCKBURNE, made up a triumvirate of Lady wits who enjoyed a great deal of the admiration of the namby pamby critics, and the indifference, and sometimes the ridicule of those whom heaven had vouchsafed to endow with taste and judgement. (p. 343)

Mrs. TROTTER, or rather Mrs. COCKBURNE, whom her biographers praise for her knowledge in the Latin grammer and logic, for embracing the Romish communion upon conviction, for her vying in metaphysics with LOCKE, for her love of her husband because he wrote an account of the Mosaic deluge, for her small stature and lively eye, produced five plays.

Agnes de Castro, a tragedy, made its appearance in 1696. It had been before treated by Mrs. BEHN, with whom this lady had better have let it rest, for it procured her neither profit nor praise, except that part of it, says an author, an Irishman probably, which contained a copy of verses to Mr. CONGREVE on his *Mourning Bride.* Her tragedy called *Fatal Friendship,* which came out in 1698, had better success, and was reprinted in her works which were published in 1751 by Dr. BIRCH. The warmest advocate, however, of this lady only says it was the most perfect of her dramatic pieces.

The *Unhappy Penitent,* a tragedy, 1701, has not left a single trace of its fate, so that we know not whether it was good, bad, or indifferent. *Love at a Loss,* same year, I am almost as much at a loss to give an account of. The writers lay its bad success to its having being printed very incorrectly, an error certainly, but not of such magnitude as materially to affect the reputation of any production. But at any rate we cannot admit it here right or wrong, for the piece was called in and correctly printed, after which it was performed with as little success as before. One more play brings us to the end of this lady's labours. It was called The *Revolution of Sweden,* and performed in 1706; but, anxious as they have been to relate the particulars of Mrs. TROTTER's life as her biographers have trod very tenderly, on the ground of her theatrical reputation, we shall imitate them and pass by this tragedy without speaking of its success. As to its intrinsic merit, those who can procure her works and chuse to take the trouble of reading it, will not find enough entertainment to require them for their curiosity. (pp. 348-49)

> Charles Dibdin, "Southern, Mrs. Pix, Mrs. Manley, Mrs. Cockburne, Lord Landsdowne, Dennis, Old-mixon, Motteaux, and Gildon," in his A Complete History of the Stage, Vol. IV, n.p., 1800, pp. 329-60.

JOHN DORAN (essay date 1864)

[*Doran was an English essayist, critic, and travel writer who wrote widely on the history of the theater. In the following excerpt, he briefly studies Trotter's career as playwright and philosopher.*]

[Mrs. Cockburn] was at first a very learned young lady, whose speculations took her to the church of Rome, from which in later years she seceded. She was but seventeen, when, in 1696, her sentimental tragedy, *Agnes de Castro,* was played at Drury Lane. Her career, as writer for the stage, lasted ten years, during which she produced five pieces, all of a sentimental but refined class,—illustrating love, friendship, repentance, and conjugal faith. There is some amount of word-spinning in these plays; and this is well marked by Genest's comment on Mrs. Cockburn's *Revolution of Sweden,* namely, that if Constantin, in the third act, had been influenced by common sense, she would have spoiled the remainder of the play.

Nevertheless, Mrs. Cockburn was a clever woman, and kept no dull household, though she there wrote a defence of Locke [*A Defence of the "Essay of Human Understanding"*], while her reverend husband was pursuing an account of the Mosaic deluge. As a metaphysical and controversial writer, she gathered laurels and abuse in her day, for the latter of which she found compensation in the friendship and admiration of Warburton. She was a valiant woman, too; one, whom asthma and the ills of life could not deter from labor. But death relieved her from all these, in 1749; and she is remembered in the history of literature as a good and well-accomplished woman; the very opposite of Mrs. Behn and all her heroines. (p. 166)

> John Doran, "The Dramatic Authoresses," in his "Their Majesties' Servants": Annals of the English Stage, from Thomas Betterton to Edmund Kean, Vol. I, 1864, Reprint by W. J. Widdleton, Publisher, 1865, pp. 163-68.

EDMUND GOSSE (essay date 1919)

[*Gosse was a distinguished English literary historian, critic, and biographer who wrote extensively on seventeenth- and eighteenth-century English literature. In the following excerpt, he relates the circumstances of Trotter's life to the development of her literary career.*]

The practically complete absence of the Woman of Letters from our tropical and profuse literature of the early and middle seventeenth century has often been observed with wonder. While France had her Madeleine de Scudéry and her Mlle. de Gournay and her Mère Angelique Arnauld, Englishwomen of the Stuart age ventured upon no incursions into philosophy, fiction, or theology. More and more eagerly, however, they read books;

and as a consequence of reading, they began at last to write. The precious Margaret, Duchess of Newcastle, hob-a-nobbed with every Muse in her amazing divagations. But the earliest professional woman of letters was Aphra Behn, the novelist and playwright, to whose genius justice has only quite lately been done by Mr. Montague Summers. Mrs. Behn died in 1689, and it seemed at first that she had left no heritage to her sex. But there presently appeared a set of female writers, who enlivened the last years of the century, but who were soon eclipsed by the wits of the age of Anne, and who have been entirely forgotten. It is to the most interesting of these "transient phantoms" that I wish to draw attention.

The extreme precocity of Catharine Trotter makes her seem to belong to the age of Dryden, but she was in reality younger than Addision and most of the other contemporaries of Pope. (p. 39)

From the beginning of her fifth year . . . , Catharine experienced the precarious lot of those who depend for a livelihood on the charity of more or less distant relatives. (p. 41)

There is frequent reference to money in Catharine Trotter's writings, and the lack of it was the rock upon which her gifts were finally wrecked. With a competency she might have achieved a much more prominent place in English literature than she could ever afford to reach. She offers a curious instance of the depressing effect of poverty, and we get the impression that she was never, during her long and virtuous career, lifted above the carking anxiety which deadens the imagination. As a child, however, she seems to have awakened hopes of a high order. She was a prodigy, and while little more than an infant she displayed an illumination in literature which was looked upon, in that age of female darkness, as quite a portent. (pp. 41-2)

She published in 1693 a copy of verses addressed to Mr. Bevil Higgons on the occasion of his recovery from the smallpox ["**Verses Written at the Age of Fourteen, and Sent to Mr. Beville Higgons, on His Sickness and Recovery from the Smallpox**"]; she was then fourteen years of age. Higgons was a young man of twenty-three, who had lately returned from the exiled court in France, where he had distinguished himself by his agreeable manners, and who had just made a name for himself by poems addressed to Dryden and by a prologue to Congreve's *Old Batchelor.* He was afterwards to become famous for a little while as a political historian. Catharine Trotter's verses are bad, but she addresses Higgons as "lovely youth," and claims his gratitude for her tribute in terms which are almost boisterous. This poem was not only her introduction to the public, but, through Bevil Higgons, was probably the channel of her acquaintance with Congreve and Dryden. (pp. 42-3)

We next find the youthful poet in relation with the Earl of Dorset, from whom she must have concealed her Jacobite propensities. Dorset was the great public patron of poetry under William III., and Catharine Trotter, aged sixteen, having composed a tragedy, appealed to him for support. It was very graciously granted, and *Agnes de Castro,* in five acts and in blank verse, "written by a young lady," was produced at the Theatre Royal in 1695, under the "protection" of Charles Earl of Dorset and Middlesex, Lord Chamberlain of His Majesty's Household. The event caused a considerable commotion. No woman had written for the English stage since the death of Mrs. Behn, and curiosity was much excited. Mrs. Verbruggen, that enchanting actress, but in male attire, recited a clever,

Agnes de Caſtro,

A

TRAGEDY.

As it is Acted at the

THEATRE ROYAL,

By His Majeſty's Servants.

Written by a Young Lady.

LONDON:

Printed for *H. Rhodes* in *Fleetſtreet*, *R. Parker* at the *Royal-Exchange*, *S. Briſcot*, at the Corner of *Charles-ſtreet*, in *Ruſſel-ſtreet*, *Covent-Garden*, 1696.

☞ Advertiſement. *The* Fatal Miſtake; *Or, the* Plot Spoil'd: *A New Play; Written by* Joſeph Haines.

Title page of the first edition of Trotter's first drama, a tragedy originally performed in December 1695 and published the following year.

ranting epilogue at the close of the performance, in which she said:—

'tis whispered here
Our Poetess is virtuous, young and fair,

but the secret was an open one. Wycherley, who contributed verses, knew all about it, and so did Mrs. Manley, while Powell and Colley Cibber were among the actors. We may be sure that little Mistress Trotter's surprising talents were the subjects of much discussion at Will's Coffee House, and that the question of securing her for the rival theatre was anxiously debated at Lincoln's Inn Fields. Her success in *Agnes de Castro* was the principal asset which Drury Lane had to set that season against Congreve's splendid adventure with *Love for Love*.

Agnes de Castro is an immature production, and shows a juvenile insensibility to plagiarism, since the subject and treatment are borrowed implicitly from a French novel by Mlle. de Brillac, published in Paris and London a few years before. The conception of court life at Coimbra in the fourteenth century is that of this French lady, and is innocent of Portuguese local colour. But, as the dramatic work of a girl of sixteen, the play is rather extraordinary for nimble movement and adroit theatrical arrangements. It is evident that Catharine Trotter was well versed in the stage traditions of her own day, and we may

wonder how a highly respectable girl of sixteen found her opportunity. The English playhouse under William III. was no place for a very young lady, even if she wore a mask. There is a good deal of meritorious character-drawing in *Agnes de Castro*. The conception of a benevolent and tenderly forgiving Princess is well contrasted with the fierce purity of Agnes and the infatuation of the Prince. Towards the close of the first act there is a capital scene of exquisite confusion between this generous and distracted trio. The opening of the third act, between Elvira and her brother Alvaro, is not at all young-ladyish, and has some strong turns of feeling. The end of the play, with the stabbing of the Princess and the accusation of Agnes by Elvira, is puerile, but was doubtless welcome to a sentimental audience. It is a bad play, but not at all an unpromising one.

Early in 1696 *Agnes de Castro*, still anonymous, was published as a book, and for the next five or six years we find Catharine Trotter habitually occupied in writing for the stage. Without question she did so professionally, through in what way dramatists at the close of the seventeenth century lived by their pens is difficult to conjecture. A very rare play, *The Female Wits; or, the Triumvirate of Poets* [see Additional Bibliography], the authorship of which has hitherto defied conjecture, was acted at Drury Lane after Catharine Trotter had been tempted across to Lincoln's Inn Fields, and is evidently inspired by the intense jealousy which smouldered between the two great houses. The success of Miss Trotter incited two older ladies to compete with her; these were Mrs. Delariviere Manley, who was a discarded favourite of Barbara Villiers, and fat Mrs. Mary Pix, the stage-struck consort of a tailor. These rather ridiculous women professed themselves followers of Catharine, and they produced plays of their own not without some success. With her they formed the trio of Female Wits who were mocked in the lively but, on the whole, rather disappointing play I have just mentioned, in the course of which it is spitefully remarked of Calista—who is Miss Trotter—that she has "made no small struggle in the world to get into print," and is "now in such a state of wedlock to pen and ink that it will be very difficult" for her "to get out of it."

In acting *The Female Wits* Mrs. Temple, who had played the Princess in *Agnes de Castro*, took the part of Calista, and doubtless, in the coarse fashion of those days, made up exactly like poor Catharine Trotter, who was described as "a Lady who pretends to the learned Languages, and assumes to herself the name of a Critic." This was a character, however, which she would not have protested against with much vigour, for she had now quite definitely taken up the position of a reformer and a pioneer. She posed as the champion of women's intellectual rights, and she was accepted as representing in active literary work the movement which Mary Astell had recently foreshadowed in her remarkable *Serious Proposal to Ladies* of 1694. We turn again to *The Female Wits*, and we find Marsilia (Mrs. Manley) describing Calista to Mrs. Wellfed (Mrs. Pix) as "the vainest, proudest, senseless Thing! She pretends to grammar! writes in mood and figure! does everything methodically!" Yet when Calista appears on the stage, Mrs. Manley rushes across to fling her arms around her and to murmur: "O charmingest Nymph of all Apollo's Train, let me embrace thee!" Later on Calista says to Mrs. Pix, the fat tailoress, "I cannot but remind you Madam . . . I read Aristotle in his own language"; and of a certain tirade in a play of Ben Jonson she insists: "I know it so well, as to have turn'd it into Latin." Mrs. Pix admits her own ignorance of all these things; she "can go no further than the eight parts of speech." This brings down upon her an icy reproof form Calista: "Then I cannot but take the Freedom to say . . . you impose upon the Town." We get the impression of a preciseness of manner and purpose which must have given Catharine a certain air of priggishness, not entirely unbecoming, perhaps, but very strange in that loose theatre of William III.

Accordingly, in her next appearance [*Fatal Friendship*], we find her complaining to the Princess (afterwards Queen Anne) that she has become "the mark of ill Nature" through recommending herself "by what the other Sex think their peculiar Prerogative" [see Additional Bibliography]—that is, intellectual distinction. Catharine Trotter was still only nineteen years of age when she produced her tragedy of *Fatal Friendship,* the published copy of which (1698) is all begarlanded with evidences of her high moral purpose in the shape of a succession of "applausive copies" of verses. In these we are told that she had "checked the rage of reigning vice that had debauched the stage." This was an allusion to the great controversy then just raised by Jeremy Collier in his famous *Short View of the Immorality and Profaneness of the Stage,* in which all the dramatists of the day were violently attacked for their indecency. Catharine Trotter has the courage to side with Collier, and the tact to do so without quarrelling with her male colleagues. She takes the side of the decent women.

> You as your Sex's champion art come forth
> To fight their quarrel and assert their worth,

one of her admirers [John Hughes; see poem dated 1698] exclaims, and another adds:—

> You stand the first of stage-reformers too.

The young poetess aimed at reconciling the stage with virtue and at vindicating the right of woman to assume "the tragic laurel."

This was the most brilliant moment in the public career of our bluestocking. *Fatal Friendship* enjoyed a success which Catharine Trotter was not to taste again, and of all her plays it is the only one which has ever been reprinted. It is very long and extremely sentimental, and written in rather prosy blank verse. Contemporaries said that it placed Miss Trotter in the forefront of British drama, in company with Congreve and Granville "the polite," who had written a *She-Gallants,* which was everything that Miss Trotter did not wish her plays to be. *Fatal Friendship* has an ingenious plot, in which the question of money takes a prominence very unusual in tragedy. Almost every character in the piece is in reduced circumstances. Felicia, sister to Belgard (who is too poor to maintain her), is wooed by the wealthy Roquelaure, although she is secretly married to Gramont, who is also too poor to support a wife. Belgard, afraid that Gramont will make love to Felicia (that is, to his own secret wife), persuades him—in order that his best friend, Castalio, may be released from a debtor's prison—bigamously to marry Lamira, a wealthy widow. But Castalio is in love with Lamira, and is driven to frenzy by Gramont's illegal marriage. It all depends upon income in a manner comically untragical. The quarrel between the friends in the fifth act is an effective piece of stage-craft, but the action is spoiled by a ridiculous general butchery at the close of all. However, the audience was charmed, and even "the stubbornest could scarce deny their Tears."

Fatal Friendship was played at the Lincoln's Inn Theatre, and no doubt it was Congreve who brought Miss Trotter over from Drury Lane. His warm friendship for her had unquestionably a great deal to do with her success and with the jealousy of her rivals. A letter exists in which the great dramatist acknowledges, in 1697, the congratulations of his young admirer, and it breathes an eager cordiality [see Additional Bibliography]. Congreve requested Betterton to present him to Catharine Trotter, and his partiality for her company is mentioned by several writers. The spiteful author of *The Female Wits* insinuates that Congreve made the looking-over of Catharine's scenes "his pretence for daily visits." Another satirist, in 1698, describes Congreve sitting very gravely with his hat over his eyes, "together with the two she-things called Poetesses which write for his house," half-hidden from the public in a little side-box. Farquhar, too, seeing the celebrated writer of *Fatal Friendship* in the theatre on the third night of the performance of his *Love and a Bottle,* had "his passions wrought so high" by a sight of the beautiful author that he wrote her a letter in which he called her "one of the fairest of the sex, and the best judge." If Catharine Trotter, as the cynosure of delicacy, at the age of nineteen, sat through *Love and a Bottle* without a blush, even *her* standard of decency was not very exacting. But in all this rough, coarse world of wit her reputation never suffered a rebuff.

Encouraged by so much public and private attention, our young dramatist continued to work with energy and conscientiousness. But her efforts were forestalled by an event, or rather a condition of the national temper, of which too little notice has been taken by literary historians. The attacks on the stage for its indecency and blasphemy had been flippantly met by the theatrical agents, but they had sunk deeply into the conscience of the people. There followed with alarming abruptness a general public repulsion against the playhouses, and to this, early in 1699, a roughly worded Royal Proclamation gave voice. During the whole of that year the stage was almost in abeyance, and even Congreve, with *The Way of the World,* was unable to woo his audience back to Lincoln's Inn. During this time of depression Catharine Trotter composed at least two tragedies, which she was unable to get performed, while the retirement of Congreve in a paroxysm of annoyance must have been a very serious disadvantage to her.

On May 1st, 1700, Dryden died, and with him a dramatic age passed away. What Miss Trotter's exact relations with the great poet had been is uncertain; she not only celebrated his death in a long elegy, in which she speaks on behalf of the Muses, but wrote another and more important poem, in which she gives very sound advice to the poetical beginner, who is to take Dryden as a model, and to be particularly careful to disdain Settle, Durfey, and Blackmore, typical poetasters of the period. She recommends social satire to the playwright:—

> Let the nice well-bred beau himself perceive
> The most accomplish'd, useless thing alive;
> Expose the bottle-sparks that range the town,—
> Shaming themselves with follies not their own,—
> But chief these foes to virgin innocence,
> Who, while they make to honour vain pretence,
> With all that's base and impious can dispense.

Honour to those who aim high and execute boldly!

> If Shakespeare's spirit, with transporting fire,
> The animated scene throughout inspire;
> If in the piercing wit of Vanbrugh drest,
> Each sees his darling folly made a jest;
> If Garth's and Dryden's genius, through each line,
> In artful praise and well-turn'd satire shine,—
> To *us* ascribe the immortal sacred flame.

In this dead period of the stage Catharine Trotter found a warm friend and doubtless an efficient patron in a Lady Piers, of whom we should be glad to know more. Sir George Piers, the husband of this lady, was an officer of rank under the Duke of Marlborough, later to become useful to Catharine Trotter. Meanwhile the latter returned to the Theatre Royal in Drury Lane, where, in 1701, under the patronage of Lord Halifax—Pope's ''Bufo''—she produced her third tragedy, *The Unhappy Penitent*. The dedication of this play to Halifax is a long and interesting essay on the poetry of the age. The author passes Dryden, Otway, Congreve, and Lee under examination, and finds technical blemishes in them all:—

> The inimitable Shakespeare seems alone secure on every side from an attack. I speak not here of faults against the rules of poetry, but against the natural Genius. He had all the images of nature present to him, studied her thoroughly, and boldly copied all her various features, for though he has chiefly exerted himself on the more masculine passions, 'tis as the choice of his judgment, not the restraint of his genius, and he has given us as a proof he could be every way equally admirable.

Lady Piers wrote the prologue to *The Unhappy Penitent* [see poem dated 1701] in verses better turned than might have been expected. She did not stint praise to her young friend, whom she compares to the rising sun:—

> Like him, bright Maid, Thy great perfections shine
> As awful, as resplendent, as divine! . . .
> Minerva and Diana guard your soul!

The Unhappy Penitent is not a pleasing performance: it is amorous and violent, but yet dull. Catharine's theory was better than her practice. Nevertheless, it seems to have been successful, for the author some time afterwards, speaking of the town's former discouragement of her dramas, remarks that ''the taste is mended.'' Later in 1701 she brought out at Drury Lane her only comedy, *Love at a Loss,* dedicated in most enthusiastic terms to Lady Piers, to whom ''I owe the greatest Blessing of my Fate,'' the privilege of a share in her friendship. *Love at a Loss* was made up of the comic scenes introduced into an old tragedy which the author had failed to get acted. This is not a fortunate method of construction, and the town showed no favour to *Love at a Loss.* The first and only public section of Catharine Trotter's career was now over, and she withdrew, a wayworn veteran at the age of twenty-two, to more elevated studies. (pp. 43-51)

[Her] *Defence of Mr. Locke's Essay on the Human Understanding* appeared anonymously in May 1702. People were wonderfully polite in those days, and Locke himself wrote to his ''protectress'' a charming letter in which he told her that her *Defence* ''was the greatest honour my *Essay* could have procured me'' [see excerpt dated 1702].

She sent her *Defence* to Leibnitz, who criticised it at considerable length. . . . Notwithstanding all this, the commentators of Locke appear, without exception, to ignore the *Defence*. . . . (pp. 53-4)

It does not appear that Catharine Trotter ever enjoyed the felicity of seeing in the flesh the greatest object of her homage [Locke]; but he occupied most of her thoughts. She was rendered highly indignant by the efforts made by the reactionaries at Oxford and elsewhere to discourage the writings of Locke and to throw suspicion on their influence. She read over and over again his philosophical, educational, and religious treatises, and ever found them more completely to her taste. If she had enjoyed the power to do so she would have proclaimed the wisdom and majesty of Locke from every housetop, and

she envied Lady Masham her free and constant intercourse with so beautiful a mind. (p. 55)

She records that, after the death of Locke, Lady Masham communicated with Leibnitz, and Catharine is very indignant because a doubt had been suggested as to whether the writer's thoughts and expressions were her own. This was calculated to infuriate Catharine Trotter, who outpours in forcible terms her just indignation:—

> Women are as capable of penetrating into the grounds of things, and reasoning justly, as men are, who certainly have no advantage of us, but in their opportunities of knowledge. As Lady Masham is allowed by everybody to have great natural endowments, she has taken pains to improve them; and no doubt profited much by a long intimate society with so extraordinary a man as Mr. Locke. So that I see no reason to suspect a woman of her character would pretend to write anything that was not entirely her own. I pray, be more equitable to her sex than the generality of your's are, who, when anything is written by a woman that they cannot deny their approbation to, are sure to rob us of the glory of it by concluding 'tis not her own.

This is the real voice of Catharine Trotter, raised to defend her sex, and conscious of the many intellectual indignities and disabilities which they suffered.

The first draft of *The Revolution in Sweden* being now completed, she sent it to Congreve, who was living very quietly in lodgings in Arundell Street. He allowed some time to go by before, on the November 2nd, 1703, he acknowledged it. His criticism, which is extremely kind, is also penetrating and full [see excerpt dated 1703]. ''I think the design in general,'' he says, ''very great and noble; the conduct of it very artful, if not too full of business which may run into length and obscurity.'' He warns her against having too much noise of fighting on the stage in her second act, and against offending probability in the third. The fourth act is confused, and in the fifth there are too many harangues. Catharine Trotter has asked him to be frank, and so he is, but his criticism is practical and encouraging. This excellent letter deserves to be better known.

To continue the history of Miss Trotter's fifth and last play, *The Revolution in Sweden* was at length brought out at the Queen's Theatre in the Haymarket, towards the close of 1704. It had every advantage which popular acting could give it, since the part of the hero, Count Arwide, was played by Betterton; that of Constantia, the heroine, by Mrs. Barry; Gustavus by Booth; and Christina by Mrs. Harcourt. In spite of this galaxy of talent, the reception of the play was unfavourable. The Duchess of Marlborough ''and all her beauteous family'' graced the theatre on the first night, but the public was cold and inattentive. Some passages of a particularly lofty moral tone provoked laughter. *The Revolution in Sweden,* in fact, was shown to suffer from the ineradicable faults which Congreve had gently but justly suggested. It was very long, and very dull, and very wordy, and we could scarcely find a more deadly specimen of virtuous and didactic tragedy. Catharine was dreadfully disappointed, nor was she completely consoled by being styled—by no less a person than Sophia Charlotte, Queen of Prussia—''The Sappho of Scotland.'' She determined, however, to appeal to readers against auditors, and when, two years later, after still further revision, she published *The Revolution in Sweden,* she dedicated it in most grateful terms to the Duke of Marlborough's eldest daughter, Henrietta Godolphin. (pp. 56-8)

Her later writings, on philosophy, on morality, on the principles of the Christian religion, are so dull that merely to think of them brings tears into one's eyes. She who had sparkled as a girl with Congreve and exchanged polite amenities with Locke lived on to see modern criticism begin with Samuel Johnson and the modern novel start with Samuel Richardson, but without observing that any change had come into the world of letters. . . .

So little mark did poor Mrs. Cockburn make on her younger contemporaries that she disappeared forthwith from literary history. Her works, especially her plays, have become so excessively rare as to be almost unprocurable. The brief narrative of her life and her activities . . . would be hopelessly engulfed in obscurity, and we should know as little of Catharine Trotter as we do of Mary Pix, and Delariviere Manley, and many late seventeenth-century authors more eminent than they, had it not been that in 1751, two years after her death, all her papers were placed in the hands of an ingenious clergyman, the Rev. Dr. Thomas Birch, who printed them for subscribers in two thick and singularly unpleasing volumes. This private edition was never reissued, and is now itself a rare book. It is the sort of book that for two hundred and fifty years must fatally have been destroyed as lumber whenever an old country mansion that contained it has been cleared out.

During all that time no one, so far as I can discover, has evinced the smallest interest in Catharine Trotter. We gain an idea of the blackness of her obscurity when we say that even Mr. Austin Dobson appears to have never heard of her. The champion of Locke and Clarke, the correspondent of Leibnitz and Pope, the friend of Congreve, the patroness of Farquhar, she seems to have slipped between two ages and to have lost her hold on time. But I hope her thin little lady-like ghost, still hovering in a phantom-like transparence round the recognised seats of learning, will be a little comforted at last by the polite attention of a few of my readers. (p. 62)

> *Edmund Gosse, "Catharine Trotter, the Precursor of the Bluestockings," in his* Some Diversions of a Man of Letters, *William Heinemann, 1919, pp. 37-62.*

MYRA REYNOLDS (essay date 1920)

[*Reynolds was an American scholar who wrote widely on English literature. In the following excerpt from her study of women writers in the seventeenth and eighteenth centuries, she examines Trotter's philosophical and theological essays and considers why the author failed to achieve an enduring reputation.*]

The most distinguished woman in the field of polemics in the first half of the eighteenth century was Catherine Trotter, better known as Mrs. Cockburn. (p. 104)

Religion and philosophy were her true field. Locke's *Essay concerning Human Understanding* was published in 1690, and among the antagonistic criticisms it called forth were three series of *Remarks* published anonymously in 1697 and 1699. Young as she was Miss Trotter pursued the controversy with the keenest interest and in 1701 she drew up a *Defence of The Essay of Human Understanding*. Mr. George Burnet of Kemney, then in Holland, and Mrs. Burnet, the wife of Bishop Burnet, were entrusted with the secret of her *Defence*, and both advised anonymous publication, agreeing with her that her youth and sex would, if known, count against a work of that nature. Her *Defence* appeared in print in 1702. Mrs. Burnet on finding that the Bishop, Mr. John Norris, and Mr. Locke

himself, were highly pleased with it, could keep the secret no longer. Mr. Locke sent Miss Trotter a present of books and a letter [see the excerpt by John Locke dated 1702] in which he expressed his gratitude for "an opportunity to own you for my protectress, which is the greatest honour my *Essay* could have procured me. Give me leave therefore to assure you, that as the rest of the world take notice of the strength and clearness of your reasoning, so I can not but be extremely sensible, that it was employed in my behalf."

A second pamphlet was entitled *A discourse concerning a guide in Controversies* and grew out of her own spiritual conflicts. Although of a Protestant family she had become a Catholic early in life, but had gradually found herself less and less in harmony with that church till 1707 when, in this *Discourse,* she announced her return to the Church of England.

The polemical years between 1701 and 1707 had been diversified by several love affairs. Mr. George Burnet of Kemney, Mr. Fenn who was an eloquent young clergyman, Mr. Cockburn, "and some others," are indicated in her letters. Miss Trotter's letters to two of these lovers, Mr. Fenn and Mr. Burnet, are nearly as polemical as her *Defence* and *Discourse*. She uses all her old Art of Logic to reason her lovers into friends. She had, in fact, no particular respect for the passion of love as a factor in human life. She apologized for having given it so important a place in her plays, for it was "not noble enough to fill a whole tragedy." When Mr. Burnet professed "the most passionate ardour of mind and soul" for her, she responded with a eulogy of "just and beneficent friendship." "It is only that niggard passion, which is distinguish'd by the name of love, that excludes all but one object from having a part in it, and is not satisfied without monopolizing the affections of the heart." She offered Mr. Burnet "due gratitude" and she surely owed him some return for the pains he took to spread the fame of her works. (pp. 107-08)

Miss Trotter's letters to Mr. Cockburn, whom she married in 1708, are also full of argument and business. If she had a deep affection for him she certainly never allowed herself to speak out. She says that their chief aim in marriage was to assist each other in performing those duties that flow from the love of God. Of the ensuing twenty years she wrote in 1738 as follows: "Being married in 1708, I bid adieu to the muses, and so wholly gave myself up to the cares of a family, and the education of my children, that I scarce knew there was any such thing as books, plays, or poems stirring in Great Britain." It was an attack on Mr. Locke that again drew her into public controversy. Dr. Winch Holdsworth published in 1720 a sermon on Mr. Locke's "false reasonings" against the resurrection of the same body. The sermon came to her hands some years later and she published in 1726-27 *A Letter to Dr. Holdsworth*. In 1727 he published *A Defence of the Doctrine of the Resurrection of the same Body*. Her answer, *A Vindication of Mr. Locke's Christian Principles,* remained in manuscript till the publication of her works in 1751. She also wrote in 1739 *Remarks upon some Writers in the Controversy concerning the Foundation of Moral Duty and Moral Obligation* which was published in 1743 in *The History of the Works of the Learned*. In 1747 she entered upon a confutation of Dr. Rutherforth's *Essay on the Nature and Obligations of Virtue*. Her *Remarks* on this *Essay* was published by Mr. Warburton with a laudatory Preface in which he spoke of her "fine genius," "clearness of expression, strength of reason, precision of logic, and attachment to truth" [see excerpt dated 1747].

From 1731 to 1748 there is a series of letters between Mrs. Cockburn and Anne Hepburn (afterwards Mrs. Arbuthnot), her niece. It is almost entirely a literary and religious correspondence and shows that Miss Hepburn's interests were on almost as high a plane as her aunt's. A list of the books they exchanged and commented on would include most of the important new works in England during the first half of the century. (pp. 108-09)

Mrs. Cockburn had a strong, clear, acute mind. The impression she made on the best thinkers in her generation is due to this fact, and, further, to the fact that she used her mentality on topics then counted vital. She was didactic, she was morally irreproachable, she was unassuming. That her editor's confident prediction of her fame [see excerpt dated 1751] has been discredited by time, that she is in reality hardly so much as a name to-day, is due partly to the oblivion that has overtaken her subjects, but also, and even more justly, to the dead level of her excellence. She has no wit, no fancy, no imagination, no sprightliness of thought, no humor. Mary Astell and "Sophia" were occasionally roused to picturesque indignation. But not so with Mrs. Cockburn. She is as cold, as orderly, as unstimulating as a formula. (pp. 107-11)

> *Myra Reynolds, "The Learned Lady in England from 1650 to 1760," in her* The Learned Lady in England: 1650-1760, *Houghton Mifflin Company, 1920, pp. 46-257.*

ALLARDYCE NICOLL   (essay date 1925)

[*Called "one of the masters of dramatic research," Nicoll is best known as a theater historian whose works have proven invaluable to students of the drama. His* World Drama from Aeschylus to Anouilh *(1949) is considered a masterpiece; theater critic John Gassner, for example, described it as "unquestionably the most thorough [study] of its kind in the English language [and] our best reference book on the world's dramatic literature," and other critics have cited Nicoll's highly original and perceptive commentary here and elsewhere. In the following excerpt from a work first published in 1925 under the title* A History of Early Eighteenth-Century Drama, 1700-1750, *Nicoll finds Trotter's later dramas noticeably flawed.*]

Among the dramatists who produced . . . plays of a mixed sort in the early years of the [eighteenth] century, three of the women writers must be noted, Mrs Wiseman, Mrs Catharine Trotter and Mrs Eliza Haywood, figures to be set alongside of the more heroic Mrs Manley and Mrs Pix. The first has but one tragedy to her credit, *Antiochus the Great: or, The Fatal Relapse*, a very dull albeit bloody play, with a strange admixture of Elizabethan, heroic and classic elements. Whincop declares that it was acted with applause. Mrs Trotter had already started her career in the seventeenth century, producing then *Agnes de Castro* and *The Fatal Friendship*. Her later work is not distinguished by any very high merits. *The Unhappy Penitent* is a dull drama, and *The Revolution of Sweden* in [John Downes' words in *Roscius Anglicanus* (1708)], "wanting the just Decorum of Plays, expir'd the Sixth Day." The latter is a poor piece of work, with a strained and chaotic plot, and passions atrophied and chill. Its only interest lies in its classic treatment of otherwise heroic subject-matter. Much finer is Mrs Haywood's *Frederick, Duke of Brunswick-Lunenburgh*, which has well-developed characters in Frederick and in Adelaid, a maiden whose passion is aroused by the neglect she supposes has been cast on her. (p. 104)

> *Allardyce Nicoll, "Tragedy: Augustan Tragedies," in his* A History of English Drama, 1660-1900: Early

Eighteenth Century Drama, Vol. II, *third edition, Cambridge at the University Press, 1952, pp. 96-113.*

W. MACQUEEN-POPE   (essay date 1952)

[*Macqueen-Pope was a distinguished English actor, manager, and theater historian whose many books vigorously promoted the London stage. In the following excerpt, he comments on Trotter's principal dramatic and philosophical works, briefly comparing them with the writings of other literary women of the day.*]

[When Catharine Trotter] was only seventeen her tragedy entitled *Agnes de Castro* was produced at Drury Lane, and she was acclaimed. She revelled in pure sentiment and romance and there was nothing in her plays of the ferocity which marked those of Mrs. Manley, in which everything was carnal love and desperation, sudden and remorseless murder. (Mrs. Manley showed great ingenuity in devising methods of extermination. In one of her plays an unfortunate man was put in a cannon and fired off like a shell. Immediately afterwards his wife, according to the authoress's stage direction, "gathered up the smoking pieces of her lord.") There was nothing like that about the plays of Mrs. Trotter, which, whether comedies or tragedies, were sentimental and full of high thought. Altogether she wrote six plays, four tragedies and two comedies. She also wrote verses in praise of Congreve. These came to the latter's attention, and friendship as platonic as that between Congreve and Mrs. Bracegirdle grew between them. Then she wrote a defence of Locke's *Essay on the Human Understanding* [*A Defence of the "Essay of Human Understanding"*], remarkable for its clarity and grip of the subject. She was a very learned young person indeed, with a most enquiring mind that led her into the Roman Catholic Church, and out again. She finally married an English clergyman (or he might have been a Scot), the Rev. Mr. Cockburn, curate of St. Dunstan's in Fleet Street. They had tastes in common, even if he was not of the Theatre. For he wrote an account of the Great Flood, which was highly approved by the learned of his day, and several other works of scholarship. Not to be outdone, Mrs. Trotter, having read some articles by eminent writers on the foundation of moral duty and obligation, wrote a most arresting series [*Remarks upon Some Writers in the Controversy concerning the Foundation of Moral Duty and Moral Obligation*] in *The Literary Journal* called *The History of the Works of the Learned*. She had no limit to her thirst for knowledge and to her powers in absorbing it, for when a book called *Essays on the Nature and Obligations of Virtue* by Dr. Rutherford appeared, she read it at once, mastered it and went on from where the Doctor had left off, her work [*Remarks upon the Principles and Reasonings of Dr. Rutherforth's "Essay on the Nature and Obligations of Virtue"*] gaining the highest commendation from the Bishop of Gloucester, Dr. Warburton, who had it published as a supplement to the original book. How this lady managed with the people of the Theatre cannot be told, but she must have had great understanding and adaptability. Maybe she just wrote her plays and then let the theatre folk get on with it. She was devoted to her husband and they had a long and happy married life. Her husband died in 1748, at the age of seventy-one and she was stricken down with grief. She mourned him deeply and she did not want to live. Indeed, she followed him very quickly in the following year. She was of quite a different type from either Mrs. Pix or Mrs. Manley, but all three were satirised together in a farce called *The Female Wits* [see Additional Bibliography], in which their abilities and weaknesses were held up to ridicule. But that is as great a compliment as can be paid to workers in the Theatre. Mrs. Trotter and Mrs. Pix both had connections with the Church, for Mrs. Trotter married a clergyman and Mrs. Pix was the daughter of one. Thus again did the closeness of Church and Stage demonstrate itself, and is it not reported that Ann and Rebecca Marshall's father was a Presbyterian minister? (pp. 131-32)

> *W. Macqueen-Pope, "First Ladies of the Pen," in his* Ladies First: The Story of Woman's Conquest of the British Stage, *W. H. Allen, 1952, pp. 126-42.*

ROBERT ADAMS DAY (essay date 1969)

[*Day is an American scholar of English literature. In the following excerpt, he closely examines the origin and structure of the anonymously published* Olinda's Adventures, *noting especially features of the novel that anticipate later developments in the genre.*]

A standard modern history of the English novel [Walter Allen's *The English Novel* (1968)] speaks of "the appearance of the novel round about 1700. Nothing that preceded it in the way of prose fiction can explain it." Though today many scholars would assert that "nothing" is too strong a term, just how much of the original fiction written under the later Stuarts could "explain" Defoe and Richardson? Most late seventeenth-century novels, it is true, are rogue biographies, scandal-chronicles, translations and imitations of French *nouvelles,* or short sensational romances of love, intrigue, and adventure with fantastic plots and wooden characters. Only occasionally was a tale published which showed that it was not examples of the novelist's craft that were wanting to inspire the achievement of a Defoe, but rather the sustained application of that craft over hundreds of pages by the unique combination of talents of a Defoe himself.

Such a novel is *Olinda's Adventures,* a brief epistolary narrative of 1693, a minor but convincing demonstration of the theory that a literary form such as the novel develops irregularly, by fits and starts, and of the truism that a superior mind can produce superior results with the most seemingly ungrateful materials. Of Defoe, *Olinda's Adventures* must appear a modest precursor indeed; but measured, as a realistic-domestic novel, against the English fiction of its day, it is surprisingly mature; and if we believe the bookseller and assign its authorship to a girl of fourteen, we must look to the juvenilia of Jane Austen for the first comparable phenomenon. (p. i)

If we are willing to admit that *Olinda* is Mrs. Trotter's work, its virtues may be explained in part by seeing it as romanticized autobiography. Olinda, like Mrs. Trotter, is a wit and something of a beauty in adolescence, a fatherless child living with a prudent mother who is anxious to marry her off advantageously, and a solicitor of favors from noble or wealthy connections. Of the details of her character and circumstances at this time, however, no information is certain, and we must rely upon two presumably biased contemporary portraits. Mrs. Trotter gets off lightly in *The Female Wits* [see Additional Bibliography]; she is represented (in "Calista," a small role) as being somewhat catty and pretentious, vain of her attainments in Latin and Greek (she has read Aristotle in the original, she says), but her moral character is not touched upon. Another account of her early life, in Mrs. Manley's fictionalized autobiography and scandal-chronicle, *The Adventures of Rivella* (1714) [see Additional Bibliography], may be entirely unreliable; but its author was certainly well acquainted with Mrs. Trotter, and what she says of her life in the 1690s, what is narrated in *Olinda,* and what Mrs. Trotter's scholarly memoirist

Thomas Birch relates are similar in outline, similar enough so that we may speculate that the same set of facts has been "improved" in *Olinda,* perhaps maliciously distorted in *Rivella.* Cleander, the Platonic friend of the novel, Orontes, the kidnapped bridegroom, and Cloridon, the inconveniently married noble lover, appear to be three aspects of the same person; for Mrs. Manley tells at length of "Calista's" relationship with "Cleander" (identified in the "key" to *Rivella* as Mrs. Trotter and Mr. Tilly). John Tilly, the deputy warden of the Fleet prison, whose mistress Mrs. Manley became and remained until 1702, first met her, she says, through Mrs. Trotter, who sought her aid in interceding with her cousin John Manley, appointed chairman of a committee to look into alleged misdemeanors of Tilly as prison administrator. Mrs. Trotter, says Mrs. Manley, was a prude in public, not so in private; she was the first, "Cleander" said, who ever made him unfaithful to his wife. Mrs. Manley goes on, with a tantalizing lack of clarity:

> [Calista's] Mother being in Misfortunes and indebted to him, she had offered her Daughter's Security, he took it, and moreover the Blessing of one Night's Lodging, which he never paid her back again. . . . [Calista] had given herself Airs about not visiting *Rivella,* now she was made the Town-Talk by her Scandalous Intreague with *Cleander.*

Whatever the truth about Mrs. Trotter's adolescent amours may have been, or whether they have any connection with *Olinda's* fictional ones, must remain a matter for speculation; but the artistic merits of *Olinda* are in no such doubt. Although technically it may be called an epistolary novel, its author is no Richardson in marshalling the strategies of the epistolary technique. Nevertheless, although it is actually a fictional autobiography divided somewhat arbitrarily into "letters," the postponement of the letter to Cloridon until the end, the introduction of what might be called a subplot as Olinda tries to promote Cleander's courtship of Ambrisia and notes its progress, the breaking off of the letters at moments of (mild) suspense, the bringing up of the action to an uncompleted present, all these show an awareness of fictional mechanics that is far from elementary. Indeed, a contemporary critic might go so far as to see in the novel's conclusion an anticipation of the "open-ended" realism of plotting so much applauded at present; for though Orontes has been got out of the way, Olinda has not yet been rewarded with Cloridon's hand by a similarly happy turn of fate, and must patiently await the demise of his inconvenient wife as anyone outside of melodrama might have to do. The contretemps and misunderstandings, the trick played on Olinda with regard to Cloridon's fidelity and her subsequent undeceiving, the closet-scene and its embarrassments, may smack of the hackneyed devices of stage comedy, but they are not clumsily handled, and they never make emotional mountains out of molehills.

Perhaps the most salient qualities of *Olinda,* in contrast to the fiction of its day, are restraint and in control. With the exception of the rather ridiculous way in which the complications are resolved at the end (Orontes's sequestration and death from smallpox), everything in the novel is planned and motivated with some care. Inclinations develop slowly and believably; the springs of action, barring a few not very fantastic coincidences and accidents, are anti-romantic—almost too much so. Indeed, such criteria of the "modern novel" as those proposed by Ian Watt are all modestly but adequately met. Most important, the situation and behavior of the heroine, her values, and the world in which she lives are (but for their sketchy development) what a reader of Jane Austen might take for granted, yet are all but unique before 1740.

Here is a middle-class heroine who is fully as moral as Pamela, but with a wry sense of humor; she defers to her mother as a matter of course when marriage is in question, yet would willingly evade parental decrees; she is capable of Moll Flanders's examinations of motive, yet sees through her own hypocrisies; she lives in London in reduced circumstances and agrees to a marriage of convenience although tempted to engage in a dashing adultery; and she endures the onset of both love and jealousy without melodramatic or sentimental posturings.

Other technical achievements of *Olinda* aside, the portrait of the heroine as she reveals herself to her confidant is the novel's most significant feature. A fictional heroine of this early date who can be sententious without being tedious, who is moderately and believably witty, who is courted by a goldsmith (even though, conformably to the times, he is named Berontus) rather than a prince borrowed from *Astrée*, and who satirizes herself soberly for scorning him, who meets her ideal lover with a business letter rather than in a shipwreck, and who levelheadedly fends him off because he is both married and a would-be philanderer, is a rarity indeed.

Olinda commends itself to the student of English literary history principally for two reasons: because it so ably anticipates in embryo so many features which the English domestic and realistic novel would develop in its age of maturity and popularity, and because we do not yet understand, and need to investigate, the cultural factors—literary, social, and economic—which prevented the kind of a achievement it represents from being duplicated with any frequently for several decades. (pp. iv-vii)

> *Robert Adams Day, in an introduction to* Olinda's Adventures; or, The Amours of a Young Lady (1718) *by Catharine Trotter Cockburn, William Andrews Clark Memorial Library, 1969, pp. i-viii.*

ROBERT ADAMS DAY   (essay date 1980)

[*In the following excerpt, Day attempts to account for the failure of Trotter and her fellow "Female Wits," most of whom had contributed a poem to the 1700 tributary collection* The Nine Muses, *to achieve strong reputations for themselves and their literary works.*]

Among the mournful cypresses metaphorically laid on the tomb of the English Poet Laureate John Dryden in 1700 was a tasteful folio pamphlet entitled *The Nine Muses*, containing laments allegedly by these deities, each in a meter and with themes appropriate to its author. The verses were by aspiring women poets, of whom most were, and must remain, anonymous; but three are identified as "Mrs. Pix, Mrs. Manley, and Mrs. Trotter." Each had had a play produced in the season of 1695-96, and they had been bound together in caricature, pilloried in a play called *The Female Wits* [see Additional Bibliography], produced at Drury Lane in October 1696. Together with Mrs. Aphra Behn, who had died but a few years earlier, in 1689, they were among the most prominent of the few women writers in seventeenth-century England.

Although these four British Muses possessed no small measure of literary talent, and though each wrote in several genres enough to fill two or more stout volumes, none of them was able to attain or at any rate to maintain the combination of a comfortable living, a respectable status in society, fame, or a general recognition of merit in literary circles, even if not with the general public. Why did our British Muses fare so ill? For fare ill they did.

After admirably competing with male playwrights through the 1670s, Aphra Behn seems to have spent the 1680s in poverty, grinding out at a frantic rate short novels, translations from the French, and occasional poems for the few pounds a dedication might bring. Her posthumous reputation, until she was rescued in the early years of this century by the eccentric scholar Montague Summers, was for nothing more than shocking obscenity, or at very least improper eroticism. Mrs. Mary Pix, for ten years a writer of farces, serious plays, and an almost unknown novel, seems to have met derision with equanimity and had some modest success; but her plays were ignored after 1706. Mrs. Catherine Trotter, author at fourteen of a remarkable little novel and at seventeen of a successful tragedy, *Agnes de Castro,* wrote four other plays with rather less success, some poems, and treatises which we shall consider presently. But after 1708, when she married an impecunious and high-minded clergyman, she was, says her biographer [Thomas Birch, in *The Works of Mrs. Catharine Cockburn* (1751)] "entirely diverted from her studies for many years, by attending upon the duties of a wife and mother, and by the ordinary cares of an increasing family, and the additional ones arising from the reduced circumstances of her husband." A political journalist and pamphleteer, Mrs. Delariviere Manley wrote five plays and at least six works of fiction. Yet she seems to have been more than glad to forsake politics for love in 1714, both in her writings, as she avers, and in life; heavily in debt and perhaps suffering from phlebitis, she was for her last ten years the mistress of Alderman John Barber, a prosperous printer, and remained silent except for a single play, some stories, and a novel which was published posthumously. Thus the Muses of King William's London, after shining briefly, were ignominiously extinguished, dying poor and obscure. Was their neglect merited, or not? Let me complicate the question by considering four facts: they wrote plays, they wrote novels, they were socially in the same rather unusual category, and they were intellectuals. The last fact first.

If our four Muses had done no more than produce a few trivial comedies, we might dismiss them with the rule *de minimis non curat lex* ["the law does not regard trifles"]: why *should* they deserve anything more than the corner of a footnote? But three of them (and Mary Pix, the exception, is an instructive exception, to whom we shall return) would rate on anybody's scale as intellectuals. Mrs. Trotter (as we noted) was almost certainly the author, at the astonishing age of fourteen, of a technically excellent novella, *Olinda's Adventures,* which had the distinction, virtually unique at the time, of appearing in France as *Les amours d'une belle angloise*; she learned French, Latin, and logic with little or no assistance; she wrote two comedies that earned the flattering attention of the playwright William Congreve, with whom her platonic friendship became well known; she wrote and published philosophical treatises, one in defense of Locke's *Essay Concerning Human Understanding* [*Defence of the "Essay of Human Understanding"*], against an anonymous attacker in the so-called "Locke-Stillingfleet controversy" of 1697, resulting in a letter from Locke [see excerpt dated 1702] which was more than merely a polite compliment. Leibniz was told about her, as was the cultivated Queen of Prussia, who referred to her as "the Scots Sappho."

Mrs. Behn wrote as her first essay in fiction a technically astonishing epistolary novel, *Love Letters Between a Nobleman and his Sister,* and her stories *Oroonoko* and *The Fair Jilt* still figure regularly in anthologies. She acquired sufficient knowledge of French to publish several book-length translations: not of frivolous fiction, but of Rochefoucauld (entitled *Seneca Unmasq'd*); of Fontenelle's *Dialogues on the Plurality of Worlds* and his translation of a history of pagan oracles, and of a work of Cowley on botany. In her preface to Fontenelle she made pronouncements on the theory and practice of translation which, though less clearly expressed, are not notably inferior to Dryden's, and some brief though rather amazing comments, concerning what would later be called Higher Criticism of Scripture. Mrs. Manley (if we except her five plays, dramatic attempts which were technically innovative, and even if we except her scandal-chronicles *Queen Zarah, The New Atalantis,* and *Memoirs of a Certain Island*) generated sufficient intellectual voltage to receive high if qualified compliments from Swift in the *Journal to Stella,* and the higher compliment of relinquishing into her hands the editorship of his political journal *The Examiner* in 1711. She wrote at least seven *Examiners,* and five or six political pamphlets praised by Swift, so that without exaggeration we may call her Swift's collaborator in an enterprise that he saw as having a weighty and serious political purpose. A biographer holds that "in open competition with the best minds, she held her own and emerged with a creditable record," and that Swift, arguably the best mind of Queen Anne's day, "treated her simply as a fellow writer." Some of her critical remarks in the preface to *Queen Zarah* have been hailed by modern critics as of great innovative significance.

Now let us briefly consider the first, second, and third points mentioned earlier. Authors of eighteen (Behn), twelve (Pix), five, and five plays respectively, they were not mere dabblers in drama; and though Catherine Trotter and Mary Pix wrote but one novel each, Mrs. Behn's collected fiction would fill two good-sized modern volumes and Mrs. Manley's three. They were not "one-book novelists." The last point is a double one: they were all of gentle, though not of aristocratic birth; and they were all, for their day, socially unmoored—that is, adrift. Mrs. Manley, daughter of Sir Roger Manley, a Royalist military governor and man of letters, was the survivor of a disastrous marriage to a cousin in adolescence. Mrs. Trotter, daughter of a naval captain and distantly related to the eminent Burnet family, was living in genteel poverty with her widowed mother, while Mrs. Behn was probably of gentle or conjecturally of illegitimately noble birth. Mrs. Pix, child of a country clergyman, was married to a merchant tailor, and she was notoriously fond of the table and the bottle.

So much for the lives: now for the documents. The authors of *The Nine Muses* are identified only by initials, and the dedicatory preface is written by the bookseller, Richard Bassett. It is pretty clear that he solicited the poems himself, to turn an honest penny; but he refrains from taking whatever advantage he might gain by naming names, he harps at length on the modesty of the fair sex, and he rather irrelevantly, it would seem (since the ladies are unknown), refers to their supposed beauty, seeming to feel that a plain or ugly female wit is shoddy goods indeed. Of our ladies Mrs. Manley is Melpomene, the Tragick Muse; Mrs. Pix Clio, the Historick Muse; and Mrs. Trotter Calliope, the Heroick Muse. All three write their elegies in iambic pentameter couplets, with an occasional triplet; they dwell respectively on Dryden's tragedies, public poems, and Vergilian translations; and except for Mrs. Trotter, who takes a witty swipe or two at such third-rate poetic translators of epic as Blackmore, Hobbes, Chapman, and Ogilby, their verses are as bad as verses can be. *The Nine Muses* is worthless in itself,

but for our purposes three facts are salient and will be reverted to. The form is old, sanctioned, respectable—the garland of elegies for a deceased worthy. The mode is classical—the elegy, replete with Great Pan, nymphs, genii, and deities. And the authors are women, modestly veiled.

Our second document is also very bad indeed. The modern editor concludes, however, that the author's animus is principally against two disquieting facts—that *The Royal Mischief* (and other recent plays by, and to a certain extent for, women) had been rather more successful than he liked, and that Mrs. Manley's heroine, supremely wicked and lustful, had out-ranted the heroines of heroic tragedy (she has an unprecedented *six* tirades to deliver) in a way that the audience liked too much for competing male playwrights' peace of mind. For something of a phenomenon had marked the theater seasons of 1695 and 1696; no less than seven plays by women had appeared—Mrs. Pix's tragedy *Ibrahim* and her comedy *The Spanish Wives,* Mrs. Manley's comedy *The Lost Lover* as well as *The Royal Mischief,* Mrs. Behn's post-humously produced comedy *The Younger Brother,* Mrs. Trotter's very popular tragedy **Agnes de Castro,** and a comedy entitled *She Ventures and He Wins* by a lady who called herself "Ariadne." *The Royal Mischief* and its sister plays were no worse than much of the trash that London was applauding in the 1690s. Mrs. Manley says bitterly and not unjustly of herself in her romanticized autobiography, *The Adventures of Rivella,* "if she had been a man, she had been without fault," and concludes tartly and probably with reference to her detention and interrogation by the secretaries of state over *The New Atalantis* in 1709, "politicks is not the business of a woman." We could multiply examples, but a few more, with reference to Mrs. Behn and of particular significance, will suffice. Her first plays, *The Forc'd Marriage* and *The Amorous Prince,* appeared with only passing reference—the pronoun "she"—to the author's sex, but in her third, *The Dutch Lover* (1673), an epistle to the reader reveals it with wry humility in a discourse where irritation clearly struggles with caution. But she makes the significant and protective statement, "Plays have no great room for that which is men's great advantage over women, *that is learning.*" However, regardless of what critics might think of her, the public went assiduously to see her plays throughout the 1670s. But in 1683, when she had turned to other kinds of writing, Dryden issued a translation of Ovid's *Heroides* by several hands, the epistle of Oenone to Paris being from her pen. Dryden said gallantly in the introduction, "I was desir'd to say that the author, who is of the Fair Sex . . . understood not Latine. But if she does not, I am afraid she has given us occasion to be ashamed who do." But the poet Matthew Prior lost his temper. In his *Satyr on the Modern Translators,* the lady is vituperatively skewered as

> our blind translatress *Behn,*
> The Female Wit, who next convicted stands,
> Not for abusing *Ovid's* verse, but *Sand's:*
> She might have learn'd from the ill-borrow'd Grace,
> (Which little helps the ruine of her Face)
> That Wit, like Beauty, triumphs o're the Heart,
> When more of Nature's seen, and less of Art:
> Nor strive in *Ovid's* letters to have shown,
> As much of skill, as lewdness in her own:
> Then let her from the next inconstant Lover,
> Take a new Copy for a second *Rover,*
> Describe the cunning of a jilting Whore,
> From the ill Arts her self has us'd before;
> Then let her write, but Paraphrase no more.

No holds barred. If a woman writer was the victim, the "slovenly butchering" of which Dryden spoke was the preferred method in satire. In the context of the times, the playwright, unless buttressed by rank and position or an eminent patron, was not taken seriously—he lived in a no man's land beneath consideration, socially and intellectually. In Dr. Johnson's words, "We, that live to please, must please to live;" and with the much-derided exception of Ben Jonson's *Works*, the haphazard textual and publishing history of Elizabethan and seventeenth-century plays gives ample supporting evidence for this statement. But Jonson is likewise important as an example: he, unlike Shakespeare, publicly plumed himself on his classical learning, and wrote comedies and tragedies ostentatiously modeled on the classics: unlike Shakespeare, he was, he hoped, the successor of Terence and Plautus, and therefore wrote *Works*—opera—not "stage-plays."

Anthropologist Mary Douglas has investigated traditional systems of taboo and concepts of dirt or pollution. She sums up her conclusions (which she applies not only to the taboos of African tribesmen, but to Hebrew dietary laws and many analogous cultural systems): "We avoid anomalous animals because in defying the categories of our universe they arouse deep feelings of disquiet." The three most important characteristics of taboo systems are extreme rigidity, simple criteria based on grossly inadequate observation, and enormous emotional power. It may seem anomalous to speak of taboo and pollution in connection with the arts, but the classical theory of genres and of literature, given at least lip-service by all in 1700, is very much to the point.

Heroic poetry, classical comedy and tragedy, history, oratory, the elegy and epistle, and satire, make up a sacred system: drama not imitative of the classics, and prose fiction, are taboo, because they were nonexistent or anomalous when the categories developed and froze. The Ancients-and-Moderns controversies in late seventeenth-century England and France are relevant here; and even that pioneering critical document, the *Traité sur les romans* of the learned Bishop Huet of Avranches (1673) spends most of its time on the novel of antiquity and on prose fiction as a variant of the heroic poem. Three or four taboo-systems operate here—that of clean and unclean literature, that of public behaviour for men and for women, that of clean and unclean literary persons, and that of classical education and higher knowledge—reserved, like the fat of beasts, for the priestly class, though Levites might partake with caution and in the fear of God. Such an anthropological view has been applied to education by Walter Ong, who aptly compares classical education, with its required mastery of Latin, to a puberty rite, an initiation, a *rite de passage:* "isolation from the family, the achievement of identity in a totally male group (the school), the learning of a body of relatively abstract tribal lore inaccessible to those outside the group." Including the lower classes (though perhaps not the occasional peasant-poet, made much of by the avant-garde) and all women.

But it would be a distortion to say that at the end of the seventeenth century European prose fiction and popular drama were merely ritually nonexistent, taboo, or unclean and therefore terrifying. Mary Douglas also points out that when "dirt" has been swept aside into its proper place and is undifferentiated, ignored, and therefore above all unclassified, it loses its power: "so long as identity is absent," she says, "rubbish is not dangerous." We now begin to see daylight if we combine literary history with anthropology and bring them to bear on the hierarchical circles of society and art. If clean literature is

bounded by the lines laid down in antiquity and if clean literary practitioners are men of position, by definition trained in the classics, clean women cannot of course practice literature for the simple reason that they never did, except for the two ancient Greek monsters Sappho and Corinna; and in the 1890s Eugene Field depicted a Midwestern *arbiter elegantiarum* as saying, "That Sappho was a gamey old girl, you know; she would have been tabooed in Chicago."

It might be objected that Dryden's famous poem of 1686, "To the Pious Memory of Mrs. Anne Killigrew," which extravagantly celebrates her as a poet and a painter, is an example to the contrary. But it is not, if we consider that Dryden knew which side his bread was buttered on. Mistress Killigrew had been maid of honor to Mary of Modena, Duchess of York and Queen to James II, she was a member of the Killigrew family, favorites of both Charles II and his brother James and proprietors of one of London's two theaters (and Dryden was a playwright); she was sister to an admiral; and most important, she died young, before she had time either to become very sinful or to accomplish very much at either poetry or painting. And her poems were published posthumously.

Of course there were exceptions; these prove the rule. Katherine Philips, "the matchless Orinda," was a gentlewoman born, married to a gentleman of wealth; her poems circulated only in manuscript, and she was furious when they were published by an enterprising bookseller. Elizabeth Elstob, who knew eight languages and published Anglo-Saxon texts and a grammar of that language, got her learning from, and lived with, her learned brother; after his death she become a poverty-stricken schoolteacher and governess. Mme. Dacier was the wife of a learned humanist and the daughter of another. The eccentric Duchess of Newcastle was a duchess; need one say more? Though she was often called "mad," no one said it to her face. Recent studies of Anne Finch, Countess of Winchilsea, make it obvious that she was torn between the desire to write and the fear that she would be condemned for seeming to seek public praise. She adopted the matchless Orinda as her model. Lady Mary Wroth, who published in 1621 a prose romance, *Urania,* containing many Petrarchan sonnets, had to withdraw it from sale and retrieve as many copies as she could when courtiers complained to King James that court scandals were depicted in it. Daughter of Sir Philip Sidney's brother Sir Robert, she had to content herself thereafter, as befitted a lady, with such praise as she might gain from the circulation of her poems in manuscript among the poets of the day and the reprinting of some of them in *The Countess Montgomery's Urania.* All were "clean" women. Mrs. Pix, the remaining anomaly, was not so at all; jolly and comfortable (*and,* after all, married), she never raised her head above the dunghill of fiction and popular drama, where she remained rooting contentedly or at least quietly. Lastly, the dramatic success of Mmes. Behn, Manley, Pix, and Trotter were short-lived. The reasons were complicated, but one at least is clear: a clean woman, except in the wicked 1670s, now piously scorned, had not yet been a successful playwright. (pp. 61-9)

Robert Adams Day, "Muses in the Mud: The Female Wits Anthropologically Considered," in Women's Studies, *Vol. 7, No. 3, 1980, pp. 61-74.*

NANCY COTTON   (essay date 1980)

[*Cotton is an American scholar who has written extensively on early English women dramatists. In the following excerpt, she surveys Trotter's literary career.*]

[Catherine Trotter] was a Scotswoman with family connections and patrons among the nobility. . . . In 1693, at the age of only fourteen, she published some verses to Bevil Higgons on his recovery from smallpox ["**Verses Written at the Age of Fourteen, and sent to Mr. Beville Higgons, on His Sickness and Recovery from the Small-pox"**] and, much more impressive, an autobiographical epistolary novel entitled *Olinda's Adventures*. The novel is remarkable for its date in technique, liveliness, and charm. *Olinda's Adventures* was translated into French and went through a half dozen English editions by 1724; the editions of 1718 and 1724 carried Trotter's name.

At sixteen she wrote her first play, *Agnes de Castro,* based on Aphra Behn's novel of that name. This tragedy shows a triangle of perfect lovers. The Prince of Portugal loves his wife's favorite, Agnes de Castro, but nobly conceals his illicit passion. Agnes is devoted to her mistress. The princess, although she discovers the prince's secret passion, continues unselfishly to love both her husband and her friend. This harmony enrages Alvaro and his sister Elvira, who love Agnes and the prince, and their machinations produce the catastrophe. Elvira stabs the princess in mistake for Agnes, then accuses Agnes of the murder. Alvaro, planning to rape Agnes, steals her from her jailors. Threatened by the princess's ghost, Elvira goes mad and stabs her ally Bianca, who then reveals the entire plot. At the last minute Alvaro kills Agnes in mistake for the prince, who is with difficulty prevented from falling on his sword. *Agnes de Castro* is written in weak blank verse; the lines end with one or two extra syllables. The dialogue of the play is peculiar. Although several characters occasionally appear on stage at the same time, there is almost never an actual conversation; usually there are only duologues and soliloquies. The total effect is of Senecan tragedy a hundred years out of date.

That a beautiful girl of genteel family, at a time when it was far from respectable for a woman to be a playwright, should enter the theatrical world at the age of sixteen is astonishing. Her action must partly be taken as a measure of the economic distress of her family. She protected herself by working anonymously; in the dedication she says she "Conceals her Name, to shun that of Poetess" [see excerpt dated 1696]. The title page of *Agnes de Castro* specifies that the play was written by a "Lady," and the dedication addresses the Earl of Dorset and Middlesex with easy familiarity: "This little Off-spring of my early Muse was first Submitted to Your Lordship's Judgment, whether it shou'd be Stifled in the Birth, or Preserv'd to try its Fortune in the World; and . . . 'tis from Your Sentence it has ventur'd thus far." The play's anonymity, its familiar dedication to a nobleman, its elevated subject, and its formal, bookish style publicized the author as a learned lady. (pp. 81-4)

In 1698 Lincoln's Inn Fields produced Trotter's most successful play, *Fatal Friendship*. This blank verse tragedy, less frigid than *Agnes,* depicts the misfortunes of Gramont and his friend Castalio. Before the play begins, Castalio has been wrongly declared a traitor and cast into prison; only payment of a heavy fine can release him. Meanwhile the impoverished Gramont has secretly married the equally impoverished Felicia (who is being wooed by his own father); their infant son is being held for ransom by pirates. Under pressure of financial need, he succumbs to his father's insistence that he marry the wealthy Lamira, who is, unknown to him, beloved by Castalio. Gramont refuses to consummate this bigamous marriage, but it sets off such a series of entanglements and mistakes that, in the last act, Gramont accidentally wounds Castalio and then stabs himself, just as a messenger brings too late the news of a royal pardon for all.

Fatal Friendship was explicitly designed to reform the stage. Trotter's dedication states that her play's "End is the most noble, to discourage Vice, and recommend a firm unshaken Virtue" [see Additional Bibliography]. There is no licentiousness and no villain; the characters are well intentioned but work at cross-purposes. Accidents bring on the disasters that Christian fortitude would have resolved. Gramont points the moral in his dying words:

> O what a Wretch was I, that could not wait
> Heav'ns time; the Providence that never fails
> Those who dare trust it, durst I have been honest,
> One day had chang'd the Scene, and made me happy.

The commendatory poems praise the play's morality:

> You stand the first of stage-reformers too.
> No vicious stains pollute your moral scene;
> Chast are your thoughts, and your expression clean [see poem
>   by John Hughes dated 1698].

George Farquhar sent Trotter a letter praising *Fatal Friendship* and "its beautiful author" and enclosed a copy of *Love and a Bottle* with the complaint that his play had been criticized for scandalizing the ladies. "As an argument of its innocence," he sent it "to stand its tryal before one of the fairest of the sex, and its best judge."

Trotter dedicated *Fatal Friendship* to Princess Anne with an appeal for royal patronage because "when a Woman appears in the World under any distinguishing Character, she must expect to be the mark of ill Nature, but most one who seems desirous to recommend her self by what the other Sex think their peculiar Prerogative." This may be an oblique allusion to *The Female Wits* [see Additional Bibliography]. If so, it is the only exception to the silence she maintained about the dramatic burlesque.

In 1700 Trotter made one of a group of women who wrote a collection of poems honoring Dryden after his death. In the same years she brought out her only comedy, *Love at a Loss; or, Most Votes Carry It*. According to the dedication [see Additional Bibliography], the play was originally intended as a subplot for one of her tragedies "when the Town had been little pleas'd with Tragedy intire." The comedy is almost as moral and reformed as her tragedies. In *Love at a Loss* each of three ladies nearly loses her man because of her own folly. Miranda's mistake is excessive coquettishness; Lucilia's, a casual youthful flirtation that led her to write some imprudent letters; Lesbia's, consummation with her fiancé after the marriage contract but before the marriage. Although there is some intrigue, some watered-down double entendre, and some railing at marriage in the older Restoration manner, the lovers solve their problems through good sense. These sensible lovers carefully point morals. Lucilia's youthful flirtation, her "childish fault," has caused her "such dangers, such anxieties, as might warn all our Sex against those little Gallantries, with which they only think to amuse themselves; but tho' innocent, too often gain 'em such a Character of Lightness, as their future Conduct never can efface." The reformed rake uses logic to prove that husbands must treat their wives well:

> For treating them with rudeness, or neglect,
> Does most dishonour, on our selves reflect;
> If that respect which their own Merit drew,

We think, by their becoming ours, less due
And as in chusing, we their worth approve,
We tax our Judgment, when we cease to love.

In the epilogue Lesbia lectures against premarital sex: ''Hands, and Seals, and Oaths cannot secure / A mind like Man's unfaithful and impure.'' The comedy was unsuccessful, which hardly surprises. *Love at a Loss* is more moral than merry.

The following year saw production of another highly moralized tragedy, *The Unhappy Penitent.* In this play, Charles VIII of France, long contracted to Margarite of Flanders, delays his marriage because he wishes to marry Ann of Brittanie. Margarite feels released from obligation by the delay and secretly marries the Duke of Lorrain, although the paragon Ann urges that Margarite first secure a formal release from her contract. Ann also urges the king to fulfill his contract, in spite of her own inclination for him. Slander and confusion ensue as a result of the machinations of the Duke of Brittanie, who hopes to marry Margarite himself. Margarite, accused of whoredom, vows to enter a convent if her honor is cleared. After the slander is exposed, her vow forbids a reconciliation with her beloved Lorrain. The play ends with a grand renunciation, Margarite going off to a convent in spite of her husband's tender appeals. The king and Ann are left not only to marry but also, considering that the king's delay caused much of Margarite's trouble, to draw rather priggish morals in the same haste-makes-waste

THE

REVOLUTION

O F

SWEDEN.

A Tragedy.

As it is Acted at the

QUEENS THEATRE

I N T H E

HAY-MARKET.

_____

_____

L O N D O N,

Printed for *James Knapton* at the *Crown* in St. *Paul's* Church-yard, and *George Strahan* at the *Golden Ball* against the *Royal Exchange* in *Cornhill.* 1706.   Price 1 s. 6 d.

Title page of Trotter's final drama (1706).

spirit as those at the end of *Fatal Friendship*. The morality of the play is contractual. Margarite violates her contract with the king, but redeems her mistake by keeping a contract with heaven.

The dedication of *The Unhappy Penitent* to Lord Halifax [see Additional Bibliography] shows Trotter ever more serious about her moral duty as a writer. In a tragedy, giving delight must be ''Subservient'' to ''forming an Instructive Moral.'' After a critical analysis of the works of Dryden, Otway, Lee, and Shakespeare, she apologizes for a defect in her play: ''The Distress is not great enough, the Subject of it only the misfortune of Lovers, which I partly design'd in Compliance with the effiminate taste of the Age.'' Rejecting love as a suitable spring for tragedy, Trotter chose patriotism as the major passion for her next, and last tragedy, *The Revolution of Sweden*. This play, which did not appear until five years later, in 1706, was the logical culmination not only of her theories of stage reform but also of her feminism.

The Revolution of Sweden is a historical play depicting Gustavus's freeing of his country from the Danes and his election as king. Interwoven with his military exploits are the adventures of two married couples; each wife is the superior of her husband. Christina, wife of the traitor Beron, disguises as a young man and fights on the Swedish side. She soliloquizes on female courage:

> Why do I dread what will enflame
> The meanest Soldiers Courage? Are our Souls too
> Like their frail Mansions of weaker frame than Mans?
> Or can the force of Custom and Opinion
> Effect this difference? 'Tis so, the Hero
> Who undaunted, faces Death midst Cannons,
> Swords and Javelins, sinks under the less
> Honourable Dangers of Pain, Disease,
> Or Poverty, below a Womans weakness:
> And we whom Custom bars this active Valour,
> Branding it with Reproach, shrink at th' Alarm
> Of War, but where our Honour's plac'd, we oft
> Have shewn in its Defence a no less Manly daring.

The other heroine, Constantia, is the wife of Gustavus's ally, Count Arwide. She argues theology with the archbishop while she is held captive by the Danes. When treachery causes her to doubt her husband's patriotism, she prefers public good to private love and accuses her husband to Gustavus. Arwide, when proved innocent, not only forgives Constantia but loves her the more for her patriotism:

> Yes, my Constantia, thy exalted Vertue
> Constrain'd my Admiration, tho' a Sufferer by it.
> O wou'd men emulate thy great Example,
> Renounce all private Ends, give up their dear
> Their warmest Passions, to the publick Safety;
> Each wou'd be happy in the common Good. . . .

Arwide describes his wife ''Not as a Woman, as a worthy Friend.'' She ''has that Softness which endears / And melts the Soul to transport: But superior / Reason holds the Reins.''

The Revolution of Sweden was unsuccessful. In 1703 Trotter had sent a rough draft or synopsis of the play to Congreve, who returned a courteous letter of detailed suggestions [see excerpt dated 1703]. The finished play ran into the very difficulties that Congreve had tactfully but rankly warned against.

> I think the design in general very great and noble;
> the conduct of it very artful, if not too full of business,
> which may either run into length or obscurity. . . .
> You are the best judge, whether those of your own
> sex will approve as much of the heroic virtue of

Constantia and Christina, as if they had been engaged in some *belle passion:* for my part, I like them better as they are.... The last act will have many harangues in it, which are dangerous in a catastrophe, if long, and not of the last importance.

In the preface [see excerpt dated 1706]: Trotter acknowledged that her desire to instruct her audience had caused her to neglect pleasing them also:

I ... cou'd never allow my self to think of any Subject that cou'd not serve either to incite some useful Virtue, or check some dangerous Passion. With this design I thought writing for the Stage, a Work not unworthy those who wou'd not trifle their time away, and had so fix'd my Mind on contributing my part towards reforming the Corruptions of it, that no doubt I have too little consider'd the present tast of the Town.

No doubt the Town would have been better pleased if the heroines, as Congreve hinted, had been "engaged in some *belle passion.*" But Trotter was sincerely single-minded in her attempt at reform and in her desire to depict heroic women.

For this reason, *The Revolution of Sweden* is interesting as an early feminist statement. It is the type of play that the Duchess of Newcastle tried to write many years earlier. Christina is the military-patriotic lady, and Constantia fulfills the duchess's ideal of the oratorical heroine, capable of arguing theology with learned prelates. In the dedication of the play to Lady Harriot Godolphin, Trotter spoke out for women's intellectual ability:

Encouraging Indulgence to the Endeavours of our Sex ... might incite some greater Geniuses among us to exert themselves, and change our Emulation of a Neighbouring Nation's Fopperies, to the commendable Ambition of Rivalling them in their illustrious Women; Numbers we know among them, have made a considerable Progress in the most difficult Sciences, several have gain'd the Prizes of Poesie from their Academies, and some have been chosen Members of their Societies. This without doubt is not from any Superiority of their Genius to ours; But from the much greater Encouragement they receive, by the Publick Esteem, and the Honours that are done them....

Trotter here refers to the fact that in 1701 the Prix de Poésie of the Académie Française had been awarded to Catherine Durand. Trotter's letters show her admiration for Durand and for other intellectual Frenchwomen such as Madame Dacier.

Catherine Trotter, herself the most intellectual of the female wits, had by this time embarked on a new literary career as a philosophical and theological writer. In this field the moralistic and didactic qualities which mar her plays found appropriate expression. Trotter had early been an admirer of Locke, and in 1703 she wrote and published anonymously her *Defence of Mr. Locke's Essay of Human Understanding.* She was closely acquainted with Bishop Burnet and his wife, who knew the secret of her authorship and revealed it to Locke himself; he sent Trotter a letter [see excerpt dated 1702] and a present of books to thank her for her championship of his theories. She also wrote religious treatises such as *A Discourse concerning a Guide in Controversies,* which was published in 1707 with a preface by Bishop Burnet [see excerpt dated 1707]. At the same time she was a voluminous letter writer, corresponding on religious, philosophical, and literary topics. For a time she corresponded with Leibnitz. Sophie Charlotte, queen of Prus-

sia, heard of her accomplishments and dubbed her the Scots Sappho.... At the age of twenty-nine, Trotter married a clergyman named Cockburn and gave up writing for twenty years. Later she wrote, "Being married in 1708, I bid adieu to the muses, and so wholly gave myself up to the cares of a family, and the education of my children, that I scare knew, whether there was any such thing as books, plays, or poems stirring in Great Britain." After rearing four children in straitened circumstances, Trotter again returned to writing: "My young family was grown up to have less need of my assistance; and beginning to have some taste of polite literature, my inclination revived with my leisure." She now presented another series of theological treatises, such as *Remarks upon the Principles and Reasoning of Dr. Rutherforth's Essay on the Nature and Obligation of Virtue,* published in 1747 with a preface by Warburton [see excerpt dated 1747]. She was still concerned about the intellectual handicaps of women:

... those restraints, which have our sex confin'd,
By partial custom, check the soaring mind:
Learning deny'd us, we at random tread
Unbeaten paths, that late to knowledge lead;
By secret steps break thro' th' obstructed way,
Nor dare acquirements gain'd by stealth display.
If some advent'rous genius rare arise,
Who on exalted themes her talent tries,
She fears to give the work, tho' prais'd, a name,
And flies not more from infamy than fame.

Her own "extensive" frame as a controversialist led to a two-volume subscription edition of her works after her death in May 1749, at the age of seventy-one. Her works were edited by Thomas Birch, who wrote her biography as an introduction partly because "her own sex is intitled to the fullest information about one, who has done such honour to them, and raised our ideas of their intellectual powers" [see excerpt dated 1751]. (pp. 103-11)

> Nancy Cotton, *"The Female Wits: Catherine Trotter,
> Delariviere Manley, Mary Pix,"* in her Women Playwrights in England: c. 1363-1750, *Bucknell University Press, 1980, pp. 81-121.*

EDNA L. STEEVES   (essay date 1982)

[*Steeves is an American scholar who specializes in eighteenth-century English and French literature, John Milton's works, and the history of feminism. In the following excerpt from her introduction to the 1982 facsimile reprint of Trotter's plays, she studies Trotter's achievement as a dramatist, emphasizing the way in which the plays exemplify her era's dramatic preferences.*]

Catharine Trotter could not by any means be considered, to employ a modern psychiatric term, an overachiever. Although in her youth she was looked upon by her contemporaries as something of a prodigy, her literary reputation waned rather rapidly, and at the time of her death her name was all but forgotten in the London theatrical world. Her plays held the stage for barely a decade, and two years after her death her first biographer [Thomas Birch] thought fit to include only one of her five dramas in his edition of her works. Her philosophical discourses, especially the essays on Locke, and her voluminous correspondence with many of the literary lights of her day show substance and ability as a writer and a thinker, greater substance and greater ability than appear in her dramatic work. Yet as a female author at a period when female authors were the common butt of satire, and as a precursor of the Bluestockings, she made her mark on the London literary scene. She was notable enough, or perhaps notorious enough, to be selected as one of three female dramatists worthy of inclusion in an anonymous satiric comedy entitled *The Female Wits* [see Additional Bibliography], which caught the taste of the town in 1704. Catharine Trotter and her contemporary Mary Pix are satirized in the preface thereto as "two Gentlewomen who have made no small struggle in the World to get into Print; and who are now in such a State of Wedlock to Pen and Ink, that it will be very difficult for 'em to get out of it." The fact that Mrs. Trotter was one of only three female dramatists chosen as the object of this satire, and that everyone knowledgeable about the theatrical scene in 1704 recognized her identity, provides evidence that her name was familiar to theatergoers at the turn of the century. Satire demands familiarity with the object of the satire. She had achieved fame—of a sort.

Histories of literature always preserve to after ages the big names; lesser lights receive shorter shrift. Yet minor writers often illustrate more clearly than major writers the characteristics of a given period: its tastes, its follies and foibles, its excesses and absurdities, its limitations. In particular, this truth applies to theatrical productions, for plays that fail to win popular applause soon fail at the box office. A dramatist, then, will mirror the taste of the audience for whom he or she writes. Mrs. Trotter's dramas provide an accurate picture of the likes and dislikes of the theatergoing public in the last decade of the seventeenth century and the first decade of the eighteenth century. That faithful reflection not only possesses its own interest but forms a substantial part of Mrs. Trotter's achievement.

Between 1696 and 1706 Catharine Trotter wrote four tragedies and one comedy. They are typical of hundreds of plays on the boards in those years. Let us consider first her ability as a tragic dramatist.

In her first tragedy, *Agnes de Castro,* she aimed at retaining the best elements of the heroic play while at the same time infusing the love-honor theme with the romantic, sentimental, and pathetic characteristics of the she-tragedy. The characters are highborn—royalty or nobility. The plot is based upon Spanish and Portuguese history. The language strives for the exclamatory, high heroic vein. Mrs. Trotter follows the trend to blank verse as the medium for tragedy, the rhymed couplet of Dryden's day having fallen into disfavor after 1680. There are strong roles for the hero and heroine and for the villain and villainess, two of the latter, in fact. Scenery is elaborate, costuming pseudo-historical. The tragedy contains a plentiful supply of gore: stabbings, swordplay, deaths, attempted suicide.

Agnes could well serve as a model heroine for the increasingly popular she-tragedy. In the moving final scene with the prince, as he affirms his never ending love for her, she hovers on the verge of a confession of true and passionate love for him. Death seals her lips before so immodest a confession can be uttered. The tone is definitely romantic and sentimental. Like Romeo, the prince prefers death to life without Agnes, and he is only dissuaded from suicide by a sense of his duty to assume the reins of kingship. The future is clear: the prince will remain ever faithful to the memory of his beloved, seeking solace in his duty to his country. On that note of high romance the play ends.

For all the blood and thunder, the madness, and the uncontrolled passions, motivation is realistically handled, the plot is well constructed, the action moves fast, and the play provides several big scenes for the whiter-than-white hero and heroine and for the blacker-than-black villain and villainess. There are

some choice opportunities, moreover, for the exhibition of the "rant" style of acting especially popular with the great tragic actresses of the day. In particular, the role of the arch-villainess Elvira gave Mrs. Knight a chance to show her mettle and to compete with the famous Mrs. Barry, the rival company's most distinguished actress of passionate heroine or deep-dyed villainess roles.

Mrs. Trotter's regard for the classical unities, shown here in her tightening of time and place, indicates her recognition of a new influence operating in the drama, an influence that within a few years will bring *Cato* before an audience receptive to classical tragedy. Although she follows rather closely the plot of Aphra Behn's novel, her source for the story of Agnes de Castro, Mrs. Trotter eliminates certain antecedent action in that novel, such as the prince's first marriage to Bianca and his early affair with Elvira, and confines the action to approximately twenty-four hours. In Behn's novel the time span is four to five years, the princess dies of grief, the prince and Agnes are then secretly married, Alvaro kills Agnes, and the prince spends the remainder of his life seeking revenge upon Alvaro. Mrs. Trotter's introduction of the princess's murder and the madness of Elvira and her confinement of events to the climactic moments in the lives of the principals add to the dramatic quality of the play.

The Fatal Friendship, Catharine Trotter's second tragedy, combines elements of the heroic play with the pathetic tragedy. The struggle between love and honor, the romantic secret marriage between the hero and heroine, the woes of the faithful, long-suffering wife, the sacrifice of the loyal comrade-in-arms for his friend, the adulterous marriage forced upon the hero, the revengeful spirit of the tigerish villainess, the plentiful spilling of blood—all constitute the stock-in-trade of 1690's tragedies.

Like all of Mrs. Trotter's tragedies, the main theme centers on the private lives of the hero and heroine. The infant son of the hero Gramont has been captured by pirates, and in order to prevent the child's death, Gramont contracts a bigamous marriage. Since the sin of bigamy would stain his character, he does not consummate this marriage. The emotional strength of the play lies in the psychological effects upon the domestic lives of the main characters who are faced with intolerable situations.

The plot provided Mrs. Barry and Mrs. Bracegirdle with the kinds of roles that their audiences expected, indeed demanded. It has been pointed out that these two virtuoso actresses appeared together in at least twenty new plays during the brief reign of William III and that these plays generally cast them in confrontation roles. The constant pairing of these two prima donnas of the stage resulted in a virtual typecasting: Mrs. Bracegirdle, the young, melting, virtuous heroine; Mrs. Barry, the lustful, passion-tossed, ranting and raving villainess. Of course, Mrs. Barry was also cast as the tragic heroine in her many varied roles; but when paired with Mrs. Bracegirdle, the two usually played confrontation scenes. They represented the Restoration audience's view of the opposite extremes of feminine psychology, and it is of interest to see a woman dramatist exploring the minds and emotions of her leading female characters. The psychological analysis is not unperceptive. (pp. xxv-xxix)

Mrs. Trotter's third tragedy, ***The Unhappy Penitent,*** like *Agnes de Castro,* combines heroics with the pathos of she-tragedy. Setting, plot, and characterization are typical of the heroic play, but the major emphasis is placed upon the misunderstandings that arise in the personal lives of the characters when love and honor come into conflict.

The dedication [see Additional Bibliography] deserves notice. In it the playwright sets forth her conception of tragedy, describing the special contributions to the genre by Dryden, Otway, Lee, and Shakespeare. She confesses to a weakness in her own play, namely, that it is chiefly concerned with the misfortunes of lovers, a subject chosen ''in Compliance with the effiminate taste of the Age.'' Questioning whether love be a proper subject for tragedy, she describes her play as designed to present a pair of doting lovers whose excess of passion is both their fault and their punishment, a lesson she feels may well move pity but does not conform to the Aristotelian standards of tragedy. Her critical comments illustrate her intellectual attainments, her wide reading, her literary eclecticism, and her perceptiveness of changing tastes in the theatre.

The Revolution of Sweden, Catharine Trotter's last tragedy, mixes love and politics and evidences her concern with and grasp of political events of the time. The source was René Aubert de Vertot's *Histoire des revolutions de Suède,* published in 1695. An English translation by J. Mitchel appeared the following year. The translator compared the history of Gustavus Vasa to political events taking place in England during the rein of William III. The fears that a foreign-born king might align himself with European powers, particularly with France, and thus threaten English independence lapsed with the advent of Anne to the throne in 1702. Yet in the same year, war with Louis XIV again broke out, and the Danish king's usurpation of Sweden could be likened to Louis' threat to the English throne. When Mrs. Trotter began writing *The Revolution of Sweden* around 1703, dramas with a libertarian theme were popular in the English theatre. It is to her credit that in this, her one attempt to write a drama based on a political theme, she has succeeded in fusing history and contemporary political feeling in an emotionally affecting tragedy. (pp. xxix-xxx)

[Trotter] refused to mold her heroine into a pattern of melting love. As the prologue, which may be from her own pen, declares:

> Invited by a Woman, every Guest
> No doubt, expects a soft Effeminate Feast,
> Has set his Appetite for tender Strains
> Of Maids forsaken, or Despairing Swains . . .
> but she by other means to pleas design'd. . . .
> To publick Virtues she'd your Souls incite.

Again, as in the dedication to *The Unhappy Penitent,* she questions whether love is a proper theme for tragedy. She holds the Aristotelian view while at the same time rather grudgingly adapting to the taste of the audience for a display of the grand passion. Hence the prologue guarantees, for the benefit of the ladies, a patriot

> In whose more tender Breast a virtuous Wife
> Rivals his Country, and divides his life.

Lastly, the ladies must surely approve a noble heroine

> Parting with Life, nay what we prize above,
> To save the Nation, vanquishing her love.

Catharine Trotter's one comedy, *Love at a Loss,* is a comedy of intrigue, with the addition of some elements of humorous comedy and of the comedy of it. It has been described [by Robert D. Hume; see Additional Bibliography] as a ''mixed'' intrigue play with new comedy leanings. Cleon and Bonsot are stock characters of the fop and the fool. Both roles suited

exactly the comic talents of Cibber and Pinkethman. The main title aptly describes the antiromantic view of marriage typical of Restoration comedy. While this play is no *Way of the World,* the witty combats between Beaumine and Lesbia possess a certain snap, crackle, and pop. Yet by the time this comedy was performed, reform is in the air, and roving sparks and gay coquettes are taking marriage vows. In fact, three marriages end this comedy. The voting contest, to determine which of two suitors the heroine should marry, is an original idea; and although the idea met with some censure, Mrs. Trotter protests in the dedication [see Additional Bibliography] that love and bright beauty alone are her theme. And she boasts that the wit is all her own, of pure English vintage, not beholden to the farce and the slapstick imported from abroad. This is far from a smutty comedy. It caters to that new formed taste that has taken place in those audiences that viewed with approval *The Beaux' Strategem,* and those that a few decades earlier had applauded *The Country Wife.*

Like hundreds of other comedies of the period, this one attempts to combine what cannot easily be combined: love and marriage are satirized, yet in the closing scene all the rakes and coquettes marry and presumably live happily ever after. Since Mrs. Trotter preferred the tragic to the comic muse, and considered this comedy a trifle, the generally high quality of wit herein comes as a surprise. The dialogue often sparkles. (pp. xxxi-xxxii)

Perhaps most significant about Catharine Trotter's achievement as a dramatist is the simple fact that she had the courage and the confidence in herself to pursue a writing career, including writing for the stage. Her plays, *although written by a woman,* were produced by the leading theatre companies of her day. The italics in the foregoing sentence are not unwarranted. (p. xxxiv)

Being a woman writer in that day constituted a hazard. The satire launched at females who dared take pen in hand was almost universal. Rarely did women writers put their names to their works. The title page of *Agnes de Castro,* for example, read, Written by a Young Lady. Even the dedication to this drama remained unsigned. Only one of Catharine Trotter's other plays bore her name on the title page, although in each instance she signed the dedication. *Agnes de Castro* is blessed with two prologues [see the excerpt by William Wycherley dated 1695], both of which beg indulgence of the play even though written by a woman. (p. xxxv)

What success she had as a dramatist . . . depended largely upon her astuteness in catching the taste of the audience, especially, one might surmise, the taste of ''the Ladies'' in that audience. The audience always knew, from the words of the prologue and epilogue, if the evening's entertainment had been authored by a woman, and in that case a special pitch for support was aimed at the women in attendance. Furthermore, Mrs. Trotter lavished her creative talents upon her women characters and did not lack ability to analyze with keen insight the female mind and heart. Her women are more realistic than her men. And her tragic heroines and villainesses gave scope to the distinctive talents of the best tragic actresses on the contemporary stage.

Two examples will serve to illustrate Mrs. Trotter's ability to portray female psychology. In *The Fatal Friendship* Felicia is secretly married to Gramont and the mother of their infant son. She discovers that her husband has taken a second wife, Lamira. Felicia does not know that he has contracted the bigamous marriage to save the life of their child, nor does she know that he has refused to consummate that marriage. Lamira is ignorant of the secret marriage of Felicia and Gramont. These facts come out in the course of a confrontation between these two women in love with the same man. (pop. xxxvi-xxxvii)

The second example is a lovers' quarrel in *The Unhappy Penitent*. The duke of Lorrain, the hero, and Margarite of Flanders, the heroine, passionately love each other. . . . Lorrain is jealous of the attentions paid Margarite by the king, to whom she was once affianced. The king has demanded the engagement continue, and the lovers move through disappointment and reproaches to a daring elopement. . . . (pp. xxxvii-xxxviii)

These sections from the two tragedies are a fair sample of Catharine Trotter's dramatic ability. The dialogue moves rapidly; the passion expressed suits the emotional situation; motive and conduct display a realistic view of human nature; the speech fits the character. From dozens of tragedies written in the late years of the seventeenth century and the early years of the eighteenth similar passages could be cited that would show these excerpts from Mrs. Trotter's pen holding up well by comparison. Her language noticeably lacks metaphor. Perhaps her mind, by bent and training logical, found a greater challenge in philosophic and critical discourse than in dramatic discourse. Her first biographer tells us that in her later years, after her marriage, she had considered revising her dramatic works, in particular, polishing the style. The cares of a wife and a mother and the long periods of absence from friends and acquaintances in the London literary world interfered with that intention. The fact remains that in a brief period of ten years, and before she reached the age of twenty-seven, Catharine Trotter had written five plays and seen them produced on the London stage, several of them performed by the leading actors and actresses of the time. In her day that was no small achievement for a woman writer. (p. xxxviii)

> *Edna L. Steeves, in an introduction to* The Plays of Mary Pix and Catharine Trotter: Catharine Trotter, *Vol. II, edited by Edna L. Steeves, Garland Publishing, Inc., 1982, pp. ix-xlii.*

CONSTANCE CLARK   (essay date 1986)

[*An American actress, director, playwright, and scholar, Clark is an authority on early English women dramatists. In the following excerpt, she surveys Trotter's major dramatic works, noting especially the author's conception of moral integrity and her marked interest in feminism.*]

If *Agnes de Castro* seems like a throwback in structure and type to earlier periods, there is one aspect about it which seems to point forward. Though the term "She-Tragedy" was coined to describe Nicholas Rowe's *The Tragedy of Jane Shore* in 1714, scholars now apply the term to Otway's plays as early as the 1680s, and to Thomas Southern's *The Fatal Marriage* (1694), which was an adaptation of Behn's novel, *The History of the Nun; or, the Fair Vow-Breaker*. *Agnes de Castro* seems of the mold, with its two heroines of unassailable virtue who meet tragic ends through no fault of their own. It has no hero per se; the Prince is well-meaning, but not particularly strong. The heroine does not even love him. Both Agnes and the Princess, however, are characters of virtue on a larger-than-live scale. Virtue supplants valor as an heroic criterion. While honor was a common preoccupation of heroines, the depth of the bond of friendship between Agnes and the Princess is extraordinary. Elvira's vengeful reaction on discovering her be-

loved loves another was a much more common reaction in the drama of the time than the Princess's mastery of her jealousy. The ideal of feminine friendship exemplifies the ideal promulgated by Trotter's idol, Katherine Philips, the concept of exquisite friendship between women.

The Fatal Friendship opened at Lincoln's Inn Fields in April or May 1698. Its dedication addressed her Royal Highness, Princess Anne of Denmark, later the Queen [see Additional Bibliography]. . . . The statement in the dedication which came under fire in [*Animadversion on Mr. Congreve's Late Answer to Mr. Collier;* see excerpt attributed to George Powell dated 1698] was likely the following:

> When a Woman appears in the World under any distinguishing Character, she must expect to be the mark of ill-nature; but most one, who seems desirous to recommend herself by what the other Sex think their peculiar prerogative.

Trotter also put forth her views of the purpose of the theatre, whose "End is most noble, to discourage Vice and recommend firm, unshaken Virtue." It is probably no coincidence that *The Fatal Friendship* was performed in the same month when Jeremy Collier's *A Short View of the Immorality and Prophaneness of the English Stage* was published. (pp. 76-8)

It is true that the real villain of [*The Fatal Friendship*] is poverty; the crisis is brought on by the hero's forced "sell-out" in marrying an heiress. This is definitely a theme anticipating the domestic drama to become prevalent in the next century. It is purely domestic in scale; no empires fall, only private lives are wrecked. The theme of the evils resulting from forced marriage hearkens back, however, to Aphra Behn, who, in her turn, was ahead of her time.

Perhaps it is a more difficult task to determine what made a play a success in that changing and fickle period than to explain the failures. *The Fatal Friendship* seems to have been championed as an example that "reformed" or moral drama could succeed. Making the hero guilty of no greater crime than impetuosity and parental disobedience (of an unreasonable parent at that) diminished the scope of the tragedy—which need not have been a fatal one. The murder is an accident. The "deus ex machina" ending of the father's sudden forgiveness and the reprieves is bitterly ironic in that it is just too late to save two essentially good young men. So, the end seems more of a mishap than a tragedy. Just what comprised tragedy bothered Trotter, and in the dedication to her next serious play [*The Unhappy Penitent;* see Additional Bibliography] she questioned whether romantic love was even an important enough concern for a tragedy.

Love at a Loss, Trotter's sole effort at comedy, opened at Drury Lane on November 23, 1700. In the dedication to Lady Sarah Piers [see Additional Bibliography], her close friend, Trotter apologizes for the play, and protects herself from too stringent criticism on three separate counts: she has never claimed to have any talent for comedy; she has not put much effort into the project; and it was ruined by sloppy printing. She claims that it was originally intended only as a comic subplot.

> I never thought of making any pretense to a talent for Comedy, but writ this when the Town had been little pleased with Tragedy intire, mingled with one of mine which since the taste has mended, appeared alone; and this lay by me a considerable time, till idleness reminded me of filling it up, thus it was placed with little care or concern for the success; not intending to establish my fame by it.

One of the three plots running through the comedy was probably intended to run parallel to that of *The Fatal Friendship.* (pp. 82-4)

Of the three plot lines which wove through *Love at a Loss,* it is probable that the more nearly serious and the one in which the female character is most fully developed was that intended to run along the plot of *The Fatal Friendship.* The Miranda/Constant plot is merely an exercise in juxtaposing two opposite humorous characters. While Lucinda's fear at being called to account for indiscreet letters written in her youth has an autobiographical ring of truth in Trotter's case, the dilemma is too slight to be used parallel to a theme with which Trotter obviously wished to make a moral statement. The lost revised version of the play may have strengthened the dominance of Lesbia's story with its improbable theme of a seduced woman who gets her man in the end. The loophole which spares Lesbia the stigma of a fallen woman is that of pre-contract, betrothal being a much stronger contract then than in modern times. But her salvation is also dependent on an enlightened, liberal partner, i.e., a reformed rake. No "Gay, roving Spark" of Restoration comedy would have married a fallen woman—even one he himself had despoiled. (p. 86)

The Unhappy Penitent, like *Agnes de Castro,* presented two highminded women who are involved with the same man and yet maintain a friendship. This time the tragedy ended in renunciation, not death. The prologue had promised: "You've a bloodless Tragedy; / Our Authoress cannot let her Heroe dye." Trotter's choice of a story based on an historical incident in which none of the principals had been killed precluded the slew of corpses that usually ended a tragedy. Trotter presented a case of basically decent people caught up in conflicts of interest, resulting in frustration and unhappiness, but without any dastardly deeds being perpetrated. What can seem from today's viewpoint contrived and priggish may well have been conscious striving on Trotter's part for a refinement of the concept of moral integrity.

Trotter's conscious effort to mold the plot and characterizations to demonstrate a moral, in keeping with her concept of the drama as a tool for instruction rather than as a mirror of life, may account for the effect of unnaturalness.

The Revolution of Sweden, Trotter's last play, was begun in 1703, but not produced until 1706. Trotter had sent an outline to Congreve for his comments, although he himself had quit writing for the stage, presumably on account of his disappointment over the tepid reception of his masterpiece, *The Way of the World* (1700). His advice [see excerpt dated 1703] was thorough and practical, but judging from the finished play, Trotter did not implement all of his suggestions. (pp. 89-90)

The play was not a success, and Trotter added a preface to the published version [see excerpt dated 1706], defending it against the critics who, she claimed, never even saw the play, or if they were bodily present were not attentive. She blamed the taste of the audience, with which she was writing at cross-purposes, and reaffirmed her moral premise.

The dedication to Harriot Godolphin was a feminist statement about the intellectual equality of women.

> There are so great Difficulties, and such general Discouragements, to those of our Sex who would improve their Minds, and employ their Time in any Science or useful Art, that there cannot be a more distinguishing Mark of a Free and Beneficent Spirit, than openly to condemn that ill-grounded Custom,

by giving Countenance and Protection to those who have attempted against it . . . such an Encouraging Indulgence to the Endeavors of our Sex, initiated by many of your Ladyship's Quality, and Merit, it might incite some Greater geniuses among us to exert themselves, and change our Emulation of a Neighboring Nation's Fopperies, to the commendable Ambition of Rivalling them in their illustrious women.

The prologue warned the audience that they were in for something of a lecture. Trotter had replaced passion in her heroines with patriotism.

> Invited by a Woman, every Guest,
> No doubt, expects a soft, Effeminate Feast
>   *   *   *
> They must a Noble Heroine Approve,
> Parting with Life, nay what we prize Above,
> To save the Nation, vanquishing her love.
>
> (p. 91)

The Revolution of Sweden was Trotter's only play after she had redirected her literary interests to philosophical treatises, and religious tracts. Her first, *The Defence of Locke's Essay of Human Understanding,* was written in 1702. By this time she was determined to marry a clergyman, and her correspondence shows she was being courted by two of them even while she was writing this play. The love between the leading characters, Constantia and Arwide, is austere, verging on the platonic. Both the heroines function on a higher plane than that of romantic love, which is not surprising since Trotter had rejected it as insufficient for tragic scope. Congreve had warned against "Harangues," and yet this was just the direction in which Trotter was directing her efforts—towards the sermonizing lecture of discourse. Such is the scene in the Viceroy's camp when Constantia engages in polemical discussion with the Archbishop, literally bringing the action to a standstill.

This play is Trotter's strongest feminine statement. The women represented are no longer even represented as dependent upon the support of a peer; each is a tower of strength unto herself. The two heroines embody two different aspects of excellence—Constantia intellectual prowess and Christina physical courage. They are also exquisitely moral. The epilogue casts an aspersion, albeit humorous, on the perils of trusting a man's promise. She is referring to a promised but undelivered prologue, but the double entendre is clear:

> Our Authoress, trusting to a Brother's Pen,
> As who among us trust no faithless Men,
> Has been deceived—But that I need not say.
> She took his word, and then—you know your way.

Although it suited neither the taste of its time nor ours, one can consider *The Revolution of Sweden* a success in the light of Trotter's perception of the purpose of the theatre. It was a platform for her feminist theories and a sort of sermon "vivant." (pp. 94-5)

> *Constance Clark, "Catherine Trotter," in her* Three Augustan Women Playwrights, *Peter Lang, 1986, pp. 35-95.*

ADDITIONAL BIBLIOGRAPHY

Carter, Herbert. "Three Women Dramatists of the Restoration." *The Bookman's Journal* XIII, No. 51 (December 1925): 91-7.

Cites *Fatal Friendship* as the best of Trotter's plays, but faults it as a specimen of tragedy. The critic concludes: "It is difficult to imagine what endowed Mrs. Trotter with distinction as a dramatist in her own time and set her above [Mary Delariviere Manley and Mary Pix]. She had not the poetic ability of the one nor the technical skill of the other. The secret probably lay in her vigorous and charming little personality."

The Female Wits; or, The Triumvirate of Poets at Rehearsal. London: William Turner, 1704, 67 p.
   Anonymous 1696 drama in which Trotter, Mary Pix, and Mary Delariviere Manley are harshly lampooned for being female dramatists. Trotter, who appears in the play as Calista, one that "assumes to her self the Name of a Critick," is particularly censured as a pretender to learning and a dramatist of little merit.

Foxton, Rosemary. "Delariviere Manley and 'Astrea's Vacant Throne'." *Notes and Queries* n.s. 33, No. 1 (March 1986): 41-2.
   Argues that Mary Delariviere Manley's commendatory poem to Trotter in *Agnes de Castro* (see poem dated 1696) provides strong evidence of a literary rivalry between the two authors.

Harman, P. "To the Author, on Her Tragedy, Call'd *Fatal Friendship*." In *Fatal Friendship*, by Catharine Trotter, pp. iii-iv. London: Francis Saunders, 1698.
   Commendatory poem honoring Trotter as a supporter of the "sinking Stage."

Hume, Robert D. *The Development of English Drama in the Late Seventeenth Century*, pp. 410ff. Oxford: Oxford University Press, Clarendon Press, 1976.
   Scattered brief references to Trotter, noting especially her role in the emergence of Augustan drama.

Lock, F. P. "Astraea's 'Vacant Throne': The Successors of Aphra Behn." In *Woman in the 18th Century and Other Essays*, edited by Paul Fritz and Richard Morton, pp. 25-36. Toronto and Sarasota: Hakkert, 1976.
   Studies *Agnes de Castro*, chiefly as it reveals the legacy of Aphra Behn's dramatic works.

Maison, Margaret. "Pope and Two Learned Nymphs." *The Review of English Studies* n.s. XXIX, No. 116 (November 1978): 405-14.
   Links Trotter with several literary portraits of young women in the works of Alexander Pope, Edward Young, and others.

[Manley, Mary Delariviere]. *The Adventures of Rivella; or, The History of the Author of the Atalantis*, pp. 64ff. London, 1714.
   Fictionalized autobiography in which Trotter, who appears as "sister Authoress" Calista, is accused of craftiness and duplicity in her dealings with the author and the public—aspersions later discredited by Thomas Birch in the biographical introduction to *The Works of Mrs. Catharine Cockburn: Theological, Moral, Dramatic, and Poetical* (1751).

Morgan, Fidelis. "Catherine Trotter." In her *The Female Wits: Women Playwrights on the London Stage, 1660-1720*, pp. 24-31. London: Virago, 1981.
   Surveys Trotter's life and literary career, emphasizing her poetry and philosophical works.

Nicoll, Allardyce. "The Theatre." In his *A History of Restoration Drama, 1660-1700*, 3d ed., pp. 1-74. Cambridge: Cambridge University Press, 1940.
   Notices *Fatal Friendship* as an example of the contemporary vogue for elaborate stage scenery.

Pilkington, Mary. *Memoirs of Celebrated Female Characters*, pp. 120ff. London: Albion Press, 1804.
   Approaches Trotter as a model of feminine virtue, claiming she is "particularly to be admired for relinquishing the flattering distinctions of an author, to fulfill those duties which are attached to the character of a wife; and she excites a greater degree of interest, superintending the education of her children, than when she was metaphysically defending the opinions of Mr. Lock."

Sutherland, James. "Drama (I)." In his *English Literature of the Late Seventeenth Century*, pp. 32-87. Oxford History of English Literature, edited by Bonamy Dobrée and Norman Davis, Vol. VI. New York and Oxford: Oxford University Press, 1969.
   Labels Trotter one of the "dreary exponents" of late-seventeenth-century tragedy.

Trotter, Catharine. "To Her Royal Highness the Princess." In her *Fatal Friendship*, pp. i-ii. London: Francis Saunders, 1698.
   Dedicatory epistle in which Trotter claims of *Fatal Friendship*: "its End is the most noble, to discourage Vice, and recommend a firm unshaken Virtue."

——. "To the Honourable Lady Piers." In her *Love at a Loss; or, Most Votes Carry It*, pp. i-iii. London: William Turner, 1701.
   Dedicatory letter of *Love at a Loss*, presenting Trotter's contention that she never pretended to a talent for comedy, spent little time composing the work, and had her intentions misrepresented by poor printing.

——. "To the Right Honourable Charles, Lord Hallifax." In her *The Unhappy Penitent*, pp. i-iv. London: William Turner, 1701.
   Dedicatory letter in which Trotter describes her conception of tragedy, adding her belief that the subject of *The Unhappy Penitent*, "the misfortune of Lovers," is an insufficient plot motive.

Williams, Jane. "The Poetesses, A. D. 1725-1750: Catherine Cockburn." In her *The Literary Woman of England*, pp. 170-88. London: Saunders, Otley, 1861.
   Biographical sketch, with emphasis on Trotter's religious beliefs. Williams finds fault with Trotter's plays but praises her intellect and zeal for moral reform: "Her reasoning powers, her comprehensive knowledge, her acute discrimination, her steadfast love of truth, and her calm, clear sense of right and wrong, always render her a formidable champion. Her eloquence has the force of manly argument, with the charm of feminine persuasion."

William Wycherley

1640?-1716

English dramatist, poet, and aphorist.

One of the foremost dramatists of the Restoration, Wycherley combined irreverent social satire and complex verbal wit to create comedies of lasting interest and appeal. His plays have attracted much controversy over the years for their candid treatment of moral—particularly sexual—attitudes and behavior, with the result that Wycherley has been alternately hailed as a force for moral regeneration and denounced as a purveyor of moral indecency. Nowhere is this controversy more apparent than with regard to the play considered Wycherley's masterpiece, *The Country-Wife,* which has garnered critical superlatives from William Archer's rejection of it as "the most bestial play in all literature" to John Palmer's praise of it as "the most perfect farce in English dramatic literature."

Wycherley was born in Shropshire and was tutored by his father until the age of fifteen. At that time the elder Wycherley (an ardent Royalist who disapproved of the strict Puritan educational system which prevailed during Oliver Cromwell's Protectorate) sent his son to France that he might continue his education and learn the graces of a gentleman in a cultured, aristocratic society. While abroad, Wycherley converted to Roman Catholicism. In 1660, with the Restoration imminent, he returned to England, undertaking a brief stint of legal studies in London before entering Queen's College, Oxford. Here he studied philosophy (though he left without taking a degree) and reconverted to Protestantism. Wycherley returned to the study of law at the Inner Temple, one of the Inns of Court in London, but his interest soon palled, though the fascination he developed for London society did not. Although little is known of Wycherley's activities during the next several years, it is surmised that after abandoning his law studies, he fulfilled various minor duties in governmental and military service and may have participated in a naval battle against the Dutch.

Although the composition dates of Wycherley's plays are conjectural, it is known that his first, *Love in a Wood; or, St. James's Park,* was performed in 1671 at the Theatre Royal in London. The play was immediately successful and Wycherley attracted the notice and approbation of London society, including that of Barbara Villiers Palmer, Charles II's mistress and soon Wycherley's own. Through her influence and his own talent and personal charm, Wycherley quickly became a favorite at court and in fashionable literary circles, his popularity continuing unabated during the next few years as his remaining plays were produced. But in 1678 Wycherley contracted a debilitating disease (the nature of which is unknown); its effects plagued him for the rest of his life, perhaps accounting for the meagerness of his subsequent literary production and probably contributing to the memory lapses from which he suffered in later years. The king provided Wycherley with the wherewithal to journey to France to aid his recovery and upon his return the following year he was offered the post of tutor to the king's son, the Duke of Richmond. Before Wycherley could begin his duties, however, he met and secretly married the widowed Lady Laetitia-Isabella, Countess of Drogheda. It was a short marriage, but one that had disastrous effects on Wycherley's life: both the marriage and the surreptitious manner in which it was executed displeased Charles, who withdrew his favor

from Wycherley; and the countess's death soon afterwards left Wycherley embroiled in endless and ruinously expensive litigation concerning the disposal of his wife's considerable fortune. Reduced finally to destitution, Wycherley was incarcerated in debtors' prison. He was released in 1686 by James II, who had succeeded to the throne following Charles's death the previous year. According to an oft-repeated anecdote, James, pleased by a court performance of *The Plain-Dealer,* had inquired after the author. Upon being informed of Wycherley's predicament, James immediately settled the dramatist's debts and bestowed a pension on him, which unfortunately came to an abrupt end a few years later when James was forced to abdicate.

Continually beset by financial difficulties, Wycherley henceforth divided his time between Shropshire and London. When he was in his sixties he befriended Alexander Pope, then a fledgling poet in his teens. At this time Wycherley was writing again for the first time in years, and he requested that Pope, whose genius he already recognized, aid him in polishing and, where necessary, revising his verses. Pope obliged, but at length the friendship cooled as Wycherley, whose poetry never matched the ease and wit of his plays, came to resent Pope's highhanded revisions and frequently supercilious comments. Nevertheless, Pope's 1729 edition of Wycherley's posthumous works indicates his continuing interest in the revision, as many of the poems included in the volume are in a different form from the versions published in Lewis Theobald's earlier edition.

Just days before his death Wycherley remarried under circumstances never adequately explained. Wycherley was as usual in financial trouble, so it is possible that he willingly entered into a reciprocal agreement with the young woman whereby he could gain the immediate funds necessary to pay his debts, with the understanding that she would be repaid upon his death with a jointure on his father's estate. This scheme had the added attraction of thwarting Wycherley's nephew, whom he disliked, but to whom he was required to bequeath the estate proper by the dictates of his father's will. There is some evidence to suggest that Wycherley, who in his old age suffered from a failing memory and intermittent periods of confusion, may have actually been trapped or intimidated into the marriage, but the truth of the matter remains unknown. Wycherley died a Catholic, having reconverted yet again, and was buried at St. Paul's, Covent Garden, in London.

To better understand Wycherley's work, it is important to place him in a historical literary context. Wycherley was both a product and an exponent of the Restoration, that period of social license which, following as it did the stifling atmosphere of the Puritan interregnum, resulted in a literature renowned for its sophisticated urbanity and licentious wit. In his own comedies, Wycherley both celebrated the hedonistic cynicism of aristocratic London society and satirized its hypocrisies and follies. His dramatic canon consists of only four plays: *Love in a Wood, The Gentleman Dancing-Master, The Country-Wife,* and *The Plain-Dealer*. In subject and incident, these plays conform to the standard conventions of the Restoration comedy of manners, with the emphasis on sexual intrigue and mistaken identity. Licentiousness, a dominant feature of all Restoration literature, is particularly evident in Wycherley's work. He dealt with sexual topics candidly—indeed, delightedly—so that the bawdiness of his plays has become nearly legendary. Amply represented in Wycherley's work are such stock Restoration characters as the roguish wit; the deceived cuckold; the conceited, ineffectual fop; and the falsely pious hypocrite. Wycherley's plays are replete with wit, a quality very highly prized during the Restoration, by which was meant not just humor or irony, but a keenness of perception that recognized the relationship between seemingly dissimilar things, a discernment of and penetration to the heart of a matter—all often expressed in elaborately fanciful similes. Such linguistic dexterity is a preeminent feature of Wycherley's work. His dialogue is invariably clever and fluent; his characters dazzle with their adroit style and verbal poise. Indeed, Wycherley has sometimes been faulted for being too clever, for occasionally sacrificing consistency of characterization for the sake of witty repartee. Wycherley's work is also characterized by pithy social satire—his most common targets hypocrisy and pretense, his most severe condemnation reserved for those who purport to be what they are not.

Critics disagree as to whether it is more accurate to identify the dramas as satire or farce. Although undoubtedly they contain elements of both, the issue leads to the question of authorial intent and the degree to which the plays should be taken as serious literature. Wycherley's work has frequently been deemed the most thematically serious of Restoration comedies; some twentieth-century scholars have argued that the plays cannot properly be categorized as typical Restoration comedies of manners, which are generally construed as clever and amusing but of negligible import. Such critics hold that beyond the witty banter and sexual innuendo of Wycherley's work lies the eternal theme of the individual in conflict with society, a theme expressed most successfully and cogently through Horner of *The*

Country-Wife and Manly of *The Plain-Dealer*, characters who struggle for sexual and personal freedom. While much recent criticism has been devoted to the exploration of this theme, particularly with regard to its implications in determining Wycherley's view of morality, many other commentators believe that such a critical approach is invalid because it is unwarranted by the evidence of the plays themselves. This debate is neatly embodied in twentieth-century critical discussion of *The Country-Wife*.

Louis Kronenberger has called *The Country-Wife* a "panoramic study of sex," and indeed a prominent aspect of the play is its sexual licentiousness. The principal plot concerns the successful scheme of the protagonist Horner to convince the men of London that he is impotent in order that he may more easily gain access to their wives. The play abounds with sexual innuendo; Wycherley's bawdiest scenes, those which have caused him to be denounced as "indecent," achieve their effect not through objectionable language or particularly suggestive action, but through witty double entendres. *The Country-Wife* was very popular during the seventeenth century as an uproarious comedy. Such serious intent as was recognized revolved around the play's satiric jabs at the hypocrisy of those who publicly profess chastity but privately enjoy extramarital affairs, and to a lesser extent around Wycherley's implicit condemnation of men who abuse or neglect their wives. Although *The Country-Wife* is deemed the bawdiest play in an age notorious for its licentiousness, it was not generally considered offensive until the latter part of the eighteenth century, when changing social and sexual mores rendered it unacceptable to the public. The last performance of the play as Wycherley had written it, until the twentieth century, was in 1753. A decade later, actor and dramatist David Garrick produced an adaptation of the play called *The Country Girl* (1766)—a considerably tamer version that deleted any mention of adultery—and it was this adaptation that was performed in the remainder of the eighteenth and throughout the nineteenth centuries. In the latter century such critics as Charles Lamb attempted to defend *The Country-Wife* by asserting that, though the world of the play is undoubtedly an immoral one, it is also a patently unrealistic one, and as such should not be subjected to the usual moral criteria. This defense was not on the whole considered valid; the prevailing nineteenth-century critical view of the unexpurgated *Country-Wife* is summed up in Lord Macaulay's contemptuous words: "In truth, Wycherley's indecency is protected against the critics as a skunk is protected against the hunters. It is safe, because it is too filthy to handle, and too noisome to even approach."

Although sporadic condemnation of *The Country-Wife*'s lewdness has lasted well into the twentieth century, in general such objections have lost their force. However, modern criticism is still concerned with the play's morality, though the nature of that concern has shifted focus. In the world of the play, which Kronenberger has described as "a society almost wholly lacking in either conscience or heart," what view of morality did Wycherley endorse? Against what, or whom, is the satire directed, the individual Horner or the society against which he rebels? To what extent, if at all, is Horner representative of his creator? Critical opinion diverges widely on these issues. Many scholars view Horner as a hero, a natural man who strikes a blow for social and sexual freedom through his rejection of narrow-minded hypocrisy and restrictive social mores. Others believe that Horner is the chief villain in what Rose A. Zimbardo has called a "world of inverted moral values," and that Wycherley intended him as a selfish, offensive example of such in a play that is essentially a satire on lust. The debate has extended to question Wycherley's moralistic intent with other characters in the play: Pinchwife has been variously interpreted as a buffoon and as an active force for evil; Margery Pinchwife as a rustic innocent, a deceiving schemer, and a "true pagan"; Alithea as a fool and as the play's "moral standard." In short, does *The Country-Wife* expound a "unique human significance that lifts [it] to the level of great art" as David M. Vieth asserted in a 1966 article, or is the play simply, as Robert D. Hume would have it, "an immensely enjoyable play in which we take almost nothing seriously"? Hume, in dismissing the moral controversy, has argued further that the play is closer to farce than to satire, and as such contains no moral message: "Delightfully bawdy and funny *The Country-Wife* is, profound it is not, and only a prude, a hypocrite, or a stuffy academician would have it otherwise." The very nature of the play thus remains unresolved, as the issue of Wycherley's morality is still as much a critical stumbling block, though for different reasons, as it was in the eighteenth and nineteenth centuries.

That, whatever else it is, *The Country-Wife* is "delightfully bawdy and funny" is clear to most modern critics, but such is not the case with Wycherley's "problem play," *The Plain-Dealer*. Ostensibly a comedy, this play's harsh satire and omnipresent sense of bitterness have disturbed many scholars. *The Plain-Dealer* is derived from Molière's *Le misanthrope* (1666), but conspicuously lacks the note of hope and idealism present in the French play. The plain dealer of the title is Manly, whose aversion to hypocrisy and pretense is extreme to the point of monomania. Manly's intense misanthropy is unrelieved by any sense of hope or the possibility of betterment, the satire of the play seeming to proceed less from a desire to instruct or ameliorate than from a pervading atmosphere of pessimism and despair. Seventeenth-century critics, after an initial period of surprise at the unconventionality of the play, preferred *The Plain-Dealer* to all of Wycherley's other plays. It was primarily on this play that Wycherley's early reputation as a moral satirist rested. The bluntness of the principal character and the savagery of his condemnation of his society were seen as a proper and courageous way to "lash this crying age," as William Congreve phrased it in his prologue to *Love for Love* (1695). Wycherley himself became known admiringly as the Plain Dealer or as "Manly Wycherley." Contemporaries lauded the fierce, straightforward satire of the play: John Dryden called it "one of the most bold, most general, and most useful Satyres which has ever been presented on the English Theatre," and John Dennis referred to it as "that excellent Play, which is a most instructive, and a most noble satire upon the Hypocrisy and Villainy of Mankind."

Later critics, not matching this early enthusiasm, have found *The Plain-Dealer* admirable on many counts, but have stopped short of wholehearted approbation, a hesitation attributable to what many have viewed as the play's nihilism. Much of the action of the play is motivated by heartless betrayal and the desire for revenge, perpetrated not only by "wicked" characters but by the protagonist Manly as well. Thus, just as Horner of *The Country-Wife* admits of conflicting interpretations, so *The Plain-Dealer*'s Manly has been found ambiguous. In his cynicism and anger, Manly has been seen—as the seventeenth century saw him—as the one honest, upright individual in a world of corruption and deceit. Alternatively, he has been regarded as a raging, irrational misanthrope whose own cruelty and inhumanity is no different from that of the world he despises. As with *The Country-Wife*, Wycherley's authorial

intent has been called into question. Is the satire of the play directed against society, Manly, or both? How can what Derek Hughes has described as Manly's simultaneous "heroic magnanimity and anarchic brutality" be reconciled? Many critics suspect that the real misanthrope of the play is not Manly but Wycherley himself. *The Plain-Dealer* lacks the detachment of *The Country-Wife*, the sense that the dramatist was able to maintain his distance even while he knew and deplored his characters' follies. It has thus been suggested that, as Wycherley's loss of perspective resulted in bitter invective rather than wit or satire, the play fails as a work of dramatic art. As Bonamy Dobrée has expressed it, Wycherley's "laughter affords no release, for it is too deeply cynical." Even with these faults—perhaps in part because of the ambiguity they create—*The Plain-Dealer* continues to fascinate. The bitterness of the work, though possibly too extreme for comedy, is both sincere and compelling; as Dobrée has said: "The play reads like a cry of despair."

Wycherley's other two plays are considered decidedly less proficient than *The Country-Wife* and *The Plain-Dealer*, though they are often studied for the light they shed on Wycherley's dramatic development. The most notable quality of *Love in a Wood* is the multiplicity of its action. Plot and subplot, intrigue and counter intrigue, combine to make *Love in a Wood* a lively—if confusing—play. The main plot turns on the fairly standard devices of mistaken identities and misunderstandings in love, while the numerous minor characters in the subplots afford much opportunity for satire against some of Wycherley's favorite targets—particularly the hypocrite and the would-be wit. Seventeenth-century critics responded favorably to the play's exuberance, but subsequent commentators have rendered a more reserved judgment. Although it is generally agreed that *Love in a Wood* shows promise of the wit and verbal dexterity that came to fruition in *The Country-Wife*, most critics believe that the play is damaged by a lack of structural unity, for the many plot lines and characters are insufficiently integrated. *The Gentleman Dancing-Master* met with a tepid reception initially and is still considered Wycherley's weakest play. This is principally due to its paucity of dramatic action; unlike Wycherley's other plays, which are crowded with movement and suspense, *The Gentleman Dancing-Master* has a single, simple plot, the outcome of which is never in doubt. The play also lacks the high-spirited energy of Wycherley's others, leading critics to note that while *The Gentleman Dancing-Master* is his least "indecent" play, it is also his least inspired.

Notwithstanding the critical contention that surrounds many aspects of Wycherley's plays, there is universal agreement with regard to the merit of his poetry, which is thought markedly inferior. Consisting mainly of satiric and bawdy pieces, the poems are thought of interest only insofar as they display, as A. M. Friedson described it in a 1967 essay, "the complex, inverted puritanism of Wycherley's vision, which . . . was likely to manifest itself in rakish amorality at one moment and moralistic indignation the next." Stylistically, the poetry fails largely because of its lack of rhythm, though the verses have also been faulted for being heavy-handed and forced. Hoxie Neale Fairchild has called them "harsh, contorted, and often incoherent."

Allardyce Nicoll has remarked that in Wycherley's work "the roué joins hands with the moralist." His work is a unique blend of farce and satire, sexual licentiousness and moral intent, encompassing the light-hearted irony of *The Country-Wife* and the trenchant savagery of *The Plain-Dealer*, the whole capped with adroit repartee and verbal wit. Perhaps then it is Wycherley's own conflicting characteristics that inspire such divergent critical responses and that account for the fact that so few critics remain indifferent to his work. H. A. Taine and John Dennis reflect this in their respective assessments of "William Wycherley, the coarsest writer who ever polluted the stage," and of William Wycherley, "the greatest Comick Wit that ever *England* bred."

PRINCIPAL WORKS

Hero and Leander in Burlesque   (poetry)   1669
Love in a Wood; or, St. James's Park   (drama)   1671
The Gentleman Dancing-Master   (drama)   1672
The Country-Wife   (drama)   1675
The Plain-Dealer   (drama)   1676
Miscellany Poems   (poetry)   1704
The Posthumous Works of William Wycherley, Esq., in Prose and Verse   (poetry and aphorisms)   1728
*The Posthumous Works of William Wycherley, Esq., in Prose and Verse, Vol. II   (poetry, aphorisms, and letters)   1729
The Complete Works of William Wycherley. 4 vols. (dramas, poetry, aphorisms, and letters)   1924

*This work contains revisions of some poems included in the earlier *Posthumous Works of William Wycherley, Esq., in Prose and Verse* which were undertaken by the editor.

WILLIAM WYCHERLEY (play date 1676)

[*The following excerpt is taken from a scene in* The Plain-Dealer, *first performed in 1676, in which Olivia and her cousin Eliza discuss their reactions to a performance of* The Country-Wife. *Wycherley uses the dialogue to comment ironically on those who professed to be shocked at the play's indecency. As the excerpt begins, Olivia and Plausible are in the midst of denigrating their acquaintances.*]

[*Olivia.*] Then, for her conduct, she was seen at the *Country Wife* after the first day. There's for you, my lord.

Plausible. But, madam, she was not seen to use her fan all the play long, turn aside her head, or by a conscious blush discover more guilt than modesty.

Olivia. Very fine! Then you think a woman modest that sees the hideous *Country Wife* without blushing, or publishing her detestation of it? D'ye hear him, cousin?

Eliza. Yes, and am, I must confess, something of his opinion; and think, that as an over-conscious fool at a play, by endeavouring to show the author's want of wit, exposes his own to more censure, so may a lady call her own modesty in question, by publicly cavilling with the poet's. For all those grimaces of honour and artificial modesty disparage a woman's real virtue, as much as the use of white and red does the natural complexion: and you must use very, very little, if you would have it thought your own.

Olivia. Then you would have a woman of honour with passive looks, ears, and tongue, undergo all the hideous obscenity she hears at nasty plays.

Eliza. Truly, I think a woman betrays her want of modesty, by showing it publicly in a playhouse, as much as a man does his want of courage by a quarrel there; for the truly modest and stout say least, and are least exceptious, especially in public.

Olivia. O hideous, cousin! this cannot be your opinion. But you are one of those who have the confidence to pardon the filthy play.

Eliza. Why, what is there of ill in't, say you?

Olivia. O fy! fy! fy! would you put me to the blush anew? call all the blood into my face again? But to satisfy you then; first, the clandestine obscenity in the very name of *Horner*.

Eliza. Truly, 'tis so hidden, I cannot find it out, I confess.

Olivia. O horrid! Does it not give you the rank conception or image of a goat, or town-bull, or a satyr? nay, what is yet a filthier image than all the rest, that of a eunuch?

Eliza. What then? I can think of a goat, a bull, or a satyr, without any hurt.

Olivia. Ay; but cousin, one cannot stop there.

Eliza. I can, cousin.

Olivia. O no; for when you have those filthy creatures in your head once, the next thing you think, is what they do; as their defiling of honest men's beds and couches, rapes upon sleeping and waking country virgins under hedges, and on haycocks. Nay, further—

Eliza. Nay, no farther, cousin. We have enough of your comment on the play, which will make me more ashamed than the play itself.

Olivia. O, believe me, 'tis a filthy play! and you may take my word for a filthy play as soon as another's. But the filthiest thing in that play, or any other play, is—

Eliza. Pray keep it to yourself, if it be so.

Olivia. No, faith, you shall know it; I'm resolved to make you out of love with the play. I say, the lewdest, filthiest thing is his *china;* nay, I will never forgive the beastly author his *china.* He has quite taken away the reputation of poor china itself, and sullied the most innocent and pretty furniture of a lady's chamber; insomuch that I was fain to break all my defiled vessels. You see I have none left; nor you, I hope.

Eliza. You'll pardon me, I cannot think the worse of my china for that of the playhouse.

Olivia. Why, you will not keep any now, sure! 'Tis now as unfit an ornament for a lady's chamber as the pictures that come from Italy and other hot countries; as appears by their nudities, which I always cover, or scratch out, wheresoe'er I find 'em. But china! out upon't, filthy china! nasty, debauched china!

Eliza. All this will not put me out of conceit with china, nor the play, which is acted to-day, or another of the same beastly author's, as you call him, which I'll go see. (pp. 113-14)

> William Wycherley, *"'The Plain Dealer'," in* The Dramatic Works of Wycherley, Congreve, Vanbrugh, and Farquhar, *edited by Leigh Hunt, Edward Moxon, 1840, pp. 102-42.*

JOHN DRYDEN (essay date 1684)

[*Regarded by many scholars as the father of modern English poetry and criticism, Dryden dominated literary life in England during the last four decades of the seventeenth century. Through*

*deliberately and comprehensively refining the language of Eliz-
abethan England in all his works, he developed an expressive,
universal diction which has had immense impact on the development of speech and writing in Great Britain and North America.
Although recognized as a prolific and accomplished Restoration
dramatist, Dryden wrote a number of satirical poems and critical
writings which are acknowledged as his greatest literary achievements. In his poems, notably* Absalom and Achitophel *(1681)*,
Religio Laici *(1682), and* The Hind and the Panther *(1687), he
displayed an irrepressible wit and forceful line of argument which
later satirists adopted as their model. In his criticism, particularly*
Of Dramatic Poesy *(1668), Dryden originated the extended form
of objective, practical analysis that has come to characterize most
modern criticism. In the following excerpt from an essay originally
published in 1684, Dryden renders his oft-quoted judgment of* The
Plain-Dealer.]

Comedy is both excellently instructive, and extreamly pleasant:
Satyre lashes Vice into Reformation, and humor represents
folly so as to render it ridiculous. Many of our present Writers
are eminent in both these kinds; and particularly the Author of
the **Plain Dealer,** whom I am proud to call my Friend, has
oblig'd all honest and vertuous Men, by one of the most bold,
most general, and most useful Satyres which has ever been
presented on the English Theater. (p. 419)

> *John Dryden, "The Author's Apology for Heroique
> Poetry, and Poetique Licence," in his* Dryden: The
> Dramatic Works, *Volume III, edited by Montague
> Summers, 1932. Reprint by Gordian Press, 1968,
> pp. 416-24.*

JEREMY COLLIER   (essay date 1698)

[*An English clergyman, Collier is best remembered for his as-
tringent dramatic study* A Short View of the Immorality and
Profaneness of the English Stage. *In the following excerpt from
that work, Collier includes* The Country-Wife *and* The Plain-
Dealer *in his condemnation of dramatic impropriety.*]

[In treating the immodesty of the stage,] I hope the Reader
does not expect that I should set down Chapter and Page, and
give him the Citations at Length. To do this would be a very
unacceptable and Foreign Employment. Indeed the Passages,
many of them, are in no Condition to be handled: He that is
desirous to see these Flowers let him do it in their own Soil:
'Tis my business rather to kill the *Root* than *Transplant* it. But
that the Poets may not complain of Injustice; I shall point to
the Infection at a Distance, and refer in General to *Play* and
Person.

Now among the Curiosities of this kind we may reckon Mrs.
Pinchwife, Horner, and Lady *Fidget* in the **Country Wife**; Widdow *Blackacre* and *Olivia* in the **Plain Dealer.** These, tho' not
all the exceptionable *Characters,* are the most remarkable. I'm
sorry the Author should stoop his Wit thus Low, and use his
Understanding so unkindly. Some People appear Coarse, and
Slovenly out of Poverty: They can't well go to the Charge of
Sense. They are Offensive like Beggars for want of Neces-
saries. But this is none of the *Plain Dealer*'s case; He can
afford his Muse a better Dress when he pleases. But then the
Rule is, where the Motive is the less, the Fault is the greater.
(pp. 3-4)

Horner is horridly Smutty, and *Harcourt* false to his Friend
who used him kindly. In the **Plain Dealer** *Freeman* talks coarsely,
cheats the Widdow, debauches her Son, and makes him undutiful. (p. 142)

Let us now see what Quarter the *Stage* gives to *Quality.* And
here we shall find them extreamly free, and familiar. They
dress up the *Lords* in Nick Names, and expose them in *Characters* of Contempt.... Lord *Plausible* in the **Plain Dealer**
Acts a ridiculous Part, but is with all very civil. He tells *Manly
he never attempted to abuse any Person,* The other answers;
What? you were afraid? Manly goes on and declares *He would
call a Rascal by no other Title, tho' his Father had left him a
Dukes.* That is, he would call a Duke a Rascal. This I confess
is very much *Plain Dealing.* Such Freedoms would appear but
odly in Life, especially without Provocation. I must own the
Poet to be an Author of good Sense; But under favour, these
jests, if we may call them so, are somewhat high Season'd,
the Humour seems overstrain'd, and the *Character* push'd too
far. (pp. 173-74)

> *Jeremy Collier, "Chapter I" and "Chapter IV," in
> his* A Short View of the Immorality and Profaneness
> of the English Stage, *1698. Reprint by Garland Pub-
> lishing, Inc., 1972, pp. 1-56, 140-76.*

ALEXANDER POPE   (letter date 1706)

[*Pope has been called the greatest English poet of his time and
one of the most important in the history of world literature. As a
critic and satirical commentator on eighteenth-century England,
he was the author of work that represents the epitome of neo-
classicist thought. All of Pope's work demonstrates his love of
restraint, clarity, order, and that often overused classical term
"decorum." His greatness lies in his cultivation of style and wit,
rather than sublimity and pathos, and this inclination shaped his
criticism of other writers. The following letter, dated April 10,
1706, is Pope's response to Wycherley's request that the younger
author "look over that damn'd Miscellany of Madrigals of mine"*
(Miscellany Poems). *Subsequent correspondence reveals the dis-
integration of their relationship as Pope's comments became more
acerbic and Wycherley's resentment more acute.*]

By yours of the last Month, you desire me to select, if possible,
some Things from the first Volume of your **Miscellanies,** which
may be alter'd so as to appear again. I doubted your meaning
in this; whether it was to pick out the best of those Verses, (as
that on the **"Idleness of Business,"**; on **"Ignorance"**; on **"Laziness,"** &c.) to make the Method and Numbers exact, and
avoid Repetitions? For tho' (upon reading 'em on this occasion)
I believe they might receive such an Alteration with Advantage;
yet they would not be chang'd so much, but any one would
know 'em for the same at first sight. Or if you mean to improve
the worst Pieces, which are such as to render them very good,
would require a great addition, and almost the entire new writing of them? Or, lastly, if you mean the middle sort, as the
Songs and Love-Verses? For these will need only to be shortned,
to omit repetition; the Words remaining very little different
from what they were before. Pray let me know your mind in
this, for I am utterly at a loss. Yet I have try'd what I could
do to some of the *Songs,* and the *Poems* on **"Laziness"** and
"Ignorance," but can't (e'en in my own partial Judgment)
think my alterations much to the purpose. So that I must needs
desire you would apply your Care wholly at present, to those
which are yet unpublished, of which there are more than enough
to make a considerable Volume, of full as good ones, nay, I
verily believe, of better than any in Vol. I. which I could wish
you would defer, at least 'till you have finish'd these that are
yet unprinted.

I send you a Sample of some few of these; namely, the Verses
"To Mr. Waller in his old Age," your new ones on the **"Duke**

of Marlborough," and two others. I have done all that I thought could be of advantage to them: Some I have contracted, as we do Sun-beams, to improve their Energy and Force; some I have taken quite away, as we take Branches from a Tree, to add to the Fruit; others I have entirely new express'd, and turned more into Poetry. *Donne* (like one of his Successors) had infinitely more Wit than he wanted Versification: for the great dealers in Wit, like those in Trade, take least Pains to set off their Goods; while the Haberdashers of small Wit, spare for no Decorations or Ornaments. You have commission'd me to paint your Shop, and I have done my best to brush you up like your Neighbours. But I can no more pretend to the Merit of the Production, than a Midwife to the Virtues and good Qualities of the Child she helps into the Light.

The few Things I have entirely added, you will excuse; you may take them lawfully for your own, because they are no more than Sparks lighted up by your Fire; and you may omit them at last, if you think them but Squibs in your Triumphs. (pp. 227-28)

> *Alexander Pope, in a letter to William Wycherley on April 10, 1706, in* The Complete Works of William Wycherley, *Vol. 2, edited by Montague Summers, 1924. Reprint by Russell & Russell, Inc., 1964, pp. 227-28.*

[SIR RICHARD STEELE] (essay date 1709)

[*An Irish-born English politician, dramatist, and essayist, Steele is best known for his journalistic enterprises. Among the many periodicals he founded and edited during the eighteenth century, the two most notable are the* Tatler *and the* Spectator, *the latter a highly popular and influential daily created in collaboration with Joseph Addison. Steele was always conscious of the moral intent and effect of his essays, and though they are often diverting and amusing, their ultimate aim is the ethical improvement of the reader. As a dramatist, too, Steele was primarily a moralist; plays such as* The Tender Husband (1705) *and* The Conscious Lovers (1722) *were instrumental in effecting the transition from the decadent, cynical comedies of the Restoration to the didacticism of sentimental comedy. In the following excerpt, Steele records his reaction to a performance of* The Country-Wife.]

This Evening, the Comedy called **The Country-Wife,** was acted in *Drury-Lane,* for the Benefit of Mrs. *Bignall.* The Part which gives Name to the Play was perform'd by her self. Through the whole Action, she made a very pretty figure, and exactly enter'd into the Nature of the Part. Her Husband, in the *Drama,* is represented to be one of those Debauchees who run through the Vices of the Town, and believe, when they think fit they can marry, and settle at their Ease. His own Knowledge of the Iniquity of the Age, makes him chuse a Wife wholly ignorant of it, and place his Security in her Want of Skill how to abuse him. The Poet, on many Occasions, where the Propriety of the Character of the Person speaking will admit of it, insinuates, That there is no Defence against Vice, but the Contempt of it: And has, in the natural Ideas of an Untainted Innocent, shown the gradual Steps to Ruin and Destruction, which Persons of Condition run into, without the Help of a good Education by which to form their Conduct. The Torment of a Jealous Coxcomb, which arises from his own False Maxims, and the Aggravation of his Pain, by the very Words in which he sees her Innocence, makes a very pleasant and instructive Satyr. The Character of *Horner,* and the Design of it, is a good Representation of the Age in which that Comedy was written; at which Time, Love and Wenching were the Business of Life, and the Gallant Manner of pursuing Women, was the best

Recommendation at Court. To which only it is to be imputed, that a Gentleman of Mr. *Wicherley*'s Character, and Sense, condescends to represent the Insults done to the Honour of the Bed, without just Reproof; but to have drawn a Man of Probity with Regard to such Considerations, had been a Monster, and a Poet had, at that Time, discover'd his Want of knowing the Manners of the Court he liv'd in by a virtuous Character, in his fine Gentleman, as he would show his Ignorance, by drawing a Vitious One to please the present Audience.

> *[Sir Richard Steele], in a review of "The Country Wife," in* The Tatler, *No. 3, April 14-16, 1709.*

JOHN DENNIS (letter date 1721)

[*Dennis was a minor eighteenth-century English man of letters who is generally esteemed for his astute, wide-ranging literary criticism. However, his several unusually abusive attacks on the character and writings of Alexander Pope have largely diminished his posthumous status in the field. In the following excerpt from a letter to William Congreve written in 1721, Dennis defends the characters of* The Plain-Dealer *from the charge that they are "too witty."*]

SIR,

I Have lately heard, with some Indignation, that there are Persons who arraign the ridiculous Characters of our late Friend Mr. *Wycherley,* for being forsooth too witty; mov'd, I suppose, by the wise Apprehension that they may be of dangerous Example, and spread the Contagion of Wit in this Witty and Politick Age; an Age so very Witty, and so very Politick, that it is always like to be an undetermin'd Question, whether our Wit has the Advantage of our Politicks, or our Politicks of our Wit.

As soon as I heard of this Accusation, I resolved to write a Defence of Mr. *Wycherley,* and to direct this Defence to you, for the following Reasons: Because you had a true Esteem for Mr. *Wycherley*'s Merit, as well as had your humble Servant; Because you are allow'd by all to be an undoubted Judge of the Matter in debate; and Because an express Vindication of Mr. *Wycherley*'s ridiculous Characters, is an implicite one of some of your own. (p. 230)

First then, Mr. *Wycherley*'s Coxcombs are really Coxcombs. And here we must observe that Fool and Wit are so far from being Terms that are incompatible or contradictory, that they are not so much as Terms of Opposition, there being several Persons who are call'd Wits, and who by the Vigour and Fire of their Constitutions are enabled sometimes to say what they call smart and witty things, who have not one grain of Judgment or Discernment to distinguish Right from Wrong, or Truth from Falshood; and that therefore the 523d Reflection of *Rochefoucault* is certainly very Just: *On est quelque fois un sot avec de l'Esprit, mais on ne l'est jamais avec du Jugement.* 'It may happen (says he) that a Man may be a Fool who has Wit, but he never can be so who has Judgment.' The Vanity of those whom they call Wits has made them pretend that there is a full Opposition between Wit and Fool, but the only true and full Opposition is between him that is a Fool, and him who is Wise. (pp. 232-33)

I desire in the next Place to observe, that as 'tis the Business of a Comick Poet to correct those Irregularities and Extravagancies of Men's Tempers which make them uneasie to themselves, and troublesome and vexatious to one another, for that very Reason, your witty Fools are very just Subjects of Comedy, because they are more troublesome and shocking in Conversation to Men of Sense, than any other sort of Fools whatsoever. Such a Fool with all his smart Repartees, as Mr. *Dryden* calls them, his snip snap, his hit for hit, and dash for dash, is but too often impertinent, impudent, insolent, opinionated, noisie, fantastical, abusive, brutal, perfidious; which shews the Solidity of that Reflection of *Rochefoucault* which is the 518*th*. *Il n'y a point des Sots si Incommodes que ceux qui ont de l'Esprit.* ''There are no Fools so troublesome as the Fools who have Wit.''

Now such are Mr. *Wycherley*'s Fools in the Comedy of the ***Plain-dealer.*** My Lord *Plausible,* Major *Oldfox,* the Widow *Blackacre,* and *Jerry,* have each of them several of these Qualities, and *Novel* has them all. He is impertinent, impudent, insolent, conceited, noisie, fantastick, abusive, brutal, perfidious. He says nothing but what a brisk Coxcomb may very well be suppos'd to say who will venture at all, and who having a good Memory keeps the top Company in a Town over-run with Wit, as *London* was at the Time of the writing of that Comedy. What is said by him and the rest in the several Scenes in which they appear, is either trifling and superficial, or utterly and ridiculously false, or appears to be a Repetition of what the Men of Sense in the Play have said before them; whereas what *Manly, Freeman* and *Eliza* say is always sensible, and is therefore always true.

As 'tis the Business of a comick Poet to paint the Age in which he lives, which if he doth not paint, he doth nothing at all, Mr. *Wycherley* had by no means shewn himself so great a Master in Comedy, as he has done, if he had not brought these witty Fools upon the Stage, because in the Reign of King *Charles* the Second they in all Places abounded. The People whom they call'd Wits were to be had every where, nay were not to be avoided, any more than Toasters, Punsters, and Newsmongers are now-a-days, but good Sense and Reason were to be found in as few Places then as they are in our Days. But now, Sir, I come to shew that the Coxcombs in the ***Plain-dealer*** are not only fairly and justly, but vastly distinguish'd from those whom Mr. *Wycherley* design'd for sensible Characters. For *Manly, Freeman* and *Eliza* every where make it appear, that with their Wit they have Judgment, and consequently make great and important Observations, and have therefore a thousand times more Wit than the foresaid Coxcombs. For he who has Wit without Judgment is but a half Wit, and therefore has but imperfect Views, and makes but superficial Reflections; whereas he who has Judgment, has home Views, and makes profound Reflections. (pp. 233-34)

All that we have advanc'd would be manifest as the Day, if we were to go thro' the principal Scenes in which the Characters of either sort appear. I know not but I may perswade my self to do that one Day, provided that what I have already said has the good Fortune to prove agreeable to you. In the mean while I cannot help making one Observation upon the Scene in the second Act, where *Novel* intends to give an Account of the Guests at my Lady *Autumn*'s Table, by which it will appear how industriously Mr. *Wycherley* avoided the making his Dramatick Persons speak out of their Characters. For *Novel* who is to give the Account is always interrupted by *Olivia,* that the Wit of that Scene may be in a more proper Mouth than his; yet so quick are the Returns, and so great is the Vivacity of that admirable Scene, that it has dazled and deluded most of his Readers, and prevail'd upon them to imagine, that *Novel* has a full share in the Wit of it, tho' he has not so much as a half quarter share in the very Dialogue of it.

Thus, Sir, I have endeavour'd to defend the ***Plain-dealer*** against the foresaid Accusation, as far as my present Avocations would give me leave. . . . At the same time I am very far from believing that the ***Plain-dealer*** is a faultless Play, for where is the Play or the Poem that is without Fault? But since these People have not hit on the true Faults, it becomes his Friends to say nothing at all concerning them. (pp. 234-35)

> *John Dennis, ''Letters on Milton and Wycherley: Letter IV, a Defence of Mr. Wycherley's Characters in the 'Plain Dealer','' in his* The Critical Works of John Dennis: 1711-1729, Volume II, *edited by Edward Niles Hooker, The Johns Hopkins Press, 1943, pp. 230-35.*

FRANÇOIS MARIE AROUET DE VOLTAIRE   (essay date 1733)

[*A French philosopher and man of letters, Voltaire was a major figure of the eighteenth-century European Enlightenment, a movement in which the principles of reason and empiricism superseded the long-established reliance on prescription, faith, and authority. As a man of diverse and intense interests, Voltaire wrote prolifically on many subjects and in a variety of genres, always asserting the absolute primacy of personal liberty—be it intellectual, social, religious, or political. Consequently, he opposed religious traditions and political organizations that he believed thwarted or curtailed individual freedom. Voltaire's most valuable contribution to literature is his invention of the philosophical* conte, *or tale, in which the story is a vehicle for an ethical or philosophical message; the most famous of these* contes *is the highly regarded* Candide *(1759). Voltaire lived for several years in England, where it is said he learned the language by frequenting English theaters; among the plays he attended were Wycherley's. In the following excerpt from an essay originally published in 1733, Voltaire comments on* The Country-Wife *and* The Plain-Dealer.]

[Mr. Wycherley], who passed his life among persons of the highest distinction, was perfectly well acquainted with their lives and their follies, and painted them with the strongest pencil, and in the truest colours. He has drawn [in ***The Plain-Dealer***] a misanthrope or man-hater, in imitation of that of Molière. All Wycherley's strokes are stronger and bolder than those of our misanthrope, but then they are less delicate, and the rules of decorum are not so well observed in this play. The English writer has corrected the only defect that is in Molière's comedy, the thinness of the plot, which also is so disposed that the characters in it do not enough raise our concern. The English comedy affects us, and the contrivance of the plot is very ingenious, but at the same time it is too bold for the French manners. The fable is this:—A captain of a man-of-war, who is very brave, open-hearted, and inflamed with a spirit of contempt for all mankind, has a prudent, sincere friend, whom he yet is suspicious of, and a mistress that loves him with the utmost excess of passion. The captain so far from returning her love, will not even condescend to look upon her, but confides entirely in a false friend, who is the most worthless wretch living. At the same time he has given his heart to a creature, who is the greatest coquette and the most prefidious of her sex, and he is so credulous as to be confident she is a Penelope, and his false friend a Cato. He embarks on board his ship in order to go and fight the Dutch, having left all his money, his jewels, and everything he had in the world to this virtuous creature, whom at the same time he recommends to the care of his supposed faithful friend. Nevertheless the real man of honour, whom he suspects so unaccountably, goes on board the ship with him, and the mistress, on whom he would not bestow so much as one glance, disguises herself in the habit of a page, and is with him the whole voyage, without his once knowing that she is of a sex different from that she attempts to pass for, which, by the way, is not over natural.

The captain having blown up his own ship in an engagement, returns to England abandoned and undone, accompanied by his page and his friend, without knowing the friendship of the one or the tender passion of the other. Immediately he goes to the jewel among women, who he expected had preserved her fidelity to him and the treasure he had left in her hands. He meets with her indeed, but married to the honest knave in whom he had reposed so much confidence, and finds she had acted as treacherously with regard to the casket he had entrusted her with. The captain can scarce think it possible that a woman of virtue and honour can act so vile a part; but to convince him still more of the reality of it, this very worthy lady falls in love with the little page, and will force him to her embraces. But as it is requisite justice should be done, and that in a dramatic piece virtue ought to be rewarded and the vice punished, it is at last found that the captain takes his page's place and lies with his faithless mistress, cuckolds his treacherous friend, thrusts his sword through his body, recovers his casket, and marries his page. You will observe that this play is also larded with a petulant, litigious old woman (a relation of the captain), who is the most comical character that was ever brought upon the stage.

Wycherley has also copied from Molière another play, of as singular and bold a cast, which is a kind of *Ecole des Femmes,* or, *School for Married Women.*

The principal character in this comedy [*The Country-Wife*] is one Horner, a sly fortune hunter, and the terror of all the City husbands. This fellow, in order to play a surer game, causes a report to be spread, that in his last illness, the surgeons had found it necessary to have him made a eunuch. Upon his appearing in this noble character, all the husbands in town flocked to him with their wives, and now poor Horner is only puzzled about his choice. However, he gives the preference particularly to a little female peasant, a very harmless, innocent creature, who enjoys a fine flush of health, and cuckolds her husband with a simplicity that has infinitely more merit than the witty malice of the most experienced ladies. This play cannot indeed be called the school of good morals, but it is certainly the school of wit and true humour. (pp. 139-41)

> *François Marie Arouet de Voltaire, "On Comedy,"* in The Harvard Classics, French and English Philosophers: Descartes, Rousseau, Voltaire, Hobbes, *Vol. 34, edited by Charles W. Eliot, P. F. Collier & Son, 1910, pp. 139-43.*

WILLIAM HAZLITT   (lecture date 1818)

[An English essayist, Hazlitt was one of the most important critics of the Romantic age. He was a deft stylist, a master of the prose essay, and a leader of what was later termed "impressionist criticism"—a form of personal analysis directly opposed to the universal standards of critical judgment accepted by many eighteenth-century critics. Hazlitt, like Samuel Taylor Coleridge before him, played a substantial role in the reinterpretation of Shakespeare's characters during the nineteenth century, and he contributed significantly to the revival of a number of Elizabethan dramatists, including John Webster and Thomas Heywood. Although he has often been considered a follower of Coleridge, he is closer in spirit and critical methodology to Charles Lamb. Like Lamb, Hazlitt utilized the critical techniques of evocation, metaphor, and personal reference—three innovations that greatly altered the development of literary criticism in the nineteenth and

twentieth centuries. For Hazlitt the ideal of any critical endeavor is not an ultimate judgment regarding a work of literature; instead, the critic serves as a guide to help determine the reader's response to certain works, or passages within those works. Perhaps the most important thing to remember when reading Hazlitt is that he was a journalist writing for the general public and that he lived from the proceeds of his pen. He was acutely aware of the abstract nature of literature as well as the limitations of his audience in understanding questions of aesthetics and style. For this reason he purposely made his criticism palatable by using illustrations, digressions, and repetitions. In the following excerpt from an essay written in 1818 and originally delivered as a lecture, Hazlitt offers a general assessment of Wycherley's plays, discussing their characterization, plot, and effect.]

Wycherley was before Congreve; and his *Country Wife* will last longer than any thing of Congreve's as a popular acting play. It is only a pity that it is not entirely his own; but it is enough so to do him never-ceasing honour, for the best things are his own. His humour is, in general, broader, his characters more natural, and his incidents more striking than Congreve's. It may be said of Congreve, that the workmanship overlays the materials: in Wycherley, the casting of the parts and the fable are alone sufficient to ensure success. We forget Congreve's characters, and only remember what they say: we remember Wycherley's characters, and the incidents they meet with, just as if they were real, and forget what they say, comparatively speaking. Miss Peggy (or Mrs. Margery Pinchwife) is a character that will last for ever, I should hope; and even when the original is no more, if that should ever be, while self-will, curiosity, art, and ignorance are to be found in the same person, it will be just as good and as intelligible as ever in the description, because it is built on first principles, and brought out in the fullest and broadest manner. Agnes, in Moliere's play, has a great deal of the same unconscious impulse and heedless *naïveté,* but hers is sentimentalised and varnished over (in the French fashion) with long-winded apologies and analytical distinctions. It wants the same simple force and *home* truth. It is not so direct and downright. Miss Peggy is not even a novice in casuistry: she blurts out her meaning before she knows what she is saying, and she speaks her mind by her actions oftener than by her words. The outline of the plot is the same; but the point-blank hits and master-strokes, the sudden thoughts and delightful expedients, such as her changing the letters, the meeting her husband plump in the Park, as she is running away from him as fast as her heels can carry her, her being turned out of doors by her jealous booby of a husband, and sent by him to her lover disguised as Alicia, her sister-in-law—occur first in the modern play. There are scarcely any incidents or situations on the stage, which tell like these for pantomimic effect, which give such a tingling to the blood, or so completely take away the breath with expectation and surprise. Miss Prue, in [Congreve's] *Love for Love,* is a lively reflection of Miss Peggy, but without the bottom and weight of metal. Hoyden is a match for her in constitution and complete effect, as Corinna, in the Confederacy, is in mischief, but without the wit. . . . Pinchwife, or Moody, (as he is at present called) is, like others of Wycherley's moral characters, too rustic, abrupt, and cynical. He is a more disagreeable, but less tedious character than the husband of Agnes, and both seem, by all accounts, to have been rightly served. The character of Sparkish is quite new, and admirably hit off. He is an exquisite and suffocating coxcomb; a pretender to wit and letters, without common understanding, or the use of his senses. The class of character is thoroughly exposed and understood; but he persists in his absurd conduct so far, that it becomes extravagant and disgusting, if not incredible, from mere weakness and foppery.

Yet there is something in him that we are inclined to tolerate at first, as his professing that 'with him a wit is the first title to respect'; and we regard his unwillingness to be pushed out of the room, and coming back, in spite of their teeth, to keep the company of wits and raillers, as a favourable omen. But he utterly disgraces his pretensions before he has done. With all his faults and absurdities, he is, however, a much less offensive character than Tattle.—Horner is a stretch of probability in the first concoction of that ambiguous character, (for he does not appear at present on the stage as Wycherley made him) but notwithstanding the indecency and indirectness of the means he employs to carry his plans into effect, he deserves every sort of consideration and forgiveness, both for the display of his own ingenuity, and the deep insight he discovers into human nature—such as it was in the time of Wycherley.... *The Plain Dealer* is Wycherley's next best work; and is a most severe and poignant moral satire. There is a heaviness about it, indeed, an extravagance, an overdoing both in the style, the plot, and characters, but the truth of feeling and the force of interest prevail over every objection. The character of Manly, the Plain Dealer, is violent, repulsive, and uncouth, which is a fault, though one that seems to have been intended for the sake of contrast; for the portrait of consummate, artful hypocrisy in Olivia, is, perhaps, rendered more striking by it. The indignation excited against this odious and pernicious quality by the masterly exposure to which it is here subjected, is 'a discipline of humanity.' No one can read this play attentively without being the better for it as long as he lives. It penetrates to the core; it shews the immorality and hateful effects of duplicity, by shewing it fixing its harpy fangs in the heart of an honest and worthy man. It is worth ten volumes of sermons. The scenes between Manly after his return, Olivia, Plausible, and Novel, are instructive examples of unblushing impudence, of shallow pretensions to principle, and of the most mortifying reflections on his own situation, and bitter sense of female injustice and ingratitude, on the part of Manly. The devil of hypocrisy and hardened assurance seems worked up to the highest pitch of conceivable effrontery in Olivia, when, after confiding to her cousin the story of her infamy, she, in a moment, turns round upon her for some sudden purpose, and affecting not to know the meaning of the other's allusions to what she has just told her, reproaches her with forging insinuations to the prejudice of her character, and in violation of their friendship. 'Go! you're a censorious ill woman.' This is more trying to the patience than any thing in the *Tartuffe*. The name of this heroine, and her overtures to Fidelia, as the page, seem to have been suggested by *Twelfth Night*. It is curious to see how the same subject is treated by two such different authors as Shakspeare and Wycherley. The widow Blackacre and her son are like her lawsuit—everlasting. A more lively, palpable, bustling, ridiculous picture cannot be drawn. Jerry is a hopeful lad, though undutiful and gets out of bad hands into worse. Goldsmith evidently had an eye to these two precious characters, in *She Stoops to Conquer*. Tony Lumpkin and his mother are of the same family, and the incident of the theft of the casket of jewels; and the bag of parchments, is nearly the same in both authors. Wycherley's other plays are not so good. *The Gentleman Dancing Master* is a long, foolish farce, in the exaggerated manner of Moliere, but without his spirit or whimsical invention. *Love in a Wood,* though not what one would wish it to be for the author's sake or our own, is much better, and abounds in several rich and highly-coloured scenes, particularly those in which Miss Lucy, her mother Crossbite, Dapperwit, and Alderman Gripe are concerned. Some of the subordinate characters and intrigues in this comedy are

grievously spun out. Wycherley, when he got hold of a good thing, or sometimes even of a bad one, was determined to make the most of it; and might have said with Dogberry, truly enough, 'Had I the tediousness of a king, I could find in my heart to bestow it all upon your worships.' (pp. 76-9)

William Hazlitt, "On Wycherley, Congreve, Vanbrugh, and Farquhar," in his Lectures on the English Comic Writers and Fugitive Writings, *Dutton, 1963, pp. 70-91.*

LEIGH HUNT (essay date 1840)

[*An English poet and essayist, Hunt was important as a literary critic who encouraged and influenced several young poets, especially John Keats and Percy Bysshe Shelley. He was a copious and facile writer who produced volumes of poetry, critical essays, dramas, translations, and, with his brother John, established the* Examiner, *a weekly liberal newspaper. In his critical essays, Hunt articulated the principles of Romanticism, emphasizing the poet's use of imaginative freedom and expression of a personal emotional or metaphysical state. Although his critical works were overshadowed by the two most prominent Romantic critics of the era, Samuel Taylor Coleridge and William Hazlitt, his essays are considered sensitive and generous to the fledgling writers he supported. Of his criticism Clarence DeWitt Thorpe states that Hunt "made a constant effort when he read his authors both to get at and analyze what was uniquely good and to ferret out and characterize what was less good or downright bad. In other words, he was habitually after specific quality." In the following excerpt, Hunt offers a brief, generally approving survey of Wycherley's plays.*]

Wycherley has justly been considered as the earliest of our comic prose dramatists, who forsook the fleeting shapes of custom and manners that were brought to their gayest head in Etherege, for the more lasting wit and humour natural to the prevailing qualities of mankind. Etherege was the "dandy" of the prose drama, and Wycherley the first man. Shadwell had glimpses "in his drink"; but he was only a gross and hasty sketcher. Schlegel has missed a general airiness in all our plays of this class, through the whole range of English comedy, and Wycherley is certainly no exception to the defect. He is somewhat heavy as well as "brawny" in his step; and when he moves faster, it is seldom from gaiety. He has "wit at will" also, but then the will to be witty is frequently too obvious, and has too artificial an air of thought and antithesis. His best scenes are those of cross-purposes, mutual exposure, or the contrast of natural with acquired cunning; those, in short, in which reflection and design have much more to do than animal spirits. His style is pure and unaffected; and clearness and force are his characteristics, in preference to what is either engaging or laughable. (pp. xviii-xix)

The idea of *Love in a Wood, or St. James's Park,* (for the Park was the wood,) was evidently suggested by the *Mulberry Garden* of Sir Charles Sedley,—a title suggested by a house of entertainment which stood on the site of Buckingham Palace, and the grounds of which, like the *Spring-garden* at the opposite corner, were resorted to by the gallants and masked ladies of the time, when they issued forth of a summer's evening like so many gnats, to buzz, sting, and make love. It turns upon a game of hide-and-seek, and other cross-purposes, between some of these "minions of the moon," and is worth little in style or plot; yet we think, upon the whole, it has been under-valued. It is not unamusing. It gives early evidence of that dislike of backbiting and false friendship, which honourably distinguished Wycherley through life; and there are the germs of two characters in it, which have been since developed by Hoadley and Sheridan,—that of *Falkland* in the *Rivals (the Valentine* of this play) and *Ranger* in the Suspicious Husband. . . . (p. xix)

[Wycherley] had manifestly gone to the same sources as Molière for the improvement of his plots, when he wrote the **Gentleman Dancing-Master**. There is a similar amusing intrigue in it to that of the *Ecole des Femmes,* carried on through the medium of an unconscious wittol, who hugs himself upon the fool he is making of the favoured lover; and the author, besides looking back to old English comedy for a Frenchified Englishman, has brought a formalised one from Spain, the favourite store-house of the comedy of the preceding age. The hero of the piece, who is made to personate a dancing-master, and to be always in motion whether he will or no, is very amusing; so is the suspicious old aunt, who sees through his incompetency: but, above all, there is an exquisite truth to nature in the egotistical effrontery of the father, who, after treating the aunt's suspicions with contempt, takes to himself the credit of making the very discovery, which she has all along been trying to beat into his head.

The **Plain Dealer,**—with the exquisite addition of the litigious *Widow Blackacre*, a kind of born female barrister, an original which he had doubtless met with in the courts of law,—is an English version, in its principal characteristics, of the *Misanthrope* of Molière, greatly improved, inasmuch as the hero is less poetically tragic, but equally contrary to nature and to the true spirit of comedy, inasmuch as he is tragical at all; and in one respect it is shockingly below the original; for it is deformed so as no other age but such a one as that of Charles the Second could suppose manhood to be deformed, and yet remain consistent with itself, by the sort of revenge which he permits himself to take on his mistress,—that of a possession of her person under the supposition of his being another man, and while he feels nothing for her disposition but hatred and contempt. Yet in this gusto of desecrated animal passion, fit only for some ferocious sensualist who believed himself as great a rascal as he thought everybody else, the wits of those days saw nothing to deteriorate from a character emphatically christened and thought "Manly,"—a name which it imparted, as an epithet of honour, to the Author himself. As to the rest, the wit put into the mouth of this much-injured Captain of the British navy is as forced, and not seldom as common-place, as the violent and solemn coxcombry of his hatred of all other vices but his own is ridiculous. Indeed all misanthropes, whatever be their pretensions in other respects, nay, in very proportion to their claims upon being thought exceptions to the generality of mankind, are, and must be, so far, nothing but stupid and immodest coxcombs, for daring to set up their supposed knowledge of themselves above the whole virtues of the rest of their fellow-creatures. In what has been charged, however, as unnatural in the characters of the two heroes of Wycherley and Molière, with regard to their believing in the goodness of one select friend and one mistress, this, we confess, appears to us provokingly true to nature; for the same arbitrary will and pleasure that trumps up a man's own virtues to himself, has only to include the first convenient man or woman it meets with in the same spotless category, and for not a jot better reason. (pp. xx-xxi)

In the **Country Wife** there are no such scenes and dialogue of continued excellence as those of *Olivia* and her visitors in the second act of the **Plain Dealer**; but the principal female character hits a point of more lasting nature, and is an exquisite

meeting of the extremes of simplicity and cunning; so that with some alterations, especially of the impudent project of *Horner,* which would have been an affront in any other age to a decent audience, this comedy outlasted the performances of the graver one. . . . (p. xxi)

[Wycherley] was so beloved in his time, as to afford a caution to sour, and therefore crude, moralists, how they put the worst construction upon what is not always best in his writings. (p. xxii)

> *Leigh Hunt, "Biographical and Critical Notices," in* The Dramatic Works of Wycherley, Congreve, Vanbrugh, and Farquhar, *edited by Leigh Hunt, Edward Moxon, 1840, pp. ix-ci.*

LORD MACAULAY   (essay date 1841)

[*Thomas Babington Macaulay was a distinguished historian, essayist, and politician of mid-nineteenth-century England. For many years he was a major contributor of erudite, highly opinionated articles to the* Edinburgh Review. *Besides these essays, collected and published as* Critical and Historical Essays *(1843), his most enduring work is his five-volume* History of England from the Accession of James II *(1849-61), which despite criticism of its strong bias toward the Whig political party, is esteemed for its consummate rhetorical and narrative prose. According to Richard Tobias, Macaulay was a writer who "feared sentiment and preferred distance, objectivity, dispassionate vision. Yet withal, he was a brilliant writer who . . . is still capable of moving a reader by sheer verbal excitement." In the following excerpt from an 1841 review of Leigh Hunt's* The Dramatic Works of Wycherley, Congreve, Vanbrugh, and Farquhar *(1840), Macaulay denounces Wycherley's plays for their immorality.*]

[We] can by no means agree with Mr. Leigh Hunt, who seems to hold that there is little or no ground for the charge of immorality so often brought against the literature of the Restoration [see excerpt dated 1840]. . . . Mr. Leigh Hunt treats the whole matter a little too much in the easy style of Lucio; and perhaps his exceeding lenity disposes us to be somewhat too severe.

And yet it is not easy to be too severe. For in truth this part of our literature is a disgrace to our language and our national character. It is clever, indeed, and very entertaining; but it is, in the most emphatic sense of the words, "earthly, sensual, devilish." Its indecency, though perpetually such as is condemned not less by the rules of good taste than by those of morality, is not, in our opinion, so disgraceful a fault as its singularly inhuman spirit. (pp. 354-55)

[Of the Restoration dramatists William Wycherley, William Congreve, John Vanbrugh, and George Farquhar], Wycherley stands, we think, last in literary merit, but first in order of time, and first, beyond all doubt, in immorality. (p. 368)

His fame as a writer rests wholly on his comedies, and chiefly on the last two. Even as a comic writer, he was neither of the best school, nor highest in his school. He was in truth a worse Congreve. His chief merit, like Congreve's, lies in the style of his dialogue. But the wit which lights up the **Plain Dealer** and the **Country Wife** is pale and flickering, when compared with the gorgeous blaze which dazzles us almost to blindness in *Love for Love* and the *Way of the World*. Like Congreve, and, indeed, even more than Congreve, Wycherley is ready to sacrifice dramatic propriety to the liveliness of his dialogue. The poet speaks out of the mouths of all his dunces and coxcombs, and makes them describe themselves with a good sense and acuteness which puts them on a level with the wits and heroes. We will give two instances, the first which occur to us, from the *Country Wife.* There are in the world fools who find the society of old friends insipid, and who are always running after new companions. Such a character is a fair subject for comedy. But nothing can be more absurd than to introduce a man of this sort saying to his comrade, "I can deny you nothing: for though I have known thee a great while, never go if I do not love thee as well as a new acquaintance." That townwits, again, have always been rather a heartless class, is true. But none of them, we will answer for it, ever said to a young lady to whom he was making love, "We wits rail and make love often, but to show our parts: as we have no affections, so we have no malice."

Wycherley's plays are said to have been the produce of long and patient labour. The epithet of "slow" was early given to him by Rochester, and was frequently repeated. In truth his mind, unless we are greatly mistaken, was naturally a very meagre soil, and was forced only by great labour and outlay to bear fruit which, after all, was not of the highest flavour. He has scarcely more claim to originality than Terence. It is not too much to say that there is hardly any thing of the least value in his plays of which the hint is not to be found elsewhere. The best scenes in the *Gentleman Dancing Master* were suggested by Calderon's *Maestro de Danzar,* not by any means one of the happiest comedies of the great Castilian poet. *The Country Wife* is borrowed from the *École des Maris* and the *École des Femmes.* The groundwork of the *Plain Dealer* is taken from the *Misanthrope* of Molière. One whole scene is almost translated from the *Critique de l'École des Femmes.* Fidelia is Shakspeare's Viola stolen, and marred in the stealing; and the Widow Blackacre, beyond comparison Wycherley's best comic character, is the Countess in Racine's *Plaideurs,* talking the jargon of English instead of that of French chicane.

The only thing original about Wycherley, the only thing which he could furnish from his own mind in inexhaustible abundance, was profligacy. It is curious to observe how every thing that he touched, however pure and noble, took in an instant the colour of his own mind. Compare the *École des Femmes* with the *Country Wife.* Agnes is a simple and amiable girl, whose heart is indeed full of love, but of love sanctioned by honour, morality, and religion. Her natural talents are great. They have been hidden, and, as it might appear, destroyed by an education elaborately bad. But they are called forth into full energy by a virtuous passion. Her lover, while he adores her beauty, is too honest a man to abuse the confiding tenderness of a creature so charming and inexperienced. Wycherley takes this plot into his hands; and forthwith this sweet and graceful courtship becomes a licentious intrigue of the lowest and least sentimental kind, between an impudent London rake and the idiot wife of a country squire. We will not go into details. In truth, Wycherley's indecency is protected against the critics as a skunk is protected against the hunters. It is safe, because it is too filthy to handle, and too noisome even to approach.

It is the same with the *Plain Dealer.* How careful has Shakspeare been in *Twelfth Night* to preserve the dignity and delicacy of Viola under her disguise! Even when wearing a page's doublet and hose, she is never mixed up with any transaction which the most fastidious mind could regard as leaving a stain on her. She is employed by the Duke on an embassy of love to Olivia, but on an embassy of the most honourable kind. Wycherley borrows Viola; and Viola forthwith becomes a pandar of the basest sort. But the character of Manly is the best

illustration of our meaning. Moliere exhibited in his misanthrope a pure and noble mind, which had been sorely vexed by the sight of perfidy and malevolence, disguised under the forms of politeness. As every extreme naturally generates its contrary, Alceste adopts a standard of good and evil directly opposed to that of the society which surrounds him. Courtesy seems to him a vice; and those stern virtues which are neglected by the fops and coquettes of Paris become too exclusively the objects of his veneration. He is often to blame; he is often ridiculous; but he is always a good man; and the feeling which he inspires is regret that a person so estimable should be so unamiable. Wycherley borrowed Alceste, and turned him,— we quote the words of so lenient a critic as Mr. Leigh Hunt,— into "a ferocious sensualist, who believed himself as great a rascal as he thought everybody else" [see excerpt dated 1840]. The surliness of Moliere's hero is copied and caricatured. But the most nauseous libertinism and the most dastardly fraud are substituted for the purity and integrity of the original. And, to make the whole complete, Wycherley does not seem to have been aware that he was not drawing the portrait of an eminently honest man. So depraved was his moral taste that, while he firmly believed that he was producing a picture of virtue too exalted for the commerce of this world, he was really delineating the greatest rascal that is to be found, even in his own writings. (pp. 384-87)

Lord Macaulay, "Leigh Hunt," in his Critical, Historical, and Miscellaneous Essays, Volume IV, *Hurd & Houghton, 1860?, pp. 350-411.*

H. A. TAINE (essay date 1863-64)

[*Often considered the founder of the sociological school of literary criticism, Taine had a profound impact on the sociological criticism of the nineteenth century, and even on the development of Marxist critical thought in the twentieth. Taine argued that a work of literature can be totally understood as a product of three influences: race, milieu, and moment. By "race" Taine meant the combined physical traits and specific mental habits of a certain nationality of people. Today, especially after the abuse of the term by the Nazis during their rise to power, race is thought a weak and constricting foundation for judging literary works. The term "milieu" according to Taine's definition, not only physical environment but also political and social conditions. It is unclear to most critics what Taine meant by the term "moment," but it is generally assumed that it is either the sum of race and milieu, or simply the milieu of a particular time. Taine's tripartite formula is severely criticized today. Although the concept of milieu retains some critical usefulness, most modern critics see it as only one aspect contributing to the direction of an individual's creative work, and by no means an adequate explanation for the greatest works of art in world history. That Taine saw it as a major force in matters of art and literature has only detracted from his standing in the history of literary criticism. In the following excerpt from a study originally published in 1863-64, Taine protests Wycherley's immorality.*]

[The] hero of [Restoration] society was William Wycherley, the coarsest writer who ever polluted the stage. (p. 357)

His style is laboured, and troublesome to read. His tone is virulent and bitter. He frequently forces his comedy in order to get at spiteful satire. Effort and animosity mark all that he says or puts into the mouths of others. . . . We find in him no poetry of expression, no glimpse of the ideal, no settled morality which could console, raise, or purify men. He shuts them up in their perversity and uncleanness, and installs himself among them. He shows them the filth of the lowest depths in which he confines them; he expects them to breathe this atmosphere; he plunges them into it, not to disgust them with it as by an accidental fall, but to accustom them to it as if it were their natural element. He tears down the partitions and decorations by which they endeavour to conceal their state, or regulate their disorder. He takes pleasure in making them fight, he delights in the hubbub of their unfettered instincts; he loves the violent changes of the human mass, the confusion of their wicked deeds, the rawness of their bruises. He strips their lusts, sets them forth at full length, and of course feels them himself; and whilst he condemns them as nauseous, he enjoys them. People take what pleasure they can get: the drunkards in the suburbs, if asked how they can relish their miserable liquor, will tell you it makes them drunk as soon as better stuff, and that is the only pleasure they have. (pp. 359-60)

Need I recount the plot of the *Country Wife*? It is useless to wish to skim the subject only; we sink deeper and deeper. Horner, a gentleman returned from France, spreads the report that he is no longer able to trouble the peace of husbands. You may imagine what becomes of such a subject in Wycherley's hands, and he draws from it all that it contains. Women converse about Horner's condition, even before him; they suffer themselves to be undeceived, and boast of it. Three of them come to him and feast, drink, sing—such songs! The excess of orgie triumphs, adjudges itself the crown, displays itself in maxims. "Our virtue," says one of them, "is like the statesman's religion, the quaker's word, the gamester's oath, and the great man's honour; but to cheat those that trust us." In the last scene, the suspicions which had been aroused, are set at rest by a new declaration of Horner. All the marriages are polluted, and the carnival ends by a dance of deceived husbands. To crown all, Horner recommends his example to the public, and the actress who comes on to recite the epilogue, completes the shamefulness of the piece, by warning gallants that they must look what they are doing; for that if they can deceive men, "we women—there's no cozening us."

But the special and most extraordinary sign of the times is, that amid all these provocatives, no repellent circumstance is omitted, and that the narrator seems to aim as much at disgusting as at depraving us. Every moment the fine gentlemen, even the ladies, introduce into their conversation the ways and means by which, since the sixteenth century, love has endeavoured to adorn itself. Dapperwit, when making an offer of Lucy, says, in order to account for the delay: "Pish! give her but leave to . . . put on . . . the long patch under the left eye; awaken the roses on her cheeks with some Spanish wool, and warrant her breath with some lemon-peel." Lady Flippant, alone in the park, cries out: "Unfortunate lady that I am! I have left the herd on purpose to be chased, and have wandered this hour here; but the park affords not so much as a satyr for me; and no Burgundy man or drunken scourer will reel my way. The rag-women and cinder-women have better luck than I."

Judge by these quotations, which are the best, of the remainder! Wycherley makes it his business to revolt even the senses; the nose, the eyes, everything suffers in his plays; the audience must have had the stomach of a sailor. And from this abyss English literature has ascended to the strict morality, the excessive decency which it now possesses! This stage is a declared war against beauty and delicacy of every kind. If Wycherley borrows a character anywhere, it is only to do violence, or degrade it to the level of his own characters. If he imitates the Agnes of Molière, as he does in the *Country Wife*, he

marries her in order to profane marriage, deprives her of honour, still more of modesty, still more of grace, and changes her artless tenderness into shameless instincts and scandalous confessions. If he takes Shakespeare's Viola, as in the *Plain Dealer*, it is to drag her through the vileness of infamy, amidst brutalities and surprises. If he translates the part of Molière's Célimène, he wipes out at one stroke the manners of a great lady, the woman's delicacy, the tact of the lady of the house, the politeness, the refined air, the superiority of wit and knowledge of the world, in order to substitute for them the impudence and deceit of a foul-mouthed courtesan. If he invents an almost innocent girl, Hippolita, he begins by putting into her mouth words that will not bear transcribing. Whatever he does or says, whether he copies or originates, blames or praises, his stage is a defamation of mankind, which repels even when it attracts, and which sickens a man while it corrupts.

A certain gift hovers over all—namely, vigour—which is never absent in England, and gives a peculiar character to their virtues as well as to their vices. When we have removed the oratorical and heavily constructed phrases imitated from the French, we get at the genuine English talent—a deep sympathy with nature and life. Wycherley possessed that lucid and vigorous perspicacity which in any particular situation seizes upon gesture, physical expression, evident detail, which pierces to the depths of the crude and base, which hits off, not men in general, and passion as it ought to be, but an individual man, and passion as it is. He is a realist, not of set purpose, as the realists of our day, but naturally. In a violent manner he lays on his plaster over the grinning and pimpled faces of his rascals, in order to bring before our very eyes the stern mask to which the living imprint of their ugliness has stuck on the way. He crams his plays with incident, he multiplies action, he pushes comedy to the verge of dramatic effect; he hustles his characters amidst surprises and violence, and all but stultifies them in order to exaggerate his satire. (pp. 362-65)

There is a character who shows in a concise manner Wycherley's talent and his morality, wholly formed of energy and indelicacy,—Manly, the "plain dealer," so manifestly the author's favourite, that his contemporaries gave him the name of his hero for a surname. . . . Wycherley took to himself in his dedication the title of his hero, *Plain Dealer*; he fancied he had drawn the portrait of a frank, honest man, and praised himself for having set the public a fine example; he had only given them the model of an unreserved and energetic brute. That was all the manliness that was left in this pitiable world. Wycherley deprived man of his ill-fitting French cloak and displayed him with his framework of muscles, and in his naked shamelessness. (pp. 368-71)

> *H. A. Taine, "The Restoration," in his* History of English Literature, *Vol. II, translated by H. Van Laun, 1871. Reprint by Henry Holt and Company, 1904, pp. 320-447.*

JOHN PALMER   (essay date 1913)

[*Palmer was an English critic and novelist. In addition to the several novels he published under his own name, including* The King's Men *(1916), Palmer coauthored numerous mystery novels with Hilary St. George Saunders under the pseudonyms Francis Beeding and David Pilgrim. From 1910 to 1915 he served as drama critic of the* Saturday Review, *subsequently accepting a similar position at the* Evening Standard. *Among his studies in dramatic criticism are* The Future of the Theatre *(1913) and* The Comedy of Manners. *In the following excerpt from the latter study,*

Palmer regards both the darker and lighter sides of Wycherley's comedy.]

From Easy Etherege to Manly Wycherley is a remarkable transition. Etherege was the expression of his period. His plays were an agreeable transcription of the life he knew. The imperturbable elegance with which his contemporaries held life, as it were, at arm's length, and gracefully postured through the seven ages, is in the plays of Etherege an unrippled reflexion. But in the plays of Wycherley there is a critical current of satire. Alone of the comic dramatists he shares in the comic spirit, though to a less extent than is commonly maintained, of Molière. In the plays of Wycherley we are frequently startled into a consciousness of moral fury, which, because it is unpremeditated, is only the more disturbing. (p. 92)

Wycherley's plays should be read . . . immediately upon leaving Etherege. Fled are the airiness, delicacy, and absolute reliance upon the finer values of style. Wycherley's phrases are less pleasing to the ear; but they bite into their topic. Here is a writer whose matter is sometimes of equal importance with his manner—here, in fact, we are not dealing with a typical figure of the time, as was Etherege. Wycherley seems a man to whom life, had he flourished in another period, would immensely have mattered—a man who, fundamentally, had an instinct to look quite through the shows of men. Fundamentally he was a Puritan. Superficially, in his life and writing, he accepted the pageant and portrayed it; but frequently the moral fury of a satirist breaks violently through the fine gentleman. (pp. 93-4)

Wycherley's main business is still with manners, not with morals; and where his moral fury intrudes it spoils rather than uplifts his comedy. Ordinarily he accepted life. But suddenly he sees clean through the spectacle that has served his turn, and breaks into a furious, confused passion of disgust. Only in this way can we explain the alternating of scenes handled in a spirit purely laughter-loving with scenes of violent rage against humanity. It is precisely this moral fury of Wycherley which is accountable for passages that have persistently disgusted the critics. There are passages in any one of the four plays which, independently of any change of attitude or manners, are revolting. Laughter is extinguished; the jester bursts irrecognisably upon us, a ferocious prophet, dredging into the filth of human nature with precisely the sombre satisfaction with which certain devout people relish the possibilities of hell. The spirit of these scenes is as far from the easy nonchalance of Etherege as from the sunshine satire of Molière. But it puts Wycherley quite definitely in touch with the French satirical school of comedy, despite the distance that is between them. More especially there are scenes where Wycherley's shrewd good humour and passing pleasure in the life of his time combine with his fundamental puritanism to produce scenes of a faintly subacid quality which agreeably suggest the manner of French comedy at its best.

The darker side of the comedy of Wycherley appears even as we scan the dramatis personæ of his first play. Alderman Gripe, even before his appearance, is obviously well-hated by the author of his being. "Seemingly precise, but a covetous lecherous old usurer of the City" is disquieting. Soon the scorpions are loosed. Alderman Gripe, betrayed by Miss Lucy into the hands of Mrs. Crossbite and her confederates, is flatly hideous. Wycherley is doing his moral worst to show vice its own image.

Love in a Wood is, for its faults, an excellent introduction to a reading of Wycherley's plays. It is prentice work. There is

no unity of style; and it is therefore possible, from page to page, to run along the whole scale of Wycherley's literary moods. The scene to which we have already alluded, in its inequitable disgust with the devil, is a prototype of *The Plain Dealer,* where, as we shall see, Wycherley's moral fervour precipitated him into one of the most unpleasant extant pieces of English literature. Thence we may gradually ascend till we arrive at scenes almost in the vein of Etherege and Congreve. As an instance of the intermediate scene, where satire is softened with humanity and seasoned with laughter—a passage in Act I, between Alderman Gripe and Mrs. Joyner may be noted; and, with an irony less bitter, the symmetrical backbiting passages between Dapperwit, Ranger, and Vincent; also the scenes where the prudery of my Lady Flippant is exposed.

At the opposite extreme from Alderman Gripe are the scenes which definitely place Wycherley in the same school with Etherege and Congreve. Dapperwit is the successor of Sir Fopling; the predecessor of Witwoud. (pp. 120-22)

Wycherley omits the finer values of style. His plays should be read rapidly, so that we may fully appreciate the quick flow of his ideas; the liveliness of their expression; the happy surprise of his best effects. Much of his laughter is simple high spirits. There is rough-and-tumble in his best comic scenes. Lightheartedness blows as a steady, purifying, and persistent wind.

Wycherley appears at his lightest in *The Gentleman Dancing Master.* (p. 125)

[It] is the merriest of Wycherley's comedies. More than any other it should be swiftly read. It is a bottle of high spirits. Once opened, it must not be allowed to go flat. (p. 126)

[*The Country Wife*] is the most brilliant of Wycherley's plays, and the most perfect farce in English dramatic literature—a whirlwind of inspired buffoonery. It lifts the reader from solid ground, and bears him to a region where laughter alone administers the law and the constitution. All questions of motive and moral value disappear. It is true that Wycherley keeps to the realistic method of his school. Mr. Horner, as Macaulay contends, is intimately modelled upon the fine gentlemen of Covent Garden. But the naturalistic method of Mr. Horner's presentation does not in the least affect Elia's fundamentally right contention that he is a native of Cloud-Cuckooland. His famous project, upon which every situation of the play so brilliantly hangs, at once puts him beyond the cool estimates of morality; and it would be absurd in a critical reader to feel towards Mr. Horner as he would feel towards an actual twentieth-century social figure of Mr. Horner's character and habits. (pp. 128-29)

Mr. Horner is an extremely dry and an entirely passionless embodiment of adventurous gallantry. Sensuously presented, with every meretricious accompaniment that a febrile imagination and a full stomach can suggest, Mr. Horner is the popular hero of the vast number of plays and romances upon which the British public persistently feeds without the least notion of harm taken. Seen in the dry light of Wycherley's classical farce, Mr. Horner is morally intolerable. Wycherley has dared to emphasize a fact invariably avoided in the modern theatre—namely, that adultery is not entirely a matter of fine phrases and exalted frenzy. Adultery is a physical fact. Like most physical facts, it may for artistic purposes be regarded comically or tragically; and, so long as all the facts are present in their due proportion, no moral harm, either way, can ensue. Mr. Horner is an active and indefatigable gallant who fulfils the artistic purpose of his being with energy and resource. (pp. 131-32)

There is a passage of *The Country Wife* which excellently prepares us for *The Plain Dealer*. Mr. Horner, admitted to the bosoms of our ladies of quality and reputation, has many opportunities to observe them at their ease. Passing the guard of their fair appearances he enables Wycherley to break into a really hideous indictment. The scene where Horner drinks with my Lady Fidget, Mrs. Dainty Fidget, and Mrs. Squeamish, and receives their confidences of the boudoir, is in Wycherley's most malignant vein. It is a serious blot upon the play; for, where we have hitherto enjoyed the dry, impersonal quality of our author's delivery, we are now conscious of a furious disgust with the world, chaotically expressed, governed by no very clear artistic purpose. It is a passage in the vein of *The Plain Dealer*, intruded into *The Country Wife*. (pp. 133-34)

Plain-dealer was Wycherley's complimentary sobriquet. Manly was accepted at the time as the embodiment of an honourable misanthropy. Virtually he was Wycherley's opportunity freely to indulge the moral ferocity which had already spoiled many scenes of his earlier plays. There are a few passages in Wycherley's best manner—notably the scenes in the second act between Olivia, Lord Plausible, and Mr. Novel. But for the most part *The Plain Dealer* is inferior work; and its indecency must frankly be admitted.

What is the precise nature of this indecency? *The Plain Dealer* is not indecent in the sense that was urged by Jeremy Collier and Lord Macaulay [see excerpts dated 1698 and 1841]. *The Plain Dealer* is exactly the reverse of any attempt to administer an aphrodisiac. It is nowhere sensuous. It is far from being a call to the pleasures of Venusberg. On the contrary, it is the deliberate attempt of a ferocious moralist to expose the vices of nature for our disgust. It is the unhappy protest against life of a man who lived semi-consciously against the grain of his nature. It is indecent in the sense that any protest against life is indecent—in the sense that any deliberate tendency to turn the seamy side without and to ignore the equitable balance of nature is indecent. (pp. 134-35)

> *John Palmer, "William Wycherley," in his* The Comedy of Manners, *1913. Reprint by Russell & Russell, Inc., 1962, pp. 92-140.*

J. MIDDLETON MURRY   (essay date 1922)

[*Murry is recognized as one of the most significant English critics and editors of the twentieth century. Anticipating later scholarly opinion, he championed the writings of Marcel Proust, James Joyce, Paul Valéry, D. H. Lawrence, and the poetry of Thomas Hardy through his positions as the editor of the* Athenaeum *and as a longtime contributor to the* Times Literary Supplement *and other periodicals. Murry's critical works are noted for their unusually impassioned tone and startling discoveries; such biographically centered studies as* Keats and Shakespeare: A Study of Keats' Poetic Life from 1816-1820 *(1925) and* Son of Woman: The Story of D. H. Lawrence *(1931) contain esoteric, controversial conclusions that have angered scholars who favor more traditional approaches. Nevertheless, Murry is cited for his perspicuity, clarity, and supportive argumentation. His early exposition on literary appreciation,* The Problem of Style *(1922), is widely esteemed as an informed guidebook for both critics and readers to employ when considering not only the style of a literary work, but its theme and viewpoint as well. In it Murry espouses a theoretical premise which underlies all his criticism: that in order to fully evaluate a writer's achievement the critic must search for crucial passages which effectively "crystallize" the* writer's innermost impressions and convictions regarding life. In the following excerpt from a review of Charles Perromat's study, William Wycherley: Sa vie, son oeuvre, *Murry assesses Wycherley's dramatic worth, stating that he is "simply boring" and his work "unreadable."*]

It is a curious and sobering coincidence that at the moment when the English Press has been busy with the tercentenary of Molière, of all the great French dramatists the one most sympathetic to our taste, a French author should have published a substantial volume on the life and work of the dramatist who has been called the English Molière—William Wycherley. Wycherley is, of course, not the English Molière; there is no such person. Congreve, who in some ways is almost as good as Molière, is quite different, while Wycherley, who had more affinity with Molière and certainly imitated his work, is too coarse in grain to be fairly compared to him.

Still, if the French critic finds no difficulty in mentioning Wycherley and Molière in the same breath, it is perhaps a little supererogatory for an English one to object. It seems like looking a gift horse in the mouth. An English Molière! We could do with one, indeed. And yet, for sanity's sake, we are compelled to refuse M. Perromat's generous offer. We accept his book with gratitude, but not his estimate of his author; and even in refusing this, we have no quarrel with his enthusiasm. It needed enthusiasm to write a book of 440 octavo pages on "Manly Wycherley." Most people would have been hard put to it to make an essay of him. And yet, without going so far as to say that M. Perromat's pages are all lively reading, we can safely assert that he has done the work for Wycherley once for all. No one else will ever want to write a book about him again.

M. Perromat is persuaded that Wycherley is a neglected author; he thinks he has been unfairly treated. . . . Wycherley has been given a fair chance during the last hundred years. The verdict has gone against him. There is no resurrecting him now.

Wycherley is dead, not because he is monstrously coarse, but because he is unreadable. Very likely he is eminently playable still; but he is too coarse to be played except by a private society behind a sported oak. Curiously enough, the very qualities which make *The Country Wife* and *The Plain Dealer* unreadable nowadays, a massive woodenness, a kind of hidebound inelasticity in the dialogue, suggest that his talent was really theatrical. Qualities which remind us so directly of Ben Jonson are pretty sure to be effective on the stage. But Wycherley cannot get on the stage nowadays; neither, alas! can Congreve. If he is to endure he must stand the test of reading. Congreve emerges triumphant; Wycherley succumbs. He is simply boring.

The Gentleman Dancing-Master is interesting, because it is concerned less than either *The Country Wife* or *The Plain Dealer* with contemporary manners. Perhaps that is one reason why it is more pleasing. But it has what no other of his plays has— what no play of Congreve has not—charm. Its charm is, however, of a very particular kind; it is a specifically Molièresque charm. It has something of the gay, irresponsible beauty of the *Ecole des Femmes*. And this is strange; for in *The Country Wife* Wycherley deliberately imitated Molière's play, while he got the plot of *The Dancing-Master* from Calderon. But Mrs. Pinchwife is not even a remote relation of the enchanting Agnes: Hippolita is, at the very least, her tomboy cousin. Moreover, besides the atmosphere and the chief character, there are some touches of real Molière comedy. When Don Diego Formal and Mrs. Caution, by their interruptions of each other, supply Gerrard with a whole series of excuses for his presence with Hippolita, we recognize the hand of the master: it is comic, and it is true.

The Gentleman Dancing-Master failed. . . . [When] we think of the plays with which Wycherley managed to renew his first success—*The Country Wife* and *The Plain Dealer*—it looks very much as though it failed simply because it was not bawdy enough. It belongs to a different kind from the others. It is English enough; Hippolita and Gerrard definitely belong to this side of the Channel. But it is not tainted, for ordinary consumption, by a procession of women who are nothing but lecherous Yahoos; and the dialogue, within the limits of Wycherley's natural stiffness, is lively and pleasant.

I believe, on the evidence of this play and its failure, that Wycherley succumbed to his age. It shows that Wycherley had at least a faint chance of becoming an English Molière, but that Caroline England did not want one. It wanted someone to supply it with *The Country Wife*. Hazlitt thought *The Country Wife* a masterpiece [see excerpt dated 1818]. It is a perfectly cold-blooded piece of nastiness. We are quite willing to believe that a riotously amusing farce might be written on the theme of a man who pretends to be a eunuch in order to seduce his friends' wives wholesale. To pretend that sculduddery cannot be amusing is simply fanatical. But it has to be exuberant; it has to be animated. . . . With explosive good humor the comic giant blows the world sky-high. But Wycherley is neither exuberant, nor explosive, nor good-humored; he is not creating a world, he is simply portraying a society. He is not playing an exquisite game, as Congreve was; he is making a record. At least we may try to believe that that is what he was doing; but one comes to suspect that he was laboriously fishing for a laugh with the only bait a Caroline audience would swallow. (pp. 760-61)

J. Middleton Murry, "An English Molière?" in The Athenaeum, *No. 4790, February 18, 1922, pp. 760-61.*

ALLARDYCE NICOLL (essay date 1923)

[*Called "one of the masters of dramatic research," Nicoll is best known as a theater historian whose works have proven invaluable to students of the drama. Nicoll's* World Drama from Aeschylus to Anouilh *(1949) is considered one of his most important works; theater critic John Gassner has stated that it is "unquestionably the most thorough [study] of its kind in the English language [and] our best reference book on the world's dramatic literature." Another of his ambitious theater studies is the six-volume* A History of English Drama, 1660-1900 *(1952-59), which has been highly praised for its perceptive commentaries on drama from the Restoration to the close of the nineteenth century. Nicoll was also a popular lecturer on Shakespearean drama and the author of several studies of Shakespeare's works. In addition, he was the longtime editor of* Shakespeare Survey, *an annual publication of Shakespearean scholarship. In the following excerpt, Nicoll briefly assesses Wycherley as artist and as moral satirist.*]

[Although Wycherley], as an artist, falls far below Etherege, as a powerful force in contemporary life [he] rises far above him. The lover of the Duchess of Cleveland, the tutor of the King's son, the husband of the Countess of Drogheda, the prisoner in the Fleet, was a quite different being from the airy ambassador, patron of a deserted *comédienne* in the Low Countries. Mr. Palmer is not far wrong in styling him a Puritan with the external veneer of a Restoration gentleman [see excerpt dated 1913]. He burst up the foetid air of the time with a force equal to that of Collier. He lashed the age with his plain-dealing

pen, lading out his disgust upon a slightly fluttered world of roués and their mistresses. He has not the style of the greater masters of the manners school, polished and fine: his wit does not overshadow his plots as does the wit of Etherege or of Congreve: yet, in scenes where his moral horror is not aroused, he can be almost as delicate as they. (p. 225)

[In *Love in a Wood; or, St. James's Park*], we are led into a world somewhat similar to that of Etherege, yet hardly so fine, and, as in the Alderman Gripe and Lucy scenes, tending to vulgarity. From the very first opening sentence of the play, however, we may see the masterly construction. The plot is ably and interestingly developed: but something remains indefinably incongruous. There is almost something of Shadwell in Wycherley's work. There is always the sense that the heart is struggling for entry into the world of the intellect.

Of like nature, though less successful, was *The Gentleman Dancing-Master* . . . in which the construction, with its opposed types of French and Spanish foppery, is even simpler than in the comedy preceding. *The Gentleman Dancing-Master* is interesting as being nearer in spirit to Etherege than almost any other of Wycherley's plays: it stands furthest in tone from *The Plain Dealer*.

In *The Country Wife* . . . Wycherley has continued in the same free easy strain. *The Country Wife* is a bright and glorious farce, in which the innuendo so successfully employed in *The Gentleman Dancing-Master* is brought to a stage of utmost perfection. The famous "China" scene of Horner is probably unrivalled in our literature, and, much as it has been condemned by moralists, can be nothing but admired for its sheer cleverness and for its swift biting humour. It has not the vulgarity which is apparent in the work of Shadwell: it is a piece of intellectualism, wherein the wit takes from the harmful effect it otherwise might have had.

The name of Wycherley, however, "manly," "brawny" Wycherley, stands not so much with these former plays, although they were enough to make the fame of any dramatist, but with a comedy almost unique in its age—*The Plain Dealer*. . . . In it the roué joins hands with the moralist, realism is mingled with artificial manners, emotions with the intellect. It satirises perfectly the infidelity and the foppishness of the time, at the very moments that it sinks to the depths of carnal viciousness. There is only one pure character in the whole of its five acts, and that is Fidelia, devoted Fidelia who follows her rough and faithless lover with a tenderness that almost draws the tears from our eyes. Everyone else is swallowed up in sense. The chief figure is, of course, Manly himself, a pessimistic hater of man's hypocrisy, and one who owes not a little to the Alceste of Molière's *Le misanthrope*. Beside him and Fidelia, with the possible exception of Olivia, Manly's former mistress, all the other characters seem mere shadows of personified qualities. Lord Plausible is simply the typical fop with nothing individual in his composition, just as Novel is the representative of the would-be wits, and Widow Blackacre of the law-mad amateurs. On women, fops, wits and lawyers indiscriminately the satire falls, intermixed with that loathsome description of passion which only men like Shadwell and Wycherley among the Restoration dramatists could give to us. Wycherley, says Congreve, was sent "to lash the crying Age," but he has lashed its sores into more fulsome aspects, until we have naught to do but turn eyes away in misery and in disgust. (pp. 225-27)

Allardyce Nicoll, "Comedy," in his A History of Restoration Drama, 1660-1700, Cambridge at the University Press, 1923, pp. 168-267.

WILLIAM ARCHER (essay date 1923)

[*A Scottish dramatist and critic, Archer is best known as one of the earliest and most important translators of Henrik Ibsen's plays and as a drama critic of the London stage during the late nineteenth and early twentieth centuries. Archer valued drama as an intellectual product and not as simple entertainment. For that reason he did a great deal to promote the "new drama" of the 1890s, including the work of Ibsen and Bernard Shaw. Throughout his career he protested critical overvaluation of older drama, claiming that modern works were in many respects equal to or better than Elizabethan or Restoration plays. Similar in prescience to his dramatic criticism is his* Poets of the Younger Generation *(1902), one of the first critical studies of many important modern English poets, including A. E. Housman, Arthur Symons, and W. B. Yeats. In the following excerpt, Archer considers both the morality and the dramatic technique of Wycherley's plays.*]

Wycherley's wit is confessed on all hands to be inferior to Congreve's, to be, indeed, somewhat lacking in grace; but it is supposed to possess a compensating vigour and pungency. His admirers take their stand upon Dryden's Alexandrine: "The satire, wit and strength of manly Wycherley." It would, no doubt, be rash to maintain that there is nothing in this judgment. Indeed, one sees readily enough, in contrasting him with Etherege on the one hand and Congreve on the other, how robustness came to be reckoned his leading characteristic. His cynicism lays about it with a weapon comparable to the cutlass of Manly in *The Plain Dealer*, that "ferocious sensualist" (as Leigh Hunt puts it) [see excerpt dated 1840] into whom he has transmogrified the exquisite Alceste of Molière. But what his contemporaries called strength very often seems to us moderns little better than laborious verbosity. Extracts are apt to do him a certain injustice, for if ever he wrote with ease and gusto it was in passages so gross as utterly to defy quotation. (pp. 183-84)

[A] favorable specimen of his wit may be found in his latest, and some say greatest, work, *The Plain Dealer*—in the scene of detraction in Act II, Sc. 1, from which Sheridan no doubt took the idea of his Scandalous College. It is too long for quotation, and is easily accessible. You will recognise in it the touch of the true dramatist, but very little that can rightly be called wit. There is humour rather than wit in the character of Novel, and in the way in which Olivia prevents him from getting a word in edgewise. Such a phrase as "most splendidly, gallantly ugly" is, at a pinch, worth remembering. So is a line of Lord Plausible's, a little further on:

Olivia.   Can anyone be called beautiful that squints?
Lord Plausible.   Her eyes languish a little, I own.

But, after making the best case we can for it, must we not allow that, in the corresponding passages in *The School for Scandal*, Sheridan immeasurably improves upon his model? There is in his wit an invention, a fantasy, a poise and a polish which Wycherley never approaches. (p. 185)

Though in technique [Wycherley] is in no way in advance of his contemporaries, we sometimes feel in his work, as I have said, the touch of a real dramatist—of a man who might have done excellent work had he not been so entirely content with the facile expedients of his age.

In his first play, *Love in a Wood*, there are three plots, not interwoven, but simply running parallel with one another.

The characters of the first intrigue are Sir Simon Addleplot, Dapperwit and Mrs. Martha. It is without interest or ingenuity, and Sir Simon's disguise is merely preposterous.

The second intrigue is that of Gripe and Lucy, with those exemplary matrons, Mrs. Joyner and Mrs. Crossbite pulling the strings. This plot is practically worked out in the one very vigorous, though disgusting scene, of the entrapping and blackmailing of Gripe.

In the third intrigue, that of Ranger and Lydia, Valentine and Christina, there is a certain ingenuity; but it turns (a) on improbable mistakes of persons in the dark; (b) on the improbable circumstance that Ranger plans to meet the pseudo-Christina at Vincent's lodging instead of his own; (c) on the coincidence which brings the real Christina there at the same moment.

Lady Flippant, the widow who is constantly denouncing marriage while hunting for a husband or a lover, wanders through all three intrigues without belonging to any of them.

The Gentleman Dancing Master is by far the least offensive, and certainly not the least able of Wycherley's plays. There is something really rather charming in the character of Hippolita; Gerrard is quite decent for a Wycherley hero; the contrast between the Francophil and the Hispanophil monomaniacs must have been really comic; and the idea of helping out the audacious attempt to pass Gerrard off as a dancing-master by making Formal resent his sister's pretension to greater perspicacity than his own, is a real dramatic invention. This is Wycherley's own idea: his debt to Calderón's *Maestro de Danzar* is, on the whole, very slight.

In spite of its merits, however, the play failed, and the reason is not far to seek. Matters began to go wrong, I conceive, when Hippolita, in the fourth act, suddenly refuses to run away with Gerrard—with no possible motive except that of furnishing the playwright with a fifth act. Then in the fifth act, the behaviour of Monsieur becomes too imbecile for tolerance; and the irruption of Flirt and Flounce, with the long and utterly preposterous negotiation between Monsieur and Flirt (a sort of topsy-turvy social essay) must have decided the failure.

In fear, perhaps, lest the play should be considered too refined, Wycherley introduced in Act IV an episode of irrelevant indecency in Prue's attempted seduction of Monsieur. Nothing leads up to it, and nothing ensues from it. Cut it out, and you would leave no perceptible gap. Like Etherege's scene at the Bear Tavern, it has reappeared in many modern French and Anglo-French farces.

Macaulay has been much derided for saying that "Wycherley's indecency is protected against the critics as a skunk is protected against the hunters. It is safe because it is too filthy to handle and too noisome even to approach" [see excerpt dated 1841]. But of *The Country Wife* this is literally true. There is one side of it, at any rate, which one cannot even investigate technically, since its technical merits depend upon the answer to questions which it is impossible to discuss.

The intrigue, however, from which the play takes its name, is not exempt from examination; and its technical merits must be pronounced very slight. The action depends entirely on Pinchwife's incredible maladroitness and stupidity; while there is no psychological coherence or consistency in Margery's state of mind. She is now densely ignorant, and again preternaturally knowing, just as the needs of a given situation happen to dictate. Pinchwife's leaving her alone at the Exchange . . . , in order to see "if the coach be at the door," and again in the letter-scene . . . , "whilst he goes to fetch wax and a candle," are technical ineptitudes far more indefensible than Joseph Surface's much-criticised exit during the Screen Scene; and the passage . . . in which Margery imposes herself upon him as Alithea, and induces him to take her to Horner's, is simply an elaborate and clumsy impossibility. The coxcomb, Sparkish, is a very coarse caricature, and the scene in which Harcourt, dressed as a "Levite," passes himself off, in spite of Alithea's protests, as his own twin-brother, is extravagant to the point of puerility. The women's drinking-bout in the last scene adds a finishing touch to the loathsomeness of what is surely the most bestial play in all literature.

Beside it *The Plain Dealer* seems almost sweet and clean; but it is technically misshapen beyond the rest of its kindred. Its first two acts consist of laboured, verbose talk, serving only to show that Olivia has (not inexcusably) betrayed her surly brute of a lover. In the third act the action stands absolutely still, while we are treated to a panorama of Westminster Hall, centring around the Jonsonian "humour" of the Widow Blackacre and her hopeful son—an episode wholly irrelevant to the main plot. In the fourth and fifth acts we have a conventional intrigue turning upon a woman dressed up as a man and a substitution of persons in the dark—the sort of intrigue which it is easy to elaborate to any extent, if you can get your audience to swallow the fundamental impossibilities. The satire of the play is sometimes coarsely effective, but dramatically I regard it as Wycherley's feeblest. (pp. 191-93)

> William Archer, "Restoration Comedy," in his The Old Drama and the New: An Essay in Re-valuation, *Small, Maynard and Company, Publishers, 1923, pp. 172-202.*

MONTAGUE SUMMERS   (essay date 1924)

[*A Roman Catholic priest, theater historian, and author, Summers was one of the foremost English scholars of Restoration drama. Maintaining that "the real test of worth of dramatic literature is performance in the theatre," he founded The Phoenix, a theatrical society which produced rarely staged sixteenth- and seventeenth-century dramas and which helped to revive the plays of William Congreve, Thomas Otway, and John Dryden, whose works Summers also edited. As the author of* The History of Witchcraft and Demonology *(1926),* The Vampire in Europe *(1929),* Witchcraft and Black Magic *(1946), and several other works on the occult, Summers was also considered an authority on witchcraft and the supernatural. His works on the occult were written from a "medieval standpoint," described by Summers as "an absolute and complete belief in the supernatural, and hence in witchcraft." In addition, he produced several scholarly works on the Gothic novel, most notably* The Gothic Achievement *(1939) and* A Bibliography of the Gothic Novel *(1940). In the following excerpt, Summers praises Wycherley's plays, finding their adroit characterization particularly admirable.*]

[*Love in a Wood*] is, indeed, an excellent comedy, and although it may be objected that there is no very close inter-relation between the two themes, the jealous love of Valentine for Christina and the business of the Gripe *ménage* ["household"], yet Lady Flippant, the ubiquitous Ranger, Dapperwit, and Sir Simon with their clandestine intrigues and cross purposes, their visits to Pepper Alley and midnight rambles in the park, their mistakes and misadventures, afford quite sufficient connexion, nor in the conduct of his neatly-balanced scenes does Wych-

erley give any one episode more importance than another. The characters are all well drawn and clearly individualized. The folly of Dapperwit is not the same as the folly of Sir Simon Addleplot; Mrs. Joyner and Mrs. Crossbite, the two old harridans, are separate and distinct; they are no mere lay figures; Crossbite, lean, sour, hatchet-faced, and sharp-tongued, is apparently the bolder and more brazen of the two. Joyner, fat, pursy, vast-bosomed and double-chinned, is hypocritically obsequious and smooth as oil, but in truth no whit the less grasping and dangerous. The two minxes, again, Lucy and Mrs. Martha, have much in common. They are both saucy and shameless; both impudently affect innocence and simplicity; they are both whores. And yet each one has her own individual characteristics: her mode of speech, her style, and diversely cunning address. (p. 30)

Alderman Gripe, his sister and daughter, his clerk and Mrs. Joyner, are English of the English. The delineation of Gripe's household is exquisitely happy, and these scenes of rich comedy give ample promise of a masterpiece to come. The characters are exactly true to life, and they are presented to us as the ripe fruit of that keen observation which is the hall-mark of a great dramatist. (p. 31)

The excellent construction of the play, an extremely rare quality in a first piece, should be carefully noted. Interest is awakened with the opening sentences at the very rise of the curtain, and the plot is developed with the greatest ease and naturalness throughout. The various threads are deftly interwoven, and although, as has been noticed above, superficially it may be supposed that the connexion between the jealousy of Valentine and the Gripe episodes is somewhat slender, a careful examination will show the care and finished art with which Wycherley has planned his succession of scenes and arranged his material. The wit of the dialogue is exceedingly pleasant and in every case agreeable to each character. Lively repartee and sharp satirical reflexions are scattered pell-mell with a bounteous hand, but in no instance has Wycherley merely interrupted his design and suspended his action to entertain an audience with a brilliant shower of dazzling bon-mots. His coxcombs and fools talk according to their folly—only they are such pure fools! And to be able thus to entertain us with the idle chatter of jays and witlings is evidence of no mean powers. (p. 32)

Upon the stage *The Gentleman Dancing-Master* seems to have been "liked but indifferently." It is difficult to account for the coolness with which so excellent a comedy was received, and one can but attribute it to the caprice of the audience. Both the plot and construction of the play are simpler than *Love in a Wood,* and although the same situation is repeated it is presented so agreeably and varied with such wit and humour that so far from wearying, it seems to gain a fresh interest as the intrigue develops. Strictly speaking the scene in the last act between Monsieur and Flirt is perhaps a little impertinent to the issue, but it is so exquisitely happy and so brilliantly written that nobody could wish it away. We may notice that Wycherley has by now a complete understanding of theatrical effect; the situations are extremely well-managed and adroit. In Hippolita we have one of the most charming of Restoration heroines. (p. 45)

[*The Country Wife*] is undoubtedly Wycherley's masterpiece of satirical comedy, as *The Plain-Dealer* is a masterpiece of philosophical comedy. In no play in the English theatre, or in any other theatre I know, is the wit more sparkling, the humour more cleverly poised, the sequence of incidents more naturally deployed; nowhere are the situations more brilliantly sustained, the characters drawn with keener observation and acuter intellectual insight and truth. It is the very acme of comedy, of its kind unsurpassable, as it is unsurpassed. (p. 46)

[Wycherley] has given us the full-blooded world of his day, the brilliant society in which he moved, their dazzling wit, their finished graces, their lively affectations, their lewd impudence, their vices, their intrigues, all without mitigation, without glozing, without excuse. The province of comedy is not apologetics. There is the hard selfishness of the gay gallant Horner, whose scheme is planned, we verily believe, as much for the sheer intellectual delight in the novelty of the adventure as for the ends to which it serves. Throughout the play one realizes that Horner's greatest joy is the knowledge of his infinite mental superiority over the silly cuckolds, who for all their busy importance and endless precautions are but puppets dancing to the tune he calls, and he pleases to pipe an amorous lay. But in my Lady Fidget he has met his match. She is every whit as clever and every whit as selfish as he. With an exaggerated care for her dear reputation she combines the morals of Messalina. Utterly egoistical and self-centred, she has no more affection for her lover than for her husband. But appearances must be maintained at all costs. And private pleasures must be satisfied—at all costs. Yet if a whore, she is a fine lady too, and a *faux pas* will meet with a frown and a rebuff. Even when on the point, one cannot write of yielding, but, of giving herself to Horner, she checks a trifling freedom in speech with "Fie, let us not be smutty." A charming creature, so long as she gets what she wants, and so long as her gallants are careful not to allow sentiment to enter in the case.

Mr. Pinchwife is a very exact figure of a man who has drunk deep of all the pleasures of town, and in whom satiety has succeeded enjoyment, and satiety disgust. He shuns his former haunts, not out of wisdom but out of moroseness, and in some rambling lone house in Hampshire fodders an exacerbated mind with the sullenness and rusticity of companions whom he despises and employments which he distastes. For his wife he takes a girl, who is not innocent but merely ignorant, and the opportunities, slight though they may be, of acquiring knowledge, which she so eagerly seizes and so obviously desires, are to him moments of the most exquisite annoyance and even bitter torment. Mrs. Pinchwife herself is young and beautiful. But she is a very child, both in the simplicity with which she blabs of her lover to her husband and the voluble delight she shows when told she has been casually admired at the theatre, as also in her bewilderment at her husband's growls and threats and violence and the cunning wherewith she circumvents his jailership when the situation gradually dawns upon her. She has the methods and morals of a schoolboy; she is as shallow and as deep as a fifth-form scholar who deludes and evades his master. There is a good deal of pathos in her situation: one feels for her as one feels for a caged bird beating his pretty breast against the bars. For those who can fully appreciate there are few lines more full of tender beauty than the postscript of the letter wherein she warns her lover against her husband: "Let him not see this, lest he should come home, and pinch me, or kill my Squirrel."

Sparkish is a coxcomb who, as the author intended, is somewhat coarsely drawn. He is not perfectly genteel, not of the line of Sir Fopling Flutter, Sir Courtly Nice, and Baron Foppington. His father, I imagine, might have been a worthy citizen, and he himself was probably born well within the sound of the bells of Bow. Yet he is a joyous moth, albeit his markings are a trifle garish, and he imitates skilfully enough the imperial butterflies.

Sir Jaspar Fidget is an important man, a very important man. One conceives him with his huge periwig, plumed hat, costly suit of plum velvet or gredalin, unwrinkled silk stockings, codfish staring eyes, round moon-like face, florid complexion, which becomes a little more mottled when he discovers his wife in Horner's embrace, but it seems she was only tickling him. An eminently respectable and respected, conventional, worldly-wise individual, and "when he is gone, there wants one, and there's an end." (pp. 47-8)

The affected prudery which professes itself scandalized at Horner's device is not worth consideration. (p. 49)

[*The Plain Dealer* is] among the most powerful and philosophical plays in English literature. The giant strength of the conception and the bold strokes of the painting cannot be denied, the brutal philosophy of some scenes may be disliked but cannot be burked. It is quite understandable that there are many who find Manly's pessimistic hatred of the vices and banalities, the shallowness and fopperies, the hypocrisy and superficiality of the society about him, delivered in too mordant a vein. He is Wycherley's Superman, and, as a superman always must, he falls into extravagance and excess. There are two, and two alone, in whom he completely trusts, his mistress and his friend. During his absence his mistress jilts and chouses him; he finds her in her drawing-room entertaining the idlest coxcombs in Town; he overhears her discussing his love with them in terms of the utmost coarseness and callousness; when he makes himself known she repels him and flouts him with the brazen impudence of a common courtesan; she listens to his reproaches with a mocking smile and leaves him with a cruel jest upon her lips; she is mercenary, too, and even though his need is pressing, she retains the jewels and money he deposited in her hands, confident he will be too proud to beg 'em again. Vernish, Manly's friend, behaves with the foulest treachery and promptly betrays him with circumstances of ignoblest dishonour and perfidy. This precious couple, man and wife, are at length unmasked, their intrigues and double-dealing exposed. And herein lies a great stroke of Wycherley's art. Another author might have plunged Manly, galled and witherwrung at being so gulled, into deeper misery and discontent; but not so Wycherley. The scales drop from Manly's eyes, and very frankly acknowledging his errors, which have been to no small extent, at least, the cause of his misanthropy, he renounces them to be made happy in the friendship of Freeman and the love of Fidelia.

The character of Fidelia Grey is very tenderly and beautifully drawn. Pure and gracious, for love's sake she follows her rough and reckless captain through perils on sea, through perils on shore. At his behest she undertakes with a breaking heart the most difficult and distasteful of functions, the rôle of Pandarus. She realizes that his attraction for Olivia is merely physical, that he is allured by the strumpet's beauty, and she who loves him for his bravery and true courage, for those sterling qualities she has perceived beneath the scurf of anger and bitter mistrust, executes all his commands save one—to leave him. In a situation of peculiar embarrassment she behaves with perfect modesty and propriety. Her loyalty and the pathos of her lot call unashamed tears to our eyes.

Olivia, who is portrayed with the most pregnant and biting strokes, is governed by self-interest and self-interest alone. The hardened assurance with which, after having confided her guilt to Eliza, she turns round, fortune favouring her, and denies all she has previously said, even accusing her cousin of maliciously inventing the whole tale, has something almost terrible in its impudence, so base and lying is she. She has no love, hardly sensuality, but merely animal passion and desire. Flamboyantly physical, she immediately captivates men, and is herself as readily attracted by them. There is in particular one acute piece of psychology which should be noted: she does not seem in the least degree fascinated by the vigour and strength of Manly, but her lust is at once stirred by the feminine graces and gentle comeliness of the disguised Fidelia. The bold abandoned woman seeks for the immaturity and softness of a bashful boy, whose embraces she craves with the most unrestrained ardour, whose kisses she snatches in a frenzy of sadistic vampirism. She preys upon the vitals of men, stripping her lovers bare and casting them aside like empty husks. A true daughter of the horse-leech, crying always, "Give, give," she is as the grave and the barren womb, as the earth that is not filled with water, and the fire that saith not "It is enough."

It is obvious that Olivia has nothing in common with Molière's Célimène, and although Wycherley has made use of *Le Misanthrope,* Manly is just as far removed from Alceste. It has been admirably put that "Wycherley has so overlaid his appropriations with the colouring of his own brilliant individuality that his play appears almost equally a masterpiece of originality as of ingenuity. It is scarcely too much to say that in *The Plain-Dealer* we are conscious of a fertility of invention, a richness of wit and satire, which make even *Le Misanthrope* seem tame in comparison."

Nor must it be supposed that Freeman in any way corresponds to Philinte. The amiable and urbane raillery of Philinte is once or twice, indeed, recalled by Lord Plausible's comments, but Philinte is a polished man of the world, exquisitely tactful and highly intelligent, whilst Lord Plausible is a supple fool. Freeman's affection for Manly seems loyal and sincere, but his scheme to secure the Widow Blackacre and the plot upon her son must be relegated to the realm of pure comedy if we are to entertain that liking for him which the author doubtless intended. It says much for Wycherley's genius that the buzzing crowd of impertinents, coxcombs, fops, chatterers, and lawyers, which circle round Manly and incessantly chafe him with their hum and sharp brize-stings, should all be so severally and entirely differentiated, should each one be a real living person, and not mere puppets to vanish away in shadowy fashion before the strong glare of his personality. The Widow Blackacre herself is, of course, supreme. As Hazlitt said: "The Widow Blackacre and her son are like her lawsuit—everlasting. A more lively, palpable, bustling, ridiculous picture cannot be drawn" [see excerpt dated 1818]. Litigation rules her life and sways every action. She can only think in legal terms, and can talk of nothing but law, of which she has all the technicalities at her fingers' ends, and to which she can immediately twist any business or any conversation. Vexatious as a dozen attorneys, and as implacable as a parson suing for his tithes, she will listen to a chancery suit as another might listen to a play, she will even purchase the defence of a case from a pure love of friction and quarrel. Her brief bag, her deeds, and her parchments are never apart from her; she is restless and resistless as the waves of the sea. We know her very looks, her sharp scolding voice, the clothes she wears, her mantle and bedraggled petticoat, the meat she eats, soused venison, and the wine she drinks. She is all bustle and pother, noise and obstruction and hurry. In fine, the Widow Blackacre is, as Voltaire wrote, "la plus plaisante créature et le meilleur caractère qui soit au

théâtre" ["the most comical character that was ever brought upon the stage"; see excerpt dated 1733]. (pp. 50-1)

Wycherley's work may be disliked, it cannot be neglected. . . . [It] is by his comedies that Wycherley will live, and it is by two of these, *The Country-Wife* and *The Plain-Dealer,* that he has assured to himself a serene immortality. These masterpieces remain unsurpassed in the English theatre, indeed few comic dramatists in any land or of any tongue have equalled, none have excelled our great and glorious William Wycherley. (pp. 63-4)

Montague Summers, in an introduction to The Complete Works of William Wycherley, Vol. 1, *edited by Montague Summers, 1924. Reprint by Russell & Russell, Inc., 1964, pp. 3-64.*

BONAMY DOBRÉE (essay date 1924)

[*An English historian and critic, Dobrée distinguished himself both as a leading authority of Restoration drama and as a biographer who sought, through vivid depiction and style, to establish biography as a legitimate creative form. Dobrée is also known for his editing of* The Oxford History of English Literature *and* Writers and Their Work *series. In all his writings, Dobrée's foremost concern was to communicate to the reader his aesthetic response to the work under discussion. In the following excerpt, Dobrée discusses Wycherley's complex, evolving attitude toward humanity as it is expressed in his four plays.*]

Perhaps no figure in the Restoration period appears so strange as that of Wycherley. What are we to make of the character of this handsome person, endowed, as Pope said, with so much of the 'nobleman look,' yet a being all angles and unwieldy muscular lumps, shot with unexpected streaks of grace? Certainly he had something of the giant deformity of Chapman, his great love of physical life, with its thew and bone and warm rushing blood, but all tinged with a deep pessimism, a fierce hatred, the *saeva indignatio* ["fierce indignation"] of Swift. He was for ever striving after the absolute, but always bewildered as to which extreme to choose. . . . Outwardly he is the outspoken witty man of fashion, admirably suited to shine in a brilliant court; yet all the while he is producing plays wherein uncouth figures rush upon the stage reviling one another as though engaged in some hopeless, desperate effort to be something absolute, whatever it may be; monsters held up to ridicule, yet which somehow have a quality that makes the laugher ridiculous. (pp. 78-9)

He is like a Dante strayed into the gardens of Boccaccio, but unable to forget for a moment the plague raging everywhere. Which of the two tugging impulses was it better to obey? On which side was he to use his vigorous intellect? It is this gnawing doubt which makes it so difficult to see what he meant by his plays, what he was trying to do. A learner in the Spanish school, unrivalled in the management of plot (here Congreve at his best is a bungler to him), he was master of the unities of time and place, but in the essential unity, that of atmosphere, he failed. Indeed, his plays, with the exception of *The Country Wife,* are the strangest hotch-potch. At one moment we are interested in the development of the story, then we are treated to an exhibition of virulent satire, now beguiled with the antics of a superbly ludicrous fop, entertained with the fencing of a coquettish tongue, or plunged into a bath of tepid romance.

It is his satire that is most interesting, and in it he differs from others who write in that vein, for his satire is never that of a prig, and it is characteristic of him that he always seems to include himself in his denunciations. Some of his writing reads suspiciously like self-flagellation . . . , as though he needed to expiate. Involved in the manners of a society he now hated, now loved, he could not forbear reviling even himself. He scourged his sensuality with a brutal whip, and like a scorpion surrounded by a ring of fire, turned his sting upon himself.

His first play [*Love in a Wood; or, St. James Park*] need not detain us long. It is obviously the work of a brilliant young man, and is not unlike a Shirley play in manner and idea, though it is much more virile. However, the intricacy of its plot, the rather clumsy handling of the humours, as in Sir Simon Addlepot or Lady Flippant, and the at times boorish repartee, make it on the whole tedious reading, though it might act more briskly. The scabrous passages seem badly aimed, as though Wycherley himself did not quite know with what object they were there. Macaulay said he attempted to make vice pleasant, but on reading this we can only think that Macaulay must have had a queer taste in vice. Its mere exposition, as in the case of Mrs. Crossbite, 'an old cheating jill, and bawd to her daughter,' unredeemed by criticism of any kind, can serve neither the purposes of pleasure or those of philosophy. That the play is full of life cannot be denied, but it lacks joyousness. Wycherley was not a poet in the sense of one who seeks for beauty, and in this play, although he did not yet hate his characters, he treated them with a cold disdain. . . . Wycherley's weapon was rounded at the point; he used, not a rapier, but a bludgeon. Vitality he had abundantly, but when he wrote this play grace was sadly lacking in him. (pp. 80-2)

''Tis not sufficient to make the hearer laugh aloud, although there is a certain merit even in this,' so Wycherley, quoting Horace, prefaced his next comedy, by now fully aware of a moral purpose. But there is little literary or moral merit in the laughter aroused by *The Gentleman Dancing Master,* for we laugh for the most part only at the farcical elements of the intrigue, and this soon becomes wearisome. In this adaptation from the Spanish, Wycherley had his technique perfected; there is only one slight flaw in a complicated structure. But no wit is needed to see his points; they are too laboured. We may take a small instance of his Frenchified fop, Monsieur de Paris, an Englishman who had spent a few months in the French capital. He enters:

> *Monsieur.* Serviteur! Serviteur! la cousine; I come
> to give the *bon soir,* as the French say.
> *Hippolita.* O, cousin, you know him; the fine gen-
> tleman they talk so much of in town.
> *Monsieur.* I know all the *beau monde,* cousine.
> *Hippolita.* Master—
> *Monsieur.* Monsieur Taileur, Monsieur Esmit,
> Monsicur . . .
> *Hippolita.* These are Frenchmen.
> *Monsieur.* Non, non; voud you have me say Mr.
> Taylor, Mr. Smith? Fi! fi! *tete non.*

It is so overdone that it ceases even to be funny. . . . (pp. 83-4)

The truth is that in these two plays Wycherley could not bear his fools; they irritated him beyond measure, and in a manner that debarred him from any sympathetic understanding of them. There was an icy deliberateness about him, an appalling consistency in his view of the characters, and it is through this that he becomes, if not a poet, at least a creator. He belongs to the prig-comedy school, but he has no personal arrogance. His satire almost reaches the level of fanaticism. It was not enough to make the spectators laugh; the poor, doubting beast felt impelled to make them brood upon their vices also. Or did he think that by steeping himself in the mud he would achieve some kind of catharsis? (p. 87)

The Plain Dealer is certainly founded on *Le Misanthrope*, but Wycherley re-thought it all, and made it into something quite different. Yet his choice must surely have been due to something in Molière's play that appealed irresistibly to him. Alceste, out of touch with the society in which he moved, how much he was Wycherley himself! Alceste who craved honesty above all things, was not this also Wycherley with his reputation for outspokenness? But *The Plain Dealer* is much more than a mere copy. For Wycherley threw himself into the character, and with his rage for the absolute came to an extreme of furious passion, imagining himself in the worst conceivable situations, so that every event would prove him right in his indignation. But this was not enough. Manly himself, with none of the hope that buoyed up Alceste to the last, incapable of that final touching appeal to Olivia that Alceste made to Célimène (though, indeed, the situation of Olivia made such a thing impossible), must be made to appear as loathsome as the rest, as untrustworthy, and much more brutal. There is no happy mean; there is no Philinte—for Freeman is an unscrupulous cozener—while Eliza, the Éliante of *Le Misanthrope*, is scarcely more than a lay figure. But on the other hand there is Fidelia, that curious evocation from Fletcherian romance, in which again Wycherley strove after some absolute. She is a delicate, hardly real figure, obviously not believed in as are the others, flitting through the play as an angel might flit through purgatory if conjured up in the imagination of a tortured soul.

This play is a strange, thorny monster, tearing the flesh of life wherever it touches it, as it were deliberately, to reveal the skeleton; an ungainly monster, sprawling all over society. Now it consists of an act in the Law Courts, an act only accidentally connected with the play; now of the grim scenes of Olivia's rape and Vernish's duplicity; now of the Widow Blackacre, a 'humour' if ever there was one; now of passages that are pure comedy of manners. And finally there is Fidelia masquerading as a man so as to follow the man she loves. How is criticism to approach this play?

Let us first compare Manly with Alceste; the former, as Voltaire said, drawn with bolder and less delicate strokes than the latter [see excerpt dated 1733]. There is no real desire in Manly for a better state of things, but rather a kind of savage delight in finding things as bad as they are. He is, in the words of Leigh Hunt, 'a ferocious sensualist who believed himself as great a rascal as he thought everybody else' [see excerpt dated 1840]. Manly would never be polite to a bad sonneteer, you never hear him hedging to avoid telling an unpleasant truth, as Alceste does . . . , for Manly would 'rather do a cruel thing than an unjust one.' It is not that he is too delicate for the society in which he moves, it is that he is not subtle enough. Take, for instance, the reactions of the two men to betrayed love. This is Alceste's despair after seeing Célimène's letter to Oronte:

> Ah, tout est ruiné;
> Je suis, je suis trahi, je suis assassiné!
> Célimène . . . eût-on pu croire cette nouvelle?
> Célimène me trompe, et n'est qu'une infidèle.
>
> [Ah, all is ruined;
> I am, I am betrayed, I am assassinated!
> Célimène . . . Would one have been able to believe this news?
> Célimène deceives me, and is naught but a faithless woman.]

This is Manly, after Fidelia reports Olivia has kissed 'him':

> Damned, damned woman, that could be so false and
> infamous! And damned, damned heart of mine, that
> cannot yet be false, though so infamous! . . . Her
> love!—a whore's, a witch's love!—but what, did she
> not kiss well, sir? I'm sure I thought her lips—but I
> must not think of 'em more—but yet they are such
> I could still kiss—grow to—and then tear off with
> my teeth, grind 'em into mammocks, and spit 'em
> into her cuckold's face.

Or contrast Célimène with Olivia. Célimène is an arrant flirt
but we are drawn to her; she is very human. Olivia, on the
other hand, is a mere depraved wretch, combining something
worse than the lightheartedness of Célimène with the false
prudery of Arsinoë. She has promised her hand to Manly, who
gives her all his wealth to keep when he goes to sea. But as
soon as he has gone she marries his trusted friend Vernish,
and between them they steal Manly's money. Within a month
of their marriage she tries to cuckold him with Fidelia, and
there is a strong presumption that she has already done so with
Novel and Plausible. Alceste proposes to revenge himself on
Célimène by offering his heart to Éliante. Such a revenge is
impossible for Manly, because, since Olivia hates him, it will
be no revenge; and so, since she will not admit him to illicit
love, he will, by a stratagem, 'lie with her, and call it revenge,
for that is honourable,' to which performance he will invite
his friends, to see her exposed. This is the man Wycherley
described in the list of characters as being 'of an honest, surly,
nice humour.' His niceties are not apparent, his surliness is
unredeemed savagery.

All through the play men are stripped naked, to reveal, not the
human animal, but the inhuman brute: the virulence is absolutely ruthless. Not a motive shown, but is to be named ra-
pacity, meanness, fear, lust (except Fidelia's), all hidden or
aided by society manners. The law is but an instrument of
money-sucking injustice supported by false witnesses; love but
physical desire; social intercourse trading in the flesh; and
friendship, well, listen to Manly:

> Not but I know that generally no man can be a great
> enemy but under the name of friend; and if you are
> a cuckold, it is your friend only that makes you so,
> for your enemy is not admitted to your house; if you
> are cheated in your fortune, 'tis your friend that does
> it, for your enemy is not made your trustee; if your
> honour or good name be injured, 'tis your friend that
> does it still, because your enemy is not believed against
> you.

This is the wild lashing of some tortured creature that cannot
understand why it is being hurt. (pp. 87-90)

Indeed, the greater part of the play is a flow of invective.
Wycherley does not preach, he indicts. To what purpose? To
redeem mankind? Hardly, for he has here no example of the
happy mean, and indicates no line of conduct to increase social
convenience. He is not the preserver of social illusions, nor
the wielder of the sword of common sense; nor does he create
a fairy world in which all that is necessary is to be comely and
to talk wittily. He is far from Etherege, he has thrown off
Molière. His laughter affords no release, for it is too deeply
cynical; it is of the kind that is man's defence against complete
disillusion, but it is too twisted to purge of discontent.

'Ridicule,' he prefaced, once more from Horace, 'ridicule commonly decides great matters more forcibly and better than severity.' But what are the great matters, and at what is the
ridicule directed? Not at society, at foibles, or vanity, but at
mankind itself. And is it ridicule for the more part? Hazlitt

surely was right when he said, 'It is a severe and poignant
moral satire . . . a discipline of humanity. . . . It penetrates to
the core' [see excerpt dated 1818]. That is how Wycherley
would like it felt. And Hazlitt also said that, 'no one can read
the play attentively without being the better for it as long as
he lives.' But an unrelieved vision of all the mean and sordid
aspects of humanity does little to free us from them. We are
likely to feel ourselves the more irrevocably imprisoned in
despondency. The play reads like a cry of despair. Wycherley
was not here among those who can stride across high mountains, and, like Zarathustra, 'laugh at all tragedies whether of
the stage or of life.' They hurt him too much.

'The satire, wit, and strength of Manly Wycherley,' Dryden
wrote; 'But is railing satire, Novel?' Manly himself asks, 'and
roaring and making a noise humour?' No, railing is not satire,
for in satire, however low the depths shown, there is always
the intense yearning for something different, a vision of the
immensely moving quality of human folly, vice, and suffering,
as in Swift. But in *The Plain Dealer* there is none of this: it is
a cry not of strength, but of weakness, the voice of humanity
outraged. But Fidelia? it will be asked. She is certainly not a
pander of the baser sort, as Macaulay splenetically called her
[see excerpt dated 1841], but a touching figure. . . . Yet there
is some excuse for Macaulay's error, because the modicum of
absolute good is overwhelmed by the flood of absolute evil
that dominates every act. (pp. 92-3)

If in his first three plays Wycherley had not yet purged himself
of the elements which interfered with the expression of his
dominating self; if he had never been sure how he wanted a
scene felt, in *The Country Wife* it is different. In it he com-
pressed all that his forceful character had shown him in Restoration society. It is the one play in the whole period equal
to *The Way of the World* in completeness of expression. It is
a masterpiece, and here Wycherley did attain unity of atmosphere. It is a staggering performance, and never for one instant
did he swerve from his point of view. From beginning to end
Wycherley saw clearly what it was he wanted to do, for now
he understood that the real point of interest in Restoration
society was the sex question. He took scenes from the *École
des Femmes* and the *École des Maris*, but the theme throughout
is the failure to rationalize sex. Horner, the principal figure,
takes a leaf out of the *Eunuchus* of Terence, and declaring
himself impotent, devotes himself to living up to his name.
From this we get the whole gallery of Restoration figures—
the jealous man who is proved wrong to be jealous; the trusting
man who is a fool to be so trusting; the light ladies concerned
for their 'honour'; the gay sparks devoted only to their pleasure;
the ignorant woman seduced; the woman of common sense
baffled—the only triumphant figure Horner himself, the type
of all that is most unselectively lecherous, and who seems to
derive such a sorry enjoyment from his success. We never
laugh *at* Horner, just as we never laugh *at* Tartufe, though we
may on occasion laugh *with* each of them. Both are grim,
nightmare figures, dominating the helpless, hopeless apes who
call themselves civilized men. Again, the absolute. Again we
feel that no mean is possible, because a mean cannot exist for
figures which seem automata animated by devils that drive
them irresistibly to an extreme—and leave them there, to laugh
fiendishly. Is it a comedy at all? Not in the ordinary sense.
The clever, cynical dialogue, the scathing irony, the remorseless stripping of all grace from man, are too overpowering.

Yet on a second reading something else seems to emerge. For
no longer is every word a curse, every phrase an imprecation.

Some other quality is there: one is tempted to say some humanity has crept in. There is, for instance, the charming figure of Alithea, trying to be honest and reasonable, the one congenial human being Wycherley ever drew. But the change is not so much in character as in feeling: the sense of torture, of evil one might say, has gone. Wycherley has shouldered the burden that was crushing him. He even tosses it aloft, displaying his huge strength in fantastic wrestlings with the hated thing. A titanic gaiety rushes him along; almost he sees life whole: if he is not reconciled, he is at least no longer personally involved.

But across this acceptance there sometimes cuts a savage snarl. When Horner asks Pinchwife whether, after all, keeping is not better than marriage, the following interchange takes place:

> *Pin.* A pox on't! The jades would jilt me, I could never keep a whore to myself.
> *Hor.* So, then you only married to keep a whore to yourself.

(pp. 93-5)

But it is wonderfully good once Wycherley overcomes his hatred, and gives free play to the impact of his stage personalities, real living beings, if distorted. How his tremendous laughter bears everything before it! (p. 95)

The actual *Country Wife* portions are not so good as the rest, perhaps because they were borrowed. There is not the conviction about Pinchwife—a rather too simplified Arnolphe—nor the reality about Mrs. Margery that vivify Horner, the Fidgets, Squeamish, and their set. The scenes are certainly sparkling with vigour and movement, full, even too full, of masterly stage effects, but somehow they are not so creatively conceived as the rest. The moral hangs too obviously upon them, and Wycherley drives it home at the expense of art. Nevertheless the whole thing is carried on with vast gusto; a torrent of life rushes through the play, so that the railing passages cease to be railing, and become part of the picture in which humanity is unfalteringly portrayed. The puppets seem now and again to show a human face, and 'while we cross his vociferous stage, the curious and unholy men and women who hurtle against us seem living beings.' Wycherley was still the moralist, but the moralist has become caught up in the artist. *The Country Wife* is a complete thing in itself. (pp. 98-9)

What are we finally to make of Wycherley? or rather, what are we to make of his masterpiece, *The Country Wife*? Somehow he has conquered life, overcome all that he loathed in it, and moulded it into a work of art. But his immense attraction for the sordid was not like that of Dostoievsky, for whom the passionate spirit in man redeemed everything. None of Wycherley's beings reach out at anything beyond immediate actuality, they have no metaphysic. They are curious symbols out of which, by some hard quality of will, he was able to make an artistic gem. It exists, it adds something to our emotions, to our knowledge, and to our aesthetic experience. Wycherley would not be subdued to what he worked in, and he achieved his result by means of not critical, but philosophic, laughter. But what a struggle it was to get there!

His figures, with their bursting vitality, their writhing in what is at once their power and their impotence, remind us not of Molière's but of Webster's. They have all the malignancy, all the *naïveté,* but not the flashes of pity. There is nothing like, 'Cover her face, mine eyes dazzle, she died young.' Nor is there the self-pity. There is no 'Thou art a fool then, to waste thy pity on a thing so wretched as cannot pity itself.' But there

is much of their defiance, with this difference; Webster's men and women are defiant because they will not submit, Wycherley's because they have submitted.

In his first plays we see Wycherley coldly, disdainfully, a little fearfully, poking with his finger the strange, crawling heap he saw the world to be. But a man such as he was could not stay at that point always; there is too much desire for a clear issue. In *The Plain Dealer* we see him shuddering on the brink; had he the courage to see life face to face without interposing barriers of rage? There is no doubt about *The Country Wife*; there he leaped in with a triumphant laugh. Once again Wycherley had dared. (pp. 101-02)

> *Bonamy Dobrée, "Wycherley," in his* Restoration Comedy, 1660-1720, *1924. Reprint by Greenwood Press, Publishers, 1981, pp. 78-102.*

HARLEY GRANVILLE-BARKER (lecture date 1930)

[*An English dramatist, actor, producer, and critic, Granville-Barker was noted for his contributions to the "new drama" movement, signaling his break from the stereotypical social comedy and melodrama of London theater. His mature plays, notably* The Voysey Inheritance *(1909) and* The Madras House *(1910), center on ideas rather than plot or action. His technique was to examine an idea from several points of view through the conversation of his characters. Among his critical works,* Prefaces to Shakespeare *(1927) is considered the most important. In the following excerpt from a lecture originally delivered in 1930, Granville-Barker disparages Wycherley's dramatic technique.*]

There has been of late much re-editing and re-valuing of Restoration drama. For the industry of the re-editing one can have nothing but gratitude. But the re-valuing leaves me, for the most part, blankly amazed. As to the comedy, I was trained in the doctrine (a compromise between Lamb and Macaulay) [see excerpts dated 1823 and 1841] that, its indecency forgiven, we should find in the best of it—in Wycherley at his best, for instance—brilliancy and wit incomparable. . . . But now it appears that Wycherley is not only a brilliant wit and a great playwright, but a stern moralist besides. (p. 118)

I, in my turn, make bold to say that this talk about the moral purpose of Restoration comedy is all stuff and nonsense, and the present claims made for the 'art' of it are not much better. (pp. 118-19)

There is a stage direction in Wycherley's *Love in a Wood* ('prentice work truly, but it has earned from its latest editor glowing praise), *They all go off in a huddle, hastily.* The play's stagecraft is summed up in that—young men and their mistresses chattering their bawdry and chasing each other through scene after scene, till one asks: How could an audience both be clever enough to understand the story and stupid enough to be interested by it when they did?

But take his maturest work, *The Plain Dealer,* that 'magnificent play' as we are now asked to call it. No matter for his pillagings from Molière and Shakespeare! They took their own goods where they found them, and would have been the last to complain. What they might have thought of his treatment of the spoils is another matter, of an Alceste turned sadistic bully and a Viola submitted to rape! But this trenches on the moral issue. Admit the brutality of it all as a fit theme for comedy, what skill or art or wit does he show in its use?

His handling of the plot has been highly praised. It has its minor unlikelihoods, in the casual comings and goings and spyings at Olivia's lodging, and in the first discovery of Manly, returned to England, visited by all and sundry, while for no reason whatever he has kept away from his betrothed nor even had her told of his return. But these are allowable enough. Not till the middle of Act III, though, does the action really get under way. Two acts and more have been spent in as much preparation and disclosure of character as a skilled dramatist could have put through in a couple of scenes. Act IV brings us to Manly's plan for revenge upon Olivia and to Vernish's unexpected arrival in the dark instead of the disguised Fidelia. An amusing situation; but as we have never set eyes on him before it has to be hurriedly explained in an aside:

> OLIVIA: Ha! My husband returned! And have I been throwing away so many kind kisses on my husband, and wronged my lover already?

Not very skilfully contrived, perhaps!

The aside does Wycherley yeoman service. It was, of course, an accepted convention; but there are ways and ways of employing it. . . .

> MANLY: So then; let's know that only; come, prithee, without delays. I'll kiss thee for that news beforehand.
>
> FIDELIA (aside): So: the kiss I'm sure is welcome to me, whatsoe'er the news will be to you.
>
> MANLY: Come speak, my dear volunteer.
>
> FIDELIA (aside): How welcome were that kind word too, if it were not for another woman's sake!
>
> MANLY: What, won't you speak? . . .

One has only to imagine this in action to see the ineptitude of the business; Manly's proximity for the kiss, his attention fixed on her, his incongruous

> What, won't you speak?

Accepted convention though it might be, nobody with any sense of the theatre would employ the aside so clumsily. (pp. 120-24)

Why, one asks, are the soliloquies (all but Vernish's) in blank verse, why those four poverty-stricken little patches stuck upon the prose area of the play? Was it because Wycherley, turning to *Twelfth Night* for his Fidelia, found Viola's

> I left no ring with her: what means this lady?
> Fortune forbid my outside have not charmed her! . . .

and the rest—self-revealing, alive in every phrase!—so said to himself: A little poetry wanted? Well, this is how it's done!

He achieves one passable line in

> And this bright world of artful beauties here . . .

but at once drops to

> Might then have hoped, he would have looked on me
> Amongst the sooty Indians; and I could
> To choose there live his life, where wives are forced
> To live no longer, when their husbands die.
> Nay, what's yet worse, to share 'em whilst they live
> With many rival wives. But here he comes,
> And I must yet keep out of his sight not
> To lose it for ever.

There would be many unexpected competitors for a prize for the worst blank verse line ever written, but I fancy that

> And I must yet keep out of his sight not . . .

would have a chance of it. (pp. 125-26)

After that he may well have resolved that prose was his mark. Nor need one deny his mastery here, while he is steering a straight dramatic course and charging his characters—and if they are characters, not mere hobby horses—with genuine self-expression. The convention is somewhat formal, but what can be better than Manly's rating of Novel?

> Then, Madam, for this gentle piece of courtesy, this man of tame honour, what could you find in him? Was it his languishing, affected tone? his mannerly look? his second-hand flattery? the refuse of the play-house tiring rooms? or, his slavish obsequiousness in watching at the door of your box at the playhouse for your hand to your chair? or his jaunty way of playing with your fan? or was it the gunpowder spot on his hand? or the jewel in his ear, that purchased your heart?

Vigorous, pungent, and well controlled! . . . And through scene after scene the vigour never slackens. His fault is, that he seldom seems to know when he has said enough for effect; he must make his point again, and yet again—and spoil it. No surer sign that a man lacks a sense of the theatre.

But what most undoes him dramatically is the dreadful obligation to be witty, and to keep on—so he seems to feel he must!—at all costs being witty. For while Wycherley has much natural passion, he has not the fineness of mind which breeds wit, and there really is not one spontaneous flash of it in the play. But, for a substitute, he can grind this sort of stuff out by the yard, and he does!

> MANLY: I was only wondering why fools, rascals and desertless wretches, should still have the better of men of merit with all women; as much as with their own common mistress, Fortune.
>
> FREEMAN: Because most women, like Fortune are blind, seem to do all things in jest, and take pleasure in extravagant actions; their love deserves neither thanks, or blame, for they cannot help it: 'tis all sympathy; therefore the noisy, the finical, the talkative, the cowardly and effeminate have the better of the brave, the reasonable and man of honour; for they have no more reason in their love or kindness than Fortune herself.
>
> MANLY: Yes, they have their reason. First, honour in a man they fear too much to love; and sense in a lover upbraids their want of it; and they hate anything that disturbs their admiration of themselves; but they are of that vain number who had rather show their false generosity in giving away profusely to worthless flatterers, than in paying just debts. And, in short, all women, like fortune (as you say) and rewards, are lost by too much meriting.

It is hardly remarkable in substance, and in method it is just about everything it should not be. It lacks clarity; the sentences are overloaded. It lacks music. . . . *who had rather show their false generosity in giving away profusely to worthless flatterers than in paying just debts!* That travelled direct from brain to pen; or if it did pass by mouth and ear, then Wycherley's ear was strangely insensitive. Worst of all, it lacks impulse and impetus, cardinal needs for dramatic speech, and of sententious speech the only salvation. (pp. 126-29)

He had, we may admit, a most demoralizing audience to work for. Its fuglemen were professed wits themselves, who wanted the wares they dealt in spread on the counter before them—an assortment to appraise—and were insensitive to anything else. And the popular themes were few, the changes to be rung on them not very various. Pimping and the pox, whoring and cuckoldry, smut and sham prudery, there is a limit to the humour that can be extracted from them. Even Manly's abuse of *decorums, supercilious forms and slavish ceremonies*—by the end of the first act he seems to have said all there is to be said on the subject twice over at least.

We have the widow Blackacre and her minor and the scene in Westminster Hall for a diversion. Certainly it is a change of subject and provides Manly with a fresh range of abuse. This is the Jonsonian comedy of Humours, for which there may be something to be said when it is Jonson's own cathartic spirit which informs it. But mere exhibition of a monomania, even the most comic, must inevitably become monotonous. Character you can develop, but not caricature. And the puppet show of lawyers in Act III, though it makes bustle enough, is pretty jejune foolery; while neither Manly—nor Wycherley—can find anything much more amusing to say about the law than that the lawyers do better by it than their clients. (pp. 130-31)

> *Harley Granville-Barker, "Wycherley and Dryden,"*
> *in his* On Dramatic Method, *1931. Reprint by Hill*
> *and Wang, Inc., 1956, pp. 117-57.*

HOXIE NEALE FAIRCHILD   (essay date 1939)

[*An American educator, Fairchild is the author of numerous essays and books on literary and religious subjects. His major works include* The Noble Savage: A Study in Romantic Naturalism *(1928), which discusses the depiction in literature of the unspoiled primitive life and its relationship to romantic naturalism, and a six-volume study,* Religious Trends in English Poetry *(1939-68), which traces religious thought and feeling in English poetry from the eighteenth to the twentieth century. In the following excerpt from the latter study, Fairchild assesses the religious values revealed in Wycherley's poetry.*]

[Wycherley] will undertake to write a poem about anything, from **"To a Lady, who wore Drawers in an Ill Hour"** to **"The Good Conscience, the only Certain, Lasting Good."** He takes pleasure in writing on opposite sides of the same subject: two of his poems are respectively entitled **"For the Publick Active Life, against Solitude"** and **"For Solitude and Retirement against the Publick Active Life."** Poetry is for him chiefly a means of displaying his paradoxical smartness in casuistry.

His favorite paradox is summed up in the title, **"Upon the Impertinence of Knowledge, the Unreasonableness of Reason, and the Brutality of Humanity; proving the Animal Life the most Reasonable Life, since the most Natural, and most Innocent."** More than once, evidently with Erasmus' *Praise of Folly* in mind, he reverts to this theme. Elsewhere, to be sure, he can advise a youth to subject his "brutish passions" to the curb of reason; but on the whole Wycherley is, for him, unusually consistent in his anti-intellectualism.

This distrust of reason is not enlisted in the defense of religion, though it was probably a main element in the modicum of personal faith that Wycherley possessed. In *The Intellectual Milieu of John Dryden*, Professor Bredvold has shown how large a part was played by fideistic scepticism in the Roman Catholicism of the seventeenth century. During his stay in France, Wycherley adopted the Roman creed, only to be reconverted to Protestantism soon after the Restoration. In the reign of James, however, he found it convenient to slip over to Rome once more. There is no evidence that he ever took the trouble of going through a second reconversion to Protestantism; indeed, there seems to be no doubt that shortly before his miserable death he received the *viaticum* ["eucharist"] as a Roman Catholic.

These spiritual experiences—if they deserve that epithet—are not explicitly reflected in Wycherley's verse. He is not, however, without ethical and even religious interests. In snarling, crabbed satires which remind one of Oldham, this friend of Charles II and of his mistresses can be very severe against the vices of the age. He can assert that atheists are more bigoted than Christians, since they cling to the one inconceivable miracle—

> That Motion is without a Mover wrought,
> That Reason's no Result of Sense or Thought;
> That Method is the blind Effect of Chance,
> And Order is without an Ordinance.

If a man like Wycherley believes in a God at all, he had best believe in an extremely amiable one. Against "an ill-natur'd Lady, who said Good Nature was Folly, and the Disgrace of Good Sense," he defends the slandered virtue. Where would mankind be now, he asks, were not God eminently good-natured? In the same spirit he addresses a clumsy but apparently sincere rhapsody **"To Love"**:

> Thou the Great Law of Nature art, O Love!
> By whom, Man first was made, does live, and move;
> Great Law of Nature! but for which, in vain,
> Religion, Justice could their own maintain.

Yet Wycherley loves to sneer at pious folk as conceited and hypocritical. Religious enthusiasm and poetical sublimity are both nonsense, and he scornfully compares them in these lines:

> As Quakers on the Spirit lay
> The Nonsense, which they preach, or pray;
> Make their dark senseless Fustian-Stuff,
> Their sole Illumination's Proof,
> So Bards of old, and present Time,
> Their Sense i' th' Clouds, will call Sublime.

This is just the tone of Samuel Butler. Again Wycherley is typically the Cavalier when he writes, in an **"Epistle to the King"**:

> And Zeal is oft the Pious Fool's Excuse,
> Whose rude Pray'r is the Deity's Abuse.

In the same poem he insists that the nonconformist preachers who attack the stage are swayed by professional jealousy; for they themselves are actors, and very bad ones, who

> Against the Play-houses so much declare,
> Cause such their Meeting-houses only are.

Scorn of dissenters is to be expected from a Restoration loyalist. Wycherley, however, delivers similar thrusts even against the Establishment in **"To an University-Wit, or Poet; who had written some ill Verses, with an ill Play or two; which, not succeeding, he resolv'd to turn Parson."** The poetaster has chosen to

> . . . damn Your Age, not to be damn'd by it.
> You'd leave Prophane and witty Poetry,
> To lie o' God's-Name, more ingeniously.

Now that he has changed his "poetic sock" for "canonical galloshes" he will fare better, since

> . . . Nonsense, Sacred, in the Pulpit is,
> Where Clergy-Fictions, Lay-men dare not hiss,
> Railing or Damning, dare not take amiss;
> Nonsense is safe still, in the House of Pray'r,
> Since there are none, who to refute it dare.

Not only dislike of Nonconformity but a more general anti-clericalism and scorn of zeal are evidently strong in Wycherley.

His poems convey no inkling of his attitude toward Roman Catholicism except for **"A Disswasive to his Mistress on her resolving to turn Nun."** He insists that the vow was

> Made in the Weakness of your falt'ring Soul,
> When Superstition did its Pow'rs controul.

But the poem should not be taken very seriously: he concludes it by saying that if she wishes to lead a truly penitential life she had better marry *him*.

Wycherley's inconsistency, combined with his readiness to say whatever will impress the reader with his ingenuity, makes it difficult to place him. . . . One may at least be grateful to him for speaking boldly on [religious] topics. . . . In a few scattered pieces, too, he shows a little more religious sense than our knowledge of his life and of his comedies would suggest. To put it very mildly, however, his poems taken as a whole are not rich in spiritual values. (pp. 9-12)

> *Hoxie Neale Fairchild, "Indifference, Negation, Scepticism," in his* Religious Trends in English Poetry: 1700-1740, Protestantism and the Cult of Sentiment, Vol. I, *Columbia University Press, 1939, pp. 3-40.*

STARK YOUNG (essay date 1948)

[*An American playwright, poet, and novelist, Young was a prominent member of the Agrarian group of Southern poets with Allen Tate, John Crowe Ransom, Robert Penn Warren, and several others, from 1928 until the mid-1930s. The aim of this school, as stated in its manifesto* I'll Take My Stand *(1930), was to preserve the Southern way of life and the region's traditional values. Young served for twenty years as drama critic for such journals as the* New Republic, Theatre Arts Monthly, *and the* New York Times, *and the best of this criticism is collected in* Immortal Shadows: A Book of Dramatic Criticism *(1948). In the following excerpt, Young rates the relevance of* The Country-Wife *to a modern audience.*]

Wycherley's plays were all produced between 1671 and 1674. By 1671 Thomas Durfey in *Sir Barnaby Whig,* is asking how, with Molière quite rifled, is he going to write? That *The Country Wife* is based partly on *L'Ecole des Femmes* and qualified by *L'Ecole des Maris* is obvious. That Wycherley, with that virile independence of his that has been mentioned so often, should depart from these French plays is to be expected. The difference between the two men is fundamental.

Molière writes for a defined and civilized society, is himself a profound social student, a popular genius, ventilated and just, rational and passionate, a ripe and equable designer in social drama. That Congreve, Ben Jonson, Shakespeare have their respective values in comedy is manifest. It is equally manifest that Molière remains outside our scope. The restlessness felt by many of the audience seeing *The Country Wife,* and a certain general indifference felt by almost everyone as to its outcome, may be partially ascribed to the fact that for us today, at least, the play has little to say as a whole; its pervading tone means very little; the spots, in either the present version or the play itself, at which Wycherley bursts into his moral *terribilità* ["dreadfulness"] are, after all, spots, where Molière's work achieves its unity from the light that falls on it from social living, and where the order and tone are the very dialect and sincerity of his nature. *The Country Wife* has been rated as the most perfect of English farces. Compared to Molière, Wych-

erley's play is footless and sunless. We should do much better to take such a play as fantastic—fantastic farce. Despite the realism of Wycherley's surface, or the shadow of his amusement, or the running brunts of his indignation, it is much better to see his hero, Mr. Horner, as extravaganza, heavy with sarcastic vindication, rich with the precision of some summer madness. The text of impotence which he announces for himself, and which thereupon serves as a focus for all the play's situations, is thus kept free for its essential farcicality. By announcing his impotence Mr. Horner opens the way for the confiding response and contemptuous indifference of the husbands and at the same time vastly enlarges the opportunities of the wives. The famous "china" motif ensues here—Mr. Horner's "china" that the ladies come to see and remain to inspect and so on and so on, with all the scandalous ringing of the changes on that theme. (p. 182)

This is an unsatisfactory piece of criticism, but so is the play unsatisfactory. Its criticism of life, once more applicable, violent and admired, is outside many of our values now. But its quality is, nevertheless, alive and actable. (p. 184)

> *Stark Young, "'The Country Wife'," in his* Immortal Shadows: A Book of Dramatic Criticism, *Charles Scribner's Sons, 1948, pp. 181-84.*

LOUIS KRONENBERGER (essay date 1952)

[*A drama critic for* Time *from 1938 to 1961, Kronenberger was a distinguished historian, literary critic, and author highly regarded for his expertise in eighteenth-century English history and literature. Among his best known writings are* Kings and Desperate Men: Life in Eighteenth-Century England *(1942), which examines British culture of that century, and* Marlborough's Duchess: A Study in Worldliness *(1969), a biography of the wife of the first Duke of Marlborough. Of his critical work, Kronenberger's* The Thread of Laughter: Chapters on English Stage Comedy from Jonson to Maugham *(1952) and* The Republic of Letters *(1955) contain some of his best literary commentaries. In an assessment of Kronenberger's critical ability, Jacob Korg states: "He interprets, compares, and analyzes vigorously in a pleasingly epigrammatic style, often going to the essence of a matter in a phrase." A prolific and versatile writer, he also wrote plays and novels and edited anthologies of the works of others. In the following excerpt, Kronenberger discusses Wycherley's sense of moral outrage and its effect on his art in* The Country Wife *and* The Plain Dealer.*]

[Wycherley and Etherege] are most alike in being most unlike the other comedy writers of the Restoration proper and in being the two best men at their trade. But they are not greatly alike for all that, and their coming together may only the more conveniently set them apart. . . . Etherege is clearly a minor writer, Wycherley essentially is not. Wycherley has a much more vigorous talent and much more violent emotions; he cannot, like Etherege, keep life under tissue paper in a bandbox; he cannot even keep life inside a drawing room or the confines of a park. His age and place in society led him to write for the theater with little restraint and with consistent coarseness and license. But in a later age he would almost certainly have turned novelist, and been more at home in the world of Fielding and Smollett. He was like them not cynical; like them robust rather than dandyfied; like them touched with humor rather than with wit; like them, essentially a social critic rather than a social chronicler. A moral misfit in his own age, wallowing in sinfulness and stammering out repentance, he displays some of that self-consuming, self-poisoning rage that we associate with Swift. He is psychologically the most interesting of the

Restoration comedy writers, and potentially the most significant. Yet only two of his four plays have any of the interest of major literature, and one of the two is to my mind a failure. Wycherley was just once able to master his age. (pp. 55-6)

As a sort of Vanity Fair of sex, *The Country Wife* is probably without a rival in Restoration or any other period of English literature. We can have nothing but praise for the fullness of the picture; nothing but praise for the force. Much of the time, moreover, the play romps wickedly from scene to scene, with a vital comic gusto, a tremendous farcical abandon. If Pinchwife with his jealousy, and Sparkish with his refusal to be jealous, are foils to each other and targets for Wycherley; so Lady Fidget, with her accomplished dissembling, and Margery Pinchwife, with her rapturous naïveté, offer an even livelier contrast; while Alithea, the nearest the play comes to a true heroine, is by no means wishy-washy. *The Country Wife* has, besides, considerable verbal explicitness. "Women of quality," Horner remarks, "are so civil, you can hardly distinguish love from good breeding, and a man is often mistaken." . . . The play is full of those similes that Wycherley is fonder of than skillful at: "A woman masked, like a covered dish, gives a man curiosity and appetite" or "Marrying to increase love is like gaming to become rich; alas! you only lose what little stock you had before."

If epigrams are not Wycherley's forte, certainly plausibility isn't. Perhaps one needn't gag too much over the characterization of the country wife (who seems almost as knowing at moments as she seems naïve at others) for she is a woman, and this is a farce. And conceivably some defense can be made for Sparkish's utter refusal to be suspicious of Harcourt or jealous of Alithea—the defense that he is a comedy-of-humors character, whose mania is a *lack* of jealousy. But at least once in the play, no defense is possible: Harcourt's dressing himself up as his non-existent priest of a brother is not only incredible but puerile. Yet this masquerade is at least at the expense of an insanely unjealous man, where Margery's dressing up as Alithea and getting Pinchwife to lead her all the way to Horner's, is at the expense of an insanely jealous one—and of her own husband to boot! One need not adduce all the evidence of this sort. The important fact is that it is so glaring and frequent that it does more than affect the play's plausibility; it badly impairs its tone. This is not a new fault in Wycherley—*The Gentleman Dancing Master* taxes our credulity quite as much. And the fault is easy to understand, if not to forgive: for Wycherley is among those robust writers with whom it is the constant movement, the composite effect, that counts; he is not dandiacal like Etherege or elegant like Congreve. He is quite the opposite—as man and writer alike, he runs to extremes, to excess. As a sex comedy, *The Country Wife* might almost be called lurid. No one seems to have reached out toward London life with a greater sense of enjoyment than Wycherley, or afterwards to have recoiled from it with a greater sense of disgust. He is the great pagan of Restoration comedy; but he is also the great Puritan.

It was not frustration that made a moralist of him, but satiety; not lofty thinking but loose living; not an appeal to ethics but a recoil from experience. He was a full-blooded man first, and only a bilious one afterwards. And as man, so was the playwright. He must first create freely and robustly; and only then harshly and mordantly criticize. The two sides of him really present one picture, but in different lights and with opposite effects, like a photograph and a negative; and they sometimes give a twofold value to a single quality. Certainly, up to a point, the thing that for centuries has most made *The Country Wife* a scandal has also most made it a sermon. There is no use pretending that Horner's famous china scene is not fully as indecent as it is amusing. There is no use pretending that a comedy that turns upon a rake's making out he is impotent is not appealing to a very definite side of its audience. We may be past the Victorian reaction of a Macaulay, who compared Wycherley to a skunk [see excerpt dated 1841], or the Edwardian reaction of a William Archer, dubbing this "the most bestial play in all literature" [see excerpt dated 1923]; we may be past it in tolerance because, for one thing, we have got past it in insight. But neither can we accept it as a mere invitation to smack our lips, and in the same breath shrug our shoulders. The question is not one of prudishness but of proportion; and though the fun far outruns the smut, the smut must—if only because it can seem so calculated—give us qualms.

But the thing, as I said, that for centuries has most made *The Country Wife* a scandal has most made it a sermon. The play is so indecent because Restoration life was so indecent. We are appalled because we were meant to be appalled; Wycherley never intended us to be enraptured. The gusto with which he painted Horner should not lead us to suppose that he meant him for a good fellow; he meant him for a bad fellow, as certainly as Ben Jonson meant Volpone. Though Margery is not without a certain appeal, we are not to suppose that because *she* was unfortunate in having Pinchwife for a husband, we would have been fortunate in having her for a wife. To the extent that the characters sharpen their wits against one another, this is legitimate and traditional comedy enough; but to the degree that they harden their hearts against all that is fair and honorable in life, this is harsh, protesting satire. No doubt a certain sort of prude could only be disgusted by this play without ever being amused. The most tolerant of us, on the other hand, could hardly be amused without ever being disgusted. But, for too long, what is revolting in the picture has been glibly confused with what is salacious. Who, however much amused by *Gulliver's Travels*, is not sometimes disgusted? But salaciousness is there not much in question—though bestiality is—hence even your prude will allow that *Gulliver* is amusing and Swift a moralist.

However Wycherley may have misused sex in *The Country Wife*, he was sound in making it the pervasive fact of his play. For through sex alone could he show what he wished to show, reflect what he wished to reflect; with sex alone could he find the right key to a callous, cold-hearted, dissolute Restoration society. Money, no doubt, made possible their way of life; but these leisure-class people were overwhelmingly concerned not with making but with spending it. Ambition doubtless played a great role in their scheme of things, but not in their day-to-day existence. These people are not, after all, the great nobility, but only the lesser fry. It was physical pleasure they cared most about—which is to say, their *own* pleasure. It wasn't simply what they did to each other, it was how they did it; not out of weakness or necessity, but out of all lack of affection and principle. We may suppose that *The Country Wife* exaggerates, but not that it misrepresents. For all that it romps like the liveliest farce, it is a serious play, a key play. One can study textbooks and source material and documents in the British Museum—as no doubt one must—to become an expert on Restoration facts. But half a library of all such things probably counts less than *The Country Wife* if one would become an expert on Restoration feeling. It hardly seems to me the masterpiece it does to Mr. Dobrée [see excerpt dated 1924]; but nothing could be more vigorously expressive, or more central to its period.

In *The Country Wife,* Wycherley not only penetrated to the center of his world, he remained close to the center of comedy also. He is not too angry to keep others from being amused; and whatever its ultimate meaning, the play is in mood a farce—much of the time, in fact, a roaring and lively farce. In his last produced play, however, Wycherley went completely out of bounds. Starting off in *Love in a Wood* with an excess of material, he wound up, in *The Plain Dealer,* with an excess of emotion. In it he lashes out too violently at the life he knew too well; too violently, indeed, to preserve the sense of that life. The play's reality crumbles beneath the playwright's rage. The picture we see painted, beyond seeming incredible, keeps calling attention to the man who is painting it. Wycherley is so anxious to indict, so determined to punish, that he wildly, feverishly, portrays all manner of crime.

Many people, to be sure, regard *The Plain Dealer* as Wycherley's masterpiece—more people, it may be, than regard *The Country Wife.* And certainly in some ways it is a staggering performance, a work crammed with vigor and talent, harsh satire and savage bite. But—at however impressive a level—it seems to me a failure as art, a failure as comedy. Under our very eyes we see its force splintering into violence, its wine turning to vinegar. For anyone to be effectively *appalled,* he must feel a simultaneous sense of horror and of truth; he must accept what only a little earlier he could scarcely have imagined. That is what we do in *The Country Wife* and fail to do here. For in *The Country Wife* we are offered a picture of a shocking but actual society, where here we are given the vision of an enraged and half-hallucinated man. Wycherley wields his club with massive force here, but with wildly faulty aim.

He begins—and so may we—with the figure of the plain dealer himself. We will postpone for the moment all comparison between Wycherley's plain dealer, Manly, and Molière's misanthrope. For this is very much Wycherley's own play; and Manly is created, not indeed in Wycherley's own image, but out of his black thoughts and lacerated moral emotions. Manly is already disgusted by the shams, the duplicities, the indecent self-seeking of London society. A sea captain who prefers honest rough weather to treacherous calms, he has acquired the sea's roughness along with its honesty, and a sea captain's confidence in his own best judgment along with his need to judge. Manly is so proud of being frank, he never asks whether he may not be brutal; is so proud of having a mind of his own, he never wonders if he may not misread things. "Now I speak ill," he says, "of most men because they deserve it; I that can do a rude thing, rather than an unjust thing." You see the virtue of his position; you see also what vast encouragement it gives him to be rude. He has reached the point of being as bilious as society is tainted; and would be not glad, but sorry, to have his opinion of it disproved. He is a little like the man one sometimes meets who thinks all literary or music critics either stupid or crazy or corrupt, so that he increasingly regards himself as infallible.

Or rather, there is *one* music or literary critic whom our man makes an exception of and swears by; just so Manly exempts from his indictment Olivia, who is his fiancée, and Vernish, who is his friend. These two he wholly admires and trusts: indeed he has bestowed all his money on Olivia—"I can never doubt," he tells Freeman, "her truth and constancy."—"It seems," Freeman answers, "you do; since you are fain to bribe it with money." And of course it is Manly's fiancée and

his friend who are destined to betray him. So far our story is familiar enough, and its irony is, if anything, too familiar. Yet it could be persuasive; and we could accept equally the poetic justice and the human injustice of the story. But Wycherley was treating of no ordinary betrayal, and of no ordinary victim. His Olivia is not just a spotted worldling, treacherous because greatly tempted, or unfaithful because easily lured; his Vernish is not one of those worldlings by education and weaklings by nature who have neither the moral starching nor the personal stamina to hold firm. By people such as these, sadly lacking in character, a man of great strength of character might easily be fooled: strength can never quite comprehend weakness. But Olivia and Vernish are not passive betrayers, or even clever compunctionless self-seekers; they are utter villains, who do not betray Manly simply for gain, but betray him gloatingly and malignantly—and in partnership. Olivia, in particular, not only commits every infamy against her suitor; she would also inflict every indignity on him—through hating him outright, as it were, rather than through feelings of guilt. Olivia has with some justice been called another Vittoria Corombonna; and when a comedy writer is brought into comparison with a blood-and-horror writer like Webster, conceivably the Comic Muse has strayed off her own preserves.

But if Olivia and Vernish are no passive betrayers, Manly is no easy victim. When he learns how Olivia has used him and what she thinks of him, we get some notion of how hellish and furious can be a gentleman scorned: Manly, still raging with desire for Olivia, and now aching for revenge, plots to possess her under cover of being some one else, and then to publish his having had her to the town at large. Thus Manly, on being made a victim, turns villain himself; and despite his hatred of dissembling, turns complete dissembler.

To be sure, Wycherley might have meant to show how, in the very act of resisting the corruption of his age, Manly so strongly felt its pressure as to be himself corrupted. But we feel that Wycherley meant no such thing—not just because of the alacrity with which Manly embarks on retaliation, but because of the alacrity with which Wycherley lets him, in succumbing to his baser self, regain the upper hand. Manly gets revenge indeed, gets back his money, gets back his right to feel that among all the depravity of London rare angels do exist. He wins, at the end, Fidelia; or rather she, poor girl, wins him, having followed him around in men's clothes for years—saying nothing and being lovesick; shipping before the mast and getting seasick; enduring Olivia's endearments when she took Fidelia for a man, and Vernish's when he learned she was a woman. Fidelia, I would imagine, has times without number been compared to Shakespeare's Viola; but the comparison is even more incongruous than it is inescapable; and Fidelia throws the play even more out of kilter than its white devil of an Olivia does.

But Fidelia is also enlightening; for Wycherley, in bringing so selfless an angel into his noisome world, is committing Manly's mistake; is himself providing so wild an exception to the rule as to raise doubts about rule and exception alike. It at least helps to *characterize* Manly, that, with so low an opinion of society in general, he should yet have so exalted an opinion of his fiancée and his friend; but it entirely stigmatizes Wycherley that of a society so monstrous he should predicate a single exception so angelic. You may urge that Fidelia is much what she is because of the role she must play in the plot; but somehow, in situations like these, blunder begets blunder, and in the very plot he chooses the author is really plotting against himself.

An early engraving of a character in The Plain-Dealer *(1676). The Billy Rose Theatre Collection, The New York Public Library at Lincoln Center, Astor, Lenox and Tilden Foundations.*

For, among other things, **The Plain Dealer** is rather absurd as a result of being set down in rage. The whole thing suggests a man, and a comedy writer, and a satirist, and an artist, who has lost control. He has seen so much of Restoration society that he cannot stomach any of it. Out of a satiety of worthless pleasure has come an excess of revulsion; the pagan in Wycherley feels such nausea that he is in a rage against himself; and the Puritan in Wycherley can only turn it into a rage against society. Wycherley's mood, like Manly's, is not just one of indignation, but of revenge; and like Manly's, his revenge is misguided, intemperate, and a reflexion on himself. There is no incident, no character, no turn or twist of plot, however vicious, however unsuited to comedy, however unintentionally comic, that Wycherley is able to forego. He paints, as a result, a picture of really lurid infamy—not from wanting to be melodramatic, only from having to be mordant. Again and again, and harder and harder, he lashes out at Restoration society; but less and less do the blows tell, does the body bleed. For instead of feeling the Restoration's hatefulness we simply feel Wycherley's hate. And when Wycherley sets about striking a balance through Fidelia, no balance is possible; being at one extreme, he can only rush to the other; against pitch black he can only set pure white.

From any point of view—comic, realistic, tragic—the final point about Manly is not the mere rightness or wrongness of his attitude, or the goodness or badness of his nature, but the violence of his methods. Moderation he looks upon as compromise; conventional good manners as hypocrisy; social adjustment as personal surrender. The pattern of extremism is always the same: the exception must be made as white as everything else is black. Out of disgust for all other political systems comes a fanatical faith in Communism; out of a sense of the incorrigible wickedness of this world comes some zealotic formula for achieving Heaven. And with it, as with Manly, is born the self-righteousness that can embark upon revenge in the belief that it constitutes justice.

Wycherley *might* have intended Manly as a Horrible Example; unfortunately he projected him as his own alter ego. Wycherley is himself fanatical here: under the guise of comedy, he resorts to melodrama; in a black mood for realism, he goes so far that nothing whatever seems real. The play can be very powerful at its best; it can be fascinating and brilliant, but never sound. It is not so much hoist by its own petard as shattered to bits by its own dynamite. The whole thing, in a way, is extraordinary. For if there is any cliché of clichés about the Restoration, it is that it represents a world of cynicism, of people who raise their eyebrows and shrug their shoulders and turn their backs. And here is a play wrecked by all lack of commonsense, of skepticism, of proportion; here at the very fount of Indifference juts up the tousled head of Fury. (pp. 66-75)

One cannot read **The Plain Dealer** without being put in mind of *The Misanthrope;* but less because of their likenesses than of their differences. (p.76)

The story [in *The Misanthrope*], or if you prefer the lack of one, has almost nothing in common with **The Plain Dealer**: the similarity lies in the situation at the outset and in the nature of the two heroes. And we may certainly allow to Wycherley a frequent power and boldness, a distinct theatrical vividness, quite lacking in Molière—because alien to Molière, quite undesired by him. For Molière did not create his misanthrope in the same savage mood with which Wycherley created his plain dealer—to lash out, despite his own misdeeds, at all the evildoing of the age. However moral Molière's purpose, he could never have adopted Wycherley's immoderate ways—his lurid twists of plot, his extravagant forms of villainy, his black-and-white view of mankind. (pp. 77-8)

Certainly no two plays so much alike at the outset as *The Misanthrope* and **The Plain Dealer** could wind up much farther apart. Their divergence is very instructive. It yields a contrast, to begin with, between comedy at its most unruffled and olympian, and satire at its most sulphurous and enraged. Where Molière is not fighting at all, Wycherley is actually fighting himself—and losing the fight, for all his prowess and strength. But quite as much as we have a contrast between the comic and the satiric spirit, we have one between moderation and excess, between the most perfect feeling for proportion in Molière and the most hopeless want of it in Wycherley. The world of *The Misanthrope* seems a completely social one; that of **The Plain Dealer** comes to seem more and more animal. As an animal world, it is often livelier, crueler, more immediately absorbing, but it will not do as a serious criticism of human life. Where the high comedy of *The Misanthrope* stands at the very borders of tragedy, the harsh, curiously maudlin satire of **The Plain Dealer** actually, I think, crosses the frontiers of melodrama. To smile, even as sadly as Molière does in *The Misanthrope,* is still to smile, if only a very little about the eyes; but to bare one's teeth like Wycherley cannot be passed off as to laugh. The lesson here is not simply that between moderation and excess, between one of the greatest of French artistic virtues and one of the worst of English artistic faults. It is equally that one cannot write comedy when one is in a mood of self-hatred born of self-indulgence. For comedy refuses to scream as an alternative to sobbing; and even satire balks at whiplashing other men's hides as a masked way of beating one's own breast. (p. 80)

> *Louis Kronenberger, "Wycherley," in his* The Thread of Laughter: Chapters on English Stage Comedy from Jonson to Maugham, *Alfred A. Knopf, 1952, pp. 55-80.*

NORMAN N. HOLLAND   (essay date 1959)

[*An American educator and critic, Holland developed a Freudian psychoanalytic approach to literature in his studies* The Dynamics of Literary Response *(1968) and* 5 Readers Reading *(1975). Holland believes that literature appeals to us because it explores yet renders manageable our unconscious fears and desires. Our response to literature is thus an intensely subjective experience; as Holland has explained, "I am advocating a criticism in which we consciously recognize that we re-create literature for ourselves" through the interaction of work and unconscious mind. In the following excerpt taken from a study Holland completed before he had fully formulated his critical theories, he discusses the theme of pretense in* The Gentleman Dancing-Master.]

Wycherley's second play was produced at the new theater, Dorset Garden, apparently in the fall of 1672. It was indifferently received then—and has been since. No one revives this play; critics rarely give it more than passing mention. Frankly, I find this hard to understand, because *The Gentleman Dancing-Master* stands out as perhaps the most ingenuous and innocuous comedy of the period. Restoration audiences received it coolly, possibly because it is less smutty than most Restoration comedies, but more probably because it was too simple for their tastes: the intrigue is not very complicated and the humor is more slapstick than verbal. But the qualities that made the Restoration dislike it are precisely the things that should make a modern critic or audience prefer it, for it is intrigue and verbal wit that make most Restoration plays hard to follow. This, therefore, should be an ideal play for revival. On its own merits, *The Gentleman Dancing-Master* has a pretty charm that contrasts with and overshadows the small amount of Restoration vulgarity that remains in it. (p. 64)

The play makes its point simply, directly, and amusingly. In the title lies the theme: the contrast between the dancing-master (one of "those tripping outsides of Gentlemen") and the true gentleman, form alone as opposed to form plus substance. Dancing itself in the play serves as one half of a sustained *double-entendre:* dancing is an outward form that cloaks the real dance of marriage—"*Adam* and *Eves* dance, or the beginning of the World," or at least of its populating. The lovers who concentrate on the substance of their relation are surrounded by absurd people who devote all their attentions to appearances: Paris, of whom, when Hippolita asks, "Is he no man?" her maid replies, "He's but a *Monsieur*"; Don Diego Formal—the name is significant—whom Paris calls a "capricious, jealous Fop" and Gerrard calls "old Formality"; Mrs. Caution, who consistently attaches more importance to the fact of chastity than to the state of mind that gives rise to it. . . . Don Diego also reverses the proper roles of social forms and state of mind, in a broader sense, of appearance and nature.

Thus, he congratulates Mrs. Caution on keeping even priests away from Hippolita:

> We are bold enough in trusting them with our Souls, I'le never trust 'em with the body of my Daughter, look you *Guarda*, you see what comes of trusting Church-men here in *England;* and 'tis because the Women govern with Families, that Chaplains are so much in fashion. Trust a Church-man—trust a Coward with your honour, a Fool, with your secret, a Gamester with your Purse, as soon as a Priest with your Wife or Daughter, look you, *Guarda*, I am no Fool, look you.

This is Wycherley's peculiarly caustic sense of humor: the ability to laugh at the whole "masquerading Age," that has given the soul the value of the body and the body the value of the soul, the ability to laugh on one side at the chaplains and the ladies who engage them and on the other at Don Diego who complains for a wrong reason.

Mrs. Caution's hypocrisy is only a more subtle version of the attention to forms that constitutes the humors of Diego and Paris. "Ha—is dere any ting in de Universe so jenti as de *Pantalloons*?" cries Paris, "any ting so *ravisaunt* as de *Pantalloons*." "I must live and dye for de *Pantaloon* against de *Spanish* hose." Marriage, compared to clothing, is a mere nothing: "Dere is not the least Ribbon of my Garniture, but is as dear to me as your Daughter, Jernie." Paris believes—almost logically—that since the French have them, the way to achieve good manners is to imitate the French, to speak one's native English with a French accent, and the like. Anything English, such as Gerrard, is *ipso facto* objectionable: "I wou'd not be judg'd by an *English* Looking-glass, Jarnie." He thus debases "Civility and good Breeding more than a City Dancing-Master." He is the real dancing-master (the outside of a gentleman), and Gerrard is the real gentleman. Fittingly, then, Monsieur is duped into bringing Hippolita her lover, standing watch for them, bringing a parson, and guarding them while they are married.

Don Diego, too, though his pretense is a little subtler than Paris', values clothing more than his daughter: "He that marry's my Daughter shall at least look like a wise Man, for he shall wear the *Spanish* Habit." Whereas Paris seeks only good manners, Don Diego seeks wisdom itself. His only mistake is to assume that by putting on Spanish clothes, beard, and oaths, one achieves "*Spanish* Care, Circumspection, and Prudence." But Don Diego is at least a shade wiser than his French counterpart. He can see Paris is "so much disguis'd"; he can see Gerrard is "a very honest man, though a Dancing master"—even if Gerrard is deceiving him as he speaks. He can at least say: "The Hood does not make the Monk, the Ass was an Ass still, though he had the Lyons Skin on; this will be a light *French* Fool, in spight of the grave *Spanish* Habit, look you." Most important, Don Diego can make a turnabout pretense at the end, to fill out the happy ending for the story.

In contrast to these absurd people who pretend almost unconsciously, stand the witty lovers who know what they are doing, even if they are impelled by the disturbing influence of love: "Love, indeed," says Gerrard, "has made a grave Gouty Statesman fight Duels; the Souldier flye from his Colours, a Pedant a fine Gentleman; nay, and the very Lawyer a Poet, and therefore may make me a Dancing-Master." It is an error to assume that the satire deals only with "nationalities." On the contrary, the satire, both in language and action, contrasts two kinds of pretense: we might call them clever and foolish, conscious and unconscious, pretense as a means as opposed to pretense as an end in itself, or more accurately, pretending in order to achieve a proper appearance with which to express one's nature as opposed to pretending in order to substitute appearances for the emptiness of one's nature. (pp. 64-7)

Hippolita, it is true, uses pretense, but she uses it to fill out a social form, not, as her father or Paris use it, to replace substance with an empty form. Hippolita creates a marriage of love, by a growth from within, whereas the real pretenders try to impose an empty marriage from without. She uses pretense to manipulate Gerrard, to bring him to her and correct his attitudes. Their relation grows from their random desires at the opening of the play, Hippolita's for "any man, any man, though he were but a little handsomer than the Devil, so that he were a Gentleman," and Gerard's desire for "a new City-Mistress." At their first meeting, their relation grows to a frank sexuality; they talk about money matters. They come to admire one another's wit when Gerrard sees Hippolita devise the dancing-master scheme. Finally, when Hippolita pretends she is penniless, she causes a real meeting of selves, free of social criteria.

On the other hand, Paris' relations with his prostitute Flirt lead from aggression on Flirt's part (like Hippolita's initiative) to a quasi-marriage, "keeping" with all the forms of marriage, settlements, maintenance, house, coach, and the rest, but without affection or cohabitation. The scene in the last act between Monsieur and Flirt adds to the general contrast in the play. Paris is blackmailed into "keeping"—explicitly contrasted to marriage—at almost exactly the same moment that Gerrard and Hippolita are being married in fact.

Not only is there this contrast between Hippolita's more or less genteel pursuit and the pursuing prostitutes: "Bailiffs, Pursevants," a press-gang to a "hot Service," there is also a continued discussion and contrast of right and wrong kinds of marriage. In addition to Gerrard and Hippolita's marriage based on love, and Monsieur's quasi-marriage, there is the Don's idea that "as soon as she's marry'd, she'd be sure to hate him; that's the reason we wise *Spaniards* are jealous." Whereas in the world around the lovers money can change a woman's very nature ("O money, powerful money! how the ugly, old, crooked, straight, handsom young Women are beholding to thee"—, Gerrard cannot part with his love, even when he thinks she is penniless. There are the marriages in which "Cuckolds by their Jealousie are made," and wives are confined to that absolute evil, the country, marriages in which the husband takes his privileges in the dark—and the wives by day." Opposed to them is Hippolita's simple announcement and Gerrard's agreement that she will have none of it: jealousy is "arrant sawciness, cowardise, and ill breeding." Some marriages are forced by parents and these, even Prue the maid can see, are bad: Gerrard and Hippolita's marriage is anything but forced. It becomes, in effect, a symbol for the harmonious marriage of appearance and nature, just as the various kinds of false marriage become symbols for false relationships between appearance and nature, the affectations of Monsieur and the Don, for example.

The general movement of the comedy parallels these contrasts: the action works through barriers of pretense toward an underlying situation. At the opening of the play, Don Diego's house constitutes a prison of folly and affectation in which Hippolita is confined like a sleeping beauty. "Around the castle," the story goes, "a hedge of thorns began to grow, which became taller every year, and finally shut off the whole estate." Before Hippolita is irrevocably fenced in (by her forthcoming

marriage to a foolish fop) Gerrard comes, though he has to break through the gallery window to get to her. The action moves further inward when Gerrard secures his entrance by the dancing-master fiction and when the lovers go into a closet to be married; the final inward movement would be the consummation after the curtain. "Together they came down the stairs and the king awoke and the queen and the entire courtly estate, and all looked at each other with big eyes." But neither Don Diego (the king?) nor Mrs. Caution (the queen?) is awakened out of pretense to a true perception of reality. The Don resolves instead on a further pretense. He makes believe he was never deceived and acts the part of the pleased father with blessings and gifts. . . . Wycherley has turned the opening situation around. Instead of being able to force the form of marriage on a loveless relationship as he had planned, Don Diego himself is forced to shape his own formal pretense to fit the inner reality given outward form in Hippolita and Gerrard's marriage. "Nature" grown into appearance scores a complete victory over appearance forced on nature.

The Gentleman Dancing-Master pictures two decent people surrounded by a world of folly. Decency means simply two things: the ability to see through to reality and the ability to make the forms one puts on reflect one's private life or "nature." Folly, on the other hand, means the substitution of appearance for one's nature, Spanish clothes for wisdom, a French accent for good breeding, or the form of marriage for the emotional basis of marriage. This kind of folly blinds its fools so they see into others no better than they see into themselves. To Etherege, folly was the confusion of private life with public front. Wycherley saw that much and more: folly represented a commitment to a life of pretense. The unconscious pretenders, Don Diego, Monsieur, and Mrs. Caution, are foolish, even to some extent evil, but without exception less happy than Hippolita and Gerrard, who pretend for a limited purpose, binding themselves temporarily to pretense to gain a permanent freedom from it. Such a contrast shapes a comic action based almost entirely on intrigue. Comedy becomes a chain of results set off by an initial discrepancy between appearance and nature or form and inner reality; for example, the loveless marriage a foolish parent tries to impose. Wycherley's unique contribution to Restoration comedy was a sense that folly, evil, and limitations to happiness were all related, that there is a right way and a wrong way. (pp. 68-70)

In *The Gentleman Dancing-Master,* both the lovers and the fools pretend, but from the wrong way represented by Diego, Paris, and Mrs. Caution, we infer the rightness of the way represented by Gerrard and Hippolita. The difference between Etherege's use of this strategy and Wycherley's is simply that Wycherley puts the right way on the stage, while Etherege either leaves it to inference or, if he does put it on stage, ironically undercuts it (Freeman as opposed to Courtall; Dufoy as opposed to Sir Frederick). With both dramatists, however, this sense of right and wrong way creates the apparently cynical and satirical tone, because they make the texture of the play the wrong way. Our reaction to the play, however, consists of contrasting the situation embodied in the language and action on the stage and an opposite state of affairs that we infer (or infer the rightness of). The very immorality of these plays impies an ethic, but an ethic of wisdom. The hero does what the villain does, and one must look inside to see the difference. (p. 72)

Norman N. Holland, "'The Gentleman Dancing-Master'," in his The First Modern Comedies: The Significance of Etherege, Wycherley and Congreve,

Cambridge, Mass.: Harvard University Press, 1959, pp. 64-72.

ANNE RIGHTER   (essay date 1965)

[*In the following excerpt, Righter discusses Horner's role in* The Country-Wife.]

Horner is the most memorable figure in **The Country Wife**, even as the Vice, with his energy, his realism, his cynicism about love, had been the memorable character in late medieval drama. Like the Vice, Horner stands completely alone in the play. Harcourt and Dorilant are his good friends; when it seems that Alithea will marry Sparkish after all, Horner has enough feeling to say to himself in an aside: 'Poor *Harcourt*, I am sorry thou has mist her'.... Yet these friends are never allowed to share the secret behind Horner's supposed impotence. Horner accepts their diffident sympathy, watches them trying to suppress the cruel jokes of Sparkish, and says nothing. Even at the end of the comedy, the nature of his pretence is clear only to people he despises: the quack, the three hypocritical ladies and (rather dimly) to Mrs. Pinchwife. Horner is a solitary, a man who has cut himself off from everyone except those female pretenders to honour who, thanks to his ruse, can sin with him joyously and still keep their reputations immaculate. For these women, Horner has profound scorn; they are devices, impersonal instruments of pleasure. Yet his purely sensual relationship with them is the only honest one he maintains.

Curiously enough, the only other character in the comedy who is at all like Horner is the country wife herself. Margery Pinchwife is hopelessly naïve and foolish; she is quite unaware of what the moral issues are. Like Horner, however, she acts purely and straightforwardly to gratify her desires. She is so much a product of the country that she has not learned that it is necessary to conceal these appetites, or to call them by other names, as Lady Fidget and her friends have learned to do so fulsomely. Mr. Horner's love is more satisfactory than that of her jealous, old 'musty husband'; she sees no reason why she should not exchange the one for the other, permanently. In fact, her public insistence upon this preference almost wrecks Horner's pretence. Mrs. Pinchwife is an amusing simpleton; Horner is both sophisticated and almost diabolically clever. Yet they have both arrived at exactly the same place, though by different roads. Their attitudes towards love are the same, Margery's because it is all she knows in the first place, Horner's because he has deliberately excluded all other possibilities. This association of Horner with the country wife makes it doubly clear that Wycherley does not intend him as the hero of the comedy. His purely behaviourist point of view is limited and distorting; like Jonson's Volpone, he is a monomaniac who pays too great a price for his undeniable success.

The trouble with **The Country Wife,** is, that although the centre of the comedy clearly lies with Alithea and Harcourt, Wycherley cannot really bring himself to believe in them. It is in their love that the conflicting claims of romanticism and the realism of a Horner are reconciled, that marriage fulfils a symbolic role. The dramatist's attention remains fixed, however, upon the negative side of the picture, upon Horner the agent of destruction, the man who flays romantic and social ideals. His behaviour scarcely accords with the truewit's standard of natural elegance and decorum; it is grotesque, one-sided and excessive, yet it dominates the comedy just the same. In its overall effect, **The Country Wife** is nihilistic. Horner is a kind

of rival touchstone to that represented at the centre by Harcourt and Alithea, wholly negative as it is positive. (pp. 78-9)

Anne Righter, "William Wycherley," *in* Restoration Theatre, *edited by John Russell Brown and Bernard Harris, St. Martin's Press, 1965, pp. 71-91.*

ROSE A. ZIMBARDO   (essay date 1965)

[*Zimbardo is an American educator and critic. In the following excerpt, she examines the satiric design of* The Country-Wife.]

[In **The Country Wife,** the] satirist does not appear as a character in the play; the adversarius is the audience, and the scenes presented before us are the satiric background. The result is that there is in the play neither a central character nor a central action. Horner is most often employed as the mouthpiece for spoken satire, for commentary upon the scene. But he does not occupy a central position, as Manly does [in **The Plain Dealer**]. He is not present in every scene. Rather, the action speaks for itself and is occasionally interspersed with scenes of commentary. Horner is not sufficiently detached from the scene to be the satirist's persona. . . . [His] position is that traditional to the parasite-satirist. He is prominent but not central. He is distinguished from the other characters by his cleverness but he is nonetheless of their number. All the characters, including Horner, serve as instruments of satire, examples used by the poet-satirist to illustrate his vision of human corruption.

As there is no central character, neither is there a central action. There are, rather, three separate actions; that which concerns Horner's disguising himself as a eunuch and his success in that enterprise, that which concerns the efforts of Pinchwife to keep his young and ignorant wife chaste, and that which concerns Harcourt's attempts to win Alithea from her misplaced loyalty to Sparkish. The actions are arbitrarily related in the relationship of characters in one action with characters in another. For example, the Harcourt-Alithea-Sparkish action is linked to the Pinchwife action because Alithea happens to be Pinchwife's sister, and to the Horner action because Harcourt happens to be Horner's friend. The lines of action are, therefore, loosely, if cleverly, linked, and none of the three predominates. Time on stage is divided almost equally among them. One's interest is directed upon one sphere of action and after the satiric point is made is shifted to another. The unity of the play, therefore, is not the unity of comedy, which depends upon a linear unraveling of theme through plot, but the unity of satire, which allows the eye to range from one to another scene of moral decay, each an aspect or dimension of the vice under consideration.

The play opens, as satire must, with a declaration of the thesis to be argued. The vice in question is lust, but not lust simply. Rather, it is lust that disguises itself, assuming one or another mask, not out of deference to morality, nor out of shame, but that it may under the protection of a disguise enjoy greater freedom to operate. The thesis is not declared directly, because there is no satiric persona in the play to speak it. It is, rather, presented graphically. As the play opens, Horner and Quack are discovered discussing Horner's plan. Horner inquires whether Quack has been diligent in spreading the rumor of his impotence. Quack assures Horner that he has, but questions the wisdom of the plan.

> HORNER: Dear Mr. Doctor, let vain rogues be contented only to be thought abler men than they are, generally 'tis all the pleasure they have; but mine lies another way.

QUACK: You take, methinks, a very preposterous way to it, and as ridiculous as if we operators in physic should put forth bills to disparage our medicaments, with hopes to gain customers.

HORNER: Doctor, there are quacks in love as well as physic, who get but the fewer and worse patients for their boasting; a good name is seldom got by giving it one's self. . . . Come, come, Doctor, the wisest lawyer never discovers the merits of his cause till the trial; the wealthiest man conceals his riches, and the cunning gamester his play. Shy husbands and keepers, like old rooks, are not to be cheated but by a new unpractised trick; false friendship will pass now no more than false dice upon 'em.

In this dialogue Horner is not expressing, as Underwood and others have suggested, the duality of art and nature; his subject is lust and hypocrisy. The "natural" Horner is a satyr, his only art the art of deception. He is a hypocrite, not a natural man, and certainly not a hero. He discards the ruse of false friendship not because it is dishonorable but because it does not work. We should not dream of suggesting that Lady Fidget is the heroine of Wcyherley's play. We are quite certain of the author's attitude toward such a lady of honor; she is a target of satire. Why, then, should we mistake his attitude toward Horner? Horner spreads the rumor that he is sexually harmless, so that he may more freely indulge his lust. Lady Fidget spreads the rumor that she is virtuous to the same end. The only difference between them is that Horner pretends a negative quality (to be harmless where he is most harmful), while Lady Fidget pretends a positive quality (to be in possession of the most grace where she is graceless). True, Horner's is the less usual disguise. It is used to attract our attention, by its very outrageousness, to the incongruity between what human beings pretend to be and what they are. In the opening scene Horner is presented as an emblem, a grotesque exaggeration of the vice we are to watch for in the play. He is, in graphic terms, the declaration of thesis.

The thesis declared, the argument of it begins. Because there are separate actions, of equal importance, that attract our attention by turn to the various aspects of the vice, the scenes maintain a degree of independence from one another. This enables the satirist to turn the vice under consideration around on all sides, to attack it from as many angles as possible. Scene after scene is presented in which some new face of the vice is presented or some aspect already presented is more deeply probed. The movement is circular and continues until all of what Dryden calls the "members" of the central vice have been presented and developed to their fullest extent.

The four faces of disguised lust that the design examines are presented by the end of the second act. First, Horner is introduced to present lust in the mask of impotence, which secures it full freedom. Then Sir Jasper enters with the "ladies of honor," who flaunt their masks of modesty and virtue. Horner, having assumed the role of malcontent-satirist, sounds the depths of their virtue and suspects it to be shallow. When the ladies have gone, he announces his suspicion to Quack, rejoicing in their disguise as well as in the efficacy of his own:

your women of honour, as you call 'em, are only chary of their reputations, not their persons; and 'tis scandal they would avoid, not men. Now may I have by the reputation of an eunuch the privileges of one, and be seen in a lady's chamber in a morning as early as her husband.

The scene that presents vice disguised as virtue is followed by a brief interlude of commentary upon the satiric background. Horner, in the company of the wits, observes and comments upon the immorality of the world. Into this commentary a new aspect of disguised lust is introduced in the person of Pinchwife. Pinchwife hides and indulges his gross carnality under the socially respectable façade of marriage. . . . Pinchwife's jealousy arises from the desire to maintain intact the socially sanctioned contract, supposedly based upon mutual regard, which provides him his mask for the indulgence of lust. He neither loves nor trusts his wife, and surely he does not esteem her. He chose her not for any virtue he admired in her but for her prime fault, ignorance, which he hoped would protect his own façade. His sole interest, throughout the play, is in forcing her to preserve his "honor" as a husband, which honor is as false as Lady Fidget's virtue or Horner's impotence. In reality, Pinchwife is not a husband but the keeper of a whore, a piece of property that he is anxious to preserve to his exclusive enjoyment. Like Horner and Fidget, he desires freely to indulge his lust under cover of a carefully sustained respectability.

The last aspect of the vice presented is lust disguised as innocence. Perhaps lust is too strong a word to describe Margery's emotion, as innocence is too imprecise to define her ignorance. Her innocence at first is genuine. However, once she has fallen in love with Horner, she develops guile, and she feigns innocence to disguise her passion from Pinchwife in the hope that she will thereby find the freedom to satisfy it.

In their first appearance the four aspects of the vice are almost purely comic—Horner's knavery, Fidget's affectation, Pinchwife's jealousy, Margery's rusticity are at first follies. However, at each successive appearance they assume more serious proportions, and by gradual stages the comic tone fades, to be replaced by the satiric. It is highly illuminating of Wycherley's method to trace the course of one aspect of the vice in its development. For example, let us consider lust disguised as virtue. Fidget and her company are wholly comic in their first appearance. They are objects of satire only in their folly of exaggeration—theirs is the "humour" of virtue which is threatened by Horner's wit. In Act II, a new dimension of their viciousness is revealed; their hidden lust, until now only suspected, is uncovered, and with it their whole perverted system of morality.

LADY FIDGET: But, poor gentleman, could you be so generous so truly a man of honour, as for the sakes of us women of honour to cause yourself to be reported no man? No man! And to suffer yourself the greatest shame that could fall upon a man, that none might fall upon us women by your conversation? but, indeed, sir, as perfectly, perfectly that same man as before your going in to France, sir? As perfectly, perfectly, sir?

HORNER: As perfectly, perfectly, madam. Nay, I scorn you should take my word; I desire to be tried only, madam.

In the system of values that prevails in the world attacked by the satiric thesis, the greatest honor accrues from building the most complete disguise of one's real motives. Horner is a man of honor because by means of his deception he has ensured free sexual indulgence not only for himself, but for "the sakes of us women of honour." His generosity is in permitting for them the same license he permits himself. Moreover, within this moral system, the "greatest shame that could fall upon a man," is to be sexually incapacitated while perfection rests upon sexual prowess. Here, as in *Love in a Wood,* Wycherley makes his satiric point in the incongruity between the heroic diction of the speakers ("I desire to be tried only, madam") and the base matter of their speech. Their style captures perfectly the duplicity of their characters. While the incongruity between vehicle and tenor produces a largely comic effect, the perverted morality of the speakers—measured as it is against the ideal of the satiric antithesis—introduces a strong satiric undertone.

The next appearance of the women of honor is in the famous "china" scene of Act IV. So farcical is the scene, and so perfectly sustained its double entendre, that we are sometimes distracted from its satiric intent by our admiration of Wycherley's technique. If we consider the scene in relation to the others in this line of action, however, we realize that the women who at first affected grotesquely exaggerated virtue, and who at their second appearances could still discuss sexuality only in heroic periphrasis, here become ardent pursuers of Horner. We must not allow the comedy of the scene to blind us to the realization that it is but a hair's breadth short of presenting the sexual act on stage. Yet, as the predatory sexuality of the women more fully reveals itself, so the mask with which they disguise it becomes more pronounced. . . . [With the last appearance of the women, in Act V,] the comic tone vanishes completely, for the women, literally and figuratively, drop their masks and do not bother to affect virtue. The stylistic tension between diction and character no longer claims our attention. Instead, satire darkens and damns more directly. Wine has robbed the women of their disguises. They abandon elevated diction and manner. Their tone coarsens and becomes sluttish. As drink loosens their tongues, they damn their husbands and compare them to "old keepers." Their talk, that of prostitutes, indicates that they think of themselves in imagery of commerce ("Women of quality, like the richest stuffs, lie untumbled and unasked for"). And finally . . . , each of them acknowledges that she has enjoyed Horner.

The same progress from comic to satiric is described in the successive appearance of each of the three other aspects of the central vice. Pinchwife's jealousy is ridiculous when he is the butt of the wits' teasing. It becomes a more serious defect when we observe him abusing his wife. In its next appearance, when he threatens "write as I tell you or I will write whore with this pen-knife in your face," it has darkened into cruel sadism. Until, at last, it is distorted into frenzy that drives him to attempt the murder of Margery—a disaster that is averted only when his reputation as husband is rescued by the public assurance of Horner's eunuchry. Following exactly the same pattern, Margery's disguise, at first so charmingly funny, leads at last to her willingness to sacrifice Alithea's reputation in order that, saving her own, she may indulge her passion for Horner. And Horner's knavery, at first so devilishly clever that it escapes our censure, degenerates into mean knavery when at last he sacrifices Alithea's true honor to the preservation of his false disguise.

The satiric thesis is complete when we see that in this world of knaves and gulls the gulls are not a jot the more sympathetic company. Wycherley preserves the unity of his design by using the gulls to "transiently lash" (as Dryden puts it) vices related but subordinate to the main vice. Sir Jasper as a husband bears some resemblance to Pinchwife; he, too, values the reputation of husband alone. It is one part of the public image of which he is so careful and so proud. Sparkish is the male counterpart of Lady Fidget; as she is a would-be lady, he is a would-be man. Her disguise is false modesty, his is false wit. He values

Alithea only as an ornament to his reputation and an addition to his wealth. Sir Jasper and Sparkish, the gulls, are then hypocrites. Their hypocrisy differs from that of the other characters only in that it does not disguise strong, animal vice. But they are as contemptible for being hollow men, masking emptiness with a bright façade, as the other characters are for being goats.

The satiric thesis, then, is presented in successively reappearing scenes of vice and folly. With each turn of the spiral, new depths of the vice under consideration are disclosed. But we do not fully gauge the depravity of this world of inverted moral values until we contrast it with the standard presented by the satiric antithesis. The opposing virtue in this play is embodied in Alithea and Harcourt. The argument of the antithesis is stronger here than in most satires. Virtue is presented as a human possibility, not a quaint reminder of the past. Alithea and Harcourt are the twin virtues that oppose the double vice of the thesis. Alithea, as her name suggests, is the truth that opposes hypocrisy; Harcourt is the romantic love that stands against lust. For every aspect of vice presented, the opposing virtue is held up for comparison in Alithea and Harcourt. For Margery's dishonesty clothed in ignorance is Alithea's sophisticated honesty. For Sparkish's foppery is Harcourt's manliness. For Pinchwife's jealousy is Harcourt's absolute faith. The scenes of vice are underscored by corresponding scenes of virtue. For example, Lady Fidget's and Horner's "perfectly, perfectly" exchange is immediately followed by a scene in which Harcourt tries to express in the disguise of double-faced diction his honorable passion for Alithea. Even though Harcourt's romantic love is the exact opposite of Horner's and Fidget's animal sexuality, Alithea will not allow even honorable love to go masked. She exposes Harcourt again and again to Sparkish. Again, the scene in which Margery disguises herself, at the risk of Alithea's reputation, to satisfy her passion for Horner is balanced by the scene in which Alithea tries to unmask Harcourt, who has come, disguised as a parson, to prevent her marriage to Sparkish. She insists upon exposing him even at the cost of injuring herself as well as Harcourt whom she has come to love. Horner, Fidget, or Margery will do harm to others by their lies in order to protect themselves. Alithea, on the contrary, sacrifices her own feeling, her love of Harcourt, to keep the contract she has made with Sparkish. Hers is the true honor which holds abstract principle above passion—the honor of the romantic heroine of pastoral that has dwindled in breadth, if not intensity, to fit the satiric design. It is against Alithea's true honor that we must measure the empty reputation of the gulls and the masked vice of the knaves.

Harcourt brings the ideal of romantic love into the design of the play. The scorn of marriage that is supposed to typify "Restoration comedy" has no place in this play. It is not marriage but false marriage that we must despise here, as we had despised it in *The Gentleman Dancing Master*. We are to scorn marriage as a commercial arrangement (Sparkish's view), marriage as a social accoutrement (the view of Sir Jasper and Lady Fidget), and marriage as the outlet for bestiality (the view of Pinchwife). These falsities must be discarded in the face of the marriage that Harcourt offers—marriage based upon romantic love. Harcourt assures Alithea that the love he offers her is "matrimonial love." He describes his passion . . . in the elevated diction of romance. He loves "with all his soul," prizing her above titles or fortune. He offers himself as the man "who can only match your faith and constancy in love," "who could no more suspect your virtue, than his own constancy in his love for you." When the test of Alithea's virtue comes, Harcourt is willing to ignore reputation, and thereby proves that his faith matches Alithea's virtue.... [Harcourt and Alithea] are the faithful shepherd and shepherdess. Although the transition in the focus of Wycherley's vision from St. George to the dragon has been effected, nevertheless in the satires, as in his first pastoral, his standard of virtue is romantic.... [Even] in *The Plain Dealer,* where the satiric vision is perfectly achieved, the ideal, though it is envisaged as a lost ideal, is romance. It is against the ideal standard of romance that we must consider the satiric thesis—Pinchwife's socially sanctioned lust, Sparkish's vanity, the bestiality of the ladies of honor, and Horner, their stud. As in all satire vice is manifested in new-fangled manners—men pose as eunuchs, women have drinking parties—while virtue lies in old-fashioned simplicity.

However, though virtue proves more attractive than vice, the satiric design must be preserved. Though the antithesis is stronger here than in Wycherley's last, most perfect satire, *The Country Wife* is, nevertheless, a well-wrought satire. Consequently, like *The Plain Dealer,* it is open-ended. Alithea and Harcourt will presumably live happily ever after in their virtue, but so will Horner, the Fidgets, the Pinchwifes live on as happily in their vice. Horner and the ladies come dangerously close to exposure, but by Quack's intervention their deception is maintained. The life of lust and hypocrisy is therefore assured both for Horner and the ladies. He has learned no more than never to trust his secret to a fool. Dorilant and Sparkish are so wrongly impressed by the example of the happy lovers that they vow never to marry. Sparkish is completely untouched by his experience: "Because I will not disparage my parts, I'll ne'er be [a husband]." His interest, as it has been from the beginning, is the façade he presents. Pinchwife learns only that the cover he had chosen to indulge his lust proves to be only an irksome burden. The example of Harcourt and Alithea is lost upon him. He has not learned what a true husband is, but only that his husband disguise is uncomfortable. He hates his wife more heartily than ever, but now he must keep her to serve the ends of reputation rather than lust. "I must be a husband against my will to a country wife, with a country murrain to me." *The Country Wife* presents the alternatives, ugly vice and beautiful virtue, but, in accordance with the demands of the satiric form, leaves the choice to the audience. (pp. 153-64)

> *Rose A. Zimbardo, in her* Wycherley's Drama: A Link in the Development of English Satire, *Yale University Press, 1965, 174 p.*

GERALD WEALES   (essay date 1966)

[*Weales is an American educator, critic, and author of children's books. Among his critical studies of modern theater are* Religion in Modern English Drama *(1961) and* The Jumping-Off Place: American Drama in the 1960s *(1969). In the following excerpt, he considers the ambiguity as well as the supposed indecency of Wycherley's plays.*]

Horner is probably the best character to illustrate the ambiguity that hangs over Wycherley's plays. He is an extremely attractive character for several reasons. The hidden *Playboy* reader in all of us is bound to identify with his sexual triumphs; the audience's fondness for the con man (from Joseph and Odysseus to the King and the Duke in *Huck Finn*) impels it to hope for the success of his scheme. He has a directness which is at once openly appealing (plain dealing is always in fashion) and insidious (we know that his plain dealing is double-dealing—

therefore, we can feel superior to his victims). He should, then, be the play's hero, but as we watch him in operation he begins to seem as foolish as the characters he manipulates. His seductions become merely mechanical. He is more like a chain smoker than a great lover. The famous china scene is one of the best jokes in dramatic literature, but we are never sure that Horner is not the butt of it. At the end of Act 2, Sir Jaspar urges Horner and Lady Fidget, "go, go, to your business, I say, pleasure, whilst I go to my pleasure, business." When Sir Jaspar speaks the line, it is the cuckold in him that bears its brunt, but by the end of the play, after Horner has sacrificed social pleasure for sexual and worked so hard for what he has got, the line, in retrospect, is almost a satiric comment on him. My description of Horner implies a greater emphasis on chronology than I intend. He is not unmasked, as Shavian characters so often are; he does not appear to be one thing and turn out to be another. He is several things at once. It is this uncertainty about how we are to react that gives the character, the play, and Wycherley's dramatic work as a whole its peculiar richness.

One of the most sensible comments ever made about Wycherley's work came from John Dennis, in *The Usefulness of the Stage* (1698): "Mr. *Wycherley* being, indeed, almost the only Man alive who has made Comedy instructive in its Fable; almost all the rest, being contented to instruct by their Characters." Dennis, preoccupied with the instructiveness of comedy, did not follow up the critical hint in this casual remark. It is not the fable in itself that gives a Wycherley play its effect; it is, as William Hazlitt implied ... the confrontation of character and incident [see excerpt dated 1819].... All four of Wycherley's plays, like most Restoration comedies, are about the quest for sex (in or out of marriage) and money (in or out of marriage). All four make a point of exposing a variety of kinds of affectation and hypocrisy. Fable should take care of the quest; character, the rest. Things are never so simple in Wycherley. His characters can be divided into three basic groups: the open and obvious comic stereotypes (the fops, the cuckolds, the social pretenders) who can be used for mild satirical points; the Horners and the Freemans, men who have presumably learned how to take care of themselves in a less-than-perfect world; the Christinas and the Fidelias, the refugees from romance, whom some critics accept seriously as vehicles for ideal honor or love. The first group causes few difficulties; the complications arise with the second and third. The Horners, as my description above suggests, succeed in a context that makes one suspicious of their success, and the Fidelias take part in incidents that make dramatic hash of their fine sentiments. One cannot even fall back on end-of-the-play rewards and punishments in a search of sure ground because, just as the incidents becloud the characters, the characters call the working out of the plot in doubt. The end of *The Gentleman-Dancing-Master* is presumably a conventional one, with the young lovers outwitting the stern father and the foolish fiancé, but after watching Hippolita for five acts, one wants to congratulate Monsieur on escaping marriage with her. This "yes-but" effect in all the plays is heightened by Wycherley's casual, even mocking use of literary stereotype and theatrical device. The plays are sprinkled with reminders that we are in a theater, perhaps none more obvious than the one at the end of Act II of *Dancing-Master* when a singer, in no way involved in the action of the play, comes on to perform; "She's come," Hippolita says, "as if she came expresly to sing the new Song...." Wycherley's characters, his plots, his subject matter, his theatrical devices are all very much a product of his time, but his double-edged use of them marks him as the most modern—that is, the most accessible to contemporary audiences—of the Restoration dramatists. (pp. xii-xiv)

At Lenny Bruce's first obscenity trial in 1962, the defense plea was that the nightclub performer was a social satirist in the tradition of Aristophanes and Swift and that the offending words were part of his satiric technique. The same defense has been made, too often, of Wycherley. In Wycherley's case, it is a plea that is neither true nor necessary. He does not use his bawdy, as Bruce does his obscene words, for its shock value; he is nearer in spirit to e e cummings in *him,* in which good humor and dramatic context milk the dirty joke of its prurience. Not that Wycherley is incapable of prurience: see **"The Answer,"** his verse reply to "A Letter from Mr. Shadwell to Mr. Wycherley," and his letter to Alexander Pope (March 22, 1705/6). The effect of even the most outrageous lines or scenes is entirely different in the plays. For example, take the exchange in Act 4 of *The Country-Wife* in which Pinchwife, having just inadvertently delivered his wife's love letter to Horner, bristles with indignation: "I will not be a Cuckold I say, there will be danger in making me a Cuckold." "Why," comes Horner's bland reply, "wert thou not well cur'd of thy last clap?" The success of that line has nothing to do with Wycherley's presumed moral stance. It is a good line because it works several ways within the play. It is appropriate to the two characters; it reminds the audience of Pinchwife's rakish past and the ludicrousness of his present possessiveness even while it illustrates the tired ironic pose that Horner so often uses. It functions dramatically within the play as a whole and within the scene itself; by exploding the pomposity of Pinchwife's threat, the line not only strengthens the audience's expectation that he will be cuckolded, but it gives them the incidental comic pleasure of seeing a windbag punctured. Most important, however, is the surprise in Horner's line. If it were blunt and nothing more, it might be as obscene as Wycherley is sometimes accused of being, and might evoke only a nervous titter from an audience. It is genuinely funny, however, because it hits the audience in two waves: first, there is the surprise of the word itself, and then, the delighted recognition of how appropriate it is. An important element in the total effect is that the author appears to be using bawdy because he finds it amusing—and somewhat special by virtue of its directness. Wycherley ordinarily works in double entendre, as in the china scene, or by incongruity in which context and line work together when they appear to be pulling apart, as when the sanctimonious lecher in *Love in a Wood* enters Lucy's house with this prayer on his lips: "Peace, Plenty, and Pastime be within these Walls." I confess that a statement such as F. W. Bateson's comment, in *Essays in Criticism,* VII (1957), on the china scene appalls me in a way that nothing in Wycherley can: "The audience, disgusted but fascinated, is quite unable to break away." To me, the scene is outrageously funny. Unless one approaches Wycherley without the defensiveness of a Bateson, half the fun of his plays will be lost. (pp. xv-xvii)

> *Gerald Weales, in an introduction to* The Complete Plays of William Wycherley, *edited by Gerald Weales, 1966. Reprint by New York University Press, 1967, pp. xi-xx.*

VIRGINIA OGDEN BIRDSALL   (essay date 1970)

[*In the following excerpt, Birdsall discusses the moral significance of the characters of* The Country-Wife.]

The Country-Wife undeniably contains elements of satire, but the satire is limited to Wycherley's own attitude toward certain of his minor characters and has nothing to do with either the attitude of the comic protagonist toward his world or the playwright's attitude toward him. Mrs. Zimbardo, for all her satiric bias, comes close to admitting this when she defines Horner as something she calls a "parasite-satirist" [see excerpt dated 1965] and, in comparing him with Manly, concludes "that while the former is lacerated by the sight of vice, the latter is amused by it. . . . The tone . . . is, therefore, always closer to comedy than that of the malcontent satirist." Unfortunately she then goes on to insist, as her own informing thesis requires, that he is nonetheless a part of the "moral decay," "the perverted morality" of the play and "a grotesque exaggeration of the vice we are to watch for." (p. 136)

It is true enough that Horner, in the conventional moral terms used by blind fools like Pinchwife and Sir Jasper, is a "lewd villain"—"a dissembler, a rogue." . . . He is possessed, as Thomas Moore once put it, of "the very esprit du diable" ["spirit of the devil"]. "Now," he mutters in one of his "villainous" asides, "must I wrong one woman for another's sake,—but that's no new thing with me, for in these cases I am still on the criminal's side against the innocent. . . . It must be so. I must be impudent, and try my luck; impudence uses to be too hard for truth." . . . The fact is that Horner, in the tradition of his comic predecessors, belongs to a different scheme of things from Alithea's (she being the innocent woman whom he must "wrong"). If he is the spokesman for vice in opposition to virtue, it is first because in his world, as distinct from Alithea's, virtue is a mere masquerade and second because he interprets good and evil in terms of his own comic oppositions of life and death, reality and pretension, freedom and repression. According to Alithea's standards of truth and rectitude, he is not a "man of honour" but precisely the "lewd villain" that Pinchwife takes him for. But he has very little to do with Alithea's sphere. Hers is a plane of romantic idealism; his, one of comic realism. So far as his unsentimental plans are concerned, innocence will have to take care of itself—a grim irony, perhaps, but an inescapable one when the life and the freedom of the natural man are the values he knows to be at stake. He is no selfless servant of mankind. He is the champion, without illusions, of every individual's right, including his own, to be what he is, and his kind of comic challenge will always be to a great extent antisocial—the challenge of the "criminal" to a society whose laws, both social and moral, are dictated by a Pinchwife, a Sir Jasper, a Lady Fidget. (pp. 136-37)

Yet Alithea, whose very name signifies *truth* (presumably in Wycherley's usual senses of both honesty and "fidelity"), remains as always a possibility in Wycherley's vision, and even skeptical libertines like Horner, who see their world with unvarnished clarity, believe in and respect her kind of honesty and innocence. But it cannot be too strongly insisted that she does *not* exist in the play as a standard against which we are to measure the "infamies" of a Horner. There is not much question, it is true, that like Christina she does represent some sort of ideal standard in the play. But it is an ideal that cannot hope to stand unchallenged above the fray, and if Horner must wrong Alithea, it is for much the same reason that Ranger must wrong Christina. The relationships are quite similar, and in each case there is the implication of reality's breaking in upon the ideal and bringing it to the test of experience.

In order to understand Alithea's particular role with accuracy, however, we must begin by determining Wycherley's central thematic concern in *The Country Wife.* The title of the play offers the opening clue, and by the end of the first act it has become clear that attention is to be focused on various kinds of wives and husbands and on the whole question of repression or tyranny as opposed to freedom in marital relationships. To Wycherley, convinced as he was at least in theory that at bottom women as well as men were by nature healthy animals, the only sin—or sickness—in male-female relationships was finally the denial of freedom in the name of morality or of civilized respectability or in the cause of a jealous possessiveness. Ideally, he felt, as the terms of Alithea's marriage to Harcourt make clear, that a "matrimonial love" based on mutual honesty and trust could lead to a mutual freedom that did not entail sexual promiscuity. But where (as almost everywhere) trust is lacking or where men and women deny their own basic natures and hide them behind false social and moral façades, there will always be the need for an irrepressible Horner to cuckold tyrannical husbands and to challenge dishonesties. Where lying and deception have become the only path to freedom, the world has become ripe for comedy, and it will take a master deceiver like Horner to bring the world back to life. (pp. 137-38)

Margery, for all her innate honesty and innocence, and indeed by virtue of it, has been trapped into marriage with Pinchwife and hence has been caught within a world in which she cannot "do what she lists" and in which, as she quickly learns, she will always be required for survival to "tell more lies." And her kind of marriage, in which she is "kept up," is set against the ideal marriage involving trust and freedom.

Alithea, however, has not easily achieved the ideal, and what the play reveals . . . is that where the question of marriage is concerned, naiveté is a dangerous quality—that its possessors are always subject to being tricked and trapped, through ignorance of reality, by the world of hypocrisies and repressions. There is always the danger that innocence will misplace its trust. And in this connection it becomes apparent that Margery and Alithea are actually parallel characters in spite of the fact that one belongs to the world of reality and the other to that of the potential ideal. Both are natural, honest women who, like Hippolita, ask only to be allowed to "take the innocent liberty of the town." . . . Alithea's innocence may be of a different kind from the simple naiveté of a Margery, but it is a form of naiveté nonetheless. In the name of her own abstract ideals of "honour" and "justice" and of her naive assumptions about love—"Love proceeds from esteem; he cannot distrust my virtue: besides, he loves me, or he would not marry me" . . . ,—she proposes to enter "freely" into a marriage in which the very freedom she cherishes will be denied her—a marriage in which she will indeed be "as one gone into a monastery, that is, dead to the world." . . . Her own ignorance of the ways of the world will then have trapped her in very much the same way that Margery has been trapped. In seeking to live according to an honorable ideal, she is thrown perilously off guard.

In short, Alithea's kind of unyielding idealism can prove in the real world of vain, mercenary, and possessive men a dangerous blindness, and by the end of the play the idealist has been thoroughly educated regarding her own folly. And meanwhile Wycherley has by no means exempted her from his irony. If she does not finally walk into the trap of her own setting, the action of the play makes it quite clear that her escape comes through no plan of her own. It is her earthy, high-spirited, realistic maid Lucy who finally saves her, and it is Lucy,

"robust creature" that she is . . . , who tells her the real truth. Accusing her mistress of "rigid honour," she declares indignantly: "But what a devil is this honour! 'tis sure a disease in the head, like the megrim or falling-sickness, that always hurries people away to do themselves mischief. Men lose their lives by it; women, what's dearer to 'em, their love, the life of life." . . . (pp. 139-40)

Lucy, who is to *The Country Wife* what Prue is to *The Gentleman Dancing-Master,* belongs to the coarse, common-sense, pleasure-oriented world of which Horner is the guiding spirit, seeing human beings for what they are and challenging misguided complacency in the interest of life. As Harcourt turns to Horner for instruction ("I am in love with Sparkish's mistress, whom he is to marry to-morrow: now how shall I get her?"), Alithea, as well as Margery, depends on Lucy; and the methods which Horner advises bear a close resemblance to those by which Lucy also achieves her ends. According to Horner, "a foolish rival and a jealous husband assist their rival's designs; for they are sure to make their women hate them, which is the first step to their love for another man . . . fools are most easily cheated when they themselves are accessaries." . . . And it is with just this same sure instinct for manipulating fools to her own ends that Lucy devises, move by move, her plan wherein Pinchwife docilely arranges for his own cuckolding and Sparkish eventually reveals himself before Alithea for the unfeeling, mercenary fop that he is. Horner, in fact, has very little to do with his successful seduction of Margery. It is Lucy, considerably better endowed with plain common sense than the over-wise Alithea, who triumphantly stages the single ingenious action which at once frees both "innocents" from their present or threatening prisons.

The association being made in the play between the current plight of Margery and the prospective one of Alithea becomes still clearer upon a closer look at the verbal parallels and the developing ironies. Pinchwife of course is repeatedly characterized as Margery's "guardian" or "keeper" and is forever being portrayed in the process of locking her up; and by the beginning of Act III, Margery has begun to think of herself as "a poor lonely sullen bird in a cage," in contrast to women like Alithea who "took their flight themselves early, and are hopping abroad in the open air." . . . What Pinchwife recognizes from the outset is that to "keep" his wife successfully, he must "keep her in ignorance" of what he calls "town-documents." . . . As Alithea puts it, "Jealousy in a husband . . . begets a thousand plagues to a poor woman, the loss of her honour, her quiet . . . nay, her life sometimes; and what's as bad almost, the loss of this town; that is, she is sent into the country. . . ." . . . The statement contains heavy ironic overtones, however, for at the same time that Margery is moving toward a release from the prison of the country and of her husband's jealousy and hence toward at least a temporary life, Alithea is, in her ignorance, moving toward the very kind of imprisonment which she most fears and is about to marry a man whom Lucy likens by implication to "a London jailer."

That Sparkish offers no better prospect for freedom than Pinchwife should, of course, have been obvious to Alithea all along had she not had her eye fixed so exclusively on the ideal as to fail to see the reality, for Sparkish has shown, as clearly as Pinchwife, that he is capable of treating a woman as little more than a piece of property. If Pinchwife thinks of Margery as his "freehold" . . . and of all women as "fit for slaves," . . . Sparkish regards Alithea as something to be shown off to feed his own vanity. "Tell me, I say, Harcourt," he says smugly, "how dost thou like her?'' . . . And again, ''go with her into a corner, and try if she has wit.'' . . . And Alithea finally has to protest, ''Sir, you dispose of me a little before your time—.'' Love to both men is ultimately just another business transaction. (pp. 140-41)

Lucy is not far wrong in seeing Alithea's kind of ''honour'' (which could prescribe for any woman marriage to such a man) as a killing disease—''a disease in the head, like the megrim or falling-sickness''—and her simile further reinforces the parallel that Wycherley is establishing between the binding effects of jealousy and of an unrealistic code of honor. The play is filled, in fact, with references to sickness and disease, all of which in one way or another suggest the health-destroying results of some particular human folly in connection with love. . . . At one point, indeed, Wycherley seems plainly to be implying that the playwright who sees human beings realistically will see them as diseased. ''Don't you give money to painters to draw you like?'' Dorilant asks Sparkish, ''and are you afraid of your pictures at length in a playhouse, where all your mistresses may see you?'' And Sparkish replies: ''A pox! painters don't draw the small-pox or pimples in one's face.'' . . . (p. 142)

More specifically, the persistent disease imagery usually associates itself with some form of repression of natural instinct. ''I have not been well,'' Margery informs her husband, ''since you told me there was a gallant at the play in love with me.'' (pp. 142-43)

It is one of the overarching ironies of the play that if Horner is to live and love freely in the diseased society to which he belongs, he can only do so by feigning disease himself. . . . What Horner's real role is to be, however, has been made clear in his opening lines: ''A quack is as fit for a pimp, as a midwife for a bawd; they are still but in their way, both helpers of nature.'' In other words, Horner has given the doctor what might be termed a fertility function, and with his aid, Horner himself will play the part for which nature intended him. . . . Horner is to be the health-giver, the curer of the disease of stifled sexuality. (In Mr. Horner's chamber, says Margery, ''methinks I should be well.'') (pp. 143-44)

Nowhere does it become clearer than in *The Country Wife* that Wycherley was no Puritan and that if he was a moralist at all, the morality that he espoused was one of naturalness and honesty. Here, as elsewhere in his writings, it is not animal appetite that he condemns but the hypocritical man or woman who, by claiming ''o'er Brute Beasts, Pow'r, or Sway,'' becomes ''more a Beast than they.'' In this regard an even worse offender than the Lady Fidgets of the world is a man like Pinchwife, who sees women as ''dough-baked, senseless, indocile animals,'' . . . who calls Alithea a ''jillflirt, a gadder, a magpie . . . a mere notorious town-woman,'' . . . and who rails constantly against the ''wicked town-life'' and against ''lewd libertines'' like Horner. The only innocence he believes in or values in a wicked world is Margery's simple ignorance, which he counts on to keep her his exclusive property. To him love is a ''little monster'' which he proposes to ''strangle.'' . . . And as if to confirm the unnaturalness of the repression he imposes on Margery, he dresses her as a boy before allowing her out into the town. While hysterically accusing virtually everyone he sees of ''beastliness,'' he emerges as little better than a ''wild beast'' himself—''D'ye mock me, sir? a cuckold is a kind of a wild beast; have a care, sir'' . . .—and proves capable of treating his wife with utter brutality: ''Write as I bid you,'' he shouts, ''or I will write whore with this penknife

in your face. . . . I will stab out those eyes that cause my mischief.'' . . . (pp. 146-47)

Into a world peopled by moralizing hypocrites like her husband and Lady Fidget, Margery with her simple honesty and innocence enters like a breath of health-giving air, and it is astounding to discover how many critics, even in our own supposedly liberated century, have seen her as simply another object of Wycherley's moral condemnation, as one more example of immorality in an immoral world. The mistake, of course, originates invariably from a failure to perceive the defiant unconventionality of Wycherley's moral stand. There does exist a ''right-way—wrong-way'' dichotomy in the play, as Norman Holland suggests, but he has drawn the line on the wrong premises (his own and not Wycherley's) and in the wrong place. Both Margery and Horner, in Wycherley's comic framework, belong in a ''right-way'' category. They are the comic hero and heroine of the piece (although Margery has to depend rather heavily on Lucy in working out her ''designs'') and each in his own way challenges the morality, the tyranny, and the hypocrisy of the world to which he belongs. Theirs, however, is the ''right way'' not in a conventional moral context but in a comic one and not because they are good or virtuous but because they are on the side of the instincts and of freedom, life, and health. (p. 147)

Margery's kind of free and ingenuous honesty of language is finally as impossible as her free pursuit of pleasure and her simple assumption that she may set aside her unsatisfactory first husband in favor of a more attractive second; and this she recognizes soon enough. She quickly learns the necessity for deceit in order to be free in a repressive society. In short, her trip from country to city becomes a trip from innocence to experience, a growing up. . . . [Her] kind of naive self-expression gives way in a civilized, adult, morality-bound society (in Wycherley's terms a fallen world, where guilt and shame are felt) to the kind of self-expression which can find an outlet only by pretending to be something it is not (as, on the level of action, Margery pretends to be Alithea).

Meanwhile, however, Horner is dealing with the social proscription upon the open expression of instincts in a way which ingeniously parallels Margery's, for he frees himself from social repressions and achieves his satisfactions by *masquerading* as an innocent—''He's an innocent man now, you know,'' says Sir Jasper . . . ; and again: ''Sister cuz, I have provided an innocent play-fellow for you there.'' . . . For him as for Hippolita the mask of innocence gives him the child's privilege of both doing and saying whatever he likes. When, for example, Lady Fidget says indignantly, ''How, you saucy fellow! would you wrong my honour?'' Horner replies with a cutting sarcasm of which she is quite unaware: ''If I could.'' . . . Safe behind his own mask, he pulls off the masks of everyone around him and exposes each for the righteous fool or the vain hypocrite that he is. And like Hippolita too he plays with words as he plays with situations, veiling his meanings behind the mask of their innocent surface appearance in order that he may voice the truths which civilized society forbids his saying openly. . . . (pp. 149-50)

All the characters in the play who are on the side of life and freedom, including Alithea, are also on the side of pleasure and of ''seizing the day,'' and all of them, unlike these ladies, know enough ''Gold to despise, for Freedom, Pleasure, Ease. / Best Ends of Wealth, and Proofs of Happiness.'' As the crucial dialogue between Lucy and Alithea in Act IV brings out, loss of liberty means not only loss of honor but loss of pleasure and even of "life," . . . and both Lucy and Horner know that if people are not to be enslaved and controlled by their moral, pretentious, acquisitive world, they must continually pit their cleverness against the enslaving forces and devise ever new means of making them cater to their own ends. (pp. 153-54)

In Alithea's sphere mutual trust in affairs of love may be the ideal path to mutual freedom, but Horner moves in a gambler's world where no one trusts anyone else and hence where freedom is to be gained only by the cleverest of tricksters. (p. 155)

In this kind of world the dance of life derives its rhythmic tensions, in effect, from the struggle of wild things to be free. As the challenger to repression and the freer of locked up passions, Horner with his irrepressible élan vital becomes the focal point for the new sense of awakened life. It is his lodging which is to provide the setting for the final "frolick," and Sir Jasper informs him that "my lady, and the whole knot of the virtuous gang . . . would come to no man's ball but yours," . . . It is to be, of course, an "innocent" ball. Glasses go round, masks are thrown off, along with inhibitions, and "innocence" is vindicated on all sides. We are witnessing, in fact, a banquet which represents at once the most complete and yet the most ironic enactment of a fertility rite to be found among the major comedies of the Restoration. "Now, sir," cries Horner, the deceiver to the end, "I must pronounce your wife innocent, though I blush whilst I do it; and I am the only man by her now exposed to shame, which I will straight drown in wine, as you shall your suspicion; and the ladies troubles we'll divert with a ballad.—Doctor, where are your maskers?" . . . It is symbolically appropriate that the doctor, the curer of disease, should be called upon by Horner to lead the dance. And if this concluding "dance of cuckolds" is imaginatively staged, Horner will stand at the vital center of the circling dancers—the phallic symbol incarnate—and will draw each of the ladies in turn into the center with him to dance a turn, for he represents, in all his impudence, the life force triumphant. (p. 156)

> *Virginia Ogden Birdsall, " 'The Country Wife'," in her* Wild Civility: The English Comic Spirit on the Restoration Stage, *Indiana University Press, 1970, pp. 134-56.*

WILLIAM FREEDMAN   (essay date 1972)

[*In the following excerpt, Freedman examines the theme of sexual and social impotence of the English male in* The Country-Wife.]

Horner's injury [in *The Country Wife*] is a symbolic one. It is meant to do more than merely expose the ladies and gull the men; it is meant to comment on one prevalent insufficiency in the Restoration world: the inadequacy, in effect the impotency, of its males. But saying does not make it so, not even for the world of the play, let alone the real one. If the impotency theme sounds only in the dialogue, speeches, songs, and Epilogue, it may be a point Wycherley wanted to make, but it can hardly be called the central idea of the play and it certainly will not have much impact on an audience. The fact is, however, that male inadequacy is central to each of the three main triangular actions of the play: Horner-hypocritical ladies-Jasper Fidget; Horner-Margery Pinchwife-Pinchwife; Harcourt-Alithea-Sparkish. And it expresses itself in a way that is likewise presaged and symbolized by Horner's ingenious stratagem and that adds significantly to the play's serious content. If Horner, to facilitate his access to the ladies of the town, publishes a report of his eunuchry, each of the male butts—Pinchwife, Sparkish, and Fidget—is in some very real sense a eunuch-

like male; each is markedly insecure in his person and each is unable to keep and satisfy a woman. Moreover, if in order to secure his private pleasure, Horner must publicly destroy himself by spreading news of his own demise as a man, each of these three expresses his impotency in a genuinely self-destructive way. It may be a sense of inadequacy that produces the inadequacy—a kind of self-fulfilling self-assessment—or it may go the other way round. But in either of its forms, the inadequate male is the self-destructive male. He is, in short, a combination of what Horner seems to be to the doctor (who knows the truth), i.e., self-destructive, and to the rest of the town (who do not), i.e., impotent. And the self-destructive behavior of these three comic butts precipitates the three main actions of the play.

Pinchwife presents the clearest and most interesting case of inadequacy and self-destructiveness, and he is no doubt at the heart of the play's exposure of both. First, Pinchwife is forty-nine years old and that, according to Restoration comic norms, almost automatically disqualifies him from sexual activity. In a society where thirty is "old," Pinchwife is strongly if not quite completely identified with the superannuated hangers-on who come under such scathing attack in this play. He is but a young wife and a few years shy of joining what Dorilant calls, "your old boys, old *beaux garçons* ["pretty boys"], who, like super-annuated stallions, are suffered to run, feed and whinny with the mares as long as they live, though they can do nothing else". . . . To make matters worse, he is married to a woman less than half his age and so falls into that enormous Restoration bag of antique husbands puffing vainly to keep up with their lickerish daughter-aged wives. But age and a mismatch are not at the root of Pinchwife's problem, for we learn through his own confession that even when younger he had never been able to keep a mistress for long. (pp. 424-25)

There are many things to be said about Pinchwife and though most of them are bad, not all are. He is, after all, quite witty, often at his own expense, and he is also candid. He is aware of his own failure as a lover and husband, admits it to Horner and does not hide it from himself. His response to the discovery of Margery's attraction to Horner exposes his plaguing sense of inadequacy. "So 'tis plain she loves him," he remarks aside, "yet she has not love enough to make her conceal it from me; but the sight of him will increase her aversion for me and love for him; and that love instruct her how to deceive me and satisfy him . . . ." . . . His solution is to compel her to write a letter to Horner proclaiming her aversion to him, and when she hesitates, Pinchwife responds with a surrogate sexual attack, a violent threat to "Write as I bid you, or I will write whore with this penknife in your face." . . . Later on, when he discovers Margery writing her own very different sort of letter to Horner, his reaction is the same—a passionate threat with his phallic substitute, the sword:

> PINCHWIFE: . . . I'll make an end of you thus, and all my plagues together.
>
>   (Draws his sword.)
>
> MRS. PINCHWIFE: O Lord, O Lord, you are such a passionate man, bud! . . .

The irony of her reply should be obvious, but Sparkish, unwittingly as always, spells it out more clearly still and reveals that while Wycherley read no Freud he knew something of sexual symbolization: "What!" he exclaims, "drawn upon your wife? You should never do that, but at night in the dark, when you can't hurt her." . . . To the dull-witted Sparkish this is wit, but to the other participants and the audience it is weightier than he knows, for it reminds us that the reason Pinchwife must draw upon his wife with his sword is that he is much less successful at "drawing" in the dark.

Pinchwife cannot satisfy his wife and he knows it painfully well, but every move he makes to secure her only serves to drive her further from his and into Horner's bed, for all his moves are compensatory, none remedial. His general plan, upon bringing his country wife to London until he has successfully married off his sister Alithea to Sparkish, is to keep her locked up and thus out of the way of the alluring web of London debauchery and to warn her against what evils lurk beyond her doors. Both plans explode in his sullen face. The effect of locking her up is, as Quack observes, "to make her but the more willing (to lie with Horner), and adds but revenge to her love; which two, when met, seldom fail of satisfying each other one way or other." . . . (pp. 425-26)

For all this, though, it is not the fact of confinement that provokes Margery to cuckold her deserving husband. It is his foolish revelation of all he would keep from her in the very act of warning her against it. Margery tells him that she despises London and wants to return to the country as soon as possible, but it is not long before Pinchwife has told her enough about London to radically change her mind. The country wife would have known nothing of Horner's fondness for her had not Pinchwife himself mentioned it. And she would have remained in countrified ignorance of the "love plays, visits, fine coaches, fine clothes, fiddles, balls, treats," that Pinchwife tolls for her as the ingredients of a "wicked town life.". . . But once he has, Margery will neither rest nor let him rest until she has seen the town, and again the jealousy born of sexual insecurity proves self-destructive; for by dressing her in men's clothes, allegedly her brother's, he leaves himself helpless to prevent Horner's kisses, offered, the rake explains, to be transmitted to the "gentleman's" sister. It is Pinchwife again who, by forcing Margery to write the scathing letter to Horner, teaches her how to write letters, a knowledge she puts to immediate use, first in a much more inviting letter to Horner which she deftly substitutes for the other (she is apparently one of those fools made clever by love), and later in one which begs Horner to free her forever from this marriage of no one's convenience. Completing this ironic pattern of self-destruction, Pinchwife delivers the first letter to Horner, thinking it the one he dictated, and in the end he does literally and directly what he has been doing metaphorically and circuitously all along: he delivers Margery herself into Horner's hands. Of course he thinks it is Alithea he is bringing to the spider's web; he can hardly be expected knowingly to offer up his wife. But he is willing to sacrifice his sister, and his motive is expressive of the tormenting sense of inadequacy that dominates and destroys all his relationships with women. "My chief reason," Pinchwife tells the audience, "is, I'd rather be akin to him by the name of brother-in-law than that of cuckold.". . . Thus it is his own sexual insecurity that impels Pinchwife to perform what Wycherley suggests is a commonplace service of husbands in Restoration society: the delivery of his wife into the gallant's bed.

Sir Jasper Fidget, the business-minded husband of Lady Fidget, and Sparkish, Alithea's wit-wouldish fiancé, do precisely the same thing and for similar reasons. Fidget is not the monomaniacally jealous husband Pinchwife is, but he is a no more satisfactory one, and he is no less the perpetrator of his own undoing. The root cause of Fidget's failure as a husband is his preoccupation with business. It is of course first, though by

no means only, herself that Lady Fidget has in mind when she complains that "wives are so neglected," for Fidget's business leaves him no time for his wife. He is a man whose pleasure, as he proudly announces, is business. At the same time, Fidget is clever enough to recognize his own inability to satisfy a woman whose "business is pleasure," and he takes compensatory action. But like Pinchwife's, his attempts to deal "prudently" with his problem produce the very result he would avoid. "Tis as much a husband's prudence to provide innocent diversion for a wife as to hinder her unlawful pleasures," he remarks in an aside; "and he had better employ her than let her employ herself.". . . This may seem like sound reasoning, but Wycherley's point throughout *The Country Wife* is that there is no substitute for the proper attention to and satisfaction of a woman, and that all attempts to find one are doomed to backfire. . . . Until they learn that Horner is no less a man than he ever was, the ladies are repulsed by the very sight of him and resist Fidget's scheme, but the wise man of business will not hear of it, and like Pinchwife he does directly what others may do in subtler ways. He personally delivers his wife and two other initially reluctant ladies into the gallant's den. To his misfortune, though he is blessed with an ignorance that prevents full discovery, it is he, not Horner, who is the eunuch.

Sparkish, the third member of the impotent triumvirate, has his own self-emasculating preoccupation. He would be a wit in all things. For a fool, however, the attempt to be a wit can only fail and the process and consequences of his failure follow the pattern set by Pinchwife and Fidget. At the playhouse, Sparkish knows, the wits are seated in the pit, and there must Sparkish sit though it means leaving Alithea with Harcourt in the box. As Sir Jasper runs off to business and leaves his wife and honor in Horner's tender care, Sparkish runs off to Whitehall to dine with the king, again leaving Alithea with Harcourt. "I know my interest, sir," he reminds Harcourt as he seeks to hide from Alithea, but in fact he knows only Harcourt's, and when at last he does leave, it is only after he has reconciled his fiancée with his "friend." Fidget at least may claim ignorance. Horner, after all, is thought by all to be a eunuch. But Sparkish can lay claim only to a colossal stupidity, for Harcourt has made his intentions glaringly clear, and there are no doubts as to his abilities. What renders Sparkish stupid, aside from his obvious natural gifts, is his determination to be a wit though he lacks the defining prerequisite. As he understands the proper order of the wit's priorities, attention to a lady takes a very low place; the pit and Whitehall take precedence. Moreover, wits are never jealous, and they love nothing quite so much as sporting with one another. Thus all of Harcourt's candid advances upon Alithea and thinly veiled insults are written off as mere jesting among fellow wits. . . . Sparkish is, as Pinchwife observes, "a pander to (his) own wife"—a description equally applicable to Fidget and to Pinchwife himself—but the warning is ignored. "Why," scoffs Sparkish, "d'ye think I'll seem to be jealous like a country bumpkin?". . . True wits, the false wit believes, act ever thus.

For all Sparkish's insensitivity, Alithea, for various reasons of honor and self-interest, is nevertheless determined to have him. At least he is not jealous, and his faith deserves fidelity in return. But Sparkish will not be diverted from his path of self-ruination. In his boundless gullibility, he accepts without question Pinchwife's report that he has just delivered Alithea to Horner, and offering her no chance to explain he betrays his jealousy and thus cuts the only bond still holding her to him. The source of his anger, however, is not simple jealousy as at first it appears to be. Rather it is the insult to him as a man of wit and pleasure: "Could you find out no easy country fool to abuse?" he howls woundedly, "none but me, a gentleman of wit and pleasure about the town? But it was your pride to be too hard for a man of parts, unworthy false woman!"... Sparkish in fact can tolerate anything but attacks upon his stature as a wit. (pp. 426-29)

Beyond everything else, Sparkish must act as his wit, such as it is, tells him wits act. This is of course the identifying mark of the Restoration false wit, but it is not enough to thus label Sparkish any more than it is enough to call Pinchwife a jealous cit and let him go. Both epithets apply, but Wycherley wants to take us beyond them—to causes and consequences and to more serious comment on the nature of Restoration society. The force that motivates Sparkish is the same as that which motivates Pinchwife and to a large extent Fidget as well. It is a debilitating sense of inadequacy. Devoid of any genuine sense of self-esteem, Sparkish is dependent for satisfaction entirely on the supposed esteem of others, and everything he does is designed to win their praise and avoid their contempt. Only a man with a fully externalized standard of self-evaluation and a man with precarious hopes of living up to it would refuse a knighthood for fear of being ridiculed on stage. But his attitude toward Alithea is more revealing still. He pushes her into a corner (in both senses of the phrase) with Harcourt only partly because he wants to demonstrate his lack of even a rudimentary jealousy. Mainly he wants Harcourt to see how clever is the woman that will be his wife, for some of the admiration for her, he is sure, will convert to envy of him. Like Pinchwife's jealousy and Fidget's business-madness, Sparkish's need to be envied and esteemed reaches pathological proportions, a condition which, like theirs, makes affection for and the satisfaction of a woman impossible. (pp. 429-30)

Sparkish is, in short, the antithesis of Horner. The genuine rake, secure in his own person and confident of his ability to perform with those who count, namely the ladies, cares nothing for the opinion of the town. In fact Horner, finding that his former reputation—the kind poor Sparkish would give everything for—bars him from the beds he wishes to share, willingly destroys the foundation of his public stature to promote his private pleasure. (p. 430)

To Horner, the able male, apparent sexual destruction enhances his actual freedom of sexual movement. To Pinchwife, Fidget and Sparkish—each in effect impotent though for different reasons—the consequences of their very real inadequacy and the search for substitutes rather than basic remedies are self-defeating and self-destructive. Each is led to do in fact what Wycherley implies a disturbingly large number of Restoration males are doing in effect: he places his wife in his rival's hands. *The Country Wife* is more than an exposé of hypocrisy or of the consequences of jealousy. More than these, and more than a delightfully vulgar comedy, which it certainly is, it is a serious comment on the self-destructive impotence, neglectfulness, and ineptitude of the Restoration male whose representative sign is the eunuch. (p. 431)

> *William Freedman, "Impotence and Self-Destruction in 'The Country Wife'," in* English Studies, *Netherlands, Vol. 53, No. 5, October, 1972, pp. 421-31.*

KATHARINE M. ROGERS (essay date 1972)

[*Rogers is an American educator and author who has combined her interests in literature and feminism in such works as* The Troublesome Helpmeet: A History of Misogyny in Literature *(1966) and* Before Their Time: Six Women Writers of the Eighteenth Century *(1979). In the following excerpt from her full-length study of Wycherley, Rogers discusses his mediocrity as a poet.*]

Wycherley had never been a poet. His ear for verse had always been undependable; as Harley Granville-Barker pointed out, "And I must yet keep out of his sight, not" could win a prize for the worst blank-verse line ever written [see excerpt dated 1930]. Even Wycherley's best verses, such as the Prologue to **The Plain-Dealer**, were defective in technique. He seemed to believe that witty sense, with some approximation of regular meter, was enough. It was enough for the Prologue to an excellent play, but not for a piece that was to stand by itself as a poem. (p. 117)

[*Miscellany Poems*] was generally condemned, as—unfortunately—it deserved. Poem after poem is merely a paradox, ingenious but not sufficiently witty to stand by itself; versification is clumsy, syntax contorted; there is none of the neatness which should grace comic or satiric verse; nor, indeed, is there a single really felicitous line. Wycherley's poems were just not worthy of publication.

The themes of the book, mostly Restoration commonplaces, show no evidence of the original thinking of Wycherley's great plays. For example, Wycherley argues that marriage is slavery, taking all the pleasure out of love ("**In Answer to a Mistress, who desir'd her Lover to Marry her...**") or that the brutes are superior to rational man ("**Upon the Impertinence of Knowledge, the Unreasonableness of Reason, and the Brutality of Humanity**"). The latter poem develops the same theme as Rochester's "A Satyr against Mankind" and Butler's "Satire in Two Parts, Upon the Imperfection and Abuse of Human Learning." Wycherley's songs, hardly distinguishable from those of the other court wits in style and subject, were probably written in the reign of Charles II. For the most part, they are adequately versified and, as Pope said, needed only to be shortened to be made presentable.

With remarkably poor judgment, Wycherley made his selection of poems in accordance with Restoration taste. Although there are some of the moral satires and stoical discourses appropriate to a formal collection, there are far too many erotic poems, typically sordid and often obscene. Readers of 1704 were understandably not interested in cumbersome epistles "**To a fine young Woman, who being ask'd by her Lover, Why she kept so filthy a thing as a Snake in her Bosom; answer'd, 'Twas to keep a filthier thing out of it, his Hand; and, that her Snake was to play with, and cool her in hot Weather; which was his Aversion**" or "**Upon a Lady's Fall over a Stile, gotten by running from Her Lover; by which She show'd Her Fair Backside, which was Her best Side, and made Him more Her Pursuer than He was before.**" The very titles indicate the unwieldiness of the poems: tolerable perhaps as ephemeral epigrams arising from some occasion in Wycherley's love life, they are hopelessly unsuitable as long epistles in heroic couplets published by an old man in an expensive folio.

Moreover, Wycherley's loss of memory and constructive power is everywhere apparent. Some poems practically duplicate each other, such as two epistles to a friend who had sent him a witty letter, explaining why he had not answered it sooner. The same arguments keep reappearing through the moral poems and satires, even, sometimes, within a single poem. None of the discursive pieces is clearly organized. Wycherley's "Preface," for example, consists of two endless paragraphs which ramble from subject to subject without transitions. The individual observations are good enough, but there is no connected argument.

There are refreshing flashes of wit every now and then, as when Wycherley wrote [in] **"Upon an Old Worn-out Picture of Justice, hung . . . in a Court of Judicature,"** "That in the Court, some Justice might appear, / Justice is still hung in Effigie there''; or, on epitaphs, that, "Since most Great Tombs their Little Guests belie, / With some such Libelling damn'd Flattery." Wit does not, however, redeem the poems as a whole, though they bristle with similes and paradoxes. Sometimes these devices are so contrived that they add nothing to the vividness or impact of a poem, such as Wycherley's comparison of the law to a weak second in a duel because it professes to help injured innocence but does not actually do so. Even when a simile is truly witty—such as, in the same poem, his comparison of law to war because it makes "Reason yield to Pow'r"—its effect is often dissipated by overelaboration: the law-war comparison is developed for forty lines. As Dryden pointed out, Wycherley was apt to display more wit than was needed, though he kindly added, "never more than pleases." (pp. 118-19)

Probably the best work in *Miscellany Poems* is **"Upon the Idleness of Business. (A Satyr.) To one, who said, A Man show'd his Sense, Spirit, Industry, and Parts, by his Love of Bus'ness."** The paradoxes are not mere empty ingenuities, as in so many of Wycherley's poems, but striking statements which are, in a way, true. Wycherley is defending the court wit's attitude against that of the serious businessman (like Sir Jaspar Fidget), who is sure that he alone is applying his talents meaningfully. The theme is developed with the wit—that is, penetration and perception of unexpected likenesses—with which contemporaries credited Wycherley.

"Your Man of Bus'ness, is your idlest Ass," the poem opens, because his hard won gains of wealth, praise, or power serve only to make him want more. Though his "Bus'ness is, to gain himself more Ease," he can never be at rest because he constantly wants more than he has: "For as one Wave, another does succeed, / So the first Bus'ness does another breed." Hence, we

> . . . Life, in quest of Sustenance, destroy,
> Our Lives so, but against our Lives, employ,
> For Bus'ness lets none, Wealth it brings, enjoy;

*   *   *

> A Sign of Emptiness then Action is,
> Circular Motion causing Giddiness,
> For Bus'ness, active Idleness is found,
> Which weakens Heads, the more 'twou'd prove 'em sound.

"The Love of Bus'ness then . . . is rather Reason's Shame, than Proof":

> Out of more Pride, to bear more Slavery,
> To lose, for more Sway, Life or Liberty.

*   *   *

> Their Wealth, Time, Life (their own not truly) so,
> Away, but out of Selfishness, to throw.

*   *   *

> Whilst Beasts are Drudges, but by Force alone,
> But only Man, of his Free-Choice, is one.

The paradoxes are true wit because they have truth: business is often but idle activity; the man of business, though motivated by self-love, is actually working for others rather than for

himself; supposedly rational man does enslave himself to drudgery as a beast never would. The poem shows shrewd insight into human nature: even the most avid, striving businessman protests that all he wants is to attain ease and peace, although the only way he could really get them would be relaxing his pursuit of gain. There are even some effective lines—"Bus'ness is the Bane of Active Life"—although the versification and phrasing are far from meticulous. One notes, for example, the expletives joining their feeble aid to the first couplet quoted ("For as one Wave, another *does* succeed . . .") and the excruciatingly unnatural word order of the couplet starting "Their Wealth, Time, Life." Wycherley did get his lines to rhyme and scan, but at such a price of awkwardness that the correctness hardly matters.

The poem sticks to its point. . . . However, it suffers from the prolixity and repetition of all Wycherley's last work. The wave simile near the beginning of the poem continues for seven additional lines which add nothing to the meaning. The idea that business is active idleness, which has been quoted, is repeated twice: "Then Bus'ness is Laborious Idleness" and "By Love of Bus'ness, idle Industry." The poem runs for six and a half large pages, and it would certainly be improved if cut to three. (pp. 121-23)

[All or most of the poems in the *Posthumous Works*] were revised by Pope; therefore it is impossible to be sure what is Wycherley's and what is Pope's. Certainly they are, on the whole, better than the *Miscellany Poems*: Pope regularized the versification, eliminated flagrant repetition, and added occasional neatly turned lines and similes. Nevertheless, these poems do not significantly differ from those in the earlier collection.

Wycherley did take Pope's advice to reduce some of his poems to maxims in the manner of La Rochefoucauld: prose epigrams revealing some usually shabby aspect of human nature. They are shrewd, if not profound, and more verbally felicitous than his poems. Many of them are merely translations from La Rochefoucauld or other writers; others repeat each other or what Wycherley had written elsewhere; others are platitudes or empty similes. Some of the maxims, however, are penetrating and well phrased. (p. 129)

The most effective poem in the *Posthumous Works* is the bitter **"The Court-Life. To a Friend, disswading him from attending for Places."** Why should we call it ambition, Wycherley asks, to obtain a place at court, where we must act in everything contrary to our mind and heart, pursue those who shun us, and gain trust by parting with virtue? . . . The whole poem is a caustic satire on the degradation and falsity of life at the center of power—even at the glittering court of Charles II. While Wycherley probably could not have produced this unassisted, even though his songs were much better than his discourses in heroic couplets, the ideas are those of the plain-dealer, who was doubtless writing from his own bitter experience. (p. 130)

Katharine M. Rogers, in her William Wycherley, *Twayne Publishers, Inc., 1972, 174 p.*

CHARLES A. HALLETT   (essay date 1973)

[Hallett is an American educator and critic. In the following excerpt, he explicates The Country-Wife *in terms of Thomas Hobbes's social philosophy of enlightened self-interest.]*

Wycherley's *The Country Wife,* although not a play one could categorize as dominated by plot, is built around three dramatic questions. Whatever suspense there is arises because the audience is eager to know, first, whether Margery will learn enough about the ways of the town to enable her to outwit her jealous husband, secondly, whether Horner can keep his wily scheme going without being caught by Sir Jasper, and finally, whether Alithea will break her contract with Sparkish and marry Harcourt. It is my contention that each of these three questions has been designed to comment upon certain notions that were basic to the theory of the social contract presented some years before by Thomas Hobbes, notions that by Wycherley's time had become part of the everyday vocabulary in court circles. On one level—the level one perceives as the play is performed on stage—the subject of the satire is hypocrisy, but on another, deeper stratum, Wycherley attacks the Hobbist society from which this hypocrisy stems. At this level, the satire is structured around key Hobbesian concepts: the war of all against all as opposed to the peace available within society, the natural state in conflict with the contractual one, liberty straining against security, power utilizing fear. Wycherley is satirizing (among many, many other things) Hobbes's assertion, and the Hobbists' belief, that the best society is the one founded upon enlightened self-interest. (p. 380)

[It] is necessary to understand what the social contract represented to the Hobbist. It not only implied unreserved submission to the will of the sovereign; it was also that which distinguished civilized man from the savage. The contract put an end to the brutish state of nature characterized by the common ownership of all things as well as to the inevitable result of such anarchy, the perpetual war of all against all. Reason had led man to accept voluntarily the terms of the covenant; he had promised to "lay down this right to all things; and be contented with so much liberty against other men, as he would allow other men against himself." . . . Although the result of the signing of the contract was regarded as universally beneficial, it fitted the cynical temper of the times for Hobbes to insist that this good had nothing to do with benevolence or self-sacrifice. On the contrary, the security of the resulting society was founded on man's omnipresent desire to further his own self-interest. Man desires pleasure; pleasure is best enjoyed in security; only a peaceful state can provide security; and such a state is only attainable through the social contract. (p. 382)

Such, in brief, was the Hobbist social theory, and it was exactly this theory of society that fired the satirical genius of Wycherley. . . . [In] the Hobbism of his society, he discovered the irresistible satiric potential of a comedy that revolved around the reactions of several characters to a contract into which they had entered voluntarily, but to which only their self-interest now tied them. No better, more universally acknowledged, voluntary, contractual agreement could he have chosen than the contract of matrimony.

As a point of contrast, Wycherley lets loose on his stage a character who knows nothing of this contract. Margery Pinchwife, though she bursts upon London from a frontier no further removed than the Hampshire countryside, is unquestionably living in Hobbes's state of nature. A monodimensional character if ever there was one, Margery is nevertheless immensely original. She is a thoroughly likable personification of the natural man who believes that he has a right to all things. (pp. 382-83)

Margery's "innocence," a strange combination of simple candor and stupidity, of guileless interest in the opposite sex and promiscuity, can be fully explained in only one way. (p. 384)

Margery Pinchwife's comic function is to proclaim unashamedly all of her desires. She embodies instinct in its purest form, unencumbered by any knowledge of custom or law. Like Hobbes's natural man in the state of nature, she acts only from self-interest. She seeks the good, but the only good she knows is pleasure. In complete contrast to Pinchwife, whose actions are governed by fear—fear of the social stigma that must be borne by the cuckold—she is boldly frank and honest. . . . And believing as she does that she has absolute freedom to seek the fulfillment of her desires, Margery is willing to love anyone who will love her in return. Thus, when she finally does meet Horner, she is determined to cast off the antiquated Pinchwife and take this "fine gentleman" in his place.

Margery has no idea of what marriage means. Though on one level she is a "country" wife, the unsophisticated girl Pinchwife went to the provinces to seek in the hopes that she would be too simple to deceive him, she goes beyond mere country ignorance to an ignorance of all social forms. Certainly country girls, even in Hampshire, could be expected to know the basic conditions of a marriage contract—to know, at least, that a woman can have only one husband at a time. Etherege's Harriet, herself a Hampshire lass, makes no attempt to collect husbands. . . . [Margery] sees no reason to return to Pinchwife, once having escaped him, if she likes Horner better. She is intelligent enough to understand that people around her are not honoring the contract; why therefore should she? In her present state of innocence, she does not realize that to evade the contract, subterfuge must be employed; thus, Horner's argument that she should return to her husband in order to "secure" their love affair is incomprehensible to her. . . . Unfortunately for Margery, however, her ignorance of the social contract and her consequent bluntness make it initially impossible for her to obtain her desires; she is constantly being frustrated in her attempts to live as though she had a right to all things by a husband who keeps her imprisoned. Ironically, it is not until the town "educates" her in the ways of circumventing such restrictions that she can become a "respectable" married woman. (pp. 384-85)

Although Margery does not understand the demands placed upon a woman by the marriage contract, the other characters in the play are very much aware of these demands. From the profligate Horner to the proper Alithea, they know, one and all, that a man and a woman, in order to have complete freedom to enjoy one another, must agree to give up their right to enjoy all other members of the opposite sex. They know that actions conceived in obedience to this law have been designated as honorable, those in contempt of it as dishonorable, and that any deviation from the norm destroys one's position in the community. Since any person motivated by self-interest would fear the scorn which would be heaped upon him should he lose his honor, all of these characters, one might expect, would staunchly adhere to the conditions of the contract.

But this is hardly the case. Wycherley does present three "women of honor": Lady Fidget, Mrs. Dainty Fidget and Mrs. Squeamish. And indeed these three women are catapulted into states of the utmost hysteria at the thought of losing their honor. In their presence, the Hobbists in Wycherley's audience might fittingly have recalled the philosopher's reference to the great majority of people who can only be held to their contracts through a "fear of the consequences of breaking their word." But somehow, though the ladies do fear "consequences," the fear is not so great as to proscribe the breaking of the contract itself. They have no intention of abiding by the marriage vow if they can break it without being punished. The difference between them and Margery lies not in their desire for pleasure, which is unabated in both cases, but in the fact that the town ladies are hampered by a consciousness of the necessity of maintaining appearances. To retain their security they must seem to be virtuous and trustworthy. The facade of virtue, the impeccable reputation, is cultivated only "to cheat those that trust us." They are constantly attempting to erect blinds behind which they can violate the contract and expand their freedom.

Horner is far more clever than these "women of honor." He is determined to live within society and to derive all the benefits from it, yet not to be restricted by any of its regulations. He knows, moreover, that everyone else would like to do as he does, that most people would prefer to free themselves from the restrictions placed upon them by the contract and are only prevented from doing so by the Hobbesian fear of losing their security. Horner's trap, therefore, in terms of the satire, is baited with the illusion that the victim can enjoy his liberty and at the same time be guaranteed his security. Since the contract does not alter the nature of individuals but merely tells them that it is in their best interest to act in certain ways, Horner, by a subterfuge aimed directly at the libidinous instincts of his victims, affords them the opportunity to act as though they were not bound by the contract, without endangering their reputations as members of the community.... Horner has the utmost contempt for the women who become his victims. He is acting solely out of that emotion Hobbes saw as the foundation of human character and therefore the one safe cornerstone of human society—self-interest. Further, it is Horner's primary intention to exploit the self-interest of others so as to escape the limitations of the social contract himself. (pp. 386-87)

Yet ironically, a certain amount of sacrifice on Horner's part is involved. The scheme does depend for its success upon Horner's willingness to scrap his own reputation. He must embrace the status of a eunuch, which in that lusty society was to be "no man at all." He must patiently endure the abuse of the indiscreet Sparkish and the unfeeling Sir Jasper. He must feign an aversion to women and, ironically, hope that his disguise fires in them a hatred for him. But with reputation—that "immortal part" of self—gone, Horner has nevertheless gained; he alone of Wycherley's characters possesses power—which Hobbes taught was the end of all men's desires. Horner recognizes the power that can come from casting off reputation altogether and sacrifices "glory" in order to gain greater pleasure. His outward personal debasement affords him a kind of omnipotence.

The lesson to be learned from Horner's charade is that as long as one is not deceived by the social contract, he can use its framework to get exactly what he would have obtained in the state of nature. Anne Righter is absolutely correct when she remarks that "Mrs. Pinchwife is an amusing simpleton; Horner is both sophisticated and almost diabolically clever. Yet they have both arrived at exactly the same place, though by different roads" [see excerpt dated 1965].

But if Horner has guaranteed security to the women of honor, what of the risk to his own security? The pivotal dramatic question of the "eunuch" plot is, after all, whether Horner's ruse will be discovered by Sir Jasper. This question must be resolved before the end of the play. Hobbes had, of course, admitted that there are always those whose passions make them rebellious. But he had argued, in making self-interest the basis of his society, that it was against reason for a man to deliberately set himself apart from society and violate its rules, because he would thereby deprive himself of its protection.

Thus unprotected, of course, he could not hope to survive. Reason would tell him that it is in his best interest to conform.... According to such argument, Horner, whose intention it is to ignore the laws that deny him the pleasures he desires, cannot reckon upon escaping detection for long; he must expect to be shortly denied the protection and security of society and to be destroyed for his effrontery. But Hobbists like Horner know better, and, in bringing Horner to the brink of discovery in his final act, Wycherley makes a wry comment upon Hobbes's naïveté. He does not believe that Horner will, as Hobbes insists, eventually be found out. (pp. 387-89)

In Act 5 events have so complicated themselves that Horner stands on the threshold of exposure. The ignorance of the husbands he has deceived, upon which he has reckoned for his security, is about to be dispelled. The cause of Horner's discomfort, it should be noted, is not the "women of honor" but Margery, who does not understand the concept of security. It is she who naïvely insists upon telling the truth and comes close to exposing the lover she is trying to protect. Horner has so manipulated all the other characters that though he has betrayed everyone, male and female alike, it is in their self-interest to allow him to go free. When threatened, they all band together to protect him, for they have more to lose than he does. The women of honor must lie for him in order to prevent detection of their own extramarital excursions. Sir Jasper must take the doctor's word or admit his own foolishness in thrusting his wife upon a rake. Pinchwife must protect himself against the loss of reputation involved in being branded a cuckold. Only the innocent, unhypocritical Margery tells the truth, for she does not realize what she has to lose. She has at this point to learn her final lesson. Of course—the point of the scene is clear—Margery's truth is not tolerated by the others; she is taught that the "correct" social response is a lie.

The moral of this closing scene is certainly not, as one critic [Rose A. Zimbardo; see excerpt dated 1965] takes it, that a man should not trust his secrets to a silly mistress; Wycherley is not aiming at teaching Horner a lesson about women. Rather, he is satirizing a basic fallacy in the philosophy that had found such ready acceptance among his peers. Wycherley does more than indicate that a society based upon self-interest is at the mercy of the clever manipulator who, by promising others their pleasure, gets them to help him to his. He also suggests that the social contract teaches men of nature not so much to give up certain pleasures in order to live in peace as to dissemble in order to obtain their natural desires. Margery, the child of nature, during the course of her acculturation learns not reasonable action in accordance with civil law, but hypocrisy. She discovers what the town ladies already know—that although one may not acknowledge his natural desires for unlimited pleasure, he can satisfy them if he dissembles.

The impression at the end of the play, then, is that although for Hobbes the war of every man against every man ends with the establishment of the social contract, the sole purpose of which is, after all, to effect peace, for Wycherley the war continues even after the signing of the contract. (pp. 389-90)

If a life-style dictated by self-interest and characterized by continued attempts to evade the terms of the marriage contract is a common element in two of the play's three plots, the third plot is unique. Wycherley's focus is still the marriage contract; indeed, the dramatic question of the third plot is whether Alithea will break her contract with Sparkish in order to gain the pleasure that would come with marriage to Harcourt. But in Alithea we find an attitude toward the marriage contract that is possible only when the self is denied full control of the personality. (p. 390)

Clearly, Alithea is to be associated with the rational beings who were to populate the Hobbesian commonwealth, but with one important qualification: it is self-sacrifice, not self-interest, that in terms of the contract results in justice and rational behavior.

The tensions that exist in the action testify to the difficulties Wycherley faced in dramatizing his theme. Certainly it was necessary for him to make Sparkish an obvious dolt or there would be nothing particularly noble about Alithea's determination to stand by him; yet if he allowed Alithea to defend such a dolt, there was the possibility that her judgment would be called into question. His awareness of his dilemma is reflected in his attempt to provide Alithea with a recognition speech that "explains" her failure to see through Sparkish. But that Wycherley's primary intent is that the audience remain sympathetic to Alithea, applauding her love of virtue for its own sake despite her misjudgment of Sparkish, is quite clear from the contrasts which he makes between Alithea and the other characters. Just how much it costs her to refuse Harcourt, for example, is suggested by the dialogue in which her maid pleads Harcourt's cause. . . . Alithea puts principle above passion, her "word and rigid honor" above her "heart.". . . Lucy, who defines honor with true Falstaffian gusto as "a disease in the head,". . . cannot understand her position. Alithea's commitment to honor as a reality rather than as opinion, which links her to those persons Hobbes discounted as "too rarely found to be presumed upon," who adhere to the contract because of "a glory, or pride in appearing not to need to break their word,". . . is also vividly contrasted with the attitudes of the ladies surrounding Sir Jasper Fidget, who are motivated alternately by fear and self-interest. These ladies wear honor as a velvet cloak to hide their tattered souls. Alithea would maintain her reputation with honorable deeds. When she says, "I must marry him; my reputation would suffer in the world else,". . . her motive is to unite appearance and reality.

Far be it from Wycherley, however, to make Alithea a sacrifice upon the altar of honor. Although honor without love is to be preferred to love without honor, a truly permanent and satisfying relationship can grow only out of some happy combination of the two. Quite predictably, therefore, the dramatic question of the love plot is resolved when Alithea is freed by Sparkish's sudden termination of the contract and her consequent discovery that he had entered into the contract under false pretenses. To effect this resolution, Wycherley introduces into the last act a trial of the two suitors for Alithea's hand— a trial which, appropriately enough, focuses upon the theme of reputation and which concludes with the bestowal of Alithea upon the man who is best able to recognize her true worth. And it comes as no surprise to the audience that this man is Harcourt rather than Sparkish. (pp. 392-93)

[It is by an] act of faith that Harcourt proves the depth of his love for Alithea and informs us that a marriage between them will have permanence. Leaving none of the doubts that Etherege fosters in our minds at the end of *Man of Mode* regarding the union of Harriet and Dorimant, Wycherley makes it clear that Harcourt and Alithea not only will marry but will respect and adhere to the terms of the marriage contract.

Each of the three dramatic questions in the play, then, contributes in some way to the satire of the Hobbist dedication to self-interest. In each, the strength of the desire for protection

and security, that is, for reputation, is weighed against the strength of the desire for pleasure; and wherever self-interest becomes the guiding principle, the desire for pleasure easily turns the balance. In the state of nature, represented by Margery, where there is no security and therefore no concern for reputation, the individual will be ruled by instinct alone; the appetites will motivate his every action. Nor does a society based upon self-interest offer much hope for the "civilizing" of these appetites, for in such a society honest instinct is merely transformed into hypocrisy, until the world becomes populated with Lady Fidgets who are ready to indulge their desire for pleasure whenever their fears are assuaged. Moreover, the same self-interest which teaches the mediocre to practice hypocrisy teaches the clever manipulator, like Horner, that he can obtain illicit pleasure without fear of reprisal if in doing so he provides others with the opportunity to do the same. In the dramatic action which focuses upon Margery as well as in that which revolves around Lady Fidget, the desire for security is easily thrown to the mat by the aggressive desire for pleasure. Only in the plot which has Alithea at its center is the desire for pleasure duly subordinated to the desire for reputation, and significantly, in this case, reputation becomes synonymous not with security but with honor. In distinct opposition to Hobbesian thought, the preferred hierarchy of values results from the determination to sacrifice one's own interest to that of an ethical principle.

If for Hobbes and his successors self-interest—tempered by reasons, which dictated that every man will make those judgments that most fully provide for his own peace and security— would work to create the best of all possible worlds, for Wycherley it was otherwise. For Wycherley, relationships based on self-interest led merely to the exploitation of others. He agrees with Hobbes that the majority of people are incapable of acting from any other motive; man *is* basically a nasty and brutish creature, self-centered and opportunistic, in other words, "warlike." But the means of controlling human egoism lay, for Wycherley, outside the realm admitted by Hobbes. Neither the sovereign, nor the laws, nor the punishments inflicted for breaking the law, nor the fear of those punishments or of ostracism will put an end to the "war" and guarantee justice. Reason can be used to circumvent each and all of these deterrents. It is the supernatural elements in human nature which Hobbes discounted, elements represented in the play by Alithea's love of virtue for its own sake and by Harcourt's act of faith in Alithea's virtue, which work toward the kind of peace Hobbes had envisioned. (pp. 394-95)

> *Charles A. Hallett, "The Hobbesian Substructure of 'The Country Wife'," in* Papers on Language and Literature, *Vol. 9, No. 4, Fall, 1973, pp. 380-95.*

W. R. CHADWICK (essay date 1975)

[*In the following excerpt, Chadwick examines characterization as a conjunct of theme in* The Country-Wife.]

The characters in *The Country Wife* can be divided into those about whom there is no argument (the Fidgets, Sparkish and Harcourt), and those about whom there is some difference of opinion (Alithea, the Pinchwifes and, of course, Horner).

Sir Jaspar Fidget is Wycherley's portrait of a new brand of business *entrepreneur*. (p. 105)

Sir Jaspar's passion for business is not prominently satirized in *The Country Wife,* but it most definitely supplies the background to and establishes the cause of the non-relationship he has with his wife. Their marriage is one of indifference, yet Sir Jaspar, a ceremonious, complacent man who clearly prides himself on his ability to manipulate others, is aware that the façade of respectability must be maintained for social reasons if for no other. He is consequently consumed by the fear, common to all husbands in Restoration comedy, of being made a cuckold. It is for this reason that he has supplied Lady Fidget with "two old civil Gentlemen (with stinking breaths too)" in order to give her the illusion of male companionship; it is also for this reason that he will not allow Dorilant to be her escort, had kept her away from Horner in earlier days, but is assiduous in his efforts to make Horner another of her gentlemen ushers now that he is, supposedly, impotent. The Fidget marriage, then, is without substance. Almost certainly contracted as a commercial enterprise, it has foundered on materialism, and Lady Fidget has every right to feel neglected.

It might appear from the last sentence that "understanding" is being sought for Lady Fidget. Wycherley, however, is no psychologist of the modern school but a Restoration dramatist, and although he clearly wishes his audience to be aware of Lady Fidget's marital situation, he does not appear to be seriously presenting this as a mitigating factor. Quite simply, it is hypocrisy that he charges her with, "that heinous and worst of Womens Crimes" as he described it in the Epistle Dedicatory to *The Plain-Dealer*. She knows . . . that a lady's main assets are virtue attended by prudence, but she is at such pains to clothe herself in righteousness that her very efforts become ridiculous. (pp. 106-07)

In Sparkish are concentrated all the usual traits of the Restoration fop. His major desire in life is to be thought a man of wit and understanding, a gentleman of breeding and elegance. His major fault is not so much that, like all his comic brothers, he lacks the necessary mental and social attributes to sustain his role but (and this is the infallible sign of the fop) that he insists on drawing attention to his non-existent "parts.". . . Thus, in order to prove he is no country bumpkin he parades his lack of jealousy, an inelegant emotion, not realizing that ostentation in any form is ridiculous; and so he loses his mistress. (p. 108)

Alithea is one of the more consistently misunderstood characters in *The Country Wife*. Most critics agree that she is as close to the normal concept of a heroine as there is in the play, but many of them add a qualification such as that "she has been stupid to accept a coxcomb like Sparkish,". . . or that she suffers from "romantic blindness,". . . or that "she must learn not to substitute a mere appearance (Sparkish's lack of jealousy) for inner nature (Harcourt's merits).". . . All these criticisms ignore the prevailing attitude towards marriage in the seventeenth century. The Marquis of Halifax, an enlightened man and a kindly father, prefaces his remarks on husbands in his somehow rather sad *Advice to a Daughter* with the following:

> It is one of the Disadvantages belonging to your Sex, that young Women are seldom permitted to make their own Choice; their Friends Care and Experience are thought safer Guides to them, than their own Fancies; and their Modesty often forbiddeth them to refuse when their Parents recommend, though their inward Consent may not entirely go along with it. In this case there remaineth nothing for them to do, but to endeavour to make that easie which falleth to their Lot, and by a wise use of every thing they may dislike in a Husband, turn that by degrees to be very sup-

portable, which, if neglected, might in time beget an Aversion.

A failure to recognize this prevailing bias as the background to Alithea's engagement to Sparkish makes her character incomprehensible and obscures Wycherley's intention of exposing the evils of contemporary marriage customs. (pp. 109-10)

[Alithea's] stand is the stand that any sensible, honourable woman of her time and class would take. And this is precisely Wycherley's point, for it is the sickness of the whole marital system, a sickness that infects not only the bad but also the good, that is the main thesis of *The Country Wife*.

There is one further point that relates to the criticism that Alithea should have reacted more quickly to Harcourt's charms. . . . [She] recognizes his external merits right away, but even so it is inconceivable that she should have broken off her marriage at the eleventh hour merely because an importunate rake urges her to. . . . As far as Alithea or anyone else can tell she is wiser to remain true to Sparkish. It is up to Harcourt to demonstrate that he has been truly smitten, which he eventually does by showing Alithea just how stupid Sparkish is, by contriving to postpone the wedding ceremony and, finally, by affirming his faith in her honour when all the evidence points in the opposite direction.

A more valid criticism of the Harcourt-Alithea scenes is that they are rather insipid in comparison with the rest of the play. One reason for this is that Alithea is overshadowed theatrically by Lady Fidget and Margery (as Harcourt is by Horner), first because her role is a defensive one, and secondly because she is a victim of the familiar law that when good and evil are brought together the good will appear dull and uninteresting— as Milton discovered in *Paradise Lost*. Then, too, Wycherley was not capable of giving Alithea and Harcourt the brilliant verbal exchanges on which the fame of the Restoration hero and heroine so often rests. Millamant, for instance, is really no more interesting as a person than Alithea; it is the superb way in which she expresses her gaiety, her affectations, her fastidiousness and so on that makes her the most famous Restoration heroine. The Alithea-Sparkish-Harcourt episodes are not without their amusing moments though, and they are of absolute thematic importance within the total scheme of the play.

Margery Pinchwife is the third of the victimized women in *The Country Wife*. Her most important characteristic is her simplicity. She is so simple that Wycherley would have us believe that she is as incapable of comprehending jealousy . . . as the Houyhnhnms lies. Pinchwife married her because she was "silly and innocent" . . . and on this basis he seems to have made an excellent choice. . . . And all the time she is good-natured and eager to please.

To this point all critics are, I think, agreed, but then a serious misconception frequently creeps in. P. F. Vernon, for example, says that Margery "develops all the brilliant cunning of a sophisticated townswoman" [see Additional Bibliography], and Rose Zimbardo echoes him when she states that "she develops guile, and she feigns innocence to disguise her passion from Pinchwife" [see except dated 1965]. T. H. Fujimura is more enthusiastic: "Mrs. Margery Pinchwife . . . is a splendid female animal, amoral, clever, sensual, who follows her natural instincts and rushes willingly into the arms of Horner"—which is a fine description of some Italian film starlet, but it does not somehow quite describe Margery. (Wilcox's criticism that she is "naturally vile" can be safely ignored.) There are two reasons why these three most recent critics of *The Country Wife* invest Margery with "cunning" or "guile," and both result from a misinterpretation of the text. The first is that Margery manages to switch the letters behind Pinchwife's back in Act IV, scene ii. A proper reading of this passage reveals that Margery accomplishes her coup more by luck than by good judgement. Everything she does is on the spur of the moment and, as in the best farce, she seems to avoid disaster by some flustered action performed at the last second. The bewilderment of her soliloquy as she works up to her plan is a clear indication of her state of mind:

> I won't, so I won't, send poor Mr. Horner such a Letter—but then my Husband—But oh—what if I writ at bottom, my Husband made me write it—Ay, but then my Husband wou'd see't—Can one have no shift, ah, a London woman wou'd have had a hundred presently; stay—what if I shou'd write a Letter, and wrap it up like this, and write upon't too; ay, but then my Husband wou'd see't—I don't know what to do—But yet yvads I'll try, so I will.

"Cunning" implies premeditated planning and there is nothing of that sort here. (pp. 110-13)

The truth is that Margery is as simple and disarming at the end of the play as she is at the beginning. She has, of course, had experiences that have induced her to change her reactions to certain aspects of her existence, but in the realms of wit and sophistication she remains essentially a child of nature. In the final act she is certain that she has solved the business of divorce (if she knows what that means) when she happily announces to Horner, "you shall be my Husband now"; and it is Horner's ultimate description of her that is the most accurate one: "Dear Ideot."

I have devoted a good deal of space to this argument because of the importance of assessing the attitude that Wycherley intended his audience to have towards Margery. If she is "cunning" then it means that she is able to look after herself to some extent and this in turn lessens the sympathy that need be felt for her. If, on the other hand, she is, as I hope I have demonstrated, consistently naive and artless (and therefore innocent) then the audience must feel compassion for her. This compassion is a significant ingredient of the final response that *The Country Wife* should evoke. G. G. Falle has noted that there is pathos in Margery's situation, but he does not quite pinpoint wherein the pathos lies. There is no need to say very much about the ugliness of her life with Pinchwife. The "caged bird" simile sums up part of it, and the distressing little postscript of her letter to Horner the rest: "Let him [Pinchwife] not see this, lest he should come home, and pinch me, or kill my Squirrel.". . . But at the beginning of the play Margery is, in her simple way, reasonably content with her lot: "I hate London; our Place-house in the Country is worth a thousand of't, wou'd I were there again"; "You are my own Dear Bud, and I know you, I hate a Stranger.". . . By the end of the play, however, she has come to look on her husband as a man who, as she says, "I loath, nauseate, and detest,". . . and she has had a glimpse of a way of life that appears to her to be more attractive than the one she had known. (This does not mean that she has become less simple, or that she has learnt anything in any deep sense.) It is in the light of these newly acquired urges that her final doom of a return to the country with her bestial husband and, more important, without now the protection that her simple acceptance of her lot once gave her, be-

comes a fate almost too appalling to contemplate. This, of course, is to imagine beyond the final curtain so the prospect can be quickly shut out. And yet the thought is there.

I do not think that it has been sufficiently realized that as much of the action takes place at Pinchwife's lodgings as at Horner's, and that in fact Pinchwife's role is the same length as Horner's. If such quantitative judgements are of significance then it means that Pinchwife and what might be called the Pinchwife influence are more important to *The Country Wife* than is usually appreciated.

Satire can evoke a limitless range of responses from the frothiest amusement to the bitterest disgust, and the satirized figures in *The Country Wife* represent a fair cross section of this range. Sparkish, I have suggested, is an amusingly vacuous creature, the Fidgets are a compound of the ludicrous and the contemptible, while Margery elicits (most of the time) an affectionate laugh. Pinchwife, on the other hand, like Volpone or Gulliver at the end of his travels, is one of those characters who inhabits the shadowy netherworld of comedy. There is little that is "funny" about Pinchwife himself; every facet of his character provokes disgust. Jealousy is his besetting vice and it so consumes him that when Horner tells him "thou art mad, Man" . . . the literal and figurative meanings merge. Pinchwife married because, he explains, "I cou'd never keep a Whore to my self,". . . and he chose a silly country girl because she would not be expensive, would not mind his age, and would not have the wit to make him a cuckold. . . . In Pinchwife's diseased world, love is evil and women ("these dowbak'd, senseless, indocile animals" . . . mere beasts of burden: "Love, 'twas he gave Women first their craft, their art of deluding; out of natures hands they came plain, open, silly, and fit for slaves, as she and Heaven intended 'em; but damn'd Love—Well—I must strangle that little Monster, whilest I can deal with him.". . . As this quotation indicates, there is a streak of physical brutality in Pinchwife. His very name, and the suggestion, already referred to, that he is not above killing his wife's pets, indicate the meanness of his small cruelties, but he often becomes more horrifyingly violent. When Margery baulks at the letter he dictates to her in Act IV, scene ii, he says, "Write as I bid you, or I will write Whore with this Penknife in your Face,". . . and later, "Once more write as I'd have you, and question it not, or I will spoil thy writing with this, I will stab out those eyes that cause my mischief.". . . In Act IV, scene iv, he draws his sword to murder her, and he also draws on Horner in the final scene. His language, too, is filled with images of physical pain, of disease and decay: "Ten thousand ulcers gnaw away their lips"; "ten thousand plagues go with 'em!"; . . . "an eternal canker seize it, for a dog"; "No, tormenting Fiend.". . . (pp. 113-16)

Although *The Country Wife* is a comedy it is fair to call Pinchwife an evil man. Indeed, all his ideas and actions are so infamous, and his language is so murderous, that he is at times close to the villain of melodrama. Yet he is not that, for he and his baleful universe of "doleful shades, where peace and rest can never dwell" perform too serious a function in the play. They provide the play with its darker colouring, its sinister background before which the more noticeable sparks of comedy dance merrily enough. And it is by means of this gloomier resonance that the intensity of Wycherley's moral commitment to his theme can be most clearly perceived.

Harry Horner must be one of the most notorious characters in Restoration comedy; he is also the subject of considerable confusion for the majority of critics. On the one hand it is acknowledged that Wycherley intended him to be the play's witty rake-hero, but on the other his cynical sexual exploits offend against moral propriety, and he is condemned with a vigour that is presumably in proportion to the outrage that the critic feels. This basic confusion of attitude can be seen in Anne Righter's essay where she begins by calling Horner (along with Dorilant, Harcourt and Alithea) one of the "truewits as opposed to the fools," a little later refers to him as a "renegade from the centre" of the truewits, and concludes by calling him a "monomaniac" whose "grotesque, one-sided and excessive" behaviour "scarcely accords with the truewits' standard of natural elegance and decorum" [see excerpt dated 1965]. But Righter is relatively restrained in her condemnation. Bonamy Dobrée calls Horner a "grim, nightmare figure" [see excerpt dated 1924]; F. W. Bateson says he is a "Grotesque or mere mechanism"; and Rose Zimbardo asserts that he is "a hypocrite, not a natural man, and certainly not a hero" [see excerpt dated 1965]. And yet he is still the truewit.

There is no good reason to suppose that Wycherley intended Horner to be a particularly unsympathetic character. It is true that he is devoted to the principle that sex is fun, that it is pleasurable to sleep with as many attractive women as possible, but there are not many members of a modern audience, any more than there would have been many members of a Restoration audience, who would disagree with him. On the other hand, to call him a monomaniac, a hypocrite, and so on, on account of his sexual escapades is to employ terms that somehow do not seem pertinent to a discussion of comic characterization. Comedy, after all, only presents that segment of an individual's nature that is required by the conventions of the genre, and to indulge in psychological analyses on this basis is inappropriate. The point can be made in other ways. If Horner is a monomaniac then so are all other heroes of sex comedies; it is their function to be monomaniacs, and therefore the use of such a heavily critical term in this context is unapt. A similar argument applies to the charge of hypocrisy. Certainly Horner is a hypocrite. So are Mirabell and Dorimant. So is Hamlet. Used in this way the term soon becomes meaningless. It is as dangerous to take comedy into the pulpit as it is to place it on the analyst's couch.

Connected with these criticisms is the charge that Horner is not only deceitful towards the corrupt figures of the play, but also towards his friends. Thus Anne Righter calls him "a solitary," a man who "stands completely alone in the play." This, again, is too dark for the case. Horner keeps his secret to himself because he knows it is wise to be circumspect in these matters. One imagines that when his ploy has run its course Harcourt and Dorilant will laugh delightedly with him over the success of his ingenuity. Such a conjecture is, of course, outside the bounds of the play, but it serves to set the relationship between the three wits into a proper perspective. They are quite clearly friends in the best sense, and it is their collective attitudes and values that Wycherley uses as a sane commentary upon the diseased society that surrounds them.

This raises the question of Horner's cynicism and the extent to which it can be said to express Wycherley's attitude towards the *mores* of Restoration society. It would appear at first sight as though Horner's contempt for his fellow man is profound and far reaching. His first words, the opening words of the play, are cynical ("A Quack is as fit for a Pimp, as a Midwife for a Bawd; they are still but in their way, both helpers of Nature"), and it is cynicism that informs his attitude towards Lady Fidget and the virtuous gang, Sir Jaspar, Sparkish and Pinchwife (but not, I think, Margery). At the same time it should be noted that Horner makes no attempt to approach Alithea, the only truly honourable woman in the play, and also that, as George Falle points out, he shows genuine concern when he hears that Harcourt has apparently lost his mistress. . . . (His betrayal of Alithea in the final scene cannot be adduced against him. He is faced with a perfect moral dilemma, in that he has to incriminate either his own mistress or Harcourt's, and there is therefore no question of apportioning blame.) His presumed respect for Alithea, then, his hopes for Harcourt's future happiness, his continued friendship with Dorilant and Harcourt, and above all his distaste for the way of life represented by the play's fools all suggest that Horner is not in fact without his ideals. It is true that little enough is seen of Horner the man of honour, but this is for the obvious reason that most of his time is spent in the company of the Pinchwifes and Fidgets against whom contempt and exploitation are understandable, though negative, methods of defence. To complicate matters even further, it must be remembered that through most of the play Horner is acting a part, that of the impotent misogynist, and therefore expresses opinions that he might not necessarily hold *in propria persona* ["in his own person"]. Taking these qualifying factors into consideration I think it would be fair to say that Horner is as cynical as Harcourt ("a Man drinks often with a Fool, as he tosses with a Marker, only to keep his hand in Use"), and as Dorilant ("I wou'd no more Sup with Women, unless I cou'd lye with 'em, than Sup with a rich Coxcomb, unless I cou'd cheat him."), and, probably, as his creator.

Although one of the aims of the preceding argument has been to suggest that Horner is not really as villainous as he has sometimes been called, it would be a mistake to leave the impression that he is a shining example of the *honnête homme* ["honest man"]. The final judgement on Horner should, I think, be that he is neither admirable or reprehensible—or perhaps it would be truer to say that he is both and they cancel each other out. His opinion of the depraved characters of the play can certainly be applauded as can his exposure of them and the comic audacity with which this is undertaken; at the same time, the nullity of his behaviour is a little disturbing, and his self-satisfaction could be considered to be disagreeable. One can certainly find room in this catholic approach to Horner for Kathleen Lynch's theory that he is himself the butt of a certain amount of satire [see Additional Bibliography]. Perhaps the most productive way of looking at Horner and his function in the play is to see him as a picaresque hero. Like the *pícaro* he is untroubled by conventional morality, and he spends his time exploiting the fools with whom he comes in contact. But the real point of the comparison is that in the picaresque novel the satire is focussed not so much on the *pícaro* himself as on the corrupt world through which he moves. This, it seems to me, is the situation in *The Country Wife* exactly. It is almost irrelevant to argue that Horner, the satirical instrument, the man by whom a depraved society is held up to ridicule, is "good" or "bad." He quite simply IS. Not to recognize this is to run the risk of deflecting attention from Wycherley's major attack on the sham of the prevailing attitudes towards love and marriage, and his exposure of the dishonesty, artificiality and misery they entail. (pp. 116-19)

W. R. Chadwick, in his The Four Plays of William Wycherley: A Study in the Development of a Dramatist, *Mouton, 1975, 208 p.*

ROBERT D. HUME (essay date 1976)

[*An American scholar, Hume is a specialist in seventeenth- and eighteenth-century English drama. In the following excerpt, he questions whether* The Country-Wife *is a satire.*]

Should *The Country-Wife* be considered 'a satire'? I am not persuaded that the play is substantially a sermon against hypocrisy, jealousy, or lust. Clearly a majority of the characters are savagely ridiculed. Margery is foolish and ignorant; Pinchwife is contemptible in every way; Sir Jaspar is an obnoxious fool; the ladies prating of their 'dear honour' draw only scorn. No doubt then the play contains a great deal of satire. We should note, however, that the objects of all the ridicule are no more than grotesque exaggerations of the commonplace butts of Carolean comedy. The violently but ineffectually jealous husband, the stupidly complacent husband, the hypocritical and lustful wives, the country innocent—all are comic stereotypes. To say that Wycherley, vastly more than Etherege, presents a degraded and often disgusting view of man and society is perfectly accurate. To call him a serious satirist is probably an exaggeration, for he never goes beyond exposing the obvious to contempt and ridicule. Never, as in Swift, is the audience made to identify itself with what is attacked. The satire is often highly amusing; almost never are its criticisms genuinely serious and thought-provoking in the fashion of Molière.

The result in *The Country Wife* is an immensely enjoyable play in which we take almost nothing seriously. Palmer exaggerates in saying that all questions of motive and moral value disappear [see excerpt dated 1933]: hypocrisy, affectation, and dissimulation enter too strongly to be ignored. Inspired buffoonery, though, is a fair description. Perhaps that phrase does less than justice to the ugliness and nasty quality often present in the play. But the critic may tend to forget just how much is plain farce. The gross character exaggerations are characteristic of farce, more than of comedy. Pinchwife is super-jealous, Sir Jaspar and Sparkish super-blind, Margery ultra-innocent, the ladies blatantly and exuberantly hypocritical. Margery dressed as her brother, Harcourt rigged out as a parson, the switched letters, the china scene, the substitution of Margery for Alithea, and the final resolution are all extraordinarily improbable and more the stuff of high farce than romantic comedy or serious satire. Delightfully bawdy and funny *The Country-Wife* is; profound it is not, and only a prude, a hypocrite, or a stuffy academician would have it otherwise. (pp. 103-04)

> *Robert D. Hume, "The Nature of the Comic Drama,"*
> *in his* The Development of English Drama in the Late
> Seventeenth Century, *Oxford at the Clarendon Press,*
> *Oxford, 1976, pp. 63-148.*

ANTHONY KAUFMAN (essay date 1979)

[*Kaufman is an American educator and critic. In the following excerpt, he explores the psychology of Manly's anger in* The Plain-Dealer.]

While few critics have totally ignored the undoubted dramatic power of *The Plain Dealer*, there has been considerable disagreement about the success of the play as a whole and its rank in the canon of English drama. Recent criticism has attempted to define more clearly the puzzling figure of Captain Manly, who is obviously the key to the play's meaning. Manly has been seen as Wycherley's alter ego—a plain speaking truewit reduced to near misanthropy by a corrupt world—and at the opposite extreme as a "mad-man," prideful and self-deceiv-

ing. Yet there is a crucial feature of Manly that has not been fully explored: his anger, its causes, and its devastating effects. I wish to suggest here that Wycherley is presenting a complex and dramatically powerful study of an exceptional man disbarred by his own anger and contempt for the world from experiencing friendship and love. Wycherley dramatizes with fascinating clarity the psychology of Manly's anger, and in a conclusion often misunderstood—indeed often dismissed as dramatically unacceptable—the catharsis of anger in the recognition of truth, loyalty, and love. (p. 119)

The question of Manly's anger has been troublesome to critics and there has been confusion as to its dramatic significance. But if we analyse this element of the play more closely than in the past, we may come to a more comprehensive and satisfying account of what I believe to be Wycherley's dramatic design. What did this playwright, noted by his contemporaries as a master of human psychology, intend in the figure of Manly? (p. 122)

[From the beginning of the play] Manly is consumed by anger as the result of his sense of human baseness, but balancing this anger is his curious, indeed remarkable, insistence that a man "can have but one friend, for a true heart admits but of one friendship as of one love." . . . Manly is portrayed as a character whose feelings of anger and resultant sense of isolation have led him to create for himself a protective illusion: that at least two people, Olivia and Vernish (the "one love" and "one friend") are . . . capable of loyalty, friendship, and love. This illusion may be understood as the psychological phenomenon "idealization," the function of which, as Charles Rycroft points out, is "to enable the ego to deny feelings of hopelessness and emptiness," which arise from a withdrawal of psychic energy from the actual world, and to evade the necessity of recognizing and resolving the ambivalence which would have to be resolved if one were to face the actual world in a healthy and productive way. Manly's idealization of Vernish and Olivia, his best and only friend, and his mistress, is of course disastrous; he is the victim of their machinations. But Manly, who sees clearly the nature of his world, whose comments on his world are perceptive and seldom wrong—is he merely deceived by Olivia and Vernish, as some critics have thought? Or is it not more likely that he *wills* to believe in the possibility that two people are exempt from social and moral degradation. In a society in which he can find no trust, where love is inevitably tainted, and friendship only self-interest, Manly arbitrarily fixes his value on Olivia and Vernish, love and friendship. Manly's illusion is psychologically sustaining, a means to evade a painful psychological situation; it also reveals a desire to simplify life and to avoid the necessity of complex discrimination. He has withdrawn from life, from feelings other than contempt and anger—but he compulsively elects to trust and to love two people.

Manly's need for idealization is related to what I believe central to his psychological make-up; Wycherley has portrayed his misanthrope as unhealthily narcissistic. And this narcissism leads to the anger which is evident in Manly up to the concluding scene. Although precise definition of the narcissistic personality and its symptoms is difficult, it is generally agreed that the narcissist typically seeks himself as a love-object. Freud's suggestion that males of the narcissistic type are typically subject to overestimation of the female is provocative; furthermore Freud maintains that the narcissistic personality will characteristically desire to *be* loved in his choice of a woman. That the search for the self in another, the overestimation, and the desire to be loved, are seen in Manly's choice of Olivia seems clear. Although Manly idealizes Vernish as well as Olivia and becomes disillusioned with him at the play's end, Vernish remains a rather undeveloped character. Manly's relationship with Olivia, however, is crucial, and Wycherley develops it at length. Olivia is apparently a notorious woman (see, for example, Eliza's telling remarks, V. i. 4ff). Indeed, Bonamy Dobrée suggests that Novel and Plausible are her lovers [see excerpt dated 1924]. Yet Manly idealizes her, the very essence of what he detests in society. Olivia well understands the need of Manly and of her other suitors to see themselves in her, and her ability to reflect her suitors' idealized sense of themselves is expressed in a revealing image: "she stands in the drawing room like the glass, ready for all comers to set their gallantry by her, and, like the glass too, lets no man go from her unsatisfied." . . . That men desire to see in Olivia their own image perfectly reveals the mythical roots of psychological narcissism.

Thus Manly's feelings for Olivia stem from his need to idealize her in order to avoid feelings of radical isolation and from his need to see, narcissistically, a reflection of himself in her and to *be* loved. If this analysis is accepted, that scene . . . in which he learns of Olivia's true feelings toward him and then feels intense rage is better understood. As Manly overhears Olivia's mockery and realizes that she despises him, pretending love only to secure his fortune, the illusion he has created is shattered and the psychological benefits of idealization are no longer available. The result must be the onslaught of the very fears that idealization helped to prevent: a sense of radical isolation and loneliness, feelings of being within an anarchical environment. He is faced with a reality which idealization has helped him to simplify and which is now seen to be complex. In short, Manly feels the proximity of feelings of despair and futility. We must note, moreover, that the scene with Olivia is a highly public scene: Freeman and Fidelia, Manly's followers, are present to witness his humiliation, as are those fops he despises, Novel and Plausible. Such humiliation is unendurable to one who like Manly possesses narcissistic tendencies, and, as Heinz Kohut points out, such types may be subject to "narcissistic rage," an intense anger and the desire to gain revenge on the one who has inflicted the humiliation. Furthermore, the desire for revenge is "limitless". . . . (pp. 122-24)

I believe that such psychoanalytic conceptions of narcissistic rage explain most fully and clearly the source of Manly's limitless rage at Olivia, an anger that in intensity of feeling goes beyond the anger of a prideful man merely duped by a clever trickster. Critics have been puzzled and indeed even irritated with Manly's intense anger at Olivia and his plans for an admittedly unpleasant revenge. But rather than cry out upon Manly as a brute, or resort to speculations about the Restoration's sense of humor, it is better, I think, to understand Manly's psychological situation—one that the playwright has taken pains to define. It is important for us to understand that Manly is portrayed as a man whose essential, vulnerable self has been intolerably wounded and whose need is for revenge—a revenge which cannot acknowledge Olivia's selfhood, her humanity, but must blot out totally what has happened. Manly's feelings are revealingly expressed as he storms out of Olivia's salon: "I'll avoid the whole damned sex forever and woman as a sinking ship.". . . That he is accompanied by Fidelia is, however, an ironic and positive foreshadowing of the fact that his development is not yet complete.

The feelings of idealization, so necessary to him, have been shaken, but for him to acknowledge this immediately is im-

possible; the psychological consequences of such realization are too painful. . . . He feels at this point confusion: disillusionment, lust, hatred. "Love," the only word he can use to describe his feelings for Olivia, undermines his sense of manhood; it forces one, he believes, into hypocrisy, knavery, cowardice—it makes one effeminate, the very antithesis of what Manly wishes to feel.

Manly's desire, painfully admitted to himself, is to make some overture to Olivia. He employs Fidelia, a girl disguised as a boy, who out of love for him has served as his "volunteer," to intercede on his behalf with Olivia. But Olivia, in a situation which recalls *Twelfth Night,* makes advances to Fidelia. Manly's confused hopes end with Fidelia's return. She is half-reluctant to inform Manly of what has happened; he is eager to learn whether Fidelia has "mollified [Olivia's] heart for me.". . . In a comic-poignant exchange, Fidelia tells Manly of Olivia's verbal abuse and perverse sexual advances. On the verge of frenzy, his incoherence a measure of the intensity of his feelings, Manly expresses the emotional confusion central to his relationship with Olivia: his lust, his need to think her true and honest, his sense of her enduring attraction, his hatred, his sense of his loss of self, his sense that love has made him cowardly, even his jealousy of Fidelia. It is a moment not easily duplicated in Restoration drama:

> MANLY: Damned, damned woman, that could be so false and infamous! And damned, damned heart of mine, that cannot yet be false, though so infamous! What easy, tame, suffering, trampled things does that little god of talking cowards make of us! But—
>
> FIDELIA: (*aside*) So! It works I find as I expected.
>
> MANLY: But she was false to me before. She told me so herself, and yet I could not quite believe it. But she was, so that her second falseness is a favor to me, not an injury, in revenging me upon the man that wronged me first of her love. Her love!—a whore's, a witch's love!—But, what, did she not kiss well, sir? I'm sure I thought her lips—but I must not think of them more—but yet they are such I could still kiss—grow to—and then tear off with my teeth, grind them into mammocks and spit them into her cuckold's face. . . .

I have no wish to exaggerate claims for this play, but in this scene's portrayal of an intelligent, powerful, yet vulnerable man's sense of betrayal and universal corruption, may we not think of Hamlet's response to the ghost's "So lust, though to a radiant angel linked, / Will sate itself in a celestial bed / And prey on garbage." Both Manly and Hamlet view the world as a disordered garden, and both have a strong sense of the disparity between what men and women appear to be and the all-embracing corruption beneath. They are especially obsessed by the possibility that a woman's beauty may conceal hypersexuality and perversion. Both at times are bitter (and witty) satirists, and both seek revenge for a woman's perverse faithlessness. (pp.125-27)

Wycherley has given us in Manly a study of anger and its causes. Yet Manly is not alone in his anger. We find in *The Plain Dealer* three important characters who in quite different ways mirror the anger that Manly feels. Olivia has played on Manly's psychological vulnerability, but it is not enough to insist that she wishes to deceive him in order to gain wealth (though that is quite true). We must see that her hatred of him is radical and centers on his very essence: his masculinity. . . . In short, Olivia loathes the "good Captain Swagger-huff," with his "boisterous sea love." Olivia is no Desdemona thrilling to the exotic adventures of the virile and marvelous Moor, nor even a Célimène, fascinated by the ''bear of merit'' (the phrase is Wyndham Lewis's), Alceste.

Throughout the play she announces her ''aversion'' to men. . . . This ''aversion,'' although in part the affectation of the coquette (''aversion'' would seem to be a ''lady's word,'') is psychologically quite true. She prefers the company of such as Plausible and Novel, those ''apes and echoes of men,'' whose effeminacy is stressed throughout the play. And it is not merely a ''comic convention'' or the necessities of plot that leads Wycherley to portray Olivia as immediately attracted to the epicene ''boy'' Fidelia upon first sight. In fact, Olivia's relations with *men* are not primarily sexual—they are exploitative and reveal her repulsion. She plays the coquette in order to gain the victory over them represented by the wealth they give her. She manipulates men, whom she instinctively senses as her enemies. In this she is sister not to Molière's coquette, Célimène, but to her much nearer relative; Mr. Horner of *The Country Wife,* whose hostility to women, his abuse and manipulation of them, are at the center of that play.

The subplot of *The Plain Dealer* presents the Widow Blackacre, a fiercely litigious woman, whose main pleasure in life is found in the law courts of Westminster Hall. She is introduced in the first act as a furious woman; she storms Manly's lodgings—to serve him with a subpoena. Freeman recognizes the woman about to enter: ''The Widow Blackacre, is it not? That litigious she-petty-fogger, who is at law and difference with all the world. . . . Manly: . . . she has no pleasure but in vexing others.'' . . . The Widow, we are told, is kinswoman to Olivia, and indeed she shares Olivia's anger; she is an obsessed personality, at war with the world. Her continual and aggressive litigation is the channel for her intense feelings. A clue to the source of her anger is revealed when we see that her ultimate horror is to be once again under ''covert baron,'' that is, under a husband's legal protection and control. When in the last act, Freeman, who has pursued her for her fortune, succeeds in forcing her into either marriage or a settlement, she complains that ''Matrimony, to a woman, is worse than excommunication in depriving her of the benefit of the law, and I would rather be deprived of life.''. . . The Widow, an energetic and aggressive woman, resents her limited role as a woman, a role she finds both confining and degrading. Neither the Widow nor Olivia modify or repent of their anger. The Widow, although forced to a financial settlement by Freeman, militantly offers legal aid to her kinswoman. In different ways, both women resent and reject the male and struggle against it through devious practices. Their aggression is often comic; it fails finally, yet their characterization is surprisingly complex (surely the Widow goes beyond a mere ''humor'' character), and their shared anger reflects that of the central character, Manly.

Although the anger of Olivia and the Widow is recognizable at once, that of another major character, Freeman, may be less apparent. His immediate source, as everyone has agreed, is Molière's Philinte. Philinte stands as foil to Alceste; his reasonable and tolerant acceptance of the way of the world sets off the extravagance, the blindness of Alceste's indictment of society, although finally Philinte may not represent Molière's final perception of the right way of social conduct and thought. Freeman is only superficially like Philinte, for unlike Philinte he embodies no philosophy of toleration and detachment. He does insist that there must be some ceremony in social life (''no professing, no ceremony at all in friendship, were as unnatural and as undecent as in religion''),. . . but Wycherley

has denied to Freeman Philinte's expression of a social philosophy which, if limited, is liberal, consistent, and coherent. Instead, Freeman advocates compliance with social forms merely for one's own self-interest, not in order that society function with amiable civility and order.

But it is important to note that beneath the ceremonious flattery of compliments and hugs, lies malice. Freeman's laughing detachment does not signal acceptance and toleration (*tout comprendre c'est tout pardonner*) [''to understand all is to forgive all''] but malice and hostility. When he says of those who practice hypocrisy and deceit in a corrupt society, ''Well, they understand the world,'' he does not forgive them their understanding nor the world its corruption. His attitude is announced in his first lines when he learns that Manly has thrust out Lord Plausible: ''Faith, I am sorry you would let the fop go. I intended to have some sport with him.''. . . And lest we think that Freeman's sport is detached, amused, and playful, we hear, a few lines later, Freeman's true attitude to those at Westminster Hall whom he has flattered: ''when their backs were turned did I not tell you they were rogues, villains, rascals whom I despised and hated?.''. . . Wycherley's design is to allow us to see Freeman's anger and hostility toward the ''world''—however that anger and hostility may be expressed through wit and laughter.

Freeman's hostility takes a more specific form. Although he can acknowledge that women ''are not all Olivias,'' often he expresses hostility toward them. . . . Critics have wondered why Wycherley did not follow his source, Molière, and portray a love relationship between Freeman and Eliza as Molière does with Philinte and Éliante. But surely Freeman's hostility towards the world and specifically towards women disqualifies him from any relationship other than the one he actually carries on: the exploitative pursuit of the rich (if old and ugly) Widow Blackacre.

There is a curious parallel among Manly, Freeman, Olivia, and the Widow; all are incapable of love owing to their anger—anger expressed in a variety of ways. Manly settles his love on a reflection of himself in Olivia; Olivia her desire on a boyish female. The Widow rejects the overtures of two suitors; Freeman pursues without either love or lust the rich, old Widow. All are at odds with their society; all feel anger—and all are disqualified from experiencing genuine love. Those other than Manly remain prey to their own psychological disabilities. Manly, of course, overcomes these feelings of anger in the recognition of Fidelia.

The ending of *The Plain Dealer* offers a baffling problem. Manly, in his discovery of Fidelia's real identity, is immediately altered: his anger and distrust of the world is seemingly dissipated by the example of Fidelia's virtue. This ending has seemed to many psychologically improbable and dramatically disastrous. Indeed it may seem akin to the typical conclusion of the so-called sentimental comedy represented by Steele's *The Conscious Lovers.* The key to the ending is obviously Fidelia, who appears to be a figure from the romance tradition (she is often said to be a recreation of the Viola of *Twelfth Night*) oddly placed in a satirical comedy of corrupt city practice. But it may be an error to believe that the romance mode must be at odds with the predominantly realistic and satirical mode of the play. We should recall that often in English comedy the two modes are thematically complementary, and this is surely the case in *The Plain Dealer,* where Fidelia as romance heroine has an important thematic function.

In Fidelia we observe the quest of the disguised girl, a quest in which she will be severely tried, proven, and at the end receive self-fulfillment in her complement, Manly. . . .

Throughout the play, Wycherley contrasts Fidelia against Olivia, whose actions, though quite understandable psychologically, are associated with the diabolic. Both women are disguised: Fidelia literally; Olivia by her shrewd playing of a deceptive role. Manly can penetrate neither disguise until Olivia deliberately drops her pretence and mocks her victim. This recognition is contrasted to that moment at the end of the play at which Fidelia stands by accident revealed. Manly has become aware of what both women are, and he sees that Fidelia embodies the perfection he had mistakenly thought embodied in Olivia.

If Fidelia seeks and finds her completion in Manly, her own action on Manly is curative: she is the means to his self-recognition and rejuvenation. In IV. i., when Manly hears from Fidelia that Olivia has attempted to seduce her and breaks out in a frenzied tirade, Fidelia has a crucial aside: "Poor man, how uneasy he is! I have hardly the heart to give him so much pain though withal I give him a cure and to myself new life.". . . Fidelia has asked to be tried, and her blood, shed in the murderous fight with Vernish, attests, symbolically to the sacrifices that she is prepared to make and the life-giving qualities she brings to a heroic but incomplete man. By carrying to Manly the news of Olivia's perverse treachery, Fidelia is the instrument of Manly's pain, but the pain is a part of his cure: painfully he will come to recognize what Olivia is and how dangerous she is. And he will recognize at once in the final scene that what Fidelia embodies is real, obtainable, and offers a new sense of himself and the world. She is the means by which he achieves an important psychological catharsis: through recognition of what she is, the explosive anger Manly contains is dissipated. And Fidelia, presented as weak throughout the play, is herself incomplete without what Manly embodies. "There is nothing certain in the world, sir, but my truth and your courage," says Fidelia. . ., and this is what Manly must and does come to recognize. Earlier in the play, at the end of Act I, Manly has asked Freeman to accompany him to Olivia's lodgings, ". . . if your weak faith doubts this miracle of a woman.". . . Now, in the last act, before him stands true faith, the "miracle of a woman" that he has sought for and always believed to exist. What we see on stage before us then is a physical action which reveals a psychological one: the violence and confusion of the darkened room, the lights and recognition, are the correlatives to the cathartic dissipation of Manly's emotional confusion, his anger, and the replacement of these by the knowledge that what he has most desired to believe in is indeed real and obtainable. Yet perhaps his discovery of Fidelia is not so much union as reunion—the restoration of faith in what he had believed in, although in a psychologically unhealthy manner, from the beginning of the play. It seems irrelevant to argue that what she represents is out of place in the corrupt world of the play, that she is the product of wish-fulfillment, or that the qualities she embodies are unobtainable. The conclusion of *The Plain Dealer* is not a concession; it is an assertion—such qualities do exist; Fidelia embodies them, and the qualities that she embodies are quite as real as those represented by her opposite, Olivia. . . . I hope that it is not improper to point out that Manly's recognition is that of Lear. It marks Manly's passage from unhealthy and unrealistic idealization to valid belief in the miracle of beauty, truth, love and virtue. (pp. 128-33)

Anthony Kaufman, "Idealization, Disillusion, and Narcissistic Rage in Wycherley's 'The Plain Dealer'," in Criticism, *Vol. XXI, No. 2 (Spring, 1979), pp. 119-33.*

DEREK COHEN (essay date 1980)

[*In the following excerpt, Cohen analyzes the role of women—which he believes has long been misunderstood—in* The Country-Wife.]

[In *The Country Wife,* Horner's pretense of impotence] is a bawdy, lecherous, hugely funny piece of locker-room humour. As a man's joke against other men, it works with unquestionable efficiency. What has not been noticed is how it is also, and with equal strength, a woman's joke of as ribald and ferocious a variety. I should like to take a new look at the play's women; at the dramatic uses to which they are put and the meanings of their responses to the protagonist. If we examine the scenes in which they appear from the perspective of their deliberate and willful participation in those scenes and not only as the merely necessary appendages to the play's overall, Horner-inspired plan, some startling facets are revealed.

The infrequently discussed "drinking scene," for example, near the end of *The Country Wife,* reveals the subversiveness of the play. As it begins, the scene shows the women as egregious a pack of moral fools as ever gathered on the stage: they are bound together by infidelity, deception and lies to their husbands and each other. And yet, with the passage of the action, it becomes ever more clear that the comedy has retained in its sinewy centre the power once again to turn the tables as the female fools reveal Horner to be a greater fool than themselves. . . . Most critics who comment on this action seem not to have noticed that the drunkenness is a deliberate pretense, unaccountably overlooking Lady Fidget's exhortation to the others to be as truthful and uninhibited as they would be "supposing we had drank each of us our two Bottles.". . . (pp. 120-22)

We have been used in comedies, particularly in Restoration comedies, to having our male characters entertaining us and each other with frank discussions about the triple delights of wine, money and sex: indeed *The Country Wife* itself furnishes several such scenes where its men talk uninhibitedly about the masculine pastimes of whoring and drunkenness. However, to find a group of fashionable women indulging themselves in conversation about the pleasures of inebriation and illicit sex is a telling twist to a theme that is as old as comedy itself. And Wycherley does his best to let us feel the spectacular impact of his innovation. The women enter Horner's lodgings with the air of being its—and its owner's—proprietors. Having compelled their defensive and helpless host to sit down with them, they proceed to treat *him* rather like the spaniel whose docility he had earlier mocked in likening that species of dog to womankind. In the midst of this crowd of grotesquely aggressive women, Horner is unusually silent. Nowhere in the play does he seem more like the object he ultimately becomes, the very plaything of a gang of female gallants. As the women grow in aggressive self-confidence they efface Horner's normally robust presence; the low point in his diminution in stature coinciding with the high point of My Lady Fidget's overweeningly boastful revelation that Horner is her lover. "They are telling ripe," . . . she mutters, then loudly announces, "this is my false Rogue," and, as significantly stated in the stage directions, she "*Claps him on the back.*" This action is powerfully suggestive in what it reveals about the altered socio-sexual roles that are now presented, and its effect is not vitiated by the hilarious consequences of the revelation.

Notwithstanding the dramatic significance of her magisterial slap on the back, it is My Lady Fidget's drinking song which contains the quintessential expression of the sex war upon which the play centers. . . .

Wine is praised as a befogger of the senses and as a beverage whose use can make marriage bearable. Men are selfish, tyrannical and vain in their treatment of women whose subordinate position makes their happiness dependent upon the men's willingness to allow it. The song urges women to vie no longer with the bottle for their husbands' attentions but, instead, to follow men in adopting drink as a means to greater happiness: through drink reality becomes blurred and more pleasant. . .; drink will enable a woman to forget her problems and will make living easier to cope with. . . . The aggrieved tone which dominates the first verse is roughly put aside in the second where it gives way to a defiant burst of contempt for men. . . . The song draws to a robust and belligerent conclusion with the recommendation that women emulate men and embrace the bottle with zest. The disdain with which the masculine world is described in the song is accompanied by an assertion of female solidarity, an assertion which seems to imply that men are inferior to women, that the power they enjoy over women is just one more of the injustices of nature and that the only recourse women have in this grossly unfair scheme of things is to get drunk (*"Because we live sober to men we submit."*)

The song, the actions, and the dialogue of this scene open to question the too readily accepted assumption that Horner is sole master and manipulator of the action. His discomfort in the action and the ladies' palpable use of him suggest very strongly that he has been hoist, if one may so put it, with his own petard. The scene throws into doubt the entire question of the extent to which Horner manipulates the world about him. In the beginning of the play as he announces his plans and expectations to Quack, his bristling self-confidence is so assured as to be infectious, and the audience is led to believe in Horner with a faith equal to his own. But by the time of this climactic scene in the plot involving Horner and his string of fashionable women, his control of events and actions is no longer indisputable. In the very last action of the play where the chief plot involving the country wife herself is brought exquisitely into conjunction with the lower plot, it seems only that Horner has manoeuvred himself into the centre of an ever-widening maelstrom of sexual entanglement which the conclusion of the China scene had hilariously indicated even he is not equipped to control ("Upon my honour I have none left now.") . . . (pp. 122-24)

Horner ironically acknowledges his victimization in his appeal for Lady Squeamish's sympathy when he laments, "Ay Madam, you see how they use me.". . . He presents himself in this complaint as a poor ill-treated eunuch for whom the women show neither sympathy nor respect. However, his own limited perception of the irony of this remark is that *he*, in fact, is using the women who, he claims, are using him. But, on a second level, perceptible more readily to the audience than to the characters on stage, Horner, the convenient phallus, has temporarily exhausted his sexual resources and has, in reality, become that impotent and useless object which the world publicly recognizes him to be.

Indeed the actions of the play counterpoint and add variations to a theme of the subjugation of men in a world which they only think they control. Women who are treated like prized objects use sex as a means of revenge against their husbands and achieve a kind of moral victory over them by making them what they most fear to be—cuckolds. Women like Alithea, on the other hand, who are appreciated for their human worth are capable of responding in kind with love, respect and loyalty. (pp. 124-25)

By way of contrast to Alithea's tenacious adherence to an idealism of mutual respect and sexual equality, the relationships of My Lady Fidget to her husband and of Margery Finchwife to hers reveal struggles for dominance. The outcome of each of these two marital relationships is a female victory. In the last line of the epilogue is a reminder of the clearer-sightedness of the women: "But . . . we Women,—there's no cous'ning us,". . . and indeed the antagonism between My Lady Fidget and her husband is a one-sided affair. With traditional masculine arrogance leavened by singular human imbecility Sir Jaspar assumes proprietorial rights over his wife. His relationship to her consists of continual efforts to placate and amuse her, while he always manifests a profound but obvious unease about his capacity to keep her faithful to him. She, however, quite overtly justifies and asserts her claims for independence from her husband. Her attitudes are crass and heartless, but expressed with such aptness and clarity that it is hard to accept her as the fool for which she is so often taken. Indeed her coyness—notably in the prelude to the China scene—seems like nothing so much as political wisdom. My Lady Fidget possesses more than a merely predatory cunning; she possesses a rare intelligence which, combined with her viciousness, makes her a formidable character whose strength even Horner seems to have underestimated. Her imagery is incisive and, when the mask of chastity is put aside, she can be as trenchant in depicting her own hypocrisy as mordant in her justification of it as Horner himself. She is her own best critic, seeing herself with as clear a vision as the most scathing satirist. . . . In social settings she is the arch-hypocrite, but—and one must admire her for it—to herself My Lady Fidget is honest and forthright, frankly using the power of hypocrisy to help her overcome the obstacles that society and nature have put in her way: "we are savers of our Honour, the Jewel of most value and use.". . . The shrewdness of such remarks suggests a far more acute personality than My Lady Fidget is usually given credit for possessing. While My Lady Fidget's husband is worldly enough to try to disguise his fear of cuckoldry, Pinchwife, his counterpart in the chief plot, is constantly giving vehement and public utterance to his suspicions of those around him and his doubts about his ability to keep his wife to himself. These fears leave him with a detestation of women and the dependent belief that although women were made to be subservient to men, love itself seduces them from this natural element. . . . One of those characters who unwittingly damn themselves each time they speak, Pinchwife provides in his credo ("If we do not cheat women, they'll cheat us") the very basis for the chief plot of the play, which centers upon the exchange of positions of dominance within his own family and which his wife effects through sheer superiority of wit and intelligence. From a subservient country wench, Margery Pinchwife begins to develop into a woman of fashionable intrigue, learning in the process to turn her husband's fears to her own advantage. Margery and Lady Fidget are more intelligent than their husbands and, like them, are unencumbered by moral sensitivity. Mrs. Pinchwife's emotions reveal themselves entirely in their physical manifestations. (pp. 125-27)

Horner, similarly devoted to the physical side of love, makes a conscious exchange of reputation, dignity and social standing for varied and continuing sexual fulfillment. Even the genial sympathy of his friends Harcourt and Dorilant makes clear that he has lost the respect of his peers. However, the contempt of his male friends is a sacrifice that Horner has made willingly and calculatedly. More surprising is the fact that even as they use him the *women*, who know that his debility is a sham, are contemptuous of Horner. In the drinking scene they treat him like a male prostitute: when they speak to each other it is as though he were not present and when they do acknowledge him—even after the revelation of his "infidelity"—their tone is such as to remind him and themselves of his servile station. He is "beast," "toad," and "Eunuch." (p. 127)

To acquire sexual license Horner consciously has decided to pay the price of subservience. The spiritual emptiness of his relationships with these women is to be recognized in the extent to which the relationship is devoid of honesty and replete with social nicety. Passing himself off as a selfless servant of womankind ("cou'd you be so generous? so truly a Man of honour, to cause yourself to be reported no man?"). . . Horner assumes an attitude of servile gallantry at the outset. (p. 129)

Perhaps even more significant, certainly more serious, is Horner's moral enslavement to the women which he unwittingly foretold early in the play with his assertion that "'tis as hard to be a good Fellow, a good Friend, and a Lover of Women, as 'tis to be a good Fellow, a good Friend, and a Lover of Money; you cannot follow both, then choose your side; Wine gives you liberty, Love takes it away.". . . The uncomfortable truth of this remark reveals itself later for Horner in his betrayal of Alithea and Harcourt, the only people for whom he appears to have anything like genuine affection or respect.

Horner owes his reputation as the play's arch-manipulator to his undeniable superiority of wit and to his enormous self-assurance, qualities eminently lacking in the men he cuckolds. What brings him down to their level in terms of his final subjection by their wives is his moral similarity to these men and his similar view of womankind, a view which is based like theirs upon time-honoured simplifications about the singular nature of the female sex. By giving Horner's last words the ring of a declaration of success, Wycherley leads us rather too easily to accept him in the light of triumph in which he finally presents himself: "But he who aims by women to be priz'd, / First by the men you see must be despis'd.". . . However, to return to the context of this remark—to the last action of the play and its accompanying spectacle—is to recognize its hollowness. Here is Horner on the precipice of imminent discovery (a discovery which must bring the whole of this society, whose binding fibre is pretense, to total collapse) wholly entrapped by his own ingenuity. In his desperation he has to turn to yet another woman for salvation; this time she is, significantly, the least of the women in the play. Of Lucy, the maid, Horner begs rescue and, in so doing, further places himself at the mercy of his erstwhile victims and playthings. She offers to "fetch [him] off" while Horner, in a passion of anxiety, entreats, "Canst thou? I'll give thee—:". . . . The uncompleted promise is heavy with suggestion. Is Horner's harem growing? And let us suppose, for argument's sake, that Lucy is old and ugly. Horner no longer has any choice in the matter. His enslavement is complete and, the bravado of the epilogue notwithstanding, our last vivid memory of Horner is of a character far more fettered than freed by sexual liberty. (pp. 129-30)

Derek Cohen, "The Revenger's Comedy: Female Hegemony in 'The Country Wife'," in Atlantis, Vol. 5, No. 2, Spring, 1980, pp. 120-30.

J. DOUGLAS CANFIELD (essay date 1980)

[*Canfield is an American educator and author who has written widely on seventeenth- and eighteenth-century literature. In the following excerpt, he analyzes how the use of religious language defines the ethics of* The Country-Wife's *characters.*]

The Country Wife is replete with ironic religious language. Nearly every character punctuates his dialogue with such apparently meaningless expletives as "Lord," "For God's sake," "damn," "Hell and damnation," and "I vow," with many variations on "Heavens," "Faith," and "The Divel." (p. 391)

In his courtship of Alithea, Harcourt . . . uses religious language ironically: He wittily employs the hackneyed language of the Christian-courtly tradition. Pretending to have only a Platonic affection for his "friend's" fiancé, he outrageously dupes Sparkish as he answers his "Catechisme": "*Sparkish*. But how do you love her? *Harcourt*. With all my Soul. . . . With the best, and truest love in the World.". . . Even, he says earlier, "infinitely well, . . . above the world.". . . Later, to thwart the marriage between Sparkish and Alithea, Harcourt disguises himself as a parson. "Well, most reverend Doctor," says the percipient and non-plussed Alithea, "pray let us make an end of this fooling." "With all my soul, Divine, Heavenly Creature," answers Harcourt. . . . He proceeds to call her "Seraphic Lady" and to swear that no one else shall marry her: "By Heavens, I'll die first.". . . (pp. 391-92)

All this is very funny and ironic. Yet Harcourt is actually courting Alithea with this language, and its unironic signification is intended for her. For . . . he is love-struck at first sight. . . . And we should remember that, in opposition to Horner. . ., Harcourt has said of the comparison between "Love and Wine, Oil and Vinegar," "I grant it; Love will still be uppermost.". . . Harcourt's language, then, while it parodies the Christian-courtly tradition, at the same time invokes that tradition to discriminate his attitude toward love from Horner's and the other characters'. And when Harcourt says, "Heavens forbid" that Alithea should marry Sparkish, or when he pleads with her "for Heaven's sake,". . . the language is witty but no longer totally ironic. It really is a kind of prayer.

In short, the relationship between Harcourt and Alithea affirms the possibility of transcendence in a transient world, where the attitude toward sex is crude, bestial, appetitive. The career of Margery epitomizes the frustration of spirit in this world, for she loves Horner with all her "soul,". . . a love that can never be fulfilled—though it may be sexually satisfied. In contrast, Harcourt and Alithea transcend that world, not just in their language but in generous action. When "all the world," including Horner, has turned against Alithea and accused her of fornication, Harcourt defends her "innocence.". . . Nor is he merely interested in her money, for Pinchwife, as her guardian, could very well deprive her of her portion if he concludes her profligate. In the end, despite all the bad marriages—and the sterile, unfruitful disdain of Sparkish . . . and Horner—Harcourt is "impatient" . . . till he be joined in a union sanctified by the grace that parson's gown ultimately represents and illuminated but not idealistically blinded by the Christian-courtly concepts of "Faith" and "constancy" and "trust.". . . As Alithea says, "Women and Fortune are truest still to those that trust 'em.". . . The line is ironically undercut by the fact that it covers up Margery's adultery. Thus Wycherley eschews simplistic solutions. Nevertheless, Alithea does not say women are "absolutely true" but only "truest" to those that trust. A relationship built on trust has the spiritual potential the Christian-courtly language in this play subtly, comically, and urbanely represents.

Even the religious expletives and witticisms of *The Country Wife* are meaningfully ambiguous. The mere number of the expletives precludes their being casual on the part of the author. As in Etherege, their being casual on the part of the characters serves to depict this world as generally hypocritical and godless. And the witticisms—for example, Horner's statement that bigots ''fear the eye of the world more than the eye of Heaven''—work only if there is still some validity to the language which establishes the satirical norm. Why else is the line funny? The bigot ought obviously to fear the eye of Heaven. The literal sense thus works against the ironic intent to create the comic incongruity. So both *are* present.

Furthermore, Horner too is a devil-figure. His favorite saying is ''the Divel take me,''. . . and at one point he exclaims, ''I cou'd adore the Devil well painted.''. . . The critic must ask why so many references to religion, in particular here to the devil, if not to form a pattern that reifies the very realm so casually and ironically dismissed—here to suggest that Horner is Satanic in his temptation of others. As such he serves as an agent of justice for those who have the wrong attitude toward love and sex and marriage. Horner himself lives in his own spiritually impotent hell: He really ''can't be'' a husband now . . . , and he can look forward to no society but that of the foolish and the meretricious. And . . . the Machiavellian Horner overreaches and almost defeats himself. Yet in a brilliant last touch of satire the audience's expectation of final poetic justice is frustrated, as if to say, the Horner is still there to punish us if we have the wrong attitude toward love. But the religious language, however witty and urbane, has subtly referred to heavens and hells beyond the play appropriate to one's behavior in it. This religious language is, after all, largely what gives Wycherley's comedy its satiric power. For it provides a moral norm with distant—but audible—metaphysical reverberations. (pp. 392-93)

> J. Douglas Canfield, ''Religious Language and Religious Meaning in Restoration Comedy,'' in Studies in English Literature, 1500-1900, Vol. XX, No. 3, Summer, 1980, pp. 385-406.

DEREK HUGHES (essay date 1982)

[*In the following excerpt, Hughes analyzes the relationships between society and instinct, language and sexuality in* The Plain-Dealer.]

Many critics have found *The Plain Dealer* hopelessly digressive and incoherent, complaining of apparent irrelevancies such as the Westminster Hall act. Those critics who have asserted the play's unity normally do so by identifying some alleged ''main theme,'' such as hypocrisy. But bald abstractions do not adequately describe the intricate principles of coherence that inform good works of art, and I should prefer to begin by drawing attention to a dramatic situation that occurs repeatedly throughout the play. This is the representation of a character engaged in frenzied, compulsive talking or noise-making. Instances are easy to find, and they figure equally in scenes that clearly advance the plot and in those that have been deemed superfluous. In his first conversation with the Widow, Manly talks with blinkered monomania about his passion for Olivia while the Widow responds with an equally monomaniacal diatribe about her lawsuit. . . . She later has a comparable bout of noncommunication with Oldfox. . ., he talking about his poems and she (as always) about her litigation, each seizing the other's words and redefining them to suit his or her humor: for example, Oldfox's epigram on a cruel mistress's decree to her lover moves the Widow to produce ''a Decree . . . drawn by the finest Clerk.''. . . We also find frenetic talking or noise when Olivia rants about the verbal associations of the name ''Horner'';. . . when she obsessively finishes the satiric portraits that Novel barely has time to start, when the Widow coaches her lawyers to speak ornately rhetorical nothings. . .; when Jerry mimics animal noises with the new toys that Freeman has bought him. . .; when Novel equates wit with ''Railing, Roaring, and making a noise''. . .; and when Oldfox binds and gags the Widow so that he might assault her ear with his acrostics. . . . (pp. 318-19)

In many of these incidents language gains an impermissible autonomy, ceasing not only to be a commonly agreed system of symbols but even to be a system of symbols at all. Though traditionally the unifying principle of society, it here serves to isolate rather than unite: Manly and the Widow shout deafly and uncomprehendingly at each other, the Widow and Oldfox alter the meaning of each other's words to suit their idiosyncratic passions, and Olivia's meditations on the word ''Horner'' treat language as a vehicle not of commonly agreed notions but of secret, private meanings. In the law courts, where the order of society should be protected, men baffle each other with nonsense for the sake of individual gain, the legal supremacy of the empty word being further illustrated when the Widow hires a forger ''to imitate exactly the flourish'' at the end of a signature. . . . And the self-sufficiency of the word is most flagrantly and obviously exemplified when Olivia claims that the ''china'' scene in *The Country Wife* has so irrevocably sullied the word that all the corresponding objects must be destroyed: words cease to be the symbols of mental images and instead usurp the status of objects.

But if language loses its traditional role as the communicative symbol of thought and reason, it compensates for the loss by acquiring some very odd and unexpected functions. Rapes, for instance, are not usually performed ''through the ear'' with ''well-pen'd Acrostics.''. . . Often (as in Oldfox's poetic rape) we glimpse a world in which all man's primitive instincts have been attenuated, their fulfillment transposed from the realm of action to that of speech. At first, Olivia's covert sexuality finds release only in her verbal play with Horner's name. If Oldfox diverts sexual passion into the *furor poeticus* [''poetic frenzy''], the Widow allows her verbose litigiousness to efface all traces of sexual or even familial instinct: she regards her suitors as an insufferable distraction from her litigation; when Jerry rehearses her case uncomprehendingly and chaotically reciting the doings of ''*Fitz, Pere,* and *Ayle*,''. . . three corporeal generations of family evaporate into the impersonal figments of law French (so impersonal that Jerry cannot at first remember the correct order of generations); and, of course, the Widow's treatment of her son monstrously subordinates all natural needs and obligations to the demands of her lawsuit, for she stifles his sexual growth and, when her legal interests require it, is prepared to declare him a bastard. . . . Indeed, when Jerry does gain freedom to indulge his animal nature, he can do so only by mocking his mother with toys imitating the sounds of ''a Duck, . . . a Boar-cat, and . . . an Owl.''. . . Here, where the human voice most obviously ceases to communicate reasoned thought, it also most obviously becomes a feeble surrogate for brute action.

Freeman's courtship of the widow is as asexual as Oldfox's, and it shows a similar conversion of the sexual into the linguistic: he first gains control over her by stealing her *writings*. . .; he completes his control by catching her in the act of forgery, a species of linguistic malpractice. . .; and the climax of the courtship is not marriage and consummation but a *written* agreement providing divorce and maintenance without the preliminary inconvenience of matrimony. . . . But lust is not the only elemental instinct that is stifled by the wild proliferation of speech, for the physical belligerence that Manly so strikingly embodies is—as he is scornfully aware—virtually absent from the effete society of London, where the beaux ''are in all things so like Women,'' . . . and ''talking Cowards''. . . conduct their combats in what are conventionally the woman's weapons: words. Manly's active aggressiveness finds its insubstantial, verbal counterpart in the railings of Olivia, Novel, the Widow, and Oldfox, and also in the harangues of the courts; for the proceedings of justice do not create an order that supersedes the anarchy of individualistic aggression but instead perpetuate the state of nature, merely attenuating the war of action into the war of noise. Importing his undisciplined aggressiveness into the halls of justice, Manly brings on himself legal writs for his physical violence and physical duels for his verbal insults. . ., the interchange stressing that the language of the courts is merely a sleazy and unheroic alternative to violence. The juxtaposition of legal language and primitive violence, indeed, dominates the second half of the play, for, as Freeman captures the Widow through the manipulation of writing, Manly gains parallel triumphs through more archaic means, avenging Olivia's false speeches of love with his silent rape and recovering *''vi & armis''* . . . the property which law cannot regain.

Wycherley's concern with the corruption of language, then, is far more elaborate and subtle than a mere concern with ''hypocrisy'' or ''pretense.'' Language in *The Plain Dealer* reveals how perplexedly man is suspended between the conditions of rational sociability and appetitive savagery. Partaking of both conditions, man can neither reconcile them nor cultivate either one exclusively, instead finding that each aspect of his divided nature hinders and frustrates the other; thus language—the principle of society—declines into uncommunicative noise, while brute appetite—the principle of savagery—is attenuated into language. The hero's contempt for the verbiage around him is contempt not only for hypocrisy but for the whole encroachment of speech upon the manly realms of belligerence and sexual conquest; it springs from his determination (doomed, as we shall see) to preserve the simple integrity of his instinctual self in a world of effete garrulity. (pp. 319-21)

[The] conflict between social role and instinctual self is most elaborately portrayed when Olivia tries to consummate her lust for her fake lover. She is haunted by the fear of interruption (that is, of the intrusion of society), and her fears are well grounded, for her husband turns up both before and during her first tryst. . ., and her second is invaded by virtually the whole cast. . . . In the final crowding of the stage, society appears as a quite literal hindrance to the pursuit of lust. In displaying the conflict between the social and instinctual self, moreover, Olivia's trysts also display with especial clarity the antipathy between instinct and the speech that distinguishes the social self. ''Take the dumb, and best Welcomes, Kisses and Embraces; 'tis not a time for ideal words,'' she urges Fidelia. . . . She does not even want Manly named during the encounter, ''for in a time of stol'n joys, as this is, the filthy name of Husband were not a more alaying sound.''. . . As she leaves for the bedroom, she protests that she did not expect to pass her time ''in talking.''. . . And, of course, the events in the bedroom

provide the clearest disjunction between man's speaking and sexual self, with the antisocial Manly silently performing the deed after Fidelia—a man only in her public trappings—has done the talking. (pp. 322-23)

The hero's disgust with society's ways is thus far more complex—and far more morally ambiguous—than a mere disdain of hypocrisy and greed, for the talk, ceremony, and money-grubbing of London embody everything antipathetic to the instinctual aggressiveness that is partially implicit in his name. His lust and belligerence issue in action, and he is regularly contemptuous of the effeminate and the cowardly; in polite society, however, lust and belligerence repeatedly evaporate into words. Manly thus hates flattery and ceremony not only because they are mendacious but because they are cowardly and servile, affronting his zeal for primitive, antipodean freedom. Early in the play he says, ''I can walk alone; I hate a Harness, and will not tug on in a Faction, kissing my Leader behind, that another Slave may do the like to me.''. . . His hatred of disguise does, on many occasions, make him an authoritative critic of a fraudulent society. But his hatred of disguise is a morally neutral passion which can also lead him to admire the naked destructiveness of lions and tigers. His initial stance makes him not so much a moral alternative to society as a logical antithesis to it, and for this reason our moral assessment of his relation to society is varied and complicated throughout the play. His indefensible usage by Olivia and others does not need documenting. But, just at the moment when Olivia appears most contemptible and Manly most wronged, Wycherley briefly alters the picture and allows her to reproach him with some dignity: ''Turn hither your rage, good Captain Swagger-huff, and be saucy with your Mistress, like a true Captain; but be civil to your Rivals and Betters, and do not threaten any thing but me here; no, not so much as my Windows, nor do not think your self in the Lodgings of one of your Suburb Mistresses beyond the *Tower*.''. . . Her charges are similar to those which Dryden's early critics leveled against Almanzor, and they suggest that society, flawed and corrupt as it may be, cannot be simply rejected and can still provide a standard whereby the heroic primitive appears perilously like an antisocial hooligan.

But there is yet another reason for the complexity with which Manly is presented, for Wycherley varies not only our response to the conflict between Manly and society but the nature of the conflict itself. For, whatever Manly's conception of himself, the play does not in fact present an inflexible antithesis between an enervated society and a virile anarch. City life may blunt man's primal urges, but—as the bouts of self-absorbed, uncommunicative speech show—it does not create a social community. Conversely, Manly turns out to have more social instincts than he at first realizes. (pp. 324-25)

If man is too imperfectly social to form a harmonious kingdom,. . . he is equally unequipped for solitary self-sufficiency. I have mentioned that the play is dominated by the recurrent dramatic situation of compulsive talking. An equally prominent dramatic motif, often combined with that of relentless talking, is provided by the interruptions that perpetually plague the characters and show how indissoluble are their ties with human society. (p. 326)

Just as the characters cannot entirely divest themselves of their social natures, so they cannot entirely escape the need for the forms and disciplines of law. The judicial regulation of the kingdom may be a chaotic sham, but the rituals of law express something that is intrinsic to nature, and throughout the play small groups of people spontaneously mimic the processes that in their larger forms are so empty of meaning. The verbal combat of Olivia and Manly in Act II becomes a formal altercation before the jury of Novel and Plausible. . . . When Oldfox and Freeman compete before the Widow for her hand, the contest naturally enough takes the form of a trial. . . . When Novel and Oldfox dispute about the nature of wit, Novel appoints Manly to "be our Judge." . . . And, most remarkably, Manly feels that his copulation with Olivia will be insufficient revenge unless he can have "Witnesses": . . . even at his most appetitive and antisocial, he still finds that he needs the customary forms of communal existence.

Why should a craving for legal form be so fundamental to man's character? The reason is that, in order to cope with the unavoidable society of his fellows, man desires some degree of certainty about their characters, motives, and actions. The rituals of law are ideally rituals of proof, and their debasement into bewildering chaos typifies a world in which empty words and meaningless forms veil the intrinsics of human existence. But the desire for certainty, though repeatedly frustrated, is inextinguishable. Manly falsely believes that he has irrefutable "proofs" . . . of Olivia's and Vernish's loyalty, and he later falsely hails Vernish as a proven friend whose "heart . . . spoke in actions." . . . Certainty turns out to be equally desirable and equally elusive when characters seek to predict the consequences of their own actions: Manly and Freeman, for instance, dispute with equally plausible reasons but opposite conclusions about the likely consequences of a plain-dealing policy. . . . And characters meet with similar difficulties when they attempt to convey certainty about their own intrinsic selves. Fidelia aspired to *show* her love for Manly not with words but with "convincing Acts/Of loving Friendship," . . . but her proofs have been negated by her male clothes, by her deceptive outer trappings. "Dear Captain, do not cast me off, till you have *try'd* me once more," she pleads; . . . (my italics), and indeed she does finally persuade him to distinguish her from *"Love, or Friend untry'd."* . . . (pp. 327-28)

But the means with which Fidelia proves herself are oddly limited and scarcely provide a universal method of assessing moral character. For the only proofs of human probity obtained in the play are the tokens that demonstrate Fidelia's sex. She cannot have cuckolded Vernish because she is a woman, and Vernish persuades himself of her femininity by fondling the "Witnesses of 't" . . .—namely, her breasts. And, when she loses her peruke in the final scuffle, her long hair makes Manly reinterpret in an instant the whole pattern of her past actions. . . . But, in a world where sexual identity is repeatedly eclipsed, even such elementary revelations of human character are rare. Indeed, even Fidelia's breasts do not free Vernish from all doubts about her sex, for, when Manly reaffirms her masculinity, Vernish starts to question the evidence of his own senses and has to remind himself of "those infallible *proofs,* her pouting, swelling breasts" (. . . my italics). That the chief moral revelation of the play should be provided by Fidelia's long, feminine hair indicates both how fully the simplest facts of human nature are generally concealed and how limited are the facts to which the eye can ever penetrate. The quest for proof that obsesses the characters is for proof not of abstract or speculative truths but of the most basic facts of human conduct. But, in this world of inane linguistic signs and empty social forms, even these are scarcely visible. (pp. 328-29)

We are now in a position to reconsider Manly's character and development. In his initial encounters with Plausible, his sail-

ors, and Freeman, Manly displays in equal measure a brusque honesty and an impatient aggressiveness. The two qualities do not necessarily demand identical responses from us, and, as W. R. Chadwick has sensitively shown . . . , each successive encounter slightly changes our assessment of the hero. But the first big complication comes in the encounter with the Widow Blackacre, who is seemingly his anti-type in her addiction to legal verbiage rather than individualistic force. But, in their antiphonal bout of egocentric shouting, they appear as puzzlingly parallel figures, each lost in language and each diverting language into the service of some private, isolating obsession. And it is chiefly in his use of language, and in his involuntary, inevitable adoption of society's linguistic habits, that Manly changes. He does remain a force of virile energy, gratifying his lust for Olivia and forcibly gaining the restitution that law denies; but his virility cannot retain its primitivistic simplicity, and he finds that his very lust entangles him in the ways of society he despises. The complexities of man's nature are nowhere better illustrated than when Manly's masculine vigor becomes an "effeminating mischief," . . . infecting him with the linguistic tricks of his effete antagonists.

When Manly first discovers Olivia's baseness, he vows to repudiate her love . . . but finds that he cannot keep his vow: his passions and words obey different laws, and he moves toward the general divorce of speech from appetite. He also falls into cursing Olivia . . . , adopting the widespread conversion of physical into linguistic aggression. In the following act, set in Westminster Hall, the ultimate home of anarchic language, Manly realizes that love is forcing him to be a hypocrite . . . , and at this point he ceases to be the champion of crude, unveiled instinct, instead furtively concealing his appetites from society's gaze. Then, immediately before the Widow instructs her lawyers in corrupt oratory, Manly urges Fidelia to use all her "Rhetorick" . . . to win Olivia for him, now making words the prime constituent of sexual conquest. And, when he later asks Fidelia to assist in his rape of Olivia, he exalts the word still further, deciding that the rape will be justifiable if he can attach the name of "Revenge" to it: . . . words here triumph over things as much as in Olivia's response to the "china" scene. In the rape itself, moreover, Manly engineers the ultimate separation of the linguistic and appetitive self, with Fidelia doing the talking while he does the copulating. The rape scene is thus both the greatest triumph and the greatest compromise of Manly's savage vigor, since he wins Olivia not through his manly actions but through words that are so unrelated to his male desires as to be spoken by a woman. Finally, in deciding that he requires *witnesses* of Olivia's shame, he shows that his elemental impulses coexist with the legalistic instinct that characterizes the whole of London society. Increasingly, the initially simple figure of the hero becomes the prime illustration of man's divided nature. (pp. 334-35)

The implication of all this is not that Manly is a hypocrite who embodies the vices that he condemns. It is that he shares the human condition: a condition in which man can be neither a solitary savage nor a socially integrated citizen. It is a condition with a vast variety of potentials, as the differing ultimate fortunes of the characters indicate, but it is the necessary foundation for whatever one makes of life. As the play's abrupt but artful shifts of genre indicate, the passions and frailties of man can result both in the nightmares of satire and the golden visions of romance. (p. 336)

Derek Hughes, "'The Plain Dealer': A Reappraisal," in Modern Language Quarterly, *Vol. 43, No. 4, December, 1982, pp. 315-36.*

JAMES THOMPSON (essay date 1984)

[*In the following excerpt, Thompson establishes how the use of language illustrates the ethical standards of* Love in a Wood.]

Today [*Love in a Wood*] seems uncontrolled, yet this energetic five-couple intrigue comedy is still impressive for a first play. And while the play does border on chaos at times, the pleasure of intrigue comedy often lies, as it does here, in the complexities and improbabilities of the plot. With a large cast of characters, and quick transitions back and forth among high, middle, and low plots, the play encompasses multitudes. There is no trick of comedy left out, and Chadwick terms the play "A Jonsonian - Fletcherian - Shirleyan - platonic - intrigue - wit - farce-comedy." Within this crowd of characters and comic devices, Wycherley has created a vast chain of speaking, from Puritan cant to heroic rant, with all the stages in between: true and false wit, plain style, and plain stupidity. This range of types of speech will be re-created in *The Plain-Dealer,* there producing a discordant noise which is harshly condemned. This play, however, is uniquely good-humored in Wycherley's canon. There are no villains and no blame is seriously attached: in fact, stupidity and selfishness, not vice and maliciousness, are the worst crimes in *Love in a Wood.* . . . In short, Wycherley's aims in *Love in a Wood* seem to be more broadly comic and less satiric than his aims in any of the other plays.

While the sharply different types or styles of speech are clearly employed in characterization, the right use of speech is not the central concern here, as it is in Wycherley's subsequent work. This simplifies our present task, because it is easier to isolate contrasting and conflicting uses or tactics of speech in this play, before Wycherley's tone becomes harsh and judgmental, and before the plays become considerably more complicated, with a whole host of interpretive difficulties. I do not believe that as yet moral order is part of Wycherley's language, though ethical aspects of speech are certainly evident here, most prominently in the ideas of decorum. (pp. 37-8)

Of the two female protagonists in *Love in a Wood,* one, Christina, argues for unswerving adherence to high-minded principles, while the other, Lydia, displays a practical adaptability, becoming what she needs to be in each situation. The rectitude of speech which Christina observes is unchanging, while Lydia's is a local rectitude, right for the moment. The words of all the characters in this play reflect widely different senses of obligation. With Joyner, for example, the proper use of speech never encompasses more than the present moment. To Christina, Valentine, Vincent, and eventually to Ranger and Lydia, the standards for speech are more rigorous: the truth of discourse ought not to alter radically from one listener to the next. The decorum of each character's speech, the way in which he adapts his words to different listeners, reveals the essence of character.

Aside from these larger ethical dimensions, decorum in its most common literary use states that all of the lines delivered by a character should be consistently appropriate to some central conception of humor, personality, or character. Assessment of character then works backwards, extrapolating from the lines some identifying qualities. In all of Wycherley's comedies, this process is simplest with his fools, for they and their language are most singular and distinctive. Their speech is obtrusive, conspicuously distorting the normative modes of speech, while the protagonists' speech is unexceptional, appearing "natural" or "correct" compared to the exaggerated or debased features of foolish talk. In *Love in a Wood,* it is Dap-

perwit's speech that stands out, calling attention to itself and serving as a false standard against which others' linguistic skills can be measured. (pp. 40-1)

The exhausting industry of Dapperwit's wit is best seen in his repartee with Lydia, where he anatomizes his each response in an aside; in the end, he must admit defeat after a vain struggle to extend his clichéd conceit on the light of her countenance: "I dare not make use again of the lustre of her face.". . . With Martha or with Lydia or in this example with Lady Flippant, Dapperwit is also unable to fit his words to his auditor: "now I call her Whore in plain english, she thinks I am jealous.". . . Sir Simon suffers from a similar inability to choose appropriate or decorous words: "A pox I must be using the words in fashion though I never have any luck with 'em.". . . (p. 42)

Dapperwit's wit is appropriately foolish in that it is always inappropriate to the moment; his wit is also appropriately foolish in its feebleness. Although wit should be striking or novel, Dapperwit's belabored similitudes are entirely predictable, and his acquaintances are so accustomed to his comparisons that Ranger calls him "Mr. or as.". . . The trifling nature of Dapperwit's bons mots reflects the conventional distinction between true and false wit; throughout Wycherley's plays and verse, by "wit" he usually means false wit. . . . True wit is paradoxically invisible, hence Restoration and eighteenth-century writers' notorious difficulty in defining it. Yet Dapperwit's highly visible wit is not just foolish; according to all definitions in *Love in a Wood,* wit is malicious. (pp. 42-3)

If wits misuse language to slander others, their praise is equally slanderous. In the tavern scene, when Vincent leaves, Dapperwit abuses him and flatters Ranger to his face. When Vincent returns and Ranger leaves, Dapperwit abuses Ranger and praises Vincent. Praise and blame, equally void of sincerity and meaning, are interchangeable for Dapperwit because they are both designed for self-elevation. . . . The self-interest of praise is evident when Joyner and Gripe try to out-flatter each other. Their stichomythic praise of each other becomes indistinguishable, while their flattery is also so exaggerated and ambiguous that it sounds suspiciously like insult. There is, in fact, little distinction, because, in Pope's version of the commonplace, "Praise undeserv'd is scandal in disguise." The self-interest of praise is most pointed in Sir Simon, who, disguised as Jonas, praises Sir Simon, that is, himself: "faith, 'tis a prety jest; While I am with her, and praising my self to her, at no ordinary rate.". . . As insult of another is really praise of self, so praise of another is really praise of self. The purpose of communication with another is lost or subverted as the language becomes entirely self-reflexive, an instrument of vanity. Like the characters wandering in the dark in act five, they end up talking of and to themselves.

Vanity is constantly present in Dapperwit's conversation; as he himself admits, "you can no more find a man of wit without vanity, then a fine woman without affectation.". . . In Dapperwit, then, Wycherley observes decorum personae: all his speeches are foolishly, amusingly empty, and so consistent with the satiric definition of wit. Thus his speech is consistent in its constant "indecorum." His overly figurative style is excessive and inappropriate, just as the substance of his remarks, self-conceit, is inappropriate. (pp. 43-4)

Wit for him is not a process but a status, a state which he is never able to maintain for long. So too, the Lady Flippant cannot maintain her image, for she has not the verbal skill to keep up in conversation. . . . Flippant expects her langauge simultaneously to conceal and reveal her intentions: impoverished and anxious to remarry, she shows herself as a rich widow, uninterested in remarriage. This lack of interest in marriage, or coyness, she reasons, will be interpreted by prospective suitors as her satisfaction with her present, ample maintenance, left by her first husband, and so attract these suitors to her fortune and her person. But, she is not skilled enough to encode such a complicated message without revealing her broken fortune and immediate need of a husband. (pp. 42-5)

Language as a social strategy or tactical weapon always betrays the less clever characters, letting them down and exposing them. While Lady Flippant is verbally unable to keep up with Ranger, he and Lydia are more equally matched. They are so well matched, in fact, and their verbal devices so similar, that communication between them often comes to a complete standstill, as it does here when his refusal to be understood meets her refusal to be understood.

> *Ranger.* Indeed Cousin, besides my business, another cause, I did not wait on you, was, my apprehension, you were gone to the Park, notwithstanding your promise to the contrary.
>
> *Lydia.* Therefore, you went to the Park, to visit me there, notwithstanding your promise to the contrary.
>
> *Ranger.* Who, I at the Park? when I had promis'd to wait upon you at your lodging; but were you at the Park, Madam?
>
> *Lydia.* Who, I at the Park? when I had promis'd to wait for you at home; I was no more at the Park then you were; were you at the Park?...

Both are lying and each knows the other is lying, but is unsure to what extent; Lydia knows that Ranger was at the Park, but she is unsure whether he knows that she knows, and Ranger knows that he was at the Park but is unsure whether Lydia knows. They each expect their words to conceal their own guilt and still elicit a revealing response. But this verbal sparring only produces echoes of their own words, and communication is frustrated as the words become less meaningful with each repetition. (p. 45)

Ranger is certainly not the only mendacious character, for, with a few obvious exceptions, they all try to deceive and cheat one another. Indeed, the complexity of the intrigue plot is generated by an extraordinary amount of lying. Such irresponsible use of language, when so many characters cannot be taken at their word, would seem to threaten to dissolve the "bond and cement of society." And yet, *Love in a Wood* is no black comedy: order is restored, inverted values are righted, and the play moves toward the formal closure of comedy, five marriages. Though speakers are shown to be unreliable, speech itself is not, almost as if Wycherley projects a language which will not allow itself to be misused without revenge. Ranger's ill luck in lying, Gripe's perpetual ill luck in hypocrisy, and Dapperwit's perpetual ill luck in wit are all eventually exposed. Characters are only able to convince themselves of their cleverness, and so they only cheat themselves, for all their crossbiting only makes everyone more suspicious. Words must be tested and validated before they can be believed here, and validation takes the form of a trial, where characters' statements are treated as if they were testimony to be evaluated. Thus Ranger's word and character are suspect due to his ill luck in lying, and he finds himself on trial:

> *Leonore.* Why do you not put him to his tryal, and see what he can say for himself?
>
> *Lydia.* I am afraid lest my proofs, and his guilt, shou'd make him desperate, and so condemn that pardon, which he cou'd not hope for.
>
> *Leonore.* 'Tis unjust to condemn him, before you hear him.
>
> *Lydia.* I will reprieve him till I have more evidence....

Valentine and Christina are also tried: "S'death, what have I giddily run my self upon? 'Tis rather a tryal of my self than her."... (p. 47)

Trials in this play are accompanied with legal language and argument, raising questions of evidence that ultimately become epistemological, asking what can be known and what must be taken on faith. Valentine's and Vincent's debate over Ranger's credibility is typically evidentiary:

> *Vincent.* Why, do you believe him [Ranger]?
>
> *Valentine.* Shou'd I believe you?
>
> *Vincent.* 'Twere more for your interest, and you wou'd be less deceiv'd; if you believe him, you must doubt the chastity of all the fine Women in Town, and five miles about.
>
> *Valentine.* His reports of them, will little invalidate his testimony with me....

Vincent's remarks turn on the distinction between inartificial and artificial proofs, or in Bacon's terms, matters of fact and matters of art and opinion; inartificial proofs are incontrovertible facts such as contracts, while artificial proofs are impressions created by the speech and depend upon the character of the speaker. Vincent establishes Christina's innocence by undermining Ranger's credibility; to Valentine, Ranger's evidence is an inartificial proof, the testimony of a sworn witness, whereas to Vincent it is a question of Ranger's character, that is, the ethos of Ranger's speech.... Ethical proof lies at the heart of Christina's defense, for she is not answering any particular charge so much as defending her character in general. Her case descends the three traditional stages of defense: the defense first questions whether the alleged event ever occurred; if it occurred, whether it was indeed a crime; and finally, if it were criminal, whether the defendant was not justified. Vincent first questions if Ranger ever met Christina, suspecting that Ranger is either lying or mistaken about the identity of "Christina": indeed, there are two "Christinas," and the skeptical repetition of the name ... underscores doubt about identity. Vincent then admits the meeting, but still denies her guilt, and when it is determined that she did break her vow to Valentine, Vincent argues that she must have been justified. In this way, Vincent forces Valentine to transcend mere questions of fact and mundane legality: Valentine must believe her word as a woman of honor, dispense with proofs, and have faith in Christina herself. (pp. 47-9)

In achieving trust or faith, Ranger and Valentine must see through the apparent and learn to discern and respect inner, true value. Though some have concluded that the prevalence of false appearances, disguise, and deceit indicate Wycherley's doubt that real, natural, or inherent values can exist, yet disguise usually fails in Wycherley's plays. There is little successful deception here, for only Joyner's schemes prosper, while Gripe's pose of piety, Lucy's of virginity, Flippant's of wealth, Sir Simon's of gentility, and Dapperwit's of wit deceive none but themselves. (p. 49)

The result of deception, disguise, and darkness in *Love in a Wood* is not confusion but clarity, for the true worth of characters is revealed at night, in the dark, when there is no constraint. In this play, as in the designs of Providence, the truth will out, in words as well as actions. (p. 50)

Trust and trial are played out in the very dialogue of *Love in a Wood,* for here Wycherley has used speech almost as a metaphor for cooperation; where Gripe, Sir Simon, and Dapperwit never hear anything beyond the echoes of their own words, their betters simply learn to listen to one another, and to believe what the other says. In the lower plot, speech is employed as a tool of suspicion and deceit, in a kind of dramatization of Perkins's *Government of the Tongue,* that encyclopedia of verbal abuse. Here, the misuse of language comes to no good, for the fools are never able to manipulate words to their advantage, but only to their exposure and disadvantage. Their exhibition of lying and swearing also serves to accentuate the cooperative uses of language achieved in the upper plot. Cooperation must be achieved even there, for at first even the more elevated characters do not trust one another, and so are unable to speak with each other. Learning to speak entails learning to listen, as happens when Valentine is forced to overhear Christina in the dark, for once without interrupting her. Worthiness, in short, comes to be identified with consideration of others, the quintessential right use of speech. (p. 53)

> *James Thompson, in his* Language in Wycherley's Plays: Seventeenth-Century Language Theory and Drama, *The University of Alabama Press, 1984, 151 p.*

ADDITIONAL BIBLIOGRAPHY

Auffret, J. M. *"The Man of Mode and The Plain Dealer:* Common Origin & Parallels." *Etudes Anglaises* XIX, No. 3 (July-September 1966): 209-22.
    Provides evidence that *The Plain-Dealer*'s Manly is a portrayal of the Earl of Mulgrave.

Beauchamp, Gorman. "The Amorous Machiavellism of *The Country Wife.*" *Comparative Drama* 11, No. 4 (Winter 1977-78): 316-30.
    Asserts that Horner, as a Machiavellian prince of sex, is unquestionably the hero of *The Country-Wife.*

Bowman, John S. "Dance, Chant, and Mask in the Plays of Wycherley." *Drama Survey* 3, No. 2 (October 1963): 181-205.
    Interesting suggestion that Wycherley's inclusion of "the movement of the dance, the rhythm of the chant, the duality of the mask" both mirrors and complements the meaning of his plays.

Dearing, Vinton A. "Pope, Theobald, and Wycherley's *Posthumous Works.*" *PMLA* LXVIII, No. 1 (March 1953): 223-36.
    Gives the background of Alexander Pope's edition of Wycherley's posthumous works and compares it with Lewis Theobald's rival edition.

Donaldson, Ian. "'Tables Turned': *The Plain Dealer.*" *Essays in Criticism* XVII, No. 3 (July 1967): 304-21.
    Analysis of paradoxes and contradictions in *The Plain-Dealer.*

Empson, William. "Honest Man." In his *The Structure of Complex Words,* pp. 185-201. Totowa, N.J.: Rowman and Littlefield, 1979.
    Study of the changing meaning of the word "honest" in various works of literature, including its significance in *The Plain-Dealer.*

Friedson, A. M. "Wycherley and Molière: Satirical Point of View in *The Plain Dealer.*" *Modern Philology* 64, No. 3 (February 1967): 189-97.

Comparison of *The Plain-Dealer* with Molière's *Le misanthrope.* The essay pays particular attention to the differences between the two plays to illustrate Friedson's contention that Wycherley's satire is directed at society rather than at Manly.

Fujimura, Thomas H. "William Wycherley." In his *The Restoration Comedy of Wit,* pp. 117-55. 1952. Reprint. New York: Barnes & Noble, 1968.
    Criticism of Wycherley's plays in which characters are classified as Truewit, Witwoud, or Witless.

Gosse, Sir Edmund. "Wycherley." In his *Silhouettes,* pp. 63-9. New York: Charles Scribner's Sons, 1925.
    Short, mostly biographical discussion of Wycherley. Gosse speculates that Wycherley's sojourn in France furnished him with the models for his dramatic characters, who are "French in essence."

Kaufman, Anthony. "Wycherley's *The Country Wife* and the Don Juan Character." *Eighteenth-Century Studies* 9, No. 2 (Winter 1975-76): 216-31.
    Classifies the character of *The Country Wife*'s Horner in terms of the Don Juan archetype and Freudian sexual psychology.

Lamb, Charles. "On the Artificial Comedy of the Last Century." In his *The Essays of Elia,* pp. 172-80. New York: A. L. Burt, 1885?
    1823 defense of Restoration comedy from the charge of immorality. Lamb contends that the world of Restoration comedy cannot be subjected to moral criteria because it is "altogether a speculative scene of things, which has no reference whatever to the world that is."

Lynch, Kathleen M. "The Period of Etherege." In her *The Social Mode of Restoration Comedy,* pp. 137-81. New York: Macmillan Co., 1926.
    Assesses Wycherley's literary debt to Molière and gauges the attitude toward Restoration society expressed in his plays.

Malekin, Peter. "'Imparadist in One Anothers Arms' or 'The Ecclesiastical Mouse-trap': Marriage in Restoration Comedy." In his *Liberty and Love: English Literature and Society, 1640-88,* pp. 15-95. New York: St. Martin's Press, 1981.
    Study of the sexual mores and social attitudes surrounding love and marriage in the Restoration era. Malekin cites examples from the plays of Wycherley and other Restoration dramatists to illustrate the link between literature and social conditions.

Marshall, W. Gerald. "Wycherley's *Love in a Wood* and the Designs of Providence." *Restoration: Studies in English Literary Culture, 1660-1700* 3, No. 1 (Spring 1979): 8-16.
    Considers *Love in a Wood* dramatically illustrative of the workings of divine Providence.

———. "Wycherley's Drama of Madness: *The Plain Dealer.*" *Philological Quarterly* 59, No. 1 (Winter 1980): 26-37.
    Views *The Plain-Dealer* as a study of obsessive thinking and behavior.

———. "The Idea of Theatre in Wycherley's *The Gentleman Dancing-Master.*" *Restoration: Studies in English Literary Culture, 1660-1700* 6, No. 1 (Spring 1982): 1-10.
    Argues that the "informing ideas" of *The Gentleman Dancing-Master* are theatrical in nature.

Matalene, H. W. "What Happens in *The Country-Wife.*" *Studies in English Literature, 1500-1900* 22, No. 3 (Summer 1982): 395-411.
    Interpretation of Horner in *The Country-Wife.* Matalene argues that Horner's scheme is motivated not by a wish to express his sexuality but by his "homosocial" desires—that is, Horner pursues sexual liaisons with women in order to achieve status with his male peers.

Matlack, Cynthia. "Parody and Burlesque of Heroic Ideals in Wycherley's Comedies: A Critical Reinterpretation of Contemporary Evidence." *Papers on Language and Literature* VIII, No. 3 (Summer 1972): 273-86.

Postulates that Wycherley experimented with a burlesque heroic mode within his comedies "to set in opposition different codes of behavior among characters who accept disparate sets of values."

McCarthy, B. Eugene. *William Wycherley: A Biography*. Athens: Ohio University Press, 1979, 255 p.
    Thorough, straightforward biography. McCarthy states that his design in the book is "to make Wycherley a little more visible, a little more knowable and enjoyable."

Muir, Kenneth. "William Wycherley." In his *The Comedy of Manners*, pp. 67-83. London: Hutchinson University Library, 1970.
    General discussion of Wycherley's plays—their sources, satire, bawdiness, and value.

Mukherjee, Sujit. "Marriage as Punishment in the Plays of Wycherley." *A Review of English Literature* 7, No. 4 (October 1966): 61-4.
    Concludes that Wycherley had such a negative view of marriage that he used it in his work as "an instrument of poetic justice" to punish his characters.

Payne, Deborah C. "Reading the Signs in *The Country Wife*." *Studies in English Literature, 1500-1900* 26, No. 3 (Summer 1986): 403-19.
    Interprets *The Country-Wife* as an expression (and perhaps indictment) of the indirect and often duplicitous communication prevalent in Restoration society, wherein language, being an inadequate indicator of meaning, was largely replaced by an intricate system of "cultural codes."

Rundle, James Urvin. "Wycherley and Calderón: A Source for *Love in a Wood*." *PMLA* LXIV, No. 4 (September 1949): 701-07.
    Details the similarities and differences between *Love in a Wood* and its Spanish source, Pedro Calderón's *Mañanas de abril y mayo*. Rundle concludes that "there is no other Restoration play that assimilates Spanish material so poorly."

Steiger, Richard. "'Wit in a Corner': Hypocrisy in *The Country Wife*." In *Tennessee Studies in Literature, Vol. XXIV*, edited by Allison R. Ensor and Thomas J. A. Heffernan, pp. 56-70. Knoxville: University of Tennessee Press, 1979.

Defines the hypocrisy so prevalent in *The Country-Wife* as a necessary, morally neutral gap between the requirements of social order and the actual behavior of individuals.

Verdurmen, J. Peter. "Grasping for Permanence: Ideal Couples in *The Country Wife* and *Aureng-Zebe*." *The Huntingdon Library Quarterly* XLII, No. 4 (Autumn 1979): 329-47.
    Examines the relationship between status and change in *The Country-Wife* and John Dryden's *Aureng-Zebe*.

Vernon, P. F. *William Wycherley*. London: Longmans, Green & Co., 1965, 44 p.
    Short but thorough examination of Wycherley's life and work.

——. "Wycherley's First Comedy and Its Spanish Source." *Comparative Literature* XVIII, No. 2 (Spring 1966): 132-44.
    Comparison of *Love in a Wood* with Pedro Calderón's *Mañanas de abril y mayo*. Vernon argues that Wycherley "borrowed with discrimination" and that "his revisions of his source reveal a consistent awareness of the play's total meaning and effect."

Vieth, David M. "Wycherley's *The Country Wife:* An Anatomy of Masculinity." *Papers on Language and Literature* 2, No. 4 (Fall 1966): 335-50.
    Analysis of *The Country-Wife* which describes the play as "centrally concerned with providing a definition of masculinity." Vieth argues that Pinchwife, Sir Jasper, and Sparkish typify failed masculinity due to sexual and personal inadequacies.

Weber, Harold. "The Rake-Hero in Wycherley and Congreve." *Philological Quarterly* 61, No. 2 (Spring 1982): 143-60.
    Compares *The Country-Wife*'s Horner to William Congreve's libertine heroes, finding Horner unusual in his natural, unadulterated, and "joyous sexuality."

Zimbardo, Rose. "Wycherley: The Restoration's Juvenal." *Forum* 17, No. 1 (Winter 1979): 17-26.
    Contends that Wycherley's plays are not comedies of manners but moral satires after the fashion of Juvenal.

Appendix

The following is a listing of all sources used in Volume 8 of *Literature Criticism from 1400 to 1800*. Included in this list are all copyright and reprint rights and acknowledgments for those essays for which permission was obtained. Every effort has been made to trace copyright, but if omissions have been made, please let us know.

THE EXCERPTS IN LC, VOLUME 8, WERE REPRINTED FROM THE FOLLOWING PERIODICALS:

The Academy, v. LIV, July 2, 1898; v. LVII, August 19, 1899.

The American Church Review, v. XXXIII, January, 1881.

The American Scholar, v. 27, Autumn, 1958. Copyright © 1958, renewed 1986 by the United Chapters of Phi Beta Kappa. Reprinted by permission of the publishers.

Anglia, v. LIV, 1930.

Archaeologia Scotica, v. IV, 1857.

The Athenaeum, n. 4790, February 18, 1922.

Atlantica & Iceland Review, v. 10, 1972. Reprinted by permission of the publisher.

Atlantis, v. 5, Spring, 1980. Reprinted by permission of the publisher.

The Catholic World, v. 25, July, 1877.

The Chautauquan, v. XXXIX, February, 1902.

Children's Literature: Annual of the Modern Language Association Seminar on Children's Literature and The Children's Literature Association, v. 6, 1977. © 1977 by Francelia Butler. All rights reserved. Reprinted by permission of Francelia Butler.

Criticism, v. XXI, Spring, 1979 for "Idealization, Disillusion, and Narcissistic Rage in Wycherley's 'The Plain Dealer'" by Anthony Kaufman. Copyright, 1979, Wayne State University Press. Reprinted by permission of the publisher and the author.

The Edinburgh Review, v. XLV, March, 1827; v. XLVI, October, 1827; v. LXXII, January, 1841; v. LXXXII, October, 1845.

English Studies, Netherlands, v. 28, 1947./ v. 53, October, 1972. © 1972 by Swets & Zeitlinger B.V. Reprinted by permission of the publisher.

The Foreign Quarterly Review, v. XXV, July, 1840.

The Freeman, New York, v. VI, January 31, 1923.

The Gentleman's Magazine, v. XXV, July, 1845 & June, 1846.

The Germanic Review, v. XXVI, December, 1951.

Harper's Monthly Magazine, v. CX, April, 1905.

Hispania, v. 67, March, 1981 for ''Picaresque Elements in Carlos de Sigüenza y Góngora's 'Infortunios de Alonso Ramírez''' by Julie Greer Johnson. © 1981 The American Association of Teachers of Spanish and Portuguese, Inc. Reprinted by permission of the publisher and the author.

Interpretation: A Journal of Political Philosophy, v. 7, May, 1978 for ''The Comic Remedy: Machiavelli's 'Mandragola''' by Mera J. Flaumenhaft. Copyright 1978 Interpretation. Reprinted by permission of the publisher and the author.

Kentucky Romance Quarterly, v. 26, 1979. © 1979 University Press of Kentucky. Reprinted by permission of the publisher.

The Literary Magazine, v. III, January, 1758.

The Living Age, v. CCCXXXIII, November 22, 1924.

Modern Language Notes, v. XLVIII, February, 1933.

Modern Language Quarterly, v. 43, December, 1982; v. 44, September, 1983. © 1982, 1983 University of Washington. Both reprinted by permission of the publisher.

The Nation, New York, v. C, February 4, 1915.

The New Englander and Yale Review, v. XV, September, 1889.

The North American Review, v. 104, April, 1867.

Papers on Language and Literature, v. 2, Fall, 1966; v. 9, Fall, 1973; v. 15, Fall, 1979; v. 18, Summer, 1982. Copyright © 1966, 1973, 1979, 1982 by the Board of Trustees, Southern Illinois University at Edwardsville. All reprinted by permission of the publisher.

Proceedings of the British Academy, v. XLIII, 1957.

The Review of English Studies, v. VI, April, 1930./ n.s. v. XXI, February, 1970. Reprinted by permission of Oxford University Press.

The Review of Politics, v. 13, April, 1951. Copyright, 1951, renewed 1979 by the University of Notre Dame. Reprinted by permission of the publisher.

The Saint Pauls Magazine, v. VIII, April, 1871.

San Francisco Review of Books, Spring, 1984. Copyright © by the *San Francisco Review of Books* 1984. Reprinted by permission of the publisher.

The Spectator, n. 51, April 28, 1711; v. 149, August 6, 1932.

Studies in English Literature, 1500-1900, v. XVII, Winter, 1977 for ''The Design of Nature in Drayton's 'Poly-Olbion''' by Stella P. Revard; v. XX, Summer, 1980 for ''Religious Language and Religious Meaning in Restoration Comedy'' by J. Douglas Canfield. © 1977, 1980 William Marsh Rice University. Both reprinted by permission of the publisher and the respective authors.

Studies in Philology, v. LIV, July 1957./ v. LXVI, April, 1969 for '' 'Fantastickly I Sing': Drayton's 'Idea' of 1619'' by Walter R. Davis. © 1969 by the University of North Carolina Press. Reprinted by permission of the publisher and the author.

The Tatler, n. 3, April 14-16, 1709.

The Times Literary Supplement, n. 1048, January 24, 1929.

Transactions of the Royal Society of Literature of the United Kingdom, n.s. v. IX, 1930.

Wascana Review, v. 9, Spring, 1984. Copyright, 1984 by *Wascana Review*. Reprinted by permission of the publisher.

Women's Studies, v. 7, 1980. © Gordon and Breach Science Publishers. Both reprinted by permission of the publisher.

THE EXCERPTS IN LC, VOLUME 8, WERE REPRINTED FROM THE FOLLOWING BOOKS:

Acton, Lord. From an introduction to *Il Principe*. By Niccolò Machiavelli, edited by L. Arthur Burd. Oxford at the Clarendon Press, 1891.

Alexander, William. From "To M. Michael Drayton," in *Englands Heroicall Epistles*. By Michael Drayton. N. Ling, 1600.

Archer, William. From *The Old Drama and the New: An Essay in Re-valuation*. Small, Maynard and Company, Publishers, 1923. Copyright, 1923, Small, Maynard and Company (Incorporated). Renewed 1950 by Frank Archer.

Ariosto, Ludovico. From *Orlando Furioso (The Frenzy of Orlando): A Romantic Epic, Part II*. Translated by Barbara Reynolds. Penguin Books, 1977. Translation copyright © Barbara Reynolds, 1977. All rights reserved. Reprinted by permission of Penguin Books Ltd.

Bacon, Francis. From *The Essaies of Sr. Francis Bacon, Knight, the Kings Solliciter Generall*. John Beale, 1612.

Bayle, Peter. From *The Dictionary Historical and Critical of Mr. Peter Bayle: M-R, Vol. IV*. Edited by Des Maizeaux. Second edition. J. J. and P. Knapton and others, 1737.

Beck, Richard. From "Icelandic Literature," in *The History of the Scandinavian Literatures*. Edited by Frederika Blankner. Dial Press, 1938. Copyright 1938 by The Dial Press, Inc. Copyright renewed 1965 by The Dial Press Inc. Reprinted by permission of Doubleday & Company.

Beckingham, Charles. From *Musarum Lachrymae; or, Poems to the Memory of Nicholas Rowe, Esq*. Edited by Charles Beckingham. E. Curll, 1719.

Bentley, Eric. From "From Leo X to Pius XII," in *What Is Theatre? Incorporating The Dramatic Event and Other Reviews: 1944-1967*. Atheneum Publishers, 1968, Limelight Editions, 1984. Copyright, 1954, renewed 1982 by Eric Bentley. Reprinted by permission of Limelight Editions.

Berthelot, Joseph A. From *Michael Drayton*. Twayne, 1967. Copyright 1967 by Twayne Publishers. All rights reserved. Reprinted with the permission of Twayne Publishers, a division of G. K. Hall & Co., Boston.

Birch, Thomas. From *The Works of Mrs. Catharine Cockburn: Theological, Moral, Dramatic, and Poetical, Vol. I*. Edited by Thomas Birch. J. and P. Knapton, 1751.

Birdsall, Virginia Ogden. From *Wild Civility: The English Comic Spirit on the Restoration Stage*. Indiana University Press, 1970. Copyright © 1970 by Indiana University Press. All rights reserved. Reprinted by permission of the publisher.

Blunden, Edmund. From *Votive Tablets: Studies Chiefly Appreciative of English Authors and Books*. Cobden-Sanderson, 1931.

Bolingbroke, Lord. From *The Works of Lord Bolingbroke, Vol. II*. Carey and Hart, 1841.

Brown, Frieda S. From *Religious and Political Conservatism in the "Essais" of Montaigne*. Librairie Droz, 1963. Copyright © 1963 by Librairie Droz S.A., 8 rue Verdaine, Genève. Reprinted by permission of the publisher.

Browne, William. From "To My Honor'd Friend Mr. Drayton," in *Poly-Olbion*. By Michael Drayton. M. Lownes, J. Browne, J. Helme and J. Busbie, 1622.

Brydges, Sir Samuel Egerton. From "Michael Drayton," in *Theatrum Poetarum Anglicanorum*. By Edward Phillips, edited by Sir Samuel Egerton Brydges. J. White, 1800.

Burnet, Elizabeth. From a letter in *The Works of Mrs. Catharine Cockburn: Theological, Moral, Dramatic, and Poetical, Vol. I*. Edited by Thomas Birch. J. and P. Knapton, 1751.

Burnet, Gilbert. From a preface to *A Discourse concerning a Guide in Controversies*. By Catharine Cockburn. N.p., 1707.

Burnham, James. From *The Machiavellians: Defenders of Freedom*. The John Day Company, Inc., 1943. Copyright 1943, renewed 1971 by James Burnham. All rights reserved. Reprinted by permission of Harper & Row, Publishers, Inc.

Butterfield, H. From *The Statecraft of Machiavelli*. G. Bell and Sons Ltd., 1940.

Dobrée, Bonamy. From *English Literature in the Early Eighteenth Century, 1700-1740*. Oxford at the Clarendon Press, 1959. © Oxford University Press, 1959. Reprinted by permission of Oxford University Press.

Dobrée, Bonamy. From *Restoration Comedy, 1660-1720*. Oxford at the Clarendon Press, 1924.

Doran, John. From *"Their Majesties' Servants": Annals of the English Stage, from Thomas Betterton to Edmund Kean, Vol. I.* N.p., 1864.

Dowden, Edward. From *Michel de Montaigne*. J. B. Lippincott Company, 1905.

Drayton, Michael. From *The Battle of Agincourt*. William Lee, 1627.

Drayton, Michael. From *Poly-Olbion*. M. Lownes, J. Browne, J. Helme, J. Busbie, 1612.

Drayton, Michael. From *The Second Part; or, A Continuance of Poly-Olbion from the Eighteenth Song*. John Marriott, John Grismand, and Thomas Dewe, 1622.

Dryden, John. From *The State of Innocence, and Fall of Man: An Opera*. H. Herringman, 1684.

Duncombe, John. From *The Feminiad: A Poem*. M. Cooper, 1754.

Einarsson, Sigurbjörn. From an introduction to *Hymns of the Passion: Meditations on the Passion of Christ*. By Hallgrímur Pétursson, translated by Arthur Charles Gook. Hallgrims Church, 1966. All rights reserved.

Einarsson, Stefán. From *A History of Icelandic Literature*. Johns Hopkins Press, 1957. © 1957 by The Johns Hopkins Press. Renewed 1985 by Stefán Einarsson. Reprinted by permission of the publisher.

Eliot, T. S. From *For Lancelot Andrewes: Essays on Style and Order*. Faber & Gwyer, 1928. Copyright 1928, renewed 1956 by T. S. Eliot. All rights reserved. Reprinted by permission of Faber & Faber Ltd.

Eliot, T. S. From an introduction to *Pascal's Pensées*. By Blaise Pascal, translated by W. F. Trotter. E. P. Dutton & Co., 1931.

Elton, Oliver. From *Michael Drayton: A Critical Study*. Revised edition. A. Constable and Company, Limited, 1905.

Emerson, Ralph Waldo. From *Representative Men: Seven Lectures*. Phillips, Sampson and Company, 1850.

Erasmus, Desiderius. From *Ciceronianus; or, A Dialogue on the Best Style of Speaking*. Edited by Paul Monroe, translated by Izora Scott. Teachers College Press, Columbia University, 1908.

Fairchild, Hoxie Neale. From *Religious Trends in English Poetry: 1700-1740, Protestantism and the Cult of Sentiment, Vol. I.* Columbia University Press, 1939. Copyright 1939 Columbia University Press. Renewed 1967 by Hoxie Neale Fairchild. Used by permission of the publisher.

Federick of Prussia. From *The Refutation of Machiavelli's 'Prince'; or, Anti-Machiavel*. Translated by Paul Sonnino. Ohio University Press, 1981. Translation © copyright 1981 by Paul Sonnino. All rights reserved. Reprinted by permission of the publisher.

From *The Female Wits; or, the Triumvirate of Poets at Rehearsal: A Comedy*. William Turner, 1704.

Fletcher, Jefferson Butler. From *Literature of the Italian Renaissance*. Macmillan, 1934. Copyright 1934, by Macmillan Publishing Company. Renewed 1962 by Mrs. Robert S. Stoddart. All rights reserved. Reprinted with permission of Macmillan Publishing Company.

Ford, Ford Madox. From *The March of Literature: From Confucius' Day to Our Own*. The Dial Press, 1938. Copyright 1938, by Ford Madox Ford. Renewed 1965 by Janice Biala. All rights reserved. Reprinted by permission of Janice Biala.

Frame, Donald M. From *Montaigne's Discovery of Man: The Humanization of a Humanist*. Columbia University Press, 1955. Copyright © 1955 Columbia University Press. Renewed 1983 by Donald M. Frame. Used by permission of the publisher.

Garland, H. B. From *Lessing: The Founder of Modern German Literature*. Second edition. St. Martin's Press, 1962. Copyright © H. B. Garland 1962. Used with permission of St. Martin's Press, Inc.

Garnett, Richard. From an introduction to *The Battaile of Agincourt*. By Michael Drayton. Charles Whittingham & Co., 1893.

Gassner, John. From *Masters of the Drama*. Third revised edition. Dover Publications, Inc., 1954. Copyright 1940, 1954 by Random House, Inc. Renewed 1968, 1982 by Mollie Gassner. Reprinted by permission of Random House, Inc.

Genest, John. From *Some Account of the English Stage from the Restoration in 1660 to 1830, Vol. II*. N.p.,1832.

Gide, André. From "Presenting Montaigne," translated by Dorothy Bussy, in *The Living Thoughts of Montaigne*. By Michel de Montaigne, edited by André Gide. Longmans, Green, 1939. Copyright 1939 by Longmans, Green and Co., Inc. Renewed 1967 by David McKay Co., Inc. All rights reseved.

Gildon, Charles. From the appendix to *The Lives and Characters of the English Dramatick Poets*. By Gerard Langbaine. T. Leigh and W. Turner, 1699.

Gildon, Charles. From *Remarks on Mr. Rowe's "Tragedy of the Lady Jane Gray," and All His Other Plays*. Second edition. J. Roberts, 1715.

Goethe, J. W. von. From *The Autobiography of Goethe, Truth and Poetry: From My Own Life, Books I.-XIII., Vol. I*. Translated by John Oxenford. Revised edition. George Bell and Sons, 1881.

Goldsmith, Oliver. From *The Citizen of the World*. J. Newbery, 1762.

Gosse, Edmund. From "Pix," in *Dictionary of National Biography, Vol. XLV*. Edited by Leslie Stephen. The Macmillan Company, 1896.

Gosse, Edmund. From *The Jacobean Poets*. Charles Scribner's Sons, 1894.

Gosse, Edmund. From *Some Diversions of a Man of Letters*.

Granville-Barker, Harley. From *On Dramatic Method*. Sidgwick & Jackson, Ltd., 1931.

Gray, W. Forbes. From *The Poets Laureate of England: Their History and Their Odes*. Sir I. Pitman & Sons, Ltd., 1914.

Greene, Thomas. From *The Descent from Heaven: A Study in Epic Continuity*. Yale University Press, 1963. Copyright © 1963 by Yale University. All rights reserved. Reprinted by permission of the author.

Hagstrum, Jean H. From *Sex and Sensibility: Ideal and Erotic Love from Milton to Mozart*. University of Chicago Press, 1980. © 1980 by The University of Chicago. All rights reserved. Reprinted by permission of the publisher and the author.

Hallie, Philip P. From *The Scar of Montaigne: An Essay in Personal Philosophy*. Wesleyan University Press, 1966. Copyright © 1966 by Wesleyan University. Reprinted by permission of the publisher.

Hardin, Richard F. From *Michael Drayton and the Passing of Elizabethan England*. University Press of Kansas, 1973. © Copyright 1973 by The University Press of Kansas. Reprinted by permission of the publisher.

Hart, Sophie Chantal. From an introduction to *The Fair Penitent and Jane Shore*. By Nicholas Rowe, edited by Sophie Chantal Hart. D. C. Heath and Co., Publishers, 1907.

Harvey, Richard. From *A Theological Discourse of the Lamb of God and His Enemies*. N.p., 1590.

Hazlitt, William. From *Lectures Chiefly on the Dramatic Literature of the Age of Elizabeth*. N.p., 1820.

Hazlitt, William. From *Lectures on the English Comic Writers*. Taylor and Hessey, 1819.

Hebel, J. William. From *The Works of Michael Drayton, Vol. II*. Edited by J. William Hebel. Basil Blackwell, 1932.

Heine, Heinrich. From *Germany, Vol. I*. Translated by Charles Godfrey Leland. William Heinemann, 1892.

Holland, Norman N. From *The First Modern Comedies: The Significance of Etherege, Wycherley, and Congreve*. Cambridge, Mass.: Harvard University Press, 1959. Copyright © 1959 by the President and Fellows of Harvard College. Renewed 1987 by Norman N. Holland. Excerpted by permission of the publishers.

Horn, Frederick Winkel. From *History of the Literature of the Scandinavian North from the Most Ancient Times to the Present*. Translated by Ramus B. Anderson. Revised edition. S. C. Griggs and Company, 1884.

Hughes, John. From "To the Ingenious Author, on Her Tragedy, Call'd 'Fatal Friendship'," in *Fatal Friendship: A Tragedy*. By Catharine Trotter. Francis Saunders, 1698.

Hume, Robert D. From *The Development of English Drama in the Late Seventeenth Century*. Oxford at the Clarendon Press, 1976. © Oxford University Press, 1976. All rights reserved. Reprinted by permission of Oxford University Press.

Hunt, Leigh. From *The Dramatic Works of Wycherley, Congreve, Vanbrugh, and Farquhar*. Edited by Leigh Hunt. Edward Moxon, 1840.

Huxley, Aldous. From *Collected Essays*. Harper & Brothers, 1959. Copyright © 1959 by Aldous Huxley. All rights reserved. Reprinted by permission of Harper & Row, Publishers, Inc.

Jacob, Giles. From *The Poetical Register; or, The Lives and Characters of the English Drammatick Poets, Vol. 1*. E. Curll, 1719.

Jenkins, Annibel. From *Nicholas Rowe*. Twayne, 1977. Copyright 1977 by Twayne Publishers. All rights reserved. Reprinted with the permission of Twayne Publishers, a division of G. K. Hall & Co., Boston.

Johnson, Samuel. From *The Lives of the English Poets: And a Criticism on Their Work, Vol. 2*. Whiteston, Williams, Colles, Wilson, 1781.

Jonson, Ben. From "The Vision of Ben. Jonson, on the Muses of His Friend M. Drayton," in *The Battaile of Agincourt*. By Michael Drayton. William Lee, 1627.

Kennedy, William J. From *Jacopo Sannazaro and the Uses of Pastoral*. University Press of New England, 1983. Copyright 1983 by Trustees of Dartmouth College. All rights reserved. Reprinted by permission of the publisher.

Kronenberger, Louis. From *The Thread of Laughter: Chapters on English Stage Comedy from Jonson to Maugham*. Knopf, 1952. Copyright 1952, renewed 1980 by Louis Kronenberger. Reprinted by permission of Alfred A. Knopf, Inc.

Lamb, Charles. From *The Works of Charles Lamb*. C. and J. Ollier, 1818.

Lamport, F. J. From *Lessing and the Drama*. Oxford at the Clarendon Press, 1981. © F. J. Lamport, 1981. All rights reserved. Reprinted by permission of Oxford University Press.

Laski, Harold J. From *The Dangers of Obedience & Other Essays*. Harper & Brothers Publishers, 1930. Copyright 1930, by Harold J. Laski. Renewed 1957 by Frida Laski. Reprinted by permission of Harper & Row, Publishers, Inc.

Leonard, Irving A. From *Don Carlos de Sigüenza y Góngora: A Mexican Savant of the Seventeenth Century*. University of California Press, 1929.

Lerner, Max. From an introduction to *The Prince and The Discourses*. By Niccolò Machiavelli. The Modern Library, 1950. Copyright 1950, renewed 1977 by Random House, Inc. All rights reserved. Reprinted by permission of Random House, Inc.

Lewis, C. S. From *English Literature in the Sixteenth Century, Excluding Drama*. Oxford at the Clarendon Press, 1954.

Lewis, Wyndham. From *The Lion and the Fox: The Rôle of the Hero in the Plays of Shakespeare*. Grant Richards Ltd., 1927.

Locke, John. From *The Correspondence of John Locke: Letters Nos. 2665-3286, Vol. 7*. Edited by E. S. DeBeer. Oxford at the Clarendon Press, 1982. © Oxford University Press, 1982. All rights reserved. Reprinted by permission of Oxford University Press.

Lukács, Georg. From *The Historical Novel*. Translated by Hannah Mitchell and Stanley Mitchell. Merlin Press, 1962. English translation copyright © 1962 by Merlin Press Ltd. Reprinted by permission of the publisher.

Macqueen-Pope. From *Ladies First: The Story of Woman's Conquest of the British Stage*. W. H. Allen, 1952.

Mander, Gertrud. From "Lessing and His Heritage," in *The German Theatre: A Symposium*. Edited by Ronald Hayman. Barnes & Noble, 1975. © Oswald Wolff (Publishers) Ltd. 1975. Reprinted by permission of the publisher.

Manley, Mary Delariviere. From "To the Author of 'Agnes de Castro'," in *Agnes de Castro: A Tragedy*. By Catharine Trotter. H. Rhodes, 1696.

Mann, Thomas. From *Past Masters and Other Papers*. Translated by H. T. Lowe-Porter. Alfred A. Knopf, 1933.

Marlowe, Christopher. From *The Famous Tragedy of the Rich Jew of Malta*. Nicholas Varasour, 1633.

McCormick, E. Allen. From "The Eighteenth Century: Foundation and Development of Literary Criticism," in *The Challenge of German Literature*. Edited by Horst S. Daemmrich and Diether H. Haenicke. Wayne State University Press, 1971. Copyright © 1971 by Wayne State University Press, Detroit, MI 48202. All rights reserved. Reprinted by permission of the Wayne State University Press and the author.

Montaigne, Michel de. From *The Complete Essays of Montaigne*. Translated by Donald M. Frame. Stanford University Press, 1958. Copyright 1948, © 1957, 1958 by the Board of Trustees of the Leland Stanford Junior University. Renewed 1986 by Donald M. Frame. All rights reserved. Reprinted with the permission of the publishers, Stanford University Press.

Morley, John. From *Critical Miscellanies, Vol. IV*. The Macmillan Company, 1908.

Murry, John Middleton. From *Heroes of Thought*. Julian Messner, Inc., 1938. Copyright 1938 by John Middleton Murry. Renewed © 1966 by Mary Middleton Murry. Reprinted by permission of Julian Messner, a division of Simon & Schuster, Inc.

Nash, Ralph. From an introduction to *Arcadia & Piscatorial Eclogues*. By Jacopo Sannazaro, translated by Ralph Nash. Wayne State University Press, 1966. Copyright © 1966 by Wayne State University Press. All rights reserved. Reprinted by permission of Wayne State University Press and the author.

Newcomb, Thomas. From "An Ode Sacred to the Memory of N. Rowe, Esq.," in *Musarum Lachrymae; or, Poems to the Memory of Nicholas Rowe, Esq.* Edited by Charles Beckingham. E. Curll, 1719.

Nicoll, Allardyce. From *A History of English Drama, 1660-1900: Early Eighteenth Century Drama, Vol. II*. Third edition. Cambridge at the University Press, 1952.

Nicoll, Allardyce. From *A History of Restoration Drama, 1660-1700*. Cambridge at the University Press, 1923.

Nicoll, Allardyce. From *World Drama: From Aeschylus to Anouilh*. George G. Harrap & Company Ltd., 1949.

O'Brien, Conor Cruise. From *The Suspecting Glance*. Faber & Faber, 1972. © 1972 by Conor Cruise O'Brien. All rights reserved. Reprinted by permission of Faber & Faber Ltd.

From "Some Account of Sannazarius and His Piscatory Eclogues," in *The Osiers: A Pastoral*. By Sannazarius. Cambridge University Press, 1724.

Palmer, John. From *The Comedy of Manners*. G. Bell & Sons, Ltd., 1913.

Pascal, Blaise. From *Pensées*. Translated by H. F. Stewart. Pantheon Books, 1950.

Phillips, Edward. From *Theatrum Poetarum*. Charles Smith, 1675.

Pierse, Sarah. From "To the Excellent Mrs. Catherine Trotter," in *The Unhappy Penitent: A Tragedy*. By Catharine Trotter. William Turner and John Nutt, 1701.

Pilcher, C. Venn. From *The Passion-Hymns of Iceland*. Edited and translated by C. Venn Pilcher. Robert Scott, 1913.

Pitkin, Hanna Fenichel. From *Fortune Is a Woman: Gender and Politics in the Thought of Niccolò Machiavelli*. University of California Press, 1984. Copyright © 1984 by The Regents of the University of California. Reprinted by permission of the publisher.

Pix, Mary? From a prologue to *The False Friend; or, The Fate of Disobedience*. Richard Basset, 1699.

Pix, Mary? From a prologue to *Queen Catharine or, the Ruines of Love: A Tragedy*. William Turner, 1698.

Pope, Alexander. From a letter in *The Complete Works of William Wycherley, Vol. 2*. Edited by Montague Summers. The Nonesuch Press, 1924.

Pope, Alexander. From *Of the Characters of Women: An Epistle to a Lady*. L. Gilliver, 1735.

Powell, George? From "To the Ingenious Mr. ——," in *Animadversions on Mr. Congreve's Late Answer to Mr. Collier*. John Nutt, 1698.

Powys, John Cowper. From *Enjoyment of Literature*. Simon and Schuster, 1938.

Priestley, J. B. From *Literature and Western Man*. Harper & Brothers, 1960. Copyright © 1960 by J. B. Priestley. All rights reserved. Reprinted by permission of A. D. Peters & Co. Ltd.

Quint, David. From *Origin and Originality in Renaissance Literature: Versions of the Source*. Yale University Press, 1983. Copyright © 1983 by Yale University. All rights reserved. Reprinted by permission of the publisher.

Regosin, Richard L. From *The Matter of My Book: Montaigne's "Essais" as the Book of the Self*. University of California Press, 1977. Copyright © 1977 by The Regents of the University of California. Reprinted by permission of the publisher.

From *A Representation of the Impiety & Immorality of the English Stage*. J. Nutt, 1704.

Reynolds, Myra. From *The Learned Lady in England: 1650-1760*. Houghton Mifflin Company, 1920.

Richardson, Samuel. From *Clarissa; or, the History of a Young Lady, Vol. IV*. S. Richardson, 1748.

Righter, Anne. From "William Wycherley," in *Restoration Theatre*. Edited by John Russell Brown and Bernard Harris. St. Martin's Press, 1965. © Edward Arnold (Publishers) Ltd. 1965. Used with permission of St. Martin's Press, Inc.

Robertson, J. M. From an introduction to *The Essays of Montaigne, Vol. I*. Translated by E. J. Trechmann. Oxford University Press, London, 1927.

Rogers, Katharine M. From *William Wycherley*. Twayne, 1972. Copyright 1972 by Twayne Publishers. All rights reserved. Reprinted with the permission of Twayne Publishers, a division of G. K. Hall & Co., Boston.

Rolleston, T. W. From *Life of Gotthold Ephraim Lessing*. Walter Scott, 1889.

Rousseau, Jean Jacques. From *The Social Contract & Discourses*. J. M. Dent & Sons, Ltd., 1913.

Rowe, Nicholas. From *The Fair Penitent: A Tragedy*. J. Tonson, 1703.

Ruffo-Fiore, Silvia. From *Niccolò Machiavelli*. Twayne, 1982. Copyright 1982 by Twayne Publishers. Reprinted with the permission of Twayne Publishers, a division of G. K. Hall & Co., Boston.

Russell, Bertrand. From *A History of Western Philosophy, and Its Connection with Political and Social Circumstances from the Earliest Times to the Present Day*. Simon & Schuster, 1945, G. Allen and Unwin Ltd., 1946. Copyright 1945, 1972 by Bertrand Russell. All rights reserved. Reprinted by permission of Simon & Schuster, Inc. In Canada by Unwin Hyman Ltd.

Sainte-Beuve, Charles Augustin. From *Selected Essays*. Edited by Francis Steegmuller, translated by Norbert Guterman. Doubleday, 1963. Copyright © 1963 by Doubleday & Company, Inc. Reprinted by permission of Doubleday, a division of Bantam, Doubleday, Dell Publishing Group, Inc.

Saintsbury, George. From "Montaigne," in *The Encyclopaedia Britannica, Vol. XVIII*. Edited by Hugh Chisholm. Eleventh edition. The Encyclopaedia Britannica Company, 1910-11.

Saintsbury, George. From "Michael Drayton (1563-1631)," in *The English Poets: Chaucer to Donne, Vol. I*. Edited by Thomas Humphry Ward. Macmillan and Co., 1880.

Saintsbury, George. From *A History of Criticism and Literary Taste in Europe from the Earliest Texts to the Present Day: Modern Criticism, Vol. III*. William Blackwood and Sons, 1904.

Samaras, Zoe. From *The Comic Element of Montaigne's Style*. Editions A.-G. Nizet, 1970. Reprinted by permission of the publisher.

Sanctis, Francesco de. From *History of Italian Literature, Vol. II*. Translated by Joan Redfern. Harcourt Brace Jovanovich, 1931. Copyright 1931, renewed 1959 by Harcourt Brace Jovanovich, Inc. Reprinted by permission of the publisher.

Sayce, R. A. From *The Essays of Montaigne: A Critical Exploration*. Weidenfeld and Nicolson, 1972. © R. A. Sayce 1972. All rights reserved. Reprinted by permission of the publisher.

Schlegel, August Wilhelm. From *Course of Lectures on Dramatic Art and Literature*. Edited by Rev. A. J. W. Morrison, translated by John Black. Revised edition. Henry G. Bohn, 1846.

Schlegel, Friedrich von. From *Lectures on the History of Literature: Ancient and Modern*. Revised edition. William Blackwood and Sons, 1841.

Selden, J. From "Upon the 'Barons Warres', the 'Epistles' and 'Sonnets'," in *Poems*. By Michael Drayton. John Smethwicke, 1610.

Smith, Hallett. From *Elizabethan Poetry: A Study in Conventions, Meaning, and Expression*. Cambridge, Mass.: Harvard University Press, 1952. Copyright 1952 by the President and Fellows of Harvard College. Renewed 1980 by Hallett Darius Smith. Excerpted by permission of the publishers.

Southey, Robert. From *The Doctor, &c., Vol. II*. Longman, Rees, Orme, Brown, Green, Longman, 1839.

Squire, J. C. From a preface to *Nimphidia: The Court of Fayrie*. By Michael Drayton, edited by J. C. Squire. Basil Blackwell, 1924.

Staël-Holstein, Madame the Baroness de. From *Germany, Vol. I*. N.p., 1810.

Starobinski, Jean. From *Montaigne in Motion*. Translated by Arthur Goldhammer. University of Chicago Press, 1985. Originally published as *Montaigne en mouvement*. Editions Gallimard, 1982. Copyright © 1985 by The University of Chicago. All rights reserved. Reprinted by permission of the publishers and the author.

Steeves, Edna L. From an introduction to *The Plays of Mary Pix and Catharine Trotter: Mary Pix, Vol. I*. Edited by Edna L. Steeves. Garland Publishing, Inc., 1982. Introduction copyright © 1982 by Edna L. Steeves. Reprinted by permission of the publisher and the author.

Steeves, Edna L. From an introduction to *The Plays of Mary Pix and Catharine Trotter: Catharine Trotter, Vol. II*. Edited by Edna L. Steeves. Garland Publishing, Inc., 1982. Introduction © 1982 by Edna L. Steeves. Reprinted by permission of the publisher and the author.

Strachey, G. L. From *Landmarks in French Literature*. Henry Holt and Company, 1912.

Strauss, Leo. From *Thoughts on Machiavelli*. Free Press, 1959. Copyright © 1958 by Leo Strauss. All rights reserved. Reprinted by permission of the Literary Estate of Leo Strauss.

Summers, Montague. From *The Complete Works of William Wycherley, Vol. I*. edited by Montague Summers. The Nonesuch Press, 1924.

Sutherland, J. R. From ''Life,'' in *Three Plays: Tamberlane, The Fair Penitent, Jane Shore*. By Nicholas Rowe, edited by J. R. Sutherland. The Scholartis Press, 1929.

Symonds, John Addington. From *Renaissance in Italy: The Age of the Despots*. Revised edition. Smith, Elder, & Co., 1904.

Symonds, John Addington. From *Renaissance in Italy: The Revival of Learning, Vol. II*. Smith, Elder, & Co., 1877.

Taine, H. A. From *History of English Literature, Vol. II*. Translated by H. Van Laun. Holt and Williams, 1871.

Taylor, Bayard. From *Studies in German Literature*. G. P. Putnam's Sons, 1879.

Tetel, Marcel. From *Montaigne*. Twayne, 1974. Copyright 1974 by Twayne Publishers. All rights reserved. Reprinted with the permission of Twayne Publishers, a division of G. K. Hall & Co., Boston.

Thompson, James. From *Language in Wycherley's Plays: Seventeenth-Century Language Theory and Drama*. University of Alabama Press, 1984. Copyright © 1984 by The University of Alabama Press. All rights reserved. Reprinted by permission of the publisher.

Tillotson, Kathleen. From an introduction to *The Works of Michael Drayton, Vol. V*. J. William Hebel, Kathleen Tillotson, Bernard H. Newdigate, eds. Basil Blackwell, 1941.

Trotter, Catharine. From *Agnes de Castro: A Tragedy*. H. Rhodes, 1696.

Trotter, Catharine. From *The Revolution of Sweden: A Tragedy*. James Knapton, 1706.

Villari, Pasquale. From *The Life and Times of Niccolo Machiavelli, Vol. II*. Translated by Linda Villari. T. Fisher Unwin, 1892.

Voltaire, Francois Marie Arouet de. From *Letters Concerning the English Nation*. Translated by John Lockman. C. Davis and A. Lyon, 1733.

Voltaire. From *Letters on England*. Translated by Leonard Tancock. Penguin, 1980. Copyright © Leonard Tancock, 1980. All rights reserved. Reprinted by permission of Penguin Books Ltd.

Warburton, William. From a preface to *Remarks upon the Principles and Reasonings of Dr. Rutherforth's ''Essay on the Nature and Obligations of Virtue.''* By Catharine Trotter. William Warburton, 1747.

Weales, Gerald. From *The Complete Plays of William Wycherley*. Edited by Gerald Weales. Anchor Books, 1966. Copyright © 1966 by Doubleday & Company, Inc. All rights reserved. Reprinted by permission of Doubleday, a division of Bantam, Doubleday, Dell Publishing Group, Inc.

Wellek, René. From *A History of Modern Criticism, 1750-1950: The Later Eighteenth Century*. Yale University Press, 1955. Copyright © 1955 by Yale University. Renewed 1983 by René Wellek. All rights reserved. Reprinted by permission of the publisher.

Woolf, Virginia. From *The Common Reader*. Harcourt Brace Jovanovich, 1925, L. & V. Woolf, 1925. Copyright 1925 by Harcourt Brace Jovanovich, Inc. Renewed 1953 by Leonard Woolf. Reprinted by permission of Harcourt Brace Jovanovich, Inc. In Canada by the Literary Estate of Virginia Woolf and The Hogarth Press.

Wycherley, William. From a prologue to *Agnes de Castro: A Tragedy*. By Catharine Trotter. H. Rhodes, 1696.

Wycherley, William. From *The Plain-Dealer: A Comedy*. James Magnes and Rich. Bentley, 1677.

Young, Stark. From *Immortal Shadows: A Book of Dramatic Criticism*. Charles Scribner's Sons, 1948. Copyright 1948 by Charles Scribner's Sons. Renewed 1976 by Lewis M. Isaacs, Jr., Executor of the Estate of Stark Young. Reprinted with the permission of Charles Scribner's Sons, an imprint of Macmillan Publishing Company.

Zimbardo, Rose A. From *Wycherley's Drama: A Link in the Development of English Satire*. Yale University Press, 1965. Copyright © 1965 by Yale University. All rights reserved. Reprinted by permission of the publisher.

ISBN 0-8103-6107-8

90000